Handbook of Markets and Economies
East Asia
Southeast Asia
Australia
New Zealand

Handbook of Markets and Economies
East Asia
Southeast Asia
Australia
New Zealand

Foreword by John O'Shaughnessy

Anthony Pecotich and Clifford J. Shultz II, editors

M.E.Sharpe
Armonk, New York
London, England

Library of Congress Cataloging-in-Publication Data

Handbook of markets and economies : East Asia, Southeast Asia, Australia, New Zealand / edited by
Anthony Pecotich and Clifford J. Shultz II.
    p. cm.
Includes bibliographical references and index.
ISBN 0-7656-0972-X (cloth : alk. paper)
  1. Marketing—Asia—Handbooks, manuals, etc. 2. Marketing—Australia—Handbooks, manuals, etc.
3. Marketing—New Zealand—Handbooks, manuals, etc. 4. Asia—Handbooks, manuals, etc.
5. Australia—Handbooks, manuals, etc. 6. New Zealand—Handbooks, manuals, etc. I. Title: East Asia,
Southeast Asia, Australia, New Zealand. II. Pecotich, Anthony. III. Shultz, Clifford J.

HF5415.33.A78H36 2005
330.95—dc22   2004017970

Printed in the United States of America

The paper used in this publication meets the minimum requirements of
American National Standard for Information Sciences
Permanence of Paper for Printed Library Materials,
ANSI Z 39.48-1984.

∞

BM (c)   10   9   8   7   6   5   4   3   2   1

CONTENTS

FOREWORD

This book has something distinctive to offer: content, organization, and clarity together with the recognition that regions and countries within regions do not stand still. It was written by experts on the countries in East Asia, Southeast Asia, Australia, and New Zealand. Normally this generates problems in reconciling different frameworks for intercountry comparisons, but this is not the case herein. In this book, contributors largely use the same framework, composed of eight systems: the system embracing the natural environment and geography; the political system; the economic system; the social system; the knowledge system; the educational system; the executive system; and the marketing system. These are the systems that enable and constrain achievement. They all need to be taken into account, which is generally not done by others, as scholars tend to fixate on just one system or a subset.

Except for the system embracing the natural environment and geography, all eight systems are social constructions, products of human ingenuity, or, in some cases, the result of imposed fetters on realizing potential. I am tempted to group all these socially constructed systems under the banner of "culture," but the term "culture" is now more commonly used to mean a "custom complex" of values, beliefs, social norms, and rules for interpreting experience and shaping actions. This was not always so. When the anthropological view of culture first came into being, the positivist climate at the time insisted that culture be confined to what was observable, that is, confined to artifacts that could be seen, heard, smelled, and touched. With the decline in positivism, the study of culture became more the study of shared beliefs, values, knowledge, meanings, and ideas—things that are discovered and inferred rather than just observed. The eight systems discussed include this view of culture and also the systems that can be described in observational terms. This is as it should be, because a country's institutions provide the context within which people live and work and within which dreams and hopes are facilitated or frustrated.

As Jerome Bruner (1990) said, psychology must link with culture, as human actions are tied to culturally shared meanings and concepts. However, the chief symbolic element in any culture is the language; the absence of a common language takes away one means of enhancing culturally shared meanings and concepts. As shown in this book, some of the countries examined suffer as a result of lack of common language.

David Landes (1998) sees culture, in the beliefs and values sense, as making the difference: success or failure is ultimately determined from within, not imposed from without. In line with this, Paul Bohannan (1995) argued that cultural meanings instilled into human beings standardize their choices just as readily, but not as unalterably, as handwriting. But we seldom slavishly follow the script embedded in cultural norms, and a society's culture is not a separate overseeing entity enforcing compliance. In a final analysis, culture is composed of the interactions of people within the culture and is shaped by those interactions. Culture and the interactions and activities that take place within the culture form an interacting system: culture constrains and guides, but culture is molded by what people do. This is also recognized in the contributions in this book.

Cultures are not made up of people who are just tokens of each other in their social behaviors: cultures produce subcultures, some of which define themselves in opposition to the dominant mores. Culture is permeable by other cultures, and the influences of these other cultures bring about cultural change: something well recognized by the contributors to this book.

It was Montaigne in the sixteenth century who remarked that, if we were not alike, we could not be distinguished from the beasts, but if we were not different, we could not be distinguished from each other. This is the same with cultures. If cultures had nothing in common, there would be no point of contact. If they were not different, we would treat them all the same. This book recognizes the similarities in imputing the framework of the eight systems on the analysis of each culture, but it also recognizes that cultures differ, in that specialist contributors have been selected for each country. Countries can be said to differ only against a backdrop of similarities. Contributors to this book spell out what is distinctive by being aware of the similarities. Such similarities do not imply a cross-cultural psychology beyond a few platitudes. As Richard Shweder (2003) argued, any cultural psychology should focus on population-based variations rather than seek the holy grail of a cross-cultural psychology. This is the position taken by the editors of this book. This does not mean that similarities are ignored. A major error of the doctrine of relativism is its failure to see that specifying differences presupposes a background of similarities, with the consequence that relativism directs us away from what we hold in common. This also is recognized in this book. If there were no commonalities, communication would be impossible.

This is an important book, not just because of the information it contains but also because it has the potential to broaden the horizons of anyone who even dips into it. Broadening horizons is what education should be about.

REFERENCES

Bohannan, Paul. 1995. *How Culture Works.* New York: The Free Press, 9.
Bruner, Jerome. 1990. *Acts of Meaning.* Cambridge, MA: Harvard University Press.
Landes, David S. 1998. *The Wealth and Poverty of Nations.* New York: W.W. Norton.
Shweder, Richard A. 2003. *Why Do Men Barbecue? Recipes for Cultural Psychology.* Cambridge, MA: Harvard University Press.

John O'Shaughnessy
The Judge Institute of Management Studies
University of Cambridge

ACKNOWLEDGMENTS

This book would not have been possible without the efforts of many people. We therefore wish to express our sincerest appreciation to all of them and, in particular, to those mentioned below.

To the authors of the individual chapters, thank you for your contributions and your patience and positive reactions throughout the revision and updating process.

Thanks are also due to Harry Briggs, Elizabeth Granda, and Angela Piliouras at M.E. Sharpe, and our copyeditor Lori Eby, who were especially helpful and supportive and were instrumental in the genesis and completion of this project.

The deans, faculty, technicians, and secretarial staff in our respective schools at Arizona State University and the University of Western Australia are thanked for their support and encouragement. Particular thanks are due to Betsy Conklin, who tirelessly searched for and double-checked statistics and assisted with formatting.

We also thank the faculty, staff, and students at the Marketing Department at the University of Split, where Anthony Pecotich was located at various periods during the completion of this text; Tom Vallely and his associates at the Harvard–Fulbright Economics Teaching Program during Clifford Shultz's visits to Cambridge and Ho Chi Minh City; and the Marley Foundation and their support of Clifford Shultz's scholarship.

We owe a major debt to our families, Katherine and Matthew Shultz, and Jan, Katherine, and Jennifer Pecotich, who were always understanding and supportive when we had to allocate time to the completion of this book, and who helped us to survive the difficult and sometimes frantic efforts to make this book a reality.

Finally, we acknowledge the marketers and consumers of East Asia, Southeast Asia, Australia, and New Zealand, who continue to move the region forward in generally positive ways, to the betterment of their nations and the global community.

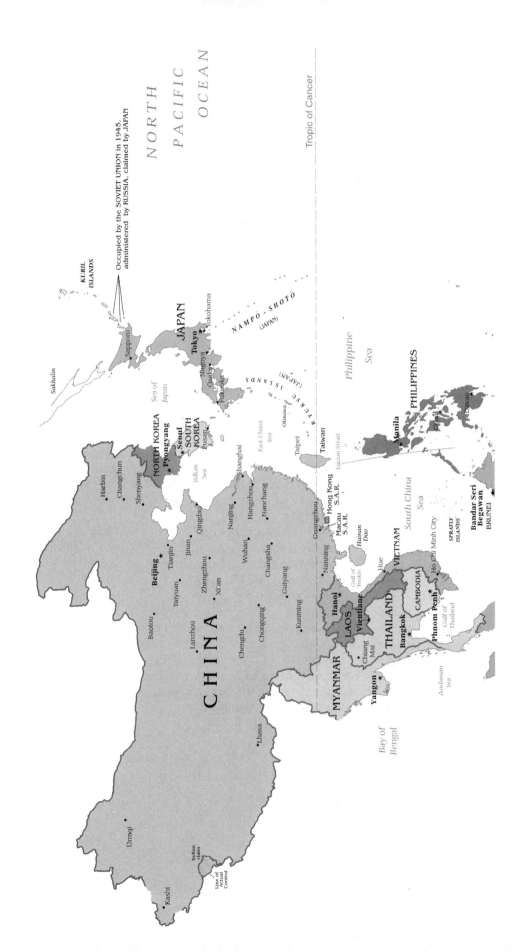

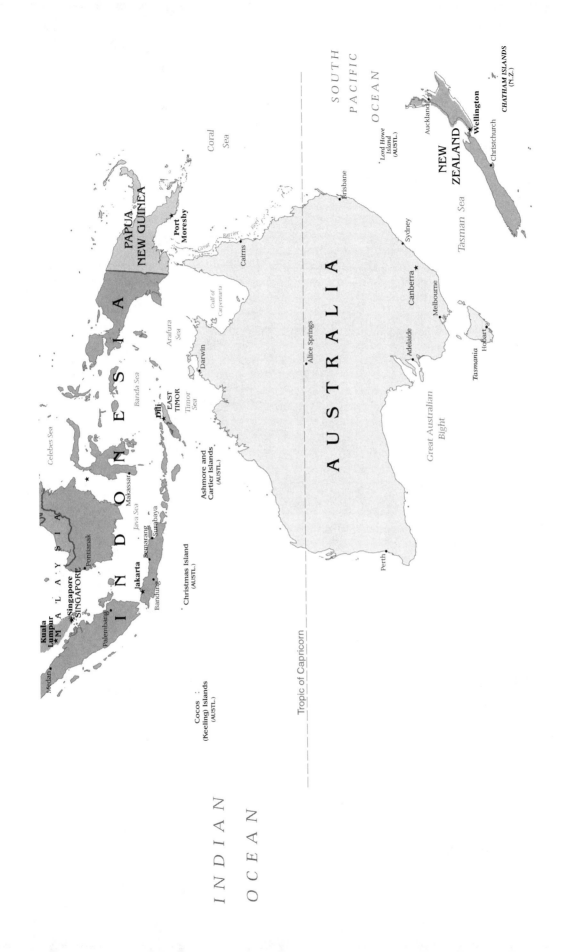

Handbook of Markets and Economies
East Asia
Southeast Asia
Australia
New Zealand

INTRODUCTION

Anthony Pecotich and Clifford J. Shultz II

Asia's ascending, if occasionally lurching, transformation continues to marvel most observers. Despite cataclysmic changes wrought by the 1997 economic crisis, the events of September 11, 2001, the global war on terror, and a tsunami, the roller coaster that describes the economic, political, and social progress of East Asia, Southeast Asia, Australia, and New Zealand (herein, ESEA, or "the region") rolls on and shows surprising resilience and progress. Though some alliances and alignments have changed, the nature of international affairs has been redefined, and marketing systems have been affected, the people and nations of the region seem determined to make the twenty-first century "the Asian Century."

The progress witnessed over the past few decades is particularly impressive when one considers that immediately after World War II (1945), much of ESEA was a scene of devastation and disorder imbued with potential for further conflict. The notion that the region was "going nowhere" was not simply based on the jaundiced assessment of those without vision but was rather the calculated evaluation of the well informed. To accentuate the true nature of the situation, Leger (1995) used the example of Korea's per capita gross national product (GNP) that, at the time, was "roughly equal to that of Haiti, Ethiopia, and Yemen and about a third less than that of India and Pakistan" (Leger 1995, 46). In the first two decades that followed World War II, there was little immediate improvement. The region continued to be characterized by colonial vestiges, the rise of brutal centrally controlled forms of government, civil wars (e.g., Korea, Vietnam, and Cambodia), poverty, and other damaging forms of internal disorder (e.g., corruption, black markets, insurrections, and various forms of political and economic repression). The full magnitude of the changes was described by Schwab and Smadja (1994, 40–41) as the rise of the "new economic world order" on whose nature they elaborate as follows:

> Perhaps . . . most spectacular . . . is the shift in the world economy's center of gravity to Asia. The extraordinary process of fast and steady growth in East Asia since the end of the 1960s has led to an overall redistribution of the world's economic power, the impact and implications of which are just beginning to be felt. In 1960, East Asia accounted for just 4 percent of world economic output. Today its share amounts to 25 percent. While GNP in Europe and the United States has grown at an average of 2.5 percent to 3 percent per year over the past twenty-five years, many East Asian countries have managed an annual average of 6.5 percent to 7.5 percent—a trend that is expected to continue beyond the turn of the century. Between 1992 and the year 2000, 40 percent of all the new purchasing power created in the

world [was] in East Asia, and the region [absorbed] between 35 percent and 40 percent of the global increase in imports. East Asian central banks now hold close to 45 percent of the world's foreign reserves, and while the United States and the major European countries keep piling up foreign debt, Japan, Taiwan, Singapore, and Hong Kong are in the remarkable position of not having any. (Schwab and Smadja 1994, 40–41)

Today, though the process is not complete, and within the region, some of the world's poorest nations still exist, the transformation, the advancement, and the potential are notable. The region is changing in ways that few experts would have forecast in 1997. The first discontinuity was due to the financial crisis in July 1997 (e.g., *Economist* 2003b; Kim and Haque 2002; Krugman 1997; Meltzer 1998; Phongpaichit and Baker 2000). The devaluation of the baht by Thailand on July 2, 1997, signaled the beginning of the crisis that led to capital flight from the region, the economic collapse of many nations, and fear of a deleterious worldwide economic impact. However, quick action by the International Monetary Fund (IMF) and implementation of tight financial policies resulted in dramatic improvements. Since then, the economic and political situation has stabilized, and gross domestic product (GDP) growth has resumed. A feature of this period has been the rising power of the People's Republic of China (herein, China or PRC) and the relative decline of Japan. It is, however, noteworthy that Japan is still an economic heavyweight in the region and the world, and that China's growth in trade has been from a small base. There is also concern with the possible effects of a downturn in China (*Economist* 2004e).

The Chinese ascendancy perhaps has been accelerated by the United States's preoccupation with events in the Middle East and Central Asia, and the concern with the growth of Islamic extremism among Muslim populations of ESEA (e.g., the United States's participation in the struggle with insurgents in the Philippines). The United States is developing closer ties with China despite the tensions associated with North Korea and Taiwan. Notwithstanding threats and counterthreats, Taiwan and the PRC are becoming increasingly interdependent, and a peaceful reconciliation in the future appears to be a distinct possibility. With regard to Hong Kong, although the optimism toward a retention of vestiges of democracy and human rights appears to be fading, integration with the mainland's political system has not been swift, and the future may not be as bleak as some postulate, for China has been undergoing a form of economic liberalization that affects social and political discourse (Abramowitz and Bosworth 2003; *Economist* 2003a, 2003b, 2004c).

During this period, the two Koreas have also become more visible on the world stage: South Korea with its highly noticeable economic growth, democratic processes, and generational change; North Korea with its devastating poverty, totalitarianism, and nuclear provocation. Despite these vast differences, the two are gingerly moving toward some form of reconciliation. The North, an economic disaster, is becoming increasingly dependent on international aid, particularly from China and South Korea. China, with its increasing economic power (three decades of economic growth) has moved toward stronger relationships with both Koreas. It has become South Korea's biggest trading partner and is vital to North Korea's existence, particularly with its energy exports.

The region's rapid recovery from the 1997 crisis and the growth of the Chinese economy has surprised many observers. Economic ties between China and its ESEA neighbors have also expanded, and China has begun to project a responsible and benign image in the region. Laos, Myanmar, and North Korea, with their isolationism and centralized dictatorial systems, remain a counterweight to progress but also show signs of change, to varying degrees, particularly in the case of Laos. Vietnam is an outstanding exception. The nation has outperformed China, with foreign direct investment (FDI) worth more than 8 percent of GDP last year (proportionally more than China), and is Asia's best-performing economy, with an average growth of 7.4 percent per year over the last ten years. The alleviation of poverty has been remarkable, from 58 percent of the population in 1993 to 29 percent in 2002 (*Economist* 2004d).

The movement toward liberal economic policies and more personal freedoms continues, for example, Indonesia's resolution of the Timor problem and the emergence of East Timor into the family of nations. The majority of the leaders of the nations in the region show a pragmatic interest in maintaining stability and economic growth and in playing a larger role in world trade. There are major uncertainties, such as corruption, insurgency, China's continuing growth, North Korea's nuclear capacity, human rights transgressions, ecological problems, public health crises, and energy shortages, that could, at any time, send the region once again into a downward spiral (Abramowitz and Bosworth 2003; Bruton 2004; Claessens, Djankov, and Lixin 2000; Easterly 2001; *Economist* 2004b, 2004c; Feldstein 2002; Fisman and Svensson 2000; Forbes 1995; Kim and Haque 2002).

There is little doubt that the region and the world face major challenges; nonetheless, our prognosis is still optimistic, and we see the economic progress initiated by the renaissance of Japan's economic power, the emergence of China, and the newly industrializing countries (NICs) as well as the growth of a group of "near NICs," as continuing. There will be problems and future discontinuities; however, we feel confident that these will be overcome, and it still seems likely that the Pacific will replace the Atlantic Ocean as the center of world trade. In essence, the region will become the world's most formidable market; the reciprocal relationship between marketing and consumers will be its catalyst. Given this ascent and importance, the purpose of this text is to provide insights to the present conditions and the future trends of the markets, economies, marketing dynamics, and consumer behavior in the various countries of the region.

EAST AND SOUTHEAST ASIA: AN INTEGRATIVE AND SYSTEMIC OVERVIEW

As a prelude to the country-specific chapters, it is necessary to address the region as a whole and to extract those aspects that are critical to the explanation of its progress. The contributors, in their presentations for each of the nations, have tended to take a regional perspective. It is not our purpose to reiterate their contributions; we will attempt to distill and to describe the major unifying themes and trends in a conceptual context. But before doing so, two issues should be addressed. The first issue is the question of regional definition, and the second is the nature of the statistical data.

The alert reader would have already noted that our region description, East and Southeast Asia, is somewhat cumbersome—hence the acronym ESEA—and that we appear to move from Southeast Asia to East Asia to the Pacific Basin, with little apparent distinction. Traditional geographers may also reject our inclusion of Australia and New Zealand, but their increasing economic integration into the region drives their inclusion. Unfortunately, the literature and common usage are such that this geographic ambiguity cannot be avoided. Many country and region demarcations are possible. Some of these classifications overlap and do not have unique contexts except in those circumstances where they describe a formal alliance or association, such as the Association of Southeast Asian Nations (ASEAN) or Asia-Pacific Economic Cooperation (APEC). Further, the history of the region has been characterized by numerous attempts to form regional alliances and the existence of contradictory (divisive and unifying) forces.

The nations differ on the bases of ethnicity, culture, language, and political and economic systems. Some of the animosities have deep historical roots spanning thousands of years. These animosities may be difficult to overcome, particularly when one notes the fairly recent military hostilities among some of them, the memory of which is deeply ingrained in the national psyches and is always a factor in international relations. The possibility of further territorial disputes is very real. Consider, for example, China, with the status of Taiwan; the wide-ranging dispute over the Spratly Islands; border tensions between Myanmar and Thailand; separatist movements; terrorism; the still unresolved Korean conflict; and the human rights problems, just to name a few potential flash points. However, the forces for integration and cooperation are also very strong and are further energized by the pragmatic attitudes of the leadership, who recognize that true progress can only be achieved through intraregional cooperation. The major trends within the region are toward international accommodation, although the conditions within many nations have not been characterized by political stability, and internal turmoil has often been the norm. The movement toward regional integration has been slow but steady, and proposals for groupings have been relatively frequent. For these reasons, the terminology and acronyms have been numerous and confusing (Chia and Pecotich 1988; *Economist* 2003b; Meltzer 1998; Pecotich and Chia 1992).

The choice we have made is based on the broad grouping of countries that are not only in relatively close geographic proximity, but that have economic and marketing futures that are inextricably intertwined. ESEA, therefore, comprises the economically developed nations of Japan, Singapore, Australia, and New Zealand; the NICs or territories such as the Republic of Korea (South Korea), Taiwan, and the states of ASEAN (Brunei Darussalam, Cambodia, Indonesia, Laos, Malaysia, Myanmar, Philippines, Thailand, Singapore, and Vietnam); and the evolving socialist economies of the region, the People's Republic of China (now integrated with Hong Kong), Cambodia, Laos, Vietnam, Myanmar, and the Democratic Republic of Korea (North Korea). Also included are Papua New Guinea and the newly formed state of East Timor.

The order of presentation of the chapters could have been based on various criteria, such as political systems (e.g., democratic versus centrally planned versus dictatorial), the level of economic development (developed versus developing), or immediate geographic proximity (e.g., Indochina: Vietnam, Cambodia, and Laos). Again, readers will note that nations fall into multiple categories. We decided to avoid classification difficulties by presenting the states in alphabetical order. This method provides an objective, unambiguous, nonoverlapping classification scheme that should be noncontroversial. The reader may then, in conjunction with this introduction, read and discuss the states in whatever sequence is most suitable for the reader's objectives.

This text contains many statistics that are used to support the assertions and to enumerate the trends. Before discussing these figures, it is necessary to provide a cautionary and exculpatory note. While statistical data, even in highly developed nations, suffer from inaccuracies and inconsistencies, in ESEA there are major problems. Even when data exist, they may be inaccessible, outdated, and sometimes distorted or deliberately misreported for political purposes. Statistics will vary according to the source and the compilers' definitions and assumptions. So, for example, the population of Cambodia is literally anyone's best guess, despite a fairly recent census (see Table I-1); such inconsistencies help to illustrate the nature of the problem: ESEA is a complex and multifaceted entity comprised of numerous forces that affect the accuracy of many measures. While this reality can be disconcerting for scholars and practitioners who need accurate data, the inconsistencies should not be allowed to cloud the overall statistical picture that has sufficiently strong power to overcome modest variances among indicators presented throughout the text.

Moreover, in this increasingly Internet-driven world in which recently calculated and regularly updated statistics are readily available from various sources, including the Central Intelligence Agency, the World Bank, Economist Intelligence Units, and governments, the contribution

Table I-1

Rudimentary Statistics for Countries of East and Southeast Asia

Country	Population estimate (million)	Population increase (%)	GDP per head (US$)	GDP growth (%)	Exchange rates (1 US$)
Australia	19.8	0.9	26,900	3.6	A$1.70
Brunei	0.36	2.0	18,600	3.0	B$1.80
Cambodia	13.1	1.8	1,600	4.5	Riel 3,912.08
China	1,287.0	0.6	4,700	8.0	Yuan 8.28
East Timor	1.0	2.13	500	18.0	See US$
Indonesia	234.9	1.52	3,100	3.7	Rupiah 9,311.19
Japan	127.2	0.11	28,700	0.2	Yen 125.39
North Korea	22.5	1.07	1,000	1.0	Won 150.0
South Korea	48.3	0.66	19,600	6.3	Won 1,251.09
Laos	5.9	2.45	1,800	5.7	Kip 7,562
Malaysia	23.1	1.86	8,800	4.1	Ringgit 3.8
Myanmar	42.5	0.52	1,700	5.3	Kyat 6.64
New Zealand	4.0	1.09	20,100	3.3	NZ$2.16
Papua New Guinea	5.3	2.34	2,100	-3.1	Kina 3.8
Philippines	84.6	1.92	4,600	4.4	Peso 51.67
Singapore	4.6	3.42	25,200	2.2	S$1.79
Thailand	64.3	0.95	7,000	5.3	Baht 42.96
Vietnam	81.6	1.29	2,300	7.0	Dong 15,325.8
Total	2,070.06				

Source: World Factbook (Central Intelligence Agency, Washington, DC, 2003), available at www.cia.gov/cia/publications/factbook/geos/cb.html.

of this book does not come so much from simplistic reporting of statistics. Rather, the contribution is found in their interpretation, in the context of the interactive and evolving marketing systems of the ESEA countries examined, and the implications for future trends in marketing and consumption.

The conceptual basis for the discussion to follow, therefore, is shown in Figure I-1, "Interactive Systems Affecting ESEA Progress" (cf. Shultz and Pecotich 1997). The figure consists of a network of elements in constant interaction. Each of these, in turn, has three aspects that are critical for its influence on the social system. This model is dynamic and is used here to illuminate and to introduce factors germane to individual country chapters, rather than to make a final and causal theoretical statement.[1]

Natural Forces

The historical basis of national wealth has emanated from natural forces, the determining elements of which are location, characteristics, and resources. The central locations of ESEA within the patterns of world trade as well as the region's vast resources have incited intense competition and colonial exploitation. However, the individual nations vary in the characteristics and extent of their natural resources that form important constraints affecting the economies, markets, and consumers. Consider, for example, China's size, topography, and arable-land-to-population ratio that raise questions about this nation's ability to administer its economy and to feed its people. Singapore, on the other hand, is densely populated with virtually no natural resources, but due to location and an organized, hard-working population, it evinces the living standards of highly developed na-

Figure I-1 **Interactive Systems Affecting ESEA Progress**

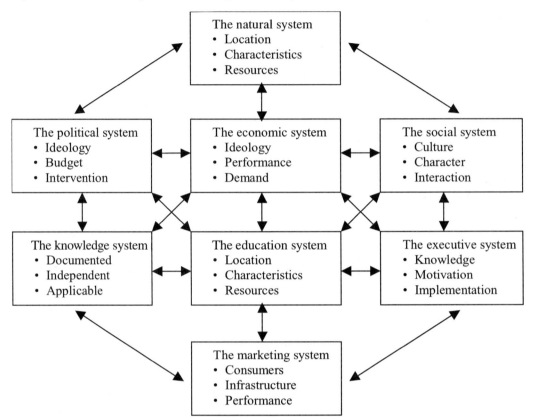

tions. Although the regional resources are plentiful and varied, centuries of exploitation and tre-mendous population pressures have inevitably led to degradation. Natural disasters—earthquakes, typhoons, droughts, floods and tsunamis, for example—also can radically disrupt environments, societies and economies. The condition of the environment presents serious problems in most of the nations and will affect their ability to enhance and to sustain life quality. Further economic progress will lead to greater stresses on air and water quality, traffic congestion, forest and fishery depletion, and soil erosion, thus creating a growth-preservation conundrum for these nations. This is one of the major challenges facing the region.

Political System

The second element is "the political system" that—guided by its "ideological" orientation as to the correct nature of the values and structures of the society—will determine the "budget" or financial allocations to various uses and, finally, will decide the extent of "intervention" in the system.

ESEA is a unique crucible of political processes and social change. Within its ambit may be found the extremes of the political spectrum, from the democratic (e.g., Australia and New Zealand) to the Stalinist authoritarian (e.g., the Democratic People's Republic of Korea, a.k.a., North Korea).

In between, one finds various forms of government, some of which have vestiges of military rule (e.g., Indonesia, Thailand, and the Republic of Korea, a.k.a., South Korea). Market socialism, market economics under the direction of single-party authoritarian rule (e.g., Chinese Communist Party, Vietnamese Communist Party, and Myanmar's State Peace and Development Council [SPDC]), is the relatively new experiment in the region. Although in some cases the progress is slow and faltering, it is not a distortion to state that tolerance for personal freedoms is a trend in most parts of the region. The noncommunist nations, such as Thailand, South Korea, and even Indonesia, have moved in the direction toward greater individual freedoms and liberties, which as institutions develop, suggests a more prosperous and peaceful future. Indonesia and the Philippines are important cases in point, having emerged from military dictatorships to form more representative democracies. The communist and socialist nations, in between periods of repression and motivated by the disintegration of Eastern Europe and the Soviet Union, are also liberalizing their institutions and, in turn, enabling more personal freedoms that are typically expressed as consumer behavior. Japan provides an interesting departure from the other models. Firmly entrenched democratic traditions have helped it to become a global economic power and also have helped it to weather more recent economic stagnation without any apparent damage to its social harmony or economic interests.

Irrespective of the trend toward political systems that enable greater personal liberties, the unsettling condition of North Korea, for example, should not be overlooked. Further uncertainty within the region may cause problems that could have a negative effect on political reforms and, ultimately, market development. Nevertheless, the growing pragmatism of the political leadership throughout ESEA suggests that the trend toward liberalization will continue. If the process is managed, and the various political transitions occur without open conflict, an auspicious future for the region is assured.

It would be a misrepresentation, however, not to state that the region contains some repressive and closed regimes, and these are not simply those labeled "communist." Many of the citizens of ESEA find themselves living in political climates that are not conducive to open dissent or the kind of "free" speech enjoyed by some of the better developed nations with longer democratic traditions. These same climates also affect the marketing and business environments. Government interference beyond the scope of agreed-upon conditions, corruption, bribery, and unethical business practices, generally, still exists. However, as stated earlier, the movement is toward economic and political systems that are more conducive to expressions of personal liberty and stable business environments. We are reluctant to categorize these trends as "democratic" in the Western sense, but it seems inevitable that further development of economic structures and greater dependence on information technologies will lead to greater freedom of interaction and expression as well as increased levels of trust within these societies.

Economic System

The "economic system" is the third element of the model. Again, the nature and influence of this system is determined by three factors: (1) the "ideology," which determines the nature, structure, and operation of the system; (2) the "performance" of the system; and (3) the "demand" for the products within the system. The dominant theme in the region is best captured by a shift to the market, and by regional and global integration, increasingly, as manifested by inclusion in the World Trade Organization (WTO).

Continuing economic reform is characteristic of the region. The socialist or command economies, to varying degrees, have liberalized their economies in an effort to achieve prosperity, with the ruling single parties retaining power. China, Vietnam, Cambodia, Laos, and Myanmar have, in different ways, sought to liberalize their economic systems and cautiously implemented reforms to move the nations toward the market system. China, in particular, has been transforming itself from a centrally planned economy into a form of decentralized market system. The moves sometimes have been hesitant and often accompanied with clampdowns on dissidents, but despite detractors, economic progress has been made. This spread of economic liberalism has brought these previously isolated nations into the world economy. Other countries, such as Indonesia, the Republic of Korea, and Thailand, on whose governments the militaries retain a strong influence, have shown flexibility in both moving toward civilian government and liberalizing the economies.

Accompanying this general trend toward the market have been the related trends of privatization, deregulation, and trade and foreign investment liberalization. Privatization and deregulation have increased the level of internal competition and placed considerable pressure on previously protected institutions, such as telecommunications and energy suppliers. While in many parts of the world, the attitude toward foreign investment is ambivalent, the consistent economic growth in ESEA has been attained through policies to stimulate foreign investment. Entry of these nations—with their over two billion people—into the international marketplace has increased competitive pressure for global financial sources. Further, the rise of the vast economic power of the region is not only being fueled by the big players, such as Japan, China, and Indonesia, with their exports to Europe and the United States, but also from within Asia, by the four Tigers (Hong Kong, Singapore, South Korea, and Taiwan). It appears that the time of region-based prosperity is fast approaching. ESEA nations are increasingly looking to their neighbors for sources of funds and, conversely, for good investment opportunities. Therefore, as they grow wealthy, they look to invest in their neighbors and so help them to move toward affluence. Although Japan's influence is well documented, newer capital exporters, such as Singapore, Malaysia, Taiwan, Korea, and China, have also emerged. The consistent high economic growth of these nations has resulted in an increase in their capacity to exert influence within ESEA and externally. Presently, about half of Asian exports are to other nations within the region, and as hinted earlier, FDI from Australia and New Zealand increasingly melds the futures of these countries with ESEA.

This welcoming attitude to foreign investment, although somewhat modified after the 1997 crisis, accompanied by a continuing deregulation of trade, has resulted in a high degree of interdependence among the economies of the region. This intraregional interdependence is being increased by the pragmatic, innovative search for new ventures that contribute to the prosperity and security of the region. Consider, for example, the Singaporean push for a growth triangle and the formation of localized trilateral links. There is also a general recognition for the need to form strategic alliances and other types of partnerships in an effort to gain a technological edge. In conjunction with this trend is the exhortation that executives must look at the market as both region and country specific. There is already considerable posturing and competition for the location of the region's center, both internationally and within nations.

Some concern, however, has been expressed that trade barriers may be coming down much faster than desired or expected. AFTA (ASEAN Free Trade Area) is in the process of expediting trade liberalization and Asia-Pacific Economic Cooperation forum (APEC) likely will move to abolish most and perhaps all trade barriers. Domestic political realities may curb this general trend, and the progress toward the free trade goals may be uneven, but it seems unlikely that it will be permanently reversed, especially as countries scramble to meet requirements of the WTO. These domestic perceptions of internal and external conditions will largely determine the pace of change. For example, the apparent desynchronization of world economic cycles (ESEA has been booming despite a mercurial Japanese economy, while Europe often seems to be on the cusp of slipping into recession) has made many of the ESEA nations more self-reliant and self-confident. In many respects, these nations now see themselves as proactive forces for economic change and development. Their leadership seems to be aware that their export orientation and high investment has brought and is likely to bring greater success than the alternatives (*Economist* 2002, 2003c; Kim and Haque 2002).

The implications for the worldwide delocalization of industrial production have also precipitated another area for concern. On the positive side, countries that were previously condemned to simple, labor-intensive manufacturing are now able to produce cost-effective and sophisticated high-tech products. Malaysia, for example, has become the world's leading producer of semiconductors and now discourages labor-intensive industries (*Economist* 2000; Masuyama, Vandenbrink, and Chia 2000; Schwab and Smadja 1994), thus making the leap to high-tech, high-productivity, high value-added industries and high wages for its citizens. On the negative side, countries that have made the strategic choice to rely on cheap labor as a competitive advantage will likely be forced to rethink and to revise their strategy. The labor-cost edge may be retained, in the short term and in relation to some external competition such as the United States and Europe, but it is not a viable foundation for a sound future within the ESEA region, where the flexible corporation may move from Taiwan to China to Vietnam and so on. Further, in some of the countries of the region, labor-cost advantages seem to vanish in the face of realities (e.g., poor infrastructure, local bureaucracy, and "voluntary payments") that accompany daily business operations. Nonetheless, the persistent growth, the size of the population, and the inevitable increase of wealth will have strong impacts on the demand for products and services.

Social System

The fourth element of the model as shown in Figure I-1 is the "social system" that consists of "culture," "character," and "interaction." "Culture" determines the most general, enduring set of values within the community. The community may, for example, place great value on business acumen and education, or it may not; it may value conspicuous consumption and wealth accumulation, or it may not. "Character" refers to the characteristics of the society, for example, the demographic structure. "Interaction" is used here as a term to indicate the extent to which the society is open or closed; that is, the extent to which freedom of interaction is afforded to members of society.

The following chapters will demonstrate to readers the vast diversity of ESEA. And while some countries are more ethnically homogenous than others (e.g., Korea), within all the nations, there exist important differences in, for example, culture, language, and religion, which preclude a simple enumeration (see, for example, Parrinder 1995). As suggested earlier, some of the differences are the sources of animosities that have deep historical roots and may be difficult to overcome (Klein, Ettenson, and Morris 1998). These differences present challenges to the further progress of not only the region but also to some of the nations, individually. It is possible that hostilities based on cultural differences and national aspirations could erupt (e.g., Indonesia, the Philippines). However, it is equally true that some of the nations in the region, at least on the surface, present a visible degree of cultural harmony and accommodation (e.g., Singapore and Malaysia). Further, the pragmatism and the positive cultural attitudes toward business and education of some of the cultural groupings suggest that a slow evolution toward cultural reconciliation may be possible. The existence of immigrant groups (e.g., the overseas Chinese) may serve not only, in the economic sense, as a source of investment but also, more importantly, as a cultural bridge between nations. The desire to minimize the potential for religious conflict (e.g., the high degree of religious tolerance in Australia, New Zealand, and Singapore) is another positive manifestation.

Concerning the "character" of the region, there are broad overarching regional tendencies that may not only describe the present but may also be predictive of the future. There is little doubt that the size, density, and growth rates of many ESEA nations make them of critical importance to the world. The region may—depending upon which nations are included—contain as much as 60 percent of the world's population while occupying only about 30 percent of the total area (23 percent if Australia and New Zealand are excluded). The region contains the world's most populous country (China, with nearly 1.3 billion people) and seven other nations with populations greater than 40 million people (Indonesia, with nearly 240 million), Japan (nearly 130 million), Philippines (84+ million), Vietnam (80+ million), Thailand (nearly 65 million), Myanmar (42+ million), and South Korea (nearly 50 million; about 70 million when considering the two Koreas together) (see Table I-1). The average annual population increase varies from 0.3 percent (Japan) to 2.9 percent (Cambodia and Laos). Although this latter rate may not seem excessive, when compared to the 0.38 percent of Europe, a stark contrast becomes evident, especially when the enormous population base of ESEA is considered, and particularly when Asia's unofficial or black-market economy is taken into account (*Economist* 2003c).

Although the region contains some of the world's poorest nations (Cambodia, Laos, Myanmar, and Vietnam), also included are several of the world's fastest-growing and most powerful economies (China, Vietnam, Japan, and Korea). Singapore is of particular scholarly interest, because its progress may illustrate the importance of trade in overcoming the problems of population density and its role as an opinion leader. The population of the region is predominantly rural (Australia, Japan, Singapore, and New Zealand are notable exceptions), and there has been a rapid rural-to-urban drift that strains the infrastructure and often leads to a disenfranchised, poor underclass. Other important demographic developments include the emergence of sex and age as determinants of future growth. Women are increasingly likely to be factors in the workforce, and women's issues generally are likely to become influential when making policy. Regarding age, although the proportion of those over the age of sixty-five is increasing (particularly in Japan and Singapore), the "youth group" (i.e., those from fifteen to twenty-four years of age) is also larger than in other parts of the world; thus, ESEA overall is younger than other parts of the world. More than half of the population is under age twenty-five compared to the populations of the United States and Europe, where the proportion is about a third and a fourth, respectively, so the demographic base for further economic growth also exists. Regional forces that typically affect population changes include migration patterns, fertility rates, and mortality and life expectancy rates. All are changing and will impact the development of ESEA. Other problems that remain to be resolved include the movement of "guest" workers and refugees, and strains to health care systems and society caused by the likes of SARS and HIV/AIDS pandemics. Rising, balanced prosperity for the region may provide the solution to or at least mitigate these problems.

Knowledge System

The "knowledge system" is the fifth element enumerated. The three components of this system are the extent to which knowledge is well "documented," that is, the degree to which knowledge in written form and in the technological facilities that serve as conduits to knowledge are readily available; the degree to which it is "independent," that is, can be relied upon to be objective and free of "ideological" influence; and finally, the degree to which guidelines for application ("applicable") may be distilled from the knowledge base. It is this system and the three systems to follow, that present some of the greatest challenges for ESEA. The leadership of the region has recognized that the passing on of "concentrated experience" in the form of recorded knowledge is critical to progress. It is becoming clear that intraregional investment needs are going to be accompanied by development of an intraregional knowledge base. It is the purpose of this text to contribute toward this development.

Education System

The "education system," presented as element six, consists of "teaching," "research," and "practice." The "practice" component is emphasized, because marketing is an applied discipline; a test of the applicability or relevance of "knowledge" is the extent to which research findings are useful and information is taught and learned. Education is also a major challenge facing the region, because the present growth has not been based on coordinated and integrated intraregional educational foundations. Education mimicry has tended to be the norm, whereby, often as not, "European models" were adopted. Some countries—Australia, Hong Kong, Singapore, and New Zealand—have used their existing systems to provide the education base for others in the region. In some instances, overseas education, whether to the better developed regional institutions or to Europe and North America, has been encouraged. Greater economic development and concomitant need for highly skilled workers will require even greater emphasis on and resource allocation for education. The ESEA governments face some critical decisions in this area.

Executive System

This leads to the seventh component of the system, which was labeled "the executive system." Essentially, this refers to the professional practice of marketing. Professionalism depends on the "knowledge" level of the executive population. The "motivation" is the extent to which the executive population will actually "implement" modern marketing practices. In many respects, the rapid growth in the region is testimony to an adequate understanding of marketing practice. The individual chapters provide ample within-nation evidence of the progress that has been made. There is little doubt that the regional orientation is toward the attainment of greater professionalism in this area.

Marketing System

The final component is the "marketing system." This component is shown to consist of "the consumers," "the infrastructure," and "performance." The region possesses some of the most well-developed marketing systems in the world—and some of the least well developed. As stated above, the growth of ESEA occurred largely because of foreign investment, cheap labor, and exports. Now the region is beginning to see itself as its own market, regionally independent and self-sustaining, but also globally linked. This inward or regional focus is partly explained by a substantial consumer base that already exists; the global orientation facilitates capital infusion, job growth, and export development. When larger numbers of consumers join the middle classes, the ESEA market may dwarf all others. Purchase patterns and consumption practices throughout ESEA suggest that this transformation is occurring much more rapidly than many observers thought possible. The marketing system ultimately enables the ethos and provisioning technology to enable national, regional, and global growth and prosperity (see Meade and Nason [1991] and Wilkie and Moore [1999] for detailed discussion on the wisdom of a systemic or macromarketing orientation).

To fully achieve this potential, the infrastructure needs are enormous. Further, and perhaps most importantly, the related specific developments vis-à-vis the marketing mix are critical: without a keen understanding of consumer needs and wants, and the market contexts in which marketers must introduce, promote, distribute, price, and support products, marketing efforts are destined to fail. Therefore, transregional development will have to include keen awareness of specific markets and consumers and mastery of marketing skills and technologies. Moreover, to attain acceptable and sustainable levels of marketing performance, environmental concerns (e.g., the need for clean technology and protection of forests and fisheries) and national and regional interests will have to be balanced. The administrative and organizational challenges are immense, and could, without resolution, destroy the potential of ESEA.

COUNTRY ANALYSES

Each chapter in this book provides a country-specific overview, vis-à-vis the elements of the previously described model, with implications for marketing and consumer developments. Furthermore, each chapter has been written or cowritten by a recognized expert and/or indigenous scholar from the country of focus. Contributors have attempted to present a balanced and focused view of the trends in each nation, while keeping a regional perspective. To assure some uniformity among chapters, throughout the review process, authors were encouraged to follow rough guidelines when organizing their manuscripts. More specifically, authors were encouraged to describe environmental or exogenous variables such as those discussed in Figure I-1 (e.g., political, economic, and social forces and systems) and to indicate their implications for marketing. Second, authors were instructed to analyze ensuing changes in consumer developments and behavior. Third, authors were encouraged to describe developments in the "macromarketing mix," that is, the aggregate trends in products, brands, services, prices, distribution, and promotion (cf. Leeflang and van Raaij 1993, 345). Authors were then requested to discuss future trends and expectations as well as to recommend guidelines for marketing management, now and into the future.

We hasten to add, however, that authors were also encouraged to accentuate arcane issues and factors that profoundly affect, and will continue to affect, marketing and consumers in their respective countries of analysis. It would be inappropriate, for example, to use precisely the same template of analysis for, say, both Japan and Cambodia. Each chapter provides materials most relevant to current and future marketing and consumer issues. Consequently, some chapters (e.g., chapter 3, Cambodia, and chapter 9, Laos) have proportionately larger amounts of text that address political forces and the resultant emergence of fledgling marketing institutions. Other chapters (e.g., chapter 15, Singapore, and chapter 7, Japan) that provide analyses of more "predictable" and economically developed countries with extensive databases on marketing and consumer trends focus more directly on specific and traditional marketing and consumer issues. Some chapters were handicapped by the absence of sound information concerning consumer behavior and marketing in the nation concerned; moreover, inevitably, no book can meet all the information needs of all possible readers, but experience and feedback suggest that our model and the authors' contributions roughly organized in response to it, can enable a wide range of readers to gain an actionable understanding of these countries, and their markets and consumers. In summary, we believe these chapters will provide readers with an introduction to the most compelling marketing and consumer issues in ESEA, today and into the foreseeable future.

Australia

The first chapter, in alphabetical order, is an evaluation of Australian consumer behavior and marketing issues, challenges, and future possibilities. It is perhaps appropriate that Australia is first, because with New Zealand, it is the most southerly of the ESEA nations and is, in some respects, a fringe member of the region. Australia, "the Southern Tiger," is endowed with natural resources, a small population, and a well-developed infrastructure. It has a Western democratic tradition that provides a stable political environment with well-established, peaceful transitory processes. The down-to-earth deeply ingrained egalitarianism, with its associated freedom of speech, is sometimes difficult for Australia's near neighbors in the North to comprehend. Nonetheless, Australia is genuinely interested in not only being a member of the region, but also in constructively contributing to the progress of its neighbors, which it has historically done. Janet McColl-Kennedy, Sharyn Rundle-Thiele, and Steve Ward, in their assessment of the economic indicators, suggest that the Australian consumer may be gaining confidence and that the economy is in a solid position. The demographic and cultural makeup of the nation suggests changes in structure and content that may have long-term implications for marketing practitioners.

Brunei Darussalam

In describing the consumer characteristics of Brunei Darussalam, Leong Vai Shiem and Tan Siew Ee provide an introduction to a small but exceptional state that is undergoing controlled change, as its government seeks to ensure a prosperous future. A monarchy founded on Islam, Brunei is, nonetheless, a modern, oil-rich welfare state with a contemporary future-directed orientation. While some may question the entrepreneurial spirit of its citizens, it is well located to take advantage of the development in the region. As a nation, it seems to be teetering on the brink of a major transformation. Its global presence is becoming more visible, as is its participation in ASEAN. Domestically, it seems to be cautiously moving toward greater democratization and economic diversification. Brunei is another ESEA nation that within its unique context is seeking a formula for a transition into a viable future, and as such, it should not be overlooked by the marketing community.

Cambodia

In chapter 3, Clifford Shultz and Don Rahtz describe Cambodia's horrific past and the present conditions that affect the country's struggle to rise from the ashes of genocide and profound economic mismanagement. The instability of Cambodia has caused many managers and investors to overlook the country as a market opportunity. Shultz and Rahtz contend that, despite the atrocities of the killing fields and ongoing political friction, newly implemented policies may lead to a brighter future. Government reform, substantial foreign investment, and consumer responses to market economics are helping to transform this war-torn nation into a viable market. Cambodian consumers remain hopeful that their country will continue to progress, but internal discord and some cynical investment practices suggest that long-term prognoses are not entirely optimistic. Nevertheless, the authors indicate that Cambodia, despite risks, is a strategically located and promising market of more than 10 million consumers receptive to many goods and services.

China

Greater China, now including Hong Kong and Macau, continues to make historic changes that directly affect more than a billion of its citizens and, increasingly, other citizens who consume many of China's exports. Pia Polsa, Stella So, and Mark Speece provide an overview of the market transition and consumer evolution in the world's most populous nation and potentially largest economy. Their reasoned arguments suggest that China, after about 5,000 years of history, has entered another period of social and economic change. The direction of the change appears to be toward the market system, democratization, and liberalization. The pace of the transformation may not be quick or consistent enough for some outside observers; however, there is no doubt that the economic reforms first implemented in the late 1970s have brought continuous growth of GDP: China is one of the fastest-growing countries in the world. As is to be expected, the consumer markets have also shown immense expansion. The accompanying social movements (e.g., from the country to the city) and other changes present both a major challenge and an opportunity for China and the world. The management of the transformation will require consummate skills, but whatever the final outcome, there is little doubt that events in China will have a major influence on the shape of the future in the region and beyond. This incisive chapter, including detailed discussion of Hong Kong as a possible predictor for trends throughout China, provides a basis for an understanding of the marketing and consumer trends in this potentially world-dominating market.

East Timor

Tony Lapsley shares a comprehensive overview of the region's newest country, East Timor. Having recently gained independence from Indonesia, East Timor is now in the process of building a nation. Lapsley includes detailed accounts of political and historical forces that led to East Timor's independence and then gives insightful overviews of the economic environment. Most welcome are the helpful discussions on East Timor's physical and human resources assets that can be leveraged to build its economy.

Indonesia

Don Rahtz and Ignas Sidik, in their chapter, "Indonesia: Transition at a Crossroads," provide a picture of the marketing situation in another giant undergoing transformation. Indonesia, one of the largest and most populous nations in ESEA, has made a transition from a poor, less developed country to a NIC. Accompanying this change has been the usual rural-to-urban drift, increasing purchasing power, and the rise of a new middle class. The government has also attempted to initiate movements of population by providing incentives for resettlement from the densely populated island of Java to less-populated areas. The projected increase in working age population necessitates that growth continue. All of this makes for a vibrant, dynamic environment with considerable potential. However, the road to true prosperity, although now open, is still long, and many problems will have to be overcome for its attainment. In particular, considerable investment in marketing education and infrastructure will be necessary. Nonetheless, Rahtz and Sidik present an optimistic portrait of a nation moving forward to take a place on the world stage that is commensurate to its size.

Japan

Tsutomu Okahashi, N. Clay Gary and Steven Ward provide a systematic evaluation of Japan, a nation that has risen from the ashes of World War II to become a dominant economic power. However, it seems that with the recent recession, the "Rising Sun" has paused; whether this pause is temporary is yet to be determined. The suggestion by the authors is that Japan is undergoing a shift from a production-oriented fast growth to a slow-growth consumption-led mature economy. This change has confused the Japanese consumer and eroded confidence. The occurrence of the recession that has come to end a period of unprecedented growth and cultural change has accentuated this confusion. While it is clear that Japan is facing a period of turbulence, the authors conclude that it is unreasonable to argue that Japan's economic prosperity has ended. The major trends of liberalization and internationalization that are also evident in Japan suggest that the nation will become more accessible to regional market entry and so, perhaps, increase the level of integration. The authors of this chapter have provided an original treatment that will challenge some of the conceptions of the nature of consumer behavior in Japan. Both the tyro and the expert on Japan will find something of value in this chapter.

Korea

According to James Gentry, Sunkyu Jun, Seungwoo Chun, HeeSuk Kang, and Gyungtai Ko, Korea is an enigma not only because of its long history of isolationism but also because of the stark contrast in the economic developments of its two constituent parts (North and South). Although culturally among the most homogeneous nations in the region, both Koreas have undergone radical changes. The communist North, while pursuing its socialist goals, has become one of the most isolated, underdeveloped nations in the world. The South, on the other hand, has shown remarkable political and economic progress in the last decade. Though reunification is presented as almost inevitable, its achievement will not be easy, and if it occurs, it will herald profound changes. The strong desire to retain cultural identities and traditions may be a delaying factor in future economic development. This chapter provides a rich source of information on these and other marketing and consumer behavior trends in the Koreas.

Laos

William Ardrey, Clifford Shultz, and Michael Keane contend that Laos's strategic location, natural wealth, and emerging consumer culture make it an opportune market as well as an integral link to regional welfare and development. However, because Laos is landlocked, has a large land-to-population ratio, and is a relatively small market of less than 6 million ethnically diverse consumers, it is often overlooked. Furthermore, the government and consumers are adjusting to the New Economic Mechanism—Laos's implementation of market socialism—and policies designed to maintain cultural and economic sovereignty in response to the influences of its larger and more commercially robust neighbors (e.g., Thailand, China, and Vietnam). Though successful marketing in Laos is not without challenges, entrepreneurship and a tenable consumer market are increasingly evident in Vientiane and other communities along the Mekong. Laos, moreover, is instrumental in many transportation and distribution networks of the greater Mekong subregion and must be included as part of the regional strategy.

Malaysia

Aliah Hanim M. Salleh, Che Aniza Che Wel, and Anthony Pecotich conclude their evaluation of Malaysia's marketing practices and consumer behavior by suggesting that within the nation, there exists a great optimism, and that the feeling of national unity has never been stronger. This optimism seems well founded, for after seven years of growth above 8 percent, the nation has ample reason for confidence. Its economic successes have been hailed in both the national and international press. In the cultural context, the ethnic groups, while still seeking to maintain their unique traditions, appear to have a strong desire for harmonious coexistence that can only lead to greater cultural understanding. However, prosperity is bringing cultural change and a new kind of consumer and is presenting the nation with major problems. To take full advantage of economic progress, a nation must develop an infrastructure and a trained workforce that will animate and direct future growth. In this, Malaysia faces its biggest challenge and is, in some respects, at the crossroads. It may continue with uncontrolled growth and face the resultant chaos, traffic jams, pollution, and environmental devastation, or it may recognize that the future does not have to imitate the worst excesses of the West and proceed to invest in infrastructure and people. As the authors demonstrate, there is evidence to suggest that Malaysia is already addressing these problems. Those interested in understanding the developments of this culturally rich and economically rapidly developing nation will find this chapter indispensable.

Myanmar

In chapter 11, May Lwin, Anthony Pecotich, and Vicki Thein provide an overview of Myanmar (a.k.a. Burma), another of the ESEA nations moving, with hope, from a problematical past to a better future. Despite continuing political problems and trade embargoes, few would disagree that Myanmar is potentially a very promising and exciting market. While the West has been negative to Myanmar's internal politics and subsequent efforts to join the world trading community, its ESEA neighbors, taking a more long-term view, have been encouraging. In particular, the members of ASEAN have taken a pragmatic, welcoming posture toward the nation. The government of Myanmar has given some indication that it intends to join the emerging developing economies in Southeast Asia by emphasizing market reform, as it moves its economy into a transitional phase. The nation is undergoing changes, and as one of the region's countries that possesses extraordinary natural riches, some common law recollections, and almost 50 million consumers, Myanmar (Burma) must have a promising future.

New Zealand

An evolutionary appraisal of consumer behavior in New Zealand, once known as "the England of the South," is provided by Roger Marshall, Mike Potter, and Christina Kwai Choi Lee. This most southerly of the nations covered in this text has undergone startling economic and social change, as necessity forced it to de-emphasize economic links with England and Europe and focus its attention on ESEA. Culturally European (particularly Anglo-Saxon) in orientation, New Zealand has undergone restructuring not only in the much vaunted economic sense but also in its internal and external social attitudes and institutions. Internally, the increase of influence of the minorities (Maori) and Asian immigration are leading to the formation of a more worldly society. This internal change has been reinforced by the necessity to turn to and understand ESEA, with its cultural richness and variety. The authors provide a current, up-to-date enumeration of the forces operating in this small but intrinsically interesting market.

Papua New Guinea

Ronald Fullerton provides an important description of culture, politics, economics, marketing, and consumer behavior in Papua New Guinea, a nation that while being on the fringes of the region can, nonetheless, benefit from regional interaction. Its unexploited resources and shifting political structure indicate that it is a market of potential. To take full advantage of regional synergy, Papua New Guinea will have to develop its infrastructure and institutions, though within the country there remains some ambivalence about making these changes. The demand for capital by other more "attractive" parts of ESEA may reduce the availability of this important resource. However, with vision, there is little doubt that Papua can join in the general economic development of the region.

The Philippines

Albert Celoza, Jane Hutchison, and Anthony Pecotich, in their chapter on the Philippines, emphasize not only economic progress but also the positive political basis for that progression. The Philippines has emerged from colonialism and political turmoil and is showing signs of the long-promised economic expansion. The most recent economic figures are compelling, and it appears that the nation is transforming from one of the world's problem areas to a growing ordered democratic state with considerable assurance for potential investors.

Singapore

Jochen Wirtz and Cindy M.Y. Chung, in their chapter on Singapore, characterize the nation as a progressive, "wealthy society with good future prospects." Singapore's economic progress has been unmatched in the region. The small, island nation with virtually no natural resources but with a central location, political stability, good management, and resourceful people has advanced to be the new vanguard of economic development in the region. Wirtz and Chung suggest that a major reason for the progress may be attributed to the pragmatic orientation of the dominant ethnic group (the Chinese), with their strong commitment to education, discipline, and industriousness. Singapore is a small market that, despite the aging of its population, will continue to grow, although perhaps at a slower rate. The evaluation of consumer and marketing trends provides an excellent resource for practitioners and academics in the region.

Taiwan

Taiwan, which could be labeled as the "fractious Tiger," is another ESEA nation that has shown progress in the last decades that has been unprecedented. Y.E. Tang, in his accomplished treatment of the changing market and consumer behavior of this nation, provides a sound basis both for an understanding of the present position as well as an indication of possible future directions. From his evaluation, it becomes clear that if political problems can be overcome, Taiwan's position as a part of greater China will assure progress well into the twenty-first century. It is expected that Taiwan, with its large foreign reserves, will play a major part in regional growth. This optimistic assessment of possibilities in relation to the external environment should not obscure the existence of internal problems and challenges that go beyond the simply political. At least in part, the existence of the large foreign reserves can be attributed to the lack of investment in internal infrastructure and social development. The time is rapidly approaching when Taiwan will have to address internal conditions before the forces of cultural and social change and consumer demand restrain future progress. This chapter should assist those seeking an understanding of the nation for marketing purposes and Taiwanese scholars and policy makers interested in the progress of this nation.

Thailand

The emergence of Thailand as an important ESEA market serves as a point of departure for "Thailand: Consumer Behavior and Marketing," by Nittaya Wongtada, Busaya Virakul, and Anusorn Singhapakdi. In a thorough, informative chapter, these authors present a cogent picture of a dynamic nation in the throes of almost uncontrolled change. They point out that although economic progress has been made, it has produced serious problems. Despite the cultural self-confidence of the Thais concerning their resilience and capacity to absorb and cope with change, the challenges emanating from pollution, poor infrastructure, and the HIV/AIDS epidemic provide ominous threats to the fabric of their society. The authors, however, present a future scenario based on the expectation that prudent marketing management may contribute positively to the evolution of an organized and progressive society.

Vietnam

Vietnam was once a country that conjured images of war and destruction. Now, with its abundant natural resources, over 80 million consumers, and a shift toward a market economy, it has become a progressive force among the market socialist states of ESEA. Clifford Shultz, David Dapice, Anthony Pecotich, and Doan Huu Duc provide an overview of the historical events that led to the transformation and the emergence of one of the most compelling markets in the region. The authors also assess the current marketing and consumer trends and portray a country that has consumers who have embraced their new market economy. For all the changes, however, including foreign investment, the proliferation of goods and retail outlets, and the explosion of consumer culture, Vietnam remains a relatively difficult country in which to be successful on a large scale. In this sense, the authors refer to Vietnam as a country full of promise but with changing laws and practices that often confuse investors and render the process of successful market penetration difficult. Despite the difficulties, the authors conclude that visionary marketers who understand the commercial, political, and legal idiosyncrasies of this market and invest for the long term stand to prosper.

CONCLUSION

Despite the vivid metaphor of a roller coaster, with the obvious implication that trends go up and down, our approach to the nations and the region has been generally positive and optimistic. The reader has no doubt detected, even in the cautionary exculpations, a strong belief that ESEA has a bright future and will ride out rough stretches to become a growing global force. Despite memories of the financial crisis (as well as some concerns that more reforms are necessary) and very real threats from corruption, terrorism, environmental degradation, and pandemics, the generally pragmatic leadership and spirit of cooperation, economic strength, and demographics have carried the region through. The region is well and moving forward once again. Further, while some restructuring is essential and will cause some stress, the fundamental economic basics exist. The population is large and growing, the labor costs are low, many entrepreneurial opportunities are still apparent, in the majority of nations GDP generally continues to rise, and societal welfare continues to improve. This "good news" will exert additional pressure on the few laggards, whose leaders will need to redouble efforts to make the appropriate changes required to catch up. It is possible that myopia and cynicism within some countries could lead to instability and even bloodshed. Our hope is that obvious benefits of market orientation, greater transparency, and regional and global integration will stimulate the necessary steps to ensure further prosperity. The individual nations in the region have little other choice; the alternative is not acceptable to their peoples or to the world community in which they are increasingly embedded. Finally, it is inevitable that as in all texts of this kind events may overtake us and perhaps even prove us wrong, nonetheless, the chapters should provide scholars and practitioners with an understanding of the underlying forces that affect the markets, economies, marketing, and consumer behavior in this rich, dynamic region.

NOTE

1. This model and the discussion of it in this chapter include excerpts from a more intricate model and discussion in Shultz and Pecotich (1997).

REFERENCES

Abramowitz, Morton, and Stephen Bosworth. 2003. "America's Changing Role." *Foreign Affairs* 82(4): 119–28.

Bruton, C. 2004. "Critical Issues for Developing Asia." *Journal of Macromarketing,* 24(2), 173–77.

Chia, Hock Hwa, and Anthony Pecotich. 1988. "Multinational Management and ASEAN Regional Development." *Asia Pacific Journal of Management* 6(1): 161–74.

Claessens, S., S. Djankov, and C. X. Lixin. 2000. "Corporate Performance in the East Asian Financial Crisis." *The World Bank Research Observer* 15(1): 23–46.

Easterly, William. 2001. *The Elusive Quest for Growth: Economists' Adventures and Misadventures in the Tropics.* Cambridge: MIT Press.

Economist. 2000. "The Tiger and the Tech," February 3.

———. 2002. "East Asian Economies: The Lost (Half) Decade," June 4: 65–67.

———. 2003a. "Learning to Love Growing China," November 27.

———. 2003b. "The Lost (Half) Decade," July 4.

———. 2003c. "Survey: Asian Finance—The Weakest Link," February 6.

———. 2004a. "Corruption in South-East Asia: Who Will Watch the Watchdogs?" February 19.

———. 2004b. "Get Well Soon," January 29.

———. 2004c. "One Country One System," April 27.

———. 2004d. "Vietnam's Economy: The Good Pupil," May 6.

———. 2004e. "Time to Hit the Brakes," May 13.

Feldstein, M. 2002. "Financial Crisis in Emerging Market Economies: Overview of Prevention and Management." NBER Working Paper series, 8837, 1–37.

Fisman, R., and J. Svensson. 2000. "Are Corruption and Taxation Really Harmful to Growth?" Firm-level Evidence, World Bank Working Paper, 1–24.

Forbes, Dean. 1995. "Towards the 'Pacific Century': Integration and Disintegration in the Pacific Basin." In *The Far East and Australasia,* 26th ed. London: Europa Publications, 24–38.

Kim, S. H., and M. Haque. 2002. "The Asian Financial Crisis of 1997: Causes and Policy Responses." *Multinational Business Review* (Spring): 37–44.

Klein, Jill Gabrielle, Richard Ettenson, and Marlene D. Morris. 1998. "The Animosity Model of Foreign Product Purchase: An Empirical Test in the People's Republic of China." *Journal of Marketing* 62 (January): 89–100.

Krugman, P. 1997. "Whatever Happened to the Asian Miracle?" Available at http://web.mit.edu/krugman/www/perspire.htm.

Leger, John M. 1995. "Rags to Riches." *Far Eastern Economic Review,* October 5: 46–52.

Leeflang, Peter, and Fred van Raaij. 1993. "The Changing Consumer in the Netherlands: Recent Changes in Environmental Variables and their Consequences for Future Consumption and Marketing." *International Journal of Research in Marketing* 10(4): 345–63.

Malkiel, Burton G., and J. P. Mei. 1997. "Why Asia's Tigers Will Roar Again." *The New York Times,* December 21.

Masuyama, S., D. Vandenbrink, and S. Y. Chia, ed. 2000. *Restoring East Asia's Dynamism.* Singapore: Seng Lee Press Pte.

Meade, W., and R. Nason. 1991. "Toward a Unified Theory of Macromarketing: A Systems Theoretic Approach." *Journal of Macromarketing* 11(Fall): 72–82.

Meltzer, A. H. 1998. "Asian Problems and the IMF." *Cato Journal* 17(3): 267–74.

Parrinder, Geoffrey. 1995. The Religions of Asia." In *The Far East and Australasia,* 26th ed. London: Europa Publications, 15–24.

Pecotich, Anthony, and C. Shultz, ed. 1998. *Marketing and Consumer Behavior in East and South-East Asia.* Sydney: McGraw-Hill.

Pecotich, Anthony, and Hock Hwa Chia. 1992. "The Role of Multinational Corporation Characteristics and Strategic Actions in the Development of ASEAN Regionalism." *Journal of Global Marketing* 5(3): 63–87.

Phongpaichit, P., and C. Baker. 2000. *Thailand's Crisis.* Bangkok: Silkworm Books.

Schwab, Klaus, and Claude Smadja. 1994. "Power and Policy: The New Economic World Order." *Harvard Business Review,* November–December: 40–50.

Shultz, C., and A. Pecotich. 1997. "Marketing and Development in the Transition Economies of Southeast Asia: Policy Explication Assessment and Implications." *Journal of Public Policy and Marketing* 16(1): 55–68.

Wilkie, W., and E. Moore. 1999. "Marketing's Contribution to Society." *Journal of Marketing* 63(Special Issue): 198–218.

CHAPTER 1

AUSTRALIA

Changing Consumer Behavior and Marketing

JANET R. MCCOLL-KENNEDY,
SHARYN RUNDLE-THIELE, AND STEVE WARD

OVERVIEW

An overview of Australia in the new millennium is presented from a marketing and consumer behavior vantage point. After a brief historical introduction, the trends in the Australian environment, together with their implications for marketing management, are presented. The Australian economic climate is discussed, followed by the demographic, social, and cultural environment in Australia and the marketing implications. Australia is presented as a developed nation that has coped well with the recent global crises and that has an economy that is in good shape for the short-term future.

INTRODUCTION AND BRIEF HISTORICAL BACKGROUND

Australia, with about 19 million people living in an area approximately equal in size to the United States (minus Alaska), is located between the South Pacific and Indian oceans. The vast majority of Australia's population can trace their origins to Europe. In the 2001 census, around four and half million Australians were born overseas, and close to three million people spoke a language other than English. In recent times, there has been an increasing proportion of Asian immigration. In 1981, around 50 percent of immigrants were from Europe, and only 2.7 percent were from Asia. By 1991, North Asia accounted for 20 percent of all arrivals compared to 20 percent from Europe (Australian Bureau of Statistics 1981, 1991). By 1999–2000, immigration from North- and Southeast Asia accounted for around 34 percent of all arrivals in Australia (Australian Bureau of Statistics 2003). As will be discussed, the changes in immigration patterns for Australia are significant, because given the low fertility rate (1.75), immigration is primarily responsible for future population growth. Changes in immigration patterns thus imply future changes in preferences and tastes and development of more diverse market niches within the country.

There is a small, yet culturally significant, indigenous Aboriginal community representing less than 2 percent of the population. Aboriginal visual and oral culture was included in the opening ceremony of the 2000 Olympics. There is worldwide interest in Aboriginal art, with motifs being used on everything from decorative ties to aircraft flown by the nation's major airline carrier, Qantas.

To understand marketing and consumer behavior in Australia, it is important to briefly consider the nation's historical development. European settlement commenced in 1788 in the form of a British penal colony. Transportation of convicts, many of whom were Irish, continued until 1840 (Hancock 1995). These convicts could gain a "ticket of leave" after serving their sentences in Australia. Thus, they formed the basis of the working class. This contrasts with the majority of free white settlers who were skilled Protestant artisans from England and Scotland who came to this new country in search of a better life. As a result, two distinct classes were emerging by the late 1800s—the Protestant urban upper class and the highly unionized and predominately Catholic labor force. There have been tensions between these groups for much of Australia's history, and many cultural values of "a fair go," egalitarianism, and distrust of authority (the tall poppy syndrome) can be traced back to conflicts between these two groups.

The great depression of the 1890s brought about high unemployment and lowered living standards. It was during this difficult time that a basic minimum wage was established to protect the workers. National identity was a key issue, and the Commonwealth of Australia was formally established in 1901, bringing together the individual colonies into a single federation (Hancock 1995). Soon after this, the "White Australia" policy was introduced. This meant that settlement was restricted to Europeans. This white migration policy continued until the 1960s, when immigrants from the Middle East as well as other European countries were allowed entry. Asian migration commenced in the 1970s, and this has continued until today, making Australia a truly multicultural society (Hancock 1995). In the 1960s and 1970s, thousands migrated to Australia to pursue their dreams, culminating, for many, in the "time of excess" of the early 1980s, when the focus was on spending. The economy went into a recession in the late 1980s, and this continued into the early 1990s. The consumer emphasis of the late 1990s was on maintaining personal relationships, obtaining value for money, and getting back to basics, including refocusing on the family and home (McColl-Kennedy 1998). At the turn of the twenty-first century, Australia experienced more positive growth, but this was tempered with a greater sense of uncertainty, with the tragic events of Bali in October 2002. Despite a hardy, historical pioneering rough-and-ready bush image, modern Australia is an urban community with a social structure centered in the cities, particularly on the east coast.

ECONOMIC CLIMATE

The economic climate of the country influences consumer behavior. Key measures of the relative health of the economy include inflation, gross domestic product, employment rates, the balance of payments, interest rates, and finally, exchange rates. The interrelationships between these and other economic factors clearly affect the well-being of Australians. As shown in Table 1.1, in recent times, Australia has enjoyed low inflation, under 2 percent, compared to over 6 percent in the 1980s and twice this in 1974. Unemployment is currently under 6 percent, down from almost 11 percent in the mid-1990s. Although the terrorist attacks on the United States on September 11, 2001, and in Bali in October 2002 have created uncertainty in the world economy, many leading economists suggest that Australia's economy remains in relatively good shape and is well placed to absorb declines in the global economy despite the recent developments.

Economic Outlook

Reforms, including fiscal consolidation (e.g., tax reforms, debt reduction, and a reduction in balance of payment deficits), financial system reform, competition, and industrial restructuring,

Table 1.1

The Australian Economy

Year	Underlying inflation rate (%)	Unemployment rate—males (%)	Unemployment rate—females (%)	Participation rate—males (%)	Participation rate—females (%)	Balance of payments	Units of US$ per A$
1974	12.5	1.2	2.5	81.8	41.5	−921	1.49
1979	6.1	5.1	8.0	78.4	43.1	−3,624	1.13
1984	6.2	8.7	8.3	75.7	44.6	−7,386	0.92
1989	6.1	6.2	7.3	75.2	50.4	−17,329	0.89
1994	2.0	10.9	10.0	73.6	52.2	−15,399	0.71
1999	1.5	7.8	7.4	72.8	53.9	−9,227	0.63
2003	2.4	5.3	6.0	71.1	54.5	−12,135	0.75

Sources: Data from Australian Bureau of Statistics (ABS), *Australian Social Trends*, Catalog No. 4102.0 (2000); ABS, *Year Book Australia*, 1974, 1979, 1984, 1994, 1999, 2003, Catalog No. 1301.1 (various years); ABS, *Consumer Price Index*, Catalog No. 6401.0; ABS, *Australian Economic Indicators*, Catalog No.1350.0 (2000).

implemented largely during the 1990s, may ensure that the Australian economy remains in relatively good shape through the first decade of the new millennium, despite the global situation. The outlook of the Australian economy suggests that Australian consumers should remain optimistic and continue to spend, thus further stimulating the Australian economy. The latest figures from the Australian Bureau of Statistics (ABS) confirm this. Consumer expenditure on goods and services for the twelve months of 1999 had increased, on average, by 6 percent in real terms (taking out the impact of inflation) from a previous survey in 1993–94 (Australian Bureau of Statistics 2000). Over the same time period, average weekly earnings had increased in real terms by 12 percent. The ten-year trend (1991–2001) for the growth of consumption expenditure, as shown in Figure 1.1, shows an average real growth of 2.2 percent per year. While it is believed that increases in real incomes have driven increases in consumption, consumer debt commitments have also increased. At the end of 1994, they stood at A$4.39 billion, and at the end of 2003 they had more than doubled to A$18.40 billion (Australian Bureau of Statistics 2004). Of concern to a consumer-driven economy like Australia has been the decline of household disposable (after-tax) income. In 1959–60, this stood at 88 percent of gross income, and by 1999–2000, it had fallen to 76 percent of gross income (Australian Bureau of Statistics 2004). The long-term viability of the present consumer boom in the "lucky country" may thus one day come to an end, if real incomes of households do not continue to increase substantially over the next few years. This will be crucial given the high levels of household debt and a declining share of disposable income.

Employment Trends

Consideration of labor force participation rates can provide marketers with an understanding of drivers of some key consumption trends. In Australia, the most important long-term employment trend has been the increase in the participation rate of women in the workforce. In 1971, this stood at 37.1 percent, and in the latest census of 2001, had risen to 55.3 percent (Australian Bureau of Statistics 1971, 2001a). This increase in the participation rate of women in the workforce has had profound demographic changes on household structures and sizes, which will be dis-

Figure 1.1 **Real Final Consumption Expenditure* Per Capita**

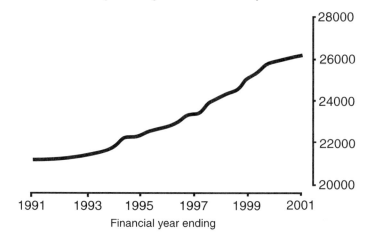

Financial year ending

Source: Australian System of National Accounts.
* Chain volume measure; reference year 1999–2000.

cussed later. On entering the workforce, women may delay having children, have fewer children, or not have children. Having more women in the workforce has also led to an increase in the number of two-income households. (In the 2001 census, around 43 percent of all families in Australia had both parents in the workforce.) The nature of consumer behavior also changes. For example, as the number of females in the workforce with dependent children increases, the requirement for convenience also increases. This is especially so given that male partners also tend to continue to work. As will be discussed in a later section on household expenditure, families are eating out more often and are buying takeout, frozen, and preprepared meals. These female labor force participation rates correspond with a growing demand for services, such as child care, dry cleaning, house cleaning, and gardening.

An increase in shopping and banking via telephone and the Internet are further examples of the importance being placed on convenience, particularly in households where both adults work full time. The Australian Bureau of Statistics (2003a) found that 23 percent of adults accessing the Internet used it to pay bills, 21 percent to access government services, and a further 15 percent to shop, up from 11 percent in 2001. Recent Internet sales in 2002 were A\$4 billion, double that in 2001 (A\$1.9 billion).

The recent deregulation of shopping hours and growth of large retail centers may be seen as a response by marketers to meet the growing demands of working women. The Australian Bureau of Statistics (2002) notes that average retail turnover per location increased from A\$17,500 in 1947 to A\$650,000 in 1992, indicating a growth in the size of retail establishments. This change has also been brought about because Australians are shopping fewer times and are spending more per shopping trip. This may also be the result of time pressures on two-income working families, and, as will discussed later, because those in full-time employment are working longer hours. The *ACNielsen Grocery Report* of 2003 found that the average number of shopping trips per year in 2002 was 134 times per year, down from 144 in 2000, while Australian shoppers spent more, on average, in 2002 (A\$42.82 per trip compared to A\$35.59 in 2000).

The second major employment trend has been the increased casualization of the workforce. During the past decade, there has been a substantial increase in the proportion of casual employ-

Figure 1.2

Growth of Casual and Other Employees, August 1988 = 100

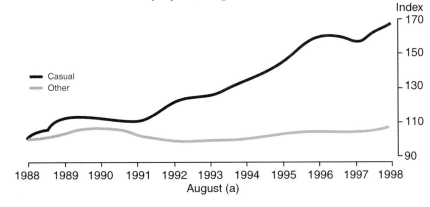

(a) For 1991, collected in July.

Source: Australian Bureau of Statistics, *Australian Social Trends,* Catalog No. 4102.0 (2000).

Table 1.2

Casual and Other Employees by Sex

	Casual employees		Other employees		Proportion of casual employees	
	August 1988 '000	August 1998 '000	August 1988 '000	August 1998 '000	August 1988 '000	August 1998 '000
Males	415.7	894.1	3,127.8	3,064.1	11.7	22.6
Females	737.3	1,052.0	1,821.2	2,234.6	28.8	32.0
Persons	1,152.9	1,946.1	4,949.0	5,298.7	18.9	26.9

Source: Australian Bureau of Statistics, *Australian Social Trends*, Catalog No. 4102.0 (2000).

ees, from 19 percent to 27 percent. Over the decade, the number of casual employees increased by more than 60 percent from 1,152,900 to 1,946,100, while the number of other employees increased slightly from 4,949,000 to 5,298,700. Figure 1.2 illustrates the growth rates. The sizeable increase in the number of casual employees has been due predominantly to a large increase in the number of casually employed males. As shown in Table 1.2, between 1988 and 1998, the number of male casual employees more than doubled, with an increase from 415,700 to 894,100. Over the same period, the number of noncasual male employees decreased by 2 percent from 3,127,800 to 3,064,100, indicating a major shift in the structure of the male workforce. Over the past decade, the number of female casual employees increased by 43 percent. Despite the difference in the rates of increase of casually employed males and females, females continued to represent a greater proportion of casual employees. In August 1998, more than half of the total casual employees were female.

The increasing casual labor force in Australia represents an opportunity for marketers who are able to tailor goods and services for this growing market segment. For example, traditional lending structures in Australia did not allow casual workers to obtain financing, largely due to their irregular incomes. Innovative lending products have recently emerged in the Australian market to cater to this market segment, and these products are generally characterized by higher fees or interest rates to counteract the increased risk to the lender. The home lending market provides a useful case study for marketers who wish to innovate and capture this growing market segment.

While the numbers of those in part-time work increased, people in full-time work reported working longer hours. In 1982, the average working hours per week equaled forty-two hours. By 2001, it had increased to forty-four hours per week (Australian Bureau of Statistics 2003b). Those working longer hours, greater than fifty hours per week, increased from 10 percent of the workforce in 1982 to 19 percent in 2002 (Australian Bureau of Statistics 2003b). This trend combined with the increased participation rates of women in the workforce means that convenience for consumers in Australia will remain an important decision criterion. It is also a key driver of the increase in demand for services.

DEMOGRAPHIC FACTORS

Key demographic factors include population size, growth, distribution, gender distribution, age distribution, and household composition. These will be discussed in this section. The size of a certain group will directly affect the market demand for products and services consumed by that group.

Population Distribution, Size, and Growth

According to the Australian Bureau of Statistics, Australia's population has grown from 3.8 million at the turn of the century to 19 million in 1999. The growth rate for Australia for the twelve months to June 1999 was the same as the overall world growth rate of 1.3 percent. This continued and steady growth will allow some product and service markets to grow, albeit slowly. Marketers considering exporting to Australia should give due consideration to the size of the Australian population. Despite the small population size, the population is concentrated, making the Australian market attractive to marketers. Australia's population is projected to grow from 19 million in 1999 to between 24.1 and 28.2 million in 2051, and up to as much as 31.9 million by 2101. Natural increase, more births than deaths, is projected to become negative between 2033 and 2046, and this is illustrated in Figure 1.3.

As shown in Figure 1.3, three estimates were made, and each series used different fertility rates and overseas migration estimates. Series I assumed a fertility rate of 1.75 and migration of 110,000; series II, 1.6 and 90,000; and series III, 1.6 and 70,000. Throughout the 1990s, Australia's annual population growth rate was around 1 percent. While similar growth rates are projected to continue for about the next ten years, these will decline to between 0.4 percent and –0.6 percent by 2051. Consequently, it is expected that many product and service markets will face declines in demand that could lead to consolidation in some markets.

As illustrated in Table 1.3, the highest growth between 1999 and 2051 is projected to occur in the Northern Territory (92 percent), Queensland (74 percent), and Western Australia (63 percent), well above the growth projected for Australia (34 percent). According to ABS projection, Queensland is projected to replace Victoria as the second most populous state between 2026 and 2038, while the population of the Australian Capital Territory (ACT) could overtake that of Tasmania between 2041 and 2047. The population of Tasmania is projected to decline. The capital cities are projected to experience larger percentages of growth than their respective balances,

Figure 1.3   **Total Australian Population: Observed and Projected**

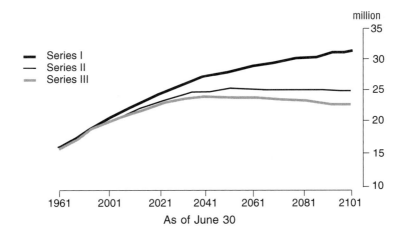

Source: Australian Bureau of Statistics, *Population Projections*, Catalog No. 3222.0 (2000).

Table 1.3

Population by State: Actual and Projected

	NSW '000	VIC '000	QLD '000	SA '000	WA '000	TAS '000	NT '000	ACT(b) '000	Australia total '000
Capital City 1999 Actual	4,041.4	3,417.2	1,601.4	1,092.9	1,364.2	194.2	88.1	309.9	12,109.2
2051 Projection	5,857.8	4,393.2	2,864.1	1,102.2	2,231.5	146.2	192.2	371.7	17,158.9
Total State 1999 Actual	6,411.7	4,712.2	3,512.4	1,493.1	1,861.0	470.3	192.9	310.2	18,966.8
2051 Projection	8,247.8	5,547.3	6,101.3	1,410.5	3,037.8	319.3	369.5	371.7	25,408.5

Source: Australian Bureau of Statistics, *Population Projections*, Catalog No. 3222.0 (2000).
    Note: NSW: New South Wales; VIC, Victoria; SA: South Australia; WA: Western Australia; TAS: Tasmania; NT: Northern Territory; ACT: Australian Capital Territory; QLD: Queensland.

resulting in further concentration of Australia's population within capital cities. Sydney and Melbourne are projected by the ABS to remain the two most populous cities in Australia at 5.9 million and 4.4 million, respectively, in 2051, followed by Brisbane (2.9 million).

    Associated with movement in the population has been considerable difference in the average income of each state of Australia. According to the ABS, Tasmania has an average income 17

Table 1.4

Regional Differences in Product Demand

Product	Best market	%	Worst market	%
Microwave ovens (percent who own)	WA	67	TAS	31
Eating in licensed restaurants (percent of population visiting)	NSW	59	TAS	46
White wine (percent of drinkers who have consumed in the last fourteen days)	NSW/ACT	51	QLD	44
Dark rum (percent of drinkers who have ever consumed)	QLD	22	VIC	9
Hair conditioner (percent who used six or more times in the last seven days)	TAS	43	QLD	30
Full-strength beer (percent of drinkers who have consumed in the past fourteen days)	NSW/ACT	40	VIC	31
Personal effects insurance (percent who have)	SA/NT	31	NSW/ACT	18
Flavored mineral water (percent who ever consumed)	VIC	45	WA	27
Bottled spring water (percent who ever consumed)	SA/NT	21	TAS	8
Corn chips (percent who ever eat)	QLD	48	TAS	36
Basketball (percent interested in)	WA	43	QLD	27
Netball (percent interested in)	SA/NT	23	QLD	15
Australian-rules football (percent interested in)	VIC	61	QLD	21

Source: AGB Consumer Market Profiles, 1992.

Note: WA: Western Australia; NSW: New South Wales; ACT: Australian Capital Territory; QLD: Queensland; TAS: Tasmania; SA: South Australia; NT: Northern Territory; VIC, Victoria.

percent below that of the national average of A$469 per week, followed by South Australia (9 percent below) and Queensland (6 percent below). States above the national average in 2000–2001 included the ACT, 24 percent above the average, and New South Wales (NSW) and Victoria, both at 3 percent above the national average. These different levels of wealth in each state are the result of population movement and greater employment opportunities in the service and government sectors of the ACT, NSW, and Victoria. As shown in Table 1.4, these differences in income and population growth in different states have created regional differences for a range of products and services.

Urbanization

Australians are generally living in closer physical proximity to each other, and in more populous urban centers. A relatively large increase in population density occurred in Australia during the twentieth century. At the start of the century, almost half the population lived on rural properties or in small towns (less than 3,000 people). In stark contrast, in 1996, most Australians (53 percent) lived in a city of close to, or more than, one million people. These city dwellers outnum-

Table 1.5

Urbanization in Australia in 1906 and 1996

	1906		1996	
Size of population center (number of people)	Number of centers	Percent of total population	Number of centers	Percent of Total population
Less than 3,000	. .	48.5	. .	18.2
3,000–9,999	54	6.3	191	5.8
10,000–99,999	19	11.7	98	13.3
100,000–539,000	4	33.6	8	9.6
950,000 or more	0	0.0	5	53.1
All population centers	77	100.0	302	100.0
		'000		'000
Total population (millions)		4,091.5		17,892.4

Sources: Australian Bureau of Statistics (ABS), *Australian Social Trends*, Catalog No. 4102.0 (2000); ABS, *Year Book Australia 1999*, Catalog No. 1301.0 (1999).

bered almost threefold those living in small towns and rural properties, whose proportion of the total population had fallen to 18 percent in 1996. This is summarized in Table 1.5.

It is important to remember that Australia remains one of the most sparsely populated nations. This has important implications for marketing managers, including small market sizes and logistical considerations. If we compare Australia with the United States, the city of Los Angeles, California, has a population that is similar in size to Australia in a far more concentrated area. Consequently, the distribution of goods in the Australian market can be considerably different when compared to more densely populated markets, such as that of the United States.

Gender Distribution

Australia was a male-dominated society at the dawn of the twentieth century. Males comprised 52 percent of the general population in 1901. By the middle of 1999, females had formed a slight majority of the general population (50.2 percent). However, today the number of females to males is about the same.

Age Distribution

The median age of the population has been steadily rising since the beginning of the 1970s due to the generally lower birth and mortality rates. In addition, women are marrying later in life and postponing their childbearing. As a result, fewer children are being born, on average, to each woman. As shown in Table 1.6, Australia's population is aging. One of the major causes of this is that people born during the baby boom (1947–61) will move into the older age groups (forty-five and over). Due to the relatively low fertility rates of the 1970s, 1980s, and 1990s, there are relatively fewer people taking their places in the younger age groups. Increasing life expectancy will also contribute slightly to the aging of the population. ABS population projections illustrated in Figure 1.4 show that the aging of Australia's population is likely to continue.

Table 1.6

Age Distribution in Australia, 1901–1999 (%)

Year	0–14	15–24	25–34	35–44	45–64	65 and over
1901	35.1	19.4	16.3	13.1	12.0	4.0
1999	20.7	14.2	15.2	15.4	22.2	12.2

Source: Australian Bureau of Statistics, *Population by Age And Sex, Australian States and Territories,* Catalog No. 3201.0 (2000).

Figure 1.4   **2051 Australia's Projected Population Age Structure**

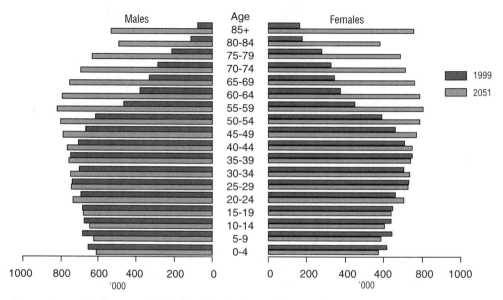

Source: Australian Bureau of Statistics, *Population Projections* (Catalog No. 3222.0).

The median age of thirty-five in 1999 is expected to increase to between forty and forty-two by 2021 and between forty-four and forty-seven by 2051. By 2051, the population aged sixty-five and over is projected to be at least double its present size, increasing from 12 percent of the population in 1999 to between 24 percent and 27 percent in 2051. The eighty-five and over age group numbered 241,100 (1.3 percent of the total population) in 1999. This group is projected to reach approximately 1.3 million in 2051, and between 1.3 million and 1.6 million in 2101. In 1999, the eighty-five and over age group was dominated by women, who made up 69 percent of the group. This proportion is projected to fall to 63 percent in 2021, to 59 percent in 2051, and to 57 percent in 2101, reflecting the increase in life expectancy of men and the narrowing gap in life expectancy between men and women.

Marketers must bear in mind that the population is aging and modify their products and service offerings accordingly. One of the largest opportunities for marketers relates to the increasing size of the forty-five and over group, as demand will increase considerably for many services, health-related products, leisure products, and holiday packages, to name a few. Consider the Australian

Pensioners Insurance Agency (APIA) that entered and gained significant market share in the Australian insurance market through innovative insurance products designed for pensioners. Benefits were offered by APIA that were highly desirable for this segment; for example, new for old replacement on all household contents. The outlook for marketers of items including durable goods and nappies or diapers is not as rosy, and these marketers can expect to face declining markets as population groups aged twenty-five to thirty-four decrease as a proportion of the total population. However, the younger age groups should not be neglected, because although relatively few children are being born per family, parents and other family members are spending a greater number of dollars per child compared with the past. It is also important for marketers to note that many Australian families, though having fewer children, will have two incomes, with around 43 percent of mothers participating in the workforce.

It is important for marketers to understand that media consumption varies greatly according to age. For example, older consumers watch a lot more television and read more newspapers than do younger segments. What they watch and read will also differ from younger consumers. Marketing successfully to older consumers will require a distinct marketing mix when compared to marketing to younger consumers. There is evidence to suggest that the older Australian population is heterogeneous. For example, the needs and behaviors of sixty-year-olds will differ from that of eighty-year-olds. As a result, marketing to segments of the senior market has the same requirements as marketing to any segment. That is, a tailored marketing mix reflecting the attitudes and behaviors of the segment will be required for each target segment.

Another notable demographic change that has recently emerged is the change in the transition to adulthood. In the 1950s, the teenage market emerged as an affluent demographic group, and marketers developed many products, both goods and services, to meet the needs of this first-time group. In the past decade, an even more important demographic group that marketers need to be aware of has been noted: the "young adults." A myriad of factors, including education, difficulties in establishing full-time employment, government assumptions that people twenty-five and under are dependent on their parents, and a lack of social pressure to marry, have all influenced the emergence of the "young adult" group. The importance of this group to marketers cannot be overstated. Traditional products targeting young adults will no longer suffice, as fundamental changes to this demographic segment have occurred. This segment now continues to live at home, whether for economic savings or convenience, or to travel to overseas destinations, rather than settle down into marriage.

Household Composition

With a female participation rate of around 55 percent and with 43 percent of couples with dependent children both working, it is clear that the majority of Australian households now have dual incomes. This phenomenon is increasing household purchasing power and the demand for luxuries such as boats, holiday homes, and second cars. There is also a greater demand for convenience products and services. Trends in household composition indicate that households are becoming smaller, and that the family with four or more children has almost disappeared, with many couples remaining childless. This is illustrated in Table 1.7. With fewer children per family, parents can spend more time working outside the home, and they can spend more of their money on purchases not relating to their children.

Factors influencing the decline in average household size include the aging of the population, the decline in fertility, the increased incidence of divorce, and the declining number of multigeneration households. Increased affluence has also played a role, in conjunction with

Table 1.7

Trends in Household Size, 1911–96

Census year	Occupants per dwelling			Total dwellings	Total population in private dwellings	Average household size
	One	Two to four	Five and over			
1911	n.a.	n.a.	n.a.	894,389	4,055,926	4.5
1921	97,620	529,744	479,646	1,107,010	4,875,428	4.4
1933	128,785	824,886	556,000	1,509,671	6,629,839	4.4
1947	152,029	1,168,781	552,813	1,873,623	7,026,760	3.8
1954	213,088	1,523,238	607,095	2,343,421	8,314,362	3.6
1961	285,360	1,743,173	753,412	2,781,945	9,870,494	3.6
1966	371,861	1,958,351	821,714	3,151,926	10,930,500	3.5
1971	497,816	2,319,179	853,559	3,670,554	10,955,250	3.0
1981	839,302	3,041,213	788,396	4,668,911	13,918,445	3.0
1991	1,130,749	3,759,850	751,797	5,642,396	15,717,020	2.8
1996	1,432,820	4,122,479	726,518	6,281,817	16,751,439	2.7

Source: Australian Bureau of Statistics, *Australian Social Trends*, Catalog No. 4102.0 (2000).
Note: n.a.: not available.

changes in housing affordability, the trend toward urbanization, and preferred living arrangements. These factors also reflect broader changes in Australian society and community attitudes and values. The number of households has grown faster than the population. This implies that consumption per household has grown more slowly than consumption per capita. Although it must be remembered that the diverse nature of family structures in Australia combined with the increased changes in economic conditions and increased participation rates of women in the workforce have created an uneven distribution of income across different types of households.

Figure 1.5 shows the composition of Australian families as of the 2001 census. It shows that a significant minority of Australian families (38.6 percent) can be thought of as traditional families of couples with dependent children. As shown in Figure 1.6, couples without children are expected by 2021 to outnumber those with children. These figures further reflect the effects of increases in the participation rate of women in the workforce, which has increased the median age of childbirth of females from 27.5 years in 1986 to 30 years by 2001 (Australian Bureau of Statistics 2003c). Recent figures suggest that around a quarter of women are likely to never have children (Australian Bureau of Statistics 2002a). This further reinforces the importance of the emerging market in Australia of DINKS (double income and no children), as well as shows that despite the fall in the size of Australian families, the market for children and youth products and services may remain healthy given the prevalence of dual-income families.

There are a growing number of single-person households, and these households clearly have different needs and wants when compared to larger households, which comprise three or more people. Product packaging will need to be suitable for small households, and single serves, in particular, will need to be available. For example, single-serve meals and individual slices of cakes are more appropriate for single-person households than households with large families. Some retailers have responded to this trend with self-service departments, where customers can select the exact number of items required.

Figure 1.5 **Family Types in Australia, 2001**

4,936,828 families

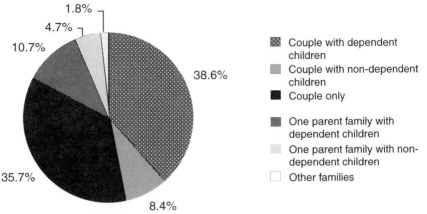

38.6%
Couple with dependent children

Couple with non-dependent children

Couple only

One parent family with dependent children

One parent family with non-dependent children

Other families

1.8%
4.7%
10.7%
35.7%
8.4%

Source: Derived from ABS (2002), *Census of Population and Housing: Selected Social and Housing Characteristics,* Australia 2001, Catalog No. 2015.0.

Figure 1.6 **Projected Family Types** (1996–2021*)

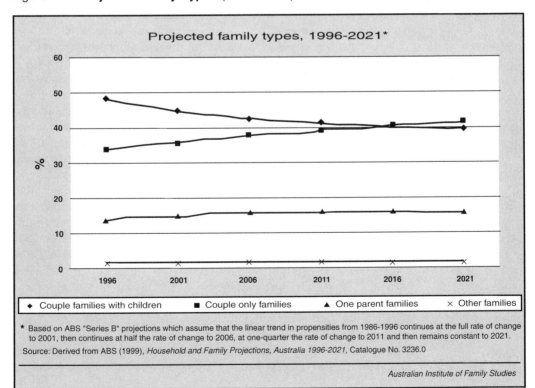

Projected family types, 1996-2021*

◆ Couple families with children   ■ Couple only families   ▲ One parent families   × Other families

* Based on ABS "Series B" projections which assume that the linear trend in propensities from 1986-1996 continues at the full rate of change to 2001, then continues at half the rate of change to 2006, at one-quarter the rate of change to 2011 and then remains constant to 2021.

Source: Derived from ABS (1999), *Household and Family Projections, Australia 1996-2021,* Catalogue No. 3236.0

Australian Institute of Family Studies

SOCIAL STRUCTURE AND CULTURE

Having discussed Australia's economy and demographics, we will now consider the social and cultural structure. In the last century, Australia has become an older, more culturally diverse, and much more urbanized society, holding wider religious affiliations and a workforce more concentrated in service-based, "white-collar" occupations.

Cultural Basics

While Australian society has undergone significant change since the 1950s, and particularly in the last twenty years, there is considerable agreement that the following are still core values of Australian society: egalitarianism, respect for the underdog, autonomy, democracy, family life, humanitarianism, "mateship," individualism, informality, and freedom. Australians have been strong believers in the rights of individuals, and many still hold to the view that they have just as much right as the next person on any given matter. This attitude, captured in the saying "Jack is as good as his master," has prevailed for much of Australia's history, certainly stemming from the early efforts to make Australia a classless society. Although modified by education, and by the increasing differences in income-earning ability and occupational status, these values are still strongly held.

One way to examine the resilience of these cultural values is to examine references made to them in two advertising campaigns, some thirty years apart. An advertising campaign for Winfield cigarettes in 1973 using Paul Hogan, a popular Australian identity and later Hollywood movie star of *Crocodile Dundee* (1986), showed the importance of mateship (his mate "Strop" was also included in the campaign), informality, individualism, and autonomy. The line "five smokes above the rest" featured in the advertisements for the brand is a reference to a cultural value of being just as good as or better than anyone else. The second advertisement for Nescafé espresso, from 2001, "Express yourself," featured another Australian larrikin, Nick Giannopoulos, another comedian of notoriety in Australia. The same sort of cultural references are used in the Nescafé advertisements, those of informality, individualism, humor, and that this Greek boy is just as good as the person next door (in this case, the reference is made to John Travolta, star of *Saturday Night Fever*). What is also interesting about comparing both advertisements is that even though the actors are from different ethnic subcultures (Australian Greek and Anglo-Australian), the cultural appeals are basically the same, for different product categories and over a time period of thirty years.

Another traditional attitude, "She'll be right, mate,"[1] is gradually being replaced by certain pessimism, largely as a result of higher levels of education and an increase in the interest in environmental issues. More Australians are reaching the conclusion that everything will not be all right if they do not start acting to conserve and protect the environment. There is also a greater interest developing in issues related to morality, ethics, total well-being (including mind and body), and spiritual matters, although for many Australians, the irreverence of humor extends to religious depictions. This is best illustrated by the T-shirt designs of Reg Mombassa from Mambo, a street and surf design and clothing business that exports many of these designs, showing the relaxed nature of the Australian culture to a global market. There has also been a trend toward a less formal lifestyle. This is evident in many facets of life, including increased demand for more informal dress, even in business, simpler home furnishings, and light entertainment. Some good examples of this include the popularity of the casual fit of clothes from Rivers (apparel store).

Table 1.8

Average Weekly Earnings (A$)

	May 1995	May 1996	May 1997	May 1998	May 1999	May 2000
All male employees: average weekly total earnings	652.70	671.50	687.10	714.50	733.00	757.70
All female employees: average weekly total earnings	429.90	441.10	457.40	468.30	483.00	504.80

Source: Australian Bureau of Statistics, *Average Weekly Earnings, States and Australia*, Catalog No. 6302.0 (2000).

Income

Table 1.8 shows average weekly earnings for male and female employees over the five years from May 1995 to May 2000. While average weekly earnings for female employees increased more than did average weekly earnings for male employees in the past year (4.5 percent compared to 3.4 percent), the level of earnings for females is still much lower than earnings for males, with average weekly earnings at A$504.80 for females compared to A$757.70 for males. While the gap between male and female earnings is decreasing, it is still large, with average weekly earnings for females remaining around 60 percent of those for men. While it might appear that cultural values of Australia are egalitarian, the reality is that there is great disparity in incomes. According to the ABS (2001), in 2000–2001, the incomes of the top 10 percent wealthiest people were four times (3.97) those of the lowest 10 percent or poorest people. A comparison of these figures with those of 1994–95 suggests that the gap between richest and poorest is increasing. The multiple of the richest 10 percent income with the poorest 10 percent income moved from a ratio of 3.77 in 1994–95 to 3.97 in 2000–2001.

Table 1.9 shows average weekly total earnings for different occupation groups and categories of employees in May 1998. Average weekly total earnings vary considerably across occupations, with persons in lower-skilled jobs tending to receive lower wages. In May 1998, full-time managers and administrators received estimated average weekly total earnings of $1,236.00, while elementary clerical, sales, and service workers earned on average $552.20. Note that the growth of many occupations with those of higher incomes occurred in the states of New South Wales, Victoria, and to lesser extent, Western Australia, explaining in part the differences in average incomes (and hence, market potential) of each state.

Expenditure

In 1998–99, Australian households spent an average of $699 per week on goods and services. The level and pattern of expenditure differs between households, reflecting characteristics such as income, household composition, household size, and location. The level of household expenditure differs between households with different main sources of income. For example, in 1998–99, households relying mainly on employee income had the highest average weekly expenditure at $866, while households with the primary source of income coming from government pensions and allowances had the lowest average weekly expenditure at $365.

Table 1.9

Average Weekly Total Earnings for All Employees in Major Occupation Groups, May 1998 (A$)

Occupation	Males	Females	All employees
Managers and administrators	1,260.60	1,015.70	1,205.30
Professionals	928.40	680.60	789.60
Associate professionals	833.20	587.70	731.90
Tradespersons and related workers	688.00	395.20	658.60
Advanced clerical and service workers	715.10	510.80	537.70
Intermediate clerical, sales, and service workers	599.90	429.30	475.20
Intermediate production and transport workers	675.30	409.20	630.30
Elementary clerical, sales, and service workers	395.30	289.90	327.30
Laborers and related workers	480.90	319.90	416.20
All occupations	729.80	484.00	610.20

Source: Australian Bureau of Statistics, *Employee Earnings and Hours, Australia*, Catalog No. 6306.0 (2000).

The pattern of household expenditure also varies between these groups. For example, households with principal sources of income from government pensions and allowances spent proportionately more than the other groups on essentials, such as current housing costs (16 percent of household expenditure, compared to 14 percent for households relying mainly on employee income) and food and nonalcoholic beverages (22 percent, compared to 18 percent for households relying mainly on employee income). Proportionately less was spent on some of the more discretionary items, for example, recreation (11 percent, compared to 13 percent for households relying mainly on employee income), and this is illustrated in Table 1.10. A comparison of the 1998–99 figures with those of 1993–94 (see Australian Bureau of Statistics 2000i) shows that the largest increases in expenditure occurred with services (25 percent) and transport (26 percent). These increases are probably due to the large number of two-income couples. For example, spending on motor vehicles was largely responsible for increased expenditure on transport, and two-income couples may have purchased more than one car per household. The increase in services can also be seen as a response to the needs of two-income families. This can be partially explained by the use of child care by about a third (34 percent) of two-income couples and, as mentioned, the use of additional services, such as gardening and a higher amount spent on education of children.

Education

At the turn of the century, fewer than one in three (31 percent) fourteen- to fifteen-year-olds still attended school (Table 1.11). Government policies, such as the extension of the compulsory school age and the need to undertake postschool education to acquire marketable skills to compete in the changing job market, have resulted in teenagers staying in the education system longer, and older Australians being more likely to be studying. In 1996, over half of all eighteen- to nineteen-year-olds (53 percent) were attending an educational institution, along with 12 percent of all Australians aged twenty years or older.

Table 1.10

Household Expenditure by Principal Source of Household Income, 1998–99

	Unit	Employee income	Own business	Government pensions and allowances	Other[a]	All households[b]
Mean gross weekly income	$	1,216	980	308	545	879
Expenditure (as percent of total expenditure)						
Current housing costs (selected dwelling)	%	14.0	12.1	16.2	10.5	13.9
Domestic fuel and power	%	2.3	2.8	3.8	2.7	2.6
Food and nonalcoholic beverages	%	17.6	18.8	21.7	16.7	18.2
Alcoholic beverages	%	3.1	3.2	2.0	2.5	2.9
Tobacco	%	1.4	1.5	2.4	0.9	1.5
Clothing and footwear	%	4.8	4.8	3.9	4.0	4.6
Household furnishings and equipment	%	6.0	5.7	5.6	7.3	6.0
Household services and operation	%	5.5	6.1	7.7	6.0	5.9
Medical care and health expenses	%	4.4	5.4	4.5	6.8	4.6
Transport	%	17.6	15.8	13.5	16.6	16.9
Recreation	%	12.7	13.1	11.2	15.3	12.7
Personal care	%	2.0	1.8	2.1	2.0	2.0
Miscellaneous goods and services	%	8.7	9.0	5.3	8.7	8.2
Total	%	100.0	100.0	100.0	100.0	100.0
Average weekly expenditure on all goods and services	$	866	745	365	638	699
Estimated number of households	'000	4,083	422	1,938	581	7,123

Source: Australian Bureau of Statistics, *Australian Social Trends*, Catalog No. 4102.0 (2001).

[a]Comprises households where the principal source of income was in the form of superannuation or annuity; interest on financial institution accounts, investments or property rent; scholarships; workers' compensation; accident compensation; maintenance or alimony; or regular income not elsewhere classified.

[b]Includes households with a principal source of income that was undefined because total income was zero or negative.

In May 1999, 5.5 million people aged fifteen to sixty-four (44 percent of this population) had completed a recognized postschool qualification, as shown in Table 1.12. This has increased over the past decades from 36 percent in 1984. Of those with postschool qualifications, one-quarter held a skilled vocational qualification (such as a trade qualification), and a further one-quarter

Table 1.11

Rates of Participation in Education, 1911 and 1996 (%)

Age group	1911	1996
5 or younger	9.1	11.9
6–11	92.5	100.0
12–13	85.2	100.0
14–15	31.2	97.4
16–17	8.7	81.0
18–19	3.3	53.4
20 and over	0.2	12.4
All ages	17.4	28.0

Source: Australian Bureau of Statistics, *Social Trends*, Catalogue No. 4102.0 (2000).

reported holding bachelor degrees. The smallest category comprised those with a higher degree, reported by 0.2 million people (4 percent of those with postschool qualifications). The twenty-five- to thirty-four-year-olds and thirty-five- to forty-four-year-olds were those most likely to hold qualifications. Bachelor degrees were the most common qualifications for twenty-five- to thirty-four-year-olds (31 percent of all those with postschool qualifications), while skilled vocational qualifications were slightly more common for thirty-five- to forty-four-year-olds (26 percent of all those with postschool qualifications).

Occupation

There has been a large shift in employment away from the primary production industries, such as agriculture, forestry, and fishing, toward employment in service industries engaged in activities such as finance, insurance, property management, health, education, and administration, and this is illustrated in Figure 1.7.

Changing Lifestyles and Attitudes

A number of major lifestyle changes have significantly affected consumer behavior. Most notable are the changing roles of men and women and an increased interest in health. With more women in the workforce, men are handling more of the shopping and housework duties traditionally performed by females. Marketers aware of these trends have responded with promotional campaigns that feature males engaged in these activities. With increasing independence and disposable incomes, women are demonstrating an increased interest in luxury goods and services, such as body massages, facials, perfumes, home decorator items, and holidays.

There is a growing segment of consumers placing greater emphasis on overall well-being, in particular, a healthier way of living. These consumers are eating less fat, salt, and sugar, and are drinking less alcohol and coffee. Marketers in Australia have already commenced responding to this trend by offering more "light," "low-cholesterol," and "low-fat" products. The 2003 *ACNielsen Grocery Report* found that 40 percent of Australians avoided foods they considered as unhealthy, while 36 percent bought more fresh chilled food. There was, however, a significant minority of Australians who only cooked when they had to (36 percent) or reported that they did not have time to cook. There is thus a large group of Australians whose food preparation is centered on convenience rather than health.

It is also clear that, according to the ABS (2003d), Australians are becoming less healthy. In 2001,

Table 1.12

Persons Aged 15–64, by Educational Attainment, May 1999

| | Age group (years) | | | | | |
Educational attainment	15–24 '000	25–34 '000	35–44 '000	45–54 '000	55–64 '000	Total '000
With postschool qualifications						
Higher degree	*2.2	45.8	81.8	83.9	31.1	244.8
Postgraduate diploma	11.2	64.4	90.5	83.9	26.6	276.5
Bachelor degree	172.5	458.3	378.1	278.4	113.9	1,401.2
Undergraduate diploma	63.5	135.8	176.6	159.6	84.0	619.5
Associate diploma	53.0	113.5	107.5	80.6	30.8	385.4
Skilled vocational	125.3	386.2	404.3	297.7	204.8	1,418.3
Basic vocational	172.3	289.2	290.2	226.4	128.5	1,106.6
Total	600.0	1,493.2	1,529.1	1,210.5	619.6	5,452.4
Without post-school qualifications						
Completed highest level of school						
Attending tertiary in May 1999	541.8	85.7	37.0	9.3	*3.5	677.3
Not attending tertiary in May 1999	336.7	436.3	337.5	304.9	184.0	1,599.3
Total	878.5	522.0	374.5	314.2	187.4	2,276.6
Did not complete highest level of school						
Attending tertiary in May1999	125.9	49.7	44.1	20.2	*5.1	245.1
Not attending tertiary in May 1999	369.0	753.4	934.3	945.7	816.2	3,818.7
Total	494.9	803.1	978.5	965.9	821.3	4,063.8
Total	1,374.6	1,326.9	1,355.1	1,283.1	1,014.1	6,353.7
Still at school	673.8	.8	1.6	0.3	0.0	676.5
Total	2,648.4	2,821.8	2,884.8	2,493.9	1,633.7	12,482.6

Source: Australian Bureau of Statistics, *Transition from Education to Work, Australia*, Catalog No. 6227.0 (2000).

* *Note:* Similar proportions of men and women hold bachelor degrees and associate diplomas. Women were more likely to have qualifications at the basic vocational, undergraduate diploma, and postgraduate diploma levels. Men were more likely to have qualifications at the skilled vocational and higher degree levels.

Figure 1.7   **Employment by Industry, 1901 and 1996**

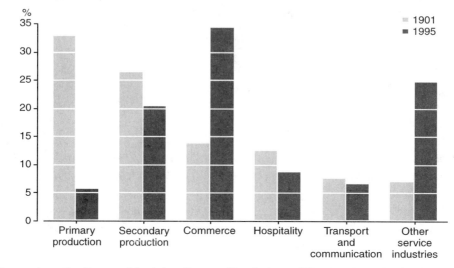

Source: Australian Bureau of Statistics, *Census of Population and Housing, Australia,* Catalog No. 2017.0 (2000).

more than 6.5 million Australians were overweight or obese. People were also more likely to engage in leisure activities that involved little if any physical activity. For example, watching television accounted for 36 percent of all free time. Average time spent on outdoor activities on weekends in 1997 was only 11 minutes for males and 8 minutes for females. It appears that Australians' concern for health extends perhaps only to what they eat, and even this is tempered by the desire for convenience.

There is a wide range of changes in Australian society that suggests that Australian consumers may be becoming less loyal. Consumers are more cynical and less trusting than in previous eras (Phillips 1999), they are more self-centered, and they tend to seek instant gratification (Neal, Quester, and Hawkins 2000). These characteristics are also displayed in many personal relationships in Australia, with partners separating because they are unwilling to put in the extra effort to maintain their personal relationships. If there is a link between social behavior and consumer behavior, there may be a decline in loyalty. It is a possibility that Australian consumers in the new millennium may be less loyal than in the past. Alternative marketing strategies may be required in the future, and the current importance of loyalty and customer retention strategies may be misguided.

Concern for Environmental Problems

The attitudes of people influence corporate decision making on environmental issues; the ABS has conducted two household surveys to gather a range of information on the views and attitudes of adult Australians on environmental issues. By relating the two sets of data, it is possible to compare the environmental views of adult Australians as they have aged; the eighteen- to twenty-four-year-olds of 1992, for example, are the same group (or cohort) being sampled as the twenty-five- to thirty-one-year-olds in 1999, seven years later. The results are highlighted in Figure 1.8.

Figure 1.8 shows that, for every age group, there has been a decline in the proportion of people concerned about environmental problems. Reduced levels of concern for environmental problems suggest that marketers should place less emphasis on environmental issues such as recyclability and reuse of products than in the recent past.

Figure 1.8 **Environmental Concerns**

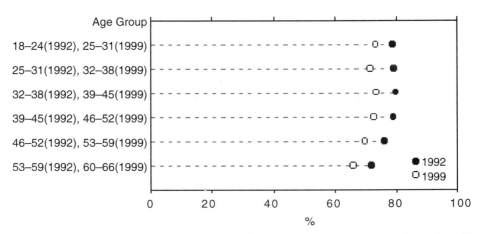

PERSONS CONCERNED ABOUT ENVIRONMENTAL PROBLEMS, Comparison of Cohorts—1992 and 1999

Source: Australian Bureau of Statistics, *Environmental Issues. People's Views and Practices*, Catalog No. 4502.0 (2000).

Immigration

According to ABS figures, Australia entered the twentieth century as an overwhelmingly Christian nation, with inhabitants who had been born almost exclusively in Australia, the United Kingdom, or Ireland. Australia ended the century with about 16 percent of its people born in other countries. While still predominantly Christian, the proportion of Australians affiliating with the Christian faith in 1996 (78 percent) was considerably less than it was in 1901 (98 percent), as seen in Table 1.13. Much of this change to the cultural composition of Australian society was generated by large-scale postwar migration and a growing tendency for Australians not to affiliate with any religion.

As mentioned, in recent times, there has been a change in immigration patterns, more from European countries to those of the southeast and northeast regions. This dramatic change in immigration has already influenced the taste preferences of both Asian and non-Asian Australians. The *ACNielsen Grocery Report* of 1993 showed a 12 percent growth in Asian foods, making it the most popular of the "ethnic" cuisines in Australia, worth around A$100 million.

As shown in Table 1.14, there are significant differences in the consumer behaviors of various ethnic subcultures within Australia. Italian households have the highest level of home ownership (around 80 percent) of any ethnic group, about double that of households of those born in Australia (around 40 percent [38.7 percent]). This is closely followed by Greek households, around three quarters (74.5 percent) of whom own their own homes. This figure is surprising, given that the average weekly income of Greek households at $811.52 is below that of Australian households at $880.66. Table 1.13 also shows that Greek, Italian, and Vietnamese households spend more on food and nonalcoholic beverages than do Australian households, yet they spend significantly less on recreation.

Such expenditure patterns may reflect the greater importance of the family and extended family in these ethnic households. The higher levels of home ownership by Greeks and Italians in Australia show the importance these ethnic cultures attach to wealth creation for future generations. For example, it is common for many Italian families to own more than one property, often accumulating one piece of real estate per family member. Property is often used as a means of

Table 1.13

Cultural Diversity, 1901 and 1996 (%)

	1901	1996
Birthplace		
Australia	77.2	77.2
New Zealand	0.7	1.7
Europe	20.0	12.9
U.K. and Ireland	18.0	6.6
Other	2.0	6.4
Asia	1.2	5.9
Other	0.8	2.2
Total	100.0	100.0
Religious affiliation		
Christian	98.1	77.9
Anglican	40.5	24.2
Catholic	23.2	29.7
Other	34.4	24.0
Jewish	0.4	0.5
Other affiliation	1.0	3.3
No affiliation	0.5	18.3
Total	100.0	100.0
	'000	'000
Total population	3,773.8	17,752.8
Indigenous population	93.0	386.0

Source: Australian Bureau of Statistics, *Australian Social Trends*, Catalog No. 4102.0 (2000).

financing retirement by both Italians and Greeks, and this is indicated in Table 1.14 by the low levels of expenditures on life insurance and superannuation by both of these groups.

Indigenous Australians continue to be a relatively small but very important part of Australia's rich cultural tapestry. In 1901, there were an estimated 93,000 Aboriginal and Torres Strait Islanders. By 1996, their numbers had grown to 386,000.

IMPLICATIONS FOR MARKETING

Australia's population is relatively sophisticated and multicultural. Consumers are generally well educated and require informative answers to their product and service inquiries. With considerable immigration over the years, first principally from the United Kingdom and Europe, and then more recently from Asia, a wide range of customs, beliefs, values, food, and goods and services preferences can be found. There are also many subcultures, namely, Aboriginal, Greek, Italian, Chinese, Vietnamese, and other ethnic populations, and so it is important for marketers to be aware that each subculture has distinctive needs and wants. The influence of subculture tends to be strongest where a significant number of the group members are geographically grouped together. For instance, in the suburbs of Kilkenny in Adelaide and Westend in Brisbane, there are large Vietnamese communities. Consumers from these groups often have preferences for particular goods and services, such as food and food-preparation items. As previously noted, the availability of goods and services catering to these subcultures' needs has changed many Australians' perceptions of food options and combinations.

While Australia could be regarded as a Christian country, an increasing proportion of consum-

Table 1.14

Ethnic Market Segments in Australia (Expenditure, Income, and
Home Ownership by Country of Birth)

Expenditure group	Australia	Italy	Greece	Vietnam
Current housing costs	95.78	62.72	73.14	96.90
Food and nonalcoholic beverages	125.37	138.90	152.58	139.39
Recreation	90.03	65.86	55.05	60.39
Superannuation and life insurance	22.59	13.64	7.79	16.66
Household characteristics:				
Average weekly household income	880.66	923.66	811.52	737.65
Percent of owners without a mortgage	38.70	79.50	74.50	30.40
Percent of population	38.70	4.60	2.20	0.90

Source: Australian Bureau of Statistics, *Consumer Expenditure Survey 1998–99*, Catalog No. 6530.0
(1999), pp. 24–25.

ers are non-Christian. Major non-Christian groups in Australia include Muslims, Buddhists, Jews, and Hindus. Practicing members of these religious groups observe certain religious days, eat or abstain from eating certain types of foods, and wear specific types of clothing. Such beliefs and customs influence consumer behavior, and marketers need to be aware of product and service requirements and to think about how products are presented to consumers, for instance, in terms of the colors used in promotional campaigns.

Although Australia's population is relatively small by world standards, it is certainly not homogeneous. It would be a mistake, therefore, to assume that Australians are exactly like the residents of the United States, and that few or no changes are required regarding products when entering the Australian market. Australia's population is aging. However, again, it is important not to think that older consumers are all alike. Targeting specific subsegments of the mature consumer segment is required. This is applicable to the other segments of the population as well.

Australian consumers are seeking increasingly more information on products and services. They expect to obtain this information quickly and are using electronic media, such as the Internet, to gather up-to-date information. Furthermore, Australian consumers want their complaints dealt with quickly and fairly. It is not sufficient in the Australian market to acknowledge a complaint; it is critical that complaints be addressed and then resolved satisfactorily.

In the new millennium, it is important to recognize that although Australia is located in the Asia-Pacific region, Australia is very much a part of the global marketplace. Marketers must ensure that promotional materials and messages are realistic, with those portrayed in the advertisements reflecting the many lifestyles of Australian consumers. Certainly, they should represent the various cultural and social groups in the population.

CONCLUSION

The new millennium is exciting yet challenging. To be successful in these ever-changing times, marketers must continue to research the Australian market on a regular basis and to thoroughly understand consumers and how to handle their complaints. Marketers should not be fooled by the generally informal behavior of Australians. Australian consumers are sophisticated, generally well educated, increasingly demanding of organizations, and generally global in outlook.

NOTES

This chapter is based on a continuation of the earlier work by Janet R. McColl-Kennedy (1998), Australia: Changing consumer behavior. *Marketing and consumer behavior in East and South-East Asia*, ed. A. Pecotich and C. J. Shultz II. Sydney: McGraw-Hill, 25–62.

    1. This is a colloquial Australian phrase meaning approximately "Don't worry, things will turn out all right."

REFERENCES

ACNielsen. 1993. *ACNielsen Grocery Report 1993* (Australia).
———. 2003. *ACNielsen Grocery Report 2003* (Australia).
Australian Bureau of Statistics. 1971. *Year Book Australia 1971* (Catalog No. 1301.0).
———. 1975. *Year Book Australia 1974* (Catalog No. 1301.0).
———. 1981. *Year Book Australia, 1981* (Catalog No. 1301.0).
———. 1991. *Year Book Australia, 1991* (Catalog No. 1301.0).
———. 1999. *Year Book Australia 1999* (Catalog No. 1301.0).
———. 2000. *Australian Social Trends* (Catalog No. 4102.0).
———. 2000a. *Australian Economic Indicators* (Catalog No. 1350.0).
———. 2000b. *Population by Age And Sex, Australian States and Territories* (Catalog No. 3201.0).
———. 2000c. *Population Projections* (Catalog No. 3222.0).
———. 2000d. *Environmental Issues, Peoples Views and Practices* (Catalog No. 4502.0).
———. 2000e. *Employee Earnings and Hours, Australia* (Catalog No. 6306.0).
———. 2000f. *Average Weekly Earnings, States and Australia* (Catalog No. 6302.0).
———. 2000g. *Transition from Education to Work, Australia* (Catalog No. 6227.0).
———. 2000h. *Census of Population and Housing, Australia* (Catalog No. 2017.0).
———. 2000i. *Household Expenditure Survey. Summary of Findings* (Catalog No. 6530.0).
———. 2000j. *Household Income and Income Distribution* (Catalog No. 2000–01).
———. 2001. *Year Book Australia 2001 Centenary Article: Household Income and Its Distribution* (Catalog No. 1301.0).
———. 2001a. *Census of Population and Housing, Australia* (Catalog No. 2017.0).
———. 2002. *Year Book Australia: Service Industries. The Changing Face of the Retail Industry: 1948 to 1992* (Catalog No. 1301.0).
———. 2002a. *Australian Social Trends* (Catalog No. 4102.0).
———. 2003. *Year Book Australia: Population, International Migration* (Catalog No. 1301.0).
———. 2003a. *Household Use of Information Technology, Australia* (Catalog No. 8146.0).
———. 2003b. *Australian Social Trends. Work* (Catalog No. 4102.0).
———. 2003c. *Australian Social Trends. Family and Community Living Arrangements: Changing Families* (Catalog No. 4102.0).
———. 2003d. *Australian Social Trends. Health: Health Risk Factors Among Adults* (Catalog No. 4102.0).
———. 2004. *Lending Finance, Australia* (Catalog No. 5671.0).
Hancock, I. R. 1995. "Australia: History." In *The Far East and Australasia,* 26th ed., 78–83. London: Europa.
McColl-Kennedy, J. R. 1998. "Australia: Changing Consumer Behavior." In *Marketing and Consumer Behavior in East and South-East Asia*, ed. A. Pecotich and C. J. Shultz II, pp. 25–62. Sydney: McGraw-Hill.
Neal, C., Pascale Quester, and D. Hawkins. 2000. *Consumer Behaviour: Implications for Marketing Strategy*, 2nd ed. Sydney: McGraw-Hill.
Phillips, M. 1999. Next Up: A Future Imperfect. *Marketing and e-Business*, March: 15–23.
Shoebridge, N. 1992. *Great Australian Advertising Campaigns.* Sydney: McGraw-Hill.

CHAPTER 2

BRUNEI DARUSSALAM

Consumption and Marketing in an Islamic Monarchy

LEONG VAI SHIEM AND TAN SIEW EE

OVERVIEW

Located on the island of Borneo, Brunei Darussalam is one of the smallest nations in the East Asia, Southeast Asia, Australia, and New Zealand (ESEA) region; however, it is also one of the wealthiest. Among the members of the Association of Southeast Asian Nations (ASEAN), it is exceptional in many ways, with a uniquely wealthy consumer market where nearly all the products are imported. As an oil-rich monarchy dominated by Islam, it is cautiously turning toward the developed world in an attempt to ensure a prosperous future. In this chapter, an attempt is made to provide an informed introduction to consumer behavior and marketing in this little-known Southeast Asian nation.

INTRODUCTION

Brunei Darussalam is one of Asia's wealthiest nations, with very high per capita income derived from its abundant oil and gas reserves. However, its gross domestic product (GDP) per capita has followed a downward trend in the past decade due to fluctuations in the world oil and gas industry, the effects of the 1997 Asian financial crisis, and the collapse of a huge local construction conglomerate in 1998. The Bruneian market is unique, very small but wealthy, with consumers of high-spending character. Nearly all products in the country are imported from abroad. It is therefore interesting to look in depth into the nature and patterns of consumer behavior in Brunei before analyzing the marketing practices in the country. The first section in this chapter focuses on the macroenvironmental factors, the importance of the natural resources of the country, which essentially shape its economic and social development programs, its demographic characteristics, the institutional aspects of the monarchical system and the national philosophy, and also, the economic and sociocultural policies of the government. The second part of the discussion turns to the relatively price-insensitive and high-spending consumers who reside primarily in the urban areas. As will be explained later, consumption patterns in Brunei are highly influenced or governed by the state philosophy: Brunei is a Malay Islamic Monarchy. Following an understanding of the patterns of consumer behavior and the marketing practices in Brunei, discussions eventually lead to the final section, which emphasizes the importance of relationship marketing and customer retention in the marketplace.

NATURAL ENVIRONMENT

Sharing the Borneo Island with the Malaysian states of Sabah and Sarawak and the Indonesian province of Kalimantan, Brunei is Borneo's smallest independent territory, with the smallest population, yet one with the highest standards of living. It is bound to the northern coastline of about 161 kilometers along the South China Sea and on all other sides by the Eastern Malaysian state of Sarawak. Covering an area of 5,765 square kilometers, Brunei is divided into four districts: Brunei/ Muara, the smallest, yet with the highest density of the four administrative districts, including the capital Bandar Seri Begawan; Tutong, a rural district housing many ethnic tribes; Belait, the oil town of the country; and Temburong, divided from the rest of the state by the Limbang district of Sarawak, and the least populated district in Brunei.

Almost 75 percent of the land area in Brunei is undeveloped and covered by tropical rainforest, with about 95.94 percent of the land area belonging to the government and the rest owned by private landowners. In 1986, of the total land owned by individuals, 94.37 percent was used for agriculture, 2.85 percent for housing, 0.25 percent for business, 2.13 percent for light and heavy industry, 0.15 percent for building, and the rest, 0.35 percent, for other land use (Brunei Government 1999). The government has allocated several sites for the development of various agricultural commodities, such as production of broilers, poultry layers, goats, cattle, deer, fruits, vegetables, and coffee, among others.

With the substantial land area covered by primary tropical rainforest, logging could be considered as one of the country's potential sources of income. Yet, logging in Brunei is still at the infancy level, and the government has set up several conservation policies and expanded the existing forest reserves. Brunei is able to forgo logging activities, compared to its neighbors Sabah and Sarawak, because of the high income generated from the oil and natural gas sector.

Brunei's most valuable resources—oil and gas—essentially shape the economic development and social structure of the country. The main exports for the country consist of three major commodities: crude oil, petroleum products, and liquefied natural gas (LNG). This sector generates more than 80 percent of the nation's income. Brunei is the third largest oil producer in Southeast Asia, with an average output of 163,000 barrels a day, and is also the world's fourth largest producer of LNG.

The government draws oil revenue for the country from its 50 percent stakes in the four companies of the Brunei Shell group. The oil industry in Brunei is monopolized by four companies: Brunei Shell Petroleum (BSP), which is essentially responsible for exploration, production, and refining of crude oil; Brunei LNG, owned jointly by the government, Shell, and the Mitsubishi Corporation of Japan; Brunei Coldgas, which purchases the LNG; and Brunei Tanker, which transports the LNG to Japan, where it is used by the Tokyo Electric Power Company, the Tokyo Gas Company, and the Osaka Gas Company (Gunn 2001). In 2001, a fully government-owned entity, Brunei National Petroleum Company Sendirian Berhad (in short, PetroleumBrunei), was formed to monitor the setting of oil and gas policies in Brunei and to act as an investment arm for the government. All of the government's assets in the respective joint venture oil and gas companies are transferred to and are managed by PetroleumBrunei (*Borneo Bulletin*, January 20, 2002). Furthermore, oil and gas exploration activities are not limited to BSP but are also undertaken by two other joint venture corporations, Total Fina Elf and Shell Deep Water Borneo Limited, which were established to explore any new oil fields.

Brunei began crude oil exportation in the early 1940s, after oil was discovered in 1929. Subsequently, the gas industry began in 1955 with the opening of the B$14 million Seria Gas Plant, and LNG exports commenced in December 1972. Since then, several oil fields have been discovered

Table 2.1

Percentage of Oil and Gas Exports to Total Exports, B$ Million (1990–2000)

Year	Petroleum crude A	Petroleum products B	Natural gas C	Oil and gas exports A + B + C	Total exports D	Percent of oil and gas to total exports E
1990	2,040.41	225.22	1,605.42	3,871.05	4,010.15	97
1991	2,024.56	206.20	1,896.88	4,127.64	4,266.97	97
1992	2,036.22	124.86	1,562.16	3,723.24	3,913.37	95
1993	1,785.57	122.66	1,591.39	3,499.62	3,632.29	96
1994	1,549.82	105.78	1,412.70	3,068.30	3,290.46	93
1995	1,475.82	110.69	1,561.40	3,147.91	3,388.27	93
1996	1,702.12	116.90	1,582.73	3,401.75	3,669.64	93
1997	1,650.07	110.34	1,859.52	3,619.93	3,970.70	91
1998	1,149.85	93.94	1,557.08	2,800.87	3,194.09	88
1999	1,875.85	93.06	1,632.56	3,601.47	4,325.14	83
2000*	3,352.17	157.28	2,532.11	6,041.56	6,733.52	90

Source: Brunei Government, *Statistical Yearbook 1993* (Brunei Darussalam: Statistics Division, Economic Planning Unit, Ministry of Finance, 1993); Brunei Government, *Statistical Yearbook 2000/2001* (Brunei Darussalam: Department of Economic Planning and Development [DEPD], Prime Minister's Office, 2001).
    *Provisional.

and exploited, and oil and gas continue to be the main exportation commodities for the country, contributing to more than 90 percent of the total exports for the country (see Table 2.1).

An Oil Conservation Policy was introduced in 1981 to preserve the country's nonrenewable resources in view of the then-unfavorable world market price of oil, and to ensure income and prosperity for the future generations of the country. The policy aimed to reduce oil production to 150,000 barrels per day (bpd) by 1988, compared to peak output of 261,000 barrels per day in 1979. However, this policy was not adhered to most of the time due to the attractive world oil prices that induced the government to produce additional oil and gas, as it is a viable source for increasing the country's revenue. For instance, following the outbreak of the Gulf Crisis in 1990, the government increased oil production to 152,000 bpd to take advantage of the higher oil price.

Brunei's exports of crude oil declined from 160,610 barrels per day at an average price of US$21.97 per barrel in 1996 to 152,000 barrels per day at an average price of US$13.43 per barrel in 1998 (Brunei Government 2000) (see Table 2.2). This was due to the financial crisis in the Asia-Pacific region, where the country's main buyers (Japan, Korea, and Thailand) reduced their purchases of oil and gas from the country. Then in April 1999, the major world oil suppliers combined to reduce the supply of crude oil for one year, limiting it to 2.1 million bpd. Following the reduction in world crude oil supply and the economic recovery in the Asia-Pacific region, the oil price increased from US$13.43 per barrel (1998) to US$27.24 (mid-2000), stabilizing at US$26–27 per barrel by the end of December 2000. When the oil price rose to US$18.57 per barrel in 1999, Brunei's oil exports increased to 174,000 barrels per day and then increased to 189,000 barrels per day in 2000 when the price peaked at US$36 per barrel. Of the country's total oil production, 96 percent was exported, while the remaining 4 percent was used for domestic consumption (Brunei Government 2000).

Table 2.2

Brunei's Exports of Oil and Gas in Quantity and Price (1995 to 2000)

| Year | Exports | | Average prices | |
	Oil and gas (thousands of barrels per day)	Liquefied natural (trillions of BTU per year)	Crude oil (US$ per barrel)	Liquefied natural gas (cif) (US$/million BTU)
1995	168	323	18.28	3.44
1996	161	321	21.97	3.67
1997	152	319	21.48	3.85
1998	151	305	13.43	2.92
1999	174	323	18.57	3.22
2000	189	333	29.71	4.53

Source: Brunei Government, *Eighth National Development Plan 2001–2005* (Brunei Darussalam: Prime Minister's Office, 2000), p. 68.

DEMOGRAPHIC CHARACTERISTICS

Census statistics (Table 2.3) placed the population of Brunei at 344,500 in 2001, a tremendous fourfold increase from 1960. The two most important factors behind this relatively high growth in population size are natural increase and immigration. It was also observed that declining crude death rate played a role in the contribution to population growth (Teo and Tan 1999). However, it was also noted that the rate of population growth has been declining over years, recording only an estimation of 1.8 percent in 2001 compared to a high of 4.5 percent in 1971. The reason behind this may be due to a fall in birthrates, and the increased number of migrant workers and their dependents leaving the country toward the end of the 1990s.

The majority of the population is located in Brunei/Muara, where the capital, Bandar Seri Begawan, is located. The commercial and government sectors are centralized in this district, and they provide better job opportunities and national facilities. Seventeen percent of the total population lives in Belait; most of them are employees of the second largest employer of the country—the Brunei Shell Group and its related companies. Tutong has 11 percent of the population, while 3 percent live in Temburong. There has been steady growth in the number of people staying in the Brunei/Muara district—from 53 percent in 1971 to 69 percent in 2001. On the contrary, the rate of growth in the Belait district has been declining, while the rates of growth in Tutong and Temburong have remained constant. This infers that people staying in the Belait district are moving over to the capital due to better job opportunities.

Brunei Malays were the dominant racial group (68 percent) in 2001. The other major group is the Chinese, comprising 11 percent of the population, while people from the indigenous group made up another 6 percent. Another group categorized under "others" includes various racial groups that consist mostly of foreign workers in the country, including Caucasians, Filipinos, Thais, and Indians. Members of these groups made up about 11 percent of the population in 2001. Over the decade from 1991 to 2001, the number of Brunei Malays grew by 34 percent, followed by "others" with 31 percent, while the Chinese and other indigenous groups grew by 29 percent and 23 percent, respectively.

According to Teo and Tan (1999), of the total 136,256 persons enumerated in the 1971 population census, some 101,511 persons (or 74.5 percent) were born in Brunei, and the remaining 25.5 percent were born outside the country. The number of local-born persons had increased to

Table 2.3

Population Indicators, 1971–2001

Population	1971[a]	1981	1991	2001[b]
Total	136,256	192,832	260,482	344,500
Male	72,772	102,942	137,616	175,600
Female	63,484	89,890	122,866	168,900
Annual growth rate (%)	4.5	3.5	3.1	1.8
Population by racial group				
Malays	89,268	125,717	174,319	233,800
Other indigenous	8,552	15,175	15,665	19,300
Chinese	31,925	39,461	40,621	52,300
Others	6,511	12,479	29,877	39,100
Population by district				
Brunei–Muara	72,791	114,231	170,107	238,300
Belait	42,383	50,768	52,957	58,000
Tutong	15,858	21,615	29,730	39,100
Temburong	5,224	6,218	7,668	9,100

Source: Brunei Government, *Statistical Yearbook 1993* (Brunei Darussalam: Statistics Division, Economic Planning Unit, Ministry of Finance, 1993); Brunei Government, *Statistical Yearbook 2000/2001* (Brunei Darussalam: Department of Economic Planning and Development [DEPD], Prime Minister's Office, 2001).

[a]In 1971, 1981, and 1991, the definition of "Malay" was changed to "indigenous population of the Malay race," which consisted of "Malay, Dusun, Murut, Kedayan and Bisaya," and the last four were included in the "other indigenous" category in previous censuses.

[b]Revised estimates.

139,167 persons (72.2 percent of the total population) in 1981 and to 184,388 persons (70.8 percent of the total population) in 1991. It was, however, also noted that in terms of proportion, the local-born population is declining. The data on foreign-born persons categorized by main country of birth showed that the neighboring country of Malaysia was the primary source of migration into Brunei. On the whole, the analysis suggested that there has been a wider spread in the country of birth of the foreign-born population. Perhaps this is due to Brunei's importation of "general" and "specialist" labor to meet the manpower needs of the growing economy. Many foreign-born workers were recruited to fill jobs that the locals rejected. For instance, at the lower rungs, many Thais and Bangladeshi were recruited to work in the construction industry, while a large number of Filipinos and Indonesians were recruited as domestic helpers. At the higher occupational levels, skilled manpower had to be recruited from countries such as Malaysia, Australia, and New Zealand.

The official religion of the country is Islam, and it is practiced by the majority of the population (75 percent in 2001). As the culture of a country is closely related to the religious practice and beliefs of one's self, it is noted that the culture of this country follows the Malay culture. All Malays are followers of Islam. Nevertheless, other religions are practiced by the various racial groups in the country. Christianity and Buddhism are practiced by the minority racial groups, with distribution composition of 9.4 percent and 8.6 percent, respectively (Table 2.4).

In general, as of 2001, the population of Brunei was characterized as young (62 percent of the population are below age thirty, with 33 percent under age fifteen, and 29 percent between ages fifteen and twenty-nine), living in the urban areas of Brunei (78 percent according to the World Bank Group [2002]), and Muslim. The ratio of male to female is almost equivalent (1,040 : 1,000) in the country, while the average number of persons in a household is six. Over a period of ten years, the

Table 2.4

Population Distribution by Religion, 1991 and 2002

Year	Islam	Christianity	Buddhism	Others	Total
Number					
1991	174,977	25,990	33,387	26,128	260,482
2001	249,822	31,291	28,480	23,251	332,844
Distribution (%)					
1991	67.2	10.0	12.8	10.0	100.0
2001	75.0	9.4	8.6	7.0	100.0
Annual growth (%)					
1991–2001	3.6	1.9	−1.6	−1.2	2.5

Source: Brunei Government, Department of Economic Planning and Development (DEPD), Prime Minister's Office (unpublished).

country's life expectancy rate has increased from 72.1 years and 76.5 years (1991) to 74.2 and 76.9 (2001) for males and females, respectively, as a result of the expansion of the primary health care system in the country and of improvements in people's lifestyles. However, the fertility rate among married women has decreased (from 3.1 percent in 1991 to 2.7 percent in 2001) due to the increasing number of women furthering education at tertiary levels and delaying marriage.

POLITICAL SYSTEM AND GOVERNMENT STRUCTURE

Brunei's form of government has been described in different ways—as constitutional sultanate, government sultanate, and absolute monarchy. This is due to the fact that Brunei's political system rests on the twin pillars of the country: the 1959 Constitution (Brunei Government "The 1959 Constitution") and the adoption of the national philosophy for the country, *Melayu Islam Beraja* (Malay Islamic Monarchy). The Brunei Constitution has to be understood in the context of the Malay Islamic Monarchy, and these two facts dominate the political system of Brunei and its government ethos.

Beginning as a Hindu-Buddhist city-state in 414 C.E., Brunei later embraced Islam. In the fifteenth and sixteenth centuries, its influence extended throughout Borneo and the Philippines. From the last quarter of the nineteenth century, Brunei steadily lost all its territories due to Spanish, British, Portuguese, and Dutch interventions. Then in 1888, Brunei was made a British protectorate. From 1906 to 1959, a British Resident held administrative power, while the Brunei Sultan's jurisdiction was restricted to Malay traditions and religion.

In 1959, Brunei's first written constitution was presented, bestowing full executive authority on the Sultan as the Head of State. The Sultan is assisted and advised by five councils; the Religious Council, the Privy Council, the Council of Ministers (the Cabinet), the Legislative Council, and the Council of Succession. In 1984, Brunei gained full political independence from the United Kingdom and has since maintained a cabinet style of government. The Sultan, also the prime minister as well as finance and defense minister, holds real political power, as the system of government revolves around him. Appointments of cabinet ministers are made at the Sultan's discretion, as the 1959 constitution states that the sultan exercises power of appointment to the councils. Therein, Brunei is an independent sovereign sultanate that is governed on the basis of a written constitution.

Melayu Islam Beraja (MIB) was declared the state ideology for the country on the day of its independence in 1984 (Brunei Government "National Philosophy"). As the name of the philosophy indicates, Brunei is a state monarchical system in style and function, which is to be guided by the teachings of the Islamic faith, and where the majority of the people in the country are of Malay descendents. The Sultan's declaration on the national philosophy on the day of Brunei's independence was as follows:

> . . . Brunei Darussalam is and with the blessing of Allah (to whom be praised and Whose name be exalted) shall be forever a sovereign, democratic and independent Malay Muslim Monarchy upon the teachings of Islam according to Ahli Sunnah Waljamaah and based upon the principle of liberty, trust and justice and ever seeking with the guidance and blessing of Allah. (Excerpt from His Majesty proclaiming the Declaration of Independence of Brunei Darussalam, January 1, 1984)

The philosophy of the MIB concept has somewhat become a model for political, economic, and social development for the country, as all projects and developments are planned and implemented according to Islamic teachings. In some respects, the ideology and visible symbolism of the state seem to reflect a balancing act between Western and Islamic pressure (Cleary and Wong 1994). The state aims to preserve the customs and traditions of the Malay culture, emphasize teachings of the Islamic faith, and administer the monarchical system. Strict Islamic teachings have been incorporated into educational and social policies around the country. This does not mean that the MIB philosophy stifles the practice of other religions; it aims to act as a vehicle to develop the country with guidance from Islamic teachings, and to enhance racial harmony and mutual respect among the peoples.

Brunei's legal system, similar to the legal systems of Singapore and Malaysia, is based primarily on English Common Law. The English judiciary system with an independent judiciary was retained after Brunei gained independence in 1984. The Ministry of Law is responsible for the legal system in Brunei, while the attorney general is the chief advisor on constitutional and legal matters (*Borneo Bulletin* 2000). The Supreme Court, the Intermediate Court, and the Subordinate Court hold the judiciary power in the country. The Supreme Court consists of the High Court and the Court of Appeal, and the Subordinate Courts comprise the Magistrate Courts. Syariah (Islamic) Courts exist side by side with the Supreme Court and deal with Islamic laws. In 1991, Intermediate Courts were established with civil and criminal jurisdiction, but these courts have no jurisdiction over capital cases.

THE ECONOMIC ENVIRONMENT

Brunei's economic environment is unique in the Southeast Asian region. The creation of wealth and income for the country is totally dependent on Brunei's valuable assets—oil and natural gas. This industry generates revenues for the government, which injects a large portion of the funds into the economy in order for the country to prosper and to improve the standards of living for its nationals. This characterizes Brunei as a "rentier state," or one suffering from the "Dutch disease" —high reliance on revenue from the oil and gas industry, which bloats the public sector, while taking on nonproductive social expenditure (Gunn 2001).

Any fluctuations in world oil prices would directly affect the government's revenue, which is the backbone of the country's economic and social development. Diversification measures had been devised to maneuver the economy from streaming down into a problematic rentier economy. However, some factors crippled the nation's progress, such as the Asian financial crisis coupled with Brunei's domestic problem—the collapse of the Amedeo Empire and the nonmaterialized expansion of the private sector.

Perhaps one would think that Brunei, with its small population size, would be able to escape from the "rentier state" condition. However, the main source of income for the country is nonrenewable, and with long-term sustainable diversification plans unrealized, together with lack of foreign direct investments and the collapse of a major construction conglomerate in 1998, the economy has been driven into a gloomy and stagnant state. Sustainable long-term diversification of the private sector is crucial to force the country's economy from its total reliance on the oil industry and to enable it to compete in the ever-changing competitive global marketplace.

At the international level, Brunei is a founding member of the World Trade Organization (WTO) and had been a contracting party to the General Agreement on Tariffs and Trade (GATT) since December 1993. Brunei's trade and investment policies are strongly linked to those of its regional trade and investment partners, principally members of ASEAN, in which Brunei plays an increasingly active role, and the Asia-Pacific Economic Cooperation (APEC) forum (WTO 2001).

Gross Domestic Product and Economic Growth

GDP at current prices for Brunei over a period of ten years, from 1991 to 2000, averaged around B$7 billion per year (see Table 2.5). For a country with a population of only 344,500 in 2001, this may imply a robust economy. However, activities in the country's economy are heavily dependent on the oil and gas industry and on the government's social and development projects.

As a small player in the world oil and gas market, Brunei does not play a significant role in the international pricing of oil and gas. The nation is a price taker; whatever price is set by the oil market, Brunei has to take, and this will be reflected in Brunei's GDP (Duraman and Opai 2002).

Figure 2.1 shows that in 1991, GDP grew by 4 percent when the country took advantage of the attractive price set by the oil market following the Gulf War crisis. It then recorded a negative growth of 1.1 percent in 1992. In the period from 1993 to 1997, the economy began to recover, recording an average growth of 3.1 percent, through contributions made by the nonoil sector, especially the service sector (Brunei Government 1999). The service sector consists of construction, wholesale and retail trade, hotel and restaurant, transport and communications, banking and finance, and other service-related business. The main thrust for the growth in the service sector was due to the numerous and large development projects undertaken by Amedeo Development Corporation (Amedeo), the nation's largest conglomerate.

Amedeo Development Corporation is a multibillion-dollar conglomerate company involved in construction and telecommunication services. Through its involvement, various sectors flourished in Brunei, namely, construction, property, and the retail industry. Many buildings and infrastructures were built and made ready for use, and several huge projects were undertaken. Then, in mid-1997, Amedeo began to experience financial difficulties due to a lack of transparency, exaggerations of funding for the projects, particularly relating to economic evaluations of the investment projects. Inquests were made on the accounts of the huge corporation. It was later uncovered that the corporation had misappropriated funds from the Brunei Investment Agency (BIA), an independent body set up to invest the country's oil revenues.

Following the collapse of Amedeo, which coincided with the region's financial crisis and the fall in oil prices, Brunei's GDP contracted 4 percent in the years 1998 to 1999. Effects of the region's crisis did not spill over much into Brunei's economic scenario, however, as foreign direct investments are not very evident in the country. The more significant factors were the decline in demand for Brunei's oil and gas from its main buyers, the unfavorable oil price, and the

Table 2.5

Brunei's Key Economic Indicators, 1991–2001

Indicator	1991	1992	1993	1994	1995	1996	1997	1998	1999	2000[a]	2001[b]
GDP, current prices, B$ million	6,620.5	6,565.1	6,585.1	6,686.2	7,394.2	7,408.6	7,627.4	6,534.0	7,144.7	7,441.1	7,619.2
GDP, constant prices, B$ million	3,750.7	3,709.4	3,728.0	3,795.1	3,910.6	3,951.5	4,093.8	3,930.6	4,031.4	4,145.3	4,206.1
GDP growth rate, %	4.0	−1.1	0.5	1.8	3.0	1.0	3.6	−4.0	2.6	2.8	1.5
GDP per capita, B$	25,415	24,515	23,833	23,502	24,980	24,283	24,262	20,223	21,605	21,989	22,117
CPI (all commodities, base = 1990)	101.6	102.9	107.3	109.9	116.5	118.8	120.8	120.3	120.2	121.7	122.4
Consumer price inflation, %	1.6	1.3	4.3	2.4	6.0	2.0	1.7	−0.4	−0.1	1.2	0.6
Exchange rates, B$: US$	1.6410	1.6513	1.6144	1.4732	1.4242	1.4106	1.6835	1.6695	1.6770	1.7370	1.8590
Total export, B$ million	4,266.97	3,913.37	3,632.29	3,290.46	3,388.27	3,669.64	3,971.70	3,194.09	4,325.14	6,733.52	4,768.98[c]
Total import, B$ million	1,922.38	2,416.02	3,054.81	2,760.48	2,959.59	3,516.47	3,153.97	2,338.33	2,250.65	1,907.80	1,577.82[c]
External trade, B$ million	6,189.35	6,329.39	6,687.10	6,050.94	6,347.86	7,186.11	7,125.67	5,532.42	6,575.79	8,641.32	6,346.80[c]
Balance of trade, B$ million	2,344.59	1,497.35	577.48	529.98	428.68	153.17	817.73	855.76	2,074.49	4,825.72	3,191.16[c]

Source: Brunei Government, *Statistical Yearbook 2000/2001* (Brunei Darussalam: Department of Economic Planning and Development [DEPD], Prime Minister's Office, 2001).

[a]Provisional estimate.

[b]Forecast.

[c]Figure only reflects from January–September 2001.

Figure 2.1   **GDP Growth Rate, 1991–2001** (%)

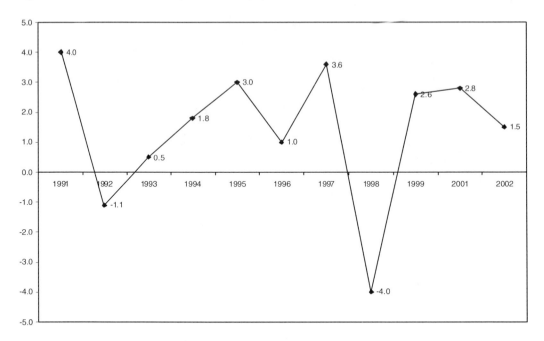

Source: Adapted from Brunei Government, *Statistical Yearbook 2000/2001* (Brunei Darussalam: Department of Economic Planning and Development [DEPD], Prime Minister's Office), p. 136.

aftermath of Amedeo's collapse. Nevertheless, the economy recorded positive GDP growth in 1999. However, this growth did not reflect the true state of the economy, as the increase in GDP was mainly due to favorable oil prices in the second half of 2000.

Sectoral Contributions to Gross Domestic Product

The essence of the GDP of Brunei is from the oil and gas industry. Sectoral contributions to GDP are divided into two main portions: the oil sector and the nonoil sector. The trend evident in Figure 2.2 is that contributions from the oil sector to GDP decreased over the years, while contributions from the nonoil sector were on the rise. In 1991, the oil sector contributed 50.4 percent to the GDP of Brunei following the outbreak of the Gulf crisis. The contribution then started to decline due to the government's conservation policy to rationalize the output of the exhaustible resource and the depressed international price for crude oil. There was a drop in the oil sector contribution to GDP in 1998 due to a reduction in demand for oil and the unfavorable oil price. Nevertheless, the oil sector picked up its contribution level in 1999 and 2000 following the increase in exports of oil due to enticing world oil prices (Brunei Government 2000).

Figure 2.2 and Table 2.6 show that the increasing contributions to GDP came from the government and the private sector. A first glance at Table 2.6 shows the increasingly important role of the private sector in the economy. However, a big portion of total GDP from the nonoil sector (about 30 percent) came from social services, including national housing, education, and health care, which are all under government control. Furthermore, most activities in the nonoil private

Figure 2.2   **Percentage Contribution of Oil and Nonoil Sectors to GDP, 1991–2000**

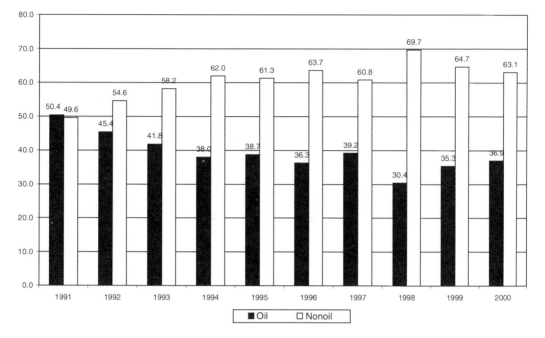

Source: Adapted from Brunei Government, *Eighth National Development Plan 2001–2005* (Brunei Darussalam: Prime Minister's Office), pp. 199–200.

sector are dependent on government's direct purchase of goods and services in the country (Shamim, Hashim, and Wahid 1997). Henceforth, contributions to GDP from the private sector revolve around government's development policies, which essentially are sustained by oil and gas income.

Table 2.6 further reveals that contributions from the primary sectors, that is, agriculture, forestry, and fishing, made up only about 3 percent of GDP in 2000, while construction, retail trade, and banking and finance played a slightly bigger role. However, it is also worth noting that they are on a declining trend since 1998. This is attributed to the slowdown in economic activities around the country: the decline of the construction industry, an increasing number of people shopping across the borders of Brunei, and the tightening of credit policies by various financial institutions in the country.

Trade and Balance of Payments

In 2000, Brunei recorded a trade balance surplus of B$4.826 billion, with exports valued at B$6.734 billion, and imports valued at B$1.908 billion (Table 2.7). Of the B$6.734 billion worth of goods exported from Brunei, nearly 90 percent (or B$6.042 billion) are contributed by the oil and gas industry, with crude oil valued at B$3.352 billion, followed by LNG B$2.532 billion, and other petroleum products at B$157 million. For the year 2000, Brunei's main destination countries for mineral fuel export were Japan (B$2.818 billion), Thailand (B$1.114 billion), Korea (B$835 million), the United States (B$344 million), and Australia (B$320 million). Machinery and trans-

Table 2.6

GDP by Kind of Economic Activity at Current Prices, 1997–2000 (B$ million)

Economic activity	1997 Total	1997 Percent of GDP	1998 Total	1998 Percent of GDP	1999 Total	1999 Percent of GDP	2000 Total	2000 Percent of GDP
I Oil Sector	2,991.7	39.2	2,139.2	30.4	2,688.1	35.3	2,951.1	36.9
II Nonoil Sector	4,636.4	60.8	4,891.3	69.6	4,927.2	64.7	5,044.4	63.1
A Government	1,713.2	22.5	1,763.9	25.1	1,783.6	23.4	1,803.6	22.6
B Private sector	2,923.2	38.3	3,127.4	44.5	3,143.6	41.3	3,240.8	40.5
1 Agriculture	153.2	2.0	162.4	2.3	158.1	2.1	160.5	2.0
2 Forestry	24.8	0.3	26.3	0.4	26.7	0.4	27.0	0.3
3 Fishing	40.3	0.5	43.2	0.6	44.8	0.6	45.3	0.6
4 Mining, quarrying, and manufacturing	252.1	3.3	266.8	3.8	292.5	3.8	313.1	3.9
5 Electricity, gas, and water	55.2	0.7	62.6	0.9	58.9	0.8	60.8	0.8
6 Construction	523.4	6.9	539.2	7.7	534.5	7.0	550.1	6.9
7 Wholesale	152.7	2.0	192.6	2.7	200.5	2.6	219.1	2.7
8 Retail trade	405.7	5.3	418.7	6.0	436.5	5.7	445.2	5.6
9 Restaurants and hotels	135.3	1.8	148.4	2.1	152.3	2.0	156.8	2.0
10 Transport, storage, and communication	347.0	4.5	372.5	5.3	385.5	5.1	391.2	4.9
11 Bank and finance	364.5	4.8	397.0	5.6	405.1	5.3	414.3	5.2
12 Insurance	115.1	1.5	122.9	1.7	125.3	1.6	127.6	1.6
13 Real estate and business services	94.3	1.2	96.1	1.4	97.5	1.3	98.6	1.2
14 Ownership of dwellings	91.5	1.2	92.3	1.3	92.9	1.2	94.6	1.2
15 Community, social, and personal services	2,067.8	27.1	2,169.0	30.9	2,135.7	28.0	2,160.5	27.0
16 Less: bank charges	216.5	2.8	218.7	3.1	219.6	2.9	220.3	2.8
GDP	7,628.1	100.0	7,030.5	100.0	7,615.3	100.0	7,995.5	100.0

Source: Brunei Government, *Eighth National Development Plan 2001–2005* (Brunei Darussalam: Prime Minister's Office, 2000), p. 200.

58

Table 2.7

Exports and Imports by Commodity Section, 2000 (B$ million)

	Exports	Percent	Imports	Percent
Food	1.59	0.02	285.44	14.96
Beverages and tobacco	0.32	0.00	46.49	2.44
Crude material (inedible)	2.00	0.03	20.39	1.07
Mineral fuel (oil and gas)	6,041.86	89.73	9.69	0.51
Animal and vegetable oil and fats	0.24	0.00	8.51	0.45
Chemicals	3.40	0.05	143.10	7.50
Manufactured goods	51.02	0.76	565.87	29.66
Machinery and transport equipment	301.43	4.48	597.57	31.32
Miscellaneous manufactured articles	324.03	4.81	226.91	11.89
Miscellaneous transactions	7.62	0.11	3.76	0.20
Total	6,733.51	100.00	1,907.73	100.00

Source: Brunei Government, *Statistical Yearbook 2000/2001* (Brunei Darussalam: Department of Economic Planning and Development [DEPD], Prime Minister's Office, 2001), pp. 56, 57.

port equipment, mainly composed of the sale of used machines or scrap metals, made up 4.4 percent or B$301.4 million of total exports, while ready-made garments worth B$324 million (4.8 percent) were mainly exported to the United States. The other commodities were of minor significance in terms of total exports. This proves that Brunei is still very much at its infancy stage in the exportation of nonoil commodities, with B$691.65 million, as opposed to the importation of nonoil commodities at B$1.898 billion.

In terms of domestic consumption, Brunei imports almost all consumer and industrial items. The nation imported about B$793 million worth of manufactured goods and articles, or 40 percent of total imports; machinery and transportation equipment came to nearly B$600 million (30 percent of total imports); and foodstuffs came to about 15 percent of total exports, or B$285 million in 2000. The country's main sources of imports are Singapore (B$505.64 million), Malaysia (B$380.28 million), the United States (B$207.45 million), Japan (B$129.4 million), and Hong Kong (B$124.96 million), comprising 26.5 percent, 19.9 percent, 10.9 percent, 6.8 percent, and 6.5 percent of the total imports, respectively.

Referring to Table 2.5, the balance of payments for the country is recorded at a surplus over the years, while Figure 2.3 illustrates that the balance of payments is consistent with total exports. The graph shows that the balance of trade peaked in 2000, at B$4.825 billion, resulting from increased production of crude oil (an average of 189,000 bpd in 2000) paralleling the favorable oil price of US$29.71 per barrel in the same period. This allows a conclusion to be drawn about the vitality of the oil and gas industry for the external trade balance of the country. On the other hand, imports have been declining since 1996, following the fall in demand for construction materials and equipment and wholesale and retail commodities due to the slowdown of the construction industry, the tightening of government budget policies, and the overall dampening of the economy.

Consumer Income and Purchasing Power

As Brunei imports most of the goods in the country, inflation is largely influenced by the price of the commodities in the exporting countries, as well as the value of the Brunei currency against the currency of its trading partners. With 1990 as the base year, Figure 2.4 shows

Figure 2.3   **Exports, Imports, and Balance of Trade, 1990–2001**

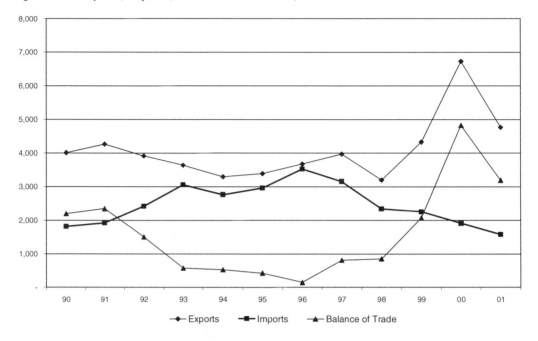

Source: Adapted from Brunei Government, *Statistical Yearbook 2000/2001* (Brunei Darussalam: Department of Economic Planning and Development [DEPD], Prime Minister's Office), p. 55.

Note: Graph shows a decline in export, import, and balance of trade toward 2001. This is due to the fact that figures are available only for the period January–September 2001 and are not representative for the year.

fluctuations in the Consumer Price Index (CPI) over a period of ten years. This was attributed to a surge of the CPI in 1995 due to the introduction of significant import duties for motor vehicles in the country. Brunei has a high car ownership ratio: with 576 cars per 1,000 people in 2001 (The Economist 2004). In the couple of months following, the government announced a substantial reduction in import duties from 10 to 30 percent to 0 to 10 percent on an estimated 700 consumer items (Brunei Government 1999). The country also began the annual Brunei Grand Sale and Discount Sales during the festive seasons. In addition, the government, through the Department of Economic Planning and Development, regulates the prices of some essential items in order to monitor price increases. These few factors led to a lower inflation rate over the next couple of years.

Brunei recorded negative CPI growth in 1998 (–0.4 percent) and 1999 (–0.1 percent). The reasons were the collapse of the Amedeo Corporation, which resulted in a few thousand foreign workers in the construction industry being sent home; a fall in domestic demand for commodities, as people went to the neighboring Sarawak towns, Miri, Labuan, and Limbang, to buy cheaper household items, as prices on imported Asian items depreciated against the Brunei dollar.

Local residents of Brunei have been enjoying relatively higher purchasing power compared to their ASEAN counterparts, Malaysia, Thailand, the Philippines, and Indonesia. Gross national product (GNP) per capita for Brunei in 2001 was US$20,400, according to *Asiaweek* (2001).[1] Local residents are able to enjoy this privilege due to various governmental policies, such as no income tax, free medical and education benefits, low-cost housing provision, and low public

Figure 2.4   **Consumer Price Index, 1991–2001**

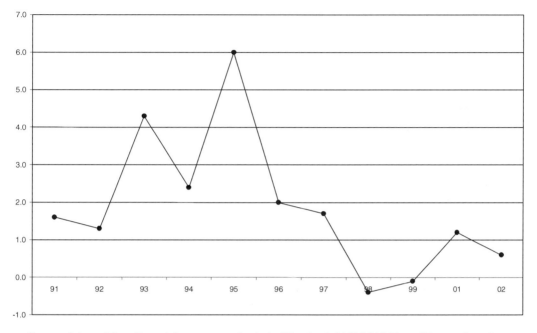

Source: Adapted from Brunei Government, *Statistical Yearbook 2000/2001* (Brunei Darussalam: Department of Economic Planning and Development [DEPD], Prime Minister's Office), p. 104.

utilities cost. In addition, most of the local residents work for the government or at Brunei-Shell Petroleum, where they draw attractive remunerations among other benefits.[2] Henceforth, with good salaries and benefits, coupled with low inflation, the local residents would have high purchasing power. This would be, and certainly is, the case before the domestic recession of recent years.

GDP per capita, as seen from Table 2.5, would, however, not be reflective of the true purchasing power of the local residents, especially from 1999 onward, as GDP for the country is a result of the increased revenue from the oil and gas sector. Following the downfall of Amedeo, various sectors in Brunei were affected. The construction industry was the worst hit (Duraman and Opai 2002). Other effects of the Amedeo collapse include the downward revision of salaries and benefits in the private sector, dampening the wholesale and retail industry, due to the retrenchment of thousands of foreign workers of Amedeo, the government's curb on public expenditures via stringent national budgetary policies, the relaxed "loan culture" of the Bruneians, which often lands them in untenable financial commitments with the banking institutions, and a steep decline in land and property prices. In brief, the decline in the CPI does not necessarily reflect higher spending power of the local residents. In fact, the declining CPI was the result of the domestic recession.

Table 2.8 shows that the monthly household income in Brunei is B$4,180. Households in the Brunei/Muara district earn, on average, a monthly income of B$4,601, which is 46 percent higher than that in Temburong. In the less-than B$2,500 monthly income category, households in the Temburong district account for the highest proportion (61.7 percent), while 28.9 percent of total households in Brunei/Muara earn more than B$5,000 per month, which is the highest in that particular category. This illustrates that there is income inequality by districts, with households in

Table 2.8

Distribution of Household Income by District and Race (1997–1998)

Monthly income group (B$)	Distribution by district (%)					Distribution by race (%)	
	All households	Brunei– Muara	Belait	Tutong	Temburong	Malay	Non- Malay
$0–$2,499	39.6	34.6	42.9	51.4	61.7	39.6	39.9
$2,500–$4,999	35.1	36.5	32.4	33.2	32.3	36.9	30.4
$5,000 and above	25.2	28.9	24.7	15.5	6.0	23.5	29.8
Total	100.0	100.0	100.0	100.0	100.0	100.0	100.0
Average	4,180	4,601	3,697	3,440	2,496	4,084	4,430

Source: Brunei Government, *Distribution of Household Income by District and Race, 1997–98* (Department of Economic Planning and Development, 2001); extracted from Hj Zulazrin Hj Mohidin, *Income and Expenditure Patterns in Brunei Darussalam* (Academic exercise, Department of Economics, Universiti Brunei Darussalam, April 2002), pp. 50, 53.

Brunei/Muara possessing the highest purchasing power, followed by Belait, Tutong, and Temburong. With regard to household income by race, the non-Malays earn B$4,430 per month, which is 8 percent higher than that of the Malays. The income inequality within the Malay and non-Malay communities in the country is only slight.

SOCIOCULTURAL ENVIRONMENT

Literacy and Education

The government provides free education to its citizens and permanent residents up to the tertiary education level. Emphasis has been placed on the nation's educational development, as policymakers in Brunei wish to expand the potentials of human resources in the country. The literacy rate for the country, consequently, increased significantly from 69.4 percent in 1971 to 89.2 percent in 1991 and to 94.5 percent in 2001 (see Table 2.9).[3] The education system is bilingual, and in 1991, those able to read both Malay and English totaled 38.2 percent of the total literacy rate compared to those able to read only Malay, Chinese, or English, at 26.9 percent, 3.8 percent, and 6.6 percent, respectively. The number of literate females also increased over a span of ten years, from 48,701 females in 1981 to 80,319 females in 1991. This represents 65 percent growth in literate females, compared to 56 percent growth in overall literate persons in Brunei from 1981 to 1991. In addition, there are more females studying in the technical or vocational colleges, institutions, and university than there are male students (2,949 males to 3,445 females in 2001).

Being a former British territorial state, the country adopted the British education system, and in the early days, almost all students who qualified for government scholarship to study abroad were sent to the United Kingdom for higher education in various tertiary institutions. The Ministry of Education monitors the primary and secondary school system in Brunei closely, and students are required to sit for the public examinations at Forms 5 and 6, where the papers are set by the University of Cambridge.

Table 2.9

Literacy by Community, 1981–2001

Community	1981	1991	2001
Malay	71,853	114,286	155,206
Other indigenous	6,159	9,315	7,867
Chinese	28,473	31,218	29,219
Others	9,457	25,636	57,258
Total	115,942	180,455	249,550

Source: Brunei Government, *Statistical Yearbook 2000/2001* (Brunei Darussalam: Department of Economic Planning and Development [DEPD], Prime Minister's Office, 2001), p. 124.

Table 2.10

Number of Students by Level of Education, 1991–2001

	1991	1994	1997	2000	2001
Total population	260,482	284,500	314,400	338,400	344,500
Student population	28.3%	29.7%	28.7%	28.6%	29.3%
Kindergarten	8,415	11,698	11,992	12,231	13,134
Primary	38,294	42,156	44,294	45,412	46,235
Secondary	24,130	27,086	29,597	33,372	34,809
Technical/vocational	1,240	1,596	1,872	2,307	2,509
Teacher training	368	422	508	406	247
Institute	314	320	385	341	516
University	891	1,138	1,498	2,867	3,369
Total	73,652	84,416	90,146	96,936	100,819

Source: Brunei Government, *Statistical Yearbook 2000/2001* (Brunei Darussalam: Department of Economic Planning and Development [DEPD], Prime Minister's Office, 2001), p. 110.

Table 2.10 shows that the number of students in the country was approximately 100,000 in 2001, accounting for close to 30 percent of the total population in the country. There are 236 schools around the country, out of which 167 are government-run, and sixty-nine are private schools. Of the total numbers of schools in the country, more than 127 are kindergarten or primary schools, while there are at least thirty-one secondary schools. This shows that the majority of the students are of kindergarten, primary or secondary levels, with 94,178 students or 93 percent of the student population belonging to those categories (see Table 2.10). To cater to the high number of students in the primary and secondary levels, the government has been training and recruiting graduate teachers from the Teacher Training College and the University of Brunei Darussalam, and building more schools and educational facilities needed to accommodate the increasing number of students.

There are six technical colleges or vocational schools that award diplomas in different technical or business fields. These technical institutions have been successful in producing mid-level professionals and technicians (Shamin et al. 1997). The University of Brunei Darussalam (UBD) was established in 1985, offering certificates, first, and postgraduate degrees. In the Sultan's *titah* (royal address) at the Fourteen Convocation Ceremony of UBD in 2002, he stressed that the production of increased graduates will give rise to more knowledgeable people and experts in

Table 2.11

Labor Force Participation, 1991–2001

	1991	1999	2000	2001
Labor force (thousands)	112.0	143.7	148.3	151.7
Males	75.1	95.3	98.2	100.3
Females	36.9	48.4	50.1	51.4
Employed (thousands)	106.8	137.2	141.3	144.5
Males	72.4	92.8	95.5	97.3
Females	34.4	44.4	45.8	47.2
Labor force participation rate (%)	65.6	64.9	65.5	66.0
Male (%)	82.2	81.7	83.1	84.4
Female (%)	46.4	45.2	46.3	46.3
Unemployed (thousands)	5.2	6.5	7.0	7.2
Male	2.7	2.5	2.7	3.0
Female	2.5	4.0	4.3	4.2
Unemployment rate (%)	4.7	4.5	4.7	4.7

Source: Brunei Government, *Key Indicators 2001* (Brunei Darussalam: Department of Economic Planning and Development [DEPD], Ministry of Finance, 2001), pp. 1, 2.

various fields, which are crucial for the development of human resources to face challenges in the world of globalization and in a knowledge-based economy or K-economy (*Borneo Bulletin* 2002b). With the emphasis placed on producing qualified tertiary students, the number of students enrolled at UBD was 3,369 in the year 2001, compared to 1,148 in 1993. Education certificates and degrees appear to be the most popular programs undertaken by the students, with 1,844 students enrolled in the Sultan Hassanal Bolkiah Institute of Education of the University in 2000 (or 64 percent of total UBD students). The number of citizens and permanent residents holding tertiary qualifications (from local and foreign institutions) increased from 16,896 in 1996 to 22,084 in 1999 (Brunei Government 2000).

Labor Force and Unemployment

Referring to Table 2.11, the labor force for Brunei in 2001 stood at 151,700 persons, of which about two-thirds were males. A big proportion of male workers (up to 65 percent of all working males) were engaged in the construction, wholesaling and retailing, and manufacturing industries, as well as in the public administration and defense service sectors. On the other hand, the number of females in the labor force grew by 39 percent from 36,900 in 1991 to 51,400 in 2001; and the overall labor force increased by 35 percent for the same period. The factor behind the increasing number of females participating in the workforce is the rise in the number of literate females seeking employment, illustrating an attitude change of societal behavior that is a residual of societal improvements.

Brunei has been dependent on the supply of foreign manpower to fill the vacancies that the locals decline. One feature of the Brunei labor market is that the locals prefer to work in the public sector due to the attractive salary scale as well as to the benefits that come with it. The government is the largest employer in the country; approximately 94 percent of the civil servants are locals, and as of September 2002, there were 39,671 people employed in the public sector, making up 26 percent of the workforce. The government implemented its "Bruneianization policy" with the establishment of the Employee's Trust Fund (ETF) and the close monitoring of compa-

Table 2.12

Working Population by Occupational Group, 2001 Census

Occupational group	Locals	%	Foreigners	%
Legislators, administrators, and managers	3,761	4.8	1,336	2.0
Professionals	8,016	10.2	2,671	3.9
Technicians and associate professionals	15,241	19.4	3,327	4.9
Clerks	14,330	18.2	1,831	2.7
Service workers and shop market sales	18,410	23.4	9,050	13.4
Skilled, agricultural, and fishery workers	577	0.7	698	1.0
Craft and related trade workers	5,510	7.0	15,435	22.8
Plant and machine operators and assemblers	3,213	4.1	3,973	5.9
Elementary occupations	9,226	11.7	29,354	43.3
Workers reporting unidentifiable	249	0.3	41	0.1
All occupations	78,533	100.0	67,716	100.0

Source: Brunei Government, Department of Economic Planning and Development (DEPD), Prime Minister's Office. (Unpublished).

nies' employment policies by the Labor Department so as to attract the locals to work in the private sector. Since then, the local share of the workforce increased from 22 percent in 1996 to 24 percent in 2000, while the foreign proportion of the workforce decreased from 78 percent to 76 percent for the same period (Brunei Government 2000). The number of locals participating in private-sector employment is expected to increase in the next couple of years following the corporatization of some government agencies, such as the Brunei Telecommunications Department, the Electrical Services Department, the Postal Services Department, and the Information Technology and State Store Department.

Table 2.12 indicates the jobs in the marketplace that are filled by both locals and foreigners in the country. It could be concluded from the information in Table 2.12 that the majority of locals hold positions as technicians and associate professionals, service and shop market workers, and positions at the clerical levels, whereas jobs at the elementary levels, such as cleaners, laborers, and production craftsmen, are filled by foreign workers. Brunei, with a small population, and with various diversification plans on hand, requires workers both quantitatively and qualitatively (Maricar 1997). This is especially so considering that there was foreign workforce participation of about 62,000 in the private sector in 2001.

However, the statistics for unemployed locals are increasing, with the unemployment rate in Brunei in 2001 at 4.7 percent, or 7,200 persons actively seeking employment. Furthermore, there are increasing numbers of graduates from local and overseas universities who are unable to find jobs or are working in environments with mismatched skills and qualifications. Factors behind this include the government's policy of downsizing employment in their agencies, the preference of locals to work for the government, and the static state of the private sector.

Social Welfare and Housing

Brunei is a welfare state. Provision of excellent welfare benefits have always been one of the top priorities of the government to uplift the standards of living of nationals of Brunei. The National Development Plan (NDP) further highlights this, where four out of the nine long-term objectives are committed to peace and security, safety, and welfare and happiness for the people of Brunei.

The following is an excerpt of the sultan's promise to his citizens, and the existing social welfare benefits are provided to the locals to this day:

> We have devoted our resources to free education, subsidized food and fuels, pensions for the aged and widowed, medical and health care including a "flying doctor" service and earnings without income tax. These and many other services are all provided to protect the children's welfare (Excerpt of the Sultan's speech at Inception to the United Nations, September 21, 1984).

Of the B\$7.3 billion funds allocated to various sectors in the Eighth NDP 2001–2005, social services received 19.93 percent of the development funds, that is, B\$1.454 billion. The categories of education, medicine and health, government housing, national housing, religious affairs, and public facilities fall under this category. Similarly, this sector received B\$1.614 billion in the Sixth NDP (29.3 percent allocation) and B\$2.384 billion in the Seventh NDP (30 percent allocation). Again, this highlights the government's commitment to upgrading the standards of living for the people of Brunei.

Medical benefits are free for the locals, and when treatments are not available in the country, citizens and permanent residents are sent abroad by the government, and expenses are fully paid. More recently, the main hospital, Raja Isteri Pengiran Anak Saleha Hospital (RIPAS), was changed from a center providing basic health care to a medical specialist and referral center. Thus, health care centers began mushrooming across the country to cater to nearby communities. With the excellent medical benefits provided by the government, and advancements in medical technology, life expectancy increased from 61.9 years to 72.1 years for males (an increase of ten years) and from 62.1 to 76.5 years for females (an increase of fourteen years) in the period from 1971 to 1991, while the infant mortality rate (children under one year of age) decreased from 27 deaths for every 1,000 births in 1974 to 6.9 deaths in 1996 (Brunei Government 1999). In fact, Brunei is comparable to other developed countries in terms of birth rate, infant mortality rate, and life expectancy (Duraman and Maricar 1995).

The importance of the family institution is emphasized as achieving a well-balanced harmonious society, and as the nucleus of a civilized society. This was emphasized by the sultan in his titah, which stated:

> The nation will be strong if this backbone is strong. Therefore it is important for families in the country to take responsibility together in planning and producing a generation that possesses virtuous values and is pious. (Excerpts of His Majesty's titah, January 1, 2002)

As part of the country's continuous effort to raise the standards of living for its nationals, housing is a sector that is prioritized in the government's development plans. It is given a budgeted fund of B\$934.6 million in the Eighth NDP, out of which B\$900 million went to national housing and B\$34.6 million to government housing. The national housing scheme aims to provide eligible citizens of Brunei an opportunity to own land and houses at subsidized prices that are payable in affordable monthly installments, while the government provides various types of accommodations for its officers and staffs at subsidized monthly rentals. In 1991, there were 40,351 houses in Brunei, an increase of about 40 percent in a span of ten years (28,860 houses in 1981). The number of households totaled 44,369 in 1991. In Brunei, it is common to have several households staying under one roof due to the culture of the people, where individuals, together with their siblings, tend to stay with their parents, even after marriage.

MIB Concept

Being a Muslim-dominated monarchy, the sultan, as the head of state for religious affairs, considers Islam his main priority. This is evident with the implementation of Islamic values in daily life in all areas and at all levels, and with the planning and implementing of all projects and developments according to Islamic teaching (Brunei Government 1999):

> The Malay Islamic Monarchy concept is actually not new but has been in existence for centuries. It is meant to show the genuine set up and features of Brunei Darussalam's government: A Malay Islamic Sultanate. As an Islamic Government, it is the best and most just for all walks of people and residents of the country, whether they are Muslims or not.

To educate the nationals of Brunei on the ideas and concepts of the country's philosophy, MIB is being taught at all educational levels in the country. In addition, to enhance and facilitate Islamic teachings, religious schools are given priority so as to complement the country's socio-economic development process, while steps are taken to integrate religious schools with conventional schools around the country. According to Duraman and Hashim (1998), the Islamic calendar of events has always had a central place in Bruneian life, both for the sake of the event and as a venue to disseminate important issues. For instance, in 1997, on the eve of the end to the fasting month in February, the Sultan reminded Muslims of the importance of complying with community responsibility through giving *zakat* (an obligatory contribution in the form of taxes on wealth). The monarch also reminded his subjects to be grateful, because there is virtually no suffering or hunger within the Bruneian community.

With the establishment of MIB as the philosophy of the lifestyle in the country, products and services in the country have to complement the rules and regulations of Islamic teachings. For instance, three local banks that exercise Islamic banking practices and offer Islamic credit arrangements to the general population have been established. Products like halal meat had come under close supervision of the religious authorities, which led to a temporary shortage in the supply of slaughtered chicken around the country (Duraman and Hashim 1998). Subsequently, this led to seizures of numerous cases of non-halal chicken meat smuggled into the country.[4] On the other hand, *haram* products could only be consumed by non-Muslims in the country.[5] Items like pork are sold only in selected shops behind dark-tinted glass or in screened-out areas of supermarkets and retail outlets, while consumption of alcohol is available only at private functions of the non-Muslims.

CONSUMERS IN THE MONARCHICAL MARKET

The Brunei market is characterized as a consumer market in which almost all commodities are imported from abroad. Brunei's world merchandise trade in 1999 was negligible in both the Asian and world markets. However, per capita merchandise trade of Brunei at about US$13,500 is high compared to its Asian counterparts, lagging only behind Singapore and Hong Kong (World Trade Organization 2000). The market is definitely small, with 0.34 million consumers, yet it is relatively wealthy. Per-unit costs of the products and services available in the market are generally more expensive compared to those of its neighboring countries due to retailers' markups and the additional costs involved in delivering the final product or service. Furthermore, the domestic market is constrained by the products and services found in the markets of its main importing countries—Singapore and Malaysia.

Table 2.13

Distribution of Households by Expenditure Level, District, and Race (1997–1998)

Monthly expenditure group (B$)	All household	By district				Distribution by race (%)	
		Brunei–Muara	Belait	Tutong	Temburong	Malay	Non-Malay
$0–$1,499	50.4	43.8	60.4	59.4	74.1	50.9	49.2
$1,500–$2,999	27.3	28.6	26.1	26.7	17.9	26.8	28.9
$3,000 and above	22.2	27.7	13.6	14.0	8.0	22.4	21.8
Total	100.0	100.0	100.0	100.0	100.0	100.0	100.0
Average	2,246	2,568	1,722	1,806	1,285	2,214	2,329

Source: Brunei Government, *Distribution of Household Income by District and Race, 1997–98* (Department of Economic Planning and Development, 2001); Extracted from Hj Zulazrin Hj Mohidin, *Income and Expenditure Patterns in Brunei Darussalam* (Academic exercise, Department of Economics, Universiti Brunei Darussalam, April 2002), pp. 50, 54.

With increased standards of living and better bargaining power, the Brunei consumers are becoming increasingly sophisticated and have greater empowerment in the marketplace. The variety of goods in the domestic market may be limited or not available, but Bruneians can still make purchases abroad, especially in the neighboring ASEAN countries. Consumers in the Brunei market are protected by the Economic Planning Unit, which monitors the prices of the goods and services, and also by the Religious Affairs authorities who ensure that products or services that are to be consumed by the Muslims abide strictly by Islamic regulations and that non-halal products are not made available to them.

The socioeconomic environmental factor plays a large role in influencing the types of products or services sought after by the consumers, particularly the concepts of the national philosophy and the economic status of the population. Until the internal and external shocks of 1997 and 1998, and the implementation of prudent budgetary policies of the government, the Bruneians have been rather insensitive to prices of commodities due to the high disposable income and excellent welfare provided by the state. Now, consumers are becoming more aware of the prices that they pay for commodities, as evidenced by the number of people traveling to the neighboring states to make purchases of household items and the declining sales in local supermarkets and department stores, as these command higher prices compared to those in neighboring states. Despite their cautious spending behavior, another emerging trend is that locals tend to readily take loans and advances to finance their purchases. This can be seen by the increasingly popular installment plans for the purchase of household appliances, cars, and expensive equipment. The vast number of credit cards granted and loans and advances in the country are approximated at B$4.198 billion, with 60 percent going to personal loans (Brunei Government 2000). Provisions for doubtful and bad debts are on the rise, but these financial advancements provide a main boost to the consumer market in Brunei. Discussions in the next section will turn to household expenditures by district and race and will reveal the consumption patterns of consumers in the Brunei market.

As seen in Table 2.13, average monthly household expenditures in the country total B$2,246. Household expenditures of those living in the urban areas (Brunei/Muara district) equal about $2,568 per month, in comparison to those in the rural area (Temburong district), who spend an average of B$1,285 per month. This indicates that households in the urban area spend twice as much as those in the rural areas, and that households in the Brunei/Muara district have the highest propensity to consume. The table also shows that households in the rural areas made up the highest percentage for expenditures in the less than B$1,500 per month bracket, while households in the urban area made up the highest proportion in the more than B$3,000 expenditure group. In terms of household expenditures by race, there is only a marginal difference between household expenditures of Malays and non-Malays. The figures revealed that a non-Malay household, on average, spends more than a Malay household, but Mohidin (2002) concluded that the Malay households generally have a higher average propensity to consume compared to the non-Malay households as a result of the lower average monthly household income drawn by the former.

With 69 percent of the population living in the capital district, this, nonetheless, reveals that a big portion of the consumer market resides in the Brunei/Muara district, and consumers in this district have a higher propensity to spend compared to those in the other districts. Furthermore, the Malays, who dominate the market making up 68 percent of the population, have a higher propensity to spend compared to the other races. The above facts show that Malays residing in the Brunei/Muara district form the biggest proportion of the consumer market. Almost all of the commercial shopping centers are located in Bandar Seri Begawan, and products or services made available to Muslims have to adhere to Islamic laws and regulations.

An estimated 20.8 percent of the population belongs to the thirty-five- to fifty-five-year-old age group. They were brought up in the era of "The Architect of Modern Brunei,"[6] and have witnessed the progress of the oil and gas sector and the development of modern infrastructures across the country, while lacking material possessions in their younger years. This group also makes up the greater part of the working population, with the majority of locals employed in the government sector. Being government employees, they enjoy the excellent fringe benefits and tend to equip their houses with the most up-to-date electrical and electronic appliances, furniture, and decorations. The majority of people who belong to this group have children and are the key decision makers in making the purchases for the largest group in the population, children and teens (42.4 percent of the total population). Additionally, this group tends to give in to the demands of their children.

Another group playing a significant role in the Brunei market is composed of young adults born between 1965 and 1981. This generation makes up 29.7 percent of the Brunei population and its members are more sophisticated and fragmented than the older generations. Young adults tend to seek out well-known brands, are better equipped with technological know-how, and are a high-spending group. This generation has received increased exposure to Western influences, for instance, from an education received overseas; increased media exposure to cable television, with channels like MTV, CNN, and HBO; availability of radio channels, like Capital FM and Capital Gold that are broadcast from London; increased access to the Internet; and exposure to Western eateries and clothing franchises, such as The Coffee Bean and Tea Leaf, McDonald's, Pizza Hut, KFC, Guess Jeans, and Levi's jeans. Although being increasingly exposed to Western culture, family-shared values and the traditional cultures are still at the core of this generation, due to high emphasis placed on the education system, the role of the family, and the influence of the religious councils.

Consumer Products

Following the broad categories of the Standard International Trade Classification (SITC), consumer products account for nearly 30 percent of the total imports of Brunei, as shown in Table

Table 2.14

Brunei's Imports of Selected Consumer Goods by Standard International Trade Classification, 1998

Product group	B$ thousand*
Foodstuffs	350,221.03
Beverages and tobacco	64,001.95
Perfume/cosmetics	13,900.26
Soaps/cleansers	16,526.38
Glassware/pottery	13,846.83
Television/radio/recorders	15,962.10
Computer equipment	34,612.07
Passenger car	119,067.07
Furniture and light fixtures	79,690.25
Clothing/apparel	47,983.10
Baby toys/game/sport	22,626.73
Total	778,437.77

Source: International Trade Centre (UNCTAD/WTO). "International Trade Statistics: Brunei Darussalam, 1998–1999." Available at www.intracen.org/menus/countries.htm.

*Figures converted to Brunei Dollars using the published rate for end of 1998, which is, 1.6695 against one U.S. Dollars.

2.14. Of these imported consumer products, foodstuffs represent the largest portion of the imports, an estimated B$350 million, or 40 percent of the consumer goods imports; followed by passenger cars worth B$119 million (15 percent of imported consumer goods); while another 12 percent (B$95.6 million) goes to furniture, light fixtures, and household electronics. The data from the table signify the country's high reliance on imported foodstuffs, high demand for passenger vehicles, and the need to fashion the home into a comfortable place. Furthermore, the data provide insights into the standards of living of the people, as the amount spent on imports of consumer products is significant for a country with a population of 345,000 people.

Table 2.15 illustrates the consumption trends of the four major racial groups in Brunei: Malay, Chinese, other indigenous, and foreigners. The average expenditure of a foreigner household is the highest in the country (B$2,847), followed by Malay (B$2,230), Chinese (B$2,139.41), and others (B$1,226). The high consumption pattern for a foreign household was attributed to "miscellaneous expenditures," at approximately 46 percent. For the four major races, household expenditures for food ranked the highest, with an average of about 26 percent; the other indigenous group spends the most in this category, accounting for 31 percent of their total expenditures.

As mentioned previously, per capita consumption for motor vehicles in Brunei is high, with expenditures for transportation constituting the second largest portion of household spending. This particular trend is unusual in the Brunei market, as consumers prioritize their transportation costs before expenditures for clothing, housing, and utilities. From Table 2.15, it can be deduced that Malays spend the most on transportation expenses, nearly equal to expenditures for food (25 percent), while Chinese spend the least in this category. Another observation worth noting is that expenditures on housing for a Chinese household make up 11 percent of their total expenditures, while it is the lowest expenditure for the Malays in this category. This is possibly due to the excellent state welfare policies provided for the citizens in the country, like the national housing scheme and government housing. On average, a Bruneian household makes its expenditures in

Table 2.15

Average Monthly Household Expenditure (percentage) by Community, 1997

Expenditure category	Malay B$	Chinese B$	Other indigenous B$	Foreigners B$
Food	559.81	558.29	383.22	633.95
	(25.09%)	(26.10%)	(31.25%)	(22.26%)
Clothing	133.96	76.01	65.08	68.38
	(6.00%)	(3.55%)	(5.31%)	(2.40%)
Housing	53.38	254.15	83.46	145.28
	(2.39%)	(11.88%)	(6.81%)	(5.10%)
Utilities	102.85	128.82	72.77	116.13
	(4.61%)	(6.02%)	(5.93%)	(4.08%)
Transport	549.69	284.45	165.19	428.9
	(24.64%)	(13.30%)	(13.47%)	(15.06%)
Durables	187.12	86.51	92.16	136.51
	(8.39%)	(4.04%)	(7.51%)	(4.79%)
Miscellaneous	644.06	751.18	364.54	1,318.29
	(28.87%)	(35.11%)	(29.72%)	(46.30%)
Total	2,230.87	2,139.41	1,226.42	2,847.44
	(100%)	(100%)	(100%)	(100%)

Source: Brunei Government, *Distribution of Household Income by District and Race, 1997–98* (Department of Economic Planning and Development, 2001); extracted from Hj Zulazrin Hj Mohidin, *Income and Expenditure Patterns in Brunei Darussalam* (Academic exercise, Department of Economics, Universiti Brunei Darussalam, April 2002), p. 123.

the following manner: food (26 percent), transport (16 percent), housing and durables (both 6 percent), utilities (5 percent), and clothing (4 percent).

Distribution and Retailing

Physical distribution of goods in the country is supported by the well-developed and extensive road infrastructure. Almost all areas in Brunei are accessible by the road system; hence, physical distribution does not hinder the delivery of goods to retailers. Conversely, the distribution channel in Brunei still takes the traditional form, where trading companies are normally involved in direct importation of consumer goods or act as main distributors for particular brands. These companies are then responsible for delivery of the goods to retailers.

According to a recent study conducted by Douty, Michael, and Yong (2002), the tenancy distribution of shops in Brunei is of a multiethnic nature. The Malay people are mostly running restaurants and feature only as partners in the other business types, such as sportswear and equipment, where they form partnerships with Indians. They also partner with Singaporean and Malaysian Chinese people in businesses such as souvenirs, antiques, building materials, irrigation equipment, and outboard engines. Chinese people as a group are spread over all business types, although there seems to be an emphasis on businesses in car sales/service, textiles/watches, footwear/bags, Chinese medicine, jewelry, tailoring, and electronic retailing. It was also observed that the Indian people run almost all the neighborhood provisional stores (*Kedai Runchit*) in the country.

Several clans of Chinese families run the handful of department stores and supermarkets in the country. However, some have not been faring well in recent years due to the high number of

Bruneians crossing the borders to shop. The number of Bruneian residents crossing to the Eastern Malaysian towns of Miri, Limbang, and Labuan to shop totals about 1.8 million, which is more than five times the Brunei population. The estimated total outflow of monies to these neighboring Malaysian states by land and sea in 2000 was about B$426 million (Anaman and Ismail 2002). With the high shopping expenditures in the neighboring states, small retailers and supermarkets in the country are finding it hard to maintain their businesses. This is evident from the low rental costs and the many unoccupied shop lots in newly built commercial areas. Furthermore, local salary earners' overcommitment to easily available bank loans, the current car-buying spree, and the departure of many immigrant workers have also contributed to the current low sales of the supermarkets in the country (*Borneo Bulletin* 2002a).

A popular trend in the retail business is the "$1.99 shop." This form of business strategy has been successful in catching the attention of consumers in the market; all items in these retail outlets cost only B$1.99, varieties of products are available and they are of relatively acceptable quality. However, other retailers began to copy this marketing concept, and many of these outlets began proliferating in the country. Competition became intense between these shops, and soon, some outlets began offering products at B$1.50, B$1.00, and then B$0.80. It appears that what seemed like a good marketing idea is eventually slowing down, with the recent closure of the first and largest "$1.99 shop" in the country.

Promotion and Advertising

Prior to the internal turmoil of 1999, not many promotional or advertising activities were seen in Brunei. The better-established companies, such as Brunei Shell Marketing, banks and financial institutions, insurance companies, and motor vehicle dealers carry out some form of advertising in the local newspapers, mostly focusing on informing the readers about their products or services. Local retailers or businesses do not place much emphasis on promoting their products or services. This is due to several factors, such as consumers' impulsive buying behavior due to their insensitivity to prices; the small market size for which retailers consider marketing activities unnecessary; Brunei's close social ties with Malaysia that make it easy to receive Malaysian television and radio broadcasts, newspapers, and magazines, and similarities in the two cultures that resulted in the thought that "whatever marketing activities are done in Malaysia will trickle over to the Brunei market"; and the fact that promotion and advertising are not priorities for businesses in Brunei, as these firms operate as importers or wholesalers in the country. More recently, there have been increasingly more sales promotion activities, still at a minimal level, by the local businesses following intense competition in the marketplace and empowerment of the Brunei consumers.

Direct Marketing

This form of marketing is increasingly popular in the Bruneian marketplace, reaching out to the two major age groups: the young adults and the thirty-five- to fifty-five-year-olds. These two groups have higher spending power in the population and are often approached by direct-sell personnel. Most firms engaged in direct marketing activities are those selling health supplements and related products, cosmetics and beauty products, and household appliances and equipment. The reason behind this increasingly important channel to reach the consumers is that almost all of the sellers are direct consumers of a particular brand or product, and the overhead costs involved in direct marketing activities are very low. These consumers have the greatest influence in introducing the product to their families and friends. However, door-to-door sales are not very popular in Brunei, and those consumers who use the direct-marketing products relay their confidence in the products to their peers. Increasingly popular direct-selling brands making their presence felt in Bruneian households are Amway, Elken, Cosway, NuLife, NuSkin, CNI, and Tupperware. It is interesting to note that Asian brands sold under this form of direct-selling method are taking a bigger share of the market previously dominated by American brands, such as Amway and Tupperware.

CONCLUSION

The outlook for the consumer market in Brunei is not expected to be very promising in the years to come. Being a "rentier state" economy, nearly all activities in the country rely on government expenditures. With free social services and an absence of income tax in the country, the Bruneian consumers are one of the highest spending groups in Southeast Asia. However, in recent years, retailers are finding it hard to make ends meet. In addition, the large outflow of monies into neighboring states means that businesses in Brunei need to provide a wide variety of high-quality goods that are competitively priced in comparison with neighboring countries. As always, the challenge is: "where are the customers?" Bringing in a variety of competitively priced high-quality goods does not ensure that retailers can sustain running the business, due to the relatively high overhead costs and the small market size.

Relationship building with customers is a special need in the Brunei market that numerous businesses in the country have been ignoring for too long. The market is no longer one in which sellers command the price and the products they sell. To retain customers, business owners need to establish good relationships with them. This is a factor needed to ensure the success of many direct-sales products in the market. In the Bruneian culture, trustworthiness in dealings is paramount. Although the Bruneian consumers are now more price sensitive, they do not mind paying a higher price for better-quality service from a retailer that they trust and with whom they have established a good relationship. In addition, in a society that is closely knit and tends to share the same core values, judgments on the reliability and trustworthiness of a business travel quickly across the market by word of mouth. The provision of excellent services to customers is one of the key ingredients in establishing good customer–business relationships.

In this small high-income market, a business must identify its niche in the marketplace in order to sustain itself in the longer run. In addition, businesses in the private sector ought to place greater emphasis on marketing activities to reach their customers and to emphasize marketing as one of the more important priorities in their business activities. In the Bruneian context, retailers have been asking "Where are the customers?" The problem is that they do not identify their target segments and position their products in the market. The government, for its part, has, however, been placing great emphasis on diversifying the economy of the country by attracting foreign direct investment and, in recent years, has been playing a very active role in assisting local retailers in churning up higher sales by organizing yearly activities like the "Brunei Grand Sales" and other sales events during festive seasons. Certainly, additional marketing and promotional activities are required by the retailers in the private sector to complement these efforts and assistance provided by the government.

NOTES

The authors acknowledge the contribution of Sara U. Douglas on an earlier work on this topic (1998, 63–92).

1. As of November 2001, of the ten ASEAN countries, only Singapore recorded GNP per capita higher than Brunei at US$24,664. GNP per capita for the remaining ASEAN countries was as follows: Malaysia, US$3,531; Thailand, US$1,984; Philippines, US$1,035; Indonesia, US$692; Myanmar, US$765; Vietnam, US$382; and Cambodia and Laos, US$280.

2. An estimated 94 percent of government employees are locals, whereas 78 percent of those working in the private sector are foreigners (Brunei Government 1999).

3. The definition of literacy used in 1991 was the ability of a person to read and write a simple letter or to read a newspaper column in at least one language.

4. It is an offense to sell chicken and meat not slaughtered according to Islamic rites, considered non-halal.

5. *Haram* are products or services that are banned in accordance with the Islamic faiths.

6. Sultan Haji Omar Ali Saifuddien III, the twenty-eighth sultan of Brunei (1950–1967), capitalized on Brunei's oil revenue to finance various development projects in Brunei and transformed a quiet backwater state into one of Asia's highest per capita income nations. To mark his contributions in transforming the country, he was regarded as "The Architect of Modern Brunei."

REFERENCES

Anaman, K. A., and R. A. Ismail. 2002. "Cross-Border Tourism from Brunei Darussalam to Eastern Malaysia: An Empirical Analysis." *Singapore Economic Review* 47.

AsiaWeek. 2001. "Bottomline: Ranked by GDP Growth," November 23. Available at www.asiaweek.com/asiaweek/magazine/yourspace/0,8782,184624,00.html.

Borneo Bulletin. 2000. *Brunei Yearbook 2000.* Brunei Darussalam: Brunei Press Sdn Bhd.

————. 2002. "Brunei's Big Oil and Gas Leap Forward Announced," January 20.

————. 2002a. "Leading Department Store Downs Shutters in Bandar," July 11.

————. 2002b. "Sultan urges University to Excellence Saying Only Best Will Do," September 8.

Brunei Government. "National Philosophy." Available at www.brunei.gov.bn/government/mib.htm.

————. "The 1959 Constitution." Available at www.brunei.gov.bn/government/contitut.htm.

————. 1993. *Statistical Yearbook 1993.* Brunei Darussalam: Statistics Division, Economic Planning Unit, Ministry of Finance.

————. 1999. *The Journey . . . Brunei Darussalam into the Next Millennium.* Brunei Darussalam: Prime Minister's Office.

————. 2000. *Eighth National Development Plan 2001–2005.* Brunei Darussalam: Prime Minister's Office.

————. 2001a. *Key Indicators 2001.* Brunei Darussalam: Department of Economic Planning and Development (DEPD), Ministry of Finance.

————. 2001b. *Statistical Yearbook 2000/2001.* Brunei Darussalam: Department of Economic Planning and Development (DEPD), Prime Minister's Office.

Cleary, Mark, and Shuang Yann Wong. 1994. *Oil, Economic Development and Diversification in Brunei Darussalam.* London: Macmillan; New York: St. Martin's Press.

Douglas, Sara U. 1998. "Brunei: Consumers in a Monarchical Market." In *Marketing and Consumer Behavior in East and South-East Asia*, ed. A. Pecotich and C. J. Shultz II, 63–92. Sydney: McGraw-Hill.

Douty, Chibamba, Pangiras Michael, and Chee Tuan Yong. 2002. "Retail Trends and Planned Shopping Centres of Brunei-Muara District Since Independence." Draft manuscript, Department of Economics, Universiti Brunei Darussalam, June.

Duraman, Haji Ismail, and Abdul A. Hashim. 1998. *Brunei Darussalam: Developing Within Its Own Paradigm.* Singapore: Southeast Asian Affairs 1998, Institute of Southeast Asian Studies.

Duraman, Haji Ismail, and Hairuni Haji Mohamed All Maricar. 1995. "Human Resources Development in Brunei Darussalam: A Phenomenal of Labor Shortage and Voluntary Unemployment among Youths." *Janang* 5 (September). Akademi Pengajian Brunei, Negara Brunei Darussalam.

Duraman, Haji Ismail, and Rosnah Opai. 2002. "Asian Economic Crisis: The Brunei Perspective." Draft manuscript, Department of Economics, Universiti Brunei Darussalam, June.

The Economist. 2004. *Pocket World in Figures: 2004.* Profile Books Ltd.

Gunn, Geoffrey C. 2001. "Brunei." In *Regional Handbook of Economic Development: The Southeast Asia Handbook,* ed. Patrick Heenan and Monique Lamontagne, 78–86. Chicago: Fitzroy Dearborn.

International Trade Centre (UNCTAD/WTO). "SITC: Brunei Imports: 1997–1998." Available at www.intracen.org/menus/countries.htm.

Maricar, Hairuni Haji Mohamed All. 1997. "Female Labor Participation and Development in Brunei Darussalam." Paper presented at International Conference on Women in the Asia-Pacific Region: Persons, Power and Politics, Singapore, August 11–13.

Mohidin, Hj Zulazrin Hj. 2002. "Income and Expenditure Patterns in Brunei Darussalam." Academic exercise, Department of Economics, Universiti Brunei Darussalam, April.

Shamim, A. Siddiqui, Hashim, A. Abdul, and Abu N. M. Wahid. 1997. "Economic and Social Policies of Brunei: An Empirical Analysis." In *The ASEAN Region in Transition: A Socio-economic Perspective*, ed. Abu N. M. Wahid. Aldershot, UK: Ashgate.

Teo, Siew Yean, and Siew Ee Tan. 1999. "Population and Labor Force in Brunei Darussalam: Patterns and Structural Changes." In *Readings on the Economy of Brunei Darussalam*. 1st ed. Brunei Darussalam: Educational Technology Centre, Universiti Brunei Darussalam.

World Bank Group. 2002. "Brunei at a Glance (November 9, 2002)." Available at www.worldbank.org/data/countrydata/aag/brn_aag.pdf.

World Trade Organization (WTO). 2000. "International Trade Statistics 2000." Available at www.wto.org/english/res_e/statis_e/stats2000_e.pdf.

———. 2001. "Trade Policy Review: Brunei Darussalam: May 2001." Available at www.wto.org/english/tratop_e/tpr_e/tp164_e.htm.

CHAPTER 3

CAMBODIA

Striving for Peace, Stability, and a Sustainable Consumer Market

CLIFFORD J. SHULTZ II AND DON R. RAHTZ

OVERVIEW

Cambodia continues to rise from the ashes of genocide and profound economic mismanagement. Despite the legacy of the killing fields, ongoing political tension, and problems associated with any poor country, relative stability and new government policies that are friendly to foreign investors are transforming this nation into a promising market economy. Positive trends include investment and development, tourism and services growth, agribusiness expansion, the emergence of some light industry, and export development. To illuminate Cambodia's economic and market renaissance, the authors frame historical developments and discuss the current political, economic, social, and market conditions that affect consumers, marketers, and policy makers; they then offer an overview of the macromarketing mix and conclude with prognoses for Cambodian consumers, markets, and managers.

INTRODUCTION

Cambodia's economic, political, and social structures have undergone cataclysmic changes that profoundly affected—and continue to affect—all domestic economic endeavors, social institutions, consumers, and perceptions of the country by foreigners as a place in which to invest and to engage in marketing activities. The accelerating pace and sustainability of Cambodia's emergence from "Year Zero" in 1975 (Ponchaud 1977) and "the killing fields" will coincide with several factors. Among them are economic and social policies, more seamless integration into the Association of Southeast Asian Nations (ASEAN), membership in the World Trade Organization (WTO), greater foreign investment and development, and the extent to which a stable consumer society emerges (Asian Development Bank 1994; Ayers 2000; Chhon and Moniroth 1999; Muscat 1989; UNDP 1991, 2002; World Bank 1992). This last factor is particularly salient to Cambodia, and it is important to mention that despite the availability of cultivable land, productive fisheries, and other natural resources, and a relatively low population-to-land ratio, Cambodia is still one of the poorest countries in the world. Moreover, unlike other countries transitioning to a more fully systemic market economy, Cambodia also must transform from a less-developed war-ravaged country to a more developed country. Compared to its neighbors,

Laos and Vietnam, also recovering from war devastation, Cambodia has a legacy of greater political volatility.

The task of managing that multifaceted process is difficult and will continue to be difficult. Simply understanding the dynamic interactions of consumers, marketers, and extant environmental conditions, as well as the evolution of the interaction process, is challenging, particularly given the convention of unreliable data in Cambodia. Prior to the last few years, fundamental economic, market, and social indicators were somewhat difficult to obtain or were often little more than educated guesses or extrapolations from decades-old statistics (cf. Chandler 1992). The availability and validity of these measures, however, has improved over the course of the last decade, revealing some positive trends, including a fledgling market economy with near double-digit growth rates. Though the rate of growth—and some might argue growth itself—may be difficult to sustain, Cambodia has maintained rates greater than most other countries in the region (e.g., *South East Asia Monitor* 2002; UNDP 2002). In a country still recovering from the carnage of genocide, many Cambodians are embracing consumer culture and looking to the future. Investors concurrently are penetrating this still somewhat uncertain market, looking for opportunities. In this chapter, we introduce geographic and cultural idiosyncrasies, examine recent historical events that created the present market conditions, and then discuss relevant trends and economic, marketing, and consumer behavior issues that investors should understand before entering the market.

GEOGRAPHIC AND CULTURAL INFLUENCES

Cambodia—or Kampuchea as the Cambodians refer to their land—is generally circular in shape, covers a landmass of over 181,000 square kilometers (about the size of Missouri) and borders Thailand, Laos, and Vietnam. It also has over 200 kilometers of coastline on the Gulf of Thailand. Cambodia has no major mountain ranges that have acted as natural barriers to invaders and traders. This physical feature and the country's proximity to navigable waterways has meant that Cambodia has always been influenced by other cultures and nations, most notably Thailand and Vietnam, but also India, Indonesia (notably Java), China, Mongolia, Japan (for a brief period during World War II), France, and now, some would contend, many donor nations.

Its borders, accordingly, have changed numerous times over the centuries. During the golden age of the Khmer Empire, circa the ninth to twelfth centuries, the kingdom extended from present-day Myanmar to the South China Sea, but expansion and annexation by neighboring states and colonial occupations have yielded the considerably smaller territory of today's Cambodia. Within today's borders is the vast Angkor temple and palace complex built during that golden era. These artifacts are regarded as some of the world's greatest historical and cultural treasures, and the importance of this site was recognized by the United Nations Educational, Scientific, and Cultural Organization (UNESCO) and was placed on the *World Heritage List;* the stark image of Angkor Wat has become the archetypal symbol for the country and is found on the national flag.

The country has abundant natural resources. The Mekong, Bassac, and Tonle rivers, which merge at the nation's capital, Phnom Penh, and the extensive canals, are important topographical influences on culture and commerce. The Tonle Sap, the largest body of freshwater in Southeast Asia, is one of the richest fisheries in the world. Fertile alluvial soil, replenished by seasonal swellings of the greater Mekong watershed, makes Cambodia a potential "rice bowl" of production. About 40 percent of the land is arable, though only about half that land is cultivated, and half of that is planted in rice. Estimates indicate that forests still cover approximately 50 percent of Cambodia, but excessive logging and other pressures on wilderness have severely degraded this resource and other flora and fauna dependent upon its preservation. Cambodia also potentially possesses substantial oil and gas deposits. There are additional physical assets, including beaches and ports, that hold tourist and industrial potential, respectively.

The climate is tropical. Monsoons are biannual; with the accompanying rainy season, they dictate many commercial and cultural activities. Weather patterns strongly influence the country's economic output and welfare; drought and floods are particularly problematic (e.g., Chandler 1992, xvi, 7). Unchecked deforestation will likely exacerbate flooding and subsequent damage.

Approximately 90 percent of the people are ethnic Cambodians or Khmer (the terms frequently are used interchangeably [*Culturgram* 1995]), making Cambodia one of the most homogeneous countries in Southeast Asia. However, the Khmers, similarly to most modern ethnic groups, are an amalgam of many peoples, with their origins likely a mixture of Mongol and Melanesian or Malay elements. Cultural forces sweeping in from India and Thailand have particularly influenced religion, architecture, language, and the arts. Theravada Buddhism is the dominant religion and affects much of daily life. The group or community is considered more important than is the individual, as are rulers and ancestors. Although Western clothing is common in Phnom Penh and other more urban areas, most Cambodians still opt for traditional clothing, such as the checked, rectangular cloth that is wrapped around the hips or worn like a kilt down to the ankles (*sampot* and sarong for women; *sarong soet* for men). A large multipurpose scarf/satchel/hat called a *krama* is also common (see also Sheehan 2000).

Chinese and Vietnamese are the largest minorities; each has traditionally been associated with the general commercial sector and fishing industries, respectively. In the distant and recent past, both groups have also been persecuted. The Chinese community less so, however, and it is re-emerging as a significant commercial force. Ethnic Vietnamese are found in increasing numbers in Phnom Penh, partly due to the importation and migration of Vietnamese women to work the entertainment trade. The remaining Cambodians are Cham Muslims (approximately 200,000) and are from various tribal groups (fewer than 100,000) typically found in Cambodia's hinterlands.

Khmer is the national language. It is from the Mon-Khmer linguistic group, is alphabetic, and is nontonal. Most Westerners find it relatively difficult to master. French was once commonly spoken, but English is clearly becoming the favored second language. Increasing influence and investment by the People's Republic of China, Taiwan, and Singapore throughout the region have also amplified interest in the Chinese language.

In summary, Cambodia possesses valuable natural and cultural resources. Its location in the greater Mekong basin and proximity to dynamic economies in East and Southeast Asia can serve the country well in the forms of investment, trade, and other kinds of economic and political cooperation. Proper development and management of those resources is contingent upon effective governance, a topic to which we now turn.

POLITICAL EVOLUTION AND STRUCTURE

One cannot fully understand or appreciate the Cambodian market and economy without revisiting political events from the past half century that have shaped the people, economy, and current and future consumer markets. Since independence from France in 1953, Cambodia has gone through a variety of political and economic regimes, as summarized in Table 3.1.

During the twenty-five-year period starting in 1970, Cambodia was engulfed in a bitter and protracted civil war, a devastating holocaust, and a costly foreign invasion and occupation. These major upheavals led to the loss of an estimated one-fourth of the population and a near total destruction of its social and physical infrastructure (e.g., Asian Development Bank 1991; World Bank 1992). There-

Table 3.1

Political/Economic Regimes in Cambodia, 1953–Present

Years	Regime
1953–70	Autocratic monarchy (Sihanouk's national socialism)
1970–75	Republic (Lon Nol Republic)
1975–78	Primitive communist system based on the early Soviet Union's War Communism ("Democratic Kampuchea," better known as the Khmer Rouge)
1978–91	Foreign-imposed communist system (the People's Republic of Kampuchea of Hun Sen/Heng Samrin/Chea Sim)
1991–93	Mandate under the United Nations Transitional Authority
1993–present	Constitutional monarchy

fore, it is important to review the changes during these periods and their impact on the economy, markets, and consumers. The following sections provide brief reviews of each of these periods.

Sihanouk's Monarchy

The early period of Sihanouk's era (1953–63) was peaceful, and Cambodia managed to record modest rates of growth, was self-sufficient in essential foods, and was a net exporter of rice (Osborne 1979; Prud'Homme 1969; Steinberg 1959). Although agriculture dominated the economy, as both source of income and source of employment, a small but budding middle class emerged, especially in Phnom Penh and some provincial capitals, such as Battambang, Kompong Cham, and the port of Sihanoukville. However, from 1963 to 1969, economic growth slowed considerably to around 3 percent, hardly enough to compensate for the increase in the population. At the same time, export surplus dwindled to a trickle, while the tax base was substantially eroded. One of the major factors behind this economic decline was Sihanouk's decision to phase out U.S. assistance and to increase the role of the state in the economy in an effort to minimize the spillover effects of the war in Vietnam. The economic and social infrastructure, although inadequate, had been developing and spreading slowly throughout the country. However, Cambodia's neutralist foreign policy ultimately led to the termination of economic, financial, and military assistance from the United States. Thus, the Cambodian government began to manage the economy. The banking and foreign trade sectors were nationalized, and the state set up a number of enterprises in the industrial and service sectors. This, in turn, led to the discontent of those businesspersons and politicians whose interests were adversely affected by the loss of U.S. assistance, especially the military. The increase in the role of the state in the economy led to increases in rent-seeking activities and inefficiency. The combination of these two problems resulted in mounting dissatisfaction among those who were most affected by the rejection of U.S. assistance and by the curtailment of the private sector. These internal factors, together with the United States' decision to withdraw its armed forces from Vietnam, provided the Cambodian military led by General Lon Nol an opportunity to stage a successful coup d'état against Sihanouk in March 1970.

The Khmer Republic

After toppling Sihanouk, Lon Nol installed a republican regime known as the Khmer Republic and attempted to return to the more liberal economic policies of the 1960s. However, the escalation of the civil war and pervasive corruption in his government quashed all hopes of an economic revival. Successive intensification of bombing and the takeover of much of the countryside by the Khmer Rouge led to the collapse of the Khmer Republic. During this period (1970–75), all production indicators fell, and soon nearly half the population was living in beleaguered cities, having to rely on airlifted food and medical supplies. Throughout the entire Lon Nol period, the government was wholly dependent on support from the United States, because its spending had far outstripped possible tax revenue (Chantrabot 1993; Corfield 1994).

The Khmer Rouge and Democratic Kampuchea

Under the circumstances, Pol Pot's Khmer Rouge forces had few problems overcoming the American-supported Lon Nol forces and marched into Phnom Penh on April 17, 1975. From this capitulation emerged Democratic Kampuchea, a regime based on the system of "War Communism" installed in the Soviet Union at the beginning of the Bolshevik revolution. The Khmer Rouge immediately and brutally proceeded to transform the Cambodian economy into Pol Pot's extreme interpretation of a communist utopia (Chandler, Kiernan, and Boua 1988; Twining 1989).

The country was sealed off, and then the cities were emptied, as the entire urban population was sent to the countryside. Everyone was obliged to live and to work on a communal basis. Much of the traditional social and economic infrastructure was dismantled; the central government was destroyed; the currency was abolished. Private property was confiscated, all economic activities became part of the state apparatus, and markets ceased to exist. Many urban dwellers, citizens associated with the previous regime ("Old People"), and educated individuals, in general, were executed or fled the country. More than a million Cambodians died from execution, exhaustion, or starvation. Urban populations were forcibly moved on short notice into slave labor camps scattered throughout the countryside of Cambodia. These slave laborers were mainly assigned to work on building the irrigation network known as the Pol Pot canal system. Work conditions were extremely inhuman. Collective manual labor for up to eighteen hours a day, with the provision of only starvation food rations, became a widespread practice. In addition, the Khmer Rouge abolished the traditional family structure and cut communication with the outside world.

In their efforts to create a new society, the Khmer Rouge ruthlessly suppressed religion by destroying Buddhist temples, which were the center of village life in prerevolutionary Cambodia. Buddhists were killed or forced to break their vows, and ritual activities were forbidden. In place of religion, tradition, and family, the Khmer Rouge instituted a political ideology that stressed new values and codes of conduct. The Khmer Rouge demanded strict adherence to these codes and new values; those who dared to challenge them were harshly and swiftly punished. Agriculture was to be the cornerstone of the economy, while industry was given only secondary attention. In virtually every area in which one could measure productivity, the quantity and quality of output were severely constrained by the highly labor-intensive methods and the implementation of ineffective administrative policies and radical production techniques. Foreign trade reverted to barter with those few countries that maintained economic relations with the Khmer Rouge.

The People's Republic of Kampuchea

On December 25, 1978, the armed forces of the Socialist Republic of Vietnam invaded Cambodia and drove the Khmer Rouge back along the border with Thailand (Leepson 1985). In January 1979, Vietnam installed a new government headed by Heng Samrin, a former Khmer Rouge general. The Cambodian government was renamed the People's Republic of Kampuchea (PRK).

Cambodia's population by this time was on the brink of starvation. The whole economy had collapsed, and there was massive movement of Cambodians throughout the country (Boua 1983).

Under the PRK, the Cambodian economy was reorganized according to the more classical type of socialist system based on a hierarchical, centrally planned organization. The new regime initially made considerable headway in rebuilding economic infrastructure and institutions, including social institutions. Families, for example, were allowed to reunite and to return to their places of origin. A central administration was reestablished; the banking system was reopened; the national currency, the riel (KHR), was reintroduced; and some factories were reassembled.

Other policies of the PRK allowed the cities to repopulate. This urbanization scheme was to introduce a new group of people who until then never lived in urban areas; they were basically subsistence farmers with limited skills and experience. They were simply referred to as "New People." The original city dwellers who had been government officials, merchants, professionals, craftsmen, and laborers—the mercantile and intellectual core of the country—had either been killed during the Khmer Rouge era or escaped to settle as refugees in many parts of the world: the United States, Canada, France, Australia, and Thailand. Some estimates suggest that over two million Cambodians were murdered or fled the country. The reconstruction efforts of the PRK were facilitated by the inflow of assistance from the former bloc of East European countries and the former Soviet Union. Many of these central-planning policies, however, were ultimately abandoned due to their rejection by the population (Vickery 1990).

UNTAC and Constitutional Monarchy

The successful conclusion of the second Paris Conference in October 1991 led to the establishment of the United Nations Transitional Authorities in Cambodia (UNTAC), under whose mandate an election was organized and carried out in May 1993. The result of the election, in which over 90 percent of the registered voters went to the polls (Siv 1998), gave a clear majority to the noncommunist parties. These parties were FUNCINPEC (Front Uni National pour un Cambodge Indépendent Neutre Pacific et Coopérative) led by Prince Norodom Ranariddh with fifty-eight representatives, BLD (Buddhist Liberal Democratic) led by former Prime Minister Son Sann with ten representatives, and Moulinaka (Mouvement de Libération Nationale du Kampuchea) led by Ros Roeun with one representative, as opposed to fifty-one representatives for the CPP (Cambodian People's Party) led by Hun Sen and Chea Sim, both former Khmer Rouge senior officials. The elected representatives established a Constitutional National Assembly, which, in turn, promulgated a new constitution. A new Royal Cambodian Government (RCG) was formed in September 1993 to take over all aspects of governance.

The RCG was a tenuous coalition with two prime ministers and two ministers of defense and interior, one each from CPP and FUNCINPEC. Political infighting continued within and among the parties in the government. Corruption was widespread and combined with an extremely low capacity of the government to manage effectively. This, in turn, allowed the Khmer Rouge to continue to challenge the government's authorities, especially in the countryside. This situation created widespread insecurity, thereby causing a delay in badly needed reconstruction and rehabilitation of the country's economy, despite the availability of a sizeable amount of financial and technical assistance from the international community. Thus, following the election of May 1993 sponsored by the United Nations, Cambodia remained economically and politically unstable. After a short period of progress, the economic, social, and political situations started to deteriorate very quickly, especially after the second half of 1994.

The 1997 Coup and Aftereffects

In July 1997, less than four years after an expensive election conducted by the United Nations, violence erupted again in Cambodia, signaling an end to dual prime ministers. Hun Sen assumed almost total control of the government. Prince Ranariddh, along with many members of the opposition and critics of the government, such as Sam Rainsy, fled the country. Violence was widespread; many feared it would spiral out of control, into a new civil war. The world community exerted pressure for new elections. The CPP finally agreed, and after an initial delay, on July 26, 1998, the Cambodian people staged a general election. Although the election was monitored by foreign (mostly European) observers, there was concern about the fairness of the process. A staggering 94.9 percent of regional business executives polled prior to the election said they did not expect the elections to be free and fair (*Far Eastern Economic Review* 1998). This concern was generated from the fact that the elections were held under the auspices of the ruling CPP. In a crowded field of candidates from thirty-nine parties involved in the elections, the CPP, FUNCINPEC, and the party of the former finance minister, Sam Rainsy, were the main contenders. The overall voter turnout was reported to be 90 percent. Thayer and Tasker captured the tension surrounding the process and the times:

> Intimidation notwithstanding, the actual voting went smoothly by all accounts. But anxiety increased as ballot counting began on July 27. By midday, Ranariddh and his top officials were privately declaring victory, after receiving initial reports from FUNCINPEC monitors around the country. By late afternoon, they were declaring fraud. (Thayer and Tasker 1998, 20)

The CPP, however, failed to win a majority of the vote, and Hun Sen was forced to create a coalition government with the opposition parties. First attempts failed, and it was not until King Sihanouk stepped in to broker a deal that a coalition government was (re)born. This particular deal was not favored by everyone, and a number of Cambodians gathered in street protests (*The Economist* 1998). The King's appeal for an end to the conflict and unified government reflected years of war weariness: "In a Cambodia that is not a state of law and not a full-fledged democracy, I have no other choice than to advise the weak to choose a policy that avoids misfortune for the people, the motherland, and themselves" (Thayer 1998, 17). Acquiescence by the antagonists provides some insight into the broad esteem for the king and his political influence. Sihanouk though has subsequently retired, replaced by his son, Norodom Sihamoni, in 2004; whether an untested new king can similarly smooth Cambodia's occasionally rough political waters remains to be seen.

Since 1998, Cambodia has been governed by another coalition dominated by the CPP and the FUNCINPEC. Rainsy's party, even though it had come in third place, was left out of the coalition. Most observers feel this ostracism was due to the CPP leadership's disdain for Rainsy. Other political parties that jostle for seats in the national assembly and senate include the Buddhist Liberal Party (BLP); Cambodian Pracheachon Party or Cambodian People's Party (CPP); Khmer Citizen Party (KCP); National United Front for an Independent, Neutral, Peaceful, and Cooperative Cambodia (FUNCINPEC); and the Sam Rainsy Party (SRP) (e.g., *World Factbook* 2003; The Economist Intelligence Unit 2003).

Much of the infighting and political intrigue that was part of the pre-1998 government remains, but the intensity is at much lower levels. An armed assault by a small group of antigovernment fighters in Phnom Penh during the early morning of November 24, 2000, apparently has been the only organized armed violence against the government since the 1998 elections. The assault occurred while both Hun Sen and Prince Ranariddh were out of the country. Authors' conversations with several sources in Phnom Penh that day revealed that there were "other aspects" concerning the ill-equipped attack that made a number of political observers and members of the opposition parties dubious about the purpose of, and who was actually behind, the attack. While this and other less dramatic events point to a continuing level of tension within the coalition, to date, the government has succeeded in providing a fairly stable environment for the country. In February 2002, the first nationwide communal (local) elections in decades were held, though not without some violence and allegations of intimidation (Dobbs 2002). Field interviews by the authors corroborated these allegations. Nevertheless, results from these same interviews also indicate that the voting public accepted the outcomes. Their fears of widespread violence have generally subsided, and, given the strong showing of the local elections in February 2002 and July 2003, the CPP and Hun Sen are now in clear control of the political environment, though the SRP interestingly received strong support from young voters (see also *The Economist* 2003a, 2003b; Un and Ledgerwood 2003).

Many observers view Cambodia as a country in perpetual political upheaval; in fact, it has had the same prime minister for more than a decade. Hun Sen has steadily solidified his hold on the political apparatus and is "fully committed to ensuring political stability" (Sereyvuth 2003, 5; see also Sen 2001 and Mydans 2002). This "stability" has generally stimulated a growing belief among local and foreign businesspersons that Cambodia has an increasingly favorable and transparent business environment, perhaps more favorable and transparent than some of its ASEAN neighbors. At the same time, and while the government pleads for financial aid, widespread rumors persist that the country's top leaders have amassed fortunes through corruption, drug trafficking, illegal logging and other nefarious activities (e.g., Kate 2004; Un and Ledgerwood 2003). Although these rumors are disconcerting, interviews conducted by the authors with current and potential investors in Cambodia reveal guarded optimism. The streets of Phnom Penh, Siem Reap, and Sihanoukville, furthermore, show obvious signs of foreign direct investment (FDI) and a consumer-based economy—tangible evidence to support this more optimistic view.

ECONOMIC ENVIRONMENT

Rebuilding a sustainable economy after genocide and decades of war remains a daunting challenge. More recently, political infighting, poor weather, and the Asian crisis all retarded growth. Despite these problems—and considering its starting point of total economic devastation—Cambodia has progressed remarkably. In 1999, the first full year of peace in thirty years, further reforms were implemented and growth resumed, but at the start of the new millennium, severe weather and high oil prices hurt agriculture and industrial production, as did declining FDI and growing debt. Modest gains, hovering around 5 percent, however, were still achieved, though some cause for concern is warranted (see also Un and Ledgerwood 2003; *World Factbook* 2003). Below, we provide a synopsis of economic development since independence and provide some sector-specific details and commentary vis-à-vis more recent trends.

From 1953 to 1970, the Cambodian economy grew in real terms on average about 5 percent per year, while the population grew about 2.5 percent per year, indicating an average per capita income real growth of 2.5 percent per year. During the Lon Nol period, the Cambodian economy registered negative rates of growth, while inflation rates reached triple digits. The beginning of a succession of upheavals in Cambodian society took place during the next two and a half decades, both in terms of its structure and behavior. One can only guess how bad economic conditions were during the Khmer Rouge years. Economic indicators from 1975 to 1980 were virtually

Table 3.2

Rate of Change of Main Economic Indicators, 1991–1994

Economic indicator	1991	1992	1993	1994
Real GDP	7.6	7.0	3.9	5.2
Domestic liquidity	28.6	17.3	20.3	16.0
Net credit to the government	35.3	200.8	19.6	6.2
Exports of goods	104.6	(23.8)	(26.5)	360.0
Imports of goods (retained)	(9.8)	37.8	61.8	92
Ratio of GDP				
Budget revenue	4.4	6.2	5.2	8.2
Budget expenditure	7.8	9.8	11.0	14.7
Current expenditure	7.4	9.5	6.7	10.0
Capital expenditure	0.4	0.3	4.2	4.7
Current budget deficit	(1.2)	(4.3)	(1.5)	(1.8)
Domestic investment	9.4	9.8	14.2	19.2
Government investment	0.4	0.3	4.2	4.7
Nongovernment investment	9.0	9.5	10.0	14.5
Financing of Investment	9.4	9.4	14.2	19.2
National savings	7.9	7.3	8.1	7.4
Foreign savings	1.5	2.5	6.1	11.8
BOP current account deficit	(1.5)	(2.5)	(6.1)	(11.8)
Gross international reserve	n.a.	1.0	2.0	2.1
GDP (billions of riel)	1,336	2,508	5,546	6,048
Gross international reserve (millions US$)	0.3	29.9	70.7	110.5

Sources: National Institute of Statistics, 2002; World Bank, 1992.

nonexistent, as the Khmer Rouge obliterated the economy. However, using anecdotal stories from those who lived through the period (e.g., Pran and DePaul 1997; Ung 2000) and information gleaned from the authors' personal interviews with survivors, the total devastation of the economy in that period becomes chillingly evident. Every postperiod economic assessment clearly points to the total collapse of the pre-Khmer Rouge economy.

In the 1980s and 1990s, Cambodia's economy passed through several phases of slump and recovery. A reduction in aid from the former Soviet Union and unfavorable weather resulted in slow growth (about 2 percent) in 1989–90. Until October 1991, economic recovery was severely hampered by civil war, by the collapse of the socialist economies in Europe, and by the lack of other sources of international support. Output, however, recovered strongly to an estimated 7 percent in 1991–92, as economic activities were boosted by the return of good weather and increased demand associated with UNTAC personnel and higher foreign exchange receipts. Beginning in 1993, the Royal Government had been "operating under the slogan '*Le Cambodge s'aide lui-même*' or 'Cambodia will help itself'" and had implemented a series of programs designed to rehabilitate the economy (e.g., St. John 1995, 266). These programs produced mixed but generally positive results, as shown in Table 3.2, which presents a summary of the main economic indicators per annum for the first half of the 1990s. Indicators were generally consistent with expectations, given Cambodia's systemic challenges. Weather conditions continued to have a pronounced effect on economic development. Severe flooding was followed by drought when the monsoon rains ended prematurely. As a result, output growth in 1994 was estimated at 5.2 percent. The low growth in production in the agricultural sector was the main cause behind this

Table 3.3

Rate of Change of Main Economic Indicators, 1995–2000

Economic indicator	1995	1996	1997	1998	1999	2000
Real GDP	8.4	3.5	3.7	1.5	6.9	5.4
Domestic liquidity	16.7	7.6	6.1	14.4	(1.5)	0.3
Net credit to the government	1.1	(3.1)	(8.1)	11.7	(6.1)	(6.9)
Exports of goods	2.4	10.1	81.0	8.3	21.8	11.0
Imports of goods (retained)	16.4	20.3	5.8	−0.1	20.4	12.0
Ratio of GDP						
Budget revenue	8.5	9.0	9.6	8.9	11.5	12.1
Budget expenditure	15.9	17.3	13.8	14.9	15.9	17.8
Current expenditure	9.1	9.8	8.8	8.9	9.6	10.3
Capital expenditure	6.7	7.6	4.9	6.0	6.3	7.5
Current budget deficit	(7.5)	(8.3)	(4.2)	(6.1)	(4.4)	(5.7)
Domestic investment	12.8	15.2	14.4	12.0	17.0	14.1
Government investment	6.6	7.1	4.8	5.7	6.1	7.3
Nongovernment investment	6.2	8.2	9.6	6.3	10.9	6.9
Financing of investment						
National savings	5.4	5.4	5.9	5.4	4.7	4.0
Foreign savings	7.2	11.7	6.6	6.0	5.7	
BOP current account deficit	(14.5)	(17.3)	(8.8)	(8.0)	(8.4)	(9.0)
Gross international reserve	1.5	2.1	2.4	3.5	3.3	2.8
GDP (billion riels)	7,274.4	7,904.5	8,735.4	10,088.6	11,150.3	11,444.1
Gross international reserve (millions US$)	192.0	265.8	298.5	324.3	393.2	501.7

Sources: World Bank, 2001, 2003; Asian Development Bank, 2003; and National Institute of Statistics, 2002.

lower than expected growth. Consequently, Cambodia was again faced with shortages in rice production to meet the population's needs. However, growth in activities in other sectors was stronger, especially in construction and logging.

Foreign aid and assistance was critical to Cambodia's rebirth and remains an important component of the economy. The initial inflows of foreign money brought by UNTAC almost doubled government revenue to 6.2 percent of gross domestic product (GDP) in 1993. Most subsequent assistance focused on implementation of the National Plan to Rehabilitate and Develop Cambodia (NPRD). The NPRD's aim was to help Cambodia "achieve a full fledged market economy" with the government as a "partner" with the private sector (Frontier Funds Management 1996, B-4). The combination of foreign assistance and the Paris Peace Accords "greatly increased public confidence" and led to a construction and housing boom that included the rehabilitation of houses, shops, offices, hotels, and restaurants (Frontier Funds Management 1996, B-5). Foreign trade and integration into the Greater Mekong Subregion also contributed to economic recovery and increased consumer choices. Asian countries were particularly helpful. As just two examples, Japanese assistance renovated Phnom Penh's ports, and Malaysian firms began construction of a free trade industrial park as part of airport rehabilitation.

The latter half of the 1990s continued a generally steady march toward economic stability and growth, but not without difficulties and disappointments, which triggered trepidation within the investor community. Table 3.3 summarizes compelling economic measures for this era. Noteworthy is Cambodia's fairly steady progress toward rebuilding its economy. Also noteworthy is the clear impact of violence (e.g., the 1997 coup). The dip in a number of the indicators demonstrates the link between perceived political stability and the well-being of the nation.

Cambodia has generally seen an accelerating increase in official financial aid. In June 2001, US$560 million was made available to Cambodia from the Consultative Group (CGAP) of multilateral and bilateral donors, which exceeded both the 1999 and 2000 figures. There also has been an increase in private investment. A significant portion of this can be traced to the tourism and garment industries, though investment patterns are erratic. The first quarter FDI in 2002, for example, dropped to US$10.1 million compared to US$28.4 million in 2000. This drop was tied to various concerns, including a slowdown in the world economy; possible shifts in lost comparative advantage vis-à-vis garments; corruption; and with the looming 2003 elections, renewed concerns about stability (see also Lintner 2001a; Un and Ledgerwood 2003).

In 1996, net inflows were US$293.6 million; in 1999, that figure had dropped to US$125.5 million (World Bank 2001). As noted above, this trend suggests lost confidence in the wake of the 1997 coup. An official boycott by the United States and other countries led to even more lost confidence. This, in turn, directly and adversely affected economic growth, at a time when Cambodia could scarcely afford it (Kevin 1998). In 2000, the entire budget deficit of about US$166 million was covered by foreign aid. The amount of foreign aid in the Cambodia GDP has grown as a percentage of the budget from 11.7 percent in 1993, to 14.4 percent in 1999, and to an even higher 16.4 percent in 2000. Cambodia received US$615 million in financial pledges in 2002; aid accounted for more than 50 percent of the government's budget (Un and Ledgerwood 2003; The Economist Intelligence Unit 2003). This trend has raised concerns within the donor community and has resulted in some changes in the allocating and monitoring of that aid. Several government officials have revealed in personal conversations with the authors a clear hope to reduce reliance on donor aid and to have the private sector become a more significant contributor to the government's budget. Revenue streams from taxes and other sources may well help to wean Cambodia from its currently heavy reliance on donor aid, but aid will be vital to Cambodia for the foreseeable future.

Inflation

Recent trends suggest inflation is reasonably well controlled. This outcome is particularly welcome, for a number of reasons; uniquely to Cambodia, however, a case can be made that inflationary pressure was a contributor to the brief resurgence of the Khmer Rouge in the mid-1990s. The rate of inflation, as measured by the Consumer Price Index (CPI), soared from about 90 percent during 1989 to over 150 percent in 1990, slowed to 88 percent in 1991, and rose again to 177 percent in 1992. The exchange rate in the parallel market declined broadly in line with the underlying inflationary pressures. Strong inflationary expectations weakened the public's confidence in the domestic currency, contributing to widespread currency substitution. The main cause behind the inflationary pressures and exchange-rate devaluation was the monetary expansion, which, in turn, was the result of fiscal deterioration. Public finances deteriorated severely during this period. While the government responded to fiscal pressures by cutting its public investment program, the overall budget deficit, nevertheless, widened and, in the absence of foreign financing, was covered by currency issued by the central bank, the National Bank of Cambodia.

By 1992, most employees in the industrial sector found it almost impossible to support households, while inflation preserved wide gaps between the living standards enjoyed by high-income earners and property owners versus those without secure sources of income. Entrepreneurs and

Table 3.4

Inflation as Measured by Change in Consumer Price Index (CPI)

Year	Change in CPI (%)	Year	Change in CPI (%)
1991	87.9	1997	7.9
1992	176.8	1998	14.8
1993	31.0	1999	4.0
1994	26.1	2000	(1.4)
1995	3.5	2001	(0.6)
1996	7.2	2002	2.4

Note: The information in this table is drawn from a variety of sources, including the Asian Development Bank, National Institute of Statistics of Cambodia, and the World Bank. Some of the data available are based on urban settings or Phnom Penh only for CPI inflation reports. At times, the author estimated reported inflation rates through the synthesizing of data from these three sources when they were dissimilar.

other private-sector businesspersons who had good fortune in both legal activities (e.g., scooter-taxis and food vendors) and illegal activities (e.g., prostitutes and smugglers) also fared well, while soldiers and civil servants saw their earning power erode or disappear. Such wage discrepancies and inflation were considered primary factors in the rising crime rates and general civil unrest of the time (The Economist Intelligence Unit 1994).

In 1993, the unsettled security and political situation up to the time of the election slowed growth in the first half of the year. Improved domestic and external confidence contributed to a rebound in the second half of the year, with growth for the year estimated at 4 percent. Private consumption accounted for an estimated 85 percent of GDP during 1991–93, and total investment is estimated to have risen from 9.5 percent in 1991 to 15.3 percent in 1993. The rise in investment resulted from a surge in public investment, as official foreign aid began to flow after the successful conclusion of the Paris agreements. There was also an increase in private investment related to inflows of FDI. National savings increased only modestly, from 7.3 percent of GDP in 1991 to 8.7 percent in 1993. Inflationary pressures improved dramatically in 1993, with an increase of 31 percent.

Inflationary pressures as measured by the CPI in 1994 declined to around 30 percent. This, in turn, helped to stabilize the exchange rate of the riel and the government. The balance of payments of Cambodia, however, continued to record large deficits and to be extremely vulnerable to domestic and external shocks. Foreign financing, especially official financing, continued to be the main source of Cambodia's financing of its overall budget deficit and the current accounts of the balance of payments. A synopsis of inflation trends from 1991 to 2001 is presented in Table 3.4.

For 2000 and 2001, the World Bank figures suggest that Cambodia actually experienced deflation, while in 2002, the inflation rate was about 2.4 percent (National Institute of Statistics 2002; Asian Development Bank 2003). The most recent inflation trend indicates that public servants and those on fixed salaries are not likely to see their purchasing power evaporate on a monthly or even weekly basis.

Financial and Legal Systems

As part of their efforts to radically restructure Cambodia, the Khmer Rouge "destroyed all records of external debt" and "destroyed" the domestic financial system (Frontier Funds Management 1996, B-7). In 1992, the World Bank supported a restructuring of Cambodia's financial system along free market lines and the reorganization of the National Bank of Cambodia. In 1994, the security environment deteriorated, and the resurgence of the Khmer Rouge adversely affected confidence, economic activity, and financial systems. The political environment remained fragile, and in July 1994, the government squelched an attempted coup; then in October 1994, the finance minister, FUNCINPEC's Sam Rainsy, was replaced by Keat Chhon of the CPP. At that point, all major economic ministries and the National Bank were each headed by CPP officials (Showcross 1994).

Part of the restructuring in the 1990s was intended to redress capital shortage, which remains a problem. Plans for a Cambodian stock exchange for local and regional companies have been discussed since 1995. At the time of this writing, much of that talk continues, but with no clear timetable for implementation. Renewed speculation suggests that an exchange may soon arrive.

The financial system continues to evolve. Initial financial-sector reforms focused on macro-economic stability; now the focus has been redirected somewhat to provide financial products that can sustain economic growth and address the needs of the population. The government continues to seek additional sources of revenue that will help reduce its reliance on donor funds. For example, in 1999, the Cambodian government instituted the 10 percent value-added tax on all goods sold in the kingdom. This tax is now fairly commonly attached to purchases in most regions of the country. Additionally, in early 2002, legislation was proposed for a 20 percent corporate tax and a 20 percent dividend remittance tax. Specific consumer-focused financial reform has not yet been implemented.

Similar to attitudes witnessed in the mid-1990s, Cambodians seem to retain "a lingering mistrust of banks and local currency" (Frontier Funds Management 1996, B-7; see also Clifford Chance 1997). Transactions in almost every market are frequently conducted in U.S. dollars. The riel is typically used only as "small change" to make up differences between the nearest dollar and the price in the exchange. The Cambodian consumer, however, has reemerged as a driver of the overall economy. In 2001, private consumption accounted for about 84 percent of the GDP. While down from 90 percent in 2000, this percentage remains substantial. The consolidation of much of that consumption in the urban centers and the high poverty rate of 36 percent reveal the need for more development work in many areas.

It can be argued that the performance of the economy remains unbalanced, and its benefits are not spread evenly throughout the society. Much of this growth has been concentrated in Phnom Penh and Siem Reap (only 10 percent of the total population), and the Cambodian economy continues to suffer from the legacy of decades of war, foreign invasion, and internal strife. Nevertheless, many economic indicators are positive, and despite events that might suggest otherwise, an objective of the government remains "to achieve a fair, just and peaceful society, and through accelerating the rate of economic growth, to raise the living standards of all Cambodians" (cf. Asian Development Bank 1994, 79).

Fundamental to that objective and the long-term health of the economy is a legal environment built to nurture the private sector (both multinationals as well as domestic small to medium enterprises [SME]), promote FDI, and facilitate citizen and consumer confidence. Just a few years ago, the Cambodian legal environment was viewed as a system in dire straits, still reeling from the aftershock of the Khmer Rouge era (see also Mydans 1998); at one point, there were reportedly only five lawyers left alive in the country. Even simple importing and exporting transactions under such legal uncertainties can impede investor enthusiasm, which, in turn, can have a chilling effect on development.

The current legal environment in Cambodia favors FDI and the active participation of foreign companies in the country's economy. Today, many observers and investors contend that Cambodia has some of the most favorable investment laws in Asia (e.g., Bruton 2001). In 1997, the Legal Affairs Division in the Ministry of Commerce was established to draft all commercial codes, act as a registry for companies, and maintain all commercial law and commercial treaties. The Council for the Development of Cambodia (CDC) is the political and commercial force in the development and enforcement protocols of commercial law. The tax rates for corporations and investments are some of the most investor friendly in the region. The tax rate has been 9 percent, but there is speculation, as noted above, that a 20 percent tax rate of corporate earnings could become law in the near future. In interviews with investors and government officials, the authors were told that compared to just a few years ago, investors have a much better opinion of the legal environment and their legal recourse in the event of commercial and contractual problems. While the legal environment has been slowly resurrected, there is still a great deal of concern about the corruption that continues to permeate certain commercial and governmental transactions.

Structure of the Economy

Cambodia's economy continues to be largely agrarian, but the trend is toward diversification, with emphases on tourism and services, construction, and light industry. Agriculture still accounts for approximately 40–50 percent of GDP, depending upon the source consulted (cf. Hach and Acharya 2002; *World Factbook* 2003), down from 55.6 percent in 1990. This shift also means that the nature and content of exports has shifted, and contributions from agriculture, still large, are down from 90 percent, during the early to mid-1990s.

Manufacturing contributes about 20 percent of GDP (*World Factbook* 2003), much of which was in value-added agribusinesses, such as the garment industry. At last count, there were more than 200 firms operating in Cambodia, about 170 of them located in the Phnom Penh area. Much of the work is in assembly and not actual textile/fabric production. Footwear is also a growth industry, and Cambodia now has over a dozen producers. Rice milling, food processing, wood products, rubber, and cement are other important industries.

Cambodia's garment industry in the late 1990s was described as being the recipient of "a gold rush mentality" by outside investors (Cochrane 1999, 8), producing considerable FDI (Johnson 2000). By renewing the 1999 bilateral trade agreement, Cambodia has increased exports to the United States at a dizzying pace. In 2000, garments accounted for about US$985 million, about 70 percent of all the exports from Cambodia (Lintner 2001b). Approximately 75 percent of that output went to popular retailers in the United States (Balfour and Prosso 2000). A number of garment producers operate in Cambodia and provide jobs for over 150,000 Cambodians, mostly young women. Efforts have been made to ensure safe and equitable labor conditions throughout the kingdom (Arnold 2001). The current bilateral trade agreement, which runs through December 31, 2004, raised the 2002 quota 15 percent from the 2001 level. Noteworthy in that deal, Cambodia was rewarded for its commitment to and performance in labor practices (*AsiaPulse News* 2002).

Cambodia has moved from virtually nonexistent trade with the United States in 1996 to recent annual exports of approximately US$1 billion. The export mix is made up largely of garments, with seafood, luggage, and jewelry being other notable contributors. The WTO accession of China (cf. Egan 1999), the new bilateral trade agreement between Vietnam and the United States, and new banking requirements, however, have raised concerns over the health of the garment industry (Russell 2001). In fact, some retrenchment has been seen (e.g., Un and Ledgerwood 2003).

The service industry is showing remarkable growth. In 1998, it accounted for about 37 percent of GDP, as compared to just 17 percent a few years earlier. The service sector is comprised of government services, wholesale and retail trade, restaurants, hotels, transport, energy, water supply, and communication. Cellular telephones are now common on the streets of most cities and are becoming affordable to a much greater portion of the population. This industry is expected to continue to expand. For example, in September 2001, China's telecom manufacturer Huawei Technologies inked a US$13 million deal to provide advanced prepaid card services and interconnection billing services with the Cambodia Shinawatra Company (a joint venture with a Cambodian ministry and a Thai company). This deal provides service not only to Phnom Penh, but also to ten other cities in Cambodia (IPR Strategic Business Information Database-pNA 2001). Tourism, per se, is now Cambodia's fastest-growing industry, with arrivals up 34 percent in 2000 and up another 40 percent in 2001 (*World Factbook* 2003). With tourists comes demand for handicrafts. The Ministry of Commerce now lists four firms involved in exporting handicrafts and producing goods for internal consumption. Some of these firms are primed to move into e-commerce as soon as the technology infrastructure becomes more reliable. The Internet is increasingly accessible, but its reliability for extended commercial activities is still somewhat suspect.

Summary and Some Thoughts on the Future

While foreign aid and assistance remain important, if Cambodia is to sustain its economy, it will need to diversify further and to leverage extant resources that provide differential advantages (Rahtz and Shultz 2001). Expansion of international trade and tourism is, therefore, vital to Cambodia's future; each will require continued increases in FDI. Indeed, tourism, if managed properly, can become Cambodia's cash cow, revenues from which can be shunted to develop other sectors of the economy. Foreign exchange accompanies tourism, as does an increase in services employment. In 2001, the growing service industry (in which tourism plays a dominant role) contributed 37.5 percent to the GDP. This contribution to the GDP is second only to agriculture, which contributed 39.2 percent (The Economist Intelligence Unit 2003). In 2000, the WTO forecasted tourist flows in the Asia-Pacific region to grow at an annual rate of 7 percent in the next decade, about double the average estimated for the world as a whole. Cambodia's piece of that is expected to grow even more. Data from the Cambodian government show remarkable growth in recent years. In 1999, there were 412,000 tourist arrivals; about 60 percent came from Asia-Pacific regions, about 25 percent from Europe, and about 15 percent from the Americas. Between 1999 and 2001, tourism numbers increased by over 60 percent (Hach and Acharya 2002), and the trend is expected to continue at an "accelerating rate" (Sereyvuth 2001). The current growth in tourism is positive, but the "mix" of tourists creates challenges. That is, a disproportionately large percentage of growth is explained by rapid growth in visits by budget travelers. Therefore, the dollar yield per tourist has dropped. This trend has implications for the strategic management of this crucial industry and the FDI it attracts.

The fragility of Cambodian tourism must also be recognized, especially for the near future. There was speculation that the late 2001 increase was driven by Asian travelers who feared visiting the United States, following the September 11, 2001, terrorist attacks. Combined with a poor economic situation in the region (Japan, in particular), this fear was exploited by Cambodia, which enticed Asian and European travelers (Wain 2002). This feeling was evident in a number of interviews conducted by the authors in Siem Riep (vicinity of the Angkor temples) in January 2002. Japanese tourists were very concerned about travel to the United States and had specifically decided to visit Cambodia, because it was, in words from one Japanese gentleman who personified the feeling of his tour group, "a much safer place than America" (Rahtz and Shultz 2002). Comparatively, just one year earlier, following the assault by a small group of antigovernment fighters in Phnom Penh during the early morning of November 24, 2000, the hotels in Siem Riep were empty of Japanese tourists. The brief upheaval in Phnom Penh resulted in numerous cancellations by Japanese tour operators. Truly, what a difference a year makes. Moreover, seemingly limited local events or uncontrollable major global events can exhibit tremendous influences on a country's "brand perception" by the outside world, which, in turn, can have significant impacts on outcomes within any given industry. In a poor, fragile country, such as Cambodia, the consequential hardships can be especially difficult.

Most indicators seem to suggest that Cambodia continues to pursue a policy of openness and economic integration (see also Chhon and Moniroth 1999). The population, however, lacks education and productive skills, particularly in the poverty-ridden countryside that suffers from an almost total lack of basic infrastructure. Fear of corruption and renewed political instability coupled with inadequate infrastructure and unskilled labor will retard more optimal growth rates (see also *World Factbook* 2003; Un and Ledgerwood 2003). Natural disasters are also potentially problematic. But if the government can deliver on promises of greater stability and transparency, the pipeline of multilateral aid and FDI will be sustained; indeed, the flow of capital will likely be expanded, thus assuring real growth into the foreseeable future.

DEMOGRAPHIC TRENDS AND SOCIETAL WELLNESS

Recent estimates now place Cambodia's population at over thirteen million people (UNDP 2002). The current social structure and demographic profile reflect the legacy of major social upheavals and warfare, thus creating a society in which the majority of the population remains illiterate and isolated. Cambodian society is radically different from "what might have been," given typical patterns seen elsewhere in the region (see also Ebihara, Mortland, and Ledgerwood 1994). A synopsis of fundamental socioeconomic indicators is found in Table 3.5.

Population growth and poverty coincide. Estimates from the Cambodian government show that a growth rate at 2.5 percent will result in a population of twenty million by 2020. Since 1999, the country's human development index (HDI) has improved, and its ranking is up from 137, which moved Cambodia above the low human development threshold of 0.50 for the first time in memory (UNDP 2002). While there is a positive trend for the HDI, which could also slow population growth, Cambodia still has some unique conditions that might negatively affect its future growth, development, and welfare.

Approximately 80 percent of the population is estimated to be involved in agriculture, typically small-scale, family-based farming. With about sixty-four inhabitants per square kilometer, Cambodia still has a favorable labor-to-land ratio. Most farmers own land, and there is no known tenancy or rural debt problem. However, access to arable land and employment as a farm laborer has its drawbacks: Cambodia still has among the highest number of embedded land mines per capita for any country in history. Not coincidentally, it also has among the highest ratios of amputees and orphans per capita. Even though many of these casualties are the results of war, death and dismemberment from contact with leftover explosive ordnance is common.

A condition that influences economic and consumer market development is the composition of the population by age group and sex. Cambodia has a dependency ratio of 0.81, which is the percentage of people between the ages of fifteen and sixty-four divided into the remaining percentage of the population. Cambodia's ratio is an extremely high number (comparatively, Singapore's is 40.4 and the U.S. ratio is 50.1). More troubling, it suggests that a large portion of the population is dependent upon others for economic support. This dependency becomes very evident in Cambodia, when one sees that nearly half the entire population is under the age of fifteen. Nearly 30 percent of the population is between the ages of twelve and twenty-two. The sex ratio of the

Table 3.5

Fundamental Socioeconomic Indicators

- Population: 13.4 million
- 84% rural/16% urban
- Annual population growth rate: 2.5%
- Human Development Index: 0.541 (121 of 162 countries)
- Population under fifteen years of age: 43% (2001)
- Literacy rate (male/female): 79.8%/57.1%[a]
- Life expectancy at birth: women, 58.6 years; men, 54.1 years
- Infant mortality/1,000 births: 95
- Under-five years of age mortality/1,000 births: 125
- Maternal mortality/100,000 births: 440
- HIV prevalence rate: 2.6% (fifteen to forty-nine years of age)
- Urban access to clean water: 51/68% Rural access to clean water: 25/39%
- Income per capita: $260[b]

Source: UNDP 2001; The Economist Intelligence Unit, 2003; *World Factbook,* 2003 (Central Intelligence Agency, Washington DC), available at www.cia.gov/cia/publications/factbook/geos/cb.html; authors' reviews of unpublished data, National Institute of Statistics, 2002, 2003.

Note: These indicators vary, depending on the source and subpopulation of interest, particularly per capita personal income, literacy.

[a]A UNESCO report with the Ministry of Education in 2000 reports adult functional literacy at 37 percent; field research by the authors leads us to conclude that the UNESCO figure is the more accurate measure.

[b]This number likely is too low, because income often is unreported or underreported.

population has been somewhat skewed by wars and executions, which took a disproportionate toll among the male population, and by the selective emigration of men. Of the population over fifteen years, about 60 percent of all people report they are married. About 11 percent of the women in this group report they are widowed. In 2000, women comprised about 53 percent of the adult population and are estimated to be around 26 percent of heads of households (see also *World Factbook* 2003; World Bank 2003). The UN Women in Development program reports that it is likely that in a large percentage of households, women play a key role in economic support (WINAP 2002). The family, though discouraged by the Khmer Rouge and ravaged by war, is very important to Cambodians. Multiple generations tend to live in one dwelling or in close proximity. Data from the 1998 census indicate that there are about 2.2 million households in Cambodia, with an average household size of 5.2 people. Table 3.6 compares age and sex data from a 1990 UNESCAP report and the 1998 Census. A slowly moving cohort effect is evident. Moreover, the older age groupings are heavily skewed toward women; that disappears in the younger cohorts in the newer data.

Still problematic is the phenomenon of internal refugees or, more accurately, displaced persons. A substantial portion of the population seems permanently displaced domestically or abroad or is internally nomadic and struggles to survive. Many of these factors contribute to still another problem: exploitation in many forms, especially human trafficking.

> Cambodia is a source and destination country for persons trafficked for sexual exploitation and forced labor. Cambodian men, women, and children who cross into Thailand, often as illegal migrants, are forced into labor or prostitution by traffickers. Cambodian children are trafficked into Vietnam and forced to work as street beggars. Vietnamese women and girls are trafficked into Cambodia for prostitution. Cambodian women and children are trafficked internally for sexual exploitation. (U.S. Department of State 2003, 43)

Table 3.6

Cambodian Population by Age Group and Sex, 1990 and 1998

Age group	1990		1998[a]	
	Percent total population	Percent female in total population	Percent total population	Percent female in total population
All ages	100.0	53.7	100.0	51.8
Over fifteen	53.1	57.3	54.5	55.7[b]
Six to fifteen	30.3	49.7	29.3	48.7
One to five	12.4	49.6	14.2	49.1
Under one	4.2	49.8	2.0	49.0

[a] The data for 1998 are from the Cambodian National Institute of Statistics. Population data for 1998 are based on the General Population Census of 1998 with a reported population of approximately 11.4 million. The last census prior to that was in 1962, when the population was reported to be approximately 5.7 million. The 1990 number reported here is based on estimates of the population from the United Nations Economic and Social Commission for Asia and the Pacific (UNESCAP). The 1990 number reported by that organization reported the total population number as approximately 8.6 million.

[b] The percentage of females in the population continues to increase as age increases. At about age forty and higher, the number of females at each age averages about 1.5 times the number of males.

Tourism and manufacturing industries offer hopes for better jobs; migration to urban and tourist centers (e.g., Siem Riep) continues to be a trend as Cambodians search for these jobs. Approximately 27 percent of the population in Siem Riep migrated from other parts of the country. The areas of the two industrial bases of the country, Phnom Penh and Sihanoukville, have 73.4 percent and 52.2 percent of their populations, respectively, comprised of migrants (National Institute of Statistics 2002, from 1998 Census data). As tourism and industry grow, one can expect these trends to continue.

To compound problems, the air of repression and violence that sometimes surrounds Cambodia is not only damaging to the country's image as a potential investment market, but it also harms the fragile social confidence needed for Cambodia to move forward. The country's future is contingent upon safeguards that enable societal trust, optimism, and the collective belief that the future can provide better outcomes for a majority of Cambodians. To those ends, in addition to coordinated and sound economic development policies and political openness, a nation's commitment to education and health are foundations to individual, economic, and societal development and, as such, are integral to Cambodia's will to move forward.

Education

The education system was destroyed by the Khmer Rouge, and the government is trying to rebuild it. Although literacy rates are among the lowest in Asia, literacy is increasing, if at a modest rate. Between 1996 and 2000, the literacy rate for men improved from 55.5 percent to 59.7 percent, but only about 25 percent of women are able to read and to write, despite literacy programs. School enrollment percentages are increasing, especially for women (rectifying the gender imbalances in education is a government priority), but the percentage of public expenditures for education remain less than adequate. That said, an ambitious building program for schools is under way. Supported by foreign aid, Cambodia has built almost 1,750 schools over the past decade. While the campaign has produced a number of buildings, often, there are not enough teachers to staff them

(Mydans 2002). Secondary education and tertiary education are also inadequate. A rising number of private education programs strive to meet increasing demands for training and higher education. This is especially evident in the burgeoning tourist industry. For example, on the road from the airport to downtown Siem Reap, there is a new Japanese language school. The school was built to meet the need for Japanese-speaking tour guides to serve the influx of Japanese tourists arriving in the province to visit the Angkor temples. In addition, some of the businesses that need skilled labor and managers increasingly use internal training programs. The Raffles Hotel training program for employees at the Raffles properties in both Siem Reap and Phnom Penh yields a number of well-trained employees at all service levels. These employees are, at times, sought and hired by the newer hotels that continue to sprout up in the Siem Reap area.

Despite positive signs, there are still broad concerns about the educational system and Cambodia's future human resources. At the tertiary education level, for example, there are questions about the competency of graduates, because degrees can be bought rather than earned. Also, in some institutions, faculty members still fear physical intimidation by students wanting to earn acceptable grades. Thus, as with so many measures in Cambodia, education statistics evoke a combination of both hope and despair.

Public Health

The Public Health system, in yet more fallout from the Khmer Rouge, continues to struggle. In 1993, it was estimated that the population-to-physician ratio was ten thousand to one (Eng 2001). Some observers think the ratio was even larger. The severe shortage of physicians remains extremely problematic. Overseas Cambodians, as in many other skilled sectors, are sought to assist. The system continues to be lacking in infrastructure, equipment, and medical personnel, at all levels. The foreign donor community is often the only health care available to the population. Health statistics are, consequently, troubling.

Average life expectancy for women may be only sixty years; men can expect to live only about fifty-five years (*World Factbook* 2003). The estimated fertility rate for Cambodia is 4.77. Maternal and infant mortality rates remain unacceptably high. Only a small minority of the population has access to real sanitation, malnutrition is still a problem for many Cambodians, and access to fundamental health services remains problematic. The maternal mortality rate is a poignant example of the result of such conditions. The rate is among the worst in the world, between 500 and 900 deaths per 100,000 deliveries (UNDP 2001). Another gender-related public health issue is wife abuse in the household; estimates are that between 16 and 25 percent of women are victims of spousal abuse (UNDP 2001). This extremely high level is attributed to years of endemic violence (Levi 1998). Multilateral aid efforts to improve these conditions are providing some hope for the future.

Despite some positive trends in public health programs, a potentially devastating cloud hangs over the health system: HIV/AIDS. Cambodia has been described as the "sickest country in Asia now at risk for a devastating spread of disease; Cambodia is seen as the epicenter of the next potential explosion of AIDS" (Mydans 2001, 1). Government leaders have expressed fears that the impact of AIDS will ultimately rival the death toll of the "killing fields." Hun Sen has gone on record to state that "AIDS has done more damage to the country than decades of war" (Vesperini 2000). General population infection rates are reported to be approximately 2.6 percent, but this number is likely lower than the actual rate of infection. The sex trade is often blamed for the spread of HIV. Over 44 percent of the prostitutes in Phnom Penh were HIV positive in 1997, and by 1999, that number had dropped to a still appalling 24 percent (U.S. Census Bureau 2000). This trend could possibly indicate that the government and the industry have begun to push more aggressively the use of condoms by sex workers. A particularly sad statistic that falls in that range is that in 1999, HIV prevalence among fourteen- to nineteen-year-old pregnant women across twenty-two provinces was 4 percent. The next few decades possibly could devastate a struggling health care infrastructure. The impact on the overall health of the population and the resultant effect on the economic and marketing environment could also have wide-ranging consequences, as resources are diverted to deal with the potential socioeconomic crisis and if investors potentially look elsewhere.

IMPLICATIONS FOR MARKETING AND CONSUMER BEHAVIOR

Given the economic, ecological, political, and social situations in Cambodia, it is reasonable to conclude that the performance of the economy is fragile but moving forward. Interactive and arcane challenges make the task of finding solutions to the multifaceted problems very difficult. Any sustainable solution to the complex problem of economic development and growth is predicated on the continued stability of the political situation. Hun Sen and the CPP have solidified their political power; in-country observations and a series of interviews by the authors over the last decade indicate that the present level of political stability will most likely continue, although with an undercurrent of discord.

The aforementioned caveats noted, opportunities for marketers in some sectors—for example, construction, infrastructure development, tourism, light industry, and agribusiness—are strong. A growing consumer market is also emerging. Commerce is increasingly obvious, especially in Phnom Penh, Battambang, Sihanoukville, and other relatively urban and tourist sites. The depth and breadth of marketing and consumption activity in Phnom Penh, for example, are almost startling and seem to symbolize the resolve of the Cambodian people to enter the global economy, despite handicaps. The streets now reveal shops that offer varieties of almost every consumer good; the riverfront promenade has numerous dining and entertainment offerings. Daily motorized and bicycle traffic flows have increased, and the fall of darkness, while still a time of wariness, does not empty the streets of people. Therefore, we submit that, with continuing political stability, marketing opportunities are no longer simply a futuristic target but are available today in several industries; others have also been cautiously optimistic (e.g., World Bank 2001). The remaining text provides a brief profile of the Cambodian consumer, macromarketing mix issues, the impact of commerce and change, and a look into the future.

Changes in Consumer Behavior: Segments and Consumer Values

The preceding text in this chapter illuminates important factors that will broadly affect consumption. But who is the Cambodian consumer? How has consumer behavior changed? What consumption patterns and consumer tendencies may marketers need to be cognizant of if they hope to succeed in this market? Several trends and indicators may lead some investors to conclude that Cambodian consumers may not be worth a heavy marketing investment. But while many Cambodians still struggle simply to survive, it would be shortsighted to conclude that this market is not tenable.

Recent observations by the authors in Cambodian markets and consumption venues (e.g., cafes, homes, and sites where consumers purchase and use goods and services) indicate that the Cambodian consumer is many people: rural and urban, young and old, male and female, traditional and more modern, poor and with some disposable income. In other words, many consumers— 36 percent of them by World Bank and CIA estimates (*World Factbook* 2003)—live in abject poverty, but a class of consumers that values the goods and services found throughout Southeast Asia has slowly emerged and is continuing to move forward. These opinion leaders are typically urban, younger, brand aware, and while perhaps poor by Western standards, have aspirations like more well-to-do opinion leaders in the likes of Bangkok, Singapore, or even the United States. For them, the standard package (cf. Keyfitz 1982) includes, for example, a motor scooter, compact disc player, cellular phone, and Western clothing, preferably adorned with a chic brand or, more likely, a pirated version of it.

The Cambodian market can be segmented several ways, but marketers fundamentally might consider the urban, emerging affluent and relatively young consumers to be prime targets. Women are also important targets, as they comprise a larger percentage of the population and are economically important to most households. Their disproportionately large employment in the garment industry has enhanced their economic clout. A significant number of women now have some disposable income and, therefore, comprise a viable target for a variety of products, especially household goods.

Another set of consumers, particularly in Phnom Penh, includes a large number of nongovernmental organization (NGO) personnel and the growing population of foreign investors. Although both groups are present throughout developing Southeast Asia, they make large contributions to Cambodia and Phnom Penh, because a substantial amount of the money in circulation in Phnom Penh is "artificial." In other words, Phnom Penh's economy has a huge infusion of money from the numerous donor organizations. This money helps to restore infrastructure and stability, generally; it also helps to fuel a Mercedes-Benz dealership, a variety of hotels and restaurants, the cellular phone market, and other markets for products and services beyond the purchasing power of the majority of Cambodians. The long-run repercussions for this artificial infusion of cash (preferably in the form of U.S. dollars), goods, and services include the rapid exposure, awareness, and diffusion of a variety of global products into Cambodian life. This diffusion process has not bypassed local opinion leaders. The net result is that urban consumers are much more aware of and receptive to new products and promotion mechanisms than one might initially surmise.

The tourist market has also brought an influential consumer group to this country (Rahtz and Shultz 2001). A few tourist archetypes are emerging. The first and individually most lucrative for marketers is the *sophisticate:* S/he is an older, well-educated, wealthy tourist who is seeking an upscale cultural experience. S/he tends to spend approximately US$500 per day on lodging, dining, art, souvenirs, and private tours. S/he lodges in five-star hotels in Siem Riep and may visit the capital for a day or two. The spin-off of money from this group has stimulated high demand for exclusive services, quality products, and artwork.

At the other end of the spectrum is the *econo-tourist:* backpackers or day-trippers. These groups do not individually contribute much revenue to the local economy, but collectively, they are lucrative visitors, contributing revenue in the forms of visas, departure taxes, and entry fees. They also provide some local infusions into the cash-based services economy. A typical day-tripper will arrive from Bangkok on a tour, visit a temple or two, and then exit the country, literally on the same day. The regional mix of this market tends to be Asian, with a growing number of Chinese. They tend to spend little on peripherals, other than on a meal with the tour group at a designated eatery. These mass-market tourists have, however, created a fairly large demand for inexpensive trinkets. Cambodian entrepreneurs have created products to service this specific type of "economy" group traveler. Those in the backpacker group are younger, from a wide array of countries; they have a similar economic impact, but they tend to stay much longer, requiring inexpensive lodging and rudimentary food and entertainment services to support their lifestyles.

Somewhere in between is a growing segment of *life-timers,* who tend to be well-educated but budget-minded tourists on the "trip of a lifetime." They tend to include a visit to Cambodia as part of a broader tour of the region. The length of stay may be a day or two but does not usually last more than three days. Typically from Europe and the United States, they tend to visit Siem Riep, with possibly a brief side-trip to Phnom Penh.

A final archetype is the *value-oriented hedonist.* This group is typically male. They come from many countries, but our interviews with hoteliers and other service providers indicate they tend to be Asian, though other regions are included. This tourist segment is, by some accounts, now one of the largest, if not the largest, client pool at many of the mid-level and lower-mid-level hotels in Phnom Penh. They also tend to frequent discos, casinos, and other entertainment establishments. This target market tends to find its demands for lodging and entertainment being underserved.

Changes in the Macromarketing Mix

The objective of this section is to present trends among the elements of the marketing mix at the national or aggregate level, that is, the macromarketing mix (Leeflang and van Raaij 1993, 353). This discussion includes inclinations for the classic marketing mix, for example, product, price, distribution, and promotion. We also include a brief discussion on market research.

Products

Cambodia's liberalized economy has changed consumer behavior and the product offerings to consumers. For most consumers, products that clothe, feed, and provide shelter are the highest priority; and because of both poverty and scarcity, most products are recycled and laterally cycled (Belk 1988). This "waste not" attitude has some positive outcomes for consumers, because products, or frequently product containers, are used time and again and for multiple purposes. We add here that marketers, perhaps, would be surprised to learn how their products and containers are used: discarded liter-sized bottles of soft drinks, for example, are used to sell gasoline. Despite poverty and the need to recycle, new-to-the-Cambodian-market products and brands that have been successful in other Southeast Asian countries are diffusing into Cambodia, and consumption of them is generally increasing.

For opinion leaders, as mentioned briefly above, favored products include goods associated with popular culture, that is, hedonic or "fun" products, such as CD and DVD players, mobile phones, and computer games. In 2000, there were over 80,000 mobile phones, somewhere between 1.5 million and 2 million radios, and over 100,000 televisions (see also *World Factbook* 2003). Other relatively inexpensive hedonic goods include tobacco products, soft drinks, and alcoholic beverages. Tobacco and liquor companies were among the first to successfully penetrate the Cambodian market. Electronics companies have also quickly penetrated urban markets. Brand images and loyalties are emerging for many products, but, in essence, products that add immediate utilitarian value, such as motorbike parts and inexpensive shoes, are well received. More hedonic goods and venues for their consumption, such as cafes, karaoke bars, television cafes, and Internet cafes, are becoming increasingly popular. Participation in the national lottery remains strong, and there is fairly active selling of tickets throughout the country.

It should be noted that because Cambodia is a large market for multilateral aid projects, construction and infrastructure materials for roads, bridges, ports, telecommunications, and buildings are sold in large quantities. These products enhance the quality of life and enable more efficient distribution of products and, thus, greater access to consumers. Several new up-market hotels and large extended-stay residence complexes have been built or restored in Phnom Penh. They target foreign investors and expatriate working professionals. Similarly, many goods and services—from bookshops to casinos—are targeted to this "investor market."

Distribution

Not surprisingly, distribution in Cambodia is still generally slow and inefficient. Poor roads and railways and a generally disparate system of marketing channels hinder distribution. Following, we provide an overview of that system, with emphasis on airports, roads, ports, and some intangible factors.

There are nineteen airports in Cambodia, but only six have paved runways. The Siem Riep and Phnom Penh airports are undergoing significant improvements to their operational capacities in terms of runway and terminal facilities. Both airports are intended to meet International Civil Aviation Organization (ICAO) standards. Pochentong Airport at Phnom Penh, which was sacked during the 1997 coup, has recently undergone rehabilitation costing US$100 million (US$20 million from the Asian Development Bank [ADB] and US$80 million from a private French firm); it is expected to be able to serve about four million passengers per year, though current passenger flow is far below projections. At Siem Riep, US$15 million worth of improvements (funded by ADB) have been made to allow larger aircraft and passenger flows.

Railways and roads must be expanded and improved. Cambodia has 603 kilometers of railways; a considerable portion of the track and roadbed is in serious need of repairs. While there are 35,769 kilometers of roads in Cambodia, less than 15 percent of those roads are paved. A portion of the nonpaved roads are impassable or nearly impassable during certain times of the year, due to inclement weather and flooding. Paved highways linking Phnom Penh with Thailand, Laos, and Vietnam are at various stages of planning. These are vital for internal distribution, as well as greater regional integration. A firm date for completion is still in question.

Sihanoukville, on the gulf of Thailand, is the primary port facility for Cambodia. Small container vessels can, however, unload shipments at Phnom Penh. The country has about 3,700 kilometers of navigable waterways. Only 282 kilometers, though, are navigable to craft drawing more than 1.8 meters. Thus, only a small portion of waterways can manage large- or medium-sized vessels—the types commonly used for large-scale commerce.

What Cambodia lacks in transportation infrastructure, it overcomes with the grit of its people. Bicycles, motor scooters, other small vehicles, and oxcarts transport many items. Larger vehicles supplied by the UN and other NGOs also lend support. Related to this grit is large-scale smuggling, especially along the Thai border. The Cambodian borders are, in essence, a sieve. This smuggling problem has prompted some businesspeople to call for turning Cambodia into a full "free trade zone." Huge amounts of timber and precious stones are smuggled across the border from Cambodia to Thailand, and, somewhat ironically, larger and better trucks are often used in this region to abet the illicit activities. Smuggling on the Thai border has been especially troublesome, because it tends to be administered, in part, by remnants of the Khmer Rouge; speculation has also implicated the Cambodian army (Thayer 1994). Cambodia's further integration into ASEAN, adherence to WTO requirements, and the subsequent opening of trade barriers will no doubt have some impact on this smuggling.

The increase in new products and the transportation of products to markets requires wholesale and retail outlets. Similar to other Southeast Asian countries, Cambodia tends to have central markets as the hubs of commerce. In Phnom Penh, for example, that central market is referred to as the "New" market, and it houses small stalls with everything from traditional Khmer textiles to televisions and computer games. New and smaller retail establishments, typically a storefront, kiosk, or shack, are proliferating seemingly everywhere consumers tend to congregate. An entire community of restaurants, cafes, and other shops has emerged across the Tonle River from Phnom Penh since the "Japanese Bridge" (so named because of the benefactors) was completed in the mid-1990s. Retailers generally range from modest street cafes and run-down hotels to electronics stores and a Mercedes-Benz dealership. Again, the likes of prestige-brand car dealerships are predominantly intended to serve expatriates, foreign investors, and members of Cambodia's power-elite, but a broader, more representative segment of Cambodians is visiting and purchasing from more diverse retailers throughout Phnom Penh and other larger communities. The arrival of inexpensive Chinese motorbikes may well signal a significant increase in traffic in Phnom Penh, but this will also increase mobility for Cambodian consumers. This increased mobility in other countries in the region, coupled with greater product awareness and purchasing power, has elicited a restructuring of distribution centers, markets, and retail establishments, which, in turn, further stimulated commerce and consumption. This emerging consumer class, with some disposable income, will demand more from the distribution system, particularly at the various points of consumer interfaces: retailers, restaurants, and cafes. These institutions will demand more from upstream suppliers, all of which will eventually render marketing channels more efficient and effective. Such systemic changes will take time; the marketing channels will remain more rudimentary than those found throughout much of the region.

Promotion

Promotion has become more sophisticated and increasingly important to the success of marketers in Cambodia. Message, medium, and overall management of the marketing communications mix must be given careful thought. Furthermore, as is the case with other elements of the marketing mix, one's promotional strategy is partly dictated by whether a company is targeting Cambodians or expatriates and members of the multilateral aid market. If one is targeting the latter, print ads in the English-language newspapers, for example, *Phnom Penh Post,* are almost requirements. Outdoor advertising is also important if one is targeting this group: brewers, airlines, telecommunications companies, petroleum companies, electronics firms, and tobacco companies are leaders in this medium. Personal selling and use of the hotel/restaurant lobby network are also imperative; the importance of person-to-person contact in Cambodia should not be underestimated. Various hotel restaurants in Phnom Penh, at Le Royale Hotel and the Cambodiana, for example, are known as "power-breakfast" meeting places where "things get done." One would expect these and other venues, such as the floating casino in Phnom Penh and the casino off the coast of Sihanoukville, to provide other personal selling, networking, and entertainment functions. Strategically placed flyers and other promotional materials in hotels, restaurants, and other consumption venues of the expatriate market are also helpful. Electronic media will become more important, but at this juncture, they are not used or preferred by most marketers.

If one is targeting Cambodians, certain rudimentary factors must be addressed. First, because of the relatively low literacy rate, outdoor advertising that displays easily interpreted symbols and images is a favored promotional tactic. Therefore, billboards with bold images and slice-of-life scenes tend to be effective. Products and brands in completely unfamiliar product classes will require ad copy that simply demonstrates utilitarian or hedonic value. It should also be noted that the lines demarking promotion and distribution are frequently difficult to distinguish in Cambodia, as evidenced by the "Marlboro store," a shop selling nothing but Marlboro cigarettes. The store's facade provided outdoor advertising and point-of-purchase reminders. On the sidewalk in front of the store, attractive young ladies—dressed in red and white Marlboro jumpsuits and standing beside their red and white Marlboro scooters, which were parked under red and white Marlboro umbrellas —have helped to reaffirm the Marlboro image recognized around the globe. Pushing the limits of effective promotion may also push the limits of propriety: Marlboro, for example, was criticized by the Western press for using an eight-year-old girl in one of its ads (Cohen 1998).

Tobacco and liquor companies, generally, have been leaders in developing promotional strategies targeting Cambodian consumers. The lessons learned from them are valuable, because brand loyalties have, in some cases, not yet been established, and in the instance of brewers, for example, the end product, beer, has not been historically popular. Annual beer consumption per capita in Cambodia is fairly low compared to other countries in the region. Brewers see this low consumption as an indicator of market *potential,* which is not a bad outlook for managers responsible for promoting other goods and services in Cambodia. The almost uniformly tried strategy to increase consumption still includes billboard advertising and the ubiquitous "beer girls," who, donned in company colors and logos and therefore making themselves virtually walking billboards, aggressively tout their brands at pubs and discos. First implemented in the 1990s (e.g., Postelwaite 1995), this promotional tactic remains popular. In addition to aggressive promotion and selling at the point of purchase, brewers and other purveyors of consumer goods are using park benches, the airwaves, and billboards to promote their goods. Bottle cap lotteries and other games, popular in the United States and other countries a generation ago, are also well liked by Cambodian consumers.

The optimal marketing communications mix varies broadly as a function of the target market: expatriate/multilateral aid market, local Cambodians, and tourists. Cambodian consumers will become more promotion savvy, but in the foreseeable future, simple outdoor and print advertising coupled with sponsorship and, for inexpensive consumer goods, sampling opportunities that create brand awareness are likely to be most effective.

Prices

The transformation to a market economy, by definition, has meant that market forces now determine prices. Although consumers were buffeted by steep price increases in the early 1990s, thanks to economic policies to control inflation and good fortune with agricultural production, prices have remained fairly stable. Prices for many products and services, however, vary as a function of the particular segment targeted. This trend is likely to continue and to reveal even greater variances as the market evolves. As noted before, almost all commerce in the markets is transacted with U.S. dollars, though credit and debit cards are gaining popularity among merchants, particularly those who cater to expatriates and tourists. Most consumers still tend to have little confidence in the riel and, similarly to consumers in other parts of transitioning Southeast Asia, they tend to save dollars, gold, or other tangible goods that will hold value over time. Barter is a common mechanism of exchange for some consumers and businesses.

Market Research

Market research tends to be fairly basic and qualitative. Most consumer-goods companies have generally categorized the Cambodian market as a developing Southeast Asian economy and have tried to replicate strategies used successfully in other countries in the region, while also trying to attend to local sensibilities. This strategy has been reasonably successful, but as the market evolves, firms are finding it necessary to collect information that is more Cambodia-specific.

Data can be collected by placing personnel in the country or by employing the services of market research and advertising firms that are now focusing on Cambodia. Whether a company hires an individual or organization to conduct market research or uses its own staff, data collection usually tends to be site-specific, person-to-person, and labor intensive, as most consumers are not familiar with questionnaires and are uncomfortable with the data-collection process, or perhaps are mistrustful of the process and how the data will be used. In addition to being labor intensive, and sometimes costly, collecting representative and accurate data can be personally demanding, even dangerous, especially in more remote areas of the country. The authors personally engaged in fieldwork in which organized thugs, political thugs, or simple bandits have terrorized communities and rendered data collection impossible. We hasten to add, however, that these precarious conditions seem to be increasingly rare, and most market researchers would be unlikely to encounter them. Nevertheless, it is important to keep in mind that when out in the field, the state of affairs can deteriorate unexpectedly.

Given the potential problems associated with the data-collection process, how does one gain an operable understanding of the Cambodian market? It has been suggested that market research in transitioning Southeast Asia requires companies to place multiskilled employees in the country of interest to collect primary data relevant to company-specific needs and objectives (e.g., Shultz 1994). Cambodia is no exception. Determining which products will sell is important, but determining optimal management of the entire marketing system, including where to sell, how to transport, promote, and price, and how to manage cultural and political influences, is equally important. Thorough on-the-ground assessments by investing firms that have examined the country's arcane conditions have led to successful enterprise development and product introductions that target consumer, multilateral aid, and tourist markets.

In summary, basic observational and qualitative market research can provide insights that will enable firms to profit in and from the Cambodian market. Thorough site research that goes beyond examination of economic indicators can pinpoint trends and future opportunities. Some international market research and advertising firms have been able to generate a variety of targeted data.

FUTURE TRENDS AND EXPECTATIONS

Cambodia is a country of beauty, danger, promise, and intrigue. It has an "edge" that investors will not likely find in many other places. This edge is, perhaps, best captured in the following text, from a Web site of a local watering hole favored by many expatriates and tourists:

> Phnom Penh, the so-called "Paris of the Far East," is a bit like the American Wild West during the 1800s, only hot and sticky too! It is not only filled with intrigue and a bit of danger, but the city attracts a lot of strange cats, many of whom come driftin' in after failing in places like Bangkok or Ho Chi Minh City. Many of these characters . . . often get in trouble by scamming expats, tourists and sometimes, ill advisedly, the locals, which inevitably leads to confrontations with Khmer authorities—or worse! This happens so frequently that many local expats and old Asia hands refer to the country as "Scambodia," or . . . "Skampuchea." (Sharky's 2003)

Despite numerous challenges—some predictable, others less so—commerce is alive and well in Cambodia. Generally strong growth in GDP, stable exchange rates, relatively low inflation (and deflation in some years), full membership in ASEAN, most-favored-nation trading status with the United States, labor agreements, imminent inclusion in the WTO, and the government's efforts to attract FDI and to promote Cambodia as a regional hub have inspired several observers to conclude that many conditions for further growth and development are reasonably good. Caution is advised, however, as the performance of the economy remains unbalanced; its overall impact is not yet spread evenly throughout the society. Much of the growth has been concentrated in metro Phnom Penh, Siem Reap, and Sihanoukville. One wonders whether some of these less-than-optimal outcomes are an evolutionary phase through which Cambodia must pass before the fruits of reform reach all Cambodians, or whether these outcomes portend greater disequilibrium and another chapter in the Cambodian epic of war, foreign invasion, and internal strife (cf. Prasso 1994).

Again, indicators suggest that Cambodia's broad goals for socioeconomic development are tenable, leading to a just society integrated into the global community, but not without massive donor assistance, political stability, improvements in infrastructure and human resources, simple luck in the form of good weather, and buoyed confidence among investors and the Cambodian citizenry that corruption is being curbed, if not necessarily eliminated. Schemes to attract FDI ostensibly geared toward development have also been proven to have rapacious effects on natural resources and have made many Cambodians and members of the world community skeptical. Timber exploitation and subsequent deforestation is just one example. To compound matters, the political climate remains infected by heavy-handed tactics to affect elections, and the long shadow of the Khmer Rouge and the on-again, off-again decision to try the surviving perpetrators of Cambodia's holocaust. All of these factors could potentially accelerate political discord and, in turn, social unrest, which would be disastrous for Cambodia, as FDI and donor aid would slow to a trickle.

One can envision a more optimistic scenario in which a degree of stability is maintained—one in which investor, donor, and consumer confidence remain reasonably strong and a middle class begins to emerge. Such a scenario is similar to comparatively successful developing economies in the region and will demand more accountability from government authorities and investors. A cycle of successes would begin to feed on itself to the benefit of Cambodia, its people, and its neighbors. An example of that emergence is provided in the following excerpts from a field interview with a young woman in Phnom Penh, just before a recent round of elections; she is a recent university graduate and a member of that emerging middle class:

> We want the same things [you want]. Honest government, good products, safety, a better life for ourselves and our children. We see what life can be. I go to Internet café; we have satellite television. I want to go to university in America. I practice English. . . . I don't like the [Hun Sen] government. I support the opposition. We have a voice. Sometimes there is trouble, but things are better. I would love to go to America for university, but I want to come back. There is opportunity here. My family is here. My mother has a business, bought some land in the country and grows [durian]. My father worries, but things are better for me and my brothers and sisters. (Shultz 2002)

A selection artifact must be addressed when interpreting that text, but finding any informant who could or would express those thoughts and feelings a decade ago would have been tricky. Now one can find many of them. The question becomes, at what point do they become a critical mass to ensure a stable and prosperous Cambodia? An answer to that question remains elusive, but there is cause to endorse the more optimistic scenario. To increase the probability of it, policies must be implemented or enforced to promote the following:

- Greater tolerance for freedom of expression and open discourse
- Literacy and technical skills
- Improvements in revenue collection
- Sustainable development programs to assure long-term prosperity and environmental protection
- Tighter controls over government expenditures
- Greater transparency and accountability by government and investors

CONCLUSION

We reiterate that, despite difficulties inherent to many developing economies, Cambodia is a viable market, with a growing number of consumers keen to participate in consumer culture. Whether marketers choose to establish manufacturing facilities in the country or to export to Cambodia should be predicated on an investor's risk and reward assessment of the country. Most country risk-assessment formulae would indicate that Cambodia is a high-risk country, though trends, including some investor success stories, reveal a less risky environment than might be expected. Cambodia provides marketing opportunities, and therefore, we consider Cambodia a "go" market, given the following considerations.

Those who have successfully entered this market have learned that the situation requires an understanding of the multiple forces that make Cambodia different from other markets and of how these forces affect management of the traditional "4 Ps" (product, price, place, and promotion) and marketing relationships. In Cambodia, managers must add five new "P"s: *predictability, prudence, patience, passion,* and *perseverance.*

In one sense, the socioeconomic and political turmoil have made Cambodia unpredictable. In another sense, marketers have learned that while they need to take into account unique Cambodian customs, habits, demographic constraints, and Byzantine politics, the market, in many ways, replicates early stages of other more established markets in the region. Therefore, with a reasonable understanding of the Cambodian condition, including the inherent risks, it can be predicted with a fairly high degree of certainty that consumers will respond positively to the types of marketing mixes used in other emerging Southeast Asian countries. Cambodia's regional and global integration suggest that a template is being laid for broader commercial endeavors, such as manufacturing and transportation, rendering them more predictable as well. Prudence and forethought, however, are required at every step. It could be argued that this recommendation is requisite for any marketing endeavor, but in Cambodia, poor judgment and carelessness may not only cripple the investor's or marketer's plans but may also result in controversy, harassment, and personal injury.

Marketing in one of the world's poorest countries requires patience. Poor infrastructure, a poorly trained labor force generally without the skills needed to succeed in today's competitive global market, corruption, and other challenges that define the Cambodian market will try the patience of the most serene manager. All of these factors indicate that passion for one's project and perseverance to assure its completion are also required. Indeed, the need for passion and perseverance to do well and to do "good" in a country that desperately needs products, services, and multisector development cannot be overemphasized.

In conclusion, those pondering whether to enter this market should know that, impediments notwithstanding, several individual entrepreneurs and large organizations have initiated projects in Cambodia that are functional, have attracted loyal customers domestically and in export markets, and, in some instances, are already profitable.

ACKNOWLEDGMENTS

The authors acknowledge support and assistance from the Marley Foundation, H.E. Roland Eng, and the staff from the Royal Embassy of Cambodia to the United States, the Cambodian Development Council, and the numerous policy makers, businesspersons, and consumers in Cambodia who gave their valuable time. We also thank Naranhkiri Tith for helpful comments on earlier drafts of this chapter, which expands Shultz and Tith (1998).

REFERENCES

Arnold, Wayne. 2001. "Translating Union into Khmer: The A.F.L.–C.I.O. Organizes in Cambodia." *The New York Times,* C1.
Asian Development Bank. 1991. *Cambodia: An Economic Report.* Manila: The Asian Development Bank.
———. 1994. *Cambodia: Economic Review and Bank Operations.* Manila: The Asian Development Bank.
———. 2003. *Key Indicators 2003: Education for Global Participation.* Manila: The Asian Development Bank.
AsiaPulse News. 2002. "USDS-US Cambodia Renew Bilateral Textile Agreement," January 10: 5.
Ayers, David. 2000. *Anatomy of a Crisis: Education, Development, and the State in Cambodia, 1953–1998.* Honolulu: University of Hawaii Press.
Balfour, Frederik, and Sheri Prasso. 2000. "Bumps in the Road to Cambodian Labor Reform: A U.S. Trade Deal Becomes a Test Case in Global Standards." *Business Week Online,* (International Edition), September 11. Available at www.businessweek.com:/@@NFK2FIcQW*EIYRQA/2000/00_37/b3698213.htm.
Belk, Russell W. 1988. "Third World Consumer Culture." In *Marketing and Development: Toward Broader Dimensions,* ed. Erdogan Kumcu and A. Fuat Firat, pp. 103–127. Greenwich, CT: JAI Press.
Boua, Chanthou. 1983. "Observations of the Heng Samrin Government 1980–1982." In *Revolution and Its Aftermath in Kampuchea,* ed. David P. Chandler and Ben Kiernan. New Haven, CT: Yale University Southeast Asian Studies.
Bruton, Christopher. 2001. US-ASEAN Business Council Conference for Investment in Cambodia, May 11, Phnom Penh.
Chandler, David P. 1992. *A History of Cambodia.* Boulder, CO: Westview Press.
Chandler, David P., Ben Kiernan, and Chanthou Boua, 1988. *Pol Pot Plans the Future.* New Haven, CT: Yale University Southeast Asian Studies.
Chantrabot, Ros. 1993. *Le République Khmère* [The Khmer Republic] *(1970–1975).* Paris: Editions L'Harmattan.
Chhon, Keat, and Aun Porn Moniroth. 1999. *Cambodia's Economic Development.* London: ASEAN Academic Press.
Clifford Chance. 1997. "Asian Financial Services Newsletter." London: Clifford Chance Solicitors.
Cochrane, Joe. 1999. "Rag Trade Blues." *Asian Business,* July: 8.
Cohen, Andy. 1998. "What You Didn't Learn in Marketing 101." *Sales and Marketing Management,* September: 202.
Corfield, Justin. 1994. *Khmers Stand Up!* Clayton, Australia: Monash University Centre of Southeast Asian Studies.
Culturgram. 1995. "State of Cambodia." Provo, UT: Brigham Young University.
Dobbs, Leo. 2002. "Spotlight: Cambodia Votes." *Far Eastern Economic Review,* February 14. Available at www.feer.com/articles/2002/0202_14/p010rbrief.html.
Ebihara, May M., Carol A. Mortland, and Judy Ledgerwood. 1994. *Cambodian Culture since 1975: Homeland and Exile.* Ithaca, NY: Cornell University Press.
The Economist. 1998. "Asia: Bunkered," September 26: 44.
———. 2003a. "Cambodia's Election," July 26: 40.
———. 2003b. "Counting on the Young," August 2: 39–40.
The Economist Intelligence Unit. 1994. *EIU Country Profile: Cambodia.* London: The Economist Group.
———. 2003. *Cambodia: Country Profile.* London: The Economist Group.
Egan, Susan Chan. 1999. "A Complex Connection: China's Government & Garment Industry." *Bobbin* November. Available at www.findarticles.com/cf_dls/m3638/3_41/59481779/p2/article.jhtml?term.

Eng, Roland. 2001. "Global Development Issues in a Changing World." *Journal of Macromarketing* 21(2): 213–216.

Far Eastern Economic Review. 1998. "Asian Executives Poll," May 28.

Frontier Funds Management. 1996. "The Vietnam Frontier Fund." Hong Kong: Frontier Funds Management Co. and Nomura International.

Hach, Sok, and Sarthi Acharya. 2002. *Cambodia's Annual Economic Review—2002* (Issue 2). Phnom Penh: Cambodia Development Resource Institute and Japan Printing House.

IPR Strategic Business Information Database-pNA. 2001. "Cambodia: Cambodian Cellular Operator Selects China's Huawei to Expand GSM Network," September 6.

Johnson, Kay. 2000. "Out of Cambodia." *Asian Business,* May.

Kate, Daniel Ten. 2004. "Under-the-Table Fees Damage Country's Image." *The Cambodia Daily,* Saturday, 3/27–28, weekend section.

Kevin, Tony. 1998. "U.S. Errs in Cambodia Policy." *Far Eastern Economic Review,* May 21.

Keyfitz, Nathan. 1982. "Development and the Elimination of Poverty." *Economic Development and Cultural Change* 30(6): 346–355.

Leeflang, Peter, and Fred van Raaij. 1993. "The Changing Consumer in the Netherlands." *International Journal of Research in Marketing* 10: 345–363.

Leepson, Marc. 1985. "Cambodia: A Nation in Turmoil." *Editorial Research Reports, Congressional Quarterly,* Washington, DC.

Levi, Robin. 1998. "Cambodia: Rattling the Killing Fields." Drawn from Project Against Domestic Violence, January 26, Ministry of Women's Affairs, Phnom Penh, Cambodia. Available at http://endabuse.org/programs/printable/display.php3?DocID98, accessed October 2, 2003.

Lintner, Bertil. 2001a. "Visited by Gloom." *Far Eastern Economic Review,* December 27. Available at www.feer.com/articles/2001/0112_27/p104econmon.html.

———. 2001b. "Kicking the Habit." *Far Eastern Economic Review,* August 2. Available at www.feer.com/articles/2001/0108_02/p052econmon.html.

Muscat, Robert J. 1989. *Cambodia: Post-Settlement Reconstruction and Development.* New York: Columbia University Press.

Mydans, Seth. 1998. "A Million Ghosts: Revenge or Justice? Cambodians Confront the Past." *The New York Times,* December 31:A1.

———. 2001. "Fighting AIDS: A New War Is Killing Cambodians." *The New York Times,* July 7: 1.

———. 2002. "Cambodian Leader Rules as if From the Throne." *The New York Times,* March 19: A1.

National Institute of Statistics. 2002. Unpublished data, Phnom Penh.

———. 2003. Unpublished data, Phnom Penh.

Osborne, Milton. 1979. *Before Kampuchea: Preludes to Tragedy.* London: Allen & Unwin.

Ponchaud, Francois. 1977. *Cambodia: Year Zero.* New York: Holt, Rinehart & Winston.

Postelwaite. 1995. "Beer Brands Battle for Market Share." *Phnom Penh Post,* May 5–18:12.

Pran, Dith, and Kim DePaul. 1997. *Children of Cambodia's Killing Fields: Memoirs by Survivors.* New Haven, CT: Yale University Press.

Prasso, Sheri. 1994. "Cambodia: A Heritage of Violence." *World Policy Journal* 11(Fall): 71–77.

Prud'Homme, Remy. 1969. *L'Economie du Cambodge.* Paris: Presses Universitaires de France.

Rahtz, Don, and Clifford Shultz. 2001. "Strategic Management of Cambodia's Tourism Industry, for Optimal Socioeconomic Development." In *Business in Cambodia,* ed. F. Brown, pp. 22–26. Washington, DC: Johns Hopkins School of Advanced International Studies.

———. 2002. Personal interview, January 3, Siem Reap and Angkor and Thom.

Russell, George W. 2001. "Society's Flimsy Fabric." *Asian Business,* December.

Sen, Hun. 2001. "Plenary Comments." US-ASEAN Business Council Conference for Investment in Cambodia, Phnom Penh, May 12.

Sereyvuth, Veng. 2001, June. Interview with authors, Phnom Penh.

———. 2003. "Government Is Fully Committed to Ensuring Political Stability for Visit Cambodia Year 2003." *Cambodian Business Review* 2(1): 5–8.

Sharky's. 2003. Available at www.sharkysofcambodia.com/skampuchea.html, accessed June 22, 2003.

Sheehan, Sean. 2000. *Cultures of the World: Cambodia.* Singapore: Times Media.

Showcross, William. 1994. "Cambodia's New Deal." Contemporary Issues Papers, No. 1. Washington, DC: Carnegie Endowment Publication.

Shultz, Clifford J., II. 1994. "Balancing Policy Consumer Desire and Corporate Interests: Considerations for Market Entry in Vietnam." *Columbia Journal of World Business* 29 (Winter): 42–53.

———. 2002. May field notes, Phnom Penh.

Shultz, Clifford J., II, and Naranhkiri Tith. 1998. "Cambodia: Transition and the Consequences for Future Consumption and Marketing." In *Marketing and Consumer Behavior in East and Southeast Asia,* ed. A. Pecotich and C. Shulz II. Sydney: McGraw Hill.

Siv, Sichan. 1998. "Return to Angkor." *Far Eastern Economic Review,* October 1.

South East Asia Monitor. 2002. "Economic Risk—Recovery to be Slow." 13(1): 16.

St. John, Ronald Bruce. 1995. "The Political Economy of the Royal Government of Cambodia." *Contemporary Southeast Asia* 17(December): 265–281.

Steinberg, David J. 1959. *Cambodia.* New Haven, CT: HRAF.

Thayer, Nate. 1994. "Log Jam." *Far Eastern Economic Review,* August 4: 55.

———. 1998. "Checkmate." *Far Eastern Economic Review,* October 1: 17.

Thayer, Nate, and Rodney Tasker. 1998. "We Are Scared." *Far Eastern Economic Review,* August 13.

Twining, Charles H. 1989. "The Economy." In *Cambodia 1975–1978,* ed. Karl D. Jackson. Princeton, NJ: Princeton University Press.

Un, Kheang, and Judy Ledgerwood. 2003. "Cambodia in 2002: Decentralization and Its Effects on Party Politics." *Asian Survey* 43(1): 113–119.

Ung, Luong. 2000. *First They Killed My Father.* New York: HarperCollins Publishers.

UNDP. 1991. *Cambodia's Rehabilitation Needs* (November 11). New York: United Nations Development Programme.

———. 2001. United Nations Development Programme, Annual Reports on Cambodia. Available at www.un.org.kh/undp/index.asp?page=publications.asp.

———. 2002. Human Development Report: Deepening Democracy in a Fragmented World. Available at http://hdr.undp.org/reports/global/2002/en/pdf/complete.pdf.

U.S. Census Bureau. 2000. HIV/AIDS Surveillance Data Base (June), International Programs Center, Population Division.

U.S. Department of State. 2003. Trafficking in Persons Report (June 11), United States Department of State, Trafficking Victims Protection Act of 2000. Available at www.state.gov/documents/organization/21555.pdf.

Vesperini, Helen. 2000. "Cambodia's AIDS Struggle." BBC News, November 30. Available at http://news.bbc.co.uk/hi/english/world/asia-pacific/newsid_1049000/1049014.stm, accessed March 18, 2002.

Vickery, Michael. 1990. "Notes on the Political Economy of the People's Republic of Kampuchea." *Journal of Contemporary Asia* 20(4): 435–465.

Wain, Barry. 2002. "Cambodia Sees Tourism Rise, Despite Sept. 11—Strategy Targeting Europe, Home Region Helped Set Record for Visitors." *The Wall Street Journal* (Eastern Edition), February 27.

WINAP. 2002. United Nations Economic and Social Commission for Asia and the Pacific. WINAP No. 26. Gender Research at the Cambodia Development Resource Institute. Available at www.unescap.org/wid/03widnews/02region/cambodia.htm, accessed March 21, 2005.

World Bank. 1992. *Cambodia: Agenda for Rehabilitation and Reconstruction.* Washington, DC: The World Bank.

———. 2001. *World Development Indicators Database.* Washington, DC: World Bank.

———. 2003. *Cambodia Rural Profile.* Washington, DC: World Bank. Available at www.worldbank.org/eapsocial/sector/rural/cambodia.pdf.

World Factbook. 2003. Central Intelligence Agency, Washington, DC. Available at www.cia.gov/cia/publications/factbook/geos/cb.html.

CHAPTER 4

THE PEOPLE'S REPUBLIC OF CHINA

Markets within the Market

PIA POLSA, STELLA L. M. SO, AND MARK W. SPEECE

OVERVIEW

A huge country such as the People's Republic of China (PRC) offers an interesting mixture of subcultures and submarkets within its national borders. The transition from a planned to a socialistic market economy adds a dimension to the diversity. To comprehend consumer behavior, it is necessary to understand the diversity of cultures, geography, economic development, and the changing purchasing power of citizens in different parts of the country. The unification of Hong Kong and Macau to the PRC further diversifies the market, because both cities have had a separate and distinguished history and economic development. To provide this understanding, the following issues are covered: geography and climate, the economic history of the PRC, the current socioeconomic environment, the demographic environment, culture, and some changes in the culture. This chapter also examines consumption patterns; macromarketing issues involving branding, price, and distribution; communications and marketing research; and concludes with some ideas on the future directions of change. Hong Kong is then discussed separately and in considerable detail. The long-term trend is convergence, but Hong Kong's consumer market will not look much like the rest of China's market any time soon. Hong Kong remains important in its own right, as an affluent, sophisticated consumer market characteristic of developed economies, and as a trendsetter that gives hints of how many aspects of China's market may develop in the future.

INTRODUCTION

China, or more accurately, the People's Republic of China (PRC), is a socialistic republic that was established on October 1, 1949. A cursory glance at this large country may give the impression that it is a single, unified, and homogeneous market of the world's largest population. However, a closer look at the PRC reveals the diversity of climate, history, culture, population, and administration in different areas. Naturally, this diversity affects consumer behavior of "mainland"[1] Chinese people and, consequently, makes marketing strategies more complex than we would assume at first glance. Part of this diversity is from the incorporation of Hong Kong and Macau under the "one country, two systems" motto that symbolizes, in the context of our discussion, that Hong

Kong is not yet much like the rest of China. The second system represented by the Hong Kong Special Administrative Region is a thoroughly capitalist, advanced, developed-country consumer market that must be discussed separately and in detail to be well understood. We devote a separate section of this chapter to this very important, distinctive consumer market.

To provide an understanding of the consumer behavior of PRC citizens, we first present the geography and climate of the nation. The variety in climate and geography has affected Chinese history and created subcultures inside the area that is currently the PRC. Therefore, knowledge of the geography and climate forms a base for an understanding of the emergence of cultural and historical differences within the PRC.

A brief look at Chinese economic history gives a further understanding of the heterogeneity of this country as well as does a presentation of the current socioeconomic environment. The current reform policies have had an uneven effect on economic development, thus enlarging the gap between the purchasing power of the eastern and western populations. However, some attempts have been made to decrease the gap as well as to diminish the income difference between urban and rural residents.

The exposition of the demographic environment explains the current differences in urban and rural areas and western and eastern regions. The country not only consists of the Han Chinese (the majority ethnic group of the population), but also of fifty-six different ethnicities with different dialects and languages. Even the Han Chinese population may be divided into different cultures (Swanson 1989) and levels of economic development. Demographic differences are crucial in understanding the market of the PRC. Due to periods of isolation during Chinese history, the general culture of the PRC has some special characteristics. These basic cultural issues are discussed, along with current levels of education and topics on gender and health. Some implications of these issues on marketing planning are presented at the end of the section.

The next section provides more detail on purchasing power by focusing on consumer income and employment issues, with an enumeration of segmentation possibilities. Based on these demographic, cultural, and employment environments, the consumption patterns of the Chinese population are discussed. Specifically, saving, single-child families, housing, household goods, eating habits, and leisure activities are discussed in detail. At the end of the section, the marketing implications are presented. The final sections take up the marketing topics of branding, pricing, distribution, word of mouth, advertising, and market research. The chapter concludes with a description of likely future developments.

A BRIEF INTRODUCTION TO GEOGRAPHY AND CLIMATE

China is located in the eastern part of Asia. The current PRC is approximately 9.6 million square kilometers of territory, bordered by mountains and deserts in the west and north, the Yellow Sea in the east, and the South China Sea in the south. China occupies one-fifth of the world's land area and one-quarter of Asia. It borders Mongolia and Russia in the north; Vietnam, Laos, Bhutan, Nepal, and Sikkim in the south; Afghanistan, Pakistan, India, and Myanmar in the west; and Korea in the east (Zhou 1992, 1).

China is characterized by contrasts in geography and climate. There are three high regions, starting from the west and approaching the eastern coast. The western part is Qinghai-Tibet Plateau, "the roof of the world." The height of this massive mountain area is typically between 4,000 and 5,000 meters above sea level. The second part is composed of the Junggar, Tarim, and Sichuan basins, in addition to the Inner Mongolia, Loess, and Yunnan-Guizhou plateaus. The average height of this part of the country is about 1,000 to 2,000 meters above sea level. The most eastern part of the country drops to less than 500 meters above sea level (Zhou 1992, 2–3). These variations in altitude partly explain the concentration of the population in the eastern parts of the PRC, which provide the most suitable living conditions. This area, though, occupies only about one-third of the total area of the PRC.

These differences in the living conditions between the east and the west are further accentuated by variations in humidity. The moist regions in the east cover about 30 percent of the land. Semimoist and semiarid areas in the central parts of the country cover about 35 percent of the land, leaving as much as one-third of the country dry. The mountainous and arid western regions have always been sparsely populated. The country can be divided from south to north into six zones in terms of variation in climate. Differences are as drastic as differences in altitude, because the warmest climate in the south is equatorial, and the coldest climate may drop to –24°C during the winter period. In between the south and the north of China, the climate can vary from subtropical to intermediate-temperature to warm-temperature areas (Zhou 1992, 4–5).

While its terrain divides China into three east–west staircases, rivers divide China into north–south regions. The PRC is crisscrossed with 50,000 rivers scattered across the western desert and mountain areas and flowing to the oceans. The most important are the three famous rivers: the Yangtze (Chang Jiang), the Yellow River (Huang He), and the Pearl River (Zhu Jiang). The Yangtze has provided fertile land for cultivation throughout history for many nations and dynasties, because it is located in the subtropical monsoon climate. The Yellow River further north was the base for the birth of ancient Chinese civilization and culture, and even today, provides a living for approximately 100 million people. The third river, the Pearl River, is famous for the recent economic development of its delta area in Guangdong province (Zhou 1992, 5–7). These large rivers have all been bases for different Chinese subcultures throughout history.

A BRIEF INTRODUCTION TO THE ECONOMIC HISTORY OF CHINA

The economic history of the PRC can be divided into four different stages according to the shifts in economic policy: centrally planned economy (1953–78),[2] planned commodity economy (1979–92),[3] socialist market economy (1993–99),[4] and postindustrialism. Table 4.1 summarizes the general stages of economic development during the last forty years. In 1997, Hong Kong was unified to the PRC as a Special Administrative Region (SAR). And, in 1999, Macau became a SAR. Though certainly part of the market that is "Greater China" (Pan 2000), their history and development are different from that of the mainland; as a consumer market, Hong Kong is still quite different, so for the most part, Hong Kong is discussed in a separate section of this chapter.

The political orientation since 1979 can also be called an "Opening Policy," as foreign investment was allowed at the end of 1978, and the planned economy restrictions were removed. Since the end of the 1970s, there have been changes not only in the applied economic policy, but also in the economic ideology. The old planned economy system was never totally abandoned, but rather, parallel new ideas cultivated a dual-track transition to a market economy (Gang, Perkins, and Sabin 1997). The objective of the reforms is to develop a system that is suitable for the conditions in China. According to some Chinese scholars, socialism did not fail, but rather, China has failed to interpret socialism in a proper way (Hsu 1991, 171). Understanding these changes in the economic philosophy or ideology is essential for fully comprehending the current situation.

Development of consumer behavior since the Opening Policy has been rapid. The reforms have led to an increase in the range of products available and to an increase in people's incomes. There has also been a growth in inflation and a change in consumer attitudes.

Table 4.1

Different Stages in the Economic Development of the PRC (except Hong Kong and Macau)

Characteristics	Economic Stage			
	Centrally planned economy (1953–78)	Planned commodity economy (1979–92)	Socialist market economy (1993–99)	Post-industrialism (2000–)
Government intervention	Direct administrative control	Diminished direct control	Indirect control	Economic law, indirect control
Orientation of business	Production oriented, plan fulfillment	Operation oriented, profitability, sales	Market oriented, profitability	Higher consumer demands
Ownership	State, collective	State, collective, emergence of private and foreign	State (still dominant in some fields of industry), collective, private (high growth), foreign	More sophisticated local players (state, collective and private), foreign (after WTO intensified competition)
Product policy	State plan	Limited freedom, meeting plan first	Autonomy	Branding (local and international)
Price	Fixed	Fixed, floating, black market	Free market price (except raw material)	Value-added pricing
Advertising	Prohibited	Allowed	Allowed	Long-term and brand effectiveness

Source: Adapted from Ying Fan, "Blending East and West, How Can Western Management Know-how Be Transferred to China's Socialist Market Economy?" (Durham: Durham University Business School, 1994); K. –A. Schlevogt, "The Branding Revolution in China." *The China Business Review* 27, no. 3 (2000): 54.

CURRENT GOVERNMENT STRUCTURE AND
THE POLITICAL SITUATION

After liberation in 1949, the government of the PRC consisted of three components: the Chinese Communist Party (CCP), the formal government structure, and the army (Spence 1990, 519). Administrative power is in the hands of the CCP, which has as its highest organ the National Party Congress. It meets every five years and functions as the Central Committee, with executive tasks. The Central Committee elects the Politburo of twenty-two members, and the Standing Committee of the Politburo. The National People's Congress (NPC) is elected every five years and represents a kind of parliament of the PRC, with a Standing Committee. The State Council of the NPC is headed by a prime minister and is composed of five vice premiers, nine state councilors, and the secretary general. A number of commissions, ministries, offices, agencies, and institutions are directly under the State Council. The administration of the People's Liberation Army (PLA) is divided in six large regions: northwest, north, northeast, southwest, east, and south-central China bureaus. The administrative structure of these units follows the hierarchical structure of the CCP and NPC.

At the local level, the PRC is divided into thirty-four provincial-level administrative divisions that are directly under the central government. These divisions are as follows: four municipalities (Beijing, Tianjin, Shanghai, and Chongqing); twenty-three provinces; five autonomous regions (Inner Mongolia, Guangxi, Tibet, Ningxia, and Xinjiang); and two SARs (Hong Kong and Macau). These divisions are further divided into 333 prefectures, 2,074 counties, and 659 cities (Zhou 1992; *China Statistical Yearbook* 2001, 3). The administrative hierarchical structure of these local units follows the form of the central governmental structure. Usually, there are provincial- and city-level bureaus for each National Ministry. For example, the Commercial Bureau executes the national economic laws and even controls local-city-level rules for local business conditions.[5] The dual reporting system to the local government and to the higher-level national ministries, creates confusing situations for lower-level authorities. For instance, national economic policies or even laws are not implemented consistently throughout the country at the local levels. Indirectly, this affects, for instance, the distribution of goods, as some health and quality inspections are locally defined.

THE SOCIOECONOMIC ENVIRONMENT

The average annual growth rate of the Chinese gross domestic product (GDP) has been high since the Opening Policy. Table 4.2 provides GDP figures from 1990 to 2000. The average growth rate adjusted with effects of price distortions in the pre-reform and early reform years has been around 10 percent (see also Gang et al. 1997).

Despite positive growth trends for the entire country, there are tremendous differences throughout the PRC. The economic environment can be roughly divided into four areas according to economic development and administrative differences: SARs; special economic zones (SEZs); larger cities, such as Beijing, Tianjin, Guangzhou, Shanghai, and Chongqing; and western parts of the PRC. The SARs are Hong Kong and Macau. Both were united with the PRC at the end of the 1990s and have a colonial and market economy history; the Chinese government promised to maintain their extant political and economic systems. SEZs are cities and areas that were first opened for foreign trade after the start of the reform policy. The purpose of these zones was to stimulate the economy and, simultaneously, to attract foreign investment. The areas were given preferential economic and political treatment, including favorable terms for investment. Conse-

Table 4.2

Gross Domestic Product (Expenditure-based)

Year	Total (Rmb bn)	Real GDP growth (%)
1991	2,166	8.0
1992	2,666	13.6
1993	3,413	13.4
1994	4,726	11.6
1995	6,145	10.2
1996	6,789	9.6
1997	7,477	8.8
1998	7,983	7.8
1999	8,386	7.3
2000	9,110	7.9
2001		7.3
2002		8.0

Source: Economist Intelligence Unit (EIU), "Country Report: China and Mongolia" (London: The Economist Intelligence Unit Ltd, 1992–2003). In EIU reports, a majority of GDP figures are drawn from national Chinese statistics. However, the World Bank has adjusted GDP numbers from 1994 until 1999 (C. A. Holz, "Institutional Constraints on the Quality of Statistics in China." *China Information* 16, no. 1 [2002], pp. 37–38).

Table 4.3

Some Economic Indicators of Cities, Open Coastal Cities, and Special Economic Zones, 2002

Economic indicator (*n*)	Per open coastal city (*N* = 15)	Per special economic zone (*N* = 5)
Gross domestic product (100 million yuan)	1,407	759
Total retail sales of consumer goods (100 million yuan)	533	258
Total wages of staff and workers (100 million yuan)	153	93
Annual electricity consumption (100 million kwh)	143	82
Total number of telephone sets (10,000 households)	199	105
Total number of cell phones (10,000 households)	233	189

Source: China Statistical Yearbook (Beijing: China Statistical Publishing House, 2003), pp. 388–89.

quently, these areas developed rapidly, prospered, and substantially increased the living standards of their people. The first four SEZs were Shenzhen, Xiamen, Zhuhai, and Shantou, all located in southeast China. Later, SEZ status was given to the island of Hainan. Even today, the SEZs are among the richest parts of the country, and their prosperity has spread to neighboring areas. One, however, should not see the SEZ or the SAR as the only lucrative markets of China. Major cities, such as Beijing, and fifteen open coastal cities[6] are also comparatively well developed. Table 4.3 shows some economic indicators for SEZs and the fifteen open coastal cities.

There also exists future market potential for less advanced parts of the PRC. In order to grasp this huge market, equal attention must be given to the lesser-known parts of China still awaiting development. In short, there are profound differences in economic development across the country that suggest important differences in purchasing power and market potential.

Table 4.4 shows the urban–rural divisions and per capita GDP grouped into coastal, central, and inland areas. At the national level, 36 percent of Chinese people live in the cities and 64 percent in the countryside. The coastal areas are the most urbanized places, as 45 percent of the area's population lives in the cities. Western inland areas, on the other hand, are less urban, as 72 percent of people in the inland areas live in the countryside. More than three-fourths of the population is concentrated in the coastal and central parts of the country, whereas 23 percent of Chinese people live in the western provinces, which constitute 50 percent of the PRC. Similarly, the GDP is concentrated in the developed coastal provinces. The average GDP per capita is 16,490 yuan in coastal areas, in contrast to the rest of the country, where the average GDP per capita is 6,462 yuan—less than half of the GDP of the coastal provinces. The growth rates for the average per-capita GDP figure between 1996 and 2001 reveal a possible future slight convergence between economic development in the inland and central parts of the country, as the growth rates are 39 percent for inland areas and 37 percent for central areas. On the other hand, the growth rate of per capita GDP for coastal areas is the highest at 42 percent.

Table 4.5 tells a similar story. Total gross domestic expenditure in the coastal regions is four times more than in the inland areas of the country and two times more than in the central areas. The ratio of investments compared to consumption is approximately equal in the eastern part of the country, while in the central and western regions, consumption counts for more than investments. The rich areas export more than import, whereas the inland areas do not produce for export but are dependent on imported goods. As a consequence, the per capita consumption in coastal areas is about 30 percent higher than in the central areas and in the western parts of the country. These figures give a general view of the uneven distribution of wealth between eastern and western parts of the PRC. Furthermore, the income inequality in rural and urban China has increased steadily since the early reform era and is one of the highest in Asia, but this varies between the provinces (Gang et al. 1997).

China's geographical economic development since 1979 can be further explained by the central government's economic development preference policy, which was implemented in four stages from south to north and from east to west. The first stage of economic development was the creation of SEZs in South China, around the Pearl River Delta, in the provinces of Guangdong and Fujian. The second development stage started at the end of the 1980s. Its focus has been on the area of the Yangtze River Delta around Shanghai–Pudong and, consequently, affected, for example, Zhejiang and Jiangsu. The third development stage occurred further north. This development has concentrated on the shore of the Bohai Sea in the Liaoning and Shangdong Peninsulas. The capital of the PRC, Beijing, will be affected by these investments, and the other large city, Tianjin, will be the essential port. The unification of Hong Kong in 1997 and Macau in 1999 with the PRC gives further economic importance to the southern parts of the country. Guangdong, Guangxi, Hainan, Macau, and Hong Kong form a significant economic area for both domestic and foreign trade.

The three preferential policy stages have widened the economic development gap of east and west. However, the current Chinese government has made efforts to decrease this gap. Two current investment projects emphasize this effort. The first is the huge investment in the Jingjiou railway from Beijing to Kowloon, Hong Kong. The regions around this transportation line benefited from the economic development the railway brought, and it also affected the central parts of the country. Provinces such as Hebei, Hunan, Shandong, Anhui, Jiangxi, Hubei, Fujian, and Guangdong have benefited from the railway. The other large investment project will bring the development further west. The Changjing–Sanxia project involves the reconstruction of the Yangtze River so that vessels from Shanghai will be able to sail all the way to Yibin city in Sichuan province. This "Golden

Table 4.4

Urban versus Rural Population and GDP Divisions in the PRC, 2002

Provinces, municipalities, autonomous regions, and SARs	Total population (10,000 persons)	Urban[a] (%)	Rural (%)	Per capita GDP (yuan)
National	**128,453**[b]	**36**	**64**	
Coastal areas				
Beijing	**1,423**	**78**	**22**	**28,449**
Tianjin	**1,007**	**72**	**28**	**22,380**
Hebei	6,735	26	74	9,115
Liaoning	4,203	54	46	12,986
Shanghai	**1,625**	**88**	**12**	**40,646**
Jiangsu	7,381	41	59	14,391
Zhejiang	4,647	49	51	16,838
Fujian	3,466	42	58	13,497
Shangdong	9,082	38	62	11,645
Guangdong	7,859	55	45	15,030
Hainan	803	40	60	7,803
Guangxi	4,822	28	72	5,099
Total	53,053	45	55	Average: 16,490
Central areas				
Inner Mongolia	2,379	43	57	7,241
Shanxi	3,294	35	65	6,146
Jilin	2,699	50	50	8,334
Heilongjiang	3,813	52	48	10,184
Anhui	6,338	28	72	5,817
Jiangxi	4,222	28	72	5,829
Henan	9,613	23	77	6,436
Hubei	5,988	40	60	8,319
Hunan	6,629	30	70	6,565
Total	44,975	33	67	Average: 7,208
Inland areas				
Chongqing	**3,107**	**33**	**67**	**6,347**
Sichuan	8,673	27	73	5,766
Guizhou	3,837	24	76	3,153
Yunnan	4,333	23	77	5,179
Tibet	267	19	81	6,093
Shaanxi	3,674	32	68	5,523
Gansu	2,593	24	76	4,493
Qinghai	529	35	65	6,426
Ningxia	572	32	68	5,804
Xinjiang	1,905	34	66	8,382
Total	29,490	28	72	Average: 5,717
SAR				
Hong Kong	678	—	—	
Macau	44	—	—	

Source: China Statistical Yearbook (Beijing: China Statistical Publishing House, 2003), pp. 65, 98; *China Statistical Yearbook* (Beijing: China Statistical Publishing House, 2001), p. 101.

[a]The division between urban and rural population is based on 2001 census data.

[b]The difference between total national population and the sum of provinces and municipalities is the number of people with unsettled household registrations and people in the SARs.

Table 4.5

Gross Domestic Expenditure by Region and Per Capita Living Expenditure, 2002

Provinces, municipalities, autonomous regions, and SARs	Total expenditure (100 million yuan)	Total final consumption	Cross capital formation[a]	Net export[b]	Per capita living expenditure	
					Urban	Rural
Coastal areas						
Beijing	**3,212**	**1,700**	**2,010**	**−497**	**10,285**	**3,732**
Tianjin	**2,051**	**990**	**1,055**	**6**	**7,192**	**2,164**
Hebei	6,122	2,819	2,661	642	5,069	1,476
Liaoning	5,458	3,031	1,836	591	5,343	1,781
Shanghai	**5,409**	**2,456**	**2,409**	**544**	**10,464**	**5,302**
Jiangsu	10,533	4,802	4,809	922	6,043	2,620
Zhejiang	7,796	3,742	3,467	587	8,713	3,693
Fujian	4,620	2,434	2,120	67	6,632	2,583
Shangdong	10,552	5,021	4,941	590	5,596	1,998
Guangdong	11,770	6,701	4,157	912	8,988	2,825
Hainan	604	331	276	−3	5,460	1,603
Guangxi	2,455	1,699	878	−121	5,413	1,686
Total	70,582	35,726	30,619	4,240	Average: 7,100	Average: 2,622
Central areas						
Inner Mongolia	1,763	1,092	848	−177	4,860	1,647
Shanxi	2,042	1,184	919	−61	4,711	1,355
Jilin	2,318	1,445	898	−25	4,974	1,680
Heilongjiang	3,829	2,288	1,322	219	4,462	1,674
Anhui	3,570	2,263	1,310	−4	4,737	1,476
Jiangxi	2,460	1,460	999	2	4,549	1,785
Henan	6,169	3,442	2,546	181	4,505	1,452
Hubei	4,861	2,670	1,995	196	5,609	1,745
Hunan	4,340	2,763	1,573	5	5,575	2,069
Total	31,352	18,607	12,410	336	Average: 4,887	Average: 1,654
Inland areas						
Chongqing	**2,020**	**1,229**	**990**	**−199**	**6,360**	**1,498**
Sichuan	4,875	2,894	1,977	4	5,413	1,592
Guizhou	1,185	890	649	−354	4,598	1,138
Yunnan	2,232	1,526	887	−181	5,828	1,382
Tibet	174	100	72	3	6,952	1,000
Shaanxi	2,036	1,109	1,107	−181	5,378	1,491
Gansu	1,165	679	539	−52	5,064	1,153
Qinghai	338	221	246	−130	5,043	1,386
Ningxia	329	249	245	−165	5,105	1,418
Xinjiang	1,598	949	864	−215	5,636	1,411
Total	15,952	9,846	7,576	−1,470	Average: 5,538	Average: 1,347

Source: China Statistical Yearbook (Beijing: China Statistical Publishing House, 2003), pp. 69, 356, 372.

[a]Data on capital formation are "highly incomplete" (C. A. Holz, "Institutional Constraints on the Quality of Statistics in China." *China Information* 16, no. 1 [2002], p. 36).

[b]Note that some provinces are unable to compile net export data (C. A. Holz, "Institutional Constraints on the Quality of Statistics in China." *China Information* 16, no. 1 [2002], p. 33).

Table 4.6

Employment and Origins of GDP by Type of Industry (percent)

Year	Employment industry			Origins of GDP industry		
	Primary	Secondary	Tertiary	Primary	Secondary	Tertiary
1952	84	7	9	51	21	29
1990	60	21	19	27	42	31
1991	60	21	19	25	42	34
1992	58	22	20	22	44	34
1993	56	23	21	20	47	33
1994	54	23	23	20	48	32
1995	52	23	25	21	49	31
1996	51	24	26	20	49	32
1997	50	24	26	19	49	32
1998	50	24	27	18	49	33
1999	50	23	27	18	49	33
2000	50	23	27	16*	52*	32*
2001	50	22	28	16*	51*	32*
2002	50	21	29	14	52	34

Sources: China Statistical Yearbook (Beijing: China Statistical Publishing House, 1995), p. 83; *China Statistical Yearbook* (Beijing: China Statistical Publishing House, 2000), pp. 54, 115; *China Statistical Yearbook* (Beijing: China Statistical Publishing House, 2001), p. 109; *China Statistical Yearbook* (Beijing: China Statistical Publishing House, 2002), p. 119; *China Statistical Yearbook* (Beijing: China Statistical Publishing House, 2003), p. 125; Economist Intelligence Unit (EIU), "Country Report: China and Mongolia" (London: The Economist Intelligence Unit Ltd, 1996–2000).

Note: In Chinese statistics, the figures for both the tertiary and secondary sectors might be inconsistent (C. A. Holz, "Institutional Constraints on the Quality of Statistics in China." *China Information* 16, no. 1 [2002], 41).

*EIU estimates.

Water Channel" will bring east and west together and provide higher income opportunities for the people living around the area.[7] Chongqing, a city at the end of the Yangtze River in Sichuan province, was given the status of municipality, and that has increased the economic development of the city and its surroundings. The most recent preferential policy stage, "Great Development of the West," initiated in 1999, has been designed to further enforce the western economic developments. This preferential policy differs from the previous ones by emphasizing market orientation, foreign involvement, limited role of state-owned industries, and social and economic balance.

The structure of the economy has also changed during the years of the PRC, following the normal trend in any developing country. Table 4.6 shows that while primary industry occupied as much as 84 percent of the total employment in 1952, its share in the year 2002 was only 50 percent. The share of secondary industry has increased during the fifty years of socialistic regime but seems to have remained stable around 21 to 24 percent during the last ten years. Tertiary industry is still increasing its share and in 2002 employed 29 percent of the workforce. In 1952, half of the GDP was produced in primary industry, while more than half of the GDP in 2001 originated from secondary industry. The share of tertiary industry from GDP has been around 30 percent during the history of the PRC.

To overcome the economic gap between the rural and urban areas, and the problem of the decreasing importance of primary industry, the government has tried to improve the economic conditions in rural areas. The reform policy of the late 1970s started in the countryside, when the government eased control, and the farmers were allowed to sell part of their production on the free market. Later, land reform allowed farmers to rent out their pieces of land if they did not wish to work them, although the land was still owned by the government. The establishment of township and village enterprises was one way to stimulate the economy in the rural areas and create employment (Rana 1993, 9). The reform of township and village enterprises was closely related to the effort to industrialize the countryside. To improve living standards in the rural areas, the government sought to facilitate the distribution of commodities while providing subsidies for agricultural products. This policy has been successful in some rural areas. For example, in Guangdong province, the rural areas are more prosperous than the urban areas, and generally, township and village enterprises have been more successful than their urban counterparts.

THE DEMOGRAPHIC ENVIRONMENT: POPULATION SIZE AND DISTRIBUTION

With a total population of nearly 1.3 billion people, China is the most populous country in the world. The growth rate has decreased from an average annual growth rate of 1.6 percent in the period from 1986 to 1990, to a more recent 0.64 percent, mainly due to the strict one-child policy (*China Statistical Yearbook* 2003, 97). The population of the PRC includes fifty-six nationalities. Ninety-four percent are Han Chinese, and fifty-five other ethnic groups comprise 6 percent of the population. Despite the small percentage of minorities, their population is substantial. For example, Zhuang, the largest minority, has a population of more than sixteen million people, which exceeds the population of many European countries. The population of the rest of the minorities ranges from ten million (Man nationality in former Manchuria) to several thousand people (*China Statistical Yearbook* 2003, 48).

Geographic Distribution

Two-thirds of the Chinese population is in the eastern and central parts of the country. For geographical and climatic reasons, these parts of the country have been the most advantageous places for agriculture and commerce. Table 4.7 shows that the coastal provinces of the country cover only 13 percent of the land, making the average population density highest in the eastern parts. China is a country of extremes. The population density of Shanghai is as high as 2,708 persons per square kilometer; but in Tibet, there are only two persons per square kilometer. Consequently, the most lucrative market for consumer goods is the coastal and central provinces, given that economic development is also the highest in these areas.

Urban Versus Rural Population

In 1992, the urban rural residence structure was 27.6 percent urban versus 72.4 percent rural (*China Statistical Yearbook* 1995, 760). In the year 2000, the urban residents counted for 36.2 percent of the total population (*China Statistical Yearbook* 2001, 101). The division between urban and rural is more complicated than before, when people could not freely move from their official residences. Nowadays, there is a large population of rural people called an urban "floating" population (cf. Wiemer 1992, 172). These people immigrate to cities, work there temporarily in less-wanted jobs, and occasionally return to their hometowns. Formally, they are still registered in their countryside residences. They form bridges between the rural and urban populations, which otherwise differ in culture and habit.

Table 4.7

Population Distribution in Coastal, Central, and Inland Parts of the Country, 2002

Provinces, municipalities, autonomous regions, and SARs	Percent of the total population (November 2000)	Area (10,000 km²)	Population density (per 10,000 km²)
National	128,453*	967.8	133
Coastal areas			
Beijing	**1.1**	**1.7**	**837**
Tianjin	**0.8**	**1.1**	**915**
Hebei	5.2	18.0	374
Liaoning	3.3	15.0	280
Shanghai	**1.3**	**0.6**	**2,708**
Jiangsu	5.7	10.0	738
Zhejiang	3.6	10.0	465
Fujian	2.7	12.0	289
Shangdong	7.1	15.0	605
Guangdong	6.1	18.0	487
Hainan	0.6	3.4	236
Guangxi	3.8	23.0	210
Total	41.3	127.8	415
Central areas			
Inner Mongolia	1.9	128	19
Shanxi	2.6	16	206
Jilin	2.1	18	150
Heilongjiang	3.0	47	81
Anhui	4.9	13	488
Jiangxi	3.3	17	248
Henan	7.5	17	565
Hubei	4.7	18	333
Hunan	5.2	20	331
Total	35.0	294	153
Inland areas			
Chongqing	**2.4**	**57**	**208**
Sichuan	6.8		
Guizhou	3.0	17	226
Yunnan	3.4	39	111
Tibet	0.2	120	2
Shaanxi	2.9	20	184
Gansu	2.0	45	58
Qinghai	0.4	72	7
Ningxia	0.4	7	82
Xinjiang	1.5	160	12
Total	23.00	537	55
Military personnel	0.3		
SAR			
Hong Kong	678		
Macao	44		

Sources: China Statistical Yearbook (Beijing: China Statistical Publishing House, 2003), p. 98; Shunwu Zhou, *China Provincial Geography* (Beijing: Foreign Languages Press, 1992).

*The difference between the total national population and the sum of provinces and municipalities is the number of people with unsettled household registrations and population in SARs (*China Statistical Yearbook* [Beijing: China Statistical Publishing House, 2001], p. 92).

Table 4.8

Age Distribution, 2002

Age	Population by age group	Percent of population
0–14	267,978	21
15–64	888,206	71
65 and over	102,767	8
Total	1,258,951	100

Source: China Statistical Yearbook (Beijing: China Statistical Publishing House, 2003), p. 104.

Table 4.9

Average Number of Persons per Household, 1985–2002

	1985	1990	1995	1996	1998	1999	2000	2001	2002
Urban household	3.89	3.50	3.23	3.20	3.16	3.14	3.13	3.10	3.04
Rural household	5.12	4.80	4.48	4.42	4.30	4.25	4.20	4.15	4.13

Sources: China Statistical Yearbook (Beijing: China Statistical Publishing House, 1995), pp. 262, 278; *China Statistical Yearbook* (Beijing: China Statistical Publishing House, 1997), pp. 294, 312; *China Statistical Yearbook* (Beijing: China Statistical Publishing House, 2000), pp. 313, 330; *China Statistical Yearbook* (Beijing: China Statistical Publishing House, 2001), pp. 305, 322; *China Statistical Yearbook* (Beijing: China Statistical Publishing House, 2002), pp. 321, 342; *China Statistical Yearbook* (Beijing: China Statistical Publishing House, 2003), pp. 345, 366.

The impact of the consumption habits of floating populations is twofold. First, urban immigrants typically send their salaries home, hence affecting the purchasing power of rural residents. Second, these immigrant people affect the social structures of the society, sometimes by creating problems such as crime, but also by bringing the urban consumption habits to the knowledge of rural consumers. It has been suggested that to truly bridge the income gap between rural and urban consumers, the Chinese leaders need to allow rural workers to absorb urban social services and get a semiofficial status in the cities (Gang et al. 1997). However, "floating" people may potentially be the future's powerful consumers, because they earn more than average and represent the rural majority of the population.

Age Distribution

As in other developing countries, the majority of the population in the PRC is young. One-third of the population is under twenty years old, and only 8 percent of the population is over sixty-five years old (see Table 4.8). Population distribution is changing because of increasing living standards, the one-child policy, and higher life expectancies.

The Chinese Household

During the last decade, the average sizes of households have constantly decreased in both the urban and rural areas, as shown in Table 4.9. In the urban regions, the one-child policy has already

Table 4.10

Type of Household (in terms of percentage of total households)

Region	Households number	Single	Married couple	Two generations	More than two generations	One generation and other	More than one generation and other
National	329.088	6	8	64	18	1	3
Beijing	22.354	8	10	60	18	1	3
Guangdong	9.709	9	5	54	26	1	5
Henan	12.488	5	6	67	18	1	3
Sichuan	14.946	7	7	61	21	1	3

Source: China Statistical Yearbook (Beijing: China Statistical Publishing House, 1995), p. 65.

had its effect on the sizes of households. This tendency may continue, even if the one-child regulations have been loosened.

Household size has been influenced by the government population policy. During the early 1960s to 1970s, the large size of the national population was believed to be the power of a nation. There were no restrictions on family size, and hence, households from that period often include as many as five or six children (Spence 1990, 685). Children born during the 1960s and 1970s are now adults, and in their turn, are building families. The sizes of their households are generally only three persons, unless grandparents are also living in the same households.

Table 4.10 gives an idea of the typical household. The most typical is a household of two generations, but today, about one-fifth of households consist of more than two generations. Some modern urban households have no children, and 10 percent of married-couple households in Beijing fall into this category. However, this often does not hold in rural homes, where children are still considered a resource, and where, despite the one-child policy, families may have more than one child and not divulge this information for official statistics. Table 4.10 provides figures for numbers of generations living in a household. More recent statistics do not provide this kind of information.

Marriage is still an important factor in Chinese society, despite some attempts to discourage it to prevent overpopulation (Spence 1990). One of these attempts, that was put in place in the 1980s, involved the revision of the legal marriage age to twenty-two for males and twenty for females (Spence 1990). It is even higher than this in some local working units. Nevertheless, only 29 percent of the population over fifteen years of age was single in 1982, and this figure decreased to 25 percent in 1990 (*China Statistical Yearbook* 2000, 97). In the latest sample survey on population (1999), 18 percent of the respondents over fifteen years of age were unmarried (*China Statistical Yearbook* 2000, 106). Practical considerations encourage marriage despite official efforts to discourage it. In many government units, such as universities, better housing is provided for married couples than for single persons. For instance, in Guangxi Teacher's College, unmarried persons share a room with one other adult teacher. However, a married couple is given a larger room. Furthermore, many young people buy their first household durable goods only after wedding, rather than investing in their comfort as single persons. During their single lives, they save in order to be able to provide good material starts for their marital lives.

These marketing implications may be deduced from Chinese demography:

- Because of purchasing power and population concentration, the most lucrative markets of the PRC are the coastal areas, but in the future, the developing central regions will be increasingly important. Potential markets for infrastructure projects increasingly include central and western regions.
- The market of young consumers is substantial.
- The decreasing size of households will affect household consumption needs.
- A good target market for promotion of household durables is provided by young couples of marriageable age rather than single persons.

CULTURE AND CULTURAL CHANGE

With its origin over 5,000 years ago, Chinese culture is one of the rare ancient civilizations that has survived and is still vital. Because China has always been, in one way or another, isolated from the other parts of the world, some features of its culture have developed independently. Naturally, many features of Chinese culture are also common to other cultures, especially in Asia, but there still exist some unique characteristics. Chinese culture is based on Confucian philosophy as well as ideas from Taoism and Buddhism. The establishment of the PRC has had a great impact, adding a third ideology, Marxism, to the factors affecting the culture. For example, the view of the woman's role has become more liberated due to the ideas of Mao Zedong, and this, along with the current one-child policy, affects the traditional role of family. In the course of the last twenty years, the Open Door Policy has changed the values of the Chinese people, despite the intention to focus only on economic development. This policy, while bringing back some old traditions, such as women staying at home, has also mixed the original Chinese values with Western ways (e.g., consumption culture). Only the future will show how deeply rooted the socialist ideas of equality have been, and to what extent the Chinese people will absorb Western ideas.

Basic Features of Chinese Culture

Culture is of critical relevance to marketers in China, because successful strategies cannot be developed without taking into account the specific features of Chinese culture. The issues associated with culture are so important, that some writers even call for special marketing theory for Chinese culture (Ambler, Lee, and Yau in Schütte and Vanier 1995). Chinese cultural values are based on interpersonal relationships and social orientation. Compared with Western cultures, Chinese culture is more collective (Hofstede 2001). Individuals are seen as existing in relationships, and some of these relationships are of special importance. Confucius defined the Cardinal Relations as those between sovereign and subject, father and son, elder brother and younger brother, husband and wife, and friend and friend. These relationships also have hierarchical patterns: a senior member to be superior to a junior one. Social order is based on everyone respecting these hierarchical relationships (Bond and Hwang 1987).

Guanxi,[8] based on personal connections, is an important factor in Chinese culture; it is not the same as the commonly used concept of relationships in Western cultures, but it is an implication of the above-mentioned collectivism. First, good guanxi in certain situations (for instance, between two countries during World War II) can affect other situations, such as business connections. As Wei-Ping Wu stated: "Good exchange within a *guanxi* network can be anything as long as it is of value to parties concerned, be it legal or illegal, corruptive or non-corruptive" (Wu 1994, 3). Hence, guanxi cannot be limited to some aspect of a relationship but in any situation can affect all other situations. Second, guanxi involves reciprocal obligation (Leung et al. 1993, 1). If

Figure 4.1 **Guanxi Network Boundaries**

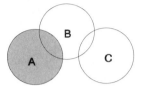

a person has received a favor, he or she is obliged to return a favor when requested. Buying back favors or services can even mean personal sacrifice. Guanxi can also be strengthened by doing favors. While giving favors, one should consider the cost of the favor, the effective component, the probability of reciprocation of the favor from the receiver, and reaction from the social network of persons involved (Bond and Hwang 1987). The four factors are important in order to reach the goal with the favor and in order to save the face of oneself and the receiver. Third, guanxi not only involves favors between two persons, but also extends obligations to entire guanxi networks (Leung et al. 1993, 1). If I do you a favor, you can pay it back by doing a favor for any one of the members of my social network, if I so order.[9] Figure 4.1 illustrates the boundaries of obligation in A's guanxi network. Through B, A is obliged to give to and also get favors from C and his guanxi network, even if the networks of A and C do not overlap.

The fourth difference between guanxi and relations in the West involves the formation of guanxi. Building up guanxi includes building immediate trust through common connections (i.e., friends, relatives, and classmates). Thus, mutual trust in a guanxi relationship can be established immediately through common connections, without any exchanges between the actors, and the exchanges do not have to be institutionalized in order to gain trust in a relationship. This differs from a normal relationship, because it exists between two parties without any episode between these parties. Guanxi exists in a latent form within one's own guanxi network, and in between the guanxi networks of members of one's own guanxi network. Hence, guanxi is a social resource.

Guanxi, as a resource or as a relationship, exists at varying levels of sentimental depth. Depth of a relationship, or guanxi, depends on the types of ties that bind people (Hwang 1987). The deepest emotional relations are bound with expressive ties that occur in primary groups, such as in families. At the other extreme are relationships with explicitly instrumental ties that are bound to attain goals other than only the relationship (Hwang 1987). In between these extremes, people are bound to relationships with what Hwang (1987) referred to as mixed ties, and they occur in relationships with relatives, neighbors, classmates, colleagues, people from the same home region, and so on. Emotional components exist to varying degrees in relationships of mixed ties. These relationships may be intimate between close or first-tier friends, or *renqing* relationships tied with an emotional bond between good or second-tier friends; ties in relationships with a romantic other, that is, with girl- and boyfriends could be classified as mixed in the early stages of a relationship, but these differ from the other mixed ties, as such relationships have a potential to evolve to primary relationships (Joy 2001). The deepest relationships in primary groups are formed by birth, but purely instrumental relationships can be strengthened.

A way of strengthening guanxi is through what is known as "face-work," which could be interpreted as a person's honor of another. The Chinese language and culture distinguish two kinds of face: *lian* and *mianzi*. A person with lian has a good moral character. The lian face is more ascribed than achieved, while the mianzi face can be achieved by building up a personal reputation by the person's own efforts. Thus, the mianzi face is more achieved than ascribed

(Harris and Yau 1994, 13; Redding and Ng 1983). Building up guanxi at any level of human behavior involves both lian and mianzi. Face-work is an important way of asking and giving favors. Favors must be requested and rejected in ways such that both partners save face (Bond and Hwang 1987). For this reason, a negative answer from a person in a Chinese culture is less direct than a negative answer in a Western context. Face-work includes enhancing one's own face, enhancing the other's face, losing one's own face, hurting the other's face, saving one's own face, and saving the other's face (Bond and Hwang 1987). The habit of giving gifts is connected to favors and has its root in the history of tributes to the imperial court. A weaker member, for example, with a lower hierarchical status in cardinal relations in the guanxi network, can pull guanxi by, for instance, giving gifts to the stronger member. The stronger member is obliged to do the favor asked if he or she has accepted the gift. Both parties have gained benefits: the weaker the favor and the stronger mianzi face through the reputation achieved in the guanxi network (Harris and Yau 1994, 12). By receiving a gift, one becomes in debt to the donor of the gift; similarly, one can give a gift, so placing the receiver in debt. Face-work through giving and getting favors in a guanxi relationship does not need immediate "equal reciprocation" from the partners involved. Years may pass before the gift giver requests a favor from the gift receiver. The importance of reciprocity also depends on the depth or type of a relationship (Joy 2001). Gift-giving traditions and habits are different in China from those in Western countries (Hill and Romm 1994; Joy 2001) and, consequently, have implications for consumer behavior.

Behavior in Chinese society is based on the individual's tendency to act according to external expectations or social norms. The objective is to maintain harmony in a group and maintain face. In Western culture, a person's behavior is based more on individual, personal, and inner values (Bond and Hwang 1987, 231). This difference in behavior affects not only management and decision making in organizations, but also consumer behavior, as purchasing decisions are made with social acceptance in mind. However, it should be noted that collectivism does not mean that a homogeneous society exists. Collectivism works within small social contexts like family, clan, or *danwei* (i.e., working unit, such as a hospital, state-owned enterprise, or university), and the nation is constituted of these smaller units. The collective units of social harmony have traditionally been the family and clan, but society is changing, and collective groups are forming outside the family. The new units are working units, regions, common education, and so on, and they form a complicated society of regional heterogeneity. This heterogeneity is further reinforced by the extreme linguistic differences between the regions.

The National Language: Putonghua and Cantonese

The official language of the PRC is Putonghua (also called Mandarin or Standard Chinese), the dialect spoken in the northern parts of the country, mainly in Beijing. The written language is the same all over the mainland, where simplified characters are used, while the traditional characters are used in Hong Kong, Macau, and Taiwan. Most of the people in the PRC understand Putonghua, because television and radio use it, but in many cases, locals are not able to speak the language. Dialects are spoken, and these often do not cross ethnic boundaries—for example, Cantonese spoken in the Guangdong province and Hong Kong may not be understood by people in the neighboring region, Guangxi. The dialect spoken in Tianjin, about 200 kilometers from Beijing, is barely understood in Beijing. Shanghai has a language of its own called Wu.

Language allows access to inner circles of regional societies. Depending on the dialect, you may be regarded as a local or an outsider. Even when Putonghua is understood, the local dialects are an advantage in marketing operations.

Table 4.11

Level of Education and Related Issues

Year	University and college students per 10,000 persons	Student–teacher ratio, higher education	Student–teacher ratio, secondary school	Student–teacher ratio, primary school
1980	11.6	4.6	17.9	26.6
1990	18.0	5.2	14.6	21.9
1995	24.0	7.2	15.9	23.3
1999	32.8	9.7	17.6	23.1
2000	43.9	12.0	18.2	22.2
2001	56.3	13.5	18.3	21.6
2002	70.3	14.6	18.7	21.0

Source: China Statistical Yearbook (Beijing: China Statistical Publishing House, 2003), p. 725.

These cultural features, which form the underlying fabric of the society, are being modified by Marxist ideologies and the current rise of consumer culture.

Education

Traditionally, education has been highly appreciated in Chinese society. Illiteracy and semi-illiteracy decreased from over three million in the year 1964 to about two million in 1990 (*China Statistical Yearbook* 2000, 97). The illiteracy rate, from the sample survey of 2000, is 6.72 percent (*China Statistical Yearbook* 2003, 99).

Nevertheless, the educational level is relatively low. One of the reasons is the turbulent time of the Great Cultural Revolution during the late 1960s and early 1970s, when some of the schools and universities were closed, and foreign-language education was abandoned. This has deprived a generation of education and is handicapping the next generation because of the lack of availability of skills, such as foreign-language teaching.

Table 4.11 shows that the number of university students per 10,000 persons has increased every year since the 1980s, indicating improvement in higher education. However, the current student–teacher ratio of 14:1 shows that there are more students per mentor in higher educational institutions. Nonetheless, this ratio is still low when compared to that of the United States in 1990, about 17:1 (*China Statistical Yearbook* 1995, 805). Interestingly, primary and secondary schools have maintained and even improved their student–teacher ratio. The educational system is also changing as a part of the general reform movement, and tuition fees are increasing; for example, the primary school fee per year may be as high as 10,000 yuan (about the annual salary of a university teacher). Also, a number of private schools are flourishing in the well-developed cities, including in Beijing, Shanghai, and Guangzhou. Consequently, much of the current urban household expenditure goes to educate children (Davis and Sensenbrenner 2000). In rural areas, where private schools are rare, education has not improved. Rural primary and secondary schools have financial problems because of limited possibilities to get means from local governments.

Gender Issues

The current national sex ratio in China is 104.31:100 (4.31 percent more men than women) (*China Statistical Yearbook* 2002, 100), but in some areas, there has been an abnormal increase in the number of males born. The highest sex ratios reported in the *China Statistical Yearbook* are 113 in

Guangxi province and 110 in Yunnan and Guizhou provinces. Several domestic surveys reported in Croll (2000) show even higher sex ratios at birth. The increase of males and male births suggests the persistence of traditional values among the population. Sons are respected and regarded as social security for the parents. Even today, most parents live in the households of their sons, and ethnographic voices prize the birth of a son. One of the reasons for an abnormal increase in the male population in the early 1990s was the tight one-child policy that has since been modified (see Croll 2000, for detailed discussion).

However, the role and status of women are in flux. The image of the "ideal female" during the early years of liberation was that of the austerely dressed socialist hero who played her equal part in the development of the New China. This is in stark contrast to the soft-skinned, fashionably dressed beauty in a well-furnished home currently appearing in printed advertisements (Hooper 1994). The freedom to express female beauty and femininity again has, in some cases, led well-off women to revert to the traditional roles of housewife and mistress, but there is also a strong emergence of professional women (*Marketing Guide Magazine* 1995). The percentage of female students at institutions of higher education has increased steadily, from 23 percent in 1980 to 44 percent in 2002 (*China Statistical Yearbook* 2003, 726). The same trend exists at the lower educational levels. There are also females who do not work for professional career reasons but do so in order to catch up with the current consumption culture (Gould and Wong 2000). Chinese females can be grouped, in addition to traditional socialist females, into traditionally modern (new rich), educated and working modern, and working-for-consumption females. All the groups consume differently for different purposes.

In Hong Kong, female consumers can be grouped into traditionalist, individualist, and prosocietalist (Sin et al. 2001). Traditionalists in Hong Kong, contrary to the mainland traditional socialist females, preserve Chinese values of family and obedience to father, husband, and son. Individualists are socioeconomically independent and are less concerned with societal issues. The mainland traditionally modern females are a combination of Hong Kong traditionalists and individualists. The last group, prosocietalists, are economically independent, behave differently from the traditional Chinese role of women, and are active in societal issues. The mainland segment of educated and working females can be analogous to prosocietalist in Hong Kong.

Health

The life expectancy of seventy-one years in China is higher than the average world figure, suggesting that the general level of health is better, on average, than for most other countries. Life expectancy is higher in China than it is in Indonesia, the Philippines, and Vietnam, is about the same as in Thailand and Malaysia, and is lower than in Singapore (*China Statistical Yearbook* 2000, 870). Health care has normally been handled at the work-unit level. For example, universities have their own pharmacies and health centers and even hospitals. Similarly, formerly state-owned factories have taken care of the health of their employees.

This situation is undergoing change. The reforms of state-owned sectors have made state-owned units responsible for producing profit, and consequently, many benefits, such as health care, have been cut. Further change in the consumption of health care products is expected in the future. Currently, health care comprises only 7 percent of consumption expenditure (see Table 4.16).

Listed below are some marketing implications of the contemporary Chinese culture:

• Face-work, through giving and receiving favors, has an impact on consumer behavior. A gift given to build up a relationship has to fit with the status of the person to whom the gift is given as well as to save the face of the donor. Hence, expensive and prestigious gifts are exchanged among Chinese people. Furthermore, clothing and choice of restaurant are considered to enhance one's status. Conspicuous consumption is a way to show off one's position in the network of one's social circle (Schütte and Vanier 1995). Reciprocal obligation implies that the receiver responds to the giver with a gift of the same value. Equal reciprocity is less explicit and important in the relationship of expressive ties (Joy 2001). On the mainland, the most popular gifts are ones that can be eaten or drunk, contrary to the Western preference for a gift that leaves a memory of its giver. The combination of the need for utility and status explains the popularity of XO cognac as a gift in the PRC, where its sales are the largest in the world.

• The collective nature of the society affects the degree of involvement in purchasing situations, particularly for products, like gifts, that are for social purposes and for which the degree of involvement is much higher (Schütte and Ciarlante 1998). A product bought for social purposes is important, because it signals the factors that give face for both receiver and giver. Such factors are price, brand name, prestige, and packaging (Schütte and Vanier 1995). The degree of involvement for products purchased for private use is low.

• Most purchasing decisions are jointly made in a social group (i.e., the family). Other reference groups that influence the decision are relatives, friends, and colleagues (*Marketing Guide Magazine* 1995).

• The major information source among Chinese consumers is most probably word-of-mouth. Trust of salespersons requires selection of trustworthy and well-connected personnel.

• A good example of the drastic change in consumer habits that are dependent on political and ideological changes on the mainland is consumption of cosmetics. The production of cosmetics has a 2000-year history in China, with production in modern China starting as early as in the 1830s (*China Market* 1992, 11). However, during the period of liberation (the 1950s and 1960s), cosmetics were considered "a remnant of capitalism" (Li 1992, 12). Despite the abandonment of cosmetics for almost thirty years, production has increased, from 200 million yuan in 1982 to three billion yuan in 1991 (Li 1992, 13); recent trends indicate acceleration in production and consumption.

• Among modern Chinese women, both the traditionalist and the independent professional, the demand for high-quality clothing and cosmetics is increasing. Similarly, convenience goods, such as fast food, kitchen appliances, and electronics, are in greater demand.

• As the cost of education and health care increases, the larger portion of household income will go to these expenses, at the same time creating a market for education and health services.

CONSUMER INCOME AND EMPLOYMENT

Table 4.12 shows that rural units other than enterprises provided a livelihood for most of the people until the reform policies were implemented in the late 1970s. In the urban areas, the only possible employment before reforms was at state-owned and collective units. Since the 1980s, there have been more alternatives for enterprise employment because of ownership reform.

The first economic reforms started in rural areas, where township and village enterprises were established. Their share of the total employment has generally increased. Private and individual companies have been encouraged with the intent to stimulate the economy and to provide self-created employment for the unemployed population (see also Xie 1991; Xiao 1993a, 1993b, Private Business Association 1993). The other new forms of companies, both in rural and urban areas, have increased their share in the employment market. Nevertheless, ownership reform has not yet been a panacea for employment problems.

Table 4.12

Employment by Urban and Rural Enterprises and State-Owned Units (percent)

Year	Total 10,000 persons	State-owned units	Collective units[a]	Foreign funded units	Other ownership[b]	Private[c]	Individual	Other	Township and village enterprises	Private	Individual	Other
		Urban							Rural			
1952	20,729	8	<1	0	0	0	4	0	0	0	0	88
1980	42,361	19	6	0	0	0	<1	0	7	0	0	68
1990	64,749	18	6	<1	<1	<1	1	0	16	<1	<1	55
1995	68,065	17	5	1	1	1	2	0	26	1	6	48
1999	71,394	12	2	1	2	2	3	8	18	1	5	46
2000	72,085	12	2	1	2	1	3	10	18	1	5	45
2001	73,025	10	2	1	2	2	3	12	18	2	4	44
2002	73,740	10	2	1	2	3	3	13	18	2	3	43

Source: China Statistical Yearbook (Beijing: China Statistical Publishing House, 1995), pp. 84–85; *China Statistical Yearbook* (Beijing: China Statistical Publishing House, 2002), pp. 120–21; *China Statistical Yearbook* (Beijing: China Statistical Publishing House, 2003), pp. 126–27.

[a]Includes collective-owned and cooperative units.

[b]Includes joint-owned, share-holding, and limited liability economic units.

[c]The difference between private and individual entrepreneurship is in the number of employees. If the total number of employed personnel is less than eight persons, the company is an individual enterprise; if there are more than eight outside personnel, the company is called "private" (Bai-san Xie, *China's Economic Policies, Theories and Reforms since 1949* [Shanghai: Fudan University Press, 1991] pp. 456–59).

Table 4.13

Average Annual Salary per Worker and Total Wage Indices for Staff and Workers

(a) Average annual salary per worker

Year	Total average annual salary per worker (yuan)	State-owned units	Urban collective units	Other ownership units
1957	—	—	—	—
1980	762	803	623	n.a.
1990	2,140	2,284	1,681	2,987
1995	5,500	5,625	3,931	7,463
1999	8,346	8,543	5,774	9,829
2000	9,371	9,552	6,262	10,984
2001	10,870	11,178	6,867	12,140
2002	12,422	12,869	7,667	13,212

(b) Total wage indices for staff and workers

Year	Total index (proceeding year = 100)	State-owned units	Urban collective units	Other ownership units
1957	120.3	114.6	155.7	—
1980	119.4	118.6	123.3	n.a.
1990	112.7	113.4	108.7	135.8
1995	121.7	117.4	115.5	140.0
1999	106.2	105.1	94.2	119.8
2000	107.9	106.3	95.5	121.3
2001	111.0	109.8	94.1	122.9
2002	111.2	107.1	95.8	129.6

Sources: China Statistical Yearbook (Beijing: China Statistical Publishing House, 1995), p. 109; *China Statistical Yearbook* (Beijing: China Statistical Publishing House, 2002), pp. 144, 145; *China Statistical Yearbook* (Beijing: China Statistical Publishing House, 2003), pp. 150, 151.

As the state-owned sector still plays a major role in urban employment, the government made a plan to reinforce government business by focusing its policies on the improvement of large state-owned companies. This plan was put into effect in 1995. The small state-owned companies are allowed to go bankrupt, and in case of malfunction, the government will allow mergers and acquisitions. The slogan is "Grasp the biggest, release the small." This policy has an effect on the retailing and wholesaling business, because the small state-owned companies control this field.

Income

Comparison of the average incomes in different enterprises shows that total average annual salary per worker is higher in other ownership groups than in the traditional state-owned and collective units (see Table 4.13). In addition, the annual salary index has generally increased over time, with some index-based blips in the late 1990s and into the twenty-first century. This shows that, although the governmental sector employs the majority of the population, nongovernmental employees have higher purchasing power. As the share of the nongovernmental sector is increasing, it is this population, employed by the nongovernmental enterprises, that will, in the future, consist of the most powerful consumers.

Not shown in the official statistics are benefits, other than salary, offered by state-owned enterprises, including holidays, clothes, dinners, and sometimes housing. Despite the increasing purchasing power of nongovernment employees, the employees and managers of the state enterprises are still an important segment for marketing.

Rural inhabitants show the lowest general income (see Table 4.15, p. 131), but their importance as consumers should not be underestimated. Some rural villages are very rich, partly because ownership reform started in the countryside. Many farmers make their livings in production or other kinds of businesses. The possibility of making money through other sources than cultivating land has given the rural population an opportunity to become a prosperous consumer group.

Unemployment

Table 4.14 shows the percentage of officially registered job seekers out of the total of officially employed persons. The current official statistics do not provide unemployment figures, but unemployment has been estimated to be high due to reforms in small- and medium-sized state-owned companies and to structural changes in the rural areas. Highly developed areas, such as Beijing, Tianjin, Zhejiang, and Guangdong, have many job seekers, leading us to conclude that the coastal areas draw people seeking work. Statistics and estimates do not tell the whole story of the unemployment situation, because there is a large population of unregistered persons; many of them establish businesses or are self-employed in other entrepreneurial endeavors. The Economist Intelligence Unit (EIU 2002, 27) uses two scenarios to calculate unemployment in China. One is somewhat generous and estimates unemployment to be 7.7 percent, and the other estimates it to be 11.5 percent.

CONSUMPTION PATTERNS

Consumer Culture and Revolution

The meaning of consumption for Chinese is not a normative goal, and in the traditional Chinese value system, consumption is perceived negatively. In the course of reform policies, these traditional values have changed, and people are more readily embracing consumer culture. However, the value system remains dual: traditional ideals are implemented to consumption, and consumption is not considered as "a terminal goal" (see also Tse 1996, 352–55).

Chinese consumption is unique on some dimensions. One such dimension is social expression (Schütte and Ciarlante 1998). Brands are increasingly used to distinguish a consumer from the social strata he or she does not belong to, and brands communicate the membership of one's own group. In a hierarchical social setting, it is important that those at the lower level do not possess valued goods before their superiors. This is particularly true for conspicuous products. Another dimension is consumption to reinforce social relationships, and Chinese people have used products to initiate, strengthen, and extend relationships. Gift giving is part of face-work and is linked to building up guanxi. When goods are bought for social purposes, involvement in purchasing is much deeper than in purchasing for private use. Utilitarian outcomes are also important, as product performance is greatly valued by Chinese consumers, perhaps more so than by American counterparts, but less so than Japanese and Korean consumers. Risk-taking, likely, would be similar among Chinese and Americans. The value dimension defined as perceived quality compared to price is strong among Chinese consumers, but the aesthetics dimension is low (see Tse 1996, for a detailed discussion on several ideas in the preceding text).

Table 4.14

Available Unemployment Figures, 2002

Provinces, municipalities, and autonomous regions	Number of employed persons (10,000 persons)	Total registered job seekers (10,000 persons)	Percentage of unemployed from employed persons (%)
National	73,740	2,684	4
Coastal areas			
Beijing	**799**	**88**	**11**
Tianjin	**403**	**125**	**31**
Hebei	3,386	109	3
Liaoning	1,842	162	9
Shanghai	**743**	**111**	**15**
Jiangsu	3,506	164	5
Zhejiang	2,835	344	12
Fujian	1,711	119	7
Shangdong	4,752	142	3
Guangdong	3,967	301	8
Hainan	341	14	4
Guangxi	2,570	50	2
Total	26,855	1,729	6
Central areas			
Inner Mongolia	1,010	31	3
Shanxi	1,417	17	1
Jilin	1,095	40	4
Heilongjiang	1,626	91	6
Anhui	3,404	58	2
Jiangxi	1,955	70	4
Henan	5,522	81	1
Hubei	2,467	118	5
Hunan	3,469	88	3
Total	21,965	594	3
Inland areas			
Chongqing	**1,640**	**30**	**2**
Sichuan	4,409	91	2
Guizhou	2,081	20	1
Yunnan	2,341	36	2
Tibet	129	1	1
Shaanxi	1,873	71	4
Gansu	1,255	29	2
Qinghai	247	29	12
Ningxia	281	22	8
Xinjiang	701	28	4
Total	14,957	357	2

Source: China Statistical Yearbook (Beijing: China Statistical Publishing House, 2003), pp. 125, 176.

Segmentation

China's economy and ideology are in transition, and living standards are changing rapidly; therefore, it can be challenging to make an accurate marketing segmentation of the entire population. A rough division can be made between the rural and urban populations, as reflected in purchasing power and consumption habits. That said, middle class and wealthy segments have emerged in large

Table 4.15

Annual per Capita Net Income in Rural and Urban Areas (yuan)

Area	1957	1980	1990	1995	1999	2000	2001	2002
Rural	73	191	686	1,578	2,210	2,253	2,366	2,476
Urban	235	439	1,387	3,893	5,854	6,280	6,860	7,703

Sources: China Statistical Yearbook (Beijing: China Statistical Publishing House, 1990), p. 272; *China Statistical Yearbook* (Beijing: China Statistical Publishing House, 1995), p. 257; *China Statistical Yearbook* (Beijing: China Statistical Publishing House, 1999), p. 311; *China Statistical Yearbook* (Beijing: China Statistical Publishing House, 2001), p. 303; *China Statistical Yearbook* (Beijing: China Statistical Publishing House, 2002), p. 319; *China Statistical Yearbook* (Beijing: China Statistical Publishing House, 2003), p. 341.

metropolitan areas, including in Beijing, Shanghai, and, of course, Hong Kong, and have been distinguishable market segments for quite some time. Several globally recognized market research and consumer packaged goods firms have had success measuring segments and accurately predicting variances in consumption habits vis-à-vis these segments. One could reasonably expect the buyer and consumer behaviors that have emerged in urban centers to serve as opinion leaders for other areas as (or if) wealth and awareness continue to diffuse to other parts of the country. However, distinct cultural idiosyncrasies in disparate regions will also drive consumer choices and practices, which brings us back to the more macro-schema of urban versus rural consumers.[10]

Differences remain salient. For example, rural consumers still buy more domestic products and have less trust in advertising than do their urban counterparts (cf. Li and Gallup 1995). Table 4.15 shows the recent average annual income differences between urban and rural populations. Urban dwellers earn almost three times more than do rural residents, whereas they earned only two times more in the beginning of the 1990s, hence, the income difference has persisted and even increased. We also add that circumspection on these and other statistics is warranted; in this context, both rural and urban income figures are misleading, because there are hidden income sources excluded from the official statistics (Gang et al. 1997), and living costs tend to be lower in rural areas.

The majority of expenditure is still allocated to the daily necessities, both in urban and rural households, as Table 4.16 shows. However, since the mid-1990s, the proportion of food has decreased from 50 percent to 38 percent in cities and from 59 percent to 35 percent in the countryside. In the cities that are more exposed to outside influences, the traditional importance of eating in Chinese culture may be declining, while other areas are gaining in popularity, for example, karaoke bars, cosmetics, traveling, pets, and movies. In both segments, the proportion of leisure and education in the total expenditure has increased.

Moreover, exceptions can regularly be found. Guangdong rural people, for example, are much richer than urban folk. However, at the moment, large numbers of rural people work in urban areas and then bring much of their earnings back to their villages. This bridge between the urban and rural populations is important. It indicates increased mobility, the likelihood of innovation, and attitude diffusion that, in turn, will affect tastes and consumer habits in both urban and rural settings.

We mentioned earlier that urban segments have emerged and continue to evolve. An extensive study of Chinese urban consumers by Gallup revealed four income segments (Cui and Liu 2001). Urban consumers can be divided into categories according to their total income: working poor,

Table 4.16

Proposition of Living Expenditure on Different Goods, 1994 and 2002 (yuan)

Living expenditure	Urban households' division of living expenditures		Rural households' division of living expenditures	
	1994	2002	1994	2002
Total per capita annual	2,851.34	6,029.88	1,016.81	1,834.31
Food	50%	38%	59%	35%
Clothing	14%	10%	7%	7%
Household facilities	9%	6%	5%	5%
Health care	3%	7%	3%	7%
Transportation and communication	5%	10%	2%	9%
Leisure time, education	9%	15%	7%	14%
Residence	7%	10%	14%	18%
Other	3%	3%	3%	4%

Sources: China Statistical Yearbook (Beijing: China Statistical Publishing House, 1995), pp. 267–76, 283; *China Statistical Yearbook* (Beijing: China Statistical Publishing House, 2002), pp. 321, 347; *China Statistical Yearbook* (Beijing: China Statistical Publishing House, 2003), pp. 345, 371–72.

salary class, little rich, and yuppies. The smallest segment (5 percent), yuppies, earns ten times more than the largest segment of working poor (55 percent). The income level of yuppies is far above average in China, about US$9,500, annually. Yuppies distinguish themselves from the other groups by being younger (on average, thirty-six years old), single, and business owners. Many of these rich people have minimum education, some of them being the youth of the Great Cultural Revolution, a period of some ten years during which schools and universities were either closed or in turmoil.[11] Nevertheless, their purchasing power is strong. They are willing to pay for branded goods and prefer foreign products but still have the highest percentage of their income in savings. As might be expected, this segment has the highest coverage rate of all consumer durables, as Table 4.17 shows.

The little rich, *xiaokang,* as the Chinese refer to this group, constitute about 15 percent of the urban population. Most of them are professionals. Even if they earn more than the salary class, their consumption habits resemble yuppies less than they do consumption of the salary class, which can be seen from Table 4.17. The salary class constitutes 25 percent of the urban population. The majority of the segment is comprised of factory workers, but many are also government employees. This segment is willing to pay for brands, even if not so many prefer foreign goods. The ownership rate of consumer durables follows closely that of the little rich and yuppies.

The majority of the Chinese urban population (55 percent) can be segmented into working poor. Most of the working poor are factory workers. Members of this segment are less eager to pay for brands or foreign products, and the ownership rates of consumer durables are the lowest, except for the ownership of private cars (Cui and Liu 2001).

Small business, *getihu,* owners can be differentiated from these segments. Even if the majority of yuppies are business owners, their consumption habits are different from the sample of entrepreneurs. Getihu owners spend the majority of their income on food (58 percent), socializing (14 percent), and children's education (10 percent) (Chow, Fung, and Ngo 2001, 201), in contrast to yuppies, who do not spend as much of their income on food.

As suggested earlier, the Chinese population can be divided geographically into economic or cultural segments; the affluent population lives in eastern areas of the country, and the poorest

Table 4.17

The Profiles of Working Poor, Salary Class, Little Rich, and Yuppies, 1997 (percent)

Segment/profile	Working poor	Salary class	Little rich	Yuppies
Age	41	41	40	36
Marital status				
Single	10	10	19	21
Married	85	87	78	78
Divorced/widowed	5	1	3	1
Occupation				
Business owners	5	6	15	29
Government employees	8	19	7	18
Professionals	14	17	21	18
Factory workers	24	23	20	14
Willing to pay for brands	44	53	43	68
Prefer foreign products	22	24	28	48
Food/eating out	49	43	42	21
Savings	12	22	19	48
Travel	1	1	7	3
Microwave oven	3	16	12	22
Compact disc player	7	13	32	55
Mobile phone	3	10	12	33
Computer	3	4	5	14
Private car	2	1	5	12
Credit card	4	11	11	40

Source: G. Cui and Q. Liu, "Emerging Market Segments in a Transitional Economy: A Study of Urban Consumers in China." *Journal of International Marketing*, 9, no. 1 (2001): 84–106.

live in the west. Cui and Liu (2000) divided urban China into "growth markets" in the south and east (Guangdong, Fujian, Hong Kong, Hainan, Shanghai, Zhejiang, and Jiangsu); into "emerging markets" in the north, center, and southwest (Beijing, Tianjin, Hebei, Shandong, Henan, Anhui, Hubei, Hunan, Jiangxi, Sichuan, Guangxi, Guizhou, and Yunnan); and into "untapped markets" in the northeast and northwest (Heilongjiang, Jilin, Liaoning, Inner Mongolia, Shanxi, Shaanxi, Gansu, Ningxia, Xinjiang, Qinghai, and Tibet). The growth markets are characterized by Min-Yue and Hai-pai cultures, favorable climate conditions, and early economic growth through SEZs, which have all escalated the economic development in the area. Min-Yue culture emphasizes mercantile entrepreneurship, while Hai-pai culture emphasizes quality of life and stylish products. The climate in the region is fertile, and the region has benefited from the policies that "let some people get rich first." The second wave of economic reforms is currently influencing the emerging markets. The north region of emerging markets is characterized by the Jing-pai culture, which emphasizes hierarchy, stability, and control in a Confucian manner. In central China, diverse cultures follow the trends set in other parts of China. The untapped markets await application of the reform policies that bring economic growth, rely on heavy industries, and are less affluent. To close the gap between the regions, the government has launched a *fubin*—"help the poor"—campaign (Cui and Liu 2000).

Chinese consumers can be divided into different consumption generations according to their historical, political, and economic experiences. Those born before 1945 have seen China's transformation to a socialist society and appreciate, therefore, socialist, nonconsumption values. This group, "a socialist generation," is austere in its consumption and has a negative attitude toward a consumption society. The following generation (born between 1945 and 1960) is called "a lost generation," because they experienced the Great Cultural Revolution. Many of them lack education and have struggled to meet the requirements of 1990s China. The last generation born after the 1960s, "a lifestyle generation," is the first group that has had a true chance to adopt the values of a consumption society often adapted from Hong Kong. Their consumption is modern and differentiated (Schütte and Ciarlante 1998).

The nature of the segmentation of China has several marketing implications:

- The yuppies and small business owners spend freely. They like to display their wealth with visible goods, such as clothing, motor vehicles, and personal adornments (Hooper 1994, 165). They also have the habit of spending enormous amounts of money on restaurants and karaoke entertainment.
- The little rich and salary class follow the consumption of the more well-off consumers, but working poor and rural consumers need to struggle to meet their basic needs.
- For a marketer of branded and foreign products, the most lucrative segments are yuppies, entrepreneurs, little rich, and even salary class, plus the "lifestyle generation." Many members of these segments live in eastern and southern China. Competition for these consumers is already tough, and competitive advantage for a marketer should reach beyond quality products and price.
- Working poor, the rural population, and the western areas, comprise the largest segment. If the economic development continues, and if the current reform policies are successful, then this segment holds great promise. Even today, due to the huge population, they are attractive, not for marketers of luxury products, but for producers of creative, cheap, and purposeful products.
- Another important group of customers for consumer goods is that of the managers charged with making decisions concerning material incentives other than money for the workers of state-owned companies.

Savings

Income figures and household expenditures do not give a complete view of Chinese purchasing power. Traditionally, the Chinese people have been encouraged to save rather than to consume (Tse 1996; Gang et al. 1997), and consequently, savings rates are high. The savings rate as percentage of GDP is almost 40 percent, the highest in the world after Singapore (*The Economist* 2001). The savings rate in Hong Kong is a bit more than 30 percent of GDP. At the same time, the number of purchases made on credit is comparatively low; but while an extensive credit card market is currently small, trends elsewhere suggest that changes could be reasonably expected. As shown in Table 4.18, the total amount of savings per capita has increased more than 100 times since the early 1980s. Even if the general savings percentage of GDP has decreased since 1995 (*The Economist* 2001), other sources show that an increase in income does not necessarily decrease the savings rate. The yuppies earn the most, but still the savings percentage of their total income is the highest at 43 percent (Cui and Liu 2001, 93).

Single-Child Market

The one-child policy has many implications for consumer habits on the mainland. The possibility of having only one child makes that child a very special treasure for the family. He or she becomes the "Little Emperor" or "Empress." Parents are willing and able to spend a great portion of their

Table 4.18

Savings Deposit Balance in Urban and Rural Households

Year	Savings deposit balance per capita (yuan)	Urban households (100,000,000 yuan)	Rural households (100,000,000 yuan)
1957		27.9	7.3
1980	40	282.5	117.0
1990	615	5,192.6	1,841.6
1995	2,449	23,466.7	6,195.6
1999*	4,735	59,621.8	
2000	5,077	64,332.4	
2001	5,780	73,762.4	
2002	6,766	86,910.6	

Sources: China Statistical Yearbook (Beijing: China Statistical Publishing House, 1995), pp. 257, 259; *China Statistical Yearbook* (Beijing: China Statistical Publishing House, 2000), p. 311; *China Statistical Yearbook* (Beijing: China Statistical Publishing House, 2001), pp. 303–4; *China Statistical Yearbook* (Beijing: China Statistical Publishing House, 2002), p. 319; *China Statistical Yearbook* (Beijing: China Statistical Publishing House, 2003), pp. 341, 344.

*The division into rural and urban is not available from 1999 to present.

income on the child's material welfare and academic success; they invest in the child's nutrition, health, education, and leisure activities (Davis and Sensenbrenner 2000; McNeal and Ji 1999).

When buying for children, parents often prefer products for educational purposes. Toys, for example, might be purchased as a reward for good grades or as a prize for a calligraphy contest (e.g., McNeal and Ji 1999). In purchasing situations for toys, children "strikingly" participate in the decision making, as Davis and Sensenbrenner (2000, 69) put it. At a very early age, four to five years old, Chinese children already independently visit stores.

While Christmas is a high season for toy sales in the Western world, the Spring Festival (Chinese New Year, comparable to Christmas) is not. Children get "gifts" from their parents, grandparents, uncles, and aunts during the Spring Festival, but these gifts are *hong bao,* small red envelopes filled with money.

For children, the most important information source for new products is TV, followed by parents and store visits (McNeal and Ji 1999). Store visits seem to be an even more important information source when small purchases, such as snacks, are concerned. In Guilin, a medium–large city in south China, small kiosks in front of schools provide small items, candies, chewing gum, snacks, pens, pencils, paper, and so on, for schoolchildren. Usually, two to three kiosks occupy the school gates to provide children with consumption possibilities during the break and after school.

Housing

In the past, housing was provided by government, that is, by the working unit to which a person belonged. The establishment of private enterprises and foreign-funded companies has changed this tradition, and the need has emerged for types of housing facilities other than those provided by the government. Furthermore, the housing reform of the 1990s encouraged residents to purchase apartments that used to be parts of the property of the working unit. For example, the Shanghai local government imposed mandatory savings plans, discounts, mortgages, and resale options (Fraser 2000), and the same types of provisions have been provided by smaller local

Table 4.19

Origin of Houses in Beijing, Shanghai, Guangzhou, and Shenzhen (percent)

City	Allocation by the working unit	Rent	Commercial houses	Buying from the working unit	Heritage from ancestors	Other
Beijing	55	20	3	6	5	11
Shanghai	37	26	4	5	11	17
Guangzhou	36	22	3	15	12	12
Shenzhen	34	5	10	40	2	9

Source: China Business Times, "Income from South to North: A Survey Comparing Family Income in Beijing, Shanghai, Guangzhou and Shenzhen," February 8, 1996 (in Chinese).

Table 4.20

Per Capita Living Floor Space in Rural and Urban Houses (m²)

Area	1980	1990	1995	1999	2000	2001	2002
Rural areas	9.4	17.8	21.0	24.2	24.7	25.7	26.5
Urban areas	3.9	6.7	8.1	9.8	10.3	15.5	22.8

Sources: China Statistical Yearbook (Beijing: China Statistical Publishing House, 1995), p. 257; *China Statistical Yearbook* (Beijing: China Statistical Publishing House, 1999), p. 311; *China Statistical Yearbook* (Beijing: China Statistical Publishing House, 2001), p. 303; *China Statistical Yearbook* (Beijing: China Statistical Publishing House, 2002), p. 319; *China Statistical Yearbook* (Beijing: China Statistical Publishing House, 2003), p. 342.

governments, such as that of Guilin. Despite the housing reform, the state retains ownership of land (Fraser 2000). Statistics, in Table 4.19 for the four main cities, Beijing, Shanghai, Guangzhou, and Shenzhen, show that the majority of the houses are still provided by the working unit. In all cities except Shenzhen, one-fifth of all houses are rented. The housing reform has been best executed in Shenzhen, where as many as 40 percent of the houses have been purchased from the unit. It has been estimated that, generally, 70 percent of previously publicly owned houses and apartments were privately owned by 1995 (see also Gang et al. 1997).

Per capita living space in rural areas is higher than in the urban areas. Table 4.20 shows that there is a significant change over time in this ratio. Even if the sizes of urban and rural houses have increased, the increase in the cities has been faster. In rural areas, there are more rooms as well as more people per household than there are in the major cities (see Table 4.21). The average number of rooms per person is higher in rural areas than it is in the most developed cities.

The Household's Bundle of Goods

The level of household equipment varies between rural and urban households, as Table 4.22 shows. There is still potential to sell such necessities as washing machines and refrigerators to the rural residents, as well as leisure goods, such as color TVs and cameras. There is still demand, both in cities and in rural areas, for cameras, videos, computers, stereos, and mobile phones. The popularity of photography indicates that demand for cameras and videos may be common, while only better-educated people purchase computers.

Table 4.21

Average Number of Rooms in a Household

City	Average number of permanent residents in a household	Average number of rooms	Average number of rooms per person
Beijing	3.41	2.27	0.67
Shanghai	3.28	1.89	0.58
Guangzhou	3.56	2.39	0.67
Shenzhen	3.51	2.89	0.82
Rural areas	4.48	5.14	1.15

Sources: China Business, "How about Chinese Life? A Survey Report of Family Consumption in Beijing, Shanghai, Guangzhou and Shenzhen." February 1, 1996 (in Chinese); *China Statistical Yearbook* (Beijing: China Statistical Publishing House, 1996), pp. 300, 312.

Table 4.22

The Rate of Some Household Durables per 100 Urban and Rural Households, 2002

Consumer durable	Coverage rate in urban household	Coverage rate in rural household
Washing machine	93	32
Refrigerator	87	15
Freezer	7	n.a.
Color TV	126	60
Camera	44	3
Bicycle	143	121
Car	1	n.a.
Electric fan	183	134
Videodisc player	52	3
Computer	21	n.a.
Hi-fi stereo	25	10
Mobile telephone	63	14

Source: China Statistical Yearbook (Beijing: China Statistical Publishing House, 2003), pp. 352, 362–63, 375.

There are some unique aspects in the consumption habits of rural consumers. Although there is a potential market for household goods, such as TV sets, motorcycles, and washing machines, it is important to note that only one brand will gain popularity. Villagers are extremely consistent in their habits and tend to purchase the same brand of product as do their neighbors. This kind of behavior is typical for rural areas and is in keeping with the collective culture and people's desire to be socially accepted. Even if the majority of the Chinese population lives in rural areas, and even if market potential for many products exists among these consumers and competition is still less fierce, research on rural consumers is, at best, suboptimal.

Nutrition and Eating Habits

Eating in China is not only about nutrition; it is also a social event. A common greeting is, "Have you eaten?" Popular gifts are edible ones. The huge popularity of Western fast-food restaurants

Table 4.23

Per Capita Consumption of Food in Urban and Rural Households (in kilograms)

	1985	1990	1995	1999	2000	2001	2002
Urban							
Grain	135	131	97	85	82	80	78
Fresh vegetables	144	139	116	115	115	116	117
Meat	19	22	19	20	20	19	23
Poultry	3	3	4	5	5	5	9
Fish	7	8	9	10	10	10	13
Liquor	8	9	10	10	10	10	9
Sugar	3	2	2	2	2	2	n.a.
Rural							
Grain	257	262	259	247	249	238	236
Fresh vegetables	131	134	105	109	112	109	111
Meat	11	11	11	15	15	14	15
Poultry	1	1	2	2	3	3	3
Fish	2	2	3	4	4	4	4
Liquor	4	6	7	7	7	7	7
Sugar	1	1	1	1	1	1	2

Sources: China Statistical Yearbook (Beijing: China Statistical Publishing House, 2001), p. 330; *China Statistical Yearbook* (Beijing: China Statistical Publishing House, 2002), pp. 328, 349; *China Statistical Yearbook* (Beijing: China Statistical Publishing House, 2003), pp. 352, 374.

is not explained by a changing diet, but rather because of the possibility for social interaction in `the restaurants. Fast-food restaurants are not just places to have a quick meal; they are places to socialize, where a "nonedible yet fulfilling experience" can be delivered (Yan 2000, 211).

Over the years, eating habits have changed, and vegetables are a smaller part of today's diet. Table 4.23 shows the change during the last fifteen years. Consumption of grain and fresh vegetables has decreased in urban and rural areas. The diet of rural residents contains more grain but less meat than the diet of urban people.

Leisure Activities

Leisure time for people on the mainland has increased steadily. Some years ago, it was common to work seven days per week. Urban residents have more leisure time than do farmers, who must tend their fields. Since May 1, 1995, a five-day workweek has been implemented in the PRC. This reform increasingly affects leisure activities and, consequently, consumption patterns.

Until recent times, the difficulty of traveling has led affluent people to spend their income on leisure activities other than tourism. Expenditure in restaurants increased by about 34 percent during 1994 (*China Business Times* 1996). Karaoke bars and discos (for the younger population) are popular, as is window shopping. During the weekends, shoppers crowd the marketplaces and shopping centers. It is, therefore, important to create a pleasant atmosphere for socialization in shopping places, and the possibility for interaction between potential consumers and salespersons (Schütte and Vanier 1995), in a similar way that Western fast-food restaurants have created a space for interaction (Yan 2000). This is the time when relations between customers, retailers, and sales representatives can be built and strengthened in a culturally acceptable way.

Though traveling abroad is not yet a common activity, internal travel is popular. Some working units sponsor holiday travel or offer it as a bonus for good workers. Similarly, companies have common traveling activities during the holidays for all their employees. However, travel within China is difficult, because it often involves long-distance trains and buses rather than the convenience of airlines. Nonetheless, tourism and travel within China and externally, and related consumer goods, have a huge market potential, particularly as standards of living increase and latent demand is released.

Below are some marketing implications based on analysis of consumption patterns:

- The high savings ratio creates a market for consumer investments and banking. Foreign banks are allowed to do business in local currency with Chinese individuals, within five years after the 2001 World Trade Organization (WTO) agreement.
- Expenditure on child-care goods is increasing.
- Rural households are larger compared with even the most-developed cities when both number of persons and space are concerned. Consequently, the requirements of rural households differ from those of urban households.
- Eating is still an important event for a Chinese family. More Western and foreign restaurants (e.g., McDonald's and Kentucky Fried Chicken) have entered Chinese markets, and have modified eating habits.
- Dining out is one of the most popular leisure activities. Restaurants have traditionally been occupied by male customers, but new fast-food outlets attract new customers, such as children, urban youth, and women (Yan 2000).
- The increase in leisure time has increased the market potential for services such as golf courses, skating areas, and ski resorts.
- Travel and tourism provide immense opportunities. Far-sighted tourist-seeking nations should enter the market now to build awareness and image and to be ready to capitalize on latent demand.
- Future high-demand markets are likely for consumer durables. As many affluent households already have TV sets, videos, washing machines, and air conditioning, high demand has turned to computers, cars, and cellular phones.
- Chinese consumers invest in real estate, particularly as housing reform and liberalization continue.
- Demand for automobiles connotes different meanings for urban and rural consumers. In many larger cities, the traffic is almost impossible to negotiate. Hence, motor vehicles are a less attractive means of transportation, but they are attractive consumption items for different purposes: cars and motorcycles can be status symbols for urban consumers. In rural areas, however, vehicles are essentially a necessity for transportation and work.

THE MACROMARKETING MIX

Branding

The consumer goods market in the PRC has been divided into three main areas: imported luxury brands, imported middle-class brands, and locally made brands (*The Economist* 1994). Foreign brands used to have a natural competitive advantage (Hooper 1994; d'Astous, Ahmed, and Wang 1995), but this has changed. This belief was so strong that some consumers did not buy products manufactured by Sino-foreign joint ventures, but preferred the equivalent, more expensive imported products.[12] In the context of Chinese culture (the history of isolation, high respect for its own capacity, and ethnocentrism), the change to preference for domestic products has been more rapid than in other developing economies. According to a Gallup survey, 62 percent of respondents connect positive quality to Chinese products, 80 percent favor local brand names, and 79 percent prefer products labeled "Made in China" over "made abroad" (Schlevogt 2000, 54). Foreign companies have used China and Chinese cultural heritage in their promotions. An example is the Chinese brand name for Revlon, which is linked to a famous Chinese poem of love between a Tang Dynasty king and one of the most beautiful women in Chinese history (Schütte and Vanier 1995). Similarly, Procter & Gamble and Unilever have used local detergent brand names (*The Economist* 1994).

The Chinese people have noticed the power of brands, and in leading universities, researchers are studying branding and brand management. Chinese leaders also have become aware of the value of a brand, and best-brands exhibitions, contests, and ranking lists have emerged in China (Schlevogt 2000). At least one Chinese brand has become a market leader. Legend covers 13 percent of the Chinese computer market, ahead of IBM, HP, and Compaq (Einhorn 1999). A local brand, Wahaha (a food company), was ranked first out of all brands in China (Schlevogt 2000). If branding "with Chinese characteristics" succeeds, future opportunities in China will be in exporting Chinese-branded products, rather than seeing China as a big potential market or a place of low production costs. Exports of top Chinese brands increased 300 percent from 1994 to 1998 (Schlevogt 2000).

In the Chinese context, corporate image is as important as brand development. Company image, however, is not based on the same criteria as in the West. *Asian Business* annually selects a company of the year using these criteria: quality of management; quality of products/services; contribution to the economy; size and type of charitable donations and establishment of educational foundations; concern shown for environment; the image projected of being honest, ethical, and a considerate employer; and potential for growth (see also Schütte and Vanier 1995). It is not only the increased wealth of shareholders that is important, but also the extent of social activities and responsibilities. In another example, a private businessperson concerned about the educational levels of private entrepreneurs used a part of the profits of his company to support teachers in developing training programs for private businesses. This may be explained by guanxi, which requires good relations in any social interaction to be shared and transferred for the benefit of other social relationships.

Packaging

Packaging is a very important signal of product quality for Chinese consumers. In addition to price and quality, packaging was found to be one of the key criteria for choosing products from among retailers (Polsa 1996). Not until recently have consumers on the mainland started to trust the quality of products, and the habit of opening the packages in supermarkets has diminished. However, even today, Chinese consumers have, when purchasing consumer durables, a tendency to open the package and test the product in the shop. This is a common habit, even if a warranty is provided for the product.

According to Yan (1994), Chinese consumers like to have complete information about a product; through this information, understanding and a feeling of security are gained. This desire is based on the importance in Chinese culture of maintaining harmony and the need to avoid counterfeits and low-quality products (Ma 1994). The search for harmony creates postpurchase behavior that is characterized by conflict avoidance and reluctance to express dissatisfaction (Schütte and Vanier 1995). Chinese consumers test the product carefully beforehand rather than voice complaints afterward. Despite this tendency, in the PRC, the number of complaints to the China Consumer Association increased rapidly over the 1990s, and had reached more than 667,000 in 1998 (Lu 2000). Today, Chinese consumers are less reticent to voice complaints and to seek redress for poorly performing products.

Only small packaged goods are affordable to many consumers. For example, shampoo is sold successfully in tiny one-use packs. Migrant workers, who do not have room to store their personal belongings, typically buy personal care products sold in small packages.

Price

The use of pricing continues to gain favor as a marketing strategy by domestic producers. For example, in the field of food production, pricing was released from state control in 1992. Traditionally, Chinese consumers are price sensitive and are used to bargaining while they shop. In the wet markets, and in the more recently established clothing markets, bargaining is a common habit, a way of shopping. A smart consumer haggles the price to an acceptable level; his or her bargaining is even appreciated by the seller. In the process, it is important that the buyer finds a solid argument for a lower price, and that the seller similarly can provide reasons for the higher price. However, in the state-owned shops, the prices were always fixed, with no bargaining possible. Currently, consumers assume that state-owned stores have cheaper products than do the private stores. This assumption is largely true, because many private sellers have a margin for bargaining in their prices.

When consumer durables and brand products are concerned, price is a less important issue. The segment that can afford these products is not price sensitive and spends more money on good-quality brands compared to lesser amounts on less conspicuous products. That said, discount brands are having an impact in these more discerning markets (see also *China Economic Review* 1994, 16).

Distribution

Chinese distribution is characterized by its fragmented structure. In contrast to the former planned-economy system, there are now, at least in principle, no restrictions concerning how a product is distributed. Since the early 1980s, a large number of retailers and wholesalers have emerged in the distribution market. At the moment, private business is encouraged by the government and is growing rapidly. However, the planned distribution system has not been abolished but remains as a base-structure for the entire distribution system. The state-owned sector has faced intensified competition, not only from the new entrants of private and foreign outlets, but because the government no longer tends to back up small- and medium-sized state-owned enterprises.

Wholesaling and retailing outlets can be categorized according to their ownership and function, as follows:

- State-owned retailers and wholesalers
- Collective retailers and wholesalers
- Private retailers and wholesalers
- Foreign retailers and, after WTO membership, foreign wholesalers.

This classification helps to divide the players into different groups and to distinguish their relative differences and strengths and weaknesses. Table 4.24 shows the importance of the respective subnetworks of state-owned, collective, and private wholesalers and retailers in 1994 and 2002. In 1994, the number of outlets at the retailer and wholesaler levels was the largest in the private sector, even though that sector covered only a fraction of the total sales volume of domestic trade. Hence, private outlets were small and functioned as convenient stalls for the nearby residents. The state-owned sector formed the most important part of the retailing and wholesaling sector in 1994. The situation was different in 2002: only 6 percent of the wholesaling outlets were private, whereas 39 percent were state-owned, and the share of the other ownership forms increased. The number of private retailers has decreased from 91 percent to 9 percent, and the share of the other ownership forms has increased. These drastic changes, however, are partly caused by measurement changes (Holz 2002).

The official statistics may not accurately reveal the reality of the evolution occurring in distribution. Field observations (Polsa 2002) reveal that private retailers are small in size, compared to collective and state-owned retailers. State-owned retailers are large outlets or department stores. They tend to be competitive because of their resources and location, but their power is diminishing, at least in some parts of the country. Collective retailers and wholesalers are medium in size, compared with the small private and the large state-owned retailers. The largest and most powerful wholesalers are the former second-level state-owned wholesalers, principally because they already formed the nationwide network during the heyday of the planned economy.

Retailers argue that private retailers and private businesses, in general, are more flexible in their ways of doing business and in reacting to fashion and consumer tastes. State-owned retailers, in contrast, have the reputation of being trustworthy but bureaucratic and inflexible. Some complain about the bureaucratic system of the state-owned companies' contracts and plans, but at the same time, appreciate their reliability. It is possible that relative newcomers in the market (those established after the 1979 reform policies), who are mainly private businesses, cannot gain the trust of consumers as easily as the old ones that have a long history; on the other hand, newcomers may more readily gain trust because they offer better goods and services. Increasing competition will force state-owned enterprises to change policies, to become more flexible, and to be responsive to customers' expectations.

Many of the old state-owned actors have a better knowledge of business and the market, but the market is changing. The guanxi of the state-owned businesses is a major asset. Old friends from production units and transportation and government offices provide valuable resources to state-owned retailers and wholesalers. Private businesspeople usually need to build up their relations from scratch. However, some government officials have established private businesses, and enjoy the relations from their former working places.

Private companies tend to differ from the state enterprises in terms of the education of employees and owners of the company. Traditionally, private businesspeople were formerly unemployed people, or farmers with no education. This is also changing, as many university students, despite their opportunities for secure government employment, are starting private businesses. Nonetheless, in general, many educated people in retailing are employed by the state-owned outlets.

As a result of the issues discussed above, the state-owned distribution channels still seem to be the most powerful. This is particularly the case in the rural interior. In the lucrative markets, such as Guangdong, Shanghai, and Beijing, nongovernment-owned firms have taken over a substantial part of distribution. Collectives have taken over markets, and some, managed by Hong Kong mother companies, have been successfully established in the PRC. At present, it might seem prudent to use the well-established state-owned channels, but one should also recognize the potential

Table 4.24

State-Owned, Collective, and Private Retailers and Wholesalers (percent)

	State-owned		Collective		Private		Foreign-funded		Other	
	1994	2002	1994	2002	1994	2002	1994	2002	1994	2002
Wholesalers										
Number of outlets* as percent of total 31,268 outlets (2002)	25	39	27	10	47	6	<1	2	1	43
Value of wholesaler sales as percent of total	67	46	28	5	0.5	6	0.5	5	4	38
Retailers										
Number of outlets as percent of total 28,751 outlets (2002)	2	23	6	13	91	9	<1	3	1	52
Value of retailer sales as percent of total	32	18	21	8	28	13		10	19	51

Source: China Statistical Yearbook (Beijing: China Statistical Publishing House, 1995), pp. 511, 522, 594; *China Statistical Yearbook* (Beijing: China Statistical Publishing House, 2003), pp. 620–21, 638–39.

*Number of outlets is referred to as "economic active units" in *China Statistical Yearbook* (Beijing: China Statistical Publishing House, 2001), p. 554, and as "outlets" in *China Statistical Yearbook* (Beijing: China Statistical Publishing House, 1995), p. 511. The term "economic active units" refers to units that have independent accounting systems. Prior to 1998, all outlets were included in the national statistics. After 1998, only those units with independent accounting praxis are included in the figures (C. A. Holz, "Institutional Constraints on the Quality of Statistics in China." *China Information* 16, no. 1 [2002], pp. 49–51). Thus, the decrease in collective and private units is partly caused by the change in ways of calculating statistics.

of the growing private and collective businesses in retailing and wholesaling. Resources that secured power for state-owned actors are also available to other businesses in a wider range than before. For example, access to transportation is currently a problem for new businesses, but in the future, new businesses may develop relations with these institutions and gain resources. In the course of banking and money market reform, financing has become easier for all types of businesses. There is also evidence that local governments do not support state-owned businesses as before, but give preferable locations and support for those businesses they believe in (Polsa 2002).

Transportation is a problem in most parts of the PRC. The central government policy has been favorable for establishing infrastructure in the eastern parts of the country, especially to the SEZs. Parts of the country that do not receive special treatment struggle with inadequate transportation and telecommunications, as Table 4.25 shows. This situation increases the state-owned businesses' power, because their guanxi gives them access to scarce infrastructure. To overcome these and other difficulties, enterprises use railroads for long-distance transportation and trucks for local transportation, or establish their own transportation systems. They also use distributors traditionally synergistic with their product lines (cf. Reinganum and Helsell 1994). This tends to favor state-owned distribution networks because of their relations to transportation officials and their knowledge of traditional distribution and warehousing.

Retailing

The following retailing outlets exist; some are more established than others:

- *Grocery stores:* located in residential areas, they sell packaged food products and other household supplies (Zhou 1993).
- *Department stores:* these have a food department, they sell packaged food products, and are officially called "General Retail Enterprises" (Hong 1990, 376).
- *Chain stores:* these are several outlets under the same organization. They have standardized management, and suppliers sell packaged food products and household supplies (Zhou 1993; *China Daily* 1993).
- *Supermarkets:* first opened in 1981 in Guangzhou and Beijing (Ho and Lo 1987), and local retailers have adopted the concept in a variety of intermediate forms.
- *Wet marketplaces:* individuals (farmers or distributors) sell fresh food products (Vernon-Wortzel and Wortzel 1987).
- *Specialty stores for one brand:* take, for example, Li-Ning stores and foreign stores, such as Benetton, Stefanel, Mexx, and Esprit.
- *Private business stores:* they are regrouped depending on the meaning the entrepreneur attaches to the business; examples follow.
  - *Private business stores* are small and large and are established to run a retailing or a wholesaling business as professionally as possible (Polsa 2002).
  - *Private welfare stores* are established by people who have no other source of income. The store, usually retailing, is established to earn a living, and the entrepreneur has no intention to increase the business or even to improve it. The primary goal is to keep the income level constant and sufficient (Polsa 2002, 146–50). The proportion of these kinds of businesses might be large, because 70 percent of private business owners in a nationwide survey said that they intend to maintain the current scale of their business (Chow et al. 2001).
  - *Private try-it stores* are established by persons who keep their secure government em-

Table 4.25

Length of Transportation Routes by Region

Provinces, municipalities, autonomous and SARs	Railways in operation (length per 10,000 km²)	Railways in operation (length per 10,000 persons)	Highways (length per 10,000 km²)	Highways (length per 10,000 persons)
National				
Coastal areas				
Beijing	**669.41**	**0.80**	**8,446.47**	**10.09**
Tianjin	**620.00**	**0.68**	**8,814.55**	**9.63**
Hebei	254.78	0.68	3,504.39	9.37
Liaoning	253.33	0.90	3,203.40	11.43
Shanghai	**426.67**	**0.16**	**10,476.67**	**3.87**
Jiangsu*	134.00	0.18	6,014.10	8.15
Zhejiang*	130.00	0.28	4,564.60	9.82
Fujian	121.17	0.42	4,512.92	15.62
Shangdong	190.33	0.31	4,935.27	8.15
Guangdong*	117.11	0.27	6,029.89	13.81
Hainan	64.41	0.27	6,140.00	26.00
Guangxi	119.35	0.57	2,447.70	11.68
Total	175.92	0.42	4,390.87	10.58
Central areas				
Inner Mongolia	48.38	2.60	567.76	30.55
Shanxi	190.63	0.93	3,725.69	18.10
Jilin	197.89	1.32	2,283.06	15.23
Heilongjiang	117.09	1.44	1,341.40	16.53
Anhui	170.77	0.35	5,195.92	10.66
Jiangxi	139.35	0.56	3,570.35	14.38
Henan	211.41	0.37	4,220.06	7.46
Hubei	132.72	0.40	4,783.22	14.38
Hunan*	137.90	0.42	4,240.40	12.79
Total	107.61	0.70	2,065.70	13.50
Inland areas				
Chongqing				
Sichuan	12.60	0.08	1,963.12	12.90
Guizhou	173.18	0.77	2,601.18	11.52
Yunnan	48.54	0.44	4,226.97	38.05
Tibet	19.76	8.88	331.33	148.91
Shaanxi	144.25	0.79	2,328.20	12.67
Gansu	51.49	0.89	893.84	15.51
Qinghai	15.17	2.06	333.38	45.37
Ningxia	112.43	1.38	1606.43	19.66
Xinjiang	17.34	1.46	518.31	43.53
Total	33.11	0.60	1,053.43	19.18

Sources: China Statistical Yearbook (Beijing: China Statistical Publishing House, 2003), p. 571; Shunwu Zhou, *China Provincial Geography* (Beijing: Foreign Language Press, 1992).
*The longest navigable inland waterways in the People's Republic of China.

ployment and run a business. Depending on the success of their business and the political environment, they may become wholly businesspersons or leave the business (Polsa 2002).

- *Foreign-funded retailers:* these are, for example, Carrefour, Metro, Wal-Mart, and Yaohan.
- *Direct-sales companies* have been forbidden since 1995, though one wonders how long this policy can or will be maintained.

Large grocery stores, department stores, chain stores, and supermarkets are mainly government-owned outlets or foreign investments. The reform in the former second-level wholesaler units emphasized building up a chain-store system at the retailer level; the network of former third-level wholesaling outlets in city districts provided good infrastructure. Some of the collective wholesaling and retailing organizations function very much like a chain-store system but do not officially carry this status. Supermarkets are a popular retailing form in the PRC. Even small private sellers have built up small self-service outlets that they call supermarkets. In general, the majority of private outlets are small neighborhood convenience stores. One popular way of distributing consumer goods is through a franchising agreement, as exemplified by Li-Ning sportswear as well as by some foreign products.

Distribution in any market is dynamic, but in a market such as that of the PRC, the change is even more evident, as a result of changing economic policies, WTO membership, and the small and medium state-owned enterprise reform. Actors emerge and disappear, new rules transform the functions of distribution, consumers' buying power changes, and the value system of the reforming economy affects trade.

These are the implications for distribution management:

- A general rule in the distribution of consumer goods is to maintain contacts at all levels of the distribution channel. Mars candies and Canpotex fertilizers (de Keijzer 1992) and Hewlett-Packard computers (*Business China* 1984) have been successful, because they have fostered relations with government units and state-run enterprises, while at the same time, regularly visiting retailers, trialing sale products through private channels, and upholding intense contacts with end users.
- Marketing to welfare retailers and wholesalers and, perhaps, also to try-it businesses, should go beyond the traditional incentives. Incentives should be social by nature, for instance, health care, insurance, and pension funds, rather than point-of-sale material and advertising support.
- The state-owned, collective, and private subnetworks, at least at the retailing level, fulfill complementary functions so that they provide different benefits for a distributor or a producer.
- Sales teams' regular visits are important to keep displays and inventory in good condition. M&M's success in distribution was based partly on an effective, well-trained sales force (see also de Keijzer 1992); in the course of the first author's fieldwork, it was discovered that a detergent producer built its offices and administered sales force teams on the premises of the most important wholesalers, to ensure close contact and cooperation.
- HP and Canpotex established service centers or information counters at the retailing level (de Keijzer 1992; *Business China* 1984).
- Finally, to overcome distribution problems, foreign companies have used the following five strategies: establishing retail outlets of manufacturing joint ventures; franchising; distribution agreements with Chinese companies; sale of the company name to existing retailers, and then managing operations under a long-term management contract (for example, the foreign firms may rent space in a large department store or in a shopping mall); and use of foreign distributors.

Word of Mouth

In China, one of the main factors affecting consumer behavior is the influence of friends, relatives, and colleagues, as the experience and knowledge of these people are respected (*Marketing Guide Magazine* 1995). The collective culture and emphases on social relations are conducive to word-of-mouth (WOM) marketing strategies; guanxi networks are effective tools for spreading information. Even though families are smaller these days, and consequently, networks of relatives are less widespread, the contemporary society provides new kinds of networks, such as working units, common education, same home region, etc.

A successful way of encouraging WOM marketing is in sales promotions at the retailer level. Supermarket cosmetics are widely promoted this way. Further, hierarchical relations in these networks make possible the use of opinion leaders. The elderly are naturally respected in all age groups and social classes. Also, salespersons are consulted and trusted (Schütte and Vanier 1995). It is also argued that WOM communication could be an important source of information among educated consumers (Schmitt 1997).

The collective society, group orientation, and hierarchical relations characteristic of China have been successfully used by a Canadian fertilizer manufacturer. Its marketing consisted of four main elements: demonstrations, farmer meetings, field inspections for leaders, and harvest field days. Provincial soil and fertilizer institutions run demonstrations for farmers, and farmer meetings and harvest field days gather the farmer's communities together. Harvest field days offer leisure activities, such as Chinese opera and cultural shows. Furthermore, the company has a long-term orientation of at least ten to fifteen years, and this has surprised even Chinese (see also de Keijzer 1992).

Advertising

Since the early 1980s, there has been a steady increase in the advertising industry in the PRC. The turnover of the advertising industry has grown rapidly and, naturally, so has expenditure on advertising. Part of the growth is the result of an increase in the cost of advertising, 20 to 30 percent for newspaper advertising and about 70 percent for TV advertising during the Opening Policy (Guo et al. 1995). Despite the increase in price, the cost of advertising in the PRC is still relatively low, making it a cost-efficient tool of marketing. The first comprehensive advertising law became effective in the beginning of 1995. The advertising regulations include prohibition of claims that play on superstitions and directions that the content of the advertising has to fit the national culture and consumer tastes (Luk et al. 1995). For example, advertising should not show scenes in which children disrespect adults.

In the PRC, TV is the medium offering the most exposure to consumers (Tables 4.26 and 4.27). After TV, consumers are most exposed to print advertisements, followed by radio and outdoor advertisements. Members of the stratum with the least education, the working poor, spend the most time listening to the radio. The effect of TV advertising is further strengthened by the fact that TV advertisements are most accurately memorized by the audience. Table 4.28 shows that consumers remember radio advertisements better than printed advertisements. Outdoor advertising has a less long-lasting effect on audience. When the actual purchasing decision is made, the effect of TV advertising is still strong but varies in different product groups.

The other mass-media promotion is not as important as information from the network of friends: the effect of friends' opinions is the next most influential agent after TV advertising for all the product groups (see Table 4.29). This reinforces our assertion that traditional cultural influences on social relations persist. In addition, the importance of exhibitions as motivation for apparel purchase reinforces the principle that Chinese consumers want to investigate consumer durables before they purchase, rather than to rely on after-sales service or warranty.

If the selection of media seems to be fairly clear, the selection of advertising agency is more complex. The preferred possibilities are as follows:

Table 4.26

Audience Exposure to Advertising Media (percent)

Frequency exposure	Daily	Often	Rare	Never
TV ad	60.7	25.0	6.6	7.7
Radio ad	14.0	36.0	41.4	8.5
Printed ad	17.7	50.9	15.0	16.4
Outdoor ad	10.5	40.0	23.6	26.0

Source: Q. G. Guo, F. Tong, H. Niu, and L. S. C. Yip, "Firms' Media Strategy in the Advertising Industry of China," in *Proceedings of the Fifth International Conference of Marketing and Development*, ed. K. Basu, A. Joy, and Z. Hansheng, June 22–25, 1995, Beijing, p. 405.

Table 4.27

Media Use per Consumer Segment (minutes per day)

Media	Consumer segment			
	Working poor	Salary class	Little rich	Yuppies
Television time	136	139	143	146
Radio time	57	40	41	42
Newspaper time	44	43	52	60
Magazine time	46	52	67	61

Source: G. Cui and Q. Liu, "Emerging Market Segments in a Transitional Economy: A Study of Urban Consumers in China." *Journal of International Marketing*, 9, no. 1 (2001): 91.

Table 4.28

Media and Audience Memory Toward Advertisement (percent)

Imprint in memory	TV ad	Radio ad	Print ad	Outdoor ad
Strong	49.9	9.3	8.2	2.5
Weak	48.1	64.1	53.4	37.0
Nil	2.0	26.6	38.4	60.5

Source: Q. G. Guo, F. Tong, H. Niu, and L. S. C. Yip, "Firms' Media Strategy in the Advertising Industry of China," in *Proceedings of the Fifth International Conference of Marketing and Development*, ed. K. Basu, A. Joy, and Z. Hansheng, June 22–25, 1995, Beijing, p. 405.

- State-owned advertising agencies
- In-house media advertising agencies
- Private advertising agencies
- Foreign-funded advertising agencies

The advertising agencies connected with government units have a close relationship with government-owned media. Private and foreign agencies are new and do not yet have a wide network of contacts with the necessary media and research institutions. It also has been argued that many agencies engage in creating advertising but cannot provide a full range of marketing services

Table 4.29

Buying Influence, Promotional Media, and Product Types (percent)

Product type	Promotional media					
	TV ad	Radio ad	Print ad	Outdoor ad	Friends	Exhibition
Household electronics	52.4	3.7	2.8	1.2	23.0	2.7
Daily necessities	37.7	9.5	4.1	2.1	14.8	3.0
Food	37.2	6.0	3.3	2.4	13.1	3.8
Apparel	29.2	7.2	7.9	2.1	12.6	1.3
Drugs	37.1	7.2	7.9	2.1	12.6	1.3
Health care	34.2	5.0	6.1	1.4	8.5	1.9

Source: Q. G. Guo, F. Tong, H. Niu, and L. S. C. Yip, "Firms' Media Strategy in the Advertising Industry of China," in *Proceedings of the Fifth International Conference of Marketing and Development*, ed. K. Basu, A. Joy, and Z. Hansheng, June 22–25, 1995, Beijing, p. 405.

(Guo et al. 1995, 404). However, relationship management can be provided by many agencies. Because media firms are in "a superior political position to advertising agencies," in many cases, they decide with whom they will deal and what kinds of advertising they will accept. Therefore, in-house media agencies provide good connections to media, but most of the time, they are unable to provide other marketing services (Luk et al. 1995, 4). Many multinational advertising agencies operate in China, serving mainly foreign-funded or joint-venture companies (Cheng and Frith 1996). They provide internationally skilled marketing services but consider their main problem to be connections to media organizations. For example, media rates may vary according to how "foreign" the advertised product is. Due to WTO membership, foreign advertising agencies are no longer required to operate in China through joint ventures.

Chinese perceptions of advertising have received attention from scholars. Early content analysis of advertising suggested that advertising messages should emphasize product performance, assurance, and technology, but less value and hedonism (Tse, Belk, and Zhou 1989). Studies in the late 1990s revealed consumption values such as modernity, youth, and status, along with persistent traditional appeals, such as group consensus, veneration of the elderly, and oneness with nature (Lin 2001). Perhaps more interesting is how Chinese consumers perceive these advertisements. Some research (e.g., Belk and Zhou 2002) indicates that Chinese consumers negatively perceive advertisements that mix Western products with Chinese traditional values or show Western values in the context of Chinese products performed by Chinese models. Chinese advertisements performing Western values are seen as vulgar; Western advertisements using Chinese traditional values are seen as unrealistic.

The following ideas could be taken into consideration when planning advertising content in the PRC:

- Identify the influential authority figures, and incorporate their images into advertising copy. In the Chinese cultural context, opinion leaders are older people, political leaders, family elders, and authoritarian types (Schütte and Vanier 1995; Lin 2001).
- Consider featuring local athletes, who are seen as having "integrity and represent the nation" (Belk and Zhou 2002), and are, thus, increasingly favored by some advertisers. Other pop culture figures are now also favored.
- Use dialects in local advertising on local TV and in local newspapers.

- Use images and emotional appeals without bombarding consumers with the "obligatory" facts and proof (Lin 2001, 90). However, "products for social usage should be advertised in a more emotive way, while those for private usage would benefit from an advertisement that reinforces habit" (Schütte and Vanier 1995, 22–23).

Market Research

Conducting marketing research in the PRC can be difficult, but it is increasingly valued, and many organizations are invoking it to make sense of the market's complexity and to develop its vast potential. The country is huge and consists of tremendously different submarkets. China may be viewed not only in terms of coastal, central, and inland areas, but also in terms of rural and urban areas and various consumer segments. Many companies have not reached the projected growth, because they have underestimated competition in the developed areas and segments and overestimated purchasing power in less affluent areas of China. The size of one submarket in China is larger than the size of an entire national market in many other countries. For example, the population of Beijing is eleven million, twice the population of, say, Finland. To overcome these problems, one needs to rely more on product- and market-specific primary data derived from both qualitative and quantitative methods, than on general statistics for the PRC. Some experts argue that it is almost impossible to rely on the results of consumer research in China. Chinese people tend to give answers that they assume the researcher wants, hence causing biases. Our experience also suggests that an efficient and reliable way to do marketing research is simply to try products within a limited market, for example, starting with some cities and slowly widening the sales area. For instance, Lu Biscuits sells packets of biscuits that include samples of most of their brands. That way, consumers taste even those biscuits that they would not otherwise pick up from the shelf, and the producer gains market information.

A number of market research agencies and consultants exist in China despite (because of?) these difficulties. For example, Gallup China Ltd. has conducted consumer-behavior research since 1994 (Li and Gallup 1995). Totally independent research is no longer allowed, and all researchers and research institutions must have Chinese partners (Tong 1999). The China Statistical Bureau provides general statistics for the PRC, although their veracity has been questioned. China is a country with huge variations and rapid changes; therefore, sample investigations of well-defined submarkets may lead to more accurate information.

Expected Changes in the Macromarketing Mix

The behaviors of Chinese consumers in the future are dependent on official government policies. Execution of these policies varies at the local level, as do the implications of these policies, although the national policy provides the framework for change in economic environment and, consequently, consumer behavior. The start of the Tenth Five-Year Plan (2001–2004) by the Fifteenth Party Central Committee indicates continuation of the current policies. The new constitution confirms adherence to the socialist road, people's democratic dictatorship, the leadership of the Communist Party, and Marxist-Leninist-Mao Zedong Thought (Li 2004). It also opens new avenues by adapting Deng Xiaoping's Theory, stressing the rule of law and giving the nonpublic economic sector better status (Yan 1999). Therefore, we can conclude that the present trends are likely to continue as follows:

- Diminishing population growth, a male-dominated sex ratio, and smaller households
- Continuing economic growth and higher consumption power

- Conspicuous consumption with a material preference
- Continuing differences in economic change consistent with east–west and rural–urban divides, but less obvious than before
- Continuing urbanization of the population
- Increasing unemployment, which will create small businesses
- Increasing leisure time, and changing leisure activities, with a wider range of possibilities
- Further "opening wider to the outside world" (see also *China Daily* 1995a, 1995b), affecting consumer tastes and habits
- Increasing reversion to the underlying traditional Chinese culture, as Marxist ideologies continue to have a decreasing effect on consumer behavior (the following issues will be affected: value of the family and social circle, role of women, education, sex ratio, and consumption patterns based on desire for social acceptance—that is, the demand for high-class products)
- Increasing availability of foreign products because of WTO membership
- Making of further steps toward modern marketing strategies but under the basic cultural constraints

Some of the changes relate to bringing in more modern marketing practices and increasing consumer sophistication; they will be partially driven by Hong Kong, as it more fully integrates into the economy of southern China. Convergence is the long-term trend, but this only partially means that Hong Kong will gradually become more like the mainland. Hong Kong is a very advanced, modern consumer market, and neither consumers nor marketers will become less sophisticated under convergence. Rather, Chinese buyers and marketers on the mainland are following Hong Kong's lead in many respects. Thus, it is important to examine Hong Kong's consumer market in some detail, both because it is a very important market in its own right, and also because many characteristics of consumers and consumer marketing throughout China will likely eventually become more like those found in Hong Kong.

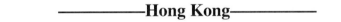

Hong Kong

BACKGROUND

Hong Kong Special Administrative Region (HK SAR), as it is known in official Chinese terminology, is located on the coast of southern China. Hong Kong was formerly a British Crown Colony that reverted to the PRC on July 1, 1997. Thus, there is considerably more Western influence on economic activities here, specifically marketing, than in most of China. As noted, many observers talk about convergence between Hong Kong and China, and this is certainly the long-term trend. However, the strong contrast between marketing and consumer behavior in Hong Kong and most of China should be clear from comparison of the two parts of this chapter. "One country" is the reality, and Hong Kong is now firmly reintegrated into China, but "two systems" is still the theme in economic activities and marketing. Convergence is not yet very far along in this sphere, and one cannot really understand how consumers behave or how marketing works in Hong Kong by examining the marketing system seen throughout most of China. In consumer behavior and marketing, convergence means, at least partially, that large tracts of China will become more like Hong Kong. The importance of Hong Kong as its own market, its strong contrast with most of

China, currently—and the fact that many aspects of marketing in China are likely to evolve toward characteristics similar to those of Hong Kong—all necessitate examining Hong Kong separately from the rest of this chapter on China.

The Hong Kong SAR is a very compact but high-spending power market. Hong Kong actually consists of Hong Kong Island (about 7.3 percent of total land area), Kowloon (about 4.3 percent of land area), many outlying islands (about 15 percent), and the New Territories. Lantau, to the west of Hong Kong Island and Kowloon, is the largest island, and it contains the site of the new airport that did not open until after the return to China. Much of the site on which the airport sits was developed through land reclamation along Lantau's north coast. All other islands are much smaller than Hong Kong Island. Lamma, just to the southwest of Hong Kong Island, is the only one of much local importance (Hong Kong Census and Statistics Department [HKCSD] 2003a).

The SAR has an area of about 1,100 square kilometers, which represents a slight but steady increase over the past two decades because of land reclamation. Although most people think of Hong Kong as a densely populated urban area, much of the territory's topography is rugged. Most of the undeveloped areas are not really useable for anything, but approximately 7.5 percent of total land area is classified as suitable for agriculture. Only about half of this is actually used for agriculture now, because opportunities in other economic sectors have become substantially better in the past two decades (HKCSD 2003a).

About 20 percent of the SAR's land area is "built-up," that is, urban. Over 98 percent of the population lives in this built-up area, which includes the north coast of Hong Kong Island, scattered areas of the south coast, Kowloon, and a number of New Towns in the New Territories. Shatin, about one-third of the way between the tip of Kowloon and the "border" with China, is the largest of the New Town urban areas (Hong Kong Government Information Services [HKGIS] 1995; HKCSD 2003a; Hong Kong Government Information Centre [HKGIC] 2003).

Hong Kong's climate is subtropical, with a hot, humid tropical monsoon season and a temperate, cooler season. Winter monsoons blow from the northeast, bringing relatively cool and dry weather from September to April. Mean daily temperature is usually lowest in January and February, at about 15.8°C. From April to September, southwest monsoons prevail, bringing very hot and humid weather. The hottest months are usually July and August, which average nearly 29°C. May to September is typhoon season, and, in an average year, five to seven tropical cyclones can be expected. Occasionally, one of these hits the territory with hurricane force. Of about 2,490 millimeters of rainfall in 2002, which was slightly above annual averages, around two-thirds fell in the period from June to September (HKCSD 2003a).

STRUCTURE OF THE ECONOMY

Hong Kong achieved some of the world's most impressive economic growth during the 1970s and 1980s. During most of the 1980s, economic growth rates ranged between 6 percent and 10 percent annually (in constant prices) and reached 14.5 percent in 1987. However, the economy slowed substantially after 1989 because of a number of factors. The Tiananmen Square crackdown in China put a temporary damper on economic growth. More importantly, China has implemented several years of austerity programs to slow its overheated economy, and the global economy went through a recession at about the same time in the early 1990s. Difficulties in Hong Kong's main markets in the West and Japan hindered Hong Kong's exports. Certainly, Hong Kong was not yet facing real difficulty, as growth remained strong by the standards of the global recession in those years. However, sentiment among the population, accustomed to roaring growth, was somewhat damaged (HKCSD 1991, 1997, August 2002).

Table 4.30

Gross Domestic Product (expenditure based)

Year	Current market prices GDP (HK$ million)	Percent change	Per capita (HK$)	Constant 2000 prices Percent change	GDP (HK$ million)	Percent change
1991	677,247		117,741			
1992	791,319	16.8	136,423	15.9	931,692	6.6
1993	912,809	15.4	154,687	13.4		
1994	1,029,773	12.8	170,622	10.3	1,045,009	
1995	1,096,263	6.5	178,078	4.4	1,085,764	3.9
1996	1,210,925	10.4	188,163	5.7	1,132,223	4.3
1997	1,344,546	11.0	207,194	10.1	1,189,966	5.1
1998	1,279,850	−4.8	195,585	−5.6	1,130,838	−5.0
1999	1,246,134	−2.6	188,622	−3.6	1,169,474	3.4
2000	1,288,338	3.4	193,299	2.5	1,288,338	10.2
2001	1,278,995	−0.7	190,188	−1.6	1,296,512	0.6
2002	1,271,082	−0.6	187,282	−1.5		

Source: Hong Kong Census and Statistics Department (HKCSD), *Special Report on GDP* (Hong Kong: Government Printing Department, Hong Kong Special Administrative Region, August 2002).

Economic growth recovered fairly well by the mid-1990s, though not to the level of the 1980s. However, Hong Kong has experienced economic decline since its return to China in 1997, partly as a result of the Asian financial crisis, which ushered in several years of severe economic problems for many economies in the region. The economy declined dramatically and has rarely posted positive growth since 1996 (Table 4.30). Figures in terms of current prices look slightly better only because the economy has seen strong deflation. Prospects were still dim at the end of 2003, after the dramatic impact of severe acute respiratory syndrome (SARS). The Asian crisis and SARS gave a painful hit to Hong Kong's formerly robust economy. It will not be easy for the territory to return to the growth rates of the 1980s or even the early 1990s. The economic shocks that popular opinion frequently blame for economic problems are not actually the underlying cause of the long term economic patterns (HKCSD 1997, August 2002).

Hong Kong's economy is undergoing structural change, and the SAR has not completely worked out its new role in China or the regional economy. By the end of the 1990s, the economy had shifted into a mature, service-oriented phase. The contributions of primary and secondary industries to economic activities dropped substantially throughout the 1990s, whereas service industries grew steadily. The economy of Hong Kong was traditionally based on trade and low-cost manufacturing. In the 1980s, it also developed into an important financial and services center for East Asia, particularly relating to China's economic interaction with the outside world (Hong Kong Information Services Department [HKISD] 2002).

Manufacturing, however, accounted for only 5.2 percent of Hong Kong's GDP in 2001, down from 15.4 percent just a decade earlier (Table 4.31). In a sense, these figures demonstrate the success of Hong Kong's economic integration with China, a trend that started well before 1997. Hong Kong is no longer very competitive in the labor-intensive industries, which was one key component fueling the rapid growth of the 1970s and early 1980s. However, Hong Kong companies remain heavily involved in relatively low-tech and labor-intensive industry. Most of this industry has been moved across the border into China to keep labor costs, and prices, low. More than 63,000 manufacturers involving Hong Kong interests have production activities in China, of which 90

Table 4.31

Gross Domestic Product by Share of Economic Activity

Economic activity	1991	1996	2001
Agriculture and fishing	0.2	0.1	0.1
Mining and quarrying	0.0	0.0	0.0
Manufacturing	15.4	6.5	5.2
Electricity, gas, and water	2.1	2.4	3.3
Construction	5.5	5.8	4.8
Wholesale, retail, trade, hotel and restaurant	25.9	25.4	26.7
Transport, storage, and communication	9.6	9.2	10.2
Finance, insurance, and real estate services	22.7	26.2	22.6
Community, social, and personal services	14.9	17.9	21.8
Ownership of premises	10.9	13.9	13.1
(Financial service charge)	–7.3	–7.3	–7.9
	100.0	100.0	100.0

Sources: Hong Kong Census and Statistics Department (HKCSD), *Hong Kong Social and Economic Trends, 1997 Edition* (Hong Kong: Government Printing Department, Hong Kong Special Administrative Region, 1997); HKCSD, *Hong Kong Monthly Digest of Statistics, 2000 October* (Hong Kong: Government Printing Department, Hong Kong Special Administrative Region, 2000); HKCSD, *Hong Kong Monthly Digest of Statistics* (Hong Kong: Government Printing Department, Hong Kong Special Administrative Region, March 2003).

percent are located in Guangdong province. In a survey of these firms, half said they would continue to increase business activities in Guangdong, shifting from Hong Kong (Hong Kong Center for Economic Research [HKCER] 2003; Chan 2002).

The British colonial government's philosophy of minimal direct involvement in the economy, along with the stable and relatively corruption-free regulatory environment, made Hong Kong a favorite regional center for financial and other business services. There has been some concern that the current administration is not defending these advantages forcefully. However, whatever erosion there may be has not been pronounced, so far. Most foreign companies are staying put, while Hong Kong has gained from an influx of Chinese companies into the SAR. By 2001, finance, insurance, real estate, and other business services accounted for nearly 23 percent of GDP (Table 4.31). Most major banks with any international presence are represented in Hong Kong. The Hong Kong stock exchange remains one of the largest outside the United States, the United Kingdom, Japan, and a few other major Western countries. A large number of multinationals have made the territory their headquarters for regional operations and remain committed to operations in the SAR (Gaeta 1995; Li 1995; HKISD 2002; Hong Kong Looking Ahead [HKLA] 2003b).

Hong Kong is also one of the primary trade centers of East Asia, particularly for China trade. Ever since China began to open after 1979, Hong Kong increasingly became the trade link between China and the outside world. In 2000, China received over 29.9 percent of Hong Kong's domestic exports and over one-third of re-exports. It also accounts for nearly 43.1 percent of Hong Kong's imports (HKCSD 2001b). Re-exports continue to rise, although domestic exports are declining, reflecting the shift in industry to China (Table 4.32). However, these figures mask the long-term shift away from Hong Kong's dominant role in China trade. As China becomes increasingly linked to the world economy, it is rapidly developing multiple linkage points. More locations are opening for intensive interaction with foreign business, and infrastructure is being upgraded so that those locations can handle bigger volumes of whatever is needed, be it port facilities for moving product or portals for moving information (HKISD 2002; HKLA 2003a).

Table 4.32

Trade and Top Trade Partners (percent)

	1991	1996	2000
Domestic exports to			
United States	27.2	25.4	30.1
China	23.5	29.0	29.9
United Kingdom	5.9	5.0	5.9
Germany	8.4	5.4	5.1
Taiwan	2.6	3.2	3.4
Total domestic exports (HK$ billion)	231.0	212.2	181.0
Re-exports to			
China	28.7	35.2	35.1
United States	20.7	20.4	22.3
Japan	5.5	6.8	5.9
United Kingdom	2.7	3.0	3.8
Germany	6.0	4.0	3.6
Total re-exports (HK$ billion)	534.8	1,185.8	1,391.7
Imports from			
China	37.7	37.1	43.1
Japan	16.4	13.6	12.0
Taiwan	9.6	8.0	7.5
United States	7.6	7.9	6.8
South Korea	4.5	4.8	4.9
Total imports (HK$ billion)	779.0	1,535.6	1,658.0

Sources: Hong Kong Census and Statistics Department (HKCSD), *Hong Kong Annual Digest of Statistics, 2001 Edition* (Hong Kong: Government Printing Department, Hong Kong Special Administrative Region, 2001).

Over the next decade, then, Hong Kong's relative importance will decline somewhat, as other parts of China, particularly the Pearl River Delta and the Yangzi Delta, catch up. Shanghai, in particular, aims to recapture its traditional role as the commercial center of China. China's entry into the WTO might further upset Hong Kong's "gateway" status between China and the outside world, as China has formally committed to opening its market, will cut import taxes substantially, and will gradually dismantle all kinds of nontariff barriers (Hong Kong Economic Information Agency [HKEIA] 2001). One of Hong Kong's claims to its dominant role in China trade has always been that no one else knows how to deal with the Chinese as well. However, as China makes it ever easier to do business in China, there is less use for this role (Wong 2002b; HKCER 2003).

On the optimistic side, Hong Kong has signed the Closer Economic Partnership Arrangement to boost its economy and to bring trade ties between China and Hong Kong even closer (Xinhua News Agency June 29, 2003; Hong Kong Lawyer [HKL] September 2003). This pact could reduce Chinese import tariffs by up to 50 percent on about 4,000 types of goods from Hong Kong exporters, which would mean a savings of millions of dollars (Chan 2002). Thus, Hong Kong continues to face economic difficulties in 2004, but its long-term position is relatively secure. The SAR is having some difficulty defining its new role, and it will not be able to hold onto its former position as essentially the only gateway to China's huge economy. Nevertheless, Hong Kong seems certain to remain a key commercial city in China, particularly for the rapidly growing Pearl River Delta area (*China Daily* HK Edition 2003; Hong Kong Trade Development Council [HKTDC] 2004).

DEMOGRAPHICS

Hong Kong's estimated population in year-end 2002 was about 6.759 million, with about 48.8 percent male (HKCSD 2002b, 2003a). This slight imbalance reflects labor emigration, which is mostly male. These figures are estimates; the last full census was in 2001, which showed that the population was 6,708,389. The population is concentrated in urban areas on Hong Kong Island, in Kowloon, and in the New Towns of the New Territories. The New Territories is the only region with rapid growth that mostly represents a population shift out of Kowloon. Although the New Territories is a large region, most of its population is concentrated in the New Towns, and very few Hong Kong residents in any area could be classified as rural. The vast majority of residents are Chinese (mostly Cantonese), and under 4 percent claim a non-Chinese language as their mother tongue (HKCSD 2002b, 2003a; HKGIC 2003).

Population growth has been slow, just 0.9 percent since 1996. In part, this slow growth is due to the fact that the increasingly affluent population is following the common trend in developed industrial economies toward small families. Marriage postponement contributes to this. The median age at first marriage for women rose from 23.9 in 1981 to 27.5 in 2001. Also, there is a significant increase in the proportion of never-married women ages forty to forty-four, which rose from 3 percent in 1981 to 12 percent in 2001. The low population growth rate is also attributable to the unfavorable economic climate since the Asian economic turmoil in 1997 (HKCSD 2001a).

Immigration from China is likely to grow somewhat, and this accounts for some of the recent growth. Prior to 1980, official policy was to grant right of abode to anyone from China who could reach Hong Kong. However, as China opened up in the late 1970s, the trickle turned into a massive flow, and nearly a half million immigrants came in the few years before 1981. Hong Kong started sending back illegal immigrants then, allowing only about 27,000 to come legally each year. China has continued the policy of keeping immigration under control and has not allowed any flood of immigrants to come into the SAR. Immigration from China rose to 150 persons per day by 2003, roughly 45,000 annually, but there seems to be no plan to increase substantially beyond that. Currently, the priority in most places is to attain family reunification (HKGIS 1995; Lam and Liu 1995; Sung and Wong 2000; HKISD 2002). It is difficult to estimate illegal immigration—arrests in 2002 were about fifteen per day, down from twenty-three per day in 2001 (HKISD 2002). Emigration was about 10,500 in 2002, about the level of several previous years, and substantially reduced from the years immediately before 2000 (HKISD 2002).

Hong Kong's population is gradually aging, also following patterns in industrial countries. The median age rose from 31.0 in 1991 to 36.8 in 2001 (Table 4.33). The percentage of people over age sixty-five increased 5.5 percent per annum from 1961 to 2001, by which time just over 11 percent of the population fell into this older age category (HKCSD 2002a, 2002b). While the youth market is still strong in Hong Kong, it is gradually shrinking as a percentage of the total population. In 2001, just 16.5 percent of the population was under fifteen years of age, down from 20.9 percent a decade earlier.

Tourism also contributes substantially to consumption in Hong Kong. In 2001, there were over 13.7 million tourist arrivals, up from 6.8 million in 1991. Tourism remains strong and continues to grow, but the structure of the industry is shifting to account for the fact that China is gradually increasing in importance as the major source of tourists. The vast majority of visitors are from East Asia, with visitors from China accounting for 32.4 percent of tourists in 2001 and Taiwanese making up another 17.6 percent. These two places and the Americas are the only major sources of tourism that have shown strong growth. Arrivals from other major regions, such as Europe, Australia and New Zealand, north Asia, and Southeast Asia have been declining.

Table 4.33

Hong Kong Population by Age and Area (percent)

	1991	1996	2001
Age group			
Under 15	20.9	18.5	16.5
15–34	36.6	33.1	30.2
35–64	33.8	38.3	42.1
Over 65	8.7	10.1	11.1
Total	100.0	100.0	100.0
Median age (years)	31.0	34.2	36.8
Area			
Hong Kong Island	22.0	21.1	19.9
Kowloon	35.8	32.0	30.2
New Territories	41.9	46.8	49.8
Marine	0.3	0.2	0.1
Total	100.0	100.0	100.0

Source: Hong Kong Census and Statistics Department (HKCSD), *2001 Population Census—Summary Results* (Hong Kong: Government Printing Department, Hong Kong Special Administrative Region, 2001).

Table 4.34

Visitor Arrivals in Hong Kong

	1991		1996		2001	
	(1,000s)	%	(1,000s)	%	(1,000s)	%
The Americas	822	12.1	1,083	8.3	1,259	9.2
Europe, Africa, Middle East	880	12.9	1,455	11.2	1,171	8.5
Australia, New Zealand, Pacific	285	4.2	425	3.3	387	2.8
North Asia	1,444	21.3	3,231	24.9	1,762	12.8
South and Southeast Asia	1,150	16.9	1,823	14.1	1,747	12.7
Taiwan	1,298	19.1	2,024	15.6	2,419	17.6
Others	41	0.6	542	4.2	532	3.9
Mainland China	875	12.9	2,389	18.4	4,449	32.4
Total	6,795		12,974		13,725	

Sources: Hong Kong Census and Statistics Department (HKCSD), *Hong Kong Annual Digest of Statistics, 2001 Edition* (Hong Kong: Government Printing Department, Hong Kong Special Administrative Region, 2001); HKCSD, *Hong Kong Annual Digest of Statistics 2002* (Hong Kong: Government Printing Department, Hong Kong Special Administration Department, 2002).

About two-thirds of visitors in 2001 were from Asia, which in terms of percentages is consistent with that of a decade earlier, although, as noted, China's share of tourism has dramatically increased over the decade (Table 4.34) (HKGIC 2003).

EMPLOYMENT, INCOME, AND HOUSING

Hong Kong's labor force stood at about 5.60 million in 2001, an increase of 1,229,000 over a decade (Table 4.35). However, the labor-force participation rate among those ages fifteen and over declined slightly, reaching 72 percent for men in 2001, although it increased slightly to

Table 4.35

Labor Force Indicators

	1991	1996	2001
Population over 15 ('000)	4,370	5,067	5,599
Labor force ('000)	2,811	3,182	3,437
Men	1,742	1,925	1,948
Women	1,068	1,257	1,489
Industrial sector ('000)			
Manufacturing	768	575	401
Wholesale retail restaurants hotels	611	757	853
Finance insurance real estate	287	409	523
Participation rate (%)	64.3	62.8	61.4
Men	78.7	76.6	71.9
Women	49.5	49.2	51.6
Unemployment rate (%)	1.8	2.8	6.2

Source: Hong Kong Census and Statistics Department (HKCSD), *2001 Population Census—Summary Results* (Hong Kong: Government Printing Department, Hong Kong Special Administrative Region, 2001).

almost 52 percent for women. These slight declines are due almost entirely to the increasing tendency for younger men and women to stay in school longer to improve job prospects and for people to retire earlier as living standards increase (HKISD 2002; HKGIC 2003).

Employment in the manufacturing sector has declined to about half the levels of 1991, but services-sector jobs have expanded. However, unemployment had risen to 6.2 percent by 2001, sharply increased from 1.8 percent a decade before, which dampened consumer sentiment in the first years of the century. Things got even worse, and unemployment was even higher, at 8.3 percent, by late 2003. Reported underemployment was 3.6 percent at that time. Other than family reunion, the government has confined imported mainland Chinese labor mainly to highly skilled areas, where it is difficult to find local employees. Local employers have to prove that the labor skills they acquire through imported labor have so far not been found in Hong Kong. This measure aims to protect Hong Kong's employment levels while still being able to satisfy labor market needs (HKCSD 2001c; HKISD 2002; *Asian Economic News* [AEN] October 28, 2003; HKLA 2003d; Wong, S. 2003).

More than one-third of the male workforce is in managerial- or professional-level jobs (Table 4.36). Accounting for about 16 percent of employment among men, craft-type jobs are still common among workers in Hong Kong. About a quarter of female workers are in managerial- and professional-level jobs. However, they are likely to be at lower levels of professional occupations than their male counterparts. The largest single category for women is clerks, about 29 percent of the jobs among women. Although it is clear that employment equality has not yet been achieved, women in Hong Kong enjoy better opportunities than they did a decade ago and substantially better opportunities than in many Asian countries. Women and men had broadly similar levels of monthly employment earnings in several occupational groups, notably in managerial- and professional-level jobs and as clerks.

Hong Kong's remarkable economic performance has resulted in living standards comparable to those in the advanced countries of the West and Japan. Living standards rose rapidly throughout the 1980s and well into the 1990s. Living standards are high and have been rising rapidly. Per capita GDP was over HK$187,282 in 2002. The Hong Kong dollar currently remains pegged to the U.S. dollar, and during the 1990s through 2001, it fluctuated in a narrow band, usually be-

Table 4.36

Working Population by Occupation

Work sector	Male	%	Female	%
Managers and administration	203.3	11.0	69.4	4.9
Professionals	130.9	7.1	63.7	4.5
Associate professionals	338.9	18.4	230.0	16.4
Clerks	152.3	8.3	406.4	28.9
Service and sales	254.2	13.8	219.8	15.7
Craft and related	299.8	16.2	9.8	0.7
Plant and machine operations	217.0	11.8	34.6	2.5
Elementary operation	243.9	13.2	368.3	26.2
Others	4.9	0.3	1.9	0.1
Total	1,845.2		1,403.9	

Source: Hong Kong Census and Statistics Department (HKCSD), *Women and Men in Hong Kong—Key Statistics, 2002 Edition* (Hong Kong: Government Printing Department, Hong Kong Special Administrative Region, 2002).

Table 4.37

Percentage of Domestic Households, by Monthly Household Income (percent)

Monthly income (HK$)	1991	1996	2001
Under 2,000	4.8	3.0	3.2
2,000–3,999	7.3	3.7	4.8
4,000–5,999	12.8	4.1	4.5
6,000–7,999	13.8	5.7	5.7
8,000–9,999	11.5	7.4	5.9
10,000–14,999	19.9	17.5	15.5
15,000–19,999	11.1	14.5	12.8
20,000–24,999	6.3	11.4	10.9
25,000–29,999	3.6	7.9	7.8
30,000–39,999	3.8	9.9	10.7
40,000–59,999	2.8	8.1	9.6
Over 60,000	2.3	6.9	8.7
Total	100.0	100.0	100.0
Median monthly domestic household income (HK$)	9,964	17,500	18,705

Source: Hong Kong Census and Statistics Department (HKCSD), *2001 Population Census—Summary Results* (Hong Kong: Government Printing Department, Hong Kong Special Administrative Region, 2001).

tween 7.74 and 7.79 (HKCSD August 2002). Many households benefit from dual incomes, because slightly more than half of all women work, which results in very high household incomes. From 1991 to 2001, the proportion of Hong Kong households earning HK$10,000 or more per month (just over US$15,000 annually) increased from only 50 percent to 75 percent (Table 4.37). The proportion earning over HK$20,000 monthly (US$31,000 annually) increased from under 20 percent to 48 percent over the past decade. About 18.3 percent of households earn over US$61,000 annually. Households also benefit from a low personal tax rate (15.5 percent; no taxes for lower income levels), so that people enjoy take-home pay, and households have considerable purchasing power. Despite the current recession, Hong Kong residents still enjoy disposable incomes among the highest in the world (HKISD 2002).

Hong Kong has acquired a reputation for very expensive housing, but this has changed since the outbreak of the Asian financial crisis and recession, which led to a slump in Hong Kong's property market. The average rents per square meter per month of Grade A private office space in the Central District on Hong Kong Island dropped from HK$682 in 1997 to HK$474 in 2001. In private retail housing, the average rents per square meter per month on Hong Kong Island decreased from HK$1,105 in 1995 to HK$858 in 2001. Yet the government still subsidizes housing for much of the population, and this public-sector competition keeps costs from going too high in the lower to middle part of the housing market. Of the 609,534 residential flats built between 1990 and 2000, about 34 percent were public housing (HKISD 2002; Wong 2002a; HKGIC 2003).

During 1997, the government took some measures to cool the property market. Tung Chee Hwa, the chief executive of the Hong Kong SAR, announced a policy of building 85,000 units of public housing per year to cool the overheated property market. Property prices fell sharply afterward, as the real estate bubble burst, and they do not seem to be rising back to the level of the 1990s, after six years of slump. How much the government policy contributed to this fall is debatable, however, and most of the sharp rollback of prices can probably be attributed to the broader economic difficulties. Anyway, such sharp drops in housing prices were also a mixed blessing, as many families ended up owing more on their mortgages than was the market value of their housing (HKISD 2002; Wong 2002a).

The government has been especially active in building the New Towns, to encourage dispersal of population to the New Territories (HKCSD 2002a, 2002b). Approximately 47.6 percent of households resided in public and subsidized rental housing blocks in 2000. Ownership of the flat in which the household lives was around 51 percent in 2000. Home purchase can be either from the private sector or through the Housing Authority Home Ownership Scheme, which allows the purchase of public housing flats. About 15.5 percent of households participated in this scheme in 2000. Median rentals in public housing and median payments under the home ownership scheme represented just about 10 percent of household income in 2001 (HKCSD 2001c, 2002a; Wong 2002a).

Although the private sector constructs some lower- and middle-income housing, much private-sector building has concentrated on the higher end of the market, where prices and rents became exorbitant by the early 1990s. Rentals of private residential flats (whole house/flat) had median rentals/payments of HK$6,500 in 2001, which represented nearly 30 percent of household income for families in them (Wong 2002a; HKCSD 2002a).

Some critics of the government point out the crowded conditions in many public housing estates, which are usually constructed in clusters of high-rise buildings. Safety and security are occasionally somewhat less than might be desired, though the government usually moves quickly to improve conditions in estates where this becomes an issue. There is certainly room for some improvement in housing conditions, but, in general, Hong Kong has made remarkable progress in providing affordable basic housing to a very densely packed population. The situation may not be perfect, but, compared with other major urban areas in Asia, the housing situation seems to be good.

SOCIAL AND CULTURAL ENVIRONMENT

In this section, we will briefly discuss several issues that have brought changes in consumer behavior over the past two decades. Education levels are very high in Hong Kong, with the result that consumers have become sophisticated and discriminating. Women have been integrated into

Table 4.38

Education Indicators for Hong Kong: Education Level (percent)

Education levels by population over age 15	1991	1996	2001
No formal schooling	12.8	9.5	8.4
Primary	25.2	22.6	20.5
Lower secondary	19.1	18.9	18.9
Upper secondary	26.7	27.7	26.3
Matriculation	4.9	6.1	9.4
Tertiary			
Nondegree course	5.4	4.8	3.7
Degree course	5.9	10.4	12.7
	100.0	100.0	100.0

Source: Hong Kong Census and Statistics Department (HKCSD), *2001 Population Census—Summary Results* (Hong Kong: Government Printing Department, Hong Kong Special Administrative Region, 2001).

the workforce and are beginning to achieve top-level positions, although there is still much progress to be made before women gain status equal to men in Hong Kong society. Concern about the environment is no longer regarded as a luxury but rather as a key issue in improving the quality of life. Finally, because of the 1997 Asian financial crisis and the political unrest in 2003, expectations have gradually been changing. This has had a major impact on consumption.

Education

Educational levels are quite high, with nine years of free and compulsory schooling. By 2001, nearly 73 percent of the population over the age of fifteen had at least a secondary education (Table 4.38). The seemingly high proportion of people without formal education (8.4 percent in 2001) or with only primary education (20.5 percent) reflects, in part, immigration from China. These immigrants generally have low educational levels, although recently, a small but increasing number of immigrants have been well-educated professional people. To further increase the education level of Hong Kong's people, the territory now has eight tertiary institutions, nurturing 16.4 percent of the population by 2001. For those who are not eligible for receiving tertiary education, the government has launched various schemes to enhance their employability and competitiveness, such as the Youth Pre-employment Training Programme (HKISD 2002; HKCSD 2003a). Demand for tertiary and continuing education is growing rapidly, and Hong Kong's education industry is gearing up to serve markets in China, as well (*The Bulletin* 2003a).

Women

Generally, feelings are mixed about how much women have progressed toward more equal treatment and opportunity in Hong Kong. Many observers feel that awareness of women's issues is generally low (e.g., So 2003), but outsiders who view Hong Kong relative to the broader context of Asia generally feel that women are much more active in economics and social life than in many other parts of the region (e.g., Marquand 2003). The government's Equal Opportunity Commission (EOC) was set up in 1996 to help ensure enforcement of laws against various forms of discrimination, including gender discrimination. Some feel much more should be done, but generally, the EOC has been fairly active and has contributed to the steady, though not always rapid progress toward upgrading women's status (*South China Morning Post [SCMP]* July 3, 2003; Wu 2001, 2002). Among other actions, the EOC initiated a court suit against the government over the issue of secondary school admissions. An EOC study concluded that the admissions procedure favored the male elite in Hong Kong. Eventually, the court agreed that the policy was discriminatory and ruled it illegal. Some observers, however, question the government's commitment to rigorous enforcement of nondiscrimination, in light of the recent failure to renew the contract of the EOC's activist chairperson (Equal Opportunities Commission of Hong Kong [EOCHK] 2003; Marquand 2003; *SCMP* July 3, 2003; Wu 2003).

Women have made substantial progress in the past several decades. In the 1960s, only about 36 percent of adult women worked (Chow 1995). As noted above, by 2001, slightly more than half of adult women participated in the labor force, and they represented over 40 percent of the total labor force. For the most part, women achieve educational levels similar to those of men. The percentage of women with very low education is larger than among men, but this is mainly due to recent immigration and reflects a characteristic of mainland Chinese society, not of Hong Kong society. The proportion of women who receive higher education, though slightly less than that for men, is rapidly catching up.

The increased rate of workforce participation in Hong Kong throughout this decade was more significant for women, in both absolute and relative terms. This can be attributed to the better educational opportunities and the increased prevalence of marriage postponement and "spinsterhood." A portion of the growth is made possible because of the increase in female foreign domestic helpers who share women's roles at home. This domestic help is usually imported labor and is affordable, even to many middle-class families. (In terms of marketing fast-moving consumer goods, one implication is that frequently, the decision maker is no longer a family member but rather a foreign maid.)

Similar to career women in other parts of the world, they must balance the conflicting demands of work and home, and they find this somewhat more stressful than do their male counterparts. There is also still some discrimination—and segregation—of some jobs by sex. Women tend to enter service industries, such as advertising, public relations, publishing, media, tourism, catering, accommodation, social services, and personnel. Despite the fact that they perform well in some male-dominated industries, such as banking or engineering, women are still sometimes not perceived to be good managers. Survey results in 2002 showed that 26 percent of top managerial positions in the private sector were held by women.

Nevertheless, while all of these problems are still substantial, women generally have good prospects in the workforce relative to those in most Asian countries, and even compared to many Western ones. They also have a number of active organizations and government offices that represent women and continue to push with some success for greater equality (Siu and Chu 1994; Ng 1995; Sun 2000; Tan Kam 2001; EOCHK 2002a, 2002b; Women's Commission of Hong Kong [WCHK] 2002).

In law and politics, Hong Kong women face the problem that much of the population is still tradition bound. Women account for only 17 percent of members of the Legislative Council, Hong Kong's highest law-making body. On lower-level district boards, they account for a similar rate, only 15 percent of members. Many of the more outspoken women lawmakers attribute the low levels of women in politics to traditional thinking among both men and women (Tan Kam 2001). About one-third of the civil service is women, but women make up only about 25 percent of directorate staff (higher-level management). However, in mid-2003, seven of the sixteen permanent secretaries, the highest-ranking officials in the civil service, were women (Hong Kong Home Affairs Bureau [HKHAB] 2003).

Traditional thinking often seems to be reinforced in the media that tend to present women in relatively traditional roles. Many mass-circulation general-interest periodicals portray a woman's place as with the family, and the publishing industry has not entirely achieved gender neutrality in textbooks. The majority of women's radio programs are devoted to family matters such as child care and housekeeping. Many women's magazines have changed little over the past decade, and still contain relatively shallow editorial content. These are usually targeted at younger women and became very successful in the 1990s. However, some local magazines did emerge, as did local and regional editions of international magazines, which have upgraded the intellectual level of the content. By Asian standards, these Hong Kong magazines are sometimes quite progressive in dealing with personal issues, such as women's sexuality. However, the content of most Hong Kong women's magazines and editions is not as risqué as many Western women's magazines (So and Speece 1991; Siu 1996; Fung and Ma 2000; Wu 2002; Young and Chan 2002; Lam 2003).

Environment

As do most major Asian cities, Hong Kong faces some serious pollution problems. In 1994, the annual average total suspended particulate in the air was 74 micrograms per cubic meter in urban areas, a figure well above government standards for clean air. Reference to figures on the Environmental Protection Department Web site (EPD 2003a) indicates that Hong Kong may have made some slight progress, as figures at most stations are normally slightly lower. However, the government classified air pollution as high for approximately half of all hours during 2003. Enforcement of air pollution controls on vehicles was lax in the early 1990s, with resistance from parts of the business community; stricter enforcement over the past decade has brought some progress in controlling this source of pollution. Particulate emissions from vehicles have dropped sharply. In outlying areas, the government was more active in forcing factories to cut air pollution, and power plant emissions were also reduced substantially over the last decade (Siddall 1991; HKGIS 1995; HKCSD 2003a; HKISD 2002; EPD 2003a).

Before the economic slowdown, some air pollution at the local level also came from dust raised by construction. In the mid-1990s, for example, many of Hong Kong's seven pollution-reporting stations at the time reported dust levels exceeding government standards, even at roof-top level, where the stations are located. This particular problem has been partially alleviated by the recession. In 1995, Hong Kong introduced air quality alerts that warn people of conditions under which those with respiratory or heart problems are advised to stay indoors. This was a critical problem for many people; respiratory problems led to 600 deaths in 1995, and asthma killed about ninety people per year at that time, one-third of them under thirty-five years of age. Such alerts have actually only been issued infrequently since. Their implementation called attention to the serious nature of the problem. While many expected the situation to become more serious, Hong Kong seems to have made some modest progress at halting the worsening air quality (AsiaWeek 1996; HKISD 2002; EPD 2003a).

Water quality was also poor in several of Hong Kong's harbors a decade ago. Again, the government started taking some action in the 1990s, sometimes more forcefully than it did with air pollution problems. In industrial areas, much progress has been made in halting the large-scale dumping of chemical waste into the sewage system or local waters. There are still many areas that are highly polluted, but substantial progress has been made. In 2002, for example, thirty-three beaches met water quality standards, compared to twenty-four in 1995. Only 15 percent of monitoring stations along rivers had bad or very bad water quality, compared to half at the beginning of the 1990s. Total metal discharge into waterways has been reduced to 2,000 kilograms per day from 7,000 kilograms per day in 1993 (Siddall 1991; HKISD 2002; EPD 2003b).

Many people in Hong Kong have become concerned about pollution. As early as 1989, a general survey found that pollution ranked as the fourth most important concern, after several worries regarding the looming return to China (Chau 1990). A survey in 1990 had nearly 20 percent responding that pollution was a "very serious" social problem, and a further 54 percent said it was "serious" (Wan 1991). A survey in 1993 showed that, among a list of environmental issues, people were most concerned with air and water pollution, but the level of concern was only moderate, not strong. People who developed more environmental awareness began to worry more about recycling, reducing waste, and reusing some materials. Younger and more educated people began to change consumption behavior, for example, by purchasing recycled or recyclable products (Chan 1994). However, even at the time of this writing, recycling is not yet a very strong trend compared to developed economies in the West and Japan.

Some observers believe that the nature of environmental problems is changing as Hong Kong undergoes structural change in the economy. For example, Hills (2002) argued that environmental problems related to production are moving to Guangdong province as Hong Kong manufacturing moves there. He cited data showing the steady downward trend in energy usage per Hong Kong dollar of output. Energy usage in Hong Kong by this measure is similar in efficiency to that in Japan and is substantially more efficient than in other developed economies of Asia, including Korea, Singapore, and Taiwan. Waste generated is steadily increasing, but Hong Kong is managing waste more efficiently, so that waste generated per capita is declining slowly but steadily. Freshwater consumption per unit of GDP generated and per capita is also declining. Although Hong Kong still has a way to go in cleaning up the environment, figures such as these indicate fairly strong progress in becoming more environmentally friendly.

Shifting the focus of environmental attention will require more use of recyclable materials in consumption, clean technologies in product usage rather than product production, and a shift away from focus on industrial waste in waste management programs (Hills 2002). Quality of life environmental issues are coming to the forefront in Hong Kong, and the government is already addressing environmental issues related to quality of life on a number of fronts. For example, it has implemented a scheme to increase the amount of green space in urban areas (HKLA 2003e). As in many other areas, the government has its critics who say that it should be more concerned about the environment. As in many other areas, there are a number of fairly active civic groups that have some ability to influence policy through public pressure and the legal system. Hong Kong has some fairly strong environmental legislation that the courts are willing to enforce. For example, in a legal battle that has gone on for several years, the Court of Final Appeal finally ruled in January 2004 that the government's land reclamation project in Victoria Harbor failed to meet the legal justification for overriding environmental legislation about harbor reclamation (HKL December 2003; *International Herald Tribune [IHT]* 2004b).

Expectations

Generally, confidence in the long-term future remained at relatively low levels during the 1990s, mainly because of political uncertainty leading up to 1997. Surveys in 1995, for example, showed that 60 percent of respondents had little or no faith in post-1997 leaders, and that 38 percent of younger people would emigrate if possible (EIU 1996). The return to China went relatively smoothly, however, and not much changed for the average citizen. Thus, consumers became more confident for several years after 1997, even feeling somewhat insulated from the Asian economic crisis for a few years. In more recent years, however, consumer confidence has been volatile, and the mood has frequently been gloomy. A number of short-term shocks, seeming recoveries, and then relapses have damaged confidence (*The Bulletin* 2001; ACNielsen February 7, 2002). Consumer spending dropped in 2002 (HKISD 2002), and SARS depressed it in early 2003 (ACNielsen June 25, 2003), but spending was recovering by late 2003 (Hong Kong Retail Management Association [HKRMA] 2003c). Overall, economic prospects seemed much better for 2004 (HKTDC 2004).

Consumers remained worried about job security and health (reflecting the economy and SARS), but sentiment was picking up strongly by the end of 2003. About two-thirds of consumers believed that the economy would improve over the next year. This was translating into greater willingness to spend, and 86 percent of respondents in an ACNielsen survey said they would be spending more on nonessentials. New clothes, out-of-home entertainment, and new technology were particularly strong categories in which they planned to buy more (ACNielsen November 26, 2003). By the end of the year, consumers were confident enough about the future to resume higher spending, and sales in December 2003 were strong (HKRMA 2003c; *IHT* 2004a). The Hong Kong General Chamber of Commerce's annual business prospects survey in October–November 2003 showed that business sentiment was also strong by the end of the year (*The Bulletin* 2003d).

PRICES AND EXPENDITURE

The Hong Kong government computes several price indices designed to summarize changes in prices for baskets of goods and services typical of different income levels. In the late 1980s and early 1990s, Hong Kong recorded inflation rates at around 10–11 percent, and the different CPIs did not diverge much from each other. By 1994, overall inflation had been slowed somewhat, so that the composite inflation rate (whole population) was about 8.8 percent (HKCSD 1995). In the 1990s, inflation diverged slightly in the different indices calculated by the government. Prices went up somewhat more strongly for many goods purchased by higher-income households, especially for housing. Prices for the sort of housing that the higher income brackets normally purchased rose at a rate of 14.6 percent in 1994 (HKCSD 1995). The inflation rate for upper-income housing remained high up until the return to China in 1997, as indicated by the CPI (Hang Seng) in Table 4.39, but the rates across the several CPI indices became more consistent on other categories of consumer expenditure.

Economic problems put a halt to inflation, and since 1999, Hong Kong has seen price deflation. Prices declined several percent annually on most goods and services, while deflation in the property markets was somewhat steeper. Consumers generally did not feel as if they gained much from deflation, especially because of the sharp decline in housing prices. The high rate of home ownership in Hong Kong led many consumers to feel that their asset base was shrinking rapidly, especially as many of them ended up owing more on their mortgages than the market value of their flats. In October 2003, housing prices were down about 66 percent from their peak in 1997 (*AEN* November 8, 2002; HKTDC 2003c). By the end of 2003, however, confidence was beginning to return, and some consumers, especially first-time home buyers, were beginning to view the more affordable housing as a benefit and began to anticipate that asset appreciation would return as the economy got back on track (United Press International [UPI] October 22, 2003). Although prices overall declined slightly in 2003, prices for some goods and services were again showing modest inflation, and public housing rents rose by over 11 percent (HKLA 2003f; Table 4.40).

Table 4.39

Prices and Change in Prices, 1996–2002

Consumer price index	1996	1997	1998	1999	2000	2001	2002
CPI (A)	97.6	103.2	105.9	102.5	99.5	97.8	94.7
CPI (B)	99.7	105.5	108.5	103.4	99.4	97.7	91.7
CPI (Hang Seng)	98.6	104.6	107.9	103.9	99.3	97.8	95.1
Percent change in prices over previous year							
CPI (A)	6.0	5.7	2.6	−3.3	−3.0	−1.7	−3.2
Food	4.0	3.7	1.9	−2.2	−2.4	−1.0	−2.2
Housing	9.4	9.1	3.1	−4.5	−6.2	−3.6	−5.7
Miscellaneous service	6.9	4.9	4.2	−0.6	#	2.7	
CPI (B)	6.4	5.8	2.8	−4.7	−3.9	−1.6	−3.1
Food	4.0	3.7	2.1	−2.1	−2.1	−1.0	−2.1
Housing	9.9	8.5	4.4	−6.8	−8.2	−2.8	−5.9
Miscellaneous service	6.5	4.8	3.3	−1.4	−0.4	0.5	
CPI (Hang Seng)	6.6	6.1	3.2	−3.7	−4.5	−1.5	−2.8
Food	3.5	3.3	1.9	−0.8	−1.9	−0.2	−1.7
Housing	11.2	10.2	6.4	−3.6	−9.9	−2.8	−5.5
Miscellaneous service	5.0	3.7	0.8	−1.7	−0.2	0.2	

Sources: Hong Kong Census and Statistics Department (HKCSD), *Monthly Report on the Consumer Price Index, April 2003* (Hong Kong: Government Printing Department, Hong Kong Special Administrative Region, 2003); HKCSD, *Hong Kong Social and Economic Trends, 2001 Edition* (Hong Kong: Government Printing Department, Hong Kong Special Administrative Region, 2001).

Notes: In the consumer price index, October 1999–September 2000 = 100; # < 0.05.

Despite relatively high inflation and worry about the 1997 issue (or perhaps because of these things), consumer spending soared during the decade leading up to the return to China, and Hong Kong became a major East Asian market for a host of foreign products. Spending increases outpaced the increase in GDP during these years. However, the economic problems of the past several years drastically slowed Hong Kong consumers' free spending ways. Overall spending has remained fairly stagnant since 2000, but the balance is shifting slightly. For example, the proportion of nonfood products to total retail sales declined from 1998 to 2001. In 2001, food retail sales increased by 2.6 percent over those of 2000, but nonfood retail sales declined by 2.5 percent. In particular, Hong Kong consumers were spending less on discretionary goods (*Euromonitor* 2003b). The latest figures suggest that consumer sentiment was improving slightly by the end of 2003, and the number of consumers planning to spend more in the near future was climbing. While retail sales were down overall for the year, in the fourth quarter, growth over the previous year's sales was seen (HKRMA 2003c).

The last extensive household expenditure survey was taken in 1999–2000, early on in Hong Kong's economic difficulties. At that time, average monthly spending was about HK$21,797 per household (HKCSD 2000a). Of course, the range of expenditure was large. Approximately 28 percent of households had monthly expenditure per person of under HK$3,750. Expenditure per head of households defined as living under the poverty level was only HK$2,520 per month, while average household expenditure among the top 10 percent of households was nearly HK$74,000 per month. Food and housing account for about 58 percent of overall household expenditure in Hong Kong (Table 4.41). On average, about 35 percent of spending is housing related, including a few percent for electricity, gas, and water. About 26 percent is for food (HKCSD 2000a; Laurent 2003; Wong, H. 2003).

Table 4.40

Consumer Price Indices and Year-on Change for Selected Product and Service Categories, November 2003

	CPI (A)		CPI (B)		CPI (C)	
	Index for Nov. 2003	Percent change over Nov. 2002	Index for Nov. 2003	Percent change over Nov. 2002	Index for Nov. 2003	Percent change over Nov. 2002
Food	94.5	−1.3	94.7	−1.2	96.0	−1.8
Meals bought away from home	96.3	−0.8	95.7	−1.0	98.4	−2.0
Food, excluding meals away from home	92.1	−1.9	92.9	−1.7	91.9	−1.4
Housing	85.6	−3.1	83.3	−6.0	81.8	−7.9
Private housing rent	81.3	−6.8	81.2	−7.3	80.0	−8.9
Public housing rent	99.5	+11.5	99.5	+11.5	—	—
Electricity, gas, and water	92.6	+1.4	94.3	+1.3	96.2	+1.1
Alcoholic drinks and tobacco	106.1	−0.4	105.8	−0.5	104.5	−0.6
Clothing and footwear	102.2	+0.9	102.5	+0.6	100.8	+5.1
Durable goods	80.3	−4.9	78.8	−5.5	80.4	−5.8
Miscellaneous goods	107.1	+2.1	107.3	+3.5	110.0	+5.9
Transport	98.2	−1.0	99.1	−0.1	99.8	+1.2
Miscellaneous services	91.5	−4.0	93.7	−3.0	94.7	−3.0
Educational services	103.8	+0.2	103.8	+0.2	105.8	+0.5
Telephone and other communications services	70.5	−15.7	67.3	−17.0	68.0	−15.3
Medical services	105.0	+4.4	103.9	+2.2	101.2	+0.7
All items	92.2	−1.8	91.6	−2.5	91.8	−2.8

Source: Hong Kong Looking Ahead (HKLA), "Decline in Consumer Prices Narrows" (News, Hong Kong Government Information Centre, December 22, 2003), available at www.info.gov.hk/gia/general/200312/22/c1e.htm accessed January 2004.

Note:

Index	Approximate proportion of population covered	Monthly expenditure range
CPI (A)	50	4,300–17,500
CPI (B)	30	17,500–30,900
CPI (C)	10	30,900–62,700

Expenditure patterns vary somewhat by expenditure level, which is closely correlated with household income. Roughly half of spending in lower-income households is for food, but, except for the bottom 10 percent of households, housing expenses account for only about a quarter of expenditure. Spending on food increases with expenditure level but declines as a percentage of budget. In the top half of households, food accounts for about 19 percent of expenditure, and in the top 10 percent of households, it is about 10 percent of expenditure. The amount spent on housing increases substantially with income and expenditure level, so that the top half of households still spend nearly half of expenditure on housing. However, the top 10 percent of households spends only about 30 percent on housing (HKCSD 2000a; Laurent 2003; Wong, H. 2003).

The recession in Hong Kong, concern that there is still poverty and a growing income gap between the rich and the rest of Hong Kong society have contributed to the gloomy outlook of many consumers. However, this should not obscure the basic fact that by world standards, Hong

Table 4.41

Average Monthly Household Expenditure by Commodity/Service

Product category	October–December 1999	January–March 2000	April–June 2000	July–September 2000	Overall
Food	24.8	26.7	25.7	25.6	25.7
Housing	34.0	31.7	31.6	31.5	32.2
Electricity, gas, water	3.3	2.5	2.5	3.3	2.9
Alcoholic drinks, tobacco	0.9	1.0	1.5	0.9	1.1
Clothing and footwear	5.1	4.6	4.6	3.4	4.4
Durable goods	3.5	4.8	4.6	5.1	4.5
Miscellaneous goods	5.0	5.1	4.3	4.8	4.8
Transport	8.8	8.6	9.7	9.9	9.3
Miscellaneous services	14.6	15.1	15.5	15.5	15.2
All categories	100.0	100.0	100.0	100.0	100.0

Number of households (average household size = 4.16)   1,624,000
Average monthly expenditure (HK$)   21,797

Source: Hong Kong Census and Statistics Department (HKCSD), *1999/2000 Household Expenditure Survey and the Debasing of the Consumer Price Indices* (Hong Kong: Government Printing Department, Hong Kong Special Administrative Region, 2000).

Kong remains an affluent society with a developed economy. One indication of Hong Kong's prosperity is the ownership of consumer electronics products, which was already extensive by the mid-1990s. Already in 1995, an estimated 98 percent of households owned at least one TV set, and 34 percent owned two or more. Three-quarters of households also owned a videocassette recorder, while 38 percent owned the more expensive laser disc player for watching movies at home (*Asian Advertising and Marketing* [*AA&M*] 1996a). Technology has moved on in the past several years, and Hong Kong consumers have kept up with it. A good indicator is that about two-thirds of all households in Hong Kong now have a personal computer (PC) in their home, and 88 percent of all PC households are connected to the Internet (HKLA 2003d).

CONSUMERS AND HEALTH CARE

General levels of health in Hong Kong are similar to the standards for most advanced industrial countries, and basic indicators compare favorably to those of other advanced economies. Life expectancy at birth for men was 78.7 in 2002 and 84.7 for women. The infant mortality rate was 2.4 per 1,000 live births, which represents substantial progress over the already low figure of 4.0 in 1997. In terms of hospital beds, doctors, and other medical personnel, Hong Kong already had good figures in 1997 and continues to make progress. For example, there were 5.2 doctors and dentists per 1,000 population, and 6.4 registered nurses (HKCSD 2003a). Even critics agree that the quality of basic medical and health services is high.

Government policy stipulates that everyone should have access to adequate medical treatment, regardless of means. In the public system, the government has recently revamped the fee structure to reduce waste and misuse of the system, but government subsidy of costs still remains at about 96 percent of costs, on average, according to government figures (HKISD 2002). Patients are free to choose between private medical care, for which they pay themselves, or public care, which has only nominal costs. The basic care in public institutions is good, but suffers from certain problems. Critics feel that the government is inefficient in service delivery, has crowded conditions, long waiting times, and impersonal services. These are fair observations, but on the other hand, the public system must provide for some 94 percent of hospital care, an expensive, but largely subsidized aspect of health care. Meanwhile, the private sector gains about 80 percent of outpatient services, and half of all consumer expenditures are in the private sector (Harvard School of Public Health [HSPH] 1999; Amersbach 2000; Ho 2002).

Medical care funding comes from the government, insurance, and out-of-pocket payments. Insurance coverage for medical and health issues has been growing rapidly but has traditionally been weak and remains probably the smallest source of funds for medical care among these three (HSPH 1999; HKISD 2002). Growth of health insurance was stimulated during the boom years of the 1990s, when comprehensive health-care insurance became an important incentive that companies used to attract and keep employees. However, this factor has been less important during the recession. Gross premiums for accident and health insurance in the first three quarters of 2003 were HK$3.2 billion, representing 18 percent of all insurance premiums. This represents an 18 percent increase in gross premiums compared to the same three quarters in 2000, but this category of insurance has been growing somewhat more slowly over the past several years than has the insurance industry overall (Hong Kong Office of the Commissioner of Insurance [HKOCI] 2003).

The majority of private expenditure is probably still from out-of-pocket expenses, rather than from insurance or benefits coverage. In 1999, 53 percent of the population had no benefits or private insurance coverage for medical expenses (HSPH 1999). Still, mainly those with expensive chronic diseases or those with low incomes showed strong preference for public hospitals and clinics. Most consumers would prefer the private sector, where they perceive service to be better (HSPH 1999; Amersbach 2000; Ho 2002).

Consumer spending on medicines in the 1999/2000 Household Expenditure Survey averaged about HK$105 monthly, or about 0.5 percent of household expenditure. Spending on medical services was HK$480, about 2.2 percent of monthly expenditure. The amounts have increased, but the patterns of expenditure have not changed substantially from the previous expenditure survey in 1989/1990 (HKCSD 2003a; Mak 2003). Low-income households spend very little out of their own pockets, because they rely mainly on public-sector health care. The proportion of those seeking private health care, and paying private-sector prices from their own pocket, increases as income increases. However, estimates indicate that total expenditure does not diverge too widely across income deciles (HSPH 1999).

Despite preferences for the private health-care sector, many consumers have low expectations when they visit a doctor or clinic, but they do expect the doctor to give them medicine. Surveys from the early 1990s show that around 80 percent want this, and they also show that the vast majority have used over-the-counter (OTC) medication before visiting a clinic. A survey of doctors has shown that 42 percent believe medication should be given for every consultation. Another survey of clinic patients found that doctors issue an average of over three different medicines per visit. But, 70 percent of respondents in this survey left clinics without learning their diagnosis (Huang 1991; Wong 1991; Hay 1992). The Harvard study in 1999 indicates that little has changed regarding these issues, which the report considers a serious weakness in the health care system (HSPH 1999).

This inability to get much information from doctors continues (HSPH 1999; Amersbach 2000) and is a major source of dissatisfaction. Consumers would like more complete information, but the health-care culture is not open about giving it. As a result, many people want to provide their own treatment if it is relatively simple. The OTC market expanded rapidly until the recession hit, especially as many pharmaceuticals shifted from prescription drugs, available only through doctors, to OTC medicines. However, trends have shifted somewhat in recent years, with many consumers not ready to shift from prescription drugs to stronger or more specialized medicines about which they feel they are less knowledgeable. The OTC market has seen only very slow growth lately, and the major pharmaceutical brands have shifted their attention to products requiring prescription. Cheaper generics or unknown brands are becoming important at the lower end of the market, and some local companies supply this market. However, the large, affluent middle class mainly demands branded products that they can trust to be effective (*Euromonitor* 2003a; Mak 2003).

The SAR government strongly backs consumer rights to information about pharmaceuticals and to safe products. Hong Kong has a fairly strict regulatory system for modern medicines and pharmaceuticals. Traditionally, there has been less attention paid to health supplements and traditional Chinese medicines, but that has been changing over the past several years. New laws and regulations, implemented since 1999, require registration of Chinese medicine practitioners and licensing of Chinese medicine traders. Many traditional medicines must also be licensed and, frequently, must demonstrate adherence to minimum manufacturing standards. Generally, such traditional medicines and supplements must follow labeling requirements, the same as other medicines and foods, including an insert describing safe and recommended usage. There are also fairly strict regulations about how all sorts of medicines can be advertised, designed to eliminate any claims that the medicines cannot substantiate with scientific proof. For example, it is illegal to advertise that any medicine can prevent SARS, because no medicine is yet known to be very effective (Ho 2003).

High living standards and educational levels also bring some awareness of health issues, as do cultural and social influences. For example, smoking peaked in Hong Kong around 1970 and has been slowly declining since. In 2000, about 14.4 percent of residents age fifteen or above smoked, down from almost 25 percent in 1984. It is not as common for adults to smoke as it is in many Western and many other Asian countries, especially among women. About 22 percent of men were daily smokers in 2000, down from 40 percent in 1982, and only 3.5 percent of women were daily smokers in 2000, down from almost 6 percent (Hong Kong Tobacco Control Office [HKTCO] 2003). Thus, diseases and birth complications associated with smoking are less common than in many other countries. Nevertheless, the higher incidence of smoking twenty years ago seems to be working its way through to mortality among middle-aged men today. One study estimates that approximately one-third of deaths among men ages thirty-five to sixty-nine could be related to smoking. Only 5 percent of deaths among similarly aged women are likely to be attributable to smoking (Lam et al. 2001).

Hong Kong started implementing regulations on smoking in public places and on marketing tobacco products at least two decades ago. By now, the regulations have become fairly strong. Advertising of tobacco products is banned from many media, smoking in most public buildings is prohibited, and packaging must carry strong warnings. Certainly, such regulations play a role in the downward trends in smoking in the SAR, but generally, there seems to be moderately good public support for regulation. For example, a survey of large restaurant owners shows that the majority of them feel that requirements to provide large no-smoking sections had either benefited business or had little effect (HKTCO 2003). Apparently, most of the public feels comfortable with some level of restriction on smoking.

The Chinese diet is an additional factor that leads to far less obesity and its associated health problems than does the Western diet. Affluence has started to change this, and there is some concern now that too many Hong Kong youngsters and some adults are becoming overweight. In 1997, an estimated 11 percent of primary school children suffered from obesity, according to a government study (Public Health and Epidemiology Bulletin [PHEB] May 1997). However, by comparison, this problem is much less prevalent in Hong Kong than in the West, and now there is a countertrend of increasing health consciousness and concern about proper diet. These few examples illustrate that the health issues in Hong Kong are similar to those in advanced, developed economies and are not similar to the situation in developing economies of Asia. Patterns of diseases and mortality are roughly similar to those in Japan and the advanced Western countries. Many things in Hong Kong's culture and lifestyle reduce the likelihood of some serious public health problems more common in the developed West. Nevertheless, some critics believe that policy has not adapted quickly enough for dealing with the continuing shift toward health needs characteristic of an aging population in a developed economy (HSPH 1999; HKCSD 2002b; Ho 2003).

Further, recently with respect to SARS, there has been some concern that some elements of traditional foods and food marketing might contribute to the spread of communicable diseases, and that the government is not capable of dealing with such emergencies. The scare over the link between civet cats and the SARS virus is just a variation on a theme that surfaces intermittently. For example, fish tanks for displaying fresh fish in restaurants and markets have occasionally been linked to typhoid, and bird flu causes occasional scares about chicken. While the bird flu scare of 2004–5 got worldwide attention, it is actually not an unusual problem, although during this period it was on a much larger scale. Hong Kong, however, was barely affected, but poultry imports from many countries were temporarily banned. The minimal impact was partly because public health officials remained on top of things; the government even has a Web site with extensive information about avian flu (HKCSD 2002b; Hong Kong SARS Expert Committee [HKSEC] 2003; Hong Kong Team Clean [HKTC] 2003; HKGIC 2004; PHEB 2004).

These sorts of problems receive front-page treatment, and the government draws criticism for not having anticipated the problem or not reacting fast enough to it. In reality, though, most such problems are isolated; once they surface, they are handled, and the problem is reduced. In 2003 SARS was the worst of these sorts of scares, and it was certainly a serious problem, causing a number of deaths. Nevertheless, it was contained fairly rapidly. It is likely to resurface on an annual basis, but the government is now experienced at dealing with it, and most projections are that it will be far less serious (HKSEC 2003). Much of Hong Kong's problem with SARS in 2003 emanated from Beijing's ineffectual responses; indicators suggest that the problem is now taken seriously, and aggressive policies to contain it in the future are likely.

Improving the food marketing system is one aspect of public health related to these issues. Over the past decade, the government has invested a lot in upgrading the physical facilities in food markets, with hygiene as well as efficiency the key goals (Speece 1994; Access Asia 2001; United States Department of Agriculture/Foreign Agriculture Service [USDA/FAS] 2003c, 2003d).

FOOD CONSUMPTION PATTERNS

The average monthly household food expenditure in Hong Kong was just over HK$5,600 in 2000, the time of the most recent detailed survey on expenditure. This represents an average of about one-fourth of household expenditure (see Table 4.41 above), and up to an estimated 60 percent of the food expenditure is made in restaurants. Households with less money spend up to half of disposable income on foodstuffs. However, Cantonese truly love to eat. As their incomes rise, they spend much more on food than needed simply to improve their diet somewhat. The

Table 4.42

Indicators of Restaurant Performance by Store Type

Type of restaurant	Number of stores	Number of persons engaged	Sales per type (US$ million)
Chinese	5,520	108,275	4,468
Non-Chinese	3,684	57,422	2,214
Fast food	1,152	36,569	1,551
Bars	594	5,296	243
Other types	603	4,214	156
Total	11,553	211,776	8,632

Source: United States Department of Agriculture, Foreign Agriculture Service (USDA/FAS), "Hong Kong HRI Food Service Sector Report 2003" [Global Agriculture Information Network, GAIN Report #HK3019.], (Washington, DC: USDA), available at www.fas.usda.gov/gainfiles/200305/145885744.pdf, accessed March 2003; based on HKCSD data.

100,000 households with highest expenditure levels spend US$1,000 or more per month on food (drawn from Speece 1994, numerous consulting projects on food products conducted by Speece and So in the 1990s, updated with additional sources as noted—HKCSD 2000a; USDA/FAS 2003b, 2003d).

Diet in Hong Kong is still thoroughly oriented toward Chinese, and especially Cantonese, cuisine. Western food, though, is becoming increasingly popular, especially in restaurants and fast-food outlets. Roughly half of the 11,500 restaurants estimated to exist in Hong Kong may have nonlocal cuisine (Table 4.42), and many Chinese restaurants seem to be putting a few Western items on the menu. Higher-income consumers are most likely to visit Western restaurants. However, fast-food restaurants are popular among all income levels. All types of restaurants have enjoyed strong growth, but fast-food restaurants have far outpaced other types (USDA/FAS 2003b).

As they become more affluent, many Chinese start eating some foods at home that one would expect to be eaten in the West, even though the style of preparation may remain Chinese. For example, pork, chicken, and seafood are the traditional meats in the Chinese diet, but beef sales have been expanding dramatically in the past decade. Lower-income households eat mostly pork, usually imported from greater China. Higher-income families eat more meat, including beef, imported from Western countries and Latin America. Fresh vegetables are traditional, but the use of Western vegetables, such as bell peppers or broccoli, has been increasing. Rice makes up a higher proportion of expenditure in less-affluent families. Higher-income families shift toward grains and processed products common in Western diets, such as bread, cakes, and biscuits (HKCSD 2000a, 2003a).

More affluent consumers are demanding more variety in food products, and younger people actively seek new products. Many people are becoming more concerned about hygiene, which affects the types of restaurants and retail stores they visit. As noted below in more detail, this is one key factor behind the shift away from purchasing fresh food in the traditional markets toward buying in the modern retail sector, mainly supermarkets. They are paying more attention to the ingredients in food and are beginning to demand complete information on package labels. Freshness, always important in Chinese cooking, has become critical to many consumers, and has led to stagnant sales of many processed products, such as canned foods (USDA/FAS 2003b, 2003d).

The high labor-force participation rate among women has also led to increasing demands for convenience. This is partly reflected in the large share of total food expenditure allocated to restaurants. In part, the need for convenience translates into the use of convenience foods in home cooking. To some extent, consumers are spending more on convenience food, such as frozen meals, and less on fresh food. Frozen dim sum sales have grown, for example, which retailers attribute to its convenience, low price, and quality. One survey showed that consumers who ate at home were buying about 20 percent more convenience and frozen food in 2002 than in 2001, reducing the consumption of fresh foods (USDA/FAS 2003d). However, convenience is also behind the increasing popularity of precut and preseasoned packaged fresh meat and vegetables. Such ready-to-cook fresh food has become more popular. The major supermarket chains have started catering to the desire for both processed convenience foods and preprepared fresh foods. Many of them have "convenience food" counters and deli counters (USDA/FAS 2003d).

Health issues started becoming important in food choice long ago. For example, organic vegetables grown in Hong Kong started gaining some acceptance in the early 1990s, despite prices that were generally 15–30 percent higher than for other produce. In 1991, a small random sample ($n = 93$) of lower-middle-class to middle-class residents showed that over one-fifth were likely to choose organically grown vegetables. Similarly, canned and packaged foods without monosodium glutamate (MSG) and beverages without artificial additives were each preferred by about 15 percent. One-quarter of respondents said they were very likely, and another third somewhat likely, to switch brands if they saw a new brand advertised that stressed green characteristics (Tong 1991). The trend has continued, and now the mass markets in Hong Kong are much more conscious of and aware of health and nutrition and environmental and food safety issues in food purchase (USDA/FAS 2003d). Packaging laws are soon likely to require more detailed nutritional information, but even at present, it is good marketing for many products to provide full information about nutritional content.

However, expanded supply of products, such as organically grown vegetables, has brought some problems with quality control. While many consumers are willing to pay a little more, in theory, for organically grown food products or many other types of foods perceived as being healthier, they do not trust the claims made about many such products. Therefore, in practice, they do not actually think the products are worth a price premium (USDA/FAS 2003b, 2003d).

Nevertheless, some products have been successfully positioned as being healthy. Milk sales, for example, surged in 2001 as a result of aggressive marketing promoting its health benefits as one of the best sources of calcium. Some Asians are lactose intolerant, so some major brands have launched lactose-reduced milk. In addition, adult consumers are concerned about fat content and are particularly interested in low-fat milk. A number of other products have successfully been positioned as being healthy, including breakfast cereals, chewing gum, soy drinks, drinks containing fruit juice, and ready-to-drink teas. Breakfast cereals and soy drinks are promoted as health food items. Marketers have been very creative in positioning chewing gum as an effective cold remedy (USDA/FAS 2003d).

This greater consciousness of health and nutrition translates into stronger consumer attention to label information. Hong Kong laws require that certain information be placed on labels of prepackaged foods, including the following:

- Name of the food
- List of ingredients
- Indication of "best before" or "use by" date
- Statement of special conditions for storage or instruction for use
- Name and address of manufacturer or packer
- Count, weight, or volume

The labeling can be in either English or Chinese, but if the package has both languages (i.e., if the product is positioned for both the more cosmopolitan and more traditional segments of consumers), then the label must contain the information in both languages. As of 2003, there were no specific requirements for the formatting of nutritional information labeling, and the information could be in the form of home country requirements, where the home country has good reporting (i.e., usually developed-country products). The government was discussing new labeling legislation in 2003 and is likely to implement more strict labeling requirements by 2005 (USDA/FAS 2003a). However, regardless of regulation, many consumers are looking for such information, and packages are likely to gain better consumer response when they include it in a format that is easy to read and understand.

Price has become relatively unimportant in buying decisions for the majority of consumers, provided that they believe they are getting the benefits they want. Surveys on a wide variety of products have shown that only a small proportion of the market is typically price oriented. The Hong Kong consumer is invariably looking for better quality, based on whatever criteria he or she considers important—freshness, nutrition, taste, sanitary conditions, and many others (Kawahara and Speece 1994; Speece, Kawahara and So 1994; Speece, So, Kawahara, and Milner 1994). Consumers trust and prefer popular brands, frequently from the West, though in recent years, local brands have become strong. One survey carried out by a supermarket chain in 2003 showed that the top ten most popular product brands were Amoy dim sum, Coca-Cola, Doll dim sum, Dreyer's ice cream, Lee Kum Kee oyster sauce, Mr. Juicy orange juice, Nestle Dairy Farm fresh milk, Nissin instant noodle, Vitasoy soy milk, and Yakult lactic drink (USDA/FAS 2003d).

Hong Kong consumers, however, are still value oriented, which means that they are ready to shift to a lower-priced alternative if they believe there is no sacrifice in quality. As local brands develop modern versions of local Chinese foods, such as frozen dim sum, many consumers shift to them, as indicated by the two dim sum brands among the top ten brands. Frequently, the local brands are cheaper, but the real reason for the shift is that consumers find them to be of good quality, and they fit into the normal diet more readily than do many foreign brands (Kawahara and Speece 1994; Speece, Kawahara and So 1994; Speece et al. 1994; Speece 1998; USDA/FAS 2003d).

One key trend in consumer spending psychology in recent years has been a shift toward value for money, in food purchases as well as across a whole range of product categories. The strong value orientation already present in Hong Kong (Speece 1998) has been reinforced by the recession, as consumers have had to learn how to save some money without substantially sacrificing their living standards. Consumers have become more sophisticated, careful shoppers and are somewhat bored with the traditional brands that cost more but are no longer perceived as delivering any substantial difference in quality (Access Asia 2001)

The recession has also fostered a slight shift toward more bulk buying. Some consumers want to save money by gaining lower unit costs without having to shift from their favorite brands (Access Asia 2001). However, limited living space in Hong Kong makes it inconvenient for most consumers to store many food products. Therefore, food products packaged in bulk do not sell very well as compared with sales in many Western markets, and smaller-sized packaged food products are generally preferred (USDA/FAS 2003d).

RETAIL SALES AND RETAIL OUTLETS

Estimated total retail trade in 2003 was about HK$172.9 billion, which represents the results of a steady decline for several years (HKCSD 2003a; HKRMA 2004). In terms of employment and

Table 4.43

Retail Stores, Employment, and Sales

	Number of establishments	Number of persons engaged	Number of employees	Sales and other receipts ($ million)
1985	48,030	168,496	109,609	73,130.8
1990	53,844	194,723	132,380	156,190.0
1995	55,895	224,651	151,553	261,364.1
1996	56,500	232,978	159,948	276,568.8
1997	53,502	244,255	170,658	283,340.6
1998	49,282	200,288	145,785	223,894.1
1999	47,841	188,371	128,617	206,257.8
2000	49,173	193,764	135,288	213,379.6
2001	49,680	194,872	135,161	206,496.7
2002	49,013	189,812	130,810	198,562.7

Source: Hong Kong Census and Statistics Department (HKCSD), *Hong Kong in Figures* (Hong Kong: Government of the Hong Kong Special Administrative Region, 2003), available at www.info.gov.hk/censtatd/eng/hkstat/fas/hes/hes.htm, accessed December 2003.

sales revenues, retailing reached its peak in 1997, when total retail trade was worth HK$283.3 billion (Table 4.43). Retailing is now dominated by the modern sector, which became strong several decades ago. During the 1980s, department stores and large chains became increasingly popular, and by the 1990s, they were well entrenched. However, in the 1990s, smaller modern specialty stores also grew rapidly. They did not usually capture much market share from the large stores, although growth of the large stores slowed. Rather, growth of these specialty stores came mostly at the expense of smaller, more traditional stores. Large stores, however, are firmly entrenched in Hong Kong's retail scene, and the traditional small-store sector is declining, though there are still numerous small, traditional stores. The trend over the past several years has been consolidation, not much growth, and a continued shift from the traditional sector and other small stores to large-scale modern retailing.

In 2000, there were nearly 50,000 nonrestaurant retail stores (Table 4.44), approximately 10,000 fewer stores than a decade earlier. Most losses were from among the numerous small stores. Still, over 96 percent of retail stores in 2000 engaged fewer than ten persons. (In small stores, especially in the more traditional sector, many of the people engaged are not employees but family members; this accounts for the discrepancy between "engaged" and "employees" noted in Table 4.43.) However, these small stores accounted for fewer than 39 percent of sales revenue. Sales are increasingly concentrated in the larger stores. In 2000, the twelve top stores with more than 1,000 employees accounted for about 25 percent of retail sales. In the 1992 figures, eight stores of this size accounted for around 11 percent of retail sales (HKCSD 1994, 2001b).

Two major chains dominate the modern sector of retailing. AS Watson & Co. Ltd. (Hutchison Whampoa) was the leading retailer in both 2000 and 2001, but Dairy Farm Management Services Ltd. was a close second and occupied the top ranking the year before. AS Watson operates Park 'n Shop supermarkets, ranked first in the supermarket subsector, and Fortress electrical/electronics/computer outlets, also first in its category. AS Watson also owns Watson's Your Personal Store chemists/druggists, which is second in its subsector. Dairy Farm owns the 7-Eleven convenience stores and Mannings chemists, which both were ranked at the top of their subsectors in 2001. They also own Wellcome, the second largest supermarket chain (*Euromonitor* 2003b).

The other main component of large modern-sector stores is the department stores. They more

Table 4.44

Indicators of Retail Performance by Store, Size

Number of persons engaged	Number of stores	Sales revenue (HK$ million)	Sales per store (HK$1,000)	Sales per person engaged (HK$1,000)	Sales per m² (HK$1,000)
<10	47,428	69,029	1,455	1,544	44,912
10–49	1,495	37,333	24,972	1,593	44,391
50–99	104	11,318	108,827	1,598	51,680
100–199	73	18,758	256,959	1,818	61,301
200–499	44	—	—	—	—
500–999	17	—	—	—	—
1,000 and over	12	41,391	3,449,250	1,763	48,926
Total	49,173	177,829	3,616	1,314	38,450

Source: Hong Kong Census and Statistics Department (HKCSD), *Hong Kong Annual Digest of Statistics, 2001 Edition* (Hong Kong: Government Printing Department, Hong Kong Special Administrative Region, 2001).

or less set the pace for many other retailers during the 1980s and into the 1990s but have lost some ground in recent years. One reason, already becoming critical before the recession, was that rents for floor space became increasingly expensive (HKRMA 2003a). This is a particular problem for large stores that makes it more difficult to operate stores with very large floor space profitably in the core downtown areas, where many were traditionally located. Another reason is that Hong Kong's recession has fostered a slight shift in purchasing away from department stores.

As have many other store formats, the department stores have established distinct images. Table 4.45 shows consumer perceptions of various department store market positioning in the early 1990s. While the images of a few stores might have shifted slightly, and a few stores have substantially reduced their presence in Hong Kong, the general pattern has not changed much. Several department stores, both Japanese and Western, such as Seibu and Lane Crawford, compete mainly in the high end of the market. The middle part of the department store market is dominated by Japanese and Western stores, although a few Chinese stores still compete. Mitsukoshi represents this strategy in Table 4.45, but most other Japanese stores, such as Sogo, Daimaru, or Tokyu, compete similarly.

These higher-end and mid-market department stores tend to be located in city centers, and many are located at major subway and metro stations, especially in TsimShaTsui (Kowloon) and Causeway Bay (Hong Kong Island). They suffered more during the recession from the combination of high rents and reduced consumer spending. The department stores are positioned slightly below this level, as lower-market to mid-market stores have more locations, and these locations are more widely spread throughout Hong Kong. These include many of the local Chinese department stores, such as Wing On and Sincere, and also several Japanese stores, such as Yaohan or Jusco (Lum 1990; Kong and Wong 1991; McGoldrick 1992; Phillips, Sternquist and Mui 1992; Kawahara and Speece 1994).

As noted, many of the stronger department stores are Japanese. By the early 1990s, eleven major Japanese department stores were present in Hong Kong, some with multiple stores, and they had captured over 40 percent of department store sales. Generally, younger consumers and those who consider themselves more modern and more concerned about their appearance tend to favor Japanese stores. They believe that the Japanese stores carry higher-quality goods than local stores and offer better atmosphere and better service. These consumers were not put off by the

Table 4.45

Consumer Perception of Department-Store Target Markets

	Percent of responders who think the target is:			
Store	Up-market	Mid-market	Lower-market	Don't know
Yaohan	3	41	55	1
Jusco	5	50	41	3
Wing On	3	41	56	—
Sincere	4	47	59	—
Mitsukoshi	23	70	10	1
Shui hing	29	50	18	3
Marks & Spencer	30	51	16	3
Lane Crawford	86	11	2	1
Seibu	52	22	1	25

Source: C.H. Kong and W.S. Wong, "An Opportunity Study for an American Department Store in Hong Kong," unpublished MBA thesis, Chinese University of Hong Kong, Hong Kong (1991), cited in Yukiko Kawahara and Mark. W. Speece, "Strategies of Japanese Supermarkets in Hong Kong," *International Journal of Retail and Distribution Management* 22, no. 8 (1994): 3–12.

Note: Seibu had opened less than a year before the survey, and some responders were not familiar with it.

perceived higher prices in the Japanese stores until the recession, but after 1997, the pricing has had some impact on the middle to higher-end stores.

Thus, much of Japanese retailing in Hong Kong has been particularly hard hit, as it relies strongly on the slightly upscale department stores. Several have withdrawn since the recession started in 1997, including Daimaru and Matsuzakaya. Yaohan also withdrew, but this had more to do with the failure of the parent company than with conditions in Hong Kong (Access Asia 2001). The few Japanese department store chains that positioned themselves as more local have suffered somewhat less from these problems, except for Yaohan, but as noted, Yaohan's problems were not mainly attributed to conditions in Hong Kong.

The concept of franchising has been catching on in Hong Kong in the past decade, in line with Hong Kong consumers becoming more affluent and more brand oriented. The number of franchise operations in Hong Kong grew from about fifty in 1992 to 130 by June 2003. Nearly 80 percent of the franchise operations in Hong Kong originate in the United States. Some local Hong Kong franchises have also developed, especially in catering and fashion wear, and some are expanding their franchises to Southeast Asia and China (Yung 2003).

In the more difficult retail market since 1997, many types of stores are suffering. Small shops that lack sufficient modern management expertise are losing sales, and a substantial number have gone out of business. Where more modern planning and management practices have been implemented, some have continued to be competitive, but even modern management cannot always overcome declining sales across the whole sector. One modern store format, the discount store, has gained a little ground during the recession. However, foreign discount stores not already present in Hong Kong have not perceived more inviting conditions, because the local stores have been good at adopting aspects of the discount format to keep their more price-sensitive customers. Carrefour, for example, a relatively recent discount store entrant, withdrew in 2000 (Access Asia 2001).

Tougher conditions have fostered some trends that will likely make the sector stronger in the future, for example, growing attention to customer service. Hong Kong has sometimes gotten a reputation for poor retail service, but the industry has been working hard to change the customer service mentality. The Hong Kong Retail Management Association (HKRMA) has taken an active role in this and has been conducting extensive mystery-shopper campaigns annually since the mid-1990s. Industry prizes and recognition are awarded to stores that score high on customer service, and the data serve as an industry benchmark to encourage others to strive for high service. HKRMA figures show substantial improvement in customer service from 1996 to 2003 (HKRMA 2003b).

Mail order and person-to-person direct selling are not popular, as consumers consider retail shopping a leisure activity. Direct sales account for less than 1 percent of total retail sales. However, direct sales have grown 5 to 10 percent annually from a small base during the recession. Many people who lost their jobs turned to direct selling, while others who suffered pay cuts joined direct-selling companies to augment their incomes (Yung 2003). Internet shopping is similarly quite small but may show slightly better long-term prospects for growth.

Food Retailing

Food retailing shows patterns similar to the general overall patterns. Total nonrestaurant retail sales of food and drinks in Hong Kong were just under HK$47 billion in 2002 and declined slightly in 2003 through the third quarter (USDA/FAS 2003d). Overall, the modern food retailing sector is becoming dominant, which is evident not so much in terms of numbers of shops but in sales. Numbers of shops continue to decline. There were around 21,000 nonrestaurant retail food establishments in 1992. Estimates for 2001 ranged from around 16,500 to 17,200 food establishments, most of which were small shops and wet market stalls. There were some eighty-two major modern-sector food retailers in 2001, but they had approximately 800 stores (HKCSD 1994; *Euromonitor* 2003b; USDA/FAS 2003d).

About 3,900 small greengrocers remained in 2001, including small neighborhood stores and wet markets (meat, fish, and produce). Small "mom-and-pop" shops sell snack foods and drink products, a similar food products mix to that of modern convenience stores. Most customers at small stores tend to be older and less educated, and to have low incomes. However, even many "modernized" Chinese shop for some foods in wet markets, primarily because they believe that many kinds of food are fresher in these markets. Wet markets move up to 80 percent of the retail sales of fresh foods. They are able to remain strong partly because they have changed gradually over the years. Newly built and renovated markets are air-conditioned, more sanitary, and more environmentally pleasant than the old ones. Many, but not all, stalls in wet markets have freezers and chilling equipment to help maintain food quality (Choy 1991; Speece 1994; *Euromonitor* 2003b; USDA/FAS 2003c, 2003d).

Although the trend toward fresh foods is still new, middle-class consumers have shifted much of their food shopping toward supermarkets. The supermarket category constitutes a small number of total retail food outlets, but its share of retail food sales rose from 44 percent in 1995 to 55 percent in 2002. This rise included an increasing tendency of supermarkets to expand their meat and produce sections, and they are now beginning to take some fresh food business away from traditional wet markets and greengrocers. The two large supermarket chains Park 'n Shop (around 244 outlets in 2003) and Wellcome (around 215 outlets) are the market leaders, accounting for around 80 percent of supermarket turnover. Both supermarkets work closely with real estate developers to open stores in strategic locations, thus maintaining their dominant market share (Kawahara and Speece 1994; *Euromonitor* 2003b; USDA/FAS 2003c, 2003d).

Many of the major nonlocal supermarkets are Japanese, located in Japanese department stores. As noted earlier, one set of Japanese stores focuses on the broad market of middle-class local consumers and defines the two major local chains as their main competition. Typical examples of these stores would be Yaohan or Jusco. The majority of the product assortment in these stores is oriented toward Chinese customers, but the stores have small sections for Japanese and Western foods, because many such items have been adopted as normal parts of the diet. This category of Japanese stores does not really compete on price compared to the local chains, and often sets trends in the introduction of new products and new merchandising techniques (Kawahara and Speece 1994; USDA/FAS 2003d).

Other Japanese supermarkets are more like specialty niche marketers. They stock a high percentage of Japanese products and target Japanese expatriates and local people who want a good selection of Japanese foods. There are also several small up-market chains (such as Lucullus and Oliver's) that cater mainly to Western expatriates and locals who have a taste for Western food products. These stores are located in major middle- to upper-class shopping districts rather than in the main residential areas. These Japanese- and Western-style supermarkets usually set premium prices and aim for up-market customers (Speece, Kawahara, and So 1993; Kawahara and Speece 1994; USDA/FAS 2003d).

In the past few years, the superstore concept has emerged, with huge stores offering the wide range of products and services that might be found in a shopping mall. For example, one Wellcome store has a floor area of 54,000 square feet. Among a wide range of products and services, it provides massage service, and a consulting office for a doctor specializing in Chinese medicine. The largest Park 'n Shop store has a floor area of 72,000 square feet and sells over 20,000 product categories ranging from snacks to electrical household appliances. Its diverse services include a drugstore with a full-time pharmacist and free Internet access to customers once they have made a minimum purchase. Some of these superstores include bargain zones, with thousands of items priced to compete directly against the bargain stores that have appeared in Hong Kong (USDA/FAS 2003d).

Restaurants must also be mentioned again briefly. Restaurant receipts were estimated at HK$48.1 billion in 2003, down from HK$56.5 billion in 1998 (HKCSD 2003a). Eating out is popular among Hong Kong Chinese, and over half the total food budget is spent in restaurants. All income levels frequent Chinese restaurants extensively. Fast-food restaurants have widespread appeal, including Western chains such as McDonald's, which is one of the largest fast-food chains (208 stores in 2003). Some local chains serving Chinese fast food are also popular. Maxims, for example, has 360 stores, and Café de Coral had 117 stores in 2003. Deli France, KFC, Pacific Coffee, Pizza Hut, and Starbucks have between thirty and sixty stores each. The slowdown that hit retailing generally during the recession has had an impact on restaurant sales. In addition, the SARS crisis in early 2003 caused drastic short-term drops in revenue, although the industry is returning to pre-SARS patronage levels (USDA/FAS 2003b).

BRANDING AND MARKETING COMMUNICATION

Hong Kong is a sophisticated consumer marketing environment, and the marketing services sector is strong. A full range of marketing services is available locally, including advertising, brand and image consulting, event organizing, public relations and corporate communications, and market research. This service sector is dominated by a multitude of major multinational marketing services suppliers, who have usually made Hong Kong their regional headquarters, but local companies also play an important role. There were over 4,500 advertising, public relations, and marketing research establishments in Hong Kong in 2003, employing over 17,000 people (Table 4.46). Although this is down somewhat from several years earlier, future prospects are for strong growth and recovery for this sector (HKTDC 2002, 2003a).

Table 4.46

Advertising, Public Relations Services, and Market Research

Number of establishments (March 2003)	4,529
Number of persons engaged (March 2003)	17,022
Business receipts and other income (2001, US$ million)	818
Value-added (2001, US$ million)	408
Exports of advertising, market research, and public opinion polling services (2001, US$ million)	818
Contribution to total services exports, 2001 (%)	2.0

Source: Hong Kong Trade Development Council (HKTDC), "Profiles of Hong Kong Major Service Industries: Marketing Services" (August 7, 2003), available at www.tdctrade.com/main/si/advert.htm, accessed March 2004.

These competitive market conditions have made branding an important issue. Hong Kong consumers are already brand conscious, a factor generally benefiting foreign brands. The huge market of Chinese consumers is also starting to become brand oriented, and this is what is really forcing Hong Kong's local businesses toward more marketing sophistication. There are many well-known Hong Kong brands, but in general, most Hong Kong companies have not traditionally been strong at product branding. Consumer brands present in Hong Kong tend to be "foreign." We include in this group a few brands from the Chinese mainland, some of which are starting to gain popularity in Hong Kong. Many of the well-known Hong Kong brands do not identify strongly with Hong Kong, for example, Giordano. They frequently believe that little advantage would come in their China markets or among international consumers from being a Chinese brand competing with a multitude of other Chinese brands. However, this failure by most local companies to develop strong brands has become an issue during recent years. Some local companies that have not traditionally worked very hard at branding are beginning to reexamine their prospects as Hong Kong's economy evolves (Access Asia 2001; *The Bulletin* 2003b, 2003c).

The major retailers, however, have developed their own strong store brand images and have begun to develop their own private-label products in recent years. They have been successful at it, and some observers view Hong Kong as one of the world's strongest private-label markets. Wellcome, Park 'n Shop, China Resources, and Jusco have often led this trend in selling their own private-label products, including, especially, food items. Fortress, a leading consumer electronics retailer, has similarly been developing its own product brands. In general, such house brands are usually positioned as good value, similar quality, but slightly cheaper. Retail prices of such private-label products are usually about 10 to 20 percent less than the most popular brand of the same product category. Many consumers perceive that the house brands are not much different in quality from many of the major brands. This has appealed to many consumers during Hong Kong's recession. One survey indicated that nearly 90 percent of Hong Kong households had bought some house-brand products in 2001 (Access Asia 2001; USDA/FAS 2003d).

Advertising

Hong Kong has one of the highest per capita advertising spending rates in the world. Total spending on advertising (adspend) grew about 8 percent in 2003 (over 2002 figures), reaching approxi-

Table 4.47

Recent Growth in Advertising Expenditure

Media	January 2003 (1) HK$ million	January 2004 (1) HK$ million	YOY % change
TV	1,241.17	1,558.62	25.6
Radio	79.95	73.21	−8.4
Newspapers	1,054.17	1,086.87	3.1
Magazines	343.13	377.79	10.1
Cinema	7.24	1.76	−75.6
Mass transit railway	68.58	65.25	−4.9
Other	25.34	45.85	81.6
Total	2,819.56	3,209.34	13.8

Sources: ACNielsen Media Research, "The Growth Momentum in Hong Kong Benefits the Advertising Industry Driving 14% Increase in the First Month" (February 26, 2004), available at www.nielsenmedia.com.hk/news.asp?newsID=214, accessed March 2004; Hong Kong General Chamber of Commerce (HKGCC), "Corporate Daily: Nielsen Media Research News Release" (March 3, 2004), available at www.chamber.org.hk/hknewsletters/news_template.asp?id=3861, accessed March 2004.

mately HK$35.8 billion (roughly US$4.6 billion), based on analysis of published rates. Total adspend was probably slightly less, because industry discounting is not usually disclosed to the research firms that track advertising. However, while there was a lot of discounting during much of the recession, the trend seems to have started pulling away from heavy discounting, as advertising demand picked up in late 2003. Adspend during the recession fluctuated widely, as consumer sentiment and spending swung from optimism to pessimism, and advertisers responded by adjusting their budgets. However, initial indications in early 2004 are that the strong growth is likely to be sustainable if there are no more major shocks to the economy, such as SARS in early 2003. Growth of year-on-year adspend in January 2004 over January 2003 was 13.8 percent (Table 4.47). Most notably, TV advertising, which accounts for nearly half of all advertising but had been flat for many of the previous several years, was recovering strongly. It posted 25 percent growth (HKTDC 2002; ACNielsen April 26, 2002; ACNielsen Media Research February 26, 2004).

Consumer worry and caution were beginning to dissipate by the end of 2003, and some of the major advertising spenders increased their budgets. While eight of the top ten categories had already been in the top ten in January 2003, some of these product and service categories drastically increased spending. Skin care products, for example, surged into first place in January 2004, with an 80 percent year-on-year increase over January 2003. Tonic ad spending was up 31 percent, supermarket adspend increased by 29 percent, and movie and entertainment ads increased by 46 percent (Table 4.48). Records and tapes and department stores moved into the top ten most prolific spending categories, with increases of 192 and 67 percent, respectively. Only overseas travel and mobile telephone services and sets showed slight declines in spending among the top ten categories, while residential real estate sales and rentals held steady (ACNielsen Media Research February 26, 2004; Hong Kong General Chamber of Commerce [HKGCC] March 3, 2004).

TV is one of the favorite media for advertising placement, partly due to its extensive penetration in Hong Kong, giving very wide reach to advertisers. Nearly every household owns at least one set, while probably about half of households own two or more. Cable and satellite TV were each available in about a fifth of households by the end of the 1990s. TV accounted for over 49 percent of adspend prior to the recession. During the recession, TV's share dropped to roughly 42

Table 4.48

Top Ten Advertisers by Product/Service Category

Product category	Adspend January 2004 (HK$ million)	YOY % change from January 2003
Skin care	145.94	80
Tonic	125.82	31
Restaurants/clubs	125.65	16
Overseas travel	109.87	−4
Supermarkets	102.44	29
Movie/entertainment	101.76	46
Residential real estate sales/rentals	100.97	1
Records and tapes	88.73	192
Department stores	82.99	67
Mobile communication services and equipment	74.51	−3

Source: ACNielsen Media Research, "The Growth Momentum in Hong Kong Benefits the Advertising Industry Driving 14% Increase in the First Month" (February 26, 2004), available at www.nielsenmedia .com.hk/news.asp?newsID=214, accessed March 2004.

percent (Table 4.49), as advertisers shifted their focus to less expensive media. Even in January 2003, TV adspend made up only 44 percent of total spending. One indication that consumer brands believe the recession is ending shows up in the shift of advertising money back to TV. At the time of this writing, TV seems to be recovering its position, accounting for over 48 percent of adspend (Table 4.47) (Access Asia 2001; ACNielsen April 26, 2002; ACNielsen Media Research February 26, 2004).

Altogether, the TV industry in Hong Kong provides more than thirty-eight channels, most of which are in Chinese, but a few are in English. It consists of two main local commercial TV broadcasters, a quasi-public broadcaster, a cable TV operator, an interactive TV service, and a number of regional satellite TV broadcasters. Hong Kong is also the home of some regional TV broadcasters, including Satellite Television Asian Region Ltd. (STAR TV), Chinese Television Network (CTN), and Chinese Entertainment Television (CETV). Hong Kong has the world's largest Chinese TV program library that helps make Hong Kong channels popular in the neighboring areas of southeastern China (HKTDC 2002).

Hong Kong is also a major publishing center, the largest in the world for Chinese-language publications, and it is home to a number of regional English-language publications. It produces more than 760 publications, including more than fifty newspapers. About ten are in English, including two highly regarded papers, *South China Morning Post* and *The Standard.* Most of the rest are in Chinese, of which a few with the largest circulations include *The Apple Daily* and the *Ming Pao Daily News, Oriental Daily News,* and *Sing Tao Daily.* There are also a number of electronic newspapers based in Hong Kong (HKTDC 2002; Yung 2003).

Newspapers are traditionally the second main medium through which advertising is placed, but the share was not close to that of TV until the recession. Newspapers' share of total adspend was about 29 percent in 1995 and had risen to 42 percent by 2000 and 2001 (Table 4.49). However, by 2003 and 2004, the share was falling again, as advertisers of consumer products began shifting back to TV and into some other smaller-share media. In January 2003, newspapers accounted for only 37 percent of adspend, and by January 2004, the share was down to 34 percent (Table 4.47). During the recession, many consumer products companies offered more promotional deals, such as coupons, that were printed in newspapers.

Table 4.49

Advertising Spending by Media, 1995, 2000, and 2001

Media	1995[a] US$ million	2000[b] US$ million	2001[b] US$ million	YOY % change
Terrestrial TV	960.61	1,492.24	1,590.73	6.6
Cable TV	n.a.	n.a.	90.87	n.a.
Radio	126.35	127.55	105.33	−17.4
Newspapers	565.53	1,312.69	1,316.12	0.3
Magazines	232.06	471.77	517.57	9.7
Cinema	6.13	1.54	7.17	366.7
Mass transit railway	50.76	n.a. (in other)	n.a. (in other)	n.a.
Other	11.79	123.59	145.71	17.9
Total	1,953.24	3,529.37	3,773.49	6.9

[a]*Asian Advertising & Marketing* (*AA&M*), "Top Ten: A Regional Ranking of Adspend and Agency Billings in 1995," April 19 (1996): 12–14.

[b]ACNielsen, "AdSpend: Hong Kong" (2002), available at http://asiapacific.acnielsen.com.au/en/AdSpend/hong%20kong.xls, accessed March 2004.

There have been several rounds of fierce newspaper wars since the mid-1990s that have affected readership and advertising expenditure. *The Apple Daily* (a Chinese-language paper) is often credited with starting one round of the wars when it was introduced, in the early 1990s, at HK$4, undercutting the HK$5 per copy price that has been standa.d in the industry for several years. *The Apple Daily* rapidly gained the number two spot in circulation. Other major newspapers cut their prices to retaliate, and some went as low as HK$2 per copy. Advertising placement increased dramatically in the newspapers that gained during the circulation wars, as advertisers took advantage of increased circulation for not much additional cost. However, the losers saw their advertising revenue decline, and this helped drive some of the smaller ones out of business. This phase of the wars ended by 1996 (*AA&M* 1996b; Hille 1996a, 1996b).

New newspaper wars erupted a few years later, because of a new major competitor and because of a surge in niche publications entering the market. The launch of *The Sun* at the end of the 1990s greatly affected *Oriental Daily News* and *The Apple Daily* (Table 4.50), and *The Sun* became the third best-selling daily in Hong Kong soon after its launch. Most other major papers have seen readership slip. While the top two newspapers have been able to keep advertising revenues growing slightly, others have suffered from the recession and because the small-niche papers are siphoning off some of the newspaper adspend to vehicles that are more specifically targeted. Many newspapers have also engaged in heavy sales promotion to keep sales up, giving free children's CDs and attracting advertising that includes coupons for big discounts or samples (ACNielsen 2002; Media Online September 20, 2002). Advertising revenue for newspapers has also tended to suffer more than many other media from short-term shocks that temporarily keep shoppers at home. For example, at the height of the SARS crisis in 2003, adspend was down about 10 percent overall but dropped 20 percent for newspapers (IFPP May 2, 2003).

Magazine and radio advertising account for smaller shares of adspend. Magazines are a key medium for several product categories, such as leisure, retail, personal items, toiletries, clothing, and watches. However, the major circulation magazines have seen slow declines in readership, although the two largest still reach half a million readers each. The market is gradually shifting to niche-market special-interest magazines. Adspend, however, remains robust across the category

Table 4.50

Newspaper Readership and Advertising Revenues

Newspaper	Readership estimates						Ad revenue January–June 2000 (HK$ million)
	July 1998–June 1999 (1,000)	%	July 1999–June 2000 (1,000)	%	July 2000–June 2001 %	July 2001–June 2002 %	
Oriental Daily News	2,551	42	2,236	36	33	34	1,425.73
The Apple Daily	1,780	30	1,615	26	23	25	1,105.36
The Sun	N/A	N/A	777	13	9	10	418.10
Ming Pao	285	5	326	5	5	4	438.06
South China Morning Post	206	3	308	5	N/A	N/A	N/A
Sing Pao	241	4	216	3	3	3	352.74
Sing Tao Daily	118	2	145	2	2	3	380.42
Hong Kong Daily News	158	3	122	2	2	2	104.57
Hong Kong Economic Times	101	2	120	2	1	2	709.28
Tin Tin Daily News	157	3	100	2	N/A	N/A	N/A

Sources: Nielsen Media Research.

(IFPP 2004), although magazines with declining circulation may see cuts in revenue. Adspend growth for magazines was about 10 percent year-on-year for January 2004, the largest for any major media except TV (Table 4.47, p. 181).

Radio is a minor medium for most important product categories. However, in certain segments, especially for younger consumers, radio plays an important advertising role. Among these consumers, listening increased during the 1990s, spurred by the popularity of Walkman®-type radios with small earphones. Pop singers and popular disc jockeys have increased the appeal. There is also some outdoor advertising, though this part of the industry is small compared to that in some Asian countries, such as Japan or Korea. Although the garish neon lights are conspicuous in Hong Kong's nighttime skyline, nearly 60 percent of outdoor adspend is actually on the mass transit railway (MTR; Table 4.47, p. 181). Most advertising on the MTR is for young adult fashion and consumer electronics. A few products also make good use of tram and bus shelter advertising, making up about one-quarter of outdoor adspend in 2001.

Advertisements in Hong Kong are among the most sophisticated in the world in terms of technological and artistic competence, though not every supplier meets the high standards. For example, advanced digital techniques are common, and the Hong Kong industry picks up advances rapidly, particularly if they come from North America or Japan. Most major advertising agencies from these countries have a strong presence in Hong Kong. Local consumers expect high-quality advertising, and they rarely respond well to ads that are not up to their high standards.

Creative appeals have largely shifted from hard sell to a softer approach that incorporates emotional appeal. This is more in line with local culture and may reflect the growing influence of locals in the multinational agencies. Relative to Western advertisements, humor seems to be less frequent. Many advertisements now reflect Chinese family values and human concern for those close to the viewer. People seem to appreciate advertisements that demonstrate warm feelings, a "people" orientation, the natural environment, and even a rural setting to provide contrast with hectic daily life. However, the recession has brought back some stronger attention to price, but the price message usually works well only when incorporated into value positioning, stressing that quality is good as well.

BEGINNINGS OF A ROLE FOR THE INTERNET

As might be expected in an advanced economy, the majority of Hong Kong consumers are integrating information technology (IT) into their daily lives at least to some extent. By late 2003, some 1,479,100 households had a PC in their home. This represents 67.5 percent of all households in Hong Kong. Among these households with a PC, nearly 89 percent were connected to the Internet, which is 60.0 percent of all households in Hong Kong. This indicates rapid growth of IT capability among consumers; one year earlier, 62 percent of households had a PC, and fewer than 53 percent of these were connected to the Internet. As might be expected, rates of using the PC are higher among younger people, better-educated persons, and students (Hong Kong Census and Statistics Department, Communications and Technology Branch [HKCSD/CTB] 2003a, 2003b; Nielsen NetRatings 2004).

Usage by consumers of some kind of electronic business service is very high, nearly 94 percent among all people ages fifteen and over. However, much usage is with what are now relatively standard technologies, such as automatic teller machines (ATMs), or payment-by-phone service (PPS). On the Internet, much usage is not for making transactions but rather for searching for information about goods and services. The use of the Internet for transactions is relatively low—about 7 percent of consumers purchased something online in 2003. This represents fairly

Table 4.51

Consumer IT Usage and Penetration in Households, Assessment Period May–August
(percent)

	2002	2003
PC penetration (among all households)	62.1	67.5
Internet connectivity (among PC-owning households)	52.5	60.0
Persons age ten and over who used PC in past year	54.0	56.2
Persons age ten and over who used Internet in past year	48.2	52.2
Users of electronic business services, age fifteen and over	92.6	93.6
Purchasers online in the past year, age fifteen and over	4.9	7.0
Registered Internet customer accounts with dial-up access (estimated, April 2003)		1,361,323
Registered Internet customer accounts with broadband access (estimated, April 2003)		1,055,571

Sources: Hong Kong Census and Statistics Department, Communications and Technology Branch (HKCSD/CTB), "Findings of the 'Household Survey on Information Technology Usage and Penetration' and the 'Annual Survey on Information Technology Usage and Penetration in the Business Sector' for 2003" (2003), available at www.info.gov.hk/digital21/eng/milestone/it_survey2003.html, accessed March 2004; HKCSD/CTB, "Information Technology" (2003), available at www.info.gov.hk/citb/ctb/english/fact/index_n.htm, accessed March 2004.

strong growth over the previous year, but the base is still so small that strong growth does not yet generate very large volume (Table 4.51; HKCSD/CTB 2003a).

Perhaps more indicative of the current state of e-business in Hong Kong is the fact that businesses in this wired city still do not use the Internet extensively. While over half of businesses have computers in their offices, and nearly half have Internet connections, only 13.5 percent have their own Web page or Web site. About half have received goods, services, or information over the Internet—in practice, this usually means that they use the Internet for information searches. Slightly less than 10 percent had actually ordered or purchased something electronically. Just over 1 percent of businesses in Hong Kong had sold anything electronically. While e-commerce transactions amounted to HK$15.6 billion, this was only about three-tenths of a percent of business receipts (Table 4.52). This represents substantial growth in just a few years—sales over the Internet were only HK$2.95 billion in 1998—but growth is erratic. In 2001, business receipts were higher than in 2002 (HKCSD/CTB 2003a; HKTDC 2003a). Partly, this represents a slow-down after the dot-com crash and retrenching by the industry and its customers; partly, it simply represents the difficulty of actually measuring such a small proportion of sales accurately.

Thus, while many observers believe that the Internet has a bright future as a channel for doing business, at present, most users use the Internet mainly for communication and information purposes. Among companies, the move onto the Internet varies by company size. About 61 percent of large companies (those employing more than 100 persons) have their own Web sites, but only 8 percent of small companies (those employing less than ten persons) have Web sites (HKTDC 2003a). However, these figures should be put into perspective. Adoption of the Internet by consumers has been slower worldwide than the hype would suggest, and Asian consumers, despite the hype, have been even slower to shift their buying onto the Internet. Thus, these seemingly low figures for Hong Kong actually represent the forefront of trends among Asian economies and are relatively advanced by world standards.

For example, one survey estimated that with 13 percent of Hong Kong firms accepting orders and payments online, Hong Kong may be in the lead for the Asia-Pacific region. An e-readiness

Table 4.52

Business IT Usage (Assessment Period May–August) (percent)

Establishments that have:	2002	2003
One or more PCs	54.5	54.8
Internet connections	44.2	47.5
Web page/Web site	11.8	13.5
Ordered or purchased electronically	7.1	9.6
Received goods/services/information electronically	45.2	51.0
Sold good/services/information electronically	1.5	1.1
Delivered goods/services/information electronically	12.1	13.6
Business receipts from selling goods/services/information electronically (HK$ billion)	22.1	15.6
Business receipts electronically as percent of total business receipts	0.43	0.29

Sources: Hong Kong Census and Statistics Department, Communications and Technology Branch (HKCSD/CTB), "Findings of the 'Household Survey on Information Technology Usage and Penetration' and the 'Annual Survey on Information Technology Usage and Penetration in the Business Sector' for 2003" (2003), available at www.info.gov.hk/digital21/eng/milestone/it_survey2003.html, accessed March 2004; HKCSD/CTB, "Information Technology" (2003), available at www.info.gov.hk/citb/ctb/english/fact/index_n.htm, accessed March 2004.

survey by the Economist Intelligence Unit ranked Hong Kong second in Asia and tenth in the world in 2003. And, specific industries have a higher Internet usage rate than the overall figures suggest. A survey by ACNielsen showed that around one-third of Hong Kong Internet users use online banking services once a week or more, making Hong Kong perhaps a more advanced Internet banking region than Singapore, South Korea, or Taiwan (all these surveys are cited in HKTDC 2003a). During the SARS crisis in early 2003, Internet usage soared, as people were afraid to go out and come into contact with others. To some extent, this boosted Internet shopping, but by June 2003 when the crisis was over, usage and shopping had fallen back somewhat compared to at the height of the crisis (Nielsen NetRatings May 20, 2003, July 31, 2003). However, some part of the gains is likely to be permanent.

Three key product categories have attracted more purchases online than most. About 36 percent of male Internet users and about a quarter of female users have bought books online. One-third of women Internet users have bought food and groceries, as have 17 percent of men. Three major supermarkets, Park 'n Shop, Wellcome, and City Super, offer grocery shopping through their Web sites. However, they are not attracting a lot of sustained interest, due to the convenience of shopping in Hong Kong, security concerns, and the cost of delivery. Computer software is the other leading product category, but this consists mostly of purchases by male Internet users. However, many online sales at present are essentially trial purchases; not all of these people become regular Internet buyers, and most do not shift the majority of their buying in the product category to the Internet. Further, no other category comes close to these rates of (trial) usage. A few, such as entertainment and tickets, music, and computer hardware (among men) have Internet purchase figures around 5–6 percent of Internet users (Access Asia 2001; USDA/FAS 2003d).

As noted, security concerns are one major barrier to consumer e-commerce in Hong Kong. Another key issue is concern about whether online retailers are trustworthy and can fulfill their promises. However, although not many consumers buy online, they increasingly use a mixed strategy, surfing for information online and then making an offline purchase (HKTDC 2003a). Thus, the Internet is becoming a major information channel for consumers. According to results of a survey at the end of 2003, roughly 20 percent of the workforce (about 685,000 people, usually white collar and professional) regularly go online at work. Most access the Internet every day, and the majority spend more than two hours a day on it, which is more than the time spent on any traditional media. It is becoming an attractive media channel for this type of target audience (HKGCC February 19, 2004).

These trends in Internet usage encouraged consumer advertisers to go online by the end of the 1990s, and slightly more than half of online adspend was targeted at consumers. About 51 percent of Internet ad revenue in Hong Kong in 2000 was from banner ads, and another 45 percent was from sponsorship (PriceWaterhouseCoopers [PWC] 2001). However, an initial upsurge in advertising spending at the end of the 1990s ended with the dot-com crash. According to the Internet Advertising Bureau Hong Kong, Internet advertising revenue was US$17.4 million in 1999 and reached US$21.4 million in the first nine months of 2000 (PWC 2001). However, by the last quarter of 2000, Internet adspend was dropping sharply and continued downward into 2001 (*Media* June 8, 2001). The long-term trend is likely a return to (somewhat erratic) growth, as online businesses recover from the dot-com crash and advertisers learn to better use the medium. The upsurge in Internet usage during SARS in 2003 reinforced the cautious return of advertising revenue to the Internet at a time when overall adspend fell because consumers were not going out to shop (IFPP May 2, 2003; Nielsen NetRatings May 10, 2003, July 31, 2003).

CONCLUSION

Over the several decades prior to 1997, Hong Kong consumers became used to ever-increasing incomes and spending power. Until the recession, they were on a huge spending spree, with a strong shift away from pure price consciousness toward very strong value and quality orientations. Many local businesses did not keep up with changing consumption habits and continued to believe that local consumers were only price conscious. Almost by default, this gave foreign products easy entry into Hong Kong. Much of the local middle class became very brand conscious, favoring, especially, foreign brands and retailers. As predicted, the economy slowed during the last years of the 1990s, and it has remained stagnant (in 1997 through 2003; Speece and So 1998). While the mood among consumers was bleak at times during this recession, there has been a hidden benefit of the difficult economic situation. Consumers have stopped wasting so much of their income frivolously and have become more careful shoppers, as they have had to learn how to preserve living standards while saving money. Despite the gloomy mood, in fact, incomes and living standards have not really declined substantially for most people—Hong Kong remains one of the world leaders in disposable household income.

Thus, Hong Kong is still a prosperous market, even though it is unlikely that the high growth rates characteristic of the 1970s into the mid-1990s will repeat often in the future. The particular advantages that helped fuel rapid growth have been diluted, including Hong Kong's unique position as a gateway to the PRC. Nevertheless, it is clear that Hong Kong will eventually adjust to its changing role in the world, and there is certainly a prosperous future in the new role. Even though Shanghai will eventually overtake Hong Kong as China's largest business center, there is no doubt that Hong Kong will retain a leading role at least over the next decade. In other words, Hong Kong consumers still have and will continue to have high incomes by world standards, but they have become much more sophisticated about how they use their money.

Hong Kong consumers developed a very high level of brand consciousness during the boom years, and upscale brands (usually foreign) did very well. Under the new economic conditions and consumer thinking, brand consciousness remains, but there is a strong shift toward value-oriented brands. These brands may still be expensive compared to some available in the market, particularly many Chinese products, but they are not as expensive as luxury brands or many other imported foreign brands. Consumers now perceive many in-house brands from retailers such as Giordano (clothing), Marks and Spencer (department store), and Park 'n Shop (supermarket) as offering better value for their money. These tend to be mid-market brands. Prospects for such local value brands are very good.

Value brands do not compete only on low prices: they are slightly cheaper than the major foreign brands, but they are not at the low end of the market. Rather, value brands are positioned as being of similar quality to the major brands, so that there is no sacrifice when buying them and saving a little money. Of course, not all consumers are convinced to shift from the major brands, but this is partly because the stronger consumer attention to value has forced many of the major brands to justify higher prices to consumers. If the justification is strong on quality and value grounds, consumers will not abandon their brands; if the price differentials cannot be justified, they will. Many local companies patiently built up their positions over the decade prior to 1997, and the payoff has come for many with this new consumer sentiment. There is also increasing competition from Chinese brands from the mainland, as companies upgrade their product quality and their marketing expertise to move into Hong Kong's middle-class value markets. Strong foreign brands will continue to find a market, especially if they are international and not overly oriented toward the pure luxury market. However, it is difficult to remain strong simply on the basis of being Western or Japanese.

The value trend is apparent in shopping and store choice as well as product brand choice. The market has not been able to support the high concentration of large foreign stores present at the end of the 1990s in the upper parts of the market. Some of the high-end stores either reduced their scope of operations or withdrew altogether. The local chains continue to expand, and small traditional stores continue to decline. Discount and wholesale/warehouse-type stores have not expanded as quickly as we anticipated, because the major local retailers learned rapidly to integrate many of the most attractive elements of the discount format to keep their middle-class customers.

Our long-term forecast remains: in the long run, Hong Kong is likely to become the services center for the economy of southeast China, with increasing economic integration into South China. This trend has already started, and this is not a small role because the Guangdong area, especially the Pearl River Delta, is one of the powerhouses of the Chinese economy. Hong Kong is just beginning to look more like a Chinese city and will gradually lose its character as an international city, but this will be a slow process. As it proceeds, Hong Kong will transform itself into a—but not the only—leading Chinese city, part of the vibrant economy of South China. There is no reason for long-term decline in the economy, or in living standards, but there will certainly be short-term adjustment difficulties, as economic restructuring moves ahead to adapt to the new situation. As noted above, into the first months of 2004, there are already indications that the economy is moving back toward sustainable growth and consumer sentiment is picking up (ACNielsen February 17, 2004). Hong Kong will remain a prosperous market full of careful, sophisticated middle-class consumers with high spending power well into the future.

NOTES

The authors acknowledge helpful comments from Bernd Schmitt. This chapter borrows heavily from and extends works by Pia Polsa and Bai Chang Hong (1998), "China, Part II: Markets within a Market," pp. 161–211; and M. Speece and S. L. M. So (1998), "Hong Kong: The Consumer Market in the 1990s," pp. 213–56.

1. We use the term "mainland" simply to denote the massive, continental portion of the PRC, with marketing systems largely distinct from Hong Kong and Macau.

2. The first five-year plan was drawn up for years 1953–1957. Before that, the economic policies of the PRC were called "the task of rehabilitating the national economy" (Hong 1990, 11–15). Hence, the centrally planned economy originated in 1953.

3. The Third Plenary Session of the Eleventh Central Committee of the Communist Party of China at the end of 1978 made a decision to change the Chinese economy into "socialist modernization" (Hong 1990, 27).

4. The economic policies and changes can be divided according to five-year plans, but the main political changes concerning the economy occurred in 1979 and after 1993.

5. Interview with the director of the Commercial Bureau of Guilin, January 3, 1996, in Guilin, Guangxi.

6. The fifteen coastal cities are Dalian, Qinhuangdao, Tianjin, Yantai, Qingdao, Lianyungang, Nantong, Shanghai, Ningbo, Wenzhou, Fuzhou, Guangzhou, Zhanjiang, Weihai, and Beihai.

7. The consequences for ecology, culture, and quality of life in the area have been criticized and widely debated.

8. Here, the words "relations," "connections," and *guanxi* are used as synonyms.

9. Cf. use of "back door" (Bond and Hwang 1987, 225).

10. It is important to remember that throughout Chinese history, there has been a huge contrast between peasants and urban dwellers, to the extent that some of the dynasties have risen and fallen when farmers have rebelled against wealthy city residents.

11. For example, two respondents in a sample of thirty-two (Polsa 1996).

12. Some studies have, though, found opposite attitudes. For instance, male consumers do not distinguish between Sino-Japanese joint venture versus imported Japanese TV sets (Bandyopadhyay and Dong 1995, 41).

REFERENCES

Access Asia Limited. 2001. "Retailing in Hong Kong: A Market Analysis." Available at www.accessasia.co.uk/showreport.asp?RptId=43, accessed March 2004.

ACNielsen. 2002. "AdSpend: Hong Kong." Available at http://asiapacific.acnielsen.com.au/en/AdSpend/hong%20kong.xls, accessed March 2004.

———. 2002, February 7. "Hong Kong Consumers Brace for Global Recession with no Recovery before Q4, ACNielsen Survey Reveals." Available at www.acnielsen.com.hk/news.asp?newsID=51, accessed December 2003.

———. 2002, April 26. "Hong Kong Advertising Expenditure Records 8% Growth in Q1." Available at www.acnielsen.com.hk/news.asp?newsID=62, accessed March 2004.

———. 2003, June 25. "Hope Fades for 2003 Rebound as Economic Concerns and SARS Weigh on Consumer Sentiment in Asia Pacific." Available at www.acnielsen.com.hk/news.asp?newsID=98, accessed December 2003.

———. 2003, November 26. "Consumer Confidence in Asia Rebounds Faster than Expected. Consumers' Major Concern Switches from the Economy to Health Issues." Available at www.acnielsen.com.hk/news.asp?newsID=107, accessed December 2003.

———. 2004, February 17. "Consumer Confidence in Hong Kong Reaches New High. More Hong Kong People Willing to Spend on Big-Ticket Items." Available at www.acnielsen.com.hk/news.asp?newsID=111, accessed March 2004.

ACNielsen Media Research. 2004, February 26. "The Growth Momentum in Hong Kong Benefits the Advertising Industry Driving 14% Increase in the First Month." Available at www.nielsenmedia.com.hk/news.asp?newsID=214, accessed March 2004.

Amersbach, G. 2000. "Health Care for a New Century. Harvard Public Health Review, Fall 2000." Available at www.hsph.harvard.edu/review/review_2000/677hongkong.html, accessed January 2004.

Asian Advertising & Marketing (AA&M). 1996a. "Profile of Hong Kong," March 8: 10.

———. 1996b. "End to HK Price War in Sight," March 22: 6.

———. 1996c. "Top Ten: A Regional Ranking of Adspend and Agency Billings in 1995," April 19: 12–14.

Asian Economic News (AEN). 2002, November 8. "H.K. Unveils Measures to Stimulate Property Prices." Available at www.findarticles.com/cf_dls/m0WDP/2002_Nov_18/94330834/p1/article.jhtml, accessed January 2004.

————. 2003, October 28. "H.K. Jobless Rate Eases to 8.3%." Available at www.findarticles.com/cf_dls/ m0WDP/2003_Oct_28/109331964/p1/article.jhtml, accessed December 2003.

AsiaWeek. 1996. "The Price of Pollution," April 26: 34–9.

d'Astous, A., S. A. Ahmed, and Y. H. Wang. 1995. "A Study of Country-of-Origin Effect in the People's Republic of China." In *Proceedings of the Fifth International Conference of Marketing and Development,* ed. K. Basu, A. Joy, and Z. Hansheng, June 22–25, Beijing, People's Republic of China, 33–38. (International Society of Marketing and Development http://home.planet.nl/~dubae000/ISMD/ pubs.html#five)

Bandyopadhyay, S., and G. Dong. 1995. "Beyond Country-of-Origin Effect: Introducing the Concept of Place-of-Origin." In *Proceedings of the Fifth International Conference of Marketing and Development,* ed. K. Basu, A. Joy, and Z. Hansheng, June 22–25, Beijing, People's Republic of China, 39–43. (International Society of Marketing and Development http://home.planet.nl/~dubae000/ISMD/pubs.html#five)

Belk, R., and Nan Zhou. 2002. "Chinese Consumer Reading of Global and Local Advertising." Working Paper, David Eccles School of Business, University of Utah, Salt Lake City.

Bond, M. H., and Kwang-Kuo Hwang. 1987. "The Social Psychology of Chinese People." In *The Psychology of the Chinese People,* ed. Michael Harris Bond. Oxford: Oxford University Press, 213–66.

The Bulletin of the Hong Kong General Chamber of Commerce. 2001. "Retail Industry Soldiers On." Available at www.chamber.org.hk/info/the_bulletin/May_2001/retail.asp, accessed January 2004.

————. 2003a. "The Business of Education." Available at www.chamber.org.hk/info/the_bulletin/march2003/ education.asp, accessed January 2004.

————. 2003b. "Discovering the Finer Things in Life." Available at www.chamber.org.hk/info/the_bulletin/ apri12003/coverstory.asp, accessed January 2004.

————. 2003c. "Branding: The Power of Market Identity." Available at www.chamber.org.hk/info/ the_bulletin/nov2003/branding.asp, accessed January 2004.

————. 2003d. "HKSAR Firms in 'Optimistic Mood.'" Available at www.chamber.org.hk/info/the_bulletin/ dec2003/biz_prospects.asp, accessed January 2004.

Business China. 1984. "HP's JV in the PRC is Second Stride in Two-Step Strategy," November 28.

Chan, Elaine. 2002. "Hong Kong Warned on Delta Challenges" (reprinted from *The Standard*). Available at www.prctaxman.com.cn/Hong_Kong_Warned_On_Delta_Changes.htm, accessed December 2003.

Chan, I. S. 1994, June. "Environmental Consciousness and Consumer Purchase Preferences: A Hong Kong Study." In *Capitalizing the Potentials of Globalisation: Proceedings of the Third Annual World Business Congress.* Penang, Malaysia, Universiti Sains Malaysia, 208–14.

Chau, Simon S. C. 1990. "The Environment." In *The Other Hong Kong Report 1990,* ed. Richard Y. C. Wong and Joseph Y.S. Cheng. Hong Kong: Chinese University Press, 491–505.

Cheng, H., and K. T. Frith. 1996. "Foreign Advertising Agencies in China." *Media Asia, an Asian Mass Communication Quarterly* 23(1): 34–41.

China Business Times. 1996. "Income from South to North: A Survey Comparing Family Income in Beijing, Shanghai, Guangzhou and Shenzhen." February 8 (in Chinese).

China Daily. 1993. "Challenge for Chain Stores," December 6, 13(3937).

————. 1995a. "Principles on Modernization Drive," October.

————. 1995b. "Process of Urbanization Speeds Up," October.

China Daily HK Edition. 2003, November 11. "Pan-Pearl River Regional Co-ordination in Blueprint." Available at www.prctaxman.com.cn/Pan_Pearl_River_Delta_Cooperation.htm, accessed December 2003.

China Economic Review. 1994. "Brand Ambitions," March:15–16.

China Market. 1992. "Fast Developing Cosmetics Production," 4: 11–2.

China Statistical Yearbook. 1990. Beijing: China Statistical Publishing House.

————. 1995. Beijing: China Statistical Publishing House.

————. 1997. Beijing: China Statistical Publishing House.

————. 2000. Beijing: China Statistical Publishing House.

————. 2001. Beijing: China Statistical Publishing House.

————. 2002. Beijing: China Statistical Publishing House.

————. 2003. Beijing: China Statistical Publishing House.

Chow, C. K. W., Fung, M. K. Y., and Ngo, H. Y. 2001. "Consumption Patterns of Entrepreneurs in the People's Republic of China." *Journal of Business Research* 52: 189–202.

Chow, I. H. S. 1995. "Career Aspirations, Attitudes, and Experiences of Female Managers in Hong Kong." *Women in Management Review* 10(1): 28–32.

Choy, Nam Wo. 1991. "Wholesale Vegetable Marketing in Hong Kong: A Perspective on Marketing Channels." Unpublished MBA Thesis, Chinese University of Hong Kong.

Croll, Elisabeth. 2000. *Endangered Daughters, Discrimination and Development in Asia.* London: Routledge.

Cui, G., and Q. Liu. 2000. "Regional Market Segments of China: Opportunities and Barriers in a Big Emerging Market." *Journal of Consumer Marketing* 17(1): 55–72.

———. 2001. "Emerging Market Segments in a Transitional Economy: A Study of Urban Consumers in
China." *Journal of International Marketing* 9(1): 84–106.

Davis, D. S., and J. S. Sensenbrenner. 2000. "Commercializing Childhood, Parental Purchases for Shanghai's
Only Child." In *The Consumer Revolution in Urban China,* ed. D. S. Davis. Berkeley: University of
California Press, 54–79.

The Economist. 1994. "How Not to Sell 1.2 Billion Tubes of Toothpaste," December 3: 63–64.

———. 2001. "Emerging Market Indicators, National Savings Rates," October 6: 114.

Economist Intelligence Unit (EIU). 1996. "Country Report: Hong Kong and Macau, 1st Quarter 1996."
London: EIU.

———. 2002. "China Country Report (September)." London: EIU.

———. 2003. "China Country Report (June)." London: EIU.

Einhorn, B. 1999. "Foreign Rivals vs. the Chinese: If You Can't Beat 'Em . . . U.S. Computer Makers Partner
with Local Manufacturers." *Business Week,* February 15: 35.

Environmental Protection Department (EPD). 2003a. "Government of the Hong Kong Special Administrative Region. Hong Kong's Environment: Air." Available at www.epd.gov.hk/epd/english/environmentinhk/
air/air_maincontent.html, accessed December 2003.

———. 2003b. "Government of the Hong Kong Special Administrative Region. Hong Kong's Environment: Water." Available at www.epd.gov.hk/epd/english/environmentinhk/water/water_maincontent.html,
accessed December 2003.

Equal Opportunities Commission of Hong Kong (EOCHK). 2002a. "Equal Opportunities Commission Annual
Report 2001/2002." Available at www.eoc.org.hk/TE/annual/01–02/index.htm, accessed December 2003.

———. 2002b. "Equal Opportunity in the Business Community." Available at www.eoc.org.hk/_File/re-
search/MLE_e.doc, accessed December 2003.

———. 2003. "Formal Investigation Report on Secondary School Places Allocation (SSPA) System." Available at www.eoc.org.hk/TE/edu/sspa/, accessed January 2004.

Euromonitor International. 2003a. "OTC Healthcare in Hong Kong." Executive summary available at
www.euromonitor.com/OTC_Healthcare_in_Hong_Kong, accessed January 2004.

———. 2003b. "Retail Trade International—Hong Kong." Executive summary available at
www.euromonitor.com/Retail_Trade_International, accessed January 2004.

Fan, Ying. 1994. "Blending East and West, How Can Western Management Know-how Be Transferred to
China's Socialist Market Economy?" Durham, NC: Durham University Business School.

Fraser, D. 2000. "Inventing Oasis, Luxury Housing Advertisements and Reconfiguring Domestic Space in
Shanghai." In *The Consumer Revolution in Urban China,* ed. D. S. Davis. Berkeley: University of California Press, 25–53.

Fung, Anthony, and Eric Ma. 2000. "Formal vs. Informal Use of Television and Sex-Role Stereotyping in
Hong Kong." *Sex Roles: A Journal of Research* (January). Available at www.findarticles.com/cf_dls/
m2294/2000_Jan/63016016/p1/article.jhtml, accessed December 2003.

Gaeta, Gordian. 1995. "Hong Kong's Financial Industry in Transition." *Columbia Journal of World Business* 30(2): 42–50.

Gang, F., D. H. Perkins, and L. Sabin. 1997. "People's Republic of China: Economic Performance and
Prospects." *Asian Development Review* 15(2): 43–85.

Gould, Stephen J., and Nancy Y. C. Wong. 2000. "The Intertextual Construction of Emerging Consumer
Culture in China as Observed in the Movie Ermo: A Postmodern, Sinicization Reading." *Journal of
Global Marketing* 14(1/2): 151–67.

Guo, Q. G., F. Tong, H. Niu, and L. S. C. Yip. 1995. "Firms' Media Strategy in the Advertising Industry of
China." In *Proceedings of the Fifth International Conference of Marketing and Development,* ed. K.
Basu, A. Joy, and Z. Hansheng, June 22–25, Beijing, People's Republic of China, 403–5 (International
Society of Marketing and Development http://home.planet.nl/~dubae000/ISMD/pubs.html#five).

Harris, P., and K. Kwok Yau. 1994. "Understanding Chinese Buying Behavior—A Cross Cultural Interaction Model." Paper presented at International Conference on Management Issues for China in the 1990s,
Cambridge, March 23–25.

Harvard School of Public Health (HSPH). 1999. "Improving Hong Kong's Health Care System: Why and for Whom?" Available at www.hwfb.gov.hk/hw/english/archive/consult/HCS/HCS.HTM, accessed January 2004.

Hay, Joel W. 1992. *Health Care in Hong Kong: An Economic Policy Assessment.* Hong Kong: Chinese University Press.

Hill, C., and C. T. Romm. 1994. "Gift-Giving Family Styles: A Cross-Cultural Study with Consumer Socialization Implications." *Australian Journal of Chinese Affairs* 14(7–8): 68–86.

Hille, Alfred. 1996a. "No End in Sight for HK Newspaper Wars." *Media,* January 19.

———. 1996b. "Apple Daily Eating Away at Readership of Rival Papers." *Media,* March 15.

Hills, Peter. 2002. "From the Problems of Production to the Problems of Consumption: Enhancing Eco-efficiency in Hong Kong." Paper presented at the *Sustainability and the City: International Symposium on Sustainable Development Hong Kong,* June 10–11, Centre of Urban Planning and Environmental Management, University of Hong Kong. Available at www.sdsymposium.org/eng/full/From%20the%20Problems%20of%20Production%20to%20the%20Problems%20of%20Consumption%20-%20Enhancing%20Eco-efficiency%20in%20Hong%20Kong.pdf, accessed December 2003.

Ho, D., and N. Leigh. 1994. "A Retail Revolution." *The China Business Review* 21(1, January–February): 22–28.

Ho, Joseph C. K. 2003. "Keeping Hong Kong Healthy." *Hong Kong Lawyer,* August. Available at www.hk-lawyer.com/2003–8/Default.htm, accessed January 2004.

Ho, Suk-ching and T. Wing-chun Lo. 1987. "The Service Industry in China: Problems and Prospects," *Business Horizons* 30(4; July-August): 29–37.

Ho, William. 2002. "Improving Hong Kong's Health Care System." *HMI World* (Harvard Medical International) March–April. Available at http://hmiworld.org/past_issues/March_April_2002/forum.html, accessed January 2004.

Hofstede, G. 2001. *Culture's Consequences: Comparing Values, Behaviors, Institutions and Organizations across Nations.* Thousand Oaks, CA: Sage.

Holz, C. A. 2002. "Institutional Constraints on the Quality of Statistics in China." *China Information* 16(1): 25–67.

Hong, Ma, ed. 1990. *Modern China's Economy and Management.* Beijing: Foreign Languages Press.

Hong Kong Census and Statistics Department (HKCSD). 1991. *Hong Kong Annual Digest of Statistics, 1991 Edition.* Hong Kong: Government Printing Department.

———. 1994. *Hong Kong Annual Digest of Statistics, 1994 Edition.* Hong Kong: Government Printing Department.

———. 1995. *Hong Kong Social and Economic Trends, 1995 Edition.* Hong Kong: Government Printing Department.

———. 1997. *Hong Kong Social and Economic Trends, 1997 Edition.* Hong Kong: Government Printing Department, Hong Kong Special Administrative Region.

———. 2000a. *1999/2000 Household Expenditure Survey and the Debasing of the Consumer Price Indices.* Hong Kong: Government Printing Department, Hong Kong Special Administrative Region.

———. 2000b. *Hong Kong Monthly Digest of Statistics, 2000 October.* Hong Kong: Government Printing Department, Hong Kong Special Administrative Region.

———. 2001a. *2001 Population Census—Summary Results.* Hong Kong: Government Printing Department, Hong Kong Special Administrative Region.

———. 2001b. *Hong Kong Annual Digest of Statistics, 2001 Edition.* Hong Kong: Government Printing Department, Hong Kong Special Administrative Region.

———. 2001c. *Hong Kong Social and Economic Trends, 2001 Edition.* Hong Kong: Government Printing Department, Hong Kong Special Administrative Region.

———. 2002a. *Hong Kong Annual Digest of Statistics 2002.* Hong Kong: Government Printing Department, Hong Kong Special Administration Department.

———. 2002b. *Women and Men in Hong Kong—Key Statistics, 2002 Edition.* Hong Kong: Government Printing Department, Hong Kong Special Administrative Region.

———. 2002, August. *Special Report on GDP.* Hong Kong: Government Printing Department, Hong Kong Special Administrative Region.

———. 2003a. *Hong Kong in Figures.* Hong Kong: Government of the Hong Kong Special Administrative Region. Available at http://www.info.gov.hk/censtatd/eng/hkstat/index2.html, accessed December 2003.

———. 2003b. *Hong Kong Monthly Digest of Statistics* (March). Hong Kong: Government Printing Department, Hong Kong Special Administrative Region.

————. 2003c. *Monthly Report on the Consumer Price Index, April 2003.* Hong Kong: Government Printing Department, Hong Kong Special Administrative Region.

Hong Kong Census and Statistics Department, Communications and Technology Branch (HKCSD/CTB). 2003a. "Findings of the 'Household Survey on Information Technology Usage and Penetration' and the 'Annual Survey on Information Technology Usage and Penetration in the Business Sector' for 2003." Available at www.info.gov.hk/digital21/eng/milestone/it_survey2003.html, accessed March 2004.

————. 2003b. "Information Technology." Available at www.info.gov.hk/citb/ctb/english/fact/index_n.htm, accessed March 2004.

Hong Kong Center for Economic Research (HKCER). 2003. "Made in PRD: The Changing Face of HK Manufacturers." Available at www.hku.hk/hkcer/prd%20index.htm, accessed December 2003.

Hong Kong Economic Information Agency (HKEIA). 2001. *Hong Kong Economy Year Book* (Series No. 41). Hong Kong: Government Printing Department.

Hong Kong General Chamber of Commerce (HKGCC). 2004, February 19. "Internet to Bring Advertisers' Messages into the Workplace." Available at www.chamber.org.hk/info/nbs/nbs_template.asp?id=3822&keyword=advertising&srch_type=appr, accessed March 2004.

————. 2004, March 3. "Corporate Daily: Nielsen Media Research News Release." Available at www.chamber.org.hk/hknewsletters/news_template.asp?id=3861, accessed March 2004.

Hong Kong Government Information Centre (HKGIC). 2003. *Hong Kong Background Information.* Hong Kong: Government of the Hong Kong Special Administrative Region. Available at www.info.gov.hk/hkbi/eng/index.htm, accessed December 2003.

————. 2004. *Prevention of Avian Influenza.* Hong Kong: Government of the Hong Kong Special Administrative Region. Available at www.info.gov.hk/info/flu/eng/, accessed March 2004.

Hong Kong Government Information Services (HKGIS). 1995. *Hong Kong 1995.* Hong Kong: Government Printing Department.

Hong Kong Home Affairs Bureau (HKHAB). 2003. "Response to U.S. Report on Human Rights 2002." Available at www.info.gov.hk/hab/press/040203usr.htm, accessed January 2004.

Hong Kong Information Services Department (HKISD). 2002. *Hong Kong Yearbook 2002.* Hong Kong: Information Services Department, Government of the Hong Kong Special Administrative Region. Available at www.info.gov.hk/yearbook/2002/ehtml/eindex.htm, accessed December 2003.

Hong Kong Lawyer (HKL). 2003, September. "The Mainland/Hong Kong Closer Economic Partnership Arrangement." Available at www.hk-lawyer.com/2003–9/Default.htm, accessed January 2004.

————. 2003, December. "Environmental Law Sharpens Its Teeth." Available at www.hk-lawyer.com/2003–12/Default.htm, accessed January 2004.

Hong Kong Looking Ahead (HKLA). 2003a. "Hong Kong an Ideal Sourcing Centre." News, Hong Kong Government Information Centre. Available at www.hklookingahead.gov.hk/news/sept11.htm, accessed December 2003.

————. 2003b. "Regional HQs Reach All Time High." News, Hong Kong Government Information Centre. Available at www.hklookingahead.gov.hk/news/oct21a.htm, accessed December 2003.

————. 2003c. "Good Response to Admission Scheme for Mainland Talent and Professionals." News, Hong Kong Government Information Centre. Available at www.hklookingahead.gov.hk/news/dec11a.htm, accessed December 2003.

————. 2003d. "PC and Broadband Penetration One of Highest in the World." Available at www.hklookingahead.gov.hk/news/dec11c.htm, accessed January 2004.

————. 2003e. "Green Light for Greening Hong Kong." News, Hong Kong Government Information Centre. Available at www.hklookingadhead.gov.hk/news/dec19b.htm, accessed December 2003.

————. 2003f. "Decline in Consumer Prices Narrows." News, Hong Kong Government Information Centre. Available at www.info.gov.hk/gia/general/200312/22/c1e.htm, accessed January 2004.

Hong Kong Office of the Commissioner of Insurance (HKOCI). 2003. "HK Insurance Business Statistics." Available at www.info.gov.hk/oci/statistics/index04.htm, accessed January 2004.

Hong Kong Retail Management Association (HKRMA). 2003a. "HKRMA Strongly Urge Landlords for Retail Rental Relief." Available at www.hkrma.org/en/pa/press/press20030425.html, accessed March 2004.

————. 2003b. "Mystery Shoppers Programme—2003 'Service Retailer of the Year.'" Available at www.hkrma.org/en/library/service/servicetrends20031231.html, accessed March 2004.

————. 2003c. "The Shopometer Survey: Improvements on Hong Kong's Spending Sentiment Continue." Available at www.hkrma.org/en/library/spending/spending20031219.html, accessed January 2004.

———. 2004. "Statistics Column." Available at www.hkrma.org/en/library/govstat/govtstats20031201.html, accessed March 2004.

Hong Kong SARS Expert Committee (HKSEC). 2003. "SARS in Hong Kong: From Experience to Action." Available at www.sars-expertcom.gov.hk/english/reports/reports.html, accessed March 2004.

Hong Kong Team Clean (HKTC). 2003. "Report on Measures to Improve Environmental Hygiene in Hong Kong." Available at www.had.gov.hk/en/public_services/team_clean_corner/final.htm, accessed March 2005.

Hong Kong Tobacco Control Office (HKTCO). 2003. "Tobacco Related Statistics." Available at www.tobaccocontrol.gov.hk/eng/loadframe.html?id=221, accessed January 2004.

Hong Kong Trade Development Council (HKTDC). 2002. "Economic Forum: Creative Industries in Hong Kong." Available at www.tdctrade.com/econforum/tdc/tdc020902.htm, accessed March 2004.

———. 2003a. "Profiles of Hong Kong Major Service Industries: Internet." Available at www.tdctrade.com/main/si/internet.htm, accessed March 2004.

———. 2003b. "Profiles of Hong Kong Major Service Industries: Marketing Services." Available at www.tdctrade.com/main/si/advert.htm, accessed March 2004.

———. 2003c. "Assessing Hong Kong's Deflationary Trend." Available at www.tdctrade.com/econforum/boc/boc031001.htm, accessed January 2004.

———. 2004. "Outlook for 2004." Available at www.tdctrade.com/econforum/hkma/hkma040101.htm, accessed January 2004.

Hooper, B. 1994. "From Mao to Madonna: Sources on Contemporary Chinese Culture." *Southeast Asian Journal of Social Science* [A Special Issue on Cultural Studies in Asia, ed. D. Birch] 22: 161–69.

Hsu, R. C. 1991. *Economic Theories in China, 1979–1988.* Cambridge: Cambridge University Press.

Huang, Chen Ya. 1991. "Medical and Health." In *The Other Hong Kong Report 1991,* ed. Sung Yun Wing and Lee Ming Kwan. Hong Kong: Chinese University Press, 311–28.

Hwang, Kwang-kuo. 1987. "Face and Favor: The Chinese Power Game." *American Journal of Sociology* 92(4): 944–74.

International Federation of the Periodical Press (IFPP). 2003, May 2. "Hong Kong Ad Spending Down 10% in Early April." Available at www.fipp.com/973, accessed March 2004.

———. 2004. "World Magazine Trends." Available at www.fipp.com/Data+And+Trends, accessed March 2004.

International Herald Tribune (*IHT*). 2004a. "Hong Kong Retail Bouncing Back." January 8. Available at www.iht.com/articles/124186.html, accessed January 2004.

———. 2004b. "Hong Kong Is Blocked on Plans for Harbor." January 9. Available at www.iht.com/articles/124374.html, accessed January 2004.

Joy, A. 2001. "Gift Giving in Hong Kong and the Continuum of Social Ties." *Journal of Consumer Research* 28: 239–56.

Kawahara, Yukiko, and Mark W. Speece. 1994. "Strategies of Japanese Supermarkets in Hong Kong." *International Journal of Retail and Distribution Management* 22(8): 3–12.

de Keijzer, A. J. 1992. *China: Business Strategies for the '90s.* Berkeley, CA: Pacific View Press.

Kong, C. H., and W. S. Wong. 1991. "An Opportunity Study for an American Department Store in Hong Kong." Unpublished MBA Thesis, Chinese University of Hong Kong.

Lam, Cindy. 2003. "Women's Magazines on the Runway." *Varsity Magazine* (Chinese University of Hong Kong, School of Journalism and Communication) May. Available at www.com.cuhk.edu.hk/varsity/0503/channels_a.htm, accessed January 2004.

Lam, Kit Chun, and Pak Wai Liu. 1995. "Labour Shortage in Hong Kong: Causes, Consequences and Policies." *Asian Economic Journal* 9(1): 71–87.

Lam, T. H., S. Y. Ho, A. J. Hedley, K. H. Mak, and R. Peto. 2001. "Mortality and Smoking in Hong Kong: Case-Control Study of All Adult Deaths in 1998." *BMJ* 323(August 2001): 361.

Laurent, C. R. 2003. *High Income Households in Asia.* Hong Kong: Asian Demographics, Ltd. Available at www.imaasia.com/AMAP/Presentation%20slides/Jun%202003%20-%20slides/Consumers-Jun03.pdf, accessed January 2004.

Leung, Thomas, Syson Wong, and Y. H. Wong. 1993. "Hong Kong Businessmen's Perceptions of Guanxi in the People's Republic of China." Paper presented at the Academy of International Business Conference, Hong Kong, June 23–25.

Li, D., and Gallup, A. M. 1995. "In Search of the Chinese Consumer." *The China Business Review* 22(5): 19–22.

Li, David K. P. 1995. "Enter the Dragon: Hong Kong's Growing Role in World Finance." *Columbia Journal of World Business* 30(2): 34–40.

Li Wuzhou. 2004. "People-Oriented Constitutional Amendments, China Today." Available at www.chinatoday .com.cn/English/e2004/e200405/p10.htm

Li, Zhang. 1992. "Regrets of the Cosmetics Market." *China Market* (4): 13, 17.

Lin, C. A. 2001. "Cultural Values Reflected in Chinese and American Television Advertising." *Journal of Advertising* 30(4): 83–94.

Lu Yong. 2000. "For Protecting Consumers' Rights and Interests." *People's Daily,* May 23. Available at http://english.people.com.cn/english/200005/23/eng20000523_41383.html

Luk, S. T. K., Li, H. Y., Guo, Q. G., and Yip, L. S. C. 1995. "The Strategic Roles of Advertising Agencies in China's Domestic Market." Unpublished Working Paper, Hong Kong Polytechnic University, Hong Kong.

Lum, Y. C. Richard. 1990. "Exploring the Reasons of Success of Japanese Department Stores in Hong Kong." Unpublished MBA Thesis, Chinese University of Hong Kong.

Ma, Chengguang. 1994. "Fake Goods the Result of Slack Inspections." *China Daily* 14, no. 4320 (December 28).

Marketing Guide Magazine. 1995, February. "Features and Trends, Characteristics and Prospects of Consumption Market in China" (in Chinese).

Mak, Rose. 2003. "Industry Sector Analysis: Pharmaceuticals." Washington, DC: U.S. and Foreign Commercial Service. Available at www.buyusainfo.net/info.cfm?id=72137&keyx=5A66B62055FB880A8ED4690CFE93C1B9&dbf=isa1&loadnav=, accessed February 2004.

Marquand, Robert. 2003. "In Hong Kong, Dissent Has a Female Voice." *Christian Science Monitor,* August 14. Available at www.csmonitor.com/2003/0814/p01s04-woap.html, accessed January 2004.

McGoldrick, P. J. 1992. "International Positioning: Japanese Department Stores in Hong Kong." *European Journal of Marketing* 26(8/9): 61–73.

McNeal, J. U., and M. F. Ji. 1999. "Chinese Children as Consumers: An Analysis of Their New Product Information Sources." *Journal of Consumer Marketing* 16(4): 345–64.

Media. 2001. "HK Dotcom Adspend Plummets 56pc in Q1," June 8.

Media Online. 2002. "HK Daily Switches Focus to Target Middle Class," September 20. Available at http://66.102.7.104/search?q=cache:6z1DGW1HvPsJ:www.media.com.hk/week/20020920.htm+%22HK+Daily+Switches+Focus+to+Target+Middle+Class%22&hl=en, accessed March 2004.

Ng, Catherine W. 1995. "Hong Kong MBA Student's Attitudes Toward Women as Managers: An Empirical Study." *International Journal of Management* 12(4): 454–59.

Nielsen NetRatings. 2003, May 20. "Online Shopping and Banking Sites Soared in Popularity as People in Hong Kong Shunned the Crowds." Available at www.nielsen-netratings.com/pr/pr_030520_hk.pdf, accessed March 2004.

———. 2003, July 31. "SARS Stimulates Ongoing Growth in Internet Usage in Hong Kong." Available at www.nielsen-netratings.com/pr/pr_030731_hk.pdf, accessed March 2004.

———. 2004. "NetView Usage Metrics: Hong Kong." Available at www.nielsen-netratings.com/news.jsp?section=dat_to&country=hk, accessed March 2004.

Pan, Yigang. 2000. *Greater China in the Global Marketplace.* Binghamton, NY: International Business Press.

Phillips, Lisa A., B. J. Sternquist, and S. Mui. 1992. "Hong Kong Department Stores: Retailing in the 1990s." *International Journal of Retail & Distribution Management* 20(1): 16–24.

Polsa, Pia. 1996. "Distribution Structure and Power—A Case of Consumer Goods in the People's Republic of China." Competitive Paper at the Annual Meeting of Academy of International Business, October 26–29, Banff, Canada.

Polsa, P. 1998. "Distribution of Consumer Goods in the People's Republic of China, An Empirical Study of Packaged Food Products (no. 43)." Licentiate Thesis, Swedish School of Economics and Business Administration, Helsinki.

———. 2002. "Power and Distribution Network Structure in the People's Republic of China (no. 106)." Doctoral diss., Swedish School of Economics and Business Administration, Helsinki. Available at http://www.shh.fi/~polsa/thesis.pdf.

Polsa, Pia, and Bai Chang Hong. 1998. "China, Part II: Markets within a Market." In *Marketing and Consumer Behavior in East and Southeast Asia,* ed. A. Pecotich and C. Shultz. Sydney: McGraw-Hill, 161–211.

PriceWaterhouseCoopers (PWC). 2001. "Hong Kong Internet IAB Advertising Revenue Report (for Hong

Kong Internet Advertising Bureau)." Available at www.pwchk.com/home/webmedia/984732922223/IAB, accessed March 2004.

Private Business Association. 1993. *A Paper Concerning the Encouragement of the Private Business.* Guilin, Guangxi: PBA.

Public Health and Epidemiology Bulletin (PHEB). 1997, May. "Student Health Service." 6(2). Available at www.info.gov.hk/dh/diseases/9705.htm, accessed February 2004.

———. 2004. "Special Edition: Avian Influenza." Available at www.info.gov.hk/dh/diseases/, accessed February 2004.

Rana, P. B. 1993, December. *Reforms in the Transitional Economies of Asia.* Beijing: Asian Development Bank.

Redding, S. B., and M. Ng. 1983. "The Role of 'Face' in the Organizational Perceptions of Chinese Managers." *International Studies of Management & Organization* 13(3): 92–123.

Reinganum, J., and T. Helsell. 1994. "To Market, To Market." *The China Business Review* 21(1, January–February): 30–4.

Schlevogt, K. -A. 2000. "The Branding Revolution in China." *The China Business Review* 27(3, May–June): 52–7.

Schmitt, B. 1997. "Who Is the Chinese Consumer? Segmentation in the People's Republic of China." *European Management Journal* 15(2): 191–94.

Schütte, H., and D. Ciarlante. 1998. *Consumer Behavior in Asia.* New York: New York University Press.

Schütte, H., and V. Vanier. 1995. *Consumer Behavior in Asia.* Euro-Asia Centre Research Series #33. Fontainebleau, France: INSEAD Euro-Asia Centre.

Siddall, Linda. 1991. "The Environment." In *The Other Hong Kong Report* 1991, ed. Sung Yun Wing and Lee Ming Kwan. Hong Kong: Chinese University Press, 403–19.

Sin, L. Y. M., S. L. M. So, O. H. M. Yau, and K. Kwong. 2001. "Chinese Women at the Crossroads: An Empirical Study on Their Role Orientations and Consumption Values in Chinese Society." *Journal of Consumer Marketing* 18(4): 348–67.

Siu, Wai-Sum. 1996. "Gender Portrayal in Hong Kong and Singapore Television Advertisements." *Journal of Asian Business* 12(3): 47–64.

Siu, W. S., and P. Chu. 1994. "Female Entrepreneurs in Hong Kong: Problems and Solutions." *International Journal of Management* 11(2): 728–36.

So, Alison. 2003. "Awareness of Women's Issues Remains Low in Hong Kong." *Varsity Online* (Chinese University of Hong Kong, School of Journalism and Communication) May. Available at www.com.cuhk.edu.hk/varsity/0503/social_issues_a.htm, accessed January 2004.

So, Stella L. M., and Mark Speece. 1991. "Gender Stereotyping in the Mass Media: A Review of the Hong Kong Situation." In *Mass Media Awareness Seminar: Mass Media and Women in the 90s.* Tien Dao Christian Media Association, Hong Kong Christian Service Communications Centre and Society of Television Awareness Training, Hong Kong, December 1990, 177–82.

South China Morning Post (SCMP). 2003, July 3. "Anna Wu's EOC Legacy is Well Worth Preserving." Available at www.skyline-technologies.com/news/0703/030703.htm#5, accessed January 2004.

Speece, M. 1998. "Value Orientation among Asian Middle Class Consumers." *Marketing and Research Today* (ESOMAR) 27(4): 156–65.

Speece, Mark W. 1994. "Wholesale Markets for Fresh Fruits and Vegetables in Hong Kong." (Technical Report No. 4), Regional Agribusiness Project, Bethesda, Maryland (USAID Contract AEP-0009-C-00–3057–00).

Speece, M., and S. L. M. So. 1998. "Hong Kong: The Consumer Market in the 1990s." In *Marketing and Consumer Behavior in East and Southeast Asia,* ed. A. Pecotich and C. Shultz. Sydney: McGraw-Hill, 213–56.

Speece, Mark W., Yukiko Kawahara, and Stella L. M. So. 1993. "Evaluation of U.S. FAS Market Development Activities in Hong Kong." Hong Kong: U.S. Foreign Agriculture Service.

———. 1994. "Imported Beer in the Hong Kong Market." *British Food Journal* 96(1): 10–18.

Speece, Mark W., Stella L. M. So, Yukiko Kawahara, and Laura M. Milner. 1994. "Beer Preference and Country-of-Origin in Hong Kong." *Journal of Food Products Marketing* 2(2): 43–64.

Spence, J. D. 1990. *The Search for Modern China.* New York: W.W. Norton.

Sun, Yun Wing. 2000. "The Pros and Cons of Implementing Equal Pay for Equal Value in Hong Kong." Paper prepared for the *Conference on Equal Pay for Work of Equal Value: International Best Practices,* Equal Opportunities Commission of Hong Kong, Hong Kong, March. Available at www.eoc.org.hk/_File/conference/EPEV/00/SUNG.rtf, accessed December 2003.

Sung, Yun-Wing, and Kar-Yiu Wong. 2000. "Growth of Hong Kong Before and After Its Reversion to China: The China Factor." *Pacific Economic Review* 5: 201–28.

Swanson, L. A. 1989. "The Twelve 'Nations' of China." *Journal of International Consumer Marketin* 2(1): 83–105.

Tan Kam, Pamela Mi-wah. 2001. "Keynote Address." Presented at the Conference on Equal Pay for Work of Equal Value: International Best Practices, Equal Opportunities Commission of Hong Kong, Hong Kong, October. Available at www.eoc.org.hk/TE/conference/EPEV/2001.htm, accessed December 2003.

Tong, Edwin Ka Hung. 1991. "A Study of the Effect of the Green Movement on Consumers' Purchasing Behaviour Towards Non-Durable Goods." Unpublished MBA Thesis, Chinese University of Hong Kong.

Tong J. 1999. "Survey Activities of Foreign-Funded Institutions Regulated." *Beijing Review* 42(45): 25–26.

Tse, D. K. 1996. "Understanding Chinese People as Consumers: Past Findings and Future Propositions." In *The Handbook of Chinese Psychology,* ed. M. H. Bond. Hong Kong: Oxford University Press, pp. 352–63.

Tse, D. K., R. W. Belk, and N. Zhou. 1989. "Becoming a Consumer Society: A Longitudinal and Cross-Cultural Content Analysis of Print Ads from Hong Kong, the People's Republic of China, and Taiwan." *Journal of Consumer Research* 15(4): 457–72.

United States Department of Agriculture, Foreign Agriculture Service (USDA/FAS). 2003a. "Hong Kong Food and Agricultural Import Regulations and Standards: FAIRS UPDATE—HK to go Nutrition Labeling." (Global Agriculture Information Network, GAIN Report #HK3040.) Washington, DC: USDA. Available at www.fas.usda.gov/gainfiles/200312/146085414.doc, accessed March 2003.

———. 2003b. "Hong Kong HRI Food Service Sector Report 2003." (Global Agriculture Information Network, GAIN Report #HK3019.) Washington, DC: USDA. Available at www.fas.usda.gov/gainfiles/200305/145885744.pdf, accessed March 2003.

———. 2003c. "Hong Kong Promotion Opportunities Annual 2003." (Global Agriculture Information Network, GAIN Report #HK3032.) Washington, DC: USDA. Available at www.fas.usda.gov/gainfiles/200310/145986208.doc, accessed March 2003.

———. 2003d. "Hong Kong Retail Food Sector Report 2003." (Global Agriculture Information Network, GAIN Report #HK3039.) Washington, DC: USDA. Available at www.fas.usda.gov/gainfiles/200311/145986786.doc, accessed March 2003.

United Press International (UPI). 2003, 22 October. "Analysis: HK Properties Tipped for Rebound. Available at http://quickstart.clari.net/qs_se/webnews/wed/aa/Uhongkong-properties-analysis.R7KD_DOM.html, accessed January 2003.

Vernon-Wortzel, H., and H. L. Wortzel. 1987. "The Emergence of Free Market Retailing in the People's Republic of China: Promises and Consequences." *Californian Management Review* 29(3, Spring): 59–76.

Wan, Po San. 1991. "The Quality of Life." In *The Other Hong Kong Report 1991,* ed. Sung Yun Wing and Lee Ming Kwan. Hong Kong: Chinese University Press, 421–46.

Wiemer, C. 1992. "Price Reform and Structural Change, Distributional Impediments to Allocative Gains." *Modern China* 18(2, April): 171–96.

Women's Commission of Hong Kong (WCHK). 2002. "Survey on the Extent and Level of Positions Taken Up by Women in the Private and Non-Governmental Sectors in Hong Kong." Hong Kong: Women's Commission. Available at www.women.gov.hk/download/executive_summary_20021115_e.pdf, accessed January 2004.

Wong, H. 2003. "The Quality of Life of Hong Kong's Poor Households in the 1990s: Cost of Living, Income Security and Poverty Situation." Paper presented at the International Conference on Quality of Life in a Global World, November 14–15. Available at http://web.swk.cuhk.edu.hk/~hwong/publication/Conference/Cost%200f%20Living_final.doc, accessed January 2004.

Wong, K. H. Raymond. 1991. "Pharmaceuticals, American Chamber of Commerce in Hong Kong, Doing Business in Today's Hong Kong." Hong Kong: American Chamber of Commerce, 309–16.

Wong, Sandy H. Y. 2003. "An Update on Hong Kong Immigration Policy." *Hong Kong Lawyer,* November. Available at www.hk-lawyer.com/2003–11/Default.htm, accessed January 2004.

Wong, Y. C. Richard. 2002a. "Public Housing Reform and Its Effects on the Private Housing Market." *HKCER Letters* 71(July/August). Available at www.hku.hk/hkcer/articles/v71/ycrwong.htm, accessed December 2003.

———. 2002b. "Shanghai: Another Hong Kong?" *HKCER Letters* 72(September–December). Available at www.hku.hk/hkcer/articles/v72/ycrwong.htm, accessed December 2003.

Wu, Anna. 2001. "Women in Hong Kong." Speech given as Head of the Equal Opportunities Commission of Hong Kong. Available at www.eoc.org.hk/TE/speech/010510e.htm, accessed January 2004.

———. 2002. "Stereotyping, Discrimination and Fair Reporting." Speech given as Chairperson of the Equal Opportunities Commission of Hong Kong. Available at www.eoc.org.hk/TE/speech/020426e.htm, accessed January 2004.

———. 2003. "The Role and Work of the Equal Opportunities Commission: Its Impact and Challenges." Speech given as Chairperson of the Equal Opportunities Commission of Hong Kong. Available at www.eoc.org.hk/CE/speech/index.htm, accessed January 2004.

Wu, Wei-Ping. 1994. "Guanxi and Its Managerial Implications for Western Firms in China—A Case Study." Paper presented at International Conference on Management Issues for China in the 1990s, Cambridge, March 23–25.

Xiao, Chen. 1993a. "Private Business Taps Advantages of State Firms." *China Daily* 12, no. 3722 (May 5).

———. 1993b. "Production Comes First in Big Ownership Debate." *China Daily* 13, no. 3912 (November 11).

Xie, Bai-san. 1991. *China's Economic Policies, Theories and Reforms since 1949.* Shanghai: Fudan University Press.

Xinhua News Agency. 2003. "First Lead: Chinese Mainland, Hong Kong Sign Closer Economic Ties Pact," June 29.

Yan, R. 1994. "To Reach China Consumers, Adapt to *Guo Qing.*" *Harvard Business Review* (September–October): 66–74.

Yan, X. 1999. "Discussion on the Amendment of China's Constitution." *Beijing Review* 42(11): 13–15.

Yan, Y. 2000. "Of Hamburger and Social Space, Consuming McDonald's in Beijing." In *The Consumer Revolution in Urban China,* ed. D. S. Davis. Berkeley: University of California Press, 201–25.

Young, Sook Moon, and Kara Chan. 2002. "Gender Portrayal in Hong Kong and Korean Children's TV Commercials: A Cross-Cultural Comparison." *Asian Journal of Communication* 12(2): 100–19.

Yung, Mei. 2003. "Hong Kong Country Commercial Guide in Macau 2004: Marketing U.S. Products & Services." Washington, DC: U.S. & Foreign Commercial Service. Available at www.buyusainfo.net/info.cfm?id=118385&keyx=BCEBE6342F4AF43E1DE58361E90B6862&dbf=ccg1&loadnav=, accessed March 2004.

Zhou, Shunwu. 1992. *China Provincial Geography.* Beijing: Foreign Languages Press.

Zhou, Yuan. 1993. "Food Chain Altering the Face of Beijing Shopping." *China Daily/Business Weekly* 13, no. 3761/28 (June 13–19).

CHAPTER 5

EAST TIMOR

Realizing Its Potential

TONY LAPSLEY

OVERVIEW

The new nation of East Timor shares the island of Timor with Indonesia. Formerly a Portuguese colony, it became Indonesia's twenty-seventh province on July 17, 1976, after a brutal invasion eight months earlier. In 1999, the East Timorese voted to end Indonesian rule in a ballot conducted by the United Nations (UN), deciding thus to resume a process of decolonization, which had begun twenty-five years earlier. East Timor is a nation in the making. Left in late 1999 with massive social, political, and economic deficits, this small Southeastern Asian nation is intent on fostering private enterprise activity as a means of generating economic and social development. This chapter provides an overview of East Timor as it enters independence, with a particular focus on its evolving economy and market, and its needs and opportunities for private-sector investment.

INTRODUCTION AND RECENT HISTORY

On December 7, 1975, Indonesia invaded the Portuguese colony of East Timor. The pretext for the invasion was the Balibo Declaration that purported to articulate the decision of the East Timorese people to integrate their homeland within the Republic of Indonesia. The declaration was a sham hastily prepared by Indonesian intelligence and signed by an unrepresentative group of East Timorese political leaders.

The Balibo Declaration (1975) called on Indonesia to "take necessary steps in order to protect" the lives of people who were "living under the terror and fascist practices of Fretilin allowed by the Government of Portugal." Fretilin, a pro-independence political party, had assumed power on November 28, 1975, after a brief civil war. The Portuguese administration had withdrawn from the territory in the initial stages of civil disorder in August. But, by late November, the major threat to peace in the territory was coming from Indonesia itself through a covert military campaign called *Operasi Komodo* (the Komodo Operation). For over a year, Indonesian intelligence had sought to subvert a process of self-determination for East Timor, which had been set in train by the Portuguese.

Indonesia's armed intervention was deplored by the UN General Assembly on December 12, 1975, and, again, by the UN Security Council on December 22. The UN called on Indonesia to withdraw and upheld the right of the East Timorese people to an act of self-determination.

In 1999, Indonesia succumbed to international pressure and permitted the establishment of a UN mission in East Timor. The UNAMET (United Nations Mission in East Timor) had a mandate to hold a "popular consultation" to determine the future status of the territory. Jakarta was offering "special autonomy" within the Republic of Indonesia or, if autonomy was rejected, withdrawal from East Timor. The pro-Indonesian, autonomy option was canvassed by the UNIF (United Front for East Timorese Autonomy—*Front Bersama Pro-Otonomi Timor Timur*) and ruthlessly supported by militia groups in each district backed by the Indonesian military. Intent on gaining votes through intimidation, the militia had already committed gross violations of human rights, including mass murder, by the time UNAMET was established in June 1999. The "no autonomy" vote, which constituted a vote for independence, was canvassed by the CNRT (*Conselho Nacional da Resistência Timorense*—National Council of Timorese Resistance), a coalition of pro-independence parties, headed by Xanana Gusmão in detention in Jakarta. The pro-independence guerrilla force, FALINTIL, had been stood down and accepted cantonment to exclude any impression that a state of civil war existed, which could jeopardize the vote.

On Monday, August 30, 1999, after several days of renewed violence and intimidation, 78.5 percent of the 451,792 registered voters courageously rejected the option of remaining within the Republic of Indonesia with limited self-government, and, thus, set East Timor on a course toward independence.

UNAMET had brought hope to the vast majority of East Timorese. Established at the request of Indonesia and Portugal in an agreement signed on May 5, 1999, the presence of the UN signaled that a just solution to the "Timor problem" was finally at hand. After years of repression and resistance within the territory and stalemated negotiations between Portugal and Indonesia, there was cause for hope. The reality, however, was that UNAMET was not fully empowered by the agreement of May 5. It had no direct peacekeeping or policing capacity with which it might seek to ensure a peaceful environment conducive to the fulfillment of its mandate. Under the agreement, responsibility for keeping the peace remained with Indonesia. The obligation was self-imposed. Jakarta was adamant that it would not surrender the peacekeeping role to an international force.

The arrangement had given cause for concern. Indonesia's armed forces, which controlled both the military and the police, had not demonstrated a capacity to maintain peace and good order in the territory. In fact, their twenty-four-year history of keeping the peace in East Timor was characterized by a gross disregard for human rights. In recent times, they had actively supported the formation of the pro-Indonesian militia units and failed to intervene in the intimidation and violence perpetrated by these groups against supporters of independence. Moreover, there was irrefutable evidence that members of the armed forces had actively participated in such activities.

The East Timorese had suffered horrifically for twenty-four years. According to Resolution 237 (1998) of the U.S. Senate, Indonesia's illegal occupation had claimed "the lives of approximately 200,000 East Timorese."[1] And, even after the vote, the suffering continued, as militia groups and Indonesian military personnel perpetrated an act of massive vandalism and violence. Hundreds of thousands of people fled for their lives into the mountains, and it is estimated that over 250,000 were taken to West Timor, the vast majority forcibly. Relief arrived on September 21, 1999, in the form of a multinational force (INTERFET), and humanitarian aid. Some weeks later, following the visit of a Joint Assessment Mission comprising UN agencies, potential donor countries, and East Timorese representatives, the World Bank reported:

> Implementation of the results of the ballot should have been an occasion for celebration. Instead, the people of East Timor were forced to watch the birth of their new country through

a haze of smoke and tears, as orchestrated violence after announcement of the ballot results wreaked physical destruction and human terror from Tutuala [in the east] to Oecussi [in the west]. It is estimated that over 75 percent of the population was displaced in the weeks following the ballot results, and almost 70 percent of physical infrastructure destroyed or rendered inoperable. (World Bank 1999d, 1)

In the vacuum that existed immediately following the violence, the CNRT used its clandestine administrative structure, which reached from the national level to the subvillage level. With the Catholic Church, this organization greatly facilitated the distribution of emergency aid and the difficult return to social order. In October 1999, the UNTAET (United Nations Transitional Administration in East Timor) was established by the Security Council to form an interim administration for the country under the leadership of Sergio Vieira de Mello, who held the dual roles of special representative of the secretary-general and transitional administrator.

THE NATURAL SYSTEM

Timor lies at the eastern extremity of the Lesser Sunda archipelago, approximately 500 kilometers northwest of Australia's Northern Territory. The island of 32,000 square kilometers is shared by East Timor and the Indonesian province of Nusa Tenggara Timur, which stretches from West Timor to Lombok, east of Bali. East Timor is bounded in the south by the Timor Sea and, in the north, by the Wetar and Ombai Straits, which separate it from the neighboring Indonesian islands of Wetar and Alor.

The country has an area of 14,609 square kilometers, making it slightly larger than Connecticut. It is divided into thirteen districts, twelve of which occupy 13,644 square kilometers in the eastern part of the island and one of which, Oecusse, occupies 815 square kilometers on the northern coast of West Timor, about 80 kilometers from the rest of the country (see Table 5.1). East Timorese territory also includes two islands—Atauro with an area of 151 square kilometers, located off the north coast some 20 kilometers from the capital city, Dili, and Jaco, just off the eastern coast, with an area of 11 square kilometers.

East Timor is 265 kilometers long and has a maximum width of 92 kilometers. Its most salient topographical feature is the Ramelau Mountain Range, which runs the entire length of the country. Seven mountains in this chain are over 2,000 meters in height, the highest being Mount Ramelau (also known as Tatamailau) in Ermera, with an elevation of 2,963 meters (*Timor Timur dalam Angka* 1997, 7). In the north of the country, the mountains or their foothills generally extend to the coast, giving way in some places to narrow plains, as is the case around Dili. In the south, there are more extensive plains, with a total area of 150,000 hectares. These stretch inland from the coast for up to 30 kilometers. In the hinterland, the sharply undulating relief is broken at intervals by plateaus totaling some 70,000 hectares. The most notable of these are the high plains around Los Palos in the east and Bobonaro in the west. The agricultural value of the south coast and inland plains is enhanced by a relatively higher rainfall.

Lying between lat 8°17' S and 10°22' S, East Timor is within the southern monsoon belt and has a tropical climate with two seasons, wet and dry. While the country is relatively small in area, there are marked variations in such climatic features as temperature, rainfall, and seasonal duration as a result of differences in elevation and location in respect to the Ramelau range. The mean annual temperature of Dili on the north coast is 27.5° C, while that of Maubisse in the highlands at 1,432 meters above sea level is 19.8° C (Keefer 2000, cited by Sandlund et al. 2001, 10). In the north coastal region, the wet season is from November to April, and it brings an annual rainfall of

Table 5.1

East Timor Area by District

District	Area (km²)	Percentage of total land area
Dili	371.60	2.5
Liquiça	548.12	3.8
Aileu	729.49	4.9
Ermera	746.00	5.1
Ainaro	798.87	5.5
Oecusse	814.66	5.6
Covalima	1,225.53	8.4
Manufahi	1,324.91	9.1
Bobonaro	1,368.12	9.4
Baucau	1,493.80	10.2
Lautem	1,702.33	11.6
Manatuto	1,705.45	11.7
Viqueque	1,780.50	12.2
East Timor	14,609.38	100

Source: Kanwil BPN Propinsi Timor Timur (National Land Board, East Timor Office) cited in *Timor Timur dalam Angka, Bappeda Tingkat I Propinsi Timor Timur dengan Badan Pusat Statistik Propinsi Timor Timur* (Annual Report with Statistics) (Dili: The Indonesian Regional Development Planning Board of East Timor and the Central Board of Statistics of East Timor, 1997), p. 3.

600 to 1,000 millimeters, while in the same period, the mountainous hinterland receives between 1,800 and 3,000 millimeters. The south experiences a longer wet season, lasting from December to June, and has an annual rainfall of 1,250 to 3,000 millimeters (Food and Agriculture Organization [FAO] and World Food Program [WFP] 1999).

The country is subject to periodic drought caused by the El Niño southern oscillation. The effect of the most recent occurrence of this phenomenon, in 1997–98, was widespread crop failure. But, even in the best of years, East Timor is "unusually dry" compared with other islands in its region, with much of its rainfall not being retained (Sandlund et al. 2001, 13). Irregular, heavy rains combine with the mountainous topography to cause high volumes of water to run off the slopes into the valleys and into the sea. This results not only in the loss of water but also in soil erosion, landslides, and, when particularly heavy downpours occur, localized flash flooding in the lower coastal areas. Rivers, which typically flow north or south off the highlands, are generally short and shallow and do not have the capacity to contain large volumes of water. Most rivers flow only during the wet season, and even then, they exhibit wide variations in volume as a result of irregular rainfall and their relatively small catchment areas.

Rain-related problems have been exacerbated by human activities. The cohesion and water-retention capacity of the soil has been diminished in many areas by an excessive harvesting of trees for timber; this was prevalent during the period of Indonesian occupation. Slash-and-burn farming is also a factor, particularly its overly zealous application, which has manifested itself in the annual burning of vegetation beyond tracts of land destined for planting. A further factor is the cutting of trees for use as cooking fuel, a necessity for low-income families who cannot afford kerosene.[2]

In contrast to the overexploitation of forests, the coastal ecosystem is "largely unspoilt" (Sandlund et al. 2001, 47). Pristine coral reefs provide protected spawning areas for sea creatures, and, combined with mountain-fringed beaches, represent a potential tourist attraction. While saltwater fish are an important food item for people living near the coast, potentially valuable fisheries remain largely untouched by the activities of traditional fisher-folk. The coastal zone, thus, has the potential, if properly managed, to provide a significant, ongoing contribution to the country's economic development.

East Timor's urban environment is small. The major urban center is Dili in the district of the same name. The district (excluding the island of Atauro) has an area of 372 square kilometers and a population of 124,427 representing approximately 20,000 households.[3] Solid waste disposal has been a problem that begs ongoing attention. The need to address indiscriminate dumping and the lack of segregation of waste in the city's dump site have been recognized. An increase in vehicles since the return to normalcy, after the establishment of UNTAET, has slowed traffic flow on the main road in the small city, but neither congestion nor vehicular pollution would seem to constitute a major problem.

East Timor shares with other countries potential sources of pollution from "sewage, harbor wastes, oil spillage, pesticides" and "industrial waste," to which its coastal zone would be particularly vulnerable (Sandlund et al. 2001, 22). But the major environmental issue at present would seem to be deforestation and the related problem of watershed management, discussed above.

> In the steep watersheds of East Timor . . . improved management of the hillsides is crucial to reduce the negative environmental impacts on local communities and population groups in the steep upland areas, in the flat rice-growing areas, as well as in urban areas. In short, the success or failure in integrated watershed management may influence the lives of all groups in East Timor. (Sandlund et al. 2001, 44–45)

Early in the UN mission, an Environmental Protection Unit (EPU) and a Forestry Division were established. Interim legislative support for these agencies has been provided. Under UNTAET regulation 2001/17, logging, export of timber, and other activities that would contribute to deforestation are prohibited. Regulation 2000/19 seeks to conserve the "biodiversity" and protect the "biological resources of East Timor" by proscribing activities that would negatively impact wild areas, endangered species, coral reefs, wetlands, and mangrove areas.

In addition to its potentially valuable coastal zone and agricultural capacity, the natural resources of the country include substantial offshore reserves of oil and gas in the Timor Sea, and possibly onshore oil reserves in the south of the country. There may also be mineral deposits, significant enough to attract extraction industries. Full recovery and economic development in East Timor will depend to a very large degree on the exploitation of its natural resources. To ensure poverty reduction and the ongoing welfare of its people, what is developed will have to be sustainable, and to be sustainable, it will have to be based on environmentally sound principles. The Directorate of Environment is well placed in the national Ministry for Economic Affairs.

THE POLITICAL SYSTEM

> I cannot envisage democratic power without the periodic renewal of mandates by means of democratic elections, without a free media, without guaranteeing the fundamental rights of citizens, without an independent and efficient judiciary, without a strong, conscious and participatory civil society and without a responsible opposition. (Alkatiri 2001b)

UNTAET was established on October 25, 1999, by the UN Security Council (Resolution 1272, 1999) with the following mandate:

(a) To provide security and maintain law and order throughout the territory of East Timor
(b) To establish an effective administration
(c) To assist in the development of civil and social services
(d) To ensure the coordination and delivery of humanitarian assistance, rehabilitation, and development assistance
(e) To support capacity building for self-government
(f) To assist in the establishment of conditions for sustainable development

The resolution vested in the special representative of the secretary-general in East Timor responsibility for all aspects of the UN's activities in the territory and the "power to enact new laws and to amend, suspend or repeal existing ones" (Resolution 1272 1999). The UN mission became, thus, the interim government of East Timor, and the transitional administrator, Sergio Vieira de Mello, the interim head of state.

From the outset, despite the urgent tasks of restoring peace and normalcy to civil society and providing humanitarian aid, the Transitional Administration was to be inclusive of East Timor. While all legislative and executive authority was exercised by the transitional administrator, Vieira de Mello committed, on November 17, 1999, in the first regulation he promulgated, to "consult and cooperate closely with representatives of the East Timorese people" (UNTAET Regulation 1999/1). To this end, a National Consultative Council was established by regulation five days later (UNTAET Regulation 1999/2). This Council consisted of fifteen members: seven from the resistance coalition, the CNRT; three from political groups outside the CNRT; one from the Catholic Church, one from the Transitional Administration; and three were other members of UNTAET.

In accordance with the provisions of the regulation, the Council established committees comprised of East Timorese and international experts in the areas of agriculture, education, environment, finance and macroeconomics, health, human rights, infrastructure, local administration, and natural resources. The committees covered the areas of responsibility of departments in UNTAET's embryonic civil service and enhanced the Council's capacity to operate as an effective adviser to the administrator.

Under Indonesian rule, East Timor was a province administered by a governor. Each of the thirteen districts (*kabupaten*) had its own administration headed by a *bupati* (administrator). There were also subdistrict (*kecamatan*) administrations coordinated by *camat* (subdistrict administrators). Below these were the traditional structures of the *desa* (villages) and the *kampong* (subvillages). Each of the levels from province to subdistrict was staffed by salaried civil servants. And, while there were provincial and district-level *Dewan Perwakilan Rakyat* (Houses of Representatives), there was no real participation in the political process by the people of an occupied East Timor, and a Golangan Karya (Golkar) (the government's chosen instrument for political action a managed organization of "functional groups") dominated Indonesia.

Although 74.6 percent of civil servants were East Timorese by the end of the occupation, "Indonesians filled top echelons in both vertical and provincial administration" in the province (World Bank 1999a, 1). Thus, there had been little opportunity for East Timorese involvement in the decision-making process through policy development and the provision of advice at any level of provincial government. In mid-2000, Vieira de Mello initiated two important measures to enhance participation.

In the early stages of the mission, the civil service was staffed almost entirely by international UN staff, because it was seeking to provide emergency services while, at the same time, being in establishment mode and also developing an effective system for the recruitment of national staff.

During the second quarter of 2000, the recruitment of East Timorese began to accelerate, but predominantly at junior levels. In July, a new, reorganized civil service, the East Timor Transitional Administration (ETTA) was established. ETTA included a cabinet comprising eight portfolios. East Timorese were appointed to the portfolios of internal administration, infrastructure, economic affairs, and social affairs (which included health and education).

The second measure initiated in July 2000 to enhance East Timorese participation in decision making was the establishment of a National Council to replace the Consultative Council. The new Council had a broader, community-based membership. In addition to the CNRT, non-CNRT parties, and the Catholic Church, representatives were now drawn from the Protestant Church, the Muslim community, women's organizations, student and youth organizations, the East Timorese NGO Forum, professional associations, the farming community, the business community, labor organizations, and each of the thirteen districts. While members were appointed by the transitional administrator, nominations were widely canvassed from each of the groups. The National Council was wholly Timorese. Its function was as follows (UNTAET Regulation 2000/24):

(a) To initiate, to modify, and to recommend draft regulations
(b) To amend regulations
(c) At the request of a majority of the Council, to require the appearance of Cabinet Officers . . . to answer questions regarding their respective functions

An East Timorese legislature was in the making.

By July 2001, 90 percent of Timorese civil servants had been recruited. Timorese now filled the positions of district administrator and deputy district administrator in each of the thirteen districts and held five of the eight cabinet portfolios. And, East Timor was preparing for its first election of national representatives. A civic education program was under way in the villages, and constitutional commissions in each district were holding consultations with local communities to inform them of the process for preparing and adopting the constitution and to obtain their input.

The resistance umbrella organization, CNRT, had been dissolved the previous month to enable its constituent parties to contest the election in their own right, and this was causing confusion at the village level. Village and subvillage chiefs had virtually all been CNRT members, and to a large degree, they saw the organization and its highly influential president, Xanana Gusmão, as the source of their authority. They were asked by the ETTA to continue to lend their support to the transitional process as local leaders until independence, when their role would be clarified by the constitution. Enormous demands were being made on the people of East Timor at all levels of civil society to participate in nation building. At the same time, they were still coping with the trauma of twenty-four years of occupation and the brutality of 1999, and were continuing to accept into the community former militia returning from West Timor, many of whom had been directly involved in that brutality. The people were responding extraordinarily well.

In the forthcoming election, voters would elect a constituent assembly of eighty-eight members, thirteen of whom would be district representatives. The remaining seventy-five seats would be determined on a nationwide basis. The constituent assembly's mandate would include the preparation of "a Constitution for a free and democratic East Timor," taking into account the results of community consultations (UNTAET Regulation 2001/2). The constitution would be adopted by the assembly with an affirmative vote of at least sixty of the eighty-eight members. The assembly would also be required to consider any draft legislation submitted by the transitional administrator. It was also mandated to become East Timor's legislature after independence, if stipulated by the constitution.

There was some trepidation in the community concerning the election, perhaps most noticeably among the long-suffering women of East Timor. Many recalled the brief but violent civil war between the two major parties in 1975—Fretilin and the *União Democrática Timorense* (UDT) (Timorese Democratic Union). All recalled the last time that they voted, on August 30, 1999, a time that was preceded and followed by horrific violence. The assembly election would be held on the second anniversary of that ballot. In response to the concerns of the people, political leaders signed a Pact of National Unity on July 8, 2001. The pact was endorsed by leaders of fourteen political parties and was witnessed by five of its strongest supporters—Xanana Gusmão, Sergio de Mello, Nobel laureates Jose Ramos-Horta and Dom Carlos Filipe Ximenes Belo (Bishop of Dili), and Dom Basilio do Nascimento (Bishop of Baucau). Two small parties, the *Partido Nacionalist Timorense* (Timorese Nationalist Party) and the *Partido Republika Nacional Timor Leste* (National Republican Party of East Timor), did not sign. The signatories to the Pact of National Unity committed themselves and their parties to, inter alia:

- respect the results of the election . . . ;
- defend the principles of non-violence . . . ;
- disseminate the practice of no-violence in relations between political parties . . . ;
- defend multi-party democracy . . . ;
- defend peace and stability, by means of a process of national reconciliation based on justice and the respect for human dignity;
- promote equality of rights and the principles of non-discrimination and non-exclusion . . . ; and
- defend the Constitution to be approved by the Constituent Assembly (Pacto Unidade Nacional Nian 2001).

On August 30, 2001, after a peaceful campaign, 384,248 East Timorese voted in an election contested by candidates from sixteen political parties and sixteen independents. Fretilin won fifty-five of the eighty-eight seats, comprising forty-three national seats and twelve of the thirteen district representative seats. The district seat for Oecussi went to an independent. The *Partido Democrático* (Democratic Party) won seven seats and two parties, the *Partido Sosial Democrata* (Social Democrat Party) and the *Associação Sosial-Democrata* (Social-Democrat Association) each gained six seats. Five parties secured two seats each, and three parties gained one seat each.

Fretilin, which had briefly governed East Timor in 1975 in the period between the withdrawal of the Portuguese and the invasion of the Indonesians, had been the dominant nationalist force during the twenty-four years of occupation. The party's parliamentary leader is Dr. Mari Alkatiri, who has been an active proponent of independence since his youth. A cofounder of Fretilin, he is an astute politician and possesses a clear vision of what his party has been entrusted to do by the people. Fretilin's macroeconomic policy, Mari Alkatiri explains, is one that will foster a free market economy and promote investment in order to create an economic environment in which poverty reduction can be achieved:

> East Timor will have a free market economy with some specific intervention of the state, mostly in social areas. Natural resources will, of course, be owned by the state and concessions will be granted to businesses. Our concern is sustainability. Poverty reduction is one of the most important tasks before us. After struggling for 24 years the expectation of the people is high. We need to fulfill that expectation and this government will give full priority to poverty alleviation. Investors will play an important role in this area through job creation. (Alkatiri 2001b)

Three weeks after the election, on September 19, 2001, a Council of Ministers was established by UNTAET regulation, which marked yet a further empowerment of East Timorese in preparation for independence. The all-Timorese Council, headed by Mari Alkatiri, as chief minister, was given a broad mandate, including responsibility for administering a reconstituted civil service, the East Timor Public Administration. It was given the power to take legal proceedings to "acquire, hold and dispose of property" and to "enter into contracts and similar agreements," with the exception of those with other states (UNTAET Regulation 2001/28). Ministerial portfolios in the Council comprised: internal administration; health; justice; finance; economic affairs and development; natural and mineral resources; foreign affairs and cooperation; water and public works; communications and transport; education, culture, and youth; labor and solidarity; and agriculture and fisheries. With the establishment of the Constituent Assembly and the Council of Ministers, East Timor had come as close to self-government as UNTAET's mandate would permit prior to a complete handover.

Notable among those who chose not to put themselves forward as candidates in the election were Xanana Gusmão and Jose Ramos-Horta. Former high-profile members of Fretilin, they have eschewed partisan politics. Jose Ramos-Horta has been appointed to the Council of Ministers as senior minister of foreign affairs and cooperation. Given his experience since 1975 as representative of the independence movement overseas and his high international profile, it is a position he is likely to retain after independence. Xanana Gusmão is certain to be elected as president, such is his immense popularity. As head of state, he will generate confidence among his people and have, thus, a stabilizing influence as they emerge from the trauma of their recent history to establish their national identity.

East Timorese evolution has been peaceful and relatively stable. The election campaign was conducted with very very few incidents, and no brutality, or violence. Political stability is a fundamental prerequisite for the development of East Timor's economy, and given the recent history of this nation, it may well be an area of concern for potential investors. The transitional administrator is confident that a durable stability has been established:

> Some cynical observers may have thought that the East Timorese lacked the political maturity, but they were proved wrong. Political stability will last. New institutions are fragile. They will require consolidation and capacity building. The overarching political framework is stable. There was a lot of skepticism over the capacity of the East Timorese to draw up a constitution. But in the Constituent Assembly we have witnessed a remarkable display of competence in debates. The Constitution will be very democratic establishing fundamental rights and a sound division of powers, respecting the independence of the judiciary. Institutions may be fragile, but the basis is very strong. (Vieira de Mello 2001)

THE ECONOMIC SYSTEM

East Timor emerges into nationhood from a position of extreme poverty. With an average per capita income of $350 in the mid-1990s (International Monetary Fund [IMF] 2000a, 3), it was one of the poorest of the Indonesian provinces and "one of the poorest areas in South-East Asia" (World Bank 1999a, 1). Thirty percent of its households, double the national average, were below the poverty line in 1996 (World Bank 1999a, 1). According to a 1997 population profile by Indonesia's Family Planning Organization, 70.59 percent of the province's 422 villages were considered to be impoverished; this compared with a national figure of 31.47 percent and was second only to Irian Jaya's 77.52 percent (Badan Koordinasi Keluarga Berencana Nasional 1998, xiv). The World Bank (1999a, 1) estimated a per capita GDP of $431 for 1996 compared with a national average of $1,153. The following year, as the effects of the Asian economic crisis began to be felt, per capita GDP declined to around $395 (Asian Development Bank 2001). While an annual revenue injection of approximately $100 million was anticipated from the exploitation of oil and gas fields in the Timor Sea (Australian and New Zealand Banking Group Ltd. [ANZ] 2001, 1), building a new nation with a viable economy would have presented immense challenges for East Timor in the best of circumstances. The events of September 1999, however, condemned the country to commencing this process from a point far below the low economic base it had anticipated. "We are starting from below zero!" leaders would tell the people in the early months of transitional administration.

The findings of the Joint Assessment Mission to East Timor revealed the economic impact of the destruction. When the Mission visited the country in October and November 1999, the civil service had been rendered inoperable. Most administration buildings had been burned, equipment had been wrecked, and files and archives had been destroyed, taken, or left to the mercy of weather. There was no central bank or any public banking system. There was, thus, no mechanism for East Timorese (wage earners or providers of goods and services) to collect monies owed by government or the private sector, and there was no access to savings. Several currencies were now in use. Activities in the important agricultural sector had been severely disrupted. Those who had controlled manufacturing and service businesses had left the country, their premises generally in ruins. There had been a sudden outflow of human resources in both the government and private sectors—non-Timorese who had held senior managerial and technical positions. Demand seriously exceeded supply and was causing hyperinflation. The World Bank's observations included the following:

> Administrative structures of the government, including revenue and budget functions, have disappeared. . . . Over 70 percent of administrative buildings have been partially or completely destroyed, and almost all office equipment and consumable materials have been destroyed. . . . Only the shell of the central bank building remains, while the public banking system was systematically dismantled: every vault of any size has been destroyed, the bank buildings have been burned or destroyed, and records and assets were reportedly removed to various parts of Indonesia. . . . Various currencies are now in circulation, including the Indonesian rupiah, U.S. dollar, Australian dollar, Thai baht, and Philippine peso. . . . Modern sectors, including manufacturing and services, were largely controlled by non-Timorese who have left the country, and suffered damage ranging from serious to complete destruction. The Timorese dominate primary agriculture, where output and incomes will be seriously affected as a result of the disrupted planting, harvest and commercialization cycles. Virtually all technical expertise was provided by non-Timorese and huge gaps in the set of skills required to sustain the modern economy have been exposed after their departure. . . . Both the public and private sectors have suffered almost total collapse in the aftermath of the violence in East Timor. The economy has been hit by a dramatic supply shock. . . . Acute shortages are leading to spiraling prices, with an ad-hoc price survey in Dili market indicating an increase in the consumer price index for poor households in Dili of some 200 percent between August and October. (World Bank 1999a-d, 1–4)

The IMF (2000a, 34) estimated that, as a result of the destruction, GDP for 1999 declined by 38.5 percent.

On December 17, 1999, a conference was held in Tokyo to consider the Joint Assessment Mission's findings and recommendations and to secure funds for East Timor's social, political, and economic regeneration and preparation for independence. Represented were more than fifty countries, the East Timorese leadership, UNTAET, the IMF, the World Bank, the Asian Development Bank, UN agencies, and nongovernmental organizations (NGOs). Donor governments pledged $523 million, of which $157 million would be dedicated to the continuation of humanitarian aid, and $366 million would be dedicated to the "support of governance and administrative capacity building, economic and social reconstruction" (UNTAET and World Bank 2000, 1). Three mechanisms were endorsed by the conference for the provision of support in this latter category.

The first is the Trust Fund for East Timor (TFET), administered by the World Bank in cooperation with the Asian Development Bank. This fund "concentrates on basic post-conflict reconstruction, including physical rehabilitation of key social and economic infrastructure, core sectoral policy development, and support to recovery of the private sector and economic institutions" (World Bank 2001). The second mechanism, the Consolidated Fund for East Timor, administered by UNTAET, supports the day-to-day governance of the country and, thus, institution and capacity building. It has been the major source of funding for the administration's budget. The third mechanism for support endorsed by the Tokyo conference is bilateral aid—funding by individual governments. The UN Development Programme (UNDP) has been a conduit for bilateral aid in such areas as environmental protection, capacity building, water supply, road rehabilitation, irrigation, and the restoration of port facilities. Six-monthly "Donors' Conferences" have followed the Tokyo conference to monitor developments, to consider program proposals, and to coordinate the provision of aid.

The restoration of payments capabilities within East Timor was achieved through the establishment of a Central Payments Office (CPO) in January 2000 (Central Payments Office 2001a). In addition to operating "one or more payments systems," the CPO's responsibilities included maintaining a secure depository for currency, ensuring the supply of banknotes and coins, and fulfilling a regulatory role in relation to banks (UNTAET Regulation 2000/6). The creation of the CPO was the first stage in the development of a central bank.

By the end of 2001, the CPO had licensed two commercial banks to operate in East Timor. They are the Portuguese Banco Nacional Ultramarino (BNU) and the Australian and New Zealand Banking Group Limited (ANZ). BNU, in addition to providing the normal range of banking services, has been an implementing partner of the World Bank's Small Enterprise Project, through which selected East Timorese entrepreneurs have received start-up loans, and it also provides a tax payment facility for the administration. As of January 2002, both ANZ and BNU had premises only in Dili. BNU, however, plans to extend its activities outside the capital in the short term. It established a branch in East Timor's second largest center, Baucau, in 2002, and offers some services in regional business centers established by the World Bank. It also operates a mobile bank, which has assisted in the Small Enterprise Program and the administration's "dollarization" program.

Since January 2000, the official currency of East Timor has been the U.S. dollar (UNTAET Regulation 2000/7). The CPO had carriage of introducing the new currency, which would replace the rupiah, which had been legal tender during the Indonesian occupation. The rationale for choosing the dollar was its strength, stability, and credibility, and its use as the major reserve currency in the world (Central Payments Office 2001b). It was envisaged that the dollar's stability would contribute to the maintenance of low inflation and interest rates and that this effect, along with its credibility, would serve to attract investment and, thus, foster economic growth. Indeed, the dollar is the preferred currency in the region for international business transactions. While the rupiah was still competing with the dollar at the lower-priced end of the market in the final quarter of 2001, the CPO's public education campaign combined with a currency exchange program was continuing to return positive results.

In November 2001, the second step was taken toward the establishment of a central bank, when the CPO was replaced by the Banking and Payments Authority (BPA) of East Timor. An autonomous authority with its own governing board, the BPA's principal objective is "to achieve and to maintain domestic price stability." In addition to protecting the purchasing power of the country's currency, it is mandated to "foster the liquidity and solvency of a stable market-based banking and financial system, to execute the foreign exchange policy . . . and to promote a safe, sound, and efficient payment system" (UNTAET Regulation 2001/30). With legislation that backs its administrative autonomy with financial independence and clearly delineates the monetary and fiscal roles in East Timor's macroeconomic environment, the BPA represents an effective mechanism for the management of the new nation's monetary system.

For the greater part of the UN mission in East Timor, responsibility for fiscal management was held, under the authority of the transitional administrator, by the Central Fiscal Authority (CFA) (UNTAET Regulation 2000/1). After the election in August 2001, the CFA's functions transferred to the Ministry of Finance in the Transitional Government. In terms of fiscal management, the challenge facing East Timor is to develop a macroeconomic environment that, at once, fosters economic development including foreign investment, facilitates the establishment of a sustainable revenue base for government, and enables real inroads to be made toward fulfilling the expectations of civil society for a new deal. The challenge is complicated by the need to demonstrate fiscal viability by mid-decade, and an expected downturn in growth in the first one or two years after independence as a result of a reduction in the international presence.

The CFA prepared two full-year (July 1 to June 30) budgets for the East Timor administration, both of which demonstrate a commitment to key social needs. In the budget for financial year 2001–2, the share allocated to education, health, and water and sanitation is over 40 percent, which will ensure "significant progress against the International Development Goals in these sectors" (Central Fiscal Authority 2001, 16). While the budget is modest, with a total expenditure across all sectors of $65 million, allocations to these areas must be seen in the context of competing priorities of high social relevance, such as defense, police and emergency services, agriculture, power, and transport. It must also be noted that education, health, water and sanitation, and other sectors receive additional (extra-budgetary) support in the form of projects under the Trust Fund for East Timor, bilateral aid, and also through the use of international staff in the East Timor Public Administration, which is funded by the UNTAET budget. This latter source is the budget for the UN mission in East Timor, which is allocated by the General Assembly from the assessed contributions of member states; the UNTAET budget and the budget of the East Timor administration are separate entities. Estimates of expenditures for 2001–2 from the above-mentioned sources are $71.7 million from the Trust Fund for East Timor, $112.8 million from bilateral donors, and $55.3 million from the Central Fiscal Authority (Central Fiscal Authority 2001, 1).

The estimated revenue from domestic sources for the financial year 2001–2 is around $25 million, which constitutes just under 40 percent of total budget expenditure. External funding makes up the deficit. The domestic revenue sources that have been established are:

- duties and taxes charged on goods imported into East Timor;
- taxes on selected services provided in East Timor;
- taxes on wage income;
- taxes on other income, including business income;

- user fees for access to government-funded facilities or for access to government-funded services;
- interest receipts;
- license and regulation fees;
- fines and penalties; and
- revenue regime applying to the oil and gas industry in the Timor Sea (Central Fiscal Authority 2001, 24).

The estimated nonpetroleum revenue for 2001–2 was $19 million, while petroleum was expected to provide $11 million. This latter amount comprises $6 million in taxes and $5 million in royalties (IMF 2001). Of these two forms of petroleum-derived revenue, only the tax receipts enter consolidated revenue and, thus, support recurrent expenditure under the budget.

In order to ensure fiscal sustainability throughout and beyond the expected two-decade life span of its offshore oil and gas fields, East Timor plans to accumulate a "major portion of Timor Sea revenues" to establish a strong investment capability. Income derived from "largely offshore" investments will be spent on a "sustainable poverty reduction strategy" (UNTAET, East Timor Transitional Government, and World Bank 2001, 17). The plan has clear implications for domestic revenue generation. As articulated to the Oslo Donors' Meeting, "it is predicated on strong growth of the non-oil sectors of the economy, providing a tax-base for revenues to cover an increasing proportion of total spending. The objective is to depend increasingly less on oil revenues and more on the private sector as the engine of growth of the economy" (UNTAET, East Timor Transitional Government, and World Bank 2001, 17).

Projections for the first three years of independence indicated a need for a total of between $154 million and $184 million in external funding to finance budget expenditure (IMF 2001). In the fourth year, 2005–6, it is anticipated that the East Timor government will fund its budget from domestic sources. The IMF takes a positive view with respect to the feasibility of achieving this objective, while, at the same time, continues to save a "major portion" of petroleum revenues:

> As the government and its donor partners are aware, the three-year budget outlook should be assessed within the context of long-term fiscal sustainability. The analysis needs to take into account the expected future oil revenue stream, which is likely to commence in 2005/ 6. It will be important to manage these revenues effectively to maintain macroeconomic stability, foster the development of the non-oil economy, and ensure sufficient savings for future generations. In this regard, the government's endorsement of a sound saving/investment strategy is welcome. (IMF 2001)

The IMF also stresses the need for strong private-sector development.

East Timor's economy is overwhelmingly agricultural. Approximately 90 percent of the population lives in rural areas, and at least 75 percent of the workforce is employed in agriculture (Pederson and Arneberg 1999, 24). Farming represents the main income source in 94 percent of villages (Suco Survey 2001, 106). The main staple crop is maize, followed by rice. Another significant staple is cassava, which because of its hardiness is an important "security crop" in lean years (FAO and WFP 1999). The rice harvest is used mostly for subsistence in 87 percent of villages; for maize and cassava the figure is around 80 percent (Suco Survey 2001, 106). Vegetable crops include taro, sweet potato, yams, peas, beans, squash, garlic, shallots, cucumbers, chilies, cabbage, and tomatoes. Also grown are coconuts, bananas, mangoes, breadfruit, papayas, candlenut, arecas, jackfruit, and tamarind (FAO and WFP 1999). Poultry, pigs, and goats are raised mainly at the household level. Surpluses of all agricultural products are sold at village and town markets. The main cash crops are coffee, vegetables, and fruit (Suco Survey 2001, 106).

Coffee has been East Timor's most important export. It provides a livelihood for approximately 45,000 "small growers," each working an average of one hectare (Moreno 2000, 9). Following the Indonesian invasion, production was controlled by PT Denok Hernandes International, a "company controlled by the Indonesian military and closely linked to former armed-forces chief, Benny Murdani" (Murphy 1999), who directed the 1975 invasion. Timorese coffee growers had no choice but to sell at the low prices determined by the government-sanctioned monopoly. In 1994, Denok's hold on the industry was broken with the formation of a national cooperative by the U.S. National Cooperative Business Association (NCBA), which has continued to be backed by the U.S. Agency for International Aid (USAID). Average annual earnings from coffee before the 1999 crisis were about $25 million (IMF 2000b). East Timorese coffee is organic and has an established niche market. The U.S. coffeehouse chain, Starbucks, for example, is a large purchaser of Timor arabica.

Any notable exports have been agricultural, though none have approached the economic significance of coffee. In the latter years of the occupation, between 3,000 and 4,000 head of beef cattle were exported. In 1997, exports included 998 tons of copra, 509 tons of cocoa, and 184 tons of kemiri nuts (or candlewood nuts) (Pederson and Arneberg 1999, 42). Sandalwood had attracted merchants from all over Asia long before the arrival of the Portuguese in the sixteenth century, but overexploitation brought this valuable resource almost to extinction during the colonial period. The amount taken out of the country in 1910 was around 900 tons, but by 1925, only 20 tons could be harvested. In the following year, the colonial authorities banned its export, thus stimulating the growth of the coffee industry (Saldanha 1994, 63). Sandalwood exports resumed in earnest during the Indonesian occupation, and it "appears that at least 150 metric tons may have been exported in some years" (Sandlund et al. 2001, 29).

The agricultural sector officially accounted for 34 percent of GDP in 1997 (Central Fiscal Authority 2001, 6). It is very likely that its real contribution was much higher, given that "large parts of the agricultural production are consumed and distributed outside of regulated markets" (Pederson and Arneberg 1999, 24). Nevertheless, agriculture has suffered severely from lack of development. The country has not produced sufficient staple foods for domestic consumption in the last thirty years (Rio 2001, 4). Forty percent of villages have reported that they experience food shortages between November and February; the figure for January is 80 percent (Suco Survey 2001, 2). In addition to the effects of unfavorable rainfall and soil quality, social turmoil, as Rio (2001, 30) notes, had "a devastating impact" on the agricultural sector "in terms of lack of market development, input supply and the climate for farmers to undertake long term investments."

The restoration of agricultural assets that existed before the crisis, including household assets, has proceeded well (UNTAET, East Timor Transitional Government, and World Bank 2001, 12). Recent initiatives demonstrate a shift in emphasis toward "demand-driven programs" and interventions to strengthen rural markets and distribution systems, including the establishment of three regional agricultural service centers that will provide "services to farmers in domestic rice marketing, sales of inputs, candlenut production, coffee marketing, and market transport," and a credit program for farmers and agrobusinesses (UNTAET, East Timor Transitional Government, and World Bank 2001, 12). In the context of further development initiatives by the Ministry of Agriculture and Fisheries within its own resources and with additional support from the Trust Fund for East Timor, bilateral aid, and the UNDP, the long-term outlook is positive:

The nation has the potential for self-sufficiency in agricultural production; it is not over-populated. We are advised by experts that coffee production can be doubled, perhaps tripled, within the existing areas of cultivation just by improving techniques. . . . Fisheries are underdeveloped. There is huge potential in this area for fishing by East Timorese and for deriving income from the granting of concessions to friendly countries. (Vieira de 2001)

Beyond more effective and efficient use of currently tapped resources, there is the scope for significant expansion in the agricultural sector. It has been estimated that less than half the land suitable for farming is now under cultivation or used for grazing (Rio 2001, 9). There would also seem to be potential for an environmentally beneficial expansion of coffee cultivation into some high-altitude areas affected by deforestation. As Moreno (2000, 11) notes in his overview of the industry, "shade is needed to establish coffee land and under such systems it promotes a combination of forestland and a cash crop," thus "solving an erosion control and deforestation problem." The country's marine resources have been underexploited. Only one village reported in 2001 that its main source of income was derived from fishing (Suco Survey 2001, 46).

Agricultural development is pivotal to East Timor's viability. Given that the vast majority of the poor are engaged in agricultural activities, development in this sector will be a fundamental element in poverty reduction and, therefore, a prerequisite to long-term social stability. A socially stable environment is a precondition for much-needed investment across the private sector and the expansion of public revenue sources.

In the buoyant economic environment generated by the presence of the UN, other international agencies, and NGOs, 719 businesses had registered for tax purposes with the East Timor Revenue Service (ETRS) by October 2001 (ETRS 2001a). As shown in Table 5.2, 424 or 59 percent of these are owned by East Timorese. Of the 295 foreign-owned businesses, the most represented countries of origin included Australia (41 percent), Indonesia (31 percent), Singapore (9 percent), and Portugal (3 percent). The U.S.-owned businesses accounted for less than 1 percent of the foreign commercial presence.

Some 820 establishments were operated by the businesses registered with the ETRS. A breakdown of these by type of activity is provided in the section on marketing. Table 5.3 shows that 211, or 26 percent, of the establishments estimated their annual turnover to be less than $10,000. At the upper level, 6 percent estimated a turnover in excess of $500,000 per year, half of these being in the over $1,000,000 category. Ninety-one percent of the establishments registered for tax purposes were located in Dili (ETRS 2001b).

While businesses registered with the ETRS are the major commercial entities currently operating in East Timor, neither the number of registrations nor the breakdown between Dili and the other twelve districts reflect the extent of activity. Commercial activities at the microenterprise level are taking place throughout the country in such areas as trade in agricultural produce at village markets, and cottage and small industries. A survey of 337 "small and medium industries," 181 of which were outside Dili, was conducted in the first half of 2001. The findings indicated that the major categories in this subsector, in terms of number of establishments, were: (1) furniture, woodworking, and sawmilling (23 percent); (2) motor vehicle and tire repair shops (17 percent); (3) traditional (*tais*) weaving, craft making, and dyeing (12 percent); (4) tailoring and garment making (12 percent); (5) bakeries, (*pao*) traditional bread shops (9 percent) (Division of Industry 2001a, 5). The Division of Industry estimated that, as of July 2001, there were over 1,300 small and medium industries operating throughout East Timor, employing approximately 8,700 workers (Division of Industry 2001b, 36).

Table 5.2

Businesses Registered with the East Timor Revenue Service by Country of Origin, October 2001

Country of origin	Sole trader	Partnership, company, other	Total
East Timor	340	84	424
Australia	67	54	121
Brazil	1	1	2
Canada	0	1	1
Indonesia	83	7	90
Malaysia	4	1	5
New Zealand	5	0	5
Portugal	5	5	10
Singapore	21	6	27
Thailand	3	0	3
United Kingdom	1	2	3
United States	0	2	2
Other	18	8	26
Totals	548	171	719

Source: Material provided by the East Timor Revenue Service, *Business Registrations* (Dili: ETRS, November 2001).

Table 5.3

Business Establishments by Estimated Annual Turnover

Estimated annual turnover	Number of establishments
Less than $10,000	211
More than $10,000 but less than $100,000	253
More than $100,000 but less than $500,000	64
More than $500,000 but less than $1,000,000	24
More than 1,000,000	24
Not available	246

Source: Material provided by East Timor Revenue Service, *Business Registrations* (Dili: ETRS, November 2001).

Note: This table refers to establishments operated by businesses registered with the East Timor Revenue Service. Several businesses operate more than one establishment.

The macroeconomic outlook is positive, with growth for 2001–2 estimated to be 15 percent (UNTAET, East Timor Transitional Government, and World Bank 2001, 16). A reduction in the international presence will have a negative impact on economic activity. However, while some observers have anticipated a "severe contraction" in the first year of independence, the IMF (2001) believes that growth in the first one to two years is "likely to be zero or slightly positive, given that there will still be a significant international presence, and indications that the recovery has become more broad-based."

THE SOCIAL SYSTEM

East Timor is in the process of establishing a demographic database. The groundwork has been completed by the national Civil Registry unit, which, in 2001, combined the tasks of electoral registration and census taking. According to data collected by the unit, the population of East Timor in November 2001 was 757,162. This figure includes 190,000 people who returned from West Timor since the suppression of the post-ballot violence in September 1999. An estimated 50,000 to 70,000 still remained in refugee camps in West Timor.

Table 5.4 provides a breakdown of the population by district. The most populous of the thirteen districts is the smallest, Dili (2.5 percent of the total land area), which has 131,000 inhabitants. The district has a population density of 353 per square kilometer, which compares to a national figure of 52 per square kilometer. Just under half of the population lives in four districts—Dili (17 percent), Baucau (13 percent), Ermera (11 percent), and Bobonaro (8 percent)—that represent 27 percent of the total land area. The population is predominantly young, with 44 percent being under the age of fourteen years and 54 percent under twenty years. Eighty-one percent of the population is under the age of forty, while only 2.4 percent are sixty-five years and above. Males (50.3 percent) slightly outnumber females (49.7 percent), but in the age groups of fifteen to nineteen and thirty-five to thirty-nine, the opposite is the case. Table 5.5 shows age and gender categories as a percentage of the population.

The life expectancy for an East Timorese is very low. In 1996 it was fifty-two years, almost eight years below the Indonesian national average (61.5 years) (World Bank 1999c, 1). As in many other developing countries, the fertility rate is high. In 1999, the total fertility rate was estimated to be around 4.6 (Pederson and Arneberg 1999, 52), that is, during their productive years, East Timorese women give birth to an average of four to five children. Infant and maternal mortality rates are also high. Precrisis estimates indicate that between seventy and ninety-five infants per 1,000 live births do not survive their first year. The mortality rate for children under five years of age is at least 125 per 1,000 live births (WHO 2000). As many as 890 women per 100,000 births die as a result of complications (WHO 2000). The maternal mortality ratio is "among the highest in the world," with higher ratios occurring only in Guinea Bissau, Eritrea, the Central African Republic, and Mozambique (Pederson and Arneberg 1999, 64).

Women have been and continue to be severely disadvantaged in East Timorese society. UNDP Representative, Finn Reske-Nielsen aptly described their circumstances as follows:

> Traditionally in East Timor, women have tended to hold only a small percentage of public service and decision-making positions. In addition, poverty in East Timor has a female face. Two thirds of women are illiterate, many have large families, tend to sick children, and have heavy responsibilities within the household and the village. As a result, women's health suffers. The fact that mothers in East Timor are amongst the most likely in the world to die as a result of childbirth is a tragedy in the twenty-first century. (Reske-Nielsen 2001)

The condition of women was exacerbated terribly by the Indonesian occupation. Not only did women participate fully in the struggle, preparing rations, carrying munitions, and acting as observers for the armed resistance forces, they also fought alongside the men and undertook various clandestine functions (Rede: Feto Timor Lorosa'e 2000). They also suffered horrifically at the hands of the occupying forces. The following excerpt from a UN report on human rights in East Timor for the period from January to November 1999 reveals that institutionalized violence against women continued in the periods before and after the Indonesian government-sanctioned ballot:

Table 5.4

Population by District, November 2001

District	Population	Percentage of total
Aileu	31,085	4
Manatuto	33,382	4
Manufahi	36,834	5
Ainaro	37,669	5
Covalima	44,195	6
Liquiça	44,620	6
Oecusse	45,864	6
Lautem	50,101	7
Viqueque	55,788	7
Bobonaro	64,113	8
Ermera	86,415	11
Baucau	96,032	13
Dili	131,064	17
East Timor	757,162	100 (rounded)

Source: Civil Registry, "East Timor Human Development Report, 2002." Dili, East Timor.

Table 5.5

Age and Gender Categories as Percentage of Population

Age category	Percent female (%)	Percent male (%)	Percent of total (%)
0–4	8.3	8.7	17.1
5–9	7.3	7.6	14.9
10–14	5.8	6.2	11.9
15–19	5.2	4.9	10.1
20–24	3.3	3.3	6.6
25–29	3.8	4.0	7.7
30–34	3.4	3.5	6.9
35–39	2.8	2.7	5.5
40–44	2.7	2.4	5.1
45–49	2.0	1.9	3.9
50–54	1.7	1.6	3.3
55–59	1.3	1.3	2.5
60–64	1.0	1.0	2.1
65+	1.2	1.3	2.4
Totals	49.7	50.3	100.0

Source: Civil Registry, "Civil Registry in East Timor: Results," presented at a press conference held by the special representative of the secretary general and transitional administrator of East Timor, Sergio Vieira de Mello, at Dili, July 2, 2001.

During the joint mission, the Special Rapporteur on violence against women heard testimonies from rape survivors and eyewitnesses to human rights violations. She found evidence of widespread violence against women in East Timor during the period under consideration. The violence was organized and involved members of the militia and members of TNI [Indonesian Armed Forces]; in some places, there was no distinction between the two as members of the militia were also members of TNI. In any event, it is clear that the highest level of the military command in East Timor knew, or had reason to know, that there was widespread violence against women in East Timor. There were cases of sexual slavery, sexual violence as a means of intimidation and sexual violence as a result of the climate of impunity created by the security forces operating in the island. (UN General Assembly 1999)

The normalization of life for the victims of the occupation, including the guarantee of economic security for the disproportionate number of widows and the families they now head, is a major challenge for East Timor. A vigorous women's movement exists and is working with the support of the international community to redress the traumatic legacy of Indonesian rule as well as the inequality that is deeply rooted in East Timorese society. The 2001 election was an important first step toward equality of access to the decision-making process, with women winning 26 percent of the Constituent Assembly seats.

The 757,000 East Timorese live in some 500 *sucos*, or villages, comprising around 2,330 *aldeias*, or hamlets (Suco Survey 2001, 8). The average number of households per aldeia is around seventy, and the average population is 325—an average of four to five people per household. The vast majority of aldeias (80 percent) do not have electricity, and in those that do, it is generally only provided for part of the day. House-to-house reticulated water systems are rare. In some aldeias (34 percent), drinking water is available from a public tap or pump, but in most (60 percent), the main sources are streams and wells. The majority of people are more than a twenty-minute walk from the nearest road and, thus, the closest access to transport. Most travel by foot to the local health clinic, an average walk of seventy minutes (Suco Survey 2001).

Since the establishment of UNTAET, community health facilities have been restored, staffed, equipped, and stocked with the support of international agencies. As of October 2001, there were over 200 health facilities (Suco Survey 2001) and five regional hospitals. The health service is modest by any comparison. Only around thirty of the 160 doctors who were working in East Timor remained after the crisis (World Bank 1999b, 1). Nurses, therefore, are the primary service providers. Initiatives in the health sector have included nationwide child vaccination campaigns, capacity building for health staff, and preliminary programs to deal with endemic diseases such as malaria and tuberculosis. Underlying the development of the national health plan is the concern whether what is put in place can be sustainable within severe human resource and budgetary constraints. The accessibility of core health services, particularly for isolated rural communities, is a major challenge.

East Timorese society is multilingual. When asked what "the main language spoken" in their village was, Timorese respondents across the country identified twenty-four languages. Of these, the most significant were Mambae (used in 23 percent of villages), Tetum (20 percent), Bunak (9 percent), and Tetum Teric (5 percent) (Suco Survey 2001, 37). Bunak and three other indigenous languages are "distantly related to Papuan languages." All the other Timorese languages belong to the Austronesian family, which also includes Malay and Indonesian (Hull 1999). Although it is second to Mambae when comparing village usage patterns, Tetum is by far the most-used Timorese language. It is the first language of the majority of the most populous sucos in Dili and is used as a lingua franca throughout most of the country. Indonesian is also widely spoken, particularly by those who were educated during the twenty-four-year occupation and those older East Timorese who worked for the government or Indonesian businesses. As a result, it is still used with Tetum, Portuguese, and English in administration and commerce.

Indonesian is being phased out and replaced with Portuguese as the language of instruction in the East Timorese education system. Portuguese was generally spoken by a relatively small number of educated people, and its use was discouraged during the Indonesian occupation. Its renaissance since the ballot can be ascribed to both historical and strategic reasons. It was history, not geography or ethnicity, that determined the borders of the postcolonial nations of Southeast Asia and elsewhere. Lines were drawn across the islands of Borneo, New Guinea, and Timor; what was Dutch became Indonesian. It was the "Portuguese-ness" of East Timor that provided the rationale for its claim to nationhood. While committed to integrating into the Southeast Asian region, the East Timor government also regards membership in the Community of Portuguese Speaking Countries (CPLP) as a strategic alliance:

> We consider our membership and inclusion in CPPLP of strategic importance. This desire is naturally derived from the history and culture shared with its seven member countries . . . , and the sharing of a common language and the sentiments expressed by the use of this language. There are also other reasons. We will not forget that these countries were the oasis of solidarity in the desert for the Resistance for many long years. To us it is a matter of strategic importance that extends the frontiers of East Timor far beyond its geographic borders. (Alkatiri 2001a)

With the Portuguese came an extremely important element of modern East Timorese society, the Catholic Church. In fact, the Dominican friars founded their first settlement in Timor some fifty years before a permanent secular presence was established in 1701, when a Portuguese governor was appointed. At the time of the invasion in 1975, Catholics represented just over 30 percent of the population, but the number increased dramatically in ensuing years. The Catholic church clearly filled important needs for East Timorese as comforter and protector during the traumatic years of the occupation. By the early 1990s, around 90 percent of East Timorese were Catholic. Not only is the Catholic Church highly influential in spiritual and moral matters, it is active in the provision of education, health, and other welfare services. The following appeal made by Dr. Alkatiri, at the swearing in of members of the transitional government in September 2001, underscores the importance of the Catholic Church's role and the respect in which it is held:

> We appeal to the Catholic Church to play a leading role in the fields of education and health. The tradition, the institutional structures and experience of the Catholic Church in East Timor are precious assets in the restoration of the ethics needed to develop our new nation. (Alkatiri 2001a)

The position of the church has been enhanced by the leadership of such prominent members of the clergy as Nobel Peace laureate Bishop Carlos Felipe Ximenes Belo, Bishop Basilio do Nascimento of Baucau, and Father Dr Filomeno Jacob—former campaign director for the independence cause, at great personal risk, and cabinet member for social services in the post-ballot East Timor administration.

Catholicism and traditional beliefs coexist in East Timorese spiritual life. Traditional ceremonies and practices mark the principal life events of birth, marriage, and death, and such vital community activities as planting and harvesting. The clan is an extremely important social unit, and its importance extends into the supernatural world. Ancestors are revered and are believed to possess the power to influence events in the physical world. The focal point for the clan, and the center of traditional spiritual life, is the *uma-lulik* (in Tetum), or sacred house. Each clan has its own *uma-lulik* that houses objects sacred to it and is the venue for ceremonies, including offerings to the spirits of ancestors. Kinship bonds and obligations are very strong and extend beyond the village from which a clan originates to those who have moved to other parts of the country.

Precolonial Timor consisted of small, independent communities or kingdoms, each with its own hereditary ruler, called a *liurai* (in Tetum). These kingdoms comprised several villages, each consisting of several hamlets. The *liurais* belonged to local aristocracies, the members of which, referred to as *dato,* performed advisory roles and acted as subordinate chiefs at the village and hamlet levels. These aristocracies survived the colonial period, though the power of the *liurais* was diminished (Twikromo, Krisnadewara, and Maryatmo 1995, 94). The progressive, albeit slow, development of an administrative system by the Portuguese culminated in a hierarchy of provincial governor, district administrator (*administrador do concelho*), subdistrict administrator (*administrador* or *chefe do posto*), head of village (*chefe de suco*), and head of hamlet (*chefe de povoação*). Under this system, the *liurais* were permitted to hold the position of village head. While this represented relegation for the *liurais,* it meant that the traditional system of governance remained largely intact below the subdistrict level (Saldanha 1994, 51). By the end of colonial rule, then, village government was still in the hands of the traditional aristocracies, as it had been long before the arrival of the Portuguese. Thus, for the vast majority of the people, there had not been any substantial social change over the centuries. The social units that meant the most to them and, therefore, from which they derived their identities were their clan, their hamlet, and their village. There was little sense of nation or nationalism, except for a small educated elite. This changed with the Indonesian invasion.

Under Indonesian occupation, the power of the traditional aristocracies was further diminished. Villages and hamlets became more formal units of the administrative structure, as they were in other provinces, and the position of village head was no longer the prerogative of the *liurais.* According to Twikromo and colleagues (1995, 96), this was because the "role and function" of the village head had changed and now required a "specific educational background." It is also highly likely that the administration saw the *liurais* as a possible impediment to social integration. Alliances of *liurais* had seriously challenged the Portuguese in various rebellions over the centuries. Despite this further decline in their power, the traditional aristocracies were still held in respect within their communities by the end of the occupation. Their status, however, had been eclipsed by national leaders.

The most significant social effect of the Indonesian occupation and the resistance against it was to extend the horizons of the people beyond the village. It is often said in East Timor, without exaggeration, that not one family was untouched by the brutality that occurred during the occupation. The iron-fisted approach did not bring about the desired result of integration but served only to alienate the vast majority of the people. The struggle to end Indonesian rule went to the roots of society; the ethic of *servisu hamutuk,* or working together, for a common cause now transcended village boundaries; resistance leaders were known and inspired loyalty and respect throughout the country; and, from town to isolated hamlet, there developed an extraordinary level of solidarity. The resistance, thus, engendered a sense of nationalism among the people and fostered the rise of a national leadership.

THE KNOWLEDGE SYSTEM

In September 1999, the great bulk of written records in East Timor were lost. Following its visit in October and November, the Joint Assessment Mission headed by the World Bank reported:

> Government archives were removed or left strewn on the grounds of public buildings at the mercy of the elements. The Mission found critical public records rotting in the burned

out shells of public buildings. A priceless stock of knowledge has therefore been lost to the public service, and will in most cases need to be reconstituted from scratch. (World Bank 1999a, 1)

The situation was exacerbated by the departure of around 7,000 Indonesian civil servants (about a quarter of all civil servants), who had held by far the majority of senior positions, and the establishment of a new UN administration initially staffed predominantly by international officers.

The first step toward filling the knowledge gaps was taken by the Joint Assessment Mission (JAM). Its reports, produced in November 1999, provided an analysis of the postviolence situation in relation to governance, agriculture, health, education, macroeconomics, and infrastructure, and a framework for recovery with estimates of funding needs. Thus, they served to inform both the UN administration and the international donor community. Since the writing of the JAM reports and the establishment of a transitional administration and the commencement of reconstruction and development, which they facilitated, East Timor has been in a state of rapid evolution from severe dependency to independence. The need to provide direction and support for this evolution and to demonstrate accountability within the administration to the UN and to international donors has generated a great deal of information about the country and its people.

Just over two years after the destruction of the greater part of its institutional memory, East Timor was establishing a National Archive and National Records Center. Information on East Timor is accessible through the Internet. The UNTAET site (www.un.org/peace/etimor/etimor) contains a large amount of material, including all legislation promulgated during the transitional administration. The World Bank site (www.worldbank.org) includes the JAM reports referred to above and donor conference progress reports. Other sources of contemporary information include the IMF (www.imf.org), UNDP in East Timor (www.undp.east-timor.org), and the East Timor government (www.gov.east-timor.org).

THE EDUCATION SYSTEM

Education was severely disrupted by the events of September 1999. The JAM estimated that "75–80 percent of primary and secondary schools [had] been partially or completely destroyed, and virtually all textbooks and school materials in the public school system [had] been removed or spoiled" (World Bank 1999d, 12). While 75 percent of primary teachers remained in the country, about 80 percent of secondary and vocational teachers, who were Indonesian, had left (World Bank 1999d, 12). East Timorese teachers, however, were found after a massive recruitment program, selection being based on the results of tests of skills, and a new curriculum and teaching materials were developed. An important feature of the curriculum was that it would phase out the use of Indonesian as the language of instruction, replacing it with Portuguese.

After an intensive rehabilitation program, the number of usable classrooms was, by mid-2001, only 14 percent below the pre-ballot level. Approximately 240,000 East Timorese children attend 900 schools, 70 percent of which are primary schools. The government operates about 80 percent of schools, with Catholic schools making up the bulk of the remainder. Student–teacher ratios are high, with the average being fifty-two pupils to one teacher (Suco Survey 2001, 1).

Tertiary education was disrupted in two ways. Thousands of students, who were studying in Indonesian universities outside East Timor, returned home, many with only one or two semesters remaining to complete their courses. Scholarship programs are being implemented to enable these students to complete their studies. Tertiary students who had been studying in East Timor literally had no university by mid-September 1999.

East Timor's university not only lost physical resources but also experienced a huge depletion of human resources. Prior to the Popular Consultation, 90 percent of academic staff of the then *Universitas Timor Timur* were Indonesian. The new university, which incorporates the former polytechnic, currently has four functioning campuses and has been staffed with the best of some 3,000 East Timorese identified as potential lecturers. There are 181 academics supported by eighty-four administration staff. About fifteen expatriate lecturers from a consortium of Portuguese universities also teach at the university in language courses and other disciplines (Martins 2001).

At the time of this writing, the new National University of Timor Lorosa'e offers courses in five faculties: agriculture, social science and political science, teaching and pedagogy, economics, and engineering. The total number of students enrolled as of the first semester of the 2001–2 academic year was 6,086. All of these students are in undergraduate courses. The university currently offers no postgraduate courses of study. Thus, the only avenue available for students seeking postgraduate study is to obtain a scholarship to an overseas university.

An Institute of Linguistics was established within the university in 2001 to foster the development of the Tetum language. Established at the same time was a National Research Center. However, the capacity of the university to undertake significant research at this stage in its development, even with such a center, is severely limited. That it is functioning at its current level is a remarkable achievement.

THE EXECUTIVE SYSTEM

East Timor's executive population is small and only just emerging with the opportunities that independence is providing. Thus far, it has been concentrated in the public sector. The establishment of a new civil service at the national level and in the thirteen districts has created an unprecedented demand for Timorese senior managers in all areas, in such positions as directors general (ministry heads), divisional directors, and district administrators. By the end of 2001, 135 Timorese had been appointed to the two highest levels of the seven-level civil service structure. There is a general lack of experience among public-sector executives, which is a legacy of the Indonesian occupation. "Many of the senior management officers have prior experience in their sectors," the Oslo donor's meeting was informed, "but due to East Timor's previous treatment as a provincial outpost, few have national policy and management experience" (UNTAET, East Timor Transitional Government, and World Bank 2001, 14). Professional development activities for this new cohort of Timorese executives have, thus far, comprised:

- Overseas study tours, courses, and work experience
- Seminars and courses at the Civil Service Academy established by UNTAET
- Knowledge and skills transfer through working with international counterparts or advisors

There is a growing demand for East Timorese senior managers in the private sector. But, private enterprise has had to compete for the small number of people possessing the requisite competencies with government, international organizations, NGOs, and aid agencies. While in the larger, foreign-owned enterprises, Timorese have tended to hold lower-level positions, there are those, such as Chubb Protective Services and the Portuguese Bank, BNU, that have taken the longer-term view and invested in the professional development of senior management. In less than two years, Chubb, one of the largest employers in the country, achieved the transition from expatriate to Timorese management.

To compensate for the lack of opportunity during the occupation and colonial rule, Timorese executives will need continued access to formal and informal professional development. The challenge in the mid-term will be to fulfill this need with minimal disruption to management in both public- and private-sector organizations. At its current stage of development, there is a significant trade-off between sending executives overseas for training and the "need to maintain a continuous management presence inside East Timor" (UNTAET, East Timor Transitional Government, and World Bank 2001, 14). Clearly, as much as possible should be done within the country, and, where formal training is undertaken, it should be through part-time programs. The University of East Timor and the Civil Service Academy, with continued international support, could make important contributions in this area.

THE MARKETING SYSTEM

The East Timorese market has experienced major distortions since 1999. The first of these began with Jakarta's announcement, in January of that year, that it would allow the Timorese people to determine the future status of the province. This resulted in an immediate buildup of pro-Indonesian militia and a campaign of intimidation and violence against suspected supporters of independence. The instability prompted the departure of thousands of Indonesians, including the dependents of government employees. The impact on the market was dramatic. "Demand patterns changed as wives and families left, reducing the market for high quality goods. Fifty percent of private distributors did not maintain stocks," while the turnover of the remainder dropped by 40–60 percent (Pederson and Arneberg 1999, 43).

At the beginning of September 1999, the market suffered a second and much more severe shock. The devastation that followed the ballot caused a complete cessation of the flow of goods and services. Warehouses and retail outlets were looted and, in most cases, destroyed or seriously damaged. The roads were the sole domain of the militia and Indonesian military, and private vehicles that had not been stolen or burnt had been taken into the mountains to be hidden. The distribution system had been demolished. The violence and massive population displacement reduced demand across all social groups to the most basic survival needs, which, for those who remained in East Timor, were met by meager supplies carried from home and what could be found in the forests, where they sought refuge.

By early November 1999, formal trading had commenced, with small amounts of fresh produce appearing at local markets, and, as already noted, excessive demand was causing hyperinflation. The market had undergone a radical transformation. Not only had commercial infrastructure been destroyed, but also the exodus of Indonesian temporary and immigrant residents was complete. This group had represented around 20 percent of the population, but its economic importance had far exceeded its size (de Almeida Serra 2000). While it had included a large number of low-income families who had come to East Timor under Indonesia's transmigration program, it had also included a high proportion of the province's middle-income residents, and the vast majority of those with the highest levels of disposable income. Members of this group had also played a dominant role in commercial activity at all levels in the province.

As the international response to East Timor's dire situation materialized, the establishment of UNTAET and the arrival of NGOs and other agencies heralded yet another shock for the fragile, reemerging market. Both the organizations and their international personnel generated a demand for goods and services that would bring about a rapid expansion of the market. The supply vacuum stimulated something of a rush by foreign businesses, the largest representation being from Australia. "Hotels," reported one radio journalist, "have burst out of the rubble, warehouses risen out of swamps, and rental car yards replaced military barracks" (ABC 2000). Foreign commercial activity was concentrated overwhelmingly in Dili. This activity began tentatively in late 1999 and began intensifying during 2000.

Construction companies and contractors (mainly electrical and plumbing) were initially attracted to East Timor by the demand from the UN and international agencies for services relating to the restoration of public-sector infrastructure and buildings. The market in this area soon extended to the private sector, with the influx of retail, hospitality, and other businesses, all of which needed to establish premises in the devastated capital. One of the most active businesses in the construction sector has been East Timor Construction, a joint venture between an Australian engineering company and an East Timorese contractor. Established in January 2000, the business employs some thirty-six expatriates and 550 East Timorese—eighty as permanent staff and the remainder on a casual basis. Its principal clients have been the UN, including elements of the Peacekeeping Force, and the Japanese aid agency, JICA. East Timor Construction's major activities have been in building construction and rehabilitation, infrastructure restoration, and the extraction of sand and aggregate. At the end of 2001, over 100 construction business establishments were registered for tax purposes (ETRS 2001a, 2001b), the great bulk of them being foreign-owned businesses.

The retail sector experienced a boom in Dili, with 229 establishments having registered with the ETRS. This does not include thousands of street and local market stalls, which have not registered, but the figure would include a large number of smaller Timorese-owned family-run businesses. Larger retail enterprises are predominantly foreign owned. Foreign entrepreneurs found a ready market for imported goods in international personnel, who generally possess high levels of disposable income. Several supermarkets were established in Dili during 2000, as well as outlets for furniture, white goods, and appliances. Hardware stores and building material suppliers also found a market, particularly among businesses in the construction sector.

The hospitality sector experienced rapid growth. Thirty-four hotels were registered with the ETRS at the end of 2001, almost all of them in Dili and foreign owned. They include prefabricated, container-type accommodations and refurbished buildings, as well as two floating hotels. One of the latter, the Thai-owned Central Maritime Hotel, has a four-star rating—the highest in East Timor. Employing 134 Timorese and twenty-nine expatriates, the hotel boasted a 92 percent occupancy rate for its 110 rooms as of December 2001. The market for hotel accommodations in East Timor has been comprised mainly of visitors to the country, predominantly for official or business purposes, and some international personnel requiring medium- to long-term lodging. The presence of expatriate staff and the steady flow of international visitors have also stimulated the establishment of numerous restaurants and cafés. Almost 100 food and beverage establishments were registered by the ETRS. While some Timorese-owned restaurants and cafés have targeted an international clientele, the majority of establishments at the higher-priced end of the market are foreign owned.

The demand for international freight services has been high. The market includes the UN and businesses, particularly those in the construction, retail, and hospitality sectors. Prominent in the area of sea freight has been a joint venture between Darwin-based Perkins Shipping and the French transport and logistics company SDV. The business offers regular freight services between Dili, Darwin, and Singapore. Other firms operating in this area include the Portuguese Agencia Maritima Euronave and the Australian AFS Projects & Logistics. The latter offers air freight, and a regular sea freight service between Dili, Surabaya, Singapore, and northern Australia. The ships sailing this route are operated by the Crocodile Line, owned by China Navigation (part of the Swire Group).

While the UN has had its own C130 Hercules for freight and personnel transport between Darwin and Dili, the private-sector market for air travel supports two airlines. The Australian company Air North operates sixteen flights weekly between Darwin and Dili using Brasilia thirty-passenger aircraft. The Indonesian Merpati Nusantara Airlines flies a Boeing-737 between Denpasar and Dili five times a week. This flight serves mainly expatriates, including UN international personnel taking recreation leave in Bali, and business travelers. A few travel agents have set up business in Dili, the most visible being a branch of the Australian franchiser, Harvey World Travel. International personnel constitute an important segment of its market with flight bookings for home leave around the world.

As noted, two banks, the Portuguese BNU and the Australian ANZ Bank, have established services in East Timor. BNU had a mission in the country as early as mid-October 1999. The absence of a banking and payments system had prompted the Portuguese government to establish a means by which its former Timorese employees could continue to receive pension payments. Before the crisis, the government had used an Indonesian bank. There was also some discussion at the time of reintroducing the escudo as the official currency. BNU opened temporary premises in Dili on November 29, 1999. By the end of 2001, it was employing sixty-two Timorese staff and six expatriates. ANZ, which opened in January 2001, had a staff of twenty-nine, including twenty-five East Timorese. During the transitional period, there has been a high demand from expatriates for money transfers to their home countries, and while the Australian dollar was the preferred currency of many businesses in Dili, there was a demand for currency exchange. Businesses have been an important segment of the market for banking services. There also appears to be a growing demand from members of the Timorese community for loans to finance the building of houses and, to a lesser extent, for business development. By the end of 2001, one of the banks had loaned a total of $2,000,000 to East Timorese clients.

The Australian telecommunication company, Telstra, established a presence very early on. It was contracted to set up communication services by the Australian Defense Force, which arrived in September 1999. It remained, after the establishment of UNTAET, providing services to the administration and other agencies, businesses, and the public. As the sole telecom provider in the country, its cell-phone service appears to have been particularly profitable. Setup costs were not high, primarily because of the limited area covered by the service, Dili and environs, and because the company was able to use its existing satellite system and Australian-based infrastructure. In February 2002, Telstra announced that it would be withdrawing from East Timor, having decided not to compete in a tender for the provision of a national telecom service (Elliot 2000). Probable reasons for the withdrawal were that going national would have required the extension of services to the less profitable rural market, and the expectation that the Dili market would contract because of the downsizing of the international presence.

The need for protective services to ensure the security of administration property brought Chubb Asia Pacific to East Timor in January 2000. The company's original brief was to manage and train Timorese security guards employed by the administration. When its contract ended, Chubb judged the market to be of sufficient size to enable it to remain. As Chubb Protective Services East Timor, the business has grown from a small group of expatriates to a Timorese-managed operation with a staff of over 750, including three expatriate advisers. Its clients comprise diplomatic missions, NGOs, government, international agencies, and owners of private residences. It is one of the largest employers and taxpayers in the country and is committed to a permanent, expanding presence.

A range of other foreign businesses has been attracted to East Timor during the transitional period. The Indonesian petroleum company, Pertamina, has returned to operate its storage facility in Dili and imports gasoline, diesel, aviation fuel, liquefied petroleum gas (LPG), and kerosene. An Australian business, Phoenix Fuels is one of several fuel distributors in Dili. Other

Table 5.6

Establishments by Type of Primary Activity/Industry, October 2001

Type of activity/industry	Number of establishments
Retailing	229
Wholesaling	85
Import–Export	75
Manufacturing	22
Transportation	28
Service	75
Restaurant/bar	96
Hotel	34
Agriculture	5
Rental/hire	17
Construction	104
Consulting	17
Other	37
Total	824

Source: Material provided by East Timor Revenue Service, *Business Registrations* (Dili: ETRS, November 2001).

Note: This table refers to establishments operated by businesses registered with the East Timor Revenue Service. Several businesses operate more than one establishment.

Australian businesses include Thrifty, a car rental firm; Wastemaster, a Darwin-based waste disposal company; and Uma Roofing, which manufactures aluminum sheeting in Dili.

This discussion on foreign commercial activity in East Timor is not exhaustive, but it indicates the scope of activity and the capacity of the market during the transitional phase. Table 5.6 provides a breakdown of the 824 business establishments registered with the ETRS by type of activity. These include establishments registered by both East Timorese and foreign residents. They do not include the many thousands of Timorese microbusinesses, such as street and market stalls, street vendors, and cottage industries. Based on available data, between 40 and 49 percent of the business establishments registered for tax purposes are foreign owned. These include the great bulk of those enterprises at the upper end of the turnover scale.

East Timor enters independence with a greatly reduced expatriate market as a result of the downsizing of the UN presence. At maximum strength, UNTAET consisted of over 12,000 international personnel. By the end of its mandate, at independence in May 2002, this figure will have been reduced by over 40 percent. A successor mission will commence operation with an international contingent comprising 5,000 military personnel, 1,250 civilian police, 300 civilian advisers and support staff working with the civil service, and a small UN administrative component. The size of this mission will be reduced gradually, as conditions permit, until the end of its mandate, which was expected to be in 2004 but has been extended until May 2005. On this date in 2005, the majority of the United Nations peacekeeping forces departed from East Timor, leaving only 130 UN administrators in the country until 2006. While it is anticipated that the international community will continue to support East Timor through such agencies as UNDP and some NGOs, and through bilateral funding arrangements, the level of extrabudgetary expenditure on reconstruction and development will have declined dramatically by mid-decade.

The decrease in international activity and the number of expatriate residents represents yet another distortion of the East Timorese market. The decline in the demand for goods and services by international organizations and their personnel will threaten the viability of some of the foreign-owned businesses. Some will seek to adapt to the new market. Owners of the Hello Mister supermarket and the Harvey Norman furniture and appliance store have indicated that they wish to remain for the long term and, consequently, "plan to change stock lines to offer more to locals at cheaper prices" (Dodd 2000). However, downsizings and closures seem inevitable. Businesses operated by East Timorese residents will be affected in two ways. Those that targeted international organizations and expatriates will face the same severe market contraction as many of the foreign-owned businesses. Those with primary markets that included Timorese wage earners will be affected by a reduction in consumption as a result of job losses.

The vast majority of East Timorese possess extremely low levels of disposable income. Forty percent of households in a survey conducted in 2000 had "incomes and expenditure of less than seven cents per person per day" (UNDP 2000). Most trade in the country is conducted at village markets, where stallholders offer surplus fresh produce and inexpensive manufactured items imported from Indonesian West Timor, such as packaged noodles, cooking oil, and clothing.

East Timorese with significant levels of disposable income constitute a small minority of the population. They include private-sector employees, business owners, and those whose salaries are government funded—civil servants, police, members of the defense force, and elected representatives. This latter group numbers less than 20,000, which represents about one-third of the pre-ballot figure. Around 90 percent of this group receives salaries in the range of $85 to $155 per month. It is doubtful that the total number of East Timorese with incomes of over $85 exceeds 7 percent of the population.

In the medium term, the domestic market will not provide a major attraction for foreign commercial activity. Much needed foreign investment will, therefore, have to be focused on external markets. Foreign investment has opened Timor Sea petroleum resources, from which, as discussed herein, East Timor will derive considerable benefits in terms of royalties and taxes. Other areas with greatest potential for development in the immediate future are the country's marine resources, tourism, and agriculture. There may also be hope for the development of mineral extraction industries.

East Timor's marine resources present an opportunity for large-scale commercial activity. Prior to the ballot, less than 1 percent of an estimated annual catch of 600,000 tons was being harvested (Pederson and Arneberg 1999, 23). Marine species with the potential for managed exploitation include tuna, skipjack, snapper, Spanish mackerel, squid, prawns, and various kinds of sea cucumbers (Brahama and Emmanuel 1996 cited by Pederson and Arneberg 1999, 14). A former center of fishing activity, Hera Port, some fifteen kilometers east of Dili, has been rehabilitated to support the small local industry. However, major development of this sector awaits foreign investment.

Tourism flourishes in the region, and there is potential for East Timor to establish a profitable tourist trade. According to an ANZ Bank report, "natural attractions such as hot springs, marine life and beaches, coupled with its rich culture and history offer potential for the tourist industry to become a valuable source of foreign exchange" (ANZ 2001, 3). A successful ecotourist industry is certainly possible. Some activity has commenced in this area through the promotion of the country's marine attractions to the international diving community by the Central Maritime Hotel in association with local diving businesses. Mainstream tourism could also be developed through effective marketing of the country's unique fusion of Mediterranean and Asian cultures, its status as the world's newest nation, and its diverse and spectacular scenery. The ANZ report noted that "The country's administration, is committed to protecting against over-development" and, thus, preserving the "attractiveness of East Timor as a Tourist destination" (ANZ 2001, 3). The majority of Dili's hotels fall below the minimum require-ments of mainstream tourists. Potential tourist destinations, such as Lospalos in the east and Oecussi and Liquiça in the west and numerous scenic locations in the mountainous hinterland, are completely undeveloped. Opportunities thus exist for major tourist projects both in and outside the capital.

While agricultural activity generally consists of subsistence farming, there are opportunities for foreign investment. The country's most profitable industry, coffee production, is underdevel-oped. Coffee plantations have been neglected, and yields are estimated to have declined from 600 kilos of parchment coffee per hectare in the 1950s to around 100 kilos at present, as a result of poor management. In addition to improving plantation management practices, there is potential for extending cultivation into areas currently affected by deforestation (Moreno 2000, 3, 11). Already well respected internationally, East Timorese coffee possesses characteristics that en-hance its marketability. It is naturally grown in the forests, and the entire national crop is organi-cally produced, which is unique among coffee-producing countries (Moreno 2000, 8). International activity in coffee production commenced in 1994 with the establishment of the national growers cooperative by the USAID-backed NCBA. In 2000, the large Portuguese coffee company, Delta Cafés, established a permanent presence in the country. Coffee will be eclipsed by oil and gas in the coming years as the country's major foreign currency earner. Nevertheless, the industry is entering a period of growth and offers opportunities for further foreign investment.

Another area of agriculture with potential for development has attracted foreign interest. East Timor Construction has plans to diversify into the sugar industry with a multimillion-dollar project involving the establishment of a sugar mill in the Lospalos district. The firm plans to export sugar products through the nearby port of Com. This enterprise is anticipated to support some 5,000 jobs in milling and plantation activities. Other crops that have the po-tential to attract investors include peanuts (groundnuts), cashew nuts, soya beans, kapok, co-conuts, cocoa, cloves, and tamarind. Timor's former major export, the overexploited sandalwood, could be nurtured back to form the basis of a profitable niche-market industry. Livestock production may also attract some investment. Before the ballot, East Timorese cattle were exported to other parts of the archipelago. As discussed, the country has the capacity to expand cattle grazing. Poultry farming has drawn some interest. At least one foreign business has established a farm, producing chicken meat and eggs for local consumption, with plans to export eggs to Australia.

The extraction of petroleum products and minerals and the process of quarrying have been flagged as possible areas of interest for foreign investors. In addition to offshore oil and gas fields, there may be onshore petroleum reserves in the south. According to one writer, the hold-ings of former Indonesian President Suharto's family in East Timor included "three onshore oil wells that were discovered in the '60s—the Suai Loro in Covalima, Aliambata in Viqueque, and Pualaca in Manatuto" and "beneath those three wells lie vast untapped oil reserves" (Aditjondro 1999). While there is seepage of petroleum-based liquids to the surface in the south of the coun-try, no credible estimate of the amount of oil in the area exists. There are also, as the East Timor Investment Institute (2001, 7) put it, "possibly economically interesting deposits of marble, gran-ite, limestone and even gold." To these can be added the presence of iron sands, copper, chro-mium, clay (red and white), bentonite, crystalline limestone, ochre, travertine, dolomite, naphtha, gypsum, phosphate, graphite, and asbestos (Pederson and Arneberg 1999, 11–12). However, there is yet to be a comprehensive survey of the country's mineral resources (East Timor Invest-ment Institute 2001, 7).

Private-sector investment will be the key to economic and social development in East Timor.

However, several issues need to be addressed in order to create an environment in which businesses are confident to commit to long-term projects. These include the "lack of: (i) skilled labor; (ii) adequate infrastructure; (iii) legislation for property rights and land ownership; and (iv) a legal and regulatory framework for business" (IMF 2001).

East Timor is not devoid of skilled people, but lack of opportunity during the period of occupation and during the colonial period has created a shortage in key areas. The government is committed to education and training, and remarkable developments have occurred in this area, given the state in which the sector was left in 1999. Further development by the government and the international community is required and assured, but the building of a skills base within the workforce will also require private-sector support. Capacity building has worked in those businesses that have undertaken it seriously, such as the BNU, ANZ, and Chubb. In the next few years, it should be regarded as a component of setup costs, offset by long-term benefits to be derived from early participation in the country's commercial development.

Infrastructure presents difficulties. Large-scale road construction was undertaken by the Indonesian government, principally to extend its sphere of control into the hinterland. The network is an extremely valuable asset to East Timor, but because of periodic rain damage, it requires an extensive, costly maintenance program. Over 1,200 kilometers of core roads had been stabilized by the end of 2001, and maintenance of these roads is being provided under village-based contracts. A program of feeder road repair and maintenance is also underway (UNTAET, East Timor Transitional Government, and World Bank 2001). Nevertheless, road transportation in East Timor is difficult, and ongoing repair and maintenance programs are essential for the country's social and economic development.

Water supply systems in Dili and district capitals have undergone basic rehabilitation programs. However, water shortages occur in some areas. Power generators in Dili have not coped consistently with the level of demand experienced during the transitional period. As of December 2001, damage to generators was causing load shedding (UNTAET, East Timor Transitional Government, and World Bank 2001). Businesses requiring a constant supply of electricity have operated their own generators, and, to avoid water shortages, some have also had bores sunk and pumps installed.

Legislation with respect to private-sector activity is urgently required. Land and property rights and disputes have been a particular problem because of the confusion created by four bases of ownership—"underlying traditional interests, titles issued in both the Portuguese and Indonesian eras, or through long term occupation" (Fitzpatrick 2001). Large-scale dispossession occurred under the colonial administration and during the Indonesian occupation, leading to competing claims for land and property. Under Indonesian rule, "most land compulsorily acquired for both public and private development was taken without due process or adequate compensation" (Fitzpatrick 2001).

The first UNTAET regulation empowered the UN to administer all property in East Timor registered in the name of the Republic of Indonesia and all privately owned, abandoned property "until such time as the lawful owners are determined" (UNTAET Regulation 1999/1). This enabled the administration, as an interim measure, to issue "temporary use agreements" to businesses with respect of such property. "Temporary use" allowed businesses to set up but, generally, did not inspire long-term commitment to a presence in the country.

Resolution of land ownership and related problems, through appropriate legislation, has been placed on the agenda of the new government. Another priority is the development of a legal framework, including an investment code, and company, contract, and bankruptcy laws. In November 2001, the transitional government established a "ministerial committee on the private sector to accelerate progress on these issues" (UNTAET, East Timor Transitional Government, and World Bank 2001, 13).

CONCLUSION

Despite the devastation of 1999, a history characterized by underdevelopment, and severe market distortions in recent years, the macroeconomic outlook for East Timor is positive. While a reduction in the international presence will impact negatively on the economy in the first years of independence, a zero or slightly positive growth rate is anticipated (IMF 2001). Political activity, since the end of the occupation, has been marked by tolerance and enthusiasm for democratic processes. Large-scale community consultation has taken place to inform the national leadership on key issues, and a government has been elected democratically and transparently without incident. Despite extreme levels of poverty and the demise of authoritarianism and summary justice, the incidence of crime is low—"much lower than in some developed countries" (UNTAET 2001).

Achievements in education and training have been impressive, but there has been insufficient time to redress the skills shortages across sectors that are derived from lack of opportunity before the ballot. The government is committed to continuing human resource development, and the international community will support this well into independence. The private sector, too, has an important role in this area. The benefits of an enlightened approach to capacity building within the business community have been demonstrated.

East Timor's location between Indonesia and Australia provides proximity to two large markets. Already flagged as a means of enhancing economic cooperation is a "triangle of development" between Indonesia's Nusa Tenggara Timor Province and Australia's Northern Territory and Queensland (Alkatiri 2001a). Meanwhile, East Timor offers investment opportunities in marine resources, tourism, and agriculture, including its proven export product, coffee. On the basis of existing data, there is also a need for extensive mineral exploration to determine the extent of deposits and the viability of extraction industries.

The government is committed to poverty reduction. Sound, sustainable strategies have been put in place to ensure that this commitment is realized, including the investment of oil and gas revenues. However, "strong private sector growth in the non-oil and gas sectors is vital to underpin poverty reduction in East Timor over the long-term" (UNTAET, East Timor Transitional Government, and World Bank 2001, iii). The government, therefore, has prioritized the creation of an environment that will attract and sustain international and domestic private-sector development:

> The Timor Sea resources should not inhibit the development of other economic sectors, namely, agriculture, fisheries and tourism. In our quest to promote economic development more rapidly, free enterprise and private sector led development shall form the essential tools of our macroeconomic strategy. In this regard, our government will, as a matter of urgency, initiate the creation of a conducive environment to encourage private enterprise. (Alkatiri 2001a)

NOTES

1. The figure of 200,000 deaths is disputed by Indonesia. On the magnitude of the genocide in East Timor, the United Kingdom's Foreign and Commonwealth Office observed: "The Indonesians themselves acknowledge that about 80,000 East Timorese died in the late 1970s, out of a population of some 650,000.

Some Non-Governmental Organizations suggest as many as 200,000, or about one third of the territory's population, died. Immediately after the invasion, East Timor's misery was compounded by a famine, exacerbated by the policy of establishing strategic hamlets and the consequent disruption of normal farming. Comparison of the last Portuguese and the first Indonesian censuses, taking into account up to 40,000 East Timorese who fled abroad, suggests a minimum figure of over 100,000 deaths" (Foreign and Commonwealth Office, London, October 1999, 4).

2. Discussion with East Timorese officers of the Environmental Protection Unit, East Timor Transitional Administration, November 23, 2001.

3. The population of 124,427 is the East Timor Civil Registry figure for Dili District, excluding the population of Atauro Island. The number of households is based on the findings of *The 2001 Survey of Sucos*, which identified 18,861 households and a population of 113,352.

REFERENCES

Aditjondro, G. 1999. "Timor: Business Interests are Behind Indonesia's Fight to Hold on to East Timor." *Sydney Morning Herald*, May 8.

Alkatiri, M. 2001a. Speech on the Occasion of the Ceremony of the Swearing in of Members of the Transitional Government of East Timor, Dili, September 20.

———. 2001b. Tim Anderson interview with Dr. Mari Alkatiri, head of government, Dili, November 30.

de Almeida Serra, A. M. 2000. *Timor Lorosa'e: construir pais no limiar do séc* (Timor Loro Sa' E: How It Is Hard to Build a New Country). Lisbon: Unidade de Estudos Asiáticos do CEsA/ISEG/UTL.

Asian Development Bank. 2001. "Country Assistance Plans—East Timor: Country Performance Assessment." Available at www.adb.org/Documents/CAPs/ETM/0101.asp.

Australian and New Zealand Banking Group Ltd. (ANZ). 2001. "Country Brief: East Timor." Melbourne, June 18.

Australian Broadcasting Corporation (ABC). 2000. "Doing Business in East Timor." *Background Briefing*, May 7.

Badan Koordinasi Keluarga Berencana Nasional (National Family Planning Coordinating Body). 1998. *Profil Kependudukan Timor Timur Tahun 1997* (The Appearance of East Timorese Demography). Dili: Kanwil BKKBN Timor Timur (East Timor Regional Office).

Balibo Declaration. 1975. November 30. An English translation is provided by the *Jakarta Post* at www.thejakartapost.com/special/os_3_doc1.asp.

Central Fiscal Authority. 2001. *The East Timor Combined Sources Budget 2001–2*. Dili: East Timor Transitional Administration.

Central Payments Office. 2001a. *Cabinet Submission: Banking and Payments Authority of East Timor Regulation*. Dili: UNTAET.

———. 2001b. *Dollarization: Implementation of East Timor's Single Currency Regime*. Programme update for East Timor Council of Ministers, November 15. Dili: UNTAET.

Civil Registry. 2001a. "Civil Registry in East Timor: Results." Presented at a press conference held by the special representative of the secretary-general and transitional administrator of East Timor, Sergio Vieira de Mello, at Dili, July 2.

Division of Industry. 2001a. *Survey of Small and Medium Industries in East Timor with Supplementary Report: Evaluation of Potential Natural and Agricultural Resources of East Timor*. Prepared by V. C. Queipo, Division of Industry, Mineral Resources and Tourism, East Timor Transitional Administration, Dili, September.

———. 2001b. *Status Report of the Industry Sector as of October 2001*. Dili: Department of Economic Affairs and Development, East Timor Public Administration.

Dodd, T. 2000. "Hello Mister: Meet Timor's Fast-Money Men." *Australian Financial Review* 29 (August).

East Timor Investment Institute. 2001. *Investment in Timor Lorosa'e*. Dili: Investment Institute, East Timor Transitional Administration.

East Timor Revenue Service (ETRS). 2001a. *An Overview of Taxes in East Timor* (Version 15.10.01). Dili: ETRS.

——— 2001b. *Business Registrations*. Dili: ETRS.

Elliot, G. 2002. "East Timorese Say Good Riddance to Telstra." *Australian*, February 19.

Environmental Protection Unit (EPU). 2001. *Environment News, January*. Dili: East Timor Administration.

Fitzpatrick, D. 2001. "Land Issues in a Newly Independent East Timor." Canberra: Parliamentary Library, Research Paper 21 2000–01.

Food and Agriculture Organization (FAO) and World Food Program (WFP). 1999. "Special Report: FAO/ WFP Crop and Food Supply Assessment Mission to East Timor." Available at www.fao.org/giews/english/ alertes/1999/SRETIMD.htm.

Foreign and Commonwealth Office. 1999. *Focus International East Timor: Historical Background.* London: Foreign and Commonwealth Office.

Hull, G. 1999. "The Languages of East Timor: Some Basic Facts." Academy of East Timor Studies, University of Western Sydney, Macarthur. Available at www.ocs.mq.edu.au/~leccles/langs.html.

International Monetary Fund (IMF). 2000a. *East Timor: Establishing the Foundation of Sound Macroeconomic Management.* Prepared by L. Valdivieso, T. Endo, L. Mendonça, T. Shamsuddin, and A. López-Mejía. Washington, DC: International Monetary Fund.

———. 2000b. *East Timor: Recent Developments and Macroeconomic Assessment.* Prepared in collaboration with the World Bank for the Donors' Conference for East Timor, Brussels, December 6. Washington, DC: International Monetary Fund.

——— 2001. Statement by Stephen Schwartz, Deputy Division Chief, IMF Asia and Pacific Department, Donors' Meeting on East Timor, Oslo, December 11–12.

Martins, M. 2001. Interview with Dr. Francisco Miguel Martins and Dr. M. Hum, vice rector of Academic Affairs, National University of Timor Lorosa'e, Dili, December 4.

Moreno, M. 2000. *East Timor Coffee: An Industry Overview.* Report for the Division of Agriculture, East Timor Transitional Administration, Dili.

Murphy, D. 1999. "Perky Future." *Far Eastern Economic Review*, February 18: 46.

Pacto Unidade Nacional Nian (Pact of National Unity). 2001. July 8. Dili, East Timor.

Pederson, Jon, and Marie Arneberg, eds. 1999. *Social and Economic Conditions in East Timor.* Oslo: Fafo Institute for Applied Social Science (International Conflict Resolution Program, School of International and Public Affairs, Columbia University, New York).

Rede: Feto Timor Lorosa'e. 2000. Statement on the Occasion of the United Nations Security Council Special Session on the Role of Women in Maintaining International Peace and Security, Dili, October 24.

Reske-Nielsen, F. 2001. Statement by UNDP Representative and UN Development Coordinator in East Timor, International Women's Day, Dili, March 8.

Rio, N. 2001. *The Status of the East Timor Agricultural Sector 1999.* Bergen, Norway: Chr. Michelsen Institute.

Saldanha, J. 1994. *Ekonomi-Politik Pembangunan Timor* (Economics-Politics of East Timorese Development). Jakarta: Pustaka Sinar Harapan.

Sandlund, O. T., I. Bryceson, D. de Carvalho, N. Rio, J. da Silva, and M. I. Silva. 2001. *Assessment of Environmental Priorities and Needs in East Timor: Final Report.* Trondheim: United Nations Development Programme and Norwegian Institute for Nature Research.

Suco Survey. 2001. *The 2001 Survey of Sucos and Implications for Poverty Reduction. Initial Analysis and Implications for Poverty Reduction.* Dili: East Timor Transitional Administration, Asian Development Bank, World Bank, and United Nations Development Programme.

Timor Timur dalam Angka. 1997. *Bappeda Tingkat I Propinsi Timor Timur dengan Badan Pusat Statistik Propinsi Timor Timur* (Annual Report of Statistics). Dili: The Indonesian Regional Development Planning Board of East Timor and the Central Board of Statistics of East Timor.

Twikromo, Y. A., P. D. Krisnadewara, and R. Maryatmo. 1995. *Persepsi dan Perilaku Kesejahteraan Hidup Rakyat Timor Timur.* Jakarta: Pustaka Sinar Harapan.

UN Development Programme (UNDP). 2000, October. *Project Brief: Creating Jobs for Urban Poor.* Dili: UNDP.

UN General Assembly. 1975. 3485 (XXX) *Question of Timor*, 2439th plenary meeting, December 12.

———. 1999. *Situation of Human Rights in East Timor.* Fifty-fourth session, agenda item 116 (c), December 10.

UN Security Council. 1975. *Resolution 384 (1975)*, adopted unanimously at the 1869th meeting, December 22.

———. 1999. *Resolution 1272 (1999)*, adopted by the Security Council at the 4057th meeting, October 25, 1999.

UNTAET. 2001. *Fact Sheet 7: Law and Order.* Dili: UNTAET.

UNTAET and World Bank. 2000. *Background Paper.* Prepared for Donors' Conference, Lisbon, June.

UNTAET, East Timor Transitional Government, and World Bank. 2001. *Background Paper.* Prepared for Donors' Meeting on East Timor, Oslo, December. Dili: United Nations Transitional Administration in East Timor in collaboration with the International Monetary Fund.

UNTAET Regulation 1999/1. *On the Authority of the Transitional Administration in East Timor*. Dili: UNTAET.
———. Regulation 1999/2. *On the Establishment of a National Consultative Council*. Dili: UNTAET.
———. Regulation 2000/1. *On the Establishment of the Fiscal Authority of East Timor*. Dili: UNTAET.
———. Regulation 2000/6. *On the Establishment of a Central Payments Office of East Timor*. Dili: UNTAET.
———. Regulation 2000/7. *On the Establishment of a Legal Tender for East Timor*. Dili: UNTAET.
———. Regulation 2000/19. *On Protected Places*. Dili: UNTAET.
———. Regulation 2000/23. *On the Establishment of the Cabinet of the Transitional Government in East Timor*. Dili: UNTAET.
———. Regulation 2000/24. *On the Establishment of a National Council*. Dili: UNTAET.
———. Regulation 2001/2. *On the Election of a Constituent Assembly to Prepare a Constitution for an Independent and Democratic East Timor*. Dili: UNTAET.
———. Regulation 2001/17. *On the Prohibition of Logging and the Export of Wood from East Timor*. Dili: UNTAET.
———. Regulation 2001/28. *On the Establishment of the Council of Ministers*. Dili: UNTAET.
———. Regulation 2001/30. *On the Banking and Payments Authority of East Timor*. Dili: UNTAET.
U.S. Senate. 1998. *Resolution 237—Expressing the Sense of the Senate Regarding the Situation in Indonesia and East Timor, Congressional Record*—Senate (May 22): S5459.
Vieira de Mello, S. 2001. Interview with Dr. Sergio Vieira de Mello, special representative of the secretary-general and transitional administrator, Dili, November 29.
World Bank. 1999a. *East Timor: Building a Nation—Governance Background Paper*. Dili: Joint Assessment Mission to East Timor.
———. 1999b. *East Timor: Building a Nation—Health and Education Background Paper*. Dili: Joint Assessment Mission to East Timor.
———. 1999c. *East Timor: Building a Nation—Macro-economics Background Paper*. Dili: Joint Assessment Mission to East Timor.
———. 1999d. *Report of the Joint Assessment Mission to East Timor*. Presented to the International Donor Conference, Tokyo, December.
———. 2001. *Trust Fund for East Timor (TFET): Report of the Trustee and Proposed Work Program for January 2002–June 2002*. Presented at TFET Donors' Council Meeting, Oslo, December 13.
World Health Organization (WHO). 2000. *Role and Function of WHO in East Timor: Plan for 2001*.

CHAPTER 6

INDONESIA

Transition at a Crossroads

DON R. RAHTZ AND IGNAS G. SIDIK

OVERVIEW

Indonesia is among the most diverse and complex countries. It has faced numerous challenges, setbacks, and triumphs. With the world's fourth largest population, it is a market that attracts considerable attention from multinational corporations, despite occasional bouts of economic and political instability. This chapter provides an overview of its geographical traits and historical developments and then provides more detailed discussion of the political, economic, marketing, and consumer tendencies and trends. While Indonesia can be considered to be at a crossroads, in many ways, indicators and author observations suggest that economic growth and increases in marketing activities and consumption are likely.

INTRODUCTION

The area that comprises present-day Indonesia has a long and vibrant history. The country—the Republic of Indonesia—first came into being on August 17, 1945, following the surrender of Japanese forces to the Allies. Indonesia subsequently has faced many challenges, setbacks, and triumphs. Its first years were marked by political negotiation and armed conflict, as the new nation strove to achieve official international recognition by the United Nations (UN), which ultimately was obtained in 1949.

Indonesia is an extraordinarily complex country. In this chapter, we provide a variety of insights built around the Pecotich and Shultz model presented in the introduction. This information is intended to give the reader a better understanding of Indonesia's diversity, its peoples, and the current business and marketing environment. The chapter is organized to provide understanding about events, issues, and phenomena before and after the Asian crisis. The turmoil of the late 1990s was so devastating that the government and world political and financial institutions continue to reexamine the Indonesian economy and seek to find ways to pull the country from its difficulties. Precrisis data reveal the progress that was being made and the optimism that was so prevalent prior to the collapse, whereas postcrisis data reveal a less optimistic condition. It is hoped that readers will ultimately be better able to make business decisions that will aid in developing Indonesia's considerable potential.

The Republic of Indonesia is one of the largest Southeast Asian nations in area. In population, it is the fourth largest country in the world and home to more than 234 million people (*World Factbook* 2003). The World Bank classifies Indonesia as a low-income country, but this classification obscures some present and near-term future opportunities. While the Asian crisis of the late 1990s had devastating effects on the Indonesian economy, the country continues to develop and is shifting from a commodity-based economy to a higher value-added manufacturing economy. Indonesia has an established and still growing middle class, with purchasing power concentrated in urban environments, which facilitates cost-effective market entry. The country is split into three submarkets, with significant differences in each submarket's consumer behaviors and purchasing power. For a wide variety of products, Indonesia is a market that offers the prospect of potential long-term growth as more people will eventually enter the middle class. On the political front, as more indigenous peoples and geographically disparate regions explore the various options available to them, the future map of Indonesia is still unclear.

Below we provide a brief overview of the natural system, including geography and climate. This section is followed by discussion of the political system and an examination of the history and broader political environment. Following that section are discussions pertaining to the economic, social, cultural, and education systems. The marketing environment is then examined by looking at the consumption patterns and some of the motivations that drive consumption. This is followed by an analysis of the traditional marketing mix variables and their use in Indonesia. Predictions about the future of marketing in Indonesia and recommended marketing strategies are then presented.

THE NATURAL SYSTEM: OVERVIEW OF INDONESIA'S GEOGRAPHY AND CLIMATE

Indonesia is an archipelago located in the Indian and Pacific oceans. It extends more than 5,100 kilometers from east to west and about 1,800 kilometers north to south and consists of approximately 17,000 islands, about 6,000 of which are inhabited. In area, these distances translate into a little less than 9,800,000 square kilometers of territory. Of that area, about 1,900,000 square kilometers is land mass, and about 8 million square kilometers (81 percent) is made up of water. Its three largest islands, Sumatra, the western area of the Irian (Papua) Island (Irian Jaya), and the Kalimantan (approximately 75 percent of Borneo, the balance belonging to Malaysia and Brunei) account for about 75 percent of Indonesia's land area. Java, the Sulawesi (Celebes), and the Maluku (Malucca) Islands make up most of the remaining land area. The capital, Jakarta, is on Java. Indonesia is perhaps most famous for Bali, a small island off the southern coast of Java.

Businesspeople usually classify Indonesia into four geographic areas: (1) Java and Bali; (2) Sumatra; (3) Kalimantan; and (4) East Indonesia, encompassing Sulawesi, Maluku, Nusa Tenggara, and Irian Jaya. The country's population and its inhabitants' incomes are distributed unevenly across these marketing areas. To give a sense of perspective, the island of Java, encompassing 7 percent of Indonesia's land area, is as large as England. Sumatra, with 25 percent of the land area, is as large as France. The Irian Jaya portion of New Guinea is about the size of Spain or California. Table 6.1 (pages 237–38) summarizes the different provinces and their population densities over the past ten years.

Much of Indonesia has an equatorial monsoon climate but exhibits substantial variation within this climate type. Around the equator, rain occurs more or less evenly throughout the year. The more northerly and southerly regions have a wet and a dry season. The northeast monsoon creates the wet season, which occurs from November to March; the southwest monsoon brings the dry season, extending from June to August or September. During the wet season, rainfall is very heavy in most areas; during the dry season, most areas become quite dry. The most easterly portions of Indonesia have a very dry season that can extend for seven months. In most of the country, humidity is usually high, averaging between 70 and 90 percent. Temperatures range from 20°C to 25°C in the evening to 28°C to 34°C in the daytime, depending on the season and elevation from sea level.

Indonesia's natural resources are vast and varied. Across the archipelago, it holds caches of petroleum, natural gas, tin, nickel, timber, bauxite, copper, gold, and silver. It also has about 14 percent of its land mass committed to permanent crops and pastureland. Within the seas surrounding the islands, there are varieties of fish and marine life that are drawn upon for both domestic and foreign food consumption and other uses. Its natural resources (particularly oil and gas) play a major role in foreign exchange (*World Factbook* 2003).

Indonesia is currently dealing with resource issues faced by many other countries in the region and elsewhere. A number of international agreements have been signed related to biodiversity, climate change, deforestation, endangered species, wetlands, and hazardous waste. Unfortunately, signing these types of agreements does not necessarily mean strong enforcement, and Indonesia's natural resources are still under an increasingly severe assault (*The New York Times* 2001).

As overall development has continued, Indonesia's wealth of natural resources from both the islands and the surrounding seas is being depleted at an increasing rate. Rain forests have been simply stripped clean or burned off to create pastureland for grazing. Smoke and haze from air pollution and a variety of waste dumping into water resources have also contributed to a degradation of the environment. The severe smoke haze that has, on occasion, covered much of Southeast Asia has its source in Indonesia.

Indonesia's once vast timber resources have continued to be exploited by both foreign and domestic companies. There have been persistent reports regarding the strong links between the government, military, police, and the large companies that allow much of the illegal exploitations of timber, fisheries, and other natural resources. There are reportedly some positive signs on the horizon, as the Ministry of Forestry has taken a stronger stand against illegal logging, and more privately funded organizations have become involved in protecting, monitoring, and evaluating resources.

THE POLITICAL SYSTEM: A BRIEF HISTORY OF COLONIALISM, UNITY, DIVERSITY, AND POLITICS

Indonesian history is a complex and colorful subject. What follows in this subsection is a brief outline of that history, based on the categorizations seen in Soetjipto et al. (1994). It provides a better sense of the political/social/religious landscape that has shaped today's Indonesia.

Pre-Republic of Indonesia

The area that is now the island nation of Indonesia is thought to have existed as part of the Asian continent three or four million years ago. The world-renowned Java man hails from the time period of connection to the main continent. At the end of the Ice Age, approximately 12,000 years ago, many of the islands emerged and make up what today comprises the Republic of Indonesia.

From its emergence up until about the sixteenth century, the area that is now Indonesia was a melting pot of Asian immigrants, traders, and a variety of indigenous peoples. Trade brought a variety of cultures and religions to the shores of the islands. As part of this trade and migration

Table 6.1

Provinces and Their Population Densities

Province	Area (km²)[a]	Percent total area	Population density/km²			Population (000)			Population as percent of total		
			1990	2000	2002[b]	1990	2000	2002[b]	1990	2000	2002[b]
Nanggroe Aceh Darussalam[c]	51,397	2.75	66	76	78	3,416	3,929	4,041	1.91	1.91	1.91
Sumatera Utara	73,587	3.89	139	158	162	10,252	11,642	11,942	5.72	5.65	5.63
Sumatera Barat	42,899	2.27	93	99	100	4,000	4,249	4,298	2.23	2.06	2.03
Riau	95,460	5.00	35	52	57	3,279	4,948	5,383	1.84	2.40	2.54
Jambi	53,347	2.83	38	45	47	2,018	2,407	2,494	1.13	1.17	1.18
Sumatera Selatan	93,083	4.92	68	74	78	5,492	6,899	7,226	3.52	3.34	3.41
Bengkulu	19,789	1.05	60	79	84	1,179	1,564	1,656	0.66	0.76	78.00
Kep Bangka Belitung[d]	16,171	0.86	56	57	820	900	917	—	0.44	0.43	—
Lampung	35,384	1.87	170	191	195	6,016	6,731	6,889	3.36	3.27	3.25
Sumatera	**480,847**	**25.43**	**76**	**90**	**93**	**36,472**	**43,269**	**44,846**	**20.35**	**21.00**	**21.15**
DKI Jakarta	664	0.04	12,439	12,635	12,623	8,228	8,361	8,382	4.59	4.07	3.95
Jawa Barat	34,597	1.83	1023	1033	1074	29,414	35,724	37,157	19.74	17.32	17.53
Jawa Tengah	32,549	1.72	876	959	977	28,516	31,223	31,786	15.91	15.14	14.99
DI Yogyakarta	3,186	0.17	914	980	993	2,913	3,121	3,163	1.62	1.51	1.49
Banten	8,651	0.46	939	996	5968	8,098	8,619	—	3.93	4.07	—
Jawa Timur	47,922	2.53	678	726	735	32,488	34,766	35,225	18.12	16.86	16.62
Jawa	**127,569**	**6.75**	**843**	**951**	**975**	**107,527**	**121,293**	**124,332**	**59.99**	**58.83**	**58.65**
Bali	5,633	0.30	493	559	573	2,777	3,150	3,230	1.55	1.53	1.52
Nusa Tenggara Barat	20,153	1.07	167	199	206	3,369	4,009	4,152	1.88	1.94	1.96

(continued)

Table 6.1 (continued)

Province	Area (km²)[a]	Percent total area	Population density/km²			Population (000)			Population as percent of total		
			1990	2000	2002[b]	1990	2000	2002[b]	1990	2000	2002[b]
Nusa Tenggara Timur	47,351	2.50	69	83	83	3,268	3,823	3,945	1.82	1.92	1.86
Bali & Nusa Tenggara	**73,137**	**3.87**	**139**	**152**	**155**	**10,162**	**10,982**	**11,327**	**5.67**	**5.39**	**5.34**
Kalimantan Barat	146,807	7.76	22	27	29	3,228	4,016	4,198	1.80	1.95	1.98
Kalimantan Tengah	153,564	8.12	9	12	13	1,396	1,855	1,966	0.78	0.90	0.93
Kalimantan Selatan	43,546	2.30	60	69	70	2,597	2,984	3,068	1.45	1.45	1.45
Kalimantan Timur	230,277	12.18	8	11	11	1,875	2,452	2,589	1.05	1.19	1.22
Kalimantan	**574,194**	**30.37**	**16**	**20**	**21**	**9,096**	**11,307**	**11,821**	**5.07**	**5.49**	**5.58**
Sulawesi Utara	15,273	0.81	162	132	134	1,762	2,001	2,052	1.38	0.98	0.97
Sulawesi Tengah	63,678	3.37	27	35	36	1,703	2,176	2,287	0.95	1.08	1.08
Sulawesi Selatan	62,365	3.30	112	129	133	6,981	8,051	8,284	3.89	3.91	3.91
Sulawesi Tenggara	38,140	2.02	35	48	51	1,349	1,820	1,935	0.75	0.88	0.91
Gorontalo[d]	12,215	0.65	68	70	716	833	859	—	0.40	0.41	—
Sulawesi	**191,671**	**10.14**	**65**	**78**	**80**	**12,511**	**14,881**	**15,417**	**6.98**	**7.25**	**7.27**
Maluku	46,975	2.48	40	26	25	1,154	1,163	1,165	1.03	0.58	0.55
Maluku Utara[e]	30,895	1.63	25	24	699	732	739	—	0.38	0.35	—
Papua (Irian Jaya)	365,466	19.33	5	6	6	1,630	2,214	2,356	0.91	1.08	1.11
Maluku & Papua	**443,336**	**23.45**	**8**	**9**	**10**	**3,483**	**4,109**	**4,260**	**1.94**	**2.04**	**2.01**
Indonesia	**1,890,754**	**100.00**	**95**	**109**	**112**	**178,500**	**205,843**	**212,003**	**100.00**	**100.00**	**100.00**

Source: BPS (Baden Pusat Statistik), Statistical Yearbook of Indonesia 2002. Excluding population without permanent residence, based on population censuses.

[a]Based on Home Affairs & Regional Ministerial Decree No. 13/2001.
[b]Population figures for 2003 are preliminary figures of population estimation, calculated using mathematical methods.
[c]Formerly D.I. Aceh.
[d]Was formed in 2000.
[e]Was formed in 1999.

activity in the earlier centuries, Hinduism, Buddhism, and Islam found homes in the island civilizations that developed.

During the early centuries, trade between the southern part of India and Indonesia led to increased cultural development that was based on Indian culture and the Hindu religion. This interaction led to a slow, peaceful spread of Hinduism throughout the region. At about the same time, Indian Buddhist traders introduced the two Buddhist sects of Hinayana and Mahayana. For example, the Buddhist Temple of Borobudur was built in the ninth century. In most cases, Buddhism permeated most levels of society, but in some of the islands, it was not accepted at lower levels. Buddhism also affected trade, as Chinese pilgrims using the Straits of Malacca on their journey to India facilitated interactions between China and parts of present-day Indonesia.

With the coming of the thirteenth century, the archipelago witnessed the introduction and spread of Islam throughout primarily the northern region. As in the case of Hinduism and Buddhism, the spread of Islam can be traced to trade activity. The peoples of the coastal regions of Java and other islands were the first to convert. Ultimately, the Hindu kings began to embrace Islam, and by around the fifteenth century, Islam had established itself as a dominant religious and political force bringing the reign of a number of powerful Hindu kingdoms (e.g., Majapahit) to an end.

Western culture and Christianity also came to Indonesia by way of trade. In the early sixteenth century, the Portuguese and later the Spanish propagated Christianity, but it did not spread too far beyond their areas of control. The Dutch, in the meantime, through the Dutch East Indies Company (VOC), were seeking to control the lucrative spice trade. Dutch traders were supported by the Dutch military and, in time (late 1600s), controlled a large portion of the region. The Dutch opted for a policy that encouraged Chinese immigrants to oversee part of their trade activities. This immigration policy ended up having a variety of implications for the modern history of Indonesia.

By the end of the 1700s, although the Dutch East Indies Company had gone bankrupt, the Dutch were well in control. The Napoleonic Wars interrupted Dutch rule in the early 1800s, and Indonesia was administered briefly by the British. Some reforms (e.g., land rights and the outlawing of slavery) took place under British rule. In agreements following the end of war in Europe, however, Indonesian interests were returned to the Dutch in 1815.

For the next century, a number of activities laid the groundwork for what is present-day Indonesia. The process began with unsuccessful regional rebellions. Those rebellions, however, seemed to have begun the process that eventually led to the rise of nationalism in the archipelago. In the early 1900s, several organizations were formed, with the goal of promoting the well-being and political power of the Indonesian peoples. Movements and organizations included Boedi Oetomo (initially an intellectual group and now extinct) and Muhammadiyah (an Islamic social and economic reform group) as early examples. The latter still plays important political and social roles in contemporary Indonesia.

In response to developing internal pressure, the Volksraad (the indigenous people's parliament) was formed under the Dutch in 1918 to give a political voice (albeit a small one) to the indigenous people of what was the Dutch East Indies. War in Europe again played a role in Indonesian history, as trouble in the Netherlands following World War I contributed to a Dutch promise of independence. It was a promise that would not be kept until after World War II.

The 1920s were full of political activity in the Dutch East Indies; more political and social organizations emerged, targeting everything from education to nationalism and independence. In this decade, staged revolts by the communist party *Partai Komunis Indonesia* (PKI) in November 1926 and January 1927 in West Java and West Sumatra, respectively, were met with force. In addition to the PKI, the government targeted other national political parties, including the Indonesian Nationalist Party (PNI). The now-extinct *Serikat Dagang Islam* (the Muslim trade association) was established around this period. It would play an important role in fostering the growth of Indonesia's indigenous businesses. The *Nadhlatul Ulama* (The Cleric Association) was another Muslim organization established in this period that still plays a strong role in Indonesia's politics and social development.

The Dutch East Indies was not immune to the global depression of the 1930s. As a provider of raw materials to a world in economic shambles, the impact was significant and painful. Political activism increased and gained momentum. Also taking place in the 1930s was the rebirth of a new PNI (*Partai Nasional Indonesia*) and the birth of several political parties, focused on obtaining more political power for the people and, ultimately, national independence.

Dutch rule again was interrupted in March 1942 by Japanese Imperial forces. While there were some initial hopes for true independence under the Japanese, those hopes were dashed. The nationalism movement received some advancement with the introduction of Bahasa Indonesia as the national language and, ultimately, a capitulation by the Japanese to a request for Indonesian civil authority. This latter outcome aided in the development of civil and political infrastructures for the future Indonesia.

The Republic of Indonesia declared its independence on August 17, 1945, following the surrender of Japanese forces to the Allies, with Sukarno as the first president. The Constitution of 1945 included the concept of *Pancasila* in its preamble. This concept has been present in one form or another through all of the regimes since 1945. Pancasila principles are to a degree based on Islamic principles but do not exclude other religions and cultures. Those principles are belief in a single supreme being (God), a general attitude of humanitarianism, nationalism (unity of Indonesia), democracy, and social justice. During the finalization of the 1945 constitution, debates over inclusions of various elements, social and religious, arose. Parts of the Islamic groups and political parties pushed for the inclusion of *Piagam Jakarta* (the Jakarta chapter) in the preamble of the constitution. The much-debated issue was centered on the phrase, ". . . the obligation for all Muslims to follow the Islamic rules and regulations . . ." Many of the founding fathers rejected the proposed charter, fearing the possibility of an Islamic state replacing the Republic. This remains a hotly debated issue, which seemingly will continue to be an issue into the future.

The years from 1945 to 1949 were, again, full of conflict. British and Dutch troops were deployed throughout the archipelago to repatriate the Japanese forces. In the ensuing four years, Dutch and Indonesian forces clashed repeatedly. Conflict continued until a final agreement was reached between the Netherlands and the new republic. An event known as "The Round Table Conference" was the culmination of that final agreement; the Republic of Indonesia achieved full sovereignty in 1949 (Ong 1997). It joined the UN a year later. The road to republican democracy, however, was to remain difficult.

The Sukarno Era: 1945–66

In the fifty plus years since the official recognition of Indonesia, the country has faced a number of crises concerning its nationalism and unity. In the 1950s, there were local revolts and uprisings fueled by regional, colonial, or political opposition to the central government. In 1955, the country held its first general elections. Thirty-eight million people participated. Sukarno's PNI party won with a slim margin in the House of Representatives. Throughout the decade, there was no single party strong enough to operate the government effectively. The result was "chronic instability," as evidenced by six cabinet changes between 1950 and 1959 (e.g., Frederick and Worden 1992). At the same time, local military officers were running their own districts across the country.

On March 14, 1957, there was a proclamation of martial law by Sukarno. In an attempt to consolidate power and to hold the country together, Sukarno created a coalition between the communist party (PKI), the military, and himself. In 1957, the PKI was growing in influence, and the government nationalized a number of foreign companies. Many of the former employees of these companies were deported. Military officers often were placed in managerial positions of the firms. In 1958, while Sukarno was out of the country, a coup (in some ways a regional rebellion) occurred, and the Revolutionary Government of the Indonesian Republic (PRRI) was proclaimed. Military forces put down the rebellion, and Sukarno returned. As an outgrowth of that rebellion and other factors (nationalization of industries, etc.), Sukarno's relations with the United States and Europe soured even more. He drew Indonesia closer to China and the Soviet Union.

In 1959, Sukarno dissolved the House of Representatives. In its place, a "Guided Democracy" was formalized. In place of the House of Representatives, Sukarno created the House of People's Representatives–Mutual Self-Help (DPR—*Gotong Royong*) in 1960. All of the house seats were appointed. In that assembly, the PKI was given a significant number of appointments. Sukarno advocated that Indonesia should be based on three ideological bases: nationalism, religion, and communism (the *Nasakom*). At that time, he was accused of being too close to the communist government of the People's Republic of China and the PKI by both a number of opponents in the region and the Western democracies.

The Suharto Era: 1966–98

Years of social and economic upheaval persisted. International conflicts with, for example, Malaysia and most Western nations, withdrawal from the UN, and Sukarno's attempts to balance the military and the PKI all erupted in 1965: Sukarno was ousted from office in a coup. It is still not clear which persons were actually involved, but the official position placed responsibility with the PKI. In the purges that followed, many PKI followers (large numbers of party members, sympathizers, and suspected communists) were killed (Vatikiotis 1994); a substantial portion of the Chinese ethnic group was also persecuted. In this bloody aftermath, Suharto emerged as the leader of Indonesia, calling his government the "New Order" (*Orde Baru*).

Some insight into "Suharto's Era" is a prerequisite to understanding current conditions as well as predicting where Indonesia may be headed in the future. Suharto markedly changed the political and economic landscape. In 1966 and 1967, relations with the West improved. Indonesia rejoined the UN and became a founding member of the Association of Southeast Asian Nations (ASEAN), and foreign aid and foreign investments poured in—all events that would have been almost unimaginable just a few years earlier. The political system became more authoritarian and dominated by the military, under Suharto's orders (MacIntyre 1990). The military kept order and maintained stability. It also played a dominant role in the economic and social systems of the country, as a number of top-level officers administered many of the nation's companies. In sum, the "dual function" of the armed forces that originated in 1958 under A.H. Nasution was reinstated (Vatikiotis 1994). Other changes included a redesigned party system. The PKI was outlawed, and a number of remaining parties were forced to merge. In 1973, four Islamic parties became the Unity Development Party (PPP), and other parties, including the PNI, merged to become the single Indonesian Democratic Party (PDI). The military's Joint Secretariat of Functional Groups (*Golkar*) played a major role in all political endeavors. In the general elections of 1971, 1977, and 1982, Golkar won 62.8, 62.1, and 64.3 percent of the popular vote, respectively (Frederick and Worden 1994). That consolidation trend continued in the following decade.

Economic and social changes also continued. For example, foreign investment from the West and diversification into non–raw-material industries began in earnest. Suharto moved toward in-clusion and consensus building among the diverse peoples of Indonesia. There was a pendulum pattern. In the beginning, Suharto relied heavily on the Chinese minority to develop the economy, and he shunned the role of Islamic parties in politics. He fostered relationships with the UN and accepted foreign aid in various forms. By the end of his era, the pattern had changed into quite a different picture. The Chinese were pushed aside to allow indigenous ethnic peoples to play major roles in the economy; Suharto embraced the Muslims by establishing the Indonesian Association of Muslim Intellectuals (ICMI). Habibie, who later became the next president, played a major role in the shift. Suharto entrusted him with bringing in the Muslim support for the government.

Six elections were held during this era. The Golkar party maintained a substantial majority after each election. Following his election to a fifth term in 1998, Suharto came under severe popular pressure to relinquish control. He left office in 1998. This pressure was partly due to the severe effect of the 1997 Asian financial crisis and the resulting social and economic turmoil. It could be argued that the Indonesian economy was the most severely damaged by the 1997 crisis. The political situation between 1997 and 2001 was chaotic (Van Dijk 2001) and included tough directives from the International Monetary Fund (IMF) and others with vested interests in Indo-nesia. During this four-year span, the people witnessed the administrations of four presidents.

Post-Suharto Era: A "New" Indonesia?

Suharto's handpicked successor, Vice President B.J. Habibie, replaced Suharto. While Habibie seemingly instituted a number of reforms related to human rights, freedom of the press, and political freedoms, there were many suspicions from both inside and outside the country in re-gards to the new president's legitimacy due to his long history of relations with Suharto. Many critics thought of Habibie as a vestige of the "New Order." Many regional conflicts started in this period, most notably, hostilities that resulted in casualties between the Christian and Muslim communities in southern Sulawesi and in the Maluku Islands, particularly in Ambon. Tensions continue to simmer. The referendum for independence in East Timor also took place during Habibie's short presidency. That referendum led to a rejection of Indonesian rule and the resultant eruption of violence.

With the end of Suharto's leadership and the loosening of controls, over 140 registered politi-cal parties became active. Forty-five new parties and the existing three parties from the Suharto era were eligible for national elections. Finally, in June 1999, a general election for the parlia-mentary seats was held. The results gave the Indonesian Democratic Party Struggle (PDI-P, chaired by Sukarno's daughter Megawati) a first-place finish, with 34 percent of the vote. Habibie's Golkar party was second with 22 percent.

In October 1999, the three top vote-getters in the popular vote faced the final step in the presidential election process, as members of the 700-seat People's Consultative Assembly met to vote on who was to be the next president. The choices for this election were B.J. Habibie, oppo-sition leader Megawati Sukarnoputri, and Abdurrahman Wahid (a popular Islamic cleric). In the final outcome, with five abstentions among the 691 votes cast, Wahid went from a third-place finish to the presidency. The final counts for Wahid and Megawati, respectively, were 373 and 313 votes. The following day, the Assembly elected Megawati to the vice presidency. She re-ceived 396 of the 700 votes from the Assembly, besting Hamzah Haz of the Muslim-based United Development Party by a margin of more than 100 votes.

The presidency of Wahid was fraught with severe domestic difficulties that at times spilled into the international arena. After a short presidency that, according to a variety of observers, lurched from crisis to crisis, an emergency presidential election was held in July of 2001. Megawati Sukarnoputri was elected president, receiving 591 votes. Hamzah Haz was elected vice president with 340 votes in the vice presidential election. The transition from Wahid to Megawati was generally peaceful.

The Political Scenery Today and Consumer Confidence

As of this writing, Megawati Sukarnoputri's presidency has been able to provide what has been termed a "stable" political environment. There have been a number of complaints from her critics about a passive and inactive presidency. It seems, however, that Indonesians are relatively happy just to have a period of calm. This comes after a period of instability in which four presidents occupied the office in about as many years. The quick accession and departure of the previous two presidents, when combined with East Timor, Aceh, and other hostile autonomy movements, had a number of observers at the time voicing extreme concern over the political future of Indonesia. That concern has subsided some in the past year, perhaps, in part, due to Megawati's "calm."

There are several positive aspects of Megawati's presidency. *The Economist* (2002a) reported that since taking over the presidency in 2001, she has been able to put together a government that includes all the major opposition parties. She has begun a series of slow-moving reforms that seem to be at least edging toward addressing such issues as government corruption, privatization, and the like. On the regional issue of autonomy and independence, there seems to be hope for averting a Balkans-type disaster as well. There is now, for example, a more optimistic expectation on the final settlement of the Aceh issue, although it may take some more time to resolve a number of "sticking points" in future negotiations.

President Megawati has not really been the instigator of any significant programs or new political movements. She and her government have, however, signaled a willingness to move in a positive direction. In doing so, she has seemed to be able to achieve a stabilized status quo in which businesses, consumers, and the general public are much more at ease than they were a few years ago when protests, riots, and bombings were prevalent.

As a seemingly direct consequence of this more stable political environment, consumer confidence and consumer spending have risen. The *Jakarta Post* (2002b) reported that in April 2002, the monthly government confidence survey by ACNielsen showed that confidence in the government rose by 2.5 percent over the previous month to 117.7 (0–200 scale, with over 100 showing a optimistic feeling, under 100 a pessimistic feeling). This rise spurred the Consumer Confidence Index (CCI) to increase to 98.8 in April, up from 93 in March of 2002—the largest increase since September 11, 2001, which continues to indicate an increasing willingness of consumers to return to their normal lives and consumption patterns.

Indonesian Government Structure

Indonesia is a republic, with three branches of government: the executive, the judicial, and the legislative. In the next few years, many more adjustments to the organization and administration of these three branches can be expected.

Executive

Heading the executive branch is the president. The members of the legislative branch elect the president and vice president separately. There is, however, a growing voice among the people and the political parties for direct election of the president and the vice president. In 2003, the legislature debated the possibility for direct election of the president and vice president, to occur in 2004 (*The Economist* 2002b). Currently, following the election of the president, the president appoints an executive cabinet of many ministers (usually more than thirty) and additional cabinet-level members, including the attorney general, state secretary, and head of the National Intelligence Agency (see also CIA 2002).

Judicial

The president appoints the judicial Supreme Court in consultation with the legislative branch. On one hand, the Supreme Court is not under the president's control. It is an independent body. On the other hand, the Minister of Justice heads the court judges, and together with the attorney general are members of the cabinet. While the legal system is based on Roman–Dutch law, over the years, this system has been modified significantly by indigenous legal concepts (*World Factbook* 2003).

The judiciary has come under significant scrutiny for its purported ties to special interests, government ministers, and the military. While recent decisions related to war crime charges in East Timor and the criminal trial for the "murder for hire" of Tommy Suharto have sent mixed signals as to the continuance of that relationship, there is a growing sentiment among those in power and critics alike that judicial independence and reform are slowly moving in the right direction.

Legislative

In the legislative branch, there is a parliament, the House of People's Representatives (*Dewan Perwakilan Rakyat*, or DPR), consisting of 500 members. Of these, 462 are elected by popular vote of the people, and the remaining 38 are appointed representatives of the military. The 700-member People's Consultative Assembly (*Majelis Permusyawartan Rayat*, or MPR) is a combined assembly of the 500 members of the House of Representatives and 200 indirectly appointed members. The MPR normally meets every five years to elect the president and vice president and act on issues related to national policy. Since 2000, the MPR has met once a year to hear the interim report from the president.

The MPR is the only body that can change the constitution. From 2000 to 2002, the MPR made changes to the Indonesian constitution four times. Currently, active military officers still have the right to serve in the government, both in parliament and in the executive branch. The military has seats (not elected) in parliament in exchange for not having the right to elect a president. For the 2004 election, however, the military agreed to withdraw from the parliament.

Provinces

As of September 2002, the country was divided into thirty-one provinces, from the previous twenty-seven provinces including East Timor. Each is headed by a governor and is further divided into second-order and third-order divisions. Some provinces have split into several new ones. For example, the West Java province is now split into two—West Java and the New Banten Province; and the Riau province split into Riau and the Riau Islands. Fifty-four of the largest cities are autonomous units. There are two special regions and one special capital city district (Jakarta). Each province (level-one region) is further divided into *Kabupaten* or districts (level-two regions).

Table 6.2

The Economy in Brief

	1990	1995	1996	1997	1998	1999	2000
Growth rate of GDP (%pa)	7.4	8.2	7.8	4.7	−13.2	0.2	4.0
Total export ($ billion)	26.8	47.8	52.0	56.2	50.4	51.2	65.4
Nonoil export ($ billion)	14.9	37.1	39.3	45.9	43.0	41.0	51.0
Total import ($ billion)	21.4	46.1	50.9	47.4	31.9	30.6	33.5
Current account (Rp billion)	−3.2	−6.8	−7.8	−5.0	4.1	4.9	3.8
Bank credit (Rp billion)	97,696	234,611	292,921	378,134	487,426	231,117	223,235[a]
Bank saving (Rp billion)	9,662	88,894	119,165	125,743	303,016	301,431	301,087[a]
Inflation rate (%pa)	9.5	9.5	7.9	6.2	5.8	20.5	3.7
Average short-term credit (%pa)[b]	24–30	14–17	14–18	15–24	19–64	9–47	9–13[a]
Foreign exchange rate US$/Rp	1,843	2,249	2,342	2,909	10,014	7,855	8,422

Source: International Monetary Fund, "Indonesia: Statistical Appendix" (2000), available at www.imf.org/external/pubs/ft/scr/2000/cr00133.pdf, accessed March 4, 2003.

[a]As of the end of March 2000.
[b]Private banks.

Outlook

Power, from the 1950s through the end of the 1990s, resided principally with the federal government. Officials of the central government headed all provincial and local governments. Outside observers felt that Indonesia's strong central government generally contributed to the country's political stability. In January 2001, the Indonesian government implemented a decentralization program, named the *Otonomi Daerah* (local autonomy). This program has resulted in a new administrative and political environment that will make the previous 357 district governments more powerful. There are indications that the number of provinces may increase in the near future. Some larger provinces, such as Irian Jaya and Aceh, have prepared themselves for splits.

THE ECONOMIC SYSTEM: A LOOK AT SOME BASIC INDICATORS

Since the 1970s, Indonesia has been attempting to make the major transition from a poor, less-developed country to a newly industrializing country. Disregarding the Asian crisis years of the late 1990s, its gross domestic product (GDP) has grown positively. In 1994, its US$126 billion GDP reflected a country that had reduced the proportion of its people living in abject poverty from 60 percent in 1970 to 15 percent by 1990. The Asian financial crisis, however, again shows its impact. Recent data suggest that approximately 24 percent of Indonesians now may be living in poverty.

The GDP now exceeds US$173 billion (World Bank 2003). Table 6.2 shows that during most of the 1990s, the GDP grew at over 6 percent per annum. The Asian financial crisis is clearly visible for the years beginning in 1997, with the low of −13.2 percent (contraction) in 1998. Data from 2000, however, suggest that a slow recovery has begun. In the economic sector, contributions were made by agriculture (17 percent), industry (41 percent), and services (42 percent) (*World Factbook* 2003). The World Bank forecast suggested an approximate 4 percent growth rate for the GDP from 2000 to 2004. For 2002, the World Bank issued data that put the GDP growth at 3.7 percent. Their forecast for 2003–2007 is slightly higher, at 4.6 percent (World Bank 2003a). Some observers, however, believe that the potentially volatile macropolitical environment will retard growth.

During the 1990–94 period, total exports were growing by 50 percent; while nonoil exports doubled, rising from 56 percent of total exports to over 75 percent. Following the financial crisis in the late 1990s, exports plummeted 31.6 percent in 1999 but increased 16.1 percent in 2000. In the first quarter of 2000, nonoil exports were at 93 percent of their precrisis levels (U.S. Department of State 2000). There is concern about the political and regulatory environment in which these activities occur. If, however, Indonesia can avoid or fix problems in these areas, it should be able to regain much of its import/export strength. As in the precrisis years, long-term growth in exports will provide jobs and a significant portion of the funds required to expand industrial output.

Indonesia was clearly hit hard by the financial crisis. Although other countries have rebounded, Indonesia is still lagging behind. Banking systems and the large corporations were badly shaken. The damage has not yet been fully repaired. As the result of the crisis, the future of the Indonesian economy remains in question. Some capital flight continues; Megawati's cabinet is trying hard to reverse this trend. There are talks to reduce or even to cut the links with the IMF.

Indonesia's economic growth still tends to be concentrated in the Western part of the nation and continues the trend followed throughout the 1980s and early 1990s (Seda and Watts 1994). In 1999, Java and Bali contributed 54 percent of Indonesia's GDP, with Jakarta alone contributing almost half (26.6 percent) of that amount; Sumatra contributed another 20.2 percent. Collectively, they account for almost 75 percent of GDP. The remaining 25 percent comes from Kalimantan (8 percent) and East Indonesia (Sulawesi, Maluku, Nusa Tenggara, and Irian Jaya—15.5 percent). These data continue to reflect the concentration of manufacturing in the West, principally in Java (*BPS* 2001).

Over the past quarter century, the Indonesian government has tried to foster economic development in the Eastern provinces. These efforts have included providing incentives for industry to locate in these provinces and encouraging emigration of farmers as well as workers. If these efforts are eventually successful, the result will be a more dispersed population and a more equal distribution of income across the archipelago. This economic migration, however, has at times run into both cultural and political roadblocks. Fallout from the economic crisis has also created funding concerns related to this goal.

One of the most important agenda items for Indonesia's government since the mid-1960s has been to control inflation. The government's goal has been to hold inflation to single digits. Table 6.3 shows inflation rates for some major classes of goods from 1990 to 2000. For most of the decade, with the exception of the years 1998–99, inflation management seems to have been mostly successful. The high rate of migration to the cities, coupled with a lag in responding to housing demand, had driven some price increases in the housing sector in the early 1990s. A return to agriculture by some of that population has eased that pressure, but property may be seen as a hedge against economic instability. As the economy comes back from the disastrous late 1990s, it will be up to the government to take action whenever the economy shows signs of returning to the years of high inflation. In 2001, the inflation rate edged up to 12.6 percent; in 2002, the number seemed to have stabilized at 11.9 percent (*World Factbook* 2003). Given past experience, current policy, and recent trends, it is reasonable to expect that single-digit (or low double-digit) inflation is likely over the next several years.

Table 6.3

Inflation Rates

Type of inflation	1990	1994	1995	1996	1997	1998	1999	2000
General price	9.5	8.5	9.5	7.9	6.2	58.0	20.5	3.7
Food	7.0	10.9	13.2	9.5	7.2	81.3	24.8	−0.005
Housing	12.4	9.4	5.8	3.4	5.7	47.5	4.9	5.6
Clothing	4.8	6.2	6.7	1.5	9.5	98.6	6.1	6.6
Other goods and services	11.6	5.0	7.2	5.5	8.7	55.0	4.9	5.4

Source: International Monetary Fund, "Indonesia: Statistical Appendix" (2000), available at www.imf.org/external/pubs/ft/scr/2000/cr00133.pdf, accessed March 7, 2003. (in percent per annum).

Employment

Historically, agriculture has been the backbone of the Indonesian economy. During the Dutch occupation, most native Indonesians worked as farmers. There was very little manufacturing in the country. Chinese and Arabs generally handled all trade activities. Trading activities were forbidden to native Indonesians, and nonnatives were not allowed to work in agriculture. Roles changed drastically over the last two decades. Indigenous and state-owned businesses started to play a major role in the economy, beyond agriculture, helping Indonesia to reach the cusp of newly industrialized country status. Though, again, the crisis resulted in reversals to many industries.

Table 6.4 shows the distribution of employment by sector from 1980 to 1999, the most recent years for which data are available. During this period, the population grew about 40 percent, from about 147 million to about 207 million. The workforce grew by about 70 percent, from 52 to 89 million. In common with many other industrializing countries, the workforce initially consisted predominantly of males; however, the proportion of females in the workforce increased from about 33 percent in 1980 to about 38 percent in 1999. There has been a slow shift from the agricultural sector to the manufacturing and wholesale, retail/restaurant, and hotel sectors. Males and females made that transition in similar proportions. As can be seen in Table 6.4, the large departure from the agricultural sector occurred between 1990 and 1995. This was a time when foreign direct investment was fueling growth in the export of Indonesian manufactured goods to the West. Some migration back into the agricultural sector has continued since 1999 with the lag in demand for exports from the manufacturing sector.

In addition to industrialization, a key government goal has been to gain and maintain independence in food production. Table 6.4 shows that the country had generally reached that objective, while the proportion of employed workers engaged in agriculture decreased. As noted previously, some of those who migrated to urban environments have returned to the agricultural sector. Integrating these returning workers has presented some difficulties. At the same time, better methods of farming, coupled with improved varieties of staples such as rice, have generally led to continued productivity increases.

Despite the large increase in the output of manufactured goods between 1980 and 1999, workers in manufacturing remained a distinct minority in the workforce. In 1990, this sector employed just 10 percent of men and 15 percent of women. Employment in manufacturing accelerated, however, during the 1980s. It grew at a rate of 4.5 percent per year in the first half of the decade to almost 7 percent during the latter half (Manning 1992). This higher growth rate extended through the mid-1990s. At the end of the decade, this trend flattened out, dropping by 0.2 percent from 1995 to 1999.

Table 6.4

Distribution of Employment, 1980–1999

Sector	Share of employment (%)			
	1980	1990	1995	1999
Agriculture	55	56	46	43
Mining	1	<1	<1	<1
Manufacturing	9	10	13	13
Electricity, gas, water	<1	<1	<1	<1
Construction	3	3	4	4
Wholesale and retail trade/restaurant and hotels	13	15	17	20
Transport, storage, communication	3	3	4	5
Finance, insurance, real estate, bus services	<1	<1	<1	<1
Community, socialized personal services	14	12	13	14
Others	<1	<1	<1	<1

Source: Central Bureau of Statistics (BPS) 2001. Available at http://bps.go.id.

These data do not capture an important part of the structural changes in workforce composition that has taken place over the last thirty years. During this period, and accelerating rapidly in the 1990s, the number of managerial and professional workers has greatly increased, especially in urban areas. As Hull and Jones (1994) pointed out, in the late 1980s and most of the early 1990s, production had been shifting structurally toward industries that require a higher proportion of managers and professionals; within industries, the share of such employees had also increased. In the post–Asian-crisis environment, however, this growth has flattened out and even receded in a number of sectors. As the economy strengthens, it is expected that the increased need for managers and skilled labor will continue to grow, albeit not at the rates of the precrisis years.

A substantial proportion of employment in Indonesia is in the informal sector, indicating an economy in which there is a labor surplus. For example, much of the employment in retail trade is as street peddlers, rather than as clerks in large retail establishments. Estimates from the World Bank in 1990, for example, put the number of people involved in the informal economic sector in Jakarta at about 65 percent. They live day to day and have virtually no safety nets. Much of the agricultural activity is basically subsistence farming, with some peddling of excess production. Table 6.5 compares the proportion of informal-sector employment in several occupational classifications in 1997 and in 2000. This proportion had decreased in every sector in the 1980s (except manufacturing), but that trend has stopped or reversed since the economic crisis. Clearly evident is the percentage increase change in the agricultural sector. This would seem to indicate a return to farming by those affected by the collapse or a downturn in the other sectors. The number of Indonesians working abroad is also increasing; they become the value creators for their village community. Despite the recent conflict in mid-2002 with Malaysia over hundreds of thousands of illegal Indonesian laborers, there are indications that this trend will continue.

While the large modern firms grew in the 1980s and 1990s, many cottage producers also emerged, making a wide variety of simple goods. In conjunction with the single proprietors, these small to medium enterprises (SMEs), drove a significant portion (especially in the local development) of the precrisis economy. These same types of firms are now, in many ways, contributing to a softening of the economic impact of the Asian economic collapse of the late 1990s and are potentially leading a grassroots economic rebound in a variety of industries. Between 1998 and

Table 6.5

Proportion of Informal Employment in Selected Sectors, 1997–2000

Main industry	1997 (0,000)	%	1998 (0,000)	%	1999 (0,000)	%	2000 (0,000)	%
Agriculture, forestry, hunting, and fishery	34,790	40.7	39,415	45.0	38,378	43.2	40,546	45.1
Mining and quarrying	875	1.0	675	0.8	726	0.8	454	0.5
Manufacturing industry	11,009	12.9	9,934	11.3	11,516	3.0	11,658	13.0
Electricity, gas, and water	233	0.3	148	0.2	188	0.2	72	0.1
Construction	4,185	4.9	3,522	4.0	3,415	3.8	3,537	3.9
Wholesale trade, retail trade, and restaurants	16,953	19.8	16,814	19.2	17,529	19.7	18,499	20.6
Transportation, storage, and communications	4,125	4.8	4,154	4.7	4,206	4.7	4.551	5.1
Financing, insurance, real estate, and business	657	0.8	618	0.7	634	0.7	888	1.0
Community, social, and personal services	12,575	14.7	12,394	14.1	12,225	13.8	9,599	10.7
Others	3	0.0	n.a.	n.a.	n.a.	n.a.	20	0.0
Total	85,406	100.0	87,672	100.0	88,817	100.0	89,824	100.0

Source: National Labour Force Survey (BPS) 1997, 1998, 1999, and 2000. Available at http://bps.go.id

2000, for example, the total number of SMEs (mostly "Establishments without Legal Entity"), in all sectors but agriculture, increased by over one million, from about fourteen million to fifteen million for the entire country. SMEs had been decreasing yearly prior to the economic crisis, having dropped from about seventeen million in 1996 to that fourteen million figure in 1998.

Ultimately, as industrialization proceeds, nonagricultural employment will again continue to grow. This means that more people will be buying their food rather than growing it. As a result, farming for profit will increase, while subsistence farming will decrease. It is expected that as this trend returns, rural incomes will increase, drawing more farmers back into the monetary economy. What the informal sector will look like in the future is anyone's guess. Political unrest and continued economic problems in Indonesia could easily derail the hope for a turnaround in the formal sectors. As in many developing societies, the SMEs may be called upon to bolster the return to a healthy economic environment.

Growth in real wages had been on a steady increase from the 1980s to the late 1990s. The collapse of the economy in 1997 took a real toll on the wage earner. As seen in Table 6.6, by 2001, a significant rebound had occurred in real wages.

THE SOCIAL AND CULTURAL SYSTEM: ONE NATION, MANY CULTURES

Indonesia is a sovereign nation that is an amalgam of some 300 ethnic groups speaking almost 600 different languages and dialects. There are several religions practiced, although Islam predominates. Since independence, Indonesia has experienced ethnic and religious strife, but at a level less evident than in some other countries with highly diverse populations. Areas like the Ambon Islands and part of Sulawesi have internal conflicts, where thousands of members of Islamic groups (mostly hard-liners) have agitated for a more traditional approach to religion.

Table 6.6

Value and Growth of Nominal Wage and Real Wage Index

	1993	1994	1995	1996	1997	1998	1999	2000	2001
All Sectors									
Nominal wages (in thousand Rp)	143.49	157.34	178.96	207.11	240.73	282.25	346.95	430.20	531.00
Real wage index (1993 = 100)	100.00	100.02	104.38	113.29	117.99	82.76	84.37	95.84	105.11
Growth (%)									
Nominal wages	23.75	9.65	13.74	15.73	16.23	17.25	22.92	23.99	23.43
Real wage index	12.32	0.02	4.36	8.53	4.15	−29.86	1.95	13.59	9.67
Agriculture									
Nominal wages (in thousand Rp)	70.70	83.35	93.58	106.57	118.77	155.25	190.513	230.308	267.593
Real wage index	100.00	107.53	110.78	118.31	118.15	92.39	94.03	104.13	107.50
Growth (%)									
Nominal wages	29.18	17.89	12.27	13.88	11.45	30.71	22.71	20.89	16.19
Real wage index	17.25	7.53	3.02	6.80	−0.14	−21.80	1.78	10.75	3.23
Manufacturing									
Nominal wages (in thousand Rp)	136.60	142.26	163.90	192.84	228.30	253.30	303.251	402.156	507.70
Real wage index	100.00	94.99	100.42	110.80	117.54	78.01	77.46	94.11	105.56
Growth (%)									
Nominal wages	34.85	4.14	15.21	17.66	18.39	10.95	19.72	32.61	26.24
Real wage index	−10.40	−5.01	5.71	10.34	6.08	−33.63	−0.71	21.49	12.17
Services									
Nominal wages (in thousand Rp)	191.68	207.00	239.10	282.28	306.02	369.54	436.80	561.69	649.89
Real wage index	100.00	98.50	104.40	115.59	112.28	81.11	79.52	93.67	96.30
Growth (%)									
Nominal wages	20.15	7.99	15.51	18.06	8.41	20.76	18.20	28.59	15.70
Real wage index	9.05	−1.50	5.99	10.72	−2.86	−27.76	−1.97	17.81	2.80
CP (1993 = 100)	100.00	109.64	119.49	127.41	142.19	237.69	286.58	312.82	352.08

Source: Central Bureau of Statistics 2001.

There are concerns, especially among foreign governments, that post–September 11, 2001 terrorists included some factions of Indonesia's Islamic hard-liners in several regions. There are several areas that could be considered in "states of conflict." Some areas, as Aceh, have independence movements. The province of East Timor, obviously, strongly pressed to be an independent state. Following a tumultuous period that included armed conflict and UN involvement, the country of East Timor, Timor Loro Sae, achieved that independence in 2002.

Speculation that Aceh and several other regions wish to follow the route of East Timor haunt the future unity of Indonesia. As the New Order centralization fades and more regionalism and autonomy issues arise, there is real concern about the maintenance of "unity in diversity" and

Table 6.7

Social Violence, 1945–99

Type of violence	1945–65		1965–98		1998–99	
	Occurrences	%	Occurrences	%	Occurrences	%
Intercommunity[a]	30	46	72	46	97	74
Community against state[b]	0	0	35	22	22	17
State against community[c]	0	0	34	22	6	5
State against state[d]	27	42	1	1	0	0
Mixed	8	12	16	10	6	5
Total	65	100	158	100	131	100

Source: UNDP (United Nations Development Programme), "Indonesia Human Development Report" (UNDP, BAPPENAS, BPS Indonesia, 2001), p. 21.
[a]Conflict or violence between community groups, ethnic groups, or indigenous groups versus migrants.
[b]Violence by communities against state institutions, including police, the parliament, or the courts.
[c]Violence by the state against the community by the police, the army, or other institutions.
[d]Conflicts between the center and the regions, including regional rebellions or separatism.

what can be considered the Indonesian culture. Table 6.7 shows the level of "social conflict" from 1945 through 1999. What is abundantly clear is the extensive rise in social conflicts in 1998–99 as compared to the previous decade in the intercommunity and the community versus state conflicts. The "Indonesia Human Development Report" (UNDP 2001), put out jointly by the UN Development Programme (UNDP) and Indonesia, speaks of a possible demise of social consensus in Indonesia that could eventually lead to a fracturing of the political, cultural, and economic entity that is today's Indonesia.

While the future cultural unity is somewhat unclear, it could be argued that there are several factors that contribute, at least in some manner, to a hope for maintaining Indonesia's unity. These are listed below:

- Indonesia's motto, *Bhinneka Tunggal Ika*, roughly translated as "Unity in Diversity," recognizes the fact of diversity as well as the need for unity and has guided much government action.
- The concept of Pancasila, articulated by Indonesia's founding father and first president, Sukarno, has been strongly inculcated in a majority of the population. Pancasila rests on five principles: belief in the one supreme god, a just and civilized humanity, unity of Indonesia, democracy guided by the inner wisdom of unanimity, and social justice for all the people of Indonesia. Though Islam is dominant, there has been, in general, tolerance of other religions. The government officially recognizes four religions: Islam, Hinduism, Christianity (Catholicism and Protestantism), and Buddhism.
- Religious fundamentalism has been actively discouraged.
- The central government has generally moved, when necessary, to limit the influence of dissident groups. Megawati recently (2002) renewed a commitment to this. Arrests, trials, and sentencings in the aftermath of the Bali bombing are signs that this may actually be occurring.
- The country adopted a single national language, Bahasa Indonesia, which is the language taught and used in schools.

The National Language: Bahasa Indonesia

During their term as rulers of Indonesia, the Dutch did not try to diffuse the Dutch language widely in the Indonesian population. Among Indonesians, only the ruling upper class and government officers spoke fluent Dutch. At that time, the ability to speak Dutch was considered a sign of breeding. Beginning in the late nineteenth century, rank-and-file Indonesians began to adopt the Malay language in addition to their own dialects. Malay became widely accepted and began its metamorphosis into the Bahasa Indonesia that became the national language after independence. Diffusion of Bahasa Indonesia after independence was fast and thorough. The new, young group of government officials that came to prominence had grown up speaking Bahasa Indonesia rather than Dutch. Although most ethnic groups maintain their own language or dialect, Bahasa Indonesia is the only official communication vehicle, and its use dominates the Indonesian media at almost any level.

The Growing Role of English and Other Foreign Languages

English has been a part of the formal school curriculum since the late 1960s for students with education beyond elementary school. It is taught at seven grade levels: three during junior high school, three more in the high school, and at least during the freshman year of college. Until the mid-1970s, however, few Indonesians spoke fluent English, because there was little need or motivation to do so. The tourism boom beginning in the late 1970s revitalized efforts to study English, as knowledge of the language could lead to a good job. The growth of foreign direct investment and joint ventures created demand for English-speaking employees. Additionally, English movies, books, and television programs had become widely available. English had become the worldwide *lingua franca* of business and was permeating Indonesian life. Furthermore, many high school graduates from the affluent upper and middle classes began to go abroad for university-level studies. By the late 1980s, Indonesia had a cadre of English-trained graduates from the United States, Australia, and the United Kingdom. Among members of the educated upper-middle class, the current trend is to have their children taught English and use it as a second language as early as in the preschool years.

In the 1990s, there had been some government reaction to the proliferation of English usage, as many domestic companies started using English brand names. In the fast-food industry, for example, indigenous enterprises continue to develop and use names such as "California Fried Chicken" in order to imitate the U.S. franchise "Kentucky Fried Chicken." Most new property developments in large cities continue to use names such as "The Regency" or "Lippo Village" to emphasize their luxury or exclusivity. In early 1995, the government began to take action to limit the use of foreign names, considering their use unpatriotic. Despite occasional expressions of government displeasure, the use of English will continue to increase. English is not expected to supplant Bahasa Indonesia as the country's established language. On the other hand, Indonesia's traditional tribal and ethnic languages and dialects are in danger of becoming extinct. In the younger generation of virtually every ethnic group, Bahasa Indonesia has replaced the traditional ethnic language as their mother language. It can be expected that many of those local dialects will become archaic over the next few decades.

English is now well established as Indonesia's second language, most notably among the upper-middle and upper classes. English-language advertising is common in newspapers and direct mail. Most executives have a good working command of English and use it extensively in domestic commerce. Again, it is doubtful, however, that English will replace Bahasa Indonesia as

Indonesia's primary domestic business language; it will remain a strong second language of business. It is likely, though, to become even more widely used, especially in advertising and business documents, such as product information brochures. An increasing amount of product information in any medium will be presented bilingually.

While not anywhere near as prevalent as the English language, Chinese has begun to gain favor among businesspeople in Indonesia. This upsurge has come from a realization that China is becoming increasingly influential throughout Asia. This trend affects not only Indonesians of Chinese origin, but also the indigenous business community. Along with the lifting of the ban of Chinese usage during the New Order and the changing face of the People's Republic of China, Chinese newspapers and radio and television programs are sprouting up in many urban regions of Indonesia.

Dynamics of Culture in Indonesia

Indonesia is the antithesis of a monocultural society, such as Japan. Many ethnic groups, languages, and dialects are spread across the archipelago. The largest ethnic group is the Javanese, which numbers almost 100 million people, more than 75 percent of whom are Muslims. The Javanese, together with the Sundanese, Balinese, and Madurese, represent about two-thirds of the Indonesian population. The smallest ethnic units, on the other hand, may consist of only a few hundred people. As a majority, the Javanese still dominate the government bureaucracy. Almost all Balinese (90 percent) are Hindus. With the exception of Bali, the west is predominantly Muslim, while the east has a substantial concentration of Christians. The predominant nonindigenous ethnic groups are the Chinese, Indians, and Arabs, each of which represents only a small minority. There are very few Africans or Caucasians in Indonesia, although in major cities, there has been an increase of Africans, Arabs, and various Westerners in recent years.

Among the nonindigenous groups, the Chinese are probably the most assimilated and, at the same time, the most visible. Most have roots in Indonesia going back several generations. Almost all have taken Indonesian names; some have become Muslim, others Catholic. Such assimilation has led to a situation in which few, especially the young, speak Chinese. The ethnic Chinese represent, at most, 5 percent of the population. Many Chinese own or manage a significant proportion of Indonesia's large business firms, and the economy in general. The Chinese population is concentrated in the urban areas of Java and Sumatra, where they engage in business, and in Western Kalimantan, where many farm or fish.

Indonesia continues to experience some of the cultural tension that inevitably accompanies economic development, as "modern" or "Western" (Euro-American) culture vies to supplement or even replace the traditional Indonesian culture. There has been a rise of various groups who are opposed, sometimes violently, to Westernization or, in some cases, even an acceptance of "modernization." Some of these groups wrap themselves in the veil of extremist Islamic teaching. The vast majority of Indonesians, however, practice a moderate brand of Islam that tolerates other religions and abhors the intolerant views espoused by a vocal few. There is some speculation that the Muslim hard-liners, although a small percentage, are tolerated by the government so that the government is not accused of being comprised of "bad Muslims." In a country that is 90 percent Muslim, politicians are very reluctant to say anything that could get them tagged with that label. Not all Muslims share this view, however; Yates (2002) quoted Ulil Abshar Abdalla, of the Islamic Liberals Network, as saying "On a personal level, . . . I also hate them in their interpretation of Islam . . . they have such black and white judgements."

In the months since the Bali bombings of October 2002, the Indonesian government has renewed its efforts to rein in the hard-liners. What the long-term outcome and approach will be is yet to be seen. As noted previously, recent arrests of a number of Bali bombing suspects and the questioning and subsequent arrests of some of the extremist clerics and their organizations, seem to support a continued effort on the part of the central government. Such efforts have also received fairly widespread support from the liberal Muslim and secular communities across the country.

What one senses in Indonesia is that while keeping touch with their traditions and faith, people generally will want to shed some vestiges of their traditional lives. It seems they generally desire the increased sense of entitlement that comes with their economic progress. The vast majority of Indonesians want to substitute new behaviors and symbols they perceive as being more consistent with "where they are going" and less consistent with "where they have been." On the other hand, during a time of rapid change, they do not want to cast themselves adrift without some anchors to a safer, though less-promising, past.

This ongoing process of cultural change that has been accompanying economic development in Indonesia is particularly complex and, at times paradoxical; therefore, the effects of change can be difficult to understand. New behaviors and symbols people adopt may be less diverse across ethnic groups than the symbols and behaviors they replace. The diversity of traditional cultures, however, makes it difficult to predict the behaviors and symbols different groups will retain. Clearly, ethnicity, religion, and their associated traditional customs all play roles in determining the new behaviors and symbols Indonesians will adopt, as well as those they will retain. At the same time, in the broader population, ethnic identity and religion are becoming less influential. This is especially true among the younger generations and, most especially, in the cities. As has been the case in some other countries, urbanization is breaking down cultural barriers and contributing to similarities in consumer behavior, as people of different backgrounds are thrown together in the workplace, the street, the supermarket, and the neighborhood.

For the most part, the direction of cultural change continues to be toward that of consumption. Indonesia has become a society in which the acquisition and display of goods is an extremely important goal. Increasingly, affluence has become the most important symbol of achievement. This is not unusual for a developing or industrializing economy. The acquisition and display of certain products is a major way of demonstrating affluence. Products that consumers perceive as symbols of affluence are, therefore, likely to be in great demand.

Government policy has been to encourage the growth of a capitalist economy. An outgrowth of this policy has been the burgeoning of an urban middle class of managers and professionals who have built their lifestyles around consumption. Consumption among this group focuses on the modern rather than the traditional and is oriented toward the Euro-American pattern (Guiness 1994). Gaining affluence and demonstrating it through consumption is a particularly important goal among younger, urban Indonesians, which is not necessarily the case with the older generation. Not all young Indonesians, however, share this view. Some are still struggling for the necessities of life.

In a work of this size, it would be impossible to capture the variety and richness of Indonesian cultural change and the symbols that accompany that change. It is possible, however, to present some examples:

- On the one hand, "traditional dress" is fast disappearing, replaced by Euro-American. The business suit and tie is gradually replacing the safari suit among urban businessmen. A domestic designer fashion industry has grown up; some are using some traditional local materials, such as batik, but the material designs and the clothing styles are not traditional, and some others are completely modern and cosmopolitan. On the other hand, there are increasing numbers of devout Muslims who adopt the "Islamic Wardrobe" and forego Western-style clothing.

Box 6.1

Ngabuburit

During the fasting month of Ramadan, Indonesian Muslims enjoy the activity of *Ngabuburit,* waiting for the sound of *beduk* during every *Magrib* to break the fast.

Another tradition is the *sahur,* the meal eaten before daybreak. The *Tarawih,* the daily religious service, follows breaking the fast.

Ngabuburit may include creative activities to pass the time. Dance courses or art classes offer cultural alternatives. For the young or young at heart, the Internet and computer games offer high-tech distractions from the hunger of the fast. Those of university age may stay awake until the sahur, going to sleep only after doing *subhuh* prayer.

Source: McCann-Erickson Indonesia, Pulse Points 2000, and McCann Pulse 2002.

- Pork is much in evidence in Bali, where most of its inhabitants are Hindus, and in areas that are heavily Chinese or Christian, but it is difficult to find in other areas.
- Many transplanted urban dwellers still consider themselves members of their ethnic group of origin and consider their birthplace as their "real" home. The typical Indonesian speaks of his or her birthplace as "my *Kampung*," a word that stands simultaneously for compound, village, or geographic area.
- After the Muslim fasting month of Ramadan, ending with the Idulfitri holiday, there is a massive exodus from the cities to hometowns or villages of origin. From Jakarta and its surrounding areas alone, it is estimated that at least two million people are making journeys to their hometowns every year. This important annual event should never be overlooked. About two weeks before Idulfitri and up to two weeks after, family, religious, and cultural issues dominate.
- Members of some ethnic groups prefer to stay in their homelands, while members of other groups tend to move into other areas. Typical quality-of-life measures are not good predictors of the tendency to migrate.
- In most ethnic groups, individuals have distinctive names that reveal their ethnic identities. Many Indonesians have names that reveal either their ethnic, geographic, or religious origins; this is often an important issue.

Who Are the Innovators of Cultural Change in Indonesia?

In many instances, cultural innovators are groups well outside the mainstream of their society. They may even be poor. In Indonesia, the innovators are from the upper-middle and upper strata of the country. Among that group, many of the leaders are those from the younger generation who have gone abroad to study, especially those who have studied in the United States. This is the group that has brought Euro-American culture to Indonesia, and along with it, such establishments as the Hard Rock Cafe and Planet Hollywood.

In the postcrisis years of the new millennium, there is a new set of young entrepreneurs and businesspeople who are continuing this drive toward Western consumerism. In the years following the Asian collapse, they bet on the rebound of the consumer economy and have made huge amounts of money in everything from selling luxury goods to the new and old Indonesian elite to taking over old government companies and reworking them to achieve success in the new deregulated environment. "Jakarta's New Titans," as *Business Week* calls them (Shari 2002), are making huge amounts of money on the desires of the population for products that support a new, more Westernized and consumer-driven lifestyle. This lifestyle drive is strongly seeded in the urban, educated, middle class, youth market of Indonesia.

Discrepancies in change, and in the facilitators of that change, in cities, towns, and rural areas, are extremely wide. Many large cities in Indonesia, especially Jakarta, are similar to their cohorts all over Asia. Western symbols, such as Western fast foods, branded fashions, foreign hypermarkets, and mega malls, have become regular parts of daily urban life, especially among the well-to-do. A quite different picture evolves in rural and poor areas. Although some foreign franchises have penetrated smaller cities, the rural areas are still in the distance. The flood of posh television programs and advertisements has created role models that are mostly still elusive to the poor, and merely, quoting a multinational advertising executive, "increasing the pain of the wound of poverty."

Women's Roles in the Indonesian Culture

Prior to independence, women in many parts of Indonesia were treated as second-class citizens. One of the famous traditional Javanese sayings about wives is "*Surga nunut, neraka katut* ([if the man goes] to heaven, she will go with him, [but if the man goes] to hell, she is to follow). As a contrast, the *Minang* people of southern Sumatra explicitly place women at the head of the family. The Minang espouse a matrilineal social system where both wealth and family name flow from mother to daughter. The wife is clearly the head of the household.

Expectations, roles, and relationships are changing. The average Indonesian woman will bear 2.6 children in her lifetime. The Indonesian government has acknowledged that women are often the victims of domestic violence. The culture, however, dictates that what occurs between a husband and wife at home is a private matter. As a consequence, such violence is mostly ignored. Women make up a substantial and increasing, albeit slowly, proportion of the workforce. In 1998, the labor force participation rate for women was 50 percent as compared to 83 percent for men. This split seems to indicate the tendency for males to focus on external jobs. A Canadian International Development Agency (CIDA) report suggested that many of those women's jobs are in the informal sector (CIDA 2002). Women's participation in the civil service had increased into the 1990s. In 2000, women made up 37.6 percent of Indonesia's civil service employees. In 2000, there were only fourteen women in rank IV/E (the highest rank in government) as compared to 212 in the same rank in 1990 (*BPS* 2001). From the early 1990s to 1998, the number of women in decision-making positions in government had fallen, with only 3 percent of women holding the ministerial-level seats (CIDA 2002). The current president is a woman, and several women have served as ministers (the highest rank in the civil service), but the proportion of women in high-ranking positions continues to be low.

During the New Order period (1967–98), wives of male civil servants, while not official members of the government, had some opportunity to affect women's roles. Each wife was required to be a member of *Dharma Wanita* (Woman's Duty), a powerful organization in Indonesia's bureaucracy. This organization concerns itself with identifying issues of importance to women and encouraging action on the issues they identify. The role of the Dharma Wanita was to lend traditional Indonesian "family values and mother's roles" into an institutional structure. This institutional structure can, at times, however, lead to difficulties in a society where Western values are making their presence felt, especially in the roles of women (Sastramidjaja 2001). With the fall of Suharto, Dharma Wanita no longer plays an important role in the society.

Younger women tend to be torn between the need to follow tradition and the more wide-open Western lifestyle. In many cases, these women will lead what amounts to a double life. They will lead one life for their family to see, and another life for themselves and their friends. This latter life tends to be the main driver for their consumption of consumer goods.

Although the women's rate of participation in the manufacturing sector compared to the men's rate is low, it has been increasing, especially among young women aged fifteen to twenty-five from poor households, rural as well as urban. Women in this age group have been shifting into factory work from domestic service, farming, or informal trade activities, and many of them leave Indonesia to work overseas. As they make this shift, they enter the monetary economy and become potential customers for products such as clothes and cosmetics. All is not rosy for these young women, however. Working conditions in the factories can be less than ideal; hours can be long, and the work can be exhausting. Health problems may appear. Typically, women earn lower wages than men and have substantially fewer opportunities for advancement. Moreover, as women move from the village to the urban factory, they lose family and other support systems that their former situations provided (see also Guiness 1994).

These types of difficulties contributed to an increase in activism for Indonesian women in both the labor and social arenas. Sen (1999) noted that many of the leaders in the labor movements of the early 1990s were women. She also notes that by the time the New Order ended with the departure of Suharto, the women's movement in Indonesia was well established in both the labor and social areas.

In today's Indonesia, more urban women, primarily those from the upper-middle and upper cohorts, are engaging in business careers. This is especially true among the Chinese minority. Data from a joint UNDP and Indonesian Government report show that in many regions of the country, the percentage of senior official, managerial, and technical staff positions that women occupy is generally somewhere between 35 and 45 percent of the total. What the exact levels of positions those women hold is not clear, but this indicates a significant role being played by women in the business and public-service sectors (UNDP 2001). A few women have reached top management. Eva Riyanti Hutapea leads Indofood Sukses Makmur, the flagship food company for the Salim Group with sales of approximately US$1.5 billion. Martha Tilaar has built a cosmetics conglomerate based on local products and brands that holds over 20 percent of the US$500 million Indonesian beauty market (Vatikiotis 2002). One of the directors of Bank Niaga, one of the largest indigenous private banks, is a woman (Dian Angreniwati Soerarso), and one can also see women in the boardrooms of such corporations as Astra Corporation, the largest public company in Indonesia, where two of the company's commissioners are women. *SWA* magazine reported that the positions held by Indonesia's fifty most powerful businesswomen are diverse. They range from CEOs of large firms (IBM Indonesia, ING-AETNA Life Indonesia, Indonesia state television, and Indofood) to editors in chief of major newspapers and other media (*Femina* and *Media Indonesia*), to senior managers of multinationals (Visa International and Merrill Lynch), to university presidents (Bina Nusantara) (*SWA* 2002). The number of women in middle management positions has been increasing rapidly, as has the number of women studying business administration in universities, both in Indonesia and abroad.

While the duality of women's traditional roles and the more modern "liberated" career path still tears at today's Indonesian woman, the ability to do both is made somewhat easier by the wide availability of comparatively inexpensive household servants. This may seemingly make it somewhat financially easier for an Indonesian woman to pursue a managerial career and a family simultaneously, as compared to women in the United States.

Box 6.2

Feminine Beauty

The advertising spent on toiletries and cosmetics in Indonesia increased by 40% from 2001 to 2002. This increase reflects the importance of physical appearance for women.

The desire for a pale (white) complexion continues to grow in popularity. Whitening creams, such as those produced by Pond's (Unilever), aid in creating the desired appearance for optimal social acceptance.

Other cosmetic products offer clean and unblemished skin. Acne is considered undesirable and almost a tragedy; a healthy, soft complexion is considered beautiful.

Source: McCann-Erickson Indonesia, Pulse Points 2000, and McCann Pulse 2002.

Marketing Implications for Indonesian Cultural Dynamics

Ethnicity and religion may appear to be promising variables for consumer segmentation. Yet they must be used with a degree of caution and appropriate insight. In periods of rapid cultural change, such as which Indonesia is now undergoing, behavior is likely to be unstable. Many consumers, especially the newly affluent, are likely to be searching for new identities and ways of expressing them.

It is also critical to distinguish the difference between correlation and causality when interpreting consumer data or observing behavior. This is especially true for products that have the potential to convey symbolic value. It is important to recognize the products and brands that may have such potential. Also of critical importance is gaining an understanding of the role of symbols in governing consumers' product choices. It is reasonable to expect that the most important kinds of symbols in an economy such as Indonesia's are symbols of affluence and modernity. An understanding of the process by which a particular good gains (and loses) its symbolic value can be a great asset for the marketer. Unfortunately, at the time of this writing, few, if any, studies have been conducted in Indonesia that might provide significant insight or guidance.

THE SOCIAL STRUCTURE SYSTEM

Indonesia is still classified as a poor country, with an average per capita annual income of US$580 (World Bank 2002). In regards to the full range of social classes continuing their march forward to economic well-being, some observers have expressed concern that Indonesia's economy may find itself "left behind" as the global economy begins to rebuild. If that is the case, the expansion of the middle class at anywhere near its precrisis levels of the 1990s is in real jeopardy for the foreseeable future.

Indonesia's Gini ratio, which reflects income disparity, is fairly low (UNDP 2001). The low ratio suggests that the income disparity between rich and poor is relatively small. This ratio has remained essentially unchanged since 1964. Furthermore, the Gini ratio for rural Indonesia (0.26) is lower than the urban area ratio (0.34). This suggests that income disparity is lower in rural

Table 6.8

Retail Prices in Jakarta of Some Commonly Purchased Goods, 1995 and 2003

Product price (in Rupiah)	1995	2003
Monthly rent or mortgage payment for household with monthly income of:		
Rp 600,000 (1995) / Rp 1,200,000 (2003)	200,000	400,000
Rp 2 million (1995) / Rp 4 million (2003)	750,000	1,250,000
Automobile (Rp million)		
Kijang (locally made, bottom of the line)	28.6	108.3
Toyota Corolla 1600 (1995)/ Altis 1800 (2003)	82.0	237.0
Mercedes Benz E 320	273.2	1,219.0
Color TV		
Sony (21″)	980,000	2,300,000
Polytron (domestic 20")	910,000	1,900,000
Electric rice cooker (1-liter size)	40,000	95,000
Electric fan (basic model)	14,000	65,000
Men's white dress shirt (basic)	15,000	40,000
Athletic shoes		
Nike (first quality)	80,000	500,000
Nike (seconds—from local manufacture)	20,000	300,000
Domestic brand	15,000	100,000
Colgate/Pepsodent toothpaste (100/120 gram)	1,600	3,500
Lux Soap (bar)	450	1,200
Gasoline (per liter)	700	1,810
Cigarettes		
Marlboro (package of twenty)	1,600	5,000
Jarum (domestic brand, package of twelve)	900	4,500
Instant noodles per serving package (basic)	300	650
Candy bar (domestic brand)	300	1,500
Rice (1 kilo)	1,000	3,500
Coke (small bottle)	500	1,500
Beer (12–16 oz bottle, domestic brand)	2,000	10,000
Bottled water (1/1.5 liter)	1,000	2,000
Cooking oil (1 liter)	1,700	7,000
Fresh pineapple (one)	500–2,000	3,000–4,000
Bananas (one bunch)	2,000–6,000	5,000–10,000
Lunch		
At a street stand (Warung)	2,000–3,000	4,000–6,000
At McDonald's or equivalent	6,000–10,000	9,000–16,000

areas. The Gini ratio tells only a small part of the story, because it does not measure the magnitude of income. In reality, however, the urban population has much higher purchasing power than the majority of the population.

Moreover, per capita incomes can be misleading indicators of purchasing power for reasons other than masking income distribution. Price levels also determine purchasing power, and the only safe route to understanding a cohort's purchasing power is to examine the price levels in some detail. Because the consumption unit for many products is the household, the number of income earners per household also affects its purchasing power. In addition, the large proportion of low-income people and the high percentage of them who work in the informal sector may result in understating this group's income; they may earn more than the estimates.

Table 6.8 shows prices, as of mid-1995, for a variety of consumer products. It also shows prices for 2002. At the prevailing exchange rate of 1995 (Rp2,270 = US$1), the prices of most necessities were low by developed country standards. A kilo of rice, for example, costs US$0.44,

Table 6.9

Socioeconomic Classes, Based on Household Expenditure (Rupiah per month)

A Market Research Firm in Indonesia						The Demographic Institute		
1995			2003			1995		
	Rp	US$a		Rp	US$b		Rp	US$a
A+	>900,000	>410	A1	>2,000,000	>240	—	—	—
A	700,000–900,000	320–410	A2	1,500,000–2,000,000	180–240	—	—	—
B	500,000–700,000	230–320	B	1,000,000–1,500,000	120–180	A	>500,000	>230
C+	300,000–500,000	135–230	C1	700,000–1,000,000	85–120	B	300,000–500,000	135–230
C-	150,000–300,000	70–135	C2	500,000–700,000	60–85	C	150,000–300,000	70–135
D	<150,000	<70	D	300,000–500,000	35–60	D	<150,000	<70
			E	<300,000	<35			

aUsing January 1995 exchange rate US$1.00 ~ Rp 2,200.
bUsing July 2003 exchange rate US$1.00 ~ Rp 8,250.

and a package of noodles cost just US$0.13. A simple street lunch could be had for under a dollar, and Coca-Cola to accompany it was only an additional US$0.22. A locally built Toyota Kijang cost US$12,600, which put it within reach of the middle class. In 2002, the situation is different. After a period of spiral, where the rupiah reached an exchange rate of over 14,000 to a single U.S. dollar, the exchange rate stabilized. As of July 2002, that exchange rate is Rp8,832 to US$1. As can be seen in the comparisons of the different products from Table 6.8, the ability to maintain a middle-class existence has become somewhat more difficult in today's Indonesia. With the turn-around of the economy, coupled with rising consumer confidence, however, there has been a renewed demand for consumer goods that has fueled a growing resurgence in consumer spending.

Economic Class

Indonesia's population is usually grouped into five socioeconomic (really economic) classes: A, B, C, D, and E. The definitions of the classes, however, are not universal. Table 6.9 presents two such classifications from the mid-1990s. A marketing research firm created one of these classifi-cation schemas. The Demographic Institute created the other classification. Both classifications are expenditure based rather than income based, and they show the expenditure range in each class in both rupiah and U.S. dollars. They form the basis for social class distinctions. In a country such as Indonesia, an expenditure-based classification is likely to provide a more accurate picture than a classification based on income. For many reasons, income data for the Indonesian popula-tion are not highly reliable. In many cases, a household's expenditures may exceed the reported income of its breadwinners. Hiding sources of income is a common practice among all socioeco-nomic classes. In making conclusions from translating income data from rupiah to other curren-cies, it is important to note the difference between the actual figures and the purchasing power of the numbers. For example, Rp100,000 is merely US$11, but its purchasing power depends a lot on the person having that amount and where that person resides.

During the 1990s, although Indonesia's officially calculated per capita income was low, *For-tune* (1994) estimated that there were more than fifteen million households having annual purchas-ing power parity between US$10,000 and US$40,000. Other observers called the *Fortune* estimate too low and claimed that the number of households with purchasing power parity between US$10,000 and US$40,000 was closer to twenty-five million in 1993. Regardless, a solid and growing middle class clearly was in place by 1993. Still other observers were more cautious. Tait (1995), for example, reported estimates of the middle-income group at 7–8 percent of the population. She placed the proportion of urban adults with the ability to spend over Rp600,000 per month (the upper half of the "B" class and above) at one in six. She also noted optimistically that the number of "A" and "B," households in Indonesia's four largest cities may have increased by as much as 49 percent between 1990 and 1994. This would suggest an increase in numbers from 2.2 to 3.4 million households. Rural incomes include incomes in rural areas adjacent to large cities. According to government statistics, just 25 percent of the rural population had monthly expenditures greater than Rp100,000 per month. In urban areas, 47 percent spent between Rp100,000 and Rp300,000 and 44 percent spent more than Rp300,000 per month.

Indonesia's middle and upper classes continue to hide incomes and protect a variety of assets. It was estimated that the collapse of the Indonesian economy in the last part of the 1990s, with devaluation and the following short-term hyperinflation, cost the Indonesian consumer about one-third of their purchasing power in the space of one year. Bresciani et al. (2002) noted that the drop in real measured wages between 1997 and 1998 was 36 percent for the urban dweller and 32 percent for those living in the rural areas. While some adjustments to that real impact were provided in the past few years, the level has still not achieved precrisis levels. In reality, the damage to the purchasing power is worse. The purchasing power has dropped to one-third of its value before the 1997 Asian financial crisis. The effect of this is worse in the middle class, which did not have assets protected from inflation. The upper cohort, however, tended to have such protection. The middle-class bundle of consumption contained a substantial proportion of imported components that pushed up costs. The lower cohort was not that deeply hurt.

The Jakarta Income Bulge

Compared with other areas in Indonesia, Jakarta of the 1990s (and in many ways still today) looked like a foreign country that was simply dropped into Indonesia. According to one source, 1993 per capita income in Jakarta reached almost US$2,500 (*Republika* 1995b) as compared to US$670 for the country as a whole. Another source estimated per capita disposable income in Jakarta at US$1,776 to US$4,200. *Asian Business* (1993) estimated that 25 percent of Jakarta's population belonged to the "A" and "B" income groups. However, there was still poverty in Jakarta. In 1991, 57 percent (1.25 million) of households in Jakarta spent at a rate of less than US$100 per month. The spending of these poorer household represented only 26 percent of the total household spending in Jakarta, while the top 24 percent represented 74 percent of total spending (*Republika* 1995a). This finding suggested that income distribution in Jakarta was more extreme than in other urban areas.

In 2002, the Jakarta bulge was still in place but at a reduced level. Tied to that was an education level in Jakarta that in 1999 showed a mean level of education of 9.7 years, while the rest of the country was generally somewhere in the range of six or seven years. The poverty rate in most parts of Jakarta is still very low compared to that of most of the rest of the country. Data show that the poverty rate is only in double digits in central Jakarta (11.9 percent): in the sections of north, south, east, and west Jakarta, those rates are 5.7 percent, 1.3 percent, 2.8 percent, and 3.2 percent, respectively. While a large portion of the rest of the country is spending about 65 to 75 percent of its income on food, Jakarta (including central Jakarta) is spending in the neighborhood of 30 to 50 percent. This is a sign of continued consumer product spending in the Jakarta area (UNSFIR 2002).

Social Class

Definitions of social class as used in Europe and the United States are usually based on differences in several facets of human life, including education, wealth, taste, hereditary background
("breeding"), and political power (Fussel 1983). These definitions work best in a mature, stable
society; they are somewhat more difficult to use in a rapidly developing and changing society
such as Indonesia. There are distinct upper and lower classes in Indonesia that meet many of the
definitional parameters; many experts have questioned, however, whether Indonesia has a true
middle class (Dick 1993). There is a lack of agreement as to whether certain groups are more
appropriately included in the middle or upper class. For example, the "large tycoons" classified
by Dick as being in the upper-middle class are economically far better off than business owners in
the immediately lower layer. The basis for classifying the large tycoons as belonging to the upper-
middle class is the argument that the only true upper class that has ever existed among Indonesians included the sultans and other nobility. Using a Euro-American definition of class, that
position is probably correct.

The consensus among Indonesian social scientists is that Indonesia's middle class is best described based on its "economic consumption behavior." Other aspects such as political goods are
less or not relevant (Dick 1993). For marketing purposes, especially in light of Indonesia's rapidly changing environment, we recommend extending this argument to other strata. Specifically,
we propose a classification system based on consumption behavior, or ability to consume. We
prefer to classify the population into economic consumption cohorts on a spectrum from upper to
lower based on their ability and desire to consume.

By the same reasoning, although top executives and intellectuals may have annual incomes in
the order of hundreds of thousands to millions of dollars, they have far less net worth than the
large tycoons, and we should, therefore, classify them separately, far from the top layer. For these
reasons, it may be more accurate to upgrade Dick's upper-middle class into upper class and then
split it into two subclasses: upper class and lower-upper class.

Not all scholars, however, agree on the above point. On Java, there was a traditional bureaucratic elite class: officials that served and reported to the sultans. Members of this bureaucratic
elite were able to gain personally from sultans' wealth and influence while serving them
(Koentjaraningrat 1985). It can be argued that these bureaucrats were the predecessors of the
modern tycoons, whose paths to riches were made smoother by their access to top levels of
government.

The Upper Cohort

The upper cohort includes two subgroups: the upper and the lower upper. The principal difference
between the two groups is net worth. Their incomes and occupations may be similar, but the
upper cohort is at the very top or most influential level of their occupations. Indonesia's wealthiest tycoons may have personal wealth in the order of hundreds of millions of dollars. Using any
relative measure, this group is part of Indonesia's upper class. Some members of the upper cohort
own the large businesses in Indonesia. Others are or have been top-level government officials or
top military officers. Since the Suharto government began, there has been a tradition of close
relationships between business, the military, and the government. It is common for government
officials to be stockholders in Indonesian businesses. While the practice is not as strong under
Megawati's current regime, there is still a definite link between government, business, and the
military.

The number of upper-cohort households is small, most likely numbering only in the thousands. Their money is new, at most, thirty to thirty-five years old. The majority of this top layer sprouted up in the early 1970s, when the Indonesian economy was in the critical stage of a structural reshaping. Most are first-generation rich, having earned their fortunes themselves quite quickly during the 1970s and early 1980s, as well as in the post-Suharto era. They include top professionals (lawyers and top executives) and some politicians. Upper-cohort members' incomes can perhaps best be described as astronomical. As a group, they act as nouveau riche, living cosmopolitan, jet-set lives. They exhibit a distinctive and quite visible lifestyle, and although small in size, this group's behavior has influenced structural changes in Indonesian lifestyle. By and large, this is a group that celebrates consumption, and the visibility of their activities serves as a model for other cohorts.

Most members of the Indonesian upper cohort enjoy luxurious living. They own large houses, luxury cars, and apartments in major world cities, and they pursue expensive hobbies, such as car and horse racing and sailing. They may collect works of art, such as paintings and antiques. Even in the postcrisis period, this layer still consumes lavishly, especially in recent years. Automobiles, for example, Porsche, Range Rover, Jaguar, and Lexus, are selected for their symbolic role. The exceptions are those who have been rich for several generations (the "established" or "old" rich). This small group is less ostentatious. After the reform in the mid-1960s, some of the established rich slid down in status to the upper-middle class.

The lower layer of the upper cohort consists primarily of top professionals, such as physicians and lawyers, top executives of large businesses who are not owners, owners of larger, but not the largest, businesses, the next-to-the-top rank of government officials, and members of parliament. Members of this lower layer of the upper cohort have monthly incomes of at least Rp20 million (US$10,000). This layer potentially has a very strong influence on the behavior of the middle strata.

The Middle Cohorts

Several definitions have emerged for middle cohorts. Dick (1993) defined two groups. The "middle-middle" includes the intellectuals, the professionals, most high-level civil servants, and entrepreneurs in medium-sized businesses. The "lower-middle" embraces a very broad spectrum of the population. In his definition, it includes, inter alia, entrepreneurs, proprietors, and managers of small businesses, rural landlords with small holdings, middle-level civil servants, and factory supervisors. Mackie (1993) recommended the term "middle-income population" to describe this diverse group. Zulkarnain, Siagian, and Ida (1993) proposed a criterion for inclusion in the middle income group: as the people within the society that have covered their basic needs (see Maslow's Hierarchy) such as hunger and security. These authors' criterion, in other words, is simply having enough resources to live above the subsistence level. Indonesia's middle cohort is actually a diverse group of various clusters cutting across several income layers, each with its own peculiarities. Mahasin (1993) offered a potentially more useful classification, dividing the Indonesian middle class into three subclasses: upper middle, middle middle, and lower middle. This approach adds occupation to income as a classifying variable.

In the mid-1990s, the upper-middle cohort's income ranged from Rp10 million to Rp20 million (US$5,000–US$10,000) per month. The collapse of the rupiah in the late 1990s severely reduced that dollar amount, as the rupiah dropped to around Rp14,000 to US$1. The recent surge of the Indonesian economy and the stabilization of the rupiah at about Rp8,000 to US$1 have given rise to at least a resemblance of precrisis purchasing power for those members who remain in this cohort. As we have noted, this cohort includes people whose societal positions have diminished as well as those who are in ascendancy. The ascendants, mostly professionals and entrepreneurs or owners of medium-sized businesses, aspire to the lifestyle of the upper class. Because their incomes limit their spending, they focus their discretionary consumption on products that are conspicuous upper-class symbols.

The middle group, composed mostly of intellectuals and middle managers, includes a higher proportion of people who seem to prefer a somewhat simpler life. This second subgroup is somewhat introverted in their consumption, is estimated to have a range of income between Rp5 million to Rp15 million per month, and may turn out to be the true lower-upper and upper-middle classes in Indonesia's future. This middle class would typically own cars, have enough income to eat out three to four times a week, and go on a shopping expedition to a supermarket (or department store) once a week and to a bookstore once a month.

The lower-middle cohort is the largest among middle-income cohorts. The income level for this group ranges from Rp0.5 million to Rp2 million with an average of Rp600,000 per month in the early 1990s (Sarjadi 1994). Although the purchasing power has sharply declined, the income level of this group does not increase as fast, probably in the range of Rp1 million to Rp5 million per month. There is thus a large gap in spending power between the lower and the middle middles; the bottom of this group is barely over the line between poor and halfway comfortable living. This group suffered significantly in the wake of the Asian crisis, as a portion of this group lost manufacturing and export-related jobs.

Members of the lower-middle class tend to be family oriented. They place great value on family development and family activities. They are very concerned about education for their children. By and large, this is a group with a firm hand on the lowest rung of the ladder. Many do not expect to climb very high on it, but they want their children to climb. While the per household consumption in this class may be low, this group is important both for its size and because it may be the model for new entrants to the middle class.

The Lower Cohort

The lower cohorts are the traditional farmers in rural areas and the poor inhabitants in urban areas, including the factory workers. The government sets a regional minimum wage for the labor force that is adjusted annually. For example, in the Jakarta area, the minimum regional wage is around Rp0.5 million per month. It is worthwhile to distinguish between the urban and rural groups. Most of the urban group work in the informal sector, albeit sporadically or, at best, day-to-day. Several household members may work. The urban cohort, however poor, is part of the monetary economy. Although any single household may have very low spending power, the cohort as a whole still represents a very large segment of the population. This urban cohort represents a distinct and valuable market for necessities, including food, clothing, and basic health and beauty aids. It is also a substantial market for basic household goods such as radios, cooking utensils, and electric fans. The urban lower cohort has access to the same goods as their more affluent neighbors, and as some escape the lower class, members are likely to emulate the behavior they see among the lower-middle cohort.

Most households in the rural lower cohort are subsistence farmers. Many have minimal contact with the monetary economy. Their only source of income comes from either selling part of their crops or finding work as informal laborers. They can buy little beyond the absolute necessities that they produce. It should be noted, however, that not all farmers are members of the lower cohort. Some, including many rice farmers, grow cash crops and form a growing rural middle cohort.

THE EDUCATION SYSTEM

Indonesia has made substantial progress in the education of its workers and managers. Between 1971 and 1990, the proportion of the population over fifteen years old with no schooling fell from 45 percent to 19 percent. Most of those with no education were from rural areas. During this time period, the proportion of the population that had completed secondary school rose from 8 percent to 25 percent. By 2000, the literacy rate for over-fifteen-year-old males had grown to 92 percent. For females over fifteen years of age, it lagged behind at 82 percent, but the trend clearly continued downward with over a 3.5 percent drop from 1996. In 1999, 90 percent of all Indonesians over ten years of age were classified as literate by the government. In 2000, Indonesian government data show that nearly 50 percent of all sixteen- to eighteen-year-olds were still enrolled in school. Education at all levels remained higher among males than females. In the future, the proportion of secondary school graduates is likely to continue its steady increase, and the gender gap will narrow.

Today, several challenges must be addressed. The World Bank articulated them:

> (i) an unsatisfactory quality of education throughout the system; (ii) the inability of the poor to afford the basic nine years of education; (iii) negative institutional incentives that impeded the efficient and equitable distribution of educational goods; and (iv) a public post-basic education system unresponsive to the rapidly changing demand of the labor market." (World Bank 1999, 1)

The World Bank report further stated what has been undertaken by the government to meet these kinds of challenges in the postcrisis environment:

- Maintaining same real level of funding for basic education as in precrisis times (1996/97);
- Launching a US$382 million "Stay-in-School" campaign in June 1998, which includes targeted scholarships for the poorest 2.6 million junior secondary children to encourage transition from primary and retention in school;
- Also as part of the "Stay-in-School" campaign, 82,000 primary and junior secondary schools in poor communities will receive block grants to compensate for the reduction in parental contributions and increases in costs of inputs;
- Supporting the above two programs is a national social mobilization effort, involving government and nongovernment organizations, and a mass TV, radio, and print media campaign. The message, extending down to the village level, is: Keep children in school.
- An effort to monitor the effect of the crisis on student outcomes is underway through a combination of rapid but representative surveys (first one in September); an independent monitoring of the scholarships and grants program; and speedy processing and analysis of the annual household-level socioeconomic survey (SUSENAS). (World Bank 1999, 1)

The long-term results of these types of programs have yet to be felt across Indonesia. Short term, there has been a continued reduction in illiteracy (in 1999, under 10 percent of Indonesians received no schooling whatsoever) and a continuing closing of the gender gap as girls continue to be offered more access to education at all levels.

Indonesia now has over 1,600 colleges and universities that service the growing education needs of its people (*BPS* 2001). Programs at these educational institutions offer all levels of degrees in a wide variety of liberal arts and sciences. Other institutes and technical training programs throughout the country also exist. A deeper look reveals an interesting fact: although there are only seventy-six (4.5 percent) state-owned tertiary schools, they absorb 50 percent of total students (1.47 million out of 2.92 million). In the past, state universities were perceived as providing better-quality education. The situation is rapidly changing. Many private universities are improving their standings quite rapidly. Foreign education also remains appealing. Top-level students who meet the academic criteria and who have the financial means still tend to study abroad, most notably in the United States, Europe, and Australia.

From 1980 to 2000, the education level of Indonesians occupying positions as professionals, managers, and supervisors also increased markedly. In 1980, for example, 31 percent of managers and supervisors had earned university degrees. By 1990, the proportion had risen to 47 percent; in 2002, that number was well over 50 percent. Educational attainment among these groups is also likely to continue increasing, as more students in Indonesia complete secondary school and increase the potential pool of university students.

THE KNOWLEDGE SYSTEM

The knowledge system briefly discussed here will focus on communication technology and access to that technology by the population, with obvious implications for expanding Indonesia's knowledge system. The three obvious technological innovations over the past few decades that have had the biggest impact on information and knowledge transference in Indonesia are (1) the Internet, (2) the satellite transmission of television, and (3) the cellular telephone. In addition to those three, there are also the infrastructure developments that allow for quicker movement of information through personal contact, printed word, or other means that require physical movement of individuals or products (e.g., roads, railways, waterways, and air transportation).

Internet

While governments, through a variety of technological means, can limit Internet access, the government of Indonesia has done little to control access on a grand scale. As a consequence, Indonesians now have access to a limitless amount of uncensored and unedited information on every conceivable subject. *Advertising Age* (2000) reported the launch of a fully foreign-funded real-time news content Web site. Indonesian Web sites with local ownership (e.g., astaga.com) offer editorial content on major political, business, and lifestyle issues relating to Indonesia. Astaga.com, however, also offers free e-mail and is expected to become a major e-commerce hub.

The extent of the use of the Internet in Indonesia is not clear. Estimates indicate that in 2002 there were twenty-four Internet service providers (ISPs) serving over 4.4 million subscribers—up from just 400,000 subscribers in 2000 (*World Factbook* 2003). Much of that usage is centered in the urban areas and in Jakarta, in particular. More recent numbers put the number of ISPs in Indonesia at 170 (fifty operable) and the number of subscribers at about 500,000, but the actual number of users approaches the 2,000,000 mark; there are also about 2,000 Internet cafés spread around the country (Setiyadi 2002). SMEs particularly seem to benefit from the Internet, and over 60 percent of SME exporters who own computers (about 85 percent of the total SME export operations) use the Internet to scan information sources worldwide for data related to business (Setiyadi 2002).

Television and Broadcast Media

Even Indonesia's most isolated islands now have access to satellite communications. Tourist hotels and resorts offer visitors a constant link to the most updated information. At the same time, local residents have that same access, if they can afford the technology for the links. Access from the satellite links to global stations is virtually limitless, with many hotels offering upward of twenty to thirty international stations for its guests. Cable News Network (CNN) and the British Broadcasting Corporation (BBC) are generally mainstays at any hotel. Schools and universities from around the world are also making use of the technology through establishment of a number of distance-learning initiatives. The most recent numbers available for the number of televisions indicate that there were about fourteen million televisions in Indonesia in 1997. There were 678 AM band radio stations, forty-three FM band stations, and about thirty-two million personal radios being used in 1998 according to the *World Factbook* (2003). In mid-2002, there were already eleven major television stations, excluding those government-owned small regional stations. In Jakarta, there are two cable television companies offering access to global stations. One of them, Indovision, uses the parabolic decoder, thus reaching most of Java Island, while the other one, Kabel Vision, uses cables that limit their access only to parts of Jakarta and its surroundings.

Telephones and Other Personal Communication Technology

In 1998, Indonesia had about 5.6 million telephone main lines in use (*World Factbook* 2003). The number of cellular telephones in use had grown to about 1.1 million in 1998, after introduction just a few short years before. The International Telecommunication Union (2002) presented data that show that 40 percent of all telephone subscribers in Indonesia in 2001 were cellular subscribers. That number translates into about 2.5 percent of all Indonesians. It is expected that the number of cellular subscribers will very soon exceed those of the landlines.

Transportation Infrastructure

Transportation is a facilitator of knowledge exchange. There is a total of about 350,000 kilometers of roads. A little under half of them are paved. There are about 6,500 kilometers of railroad roadbed. That number includes a mix of both narrow and wide-gauge track. There are about 21,500 kilometers of navigable waterways, with the majority of those being on Sumatra, Kalimantan, and Irian Java. There are 631 airports with a variety of runway lengths. Of those 631, only 153 are paved, and of those paved runways, less than twenty of them can take large commercial jets (*World Factbook* 2003).

This is just a brief summary of the level of transportation infrastructure. Indonesia possesses a limited but developing capability to disseminate knowledge to its population and to expand its knowledge system. The government of President Megawati has shown a willingness to allow a more open exchange of information between the press and the populace as well. Unfettered access to the Internet and other global sources of information will allow Indonesia to move forward in the more global environment.

THE MARKETING SYSTEM: CONSUMER BEHAVIOR AND MARKET CONDITIONS

The following section describes the modal consumption patterns that are emerging in the country. It should be noted that there are significant differences across income and certain ethnic groups and between urban and rural households. Prices will be presented in rupiah, which at the time of this writing is considerably less valuable than it was prior to the Asian crisis. According to Spike Braunius, President of Sara Lee Indonesia, " . . . (everything) feels very expensive (in Indonesia)

Box 6.3

Japanese Influences in Jakarta

Despite the occupation of the forces of Japan in the 1940s, influences of Japanese culture and brands are now welcome in the urban areas of Indonesia, particularly in Jakarta. These preferences begin at an early age.

Children enjoy Japanese comic books and characters. These include *Doraemon*, *Pokemon*, and *Kobochan*. Indonesians, who believe in mysticism, often relate better to the heroism and magic of Japanese cartoons than to the antics of American characters.

Clubs in Jakarta and other cities offer the popular Japanese *karaoke* as an entertainment option for older teens and working adults. Song offerings include those in Indonesian, English, Korean, and other Asian languages.

Japanese foods and restaurants are also prevalent throughout the city of Jakarta. These include franchises, such as *Hoka Hoka Bento* or others, offering a wide range of Japanese menu items.

Japanese traditional culture appears as Jakarta's residents strive for better health. *Aikido*, a Japanese martial art, has been in Indonesia since the early 1980s. Massage parlors offer shiatsu, a Japanese therapy with origins in China. Those seeking strength and flexibility may practice yoga, a Japanese form that encourages awareness of the body.

Source: McCann-Erickson Indonesia, Pulse Points 2000, and McCann Pulse 2002.

because the rupiah is weak" (Personal communication 2004). The quality of life did not, however, drop as much as some might have thought. Indonesians have adapted well in the postcrisis period, although in a tough way, mostly by reducing their bundle of consumption goods. Slow recovery, however, is evident.

Housing

Prior to the mid-1990s, almost all Indonesians, whether center-city, suburban, or rural dwellers, lived in single houses. Housing prices vary significantly based on location and size. In rural areas, houses are relatively inexpensive. In the larger metropolitan areas such as Jakarta, Bandung, or Surabaya, a small house typically stands on a lot of not more than 20 to 80 square meters. The house alone would range from 15 to 70 square meters in size. Land costs for such houses range between Rp300,000 to Rp1,000,000 per square meter, and the house alone would cost from Rp30 million to Rp150 million. The higher economic cohorts typically have larger, more spacious houses. These houses usually stand on lots 100 to 400 square meters. Houses built on such lots can range in cost from Rp200 million to Rp3 billion, including the land. The upper cohorts are likely to live in houses costing at least Rp2 billion. A top-of-the-line house in the most expensive cities, such as in Jakarta, can cost more than Rp10 billion (US$1.1 million in mid-2002). These price ranges show the very wide gap in purchasing power discrepancies among the haves and the have-nots in Indonesia.

In urban areas, it has been customary for owners of small businesses, especially retailers and craftsmen, to live on the same premises as their businesses. Buildings combining stores or offices and living premises are called *ruko* (*rumah-toko* = house and store) or *rukan* (*rumah-kantor* = house and office); they are the Indonesian version of the "shophouse" found throughout Asia. Such buildings are usually two to four stories high, with land areas of 50–100 square meters, and are located on main streets. The building takes up virtually all the land area except for a sidewalk in front. The first floor houses business activities, while the upper floors are living areas. Because of their larger land and building size, shophouses are relatively expensive. For example, in a new suburb 20 kilometers from the east side of Jakarta, the smallest ruko (three stories with 90 square meters of land area) sold for Rp150 million, while the top-of-the-line ruko with 170 square meters of land in the prime area of Jakarta might cost Rp3 billion.

Beginning in about 1994, high-rise apartment buildings began proliferating throughout Indonesia, especially in Jakarta. Apart from the unfamiliarity of living in small spaces in high-rises, many Indonesian families find them unattractive because of their high prices. A good apartment in a prime Jakarta location would be priced at Rp14 million to Rp27.5 million per square meter. Escalating land costs in Jakarta are making this less-attractive option more of a necessary choice; the land cost for a single-family dwelling in a good location is becoming out of reach.

Another recent urban trend is the development of high-rise apartment buildings for the poor. These developments are an attempt to solve two problems. One is to get rid of unsightly slums, some of which may be in prime residential or business areas. The other is to free the valuable land the slums occupy for other uses. Although these low-cost high-rises were small in number in 1995, in the future, it is believed that such housing will continue to become more important. Again, the disruption of government funding in the postcrisis era has played a role in the diffusion of such developments.

In rural areas, land and houses are much cheaper than in the cities. Although poverty has been significantly reduced since the early 1970s, rural households are markedly different from urban households. Most rural families are farmers. Some have their own farms, but many work only as farm workers, typically on a profit-sharing basis. Many houses in rural areas are not built with bricks and cement, as is the case with most urban dwellings. The rural poor are likely to live in houses made from materials for which they can forage rather than buy. Typically, such houses have walls made from bamboo mats. The floors of these houses are simply the earth. The proportion of houses with cement floors and brick walls, however, is increasing, as more farmers enter the monetary economy. With continued economic development, the rural dwelling will become more like its urban counterpart.

The Household's Bundle of Goods

Households can spend funds on acquiring goods once they have satisfied their food and housing needs. Generally, when the proportion of household income spent on food falls below 50 percent as per capita income reaches around Rp300,000, people begin to consume durable goods.

Indonesian households have experienced major changes in their aspirations for household durable goods. This is a result of the increasing availability of consumer goods over the last decade as well as increased purchasing power. Consumer durables such as stereos, refrigerators, air conditioners, and televisions were considered luxuries just ten to twenty years ago. By the mid-1990s, these items had become common household possessions. Table 6.10 lists some of the durables typically owned by urban households of different income cohorts. As this table shows, even the lower-middle cohort is likely to have a respectable inventory of durable goods. Higher-

Table 6.10

Durable Goods Inventories and Economic Cohort

Socio-economic Class	Typical occupation	Household income level	Urban
Upper-middle	Top professionals, intellectuals, medium entrepreneurs	10+ million	2+ cars Medium house (300–800 square meters building area) Large TV (35″+, more than one TV at the house) Quality home theatre and sound system Vacation home Luxurious watches Upper-scale furniture
Middle-middle	Small entre-preneurs, upper-level government officials	10 million	Passenger car or multipurpose car (up to two cars) Small house (100–400 square meters of building area) Larger refrigerator Larger TV (27–31″) Home entertainment Personal computer Air conditioner Excellent garden
Lower-middle	Supervisors, junior managers, middle civil servants, rich farmer, small rural landlord	2.5 million	Small and low-end multipurpose/passenger car Smaller house (50–100 square meters of building area) Small refrigerator Small/medium TV (14–20″) Inexpensive hi-fi and sound system VCD player Washing machine (basic model) Electric fans Selected kitchen appliances

Source: Authors' estimates based on several unpublished market research studies.

income groups have both broader inventories and more expensive models of goods held by the lower middles.

The same is true of other durables. There are two aspects of Indonesian durable goods consumption. It is critical that marketers recognize both in their choice of products and positioning for this market. The first is technological leapfrogging, the desire to have the very latest technology. In consumer electronics, Indonesia is a late adopter country but with an inordinately high proportion of the most technologically advanced products of their types. Many Indonesian households will simply skip the older product and select the very newest for their first adoption. There is little and diminishing interest in anything that smacks of "old technology." It is fair to say that the high level of Japanese penetration in the consumer electronics and other durables market has contributed to this phenomenon. For example:

- When choosing a means of showing movies at home, they are more likely to pick a DVD player than a VCR. There is an abundance of DVD rental shops in urban areas.

- One-hour mechanized processing of color film is commonplace.
- Jakarta has several well-developed cellular phone systems.
- There is an apparent preference for newer electronics over the older "electrics."

The second aspect of Indonesian durable goods ownership is the somewhat more limited penetration of labor-saving devices and modern kitchen appliances than might be expected. Every household with electricity has its electric rice cooker but may have little else. There are still servants to do the household's laundry and to do the cutting, grinding, or mashing of food that may accompany the preparation of a meal. In addition, door-to-door vendors as well as an abundance of take-out establishments can supply the components of a meal at very low cost. It is likely that the expected diminishing availability of servants will increase demand for household labor-saving devices.

Health and Fitness

Indonesians are more concerned about health than they were twenty years ago. However, Indonesians may define "healthy" in a different way than Westerners might. For example, a senior Dutch marketing executive working in Indonesia recalled that she was surprised that a bowl of salad was not seen as a symbol of health in a recent qualitative study that she administered. Instead, the respondents said that a dish of rice and fried chicken were considered "healthy."

Beginning in the early 1980s, fitness centers sprouted in many large urban areas. In the 1990s, fitness centers had become a visible part of urban life, especially for the younger generation. Stores featuring home exercise equipment continue to be in practically every shopping mall. Aerobic exercise (such as jogging and bicycling) is very popular. In almost all urban areas, people gather in the cities' parks and main streets to jog and to cycle. Because of the heat and humidity, these activities start very early, at about 4:30 A.M. and finish about two hours later, at around 6:30 A.M. Tennis and badminton are popular. The number of golf courses is increasing rapidly in many urban areas.

Cigarette smoking is still prevalent, but less so among younger people, though the tobacco industry targets young consumers. Tobacco companies use a variety of marketing tactics. Such schemes as giveaways and personal promotions are in use. The government has required a warning statement to be included in cigarette packages and instituted a ban for explicit advertisements of tobacco products in most media. Television has currently escaped a total ban.

A wide variety of vitamin and mineral supplements is much more visible and much more widely available than in the early 1980s. Both multinational and some domestic pharmaceuticals companies are actively promoting the use of a broad range of nutritional supplements. The result has been steadily increasing demand; growth of this market has been limited only by income.

Self-medication for a variety of real and imaginary ailments is very popular. For many ailments, modern and traditional treatments coexist. The traditional treatment, *jamu*, consists of herbal remedies derived from the very wide variety of indigenous botanical substances available in the country. There are jamu for treating everything from colds to infertility. Vendors in street markets all over Indonesia sell prepackaged and labeled jamu. It is inexpensive (Rp500–Rp1,500 per packet) and does not require a prescription. Any over-the-counter (OTC) medication that does not contain modern pharmaceutical ingredients is considered by the government to be jamu.

Modern pharmaceuticals are also widely available. Virtually every multinational pharmaceuticals company markets its products in Indonesia, and there are domestic marketers as well. Consumers can purchase both OTC and many ethical (prescription-only) products without a physician's prescription. Ethical pharmaceuticals are distributed only through *apotiks* (pharmacies/dispensaries), while even small neighborhood stands sell popular OTC medication. In the OTC market, there is strong competition between domestic brands and foreign brands.

Nutrition and Eating Habits

The traditional Indonesian diet is a nutritional and health paradox. On the healthy side of the ledger, rice has always been the basic staple, supplemented by some vegetables and a bit of fish or meat. Soybeans in cake form (*tahu*) or fermented (*tempe*) have been a major source of protein. Tropical fruits are also abundant. On a less healthy note, the use of coconut milk or cream, heavy in saturated fat, is ubiquitous. *Padang* food, popular throughout the archipelago, combines coconut milk and meats. Frying and stewing are the preferred cooking methods for Padang food. The two national dishes are *nasi goreng* (fried rice with accompaniments) and *sate* (little skewers of meat)—the first is fried with hot spices, and the second is served with a sauce of coconut milk and ground peanuts. *Krupuk*, a wide variety of fried crackers, are also popular everywhere.

Echoing the heightened interest in fitness and nutritional supplements, Indonesians' food habits are also changing. There is more awareness of the fat and cholesterol contents of traditional foods and increasing concern for limiting one's caloric intake as well as fat content, especially in the upper-middle class and above. The following discussion will identify some of the changes taking place and will suggest that the changes signal potential opportunities to introduce new food products.

Eating out (in this case eating outside) is common. Every city neighborhood and every tiny village will have a collection of small stands with a few crude tables, stools, or benches in front that sell a variety of local dishes. In addition, there are traveling food vendors who go from house to house, each offering the vendor's particular specialty. Prices at the stands and from the vendors are so low that they compete with home-prepared food.

People typically eat three full meals per day: breakfast, lunch, and dinner. If taken at home, all three meals are fully served at the dining table. A typical Indonesian meal consists of rice and several accompanying foods served family style. Each region has its own cuisine. The most notable are the previously mentioned Padang foods (spicy and coconut milk and chili based), *sunda* food (*fritures* with fresh vegetable), *yogya* and *solo* food (spicy, sweet), and *madura* (famous for *sate*) food. Tea (plain or sweetened) or soft drinks accompany most meals. Most Indonesians love sweetened tea. In fact, bottled sweetened teas are the most popular drinks. An indigenous firm introduced this category in the late 1970s with the brand "The Sosro." Even Coca-Cola has not been able to upstage this brand in Indonesia.

Many start the day with a breakfast of *nasi goreng* (fried rice), *nasi soto* (rice served with various other ingredients as a soup), or plain rice served with leftovers from the previous night's dinner. Older middle-cohort people who were raised under the Dutch influence may have a continental breakfast: white bread with butter and chocolate rice (*muisjes*) or jam.

Some breakfast habits are changing. A recent survey conducted among middle-class residents of South Jakarta found that almost 30 percent usually skip breakfast. Instant noodles are becoming increasingly popular as breakfast food (total sales of instant noodles reached US$600 million annually). Strangely enough, cold cereals are entering the breakfast menu of many urban middle-class families.

In some of the smaller cities, such as Solo, Semarang, and even Surabaya (the second-largest city in Indonesia), it is still a common practice to eat breakfast in small restaurants, food stores, or from street-side food sellers. In rural areas, it is customary to eat a light breakfast such as steamed yams or bananas at home or to buy their breakfast (rice based) from street peddlers. Poor farmers' families may skip breakfast and have brunch instead, taking only two meals a day.

In sum, there is a trend, especially in the large urban areas, toward, faster, lighter breakfasts including more nontraditional foods. This trend reflects both the heightened interest in nutrition and the time pressures accompanying an urban work environment. We expect the trend to continue. With patience and sound marketing, we expect cereals, especially high fiber, to catch on as well.

People spend more time at lunch than at breakfast, though not nearly as much as in the past. Factories and offices have lunch breaks. Some factories provide subsidized or even free lunches for their workers. In those factories where lunch is not provided, workers buy their lunches from nearby food peddlers. These peddlers appear wherever there is potential business to be had. Office workers and managers usually go to nearby fast-food outlets, restaurants, or fast-food courts in malls. It is uncommon for people to bring their own lunches to work. In rural farming areas, wives may bring the meal and the children to wherever in the fields their husbands are working, and the family eats together.

As recently as twenty years ago, it was customary to have a siesta or nap after lunch. Offices and stores closed, and people went home for lunch and a nap. Government offices closed for the day at 2:00 P.M.; stores reopened at 5:00 or 6:00 P.M. In some of the smaller cities, such as Solo, a small town in central Java, there are still some traces of this practice. As school ends at 12:30 P.M., mothers who do not work wait for their children to return from school so that they have their lunch together.

Traditionally, dinner is an important family event. Most families try to eat dinner together. The best foods are served during this meal. A typical dinner includes rice, two to five different accompanying foods, *krupuk*, drinks (usually iced tea, iced water, or orange juice), and dessert (most likely fresh fruits, such as bananas, melons, or oranges). Families sometimes go out together to eat in restaurants. Family togetherness at dinner has become a less-frequent event, especially among the more affluent. Long working hours and long commutes make it more difficult for the breadwinner(s) to make it home in time. The children in the family are also busy with school-related group work, sports, and other activities. Therefore, real family dinners are tending to take place principally on weekends. The weekend may well include a shopping expedition or two; if so, the family will have its meal together on the way to or from shopping. The custom of three meals a day consumed at home by the whole family, together, is disappearing.

Eating out has changed the composition of meals. Foreign foods, especially fast foods, have become part of the Indonesian diet, especially in urban areas and especially among children. The United States, for example, has contributed McDonald's, Kentucky Fried Chicken, (Church's) Texas Fried Chicken, Dunkin' Donuts, Wendy's, Pizza Hut, among others. Local entrepreneurs have also developed fast-food chains based on U.S. concepts, such as the previously mentioned California Fried Chicken (100 percent Indonesian owned). Es Teler 77 and other slightly more up-market foreign restaurants, including Tony Roma's (United States) and Crystal Jade (Singapore), have entered larger cities, especially in Jakarta. Indigenous restaurant chains featuring Indonesian food are also sprouting up everywhere, such as Nyonya Suharti Fried Chicken, Bakmi Gajah Mada, and Ayam Bakar Wong Solo. As compared to the precrisis period, the quality and the variety of many restaurants and other upper-market food outlets have improved considerably. Coffee shops are common in the urban areas. Foreign shops such as Starbucks (United States) and Coffee Beans (Singapore) as well as local chains such as Excelso or Independent stores are sprouting. A food revolution is well underway, starting first at the large cities and spreading rapidly to the smaller cities and beyond.

Accompanying the fast-food revolution is a marked increase in the variety of processed foods available in the marketplace. There are, for example, several brands of ready-mixed seasoning packets for making traditional Indonesian dishes. Condiments traditionally made fresh come in plastic squeeze bottles. Supermarket shelves display foreign foods in processed forms, both Asian and Western.

Leisure Activities

The newspaper reading habit is highest in major cities, especially in Jakarta. The low rates of newspaper reading outside Jakarta result from several factors. Illiteracy is higher in rural areas, newspapers are national and contain little local news, print media are less widely available in rural areas, and newspapers are expensive for most lower-income people (approximately Rp75,000 per month). This picture may change in the future, when the costs for newspapers may be lower, and regional editions may be allowed.

Television is the most popular medium across Indonesia. Changes since 1991 probably understate television usage in 1995. In 1991, only state-owned television could reach all parts of the country. Private television stations existed only in the Jakarta and Surabaya areas, and there was only one private station, RCTI (Jakarta) or SCTV (Surabaya), in each area. By 1995, there were three additional private stations—Indosiar, ANTEVE, and TPI—bringing the total to six available stations. By 2002, there were four more television stations, bringing the total to eleven stations. In addition, each province provided its own regional programs.

Indonesians seem to develop tastes for certain types of entertainment. Movies such as *Harry Potter*, for example, were not as popular in Indonesia as in other countries. Indonesians love soap operas. It is interesting to note that television series from the United States were no longer as popular as they were in the early 1990s. Local series and, especially, series from Spain are very popular in the middle-middle class and classes lower than that level. Recently, television series from Taiwan and South Korea, such as "Meteor Garden," have gained tremendous popularity.

One notable leisure activity among the more affluent is golf. To give perspective, at the end of 1992, greater Jakarta had just ten golf clubs, four of which were public courses. In 1993, another six courses opened (*The Economist* 1993). Prior to the crisis, a number of new golf clubs were under construction, and most major cities now have at least one golf course.

Consumer Credit and Consumer Banking

Credit cards have become part of the lifestyle for much of the middle class, especially in urban areas. In addition to global cards such as Visa, MasterCard, American Express, and Diners Club, national cards have flourished. One of the most successful national cards is the BCA card issued by Bank Central Asia. As of March 2002, the number of cards circulating in Indonesia was estimated to exceed 3.44 million, an increase of 16.7 percent over the last twelve months (Abdullah 2002).

The deregulation of the banking system that took place in the early 1990s coupled with the more consumption-oriented lifestyle of the middle class have fostered the use of consumer loans. Many banks and other financial institutions now offer consumer financial products that simply did not exist fifteen years ago. For example, home equity loans have become popular in large cities. First introduced by Citibank Indonesia several years ago, this flexible loan is commonly offered by many banks. Some stores, like the indigenous supermarket chains such as Hero, have even issued their own store cards. Although there were some setbacks in the banking industry as a result of the 1997 Asian crisis, consumer banking does not seem to be much affected. The use of Internet banking, although still covering only a limited number of customers, is also on the rise.

Indonesians have become more sophisticated in handling their money. More families and individuals use banking services. This trend has penetrated smaller towns all over Indonesia. Savings accounts, in particular, are popular, especially when supplemented with an automated teller machine (ATM) card. For example, Bank Central Asia (BCA), the market leader for consumer banking, had more than eight million customers using their ATM cards by the end of 2001. ATMs are found throughout urban areas.

Most Indonesians purchase cars and houses using consumer credit. Car loans are usually financed by consumer banks or by car credit companies. Loans for household appliances are popular for the lower- and lower-middle-income groups. Stores selling consumer durables on credit have existed since the mid-1970s. In addition to banks and credit companies, Indonesian consumers can finance their purchases by using credit facilities offered by employee cooperatives. Another option is simply to use credit cards. Most major banks pursue this market aggressively. In rural areas, there are many traveling entrepreneurs (one-man "stores") that sell household appliances on credit, collecting on each subsequent visit. The availability of consumer credit coupled with consumers' evident willingness to make use of it will accelerate development of consumer durables markets at a rate faster than income increases alone would allow. As a household's income increases, its perceived debt capacity also increases. In a society with a consumption-oriented lifestyle, consumers are more likely than not to use their expanded debt capacity.

THE MARKETING MIX IN INDONESIA

Products, Branding, Consumption, and Image

Consumer goods and brands in Indonesia are produced and marketed by domestic and multinational companies. There tends to be a two-tiered market for most brands. In the top tier are the brands owned by multinational firms. They are typically more prestigious and more expensive and are perceived by consumers to be of higher quality than the lower-tier domestically owned brands. In actuality, the two tiers may offer identical performance; it may be perception rather than reality that guides consumers' judgments.

As consumers become more affluent, a phenomenon called brand shedding appears. With affluence, consumers may shed the domestic brands they grew up with and adopt the more prestigious multinational brands. This may occur even if the domestic brand is as good as the multinational; it is a matter of symbolism, not performance. However, in many product categories, indigenous brands have succeeded in replacing some foreign-owned brands; a good example is the cosmetics industry. Local brands dominate the astringent category, whereas in hand and body lotions, foreign brands dominate, but some indigenous brands have pushed into the top ten brands. This situation seems to be inconsistent with the notion of brand shedding and thus requires closer examination. In a product category with a broad base of consumer use extending across economic cohorts, the bulk of users may be from lower economic cohorts simply because the lower cohorts contain more people. Many of them may shed their present brands as their incomes increase, which will have implications for market share for both domestic and multinational brands.

Another interesting development was the introduction of many flanker brands during the postcrisis period to prevent brand switching. For example, in the detergent category, So-Klin, the leading local brand, introduced Daia as its second brand to capture customers searching for a better price. They were successful, and Unilever introduced Surf as its second brand to protect

Rinso. All four brands coexist. Another development was the introduction of smaller, low-cost packaging, such as shampoo sold in small sachets and no-frill refill packaging to reduce consumers' costs. In the bulk sales business market, many marketers provided larger packaging with larger quantities of the products to reduce costs.

Price

Traditionally, Indonesians are price sensitive and trained to bargain when they shop. More stores, however, are switching to fixed prices, and in them, there is absolutely no price negotiation. Examples include supermarkets, department stores, and stores located in upscale locations—in short, most modern retailers. So, now there are two price segments among consumers. Those seeking convenience are price takers. They search for stores with an image of "dependable price setter" and shop happily in those establishments. The others are more price sensitive or prefer to bargain shop at "negotiable price stores." This price segmentation applies to shopping for most consumer durables, garments, and fresh produce. There are indications that, increasingly, urban consumers are price takers, a trend that should become stronger in the future, especially among the young and affluent. On the other hand, in rural and smaller urban areas, negotiable price practices are likely to continue for the next few decades.

Distribution

Distribution and its regulation are broadly determined by whether a product is classified as a commodity or some other good. Distribution of commodities such as sugar, rice, cement, steel, flour, and cloves is heavily regulated. Distribution of most other goods is less regulated. Furthermore, foreign manufacturers, even if producing in Indonesia, cannot sell directly to retailers; they must use independent distributors. Foreign retailers must have domestic partners.

Traditional and modern distribution channels exist side by side. The modern system includes outlets such as large self-service supermarkets, convenience stores, and department stores. Traditional outlets range from small individually owned stores to street stands. Although in many urban areas there is a shift from traditional outlets to modern outlets, in rural areas, the traditional distribution system still accounts for the majority of sales.

Recent developments in modern distribution outlets in Indonesia, interestingly, are almost exact replications of outlets found in the United States and other industrialized countries. It seems that while the traditional distribution system is unchanged, the modern distribution system has leapfrogged forward to include the most advanced forms in use anywhere. Modern outlets include retailing not done in stores, such as direct marketing and telemarketing. These developments are expected to continue at an increasing speed as they continue to penetrate a wide variety of markets.

Packaged Goods Distribution

Packaged consumer goods are typically distributed through small stores. Such stores can range from shacks to multilevel department stores. The shack may have only two square meters of floor area set up along the street pavement; these are called *warung*. The larger store may sell many items, not unlike the general store of nineteenth-century America. Most traditional stores are full-service rather than self-service based. Table 6.11 lists several types of small stores and describes their physical forms and the merchandise lines they carry. To give some idea of the breadth and

Table 6.11

Some Types of Traditional Small Stores

Local name	Physical form	Assortments
Warung rokok	A very small shack, usually 2 square meters floor area, 2 meters high	Cigarettes, limited over-the-counter products (cold tablets, shampoo, etc.), soft drinks, bottled water, snacks (50–100 items)
Warung	Small store, usually 25–50 square meters, one story, sometimes built in front of residential houses, sometimes in "shopping areas/streets"	Similar to warung rokok but with more complete product assortments (100–500 items)
Warung nasi	Traditional food stores	Food (usually ethnic), also serve soft drinks
Toko kelontong	Larger than warung, mostly stand-alone units in "shopping areas/streets"	Similar to warung plus some clothing, toys, canned foods; product assortments may vary from store to store
Toko P&D*	Size similar to toko kelontong	Specialize in food and beverages, including breads, cakes, and local fresh snacks
Toko elektronik	Size similar to toko kelontong	Mostly electronics

*From Dutch: *provision en dranken* food and drink store.

number of outlets in Indonesia, Unilever, the acknowledged market leader, distributes either directly or indirectly to over 300,000 retail outlets.

There are two ways for a manufacturer to reach these traditional outlets. One is to go through a chain of distributors. The manufacturer sells to a national distributor, and then the national distributor sells to a regional (provincial) distributor, who then sells to local distributors. The local distributor sells to local wholesalers. They, in turn, sell to the ultimate outlets or the warungs. There are many firms that act as exclusive distributors at the national level for specific products such as PT Indomarco, PT Wicaksana, PT Tempo, and PT Borsumij Wehry. These firms then appoint regional or provincial distributors, who then appoint the next distributors in the supply chain.

The other distribution channel is through canvassing. In this system, the distribution company can either be owned by a manufacturer that sets up its own direct distribution channel or by a general wholesaler that sells directly to the final outlets. Typically, a canvassing firm has a fleet of small trucks or motorcycles with a box in the back for the truck canvasser. Each truck carries a driver and a salesperson who also acts as a collector. Each truck starts a canvassing trip by leaving the manufacturer's warehouse with the truck filled with inventory.

The salesperson determines the trip route, stopping at each warung or toko along the way. At each stop, the salesman checks the outlet's inventory (not unlike rack jobbers in the United States), places new inventory, issues an invoice, and collects payments for cash purchases or for outstanding past invoices. While the sale made at each outlet may be very small, the very close distance between outlets coupled with the very low salaries paid to the salesperson and driver make this system economically feasible. Whether or not it will be sustainable in the future is not known.

Unilever is using a variant of this system to sell its Wall's Ice Cream in Jakarta. It is a system that is reminiscent of the Good Humor Ice Cream channel in the United States. It has a fleet of tricycles, each equipped with an insulated plastic box, from which the driver sells ice cream novelties directly to consumers. Before the introduction of this system, ice cream for immediate consumption was not extensively distributed, because most of the small warung that would have been the natural outlet could not afford freezers. Once again, low labor rates make the Unilever/Wall system possible. It seems that indigenous distributors may be able to maintain a differential advantage based on current infrastructure, costs, and their closeness to local cultures and habits, perhaps regardless of efforts by foreign firms.

Fresh Produce

Most fresh produce is distributed through a traditional system. Farmers have two alternatives for marketing their produce. They can sell directly to local (usually rural) markets. Or, they can sell to traders who bring the fresh produce to urban areas. In every city, there is a *pasar induk* (main market), where produce wholesalers sell either to lower-level distributors or directly to final retailers. Fruit is distributed somewhat differently. Some fruit goes through the same system as fresh produce, but some also goes to special areas that sell fruit in street-side shacks. These areas are usually specialized. A row of shacks might sell, for example, only bananas. The vast varieties of bananas available in Indonesia make such specialization possible. Other recent developments in urban areas include fruit shops that exclusively sell a particular variety of fruit, and in urban residential areas with no immediate access to a fresh market, vendors bring fresh produce and meats on moveable carts. These vendors are called *Tukang Sayer* (literally, "The Vegetable Man").

Consumer Durables

Channels for durables are typically shorter than those for nondurable consumer products. Durables are sold in chain stores, stores dedicated to electronics, and even in market stalls. Many manufacturers appoint exclusive distributors. For imported products, parallel imports are a critical concern. For example, firm A may have exclusive rights to distribute imported products from manufacturer B. At the same time, an independent distributor may, on his own, import the same manufacturer's products from a distributor in Singapore or Hong Kong. Products from the different sources compete with the parallel imports usually offered at lower prices.

Warranties and after-sales service are becoming more important to consumers. As they become more experienced, they become more demanding, and they possess more knowledge about their rights as consumers. In theory, this should work in favor of the appointed distributor; if Indonesia repeats the U.S. experience, it will not. Independent providers of after-sales service blunted the competitive edge held by appointed distributors.

The Emergence of a Modern Retailing Sector

The 1990s brought a boom in modern retailing mostly in urban areas. Almost all types of modern retail establishments now exist in Indonesia's urban areas. Supermarkets, department stores, and ultramodern shopping malls are part of everyday urban and suburban life. Family weekend mall shopping has become a very popular activity in most medium-sized or larger cities in Indonesia.

Foreign-owned chains have entered the retail market, using local partners. Indonesian-owned chains have appeared practically everywhere. Table 6.12 presents a list of some of the major retail players classified by country of origin.

Table 6.12

Some New Store Types and Their Owners

Type of store	Foreign-owned brand	Indigenous brand
Megastore	Makro (The Netherlands), Carrefour (France)	Goro, Alfa, Indogrosir
Department store	Sogo (Japan), Metro (Singapore)	Matahari, Pasaraya, Ramayana, Robinson
Supermarket	Sogo	Hero, Gelael, Superindo, Indomarket
Restaurant	Pizza Hut, Tony Romas (United States)	Ayam Ny, Suharti
Fast food/coffee shop	Kentucky Fried Chicken, McDonald's, Burger King, Wendy's, Starbucks (United States), Coffee Beans (Singapore)	Es Teler 77, California Fried Chicken, Café Excelso
Specialty store	Ace Hardware, Shop (United States), Guardian (Singapore)	Optik Melawai, Gramedia

The growth of these chain stores is one of the most important trends in Indonesian retailing. They bring distribution efficiencies by shortening channels and increasing order sizes. They facilitate entry into the market by taking over some of the distribution and promotion functions manufacturers previously had to perform. They also facilitate a shift in channel power from manufacturer to retailer.

Promotion/Marketing Communications

Direct Marketing and Telemarketing

A somewhat unreliable and overburdened telephone system has limited the growth of telemarketing; direct marketing using catalogs or television commercials has been growing rapidly. Indonesians with cable televisions have access to the offers presented on CNN; advertisers frequently fill orders based on their offers in Indonesia. The Indonesian Post Office has set up a special unit to assist direct marketers in filling orders.

Direct marketing may become a particularly important channel for reaching rural consumers, as this population is so widely dispersed. After the government partially lifted the ban on direct marketing, it was predicted in the mid-1990s that direct marketing would sweep the country. We have not yet seen evidence of this outcome.

Foreign multilevel marketers such as Amway, together with a variety of indigenous companies, are already in operation. Various indigenous firms market kitchenware, health and beauty aids, and a myriad of other product lines. Multilevel marketers appeal primarily to the lower-middle cohort. Incentive arrangements make it easy to recruit salespeople. Because many women in this population segment are housewives, salespeople can conveniently reach them.

Advertising

Advertising has become the most important promotional tool for Indonesian businesses. Both multinational and local firms use it extensively. Unilever, with at least one leading brand in virtually every important consumer goods category, is far and away the heaviest spender, but indigenous marketers can compete with the multinationals. During the first quarter of 2002 (January to March), advertisers spent US$221 million, a 34 percent increase over the same period in 2001; the largest increase in the Asia-Pacific region. This amount was still too low. Singapore, for example, a small country with 3.5 million people, had almost the same level of advertisement spending (US$221 million versus US$202 million) in the same period (*ADOI* June/July 2002).

In the earlier days of the Suharto government, regulations forbade advertising on television. The government believed that advertising encouraged consumption, and that it was more important for people to save than to consume. That attitude has changed. The government now believes that the desire to consume is an important motivation for people to enter the workforce. It also believes that building a mass consumptive society will help break down ethnic barriers and contribute to a united country.

Television has rapidly become the advertising medium of choice, followed by radio. Newspapers are less important, while magazines are growing in importance for products that target specific consumer segments. The government, however, prohibits cigarette advertising in newspapers.

One of the leading and most successful advertisers is Indofood. It has used television and radio advertising effectively to build its brand of instant noodles, Indomie, into the largest-selling brand in the country. The Indomie name is synonymous with the category. Indofood incidentally leveraged its home-country advantage, capitalizing on different local taste preferences by introducing various local and ethnic flavors for the simple instant noodle.

Sales Promotion

The use of consumer sales promotion is popular in Indonesia, especially in rural areas. Marketers participate in village fairs or appear at weekly markets. A group of traveling players might perform a skit, which would be a "live commercial" for the product. Providing samples at such events is common. The advent of satellite television has made these "live commercials" less important.

Sweepstakes and contests are popular, as are giveaways or premiums. A typical giveaway is a dinner plate or glassware. Bundled goods packaging, for example, a bar of soap as a giveaway with a bottle of shampoo, is also popular. Marketers have not used coupons placed in the media to the extent that they are used in the United States. One reason is that, given the large number of very small stores, redemption costs could be very high. The growth of chain stores could significantly increase the use of coupons, although the decrease in use of coupons in the United States for various reasons may preclude any widespread application, if Indonesia follows that trend.

The growth of malls and chain stores is facilitating the use of point-of-purchase (POP) displays and in-store sampling. In many cases, an attractive young man or woman is present at a POP display to answer questions and to encourage purchase of the product. Foreign-brand products such as liquors are commonly promoted in this manner. This form of promotion is a particularly effective way to introduce new products, especially food products. The trend toward stores using fixed-price sales has increased the use of price promotion. Periodic or seasonal sales are fast becoming the norm for chains, which can use the newspaper or television to advertise these events. With increasing retail competition, the use of price promotion will inevitably increase.

Market Research

Secondary and primary data are used to make marketing decisions in Indonesia. The acquisition and application of secondary data can be problematic. The most reliable data are published annually by Indonesia's *Central Bureau of Statistics*. The Bureau's reports become available in the middle of the year and can be purchased for relatively low prices. The data are usually presented at a high level of aggregation and are typically used for making policy and welfare evaluations, rather than firm- or brand-level marketing strategies. Mass-market information is also increasingly available, but one needs to be careful in purchasing such reports. Higher prices do not necessarily have a positive correlation with information quality. Industry studies from a variety of sources are also available. As noted, though, purchasers should be sensitive to the possibility of extreme variability in the reliability and validity of research from these providers.

Marketing research firms have filled an obvious void since the early 1980s; there are generally two types of firms operating in Indonesia: independents (e.g., ACNielsen) and advertising agencies. In addition to firms dedicated to conducting consumer research, there are firms that collect industry information (e.g., PDBI and Indoconsult) and conduct economic forecasting. Most of them are located in Jakarta, although their operations may be anywhere in Indonesia, depending on clients' interests. Market research trainers from firms such as the Burke Institute from the United States have also appeared in Jakarta on a periodic basis.

Focus group discussions are popular and are almost invariably followed by a descriptive survey. The most popular statistical method is cross-tabulation. Statistical information, such as confidence levels and t-test scores, is not usually reported. More advanced techniques such as multidimensional scaling and factor analysis have also been utilized.

The fees charged for market research field projects vary. Low-end projects may cost approximately US$2,500, and high-end projects may cost several tens of thousands of dollars. Sample size and representativeness and the complexity of the research questions and analysis are usually the factors that determine prices.

Many of the leading consumer goods companies, such as Konimex and Kalbe Farma, are increasingly emphasizing data from market research to devise marketing strategies and marketing mix decisions. Multinationals Unilever and Procter & Gamble similarly rely heavily on market research. As the number of marketing practitioners who have formal training in marketing increases, use of marketing research continues to increase. Stiffer competition, higher marketplace complexity, the emergence of mass retailers—some of whom are using scanners—will also drive the need for more and better research. Higher-quality work and more providers will be evident. All these developments, we believe, will come quickly.

Expected Changes in the Macro- and Micromarketing Mix

Indonesia is beginning to experience many of the marketing mix changes that accompany economic development. Clearly, for most goods and services, Indonesia is already a buyer's market. Apparently, Indonesia has passed through the initial adjustment period following the severe 1997 Asian crisis and is now entering what could be considered a transitional stage. The market will become more turbulent and more complex as consumers learn new roles and have more choices. As deregulation continues, making it easier for more foreign as well as domestic firms to enter the market, competition will increase further. Change will be the only constant. Some of these expected changes are outlined below.

- The role of brands will increase in importance for a time, as consumers use brands as guarantors of value. As consumers become more experienced and able to distinguish similarities and differences, the guarantor function that brands serve will become less important to consumers.

- Opportunities to build new brands are now excellent because of the large numbers of households entering the middle class. These opportunities will diminish, however, as the market grows and more brands become established. As any market matures, brand building becomes more difficult.
- Products and brands with symbolic value, especially those that are symbols of affluence, will continue to be very important. However, such products and brands will quickly lose their symbolic value if they are too widely adopted by consumers.
- In building a brand, especially a brand that has potential symbolic value, the quality of the brand's customers in the brand's formative stages is more important than its quantity.
- The consumer information environment will become much richer and broader. The availability of foreign television programs, either by cable or by satellite dishes, makes product information from other countries, some directly from commercials, readily available to Indonesian consumers.
- Proliferation of products and brands will persist until market growth slows. Domestic firms are introducing new products at a growing rate, multinational firms are expanding their offerings, and more multinational and other foreign firms are entering the market.
- The time lag between the introduction of a new product anywhere in the world and its first appearance in Indonesia will continually shorten and then disappear. If the originator does not enter the market directly, an imitator will.
- A modern retailing sector composed of large chain units, malls, and strip centers will continue to develop rapidly, in the small cities and suburbs as well as in the largest cities.
- The continuing growth of chains will shift distribution channel power from manufacturer to retailer.
- As long as factory wages remain low and unemployment remains significant, warungs and other forms of small retailing and peddling will persist. The warung will remain an important distribution channel for reaching both lower-income urban consumers and rural consumers.
- In new neighborhoods housing the emerging middle class, convenience stores such as those found in the industrialized countries will replace the warung as the neighborhood outlet for convenience goods and will be a more central component of every marketing strategy.
- Consumers' desires for the very latest technology will persist, and high-tech consumer products will be in demand.

In summary, Indonesia continues to attract multinational corporations with the world's fourth largest population: "Despite poverty, political turmoil, and religious strife, consumers still consume" (Shari 2003, 38). Multinationals now provide most of Indonesia's leading household brands; foreign companies produce the top-selling bottled water, soy sauce, and tea. However, with increasing competition from China in labor-intensive industries, multinationals must adopt strategies to deal with the potential downturn in demand. The need for effective, creative, and locally sensitive marketing will intensify. Unilever, as an example, has recently signed agreements with 12,000 wholesalers that will reach 800,000 traditional small vendors. Creative distribution includes using motorcycle saddlebags to sell bottled Lipton iced tea where narrow roads prohibit conventional vehicles.

A FINAL THOUGHT

In this chapter, we have tried briefly to provide the reader with better insight into the consumer environment that is today's Indonesia. As noted at the beginning, diversity acts as both the strength and the weakness of Indonesia. This diversity is present in its geography, peoples, cultures, and almost every domain addressed in the Pecotich and Shultz model.

What the future will hold for Indonesia is still not clear. Two very significant events in the very recent past, however, have the potential to influence that future in both the near and long term. One is a monumental "act of God" and the other an insidious "act of man." Both reverberated not only in Indonesia, but around the world. Both also have shaped the way in which the world views and relates to Indonesia and the way in which Indonesians look at themselves. They are, of course, the December 2004 earthquake and tsunami and the bombings in Bali and Jakarta over the past few years. The prior wreaked massive devastation on the Indonesian province of Aceh and left more than 100,000 dead. The bombings that started with the Bali bombing that killed more than 180 people (mostly Australian tourists) in October 2002 devastated the tourism industry on an island that relied on tourism for about 80 percent of its revenue.

While the tsunami, by far, dwarfs the level of human loss and suffering caused by the bombings, some are downplaying the significance of the tsunami's long-term negative impact on the overall economic and consumer well-being of Indonesia. Some see the Bali and Jakarta bombings having a much greater impact on the economic well-being of Indonesia (Samual 2005). This is for a number of reasons. First, the Aceh province in 2003 contributed under 3 percent of Indonesian GDP. Additionally, the main industries of the Aceh area (oil and gas) remain mostly intact. Finally, the international community has expressed a strong commitment to the government and people of Indonesia to help rebuild the devastated infrastructure of the region. This last piece may, indeed, offer an impetus to development in the region and ultimately contribute to peace between the Aceh rebels and the Jakarta government. Such a peace will clearly provide an environment where the consumer market can flourish.

The bombings in Bali and Jakarta, on the other hand, have the potential to keep needed foreign direct investment out of the country. The bombings have shocked and saddened most Indonesians, yet there are certain extremist groups that continue to pursue the violent path in the rejection of Western influence. While the economy has been staggered by the flight of foreign direct investment and the downturn of the tourism industry, long-term prospects for economic recovery are uncertain. Furthermore, the future political map of the country is linked to economic issues. As various regions reevaluate the well-being of their populations, the decision to follow in the "Balkanization" steps of the former Yugoslavia or to pursue the Pancasila within the political entity that is Indonesia will need to be addressed. These decisions will ultimately shape the consumer, business, and political landscape of the archipelago.

REFERENCES

Abdullah, Riksa. 2002. "Still Large Room for Further Expansion," *The Jakarta Post,* September 1. Available at www.thejakartapost.com/Archives/ArchivesDet2.asp?FileID=20020901.E02, downloaded February 23, 2003.

ADOI. 2002. "Asia Pacific Poised for a Great Year Ahead," June/July: 46.

Advertising Age. 2000. "First U.S.-Funded News Web Site Launches in Indonesia," February 14 (available at www.adage.com/news.cms?newsId=14371, downloaded March 17, 2002).

Asian Business. 1993. "Indonesia and China: The Retail of Two Cities," October: 12–14.

BPS (Baden Pusat Statistik). 2001. *Statistical Yearbook of Indonesia 2000.* Jakarta.

———. 2002. *Statistical Yearbook of Indonesia 2002.* Jakarta

———. 2003. "BPS: Statistics Indonesia." Available at www.bps.go.id/index.shtml.

Bresciani, Fabrizio, Gershon Feder, Daniel O. Gilligan, Hanan G. Jacoby, Tongroj Onchan, and Jaime Quizon. 2002. "Weathering the Storm: The Impact of the East Asian Crisis on Farm Households in Indonesia and Thailand." *World Bank Research Observer* 17(1): 1–20.

Central Intelligence Agency (CIA). 2002. "CIA Directory of Chiefs of State and Cabinet Members of Foreign Governments." Available at www.cia.gov/cia/publications/chiefs/chiefspdf/April2002ChiefsDirectory .pdf, downloaded August 17, 2002.

CIDA (Canadian International Development Agency). 2002. "Department of Foreign Affairs and International Trade—Asia-Pacific." Available at www.dfait-maeci.gc.ca/asia/menu-en.asp, downloaded August 17, 2002.

Dick, H. W. 1993. "Refleksi Lanjutan terhadap Kelas Menengah." In *Politik Kelas Menengah Indonesia*, ed. Richard Tanter and Kenneth Young, pp. 67–76. Jakarta: LP3ES.

The Economist. 1993. "Among the Rich." February 6: 42–43.

———. 2002a. "Indonesia: Trading on Her Father's Image." April 11. Available at www.economist.com/ displayStory.cfm?Story_ID=1079838, downloaded August 17, 2002.

———. 2002b. "A Direct Insult: After 57 Years, Can't Voters Be Trusted to Make a Sensible Choice?" (From *The Economist* print edition, July 11). Available at www.economist.com/displaystory.cfm ?story_id=1227923, downloaded August 17, 2002.

Fortune. 1994. "The Big Rise," International edition, May 30: 40–46.

Frederick, William H., and Robert L. Worden. 1994. *Indonesia: A Country Study (Area Handbook)*. Baton Rouge, LA: Claitor's Law Books and Publishing.

Fussel, Paul. 1983. *Class*. New York: Ballantine Books.

Guiness, Patrick. 1994. "Local Society and Culture." In *Indonesia's New Order*, ed. Hal Hill, pp. 267–304. Honolulu: University of Hawaii Press.

Hull, Terence H., and Galvin W. Jones. 1994. "Demographic Perspectives." In *Indonesia's New Order*, ed. Hal Hill, pp. 123–44. Honolulu: University of Hawaii Press.

IMF. 2000. "Indonesia: Statistical Appendix." Available at www.imf.org/external/pubs/ft/scr/2000/ cr00133.pdf.

International Telecommunication Union. 2002. Available at www.itu.int/ITU-D/CDS/Country_Data.asp ?Country=INS, downloaded March 17, 2003.

The Jakarta Post. 2002a. "Muslim Liberal Takes on Militants in Indonesia," September 2:3.

———. 2002b. "Consumer Confidence Continues to Rise: Danareksa," May 29. Available at www.thejakartapost .com/Archives/ArchivesDet2.asp?FileID=20020529.N03, downloaded August 1, 2002.

Koentjaraningrat. 1985. *Javanese Culture*. Singapore: Institute of Southeast Asian Studies and Oxford University Press.

MacIntyre, Andrew. 1990. *Business and Politics in Indonesia*. St. Leonard, Australia: Asian Studies Association of Australia.

Mackie, James A. 1993. "Uang dan Kelas Menengah." In *Politik Kelas Menengah Indonesia*, ed. Richard Tanter and Kenneth Young, pp. 105–35. Jakarta: LP3ES.

Mahasin, Aswab. 1993. "Kelas Menengah Santri: Pandangan dari Dalam." In *Politik Kelas Menengah Indonesia*, ed. Richard Tanter and Kenneth Young, pp. 151–59. Jakarta: LP3ES.

Manning, C. G. 1992. "Survey of Recent Developments." *BIES* 28(1): 3–38.

The New York Times. 2001. "Selling the Forests," December 29 (late edition, final section A): 32.

Ong, Hok Ham. 1997. "Economic Outlook of Indonesia in the Pre-independence Era." In *Indonesia's Economy Entering the Third Millenium*, vol. 1. London: International Quality Publication.

Republika. 1995a, January 4. "Berebut perhatian kaum remaja." 3(1): 7.

———. 1995b, January 25. "Bertahan atau banting setir?" 3(2): 7.

Samual, David E. (2005) "Economic Ramifications of the Aceh Disaster," *The Jakarta Post*, January 7. Available at www.thejakartapost.com/Archives/ArchivesDet2.asp?FileID=20050107.E02

Sarjadi, Soegeng. 1994. *Kaum Pinggiran Kelas Menengah Quo Vadis?* Jakarta: Gramedia Pustaka Utama.

Sastramidjaja, Yatun. 2001. "Sex in the City." *Inside Indonesia* April–June(66). Available at www.insideindonesia.com/edit66/yatun.htm, downloaded August 16, 2002.

Seda, Frans, and Donald W. Watts. 1994. "Kerjasama Ekonomi Northeastern Territory / Indonesia Bagian Timur." In *Melebarkan Cakrawala: Australia dan Indonesia Menuju Abad ke* 21, pp. 163–239. Jakarta: Pustaka Sinar Harapan.

Sen, Krishna. 1999. "Women on the Move." *Inside Indonesia* April–June (58). Available at www.insideindonesia.com/edit58/women1.htm, downloaded August 16, 2002.

Setiyadi, Mas Witrantoro Roes. 2002. "e-Commerce for Rural and SMEs Development in Indonesia." Presented at the *Workshop on Electronic Commerce Policy and Regional Cooperation*, Bangkok, Thailand,

June 19–21. Available at www.ecommerce.or.th/APEC/workshop2002/full-notes.html, downloaded March 13, 2003.

Shari, Michael. 2002. "The Beauty of the Business." *Far Eastern Economic Review Online,* July 25. Available at http://proquest.umi.com/pdqweb?Did=000000135407041&Fmt=3&Deli=1&Mtd=1&idx=, downloaded August 17, 2002.

———. 2003. "Consumer Heaven? Global Giants are Finding a Rich Market in Indonesia." *Business Week Online* March 24. Available at www.businessweek.com/magazine/content/03_12/b3825112_mz033.htm, downloaded March 26, 2003.

Soetjipto, H., W. A. Karamoy, M. S. Wuryani, et al. 1994. *Indonesia 1995: An Official Handbook.* Department of Information, Directorate of Foreign Information Services, Perum Percetakan Negara RI.

SWA Magazine. 2002. "The Most Powerful Business Women," February 21–March 6.

Tait, Nikki. 1995. "In Search of Big Spenders." *Financial Times Survey Indonesia,* June 9: VI.

UNDP (United Nations Development Programme). 2001. "Indonesia Human Development Report." Available at www.undp.or.id/pubs/ihdr2001/index.asp, downloaded August 17, 2002.

UNSFIR. 2002. "United Nations Support Facility for Indonesian Recovery, Monitoring Database." Available at www.unsfir.or.id/monitoring.php, downloaded March 19, 2003.

U.S. Department of State. 2000. "FY 2000 Country Commercial Guide: Indonesia." Available at www.state.gov/www/about_state/business/com_guides/2000/eap/indonesia_CCG2000.pdf, downloaded April 24, 2002.

Van Dijk, Kees. 2001. *A Country in Despair: Indonesia between 1997 and 2001.* Leiden, The Netherlands: KITLV Press.

Vatikiotis, Michael R. J. 1994. *Indonesian Politics Under Suharto,* rev. ed. London: Routledge.

———. 2002. "The Beauty of the Business." *Far Eastern Economic Review Online* July 25. Available at http://proquest.umi.com/pdqweb?Did=000000140968221&Fmt=4&Deli=1&Mtd=1&idx=, downloaded August 17, 2002.

World Bank. 1999. "Social Policy and Governance in East Asia and the Pacific Region, Education in Indonesia." Available at www.worldbank.org/eapsocial/countries/indon/educ1.htm, downloaded April 24, 2002.

———. 2002. "Key Social and Economic Indicators: Indonesia." Available at http://lnweb18.worldbank.org/eap/eap.nsf/2500ec5f1a2d9bad852568a3006f557d/4e713c3e61dc2bbb472569af001857ad?OpenDocument, downloaded March 20, 2003.

———. 2003. "Indonesia Data Profile." Available at http://devdata.worldbank.org/external/CPProfile.asp?SelectedCountry=IDN&CCODE=IDN&CNAME=Indonesia&PTYPE=CP, downloaded September 20, 2003.

———. 2003a. "Indonesia at a Glance." Available at http://siteresources.worldbank.org/INTINDONESIA/Resources/Country-Data/IndonesiaataGlance.pdf, downloaded December 2004.

World Factbook. 2003. Central Intelligence Agency, Washington DC. Available at www.cia.gov/cia/publications/factbook/, downloaded September 20, 2003.

Yates, Dean. 2002. "Muslim Liberal Leader Takes on Militants in Indonesia." Available at WorldWide Religious News Web site http://216.239.39.104/search?q=cache:C_v2FnQITW4J:www.wwrn.org/parse.phppercent3Fiddpercent3D6077+percent22they+have+such+black+and+white+judgements.percentE2percent80percent9D&hl=en&start=1&ie=UTF-8, downloaded March 20, 2003.

Zulkarnain, Happy B., Faisal Siagian, and Laode Ida. 1993. "Preface." In *Kelas Menengah Digugat,* ed. Happy B. Zulkarnain, Faisal Siagian, and Laode Ida, pp. 9–26. Jakarta: Fikahati Aneska.

CHAPTER 7

JAPAN

A Crisis of Confidence in the World's Second Largest Economy

TSUTOMU OKAHASHI, N. CLAY GARY, AND STEVEN WARD

> The fatal blow to conventional wisdom comes when the conventional ideas fail signally to deal with some contingency to which obsolescence has made them palpably inapplicable.
>
> ——John Kenneth Galbraith, *The Affluent Society*

OVERVIEW

Japan continues to exist in the doldrums of a sluggish economy; however, it can be argued that Japan is on an evolutionary course into a more modern and competitive marketplace for the consumer. The country is opening up to new economic, political, and social realities. There are tectonic changes in retailing and distribution that have closed the gap between manufacturers and the marketplace. Increasingly, the consumer is becoming *the* key player in the consumer and provider dyad. This right to choose comes at the price of greater uncertainty. The new realities as the marketplace evolves mean that foreign marketers will continue to see ever-increasing access into the "Land of the Rising Sun," as that sun continues its rise back.

INTRODUCTION

In the Japan of the early twenty-first century, if the conventional wisdom has not yet received its knockout punch, it is certainly on the ropes. Although indisputably a first-rate economic power with enduring traditions, Japan has remained mired in economic, political, and social stagnation. The fast-growth, production-led economic miracle that was Japan of the 1970s and 1980s has given way to a slow-growth, consumption-led mature economy that has struggled by fits and starts to avoid deflation for most of the last decade. Once characterized by the West as "Japan Inc.," an invincible mercantilist juggernaut, poised to rule world markets, the Japanese economy, while indisputably one of the world's largest, is looking far less likely to be a leader of future economic expansion any time soon.

Consumer confidence, measured by a variety of surveys, has been befuddled by this new state of affairs, alternately rising and falling from one month to the next in response to media reports that seem to change with the weather. To blame are frequent contradictions between the official media statements and actions of Japan's highly respected bureaucracies. Japanese officialdom's propensity for optimism, founded on a postwar history of three full decades of galloping economic growth and rising prosperity, has been cruelly betrayed by stark realities time and again during the last decade.

The fundamental realities of the state of the Japanese economy, today, have changed little since 1998. The bad debt problems in Japan's banking industry, a continuing bear market in the financial sector (notwithstanding a brief "dot-com" rally), and deflating real estate and asset values are all well known. Worldwide demand for Japanese-made consumer durables, once expected to grow without limit, remained flat due to the high yen and the increasing quality and popularity of cheaper products from China, South Korea, and elsewhere. Although many of Japan's blue chip manufacturers boast solid balance sheets and report good earnings on a regular basis, there continues to be crisis among much larger ranks of second-tier companies that do not have the technology, business prowess, or cash reserves to remain competitive globally. Bankruptcies and layoffs in this sector of the economy have steadily spread the understanding that the traditions of corporate Japan and its lifetime employment system, the foundation of Japan's postwar "economic miracle," were giving way to a more fluid, merit-based employment market with far less job and income security for the average white- or blue-collar consumer.

Against this backdrop, the reform of Japan's postwar political system, long dominated by the Liberal Democratic Party, continued to stagnate under the leadership of Junichiro Koizumi. Originally touted as a kind of populist reformer–savior, the Koizumi administration has fared no better than any previous administration in achieving the financial and monetary reform commentators both domestically and abroad have been clamoring for since the first precipitous declines of the Tokyo Stock Exchange's Nikkei Index in 1990.

On the foreign policy front, the more active role of Japan's military in support of U.S. forces in the "War on Terrorism" notwithstanding, Japan's role in international politics and its close security ties with the United States remain in a state of transition, with no clear future policy directions in sight.

The fabric that has held Japan together over much of its modern history has begun to show signs of wear. Stagflation has been the nemesis of the Japanese economy for most of the past decade. The once vaunted "company man for life" economy has slowly started to fray, as long-term employees are seeing their jobs eliminated in restructurings and corporate stream-lining. As a consequence, there is a growing uneasiness in the middle management and other salaried ranks as to the commitments of their employers to their (the employees) long-term well-being.

Immigration has also changed the face of the Japanese landscape. In parts of urban centers, in particular, one can now see a fairly broad cross section of immigrant groups from such places as China, Southeast Asia, and even Africa. Often, these new immigrants are found working in the low-end, unskilled labor types of jobs. For example, in parts of Tokyo, one may find an African from Nigeria acting as a "hawker" for one of the entertainment establishments; he also tends to live in the lower-end neighborhoods and may live with many roommates to try and offset the high cost of rents in the urban centers.

A dozen years ago in Tokyo, it was rare to see homeless men and women. One could make the assumption that the few homeless were either mentally ill or had other types of social or physical disabilities that led to them being dismissed, or dismissing themselves, from the mainstream of society. When walking through the parks and streets of Tokyo in 2005, however, it was not that uncommon to see homeless men and women. Still, these people tend to be adults (both young and old) instead of whole families, which is sometimes seen in other countries.

One also walks through the parks at night now with a growing trepidation concerning the possibility of being assaulted. This is a thought that would not have crossed one's mind in the late 1980s and earlier. The country as a whole, but more clearly in the urban centers, has experienced an increase in crime. A portion of that increase is violent. The school environment has not been immune to this increase in crime. In schools, physical violence and stabbings have been reported, where once such things were unthinkable.

In 1973, the annual total in Penal Code offenses reported (homicides, armed robberies, and other crimes of a cold-blooded or brutal nature; assaults, bodily injuries and other violent crimes; burglaries, white-collar crime, gambling, and sex offenses) bottomed out at less than 1.2 million. Although punctuated by a series of ups and downs thereafter, in 2000, the total increased to 2,443,470, its highest level since the end of World War II (Ministry of Public Management, Home Affairs, Posts, and Telecommunications 2001).

While what to make of the state of the state may not be a quotidian undertaking, the man-in-the-street knows something large is afoot. There is a sense of change, some might even say foreboding, that seems to waft through the boardrooms, halls of political power, and the streets themselves about the coming years for Japan. There were growing doubts of the conventional wisdom that Japan would always be a safe, peaceful country with a level of social harmony championed as a triumph of Asian values. The Sarin gas attack on Tokyo's subway system by a religious cult nearly a decade ago provided a glimpse of tensions emerging in step with the disintegration of consensus on social and cultural mores. On another front, the government's relief efforts in response to the catastrophic earthquake in Kobe came under attack in the media for being slow and clumsy, highlighting a growing lack of confidence in the effectiveness of the country's paternalistic bureaucracies.

In short, the recession is undermining conventional wisdom in every facet of Japanese life. In turn, the face of the consumer marketplace is changing in ways that make conventional wisdom inapplicable for the Japanese consumer. Thus, a reassessment of consumer behavior in Japan is now particularly timely.

THE JAPANESE CONSUMER: CONVENTIONAL WISDOM

The conventional wisdom on Japan is that it was different: an island country with a history that reaches back to antiquity and inhabitants with homogenous ethnic origins, a single common language, and unique culture and customs. When it came to consumer markets, Japan was similarly unique, a place in which historical relationships and collective prosperity took precedence over individual financial gain. Japan's homogenous consumers were inscrutably complex, finicky, and fickle in their tastes. Due to the high quality of Japanese products, they were likely to prefer Japanese products to imports, with the exception of import luxury goods or fashion designer brands not available in Japan. All of this was undeniably accurate, but even as marketers worldwide were coming face-to-face with this conventional wisdom on the Japanese consumer, the seeds of change were already being sown. The so-called bubble economy of 1986–1990 did much to cultivate these seeds, revealing that Japanese consumers, when left to their own devices, can show the same propensities for status, luxury, and greed as consumers in other markets. In the aftermath of the bubble economy period, consumers, especially the young, are showing similarly comprehensible growth into mature, marketing-wise value seekers, not so easily duped by hype as once supposed.

THE BUBBLE ECONOMY

Japan's speculative bubble economy was the crowning moment in Japan's ascension into the ranks of the world's economic elite. It was a heady time for Japan. The growth rate of its traditionally high-growth economy, fuelled by a soaring yen, accelerated even further, in defiance of the laws of economic gravity. It has been noted that Japan grew by the equivalent of the GNP of Korea each year during the bubble economy, and by the end, it was "one France larger" (Wood 1993, 181). This unprecedented growth brought with it the spotlight of worldwide attention. After four decades of Japanese businessmen traveling overseas to visit factories and learn from the West, during the 1980s, it was Western managers and academic gurus who came to Japan to pay homage to and glean the secrets of Japan's "economic miracle."

The bubble was a boon to Japanese consumers. The strong yen, the expansion of consumer credit, the repeal of an exorbitant luxury excise tax, and broad liberalization of import restrictions, gave the Japanese middle class access, for the first time, to every imaginable kind of luxury imported good, from bejeweled watches to expensive designer handbags. A nearly threefold increase in foreign travel, mostly from increased demand for holiday travel by young singles, rapidly expanded exposure to foreign cultures and ideas, thereby accelerating a diversification of values and lifestyles.

Yet, Japan Inc. was, even during its economy's finest hour, accumulating a bad debt overhang due to rampant speculation in securities markets and real estate. Meanwhile, a boom in Japanese auto and electronics industries' investment in new production capacity unhappily coincided with the downturn of worldwide demand. When these problems came to a head with the crash of the Tokyo Stock Exchange in 1990, Japan Inc. went into a state of shocked denial that it is still coming to terms with Wood (1993, 7), wryly noted:

> Isaac Newton actually arrived in Japan in 1990. His presence did not prove a pretty sight in a country where too many people had concluded that the laws of gravity, when applied to their own [economy], had somehow been suspended.

Unwillingness to accept the laws of gravity meant that many of the changes most commentators believe are required for Japan to restore economic stability are still being postponed, at the time of this writing. And the consensus of most is that the postponement has significantly damaged the country's potential for growth in the long term.

But, as Wood and others also predicted, greater convergence with the international marketplace has been occurring at a steady pace. Purchase of Japanese corporate and real estate assets by foreign entities has become commonplace, as evidenced by such high-profile mergers and acquisitions (M&As) as Ripplewood Holding's purchase of Long Term Credit Bank, one of the leading instruments of Japan Inc.'s central economic planners during the postwar economic miracle. Under Ripplewood's management, the former industrial lender has been renamed *SHINSEI* Bank (meaning, literally, "new life" bank, in Japanese) and is focused increasingly on the consumer retail banking business. The influence of these types of major corporate M&As on the economic and business culture will undoubtedly be broad and lasting. For foreign marketers, this should mean a broad expansion of opportunities in Japan in the coming years as the strong yen, continued deregulation and reform of the distribution system, and diversification in consumer values clear the way for greater foreign product participation in the consumer marketplace.

What follows is an attempt to present the conventional wisdom about the Japanese consumer side-by-side with powerful evidence that this wisdom is no longer applicable to current realities. The goal will be not to create a substitute conventional wisdom but to understand where consumer behavior has been and to suggest the directions changes in consumer behavior and marketing will take during the years to come.

THE ECONOMIC ENVIRONMENT

The economic environment, for years precarious and unpredictable, looked particularly bleak in 2004. Forecasting is always complicated by the Japanese bureaucracies' ever-sanguine interpretations of their voluminous data on Japanese economic life. Having presided over Japan's economic miracle, the Economic Planning Agency (EPA), the Bank of Japan (BOJ), the Ministry of International Trade and Industry (MITI), and others are not accustomed to making pessimistic predictions. During what in 1995 had become a four-year slump, the EPA and the BOJ prematurely proclaimed that the recession was, in fact, over several times, only to watch the economy slide further.

From 1995 to 2000, the economy continued to make sluggish progress, with real GDP growth averaging just around 1 percent per year (*Euromonitor* 2000). This included a major recession in which growth contracted –2.5 percent in 1998. The economy in 2002 remained at a standstill, with growth hovering at around 0.3 percent (BFI 2003). No comment is necessary on the negative impact of such a result on consumer confidence.

Decline of "Lifetime" Employment

Most observers expect lifetime employment to come under increasingly direct pressure. A survey conducted by the leading Japanese advertising agency, Dentsu Inc. (1993), in the fall of 1993 revealed that as many as 57 percent of all Japanese believe fewer people will work for only one company until retirement. Meanwhile, 90 percent responded that developing specialized skills and expertise would be important in the future. This reflects the growing belief that the future will call on employees to take the initiative in building and maintaining skills that make them viable employees.

Current economic observers have likened the current employment situation to an ice age, where companies are no longer hiring vast numbers of young college graduates. According to the Ministry of Education in 1998, some 82,000 graduates in different areas of specialization could not find work in Japan. This total of unemployed *ronin* (masterless samurai) was a record high. There is now an increasing employment practice of only hiring graduates when they are needed rather than hiring these people en masse each spring. This is a fundamental change in what had been a time-honored tradition—a change that is as much social as it is economic.

Another change has been an increase in the labor force of workers ages 55 or over. That proportion of the workforce has increased from 15.1 percent to 20.7 percent and is expected to continue to increase in Japan (Ministry of Labor 1999). One could speculate that there are two elements at play here. First, the tendency of managers to keep the "old guard" in place out of loyalty and at the cost of the new hires. The second element is, simply, the aging population demographics in Japan. There is also a tendency among employers to reduce wage costs by reducing the number of employees and using temporary dispatch services and temporary dispatch workers. The number of people registered as temporary dispatch workers, for example, increased from 87,000 to 860,000 in 1998.

Employment Outlook

Due to corporate efforts to ease the shift to a more fluid employment structure, nominal unemployment remains low by Western standards. Table 7.1, as an example from just one industry, TV production, shows that Japanese consumer durables manufacturers are steadily moving produc-

Table 7.1

TV Production Location

Year	Domestic (%)	Overseas
1984	58.2	41.8
1985	61.2	38.8
1986	52.8	47.2
1987	51.3	48.7
1988	45.3	54.7
1989	39.9	60.1
1990	37.2	62.8
1991	34.1	65.9
1992	28.1	71.9
1993	28.0	72.0
1994	22.2	77.8
1995	18.2	81.8
1996	12.9	87.1
1997	14.8	85.2
1998	13.3	86.7
1999	8.5	91.5

Source: Asahi Shimbunsha (1995, 2002), Asahi ki wado (Asahi Keywords), Tokyo.

tion overseas, primarily to Southeast Asian countries that offer cheaper labor. In the midst of this seismic shift, retraining for intracompany transfer and outplacement programs in the manufacturing sector have helped minimize the extent of layoffs of blue-collar workers. Nevertheless, at nearly 4.9 percent, unemployment in 1999 was a historical high for Japan (Ministry of Labor 1999), and in 2003, the rate was near 6 percent. Even this figure, shocking in historical terms, may be artificially low due to the phenomenon of *shanai shitsugyou* or "intracompany unemployment," which is another term for white-collar overstaffing.

Wood (1993) asserted that overstaffing is partly due to overhiring in the 1980s and an acceptance of the "myth of a labor shortage," a favorite precept of the conventional wisdom of the day. Director and vice president of Bain & Company, Japan, Shintaro Hori (1993), concurred with this analysis, asserting that Japan's service sector tolerates levels of employment that would be considered unusually high in other countries. Hori (1993) once estimated that 5–6 million Japanese white-collar workers are redundant. If these jobs were eliminated outright, unemployment would soar to over 10 percent, although this would be highly unlikely due to the tacit commitment to lifetime employment.

Rather than eliminate jobs outright through layoffs, Japanese firms have quietly used a variety of tactics to decrease their white-collar payrolls. The gradual rise of both voluntary and compulsory early retirement programs, transfers to lower-paying subsidiaries, merit-pay systems, and cutbacks in annual hiring of new college graduates are all evidence of these efforts. Some companies have used more novel approaches to manage staff budgets. One of these approaches is the use of a "discretionary work system." Here, Japanese employees, such as research and planning staff, work at their own discretion and are considered to have worked for an agreed-upon number of hours, regardless of the number of hours they may have actually worked. Job sharing is also used as a means of protecting employment. Other efforts to avoid further unemployment include the reduction of hours by workers. That is, the length of the legal work week has been decreased. Meanwhile, government surveys reveal that Japanese worker attitudes toward employment are

Table 7.2

Income Distribution (percent share of GDP, 1990)

Lowest 20 percent	Second 20 percent	Third 20 percent	Fourth 20 percent	Top 20 percent	Top 10 percent
8.8	13.2	17.4	23.1	37.5	22.4

Source: Christina A. Genzberger et al., *Japan Business: The Portable Encyclopedia for Doing Business with Japan* (San Rafael, CA: World Trade Press, 1994), p. 172.

more liberal. Japanese workers are more willing to change jobs. Although some job changing may be due to corporate outplacement, there is greater willingness for Japanese workers who are disgruntled with pay and conditions in one job to look for greener pastures elsewhere.

Despite corporate attempts to reduce the pain of the changing employment structure, if estimates of the slack in white-collar employment are even half right, and if the economy continues to be sluggish over the near- to mid-term, greater dislocation is undoubtedly in store. The brunt of it would be borne by Japan's young people. This was foreshadowed a decade ago, when a record 150,000 new university graduates were not hired by any company to which they applied. Many had offers withdrawn by companies who belatedly realized they could not afford to make lifetime commitments. In Japanese society, which tacitly assumes universal employment, there is the threat of stigma for these young people. Should expectations of universal lifetime employment be betrayed, resulting in higher structural unemployment, there would be a potential for the emergence of a Japanese "Generation X," an economically disenfranchised generation of young people, raised in affluence but with significantly dimmer financial prospects than their elders. Chats with younger consumers and even the young service industry employees, in the shops and on the streets of Tokyo, suggest this emergence is already underway.

Income

Japan has had the most equitable distribution of wealth among the advanced industrial countries, as shown in Table 7.2. These figures reinforce the belief of the Japanese that they belong to the middle class; even after the severe recessions of the post-1992 era, around 90 percent believed themselves to be middle class (*Euromonitor* 2000).

The current economic difficulties in Japan are also reflected in a trend developing since the mid-1990s of lower household incomes. Household expenditure has also subsequently declined to its lowest level since the recession of 1980–81 (see Table 7.3). This downward trend is likely to continue. Although the Japanese household savings rate remains the highest among the advanced countries, consumer debt has risen considerably since the 1980s. Consumer confidence surveys, moreover, show lowered expectations for positive income growth, employment, and living standards.

As the white-collar employment situation suggests, future prospects for nominal income growth are not bright for the majority. On the other hand, the increased fluidity of the labor market and the decline of seniority-based compensation will mean greater opportunities for talented employees. Many commentators have noted that record sales in Japan for brands such as Louis Vuitton in 2000 and 2001, and record waiting lists of potential buyers for Toyota's new Lexus models in Japan, point to a growing upper-middle class comprised of men and women in their thirties and forties with specialized talents to command higher compensation than the average white-collar

Table 7.3

Average Monthly Salary of Nationwide Nonagricultural Households

Year	Net income Net Income (yen)	Net expense Net Expense (yen)	Net income change after inflation (%)
1975	236,152	186,676	2.7
1980	349,686	282,263	−0.6
1985	444,846	360,642	2.7
1990	521,757	412,813	2.0
1991	548,769	430,380	1.8
1992	563,855	442,937	1.1
1993	570,545	447,666	0.1
1994	567,174	439,112	−1.1
1998	494,884	351,935	−0.7
1999	481,578	345,121	−2.7
2000	470,982	341,335	−2.2

Sources: Management and Coordination Agency (1995); Management and Coordination Agency, *Employment Structure of Japan, 2001* (Tokyo: Employment Sector, 2001).

Table 7.4

Inflation Rate

Year	Inflation (%)
1971	6.4
1980	7.8
1990	3.1
1991	3.3
1992	1.7
1993	1.3
1994	0.7
1995	−0.1
1996	0.1
1997	1.7
1998	0.6
1999	−0.3
2000	−0.6

Source: Euromonitor, "Consumer Lifestyles in Japan: Integrated Market Information System" (2000), August, p. 34.

employee and the desire to spend their high disposable incomes to enjoy the finer things in life. Greater social acceptance of job-hopping in the face of the decline of lifetime employment gives these new-generation professionals the confidence to move from one employer to another in order to profit from this more merit-based approach to compensation.

Inflation

Table 7.4 shows that inflation has declined dramatically since the bursting of the bubble economy. Continued price destruction, and the looming threat of debt deflation, described earlier, has re-

Table 7.5

Birth Rate

Year	Rate (%)
1960	2.00
1970	2.13
1980	1.75
1990	1.35
1995	0.99
2000	0.92

Sources: Ministry of Health and Welfare, *Population Projections for Japan 1991–2090* (Tokyo, 1992); Ministry of Health and Welfare, *Vital Statistics* (Tokyo, 1995); *Euromonitor*, "Consumer Lifestyles in Japan: Integrated Market Information System" (2000), August, p. 4.

sulted in deflation in the past two years 1999–2000. *The Economist* estimates that prices in Japan are falling at the rate of 1 percent per year. While deflation points to a continued recession in Japan, it also has cushioned the decline of nominal wages by increasing the purchasing power of available incomes of households. For example, young Japanese couples in 2003 could find 0 percent financing on apartments in Tokyo and other cities. Deflation, however, encourages consumers to save, not spend. For companies in Japan, deflation is a nightmare, with the amount of debt increasing over time. This further limits any expansion of business activity and reduces future employment prospects, thus eroding consumer confidence in the future.

THE DEMOGRAPHIC ENVIRONMENT

That Japan is an ethnically homogeneous country is generally well-known. Nevertheless, the rising number of legal and illegal residents is contributing to greater ethnic diversity in urban areas. People from other Asian countries are frequently brought to Japan on labor contracts with small industrial firms to do the so-called Three-K jobs. The Three Ks are *kitanai* (dirty), *kitsui* (hard), and *kiken* (dangerous). Demand for such foreign laborers is expected to increase as Japan shifts increasingly to a service-oriented economy, and younger Japanese are less willing to take these kinds of jobs. Moreover, given the trend toward lower birth rates (see Table 7.5) and as little population growth is expected (see Table 7.6), one could reasonably conclude that the demographic profile of Japan will become less homogeneous.

Age Distribution

In 2000, 17.3 percent of Japan's total population was sixty-five years of age or older, having increased rapidly from just over 10 percent in 1987. With average life expectancies in Japan among the highest in the world at eighty-one years for women and seventy-five years for men, the ratio of senior citizens will continue to increase sharply and is expected to be more than 25 percent by 2020. The population of those ages fifteen years and under is expected to remain fairly constant, at about 15 percent, as shown in Table 7.7.

The *Dankai* Generations

An important feature to note in Japanese demographic composition is the existence of two huge baby-boom generations. They are commonly known to marketers as the *Dankai* generation and

Table 7.6

Population Growth

Year	Average annual growth rate (%)
1971–80	1.3
1981–90	0.5
1991–2000	0.3
2001–2010*	0.2
2011–20*	–0.2

Source: Ministry of Public Management, Home Affairs, Posts and Telecommunications, 2000 Census.
*Projected.

Table 7.7

Projected Age Distribution of the Population

Age	1995	2000	2010	2020
0–14	16.0	14.6	16.4	15.5
15–64	69.4	67.9	62.4	59.0
>65	14.5	17.3	21.3	25.5

Source: Ministry of Health and Welfare (2002).

their children, the Dankai junior generation. Although each represents only a four- or five-year period, not full generations in the strict sense, these two groups are considered to be opinion leaders for broad segments of the population and are tracked closely by marketers for clues to changes in consumer behavior.

Members of the Dankai generation are the children of Japan's post–World War II baby boom. Some nine million strong, they are currently in their mid-to-late fifties. This means their ranks are now the upper-echelons of corporate Japan. The Dankai were the driving force behind Japan's student protest movement in the late 1960s and early 1970s. They challenged authority on a variety of issues, including the country's support of the U.S. war effort in Vietnam. Although they eventually settled down into jobs within the Japanese establishment, the Dankai have remained proud of their self-styled maverick image. They perceive themselves as having made constructive changes in Japanese society by actively supporting government and corporate policies to encourage more individuality, greater internationalism, and shorter working hours. As Kawakami (1993) noted, while they have, on the surface, been able to adapt to the corporate establishment, because Dankai distrust the establishment, they have a strong belief that "work is not everything," and their strongest loyalties are to their families, not their companies.

Although the leisure boom is a relatively new consumer trend, it has been argued that the "all-work no-play" philosophy of the Japanese workforce actually began to change in the early 1970s when the Dankai generation entered the workforce. Dentsu Inc.'s Teizo Tsutsumi (Denstu 1986, 17) has argued that the Dankai led the revolutionary shift in Japanese worker behavior from "ant-

Table 7.8

National Average Working Hours per Person

Year	Average working hours (hours/month)
1960	202.7
1965	192.9
1970	186.6
1975	172.0
1980	175.0
1985	175.8
1990	171.0
1991	168.0
1992	164.3
1993	159.4
2000	154.4

Sources: Ministry of Labor, *Monthly Labor Survey* (Tokyo, 1995); Ministry of Labor (2000).

like" to "grasshopper-like," taking his metaphor from Aesop's fables. Whereas the ant works himself to the point of death to gather food for tomorrow, the grasshopper prefers to enjoy today and lets tomorrow take care of itself. Table 7.8 shows the steady decline in average annual working hours by Japanese workers since the Dankai entered the workforce in the early 1970s.

From a consumer behavior perspective, it is interesting to note that Honda and Sony, innovative mavericks of the Japanese corporate establishment, are brands that are closely associated with and favored by the Dankai generation.

Members of the Dankai junior generation are the children of the Dankai generation. Born between 1970 and 1973, Dankai juniors number more than 8 million. Now in their mid-thirties, they are becoming the center of the workforce and are exerting their adult and family spending power on the marketplace. Their consumer behavior will be discussed in more detail later.

EDUCATION

The education system has five stages: kindergarten (one to three years in duration), elementary school (six years), middle school (three years), high school (three years), and university (generally four years). There are also junior colleges offering courses of study of two or three years in duration, though these are predominantly for women. In addition, many universities provide post-graduate courses for advanced studies.

Primary and middle school education is free and compulsory. However, in 2000, 97 percent of all students entered high school, a ratio similar to that of the United States, indicating that high school is, in fact, an essential part of a child's education. Of all high school students, 45.1 percent continued on to two-year women's colleges or four-year universities (Ministry of Education 2000). This is a smaller ratio than that from the United States, where nearly half of all students enter university, but more than that from western European countries, where averages range between 20 percent and 30 percent.

Private schools exist at all stages of the system. As of 1994, as many as 80 percent of children in kindergartens and 73 percent of students in universities were enrolled in private institutions, and 30 percent of all high school students were attending private schools. Traditionally, educational background has been an important factor in Japan's lifetime employment system. In order to land a job in a top-ranking company, it is necessary to be graduated from a top-ranking university, a qualification that is dependent, in turn, upon graduation from a top high school and middle school. Thus, students generally attend private entrance examination, or "cram" schools. These schools, which provide supplementary, after-school instruction to help students enter the schools of their choice, exist at all levels, from nursery school through university.

Because even public high school education is not free, and due to the connection between educational background and employment, household educational expenses are uniformly high. A 1995 survey by Sanwa Bank indicated that the cost of sending one child to private schools from nursery school through university cost approximately US$264,000. The typical cost for a child who attends only public institutions is US$114,000. These daunting costs, which have continued to rise, coupled with generally high child-rearing expenses, may be a factor in the declining birth rate.

The post–World War II education system was designed to produce an obedient workforce with uniform training, knowledge, and values. This system has been credited with creating the efficient worker culture necessary to achieve Japan's economic miracle. However, there is an overwhelming consensus in favor of education reform. The fierce "examination hell" that students go through to gain places in the best schools has long been decried for placing undue stress on children at an early age. Also, institutionally encouraged bullying of students judged by teachers to be "different" from others has come under attack. A 1995 independent report on the need for education reform stated that 97 percent of Japanese agree that education needs reform. Top reasons cited included "intensity of entrance examination system" at 60 percent, "increasing bullying" at 37 percent, "problems with the quality or nature of instruction" at 35 percent, and "too much emphasis is placed on in-school education" at 32 percent. Perhaps more importantly, it has been argued that the increasingly competitive international business environment demands a more diverse workforce with specialized skills and the intellectual flexibility to make quick decisions.

In the early 1990s, the Ministry of Education began to reform the education system to address these issues. Reforms included deemphasis of rote memorization of a uniform body of common knowledge, a new emphasis on out-of-classroom learning experiences, and greater tolerance for individual differences. Schoolchildren have had two Saturdays off per month as the first step toward the implementation of a five-day school week. The stated purpose of cutting school hours is to provide students the opportunity to pursue extracurricular activities, with a view to producing better-rounded adults. In addition, as many companies implemented a five-day workweek during the 1980s, children can now spend more time with their families.

CHANGES IN THE TRADITIONAL FAMILY

According to collective cultural memory, prior to World War II, most Japanese lived in an extended family of three or more generations. Statistics tell a slightly different story, as we will discuss later, but the multigenerational family certainly played a key role in society in the early twentieth century. In adherence to Confucian traditions that entered Japan via China and Korea, family relationships were governed by a rigid hierarchical system. The elderly members of the household held an honored position, and parental authority was strong. As the nominal head of the household, a father commanded special respect and obedience from his children and his wife. However, the de facto head of household affairs would be his mother, who would manage all household affairs, including the budget.

Upon marriage, a new bride was expected to live with her husband's family and faithfully obey her parents-in-law, for whom she would be the primary caretaker in their old age. The

Table 7.9

Persons per Household

Year	Persons per household
1960	4.14
1970	3.41
1975	3.28
1980	3.22
1985	3.14
1990	2.99
2000	3.00

Sources: Management and Coordination Agency, *1990 Population Census of Japan* (Tokyo: Employment Sector, 1992); *Euromonitor*, "Consumer Lifestyles in Japan: Integrated Market Information System" (2000), August, p. 22.

young housewife served what amounted to a Cinderella-like apprenticeship to an often strict and unforgiving mother-in-law. From her mother-in-law, the young housewife learned how to keep house, manage the family budget, and cook. Typically, she could never do enough to please, especially if she failed to bear a grandson for her mother-in-law. Strained relationships between young wives and mothers-in-law are still popular subject matter for today's television dramas.

Changes in Household Composition

Rapid economic growth and urbanization have wrought major changes in the traditional family. There has been a sharp decline in the number of persons per household, which now stands at less than three people, down from 4.14 in 1960 (see Table 7.9).

Urbanization has resulted in a decrease in the number of extended families in rural areas, as children left home to attend universities and take jobs in the cities. In the cities, expensive and smaller housing has led to much lower percentages of extended families in urban areas. Extended families accounted for 36.5 percent of all households in 1955, but this ratio has declined steadily, dropping to 15.7 percent in 2000. On the other hand, the number of one-person households has skyrocketed from 3.4 percent in 1955 to 25.6 percent of households in 2000, reflecting a continuing long-term trend of urban young professionals and elderly increasingly living alone in so-called one-room mansions. Meanwhile, the number of nuclear families, comprised of parents and children, which had gradually increased to 63.3 percent by 1980, had declined slightly to 58.7 percent by 2000 (see Table 7.10).

As women increasingly opted for full-time careers, the number of double-income-no-kids (DINKs) households increased during the 1990s, as suggested by the relatively stable figure for earners per household through 1995, despite the declining number of persons per household. However, the rising unemployment rate has taken a toll on the earners per household, as seen in the year 2000 (Table 7.11). Also, with the decline of the extended family, the number of elderly living alone is rising. The number of households in which the householder is over sixty-five years of age increased from 2.2 percent in 1955 to 13.2 percent in 1994 and to 17.3 percent in 2000 (Ministry of Health and Welfare 1995a).

Compounding changes in household size and composition is the previously discussed declining birth rate. The aforementioned rise of one-person households and DINKs households and the

Table 7.10

Type of Family (%)

Year	Nuclear family	Extended family	One-person household
1920	55.3	38.2	6.0
1955	59.6	36.5	3.4
1960	60.2	34.7	4.7
1970	63.5	25.4	10.8
1980	63.3	20.7	15.8
1990	61.8	17.8	20.2
2000	58.7	15.7	25.6

Source: Management and Coordination Agency, *1990 Population Census of Japan* (Tokyo: Employment Sector, 1992); Management and Coordination Agency, *2000 Population Census of Japan* (Tokyo: Employment Sector, 2000).

Table 7.11

Earners per Household

1970	1.64	1995	1.54
1975	1.59	1996	1.52
1980	1.55	1997	1.53
1985	1.56	1998	1.49
1990	1.60	1999	1.47
1991	1.63	2000	1.41
1992	1.62	2001	1.37
1993	1.60	2002	1.32
1994	1.56		

Source: Ministry of Public Management, Home Affairs, Posts and Telecommunications (2002).

tendency to delay marriage are closely related to this trend. The high cost of child-rearing and education, combined with the decreasing average size of housing, is discouraging some people from marrying and from having children.

Another reason for the decline in the birth rate in Japan is the reluctance of Japanese women to marry. This is important, because only 1 percent of Japanese children are born out of wedlock. The wife of an eldest son is, by tradition, expected to live in the family home and look after her parents-in-law. Therefore, eldest sons are not particularly attractive prospects for the young, increasingly educated and prosperous Japanese women. This has also given rise to a group of Japanese women, termed "freeters" or "parasite singles," estimated to make up 10 percent of those who are twenty to thirty-four years of age, who prefer to stay at home with their parents. These Japanese women are less likely to pursue conventional employment and seem to drift from job to job. They are, however, likely to have larger disposable incomes than women in the past. The rise of this demographic group explains, in part, the development of fashion and cultural industries in Japan, in the latter half of the twentieth century.

For working women, a lack of sufficient affordable child-care services is another major deterrent to childbearing. The Japanese government predicts the birth rate will rise to 1.61 percent by 2025, but with the declining number of people in their childbearing years and in the absence of cogent public and private-sector programs to encourage childbearing, these figures may be optimistic. According to the government's statistics, the population of Japan is expected to peak at 127 million people in 2010 before entering a precipitous decline to just over 100 million by 2050 (Ministry of Public Management, Home Affairs, Posts, and Telecommunications 2001). This population trend likely will require the government to encourage greater immigration to maintain the relative competitiveness and prosperity of its economy. Already, long-term foreign residents of Japan are noting a significant reduction in the red tape required to obtain long-term residence visas.

As a result of the demise of the extended family and the increasingly long life expectancy of the Japanese, the ratio of households consisting only of people aged sixty-five or older jumped from 2.2 percent in 1955 to 13.2 percent in 1995 and to 17.5 percent in 2000 (Management and Coordination Agency 2000a). In three-generation households, grandparents enjoyed an honored role, and children and grandchildren were committed to taking care of grandparents until death. However, younger Japanese are far less inclined than previous generations to honor this commitment of taking care of their elders. The emergence of the young woman who has decided to spend income on herself, for clothes and travel, rather than saving and caring for the family is one such indicator of this trend (see discussion below under "Gender Issues"). In greater Tokyo, Chiyoda Ward is currently considering a new tax on apartment buildings containing a majority of one-room apartments. The tax is defended on the grounds that it is intended to discourage the breakdown of the multigeneration household. Whether such measures will actually result in fewer elderly living alone remains to be seen.

The dramatic shift toward one-person households has not yet been sufficiently reflected in official statistics on Japanese consumers. Some researchers pointed out that single-person households are ignored in the "Annual Report on Family Income and Expenditure Survey," the most widely used source of data on Japanese consumer behavior (Suzuki and Kirishima 1995). This is significant, because many one-person households are comprised of singles under thirty years of age, who, free of the burden of high child-rearing and educational expenses, have high disposable incomes to spend on advanced consumer durables, such as personal computers and overseas travel. Major factors in the rise of one-person households are declining average living space per family and a growing preference for privacy and independence, which encourages many children to live on their own. The rising average age of first marriage, 28.7 years for men and 26.4 years for women in 1999, will contribute to further increase in the number of one-person households (Ministry of Public Management, Home Affairs, Posts, and Telecommunications 2001).

Supporting the continued growth of one-person and DINKs households are the diffusion of modern household appliances, the expansion of the instant and frozen-food industries, and the proliferation of home delivery services for everything from mineral water and fresh vegetables to dry cleaning and pizza. These conveniences allow one-person households and DINKs to balance busy work schedules with their broad leisure interests. Meanwhile, in more traditional families, these conveniences have freed housewives to take part-time jobs, enroll in courses at community centers or continuing education programs at universities, or participate in volunteer activities. A synopsis of changes in monthly income and expenses and, hence, consumption is found in Table 7.12.

Gender Issues

The revision of the Civil Code in 1947, which gave women equal legal status with men in all aspects of life, was the first step toward abolishing the patriarchal character of the family. As in Western countries, an increasing number of women are now entering the workforce. In 2000, women accounted for 40

Table 7.12

Monthly Income and Expenses in Yen (nationwide nonagricultural households)

	1970 Yen	%	1980 Yen	%	1990 Yen	%	1994 Yen	%	2000 Yen	%
Income	112,949		444,846		521,757		567,174		560,954	
Living expenses:	82,582	100	238,126	100	331,595	100	353,116	100	317,113	100
Food	26,606	32.2	66,245	27.8	79,993	24.1	81,513	23.1	73,844	22.3
Housing	4,364	5.3	11,297	4.7	16,475	5.0	22,446	6.4	20,787	6.5
Utilities	3,407	4.1	12,693	5.3	16,797	5.1	19,150	5.4	21,477	6.8
Clothing	7,653	9.3	17,914	7.5	13,103	4.0	13,239	3.7	16,188	5.1
Furniture	4,193	5.1	10,092	4.2	23,902	7.2	21,963	6.2	11,018	3.5
Medical care	2,141	2.6	5,771	2.4	8,670	2.6	9,474	2.7	11,323	3.6
Transport and communications	4,550	5.5	20,236	8.5	33,499	10.1	37,301	10.6	36,208	11.4
Education	2,212	2.7	8,637	8.5	16,827	5.1	18,988	5.4	13,860	4.4
Recreation	7,619	9.2	20,135	8.5	31,761	9.6	34,549	9.8	32,126	10.1
Other	19,837	24.0	65,105	27.3	90,569	27.3	94,491	26.8	80,302	25.3
Net income	103,634		305,549		440,539		481,178		470,902	
Net savings	13,480		39,714		74,526		85,503		98,908	
Living expenses as a percent of net income		79.7		77.9		75.3		73.3		67.3

Source: Management Coordination Agency, *Annual Report on the Family Income and Expenditure Survey, 1994* (Tokyo: Employment Sector, 1995); Management Coordination Agency, *Annual Report on the Family Income and Expenditure Survey, 2000* (Tokyo: Employment Sector, 2000).

percent of the total workforce. This percentage gradually increased from 38.7 percent in 1980 (Ministry of Public Management, Home Affairs, Posts, and Telecommunications 2001). The number of women in full-time employment over the same period has increased by 6.2 percent. Even in the continuing recession, women's employment grew by 2.5 percent (*Euromonitor* 2000). A main reason for this increase in the number of women workers is rising educational levels, but the lower cost of women employees cannot be ignored as a factor. The average wages of women employed in companies staffing more than thirty people are around half those of men (*Euromonitor* 2000).

Despite this lower average earning potential, the rising numbers of young women in the full-time professional workforce are undoubtedly the reason pop-sociological writings on the phenomenon of "parasite singles" tend to focus on working women. As mentioned, parasite singles are said to be single working adults who continue to live as dependents in their parents' homes well into their twenties or thirties. Irrespective of the trend toward one-person households, research indicates that as many as 62 percent of men and women between the ages of twenty and twenty-four are parasite singles. While, in general, men and women are parasite singles in equal numbers, the lower average wages for women have resulted in a tendency for parents to forego asking female parasites for assistance with household expenses more often than their higher-paid male counterparts. As a result, all of a female parasite single's income tends to be disposable, contributing to a popular image of the parasite single as "twenty-six years old, beautiful, drives a BMW, carries a $2,800 Chanel handbag . . . (and) vacations in Switzerland, Thailand, Los Angeles, New York and Hawaii" (Takahashi and Voss 2000).

Certainly, the number of women committed to long-term employment continues to increase, as shown by a decrease in the number of women who quit their jobs for reasons due to birth or marriage. This number decreased from 22 percent in 1977 to 7 percent in 1992. Women in the workforce are more educated than in the past, with the number of female graduates with two- and four-year college degrees increasing to 22 percent in 1987, up 9 percent from 1977. Moreover, the number of female graduates of four-year universities reached 57.1 percent of the total number of four-year graduates in 2002, up from 18 percent in 1970 (Management and Coordination Agency 2002a). Nevertheless, there is evidence that corporate freezes on new hires during the recession have hit women harder than men. Of female four-year college graduates, 16.3 percent were unable to secure an offer of lifetime employment in 1994 as compared to 9.9 percent for males (Asahi Shimbunsha 1995).

The increase of women in the workforce has also had a profound effect on marriage. A survey by the Prime Ministers Department in 1997 found that around 66 percent of respondents believed women were marrying later in life because they were "more financially independent now." Marriage rates have also fallen from 7.2 per thousand in 1977 to 6.1 per thousand in 2000 (*Euromonitor* 2000). A reduction in marriage rates has affected fertility rates, which have fallen from 17,551,030 in 1977 to 11,726,000 live births in 2000 (*Euromonitor* 2000). These changes have a continuing effect on family structures. Note that one of the main reasons for not having children is the high cost of education. This suggests that in the continued economic downturn, we are likely to see no changes in the trend toward growth in single-person households or in the phenomenon of parasite singles (both males and females).

The other important aspect of change has occurred within more "traditional" salaryman-headed households. Given the long working hours and commuting times of their husbands, these housewives have taken control of their home lives and make most of the important household decisions, including those regarding finances and children's education (McCreey 2000). However, the actual rearing of their children is increasingly left to others, as children from kindergarten to university age attend extra cram schools and thus spend large amounts of time away from the family home. So-called play-education mothers want to make the most of the leisure time they have while their husbands and children are out of the family home. As McCreey (2000) suggested, they comprise an important market for cultural activities, such as theater and gallery attendance, and provide lavish opportunities for the luxury goods market. Increasingly, these are women who have worked and have their own personal savings, which adds to their independence.

Breakdown of Traditional Family

Although still low, the divorce rate is rising, reflecting the breakdown of the traditional family (*Euromonitor* 2000). One reason for this may be the long hours fathers typically have away from the home due to long working hours and work-related social commitments. During the recession, media reports focused on the difficulty some fathers have in integrating themselves into family life now that overtime hours and time spent wining and dining customers have decreased. A spate of television ads depicted former "workaholic" fathers feeling out-of-place in the home or in family settings. Older men, having spent little time at home during their work careers, have especially difficult times getting along with their wives upon retirement. Referred to as *sodai gomi*, or oversized garbage, by their wives, such men had become strangers in their own homes by the end of their work careers. Among younger generations of fathers, however, there is a stronger desire to balance work and family, Also, one positive side-effect of the recession has been that fathers are spending more time at home and are enjoying leisure activities with their families.

MATERIALISM, THE ENVIRONMENT, AND HEALTH

It has been noted by many commentators that, if the Japanese government's mission after World War II was to catch up with the West, economically, the dream for the average Japanese worker was to catch up to the lifestyle of the American middle class in terms of durable goods ownership. The U.S. occupation forces gave Japan its first exposure to everything from Coca-Cola and instant coffee to Levi's, and the U.S. image as an affluent middle-class consumer culture had enormous appeal. While it has been noted that aspirations for the American lifestyle have declined since the late 1980s, trends from America and Europe still have a major influence on popular consumer culture in Japan, especially among the young (Dentsu Inc. 1994). It is worthwhile taking a look at changing attitudes toward material wealth during the previous two decades.

During the 1970s, the so-called Three Cs ("car," "cooler," and "color TV") were the leading icons in the rush to achieve a middle-class standard of living. Along with the cultural emphasis on conformity to the group, the obsession with the American middle class may be one of the reasons for Japan's oft-noted middle-class consciousness. As Japan became more affluent, the government sought to nurture the emergence of this consciousness, as well as relative real equality in the standard of living. Thus, it is not surprising that annual polls on the life of the nation, conducted by the Prime Minister's Office since 1964, have consistently indicated that an overwhelming majority of the people feel that they belong to the middle class. And, as discussed earlier, among the advanced countries, Japan has the greatest equality in the distribution of wealth. It will be interesting to see how this consciousness will be reconciled with the aforementioned potentially greater disparities in wealth as trends such as merit-based compensation progress.

Until the 1980s, even as affluence continued to increase, the realities of declining size of the average home and the high cost of housing, coupled with the highest consumer prices in the world for daily goods, dictated a relatively austere lifestyle for the average Japanese. Ariga and Gary (1990), for example, cited a survey by the Japan Economic Research Center that showed that at this time, 76 percent of Japanese believed that they would never own their own homes. Thus, the strong yen, the deregulation of import and luxury goods markets, and the expansion of consumer credit during the late 1980s' bubble economy gave many Japanese consumers the opportunity to enjoy their country's affluence for the first time. Having satisfied their material goals in terms of consumer durables, consumers moved on to designer brands, foreign travel, and other luxury items previously beyond their reach.

The expansion in the range of choice during this period, due to the influx of imports and Japanese durables manufacturers' product diversification strategies, created an emphasis on differentiation of lifestyles through consumption. In addition, greater access to luxury goods created a boom in expensive lifestyle products with high-class images. This explains why studies in the 1980s indicated that Japanese consumers looked at consumption as a means of self-expression and self-realization. It has been noted that self-expression through consumption has allowed the average Japanese to build an independent identity in personal life while maintaining conformity with society in public or professional life. For both men and women, one's choice of imported fashion brands became a primary means of creating an individual identity, allowing the latest styles from Europe and America to take hold quickly.

Since the bursting of the bubble economy, however, consumer attitudes toward material goods have begun to change. For one thing, consumers are less conscious of images of status and luxury and, in turn, with high fashion, per se. While consumption remains a key means of self-expression, consumers seem more comfortable with down-to-earth lifestyle goods. Moreover, rather than focusing on what a chosen brand will mean to others, they are basing decisions on which brands to buy based on whether or not a brand fits one's self-image. This is a subtle, but important, change from "me-too" consumption style, to a more thoughtful, personal, and truly individual style (Ohashi 1989; Denstu Inc. 1994). This change will be discussed further in the section on consumer behavior.

Japanese workers traditionally had little free time for leisure due to long working hours. Moreover, the corporate work ethic dissuaded workers from taking their full allotment of paid vacation for fear of incurring the disapproval of both coworkers and superiors. However, since 1970, both regular working hours and overtime hours have declined steadily. Furthermore, from the Dankai generation onward, Japanese workers have become more leisure oriented and are willing to take holidays to enjoy the fruits of their labor. According to an annual survey by the Leisure Research and Development Center, the number of Japanese workers who say they stress leisure time more than their careers increased from 27.1 percent in 1985 to 32.7 percent in 1994. Those who stress career over leisure time fell from 44.4 percent to 38.7 percent over the same period, while those who seek a balance between career and leisure rose slightly from 27.5 percent to 28.3 percent.

The strong yen has made overseas travel a particularly popular and attractive leisure pursuit. Peak demand for overseas travel tends to focus on three national holiday seasons—*O-shogatsu* (New Year's), the "Golden Week Holidays" in May, and the *O-Bon* holiday week in August— indicating that workers are still somewhat reticent to take long vacations during nonholiday seasons. Yet, the rise of cost-consciousness among consumers has also produced higher demand for foreign travel during periods when airfares are lower, immediately before and after peak travel seasons. The increase in the number of new carriers in the airline industry has also given the Japanese air traveler some options for "value travel" that they had not previously enjoyed.

Internationalism and Materialism

Internationalization due to increased foreign travel, lower prices on imports due to the high yen and deregulation, and the increased pace of exchange of popular culture through mass media, will accelerate the convergence of the Japanese consumer culture with the global consumer culture. Yet, aspects of Western materialism are often adapted in unique ways to the Japanese lifestyle. In a nation where less than 1 percent of the population is Christian, Christmas has become an important festival in Japan. For many years, there has been a custom of fathers bringing home special "Christmas cakes" for their families. In some families, children can expect to receive Christmas gifts from their parents. For young singles, Christmas has strong romantic connotations, and having a date for Christmas night is a major concern. East Japan Railways' "Santa Claus Express" advertising in recent years dramatizes this trend. The Bullet train has been promoted as a means for young lovers working or attending school in different cities to get together for Christmas, and past ads have depicted lovelorn couples enjoying an evening of bliss together. Couples often exchange expensive gifts and may choose from a variety of "Christmas Date courses" at major hotels. The courses usually include a formal Western-style meal, combined with entertainment and a night's accommodation. Typically, reservations must be made months in advance. In 1993, Christmas-related sales in Japan were down 5 percent on the previous year due to the recession but still amounted to 5.85 billion (Anonymous 1994).

In the future, Japanese youth are expected to lead the greater convergence with Western materialism. Kenichi Ohmae, former partner in McKinsey & Company's Tokyo office, believes that Japan's young people, whom he calls "Nintendo Kids," have a way of perceiving the world that is different from their elders but that is similar to how young people in other countries perceive it. Having grown up playing sophisticated video games, Nintendo Kids "have learned to revisit the basic rules of their world and even to reprogram them if necessary" (Ohmae 1995, p 18). Noting that this kind of thinking is "alien to Japanese culture," Ohmae predicted that Nintendo Kids will use technology to reach out to their multimedia peers in other countries (Ohmae 1995). It is certainly true that Japanese kids now often listen to the same music, watch the same American movies and TV shows, and have the same sports heroes as other Nintendo Kids throughout the world.

Environmental Concerns

Despite the continuing influence of animistic religions such as Shinto and Buddhism, concern about the environment in Japan is much lower than that shown in Western countries. According to a Gallup survey quoted by Simon (1992), only 40 percent of Japanese consumers avoided environmentally harmful products, compared to 57 percent in the United States, 81 percent in Germany, and 75 percent in the United Kingdom. Involvement in environmental groups was only at 4 percent of those surveyed. Meanwhile, *The Japan Times* cited a 1995 survey by the Environment Agency that indicated that 58 percent of Japanese in their twenties said they would change their lifestyles to help the environment. Willingness to change lifestyle for the environment was even higher for those in their seventies, at 88 percent. Yet, none of those over seventy and only 18 percent in their twenties said they would be willing to pay more for ecologically friendly products. Thus, in spite of the relatively high stated willingness to change lifestyles for the environment, this and other surveys reveal that the Japanese people, in general, are actually doing very little for the environment in practice; many do little more than separate their garbage for recycling (cf. Daiwa House Industry Company Ltd. 1994).

Nevertheless, a growing number of products on the market make environmental claims, and the market for environmentally friendly products is expanding, as mainstream acceptance of imported eco-chic brands, such as "The Body Shop" and "Origins," demonstrates. It is fair to assume that interest in and commitment to buying environmental products will continue to grow in the future, roughly in line with similar trends and fads in Europe and America.

Health

Westernization, urbanization, and increasing affluence have increased the stress of daily life and changed eating habits dramatically. In spite of the longest life expectancy in the world, Japanese are generally less healthy, primarily because of increasingly Westernized eating habits. For example, registered cancer patients in 1993 had jumped to 200,000 from 130,000 in 1983; the number of people in their forties who receive a clean bill of health at regular medical checkups declined to only 19 percent in 1994 compared to 31 percent ten years prior (see also Ministry of Health and Welfare 1995a; Nihon Keizai Shimbun 1995b).

Despite these ominous statistics, surveys show that Japanese are relatively ambivalent about their health, neither greatly concerned nor completely confident. A 1994 survey by Sumitomo Life Social Welfare Services Foundation of working men and women thirty to fifty-nine years of age reported that only 25.7 percent say they lack confidence about their health against 24 percent who are confident about their health. Meanwhile, 51 percent were noncommittal, claiming neither to have nor lack confidence. Women who say they lack confidence make up 36 percent, while men who lack confidence total only 15 percent. When asked when they tend to worry about their health, 30 percent responded upon the death of an associate. This response was highest for those in their fifties, at 37 percent (Sumitomo Life Social Welfare Services Foundation 1994).

A later survey by the Prime Minister's department found that care with diet (66 percent) and getting enough sleep and rest (59.6 percent) were seen as the main means used to improve health. In terms of fighting stress, the Sumitomo survey of 1994 found that 42 percent of men cited drinking and smoking as a means to fight stress, compared to 34 percent who cited sports activities. Women tend to fight stress through social activities, such as chatting with friends (66 percent) and shopping (46 percent). The younger Japanese consumers fight stress through a greater reliance on *iyashi* (the importance of healing and relaxing). This has been used to explain the boom in aromatherapy, herbal remedies, pets, and holidays at hot springs or the beach. This is particularly so with the *Hanako* (or, disparagingly, the parasite singles), or young, female office ladies, aged eighteen to twenty-nine.

Despite concern over the health consequences of changes in the traditional diet, eating habits are becoming increasingly Westernized and convenience-oriented. A survey by the Ministry of Health and Welfare (1992) showed that the use of precooked food in Japanese households was extensive. While only 2 percent of housewives use some kind of precooked food as a main dish everyday, 13 percent of housewives now use some kind of precooked food as a main menu item once or twice a week. Meanwhile, 15 percent use precooked food everyday as a side dish, and 30 percent use precooked food as a side dish once or twice a week (Ministry of Health and Welfare 1992b). At the same time, eating out of the home is on the rise over the long term, although with the recession, a slight decline in spending on meals outside the home has been seen. Figures for use of convenience foods and eating out are significantly higher for DINKs and one-person households.

At this time, the antismoking movement is relatively weak in Japan, although an increasing number of companies are implementing restrictions on where and when employees may smoke. Airports are now smoke-free, except in "smoking zones" that are either exhaust fan areas or closed rooms. Trains operate a decreasing number of smoking cars on their intercity rail service. Also, restaurants are increasingly offering nonsmoking sections, something that had been unheard of in the past. Cigarette advertising is permitted in public places but has now been phased out on television.

While exercise is touted in the West as a means to better health, the trend has not caught on as much in Japan. Compared to ten years ago, on a typical morning in Tokyo, one can see a slightly larger number (but still very small) of Japanese out for morning runs. There is also some interest in health clubs, but compared to the West, there is a rather small number of Japanese who "work out" on a regular schedule. If one passes many of the larger urban parks in the morning, though, the early morning exercise routines of the older Japanese can still be seen.

CONSUMER BEHAVIOR

Ten years into Japan's recession, the fact remains that unemployment, while at historical highs, has not reached levels that would ordinarily be expected in a recession in the United States, for example. The yen skyrocketed to a historical high, briefly eclipsing the 80 yen to the U.S. dollar over the summer of 1995, badly pinching profits for exporters, but by fall 1995, it had eased and stabilized at the 100 yen to the dollar level. By fall 2003, the exchange was still approximately 105 yen to the dollar. For the time being, a serious crisis had been avoided. However, the lack of a concrete plan for resolving the bad debt crisis in the banking industry, the declining real estate prices, and a stagnant stock market are dark clouds on the economic horizon.

On the other hand, it is clear that consumer values have changed significantly since the recession took hold, and not all of these changes are merely a product of the purse strings being tightened to weather the recession. Some of the changes are, in fact, due to the greater maturity and experience of Japanese consumers. These changes will be discussed in detail in the next section.

Changes in Consumer Behavior

During the early 1990s, consumers became far more conscious of price than they were during the 1980s. So-called price destruction, deflationary pressure on retail prices due to reform of the distribution system (Tanzer 1992), and cheaper import prices due to trade liberalization and the high yen have given rise to greater price competition (Eisenstodt 1992). Consumers, in turn, learned to take advantage of this trend by shopping around for better prices when making big ticket purchases. This is a major change, because during the bubble economy, high price was associated with prestige, and thus, a high price tag was an important component of a brand's value.

At the same time, diversification of consumer values is expected to create greater differences in the ways individual consumers spend their money. A report by Dentsu Inc. (1993) suggested that Japanese will become less conformist in their behavior in the future; individuals will develop their own unique "lifestyle fundamentals" by which they determine their spending priorities. This trend is clearly evident in the Hanako and Dankai junior segments.

The youth fashion market consists of a series of short-term fads and styles. What characterizes these fads is individualism, young people constantly seeking a unique identity and enhancement of their looks. The birthplace of many Japanese fads is Shibuya, Tokyo's youth-orientated shopping mecca. Most of the trendsetters are popular Japanese celebrities. For example, the *Ganguro* fashion trend was started in 1998 by Amuro Namie, lead singer of the pop group called The Super Monkeys. The basic look of this trend was that of a dark tan, bleached-blonde hair, high platform shoes, and heavy makeup. By 1999, this trend evolved further into *Gonguro,* which featured even more extreme tanning and a California-girl style of dress. By summer 2000, this trend subsided as Hamasaki Ayumi, a pop singer with extremely light skin, grew in popularity. Her fans would stay out of the sunlight, whiten their skin, and bleach their hair. These examples reveal the nature of the youth culture in Japan, where short-term trends are quickly adopted and then die out suddenly to be replaced by the newest fad.

Expectations about products are also changing. Especially for consumer durables, the emphasis is increasingly on such factors as design and ease of use, rather than on high-tech bells and whistles. These changes will be discussed further in the section "Changes in the Macromarketing Mix."

Table 7.13

Savings Rates as a Percentage of Disposable Income

1975	14.8	1994	17.8
1980	13.0	1995	13.7
1985	12.9	1996	13.4
1990	16.9	1997	12.6
1991	17.9	1998	12.8
1992	18.2	1999	11.9
1993	17.0	2000	12.1

Sources: Management and Coordination Agency, *Annual Report on the Family Income and Expenditure Survey, 1994* (Tokyo: Employment Sector, 1995); *Euromonitor*, "Consumer Lifestyles in Japan: Integrated Market Information System" (2000), August, p. 34.

Consumer Credit

In seeming contradiction to the trend toward greater consumption, Japanese maintain the highest savings rate among the advanced countries. Despite greater spending on leisure and imported goods during the 1980s, the savings rate rose due to dramatically increased income from overtime hours and bonuses during the economic boom. Another factor is that older, more conservative consumers at the top of the seniority pyramid, hence, those with higher incomes, tend to lead far more austere lifestyles than younger Japanese. Since the recession began, savings as a percentage of income has continued to rise due to the combined forces of lower retail prices and greater consumer price consciousness, which has curtailed consumer spending. Also, Japan's unprecedented low interest rates also mean that the return on savings is lower in Japan than anywhere else in the world, compounding the sense of urgency to save even more. A case in point came during the early years of the recession, in 1994, when a tax rebate intended to stimulate consumer spending backfired. Instead of greater consumption, the rebate resulted in increased savings. In the decade since the 1990s, despite some fluctuations and a modest downturn, savings have remained high (Table 7.13).

Consumer debt, however, generally, has continued to rise during the last decade, from 63.1 trillion yen in 1990 to 66.8 trillion in 1999. Credit cards issued annually increased from just less than 87 million cards in 1984 to more than 220 million in 1994, and they are now a commonplace item in the billfolds and purses of Japanese of all ages.

Consumption

The Japanese household over the past couple of decades has had substantial increases in real income, but as previously mentioned, they have also faced a high cost of living. As can be seen in Table 7.12, the percentage of living expenses to total income, for example, has declined from 79.7 percent in 1970 to 67.3 percent in 2000. Food still accounts for a large proportion of living expenses for the average Japanese household. It accounted for 22.3 percent of living expenses in 2000, down from 32.2 percent in 1970. The disproportionately large ratio is due to traditionally high distribution costs and price supports for Japan's heavily protected agricultural sector. However, food prices will decline further in the future due to continued deregulation. And despite the perception, pervasive throughout the 1980s, that the Japanese palate was too finicky to readily accept imported foodstuffs, there is clear evidence that the Japanese consumer is highly receptive to less-expensive imported agricultural products. Imported beef is an excellent example.

Prior to liberalization of beef imports in April 1991, Japanese consumers had a distinct prejudice against it. According to an Economic Planning Agency report, quoted in Fields (1990), only 15 percent of respondents found imported beef "tasty," versus 36 percent who said it was "not tasty." Between 1988 and 1993, however, the percentage of imported beef as a component of total beef consumption nearly doubled from 28 percent to 55 percent, 99 percent of which was imported from America and Australia. Aggressive trade marketing and consumer advertising campaigns by government-backed beef export organizations from both countries have supported the growth in demand. The top three reasons for buying imported beef were its "inexpensive price" at 88 percent, "wide availability in stores" at 45 percent, and "good quality" at 13 percent (Japan Meat and Poultry Association 1994). Thus, it can be rationalized that despite the perceived superior quality of domestic beef, demand for imported beef has expanded because it is less expensive and is perceived as being "tasty enough." In a variety of formerly regulated product categories, cheaper imports can be expected to make similar inroads into the market shares of domestic products.

The increasing participation of women in the labor force may have contributed to the rise in expenditures on eating out. Expenditures on eating out rose from 9.1 percent of leisure expenditure in 1965 to 16.9 percent in 1990, but the recession has had a braking effect on this trend, and expenditure remained relatively stable between 1990 and 1994.

The other major increases in consumer expenditures over the last couple of decades were on transport and communications, which increased from 5.5 percent of living expenses in 1970 to 11.4 percent in 2000, and education, which increased from 2.7 percent in 1970 to 4.4 percent of living expenses by 2000. Education expenses can be expected to remain high due to the increasingly competitive employment market. Dentsu Inc.'s (1994) *Consumption in the Heisei Era* survey revealed that 71 percent of Japanese between the ages of eighteen and fifty-nine intend to further their education with the objective of "self-improvement," which they see as a necessary hedge against increasing uncertainty.

Despite the long working hours faced by most Japanese workers, recreational expenditure as a percentage of living expenses increased dramatically from 17.4 percent of living expenses in 1965 to 24.4 percent of living expenses in 1990. As was previously suggested, the largest increases in the share of the leisure yen is with eating out and with self-improvement and experiential consumption, such as "recreation" and "tours." Expenditure on "tours," which includes both domestic and overseas travel, has increased dramatically in recent years. Recreation expenditure increased from 15 percent to 20.9 percent of leisure expenditure over this same period. The large expenditures on "recreation" and "tours" may reflect the interest of the Japanese consumer in self-actualization rather than in material benefit (Ohashi 1989). Expenditure on durable goods comparatively remained constant at around 4–6 percent of total recreational expenditure over the last few decades.

Youth consumption trends, meanwhile, are focused heavily on leisure. Many teens have part-time jobs, or *beito* (from the German *arbeit*). Tully described Naoshi Saito, a seventeen-year-old student whose beito with a moving company ("riding around the streets of Tokyo with the drivers, reading complicated maps of the city's streets") pays him the equivalent of US$855 per month (Tully 1994, p. 24). Because Japanese parents typically support their children until graduation from university, all such income is disposable and is used on clothes, CDs, DVDs, mobile phones, and leisure activities. International sports such as soccer and basketball have been especially popular with youth in the 1990s. Japan's professional soccer league, the J-League, markets heavily to teenagers, as do international sports shoes and apparel companies, such as Nike and Reebok. Soccer's World Cup, cohosted by Japan and Korea in 2002 and thus requiring several of the matches to be played in Japan, was phenomenally popular and resulted in the marketing and consumption of many products and services directly tied to this global event.

A darker side of the drive by youth to acquire status goods can be seen in the number of young Japanese who work part-time in the nightclubs to earn money for consumer goods. In the clubs of Tokyo, in such places as Shibuya and Roppongi, college students and daytime clerks from the retail trade may be found dancing and working the tables of different clubs. When asked about their reason for working in such places, the answer is usually "to buy clothes and accessories to support my social activities" (Rahtz 2003).

Overseas Travel

The strong yen generally makes overseas travel more affordable than domestic travel. In 1997, the number of Japanese traveling abroad peaked at 16,803,000 (*Euromonitor* 2000). Ohmae (1995, 154) noted in 1995 that "flying round-trip between Tokyo and Okinawa now costs more than flying between Tokyo and Chicago." Particularly alluring are lower prices for shopping, fine dining, and leisure activities, such as golf and scuba diving, all popular Japanese pastimes that can be more cheaply enjoyed overseas than in Japan. This situation has prompted a recent advertising campaign by the Guam Visitors Bureau that uses the slogan: "Rather than a distant Japan, come to nearby Guam." The campaign draws attention to the fact that for less money and in about the same amount of time it takes to go to Okinawa, Japan's southernmost resort island, urban Japanese can travel to Guam. Nearly fourteen million Japanese traveled overseas in 1994, more than nine million for tourism, more than one million to visit relatives, and nearly 300,000 for honeymoons. In 2001, that number was almost seventeen million. A year earlier, that number was higher (17.8 million), but the terrorist attacks of September 11, 2001 contributed to the drop, with about 64 percent of those traveling for tourism (JATA 2002a). Nearly a decade ago, the average overseas traveler spent 431,000 yen per trip, including 112,000 yen for shopping (Japan Travel Bureau Overseas Travel Development 1995), but that number has been on a downward slide. In 2000, it was down to 309,000 yen (JATA 2003b). Over the past ten years, the average duration of those trips remained fairly constant, about eight days.

CHANGES IN THE MACROMARKETING MIX

The marketing mix is undergoing revolutionary changes that are making Japanese consumers more value conscious. Three main factors have combined to cause this revolution in Japanese marketing. The first is greater choice in terms of price, cultivated largely by greater retail competition due to deregulation (De Rosssario 1993; Holyoke and Glasgall 1994). Direct marketing is also becoming a more accepted means of distribution, because consumers are placing a lower priority on the kind of fawning and costly service traditionally provided by Japanese retailers (Nakanomyo 1990). A second factor has been the recent slowdown in the Japanese economy, which has made consumers more careful about how they spend their money (Miller 1992). A third has been the diversification of consumer values over the long term, which is making consumers more heterogeneous in their spending priorities (Ohashi 1989).

Products

Significant changes have occurred in consumer expectations for products during the last ten years, particularly with consumer durables. During the 1980s, consumer emphasis on lifestyle differentiation through consumption fueled the success of Japanese manufacturers' much-touted strategies of offering wide product ranges, high product variation, and rapid innovation through lightning-quick product cycles. New products were automatically perceived as superior, and the more leading-edge features a product boasted, the greater the premium it could command (Yoshimori 1992).

The Honourable Japanese Consumer (March 1990, p. 8) quoted a senior Japanese business-man, Mr. Toshifumi Suzuki, chairman of the Japanese Franchise Association, who offered the following insight on this phenomenon:

> They say that today's consumer is individualistic, diverse in thinking and tastes. I say con-sumers have been more sheep-like in their attitudes. The reason their buying habits look diversified is the extremely short product lifecycle of most popular products. Makers put new versions on the market so quickly these days. They don't trust their own judgment. That's why they tend to buy brand name products. From childhood, they've been dressed in uniforms and their individuality has been carefully killed off.

Yet, even as Suzuki was making this comment, consumers had begun to realize that sheep-like behavior could lead to bad purchase decisions. Increasingly short product cycles also meant that when a new model hit the market, there were bargains to be had on the previous model. Moreover, aside from minor changes or added functions, the basic performance specifications of air conditioners, for example, did not change significantly from model to model. These facts, coupled with increasing value consciousness, have made consumers far less willing to pay a premium for trivial product enhancements. This has been a boon to discounters and consumers who are willing to buy older models in exchange for savings, which can be spent on other lifestyle priorities, such as leisure.

Stalk and Webber (1993) argued that because all Japanese companies followed the same strat-egy, differentiation became a commodity, not a persuasive value-added feature. Moreover, the authors argued that Japanese manufacturers in the 1980s substituted a scattershot approach to production as a substitute for the hard work of real marketing. As long as the bubble economy in Japan made money cheap and consumer demand grow, it made little difference that manufactur-ing operations were unconnected to consumer needs.

During the early 1990s, manufacturers streamlined product lineups and lengthened product cycles. Nissan received favorable publicity from the auto industry press when it launched its new subcompact, the "March," with the declaration that there would be no model change for eight years. Toyota, at the same time, was reducing the varieties of the Corolla from eleven to six. In the electronics industry, Sony ceased offering twenty-seven- and thirty-one-inch televisions, and Matsushita began streamlining its 220 television models and sixty-two VCR models, "recogniz-ing that only 10 percent sold well" (Stalk and Webber 1993, 98).

Fast-moving consumer goods giants Kao and Lion are also scaling back on their product line-ups. With fast-moving consumer goods, one of the influences has been point-of-sale (POS) infor-mation systems that supply retail chains with up-to-the-minute data on what sells and what does not, giving them significant power to dictate to manufacturers what they will sell and what they will not. Another factor that will place limitations on the speed with which manufacturers can bring new products to the market over the long term is the stricter product liability law imple-mented in 1995.

Table 7.14

Dankai Junior's Favored Product Values

Simple	68.8	Major	19.2
Natural	44.4	Rich	14.3
Down to earth	43.2	Stimulating	13.5
Intelligent	31.6	Genki	12.8
Basic	29.3	Novel	10.2
Unique	29.3	Luxurious	7.2
Orthodox	23.7	Minor	6.8
Profound	19.9		

Source: Dentsu Inc., *ROMANJI-JAPANESE* (Study of the Baby Boomer Jr. Generation) (Tokyo, 1992).

DANKAI JUNIORS AND THE PRODUCT MIX

Coming from the Dankai junior generation, with members born between 1970 and 1973 and onward, Japan's youth are more savvy, independent, and confident consumers. The Dankai juniors are the first generation to have grown up with their own color TVs, CDs, and DVD players, and air conditioners in their own rooms. They, like Ohmae's Nintendo Kids below them, help their parents make many decisions about what products to buy. The recognition of this fact led to a Mercedes-Benz ad for their new value-for-money-oriented C-Class. It featured a stern, conservative father, next to his young, trendy son, declaring, "It was my son who recommended I buy the new C-Class." This generation may be affluent and lethargic, but they are also smart consumers. The values of these consumers are the values of the current age. They gather a great deal of product information from a variety of sources. Just like the youth in the United States, they are "Net savvy" and "wired." They are changing the kinds of products manufacturers offer and how they offer those products to the market. An example of this is the *puchi-kure* camera from Casio, which is pocket-sized and prints out instant images from a miniature thermal printer inside the camera. Its main benefits are being digital, editable, bendable, and stickable. It is also a highly personalized device and shows the effect of the Dankai juniors' consumer behavior on the design of products in Japan.

Fashion has also changed, as young consumers require less status recognition and focus more on comfort and value for money. Even university students in the 1980s aspired to ostentatious fashion brands such as Armani, Chanel, and Louis Vuitton; "casual dress" standards were quite formal. In the 1990s, however, laid-back, outdoor-oriented brands such as L.L. Bean and Eddie Bauer stole the fashion show (Miller 1993). Table 7.14 reveals that product values that appealed to young people in the 1990s tended toward "simple," "natural," and "down-to-earth." In the 1980s, popular values with the young would have been "rich," "stimulating," "novel/original," and "luxurious." These latter values plummeted to the bottom of the list in the 1990s. This change was not lost on the domestic fashion industry, which now offers a number of "outdoor casual" fashion brands.

Consumer Reactions to Price

According to the Statistics Bureau, the national average consumer index stood at 101.5 in 2000 (in 1995, it was 100), registering a decrease of 0.7 percent from the previous year, marking the second consecutive year-on-year decline. This is attributable to lower prices of fresh food and manufactured goods, such as consumer durables and textile products (Ministry of Public Management, Home Affairs, Posts, and Telecommunications 2001). While Tokyo still ranks tops in many categories as the world's most expensive city, the last ten years have been characterized by modest declines or at least relatively stable prices for most items.

The resulting change in Japanese consumers' attitudes toward prices is best summarized by comments made by an ex-prime minister, Kiichi Miyazawa, who noted: "What Japan has learned throughout this recession is cost-consciousness." Three major economic and political events have elevated the position of price on the Japanese consumer's priority list. First, the appreciation of the yen (in the long term) has lowered the prices of many imports. Second, there has been great pressure from major trading partners, particularly the United States, for the Japanese to open their markets. This has allowed greater product competition, which has further increased price competition. Retailers and manufacturers have had to reduce prices because of this in order to revive consumer spending during the recession. Finally, changes in distribution due to deregulation and new information technology have increased competition among retailers, also contributing to lower prices.

Where prices have decreased, the cause is often due to a broad structural reform of Japan's once Byzantine distribution system rather than due to the recession, per se. Japanese have coined the term "price destruction" to describe these de facto price reforms. Availability of cheaper import products and the rise of discount shops have led a shift toward "open pricing," wherein retailers accept the risk for unsold products in exchange for the right to price them as they see fit. This is in stark contrast to the system that was prevalent throughout the 1980s, whereby the manufacturer agreed to buy back unsold products in exchange for the retailer maintaining a hard line on manufacturer-suggested pricing. According to the conventional wisdom, consumer respect for traditional relationships made them not only tolerant of exorbitant prices at their neighborhood electronics shops, but also decidedly scornful of the discount appliance stores. However, counter to this "wisdom," discount stores were rapidly multiplying, even as the same wisdom predicted their doom. In the early 1990s, a watershed period in the rationalization of the Japanese wholesale and retail industries, the number of independent electrical retail chains in Japan trebled to 2,000, and prices of consumer electronics fell by an average of 30–40 percent (cf. Tanzer 1992; Management and Coordination Agency 1995).

Distribution

Perhaps one of the most important changes that occurred over the last twenty years in Japan is the rationalization of Japan's distribution system. The reform is a work in progress, to be sure, and even now there are sectors of the economy in which wholesale and retail systems remain outmoded, confusing, economically inefficient, and unfair to consumers, but major changes are evident. Below, we will outline some of the traditional features of the distribution system, along with recent changes.

The Japanese distribution system has been characterized by a profusion of tiny retail stores and vast, powerful wholesale trading houses. On a per capita basis, Japan has more retail outlets than any other advanced country. In 1991, Japan had 14.3 retail outlets per 1,000 people, compared to 8.4 in the United Kingdom and 6.7 in the United States (Ariga, Gary, and Nishimaki 1991). Many of Japan's retail outlets are small stores employing only one or two people. In 1988, for example, the total number of retail outlets in Japan was 1,620,000, with more than half employing one to two people (Nakanomyo 1990). Small neighborhood merchants traditionally enjoyed the loyal patronage of people in the local community; however, the total number of retail outlets has gradually declined since 1985.

As noted above, many changes in the retail scene have their origins in deregulation, which has given retailers more flexibility in responding to emerging consumer needs. For example, urbanization and the growing number of women in the workforce have increased the need for longer store hours. Thus, twenty-four-hour convenience stores have increased in number rapidly, with the rollback of restrictions on store operating hours. Growth in the number of supermarkets has been fueled by the revision of zoning regulations originally designed to protect neighborhood merchants. As the number of suburban supermarkets in large shopping complexes has multiplied, the higher prices, shorter business hours, and limited product selections of neighborhood merchants have increasingly put them out of favor with busy, mobile urban consumers who have no strong neighborhood loyalties. Another factor has been that, whereas traditional Japanese housewives could make frequent trips by bicycle to the neighborhood store, working women cannot. Thus, supported by the widespread ownership of both large refrigerators and automobiles, Japanese consumer grocery shopping patterns are changing. Increasingly, working women drive with their husbands to supermarkets in large suburban shopping centers to do their grocery shopping once a week, or less. Meanwhile, consumers can rely on the growing number of convenience stores to pick up odds and ends between major shopping trips (cf. Ariga, Gary, and Nishimaki 1991).

The traditional system was a pyramid with large manufacturers on top, and, in descending order, a "contract" wholesaler, a second-tier wholesaler, and neighborhood retailers at the bottom. A complex system of processing fees, margins, and rebates resulted in 38 percent of consumer prices paying for distribution (Fuji Keizai Corporation 1994). For the small retailer, refusing to follow the manufacturer's suggested price, in the absence of an agreement with a wholesaler for another manufacturer, could be suicidal. On the other hand, there were many benefits for honoring the system. For example, retailers could expect a full refund from the manufacturer for unsold stock. For merchants who agreed to be exclusive manufacturer chain stores, there were even more benefits. For example, manufacturers would pay for the promotional expenses, provide additional sales staff, and accept IOUs from chain-store retailers. Shiseido, a Japanese cosmetics company, did 70 percent of its sales through its 25,000 tied or affiliated stores (Morris 1994). It is not surprising that these sorts of arrangements are often perceived by foreign manufacturers as being a significant trade barrier.

The growth of huge supermarket and convenience store chains has been one of two key factors in the deterioration of the traditional distribution system. Sales by large retailers such as Ito Yokado, Daiei, Seiyu, and 7–Eleven Japan became such a large component of total retail sales that manufacturers could no longer effectively enforce the manufacturers' suggested retail pricing system. Such chains began to insist on dealing directly with the manufacturer, cutting out the wholesalers and sharply reducing distribution costs. These savings, in turn, they passed on to consumers who gladly accepted the opportunity to save money on their favorite products (Morris 1994). In addition, supermarkets now put pressure on manufacturers' prices by selling private or house brands, sourced through manufacturing contracts with companies in other Asian countries with cheaper labor costs. Import deregulation and the high yen have contributed to extremely competitive prices for private-brand products.

Technologies such as POS computer systems have also aided large retail supermarket chains in gaining the upper hand on manufacturers. By arming large retailers with up-to-the-minute data on product sales, POS systems give retailers significant leverage to dictate the product lines they will carry and the prices. This is a dramatic change from the days when a manufacturer with a top-selling product line in one category could force a small neighborhood grocer to carry its low-selling lines in other categories at the exclusion of other manufacturers' trips (Ariga, Gary, and Nishimaki 1991).

The second key factor has been an increase in the number of discount stores that liquidate manufacturer's excess inventories. During the 1980s, the inefficiencies of the traditional system contributed to price destruction, as manufacturer production levels outstripped demand, producing a glut of inventories. There were also a greater number of unsold products that manufacturers were required to buy back from retailers under the traditional system described above. This inventory pinch coincided with deregulation of retail zoning laws, which spurred rapid growth in the number of large-scale discount stores specializing in electronics, for example. As mentioned previously, within two years of deregulation of the retail industry in 1990, the number of independent electronics retail chains in Japan trebled to more than 2,000 and prices of consumer electronics fell markedly.

Thus, as a result of all of these changes, today, Japanese consumers enjoy lower prices and a more competitive retail sector offering a greater degree of choice. For foreign marketers and retail chains, there has been far greater access to the marketplace. This is a marked change from the days when protective government bureaucracies cited worries over the "acceptability" of foreign brands to Japanese consumers as an excuse for restricting their entry to the market. In the consumer marketplace of the twenty-first century, the success or failure of foreign products in Japan is predominantly being determined by market forces.

Vending Machines

Although not new, automatic vending machines are probably a more important distribution channel in Japan than anywhere else in the world. Numbering in the tens of millions, Japan's ubiquitous automatic vending machines hawk an astounding variety of goods, including such common products as soft drinks and cigarettes, as well as less common ones such as beer, CDs and videocassettes, and even fresh flowers. It is estimated that 50 percent of all alcoholic and nonalcoholic canned beverages are sold through automatic vending machines. The use of automatic vending machines was the key to the success of the Coca-Cola Japan Company, which, as an exception to foreign-affiliated companies in Japan, has long been one of the leading soft drink companies in Japan and is a feared competitor in the industry (Ariga, Gary, and Nishimaki 1991).

Direct Marketing

Direct marketing grew rapidly during the 1980s and 1990s in Japan. Although generally not thought of as being as prevalent as in Europe or the United States, a variety of forms of direct marketing, television shopping, and e-commerce are growing steadily in Japan.

Large retail institutions in Japan have also been developing their own specialized forms of direct marketing. Matsuzakaya, a leading retail company, has set up a satellite link with a German department store and mail order group to provide an online catalog. The Seibu department store chain has set up a number of videotext catalogs and ordering systems in special kiosks throughout railway stations in Japan, and in the future, possibly in the trains themselves.

The increasing popularity of direct marketing in Japan may be due to both demographic and technical factors. As already mentioned, more women are now entering the workforce, there is a greater willingness of young people to buy depending on trust and experiment, and there is an aging population that is becoming more interested in convenient ways of shopping (Sanghavi 1988). Technically, the introduction of toll-free phone numbers and credit cards has greatly

Table 7.15

Advertising Expenditure by Medium, 1992, 1998, 2000, and 2003

Media	Advertising expenditure (in billions of yen)				Component percentage			
	1992	1998	2000	2003	1992	1998	2000	2003
Major Media								
Newspapers	1,217.2	1,178.7	1,247.4	1,050.4	22.3	20.4	20.4	18.5
Magazines	369.2	425.8	436.9	403.5	6.7	7.4	7.2	7.1
Radio	235.0	215.3	207.1	180.7	4.3	3.7	3.4	3.2
Television	1,652.6	1,950.5	2,079.3	1,948.0	30.3	33.6	34.0	34.3
Subtotal	3,474.0	3,770.3	3,970.7	3,582.2	63.6	65.3	65.0	63.1
Sales Promotion								
Direct mail	222.2	315.5	345.5	337.4	4.1	5.5	5.6	5.9
Flyers	323.2	408.2	454.6	459.1	5.9	7.1	7.4	8.1
Outdoor	375.4	319.6	311.0	161.6	6.9	5.5	5.1	4.6
Transit	267.2	243.8	245.0	237.1	4.9	4.2	4.0	4.2
POP	146.7	164.4	169.5	172.5	2.7	2.9	2.8	3.0
Telephone directories	160.0	185.1	174.8	152.4	2.9	3.2	2.9	2.7
Exhibitions/screen displays	481.0	331.2	353.5	321.6	8.8	5.7	5.8	5.6
Subtotal	1,975.7	1,967.8	2,053.9	1,941.7	36.2	34.1	33.6	34.1
New Media	11.4*	33.0	85.6	160.2	0.2	0.8	1.4	2.8
Total	5,461.1	5,699.6	6,110.2	5,684.1	100.0	100.0	100.0	100.0

Sources: Dentsu Inc., *Shohisha jikkan chosa* (Dentsu Bi-Monthly Consumer Confidence Survey) (Tokyo, 1995); Dentsu Inc., *Raw Data*, p. 17 (Tokyo, 2003); *Euromonitor*, "Consumer Lifestyles in Japan: Integrated Market Information System" (2000), August, p. 72.
*Includes satellite Internet media.

facilitated the development of direct marketing in Japan. In the future, media such as broadband Internet, cable TV videotext, and "smart cards" (containing memory chips on which customer information can be stored), should greatly encourage the further development of direct marketing services.

Advertising

In 1992, and for the first time since 1965, Japanese advertising spending fell by 4.6 percent to 5.5 trillion yen. This came as a shock to an industry that had been accustomed to seeing advertising expenditures grow. The recession and manufacturers' focus on internal restructuring were the key factors in the decline. Table 7.15 shows that in the latter half of the 1990s, the split of advertising expenditure among the four major media of television, newspapers, radio, and magazines remained fixed, at around 30 percent for television, 20 percent for newspapers, 3–4 percent for radio, and 7 percent for magazines. Collectively, advertising in these media accounted for around 65 percent of total promotional expenditure in Japan. By 2003, however, advertisers were increasingly favoring television, at a cost to newspapers, with allocations over 34 percent and less than 19 percent, respectively. Advertising in the four major media dropped to about 63 percent.

There is prima facie evidence of a trend in Japan, as in other countries, to shift more marketing communications spending to sales promotion, sponsorship, and direct marketing; though the figures in Table 7.15 raise questions about the extent to which this trend is truly occurring. The trend toward integrated marketing communications (IMC) and relationship marketing, however, un-equivocally has increasing influence in Japan.

Media Planning

IMC-style media planning in Japan is somewhat hampered by some key differences from the United States. Cable networks, for example, are relatively small in terms of subscribers and are limited in geographic scope. Although multichannel satellite TV subscription is on the increase, the highly segmented targeting of television audiences possible in the United States is not yet possible in Japan. Moreover, television audience rating services in Japan only recently introduced individual viewership data in addition to household ratings. Therefore, clear segmentation of television audiences is not yet easy, and commercials tend to target broad segments of the population.

Nevertheless, television is the most popular medium for advertisers and is extremely expensive (due to high viewership of Japan's five national commercial networks and traditionally high demand for commercial slots). Newspapers, meanwhile, are a popular medium for advertisers, because of high readership levels and the long commutes of most Japanese workers. The morning edition of the *Yomiuri Shinbun,* for example, has a national circulation of more than nine million. Because white-collar workers in Tokyo still face an average commute of seventy minutes or more each way between home and the office, they have ample time to read print media (cf. Ariga and Gary 1990). Magazines allow greater segmentation due to many magazines' tight targeting of both demographic and psychographic reader segments. One magazine, for example, targets marriage-minded young single women from affluent families who live with their parents and do not work. Radio is also important and is considered good value for the money spent. Outdoor and transit media are also important and will be discussed in the context of the total campaign.

A typical Japanese ad campaign targeting businesspeople might kick off with a commercial on one of the popular late-night news analysis programs on network television. The next morning, a full-page ad elaborating on the TV commercial might run in the *Japan Economic Journal* (Nikkei), read by many businesspeople on their way to work in the morning. At the same time, ads would be placed on in-train advertising boards on key white-collar commuter rail lines. Later in the week, more ads might appear in weekly news and general interest magazines commonly read by the business target. This might be combined with an evening rush-hour promotional event in an outdoor square near one of the hub stations of the commuter rail system. This kind of integrated, multilayered approach can be used to reach the target from many different angles during a single twenty-four-hour period, increasing campaign reach, frequency, and awareness percentages in an extremely short period of time.

Television Advertising Content and Tone and Manner

Due to the prevalence of fifteen-second spots in Japanese television formats, television advertising has traditionally focused on creating memorable images and evoking emotional responses in a short period of time. Mitsubishi, for example, ran a successful campaign featuring an Australian frill-necked lizard. Such memorable images are used to link and unify advertising run simultaneously on TV, in national newspapers, magazines, metro-transit posters, and outdoor signs. The role of print media is to provide detailed product specifications and information on price and sales outlets that cannot be provided in a fifteen-second TV spot (Syedain 1993–94).

Hiroshi Tanaka of Dentsu Inc. also attributed the use of seemingly irrelevant imagery in TV commercials to differences in the way Japanese process messages. Citing a 1987 study on advertising messages in Japan, Tanaka (1993) argued that Japanese tend to process information top down instead of bottom up. Top-down processing means developing a whole impression of the target object first and evaluating it as good or bad before focusing on the details, whereas bottom-up processing refers to building a total impression from consideration of the parts. By extension, Japanese people would seem to be less concerned about the logical reasoning of commercial messages than, say, Americans might be (Tanaka 1993).

Thus, indirect, image-oriented advertising may be used more often in Japan than in other countries. Indeed, 73.3 percent of Japanese commercials can be classified as indirect, image-oriented, soft-sell commercials, as opposed to 50.9 percent for the United States. However, it is not necessarily true, as has been argued in the past, that Japanese reject direct, logic-oriented, or hard-sell commercial messages. A study by Matsui found no differences in the communicative effectiveness on brand awareness and purchase intention scores between direct and indirect expressions in Japan; this seems to contradict the conventional wisdom that states that indirect forms of advertising expression are preferred by consumers in Japan (Tanaka 1993). Many of these indirect advertising campaigns use American celebrities not as endorsers, but as part of the visual branding of the product. For example, ZZ Top, with their American-style brand of music and unique Z-shaped guitars, are used as a novelty and contrast for Honda's Z minicar. Brad Pitt, the American movie star, served as a credible spokesperson to endorse or to Americanize the brand using the name "Roots," a popular American TV series.

Comparative Advertising

Some argue that many advertising preferences attributed to Japanese consumer tastes are, at best, outdated, and, at worst, the product of Japanese manufacturers' cartel-like competitive practices. George Fields, former chairman of ASI-SRG Japan, charges that for too long, Japanese corporations have assumed that their own values were shared by the consumer. While no law exists against comparative advertising, there has been a tacit agreement among advertisers that direct competition for the consumer's allegiance through comparison of product benefits would be avoided. This agreement was veiled under the claim that the overt knocking of a competitor went against Japanese cultural values and would not be tolerated by the consumer (Fields 1993).

Fields noted that, contrary to the consumer values argument against it, comparative advertising campaigns by Pepsi and General Motors have been implemented without obvious damage to those companies' reputations with consumers. Yet, while Japanese computer maker NEC ran a campaign demonstrating its PC's superiority to the IBM PC in processing Japanese text, the broad sweeping effects of Japanese–Japanese comparative campaigns are to be determined.

Advertising and Price

Another interesting development of note in advertising is that price is playing an increasingly important role in advertising expression, in line with increased price consciousness of consumers. The conventional wisdom suggests that prominent references to price in advertising are a "hard-sell" tactic, which would be an insult to consumer sensibilities. Nevertheless, auto importers made major inroads into a slumping auto market in 1994, primarily due to aggressive price-oriented campaigns. Fast-food giant McDonald's, which pioneered the industry in Japan, has also leveraged its price advantage due to cheap materials sourced overseas to make price a central part of its marketing mix, offering "value meals," including a hamburger, fried potatoes, and a soft drink at a low price, and even advertising "100 Hamburgers," the lowest price in the industry. McDonald's competitors have been forced to respond with value campaigns of their own.

Corporate Branding

Strong corporate branding is another traditionally important feature of Japanese advertising that is undergoing change. Rather than spending time and marketing resources to build stand-alone product brands, Japanese advertisers have tended to focus on maintaining the consistency of the advertising tone and manner across their entire product portfolios. Thus, brand equity is measured on the corporate level, not at the product level, and the corporate logo plays a prominent role in many product ads.

An example of strong corporate branding in Japan can be seen in some of the products directed at the youth market. It is this market, in particular, where there is real concern about matching lifestyle with the brand. The Gap has tried to create a full relationship with its target market through a variety of IMC elements. Their success has been mixed, but generally, there is a clear recognition in the youth market of what Gap is all about. DoCoMo launched a new generation of wireless telecommunications products and succeeded in establishing a strong brand identity with the young Japanese consumer through a variety of relation-building marketing activities. Disney continues a clear presence with over seventy stores throughout Japan. Some Japanese firms have used the equity of the international brand as a clear way to success in building their own business portfolios. The following is taken from the Web site of Dean & DeLuca (a gourmet food retailer that recently opened its second store in Japan) touting their Japanese partner, Itochu Corporation:

> With annual revenues ranking among those of the world's largest corporations, Itochu Corporation is a globally integrated trading company with offices in over 80 countries and operations spanning a broad spectrum of industries. Developed during 140 years of business, Itochu offers unparalleled scope and diversity in every market—retail, finance, media, technology, and trade—in helping companies cross into the international business arena. As master licensee or sole importer, Itochu maintains a significant portfolio of key brands in Japan including Giorgio Armani, Bvlgari, Guess, J.Crew, Nautica, Paul Smith, Tommy Hilfiger, Tumi and Vivienne Westwood. (Dean & DeLuca 2002)

There are two important reasons for the focus on corporate branding in Japan (cf. Tanaka 1993). First, it reflects the cultural emphasis on relationships. A bond comprised of familiarity, trust, and reciprocity between the consumer and those who provide the products used by the consumer in his home has been a traditionally important cultural pact. Japanese consumers in a former age preferred to buy goods from a neighborhood merchant, who would be likely to reciprocate the patronage, rather than buy from an unfamiliar merchant in another neighborhood. Similarly, today, Japanese working for a major bank with business ties to a particular brewer are likely to be loyal drinkers of the brewer's product, and the brewer's employees are likely to deposit their salaries with the bank. Thus, unlike in Western countries, the product maker in Japan has had greater importance than the values the product stands for.

A second important aspect of corporate branding is that it has facilitated what Stalk and Webber (1993) referred to as scattershot marketing. When the corporate branding approach is used instead of stand-alone branding, quick scrapping and building of product brands is possible at a minimum marketing cost (Tanaka 1993). Nevertheless, even large, traditional marketers such as Kao are beginning to reconsider their devotion to this time-honored practice. For example, Kao, which formerly marketed everything from shampoo to floppy disks under their corporate name, has moved toward stand-alone brand strategies through gradual deemphasis of the corporate name in advertising and packaging for its Sofina skin-care line (see also Okahashi 1995).

Sales Promotion

As shown in Table 7.15, sales promotion expenditures from 1992 to 2000 made up about one-third of total media expenditure in Japan. Share of expenditure across a range of media for this type of promotion expenditure remained constant over this same period. In 2000, 5.6 percent of the total promotional budget was spent on direct mail, 7.4 percent on newspaper and magazine flyers, 6.3 percent on outdoor advertising, 5.1 percent on transit advertising, 2.8 percent on POP advertising, 3.2 percent on telephone directories, and around 5.8 percent on exhibitions and trade displays. Given that the long commuting times of the Japanese consumer are likely to continue, the popularity of transit advertising and flyers as means of sales promotion is likely to continue. The greater level of price discounting and competition in the retail sector should lead to an increase in POP and direct mail expenditures.

Market Research

In 1991, there were sixty-nine market research organizations in Japan employing, on average, forty-two people. In the past, market research was not considered an important adjunct to the marketing strategy of Japanese companies (Nishikawa 1989). However, the numbers of market research organizations, total employees in the field, and average employees per firm have risen steadily since 1987. This reflects increasing emphasis on market research in light of the changing competitive environment, in terms of product strategies, value consciousness among consumers, as well as diversification of consumer values as a whole.

FUTURE TRENDS AND EXPECTATIONS

Economic Trends

The near- to midterm future of marketing and consumer behavior is inexorably linked to how rapidly Japan's current bad debt crisis can be remedied and the real estate price slide halted. If further delay occurs, there are great risks to political and social stability, as the 1995 Sarin gas attack on the Tokyo subway system, however indirectly, attests. Certainly, all evidence points to the need for Japan Inc. to bravely swallow the bitter pill on which it has been choking for the last few years. If Wood's (1993) warning of the threat of the economy entering a depression-like debt-deflation spiral seemed merely the alarmist assessment of an ill-informed foreigner, there were many Japanese who also shared his view:

> The government's delay in solving the bad debt problem, along with the increasing defla-
> tionary trend, has sowed the seeds of widespread pessimism and sent land prices into a
> downward spiral. The situation looks so much like [the Great Depression] that I don't want
> to think about it. (Kudo 1995, p 10)

There is a growing feeling that reforms to date in government and industry have only just scratched the surface of what must be done to complete the transition to the post-bubble era. Some poignant assessments of problems with the financial industry still accurately describe the current situation in many sectors of the Japanese establishment:

> Instead of responding to adversity, meeting the challenge, and moving on, senior managers in Japan's leading financial institutions are more like frightened rabbits caught at night in a car's headlights. Confronted by the unfamiliar and used to being told what to do by the overweening Ministry of Finance, they are frozen into inaction. Not knowing how to respond, they have decided to do nothing, hanging on in the forlorn hope that the problem will go away. (Wood 1993)

This echoes a comment made by former MITI vice minister, Amaya, that Japanese bureaucrats were like racing greyhounds who had chased the rabbit of economic development with great speed and grace ever since the end of World War II (Amaya 1989). Now, having crossed the finish line, and finding no more rabbits in sight, the bureaucrats do not know which way to turn.

Ultimately, the restructuring of Japanese banking, finance, and manufacturing in response to the bursting of the bubble economy, along with a continued strong yen and *gaiatsu* (foreign pressure), for deregulation and reform of trading practices, should greatly encourage the transformation of Japan from a producer to a consumer economy; indeed, as we indicated earlier, there is some evidence that this transformation is underway. But, in the near term, it is likely that broader consumer confidence will remain low, especially in view of the rough waters ahead for personal income.

Demographic Trends

The key demographic issues are the aging of the population and the deterioration of its health, which will place unprecedented stresses on the nation's workforce and the social welfare and health infrastructure. Japan enjoys the highest life expectancy in the world, but survival rates among the old are low, which, in turn, puts an ever-increasing and costly burden on the health care system (cf. Reuters 1995; Nihon Keizai Shimbun 1995b). Thus, determining cost-effective ways to care for a growing and increasingly infirm elderly population remains a central concern. On the upside, there clearly will be major market opportunities for goods and services designed to meet the needs of the elderly.

Another important demographic trend to watch will be the increasing education and workforce participation levels of women. As discussed earlier, women workers have fared worse than men during the recession. Whether or not women make real gains in terms of salary and opportunities for promotion will be a telling indicator of the degree of change in gender roles in Japan's traditionally male-oriented work culture. It will also determine the degree to which expenditures are made on services by Japanese households and such things as growth in the use of convenience food products.

Cultural Trends

The desire for social harmony and the collectivist spirit is rapidly being replaced by a greater degree of individualism. How the balance can be struck between these competing forces will be a critical issue at every level of society. Yet, it is clear that for individuals, the demise of the lifetime employment system, the reduced working hours, and the gradual withdrawal of corporate funding for employee leisure facilities and other benefits will undoubtedly change the way leisure

Table 7.16

The Twenty Most Frequently Used Words in Advertising Copy in the Last Forty-Five Years

1	*Watakushi* (I)	999
2	*Hito* (person)	980
3	*Otoko* (man)	697
4	*Onna* (woman)	560
5	*Nihon* (Japan)	556
6	*Anata* (you)	515
7	*Shin* (new)	445
8	*Haha* (mother)	337
9	*Natsu* (summer)	336
10	*Jidai* (era)	316
11	*Sekai* (world)	313
12	*Chichi* (father)	312
13	*Nomu* (drink)	292
14	*Nen* (year)	259
15	*Terebi* (TV)	249
16	*Amerika* (America)	240
17	*Iro* (color)	239
18	*Kyo* (today)	217
19	*Utsukushii* (beautiful)	215
20	*Me* (eye)	213

Source: John McCreey, "Japanese Consumer Behavior: From Worker Bees to Wary Shoppers," in *ConsumAsia Book Series,* eds. Brian Moeran and Lise Skov (Richmond, UK: Curzon Press, 2000), p. 43.

time and money are spent. The number of Japanese traveling abroad has quadrupled since 1975, which means greater exposure to the products, services, and lifestyles of other countries. Coupled with the increased penetration of Japanese markets by foreign products, this will mean greater diversification of tastes and preferences, as well as an expansion in the range of consumption choices available to the average consumer. Meanwhile, now that Japanese material goals in terms of consumer durables have been largely satisfied, consumers will continue to shift their priorities toward lifestyle goods and services and leisure pursuits.

Many of these changes in Japanese values have been reflected in advertising over the past forty-five years. Table 7.16 provides a list of the twenty most common words in advertising copy over the same period. McCreey (2000) noted that the use of such words or themes indicated the greater recognition of women in society, at the expense of men, the movement toward more individualistic values (as shown by the most common word used in advertising copy), and the continued fascination with American culture.

Consumption

As mentioned, the proportion of expenditure on food is expected to fall; recreational expenditure is likely to increase. Expenditure on eating out is expected to continue to rise as labor force participation of women increases. Meanwhile, consumer credit is clearly a permanent part of the Japanese consumer environment. Constraints put on bonuses and overtime payments by many Japanese corporations may provide an added incentive for the use of credit.

Potentially lower real estate prices over the midterm may mean that younger Japanese, to whom owning a home of one's own once seemed a pipe dream, may become increasingly thrifty in order to buy homes at earlier ages. Cheaper imported building materials are already making inroads into a once well-protected housing market. It has also been argued that reforming the archaic zoning regulations would be helpful. For example, some policy makers still prefer to reserve land near Tokyo for agriculture; this land might be better used for housing, which, in turn, would enable more families to own homes, or own larger homes (cf. Ohmae 1995). A dramatic change in the size of housing consumers can afford would have broad implications on consumption habits for other goods and services.

MARKETING MANAGEMENT

Internationalization

Internationalization of the Japanese economy is well underway and accelerating. It has been noted that as foreign products in all categories become more accessible, Japanese consumers show increasing willingness to shrug off traditional prejudices against non-Japanese products. Meanwhile, unprotected by trade restrictions and spurred on by the intensifying global competitive environment, Japanese manufacturers' products will increasingly be made to world-market specifications, not specifications that please an insular and unique domestic consumer. The implications of this should be continued through deregulation and greater competition in the retail sector, lower prices for consumers, and continued emphasis on value for money. Ohmae suggested that "Japan's leaders are trying to hold back a future that has already arrived . . . and the Japanese consumers will continue to pay for their obstructionism" (Ohmae 1995, 161). While the shift toward internationalization has met resistance, it continues. Where to strike the balance between Japan's traditional insularity and the need for industry to continue to internationalize will remain an important issue in the years to come.

Packaging

Packaging is likely to remain an important consideration of product strategy in Japan. Sherry and Carmargo noted the following:

> Packaging, or wrapping (*tsumi*), has a venerable history in Japan. It has been an art for ten centuries. Not only does it play a central role in a range of spiritual and cultural aspects of Japanese life, but it has become an end in itself insofar as the symbolic and monetary value of the package often exceeds that of its contents. (Sherry and Carmago 1987, 174)

Packaging, therefore, will likely remain an important product attribute for many consumers, despite the pressure that economic factors and greater foreign imports may have in reducing costs. Moreover, many Japanese manufacturers' focus is on excellence in aesthetics, which can be a crucial competitive edge against which foreign marketers have to contend (Peters 1994). Even the most inexpensive and familiar products may emphasize innovative packaging aesthetics. Aesthetic and cleverly packaged popular products at the time of this writing include two types of instant noodles. The first is the ultimate pot noodle vintage, whereby the information on the package encourages consumers to store in a cool place, wait until 2010, open the aluminum can, simply add boiling water, and taste the future. The second is an "iNoodle" to rival "iMac" in all its skeletal glory, revealing important product characteristics of this low-involvement consumer necessity. Even breath mints appear in stylish, oddly shaped packaging and have ridiculous names to capture attention; disproportionately large and incongruous (to an English speaker) words such as "I My Me" and "She Her Her" are seen on the labels.

Price Consciousness

Market restructuring, competition, and consumer savvy should continue to have a marked effect on lowering prices in many product categories. Despite recent price declines, Tokyo consumer prices remain among the highest in the world, and there will be considerable downward pressure on prices in the near- to midterm, particularly in view of similar downward pressure on household incomes. Value is the key word for many Japanese consumers these days. This will mean that consumers in Japan will remain cost conscious in obtaining the best value for their money for the foreseeable future. That is also translating into more use of the Internet as a distribution channel to acquire goods, as it allows global sourcing outside of the traditionally higher-priced local markets.

Distribution

Japan is currently experiencing a retail revolution. Expected is greater use of specialist discounters by Japanese consumers and an increase in the popularity of Western chain stores, such as Toys 'R Us. Changes in the Large-scale Retail Store Law, ostensibly designed to protect small stores, will actually encourage the shift toward large-scale retail stores. Direct marketing (Internet and other media) will continue to grow, given the high level of development of technology and the widespread use of credit cards. Japanese consumers continue to shop on the Internet in increasing numbers, as broadband technology expands throughout the country. Further impetus will come from changes in demographics, such as the rising number of senior citizens and working women, that make shopping by catalog, the Internet, or by increasingly popular television shopping programs as necessary as it is convenient.

Advertising and Media

Although some would argue that marketing communications campaigns have long been executed in the integrated manner described previously, the diversification of consumer lifestyles and changes in macromarketing factors are putting pressure on Japanese brand managers and their advertising agencies to achieve the kind of total integration, pinpoint targeting, and cost performance promised by the IMC tools currently being imported from the United States and implemented in Japan. Many changes to the industry continue to unfold in the advertising industry; major advertisers continue to put greater pressure on advertising agencies to provide new and better consumer targeting data as justification for their media plans. The evolution of media, particularly cable TV and interactive media, will undoubtedly play a more important role in the way campaigns are designed and targeted.

CONCLUSION

Despite justifiable concerns on many issues that affect the economy, marketing, and consumption, there are no grounds for arguing that Japan's economic prosperity is over. In the 1990s, reports of improved corporate performance due to restructuring were already beginning to filter in. The bad-debt problem will inevitably be resolved, albeit not without suffering. And, Japan's new consumer-led marketplace undoubtedly will be vibrant.

The day of reckoning has arrived, and eyes are opening to new economic, political, and social realities. These realities demand a broad revision of the conventional wisdom about Japanese consumers. Deregulation has effected changes in retailing and distribution that have closed the gap between manufacturers and the marketplace. Increasingly, it is the consumer who has the power to determine the winners and losers at the storefront. This right to choose comes at the price of greater uncertainty. Increased competition is already eroding the safety net of lifetime employment, for example. Increased competition will also mean greater access to the Japanese market for foreign marketers. Internationalization of the marketplace means that the Japanese marketing system will intertwine more seamlessly with global marketing systems. This interconnection will create new opportunities in Japan. Even as new markets in China, Southeast Asia, India, and other parts of the world beckon, Japan, for its part, will be a more accessible and inviting consumer marketplace than it was in the past. For the Japanese consumer, the sun is no longer rising, and it is not setting. Rather, it has reached midday, with the prospects of blue skies, albeit cloudy at times, ahead.

ACKNOWLEDGMENTS

Don Rahtz provided helpful comments on this manuscript, which builds on that by Okahashi, Gary, and Cornish-Ward (1998); the authors acknowledge helpful support provided by Dentsu, Inc.

REFERENCES

Amaya, Naohiro. 1989. "Time to End the Greyhound Era." *Shizuoka Shimbun*, November 11: 2 (Tokyo).
———. 1993. "The Enigma of Japanese Advertising." *The Economist*, August 14: 59–60.
———. 1994. "The Best and Worst Times for the Japanese Consumer." *Focus Japan*, December: 1–2.
Ariga, Masaru, and Clay Gary. 1990. *Seven Crucial Viewpoints to Understand the Japanese Consumer.* Tokyo: Marketing Planning Department, Dentsu, Inc.
Ariga, Masaru, Clay Gary, and K. Nishimaki. 1991. *Mass Retailing to the Japanese Consumer.* Tokyo: Marketing Planning Department, Dentsu, Inc.
Asahi Shimbunsha. 1995. *Asahi ki wado 95–96* (Asahi Keywords), Tokyo.
BFI. 2003. "Japan: GDP Expanded by .03% in 2002." Eco Flash, BFI Economic Research, February 14, #03–082. Available at http://economic-research.bnpparibas.com/applis/www/RechEco.nsf/0/ 3C6F153F4805D17580256CCD0036B687/$File/Ecoflash082_english.pdf?OpenElement.
Daiwa House Industry Company Ltd. 1994. "Ekoroji to Seikatsu" (Ecology and Lifestyle Survey Report). Tokyo: Dentsu Inc.
De Rossario, Louise. 1993. "Retailing: Sell'em Cheap: The Japanese Discover No-Frills Electrical Goods." *Far Eastern Economic Review*, February 4: 44–45.
Dean & Deluca. 2002. "Itochu International and Dean & Deluca Form Strategic Alliance." Available at www.deandeluca.com/cgi-bin/ncommerce3/ExecMacro/store/about_us.d2w/report. Accessed September 10, 2002.
Dentsu Inc. 1986. *Ari gata ningen. Atarashi seikatsu wo tsukame* (Ant-like People and Grasshopper-like People: Understanding the New Tokyo). Dentsu Marketing Study Group Report. Tokyo: Yosensha Publishing Inc.
———. 1992. *ROMANJI-JAPANESE* (Study of the Baby Boomer Jr. Generation), Tokyo.
———. 1993. *Hesei shohi tenbo* (No life No Consumption: Consumption in the Heisei Era), Tokyo.
———. 1994. *Hesi shohi tembo Rasen shijo no haken* (Consumption in the Heisei Era: Discovering the Spiral Lifestyle Market). Tokyo.
———. 1995. "Shohisha jikkan chosa" (Dentsu Bi-Monthly Consumer Confidence Survey). Tokyo.
———. 2003. Raw Data. Tokyo.

Economic Planning Agency. 1994. "Degree of Satisfaction with Living Situation." Tokyo.

Eiesenstodt, Gale. 1992. "Value for Yen." *Forbes*, April 27: 78–79.

Euromonitor. 2000. "Consumer Lifestyles in Japan: Integrated Market Information System," August.

Fields, George. 1990. "Buy Domestic or Buy Foreign? What's the Story in Japan?" *Tokyo Business Today*, July: 11.

———. 1993. "Can It Be? Comparative Advertising Sprouting in Japan?" *Tokyo Business Today*, April: 41.

Fuji Keizai Corporation. 1994. *Ryustu Shin Jidai no genjo to shorai tenbo* (New Age for Distribution: Current Realities and Future Prospects). Tokyo: Fuji Keizai Corporation.

Holyoke, Larry, and William Glasgall. 1994. "A Bargain Basement Called Japan." *Business Week*, June 27: 14–15.

Hori, Shintaro. 1993. "Fixing Japan's White Collar Economy: A Personal View." *Harvard Business Review* (November–December): 157–72.

Japan Association of Travel Agents (JATA). 2003a. "Purposes of Japanese Travelers." Available at www.JATA-net.or.jp/english/materials/2002/materials0205.htm. .Accessed on October 21, 2003.

———. 2003b. "Average Overseas Spending by Japanese." Available at www.jata-net.or.jp/english/materials/2002/materials0208.htm. Accessed on October 21, 2003.

Japan Marketing Association. 1993. *White Paper 1993*. Tokyo.

Japan Meat and Poultry Association. 1994. *Yearbook of Meat and Poultry '95*. Tokyo.

The Japan Times. 1995. "Elderly Will Alter Lives to Aid the Earth," November 8: 4.

Japan Travel Bureau. 1995. *JTB Report 95. All About Japanese Overseas Travelers*. Tokyo: JTB, Overseas Travel Department.

Kawakami, Seiji. 1993. "Tamesareru dankai no sedai no tsuyosa to yowasa" (Strengths and Weaknesses of the Dankai Generation: The Test Lies Ahead). *ZAIKAI Special Spring Edition, Zaikai Research Insititute Ltd.*, January 19:72–75.

Kishii, T. 1983. "Message Versus Mood—A Look at Some of the Differences between Japanese and Western Television Commercials." In *Japan Marketing and Advertising Yearbook 1988*, pp. 51–57. Tokyo: Dentsu Inc.

Kudo, Yasushi. 1995. "No Bottom in Sight." *Tokyo Business Today*, November: 10–15.

Management and Coordination Agency. 1995. "Annual Report on the Family Income and Expenditure Survey, 1994." Tokyo: Employment Sector.

———. 2000a. "Employment Structure of Japan, 2000." Tokyo: Employment Sector.

———. 2000b. "Annual Report on the Family Income and Expenditure Survey, 2000." Tokyo: Employment Sector.

———. 2000c. "2000 Population Census of Japan." Tokyo: Employment Sector.

———. 2001. "Employment Structure of Japan, 2001." Tokyo: Employment Sector.

March, Robert M. 1990. *The Honourable Consumer: Marketing and Selling to the Japanese in the 1990s*. Adelaide, Australia: Longman Professional.

McCreey, John. 2000. "Japanese Consumer Behavior: From Worker Bees to Wary Shoppers." In *ConsumAsia Book Series*, eds. Brian Moeran and Lise Skov. Richmond, UK: Curzon Press.

Miller, Karen Lowry. 1992. "How Can You Call This a Recession?" *Business Week*, April 27: 58.

———. 1993. "You Just Can't Talk to These Kids." *Business Week*, April 19: 104–6.

Ministry of Education. 2000. "Statistics." Available at www.mext.go.jp/english/statist/index01.htm, downloaded March 13, 2003.

Ministry of Health and Welfare. 1992. "Food and Processed Food Survey." Tokyo.

———. 1995a. "Report on Comprehensive Survey of Living Conditions." Tokyo.

———. 1995b. "Vital Statistics." Tokyo.

Ministry of International Trade and Industry. 1992. *Census of Commerce, 1991*. Tokyo.

Ministry of Labor. 1987. "White Paper on Women Workers." Tokyo.

———. 1995. "Monthly Labor Survey." Tokyo.

———. 1999. "Monthly Labor Survey." Tokyo.

Ministry of Public Management, Home Affairs, Posts, and Telecommunications. 2001. *Statistical Handbook of Japan*. Tokyo.

Morris, Kathleen. 1994. "Adam Smith in Tokyo." *Financial World*, January 4: 22–24.

Nihon Keizai Shimbun. 1995a. *Bonasu konnatsu 1.7 percent, zo sannen buri purasu* (Summer Bonuses Up by 1.7 Percent). Tokyo: Nikkan Kogyo Shimbun Company Ltd.

———. 1995b. "Chouju sekai-ichi ni kenkou huan no kage" (The Shadow of Ill Health Looms Over the World's Longest Life Expectancy). *Japan Economic Journal*, September 22: 17.

————. 1995c. "Nen-go no seikatsu 'kurushi naru 4 wari" (Standard of Living Will Decline, 40 Percent Believe), September 24.

————. 1995d. "Koukou kara daigaku made, heikin de 932 man en" (From High School to University an Average of 9.32 Million Yen), October 25:3.

Nishikawa, Toru. 1989. "New Product Planning at Hitachi." *Long Range Planning* 22 (4): 20–24.

Ohashi, Terue. 1989. "Marketing in Japan in the 1990s: Homing in on the Holonic Consumer." *Marketing and Research Today*, November: 220–29.

Ohmae, Kenichi. 1995. "The Triad World View." *Journal of Business Strategy* 7 (4): 8–18.

Okahashi, Tsutomu. 1995. "Relationship Marketing in Japan Is a Tradition or a New Trend?" Presented at ESOMAR TRIAD 2000, June 13, New York.

Okahashi, Tsutomu, N. Clay Gary, and Steven Cornish-Ward. 1998. "Japan: High Noon for the Rising Sun—New Realities and Forces of Change in a Mature Consumer Market." In *Marketing and Consumer Behavior in East and South-East Asia*, ed. A. Pecotich and C. Shultz, pp. 315–70. Sydney: McGraw-Hill.

Peters, Tom. 1994. *The Pursuit of Wow!* New York: Random House.

Prime Minister's Department. 1997a. "Public Opinion Survey on the Participation of the Sexes in Society."

————. 1997b. "Public Opinion Survey on Sports and Physical Fitness."

Rahtz, Don R. 2003. "Views from the Streets of Tokyo." Unpublished Research Paper, The College of William & Mary, Williamsburg, VA.

Reuters News Service. 1995. "Americans Over 80 Years Old Found to Outlive the Elderly of Other Nations." *Japan Times*, November 3: 3.

Sanghavi, Nitin. 1988. "The Japanese Yen for Non-Store Retailing." *Direct Marketing*, April: 24–28.

Sherry, John F., and Eduardo G. Carmargo. 1987. "May Your Life Be Marvellous. English Language Labelling and the Semiotics of Japanese Promotion." *Journal of Consumer Research* 14 (September): 174–87.

Simon, Françoise. 1992. "Marketing Green Products in the Triad." *Columbia Journal of World Business* 27 (4): 268–85.

Sumitomo Bank. 1988. *Salaried Men's Health and Stress.* Tokyo.

Sumitomo Life Social Welfare Services Foundation. 1994. *Health Survey of Middle Aged People.* Tokyo.

Suzuki, Toshi, and Kazutaka Kirishima. 1995. "Shinku tanku no me. Kakudai suru wakamono shohi shijio" (From the Eyes of a Think Tank. The Expanding Youth Consumption Market). *Nihon Kogyo Shimbun*, March 7: 20.

Syedain, Hashi. 1993–94. "Understanding the Inscrutable." *Marketing Director International* (Winter): 19–21.

Takahashi, Hiroyuki, and Jeanette Voss. 2000. "Parasite Singles: A Uniquely Japanese Phenomenon?" *Japan Economic Institute Report* 31 (August 11).

Tanaka, Hiroshi. 1993. "Branding in Japan." In *Brand Equity and Advertising. Advertising's Role in Building Strong Brands*, ed. David A. Aaker and Alexander L. Biel, pp. 51–63. Hillsdale, NJ: Lawrence Erlbaum.

Tanzer, Andrew. 1992. "A Message from Akihabara." *Forbes*, June 8: 42–43.

Tully, Shaun. 1994. "Teens. The Most Global Market of Them All." *Fortune International*, May 16: 24–29.

van Wolferen, Karel. 1990. *The Enigma of Japanese Power.* New York: Vintage Books.

Wood, Christoper. 1993. *The Bubble Economy: The Japanese Economic Collapse.* Tokyo: Charles E. Tuttle.

Yoshimori, Masaru. 1992. "Sources of Japanese Competitiveness: Part II." *Management Japan* 25 (2, Autumn): 31–36.

CHAPTER 8

KOREA

Two Countries, Sharp Contrasts, but a Common Heritage

JAMES W. GENTRY, SUNKYU JUN, SEUNGWOO CHUN, HEESUK KANG, AND GYUNGTAI KO

OVERVIEW

South Korea experienced nearly unprecedented economic growth in the last half of the twentieth century before weathering a devastating economic crisis at the end of that period, while the North lost its economic lead over the South in the 1950s and has become isolated politically and economically. Yet the two Koreas share an old, unique culture, and the likelihood of eventual reunification is great, despite saber-rattling from Pyongyang. In this chapter, the changing consumer environments in the two Koreas will be discussed with coverage of historical, cultural, economic, and political forces that underlie those changes.

INTRODUCTION

Korea is an enigma. On one hand, there is tremendous appreciation for tradition. Its history is a long one, as Koreans refer to "five thousand years of Korean civilization" (Hoare and Pares 1988). At the same time, Korea has changed enormously in the past decade. Korea is split into parts, which would seem to be radically different at first. North Korea (or, officially, the Democratic People's Republic of Korea) is one of the few surviving communist nations. The loss of support from the former USSR and, to some extent, China has made it become an even more isolationist extension of the "Hermit Kingdom," the name applied to the Korean peninsula due to its policy of exclusionism during the period of *Chosun* (1392–1910). On the other hand, South Korea (or, officially, the Republic of Korea) has blossomed into one of the major players in the global economy. From 1960 to 1990, South Korea was the second-fastest-growing economy (International Strategies 1994). At the same time, both Koreas remain one of the most unified areas in the world—probably only the Japanese are as homogeneous in terms of racial origin and national identity as the two Koreas (Clifford 1994). Further, despite its global presence, South Korea also demonstrates remnants of its Hermit Kingdom roots; for example, Templeman and Nakarmi stated "Korea's market is so hermetically sealed that it makes Japan's market look positively open" (1994, 6). As will be noted, though, the economic crisis of the late 1990s served as an impetus for the South to open its economy somewhat.

BRIEF HISTORICAL PERSPECTIVE

Korea's long history has seen it dominated by several foreign powers, especially during the twentieth century. Pressure to open Korea came from Western powers in the 1860s after China had been opened for trade in the 1840s and Japan in 1854. Japan opened Korea by force in 1876 and later occupied the peninsula in the first decade of the twentieth century with the tacit agreement of the United States and Great Britain, who feared further Russian expansion into East Asia (Hwang 1993).

From 1910 to 1945, Japan dominated Korea. During the colonial era, Korean trade was almost solely with Japan: 85 percent of exports went to Japan, and 73 percent of imports came from there. After the attack on Pearl Harbor, Koreans became wartime resources for the Japanese, as both men and women were forced to work eleven-hour days and seven-day weeks supporting the war effort. In 1943, Koreans were prohibited from using their own language and were forced to read only Japanese newspapers, books, and magazines. They were even compelled to change their family names into Japanese (Hwang 1993). There is good reason for the antipathy and even hostility still held by many Koreans for the Japanese. In October 2001, the prime minister of Japan, Junichiro Koizumi, offered a "heartfelt apology" to South Korea for his country's occupation of the peninsula and World War II (*The Economist* 2001c).

Korea was split by the Western powers (Russia and the United States) as a temporary expedient determined by the occupying forces. However, the idea of dividing the Korean peninsula had originated as early as 1593 at the time of a Japanese invasion. China and Japan discussed splitting the eight Korean provinces, with the northern four being ruled by the King of Korea and the remaining four being ceded to Japan. The negotiations failed, though, and the war continued. The Japanese–Russian conflict at the turn of this century also involved negotiations concerning the division of Korea, with Russia attempting to select the thirty-ninth parallel as the dividing line between the spheres of influence of the two nations. Again, no agreement was reached, and the war was continued (Kim 1992).

The Korean War devastated both parts of the country. Some three million Koreans, nearly one of every ten people, were killed, and over 40 percent of all industrial installations were heavily damaged. The North's economy rebounded faster than that of the South, despite the fact that postwar aid was at least seven times greater for the South (Kim 1992). The American military government's attempt to impose a full market economy in the South did not work well in a Confucian culture. Further, U.S. planners resisted reforming the colonial legacies and gave political support to the tiny Korean aristocracy that the public saw as having collaborated with the Japanese. In the North, the USSR kept a relatively low profile and backed Kim Il Sung, a hero of the anti-Japanese resistance. By the end of 1946, the North had undertaken land, labor, and women's rights reforms, and Soviet troops were withdrawn by the end of 1948 (Cummings 1997).

While Western powers established the two Korean states, Eastern powers played a more decisive role in shaping the developmental courses selected. South Korea dropped the U.S. model of development in the 1960s for the Japanese model, adopting the principle, "Do what the Japanese have done, but do it cheaper and faster." The choice of the Japanese model over the American model may have been due, in part, to the fact that Park Chung Hee, the military strongman who commanded South Korea from 1961 until his assassination in 1979, was educated in Japanese military academies (Mallaby 1995). Similarly, North Korea replicated itself after the Stalinist model during the late 1940s and 1950s, but then was influenced more by the Chinese communist model (Kim 1992).

POLITICAL ENVIRONMENT

Though the emphasis of this chapter is on economics, marketing, and consumption, it would be fruitless to discuss the two Koreas without confronting political issues. One only needs to consider the role of defense spending in the two nations to realize the strong interface between politics and economics. The combined countries have the world's fifth largest number of military personnel and are thirteenth in military spending. Military spending in the South is $19.9 billion (3.2 percent of its gross national product [GNP]), while the North spends $4.3 billion or 29 percent of its gross output value of social production (GVSP) (*Asia Source* 2001). South Korea continues to seek a self-reliant defense capability, but North Korea maintains its numerical superiority over the South in military forces. According to data reported by the South Korean Ministry of Defense in 1999, the size of the military force in the South is 690,000 (Army, 560,000; Navy, 67,000; Air Force, 63,000) while the size of military force in the North is 1,170,000 (Army, one million; Navy, 60,000; Air Force, 110,000). North Korea has the ability to conduct limited guerilla warfare, mobilize the entire population rapidly in an emergency, and wage an all-out war effort with little notice. One of the few reliable export industries in the North has been its arms industry.

The Korean War and the nearly constant state of tension between the two countries since are indicants of the focus on one another in terms of most policy decisions. However, there are indicators that situations are changing in both countries. The South has become more democratic since the 1987 and especially since the 1993 elections. In fact, after those pivotal elections, in which the first nonmilitary president was elected, Chalmers Johnson states, "[South] Korea is without doubt the most democratic country in Asia right now" (cited in Clifford 1994, 330). By and large, South Koreans are free to say and write what they think. In 1990, they were not (*The Economist* 1990c).

The political situation in North Korea is changing as well, in part due to the death of its long-time leader Kim Il Sung (Bracken [1995] noted that his son Kim Jung Il lacked his father's widespread support in the regime and also in the larger society as a whole), but more due to the changing political environment globally. Though the *chuche* ("self-reliant") ideology of autonomy was adopted by Kim Il Sung as early as 1955, North Korea has relied heavily on the former Soviet Union and the People's Republic of China for both political and economic support. The Soviet transformation forced North Korea to rethink its political future. Even before the fragmentation of the USSR, South Korean leader Roh Tae Woo met with Mikhail Gorbachev in San Francisco in 1990, an event that the *The Economist* (1990c) called the "most significant event in Korean diplomacy since the Korean War." By meeting with the South, Gorbachev gave the clear signal that the USSR would no longer support (either financially or militarily) the North's aggressive stance against the South. Further, despite all of the ideological ties between the North and China, as early as 1990, China had six times the level of trade with the South as it did with the North (*The Economist* 1990c). Former President Roh created a second historic meeting in September 1992, when he visited Beijing (Nakarmi, Brady, and Curry 1992).

While the South Korean economy continued to grow rapidly, the North's economy shrunk by 25 percent between 1990 and 1994 (Mallaby 1995) and has continued to have negative growth since then. The closed environment in Pyongyang makes it very difficult to get an accurate reading of what is transpiring. Breen quoted a Western intelligence source in Seoul as acknowledging, "Different observers see it differently" (1990, 44). The political divisions between countries run deep, and the rhetoric observed in the world press offers only rare glimpses of conciliatory statements. It would appear that the North Korean economy is in such a poor state that the North cannot continue long on its own. Whether it will react violently with another invasion into the

South or whether it will move slowly toward reunification remains to be seen; Bracken phrased this question as whether "the end for Pyongyang [the capital of North Korea] comes with a bang or a whimper" (1995, 63).

Certainly, the changing global relations are providing impetus for change. Understanding the political environment in the two Koreas clearly provides one with greater appreciation for the delicacy of the agreement reached August 13, 1994, concerning nuclear issues. North Korea removed its U.S. trade ban as part of the August agreement. The South too made conciliatory gestures; for example, *The Economist* quoted the South Korean President Kim Young Sam as saying, "The problems of the North are our own problems. We must always be prepared to cooperate with our brethren" (1994a, 32).

An inter-Korean summit was held in Pyongyang in June 2000. The meeting of leaders of the two countries was the first since the division of the peninsula. Even though the summit has not yet produced a military relaxation between the two Koreas, progress was made toward a reconciliation of the North and the South. Many interpret the summit as a signal of a change in North Korean policy away from the ideology of chuche in order to avoid a breakdown of its economy (Wehrfritz 2000). The summit did result in increased inter-Korean exchanges and cooperation in 2000. Active promotion of inter-Korean exchanges led to two exchange visits by family members who were separated when the North and South were divided. Through the visitor exchange program in 2000, 7,280 South Koreans visited the North, and 706 North Koreans visited the South (Nam 2001a). Still, nuclear saber-rattling from Pyongyang continues to worry South Korea and the world community, more broadly; as of this writing, Pyongyang's nuclear weapons program continues to dominate diplomatic dialogue (e.g., *The Economist* 2003).

The political situation in the Koreas has served to raise even more questions than usually exist concerning the validity of economic statistics reported by developing countries. Such statistics are often called into question in many parts of the world, but this may be especially true with the Koreas, given their continuing battle for prestige in the world community. As Hwang (1993) noted, there has been (and continues to be) a serious lack of published data for North Korea, while there is a wealth of published data and statistics from South Korea. Chung (1986) asserted that withdrawing information has been one of North Korea's main means of concealing unfavorable developments. For this reason, our discussion of the South's economy will be far richer in detail. But even here, one must be quite careful. Hwang (1993, 100) noted that economic data with political implications (income distributions, credit rationing, etc.) must be handled with care. Similarly, Halladay (1989) noted that official Pyongyang claims were often exaggerated but that Western and Seoul downgradings of the North were usually also inaccurate.

A case in point is the reporting of North Korean agricultural output. In the 1990s, the South Korean state-run Rural Development Administration consistently estimated that the North's grain harvest was well below the level needed to prevent food shortages. The estimates were compiled from studying crop yields in border areas and from studying weather patterns. For example, Table 8.1 shows the consistent discrepancies between supply and demand, as reported by South Korean sources. On the other hand, the North Korean–controlled media yearly boasted bumper crops. Hwang (1993) and Merrill (1989) found the North's agricultural achievements to be impressive, especially given its unfavorable climate and terrain. Thus, we will attempt to provide an objective evaluation of the marketing systems in the two countries but have to acknowledge that our "facts" may well be misrepresentations of the actual circumstances.

Table 8.1

Food Demand and Supply in North Korea (in billions of tons)

	1992	1993	1994	1995	1996	1997	1998	1999
Demand	57.6	56.9	57.6	58.0	57.8	58.3	54.1	55.1
Supply	44.3	42.7	38.8	41.3	34.5	36.8	34.9	38.9
Shortage	13.3	14.2	18.8	16.7	23.3	21.4	19.2	16.2

Source: South Korean Ministry of Unification, September 1999.

THE ECONOMIES OF THE KOREAS

Comparing the economies of the North and the South is a complex task, and, as will be indicated, there is little consensus on the pertinent numbers. It is clear, though, that the South is doing much better now, and that those performances were reversed in the 1960s. One problem in comparing the economies is that the countries use different measures. The South uses GNP data that includes both productive and nonproductive (service) sectors in its measurement. The North uses GVSP data that includes intermediate material inputs except for goods consumed within the same enterprise but does not include nonproductive sectors. To complicate matters, because the North Korean currency is not convertible, there are multiple exchange rates to use in the analyses. Hwang (1993) found that the North led the South in per capita GNP until 1985 if the official exchange rate is used, but only until 1974 if the trade exchange rate (which is more than twice the official rate) is used. Meanwhile, Seoul claimed that it overtook the North in 1969, while the U.S. CIA claimed this happened in 1976 (Hwang 1993).

Today, the North Korean economy is in shambles, suffering from critical shortages of food, energy, and hard currency, with an increasing number of people moving dangerously close to famine and some 70 percent of factories halting their operations (*The Economist* 2003; see also Kim 1998). Forty percent of North Koreans are undernourished, putting North Korea behind only the Congo and Tanzania (*The Economist* 2001c), and it was the largest recipient of the United Nation's World Food Program's food aid in mid-2001 (*The Economist* 2001e).

In spite of its desperate economic conditions, North Korea has continued to attempt to improve its economy by developing better relationships with South Korea and the United States. For example, tourism efforts such as Kumgang Mountain sightseeing have become a stepping-stone for mutual economic efforts between the North and the South (Kim 2001), and the North has cautiously initiated some special economic zones that permit market-determined prices therein; in addition, the North continues talks with the U.S. government in hopes of having economic sanctions lifted in exchange for suspending the launching of test missiles (Rubin 2001; *The Economist* 2003).

South Korea's "miracle economy" started showing signs of trouble in late 1995 and early 1996 with downturns in the semiconductor, metals, and petrochemical industries (*The Economist* 1997c). Also, Korean banks started reporting large losses on loans to *chaebols* (large Korean conglomerates). Thirteen of the top thirty chaebols lost money in 1996, before the Asian meltdown. Manufacturing wages had increased to the point that they were 30 percent higher than those in Britain (*The Economist* 1997c). The Southeast Asian currency problems in October 1997 added to the uncertainty in the South Korean financial markets, and the exchange rate for the won plunged 27.5 percent against the U.S. dollar in November 1997. By December 1997, it had lost

Table 8.2

Debt-to-Equity Ratios for Various Countries

Year	Country				
	Korea	Japan	Germany	Taiwan	United States
1980	5.0	3.5	1.9	1.7	0.5
1984	3.6	2.7	1.7	1.5	0.6
1988	3.0	2.0	1.6	1.2	0.8
1992	3.3	1.8	1.6	0.9	1.0
1995	3.0	1.7	1.6	0.8	1.0
1997	4.0	n/a	n/a	n/a	n/a

Source: Dongchul Cho, "Recovering from the Crisis: Where Does the Korean Economy Stand?" *Korea Journal* 38, Autumn (1999): 183.

40.3 percent of its value from the same month in 1996 (Yi 1999). Real gross domestic product (GDP) contracted by 5.8 percent in 1998 due to a drastic fall in investment (–21.6 percent) and sharp cutbacks in private consumption (–8.9 percent). Unemployment, which had been around 2 percent in the period 1995–1997, peaked at 8.7 percent in February 1999 (Yi 1999). The depth of the economic discontinuity can be seen in tourist statistics: in 1997, 108,000 South Koreans visited New Zealand; in 1998, that number dropped to 18,000 (Thyne and Lawson 2001). Shim and Cho (2000) found that consumers reacted to the crisis by becoming more utilitarian in their purchases of clothing and by changing their patronage from department stores to cheaper stores (discount stores and mass merchandisers).

Multiple factors interacted to cause the economy's crash. For instance, Yoon (2000) asserted that corruption was the principal cause of the financial crisis, reporting survey results indicating that 97 percent of Koreans saw corruption in Korea as being serious. On the other hand, Cho (1999) pointed to the over-leveraged financial structure of the Korean corporate sector as the chief reason (very possibly, the two causes may overlap). As Table 8.2 indicates, the debt-to-equity ratios in Korea had been much greater than those of Japan, Germany, Taiwan, and the United States in the last twenty years. Cho (1999) further pointed to the close government and chaebol relationships, and the implicit bailout policy of the government that eliminated the threat of bankruptcy—the essence of market economy discipline. While smaller chaebols were allowed to fail, four of the five largest (Samsung, Hyundai, LG [Lucky Goldstar], and SK) were supported after agreeing to a number of reforms, such as providing consolidated balance sheets, reducing debt-to-equity ratios, and eliminating cross-loan guarantees among subsidiaries (Cho 1999). Daewoo, however, lost its government support in 1999, and it was broken into smaller parts. Korea's financial sector was rehabilitated. Of the thirty-three commercial banks, five were ordered to close and eleven to restructure. Of the 377 non-bank financial institutions, thirty-four were closed, twenty-one suspended operations, and eleven had to restructure.

Early outside estimates were that South Korea would need to borrow US$60 billion in November 1997 to avoid bankruptcy (*The Economist* 1997b). Korea actually borrowed $19.6 billion from the International Monetary Fund (IMF) in 1997 but paid the loan off in the summer of 2001. It still owed $10.7 billion borrowed from the World Bank and the Asian Development Bank but had built its foreign-exchange reserves to nearly $100 billion by August 2001. The banking sector is still plagued with bad assets, as three out of every ten manufacturing firms surveyed by the Central Bank were failing to generate enough cash to pay interest on their debts (*The Economist*

Table 8.3

Per Capita Income Distribution in 1988

Percentage of population below	Income Level	
	South Korea	North Korea
0–10	648	720
10–20	1,264	900
20–30	1,684	1,000
30–40	2,010	1,100
40–50	2,349	1,200
50–60	2,755	1,300
60–70	3,211	1,400
70–80	3,818	1,500
80–90	4,850	2,000
90–100	8,897	4,200

Source: Byoung-Lo Philo Kim, *Two Koreas in Development* (New Brunswick, NJ: Transaction, 1992), p. 95.

2001a). Yet, banking reforms had been sufficiently successful that *The Economist* concluded that South Korea was among only three East Asian countries (along with Singapore and Hong Kong) where banks "work at all as they should—intermediating financial flows" (2001f, 65–66).

At the turn of the twenty-first century, South Korea was one of the few East Asian countries with positive economic growth (*The Economist* 2001f). In 2001, South Korea's GDP was nearly one-quarter bigger than in 1996, before the meltdown. It managed this turnaround despite the downturn in the United States, through impressive growth in domestic consumption (*The Economist* 2001c).

Income

The income distributions in the two countries are summarized in Table 8.3. It appears that the poor (lowest 10 percent) in the South may have had less than the poor in the North; on the other hand, 90 percent of the South was above the median income in the North and 70 percent of the South had incomes comparable to the top 20 percent in the North. Again, it should be noted that data from both Koreas may need to be viewed with skepticism. Breen (1990) noted that officially Pyongyang claimed its annual per capita income to be US$2,500, but one UN official said the figure was around the US$1,000 mark, and a diplomat from Beijing who had been assigned to the North said that its per capita income was "definitely" below China's figure of US$450. The Bank of Korea estimated the per capita income in North Korea to be US$757 in 2000.

Confucianism (plus Communism in the North) has worked to reduce the disparity of incomes in both Koreas. In 1970, by one measure, South Korea had a more equal income distribution than Japan or the United States (*The Economist* 1990a). Clifford (1994) also notes this strong egalitarian tradition and acknowledges that the division between rich and poor is not that great. He also notes that there is great reliance by government on the use of slogans and symbols calling for sacrifice; frugality sometimes resembles a religion.

Both countries have somewhat inflexible class structures. In the South, as in the United States, blue-collar workers have had little opportunity to move into management, as a hierarchical system has been generally accepted (Clifford 1994). In the North, every individual is classified into one of fifty-one categories according to his or her *sungboon* (the family's class background). The highest group includes anti-Japanese guerrilla fighters and their families; orphans of parents killed in anti-Japanese activities or in the Korean War; and the families of party members, government officials, and military officers. The elite receive preferential treatment in the acquisition of food and other consumer goods. Those at the bottom of the ladder include descendants of landlords, capitalists, rich peasants, collaborators with the Japanese, and members of religious groups, as well as the families of persons who fled to South Korea (Kim 1992). Persons with good sungboon find their entry into the best schools and their rise in the bureaucracy facilitated. Those with a bad sungboon have little chance for a good education or a good job. Because family background is passed on from parents to children, stratification is rigid, and there is little evidence that opportunities for those at the bottom of the ladder are improving.

Employment

Employment levels in both countries have traditionally been high, in part because of the close interface between business and the government. In the North, a "paradise on Earth" was built: no taxes, no crime, no beggars, no unemployment, and no corruption. The price for this paradise was no television, no refrigerators, and a lack of decent clothing and comfortable housing (Kim 1992). Historically, urban workers usually worked six days a week with fifteen days of paid vacation a year. Farmers had every first, eleventh, and twenty-first day of the month off. Most white-collar workers (with the exception of those in the teaching profession) engaged in some sort of manual labor, such as digging ditches every Friday, and Saturday was "education day" (indoctrination) for all people (Chung 1986).

More recent evidence indicates that work conditions in the North have not changed. According to Young Kim (www.kimyoung.co.kr), who is a recent refugee from the North and now an entrepreneur in the South, officially, North Korea has adopted an eight-hour workday, shortened to six to seven hours for difficult hours or for women with more than three children. However, in reality, most men are in the workplace for thirteen hours a day, from 7 A.M. to 8 P.M. Officially, two of the thirteen hours are allocated for ideological education, but in practice, the education usually exceeds two hours, and workers often do not get home until 10 P.M. In 2001, the (South Korean) Ministry of Unification noted that North Korean workers are to have fourteen days of paid vacation each year, but that absenteeism is high, as many factories are closed and those open often no longer receive an allocation of food to feed their workers, due to the current economic problems.

Prior to the mid-1980s, wage rates in the South were quite low, helping exports to be price-competitive in global markets. Trade unions lacked power, as union membership included only a small percentage of the workers (about 7 percent in 1985). Many firms did not accept trade unions. In the 1980s, holidays were limited to a weekly rest day and public holidays, and employers sometimes obligated employees to put in extra hours in order to meet production peaks (Hoare and Pares 1988). The incentive systems usually included seasonal bonuses, which were uniform and not tied to performance (Yoo and Lee 1987). Similarly, promotion was based primarily on seniority and not on performance. South Korean employees retire between the ages of fifty-five and sixty-five (depending on the profession; for example, teachers retire at age sixty-two and professors at age sixty-five), receiving a lump sum retirement allowance.

In the late 1980s, there were dramatic changes in the South's labor market policies. As the result of an increase in demand for democratization in the South, labor became unionized, and wages rose dramatically, while some industries requiring heavy manual labor experienced a labor shortage (Oh 2000). This brought an end to the relatively cheap, high-quality, and cooperative Korean labor force. The heaviest losers were key export markets such as electronic equipment,

Table 8.4

Annual Numbers of Hours Worked

Country	1990	2000
Republic of Korea	2,514	2,474
United States	1,943	1,979
Japan	2,031	1,842
Spain	1,824	1,812
United Kingdom	1,767	1,720
Finland	1,728	1,691
Germany	1,573	1,480
Norway	1,432	1,376

Source: American Demographics, "The Laboring Masses," November (2001).

textile fabrics, iron and steel, miscellaneous manufacturing, and nonmetallic metals (Clifford 1994). Steel, one of Korea's early success stories, is a typical case. Production costs of cold-rolled steel products were only three-quarters of the Japanese levels in 1988, but by 1993 had risen to nearly 90 percent of Japan's. Rising wages also priced the shoe manufacturers of South Korea out of world markets (Clifford 1994).

The government's reaction to the downturn in the early 1990s was a campaign launched in 1991 urging citizens to work more (an extra thirty minutes a day), save more (another 10 percent of income), export more, produce more, and live a more frugal life. This campaign may have been successful, as Koreans at the start of the twenty-first century work more hours than their counterparts in other industrialized countries, as shown in Table 8.4.

In 1997, despite strong opposition from the federation of labor unions, the government implemented a new labor law that focused on labor market flexibility to facilitate company restructuring and the expansion of a social safety net to help unemployed workers (Oh 2000). The new law allowed employment adjustments in such situations as business transfers, acquisitions, and mergers in order to avoid financial difficulties.

Prices and Credit Policy

In North Korea, a commodity's price is determined not by the demand and supply mechanism but arbitrarily by the central planners who seek to control the demand for and supply of commodities. Therefore, the price of a commodity is not relevant, in many cases, to the actual value of that commodity. Based on so-called socially needed labor time, which represents the average quantity of labor put into the production of the good, the price is determined so as to raise labor productivity, increase cost-effectiveness, and reflect savings in the use of raw materials and consumers' living standards (Hwang 1993; South Korean National Intelligence Service 1999).

Consistent with other command economies, labor inputs are not necessarily the unique basis for the determination of price. Prices for consumer goods are frequently set at levels distinct from their (production-oriented) actual values. For example, in 1999, rice was priced at $0.08 per kilogram, less than one-fifth of the actual production costs. In general, prices for nondurable consumer goods are subsidized, while prices for durable and luxury goods greatly exceed their production costs (South Korean National Intelligence Service 1999).

In general, all prices in the North are controlled by the government except for those for agricultural products in the farmer's market (flea market) on the first, eleventh, and twenty-first days of the month. Most prices are set by the State Price Establishment Committee, which then distributes price lists to resellers. Exceptions to this process include goods produced by regional business units, in which case, prices are set by Provincial Price Bureaus (South Korean National Intelligence Service 1999).

More recently, the economic problems of the North have resulted in a closer alignment of price and value. As the economic situation in the North worsened in the 1990s, the government lost control of the price of commodities, because the economy could not provide people with the necessities of life. Lim (2001) reported that people in the North even traded houses (that are rented from the government and not owned) in the private market to make a living. Thus, people in the North have become more familiar with the price and value relationship for commodities in private markets.

Pricing in the South is more market oriented. A World Bank study in 1983 showed that South Korea had one of the least price-distorting regimes in the world. With the increase in wages after the mid-1980s, prices rose, especially as increasing attention was paid to domestic demand as opposed to exporting. The government's rice-buying prices rose 30 percent from 1988 to 1990 (*The Economist* 1990a). Inflation rose as high as 12 percent following the wage increases (Nakarmi 1991) but was brought down to 4.5 percent by 1992 (International Strategies 1994).

The South Korean government rationed the flow of credit (Hoare and Pares 1988), making funds available for business expansion but restricting credit access in consumer markets, especially the supply of credit for house buying. Mortgages were scarce and difficult to get for more than 20 percent of the value of a house or apartment (*The Economist* 1990c); however, since the restructuring of the banks due to the economic crisis of the late 1990s, mortgages have become more common.

In early 1995, in order to cool down the economy, the government dictated that banks could no longer issue credit cards to people less than twenty years of age, university students, or workers during their first year on the job. This was seen largely as a symbolic gesture, as this segment did not spend nearly as much as their elders. Most people reacted positively to the policy, as there was a fear that the free-wheeling youth market would undermine the social order (*The Economist* 1995a). Overall, though, credit cards have become very common in South Korea, as over forty-three million had been issued there by 2000. After the economic crisis, the government began encouraging the use of credit cards. The share of sales at department stores via credit cards increased from 51 percent in 1998 to 70 percent in 2000, while the share of credit card sales in discount stores increased from 27 percent in 1998 to 51 percent in 2001 (Korea Department Stores Association 2001).

Government/Business Interface

In the North, a controlled economy exists; business activities are government run. In the North Korean command economy, the priorities of production are ranked down from public goods, producers' goods, light industry goods, and lastly, consumer goods, so that consumer preferences on the micro level were neglected (and still are) for the sake of the macro-level targets of the planners (Hwang 1993). In the South, there is also a strong history of government playing a dominant role in business. Park Chung Hee decided in the early 1960s that the correct path for development was to favor a few companies (now known as chaebols) with carefully channeled credit and subsidies. In return for these favors, the firms had to meet the government's expectations (*The Economist* 1990c). Business has existed at the pleasure of government and has been expected to put national development ahead of private desires (Clifford 1994). As a result, the economic power in the South has been quite concentrated; ten of the country's firms were responsible for more than half of its exports in 1990 (*The Economist* 1990c). The concentration of the workforce has been reflected by the very low ratio of companies to population in South Korea: 0.7 percent, compared to 4.4 percent in the United States, 5 percent in Japan, 4.1 percent in the United Kingdom, and 2.5 percent in Taiwan (Park 1994). The authorized *Handbook of Korea* in the 1987 edition stated, "The national economy can be divided into two parts: the government sector and the private sector functioning under the government's policy" (Hoare and Pares 1988).

There are similarities between the Korean chaebols and the Japanese *zaibatsus*; for example, both names are derived from the same Chinese characters and both are loosely translated as "conglomerates" (Chang 1988). But the close government/business relationship in Korea ("Korea Inc.") differs from that of "Japan Inc.," which reflects a consensus of equals. Traditionally, Korea Inc. has seen more government leadership, largely due to the Korean government's strong control over access to credit, whereas the large Japanese zaibatsus often have their own banks from which they can obtain credit (Yoo and Lee 1987).

Chang (1988) used the acronym FARS (family, alumni, regional, state relationships) to explain the intricate nature of chaebols. Unlike the zaibatsus, most chaebols (with the possible exception of Daewoo) are dominated by the founding families and appear to be able to continue to do so. There has been a strong preference for employees who have attended the right schools (Kyunggi High School and Seoul National University). For example, seven of the nine inner-circle executives at Daewoo in the 1980s were graduates of Kyunggi High School. Chang (1988) noted that 62 percent of the top executives of the seven largest chaebols were graduates of Seoul National University. Similarly, most top executives of the chaebols have come from the same geographic region of Korea as the founders.

The political influence of the chaebols has diminished with the election of nonmilitary leaders. Former President Kim Young Sam's lifting of sanctions for trade with North Korea was intended to allow small and medium-sized South Korean companies to venture North rather than the chaebols. Unfortunately, the chaebols were more likely to have the funds needed and the willingness to take the risks needed to establish large-scale trade (*The Economist* 1994e). On the other hand, public resentment toward the chaebols and the rich families that control them has made it politically expedient to push them around (*The Economist* 1990b). There are indications that the government pressure on the chaebols changed the nature of business even before the economic crisis of the late 1990s, as the percentage of sales in more competitive markets (i.e., markets where the top three firms had a market share less than 50 percent) increased from 26 percent in 1981 to 37 percent in 1992.

The most evident split between the chaebols and the government occurred when Hyundai's founder Chung Ju Yung stood in the presidential elections in the early 1990s. He was the first to break the unwritten rule by being a political opponent of the government. He had irritated the government by being the first prominent businessperson to visit the North in 1990, and in October of that year, Hyundai was singled out for tax evasion. In 1992, he attempted to make public the collusion that existed between chaebols and government by providing details of millions of dollars in payments to Korean politicians, including Roh Tae Woo's government. Roh admitted receiving the money but said that it was spent on the "needy" (Nakarmi 1992). In the early fall of 1996, former presidents Chun Doo Hwan and Roh Tae Woo were imprisoned for their roles in a 1979 military coup and the 1980 massacre of pro-democracy demonstrators in Kwangju. Further, the heads of eight chaebols were given prison terms for bribing Roh, four of which were subsequently suspended (Lee 1996). The government/chaebol interface became even more complex in late 1996 with the collapse of Hanbo Steel and the subsequent charges made against former President Kim Young Sam's son for his role in that failure (*The Economist* 1997a). Kim Woo Choong, once Korea's most honored businessman, saw his Daewoo chaebol encounter enormous problems and faced fraud charges for creating fictitious profits, covering up failed ventures, and creating a London-based slush fund that diverted money from Daewoo's trading company (Moon 2001a).

Barriers to Trade

The North Korean market has been closed to much of the world since its inception. In 1987, North Korea began to let Western tourists visit, and in 1989 reported that 25,000 tourists had visited from Western Europe, Australia, Canada, and Hong Kong (Breen 1990). The North Korean Tourist Organization reported that the number of foreign visitors increased to 117,500 in 1992 and to 130,000 in 1998. In 1992, 85 percent of the visitors were from East Asia and the Pacific Rim, with 11 percent from Europe and 2 percent from the Americas. But the North is not a tourist's dream. The facilities for tourism are in place, as Pyongyang is a clean city with wide streets and a new streetcar system, and it has several modern hotels, monuments, museums, and scenic parks. However, tourism revenues dropped drastically with the disintegration of the Russian economy. One of Pyongyang's finest hotels, the Koryo, has 500 rooms, but a visitor in 1991 found only thirty-five of them occupied. Similarly, the Hyangsan Hotel situated in the northwestern hills of Pyongyang was found not to have a single overnight guest one summer night in 1991 (Gluckman 1991). Conditions did not improve greatly in the next decade. *The Economist* (2001g) warns that you may be the only guest when you check into a forty-five-story, 500-room edifice. Get off on the wrong floor, and you may find yourself in total darkness, as they see no reason to light unused corridors. The radiators in your room may not work, and it is common to see people eating with their coats and gloves on if there is a power cut.

The "opening" of North Korea to visitor exchanges with the South has fostered increased flows of South Koreans to the North. Overall, though, it appears that while the North would like to have the revenues possibly generated by tourism, they are still scared of the possible cultural contamination it might bring. Western tourists lucky enough to get a visa are accompanied at all times by official guides wearing Kim Jong Il badges. South Korean tourists are not allowed to talk to any North Koreans (*The Economist* 2001g).

Since 1988, Seoul has allowed indirect trade with the North, with each chaebol allowed to buy a little under $200 million per year of gold, zinc, fish, and rice liquor, shipping it via China or Hong Kong (*The Economist* 1994d). Table 8.5 provides a summary of the growth in trade between the two Koreas. The fact that inter-Korean trade has been on the rise indicates that the two Koreas have started cooperating with each other (*Business Korea* 2000). In spite of South Korea's economic recession, inter-Korean transactions reached a record high of US$333.4 million in 1999 (*Business Korea* 2000). After the June 2000 summit, more South Korean companies have entered North Korea, where cheap and plentiful labor is available. In the early days of trade between the two Koreas, trade was limited to agriculture and fishery products and mineral products. However, more recently, trade has diversified to include textiles, electronic equipment, and machinery (KOTRA 2001b). Information-technology (IT)-related economic cooperation between the two Koreas has expanded, due in part to the North Korean IT workforce being well educated and capable of communicating in their common language with the South (Nam 2001b). Similarly, the South exports raw textile materials to the North and then imports the finished textile products, taking advantage of the relatively cheap labor supply in the North. The inter-Korean trade amount

Table 8.5

Trade between South and North Korea (Unit: US$1,000)

Year	Import			Export			Total		
	Cases	Number of items	Amount	Cases	Number of items	Amount	Cases	Number of items	Amount
1989	66	25	18,655	1	1	69	67	26	18,724
1990	79	23	12,278	4	3	1,188	83	26	13,466
1991	300	44	105,719	23	17	5,547	323	61	111,266
1992	510	76	162,863	62	24	10,563	572	100	173,426
1993	601	67	178,167	97	38	8,425	698	101	186,592
1994	827	73	176,298	495	92	18,249	1,322	159	194,547
1995	1,124	105	222,855	2,720	174	64,436	3,844	265	287,291
1996	1,648	122	182,400	2,980	171	69,639	4,628	280	252,039
1997	1,806	140	193,069	2,185	274	115,270	3,991	385	308,339
1998	1,963	136	92,264	2,847	380	129,679	4,810	486	221,943
1999	3,089	172	121,604	3,421	398	211,832	6,510	525	333,437
2000	3,952	203	152,373	3,442	505	272,775	7,394	647	425,148
Subtotal	15,965		1,618,546	18,277		907,671	34,242		2,526,217

Source: KOTRA, "Intra-Korean Trade by Years," September 2001 (available at http://crm.kotra.or.kr.main).
Note: The amount (US$237,213,000) of rice aid was not included in the export amount of 1995.

is the third largest for North Korea, after China and Japan, and accounted for 22 percent of the North's trade in 2000 (*Business Korea* 2000.

One obvious problem in trade between the Koreas is the lack of a hard currency; as South Korean firms have noted, how much zinc and rice liquor does one need (*The Economist* 1994d)? Further, North Korean quality standards have been found to be below those of the South. For example, Breen (1990) reported an instance when an entire shipment of coal from the North was of a significantly lower grade than specified and was returned. For the North, importing does not present quality problems but rather image problems. Electronics imported from the South were stripped of their brand names by authorities in Pyongyang in order to prevent its citizens from perceiving that the South is capable of producing more sophisticated products (Breen 1990). Nam (2001c) indicated that this perspective still dominates, as the North has focused on its exports, and noted that domestic sales of imports are "exceptionally allowed."

In the late 1990s, the economic situation in North Korea deteriorated to the extent that the country realized that it could no longer maintain a closed economic system. The shortage of food due to a severe drought starting in 1996 made the North ask for foreign aid from Western countries and the South. Even though there has been no observable change in economic policy regarding foreign trade, the North has made diplomatic efforts to improve relations with Japan, the United States, and the South (Kim 2001).

Remnants of the Hermit Kingdom legacy are also evident in the South. Its export-driven economic policies reduced its attraction as a consumer economy, though the liberalization in the 1980s changed matters somewhat. In order to manage trade deficits, the South's government used a variety of tariff and nontariff barriers. While tariffs have been falling in general, duties remained very high on high-value and value-added agricultural and fisheries products (International Strategies 1994). During the period of high inflation in the early 1990s, the South placed limitations on the number of "luxury" goods (Kraft and Chung 1992).

In 1997, tariffs on cars resulted in a comparably priced Ford car (to a Hyundai in the United States) to sell for $2,600 more than the Hyundai in Korea. Additionally, Korea added special excise taxes (ranging from 10 to 20 percent) for imported "luxury" goods such as coffee, refrigerators, and televisions (*The Economist* 1997b).

Nontariff barriers have posed greater problems, especially in the early 1990s. Frustration was encountered due to the complicated licensing requirements, the inspection of industrial goods, and "special laws" that gave line ministries broad powers to "stabilize" markets by controlling imports (International Strategies 1994). In 1990, Korean importers were slapped with strict new guidelines that raised the prices of foreign goods to extraordinary levels; a General Electric refrigerator selling for about $1,600 in the United States cost $4,200 in Korea. The government went so far as to send its tax inspectors to dig into the records of Koreans who bought imported cars and even those who went salmon fishing in Alaska or golfing in Hawaii (Nakarmi 1991). The tax audits of people buying imported cars stopped in 1993, though more subtle forms of intimidation continued. As a consequence, only about 2,000 import cars were sold in 1993 in a market of about one million cars (Templeman and Nakarmi 1994). The sales of import cars peaked in 1996 at 10,300, shrunk to 2,075 in 1998 during the economic crisis, and then rebounded with estimated sales of 12,000 in 2001.

In March 1990, the Korean government announced that retailers must display two prices on certain retail products. The first price was the ex-factory price for domestic goods or the customs clearance price for imported goods; the second was the retail price. Because of the difference in the composition of the ex-factory and the customs clearance price, the markup on imported goods appears higher, making them less attractive to Korean customers (International Strategies 1994). This dual price-tag policy has since been discontinued.

In 1992, authorities detained a shipment of $250,000 worth of Snickers and Skittles candy at the port of Pusan. The imported candy lacked a quarantine certificate testifying that the sweets adhered to new "internal guidelines," although these candies had been imported for several years with no problems. The guidelines were never made public (Clifford 1994).

The existence of bureaucratic barriers continued into the Kim Young Sam administration. In June 1993, just four months after Kim took office, prosecutors arrested seven executives from Amway and Sunrider International. Sunrider's top executive in Korea was jailed for operating a multilevel, or pyramid, sales network, which special prosecutor Kwak Young Chul said could lead to "serious social disorder" (Clifford 1994).

Citibank's experience in the early 1990s reduced interest in South Korea on the part of other U.S. financial institutions. Authorities insisted that its cash machines could only operate during normal banking hours, that it could not join a national payment network, and that each branch had to be capitalized and operated as if it were a separate bank, with separate reporting and operating structures (Clifford 1994). However, financial market accessibility improved, and by August 1994, seventy-four foreign banks, thirty-nine foreign securities firms, and twenty-eight foreign insurance companies had entered South Korea and been accorded full national treatment. As noted earlier, there was much attrition in the banking sector during the economic crisis of the late 1990s. Citibank, by the way, persevered, and in 2000 was by far the most profitable of the forty-four remaining foreign banks in Korea (Financial Supervisory Service 2001).

In the last half of the decade of the 1990s, the government of South Korea made progress in gradually opening its market to foreign investment. About 98 percent of the industrial areas and 62 percent of the service areas are now open to foreign investment. Foreign businesses operating in South Korea may now purchase land and housing for their staffs without obtaining government approval. As late as the early 1990s, Korea was receiving a relatively small amount of foreign direct investment (FDI) compared with other countries in the region. During 1988–1992, Korea received $5.5 billion in FDI compared with $87.6 billion for China, $30.4 billion for Thailand, $24.7 billion for Malaysia, and $9.1 billion for Taiwan (International Strategies 1994).

Former President Kim Young Sam initiated many changes aimed at attracting foreign investment. In July 1994, the Ministry of Finance announced a special corporate profit tax exemption for a period of five years for new high-technology businesses created by foreign corporations in Korea. Further, Holstein and Nakarmi noted that the return of many U.S.-trained Ph.D.s was "tilting the balance away from an inward-looking, relatively closed nation toward one that is eager to play a larger international role" (1995, 63). For example, the won has become convertible, and there is no limit to portfolio investment in firms listed on the Korean Stock Market. There is a limit of 30 percent in equity ownership by foreigners of public enterprises.

FDI increased greatly during and after the economic crisis. In fact, there have been more foreign-invested companies registered since 1996 (4,207 companies) than in all the previous years combined. During the period between 1999 and 2000, an increase in this trend was shown, with over 2,000 new foreign companies being registered in Korea in 2000. In 2000, FDI in Korea was $16 billion, compared to $41 billion in China and $64 billion in Hong Kong (Ministry of Finance and Economy 2001).

While the United States has continued to be the primary source of foreign investment with 494 new registrations in 1999–2000, the great increase in Chinese/Hong Kong investment is noteworthy. China, Hong Kong, and Taiwan had 488 new registrations in the period from 1999 to 2000. Japan, Pakistan and Malaysia followed with 332, 81, and 60 new registrations, respectively (KOFANET 2001).

Korean–Japanese Trade Relations

Despite ill will lingering from the colonial period, both Koreas experienced more dependence on the Japanese than any other country in the 1970s and 1980s (Kim 1992). In May 1955, leftist Koreans in Japan formed an organization named *Choch'ungnyon*, and this organization was soon brought under the direct control of North Korea. The organization was designed to capture the leadership of all the Korean residents (amounting to some 600,000) in Japan. Gradually, relations with Japan deteriorated in the 1960s as Japan's economic ties with South Korea improved. In 1972, Japan sent a goodwill mission to Pyongyang, which marked a new stage in bilateral agreements. Kim Il Sung indicated that the normalization of relations between Japan and North Korea would not be hampered by the existing relationship between Japan and South Korea. Japan's official policy has been that of pursuing a "two Koreas" policy (Eisenstodt 1990).

In 1989, Japanese/North Korean trade came to almost $500 million and involved more than forty joint ventures; yet this was a mere trickle compared with Japanese/South Korean trade ($30 billion at that time). Still, the Japanese trade was of immense importance to North Korea. Much of the trade involved small firms owned by Koreans in Japan (Eisenstodt 1990). In 1989, the volume of trade with Japan was second only to the USSR, and larger than that with China (Kim 1992). North Korea's total trade with Japan amounted to US$467 million in 2000, an increase of 32.1 percent over the previous year but still less than the peak amount of US$594 million in 1995 (KOTRA 2001a). This fluctuation in the amount of trade can be attributed in part to Japan's relatively weak economy since 1991. The Japanese government has donated food (principally rice) to the North via the World Food Programme (Kim 2001), and this food aid is expected to have a positive effect on ongoing negotiations between the North and Japan for establishing diplomatic relations. In the first half of 2001, imports from Japan exceeded $600 million (most of it rice), while exports to Japan were barely over $100 million (KOTRA 2001a).

In contrast to the appearance of South Korean dependency on the United States, the South's trade volume with Japan is 1.7 times larger than that with the United States. With the yen up 13 percent against the South Korean won in 1993 and 1994, Seoul was able to boost exports by 7.3 percent, helping to cut its overall trade deficit by nearly 70 percent, to $1.5 billion. But, as Korea is heavily dependent on Japan for capital goods and components for its exports, Japan's trade surplus with Korea ($4.7 billion through May 1994) widened (*Business Week* 1994a). This trade imbalance has continued, as the South Korean trade deficit with Japan was $11.3 billion in 2000, with imports of $31.8 billion and exports of $20.5 billion (KOTRA 2001a).

The IMF fund's bailout program mandated that the South Korean government open most markets to Japan. Since 1978, South Korea's import-diversification policy had been designed to redirect its trade deficit with Japan and had given preference to imports from countries with which it had more balanced trade relationships, by restricting the import of similar items from Japan (Lee 1999). In 1988, the number of banned Japanese products reached a peak of 344, including VCRs, large-screen TV sets, cameras, and cars. Since 1999, Japanese cultural products such as films and music have also been allowed to enter South Korean markets.

Trade between North Korea and China

In 1990, North Korea–China trade accounted for only 10.1 percent of total North Korean trade. However, the ratio and importance of trade with China increased to 30 percent in 1991, when China emerged as North Korea's largest trading partner. China provides North Korea with exports at favorable prices as well as other forms of aid. North Korea has posted substantial deficits in its trade with China since 1990. The cumulative trade balance deficit amounted to US$3.8 billion during the 1990s (total imports from China: US$5.1 billion; and total exports to China: US$1.3 billion). The reason why the trade balance deficit is so large is because North Korea imports major items like machinery, chemicals, textiles, and necessities, as well as strategic supplies (food and fuel). Meanwhile, its exports to China were very limited. It is projected that the North Korean trade balance deficit is not likely to improve for a while, because its products are gradually losing competitiveness in China, except for commodities (Chang 2001).

DEMOGRAPHIC AND SOCIAL ENVIRONMENT

Population

Koreans are changing. For example, they are getting bigger: fourteen-year-old [South] Korean boys in 1990 were five inches taller than those of 1965 (*The Economist* 1990c), and the average weight of thirteen-year-old males increased by 11 kilograms to 51.7 kilograms from 1980 to 2000. In 1910, the population of Korea was said to be over thirteen million, while in the early 1920s, it was just over seventeen million. A census in 1949 gave the population of South Korea as just over twenty million, compared to the current level of 47.5 million in 2001 with a 0.8 percent growth rate (United Nations Statistics Division 2001). The population of the North was about 23.7 million in 1999 with a 1.6 percent growth rate, and 61 percent of the population is in urban areas (United Nations Statistics Division 2001). See Table 8.6 for a comparison of population figures for North Korea and South Korea in various years.

Table 8.6

Population in Millions

Year	South Korea	North Korea
1945	16.0	9.9
1946	19.4	9.3
1953	21.6	8.5
1989	43.1	21.0
1992	43.7	22.3
2001	47.5	21.7
2002	47.6	22.4

Source: Byoung-Lo Philo Kim, *Two Koreas in Development* (New Brunswick, NJ: Transaction, 1992), 95; *Asia Source*, "Asia Profiles," October (available at www.asiasource.org/profiles); Economist Intelligence Unit, *Country Report: Korea* (London: Economist Intelligence Unit, 2003).

In 1962, the South Korean government introduced the national family planning program, which successfully reduced the annual population growth rate from 3 percent in the 1950s to 1.6 percent in the 1970s. Despite such efforts, the population of Korea has continued to grow. This growth will significantly increase a population density that is already the world's third highest, following Bangladesh and Taiwan (Whang 1991). Many Korean towns had "population clocks" that, by regularly showing the rate of population increase, were supposed to help slow it down (Hoare and Pares 1988). Traffic in the average Korean city was heavier than in Western cities in the 1990s, even though many people walked or rode bicycles in order to have greater flexibility of movement (Choe and Pitman 1993).

The school-age population (five to nineteen years of age) decreased from 35 percent of the population in 1980 to 21 percent in 2000, reversing the growth trend of the previous two decades (Korean National Statistical Office 2001a). The aged population has grown at an annual rate of about 3.7 percent, with those over age sixty-five comprising 7.3 percent of the population by 2000 (Korean National Statistical Office 2001a). Life expectancy at birth improved from fifty-three years in 1960 to seventy-three and seventy-two years in South and North Korea, respectively, in 1999 (United Nations Statistics Division 2001). The total fertility rate for the South was recorded as 4.2 in 1970 and 1.6 in 1999, while for the North it was 5.4 and 2.0 in the corresponding years (United Nations Statistics Division 2001).

Immigrants

Traditionally, there have been almost no ethnic divisions in South Korea, other than about 20,000 Chinese. Since the late nineteenth century, there has been a small Chinese minority, mainly concentrated in Seoul. Even this Chinese minority is dwindling, due in part to bureaucratic barriers such as for nationalization—one must have a Korean sponsor them, a good job, and over $60,000 in cash. The stores in the "Chinatown" area of Seoul (Myong-dong) now are run by Koreans (*The Economist* 1996). Other than for the diminishing Chinese minority, Korea is inhabited by people who display few regional differences, either physical or cultural. Only in Cheju are there speech patterns and cultural practices noticeably different from those elsewhere, and even these are minimal (International Strategies 1994). In the last five years of the twentieth century, though, 65,000 foreign households moved to South Korea, an increase of 281 percent over the 1995 level (Korean National Statistical Office 2001a).

Education

The adult literacy rates in both Koreas reached over 98 percent in 1988. North Korea has spent more time in ideological education of students (Kim 1992). In 1990, over 37 percent of South Koreans and 23 percent of North Koreans got at least some higher education (compared to 60 percent of Americans, 45 percent of Taiwanese, and only 22 percent of Britons) (*The Economist* 1990b). In 2000, nearly 70 percent of South Korean young adults obtained some college education (*The Economist* 2001e). Education has played an important role in South Korea's postwar modernization, primarily because of the almost blind faith in the value of educational attainment among Korean people (Whang 1991). Students in South Korea attend class 222 days a year compared to 180 in the United States and 188 in Canada (International Strategies 1994). This reverence for education (and the equating of education with the ability to pass standardized tests) is a holdover from Confucianism. In mathematics tests administered by the Educational Testing Service to thirteen-year-old students from a variety of countries, including the United States, Koreans ranked first in each of the five categories of problems (Clifford 1994). However, densely populated South Korea has not been able to offer free government education for every child at all levels. Six years of free schooling have been provided since 1959, and, more recently, free schooling was extended to middle school.

Traditionally, gratitude is shown to elementary and junior high teachers by parents in appreciation for the teachers' services to their children. At least once a semester, a parent (usually the mother) meets with the teacher to discuss the child's progress and then usually will hand over cash in a white envelope to the teacher. This gift giving is generally a token of appreciation, but on occasions, donating parents will expect certain favors for their child. Some teachers may take the gifts for granted and may go as far as suggesting to delinquent parents that they should visit the class (Chang, Chang, and Freese 2001).

Private education is pervasive, and spending on private education has not been sensitive to changes in income. Total expenditures for private education accounted for 6 percent of GDP in 1997; private education is a critical issue in Korean families, as Chung (1999) found that spending on private education could be as high as 45.6 percent of total family spending. Spending on private education did not decrease during the period of economic crisis and lowered incomes, unlike spending on clothing, food, and leisure (Chung 1999).

The emphasis on private education reflects concern with the quality of public education. More recently, Korean parents have become vocal about their concerns with the educational system, such as large classes, rote learning, and a rigid curriculum devised by bureaucrats. In 1998, parents successfully sued the government to allow high school students over the age of fifteen to study overseas, and since then, tens of thousands of Korean youngsters have headed to North America, Britain, or Australia to study. President Kim Dae Jung recognized the problem, as he had changed his Education Minister six times between the time he had taken office in 1998 and August 2001. The government has promised to spend $12.8 billion in the period 2001 to 2004 to hire 23,600 teachers, reducing high school class sizes from forty-three to thirty-five. Additionally, instructors are to be trained to teach more creativity and to encourage discussion (Moon 2001b).

Health Care

North Korea claims to spend far more effort and money on health and to have a much higher ratio of doctors to population than the South (twenty-four per 10,000 people compared to ten per

10,000 people). But the North's definition of "doctor" does not always make it clear whether he or she is a licensed doctor who has received a regular education at medical school (Hwang 1993).

In 1999, the South Korean Ministry of Unification estimated that there were 32.5 physicians and pharmacists per 10,000 North Koreans (compared to an estimated 31.5 in the South). In the South in 1999, there were 70,000 physicians, 17,300 dentists, 390,000 nurses, 49,200 pharmacists, and 11,300 Oriental medicine doctors. In 1992, the South had thirty-two hospital beds per 10,000 people (*Asian Business* 1992). By 1998, the number of hospital beds per 10,000 South Koreans had dropped to 5.1, compared to 2.9 in China and 16.2 in Japan (World Bank 2000). South Korea is able to provide all Korean citizens with comprehensive health protection, a pension for those who were hired in firms with five or more employees, and public support for those with low incomes.

Family Relations

Two-generation families have been common in South Korea, with three-generation families common in North Korea. However, in South Korea, the nuclear family is becoming the dominant type of family. During the 1975–1980 period, the numbers of one- and two-generation families increased by 47.2 percent and 19.1 percent, respectively, while three-generation families increased only 2.7 percent during the same period (Hwang 1993). The proportion of households with grandparents dropped from 19 percent of the households in 1970 to 9.5 percent in 1990. Consistent with global trends, household size in the South has continued to decrease. While a small majority of households in 1995 had four or more members, by 2000 that percentage had dropped to 44 percent. About 21 percent of Korean households had three members, 19 percent had two, and 16 percent were single-person households (Korean National Statistical Office 2001a).

In the North, families are organized into groups of five, sharing a bathroom, eating together, and spying on each other. Disloyalty to the government results in time in labor camps, while loyalty may be rewarded with party membership, which can lead to material benefits (Mallaby 1995). In South Korea, men marry around the age of twenty-seven, while women are married at about age twenty-four. Love matches have become quite common, with parents giving their approval for such marriages.

Traditional family values are still prominent. The family has an essential role as the forum of worship of the ancestors and guarantors of the ancestral lineage. Perpetuation of the male line is a duty of each new generation, as is the proper observance of mourning rites for deceased parents. Traditionally, a woman's chief function and desire has been to produce a male heir for her husband's family. The husband's family and its needs still take social precedence over the wife's. Headship of a family still passes to the eldest son, and it is his duty to look after a widowed mother and any unmarried siblings.

Preferences for sons are common to men and women in their fifties but greatly differ between men and women in their twenties: for those who are in their fifties, 82.4 percent of men preferred sons, and 81.3 percent of women preferred sons as well; for those in their twenties, 47.7 percent of men preferred sons, while only 15.4 percent of women preferred sons (*LG Ad* 1997).

Wives play the dominant decision-making role for most consumer decisions. Most purchases for husbands are made by their wives; joint husband–wife decisions about these purchases are less likely than decisions made by wives but are more likely than husband-only decisions. Wives are the clear decision makers for their own purchases, while children have primary say in purchases for themselves, followed by joint mother–child decision processes. These patterns are especially true for consumer nondurables, as joint husband–wife decision making is common in the case of consumer durables (*Media and Consumer Research* 2000). Na, Son, and Marshall also found that wives have a lot of say in decisions for themselves and the children, but decisions to buy items for general family use, such as a car, are still heavily male dominated. Overall, they concluded, "not only do Korean women have significant autonomy, but they are swiftly gaining more" (1998, 573).

The socialization of children among Koreans is a primary concern. Koreans have a great respect for learning, and Korean children are under tremendous pressure to attain high academic achievement. In fact, Hupp, Lam, and Jaeger (1992) report a study finding that 24 percent of Korean immigrant parents listed the most important reason for their immigration to the United States as being the desire to give their children a better education. Hupp et al. (1992), in a study comparing play activities of one-year-olds in Anglo and Korean-American families, found that Korean parents intervened significantly more during the play sessions than did the American parents. The Korean parents perceived that their children had a desire for more adult guidance and wanted to be less independent than did the American parents. Independent exploration was appreciated far more by Anglo parents.

Divorce is now legally permissible and is becoming more frequent, though it was initially viewed askance socially (Hoare and Pares 1988). Divorce is not regarded as shameful for the younger generation: about 70 percent of women in their twenties said divorce is not shameful, while about 46 percent of men in their twenties expressed similar views (*LG Ad* 1997).

In 1990, a court decided to allow divorced women access to their children. In 1993, a divorcee whose husband had died won custody of her children despite the fact that she was an adulteress. Previously, it was always assumed that the dead husband's parents had a prior claim. Adulterous women have also gained the right to receive alimony, after they have completed their prison terms for breaking their marriage vows. By 1994, one out of every seven South Korean marriages ended in divorce, a threefold increase since 1972 (*The Economist* 1994b).

Gender Relations

Females, in accordance with Confucian ideals, are given family-centered, informal instruction in the virtues of diligence, frugality, and chastity. Traditionally, a woman's existence was meaningful only in terms of her relationships with men: she was a man's daughter, a man's wife, and finally, if lucky, a man's mother (Hyde 1988). Legally, women are equivalent to men, as there is universal suffrage at twenty years of age (International Strategies 1994). The constitution of 1948 introduced a Family Law that sought to impose a measure of equality on customary family relations (Hoare and Pares 1988). Still, gender norms have been slow to change. For example, traditionally, wives did not accompany their husbands to parties, and they were frequently excluded from business entertainment (Choe and Pitman 1993).

In both North and South Korea, men occupy most top jobs in the civilian economy. This is particularly true in top jobs in government and industry. In 1992, women made up about 48 percent of the North Korean total workforce and about 45.5 percent of the industrial workforce in South Korea (Hwang 1993). The *Yearbook of Labor Statistics* in 1999 indicated that female participation had increased in South Korea to 49.5 percent, compared to 50.4 percent in Japan, 47.8 percent in France, 43.0 percent in the United Kingdom, and 59.8 percent in the United States.

In general, the female workforce is still quiescent, and a considerable discrepancy exists between male and female average wages. Women's problems used to stem partly from negative attitudes among both men and women toward female participation in work outside the home. (A nonworking wife was interpreted by some as a sign of a man's good financial standing.) Their

Table 8.7

Role of Women in the Workforce, Globally

Country	Seats in parliament (%)	Percent female administrators and managers (%)	Percent female professional and technical workers (%)
South Korea	4	4.7	32
Japan	9	9.5	44
United Kingdom	17	33	45
United States	13	44	53

Source: United Nations Development Programme, *Human Development Report 2000* (Oxford: Oxford University Press, 2000).

poor status is reflected in their relatively low earnings, and in their general absence from managerial and decision-making grades. For example, the Ministry of Labor noted that the female-to-male wage ratio in 1999 was 0.63, increasing from 0.53 in 1990. Table 8.7 shows the female participation rates in higher administration in 2000 across several countries. The likelihood of South Korean women participating in managerial roles is about half that of Japanese women, and far, far less than for women in the United Kingdom and the United States.

Men and women have very different views about gender norms (*LG Ad* 1997). Men have stronger beliefs that housekeeping is the woman's role, even if she is employed, than do women, and the divergence in this belief is greater among the younger generation: for those who are in their twenties, 45.6 percent of men responded that housekeeping is a woman's role, even if she is employed, while 15.4 percent of women responded similarly; for those who are in their fifties, 64.6 percent of men agreed, while 55 percent of women agreed. Both men and women agree that it is good for women to work outside the home; about 80 percent of women think it is good for a woman to have a job, which is higher by 20 percent than what men responded (*LG Ad* 1997).

There are other indicants that times are changing. During the summer of 1994, the hottest in Korea since the turn of the century, there was a fad among young South Korean women to wear cropped t-shirts that left the midriff exposed. A policeman in Kwangju arrested two twenty-somethings for flaunting their belly buttons in the street. What came as a surprise was that a judge threw the case out, ruling that the flashing of a female navel was not indecent. An equal opportunity law was passed in 1987, but the maximum penalty inflicted on firms that openly recruit only men for any post more responsible than tea-serving has been a modest one million won ($1,250). Bosses can draw two years in prison for paying different wages for the same work, but none has yet done so. In April 1994, a professor at Seoul National University was ordered to pay 30 million won ($37,500) in damages to a female assistant who claimed she had been fired for resisting his advances. This was Korea's first successful sexual harassment suit (*The Economist* 1994b).

Crime

The rate of violent crime in South Korea is relatively low: 1.4 murders per 100,000 population per year, virtually unchanged since 1960. In the United States, the rate is 9.4, in France 4.5. But the South's government became concerned about growing violence, and fifteen convicted killers who happened to be on death row at the time, were hanged in 1994 (*The Economist* 1994c). By 1999, the homicide rate in South Korea had increased to 2.1 per 100,000 people, compared to 1.1 in Japan, 2.8 in the United Kingdom, 3.7 in France, and 4.5 in Canada. A similar pattern was observed in the total number of crimes per 100,000 people: 3,748 in South Korea; 1,671 in Japan; 6,096 in France; 8,453 in Canada; and 9,823 in the United Kingdom (United Nations Human Development Report 1998).

CULTURAL ENVIRONMENT

The typical South Korean consumer lifestyle is still conservative and traditional. The majority of Korean consumers are conservative in their clothing consumption patterns, while fashion-oriented consumers are a minority (about 19 percent of the respondents; Park 1996). In general, the consumption patterns of most Korean consumers are conservative and rational and are dominated by traditional values (Park 1996). This convenience-value orientation in consumption patterns has been stable and even increased after the Korean economic crisis, which was associated with a decline in the consumption of fashionable products and well-known brands (Park and Choi 2000).

In contrast to the older generations, those between thirteen and twenty-three years old are more liberal, are very clear about what they like or dislike, are self-assertive and unwilling to follow others, value self-achievement, and are willing to compete in order to reach their goals. The younger generation is more fashion-oriented, is more variety-seeking, and tends to purchase compulsively. The fast diffusion of the Internet in Korea and the younger generation's heavy use of it appear to be a cause of the liberal attitudes and consumption patterns. Those who use the Internet and are classified as "netizens" showed a greater tendency toward liberal attitudes and materialistic consumption patterns than non-netizens, even when age was held constant (*LG Ad* 2000).

Inglehart (1997) found Korea to have the widest generation gap (in terms of values) in the forty-three countries he studied. Changing values over time was the topic of the study by Na and Cha (2000), who compared data obtained from twenty-year-olds and fifty-year-olds in 1979 and then in 1998. This approach allowed the investigation of generational differences as well as differences due to aging. Filial piety was of less import to the younger generation in 1979, but of much less import to it in 1998 (indicating an increasing generation gap). At the same time, there was evidence of a changing interpretation of "filial piety," as the younger group in 1998 was much more likely to see being successful as a proper means of showing filial piety.

Values that were seen as being more important than they were in 1979 were placing emphasis on self and family (as opposed to nation), correcting one's superiors, valuing modesty over ostentation, viewing the occurrence of "losers" as inevitable, deemphasizing female chastity, believing women should pursue careers, and believing that both sets of in-laws should be treated equally. Values that saw little change in importance were demanding correction rather than forbearing, choosing the future over the past, and perceiving traditional customs as being beneficial. Besides issues concerning filial piety, the values associated with the largest increases in the generation gap over the period studied were favoring distinctions based on function rather than hierarchy, the deemphasis of female chastity, and preference for pursuing a full lifestyle over a pure lifestyle (Na and Cha 2000).

Religion

The North Korean culture is characterized by the absence of any significant religion, an overflowing phenomenon by contrast in South Korea. Instead, Kim worship (the reverence for Kim Il Sung) took on a religious fervor, and in some homes, his picture stood on the altar where tablets of ancestors once stood (Kim 1992). Lee (1995) reported that this reverence of the North's leader is especially strong among the less educated, but that even the more educated never failed to respect their leader. North Koreans wear Kim badges on their lapels in the same way that Catholics wear crucifixes (Mallaby 1995). Kim (1998) noted that no other state in modern times has expended as much scarce human and natural resources in building so many monuments to Kim Il Sung; one Japanese estimate was as many as 50,000. At the International Friendship Exhibition, a marble palace in the hills, you can marvel at the over 100,000 gifts with which foreigners have shown their admiration for the father and son Dear Leaders, including a bulletproof limousine from Stalin (*The Economist* 2001g).

Two Christian churches opened in 1988 and one in 1989, and the estimates of the number of Christians in North Korea have varied widely from some 770 to 10,000 (Kim 1992). By 2001, the number of religious adherents had increased to 38,000. Cheondogyo had the most followers (15,000), and their status in the country was quite high. There were sixty Buddhist temples in the North, and an estimated 10,000 adherents. There were also an estimated 10,000 Christians in the North (most of them Protestants), and thirty ministers. There were an estimated 2,000 to 4,000 Roman Catholics, but only one Catholic church offering a simple mass for 100 to 200 followers, with no priest or nun present (www.unikorea.go.kr).

In South Korea in the early 1990s, religious adherents were estimated to be 48.6 percent Christian, 47.4 percent Buddhist, 3 percent Confucianist, plus small numbers of pervasive folk religion (Shamanism) and Cheondogyo (religion of the heavenly way) (International Strategies 1994). In 1999, the Korean Statistical Office estimated that 54 percent of the population was religious, with 49 percent of those being Buddhist, 35 percent Protestant, 13 percent Roman Catholic, 1.2 percent Confucians, 0.4 percent Won-Buddhist, and 0.1 percent Cheondogyo. The elderly are more likely to be Buddhist, while the youth are more likely to be Protestant.

Many Koreans, old and young, still cling to the age-old belief in spirit possession and destinies written in the stars. There are no statistics on how many share this faith. But one telling sign is that churches and wedding halls were booked solid months in advance for October 23, 1994, which fortune tellers touted as one of the luckiest dates ever for a wedding. Though most of the population is Buddhist or Christian, many hedge their bets, seeking help from other spiritual advisors too. The Reverend Chun Ji-Seok of the Christian Academy estimates three of ten Christians turn to shamans and fortune tellers in times of need (*Lincoln Journal Star* 1994).

One difference in the economic history of the two Koreas has been the growth of Christianity in the South and the development of more assertive and ambitious mind-sets among those adherents. Numbering only 1.2 million in 1957, the number for Christians is now similar to that for Buddhists. In contrast, Christian missionaries have failed to convert more than a scant 1 percent of the people in neighboring Japan. The popular explanation is that Koreans turn to the gospels because they have suffered so much. As an indication of the increasing role of Christianity, ex-President Kim Young Sam is a Presbyterian (*The Economist* 1994f).

Confucianism

The economic rise of East Asia has brought Confucianism much attention recently. Some academics have looked to culture for an explanation of the economic success and concluded that "Confucian ethics," stressing the claims of the community over the individual, are the key. Part religion, part ethical code, part social ritual, and part political philosophy, Confucianism remains an elusive concept. It has become a code word for a set of "Asian" values: commitment to education and family loyalty, and a quiescent attitude to authoritarian rule, where the government assumes the role of the father in a family. One reason for the reassertion of Confucian values is that people often turn back to old beliefs in times of rapid change. As divorce rates and delinquency rise in Asia, as voters become less acquiescent, so fathers and rulers insist that the old, obedient ways are best (*The Economist* 1995b).

The Confucian ethic is evident in the people's general attitudes. On the other hand, the generalization of Koreans as typical Asians may be a gross oversimplification. For example, Alston (1989), Dubinsky et al. (1991), Hupp et al. (1992), and West (1989) note that Asian countries, such as Japan and South Korea, should not be viewed as a single homogeneous entity with respect to business conduct.

The Confucian culture has been credited as being a major part of the remarkable success of South Korean development. One wonders how the same Confucian culture that is practiced in both Koreas can yield such different results. Confucianism as a religion is not actively practiced in either Korea today. One important aspect of Confucianism as an ideology is the emphasis placed on effort. Working hard is valued immensely, meaning that the actual process of being industrious is as important as the result. The same Confucian value system held by the two Koreas has produced two fundamentally different outlooks toward development. For example, Korea has historically emphasized the importance of the Confucian belief in scholarship over commerce and material things. Traditional Confucian ideology disdains commercial activities; this tradition was easily carried on in North Korea, where communism disdained commercial and service activities. People were mobilized not by material incentives but by moral exhortation. In South Korea, pluralistic values help explain the extraordinary commercial bustle, the materialism, and conspicuous consumption of the people. Christians have been somewhat overrepresented in the entrepreneurial population in South Korea, introducing the notion that commercial activities can lead to one's personal salvation (Kim 1992).

Confucianism is influential with Korean college students, but Western values are also being adopted. Korean students value acquiescence and modesty, are sensitive to others' appraisals, and base their behaviors on tradition and customs more than do Canadian college students. At the same time, Korean students pursue the realization of one's self-identity and are as present-time-oriented as Canadian students (Chae 1999).

Korean/Japanese Cultural Similarities and Differences

Westerners may tend to lump Japanese and Koreans together. Both cultures share Confucian traditions. For instance, like the Japanese, Koreans say of their society that "the nail that sticks out gets hammered down" (Clifford 1994). But, compared to the Japanese, Koreans are much franker and do not have the same degree of outward politeness. Koreans are more emotional, more openly distrustful, and more willing to act on that distrust (Clifford 1994).

Despite many outward similarities in business culture, Korea is not a second Japan. Korean companies are much more confrontational in their dealings with each other and with the government than their Japanese counterparts. Korean employees are also less loyal to their firms than the American image of Japanese workers. It is not unusual for Korean middle managers to work in several companies over the course of their careers (International Strategies 1994). This mobility may be due, in part, to the rapid growth of the Korean economy, creating competition for middle management personnel.

Further, business decision-making processes differ from those in Japanese firms. Unlike their Japanese counterparts, Korean companies are still young enough to be led firmly from the top. The Japanese system of *nemawashi* (coming to decisions by a sort of collective consent) is unknown (*The Economist* 1990c). For example, Lee (1989) asserts that Korean workers tend to

Table 8.8

Hofstede's Findings for Korea, Japan, and the United States

Dimension	Ranking of the country on the dimension		
	Korea	Japan	United States
Power distance	27/28	33	38
Uncertainty avoidance	16/17	7	43
Individualism	43	22/23	1
Masculinity	41	1	15

work within a top–down authoritarian structure and require a higher level of definition in their job structure to avoid suffering from role conflict than do Japanese workers.

Comparison on Hofstede's Cultural Dimensions

Hofstede (1984) compared work attitudes of IBM employees across fifty-three countries, uncovering four underlying dimensions: uncertainty avoidance, masculinity/femininity, individualism/collectivism, and power distance. As can be seen in Table 8.8, Korea and Japan are quite similar in terms of power distance and uncertainty avoidance and have higher levels than does the United States. On the other hand, Korea is much more collective than Japan, which is itself much more collective than the United States. Japan was found to be the most masculine country in the world, while Korea is relatively feminine, with the United States falling in between. ("Masculinity" in the Hofstede schema relates to an emphasis on work goals and work-related assertiveness as opposed to personal goals and nurturance.)

Interpersonal Interactions

In Korea, there are many rituals of courtesy, formality in behavior, and customs regulating social interactions. Hard work and piety are valued characteristics. Compliments and honors are graciously denied. Friendship is valued and respected. The Korean method of social intercourse consists of one pretending to like something though it is bad and pretending to dislike it though it is good (Kim 1975). Many decisions of Korean consumers are made under heavy influence from the group with which they are interacting, such as the extended family, neighbors, friends, co-workers, and even people in the overall society. For example, it is not unusual to find that many Korean people living in the same area (e.g., an apartment building) use the same brand of detergent (Lee and Green 1991).

Respect for Age

It is not a coincidence that the majority of Koreans like autumn best, while most Americans prefer spring. Philosophically speaking, spring is the time of youth, and autumn is the time of old age. Americans generally consider youth as the best time of life and accept old age with reluctance (Kim 1975). Reaching the age of sixty has long been a triumphant moment in a Korean's life. Respect and a large measure of personal freedom become one's due, whether male or female. This used to be the age when women could start to smoke in public. The sense of pride was especially strong in earlier days when average life expectancy was lower. Now, with life expectancy over seventy, the sixtieth birthday is no longer so remarkable, but it is still a time for congratulation.

Financial support of the elderly has traditionally been left to families but will increasingly be met now by a network of pension systems. Not all old people will be cared for by families, and day centers and residential homes started appearing in the late 1980s (Hoare and Pares 1988).

Relationship with Nature

Western people look for the beauty discovered in humanity, while nature is the background for humanity. Koreans have the opposite perspective. While most Western magazine covers show human beings, most Korean magazine covers show nature without a human being in the background (Kim 1975). Despite this profound respect for nature, air and water pollution is a problem in South Korea, especially in the densely populated cities. Over 80 percent of the people live in cities (World Bank Indicators 2000). Environmental pollution issues have attracted attention from the Korean government and from consumers. The Korean government introduced Climate Mark in 1992, which informs consumers about products with low levels of contamination; Recycle Mark in 1995, which discerns recyclable products; and the Energy Efficiency Rating in 1995, which gives the energy efficiencies of electronics and automobiles. The Energy Efficiency Rating is used the most by Korean consumers followed by Climate Mark and Recycle Mark. Environmental issues are acknowledged more by younger, more educated, and high-income-earning consumers, who are, in turn, more sensitive to the purchase of contamination-free products (Kim and You 2000).

CHANGES IN THE MACROMARKETING MIX

Comparison of the Two Koreas

In North Korea, heavy industry is in the domain of the central government, which also manages large factories producing consumer goods, such as textile mills. However, most consumer good and food-processing industries are run by local governments. The production of television sets, refrigerators, wristwatches, clothes, and other consumer goods such as toothpaste show remarkable contrasts between the two Koreas. South Korea by far surpasses North Korea in the production of such consumer goods (Kim 1992).

The January 1995 issue of *Shin Dong-A* presented a comparison of the two economies (Table 8.9). Marketing in North Korea occurs in accordance with the state plan. The types of marketing are classified according to different ownership types, with differing price systems applying to each. For example, different wholesale price structures exist for transactions between two state-run enterprises and from those transactions between a state-run enterprise and a cooperative organization. Markets are divided into state-run markets, cooperative markets, and farmers' markets. In the state-run market, wholesale trade of industrial products dominates, with occasional retail transactions also occurring. The cooperative market includes the farmers' cooperative market, the producers' cooperative market, and the marine products cooperative market, as well as such entities as barbershops and public bathhouses (Hwang 1993).

To some extent, North Korea's opening of markets has resembled China's. But the Chinese have policies designed to activate the domestic economy by expanding the market price system. In the early 1990s, Pyongyang took to reform its domestic economy, which comprises:

- the expansion of farmers' markets;
- direct sales stores;

Table 8.9

Comparison of the Two Korean Economies in 1992

Item	Unit	North Korea	South Korea
Oil imports	10,000 tons	152	6,930
Crops produced	10,000 tons	427	621
Rice	10,000 tons	153	533
Fish	10,000 tons	114	329
Steel	10,000 tons	179	2,865
Cement	10,000 tons	475	4,265
Fertilizer	10,000 tons	139	399
Cars	10,000	1.04	172.5
Telephone lines	10,000	40	1,529
International airlines	Number	4	51

Source: Shin Dong-A, Kim Jung Il and North Korean Encyclopedia (Seoul: Dong-A Il Bo, 1995).

- the recent permission for working people to buy goods at the Nakwon ("Paradise") stores in urban areas;
- the introduction of a productivity-linked payment system in the production of consumer goods;
- an autonomous business management system in factories; and
- a material incentives system (Hwang 1993).

Basic Consumption in the Two Koreas

The lack of data on North Korea often results in the reliance upon defectors for a portrayal (possibly biased) of conditions there. Lee (1995) reports that flea markets operate every ten days (the first, eleventh, and twenty-first of each month), and farmers are allowed to barter their possessions there. However, products of greater value are likely to be traded in the black market, which is run largely by the small Korean Chinese minority.

For the South, statistics are more abundant. Table 8.10 shows how the expenditure patterns have changed from 1973 to 2000. Penetration of consumer durables from a nationwide survey in January 1994 was: color TV, 99.5 percent; audio systems, 81 percent; refrigerators, 99.3 percent; VCRs, 75 percent; washing machines, 92 percent; air conditioners, 14 percent; personal computers, 33 percent; and cars 45 percent.

In spite of the economic crisis, South Korea saw huge increases in the acceptance of technology at the end of the twentieth century. For example, the number of mobile phone subscribers increased from fifteen per 100 persons in 1997 to thirty in 1998 and then to fifty in 1999. Thus, Korea had a higher penetration rate of mobile phones than much of the developed world: forty-five per 100 Japanese, thirty-six per 100 French, thirty-one per 100 Americans, twenty-three per 100 Canadians, and 3.4 per 100 Chinese (Korean National Statistical Office 2001b). This growth in mobile phone users may reflect Korea's (possible temporary) leadership in third-generation mobile telecom, using the CDMA2000 format. It appears that Japan and Europe see a rival technology (W-CDMA) as the superior format (*The Economist* 2002).

Subscriptions to cable television in Korea more than doubled in the period between 1998 and 2000 to 2.5 million households. The number of personal computers in Korean homes has also increased rapidly, from twenty-one per 1,000 persons in 1992 to sixty-two per 1,000 persons in 1999. Koreans had far fewer passenger cars per 1,000 people (165) than other countries in the

Table 8.10

Composition of Household Consumption Expenditures (%)

Item	South Korea	North Korea
Food and drink	36.0	44.0
Clothing and footwear	7.6	33.0
Housing	20.0	0.7
Fuel and power	6.5	4.0
Household equipment	4.2	2.4
Health, education, etc.	25.7	15.9

Source: Byoung-Lo Philo Kim, *Two Koreas in Development* (New Brunswick, NJ: Transaction, 1992), p. 99.

developed world (486 in the United States, 455 in Canada, 384 in Japan, and 392 in the United Kingdom) (Korean National Statistical Office 2001b).

Food

In 1985, the World Bank estimated that the North's food intake was slightly higher, at 130 percent of the daily calorie requirement per capita, than that of the South, at 125 percent. In the North, food is either rationed by the government or distributed in rural areas according to each member's work contribution (Hwang 1993). *The Economist*'s review of North Korea as a tourist destination noted that the cuisine, even for paying customers, is very bland, unlike the "fiery and exhilarating" cuisine of the South. Shortages of even the most basic ingredients meant that the North's only contribution to world cuisine is a bland version of *kimchi*—"a cabbage dish that is supposed to be hot, but in this case isn't" (*The Economist* 2001g, 51).

As Table 8.11 indicates, the percentage of income spent on food in the South declined steadily in the period from 1970 to 2000. The total number of daily calories increased from 2,485 in 1980 to 2,853 in 1990, and to 2,941 in 1999. This compared favorably to the 1998 levels in the Philippines (2,288), Thailand (2,463), and India (2,466), but fell short of levels for Japan (2,874), China (2,973), Canada (3,167), the United Kingdom (3,256), France (3,541), and the United States (3,757) (Korean National Statistical Office 2001b).

The majority of Korean consumers favor domestic foods, while those who favor dining out and foreign foods are a minority (Park 1996). Food consumption outside the home became relatively less common during the economic crisis but has become an increasing phenomenon, as, in 2000, expenditures on meals outside the home accounted for 39 percent of the consumption for food and drinks. Most of the expenditures were for Korean, fast food, and snack bars, as only 2.4 percent and 1.2 percent were spent at Chinese and Western restaurants, respectively (Korean National Statistical Office 2001b). By 1993, 66 percent of households in the South had eaten at fast-food restaurants, though there was strong variance across age groups (36 percent of those in their fifties versus 87 percent of those in their twenties). KFC was the most likely to have been experienced (56 percent), followed by Pizza Hut (40 percent) and McDonald's (38 percent) (Choe and Pitman 1993).

In 1999, Lotteria was the market leader with sales of $270 million, followed by Our Home ($235 million), Samsung Everland ($185 million), Cheiljedang ($153 million), McDonald's ($146 million), BBQ ($138 million), Pizza Hut ($138 million), KFC ($108 million), Popeye's ($90 million), and Shinsegae ($83 million). Lotteria had one-third of the fast-food market in 1999, followed by McDonald's with 18 percent, BBQ with 17 percent, KFC with 13 percent, Popeye's with 11 percent, Burger King with 5 percent, and Hardees with 2 percent. In the relatively small (but growing) Western family restaurant market, TGI Friday's was the market leader with 25 percent, followed by Bennigans (18 percent), Cocos (18 percent), SkyLark (14 percent), Marche (8 percent), Tony Roma's (5 percent), Outback (5 percent), VIPs (5 percent), and Sizzler (4 percent). Pizza Hut had nearly two-thirds of the pizza market, followed by Pizza Mall with 13 percent and Domino's with 11 percent (Korea Super/Chain Store Association 2000).

Housing

All housing in the North is either state or cooperatively owned (Hwang 1993). The government controls the allocation of housing, which varies according to the person's position or rank. Rent varies depending on the size of the house, but constitutes only about 0.3 percent of living expenses (and in no case should exceed 3.0 percent). In rural areas, houses are provided free (Peace Institute 1997). The quality of houses in North Korea is far lower than that in South Korea. According to a videotape report, the two-bedroom apartment of one upper-middle-class family was strikingly small, and eight family members including four relatives lived there (Kim 1992). Most dwellings in the North are either flats or (rented) terraced houses. The living space per general worker family is 26.4 square meters (8 pyong), and this is equivalent to 5.3 square meters (1.6 pyong) per individual, varying from 4.5 square meters for ordinary citizens to 13.2 square meters for party officers (Peace Institute 1997). This compares to the housing space levels (in square meters) in South Korea: 1970, 35.9; 1975, 41.4; 1980, 45.8; 1985, 45.3; 1995, 80.5; and 2000, 81.5. The living space per capita was 6.8, 8.2, 10.1, 11.1, 17.2, and 20.1 square meters per individual (Hwang 1993; Korea National Statistics Office 2001a).

In housing decisions in South Korea, the majority values convenience, while those who favor aesthetic values are a minority (Park 1996). In 2000, 50 percent of the South Korean population lived in a house, while 37 percent lived in an apartment. Apartment living is increasing relative to house residence. The average number of rooms per household was 3.4 in 2000, up from 3.1 in 1995 (Korean National Statistical Office 2000). At the same time, the number of residents per room has decreased from 2.3 in 1975 to 1.8 in 1985 and to 1.1 in 1995. Similarly, the presence of a modern kitchen increased from 18 percent in 1980 to 53 percent in 1990 and to 85 percent in 1995. Access to running water in the home increased from 42 percent in 1974 to 67 percent in 1985 and to 90 percent in 1995 (Ha 1999).

Advertising

The remainder of the discussion of the macromarketing mix will concern only South Korea. The basic media for advertising in the South are, in order of importance, newspapers, television, radio, magazines, and movies. Total advertising expenditures in 2000 were 5.9 trillion won (an increase of 27 percent from 1999). Newspapers' share was 36 percent (down from 44 percent in 1992), TV 28 percent (up from 25 percent in 1992), with radio and magazines having 4 percent and 3 percent, respectively (down from 5 percent for each in 1992) (Cheil Communications 2001; Han and Chang 1994). Ad expenditures have varied by industry, with TV being the dominant medium for advertising food and beverages, drugs, clothing, cosmetics and detergents, computers, and home appliances, while services, entertainment, books, construction, education, and retailers spend more on newspaper advertising (Cheil Communications 2001; Han and Chang 1994).

Koreans get their news (in order of frequency) from TV, newspapers, magazines, and radio.

Teenagers rely on TV more than do other age groups. The ad exposure rate for males is highest on TV followed by newspapers, magazines, and radio, while females are exposed to more radio ads than magazine ads. TV penetration is 99.9 percent, and 48.7 percent own more than two TVs. Koreans watch TV an average of two hours and 35 minutes a day on weekdays, three hours and 37 minutes on Saturday, and four hours and 22 minutes on Sunday. In general, dramas are the most watched shows, followed by news, variety shows/entertainment, sports, and movies. Males in their thirties or older watch news most; males in their twenties watch sports most; and males in their teens watch variety shows/entertainment most. Females in their twenties or older watch dramas most, while females in their teens watch variety shows/entertainment most. There is disagreement between husbands and wives as to the perception of who has greater voice over channel selection: husbands across all age groups think they have greater voice than do their spouses; wives in their twenties and fifties think they have greater voice, while wives in their thirties and forties think their husbands have greater voice. Mothers perceive children have more influence on channel selection than do fathers (*Media and Consumer Research* 2000).

The political, financial, and society sections of the newspaper are the favorite sections for males in their thirties or older; females in their thirties or older prefer the society and financial sections; and both males and females in their teens and twenties prefer the entertainment and sports sections. The newspaper ad exposure rate is higher for females (59.3 percent) than males (47.3 percent). For males, the ad exposure rate is highest for teens and decreases with age; for females, the ad exposure rate is highest for those in their thirties followed by those in their twenties, forties, teens, and fifties (*Media and Consumer Research* 2000).

Among the more than 100 advertising agencies approved by the Korea Broadcasting Advertising Corporation (KOBACO), over thirty agencies are in-house (affiliates of local business conglomerates or parent companies), and half of the top thirty agencies in terms of billing amount are in-house agencies of chaebols. Over twenty agencies have foreign-investment or technical cooperation, among which six are locally established multinational agencies in joint-venture arrangements. Broadcasting advertising has been wholly controlled by the KOBACO, which designates official broadcasting ad agencies every year and pays agency commissions that it determines. In 1992, ninety-five agencies were selected as official KOBACO agencies, including fourteen newcomers (International Strategies 1994).

The Korea Newspaper Advertising Association approves official advertising agencies for newspapers every year. As of December 31, 1991, the number of designated agencies was forty-six. About sixty newspapers and 2,200 magazines are available in the local market. Han and Shavitt (1994) performed a content analysis of magazines in Korea (*Wolgan Chosun* and *Yosong Donga*) and comparable U.S. magazines (*Newsweek* and *Redbook*). U.S. ads were rated significantly higher in individualism, while Korean ads were rated higher in collectivism. In an experiment, U.S. subjects were more persuaded when the ads presented individualistic rather than collectivistic appeals, whereas Koreans were more persuaded overall when the ads presented collectivistic rather than individualistic appeals. Wilcox et al. (1996) failed to replicate this finding.

Keown, Jacobs, and Ghymn (1993) performed a systematic content analysis of Korean, U.S., Japanese, and Chinese mass media advertising. Korean television ads were more likely to promote nondurables than was the advertising for the other countries. Korean radio ads were also more likely to promote nondurables than were U.S. or Chinese radio advertising, but the levels were similar to those of the Japanese. Korean newspaper advertising was more than twice as likely as the newspaper advertising in the other countries to promote consumer services.

Both Japanese and Korean television ads were about twenty seconds long, compared to thirty-second ads in the United States (with Chinese ads ranging between twenty and sixty seconds).

The nature of Korean television advertisements differed from the other three countries; they informed the viewer of attributes and functions, while the ads in the other countries informed of the existence of the product and its attributes. Like Japanese television ads, demonstration formats were common in Korean television ads. Testimonials were used less frequently in Korean television ads as compared to Japanese and U.S. ads (Keown et al. 1993).

Nearly all Korean television ads show or name the product, and the logo is shown in 84 percent of the ads. Voice-overs are used in most ads, with the voice-over being male in two-thirds of the cases. In fact, the product is more likely to be shown in Korean ads (97 percent of the time) than in the other three countries, and the product is shown in use in 50 percent of the cases. People are used in commercials 60 percent of the time, with only males in the ads or a mixture of males and females (female-alone presentations occur only 7 percent of the time). Price is mentioned more (63 percent of the time), but slogans are used less than in Japanese and U.S. television ads. Korean advertising had about half the informational cues of U.S. commercials (Keown et al. 1993).

A survey conducted by KOBACO indicated that about 60 percent of Koreans think advertising is useful, and 73 percent think that advertising is entertaining, while 47 percent perceive advertising is untrustworthy, and 70 percent think that there are too many advertisements (*Ad Information* 2001).

Context in Advertising

Gudykunst, Yoon, and Nishida (1987), Hall (1976), and Kim (1985) indicated that Korean language and communication are high context, meaning that indirect and ambiguous messages tend to be utilized. Kim, Pan, and Park (1998) operationalized the "context" construct, and found that Koreans, as compared to Americans, have more difficulty thinking in new and unfamiliar situations, feel that things are changing too fast, are not excited about learning new ways to think, and would try to avoid situations where in-depth thinking is required. Taylor, Wilson, and Miracle (1995) found that low context brand differentiating messages were present in only about 3 percent of the commercials coded. They found that Korean students like brand differentiating messages as well as more high context messages, but it may be that they were attracted by the novelty of the approach.

Use of Humor

Alden, Hoyer, and Lee (1993) found that Korean television ads had a lower percentage of humor (57 percent) than did those from Germany (92 percent), Thailand (82 percent), and the United States (69 percent). In those studies, humor was defined as incongruent contrasts. The two nations high on Hofstede's collectivism dimension (Korea and Thailand) had a substantial number of humorous ads with three or more central characters, whereas the two that were low (United States and Germany) had substantially fewer ads with three or more characters. Further, the cultures high on power distance (Korea and Thailand) had more ads with characters of unequal status than countries low on this dimension (Germany and the United States).

Distribution

Retail distribution in South Korea is complicated, as the majority of outlets are small one-family stores, stalls in markets, or street vendors. However, there are many middle-sized department stores in Seoul and Pusan, and the chain store and supermarket concept developed rapidly in the

Table 8.11

Trends in Household Consumption in South Korea, 1973–2000

	Percentages		
Item	1973	1992	2000
Food and drink	48.7	30.4	27.4
Clothing and footwear	10.1	8.0	5.6
Housing	2.7	4.2	3.5
Utilities	6.4	4.1	5.3
Furniture/home appliances	2.1	5.5	3.6
Medical care	2.9	5.4	4.3
Education/entertainment	10.9	13.3	16.4
Transportation/communication	5.0	9.2	16.0
Other	11.1	20.1	17.8
Total	100.0	100.0	100.0

Source: Korean National Statistical Office, "Population and Household." 2001 (available at www.nso.go.kr.eng).

1990s. In 1994, there were approximately 12,000 supermarkets throughout the country, including 2,400 in Seoul; however, none of the supermarkets was truly large by common U.S. standards. Foreign participation is prohibited in seven service sectors, including retailing of tobacco, antiques, arts, and publicly consumed alcoholic beverages (International Strategies 1994).

Wholesalers have tended to dominate the distribution channels and often dictate terms to manufacturers. It is common for the wholesaler to obtain considerably longer credit terms from the manufacturer than are extended to the retailer, sometimes allowing the wholesaler to earn substantial interest on the differences (International Strategies 1994). The distribution industry represents 10 percent of South Korea's GDP and 18 percent of employment as of 2000. However, the industry was slow to grow, as it has been regarded as a nonproductive industry for a long time. As late as 1994, 91 percent of retail businesses employed fewer than two persons, and 78 percent of the businesses operated had floor-space smaller than 10 pyong (about 33 square meters) (International Strategies 1994).

The dominant retail type in the South is the department store, with total sales five times greater than convenience stores and almost 100 times greater than supermarkets. Of department store sales, 45 percent is from clothing, 19 percent food and beverage, and 8 percent electronics (*Korea Chamber Weekly*, July 25, 1994). In 2001, there were over ninety department stores in Korea, with Lotte having the most (fourteen), followed by Hyundai (twelve), New Core (eleven), Shinsegae (seven), and Galleria (seven) (Korea Department Stores Association 2001).

New types of businesses, such as discount stores, general merchandise stores, or hypermarkets, have been introduced. In May 1989, 7-Eleven opened its first store in Korea to become the first foreign convenience store, followed by Lawson and Circle K. The opening of discount stores was initiated by Price Club in 1994; at the time, this was the result of a joint venture between Shinsegae and Costco. This was followed by the entry of Macro and Carrefour in 1996, and by Home Plus in 1997, a joint venture between Samsung and Tesco. WalMart entered the Korean retail industry by merging with Macro in 1998 (Lee and Shin 2001; Nakarmi 1995). In 2001, there were over 200 discount stores in Korea, with E-Mart having the most (thirty-four), followed by Carrefour (twenty-one), Magnet (twenty), Kim's Club (twenty), Home Plus (eight), Wal-Mart (eight), Hanaro Mart (five), Costco (five), and Grand Mart (five).

TV home shopping was introduced to the Korean market in 1995 and has been successful because of the increasing penetration of credit cards, the growth of the cable TV audience, the relatively low prices, and the convenience offered. LG home shopping and CJ39 home shopping took the early lead, but now face competition from Hyundai home shopping, Woori home shopping, and Nongsusan TV. Internet sales are expected to increase rapidly, as the number of Internet users in Korea has grown rapidly (Korean Department Stores Association 2001).

However, expensive land prices and the unique environment of the local distribution industry may be negative factors for foreign companies planning to start any large-scale operations in Korea. The Korean government deregulated restrictions on land acquisition in 1993. In terms of construction, the restrictions on the construction of sales facilities larger than 40,000 square meters were removed in 1994 under the "Metropolitan Area Maintenance Plan Law" (International Strategies 1994). In addition to these structural barriers, foreign retailers have to deal with Korean ethnocentrism, which results in more positive attitudes toward domestic retailers than toward foreign ones (Lee and Shin 2001). Similarly, Hong and Yi (1992) and Ulgado and Lee (1998) found that Koreans place more importance on the country of manufacture than do Americans.

Liberalization of investment in wholesale/retail business may prevent further trade distortions caused by the distribution network. Some major Korean department stores are linked to chaebols, which are also often manufacturers of consumer goods carried in the stores. Consequently, they are interested primarily in selling imported goods that complement their own product lines. Other manufacturers have set up franchised distributors.

CHANGING TRENDS

Intellectual Property Protection

One of the most serious problems for U.S. business in South Korea has been the protection of intellectual property. In 1992, South Korea was placed on the priority watch list for its lax protection of intellectual property rights (IPR), and enforcement remains a problem in several important areas, including copyrights, three-dimensional characters, and confidentiality of required government documentation. The U.S. government has pressured the Korean government to recognize the need for better protection of intellectual property, and, as a result, several task forces were formed to root out piracy of software and trademarks and other IPR infringements (International Strategies 1994). While Koreans counterfeit foreign brands, at least they do it well. One Singaporean informant on the detection of counterfeits by consumers noted that "Korea is known to be the best at producing exquisite imitation goods. Hong Kong is second followed by Thailand" (Gentry et al. 2001). Similarly, a Malaysian Chinese female in Singapore praised the quality of Korean counterfeits:

> The wallets nowadays are better replicates of the originals and are made from real leather. Besides, they are not really that cheap as well. [How much did your wallet cost?] About S$50. But the quality of the fake Prada wallets here in Singapore as not as good as the ones in Hong Kong and Korea. I bought a Louis Vuitton wallet from Korea three years ago and the leather is still good. (Gentry et al. 2002)

Also, a white British male in his mid-thirties claimed to be somewhat of an expert on counterfeits, and he liked those from Korea:

I have come across better and closer replicas in some Asian countries. I have traveled quite a bit in Asia and I can tell you that some countries are better known than others in counterfeiting products. [Can you give me some examples?] Well, countries like Thailand, Korea, and Hong Kong have pretty good quality counterfeits while the ones in China and Indonesia are very poorly made. [What about Singapore?] Not really fantastic, I am afraid.

Changing Technology

One of the South's assets for building future growth is its engineering population. As the Korea Institute for Industrial Economics and Trade (KIET) pointed out, in 1994 there were almost eighty engineers per 100,000 Koreans, compared to seventy-two in Japan and forty-one in the United States (*Business Week* 1994b). Signs of technological progress are common. Huge machines are eating through the hills south of Seoul to make way for a track that will carry Europe's famous *trains à grande vitesse*. The trains will link Seoul with Pusan, 270 miles south, at a projected cost of $13.4 billion. Additional new technology included a $5 billion Seoul airport at Inchon (now completed), thirty new power plants, including several nuclear ones (total investment of $50 billion), and a $1.2 billion mobile telecom network (Holstein 1994).

Some of the rush to new technology is confronting Koreans with cultural problems. For example, cable television has come to Seoul, providing access to movies, sports, home shopping, and news twenty-four hours a day. Satellite dishes are also becoming common, bringing Japan's NHK and Hong Kong's STAR-TV into homes. The government is attempting to limit culture shock by requiring that cable channels must have at least 70 percent domestically produced programming, while sports and documentary channels have a 50 percent quota (*Lincoln Journal Star* 1995).

CONSUMER ISSUES

There is little "consumer culture" in the North, even for tourists with money. Most store shelves are relatively empty, with the only readily available items being books written by Kim Jong Il (*The Economist* 2001g). Our discussion of consumer issues in the South tends to focus on differences rather than similarities. To some extent, there is value in this approach, as it may reduce tendencies on the part of Western marketers to be ethnocentric. However, similarities have been reported as well. Hafstrom, Chae, and Chung (1992) found that several consumer decision-making styles used by young U.S. consumers are similar to those used by young Korean consumers. Lee and Green (1991) found that U.S. and Korean students identified the same set of six salient attributes with regard to their purchase of sneakers: price, style, comfort, brand, durability, and color. In general, research has consistently found evidence of a relatively homogeneous youth market globally, including studies comparing Korean and U.S. youth markets.

Information Search

Whang and Min (1978) found that consumers in the market for refrigerators considered very few brands, visited few stores, and relied heavily on neighbors and family for information. On the surface, this would indicate lower levels of consumer search by Koreans. However, Olshavsky, Moore, and Lim (1988) noted the role that structural forces play:

- Only four brands of refrigerators were available in Seoul and few brands were imported.
- Some types of in-store information (i.e., point-of-purchase materials and catalogs that sys-

tematically display the available brands, models, and product characteristics) available in the United States were not available in Korea.

- The average household size was far greater in Korea than in the United States.
- Exclusive dealership for refrigerators was more common in Korea, making the distance to stores greater.
- There was little price variation across such dealerships.
- There was far greater reliance on mass transportation and less family car ownership in Korea.

While the retail market in South Korea has changed greatly since the Olshavsky et al. (1988) study was conducted, all indications are that Korean consumers still search systematically, similarly to most consumers in the developed world.

Innovativeness

In a study of college-aged consumers in five countries (Korea, the United States, Senegal, India, and Thailand), Tansuhaj et al. (1991) found Koreans to be more willing to adopt new technological products but less willing to adopt new media products, entertainment offerings, and fashion products. Similarly, Koreans indicated that they were less likely to buy new products, less likely to seek advice about new products (with the exception of Thais), and less likely to give advice about new products. Characteristics offered as explanations for these findings were that, among the five cultures, Koreans had relatively high levels of fatalism, traditionalism, and religious commitment. While these findings no longer describe the youth market in South Korea, we believe that they are still applicable to the older generation.

Gift Giving

Koreans' strong motivation not to "lose face" is reflected in their consumption behavior. They exhibit a strong tendency to purchase a product with price, brand, and packaging that match their social position and reputation in order not to lose face. For example, in gift-giving behavior, Koreans usually purchase products as gifts that are expensive enough to match their income or the receiver's status so that the gifts can maintain the face of the receiver, and so that the giver does not lose face at the same time (Lee and Green 1991). Teachers receive gifts from children and parents, who feel indebted to them. The hierarchical gift-giving practices in Japan can also be found in Korea. In contrast, Americans tend to exchange gifts with only close family members and friends, and do not usually give gifts to their superiors (Green and Alden 1988). Park (1998) found that, relative to Americans, Koreans report more gift occasions, a wider exchange network, more frequent giving of practical gift items, more social pressure to reciprocate, and more frequent workplace gift giving.

Howe (1988) observed that entertaining guests in Korea was usually more lavish than the host can really afford in order to save the host's face as well as the guest's. Usually, gifts should not be opened in the presence of the giver and should always be wrapped, especially if the gift is money. Gift giving is considered nothing more than a display of good manners and only spoken thanks is required in return. If someone gives a substantial gift—something that required some time and thought to buy—it is good manners for the giver to apologize for its insignificance, whatever its value. This is intended to relieve the recipient from feeling indebted. One of the most distinctive differences in gift giving is that Koreans use cash gifts much more often than do Americans. For example, it is conventional to give a cash gift for weddings and funerals. Also, it is common for Korean adults to give some money to children or very old family members when they visit the home of people with whom they have a very close relationship. Such a gesture is perceived as an expression of kindness and thoughtfulness. It is a Korean custom to give money to children on New Year's Day when they bow deeply and say the New Year's blessing to their parents, relatives, and close adults (Howe 1988).

Social Roles

Lee and Green (1991), in a study of sneaker purchases, found that U.S. and Korean respondents identified friends and family as two of the most influential referent individuals or groups in the purchase of sneakers. But the third influential referent for Koreans was the store salesperson, while it was the boy/girl friend for the U.S. respondents. The social atmosphere in Korea discouraged students from having extensive interaction with the opposite sex during the college period. Also, Lee and Green (1991) found that social norms are more important than attitude in the determination of behavioral intentions for Koreans, while U.S. respondents use attitude as the primary determinant (in the purchase of sneakers). The relative importance of social norms would seem to be very applicable in the current Korean marketplace.

FUTURE TRENDS

Reunification

The overriding future concern for all Koreans is the reunification of the two Koreas. Reunification, whatever its timing and however it occurs, will come. Whether it comes with a bang or a whimper, it will change the country profoundly. As noted earlier, both the North and the South have made some conciliatory gestures. Lucky Goldstar was asked to take over the North's largest steelworks, as North Korea needs the trade and investment. It already has a special economic zone designed for foreigners, although, observers note, it is in the far north, well away from big centers of population.

The biggest obstacle to more trade and investment may be opinion in Seoul. Conservatives worry that the North's regime will be propped up by South Korean companies and that technology transferred to Pyongyang could be used to guide missiles more accurately on to Seoul. For its part, the North continues to rattle sabers. For example, in February 1995, its defense ministry announced that the North had produced and deployed along the border a new kind of tank and some new artillery, and that they were building submarines and high-speed hovercraft. There is evidence that the South is still very tense. In 1994, after the death of Kim Il Sung, some southern students built altars to him. While most in the South saw this as harmless folly, the government incarcerated the altar-builders (*The Economist* 1995b).

However, the South has paid careful attention to the economic problems associated with the German reunification and apparently is not interested in driving the North's economy to ruin (Hwang 1993). In order to create the North's economic dependence on the South, there has been an effort to create a "Greater Korea," which also includes neighboring regions of China and Russia, where three million ethnic Koreans live. Already, signs in China's Shandong Province, directly across the Yellow Sea from the Korean peninsula, are written in Korean, as the number of Korean companies there increases. This so-called *Nordpolitik* strategy is merging technology and capital from the South with the rich natural resources of Northeast Asia. The inclusion of the North in the concept of Greater Korea is evidenced in such dealings as the plan to lay a gas pipeline from Yakutsk in eastern Russia to South Korea, through North Korea. Daewoo's Kim

Woo Chung was able to persuade former Russian President Boris Yeltsin, former South Korean President Roh Tae Woo, and North Korea's leader Kim Il Sung to agree to the transaction (Nakarmi, Brady, and Curry 1992). The dynamics of the two Koreas' relationship continues to be increasingly complex; in 1996, the North had to acknowledge the sending of spies via submarine to the South and then saw one of its highest officials, Hwang Jang Yop, defect to the South via Beijing (*The Economist* 1997a).

Despite subtle preparation economically for reunification, there is recognition that the process in Korea is likely to be much more complex than in Germany. There were at least four West Germans to share the burden of each East German, but South Korea has only two people for every North Korean. A study conducted at Korea University put the cost of moving the North's economy to the South's level at $1.2 trillion, four times South Korea's GNP at the time (Mallaby 1995). "The Germans argue that they will need at least a generation to alleviate the problem. Our situation is much, much worse than Germany's" (Kim 1994, 91).

There is much economic incentive for reunification, as the two Koreas have always offered each other what is needed. Before the division of Korea, northern Korea had 75 percent of the heavy industry, while southern Korea had almost 75 percent of the light industry. Today, the specific problems faced by each state are "complementary"; that is, they have the potential to be each other's best markets. For example, in trade, South Korea could probably become more efficient by importing North Korean fishing and mining products, while the North could import capital and technology from the South. The North could probably become more efficient by reducing its agricultural population. Capitalist South Korea could do so by relocating some of its wasteful service population.

More recently, North Korea's weakening economy has made it more willing to enter negotiations. For example, its 1999 petroleum production was estimated by the Bank of Korea to be about one-sixth of the 1991 level, its electricity production in 1999 was 70 percent of that in 1991, and its coal production was roughly two-thirds of that in 1991 (Chun 2001). Admittedly, it is not inconceivable that this source would be biased in its estimates of current economic activity. As discussed earlier, in June 2000, the two Koreas held joint summit talks. From the summit and subsequent working-level talks, the South pledged to supply the North with large quantities of Thai rice, Chinese corn, and fertilizer. South Korean firms were allowed to take part in North Korean social overhead capital projects, including the construction of roads and railways, and to accelerate ongoing joint ventures in automobiles and electronics. Efforts were made to avoid double taxation. With the economic downturn faced by its traditional trade partners (Russia and China), the North has come to view the South and the United States as its main sources of economic aid, facilitating the negotiation process. On the other hand, the two Koreas had very different goals in negotiation. Kim Jung Il's goals included maintaining political control over North Korean society, while South Korean goals included the development of reasonable common grounds for reunification (Chun 2001). On the surface, these two goals would seem to be incompatible.

President Bush's more aggressive stance on the North resulted in the North's breaking off talks with the South in March 2001. Only when the primary advocate (Lim Dung Won) for President Kim Dae Jung's Sunshine Policy with the North was about to be forced out of office (he was despite Kim Jung Il's conciliatory efforts) in September of 2001 did the North attempt to keep communication with the South alive (*The Economist* 2001b). A possible restart of the talks was delayed further in the summer of 2002, when warships from the North and South fired on each other in disputed waters in the worst conflict between the two countries. A South Korean ship sank and four sailors died. Besides providing another barrier to the resumption of talks, the clash resulted in the South postponing new business contacts and suspending rice shipments to the famine-stricken North.

As a unified nation, Korea would be the world's twelfth most abundant country in labor force and the world's twentieth wealthiest country in size of the economy. The wasteful military defense burdens could be diverted to the construction of a powerful economy. As noted in the German unification, many North Koreans might face unemployment for the first time ever. Noland (1998) predicted that, in light of its domestic policies and geopolitical position, North Korea is likely to muddle through, supported by China (and possibly Japan and South Korea), who would like to avoid its collapse. Similarly, *The Economist* (2001e) predicted that the chief contributors to the UN World Food Programme's North Korean aid efforts (the United States, Japan, and South Korea) will not let North Korea slide into a famine.

Korea's Role in a Global Economy

Even if the reunification goes smoothly, Korea's adaptation to the global economy may create problems, given its Hermit Kingdom heritage still evident in both states. Whang (1991) discusses the arising conflict caused by Korea's need to preserve its national and cultural identity during the process of internationalizing the economy. The integration of the Korean economy into the rest of the world will likely cause an identity crisis for Korea, unless its unique national spirit is reflected consistently in both its internal societal management and its external relations.

Clifford (1994) asserted that Koreans would not easily dispense with their xenophobia and the sense of being a unique people. Ingrained nationalism and a rigid sense of hierarchy (the hypersensitivity to title, status, and educational background) are evident in both states. South Korea was virtually alone among developing nations in its ability to chart a high-growth trajectory while strictly limiting foreign control of the economy. "But what was a point of national pride now threatens to shut Korea out of an increasingly integrated world economy" (Clifford 1994, 334).

Fukuyama (1995) argued that Korea is a low-trust society because of a low level of trust outside strong-tie relationships. Y. H. Kim (2000) noted that despite Korea's development as a capitalistic nation, the importance of the old-boys' network had not diminished. The three most important ties are still family, region, and school. But changes are taking place. In the late 1990s, apparel manufacturer FILA ran an advertisement at a time when Koreans were lining up to donate gold to boost the nation's foreign exchange reserves. Over $2 billion in gold was donated (S. K. Kim 2000). "The ad asked which of two companies contributed more to the Korean economy— a Korean firm that sets up a factory in a foreign country, employs foreign workers, and deposits the earnings in a foreign bank—or a foreign company that builds a factory in Korea, employs Korean workers, and deposits the earnings in a Korean bank?" (Y. H. Kim 2000, 172). This ad certainly ran counter to the sentiment that purchasing foreign foods was unpatriotic; the fact that the ad was allowed to air also reflects a liberalization of policy.

The economic crisis of the late 1990s and the intervention by the IMF forced South Korea to make many needed changes. Even before the economic crisis, there was evidence (Nakarmi 1995) that the chaebols were restructuring in order to be more competitive in world markets. The Hyundai group considered divesting; Samsung tried to increase sales internationally to 30 percent of the total up from 20 percent; and Daewoo concentrated on developing markets. Former President Kim Young Sam pressed for changes in the ownership structure of the chaebols. The founding families own about 10 percent of the groups' total capital, while they control more than 40 percent. In 1995, the government started making it harder for chaebols with more concentrated ownership to raise funds and to pursue new businesses (Nakarmi 1995).

As Korea has opened itself to the world, it has paid a price in terms of facing change in traditions. For example, hosting the Olympic Games in 1988 resulted in an increase in tourism since (Berry 1989). As a partial result of sponsoring the games, Visa card membership has more than doubled in South Korea since the games. The exposure helped Visa tack 4 percent onto an already commanding 57 percent share against its prime competitors (Berry 1989). However, despite opposition to changes in culture, since early 1994 but especially in the last years of that decade, there have been many signs that Korea is proceeding with plans to bring its foreign-investment laws, trade codes, and capital markets in line with international standards of openness.

Possibly an even more important "opening to the world" occurred in the summer of 2002 when the South cohosted the World Cup with Japan. The fact that the South Korean team was the first from Asia ever to reach the semifinals generated extraordinary football frenzy and made the team's Dutch-born coach Guus Hiddink a cult figure and management guru. After the Korean loss to Germany in the semifinals, an estimated seven million people (one out of every seven people in the country) were out in streets across the country in one of the biggest parties ever seen in Asia.

On a very pragmatic level, the World Cup was not that successful financially, as foreign fans did not come in the expected numbers, despite huge investments in hotels and facilities. For example, Cheju Island, one of Korea's biggest tourist attractions, had fewer domestic and foreign tourists during the World Cup than during the same period in 2001 (*The Korea Economic Daily* 2002).

However, the indirect economic effects appear to be phenomenal. The Hyundai Research Institute (2002) predicted that the World Cup would stimulate the construction, broadcasting, advertising, tourism, and sports industries in the short run, and would have positive long-term effects on the home appliance, computer and Internet, communication, leisure and health, and financial industries. The institute estimated that the direct and indirect effects of the World Cup amount to $21 billion, including increased consumption, an increase in the brand value of Korea, and an improvement in the image of Korean companies.

Another clear result of cohosting the World Cup (and of the home team's performance) was the increase in national pride and self-confidence. The Hyundai Research Institute (2002) predicted that the World Cup would provide momentum for the so-called Red Spirit, which encompasses a positive, open-minded, flexible, cheerful, and self-creative orientation that can foster the social development of Korea. In fact, a survey conducted by the Korean Research Institute following the World Cup shows that Koreans are more proud of the country, more confident in the potential of the country as well as in their own potential, and more trustful of their people due to the World Cup (Maekyung 2002).

At the root of present chaos in the housing market and in labor-management relations is the desire for a higher standard of living. Koreans want to spend more on cars, on houses, on telephones, on washing machines, and on all the other baubles their counterparts in Europe and America spend their time working on to buy. Before the economic crisis, this was evident in the form of feverish crowds in department stores, and from the clogging of Seoul's roads with new cars that middle-class people were beginning to be able to afford (*The Economist* 1996). At the same time that there is strong evidence that Koreans consumers see that they are entitled to "things" and leisure because of the deprivations suffered in the past, frugality appears to be embedded in their psyches. S. K. Kim summarized the current status: "It is still premature, despite its rapid expansion, to argue that South Korean consumers have been taking an active role in creating their self-identity through consumption, as much of the expansion remained at the level of accumulating household and other durables" (2000, 76). While some consumer desires have been stifled in the South, this situation is still far superior to that being experienced in the North.

CONCLUSION

The two Koreas have demanded a great deal of attention from the rest of the world. North Korea has been viewed in the West as a "rogue nation," capable of instigating nuclear warfare. South Korea has had one of the fastest-growing economies in history.

The 1990s confronted both countries with strong discontinuities. The North's reliance on the former USSR for political and economic support dissipated with the breakup of the Soviet Union. China continues to be supportive, but its entry into the world economy has seen it develop trade with the South at far greater levels than its trade with the North. The North's economy is in shambles, as it is in dire need of food aid to feed its people. Increasingly, that aid is coming from Japan, the United States, and the South.

For its part, the South suffered its own economic crisis in the mid to late 1990s, requiring massive amounts of financial aid. A restructuring of the financial sector has taken place, and the South has taken steps away from its preferred stance of independence to become more integrated in the global economy. Korea has opened its doors to the world: South Korean companies are now faced with tougher competition from foreign companies in the domestic market, and the North Korean government is intrigued by the slow but inevitable inflow of capitalism.

Reunification looms for the two Koreas, but it is likely that the process will be slow. While the importance of "face" to all Koreans is understandable from a cultural perspective, Westerners with short-term time horizons may interpret some of the political actions (and inactions) by the two countries as stubbornness. It is likely that separate Koreas will continue to exist for some time, but "cooperation" is a term being used far more frequently by both sides. Thus, we expect to see gradual movement toward reconciliation.

The importance of the military to both nations has been a barrier to the development of consumer societies. Similarly, the governments' dominance of business and their directed development policies have retarded the growth of consumer societies. The South showed signs of movement toward a consumer society in the 1990s, despite economic downturns in the decade that resulted in more "frugal" orientations on the part of consumers. But the experience of a less restrictive consumer environment is not one easily forgotten, and the South is continuing to move toward a consumer society. Movement in such a positive (for consumers, anyway) direction in the North is very unlikely. Thus, while North Korea has avoided changes in consumer culture, the South's consumer culture is buffeted a bit by, on one hand, the government's past encouragement of conservative and traditional and, on the other hand, its promotion of Western-oriented consumption patterns.

ACKNOWLEDGMENTS

The authors thank Ju Young Park for his comments on an earlier draft of this chapter.

REFERENCES

Ad Information. 2001. "KOBACO," October: 134–38.
Alden, Dana L., Wayne D. Hoyer, and Chol Lee. 1993. "Identifying Global and Culture-Specific Dimensions of Humor in Advertising: A Multinational Analysis." *Journal of Marketing* 57(April): 64–75.
Alston, Jon P. 1989. "'Wa,' 'Guanxi,' and 'Inhwa': Managerial Principles in Japan, China, and Korea." *Business Horizons* 32: 26–31.
American Demographics. 2001. "The Laboring Masses," November: 56.
Asia Source. 2001. "Asia Profiles," October. Available at www.asiasource.org/profiles.
Asian Business. 1992. "South Korea: Statistics," 28(June): 43–44.
Berry, Jon. 1989. "Asia Minors." *Adweek's Marketing Week,* July 17: 32–40.

Bracken, Paul. 1995. "Risks and Promises in the Two Koreas." *Orbis: A Journal of World Affairs* 39(1): 55–64.

Breen, Mike. 1990. "Pyongyang Opens the Door a Crack." *Asian Business* 24(June): 44–46.

Business Korea. 2000. "Inter-Korean Economic Cooperation," July: 24–27.

Business Week. 1994a. "Korea's Export Boom Is Hurting—and Helping—Japan," August 8: 6.

———. 1994b. "South Korea: The New Titan of Technology," Advertising Supplement, November 28.

Chae, Jung Sook. 1999. "A Cross-Cultural Study of Lifestyle: Focusing on the Lifestyle Traits of Korean and Canadian Students." *Journal of Consumer Studies* 10(1): 79–98.

Chang, Chan Sup. 1988. "Chaebol: The South Korean Conglomerates." *Business Horizons* March–April: 51–57.

Chang, Chan Sup, Nahn Joo Chang, and Barbara T. Freese. 2001. "Offering Gifts or Offering Bribes? Code of Ethics in South Korea." *Journal of Third World Studies* 18(1): 125–39.

Chang, Sang-Hae. 2001. *Current Status of Economic Exchange between North Korea and China and Prospects for Exchange.* Seoul, Korea: KOTRA.

Cheil Communications. 2001. *Cheil Communications*, March, Seoul, Korea.

Cho, Dongchul. 1999. "Recovering from the Crisis: Where Does the Korean Economy Stand?" *Korea Journal* 38(Autumn): 179–97.

Choe, Sang T., and Glenn A. Pitman. 1993. "Conducting Business with Koreans." *Marketing Intelligence and Planning* 11(2): 44–46.

Chun, Chaesong. 2001. "North–South Relations Viewed from the Perspective of the Recent Transformation of the Cold War Order in Northeast Asia." *Korean Journal* 41(2): 28–58.

Chung, Joseph S. 1986. "Foreign Trade of North Korea: Performance, Policy, and Prospects." In *North Korea in a Regional and Global Context*, ed. Robert A. Scalapino and Hongkoo Lee, pp. 78–114. Berkeley: Center for Korean Studies.

Chung, Young Sook. 1999. "Impact of Private Education Expenditures on Consumption Patterns." *Journal of Consumer Studies* 10(4): 61–74.

Clifford, Mark L. 1994. *Troubled Tiger: Businessmen, Bureaucrats, and Generals in South Korea.* Armonk, NY: M. E. Sharpe.

Cummings, Bruce. 1997. *Korea's Place in the Sun: A Modern History.* New York: Norton.

Dubinsky, Alan J., Marvin A. Jolson, Masaaki Kotabe, and Chae Un Lim. 1991. "A Cross-National Investigation of Industrial Salespeople's Ethical Perceptions." *Journal of International Business Studies* 22: 651–70.

The Economist. 1990a. "When Democracy Hits the Purse," March 10: 36.

———. 1990b. "Two Paths to Prosperity," July 14, 19–20: 2 2.

———. 1990c. "A Survey of South Korea," August 19: 1–20.

———. 1994a. "The Koreas: Up to a Point," August 20: 32.

———. 1994b. "The Battle of the Belly Button," September 24: 39.

———. 1994c. "Shop till You Drop," October 15: 44.

———. 1994d. "Cousins Less Removed," October 22: 38–39.

———. 1994e. "Into the Hermit Kingdom," November 12: 81.

———. 1994f. "Blessed Are the Rich," December 10: 35.

———. 1995a. "Down with Youth," January 14: 35.

———. 1995b. "Confucianism: New Fashion for Old Wisdom," January 21: 38–39.

———. 1996. "The Vanishing of Chinatown," August 3: 34.

———. 1997a. "Korea's Twin Crises," February 22, 42–45.

———. 1997b. "South Korea's Firms: Kia Keels Over," July 19: 55–56.

———. 1997c. "South Korea Manufacturing: The Giants Stumble," October 18: 67–68.

———. 2001a. "Pressures on South Korea: A President in a Hurry," September 1: 36.

———. 2001b. "Fraternal Meetings: Signs of a Thaw on the Korean Peninsula," September 8: 45.

———. 2001c. "The World This Week," October 20: 8.

———. 2001d. "Malnutrition: Hunger Strikes," October 20: 76.

———. 2001e. "Hunger in North Korea: Also with Us," November 10: 40.

———. 2001f. "East Asian Economics: Another Bout of Flu," November 24: 65–66.

———. 2001g. "Unusual Excursions: Destination North Korea," December 22: 51–52.

———. 2002. "Mobile Telecom: 3G by Any Other Name," January 19: 60.

———. 2003. "Hell-bent," May 3: 11–12.

Economist Intelligence Unit. 2003. *Country Report: Korea.* London: Economist Intelligence Unit.

Eisenstodt, Gale. 1990. "Hold the Applause." *Forbes*, October 1: 182–83.

Financial Supervisory Service. 2001. www.fss.or.kr.

Fukuyama, Francis. 1995. *Trust: The Social Virtues and the Creation of Property.* New York: Free Press.

Gentry, James W., Sanjay Putrevu, Clifford Shultz II, and Suraj Commuri. 2001. "How Now Ralph Lauren? The Separation of Brand and Product in a Counterfeit Culture." In *Advances in Consumer Research*, Vol. 28, ed. M. Gilly and J. Meyers-Levy, pp. 258–65. Valdosta, GA: Association for Consumer Research.

Gentry, James W., Sanjay Putrevu, Jonathan Goh, Suraj Commuri, and Judy Cohen. 2002. "The Legitimacy of Counterfeits: Consumers Choosing Counterfeit Brands and Tourists Seeking Authentic Counterfeits." Working Paper, University of Nebraska.

Gluckman, Ron. 1991. "Profit versus Paranoia." *Asian Business* 27(November): 23–24.

Green, Robert T., and Dana L. Alden. 1988. "Functional Equivalence in Cross-Cultural Consumer Behavior: Gift Giving in Japan and the United States." *Psychology and Marketing* 5(2): 155–68.

Gudykunst, William B., Young-Chul Yoon, and Tsukasa Nishida. 1987. "The Influence of Individualism/Collectivism on Perceptions of Ingroup and Outgroup Relationships." *Communication Monographs* 54(September): 295–306.

Ha, Seung-Kyu. 1999. "Urban Growth and Housing Development in Korea: A Critical Overview." *Korea Journal* 38(Autumn): 63–94.

Hafstrom, Jeanne L., Jung Sook Chae, and Young Sook Chung. 1992. "Consumer Decision-Making Styles: Comparison between United States and Korean Young Consumers." *The Journal of Consumer Affairs* 26(1): 146–58.

Hall, Edward T. 1976. *Beyond Culture.* Garden City, NY: Anchor Press/Doubleday.

Halladay, Jon. 1989. "The Economies of North and South Korea." In *Two Koreas—One Future?* ed. John Sullivan and Robert Foss. Lanham, MD: University Press of America.

Han, Min Hee, and Dae Ryun Chang. 1994. *Advertising Management.* Seoul: Hak Hyun Sa.

Han, Sang-Pil, and Sharon Shavitt. 1994. "Persuasion and Culture: Advertising Appeals in Individualistic and Collectivistic Societies." *Journal of Experimental Social Psychology* 30: 326–50.

Hoare, James, and Susan Pares. 1988. *Korea: An Introduction.* London: Kegan Paul International.

Hofstede, Geert. 1984. *Culture's Consequences: International Differences in Work-Related Values.* Thousand Oaks, CA: Sage.

Holstein, William J. 1994. "Building the New Asia." *Business Week,* November 28: 62–68.

Holstein, William J., and Laxmi Nakarmi. 1995. "Korea." *Business Week,* July 31: 56–63.

Hong, S., and Yongae Yi. 1992. "A Cross-Cultural Comparison of Country-of-Origin Effects on Product Evaluation." *Journal of International Consumer Marketing* 4: 49–71.

Howe, Russell Warren. 1988. *The Koreans: Passion and Grace.* New York: Harcourt Brace Jovanovich.

Hupp, Susan C., Shui Fong Lam, and Janice Jaeger. 1992. "Differences in Exploration of Toys by One-Year-Old Children: A Korean and American Comparison." *Behavior Science Research* 26(1–4): 123–35.

Hwang, Eui-Gak. 1993. *The Korean Economies: A Comparison of North and South.* Oxford: Clarendon Press.

Hyde, Georgie D. M. 1988. *South Korea: Education, Culture and Economy.* New York: Macmillan Press.

Hyundai Research Institute. 2002. *The Development Strategy and Policy for the Post World Cup*, June 25.

Inglehart, R. 1997. *Modernization and Postmodernization: Cultural, Economic, and Political Change in Forty-three Societies.* Princeton, NJ: Princeton University Press.

International Strategies, Inc. 1994. "Republic of Korea." Export Hotline, Boston, MA.

Keown, Charles F., Laurence W. Jacobs, and Kyung-Il Ghymn. 1993. "Content Analysis of Major Mass Media Advertising in the United States, Japan, South Korea and China." *Asian Journal of Marketing* December: 31–43.

Kim, Byoung-Lo Philo. 1992. *Two Koreas in Development.* New Brunswick, NJ: Transaction.

Kim, Dae-jung. 1994. "The Impact of the U.S.–North Korean Agreement on Korean Reunification." *Korean Journal of Defense Analysis* 6 (Winter): 85–100.

Kim, Donghoon, Yigang Pan, and Heung Soo Park. 1998. "High- versus Low-Context Cultures: A Comparison of Chinese, Korean, and American Cultures." *Psychology & Marketing* 15(6): 507–21.

Kim, E. H. 1985. *Korea: Beyond the Hills.* Seoul: Seoul and Samwha Printing Co.

Kim, Eun Ji, and Doo Ryun You. 2000. "A Study of the Purchasing Behavior of Consumers toward Environmentally Labeled Products." *Journal of Consumer Studies* 11(3): 41–58.

Kim, Jang-Han. 2001. "North Korea's Economy and the Prospect of its Overseas Economic Policy in 2000." Available at www.kotra.or.kr/main/common_bbs.

Kim, Ki-hong. 1975. "Cross-Cultural Differences between Americans and Koreans in Nonverbal Communication." *East–West Culture*, 8: 39–53.

Kim, Samuel Soonki. 1998. "The Future of the Post Kim Il-Sung System in North Korea." In *The Two Koreas and the United States*, ed. Wonmo Dong, pp. 32–58. Armonk, NY: M. E. Sharpe.

Kim, Seung-Kuk. 2000. "Changing Lifestyles and Consumption Patterns of the South Korean Middle Class and New Generations." In *Consumption in Asia: Lifestyles and Identities*, ed. Beng-Huat Chua, pp. 61–81. New York: Routledge.

Kim, Yong-Hak. 2000. "Emergence of the Network Society: Trends, New Challenges, and the Implications for Network Capitalism." *Korea Journal* 39 (Autumn): 161–84.

KOFANET Data Consulting Information. 2001. Korea Foreign Company Associate, February 15. Available at www.kofa.org.

Korea Economic Daily. 2002. "The Economic Impact of the World Cup: Host-Cities Are Just a Mild Breeze," June 27.

Korea Super/Chain Store Association. 2000. *The Yearbook of the Distribution Industry.*

Korean Department Store Association. 2001. *Journal of Distribution,* November.

Korean National Statistical Office. 2001a. "Population and Household." Available at www.nso.go.kr/eng.

———. 2001b. "Social Indicators in Korea." Available at www.nso.go.kr/eng.

KOTRA. 2001a. "Intra-Korean Trade by Years." Available at http://crm.kotra.or.kr/main.

———. 2001b. "Structure of Export & Import Items for CPT." Available at www.kotra.or.kr/main/info/nk/eng.

Kraft, Frederic B., and Kae H. Chung. 1992. "Korean Importer Perceptions of U.S. and Japanese Industrial Goods Exporters." *International Marketing Review* 9(2): 59–73.

Lee, Catherine Keumhyun. 1996. "Unfinished Business: Kim Sends the Chaebol a Message." *Business Week,* September 9: 56–57.

Lee, Chan-sam. 1995. "Ohk-Wha Comrede, Don't Wait for Me." *Sung Ang Daily Newspaper* January 10: 1.

Lee, Charles S. 1999. "Buyers' Market." *Far Eastern Economic Review,* July 1: 45.

Lee, Chol, and Robert T. Green. 1991. "Cross-Cultural Examination of the Fishbein Behavioral Intentions Model." *Journal of International Business Studies,* September: 289–305.

Lee, Dongdae, and Changhoon Shin. 2001. "Role of Ethnocentrism in Consumer Attitude Formation toward Retail Stores." *Journal of Consumer Studies* 12(1): 1–15.

Lee, Hak Chong. 1989. "Managerial Characteristics of Korea Firms." In *Korean Managerial Dynamics*, ed. K. H. Chung and H. C. Lee, pp. 147–62. New York: Praeger.

LG Ad. 1997. March: 58–62.

———. 2000. May–June: 49–57.

Lim, Kumsook. 2001. "The Direction of the Innovation of a Price System in North Korea." *Reunification Economy*. Available at www.nk-infobank.com.

Lincoln Journal Star. 1994. "South Koreans Hedge Their Bets on the Occult," November 18: 20.

———. 1995. "Cable TV Wires in S. Korea," March 2: 5.

Maekyung. 2002. "The World Cup Built Confidence," July 9.

Mallaby, Sebastian. 1995. "The House that Park Built: A Survey of South Korea." *The Economist,* June 3: 1–18.

Moon, Ihlwan. 2001a. "Kim's Fall from Grace." *Business Week,* February 19: 50–51.

———. 2001b. "A Long Trip to School." *Business Week,* August 27: 62–63.

Media and Consumer Research. 2000. KOBACO, Seoul, Korea.

Merrill, John. 1989. "North Korea's Halting Efforts at Economic Reform." Paper presented to the Fourth Conference on North Korea, Seoul, August.

Ministry of Finance and Economy. 2001. Available at www.mofe.go.kr.

Ministry of Unification. 2001. Available at http://unibook.unikorea.go.kr

Na, Eun-Yeong, and Jae-Ho Cha. 2000. "Change in Values and the Generation Gap between the 1970s and 1990s in Korea." *Korea Journal* 39(Spring): 285–324.

Na, WoonBong, Young Seok Son, and Roger Marshall. 1998. "An Empirical Study of the Purchase Role Structure in Korean Families." *Psychology & Marketing* 15(6): 563–76.

Nakarmi, Laxmi. 1991. "Korea Throws Open Its Doors." *Business Week,* July 29: 46.

———. 1992. "A Chaebol Plays Hardball and Roh Wae Too." *Business Week,* February 24: 50.

———. 1995. "A Flying Leap toward the 21st Century?" *Business Week,* March 20: 78–80.

Nakarmi, Laxmi, Rose Brady, and Lynne Curry. 1992. "Can Korea Unite and Conquer?" *Business Week,* November 16: 52–54.

Nam, WooSuk. 2001a. "Overview of Inter-Korean Exchanges and Cooperation for 2000." KOTRA (available at www.kotra.or.kr/main/common_bbs).

———. 2001b. "Current Status of Inter-Korean Economic Cooperation in the IT Field, Tasks and Future Outlook." Available at www.kotra.or.kr/main/common_bbs.

———. 2001c. "Sales Conditions in North." Available at www.kotra.or.kr/main/common_bbs.

Noland, Marcus. 1998. "The Economic Situation in North Korea." In *The Two Koreas and the United States*, ed. Wonmo Dong, pp. 19–31. Armonk, NY: M. E. Sharpe.

Oh, Boosu. 2000. "Labor Market in Korea." Available at www.kisc.org.servlet.

Olshavsky, Richard W., David J. Moore, and Jeen-Su Lim. 1988. "An Information Processing Interpretation of Cross-National Consumer Characteristics." *Journal of Global Marketing* 1 (Summer): 2 5–40.

Park, Seong Yeon. 1996. "The Type and Characteristics of the Korean Lifestyle." *Korean Marketing Review* 11(1): 19–34.

———. 1998. "A Comparison of Korean and American Gift-Giving Behaviors." *Psychology & Marketing* 15(6): 577–93.

Park, Seong Yeon, and Shin Ae Choi. 2000. "Longitudinal Study of Economic Change and Lifecycle Trend." *Korean Marketing Review* 15(3): 1–18.

Park, Untae. 1994. *Korea's Economic Development*. Seoul: Kyung Yeon.

Peace Institute. 1997. *Handbook of Unification*.

Rubin, James P. 2001. "No Time to Delay on North Korea." *The Washington Post,* May 18.

Shim, Soyeon, and Pil Gyo Cho. 2000. "The Impact of Life Events on Perceived Financial Stress, Clothing Specific Lifestyle, and Retail Patronage: The Recent IMF Economic Crisis in Korea." *Family and Consumer Sciences Research Journal* 29(September): 19–47.

Shin Dong-A. 1995. *Kim Jung Il and North Korean Encyclopedia*. Seoul: Dong-A Il Bo.

South Korean National Intelligence Service. 1999. Available at www.globalsecurity.org/intell/world/rok/nis.htm.

Tansuhaj, Patriya, James W. Gentry, Joby John, L. Lee Manzer, and Bong Jin Cho. 1991. "A Cross-National Examination of Innovation Resistance." *International Marketing Review* 8(3): 7–20.

Taylor, Charles R., R. Dale Wilson, and Gordon E. Miracle. 1995. "The Impact of Brand Differentiating Messages on Effectiveness in Korean Advertising." *Journal of International Marketing* 3(1): 31–52.

Templeman, John, and Laxmi Nakarmi. 1994. "For Korea, A Taste of Its Won Medicine." *Business Week,* April 4: 6.

Thyne, Maree A., and Rob Lawson. 2001. "The Design of a Social Distance Scale to be Used in the Context of Tourism." *Asian Pacific Advances in Consumer Research* 4: 102–7.

Ulgado, Francis M., and Mookyu Lee. 1998. "The Korean versus American Marketplace: Consumer Reactions to Foreign Products." *Psychology & Marketing* 15(6): 595–614.

United Nations Human Development Report. 1998. *Korea Human Development Report 1998*. Online edition available at http://hdr.undp.org/reports/detail_reports.cfm?view=147.

United Nations Statistics Division. 2001. "InfoNation." Available at www.un.org/cgi-bin/pubs/infonatn.

Wehrfritz, George. 2000. "A 'New Day' in Korea." *Newsweek,* June 26: 36–41.

West, Philip. 1989. "Cross-Cultural Literacy and the Pacific Rim." *Business Horizons* 32: 3–17.

Whang, Eui R., and Buyng M. Min. 1978. "A Study of Brand Choice Behavior." *Research Bulletin* (Korean Institute for Research in the Behavioral Science) 11(March).

Whang, In Joung. 1991. "The Korean Economy toward the Year 2000." In *A Dragon's Progress: Development Administration in Korea*, ed. Gerald E. Caiden and Bun Woong Kim. West Hartford, CT: Kumarian Press.

Wilcox, Julie Scott, James W. Gentry, Gyungtai Ko, Michael Stricklin, and Sunkyu Jun "Advertising Presentations of the Independent versus Interdependent Self to Korean and U.S. College Students." *Advances in International Marketing,* Vol. 7, 1996, 159–74.

World Bank. 2000. *World Development Indicators*. Washington, DC.

Yearbook of Labor Statistics. 1999. Available at http://laborsta.ilo.org.

Yi, Insill. 1999. "Mid-Term Evaluation: The Korean Financial Crisis." *Korea Journal* 39(Autumn): 271–314.

Yoo, Sangjin, and Sang M. Lee. 1987. "Management Style and Practice of Korean Chaebols." *California Management Review* 29(Summer): 95–110.

Yoon, Sanchul. 2000. "Anticorruption Movement in Korea: Focusing on International Influences and Internal Political Context." *Korea Journal* 39(Autumn): 185–216.

Chapter 9

LAOS

Emerging Market Trends and the Rise of
Consumers and Entrepreneurs

William J. Ardrey IV, Clifford J. Shultz II, and Michael Keane

OVERVIEW

Laos is emerging as a growing player in the development of the vibrant Mekong Region. Long isolated and dependent on foreign donor assistance, Laos continues to liberalize policies and to move from central economic planning to a more market-oriented economy. A resulting growth cycle has stimulated commerce, improved the purchasing power and choices of many consumers, and has generally improved socioeconomic conditions. These improvements are contrasted with delays in the reform process, which create a drag on the initial success of the New Economic Mechanism (NEM). Further structural changes, including more robust incentives for foreign investment, human resources development, and more banking and monetary policy reforms, are still needed. In this chapter, we review the important trends vis-à-vis socioeconomic development, marketing, and consumer behavior, and discuss implications for an appropriate marketing mix for entering and further developing Laos.

INTRODUCTION

Laos, officially the Lao People's Democratic Republic (LPDR), is a least-developed country (LDC), cautiously transitioning from a centrally planned economy to a more market-oriented system. After initial, if modest, successes, the economy, markets, and consumers of Laos have been substantially affected by various forces—largely, the negative economic contraction and currency depreciation caused by the economic downturn from 1997–1999 and then the post-2000 restoration and recovery. Still, a number of legacies continue to create a drag on further economic development and consumer and business emancipation. The first is the legacy of the Vietnam War, or more accurately, the Indochina War. The second is the legacy of a rather immobile political system that has led to the entrenchment of authoritarian leaders with close ties to the military, whose reforms lag behind those seen even in the region's other transitioning economies, China, Cambodia, and Vietnam. The immobility has also led to signs of political dissatisfaction in this one-party state. The third principal legacy is the simple isolation and poverty of a landlocked country, making education and infrastructure expensive to extend to the majority of the population who reside in the countryside. Finally, Laos has a healthy concern for the cultural, linguistic, and economic strength of its powerful neighbors, particularly Thailand, which continues to have a strong influence on Laos through the reception of Thai television, a popular family entertainment in linguistically similar Laos. This concern also retards cooperation and development. These factors have constrained socioeconomic development and regional/global integration. Despite them, however, private businesses and individual consumers have begun to benefit substantially from policy changes. A vibrant, small-business sector has emerged—especially around Vientiane and regional business centers—capitalizing on pent-up consumer demand. Trade is on the rise, and a more outward, globally integrated focus is evident. Laos, nevertheless, remains one of the poorest countries; however, its national economic plans call for "graduation" from LDC status by 2020 (e.g., Litner 2003; Xinhua 2001a).

Below, we briefly describe the land and people of Laos. We discuss the economic environment, with particular emphasis on salient trends affecting the dynamics of enterprise development and the emergent consumer society, as well as the marketing and consumption of products and services made possible by the NEM, and by further reforms instituted during the Seventh Party Congress in March 2001. Conclusions for marketers and businesses seeking to invest and to operate in the LPDR form the final discussion of this chapter.

GEOGRAPHY, LAN XANG, AND THE EMERGENCE
OF MODERN LAOS

Laos remains, by most accounts, one of the most enigmatic countries in Southeast Asia. It is 236,800 square kilometers of landlocked, mountainous terrain, dense forests, and flood plains, with a large area-to-population ratio and a long monsoon season. It is inhabited by sixty-eight ethnic groups, many of which are isolated culturally as well as geographically. Surrounded by Myanmar, Thailand, China, Vietnam, and Cambodia, and with the Mekong River running its length, the geographic position of Laos has greatly determined its fate: Laos has been divided, conquered, colonized, bombed,[1] and dominated by more powerful Asian and Western powers, numerous times (e.g., Steinberg 1987; Than and Tan 1997). Indeed, over the centuries, the landmass within the political boundaries of present-day Laos regularly has been administered by various non-Lao powers.

Humans have inhabited the terrain for thousands of years. Migration patterns from various directions resulted in the present ethnic diversity, but most Lao[2] can trace their roots to Tai peoples who emigrated from Yunnan province in China. The most significant history seems to have begun in the early fourteenth century and coincided with the deterioration of the Khmer empire. Notable were the contributions of Fa Ngum,[3] a Lao King who united the Kingdom, made Buddhism the state religion, and named the sovereignty Lan Xang,[4] "Land of a Million Elephants." A golden era that produced many palaces, libraries, temples, and monuments lasted until the middle of the eighteenth century. An eventual inability to find an appropriate male heir to the throne and foreign invasions ushered in the kingdom's decline. By the end of the nineteenth century, France had established a protectorate in Laos but did little to develop the country. Japanese forces briefly occupied Laos during World War II; however, at the War's end, France regained control, despite efforts by the Lao Issara (Free Laos Movement). French administration ended, and full sovereignty was granted to Laos in 1953 (see also Mansfield 1998).

Internal discord coupled with turbulent political and military crises strongly and adversely affected Laos for the next two decades. With the combination of the Congress of People's Deputies meeting, the abdication of the king, and the proclamation of the socialist Lao People's Democratic Republic, a new governmental system was established in 1975; the political structure of that system still, essentially, exists today. Initial policies of the LPDR included central economic planning, import substitution, and agricultural collectivization. Many socioeconomic difficulties ensued, including decline in many production sectors, a drop in Western aid, dependence upon the former Soviet Union, devaluation of the kip, various forms of privation, and the flight of some of the most talented human resources.

By the late 1980s, poor economic performance, the collapse of the former Soviet Union, and the positive experiences of China and Vietnam in promoting economic transition and the apolitical freedoms that transition required, led to "softened authoritarianism" and the New Economic Mechanism (Ljunggren 1992, 11). This shift also included a more elastic foreign policy, such as economic integration and "Treaties of Friendship and Cooperation" with neighbors Thailand (in 1991), Cambodia (in 1992), China (in 1994), Myanmar (in 1994), and stronger ties with Vietnam (a similar treaty was already signed with Vietnam in 1977). Laos became an observer, then a member of the Association of Southeast Asian Nations (ASEAN) by 1997, and was also linked directly to Thailand via the Australia-financed "Friendship Bridge," during the period from 1994 to 1995. ASEAN membership forced a reduction on tariffs and taxes and also demonstrated to the leadership the positive changes of economic transition and foreign investment by Malaysia, Singapore, Vietnam, and China.

Today, the Lao government represents its position on international engagement as one in which it will consistently apply a policy of peace, friendship, and cooperation with all countries. This *Realpolitik* includes efforts to improve English proficiency among its citizens, to enhance higher education, and to participate in constructive engagement in various forms, such as educational exchanges, aid projects, and foreign direct investment (FDI). Thus, modern Laos increasingly participates in the global economy, but a regional focus still dominates trade and diplomatic relations. Internal geographic and cultural tendencies coupled with proximity to particular neighbors also affect the country and its outward orientation. For example, northern Laos is being drawn into close trade with Yunnan, and products from China dominate the markets. The center and south of the country have been pulled toward trade and the consumer culture of Thailand. The eastern border is dominated by trade with and political urgings from Vietnam; and with the signing of the U.S.–Vietnam Bilateral Trade Agreement, stronger trade with Vietnam is predicted. Computers, the Internet, and other advancements coincide with this trade and the arrival of a large donor and expatriate community; together, with an accelerating increase in tourism, these have contributed to a more outward or global orientation in Vientiane and the central provinces (see also *Bangkok Post* 2001; Economist Intelligence Unit 2003).

In summary, modern Laos is following the lead of its transitioning neighbors in struggling to catch up with the rest of the world. External shocks and internal political caution have dampened the pace of change (e.g., Kazmin 2003), but low exchange rates and a commitment to increased cooperation, trade, and economic development have sustained positive growth and development, all of which bode well for modern Laos. A synopsis of basic physical and socioeconomic indicators is provided in Table 9.1.

THE ECONOMIC ENVIRONMENT

The current Lao economy is rooted in the demise of its donor states and the subsequent economic reforms initiated in 1986. Serious economic reform was created through the initiation of the Fourth Party Congress slogan, *pean pang mai* or "new thinking," ending the collectivization of agriculture and permitting private-sector development. As noted above, this policy has been termed the New Economic Mechanism (NEM). The NEM has created gradual economic prosperity. The leadership of the LPDR is following the economic restructuring policies of its neighbors, China and Vietnam,

Table 9.1

Basic Physical and Socioeconomic Indicators

- Land Area: 236,800 square kilometers (EIU 2003)
- Population: 5.4 million (mid-year 2001) (EIU 2003)
- Annual population growth rate: 3.4% (2001) (EIU 2003)
- Main cities (with populations): Vientiane (555,100); Savannakhet (711,500); Pakse (531,000); Luang Prabang (386,400).
- 76% rural–24% urban (2001) (EIU 2003)
- Average annual income per head: US$320 (2002) (EIU 2003)
- GDP per capita: US$326 (2001) (UNHDR 2003)
- Primary economic activity: agriculture (50.09% of GDP in 2001), with some light industry and services (EIU 2003)
- Population under sixteen years of age: 50% (2002)
- Adult literacy rate (age of adulthood not defined): 50% (2001) (EIU 2003)
- Adult literacy rate (ages fifteen and above): 65.6% (2001) (UNHDR 2003)
- Female adult literacy rate (ages fifteen and above): 54.4% (2001) (UNHDR 2003)
- Male adult literacy rate (ages fifteen and above): 76.8 (2001) (UNHDR 2003)
- Currency exchange: 1$US = 10,619 Lao kip (first quarter 2003 average) (EIU 2003)

Sources: Economist Intelligence Unit (EIU), *Laos: Country Profiles* (London: EIU Publications, 2003); interviews with Lao authorities (2002); United Nations Development Programme, *Human Development Report*, Indicators (2003).

and to a lesser degree, Cambodia. The first round of reforms (1987–1997) involved improvement of macroeconomic management, including monetary, fiscal, financial, and trade reforms. A primary policy focus was price reform, which permitted agriculture to return to the responsibility of farmers. Another important positive outcome included a successful hydropower program to export electricity to neighboring countries in return for valuable foreign exchange, and privatization of some state assets. The second round of reforms (1998–2001) involved microeconomic efficiency, including privatization and performance enhancement at state-owned or controlled banks, industries, and government offices, as well as policies to improve the living standards of consumers. Broadly, the NEM has sought to improve living standards, to reform legal and regulatory frameworks, and to clarify the role and function of government and markets. The government privatized many nonessential consumer companies but held on to some valuable assets such as Lao Tobacco. These policies are detailed in Table 9.2 in the areas of systemic, stabilization, and trade policy reforms.

Based on a synthesis of materials and personal communications by the authors with Lao authorities, the goals of these policies were eightfold, namely, as follows:

1. Improve food production.
2. Eliminate slash-and-burn agriculture.
3. Improve commodity production.
4. Develop infrastructure.
5. Develop rural areas.
6. Widen economic cooperation and trade relations.
7. Build service sector.
8. Develop human resources.

Pursuits of policy reforms for the goals listed above were quite ambitious from 1990 to 1996, with important advances made in the areas of rural and agricultural reforms, fiscal policy changes,

Table 9.2

Summary of Reform Program in Laos

Policy area	Date of introduction	Implementation
Systemic: Agriculture	1987–1992	Permitted long-term land leases, ended collectivization and self-sufficiency policies
Systemic: Trade	1984–1987	Removed internal trading and pricing controls
Systemic: Enterprises	1989–1995	Allowed for privatization of many state owned enterprises
Systemic: Factors and foreign direct investment	1988–1994	Labor market restrictions reduced, foreign investors and private business legally protected
Systemic: Role redefinition	1988–1991	Banking system separated from state, tax and treasury centralized, mixed economy constitutionally protected
Stabilization: Fiscal	1988–1995	Tax systems, public expenditure controls, civil service reduced
Stabilization: Monetary	1988–2001	Attempts at inflation control and monetary stability
Trade: Liberalization	1988–2001	Quantitative restrictions and excessive import/export taxes eliminated, trading partners diversified
Trade: Exchange rates	1988–2001	Devaluation and controlled flotation of kip

Source: M. Than and J. Tan, "Introduction: Laos Transitional Economy in the Context of Regional Economic Cooperation," in *Laos' Dilemmas and Options*, eds. M. Than and J. Tan (Singapore: ISEAS, 1997); Y. Bourdet, *The Economics of Transition in Laos* (Northampton: Elgar, 2001).

labor market adjustments, reduction of regional disparities, and macroeconomic adjustment (Bourdet 2000). Freeman (2000) argues that the economic reform process stalled in the late 1990s. Moreover, the reliance on donor assistance has created noteworthy pressure from agencies such as the Asian Development Bank, the International Monetary Fund, the World Bank, and national donors for faster reform, which has been resisted by an immobilist faction in the Lao leadership (McFarlane 2001). The conservative approach created slow but steady economic growth—and manageable political discord—stirring the leaders and some observers to conclude that the pace and scope of the reform movements were ideal:

> [Laos] has been more fortunate in a number of aspects. It has not suffered from drastic economic and social disruptions caused by internal strife and warfare, as Cambodia did for a large part of the past two decades. Also, the Laotian economy has not borne the burdens arising from an embargo on trade, financial or other relationships by the United States and other countries, plus an adverse ripple effect on third countries and institutions, as Vietnam did during most of the same decades. It is, moreover, blessed with perhaps the most abundant natural resources among the Indochinese economies. (Nam 1997, 267)

The economic environment has evolved from an inward-looking, centrally planned, socialist framework, to a market- and export-oriented system. The NEM has enabled economic growth, boosting the real incomes and living standards of most Lao consumers, as detailed in sections below. Key gross domestic product (GDP) growth rates from 1998 to 2000 were as follows: agriculture, 6 percent; industry, 10 percent; services, 10 percent; and overall GDP, approximately

7 percent. Despite considerable progress, Laos nevertheless remains a poor country, with less than US$400 GDP per capita. Agriculture continues to comprise some 60 percent of domestic production (World Bank 2002). The Lao economy remains fragmented, with fewer supportive institutions found implemented by its neighbors (e.g., Vietnam) and not yet fully monetized.

Since 2001, significant success has been achieved in diversifying the trade relationships of the economy and in building a services sector. The balance between trading relations with Vietnam and Thailand was stabilized, and the move toward Western trading partners and investors and away from Eastern European trading partners was complete (Bourdet 1996, 1997, 2000, 2001). The overall macroeconomic conditions improved as the government regained control over fiscal and monetary policy, improved tax revenue collection, reduced public expenditures, instituted credit policy reforms for banks, and absorbed liquidity through the sale of treasury bills. The resultant 6–7 percent GDP growth rate from 1999–2001 decreased the budget deficit and decreased inflation to approximately 10 percent. Industry and services grew at a 5–6 percent rate, whereas agriculture grew at a slower rate but remained resilient in the face of external trade and economic shocks (*The Economist* 2000, 2001; Tass 2001; *Vietnam News* 2001).

The state has moved from economic planner to economic facilitator; that shift is very clear in agriculture. Government policies permitted the importation of chemical fertilizers, which somewhat alleviated the reduced output during the 1999–2001 period. The wide divergence of performance in the forestry sector highlights the environmental concerns around deforestation and land encroachment. Illegal logging, slash-and-burn agriculture, and general unorganized forestry management continue to threaten the fairly environmentally friendly government policies toward the forestry sector (see also Domoto 1997 for earlier observations). Natural resources, such as minerals, and especially hydropower, continue to offer employment, foreign exchange, and cash export opportunities for Laos.

Regarding trade and foreign investment, liberalization has led to increased importation, including consumer goods, which increases the trade deficit. For the lowest value-added and simplest manufacturing industries (e.g., textiles and garments), Laos has become competitive as a low-wage destination for foreign investors. However, for higher-value and technological manufacturing, Laos has not emerged as having sufficient infrastructure to attract the attention of major foreign investors; until very recently, Laos remained at the bottom of the rank-order as a destination for FDI in Southeast Asia (Bartels and Freeman 2000). Foreign investment has increased markedly, however, particularly in the energy sector (Thayer 2003; LPDR 1995, 2001), and the government has announced intentions to launch its first communications satellite (Reuters 2002).

The devalued kip has proven a boon for farm exports from 2000 to 2002, as well as for export of kits for motorbikes and simple machinery that are assembled in Laos due to the very low labor costs (Economist Intelligence Unit 2003; see also Joyeux and Worner 1997). Unfortunately, agricultural irrigation is not widespread, and the importation of fertilizer was constrained until 2000, making the farm sector very dependent on weather patterns. When good weather creates good harvests and exchange rates favor exports, as in 2000, farmers, not surprisingly, prosper (Bourdet 2000).

Investors, marketers, and consumers are better off in many dimensions, but also face a more uncertain economic environment (see also Thayer 2003). The rudimentary agricultural economy ties over half of consumer spending and income to the performance of that economy, or the whims of aid donors who contribute a large share of Laos's GDP. Close examination suggests economic performance really has only been strong in certain regions, for example, the Vientiane municipality and integrated cities and farms around the Mekong or in the northern and central regions with infrastructure links to Thailand, China, and Vietnam. Macroeconomic stability is still problematic, compared to other transitioning countries such as Vietnam and China. Yet, in 2005, the government expects economic performance and growth rates of 7–8 percent, with concurrent positive effects on consumption and marketing activities in Vietnam. In summary, the domestic political support and economic capacity for Laos to sustain NEM reforms and to further promote regional and global economic integration remains unclear, though the overarching trends should leave domestic consumers and businesspersons, as well as foreign investors, guardedly optimistic that Laos will continue to progress in generally predictable ways, consistent with global standards of marketing and development. We now turn to important trends and drivers that must be nurtured to sustain economic growth.

SALIENT TRENDS AND ECONOMIC DRIVERS

Perhaps the most obviously important positive trends are entrepreneurship, banking, regional integration, and consumer emancipation. Each is discussed in some detail, though we add that the long-term welfare of each is dependent upon one or more of the others.

The NEM created an environment conducive to entrepreneurship (Radetzki 1994; see also Siphandone 2001; Worner 1997). A vibrant, small-business sector has emerged, especially around Vientiane, regional business centers, and areas that are conduits to emerging commercial hubs, China and Vietnam (see also Park 2000). Dana (1994) and Bartels and Freeman (2000) have documented the growing, if unsteady, importance of small businesses and entrepreneurial firms in Laos to create employment and income and to establish a business climate receptive to foreign investors. The Lao constitution and legal code both give clear protection to this private-sector activity by domestic businesses (e.g., PriceWaterhouseCoopers 2001); it has been argued that Laos has had one of the clearest legal frameworks in the region regarding ownership of land, rights of women to work and to own land and other resources, and the ability for entrepreneurs— including minorities—to engage in business activities (Flipse 1992). Dana noted that many entrepreneurs in Laos have been women or ethnic minorities, due to the strong influence of Therevada Buddhism and predominant Lao culture, wherein "the belief system functions against the fostering of entrepreneurial spirit among Lao men. . . . Lao men tend to refrain from business activity," (1994, 95). However, recent fieldwork by the second author of this chapter indicates that this tendency is changing. Light industry, agriculture, services, petty trading, and import–export petty trading with Vietnam, China, and Thailand all evince improvements by entrepreneurial businesses. The growth of a cash-based economy in and around cities such as Vientiane also has helped to create a growing entrepreneurial class (Bourdet 2001). For the agricultural sector, a return from collective agriculture to household responsibility with protected land tenure has been a significant boon to farming and agricultural entrepreneurship, such as livestock raising, export vegetable crops, and petty trading in the countryside cash economy (see also Than and Tan 1997; Ardrey, Pecotich, and Shultz 2002). Though many of these endeavors remain small family-oriented production facilities, some have become value-added small to medium-sized enterprises, which are crucial to Laos's future development and prosperity. In order to grow, these businesses must have access to capital provided by reliable financial institutions.

Banking has improved since the Fourth National Conference on Banking, in January 2000, rescued the banking sector from potential collapse caused by the Asian financial crisis of the late 1990s. Now, it is possible for businesses to finance purchases more easily, while consumers have credit services available to finance purchases of motorbikes, washing machines, and home improvements, although these services tend to be limited geographically to the central provinces. The three state-owned commercial banks in the north, Setthathirath, Lanexang, and Alounmay, were merged into a single Lanexang Bank; a similar process in the south created May Bank, while the state-owned Banque Commerce Extérieur Lao remained an independent entity. Though not resolving certain outstanding issues (such as clearer reporting of balance sheets or provisions to fund the overdue loans granted to, but not repaid by, struggling state-owned industries), the merged organizations had sufficient strength to continue operations and actually earn profits (Economist Intelligence Unit 2003). Banks have also offered attractive, short-term bank bills and investments to soak up liquidity and reduce inflation, creating a savings option for consumers who traditionally hoarded wealth in gold, consumer goods, or in kind (Fry 1997). Laos, however, continues to suffer from a low savings rate (less than 5 percent of GDP) and a banking system that has difficulties serving consumers and businesses in the countryside. However, during the 1999–2000 period, the merged banks reported operating profits, the growth in tourism led to an improvement in foreign exchange holdings, and the slow but gradual reform process has made banking reform a priority for post-2001 plans by the Seventh Party Congress (Bank of the LPDR 2000).

Recent regional integration has gradually led to foreign investment and consumer emancipation, as investors have become legally protected, and choices and options open to consumers have increased dramatically. Thailand clearly remains a critical trading partner; however, Laos has continued to mitigate its dependence on Thailand through important agreements with Vietnam and China, which include barter as well as cash-payment options for trade (*The Economist* 2001). Barter agreements with Vietnam, whereby Laos exports motorbike assembly kits in return for consumer goods, could boost cross-border trade to over $400 million annually, and permit cash-constrained Laos to acquire more consumer goods from its neighbors. Recent site interviews by the authors and observations in many markets indicate that growing trade, generally, and particularly with Vietnam, Thailand, and China, has led to an improvement in the breadth and depth of garments, footwear, bicycles, foodstuffs, handicrafts, and other consumer goods available to Lao consumers. Tourism growth, the Internet, and satellite television have brought exposure to tastes and goods desired by foreign customers; tourism, per se, has helped the service economy to grow. FDI has also created more goods for local consumers, and an expatriate segment of non-Thai opinion leaders influencing consumption in urban areas (Bartels and Freeman 2000; Xinhua 2001b). Consumer trends follow a pattern of "convergence" of spending decisions among other transition economies in Southeast Asia (Park 2000), with standard packages of consumer goods, including motorbikes, white goods, and other products, and are described as follows:

- Gradual economic prosperity and consumer freedom of choice
- Gradual move away from subsistence agriculture and toward a cash economy and consumer culture (see also Worner 1997)
- Gradual stimulation of a middle class and a private sector with increased purchasing power, while moving away from consumer dependence on low government salaries
- Gradual segmentation of markets
- Gradual diversification of consumer opinion leadership that still includes Thailand, but also looks toward China, Vietnam, Japan, and Western consumer cultures

Laos has continued a regional focus, with special emphasis on foreign investment from other ASEAN nations (UPI 2001). Since 1988, over 860 foreign invested projects totaling $7.1 billion have been created, in areas such as hydropower (seven projects), telecoms (seventeen projects), hotels and tourism (forty-six projects), processing (thirty-eight projects), mining and gems (thirty-one projects), agriculture (eighty-nine projects), garment manufacturing (ninety projects), and services (157 projects). Leading investors in 2001 were Thailand ($2.9 billion invested), the United States ($1.4 billion invested), and South Korea ($636 million invested). The current focus of ASEAN investment suggests that Laos will have the resources necessary to transform an agrarian economy.

Finally, consumer emancipation and the introduction of choice and market forces into the household level have taken root in Laos, albeit in some segments of the population more than in other segments. Consumption of more modern goods associated with a global economy takes place in "integrated" regions along the borders with China, Thailand, and Vietnam, where consumer goods are available (cf. Adams, Kee and Lin 2001; Xinhua 2001a). In the rural areas and the poor southern provinces, isolation, poverty, and low population density make distribution of consumer goods problematic. Greater awareness and rising incomes among certain segments have elicited consumer desire; entrepreneurs provide desirable products for consumers. This relationship is significant, because previous restrictions on the market freedoms of Laotian citizens and economic ties to the former Soviet Union led to capital flight, departure of technically trained specialists, and ultimately the demise of the middle class, especially during the 1975 post-revolutionary period.

The first choice of consumers typically has been to purchase the land on which their household organizes its economic functions, and this has created cash for consumption of goods and services (Bourdet 2001). However, beyond Vientiane and other centers, marketing and consumer behavior in Laos, and social interactions in general, remain somewhat difficult to observe (Adams, Kee, and Lin 2001). Consumers in the central regions and consumers belonging to the dominant Lao Loum ethnic group have tended to be more prosperous and to have more choice in products and services, with disposable incomes twice those of their counterparts in the countryside (Chamberlain 1999). Also, expatriates working in Laos and the nearly one million tourists who now visit annually expose many Lao consumers to ideas, products, brands, and trends (Park 2000; Sayavong 2001; Sluiter 1993). This fuels demand for goods and services and stimulates local opinion leadership, which in turn, stimulates market activity, individual wealth, and tax revenue.

INFLATION

Laos has faced high inflation since the implementation of the NEM, as noted in Table 9.3, which also includes measures for real GDP growth. The first of these shocks came in the 1986–1989 period, when inflation grew from 6 percent to 76 percent, placing huge stresses on economic development. Fiscal austerity and monetary discipline measures by 1990 reduced inflation to 35 percent; not until 1995 was inflation controlled at a rate under 10 percent through a combination of more effective macroeconomic policies and official development assistance (ODA). The second inflationary shock was the financial crisis from 1997 to 1999, which partly caused the government to retreat from fiscal and monetary austerity; inflation rates in 1997 and 1998 were 19 percent and 142 percent, respectively. A return to fiscal and monetary austerity and some positive agricultural and industrial figures permitted the government to gain some control over inflation in 2000, however, at an annual rate of 25 to 30 percent inflation remains problematic.

Inflation has a number of structural problems that lead to continued pressure on consumer prices. The first is the attractiveness of exporting rice and other agricultural products, which creates scarcity and shortages of basic foodstuff within Laos. A second structural problem contributing to inflation includes bottlenecks in the labor market, where workers with even limited technical skills are in high demand (Bourdet 1996). A third structural problem is credit rationing, with the government waffling between credit restrictions on lending, then reversing these decisions for policy reasons to prop up inefficient state firms, to make irrigation and other capital

Table 9.3

Inflation and GDP Growth

Year	Inflation (%)	Real GDP growth (%)
1987	6.6	−2.9
1988	14.8	−0.7
1989	59.5	14.3
1990	35.7	6.7
1991	13.4	4.0
1992	9.8	7.0
1993	6.3	5.9
1994	6.8	8.1
1995	19.4	7.0
1996	13.9	6.8
1997	19.3	6.5
1998	87.4	4.0
1999	128.5 (EIU 2003)	7.3 (EIU 2003)
2000	25.1 (EIU 2003)	5.8 (EIU 2003)
2001	7.8 (EIU 2003)	5.7 (EIU 2003)
2002	10.6 (EIU 2003)	5.7 (EIU 2003)
2003 (forecast)	10–20 (EIU 2003)	5–6 (EIU 2003)
2004 (forecast)	10–20 (EIU 2003)	5–6 (EIU 2003)

Source: Y. Bourdet, *The Economics of Transition in Laos* (Northamption: Elgar, 2000); Economist Intelligence Unit, *Laos: Country Profiles* (London: EIU, 2003).

improvements, and to continue printing money to make up shortfalls in the government budget. Fiscal austerity (deficits already exceed 10 percent of GDP) constrains the ability of the government to borrow additional funds, creating money supply pressures and pushing inflation still higher. Consumers remain faced with uncertain and inflationary trends and wonder about the purchasing power of their kip, which invokes little confidence in the national currency and forces many Lao to save and to spend in baht, dollars, gold, or consumer goods. Prices and variances in prices for some staples are seen in Table 9.4.

INCOME AND EMPLOYMENT

Laos has plans to grow past its status as an LDC, to eradicate poverty, and to triple per capita income to $1,200 per annum by 2020, but the income per capita remains modest, despite gains resulting from the NEM (e.g., Thayer 2003). Currently, low incomes are partly explained by employment patterns: approximately 75 percent of the workforce is engaged in agriculture, which contributes about 50 percent of GDP (Economist Intelligence Unit 2003). These percentages will decline, as Laos develops its manufacturing sector; with manufacturing jobs typically come higher wages. FDI has, in fact, created thousands of jobs since the NEM began, yet there are a number of constraints that will prevent Laos from soon becoming another "tiger" economy, with workers earning wages at rates found in Thailand or Malaysia, despite renewed emphasis on education and skills acquisition.

Among the constraints faced in Laos are the following. Almost half the population lives below the national poverty line; without remedying this crippling problem, Laos cannot truly progress. Second, rates of inflation and currency exchange often affect purchasing power, and because the economy is heavily oriented toward Thailand, many Lao were hit hard by the regional economic

Table 9.4

Market Prices of Food in Vientiane Municipality and Countryside (in kip)

Item	Vientiane 1996	Vientiane 1997	Vientiane 1998	Vientiane 1999	Country-side 1999
Rice (kg)	500	661	1,670	2,641	2,521
Vegetable (kg)	471	652	1,129	2,396	2,537
Meat—pork (kg)	2,665	2,779	5,389	16,118	13,699
Meet—beef (kg)	2,400	2,834	5,495	15,823	1,352
Fish, fresh (kg)	2,975	3,490	5,863	14,486	12,566
Egg (one)	82	97	214	470	502
Petrol (litre)	297	397	715	1,745	1,807
Paper notebook	250	250	408	1,117	1,077
Cigarettes	330	390	738	2,154	2,409

Source: LPDR, *Basic Statistics of the LPDR 1975–2000* (Ventiane: State Planning Commission and National Statistical Center of the LPDR, 2001).

downturn, as the kip depreciated greater than even the Indonesian rupiah (Freeman 2000). Interesting income trends ensued. Some agricultural exports grew, as did incomes for some farmers with access to export markets, but for urban dwellers, especially state employees who became accustomed to purchasing imported goods, inflation devalued their real income at the same time currency fluctuations made imported consumer goods more expensive (Bourdet 2001). Agricultural workers using more modern techniques and with access to international markets have seen annual wage increases exceeding 8 percent. State workers, held to fixed salaries and fixed annual wage increases of less than 5 percent, have been hit the hardest by a combination of inflation, low salary increases, and layoffs, which are becoming more common under the NEM reform policies (Chamberlain 1999). Some northern and central agricultural workers, including those employed in forestry and animal husbandry, continue to benefit when they have access to foreign markets (e.g., agribusinesses along the Mekong River), but they struggle in isolated areas. Workers employed in the construction, tourism, and ODA industries, almost exclusively in urban areas, generally have benefited. Garment, coffee, and power exports have created some of the most lucrative employment opportunities, as these industries have remained vibrant throughout the various economic downturns, though coffee has recently taken a downturn. ODA now comprises over 20 percent of GDP, and tourism contributed over US$120 million in 2001, offering valuable jobs to workers in the service sector. Slightly less than 20 percent of the population works in urban areas, with many now willing to migrate and to work in boom sectors such as tourism and garment manufacturing. On the upside, the growth of income disparity has stabilized, but urban incomes remain approximately twice the incomes in the countryside (e.g., Bourdet 2001; Chamberlain 1999), and most Lao consumers in the center and north of the country are becoming wealthier, but at a gradual pace.

Another constraint is the low technical sophistication of the labor force. Laos, accordingly, tends to receive investment only for the simplest and lowest value-added manufacturing and processing enterprises (Bartels and Freeman 2000). The present dearth of skilled and highly educated workers suggests Laos is creating a predominately "blue-collar" segment of workers/consumers, and at a more rapid rate than in neighboring countries. Comparatively lower wages result. Moreover, serious deficiencies exist in accountancy and information technology (PriceWaterhouseCoopers 2001). A closer look at the labor force reveals a preponderance of small farmers, animal husbandry specialists, and also, increasingly, immigrants from China and Vietnam. Many ethnic groups and hill tribes do not actively participate in the formal economy or even any kind of parallel cash economy. Lao in the southern provinces generally have not benefited from infrastructure and employment opportunities; they also have not seen substantive increases in incomes.

Underdevelopment has caused a large segment of the population to be unable to buy the standard 2,100-calorie daily requirement for good health and nutrition. Thus, as elsewhere, income creates separate market segments: a subsistence consumer group in the southern and upland regions and a more modern consumer culture in the northern and central regions, where incomes are higher than the national average. Certain hill tribes and ethnic groups engaged in slash-and-burn agriculture still retain barter and trade systems and do not account for income and wages in U.S. dollars or kip (Chamberlain 1999), but transactions, including wages, are sometimes conducted or paid in cash rather than by barter or government-issued coupons.

Two important caveats to income and employment trends must be noted. The first is the difficulty in compiling accurate data, because unemployment is likely underreported in Laos. The second problem is that of "underemployment," including large farming households that remain idle for much of the year, between harvests. The Lao economy of the countryside is less dynamic than, say, Vietnam's, where many state and agricultural workers have second jobs in the private sector to supplement their incomes. In Laos, entrepreneurship as a full-time career or supplemental job is only recently emerging in the countryside. Also, these small businesses tend to be managed by women on a part-time basis, rather than be full-time family businesses, as is common in Cambodia and Vietnam (Ardrey, Pecotich, and Shultz 2002; Dana 1994; McVey 1992; Shultz 1994; Steinberg 1987).

One must place income in the context of local purchasing power. Economists use various measures when attempting to quantify the purchasing power of Lao consumers. Traditional per-capita GDP or income measures may underreport the success of specific market segments, such as the prosperous geographic segment of the Vientiane municipality, and certain cities that trade regularly with Vietnam, China, and Thailand. While traditional measures place income at approximately $400 per consumer, Park (2000) evaluates Laos more favorably, demonstrating a convergence among rich and poor ASEAN nations based on purchasing power parity (PPP), which may be more useful when evaluating the ability of Lao consumers to spend in an inflationary environment with unclear currency exchange rates. Estimates indicate that per capita PPP income in Laos exceeds US$1,300, bringing the spending power of consumers more in line with other more promising, emerging economies.

In summary, an interdependent and occasionally unique set of factors affect income and employment in Laos. Currently, the average income remains modest, and there are limited job opportunities, but some Lao already enjoy purchasing power that enables consumption of numerous goods, beyond subsistence. As constraints subside, real purchasing power growth will increase more rapidly, particularly for steady urban workers in dynamic sectors and rural workers connected to export markets, pending weather patterns, commodity prices, and exchange rates.

NATURAL ENVIRONMENT

Natural resources are among the most important to Laos's economic rebirth, particularly forests, rivers, lakes, farmland, and minerals. These resources are threatened by slash-and-burn agriculture, overfishing and deforestation, and overfertilization leading to water contamination. "External" threats include overlogging and strip mining by foreign investors, clandestine logging by smugglers and unauthorized traders, and businesses focused on short-term gains at the expense of natural resources and long-term welfare of the country and its citizens (Domoto 1997). Official Lao policy is to remain committed to controlled and sustainable development, though problems with surveillance, enforcement, and rank opportunism will challenge this policy.

Mass tourism, while helpful in many ways, also threatens. Lao leaders are concerned about degradation of Lao culture and natural resources, as well as potential threats to government authority that potentially accompany a massive influx of people with new ideas, values, products, and purchase patterns. Ecotourism and efforts to invoke sustainable development have become increasingly important to the leadership (Economist Intelligence Unit 2003). The country is also cooperating with regional and global neighbors to coordinate environmental protection, to eradicate opium poppy production (cf. Thayer 2003), and to commence other initiatives intended to sustain the environment and to bolster life quality and future prosperity.

THE DEMOGRAPHIC AND CULTURAL ENVIRONMENT

In the following text we discuss the people of Laos. Particular emphasis is placed on the demographic structure and trends, as well as cultural influences that shape attitudes and behaviors.

Population

The population of Laos is relatively small—5.4 million people—and widely dispersed throughout the countryside. Laos, in fact, has the lowest population density in Southeast Asia, with approximately twenty persons per square kilometer. About 40 percent of the entire population lives in Savannakhet, Champassack, and Vientiane (city and province). In addition to being isolated and relatively young—over half the population is under twenty years of age—Lao traditionally have preferred not to migrate from their home provinces. We have hinted that NEM and its socioeconomic outcomes will substantially affect extant traditions and migratory patterns. Regional economic integration and comparative urban prosperity have stimulated internal migration to cities and border-trade areas, though this migration has not been profound. Chinese and Vietnamese immigrants also continue to settle in Laos. Nonetheless, the total population remains relatively small, young, dispersed, and focused on subsistence farming and family survival. Statistics on physical dispersion of the population in specific provinces are found in Table 9.5.

The annual population growth rate approaches 2.4 percent, compounding problems associated with a disproportionately young population (see Table 9.6). Down from 2.9 percent in 1997, the growth rate is still high, and the dependency ratio strains resources for health, education, and job creation. Young people enter the job market at an increasingly rapid rate and begin their own families, which further stresses the health and educational systems. The pressure on the physical and institutional infrastructure remains a challenge, and immigrants from China and Vietnam exacerbate this pressure.

A poor country with a young, largely rural population and inadequate infrastructure not surprisingly produces alarming measures for health and wellness, as seen in Table 9.7. Mortality rates, life expectancies and other fundamental indicators indicate Laos indeed is among the most disadvantaged countries in Asia. Within Southeast Asia, Laos ranks near the bottom on the Human Poverty Index and the Human Development Index (World Bank 2002).

Sex Roles

According to official policy and common practice, there is no formal discrimination against women in Laos. Lao women enjoy inheritance and land title rights, and neither female infanti-

Table 9.5

Population by Province

Province	Population
Savannakhet	683,000
Champassack	477,000
Vientiane municipality*	519,000
Luang Prabang	385,000
Vientiane province*	341,000
Oudomxay	198,000
Khammouang	279,000
Houaphan	232,000
Saravane	237,000
Xieng Khouang	191,000
Sayaboury	195,000
Bourikhamsay	172,000
Phongsalay	149,000
Huang Namtha	125,000
Attaptu	93,000
Bokeo	114,000
Sekong	69,000
Special Xieng Hongsa Region	87,000

Source: Laos United Nations Mission (1996; 2001).

*Unofficial sources indicate population in the Vientiane province and the Vientiane municipality and capital region have experienced a sizeable population increase through both migration and immigration from China and Vietnam in the 1998–2002 period.

Table 9.6

Age Distribution in Years

Age	Thousands	Percent of total
0–9	1,501,3	30.9
10–19	1,123.7	23.1
20–29	747.8	15.5
30–39	580.1	12.0
40–49	358.9	07.4
50–59	257.1	05.3
60+	276.8	05.8

Source: LPDR, *Basic Statistics of the LPDR 1975–2000* (Vientiane: State Planning Commission and National Statistical Center of the LPDR, 2001).

cide nor a marked preference for sons exists among the majority of the population and ethnic groups. It is common, however, for "fewer family resources to be expended for female than male children" (Thant and Vokes 1997, 171) and for women to work in the home while male children attend school. Laos remains ranked poorly on the global Gender Development Index, but this inequality is gradually subsiding, due to government policy, ODA funding, and market opportunities (Worner 1997).

The Lao population is heterogeneous, with differences in gender equality varying across ethnic and cultural groups. Since the 1990s, economic migration among males has left the balance of

Table 9.7

Poverty, Health, and Wellness Indicators

Indicator	Value
Human Development Index	.525 (2001) (UNHDR 2003)
Human Poverty Index Rank	66 (UNHDR 2003)
Human Poverty Index Value	40.5 (UNHDR 2003)
Human Development Indicator Rank	135 (UNHDR 2003)
Life expectancy at birth	52 years
Infant mortality	8.7/100
Mortality, under five years of age	13/100
One-year immunization	98%
Access to safe drinking water	52%
Access to sanitation	28%
Population per doctor (Vientiane municipality)	1:1089
Population per doctor (rural countryside)	1:12,600
Average household size	10

Source: Permanent Mission of the Lao PDR to the United Nations (2002), United Nations Development Programme, *Human Development Report*, Indicators (2003).

men and women unequal in many regions, with women outnumbering men. For ethnic groups practicing semimigratory lifestyles, education and equality for women remain problematic. Across all ethnic groups, women typically handle cultivation and marketing of family produce, whereas men build, hunt, fish, and clear fields. Among the majority Lao Loum, "women's status is somewhat lower than that of men, but women are important decision makers within the household and manage much of the family economy" (Thant and Vokes 1997, 174). Among the Lao Theung (peasant farmers) and hill tribal cultures (slash-and-burn migratory cultures), the status of women remains constrained by poverty, isolation, traditional practices, and difficulty in accessing education and markets.

Two important trends have emerged. The first is the improved education of younger women since the 1990s; the second is the higher status of women as household decision makers and economic contributors among the urban and lowland Lao Loum ethnic groups (Ardrey, Pecotich, and Shultz 2002; see also Thant and Vokes 1997). Among urban and lowland females, women over thirty years of age see fewer than 20 percent of their numbers typically having any significant education, whereas over half of women under nineteen years of age have between four and ten years of formal education. Women tend not to be well represented among senior officials or business executives. The largest numbers of employed women are found in agricultural and fishery occupations, low-level clerical and services sectors, and small-scale entrepreneurship; women also are not well represented in education, technical positions, and other professions (Adams et al. 2001; Dana 1994).

Religion

Lao are principally Therevada Buddhist. Upland tribes may be Buddhist, Christian, Muslim, or animist. Christian seminaries were officially closed in 1975, although the government has recently become more accommodating toward all religions and reopened many churches. The government is increasingly sensitive to the needs of the Buddhists in the country, and Buddhism is constitutionally protected under Article 9, along with other "lawful" religious practices. To most Lao, Buddhism is more than religion, it is a deeply important cultural and historical facet of life, and Buddhist rituals, symbols, and traditions are enduring and powerful (see also Swearer 1980). With its emphasis on spiritualism and collectivism, Buddhism perhaps may mitigate the effects of a growing consumer culture and its materialism (see also Dana 1994, for earlier observations).

Household Size

Three generations of families under one roof are common throughout Laos; among upland tribes, larger households can be found. The high fertility rate combined with declining infant mortality often creates even larger and younger families. In Vientiane, for example, women commonly bear as many as seven children, whereas Luang Mamtha women typically bear only four children. Despite such regional variances, a typical Laotian household is comprised of ten members. Few Lao men, and even fewer Lao women, live alone or without children. Farming families continue to find large households expedient, whereas more modern urban families see benefits in smaller families.

The peasant family remains a principal economic engine for development, since the Fifth Party Congress in 1991. Over two-thirds of households are located in rural areas. As indicated previously, a high dependency ratio affects the Lao economy; that is, a small number of working family members must support large numbers of children and elderly relatives. This household composition and dependency ratio affects purchase patterns. Households frequently have their own vegetable plots and livestock, permitting barter and food subsistence outside a cash economy. This can act as a cushion for consumers in bad times, but can also be a constraint in a purely cash economy based on "national markets," wherein consumers deal with distant others, rather than purely in-group members. For more expensive purchases, such as motorbikes and washing machines, large households can be advantageous, as numerous generations can "pool" financial resources. It is, therefore, common to buy and to share, collectively, one or two motorbikes or other "necessities." Expensive or nonessential purchases cannot be made by most Lao households without pooling resources.

Health

Health and nutrition remain problematic for Laos, with many consumers suffering from malaria, malnutrition, and limited access to health care. Life expectancy and infant mortality compare unfavorably with Vietnam and Myanmar, for example (Economist Intelligence Unit 2003). War, poverty, underdevelopment, and infrastructure challenges have adversely affected public health, and government and ODA institutions continue to lack sufficient resources to remedy deficiencies. Many medical doctors departed Laos after 1975, and the country has been challenged to replace and to train new generations of medical specialists.

Poor sanitation, recurring malaria and other tropical and water-borne diseases, and difficulties in accessing and changing health behavior in remote regions continue to challenge the Lao health sector. Low population density and a lack of currently trained personnel make health care expensive to administer. The government has taken steps to remedy this situation and cooperates with other Mekong countries in attending to public health issues such as HIV-AIDS, malaria, and family planning. Government cutbacks in spending, however, retard attracting and retaining skilled health care professionals, although the total number of hospitals (2,000) and hospital beds (12,000) represent improvements.

Consumers are challenged to find the resources for spending in two important areas. The first involves family planning, where contraception is relatively expensive for poor households. In urban areas, smaller families are becoming more desirable. Similarly with antimalaria drugs and other medicines, rural families find it problematic to earn the income for these expensive but critical items. Donor aid covers many of the basic charges for such services, supplemented by public health programs; however, doctors and health care workers are still forced to charge for many services.

Low health standards, in comparison with other developing countries, create a number of impacts on consumer behavior. First, consumers who are ill or partially disabled (e.g., malaria sufferers) face constrained earning potentials and thus have less income. What income they have tends to be spent on medicines. Also, the costs of improving health care are increasing beyond the budgets of many Lao. Nevertheless, spending on medicines, health care, family planning services, contraception, and basic health services is a growing area of importance for consumers.

Education

Policies exist to improve education. Due to limited resources, national priorities focus on extending primary education to all citizens, and this often is at costs to secondary and tertiary education (Siphandone 2001). The educational system in Laos remains challenged by demography, geography, inadequate funding, and neglect. Population pressures combined with uneven economic growth compound such problems. Less than 40 percent of females in the upland areas, for example, have access to education; among some of the sixty-eight ethnic groups officially recognized, neither women nor men attend school. Human resources will be difficult to develop under such conditions; without improvements, economic development will be impeded.

Adult literacy has improved to 50 percent for males and 35 percent for females, particularly as more Lao participate in formal education. School enrollments for ethnic minorities, however, are far lower than for the majority Lao groups. Adams et al. (2001) determined that 23 percent of dominant Lao ethnic groups have never attended school, whereas higher percentages of ethnic tribes have never attended school, such as the Phutai (34 percent never attended), Khmu (56 percent never attended), Hmong (67 percent never attended), Kor (96 percent never attended), and Musir (96 percent never attended). Part of this problem is that Lao, the language of instruction, is only spoken well by some 50 percent of the national population.

Educational challenges stem partly from underdevelopment and low funding, but have roots in the history of the educational system. In the 1800s, educational access was segmented by religion, as Buddhist temple schools were the most common provider of education to boys and girls. Upland tribes, which generally were not Buddhist and had no access to these schools, remained illiterate. Modern schooling was not established until 1907, and under French administration, higher degrees were principally granted in Hanoi, between 1907–1925. By 1964, Laos boasted of 147 primary schools with 14,712 students. However, colonial policies favored European pedagogy and hindered the expansion of Buddhist temple schools and domestic schools previously funded by the monarchy. By 1975, through the initial independence period, the educational system expanded, with over 6,000 teachers and 240,000 students engaged in primary education. High schools and universities were only available in the Vientiane municipal region surrounding the capital (Permanent Mission of the LPDR 2002; PriceWaterhouseCoopers 2001).

The communist system affected education through emphasis on education of the masses at the primary level and on the eradication of illiteracy. Important developments included (1) linking educational development to national socioeconomic development; (2) developing a competency in the sciences; (3) training cadres in science and economics; and (4) extending education to isolated areas. University training was principally conducted through cooperative agreements with Cuba, Vietnam, the former Soviet Union, and through Eastern European vocational schools. In 1991, the Fifth Party Congress focused educational policy on improving relevance to the business and government needs of the economy, improving teacher training (and salary and support payments), and expanding access to education for remote ethnic groups. By 2000, enrollment targets for primary school (715,000), secondary school (120,000), and upper secondary schools (42,000) were complemented by ambitious goals for vocational training and planning for future basic university education for selected high school graduates. A recurring problem is that of dropout rates at all levels, leaving many Lao partially educated and without certificates or diplomas.

In the 2001–2002 period, educational priorities pursued by the government and external donors focused on the four areas of preschooling, general education, vocational and technical education, and adult education (for both vocational skills and literacy building). Also, the government is working to recruit and to train minority teachers, as many minority students have special needs, language challenges when receiving instruction in the Lao language, and unfamiliarity with customs outside their local and ethnic environs. Lao education continues to suffer from low investment in real terms, inefficiency, poor access to schools, low teacher quality, and gender inequity. Attending school remains a novel experience for Lao, and the habit and support for learning remains problematic for most families and individuals. The lack of broad exposure to modern concepts, written materials, the Internet, and other global educational trends will continue to impede Lao citizens until family habit to support education evolves to mirror tendencies seen in more developed Southeast Asian countries.

The transition to a developed and market economy has required additional technical training and university education. With Japanese government assistance, Laos has created universities for teacher training, economics training, and general university education. Budgetary allocation for education, initially low during the first phases of economic reform, has increased in the 2000–2 period. In theory, education is compulsory from ages six to sixteen; however, the Lao Loum ethnic group is more receptive to formal education for their families. All levels of education, from kindergarten to technical training, are now widely available.

The impact on adult literacy has been gradual improvement; however, literacy remains low by international standards. Depending on the source, the literacy rate is between 60 and 83 percent among adults (even 60 percent may be optimistic), with men disproportionately more literate than women, depending on the region. In rural areas, women especially have difficulty accessing schools, and only 25 percent of many ethic groups study beyond primary school. Teacher training remains problematic, and many teachers leave the education profession for more lucrative employment in industry. The Lao government has made education and human resources development priorities for the nation; clearly, challenges are daunting.

Ethnicity

The Lao population is diverse and includes sixty-eight ethnic and linguistic groups. Ethnic Lao comprise 60 percent of the population, followed by Phoutheng "Khan" minorities (15 percent), Tribal Thai minorities (20 percent), and Hmong, Yao, Khmu, and others comprising the remainder of the population. These various groups can be simplified into three broad consumer cultures, namely, lowland peasants, upland tribes, and modernizing urban dwellers.

Lowland Peasants

This group uses cash and money as mediums for exchange, has basic literacy and primary educational skills, and is primarily engaged in agriculture, petty trading, and animal husbandry. This segment is exposed to marketing messages through television, radio, newspapers, and communal access to telephones, transport, banking, and communications infrastructures.

Upland Tribes

This diffuse group is geographically, linguistically, religiously, and culturally isolated, involved in gathering, slash-and-burn agriculture, logging, and subsistence farming. The diverse cultures within this segment often prefer barter to cash and have difficulty accessing modern infrastructures of banking, transport, and communication, including television and newspapers.

Modernizing Urban Dwellers

Members of this growing group, principally found in the Vientiane municipality, at other points along the Mekong river, and in Vietnam, China, and Thailand trading towns, tend to hold salaried jobs or regular income-earning activities, retain exposure to modern consumer culture, encounter tourists and foreign visitors, and have regular access to mass media. Cash is the medium for exchange, and access to banking, telecommunications, individual transportation (cars, bicycles, and motorbikes), and advertising messages increases.

Trends toward regional integration are pushing these cultures toward modernization in three different ways (McFarlane 2001). First, the lowland peasant culture is overlapping the modernizing urban culture. More workers are leaving farms for salaried jobs, and NEM reforms have reduced state jobs and forced consumers to rely heavily on the market for jobs and cash wages. Regional integration has permitted more non-Lao goods, tourists, and services to enter Laos. Western brands and services, from banking services to soft drinks, can now be bought throughout the northern and central provinces; and fast-moving consumer goods, ranging from condoms to candy, can be bought in the isolated areas. Ethnic divisions are slowly giving way to common consumption patterns in many areas of the country.

These three cultures can be further subdivided into ethnic market segments. Lowland peasants stem from the dominant Lao Loum culture, residing in the valleys along the Mekong River, practicing wet rice agriculture and cash crop activities. Increasingly, these ethnic participants in peasant culture are being drawn into the modernizing urban culture growing around the Mekong River trade. The upland or tribal cultures are comprised of two principal ethnic groups, the Lao Theung and Lao Soung, along with other minority tribes such as the Hmong. Lao Theung, or upland Lao, are generally continuing slash-and-burn agriculture and resist attempts at resettlement, education, and integration fostered by the government and donor agencies. The Lao Soung peoples are cash crop cultivators, including opium growers, and hold to traditional practices and cultural isolation, although they appreciate the monetized economy (Kittikhoun 1996).

Ethnicity is broadly described in Table 9.8. It should be noted that Lao Loum dominate much of the business and government, with other groups increasing their participation in modern society.

Official policies of the LPDR are nondiscriminatory, with equal opportunity for all ethnic groups. Outreach efforts are increasingly made to recruit more teachers, government officials, and politicians from the ethnic tribes. Financial and infrastructure constraints have made this policy difficult to put into practice; nonetheless, key ministers, such as the Interior Minister, and

Table 9.8

Ethnic Groups in Laos

Ethnicity	Percentage	Characteristics
Lao Loum	60	Occupy lowland plains and Mekong river valley; dominant ethnic group; involved in government and trade
Lao Theung	22	Mountain slope and upland dwellers; moderate contact with monetized economy and consumer culture, subsistence and cash crop agriculture and animal husbandry.
Lao Soung	10	Mountaintop dwellers, isolated and cut off from most standard education and monetized economy, save for small pockets of loggers, gem miners, smugglers, and narcotics trade participants
Other	8	Hmong and Yeo tribes, returning exiles, immigrants from China and Vietnam, Chinese traders, expatriates, etc.

Source: Lao United Nations Mission, "Basic Data and Economic Indicators," Permanent Mission of the LPDR to the United Nations (2002).

many supporters of the Communist movement stem from ethnic minority tribes and hold high positions in government. Minority tribes are now encouraged to participate in government (Dommen 1995). Most officials, however, are males from the Lao Loum ethnic group who comprise the majority of the ruling political party.

Cultural Protection

Lao is the official language and thus is the language of instruction, although the country officially recognizes some sixty-eight ethnic groups with unique cultures and languages. Laos has created an official Lao Tourism Development Coalition to ensure that the national culture and indigenous minority cultures are protected as Laos opens to the outside world. The lesson of Thailand is used as an example of overly rapid development, with a host of social problems, such as AIDS, prostitution, and drugs, which accompanied economic development.

Lao leadership has a priority to develop the nation, while still protecting national cultural traditions. As consumer culture becomes more normative, concerns increase over cultural imperialism, commercial domination, or de facto annexation by Thailand. Laos is surrounded by powerful neighbors and hosts an increasing number of tourists, businesspersons, and aid workers. The problem of Thai influences is especially strong for historical and linguistic reasons (Chanthavong 1997). At various times in history, Thailand has annexed Laos. Linguistically, the languages are similar, and many urban consumers tune in regularly to Thai television, which also provides exposure to advertising and marketing messages (Evans 1999). As Laos becomes more embedded in the global economy, other cultural forces and traditions will become apparent; many will be helpful, some will be disruptive.

CHANGES IN CONSUMER BEHAVIOR

The preceding text introduces readers to various forces that affect consumer behavior. Below, we discuss some of the changes in consumers and their behaviors that are occurring in transitioning Laos.

Materialism

Laos, nestled in the middle of a dynamic region and now open to FDI and global telecommunications, is increasingly exposed to a wider range of people, companies, products, brands, and media that promote consumption and the advantages (trappings?) of material possession. Households are growing beyond the local barter economy into a cash economy for goods and services. This trend has influenced consumption patterns, although the extent to which Lao have embraced materialism and consumer culture varies by geographic, ethnic, and behavioral segments throughout the country. Consumer culture along the vital trading link of the Mekong River, in the Vientiane municipal region, and in major China–Thai–Vietnam–Lao trading cities has evolved more rapidly compared to more isolated geographic regions. In many areas of rural Laos, consumer culture is not yet firmly entrenched. But, as development expands and rural Laos becomes less isolated, consumers gain awareness of how their neighbors live, work, own, and spend. Gaps between Laos and other ASEAN nations will drop. The Lao Loum ethnic group, which has made the transition to the market economy most successfully, will likely continue to prosper and continue to adopt modern purchasing and spending patterns for motorbikes, televisions, and services, as experienced in China and Vietnam during their transitions.

Consumerism is unlikely to grow into rank materialism, as certain checks exist in Lao politics and society, including the official socialist philosophy and a fairly devout Buddhist population, neither of which favor individualism or conspicuous consumption. Another factor is isolation. Many villages are remote—especially during monsoon seasons—and market trends to, and through, them move slowly. Also, many families remain focused on survival and cooperative agriculture. All these factors and trends provide pressures against individualism, materialism, and excessive consumption. That said, recent observations suggest that a new consumer order may be unfolding:

> As the workday ended, young and old Lao begin to congregate along the newly refurbished promenade that runs along the Mekong, in Vientiane. Most people were gravitating to a number of new shops, restaurants and cafes that had emerged, post NEM. I chatted with a young man who was wearing a replica of the Croatian national soccer jersey. Fashionable sunglasses were perched on his gel-laden, spiked hair, and he wore newer sneakers that clearly were counterfeit iterations of Nike. No matter, he likes them; he guessed they came from Thailand or China. The young man straddled his new motorbike, which apparently was designed in Japan, made in China and distributed through Vietnam. He was preparing "to play some football [soccer], before [the evening's telecast of] the World Cup," which he intended to watch with friends at a local pub/restaurant, and which would be beamed to Laos, from Korea and Japan, complete with all the advertisements of the global sponsors and their brands. He knew almost all these brands, well; he liked them, too. Before his match, we chatted a bit more—his English was quite good—and watched about 60–70 Lao women gather in an open pavilion. Soon they began to stretch, twist, jump, and gyrate. Each woman was clad in various hues of fluorescent spandex tights and followed the lead of the aerobics instructor and the pulsating rhythms of blaring "techno" pop-music. Saffron-draped monks and other folk nonchalantly strolled by or watched nonplussed from cafes, with soda-pop, beer or tea in-hand . . . (Shultz 2002, notes)

Finally, concerns over mimicking Thailand too closely will constrain shameless materialism, if only because the Lao government will encourage cultural distinctiveness and will rein in Thai businessmen, who Lao generally consider to be disingenuous at best (cf. Than and Tan 1997). Thus, while many Lao consumers will become more materialistic, various cultural and governmental forces will discourage levels that many Lao believe are endemic to Thailand. At the same time, greater access to global information networks means that Lao consumers will also develop a more global sense of the boundaries for materialism, and their consumption patterns will change accordingly.

Consumer Expectations

Lao consumers with access to information and infrastructure will continue to expect higher standards of living, and more goods and services upon which to spend their growing incomes. Over 40 percent of imports into Laos are consumer goods, and an additional 4 percent of imports are spare parts and accessories for the increasingly popular motorbikes used as the favored mode of transportation (cf. Economist Intelligence Unit 2003). Consumers are increasingly participating in a more modern cash economy and formal credit systems; they are exposed to foreign ideas and brand names, and are benefiting from a gradually more open political climate. Diffusion of information technologies and an increase in tourism to the country provide additional contact with current trends and global consumption patterns. All these factors stimulate consumer expectations, especially in Vientiane municipality, border towns, and towns along the Mekong. In sum, Lao policies are slowly fostering the growth of an educated, wealthier class of consumers, and quality of life is expected to improve through consumption of a growing range of products and services from foreign and domestic sources.

Challenges and long-term problems, however, remain. Most pressing among them are population dispersion, a largely uneducated workforce, underdeveloped infrastructure, and a disproportionately large number of consumers with low incomes. More expensive products and services are still beyond their reach. Nevertheless, rural consumers, who were able to participate in the benefits of NEM and export businesses, have also seen incomes rise, along with expectations. Only the most distant and most culturally traditional consumers are unlikely to participate in the benefits of the NEM, and thus hold to their existing expectations for subsistence agriculture and basic tools for survival.

If economic growth is unable to keep pace with consumer expectations, dissatisfaction will likely occur. New roads, telephone lines, and other infrastructure improvements will make communication easier within Laos and with neighboring transition economies that have prospered more rapidly (see also Shultz and Pecotich 1997). Goods, ideas, services, and quality standards from other countries will continue to flow into Laos, along with consideration for top Asian- and Western-branded goods. Consumers, in general, will expect more sophisticated products and services, and only Lao in the most remote hinterlands will not have raised expectations.

Market Segmentation Trends

We have alluded to emerging market segments, most notably determined by income, employment, geography, ethnicity, and political influence. As Laos becomes more prosperous and experiences social changes forced by the market, consumption patterns become more diverse, and the number and structure of segments are increasing. Table 9.9 provides an overview of these increasingly diverse segments.

Regional differences in political influence, professional standing, purchasing power, and ac-

Table 9.9

Emerging Segmentation Determinants

Segment	Principal of segmentation
Geographic	Northern versus southern Thai border town/Vietnam border/China border Urban versus rural Highland versus lowland
Ethnic	Lao Loum/Lao-Thai/Lao-Chinese/hinterland tribes
Purchasing power and political influence	State salaried workers and party cadres Joint venture workers Small entrepreneurs Wealthy traders, newly rich, party officials
Societal orientation	Buddhist versus former Communist; secular urban elite
Age	<19 years 19–35 35+
Sex	Male versus female

Source: Lao United Nations Mission, "Basic Data and Economic Indicators," Permanent Mission of the LPDR to the United Nations (2002).

cess to urban or trading-center markets will be consequential in the foreseeable future. Furthermore, as government cadres and state employees generally have seen real incomes decline due to inflation and NEM restructuring, professional and social standing may lead to reduced incomes, compared with successful farmers and traders. High-status professionals—such as teachers, doctors, and medical workers—have seen their incomes constrained, sometimes through government salary restrictions, and have had difficulties earning outside income; they also increasingly leverage their education and skills in moonlighting capacities to generate additional income. Sex roles may grow in importance (cf. Dana 1994), as Lao women have tended toward entrepreneurship and trading and now have some disposable income. Age is a particularly important segmentation criterion. The large younger segment tends to be more "wired" to information technologies, which facilitates the diffusion of goods and services synonymous with popular culture. Indeed, the previously described soccer player—wired to the Internet, satellite broadcasts, and global brands— is the archetype of this segment.

Profession-based segments that resulted from the NEM are found in Table 9.10. Although many segments remain somewhat nebulous—e.g., the moonlighting state employee who quadruples his or her income through an entrepreneurial endeavor—trends suggest there are attractive market segments in Laos, and somewhat predictable buyer behaviors from which sensitive and savvy marketers can profit. Economic conditions have progressed such that many consumers regularly purchase more than subsistence products. Moreover, many Lao are wealthier than official statistics indicate, as many transactions go unrecorded. Estimates of purchasing power at approximately $1,300 mean many urban dwellers and some farmers and border traders have disposable income. Obvious signs of relatively expensive products in shops and in use by Lao consumers indicate pockets of wealth.

Table 9.10

Market Segments under NEM Reforms

Segment	Characteristics
New entrepreneurs	Service sector and tourism Businessmen, joint-venture partners Foreign local partners; women entrepreneurs
New private-sector employees	Garment manufacturing managers and workers; transportation, power generation, tourism workers, factory workers in joint-venture and foreign firms
Traders and middlemen	Increasingly oriented to China and Vietnamese border towns, Thai and Mekong River traders, exporters, "smugglers"
Private agricultural workers	Increased cash earnings plus household economy in-kind earnings; spending preferred over saving; savings and trading in-kind and through barter; export opportunities abound due to low kip exchange rates 1999–2002
State workers	Workers retained after restructuring still have many state benefits, such as housing and other subsidies; still struggle to keep pace with inflation
Collective state farmers	Salaried workers paid principally in-kind or with ration coupons; constrained to participate in money economy or consumer culture; underutilized and underemployed
Traditional cultures	Avoid cash economy; prefer tradition; some communal exposure to brands and products through communal viewing of television when in towns

Source: LPDR, *Basic Statistics of the Lao PDR 1975–2000* (Vientiane: State Planning Committee National Statistical Center, 2001).

CONSUMER SAVINGS AND CREDIT

Financial services reform began in 1988, when a two-tier banking system was created, leaving the central bank as principal regulator and permitting state-owned commercial banks to provide financial services. Currently, financial services remain in their infancy for Lao consumers, who typically access state-owned commercial banks and, in major cities, have opportunities to use foreign bank branches. Foreign banks (principally Thai owned) are restricted to the Vientiane municipality. Insurance, via the state Assurance Générales du Laos, is also available to consumers. Most banking products offered to businesses and consumers are very short-term loans and bank deposits. Competing with the state-dominated banking sector is "a thriving informal capital market, including private money lending and revolving-credit circles" (Economist Intelligence Unit 2003, 59). With the growth in a cash economy, bank savings practices have increased, as has the ability of local consumers to access credit cards, although both services are limited to the northern and central geographic segments.

Domoto (1997) observed that the financial sector is fragmented, disorganized, and remains "not fully monetized." Over 50 percent of the assets of Lao banks, and over 90 percent of bank savings deposits, reside in the Vientiane municipal region. Because of the recurring provision of foreign ODA, constituting as much as 15 percent of the nation's GDP, the necessity to mobilize domestic savings has not been a priority. Also, state banks have a recurring and serious problem with nonperforming loans, exceeding 25 percent of total assets, creating solvency challenges for the banking system. Both serious banking reform and planned stock exchanges remain distant prospects. However, modern banking services are emerging slowly in the Vientiane region, based on market forces. To date, the high rates of domestic investment have been financed through borrowing from foreign lenders. Most of these loans are at concessionary rates; however, the shortfall has been continuous for over a decade. In addition, state-owned commercial banks have continued policy-based lending decisions in spite of nonperforming loans and questionable efficiency. At present, the banking system is receiving an important focus of attention from the senior leadership to ensure continued stability.

Domestic savings will need to originate from private sources, including deposits from small savers and businesses in commercial banks. Fiscal reforms are being made concurrently to banking-sector reforms to ensure continued price stability, improved savings mobilization, and clearer understanding and management of credit risks by public and private banks. For consumers, this will translate into improved banking services and a choice between informal money lenders and credit circles, as well as state-owned banks, in addition to foreign commercial bank branches operating fully in the private sector.

Consumer Credit

Credit to businesses and consumers remains rationed by the government through its ongoing efforts to control inflation. Consumer credit has only recently been contemplated as part of ongoing banking reforms. Banks are also uncommon for savings mobilization and informal credit circles, and agricultural credit cooperatives are the norm in Laos rather than formalized banking institutions. Wealth is stored collectively in cash, gold, rice, or even consumer goods during times of high inflation. By 1998, basic consumer services for credit and savings became available through national banks and also through Thai joint-venture banks in the Vientiane municipality. By 2001, restructurings of loss-making banks have confined modern banking services to the capital region.

Consumer credit cards, short-term loans to entrepreneurs, and installment programs with low down payments (for such products as motorbikes) have become commonplace in many urban and border town areas. Also, for agricultural purposes, the Bank of the LPDR has empowered the Agricultural Bank and Laos Commercial Bank to make loans to farmers at concessionary rates. Informal money lending, especially among ethnic Chinese, remains commonplace.

CHANGES TO THE MACROMARKETING MIX

The continuation of the NEM reforms, slowed during the 1997–1999 period, has been assured since 2000. This renewed push has made a substantial impact on the macromarketing mix. An overview of the trends for the mix of products, place and distribution, promotion, pricing, customer service, and market assessment are provided below. The growing importance of communications and marketing research are stressed.

Products

Prior to the launch of the NEM, command economics and state-owned production resulted in few product and service choices for consumers. This condition has rapidly changed in relatively urban environments and provinces bordering the Mekong River and rapidly developing neighbors. More goods are available, and credit is often available from official or unofficial sources to finance purchases. A range of products and services is described below, from local goods to inexpensive Vietnamese and Chinese goods, to services and entertainment available to consumers.

Local Goods

Most staples, such as unprocessed food, rice, and simple clothing and shoes, are produced domestically. National beer, tobacco, and foodstuff manufacturers have expanded product lines and improved standards, marketing, and advertising. Beer Lao, fresh local beer, and locally packaged food products are maintaining market share, and in some instances capturing market share, compared with imported brands. The presence of counterfeit Western brand names has also become more obvious, though their origins are not necessarily Laos.

Chinese and Vietnamese Products

Increased road and air links with China and Vietnam have contributed to growth in imported products, including bicycles and motorbikes, electronics, textiles, and numerous other consumer goods. China still buys over 5 percent of Laos's exports, provides 11 percent of Laos's imports, and remains an important trading partner. Vietnam's cross-border trade was expected to top $400 million annually by 2004. Construction equipment, labor, and transport and infrastructure materials, as well as cheap plastic toys and gifts remain common imports.

Thai Goods

Physical proximity and cultural compatibility with Thailand make Laos a natural market for Thai goods. Demand is stimulated through Thai advertising and other forms of marketing communications; the similarity of language and written script makes consumers aware and impressionable. Thai goods, television shows, media, and services (e.g., banking) are generally perceived as being of higher quality than Lao goods. However, because the possible dominance of Thai culture remains a concern, some consumers search for other countries of origin when seeking to make purchases.

Expensive Foreign Imports

The small segment of wealthy consumers, plus the growing expatriate market, demand foreign and imported goods associated with or produced in developed countries. Japanese, European, and American brands are perceived as being of high quality. Laos is increasingly viewed as an attractive target by marketers, and the types and varieties of high-end products are increasing. While automobile imports remain less common in comparison with other transitioning economies, proliferation of other relatively expensive goods and services follows patterns seen in Vietnam and China. Some of these goods enter the Lao market through legitimate channels; many are smuggled.

Services

Services have flourished under the NEM. Taxis, airlines, tour guides and agencies, hotels, cafés and restaurants, Internet cafés, telephones, and media are increasingly available to consumers. Newspapers and print media are less commonly consumed due to literacy rates, but this problem is expected to be remedied. Increasing the scope, availability, and quality of services has become a priority for Laos, for both government services (education, medicine) and tourism-level services (hotels and restaurants). This sector has grown markedly, and increasing investment has gravitated toward it because of fundamental opportunities and in response to Laos's National Development Strategy.

Entertainment

Entertainment, a subset of services, has shown remarkable signs of life in the last decade. In the countryside, entertainment ranges from buying a ticket to watch Thai television, to karaoke, to traditional entertainment such as singing and storytelling. In the cities, movies, ice cream shops, dance halls, aerobics pavilions, videos, video games, and music halls are now available, as is a rudimentary "café culture" and, increasingly, an Internet café culture. Chinese-exported soap operas and popular music and culture are also growing in influence, as are Vietnamese education and cultural media.

To summarize, new products, services, and brands are entering Laos at an accelerating rate; Laotians have become increasingly discriminating when choosing among price, quality, country of origin, and marketing messages/labels. Competition and domestic reforms have improved quality and variety of Lao goods and services. Domestic and export consumption of both generally have increased. Garments, for example, are exported to the United States, Japan, and Canada in addition to being consumed locally. Growing economic trends and disposable income, as well as newly wealthy middle-class and upper-class segments, create additional demands for many locally manufactured goods, imports, and new services. The Lao demand for most goods and services marketed elsewhere in Southeast Asia is expected to accelerate further.

Successful product management in Laos should consider the following recommendations:

- Products should be durable, have long shelf lives, and should be sturdily packaged.
- Labels should clearly identify what the product does and include illustrations, where appropriate.
- The Thai language and alphabet can be used in addition to Lao languages; even globally recognized brands will benefit from packaging that includes Lao text, images, and symbols.
- In some categories dominated by multinational corporations, new products from non-Thai or Lao sources are increasingly preferred; however, brief instructions translated into Lao or Thai are helpful.
- Joint-venture products should identify the made-in-Laos component. Despite the growing presence of global brands, when given the choice, Lao consumers will often prefer to purchase Lao products, particularly those steeped in tradition, such as clothes and foods.

Prices

Pricing policy is one of the most significant outcomes of the NEM. Prior to the NEM, pricing was set by government decree rather than by market forces. Now, prices are negotiated, and the government protects the ability of sellers and buyers to set prices based on the market mechanism (see also Ljunggren 1992). The freeing of prices has also led to frustration among many consumers, as both inflation and poverty have combined to make some goods more expensive. Also, the procurement prices used by some remaining state industries are "rationalized," creating artificially low prices for some staples and locally manufactured goods. Although a considerably freer market exists, government pricing, inflation, and problematic exchange rates often distort actual consumer prices for some segments.

Segmentation and pricing strategies are clearly linked, and foreign firms must be sensitive to this relationship. Moreover, the institutionalization of consumer credit, through fledgling banks and informal credit circles, has permitted larger individual purchases; it also helps households that choose to pool resources when purchasing communal television sets, motorbikes, or telephones. Many transactions still necessitate cash and are discouraged by high prices. Moreover, without further improvement of the banking system, methods of storing wealth remain constrained, and spending tends to be preferred over savings. Except for consumption of increasingly high-priced goods, few mechanisms exist to absorb the cash/wealth enabled by the NEM.

Place and Distribution

"Easy" points of distribution remain the major trading areas along the Mekong River or in the Vientiane and Luang Prabang regions. Distribution to and through the majority of Laos suffers greatly from geographic and infrastructure constraints, a long rainy season, low population density, and mobile target markets (i.e., nomadic tribes). Much of the population is not served by adequate roads, televisions or television signals, or railways. Many regions remain highly fragmented, and lack of communication systems creates a need for numerous intermediaries. These factors conspire against low transportation fees and timely delivery of goods and services.

Small, family-owned shops or distributors, traditional markets, and traveling traders, are the common methods of distribution for Laotian consumers. Marketing managers of developed firms must target common distribution points and then let local systems distribute to end consumers. This arrangement is not likely to change in the foreseeable future.

The transportation infrastructure, which will positively affect distribution, is a high priority for the Lao government and donor organizations. Since 2000, many more provinces and townships have become more accessible. The growth of tourism has encouraged better road links. Perhaps most importantly, Laos is at the heart of the greater Mekong region, and cross-border trade continues to increase despite the aforementioned challenges. ASEAN and ASEAN Free Trade Area (AFTA) involvement has spurred regional cooperation to improve rail, river, and air links, as well as road connections. Costs and bureaucratic encumbrances are dropping. Further improvements to infrastructure and distribution mechanisms will likely have the effects discussed below.

Information Reach/Product Reach

The diffusion of information technologies creates greater consumer awareness; more open policies create more internal and external trade. Growing economies and citizen awareness throughout the region, including Laos, will continue to drive infrastructure development and to enhance distribution efficiencies and effectiveness. We already witnessed this trend in agricultural products, consumer goods, and tourism. This trade, in turn, will drive yet more infrastructure development, which further abets more trade.

Trading Center Development

An outcome of the preceding dynamic will be the emergence of trading centers. Growing sophistication in terms of brand, product, and country of origin awareness has extended to towns along the Mekong, on the Thai and China borders, and increasingly along Vietnam's border. New roads and infrastructures make an increasing number of towns accessible for distribution of various products. Greater mobility to these towns will help to create hubs or trading centers (McVey 1992; LPDR 1999; UNDP 1997).

Exposure to and Consumption of More Types of Goods

Laos has become a media target, a tourist destination, a market target, and is expanding as a distribution network throughout the Greater Mekong countries of Cambodia, China, Thailand,

Vietnam, and Myanmar (Than 1997). These factors create still more exposure to goods, more consumer demand, more efficient distribution mechanisms to meet this growing demand, and more consumption.

Marketing Communications

The marketing communications mix of Laos has grown to include the Internet, as well as English- and French-language expatriate newspapers, in addition to local newspapers, magazines, and television broadcasts. Point-of-sale materials, sampling, radio, and flyers/brochures are increasingly used in trading centers. It must be noted that, as of this writing, media remain under government control, including advertising copy; however, the authorities now recognize the importance of advertising and other forms of marketing communications. Consumer capabilities to process marketing information depend largely on exposure to media, familiarity with advertising, culturally sensitive ad copy, literacy, and, for the illiterate, ad copy that persuades, creates images, or reinforces, often without written text.

Consumer knowledge of many new products and services remains constrained by underdevelopment, isolation, and literacy issues. Receptivity to foreign brands is growing, driven by the increase in media and the improvements in trade and tourism links. Similar to their ASEAN neighbors, local consumers are receptive to foreign brands. The government has few domestic industries to protect, so brands such as Coca-Cola, Sony, Honda, JVC, Singha, Marlboro, and Microsoft circulate openly. With such a large percentage of the population under age sixteen, competing for brand awareness has become intense, as marketers attempt to educate a new generation of consumers about foreign and domestic brands.

We have suggested that brand awareness is rapidly diffusing throughout Laos, but the relatively slow pace of reforms, compared to, say, China and even Vietnam, means that consumers may be less aware of new and established brands. Consumers, therefore, will increasingly rely on marketing communications to obtain information, with hopes of making informed choices for what eventually will be a large number of purchase decisions. And as consumers become wealthier, brand promotion will be rewarded.

The integration of various media to communicate with consumers in a clear and understandable way is critical to success. For the growing segment of young, urban consumers, Internet cafés, sponsorship of popular events, and youth magazines are appropriate methods; posters and point-of-sale print materials will become increasingly important. In rural areas, posters and placards with pictures and brief descriptions will have superior results compared to dense advertising copy. Private and joint-venture newspapers, local state television and radio, and, in many regions, Thai television and radio stations provide market and consumer information. Radio, television, and telephone penetration is growing throughout much of Laos. Thai–Lao joint-venture television broadcasts bring increasingly high-quality programming to consumers; cable and satellite broadcasts will expand programming even more (Reuters 2002). In summary, Laos is on the cusp of a multimedia growth spurt that will afford new opportunities to communicate with Lao consumers, but fundamental ad copy and communication guidelines will likely remain the same.

Market Research

Market research in Laos is growing in importance and sophistication. International market research firms continue to operate, as do major management consulting firms; at the same time, the government has updated the accuracy and timeliness of its statistical reporting. Government data, however, tend to focus on macroeconomic indicators. Private-sector research is needed for timely, detailed analysis of local market conditions. Certain segments are profitable in Laos, and efforts to plan, implement, and control consumer marketing efforts will benefit from additional research.

Collecting accurate data from consumers can be problematic. The UNDP (1997), for example, found that surveying Lao women is often challenging for cultural reasons and because of unfamiliarity with market research techniques. Rural consumers are often uncomfortable speaking with unfamiliar researchers about personal issues related to savings, spending, and income and consumption patterns. Reporting positive information about income and consumption could draw the attention of taxation or other authorities, making accurate information collection problematic. Fieldwork by Shultz in the summer of 2002 indicates that valid consumer attitudes and market trends are becoming easier to measure, particularly in urban settings. Nevertheless, as argued elsewhere in this volume (see chapter 18, "Vietnam"), a clear understanding of the intricacies of the local marketing system in which the investor must succeed may be best achieved by placing multiskilled employees, in country, for an extended period, to collect primary data relevant to company-specific needs and objectives (see also Shultz 1994). Determining which enterprises to commence and products to sell is a challenge, because Lao consumers may not immediately discern the utility of the product or service, and key aspects of the marketing system in which an investor must function may vary from those familiar in, for example, Thailand or Vietnam. Furthermore, determining not only which products or services to sell, but where to sell them and how to transport, merchandise, promote, and price them also require considerable, Laos-sensitive market research. In addition to extended, systemic fieldwork, note too that managers of many local, joint-venture, and foreign-invested firms in ASEAN countries informally share market information (see also Vu and Speece 1995).

FUTURE TRENDS AND EXPECTATIONS

Analysis of historical events and recent economic and market data indicates Laos is a growing, increasingly accessible and profitable market (Than 1997). Movement toward regional integration, improved performance under NEM, and ongoing political stability predict future progress. Continued regional harmony and economic integration, FDI, foreign aid and technical assistance, and domestic growth combine to raise the national income and consumer purchasing power. The abundant natural resources, willing human resources, and cultural treasures of the country are being developed, and many of the current exports—hydropower, rice, garments, forestry products—are sustainable. The historical experience of dependency on foreign powers, such as Thailand, France, and Vietnam, suggests a balanced approach to development with a gradually increasing reliance on world markets, technical talent, resources, and infrastructure investment.

Consumer Behavior Trends

Principal trends affecting consumer behavior include growing awareness and wealth of Lao consumers, greater market access by foreign companies, and Laos's greater integration with the region. Awareness, access, and purchasing power have combined to create an increasingly robust consumer culture in urban and trading centers. Retail stores, distribution points, and trading will remain largely family dominated, with increased alliances, joint ventures, and marketing initiatives with larger and foreign-owned companies. Segmentation by purchasing power, income, and geography will continue to receive attention from marketers; however, new psychographic and behavioral segments will become apparent, and efforts will be redoubled to measure and to track them. A "youthful globally wired segment" (our less-than-elegant description) is already obvious in Vientiane, as exemplified by the previously described young soccer player. Similar to other transitioning countries, this youth and his peers will be opinion leaders for the larger market. Broad consumption patterns will still be oriented toward the purchase of necessities—for example, housing, clothing, and food—but even in these purchases, we already see more hedonic consumption patterns in the forms of more ornate homes, "modern" fashionable clothing, and restaurants of varying cuisines. The motorbike, once a luxury item, is increasingly a necessity, as are the television, CD/DVD player, and mobile phone.

The market will continue to develop, and retailers and advertisers will need to become more sophisticated to match the growing sophistication of consumers and to keep them loyal. One outcome of this consumer/brand/retailer dynamic is greater use of global tactics to sell to and to communicate with consumers, but—and somewhat counterintuitively—locally sensitive niches will remain important and perhaps will grow. Thus, some brand managers and retailers will succeed by making their products and institutions seem "more Lao." If trends follow our observations in other transitioning economies in the region, such market incongruity of sorts, and certainly market complexity, seem inevitable.

Regional integration among the Greater Mekong countries has created a more open environment for the exchange of goods, services, workers, traders, and exporters (see also Lee 1994). Laos has benefited from this integration. Cooperation in the forms of many new policies and tangible outcomes in the form of FDI and infrastructure—including favorable rail and road links—bring together peoples and consumption patterns; Lao consumers will increasingly purchase a standard package of goods and services, including many elements listed above. Isolation and poverty previously rendered Laos a virtual nonmarket for consumer goods. Now, a consumer market has emerged, as have unique segments. The Lao market is now easier to reach for firms targeting the Mekong region as a whole. While unique cultural tendencies will be very important—and for some consumer segments even more important—a global or at least a regional approach to marketing will become increasingly advantageous to marketers targeting Laos. (See Steinberg [1987] for an interesting and prescient regional prognosis, with implications for Laos.)

Changing Government Role

The Lao government has been cautious when implementing reforms; however, the legal environment for the protection of property ownership, market activities, advertising, land ownership, and trade is among the more comprehensive among transitioning economies. Development remains a national priority, but a cultural imperative for balanced development is critical. The "social evils" witnessed in neighboring Bangkok, and even Ho Chi Minh City, remain a concern for authorities. Also, the environmental degradation experienced by some neighboring nations suggests that the government will move carefully but steadily when continuing reforms.

The reality is that economic prosperity will come before comprehensive political freedom. The government has made concrete steps toward expanding trade and friendship with other nations, eliminating religious persecution and gradually easing control over the local Buddhist clergy, inaugurating major cooperative initiatives with ASEAN partners and China, and even exploring ways to leverage the popularity of the ancient monarchy. At last, the encouragement of tourism, entrepreneurship, cross-border trade, and export of agricultural commodities and some value-added products has been recognized as critical to development. New products, businesses, tourists, and services are now welcomed into Laos, so long as the local authority, environment, and culture are adequately protected.

The political situation in Laos faces challenges, as reformers within the Communist party seek to accelerate change and growth, counterbalanced by "immobilist" and conservative elements. This is common throughout transitioning Southeast Asia. The government remains challenged to make tough decisions on banking, education, FDI, corruption, and cultural protection. A balanced and gradual view toward modernization can be expected, with growing consultation with mass organizations to permit increased input from the population vis-à-vis the direction of reforms. In general, Laotians believe that quality of life is improving, and this is an important component of government legitimacy.

Implications for Marketing Management

Laos remains a small market. It lags behind many of its neighbors in terms of size and development. Nonetheless, trends indicate it is becoming a viable market, and as part of a strategy to access the Greater Mekong Region, Laos perhaps has never been more attractive to investors. Some management implications follow.

Broadly Consider the Market

Our primary focus has been consumer markets; business markets, government markets, and infrastructure projects also continue to grow and to present numerous opportunities. Thus, one must consider the Lao market, broadly, as opportunities exist in many sectors. Most Lao consumers and businesses are concentrated primarily in the central, south, and urban and trading areas. Moreover, the newly prosperous farmers in the countryside can now more easily travel to towns and cities to acquire goods. Most marketing activity, not surprisingly, is concentrated in these areas. Investors should also keep in mind the trend toward a Greater Mekong Region and conceivably an eventual Greater Mekong Market. A presence in Laos then will provide access to, or supplement marketing efforts in, Cambodia, China's Yunnan Province, Myanmar, Thailand, and Vietnam. Even if Laos, per se, still does not provide a critical mass of consumers for some investors, this new, enlarged market may be more enticing, and Laos is an integral part of it.

Ride the Demographic Wave

Laos has a young population that is growing in affluence and sophistication. Although still relatively poor by Western standards, it is an influential segment developing fast enough to warrant targeted marketing. Economic and education trends suggest that the current cohort of young consumers will become increasingly mobile and wealthy; simple, specific advertising and promotions today will pay off in the near future and will help to establish sustainable brand loyalties. Given this segment's connection to global events, via information technologies, and given trends of youth markets observed in other transitioning economies, it is reasonable to expect similar consumption patterns and brand preferences to emerge. The "act local" marketing axiom will remain salient, however, even for these youthful and wired consumers.

Maintain Government Dialogue

The Lao government is increasingly ambitious in its development plans and welcomes foreign investors. Some businesspersons find less "red tape" and hindrances, compared with some provinces in Vietnam, and the process of opening up to the outside world has had a generally favorable impact on Laos. Nevertheless, recognition of high military involvement in government, continued reliance on socialism as the governing political philosophy, and resistance of the government to rapid political change must be recognized by marketers (see also Dommen 1995). Leaders will continue NEM policies to improve consumer access to goods and services. However, this will occur according to the government's direction and timing. Joint ventures with state companies will remain an option for some investors entering the market.

Identify Local Partners

The complex society and multiple cultures and languages of Laos suggest a renewed focus on locating good partners. While, previously, low education and technical standards made this problematic, the country now has five years of solid growth, positive experiences of local workers who cooperated with international companies and aid agencies, growing use of French and English languages, and higher technical skills. Universities can now supply graduates with functional competence in economics and business, and companies have been able to recruit capable workers from educational institutions. The quality of local partners has improved, permitting better market access and profitability.

Invest in the Lao People

In the end, the Lao people will determine the welfare of the country and the prospects for its market development. Accordingly, Laos has accelerated efforts to develop human resources. Investors must also play a role toward this end. New and prospective employees have more and better skills, but will still likely be constrained by suboptimal knowledge of modern marketing and other business concepts, such as auditing, depreciation, finance, and advertising. Efforts to develop the skills of local workers, however, have paid off handsomely for companies committed to this growing market. And, they are increasingly welcome—especially non-Thai Asian and Western firms that help to counterbalance the influence of Thailand.

NOTES

The authors acknowledge the support of staff from the Permanent Mission of the Lao PDR to the United Nations, the Embassy of the Lao PDR to Vietnam, and members of the Faculty of Economics and Management at the National University of Laos. The authors also thank Khamlusa Nouansavanh and Karen Adams for assistance and helpful comments on early drafts of this chapter.

1. To put this in perspective, during the period of the Vietnam/Indochina War, consider that the United States "dropped more bombs on Laos than they delivered over all of Europe during the Second World War" (*The Economist* 2001, 5).

2. The terms "Lao" and "Laotian" are generally regarded as interchangeable.

3. Fa Ngum has taken on particular significance, because the government has tried to attach itself to ancient Lao Royalty, with hopes of enhancing its legitimacy and of distancing Laos from the influential Thai Royalty.

4. Also spelled Lane Xang.

REFERENCES

Adams, D., G. H. Kee, and L. Lin. 2001. "Linking Research, Policy and Strategic Planning to Educational Development in the LPDR." *Comparative Education Review* 24(May): 220–28.
Ardrey, William, Anthony Pecotich, and Clifford J. Shultz II. 2002. "Entrepreneurial Women as Catalysts

for Socioeconomic Development: Issues, Policies and Answers in Transition Economies." Working Paper, Arizona State University.

Bangkok Post. 2001. "Laos Economy Surges Ahead," May 24, A3.

Bank of the LPDR. 2000. Annual Report. Vientiane, Bank of the Lao People's Democratic Republic (unaudited figures).

Bartels, Frank, and Nick Freeman. 2000. "Multinational Firms and FDI in Southeast Asia." *ASEAN Economic Bulletin* 27(5): 324–33.

Bourdet, Yves. 1996. "Laos in 1995: Reform Policy Out of Breath?" *Asian Survey* 36(1): 89–96.

———. 1997. "Laos in 1996: Please Don't Rush!" *Asian Survey* 37(1): 72–77.

———. 2000. *The Economics of Transition in Laos.* Northampton: Elgar.

———. 2001. "Laos in 2000: The Economics of Political Immobilization." *Asian Survey* 41(1): 164–70.

Chamberlain, J. R. 1999. *The Social Impact of the Economic Crisis on the Lao PDR.* Manila: Asian Development Bank.

Chanthavong, Saignasith. 1997. "Lao-Style New Economic Mechanism." In *Laos Dilemmas and Options,* ed. M. Than and J. Tan, pp. 28–47. Singapore: ISEAS.

Dana, Leo. 1994. "Small Business in a Non Entrepreneurial Society: The Case of the Lao People's Democratic Republic." *Journal of Small Business Management* 33(3): 95–98.

Dommen, Arthur. 1995. "Among Generals, Among Friends: Laos in 1994." *Asian Survey* 35(1): 84–91.

Domoto, Kenji. 1997. "Environmental Issues in Laos, Balancing Development with Preservation." In *Laos Dilemmas and Options,* ed. M. Than and J. Tan, pp. 309–25. Singapore: ISEAS.

The Economist. 2000. "Gooseflesh: Mystery Bombings in Laos," December 16: 4.

———. 2001. "No Dissent: Laos's Uncritical Friends," April 28: 5.

Economist Intelligence Unit (EIU). 2003. *Laos: Country Profiles.* London: Economist Intelligence Unit Publications.

Evans, Gary. 1999. *Laos: Culture and Society.* Chiang Mai: Silkworm.

Flipse, Mary. 1992. "Asia's Littlest Dragon: An Analysis of the Laos Foreign Investment Code and Decree." *Law and Policy in International Business* 26(Winter): 199–237.

Freeman, Nick. 2000. "Laos Economics of Transition Commentary." *ASEAN Economic Bulletin* 27(December): 346–47.

Fry, Maxwell. 1997. "Savings, Investment & Economic Growth in Laos." In *Laos Dilemmas and Options,* ed. M. Than and J. Tan, pp. 61–83. Singapore: ISEAS.

Joyeux, Roselyne, and William Worner. 1997. "Stabilisation Policies and Exchange Rate Determination in Laos." In *Laos Dilemmas and Options,* ed. M. Than and J. Tan, pp. 195–201. Singapore: ISEAS.

Kazmin, Amy. 2003. "Laos Jailings Deepen Doubts of Aid Donors," *The Financial Times,* July 10: 6.

Kittikhoun, H. E. 1996. Interview with Author, Permanent Mission of the Lao PDR to the United Nations, New York City (December).

Lee, T. Y. 1994. "The ASEAN Free Trade Area: The Search for Common Prosperity." In *Asia Pacific Regionalism,* ed. R. Garnaut. New York: Harper.

Litner, Bertil. 2003. "Laos: Aid Dependent." *Far East Economic Review,* July 3: 45.

Ljunggren, Borje. 1992. "Marketizing Economies under Communism: Reform in Vietnam, Laos and Cambodia." Doctoral thesis, Southern Illinois University, Carbondale.

LPDR. 1995. "World Summit for National Development." Vientiane: Government Annual Reports Government of the Lao PDR.

———. 1999. "National Development Statistics." Vientiane: Government Annual Reports Government of the Lao PDR.

———. 2001. *Basic Statistics of the LPDR 1975–2000.* Vientiane: State Planning Commission and National Statistical Center of the Lao PDR.

Mansfield, Stephen. 1998. *Laos.* Singapore: Times Books International.

McFarlane, Bruce. 2001. "Politics of the World Bank-International Monetary Fund Nexus in Asia." *Journal of Contemporary Asia* 34(8): 214–21.

McVey, Ruth. 1992. "The Materialization of the Southeast Asian Entrepreneur." In *Southeast Asian Capitalists,* ed. R. McVey, pp. 112–21. Ithaca: Cornell University SEAP.

Nam, N. V. 1997. "External Assistance and Laos." In *Laos Dilemmas and Options,* ed. M. Than and J. Tan, pp. 267–79. Singapore: ISEAS.

Park, Donghyun. 2000. "Intra-Southeast Asian Income Convergence." *ASEAN Economic Bulletin* 17(3): 285–91.

Permanent Mission of the Lao PDR to the United Nations. 2002. "Statistical Information Fact Sheet." New York: Embassy of the Lao PDR.

PriceWaterhouseCoopers. 2001. *Lao PDR Capabilities & Services.* Hanoi: PriceWaterhouseCoopers Economic Publications.

Radetzki, M. 1994. "From Communism to Capitalism in Laos: The Legal Dimension." *Asian Survey* 34(8): 799–808.

Reuters. 2002. "Laos Says to Launch First Satellite within Two Years." *Reuters News Service,* July 8.

Sayavong, C. 2001. "Comments of Laos Commerce and Tourism Vice Minister." From www.comtexnews.com, accessed May 9.

Shultz, Clifford J. II. 1994. "Balancing Policy, Consumer Desire, and Corporate Interests: Considerations for Market Entry in Vietnam." *Columbia Journal of World Business* 29(Winter): 42–53.

———. 2002. Raw data from author's notes, May, Vientiane.

Shultz, Clifford J. II, and Anthony Pecotich. 1997. "Marketing and Development in the Transition Economies of Southeast Asia: Policy Explication, Assessment and Implications." *Journal of Public Policy & Marketing* 16(1): 55–68.

Siphandone, Khamtay. 2001. Comments of the President of the Central Committee, Seventh Party Congress Documents (March 12).

Sluiter, Elizabeth. 1993. *Lives and Times of a River: The Mekong Currency.* Bangkok: Asia Books.

Steinberg, David J. 1987. *In Search of Southeast Asia.* Honolulu: University of Hawaii Press.

Swearer, Donald. 1980. *Buddhism in Society in Southeast Asia.* Cambridge: Cambridge University Press.

Tass. 2001. "Cooperation with Laos Important in Russian Southeast Asian Policy." Tass News Agency, August 17.

Than, Mya. 1997. "Laos' External Trade." In *Laos Dilemmas and Options*, ed. M. Than and J. Tan, pp. 242–67. Singapore: ISEAS.

Than, Mya, and J. Tan. 1997. "Introduction: Laos Transitional Economy in the Context of Regional Economic Cooperation." In *Laos Dilemmas and Options*, ed. M. Than and J. Tan, pp. 1–22. Singapore: ISEAS.

Thant, Myo, and Richard Vokes. 1997. "Education in Laos." In *Laos Dilemmas and Options*, ed. M. Than and J. Tan, pp. 154–95. Singapore: ISEAS.

Thayer, Carlyle. 2003. "Laos in 2002: Regime Maintenance through Political Stability." *Asian Survey* 39(1): 120–26.

UNDP. 1997. "UNDP Briefing Note: The Lao PDR." New York: United Nations Development Program.

UPI. 2001. "Southeast Asia Pushes Free Trade." United Press International, July 20.

Vietnam News. 2001. Various articles and trading statistics on Lao–Vietnam cooperation and ministerial visits, December 1–5.

Vu, T., and M. Speece. 1995. "Marketing Research in Vietnam." *Journal of International Marketing and Marketing Research* 21(3): 145–60.

World Bank. 2002. *World Development Indicators.* Washington: The World Bank.

Worner, William. 1997. "Lao Agriculture in Transition." In *Laos Dilemmas and Options*, ed. M. Than and J. Tan, pp. 84–125. Singapore: ISEAS.

Xinhua. 2001a. "Tourism Grows Fast in Laos." Xinhua News Agency, May 9.

———. 2001b. "Vietnam, Laos to Further Strengthen Trade Relations." Xinhua News Agency, June 24.

CHAPTER 10

MALAYSIA

Toward Prosperity with Harmony and Diversity

ALIAH HANIM M. SALLEH, CHE ANIZA CHE WEL, AND
ANTHONY PECOTICH

OVERVIEW

Malaysia, "Asia's tiger with a vision," has just completed another period of noteworthy economic development and political transition that has moved the nation another step toward prosperity. In this chapter, an attempt is made to enumerate and explain the sources and the nature of these changes. Their impact and likely future manifestations are also evaluated with a particular emphasis on consumer behavior and marketing aspects. The general conclusion is that Malaysia has once again sailed through troubled waters and is in a unique position of political stability and national unity that forms a solid platform for future "prosperity with harmony and diversity."

INTRODUCTION

> As you sit over your chicken *rendang*, with perhaps a dish of *kway teo(w)* lined up for afterwards, the food court on the second floor of the Kuala Lumpur City Centre (KLCC), in the shadow of the soaring Petronas Towers, is a fine place to observe everything that works best about Malaysia. The names of the various stalls—Nasi Padang, Hainanese Chicken Rice, Panggang Delights, North & East Indian Cuisine—are the gastronomic manifestation of Malaysia's extraordinary multiculturalism. Nowhere else in the world can you find the dominant ethnic group (here, the rendang-loving Malays, who make up about 53 percent of the population) living so amicably with such a big and economically powerful minority (the kway teo[w]-eating Chinese, about 26 percent, not to mention the Indians, another 8 percent). (*The Economist* 2003, 3)

Despite the latter qualifications, and with full recognition of the problems, the above quote captures the essence of our chapter title. The Federation of Malaya was expanded into a Federation of Malaysia in 1963 with the inclusion of Singapore, Sabah, and Sarawak. (Singapore was excised from the Federation in 1965.) Malaysia is a land of diversity—diverse races, cultures, languages, and religion. Yet, Malaysia is one of the most stable nations in the region, and an emerging industrial power to be reckoned with. It is the leader in the affairs of ASEAN (Association of Southeast Asian Nations) and a respected voice in world affairs. In this chapter, we attempt to update and redevelop the earlier work by Salleh, Teo, and Pecotich (1998) so as to provide a new overview of a progressive nation.

THE NATURAL ENVIRONMENT

Malaysia is a complex country with an area of 329,733 square kilometers, which is divided into two separate territories. West Malaysia is a long finger-shaped land known as the Malay Peninsula (eleven states), surrounded by the South China Sea. East Malaysia consists of Sabah and Sarawak, and it forms a strip along the northern coast of the island of Borneo, 700 kilometers across the South China Sea. The eleven states of Peninsula Malaysia, along with Sabah and Sarawak, form the Federation of Malaysia. The major seaports of Peninsula Malaysia are those at Penang and Port Klang. Kuching, Sibu, and Miri are the main ports in Sarawak, and Labuan is the principal port of Sabah.

A country of contrasts, Malaysia's geographic position is in the heart of Asia, where it straddles the major trading routes of the Asian continent. This has resulted in a rich and varied population touched by many cultural traditions. The ethnic Malays live alongside Chinese and Indian people as well as other minorities. In East Malaysia, for example, indigenous tribes (such as Dayak, Iban, Jakun, Bidayuh, Penan, Kadazan, and Murut) still live in the longhouses in remote forest inland areas, whereas in West Malaysia, modern cities are common, and people's lifestyles are similar to those in Europe or the United States (Rowell 1996).

In West Malaysia, a central chain of mountains divides the country into geographical regions. The mountains separate fertile lowlands to the west from a narrow belt of the eastern coast. Human activity on the western plain has transformed the landscape. Both the rural areas and the towns and cities are heavily populated. There are many Malay villages surrounded by rice fields. Rubber and palm oil estates alongside tin mines help to make this an industrial zone (Rowell 1996). Toward the east and south of the central chain of mountains, the second lowland region takes on a different character. This area is less developed, poorer, more rural, and less densely populated. The majority of people living in this area are Malays, whose activities are based upon small-scale farming and fishing. The mountains provide a hostile rocky environment (usually limestone) at the summits, while the slopes are cloaked in vegetation that is difficult to penetrate, making human habitation difficult and sparse.

The coastal plains of East Malaysia are characterized by mangrove swamps that rise into mountains on the border with Indonesia. Flowing across the landscape to the coast are large rivers, such as the River Rajang in Sarawak and River Kinabatangan in Sabah. In East Malaysia, the water has worn away the rock, and huge caves have appeared. The cave systems at Niah and Mulu in Sarawak are still being discovered, and some, such as the Sarawak Chamber, are the biggest in the world. In Sabah, Mount Kinabalu is the highest mountain between the Himalayas and New Guinea.

The tropical climate of Malaysia is characterized by high temperatures and humidity throughout the year. Temperatures rarely fall below 20° C (even at night) and usually climb to 30° C or higher during the day. Rain falls throughout the year, with at least some precipitation on 150 to 200 days, but this rarely lasts all of each day. In West Malaysia, the wet season occurs on the west coast from September to December and, on the east coast, where it is more pronounced, between October and February. In East Malaysia, the rain is even heavier, and flooding is common.

Table 10.1

Malaysia and Its Neighbors

Selected indicators 2001	Malaysia	Indonesia	Philippines	Singapore	Thailand
GDP per person, $	3,640*	680	1,050	24,740	1,970
Life expectancy years	71.7	65.9	67.7	78.8	68.9
Health care spending, % GDP	2.5	2.7	3.4	3.5	3.7
Computers per 1,000 people	13	1	2	51	3
Mobile phones per 100 people	31	3	15	72	12
Electricity (kWh) used per person	2,474	345	454	6,641	1,352
Cars per 1,000 people	147	12	10	122	27

Source: The Economist, "The Changing of the Guard: A Survey of Malaysia," April 5(2003): 4.
*Malaysia's GDP per person, updated for 2005 is US$10, 450 (at purchasing power parity), ranked as the top sixth Asian country on this measure (the Economist Intelligence Unit's quality of life index, reported in *The Star–Nation*, 23 April 2005, p. 2).

THE ECONOMIC ENVIRONMENT

Since its inception, Malaysia has achieved remarkable economic success (*The Economist* 2003). This has, of course, not been achieved without costs, and at times, there have been major setbacks (such as the financial crisis). There is still much to be done, for Malaysia is a developing nation (average income under $4,000 per head), but the progress and well-being are visible and real. For example, it can be seen in Table 10.1 that on a number of selected indicators, Malaysia compares favorably to most of its neighbors in the region.

Gross Domestic Product, Inflation, Employment, and Trade

Gross domestic product (GDP) is one of the commonly used indicators of national economic well-being. Malaysia recorded a GDP annual growth of 8.1 percent for the period of 1991–93, and 8.0 percent for the 1994–95 period. Between 1988 and 1992, its GDP increased between 8 and 10 percent each year up to 1996 (*Mid-Term Review of the Sixth Malaysia Plan* 1993). The regional financial crisis, which started in mid-1997, caused GDP to decrease by 7.5 percent in 1997. It worsened during the crisis, resulting in a 6.7 percent contraction in GDP. By 1999, the economy had begun to recover, and the GDP showed a positive growth of 4.3 percent (*Economic Report 1999/2000*). Although, since then, there have been "peaks and troughs," the average growth has been around 6 percent. Malaysia's economy expanded 5.1 percent in the third quarter of 2003. The GDP growth for the full year of 2003 was 4.5 percent, against a 4.1 percent expansion in 2002 (Department of Statistics Malaysia 2003). The GDP is expected to grow 5.5–6.0 percent for the year 2004 (*Economic Report 2003/2004*).

In the early days, Malaysia was considered an agro-based economy—from 1980 to 1990, agricultural GDP increased by an annual average of 3.8 percent (Moore 1994). In 1999, the agricultural sector contributed 4.6 percent GDP and 16.0 percent of employment, and 3.8 percent and 15.5 percent, respectively, in 2000 (*Utusan Malaysia Online* 2002). The manufacturing sector has become the leading source of revenue for the country since 1987, providing an estimated 18.2 percent of GDP and 26.5 percent of employment in 1996. However, its percentage of GDP decreased to 10.4 percent and 13.7 percent in 1997 and 1998, respectively, concurrent with the economic crisis. Since then, the manufacturing sector has recovered and now accounts for about a third of the GDP, with a robust 8.5 percent growth in the third quarter of 2003. The services and agriculture sectors expanded 4.2 percent and 6.2 percent, respectively (Department of Statistics Malaysia 2003).

Inflation has historically been low at about 3–4 percent per annum, and poverty has been reduced significantly to below 10 percent of the population (Ramon 1997). Inflation rate, as measured by the annual rate of increase in the Consumer Price Index (CPI), continued to decelerate from a high of 6.2 percent in June 1998 to 2.1 percent in September 1999. On average, the CPI increased by 3.0 percent during the first months of 1999, compared to a 5.2 percent increase during the corresponding period of 1998 (*Economic Report 1999/2000*). The rate of inflation in 2003 was 2 percent. This is expected to remain low due to excess capacity and low export prices (Asian Development Bank 2003).

As shown in Table 10.2, the unemployment rate in 1995 stood at 3.1 percent and decreased to 2.5 percent and 2.4 percent in 1996 and 1997, respectively. However, it increased to 3.2 percent in 1998 and went to 3.0 percent in 1999 and 2000, respectively. It further increased to 3.6 percent in 2001 and declined slightly to 3.5 percent in 2002 and 2003. Optimistically, it is estimated that the unemployment rate will decrease again in 2005 to 2.7 percent (*Economic Report 2003/2004*). The agriculture (agriculture, forestry, livestock, and fishing) sector showed a declining percentage of total employment. The sector contributed 18.66 percent to the employment rate in 1995, it then decreased to 15.18 percent in 2000, and it was forecasted to decrease further to 12.03 percent in 2005. The manufacturing sector showed growth in this period from 25.34 percent in 1995 to 27.09 percent in 2000, and it was forecasted to grow further in 2005 (*Economic Report 1999/ 2000*). This emphasizes the importance of the manufacturing sector to the economy—it contributed nearly half of the total employment for this period.

The services sector displayed strong growth, particularly in the finance, insurance, real estate, and business services subsector, of 8.8 percent in the first quarter of 2002 compared to 12.5 percent during the fourth quarter of 2001. Value added in the manufacturing sector recorded a significantly lower decline of –2.1 in first quarter 2002 compared to –8.4 percent during fourth quarter 2001 following improved external conditions and sustained domestic consumption (Bank Negara Malaysia, 2002).

Malaysia has historically favored free trade and is heavily dependent on export, with an export-to-GDP ratio of 108 percent in 2000. Electronics and electrical machinery were the principal exports in 2000 (60.6 percent) followed by petroleum and liquid natural gas (7.6 percent) and chemical products (3.9 percent) (*Utusan Malaysia Online* 2002). In 1996, the overall balance of payments was RM6.24 billion, which decreased to (RM –10.89 billion) in 1997 due to the economic crisis. The overall position of balance of payments improved in 1998 to RM40.3 billion (Economic Planning Unit 2000). The turnaround in real GDP growth has been accompanied by a further strengthening of the balance of payments position as well as lower rate of inflation. Boosted by a stronger volume of exports, which continued to outpace imports, and external trade position recorded a surplus of RM46.2 billion in the first eight months of 1999. These visible surpluses continued to 2003, and as a result, the nation's external reserves held by Bank Negara Malaysia (BNM) are expected to remain strong.

The Impact of the 1997–98 Regional Financial Crisis

Although the impact of the Asian regional financial crisis of 1997–98 was widespread, its specific effects on particular nations were differential. In Malaysia, the most immediately visible effect

Table 10.2

Employment and Labor by Sector

Sector	1997	1998	1999	2000	2002	2003	2005
Labor Force ('000)	9,038.2	8,880.9	9,010.0	9,572.5	10,198.8	10,514.9	11,161.9
Change (%)	(4.6)	(–1.7)	(1.5)	(6.2)	(3.1)	(3.1)	(16.60)
Employment ('000)	8,817.4	8,596.9	8,740.7	9,271.2	9,840.0	10,150.0	10,858.9
	(4.6)	(–2.5)	(1.7)	(6.0)	(3.2)	(3,2)	(17.12)
Unemployment rates (%)	2.4	3.2	3.0	3.1	3.5	3.5	2.7
Agriculture, forestry, livestock, and fishing	1,468.2	1,401.1	1,399.2	1,407.5	1,405.5	1,403.0	1,306.5
	(16.65%)	(16.29%)	(16.00%)	(15.18%)	(14.9%)	(13.8%)	(12.03%)
Mining and quarrying	41.7	42.2	41.9	41.2	42.2	42.8	42.3
	(0.47%)	(0.49%)	(0.48%)	(0.44%)	(0.3%)	(0.4%)	(0.38%)
Manufacturing	2,374.5	2,277.1	2,368.3	2,558.3	2,679.8	2,814,9	3200.3
	(26.93%)	(26.49%)	(27.09%)	(27.59%)	(21.7%)	(27.7%)	(29.47%)
Construction	876.1	809.7	803.8	755.0	782.1	794.6	880.1
	(9.94%)	(9.42%)	(9.19%)	(8.14%)	(9.5%)	(7.8%)	(8.10%)
Finance, insurance, business services, and real estate	428.9	417.8	420.3	508.7	607.2	635.3	647.3
	(4.86%)	(4.85%)	(4.80%)	(5.48%)	(6.7%)	(6.3%)	(5.96%)
Transport, storage, and communication	433.6	435.3	441.9	461.6	508.6	522.8	552.7
	(4.92%)	(5.06%)	(5.05%)	(4.97%)	(5.2%)	(5.2%)	(5.08%)
Government services	873.0	874.8	876.5	981.0	994.5	1,026.1	1070.3
	(9.90%)	(10.17%)	(10.03%)	(10.58%)	(10.4%)	(10.1%)	(9.85%)
Other services	2,321.4	2,339.0	2,388.7	2,557.9	1,036.8	1,082.9	3,159.4
	(26.33%)	(27.21)	(27.33%)	(27.58%)	(15.1%)	(10.7%)	(29.09%)
Total	8,817.4	8,596.9	8,740.7	9,271.2	9,840.0	10,150.1	10,858.9

Source: *Economic Report 1999/2000* (Kuala Lumpur: Percetakan Nasional Malaysia Berhad).

was on the currency, which lost about 40 percent of its value within half a year. A 40 percent devaluation of the ringgit is equal to a reduction of per capita income from US$5,000 to US$3,000. In total GDP terms, this amounted to approximately US$40 billion yearly. At the same time, more than US$100 billion was wiped out from the stock market. In total, the nation lost about US$140 billion a year (Mohamad 1999). Malaysian economic growth measured in terms of real GDP contracted. The impact of the financial crisis on economic growth became evident toward the end of 1997 when the real GDP began to slow and registered a negative growth for the first time since 1985. As a result of the contraction in economic growth, per capita income declined by 1.8 percent to RM11,835 compared with RM12,051 in 1997 (*Utusan Malaysia* 2001).

The contraction of GDP resulted in slower employment growth and increased unemployment as well as retrenchment. However, the unemployment rate did not reach an alarming level, because many industries facing labor shortages were capable of absorbing retrenched workers. Employment declined in 1998 by 3.0 percent compared to positive growth of 4.9 percent in 1996 and 4.6 percent in 1997. The largest decline was in the construction sector at –16.9 percent, while the manufacturing sector was at –3.6 percent. The total number retrenched was 19,000 workers in 1997. Between January and December 1998, the total number of workers retrenched was 85,865. Many of these retrenched workers were absorbed into the manufacturing, plantation, and services subsectors that continued to experience labor shortages. The unemployment rate, however, increased from 2.6 percent in 1997 to 3.9 percent in 1998 (*Utusan Malaysia Online* 2002).

Private investment generally contracted mainly due to uncertainties arising from volatile exchanges rates, decline in both local and external demand, existence of excess capacity, and the tight liquidity position encountered since the onset of the financial crisis in July 1997. Foreign direct investment (FDI), measured in terms of the value of applications in the manufacturing sectors and applications for the investment incentives from the hotel, tourism, and agricultural sectors to the Malaysian Industrial Development Authority (MIDA), showed a declining trend over the period between January and December 1998.

The exchange rate of the ringgit vis-à-vis major currencies declined. The ringgit depreciated by 40 percent against the U.S. dollar between July 1, 1997, and December 31, 1997. It was at its lowest level in January 1998. The Kuala Lumpur Stock Exchange Composite Index (KLSE CI) declined by 44.9 percent during the period between July 1, 1997, and December 31, 1997. After a slight recovery in the first quarter of 1998, the index slid to an eleven-year low of 262.70 points on September 1, 1998. Between July 1, 1997, and September 1, 1998, KLSE market capitalization fell by 76 percent to RM181.5 billion (Okposin and Ming Yu 2000). Movement of stock prices on the KLSE were affected by several factors, including exchange rate fluctuations, developments in regional economies and sharp loss of confidence in emerging market by international investors. The corporate sector was adversely affected by the crisis, reflecting the decline in the number of new companies registered and the increase in the number of closures (Okposin and Ming Yu 2000).

The rate of nonperforming loans (NPLs) in the banking system increased, pursuant to a slowdown in economic activity as well as an increase in interest rates, which raised the cost of funds to as high as 20 percent per annum in early 1998. Corporate governance covers the rules, standards, and guidelines that govern the behavior of corporate owners, directors, and managers as well as defines their duties and accountability to investors. While there is room for improvements in the corporate governance framework, significant attention was drawn only to the issue as the crisis unfolded.

The incidence of poverty among Malaysians decreased from 8.9 percent in 1995 to 6.1 percent in 1997. However, efforts to maintain this rate of reduction were affected in 1998 due to the economic downturn. As the economy contracted, there were limited employment and income-earning opportunities. Coupled with the increase in inflation rate, the incidence of poverty increased to 7.0 percent in 1998 (Okposin and Ming Yu 2000). Furthermore, the drastic decline in shares and the values of property severely negatively affected the consumption patterns of Malaysians. The poor performance of KLSE also seriously constrained the ability of the corporate sector to procure financing through the stock market. The fall in the prices of shares and property adversely affected the value of collateral provided by businesses for the loans they procured. The increase in interest rates following the crisis brought further hardship to the public at large as well as businesses in terms of higher debt service commitments. For instance, a family having to service a housing loan or an overdraft of RM100,000 had to pay about 20 percent more in monthly repayments (Okposin and Ming Yu 2000).

The impact of the economic downturn on share prices and corporate performance also adversely affected the share of Bumiputra ownership in the corporate sector in 1998, which fell below the 1995 level. Reflecting the broad-based effects of the slowdown in business activities on all Malaysians, the share of Chinese ownership also declined, while the Indian share remained at the 1995 level (Okposin and Ming Yu 2000).

Currency depreciation affected the capacity to pursue education abroad. Institutions offering financial assistance for education abroad, including the government, either stopped the aid or reduced it drastically, as most were dependent on government assistance. Generally, as the cost of education abroad increased sharply, more students had to pursue their education locally.

A Malaysian Central Bank report stated that throughout 1998, the crisis countries underwent structural adjustment, namely, banking-sector consolidation and recapitalization and resolution of the NPLs. By strengthening prudential regulation and supervision, corporate restructuring and governance gained momentum. The economic recovery has been underpinned by policies initiated by the National Economic Action Council in line with its National Economic Recovery Plan as well as other favorable domestic and external developments. The imposition of selective exchange control and the pegging of the ringgit at RM1 = US$0.2632 (US$1 = RM3.8) since September 2, 1998, brought stability and, consequently, confidence in the financial market (*Economic Report 1999/2000*).

Reforms introduced by the government to strengthen and restructure the banking system have enabled the banking sector to carry out its intermediation function more effectively and, thereby, support the economic recovery process. These policy initiatives, coupled with the strong increase in external demand following improvement in economic conditions in East Asia as well as continued robust growth in the United States, have spurred output increases, especially in the manufacturing sector. A recovery in agricultural output, underpinned by a significant improvement in palm oil yield, also contributed toward the positive growth in the economy.

Danaharta, an asset-management company set up to deal with banks' NPLs, and Danamodal, set up to inject capital into ailing banks, seemed to have been successful, as planned. Since its establishment in June 1998, Danaharta has acquired a portfolio of NPLs totaling RM88.03 billion (value of loan rights acquired [LRA]). Of this, 81 percent of the NPLs with an LRA value of RM39.12 billion (and the gross value of RM40.89 billion) are undergoing various recovery measures, with expected returns of RM23.21 billion (expected recovery rate of 57 percent). In June 2001, the default rate stood at 14 percent (Pengurusan Danaharta Nasional Berhad 2001). The unresolved NPLs amounted to RM8.91 billion. Danaharta restructured or approved for restructuring almost all of the NPLs under its purview. Capital injection by Danamodal into the banking institutions was maintained at RM2.1 billion as of the end of March 2002. The Corporate Debt Restructuring Committee (CDRC) achieved considerable progress in resolving debt restructuring (Bank Negara Malaysia 2002).

Table 10.3

GDP Growth Rates[ab] for East Asia Countries: Pre-Crisis (1996) and Revised Estimates for 1999 and 2000.

Country	1996	1997	1998	1999	2000	2001	2002	2003
Hong Kong	4.9	5.3	− 5.1	− 1.3	3.1			
Indonesia	7.8	4.6	− 13.7	− 4.0	2.5			
Japan	n.a.	1.4	− 2.8	− 1.4	0.3			
Malaysia	*8.6*	*7.7*	*− 6.7*	*1.0***	*2.0*	*(−1.4)*	*6.1*	*7.8*
Singapore	6.9	8.0	1.5	0.5	4.2			
South Korea	7.1	5.5	− 5.5	2.0	4.6			
Taiwan	5.7	6.8	4.9	3.9	4.8			
Thailand	5.5	− 0.4	− 8.0	1.0	3.0			

Source: Selvarajah, T. Christopher (*Jurnal Pengurusan*, 1999). From International Monetary Fund (reported in *Star Business*, April 26, 1999 and Reuters report in *New Straits Times–Business*, May 24, 1999, p. 21).

[a]Growth rates are calculated based upon inflated adjusted GDP
[b]Up to early July 1999, the Malaysia Central Bank has revised Malaysia's 1999's GDP to be 4.3 percent.

Among those countries most severely hit by the currencies crisis, Malaysia seems to be one of the first to see recovery remedies bearing fruit, as suggested in Tables 10.1 and 10.3. It is likely that Malaysia will gradually return to healthy growth over the next three to five years. Alongside Asia's dynamic growth, Malaysia is expected to sustain its competitiveness. As growth is seen again, it may be on top of a much more robust business framework that could sustain further growth for several decades.

Aftermath of September 11, 2001

Malaysia's open economy, dependent on exports, is particularly sensitive to cataclysmic international events. Exports, the engine of the country's economic growth, formed 108 percent of its GDP in 2000. The United States is the largest export destination (20 percent or RM39.7 billion, January–July 2001); 54 percent (RM21.5 billion) of exports are dependent on air transportation. Electrical and electronic appliances are a major export (75 percent) to the United States (*Utusan Malaysia Online* 2002). Therefore, the closing of major airports around the world had an immediate impact on Malaysian exports, in addition to losses suffered by its national carrier, Malaysian Airlines System (MAS), and the hospitality industry, especially the tourism sector.

However, it is speculated that American response to this crisis will determine the direction and intensity of the impact on Malaysia. The nation experienced positive growth in 2001 and 2002 as evidenced by the following:

> Strong economic and financial fundamentals, such as, international reserves of Bank Negara Malaysia (BNM) increasing further to RM124.5 billion (US$32.8 billion) in May 2002, adequate to finance about 5.5 months of retained imports, being 5 times the value of its short-term external debt.

1. Malaysia's total external debt position amounted to RM175.6 billion (US$46.2 billion) as at end-March 2002, equivalent to 57 percent of GNP. The federal government financing requirements are primarily met from domestic non-inflationary sources. Nevertheless, tak-

ing advantages of favorable market conditions, the Federal Government reopened its US$1 billion, 7.5 percent Notes due 2011 by an additional US$750 million in March 2002. Interest spreads on Malaysia's benchmark securities have tightened. The spread on Malaysian Notes due 2009 narrowed to 149 basis points at end-April 2002. The Federal Government's external debt continued to account for a small share (15.4 percent) of total external debt. Total short-term debts also remained low, at 15.3 percent of total external debt.

2. Malaysia continued to operate under full employment. The number of retrenched workers was 10,083 persons in the first quarter, with retrenched mainly in medium-sized manufacturing companies, which produced low-end electronics and electrical products on a contract basis for the larger firms. Reflecting consumer expectations of better job market conditions, the MIER Employment Index rose by 20.2 points to 106.3 points from 86.1 points in the fourth quarter of 2001.

3. Inflation remained low with the Consumer Price Index (CPI) rising by 1.4 percent. In March, inflation edge up largely due to the one-off price adjustment in telephone service charges. Excluding these telephone charges, inflation would be lower at 1.1 percent. In August 2001 the rate increased only 1.3 percent compared to a year earlier.

4. Political stability; the main factor considered by the investor is the security of their investment and the confidence of achieving profit.

Monetary conditions supported the economic recovery—the relative price stability combined with the solidity in the financial markets have created an environment conducive for sustaining business activity and consumer confidence. Total loans outstanding extended by the banking system increased by RM5.7 billion during the quarter. On an annual basis, loans outstanding rose by 4.6 percent at end-March 2002 (3.6 percent at end-December 2001). Nevertheless, overall financing through the banking system and PDS raised by the private sector was slightly lower at RM4.3 billion during the quarter (4Q 2001: RM6.5 billion) because of higher redemptions and conversions to equity in the PDS market. Financing through the equity market was significant in the first quarter. Improved investor confidence prompted thirteen successful initial public offerings (IPOs), amounting to RM353 million on the property, industrial and technology sectors. (*Utusan Malaysia Online—Rencana* 2002; Bank Negara Malaysia 2002)

Economic conditions improved further in the first quarter of 2002. The Malaysian economy expanded by 1.1 percent in the first quarter (4Q 2001:-0.5). The recovery was mainly driven by strong consumption spending and was supported by the improved external demand following the general overall recovery in the global economy. Reflecting the cumulative effects of expansionary monetary and fiscal policies and the recovery in imports, private consumption, which accounts for almost half of GDP, increased by 2.5 percent. Public consumption continued to register a strong increase of 13.4 percent, reflecting implementation of fiscal stimulus during the quarter, including the 10 percent salary adjustment for civil servants and higher expenditure on supplies and services (Bank Negara Malaysia 2002).

Privatization has now emerged as a key policy thrust. Major public utilities have been or are in the process of being privatized. Electricity, telecommunication, water, sewerage, shipping, ports, airports, airlines, railways, and many major highways have also been privatized. More of the over 1,000 government-owned companies and statutory bodies are either being corporatized or privatized. The universities are getting ready for corporatization, while many private educational institutions have sprung up within the context of privatizing tertiary education. Ostensibly, privatization has enabled the government to reduce its expenditure and to cut down on borrowing for public investment in infrastructure. A classic example is the North–South Highway, which was entirely privatized. In the period between 1983 and 1999, a total of 464 projects were privatized—345 existing projects and 119 new projects. The privatization projects have reduced capital expenditure by RM129.1 billion, with the elimination of 106,360 jobs from government payroll.

The Future: Economic Aspects

The outlook for the future is optimistic, and a further strengthening of the Malaysian economy is expected. The nation has weathered some storms, but through good economic management, it is showing signs of a continuing recovery. To a nation that depends on exports, much will depend on the international trade environment and, particularly, the big players on the world trading stage. Although some recent indicators for the United States remain positive, there is some softening in selected data in April 2002, and the situation remains problematical. In Europe, there have also been signs of improvement in sentiment as well as production benefiting from improved export performance. The regional economies are also showing signs of steady improvement, given the strong linkages with the industrial countries (Bank Negara Malaysia 2002).

On the home front, indicators point to continued domestic driven growth. Capacity utilization has improved, and earlier expectations of a recovery in investment remain unchanged. The positive growth of this index suggests that the Malaysian economy will continue to expand. The MIER Consumer Sentiments Index and Business Conditions Index continue to gain, indicating that recovery is on track (Bank Negara Malaysia 2002).

However, there is some nervousness arising from the political and economic uncertainties in the short term, but it is expected that over the medium to longer term, investors will take a more positive approach toward Malaysia in view of its strong fundamentals and economic management (see also *The Star—Business* 2002a). Competition for FDI from China is likely to continue, and the slowing of the electronics sector as well as the necessity to comply with new regional and World Trade Organization (WTO) trading rules are challenges that are already being faced. The strategies being developed include a reduced dependence on manufacturing, a reemphasis on the commodities (palm oil, rubber, and crude oil) that made Malaysia rich, an attempt to "climb the value chain" in electronics, and a new focus on services such as tourism (*The Economist* 2003). Malaysia is fortunate in that it has a relatively large domestic market, the development of which may reduce the impact of international uncertainties.

A smooth transition of power from Prime Minister Tun Dr. Mahathir Mohamad to his successor, Deputy Prime Minister Datuk Seri Abdullah Ahmad Badawi, according to the stated timetable, would greatly help to ensure continued stability in the economy and bright prospects for the KLSE (*The Star—Business* 2002a).

POLITICAL ENVIRONMENT

Malaysia has enjoyed a long period of democracy and political stability with the rule of the Barisan Nasional (National Front) coalition of political parties since its independence in 1957. Barisan Nasional was born from the alliance of United Malays National Organization (UMNO Baru), the Malaysian Chinese Association (MCA), and the Malaysian Indian Congress (MIC). UMNO Baru is the dominant party in ruling the Barisan Nasional coalition. Each of the main races has tended to congregate in its own political party. Barisan Nasional has easily retained its majority in parliament throughout the nine elections held since independence.

The historical attempt to even out the economic development among the races has been one of the dominant issues of policy making in Malaysia since the 1970s. However, after the race riots in May 1969, the main goal of the state was to carry out the New Economic Policy (NEP) of 1970. The government extended all types of control to Bumiputra (the indigenous Malays and some native tribes—"sons of the soil") and non-Bumiputra capitalists, and it advocated profitability as the criterion of running state enterprises. There are two basic objectives of NEP: (1) to reduce poverty and inequality among different sections of the Malaysian population and (2) to abolish inter- and intraracial concentration of monopolistic economic power as revealed in various business professions and enterprises. The NEP was based on the principle of capitalist development to generate a surplus for capital accumulation and to possibly change the existing system of production relations. Although it was an attempt to eliminate the racial identification of any class, it was not primarily designed to be a policy on class relation, per se. However, in implementation of the NEP, one could discern the slow emergence of Malay bourgeoisie loyal to the state, and also side by side, the growth and consolidation of Chinese capitalism as a reactionary backlash (Ghosh 1998).

Although there is still much to be done, the NEP has achieved its objective in eradicating poverty and restructuring the Malaysian society. The economic prosperity achieved in the 1970s enabled the administrations of Tun Abdul Razak, who succeeded Tunku Abdul Rahman as premier in 1970, and Tun Hussien Onn, who took over on the death of Tun Razak in 1976, to make considerable progress toward these ends. At the same time, Malaysia established a more independent foreign policy, helping to found ASEAN in 1967, recognizing Communist China in 1974, and identifying the nation with the nonaligned countries of the Third World (*Information Malaysia 2000 Yearbook*).

The 1980s brought new political directions and economic challenges. During the administration of Tun Dr. Mahathir Mohamad, starting in 1981, there has been a search for new sources of support and development, a bold policy of heavy industrialization was initiated (the national car, a steel industry, and oil refineries), and an aggressive foreign policy was put in place asserting the interest of the undeveloped south versus those of the developed nations in the north. The world was stunned by the announcement made by the Malaysian Prime Minister, Tun Dr. Mahathir Mohamad, on June 23, 2002, of his intention to retire from any position in the government and party after twenty years of involvement in the government (*The Star—Business* 2002a). Tun Dr. Mahathir's long career had its ups and downs, but even in crisis situations, he was successful, including during the 1997 financial crisis and 1998 Anwar episode. As analysts predicted, the transition of power from Tun Dr. Mahathir Mohamad to his successor, Deputy Prime Minister Datuk Seri Abdullah Ahmad Badawi, has been smooth, according to schedule, and appears to have ensured continued stability in the economy. Malaysia's new premier, Datuk Seri Abdullah Ahmad Badawi, busily fine-tuning what he believes is a successful system, wants moderation in all future government functions, pointing out that many of these events were "way too elaborate" (Asia Times Online Co., Ltd. 2003).

INVESTMENT CLIMATE

Malaysia's economic development has been based on FDI. Incentives still exist for investment in the manufacturing, agriculture, and hotel and tourism industries, for research and development (R&D) and training. These incentives are contained in the Promotion of Investment Act, 1986, and the Income Tax Act, 1967. The incentives are designed to grant partial or a limited extent of relief from income tax. All investors, both local and foreign, have to apply for a manufacturing license under the Industrial Coordination Act. Projects are appraised according to their merits, and there is no discrimination. The following are aspects of policy that may be of interest to foreign investors:

1. In manufacturing, joint ventures between Malaysians and foreigners are preferred. The extent of foreign capital ownership allowed depends on the nature of the project. If a project is dependent to a very large extent on the Malaysian market of nonrenewable Malaysian resources, then the government would require that such a project have a substantial Malaysian majority ownership.

2. For substantially export-oriented projects, consideration may be given to foreign majority ownership, and the extent of such a majority will depend on the merits of the individual projects, its location, the nature of the products manufactured, the level of technology involved, and the number of similar projects already established. In the past, the government has even allowed 100 percent ownership for wholly export-oriented projects.

3. It is the government's view that joint ventures are the best means of serving long-term interest of both foreign investors and Malaysians, and 100 percent foreign ownership is not encouraged.

4. The Ministry of International Trade and Industry is prepared to be flexible in the stipulation of foreign equity participation to ensure that the project is mutually beneficial to Malaysia and the foreign partners.

5. Similar to policies of other nations, Malaysia's policy is to develop its own people and to increase their skills by training and their welfare by employment. Notwithstanding this, Malaysia allows foreign companies to import personnel in areas where there is a shortage of skilled Malaysians. In addition, foreign companies are allowed to have certain key posts be permanently filled by foreigners to safeguard their interests.

6. The Malaysian Government follows a liberal exchange control policy. Foreign investors can bring from abroad for approved projects and are allowed to remit overseas capital and profits with minimal government control. Malaysia has acceded to Article VIII of the International Monetary Fund's Articles of Association, and free transfer funds for international transactions are assured.

7. An appropriate royalty or technical assistance fee rate will be considered according to the level of technology involved. However, the amount of the fee will depend on the merits of the application and other factors, for example, the technology level to be transferred, the nature of the project, and relevance to Malaysia's industrial needs.

8. Malaysia does not encourage payment for the simple transfer of technical know-how, but rather, payments must be related to production performance. Foreign companies interested in granting likenesses to Malaysian companies are bound to the following terms in licensing agreements: (a) the licensor shall not restrict the marketing territory of the licensee; (b) the term of the licensing agreement approved is fifteen years, and any renewal thereafter is subject to prior approval; (c) the applicable law is the Law of Malaysia and disputes settled by arbitration in Malaysia; (d) the know-how transferred through the licensing agreements must also include information on improvement development made by the licensor during the period of agreement; (e) any taxes or duties imposed on the payment or any of the fees should be borne by the local manufacturing company/companies; and (f) direct costs associated with training programs conducted by the licensors for local personnel should preferably be borne by the licensors.

9. Malaysia welcomes foreign investment, and the government has introduced a policy to protect investors. The protection has many forms, but fundamentally it involves Equity Owner-

ship Guarantees, Investment Guarantee Agreements, Convention on the Settlement of Investment Disputes, and establishment of the Regional Centre of Arbitration.

Foreign Investment in Malaysia

During the pre- and post-independent periods (before and after 1957), investment was concentrated in agricultural and extractive industries. Agriculture, rubber plantations, tin mines, and basic transportation infrastructure received the major portion of FDI. In the late 1960s and early 1970s, FDI was utilized in import-substitution industries of which consumer goods and intermediate goods were the major recipients. Between the mid-1970s and 1983, FDI was concentrated in petroleum, gas, electronics, and textiles. During the period of recession, foreign investment was severely curtailed and focused on basic metals and transport sectors. After the end of the world recession, and particularly since 1988, foreign investment was mainly directed to export-promoting industries.

Over the years, there have been some structural changes in the utilization pattern of FDI. For instance, basic metal products and transport equipment received the major share of foreign equity in 1985. However, in 1990, a greater proportion of foreign investment was concentrated in electrical and electronics products and basic metals. In the early part of the 1990s, most of the foreign investment was utilized in electrical and electronics industries and in textiles and textile products. Recently, foreign investment is being utilized mostly by the manufacturing sector.

Malaysia has been fortunate in that it has been an attractive recipient of FDI due to its political and economic stability and a carefully acculturated system of peace and tolerance (cf. Ghosh 1998). Between 1960 and the early 1970s, Malaysia received an average of RM200 million to RM300 million per year. The amount of foreign investment increased to RM1 billion annually during the period 1974–79 (Ghosh 1998). During the world recession, foreign investment declined; however, it picked up again from 1988 to the level of RM8–RM10 billion. The World Bank Annual Report (1993) indicated that Malaysia was the third largest recipient of FDI after Mexico and China.

FDI during the years 1990–97 was mostly directed into the manufacturing sector (accounting for 65 percent), followed by the oil and gas sector (18 percent), services (10 percent), and property (7.0 percent). Since 1998, FDI has been more broad-based, with the manufacturing sector share dropping to 43 percent of the total FDI inflows during 1998 to 2000, when the share of the oil and gas sector remained sizable at 19 percent of the total, while investment in the services sector rose to 35 percent, mainly in financial services, trading, and marketing, communication, and IT-related services (*Economic Report 1999/2000*). Malaysia is now targeting knowledge-based FDI, as most capital-intensive industries have already established their presence. The knowledge-context activities are to be centered in areas involving the Multimedia Super Corridor (MSC) and medium-sized industries, adding other areas including petrochemicals, electronics, and value-added resource-based products (Xinhua News Agency 2001c).

Foreign investment in the MSC approved by the Multimedia Development Corporation (MDC) more than doubled to 4.2 billion ringgit (US$1.1 billion) in 2000 up from that of 2.0 billion ringgit (US$0.52 billion) between 1997 and 1999. With a favorable political and business environment, Malaysia continues to attract FDI and continues to meet the target of securing 8.8 billion ringgit (about US$2.3 billion) in foreign investment each year (Xinhua News Agency 2001a, b). However, FDI is not bereft of problems; it has created uneven development in the manufacturing sector and has changed the structure of manufactured exports. Although it has brought many structural changes to the economy and has positively contributed to domestic capital formation, recently it has been blamed for balance of payment problems.

In first quarter 2002, there continued to be inflows of funds for investment. In an environment of modest global economic recovery and continued excess capacity, gross inflows of FDI moderated to RM2.5 billion in the first quarter. Investments are in the manufacturing and services sectors. On a net basis, FDI recorded an outflow of RM0.3 billion due to repayment of loans as well as a reduction in the share capital of foreign-owned banks. Portfolio investment, on the other hand, turned to record a net inflow of RM3.2 billion, as investor sentiment was buoyed by improved economic prospects and progress in the restructuring of several large corporations. International rating agencies have upgraded Malaysia's sovereign rating outlook to positive from stable (see also Bank Negara Malaysia 2002).

TECHNOLOGICAL ENVIRONMENT

Malaysia has embraced the Information Age with its promise of a new world order, where information, ideas, goods, and services move across borders in the most cost-effective and liberal ways. As the traditional boundaries disappear, and as companies, capital, consumers, and cultures become truly global, new approaches and attitudes to business are required. Thus, Malaysia has chosen to be open and pragmatic in dealing with the changes and the challenges of becoming a fully developed mature and knowledge-rich society (*Information Malaysia 2000 Yearbook*). To achieve Vision 2020, a national agenda that sets out goals and objectives for long-term development, Malaysia has embarked on an ambitious plan to leapfrog into the Information Age by providing intellectual and strategic leadership.

The MSC was created in Malaysia and consists of a fifteen kilometer by fifty kilometer zone extending south from the capital city of Kuala Lumpur. The main purpose of this corridor is to create a suitable environment for companies that want to create, distribute, and employ multimedia products and services (Ghosh 1998). The MSC brings together three key elements: a high-capacity global telecommunications and logistics infrastructure, new policies and cyber laws, and an attractive living environment. Seven multimedia industries have been targeted for development by the year 2000 to rapidly catalyze the growth of the MSC and accelerate Malaysia's progress toward Information-Age leadership. The seven industries are as follows: electronic government (paperless work); smart school (having access to the Internet); telemedicine (for the development of the health care system); R&D clusters (for collaborating research activities between corporations and universities); national multipurpose smart card (to serve as a national identity card); borderless marketing centers (for companies to serve their customers); and worldwide manufacturing webs (to control, monitor, and deliver operational support to regional networks of design, manufacturing, and distribution centers).

The MSC has been designed to allow corporations to test the limits of technology and prepare themselves for the future. It is hoped that this will accelerate Malaysia's entry into the Information Age, and through it, help actualize Vision 2020. Set to deliver a number of sophisticated investment, business, R&D, and lifestyle options, the MSC will act as the following:

1. A vehicle for attracting world-class technology companies to Malaysia and for developing local industries
2. A multimedia utopia offering a productive, intelligent environment within a multimedia value chain of goods and services
3. An island of excellence with multimedia-specific capabilities, technologies, infrastructure, legislation, policies, and systems for competitive advantage
4. A test bed for invention, research, and other ground-breaking multimedia developments spearheaded by seven multimedia applications

5. A global community living on the leading-edge of the information society
6. A world of smart homes, smart cities, smart schools, smart cards, and smart partnerships

Companies that want to join MSC can apply to the MDC for "MSC status." This status will entitle the companies to operate tax-free up to ten years or receive a 100 percent investment tax allowance, and enjoy other incentives and benefits backed by the Malaysian Government's Bill of Guarantees.

The MSC brings together three key elements: (a) a high-capacity global telecommunication and logistics infrastructure built upon the MSC's 2.5–10 GB digital optical fiber backbone and a massive, new international airport; (b) new policies and cyber laws designed to enable and encourage electronic commerce, facilitate the development of multimedia applications, and position Malaysia as the regional leader in intellectual property protection; and (c) an attractive living environment planned with careful zoning plans integrating infrastructure mega-projects with green reserves to create environmentally friendly, intelligent urban developments.

UNDERSTANDING MALAYSIAN CONSUMER BEHAVIOR

The Malaysian Consumer: Demographics

Total Population and Growth

The total population of Malaysia, according to the 2000 census, was 23.27 million compared to 18.38 million in 1991, thus giving an average annual population growth rate of 2.60 percent over the 1991–2000 period. This rate was similar to that from 1980–91. If a 2.60 percent annual growth rate is assumed, the total population would stand around 24.51 million in 2002. State-wise, Selangor had the highest growth rate of 6.1 percent for the period of 1991–2000, followed by Sabah (4.0 percent), the Federal Territory of Labuan (3.6 percent), and Johor (2.6 percent). Among the states that experienced very low growth rates were Perak (0.4 percent), Perlis (0.8 percent), and Kelantan (0.9 percent).

Population Distribution and Urbanization

In terms of population distribution by state in Census 2000, Selangor was the most populous state (4.19 million), followed by Johor (2.72 million) and Sabah (2.60 million). Their share of the total population of Malaysia was 18.0 percent, 11.8 percent, and 10.6 percent, respectively. The least populated states were the Federal Territory of Labuan (0.08 million or 0.3 percent) and Perlis (0.20 million or 0.9 percent). With respect to urbanization, it is observed that the proportion of urban population had increased to 62.0 percent in Census 2000 from 50.7 percent in 1991. States with very high proportions of urban population were the Federal Territory of Kuala Lumpur (100 percent), Selangor (87.6 percent), and Pulau Pinang (80.1 percent). Conversely, the states with low urbanization levels were Kelantan (34.2 percent), Perlis (34.3 percent), and Kedah (39.3 percent) (see Table 10.4).

Age

The proportion of population of Malaysians below fifteen years of age in Census 2000 was 33.3 percent compared to 36.7 percent in 1991. State-wise, this proportion was very low in the Federal Territory of Kuala Lumpur (25.6 percent), Penang (26.9 percent), and Selangor (30.5 percent). At

Table 10.4

Population[a] by State, 1990, 1995, 2000, and 2005

State	Number ('000)				Average annual growth rate		
	1990	1995	2000	2005	1991–95	1996–2000	2001–5
More Developed States	**10,007.1**	**11,490.0**	**13,117.4**	**14,893.0**	**2.8**	**2.8**	**2.5**
Johor	2,121.3	2,422.0	2,721.9	3,020.0	2.7	2.4	2.1
Melaka	531.6	600.0	634.1	681.0	2.5	1.1	1.4
Negeri Sembilan	713.7	804.0	858.9	907.7	2.4	1.3	1.1
Perak	1,980.6	2,036.0	2,109.7	2,182.0	0.6	0.7	0.7
Pulau Pinang	1,114.5	1,179.0	1,307.6	1,452.2	1.1	2.1	2.1
Selangor[b]	2,331.4	3,210.0	4,175.0	5,069.0	6.6	5.4	4.0
Wilayah Persekutuan Kuala Lumpur	1,214.0	1,239.0	1,370.3	5,581.0	0.4	2.0	2.9
Less Developed States	**8,094.9**	**9,194.0**	**10,088.7**	**11,143.3**	**2.6**	**1.9**	**2.0**
Kedah	1,357.8	1,501.0	1,652.0	1,791.4	2.0	1.9	2.0
Kelantan	1,184.4	1,286.0	1,314.9	1,384.0	1.7	0.5	0.5
Pahang	1,058.2	1,200.0	1,290.0	1,365.1	2.6	1.5	1.1
Perlis	187.2	197.0	204.5	213.2	1.0	0.8	0.8
Sabah[c]	1,817.6	2,267.0	2,656.4	3,112.5	4.5	3.2	3.2
Sarawak	1,699.5	1,908.0	2,071.8	2,300.1	2.3	1.7	2.1
Terengganu	790.1	835.0	899.0	1,013.0	1.1	1.5	2.4
Malaysia	**18,102.0**	**20,684.0**	**23,266.0**	**26,036.2**	**2.7**	**2.4**	**2.3**

  [a] Population data refer to mid-year population.
  [b] Includes Wilayah Persekutuan Putrajaya.
  [c] Includes Wilayah Persekutuan Labuan.

the other end of the spectrum, this proportion was high in the states of Kelantan (41.5 percent), Terengganu (40.3 percent), and Sabah (38.4 percent). This inverse relationship can be due to higher birth rates in states recording higher rural poverty. Conversely, the proportion of population aged sixty-five and over in the Census 2000 was recorded at 3.9 percent compared to 2.7 percent in 1991. Consequently, the median age for Malaysia increased from 21.9 years in 1991 to 23.6 years in 2000. All these different age parameters point clearly toward continuation of the trend of population aging in Malaysia (see Table 10.5).

Gender Roles

Census 2000 revealed that for Malaysia as a whole, men outnumbered women, a pattern similar to that observed in 1991. In Census 2000, there were 104 males for every 100 females, a marginal increase over a gender ratio of 103 in 1991. In Census 2000, the ratio of males to females was relatively high for the Federal Territory of Labuan (110), Pahang (110), Johor (107), Sabah (107), Negeri Sembilan (105), Selangor (105), and Terengganu (104). On the other hand, women outnumbered men in the states of Perlis, Penang, and Kedah. The outnumbering of men by women is particularly noticeable in the sixty to sixty-four year age group; the gap widens with advancing age. This is expected given that female life expectancy is higher than that of males.

A study by Malar and Ahmad (1997) examined the existence of female role portrayals in

Table 10. 5

Population Size and Age Structure, 1995–2005

	1995	Percent	2001*	Percent	2005	Percent	Average annual growth rate (%) 7MP	8MP
Population	20.68		23.27		26.04		2.4	2.3
Citizens	19.68	100.0	22.04	100.0	24.66	100.0	2.3	2.3
Bumiputera	12.47	63.3	14.56	66.1	16.59	67.3	3.2	2.6
Chinese	5.22	26.5	5.58	25.3	6.04	24.5	1.4	1.6
Indian	1.49	7.6	1.63	7.4	1.78	7.2	1.8	1.8
Others	0.50	2.6	0.27	1.2	0.25	1.0	−12.7	−1.1
Non-citizens	1.00		1.23		1.38		4.3	2.4
Age Structure								
0–14	7.25	35.0	7.71	33.1	8.15	31.3	1.2	1.1
15–64	12.71	61.5	14.62	62.9	16.77	64.4	2.8	2.8
65 and above	0.72	3.5	0.94	4.0	1.12	4.3	5.3	3.6
Dependency Ratio	62.7		59.1		55.3			
Median Age (years)	22.8		23.9		25.3			

*Estimates based on the preliminary count of the Population Census 2000 and adjusted for under-enumeration.

advertisements in Malaysia that portray women and men in different roles. These differing roles are those concerning their credibility ("men as authorities"), interdependent roles ("women are dependent," "men are independent"), and their location (men were portrayed in occupational settings and women at home). Even though respondents comprised 200 Universiti Putra Malaysia and Universiti Kebangsaan Malaysia undergraduates, there was evidence that male and female viewers significantly differ in their perceptions of female role portrayals in television advertisements. (Variances in ethnicity were also found to account for differing perceptions.) Certain portrayals of women in television advertisements were considered offensive, particularly by female viewers, and they felt that there is a need for a change in such portrayals.

Marital Status

Census 2000 also revealed that young adults tend to marry at later ages than before. Consequently, the proportion of single persons ages twenty to thirty-four years continued to increase between 1991 and 2000 from 43.2 percent to 48.1 percent. Among females twenty to twenty-four years of age, 68.5 percent were single in 2000 compared to only 60.2 percent in 1991. A similar pattern is also observed for females in the twenty-five to forty-three year age group, as well as among males. The tendency of young male adults to marry at later ages is indicated by the mean age at first marriage that rose from 28.2 years in 1991 to 28.6 years in 2000, while for females the increase was from 24.7 years to 25.1 years over the same period.

Ethnic Composition

The Malaysian population is multiethnic, which makes it a heterogeneous and diverse market. The Census 2000 accounted the total Malaysian population to be 23.27 million, of which

94.1 percent were Malaysian citizens. Of the total Malaysian citizens, Bumiputras comprised 65.1 percent, Chinese 26.0 percent, and Indians 7.7 percent. This shows that the Bumiputra population has grown faster during the nine-year period, vis-à-vis other ethnic groups, as 1991's figures were 60.6 percent, 28.1 percent, and 7.9 percent, respectively (www.statistics .gov.my).

Non-Malaysian citizens totaled 1.39 million (or 5.9 percent) in Census 2000 compared to 0.81 million (or 4.4 percent) in 1991. The statistics on foreign workers in Malaysia is understated, as there are millions of illegal workers in the country. But, with the increasingly stern measures put in place by Malaysian immigration officials, their influx in such high numbers in the pre-1997 boom years is expected to be arrested. Most foreigners are expatriates in the professional services and manufacturing sectors, while a majority of Indonesian, Bangladesh, Thai, Philippines, and Myanmar workers are employed in the plantation, construction, and services (including domestic services) sectors. In Sarawak, the predominant ethnic group in Census 2000 was the indigenous Ibans. This group accounted for 30.1 percent of the state's total Malaysian citizens, followed by the Chinese (26.7 percent), Malays (23.0 percent), and Dayak, Murut, and other indigenous minority races. Similar data for Sabah showed the predominant ethnic group as being the natives Kadazandusun (18.4 percent) followed by Bajau (17.3 percent) and Malays (15.3 percent).

Religion

In Malaysia, religion is highly correlated with ethnicity. Islam is the most widely professed religion, with its proportion of the population increasing from 58.6 percent in 1991 to 60.4 percent in 2000. As a multicultural and heterogeneous society, the nation also has a proportion of its populace embracing other religions, such as Buddhism (19.2 percent), Christianity (9.1 percent), Hinduism (6.3 percent), and Confucianism/Taoism/other traditional Chinese religions (2.6 percent). The practice of Islam is also influenced by social traditions and conventions of the Malay culture, which are even older than Islam itself in Malaysia (Noor 1999). The ultimate concern in life is to please God by following His teachings in order to attain optimal well-being in both the present life and the hereafter (where the afterlife will take on an infinitely enduring dimension and, therefore, will be paramount to the present life, which is merely temporary). To achieve this goal, one has to cleanse oneself by suppressing selfish desires.

The Chinese generally adhere either to Buddhism or to Confucianism or, to a lesser extent, Christianity. Confucianism has been the dominant value system and teaches that one should strive for prosperity for the common good, rather than for individual welfare. Buddhism and Confucianism appeal to the intellect. A popular version of Taoism is considered the "religion of the masses." It venerates a multitude of gods, each with his or her own powers. Gods are simpler to grasp than the refinements of Buddhism philosophy. Regional and local gods, provincial heroes and deities, and worthy ancestors hold places in the Chinese temple.

The Indians are mostly of the Hindu faith. Christianity, however, cuts across all races (except Malays) but enjoys a much smaller following; British colonial officers were predominantly Christians. While Islam is the official religion as enshrined in the Malaysian Constitution, religious freedom is allowed and prevails (consistent with Islam, professing high tolerance toward other religious and cultural practices). It is a common sight in Kuala Lumpur, for example, to observe many a mosque, temple, or church be frequented by throngs of worshippers, signifying a high level of religious consciousness among Malaysians. Every major religious festival is celebrated and marked with official public holidays throughout the year, and the concept of open houses, where hosts celebrating "Hari Raya" or "Gong Xi Fa Chai" and welcoming guests of all ethnic groups has become a truly Malaysian tradition.

Languages

Languages vary widely from Malay, English, Chinese, and Tamil to Kadazan, Murut, and aboriginal, or *orang asli*. Of course, within Malay and Chinese languages, many dialects are spoken. For Malays, dialects vary widely according to locality, where they can be distinctly identifiable whether one speaks Kelantanese, Terengganu, or northern Malay (dialects indigenous of Perlis, Kedah, or northern Perak) or the more (formal) literary southern Malay dialect (of Johore-Singapore-Riau origin). Most popular Chinese dialects spoken include Hokkien, Hakka, Cantonese, and the formal, literary, Mandarin. Because language is the foundation of culture, it is thus easy to understand why there is such a wide range of cultures permeating the Malaysian scene. However, Malay has been designated as the official and preferred language of communication in the public sector, including government civil service, national-type schools, public universities, and other government-owned agencies.

However, English is used rather extensively, especially as it is being considered as the lingua franca in business circles. Increasingly, English has been gaining recognition as the accepted language to be "IT-advanced" and digitally connected, globally. Since the colonial era when English-medium schools were in place, the Malaysian national educational policy, particularly since 1970, has institutionalized the importance of the Malay language, by running government national-type schools to replace the English-medium school system. This exists beside privately run Chinese-medium and Tamil-medium schools, which still prevail. In the government national-type school (primary to secondary schooling), the pupil goes through eleven years of precollege education with Malay as the medium of instruction, besides eleven years of English as a mandatory subject. Recently, following public concerns about the decline of the average Malaysian's proficiency in English, plans are in place to teach selected subjects, such as science and mathematics, in English in primary and secondary government national schools.

One concern confronting the proponents of the "multicultural Malaysia" ideals is the need to attempt to arrest the racial divide that persists (Jaffar 2002). Despite the National Education Policy and the National Education system designed for national multiracial integration, only 2.1 percent of Chinese and 4 percent of Indian parents send their children to government national schools at the primary level (ages seven to twelve). As many as 910,000 Malay (Muslim) parents send their children to private religious schools. Thus, " . . . the paths of those millions of children will never cross. . . ." (Jaffar 2002, 10). In fact, Malaysia is a country that practices liberal education policies, especially pertaining to language, when one notes that even where 75 percent of Singapore's population is Chinese, schools teaching entirely in the Chinese language no longer exist there. Malaysia, comparatively, is regarded to have Southeast Asia's most comprehensive Chinese-language system of education, where Chinese educationists are very influential in the political and business communities.

The recent implementation of the vision school concept, where a national (Malay-medium) Chinese and Tamil school operates within one integrated complex of shared facilities in one vicinity, hopes to narrow this racial divide. The point is, after the 1969 racial riot, racial issues have been addressed nationally with a mix of social engineering, patriotism, and slogans. The lesson to be learned is that any initiative to bind the ethnic groups together should be attempted (Jaffar 2002).

SOME STUDIES ON CROSS-CULTURAL CONSUMER BEHAVIOR IN MALAYSIA

Perceptions on Product Branding

Nik Rahimah Nik Yacob (1991) surveyed a sample of 203 Malaysian consumers in Kuala Lumpur, Selangor, and Negri Sembilan, to attempt to understand the determinants of product symbolism by positing significant influences of ethnic and gender subcultures. Product symbolism was measured by asking the Malay and Chinese respondents to provide general impressions of someone wearing a specific branded product, Levi Strauss jeans (a conspicuous consumer product with symbolic meanings), available in many varieties and relatively expensive in Malaysia. The findings showed that consumers ascribed distinct product meanings on twenty descriptors to measure product symbolism. There were significantly different product meanings between male and female responses, but no evidence was found to show significant ethnic subcultural influence on product symbolism.

Md. Nor Othman and Aik Shian Heng (1997) investigated brand selection decisions for the purchase of durable products such as electrical appliances. Based on the products' performance dimensions, they found that significantly more Chinese consumers chose brands because "they work well" and they are more likely to be concerned with the attractive style and appealing colors, whereas the Malays generally are motivated by "the perceived best brand." Other interesting findings point to only two to three brand preferences for such purchases, with product performance, affect, and normative factors in decreasing order of importance, as brand selection criteria. One's spouse was deemed to be the most important "other person" to influence the buyer, further attesting to the need to understand marital role power-play in influencing household purchase decisions.

In their study on consumer perceptions of celebrity advertising for branded products, Zabid and Jainthy (2001) found that there were significant differences among the Malay, Chinese, and Indian consumers in their attitudes toward advertising using celebrity endorsements. It was also found that Malays were able to identify celebrity advertisements better than the other ethnic groups, where they tended to recall the specific products better. Significant differences also emerged among Malays, Chinese, and Indian consumers in associating the celebrity with the product they endorsed, such as Siti Nurhaliza with Maybelline cosmetics, Camelia with L'Oreal cosmetics, and Yusni Jaafar with Labour brand cooking oil. This implies that usage of celebrity endorsements appears to be more effective in reaching and appealing to targeted Malay segments for particular branded products. Overall, the study found that 47.9 percent of respondents agreed that advertising using celebrities positively influenced them toward product selections or purchase decisions, and this was particularly so among Malays.

Shopping Behavior and Perceptions of Loyalty Patronage

M. Z. Osman (1994) studied the influence of Malaysian lifestyles on loyalty patronage behavior. Surveying 215 Kuala Lumpur residents, four lifestyles (fashion-conscious, tradition-bound, ethnic-bound, and innovativeness) were examined in relation to clothing purchase at selected retail organizations. There was statistical evidence to show that only the ethnicity and innovativeness variables were strongly correlated with loyalty patronage. It was expected that the fashion-conscious would be discerning shoppers not easily developing loyalty to any particular store. Also, because it is still affordable to tailor one's clothing in Malaysia, rather than buy ready-made clothes at stores, this may also explain why the tradition-bound and fashion-conscious lifestyle consumers are not likely to be highly loyal to a particular store. One's ethnic-bound lifestyle was found to strongly influence loyalty patronage to a particular clothing store. Interestingly, this implies that it would be beneficial for retail store managers to break this ethnicity polarization, so that their merchandise can be perceived by customers to cater to a bigger market, rather than for customers confined to a certain ethnic group. This finding also demonstrates that even "ethnically differentiated" shopping outlets prevail in Malaysia.

Rahman (2001) advanced further into profiling Malaysian shoppers through retail brand lifestyle orientations. Through systematic sampling of 400 female shoppers in Kelang Valley shopping complexes housing six flagship department stores, her attempt to cluster shoppers was not successful. She attributed this to not knowing whether her respondents understood the meaning of "retail brands." She found that her sample of Malaysian shoppers perceived that there was a difference between "retail brands" and "(store)-owned brands." In fact, they were confounded with the term "retail brands." Furthermore, they did not perceive any difference between "retail brands" and "international brands." Given that shoppers' understanding and attitudes toward retail branding was so poor, it is not surprising that the attempt to cluster retail brand orientations into several categories was not successful.

To determine country-of-origin effects, Mohamad, Ahmed, Honeycutt and Tyebkhan (2000) examined the effect of country image on Malaysian consumer preferences in terms of product innovativeness, design, prestige, and workmanship. It was found that for garments, Malaysians prefer local over imported goods. Consistent with previous research, evidence suggests significant consumer preference and positive image perceptions for products originating from the United States, Japan, France, and Italy. Managers are recommended to utilize country-of-origin as a strategic tool to position and market both locally manufactured and imported goods.

An earlier study by Zabid, Samsinar and Siti Hawa (1996) showed a similar preference for local over imported goods over a wider array of shopping goods. Second preference was shown for goods of Japanese origin (particularly for electrical goods, home appliances, and toys), followed by those from the United States (such as furniture, footwear, and snack food) and France (such as perfume and clothing). These findings have to be tempered, because the consumer's first preference for locally made goods may not reflect actual purchasing behavior, which is constrained by many factors. These factors include purchasing power, product availability, limited knowledge of foreign-made products, and sociodemographic profile of the 116 respondents surveyed in the Kuala Lumpur area.

In the international arena, the issue of "adoption versus adaptation" becomes paramount. For instance, how would a marketer identify where standardization is possible and where the need to "act local" is necessary? This issue was investigated by Hult, Keillor, and Hightower (2000) in the context of comparing key product attributes between a developed market (i.e., France) and an emerging market (such as Malaysia). Potential differences among sixteen "sought for" product attributes were examined. The analysis explored how these attributes change across the convenience, shopping, and specialty good categories. Even though a two-country study such as this has limited applicability of its findings, the evidence points toward a fully integrated global consumer market that does not generally apply across different levels of market development. The results of this study show that the ability to implement a global marketing strategy across a variety of market types hinges upon the ability to implement the "think local, act local" strategy. Consequently, researchers suggested that when developing and implementing innovative products for market adoption, market-driven organizational learning becomes a vital component of global strategy.

The Malaysian Quality of Life

After achieving two decades of high growth averaging 7 percent to 8 percent per year, the 1997–98 regional financial crisis stifled growth for a short period. Speculators lost millions; the daily lives of average citizens were made more difficult. Many small financial institutions were restructured to reconsolidate the strength of the financial industry, causing thousands of job displacements. However, a silver lining was provided by the expenditure motivated by hosting the Commonwealth Games in September 1998. Malaysia was the first nation to host the Commonwealth Games outside of the main English-speaking Commonwealth group. The building of world-class facilities such as the Kuala Lumpur international airport, a new national sports complex, the new F-1 Sepang circuit, and other essential transport and telecommunications infrastructures was a big step toward qualification for advanced nation status, as enshrined in Malaysia's Vision 2020.

The world's tallest building (the Petronas Twin Towers at KLCC) was built, further enhancing Malaysia's attractiveness as a tourism destination and providing a visible symbol of progress on the global landscape. Computer penetration usage increased from 5 percent in 1993 to 13 percent in 1999; 480,000 new household subscribers were recruited with services launched by two new Internet providers, "connecting" many Malaysians via their personal home or office personal computers or college or school or cybercafé networks (Hew 2000). The Malaysian government's ambitious MSC project, covering a fifteen kilometer by fifty kilometer zone between Kuala Lumpur and the Kuala Lumpur international airport launched in 1995, has recorded participation of hundreds of international companies, exceeding its targets. This special project was designed to develop Malaysia as a future global leader in information technology.

In line with the government's aim of making Malaysia a regional center of excellence for education and responding to the growing market for education by the thriving college-age population, up to October 2003, the country boasted eleven public universities, seven university-colleges, ten private universities, six private university-colleges, and 700-odd private colleges, approved by the Malaysian Education Ministry to confer academic degrees and diploma/certificates. Gearing toward becoming a knowledge-based society, the number of television stations rose from three (in 1993) to five (in 2000), and two cable and satellite television broadcasters (including Astro) now offer up to thirty channels to about 791,000 subscribers (comprising 17.4 percent of total households). Also, 71 percent of total households in 1998 owned fixed telephone lines compared to 1993's penetration of only 44 percent. Mobile telephone ownership recorded a dramatic 600 percent increase in 1998, over 1993's ownership rate, with, currently, six telecommunication service providers offering six digital services (Hew 2000).

A Malaysian Quality of Life (MQL) 1999 report by the Economic Planning Unit (EPU) of the Prime Minister's Department developed a MQL index comparing changes between 1980 and 1998. The sum MQL index score of 86.22 for 1980 increased by 22.6 percent to 105.71 for 1998. This is attributed to improvements in MQL scores for this eighteen-year period, for eight out of the ten measures, notably for income and distribution (37.7 percent increase), education (36.5 percent increase), family life (33.2 percent increase), health (31.6 percent increase), and transport and communications (29.1 percent). The two casualties were public safety (–8 percent) and the environment (–2.8 percent). The overall incidence of poverty decreased from 49.3 percent of total households in Peninsular Malaysia in 1970 to an estimated low of 7.6 percent of total Malaysian households in 1999 (Economic Planning Unit 2000). While the incidence of rural poverty is markedly higher than urban poverty, these statistics have been consistently decreasing every year, from 58.7 percent of households in 1970 recording incidence of rural poverty to 11.8 percent of households in 1998. For incidence of urban poverty, the figure dropped from 21.3 percent of households in 1970 to a mere 2.4 percent in 1998. This indicates that the NEP objective of eradicating poverty is bearing fruit, with relentless endeavors over the years toward this end (for further exploration, see Tables 10.1, 10.3, and 10.6).

In short, the pace of change during the years from 1995 to 2001 has been brisk and dynamic. This implies visibly changing lifestyles with significant impact on consumer behavior in Malaysia. The most important changes are discussed in the next section.

IMPORTANT TRENDS AND IMPLICATIONS FOR MARKETING AND THE INDUSTRY

The Mahathir Generation

Malaysia's population is 23.27 million. Of the total population, 33.3 percent were under the age of fifteen, while 62.9 percent were in the age group of fifteen to sixty-four years, and 3.9 percent were over sixty-five years of age. About 45–50 percent of the population is estimated to be less than twenty-two years old. This percentage included those born in 1981, when Tun Dr. Mahathir Mohamad, Malaysia's fourth prime minister, first held the reins of the nation's supreme political leadership. It can be conjectured that an entire generation grew up in the Mahathir era over the twenty-two years he served as prime minister, before his retirement in October 2003. The age group of less than fourteen years has been growing at 1.4 percent a year, on average, since 1990. In 1990, this age group, consisting of children and young teenagers, occupied 37.4 percent of the population. This figure was 34.5 percent in 1997 and 34.0 percent in 1999 (EPU estimates for 1999).

This phenomenon shows that the trend in dominance of a young population will likely continue for at least another decade. Members of the "Mahathir generation" are now in their early twenties, and the hopes and dreams of this small yet feisty nation rest upon the shoulders of this generation, for they hold the key to its success in the future (Noor 2002, 10). For two decades, this generation enjoyed certain luxuries virtually absent in many other emerging nations. Certain preferential treatment was given to the Bumiputras with the intention of narrowing the economic gap between Bumiputras and non-Bumiputra groups and to reduce occupational and material wealth identification along racial lines. However, such policies cannot be sustained indefinitely, for even a young nation has to wake up and be resilient.

Dominance of a young population has interesting marketing implications. Zaharah Bakar (1991) surveyed Klang Valley household family life cycle categories, whose sociodemographic characteristics resembled the national ethnic composition. She found that 58.4 percent of the 1,500 families sampled were in the "full-nest with children" category. The average household size was five members, consisting of two adults and three children. Whether the present household size and composition have vastly changed from Bakar's study has not been found in any recent study. Specifically, 29 percent of the households in the above survey were composed of those ages twenty-five to thirty-five years, married for less than ten years, with several children, including their youngest child under six years of age. Another 29 percent were older married couples with older children. For these two largest segments, *The Star* (1995) valued the Malaysian children's market to be worth RM28.38 billion annually in the influence market (such as in fast-food franchise restaurants, milk products, toys, and educational products) and another RM1.55 billion in the primary market (such as teenage clothing, sports and fashion items, tuition classes, and video games). Also, considering the relatively higher savings rate of Malaysians, there is a high potential demand for child education and savings plans. With the typical Malaysian variety-seeking

Table 10.6

Malaysia's Position vis-á-vis Selected Countries—Selected Economic and Quality of Life Indicators

Country	Real gross domestic product (% annual growth) 2000 (f)	distribution of GDP (percent)		Urban population as % of total population (1998)	Total employment ('000s)	Employment by sector (% of total employment) services	1997 Life expectancy		1998(e) GNP per capita (US$)
		Exports	Imports				Males	Females	
World	3.4								
United Kingdom	2.4	29.0	29.0	89.3	26,870	71.1	75.0	80.0	21,400
United States	2.6	12.0	13.0	76.6	130,730	73.2	73.0	79.0	29,340
Singapore	5.0	215.0	201.0	100.0	1,830	69.5	73.0	79.0	30,060
South Korea	5.5	38.0	38.1	84.0	21,050	66.4	69.0	76.0	7,970
Indonesia	2.6	28.0	28.0	38.0	85,700	16.7	63.3	67.0	680
Malaysia	**5.0**	**114.4**	**92.6**	**55.1**	**8,817**	**46.0**	**69.6**	**74.5**	**3,093**
Philippines	3.5	56.0	67.0	57.0	27,890	42.9	67.0	70.0	1,050
Thailand	4.0	47.3	47.0	20.6	32,230	29.1	65.1	71.6	2,200
China	6.0	22.0	17.0	31.9	696,000	24.2	68.0	71.0	750

Country	Daily newspapers per 1,000 people (1996)	Mobile phones per 1,000 people (1997)	Personal computers per 1,000 people (1997)	Internet hosts per 1,000 people (1999) (1/)	High-technology exports (US$ million) (1995)	High-technology exports—% of manufactured (1997)
United Kingdom	332.0	151.0	242.4	24.10	79,256	41.0
United States	212.0	206.0	406.7	113.20	181,233	44.0
Singapore	324.0	273.0	399.5	21.00	69,249	71.0
South Korea	394.0	150.0	150.7	4.00	47,805	39.0
Indonesia	23.0	–5.0	8.0	0.08	3,615	20.0
Malaysia	**163.0**	**113.0**	**46.1**	**2.13**	**37,072**	**67.0**
Philippines	82.0	13.0	13.6	0.12	2,986	56.0
Thailand	65.0	33.0	19.8	0.34	14,826	43.0
China	23.0(3/)	10.0	6.0	0.01	24,393	21.0

Source: Economic Planning Unit, *The Malaysian Economy in Figures 2000* (Kuala Lumpur: Prime Minister's Department, 2000). Compiled from various international sources such as *The Europa World Yearbook 1998*, *The World Competitiveness Yearbook 1998*, *World Development Report 1999/2000*, *Human Development Report 1999*, *World Economic Fact Book 1998/99*.

behavior for food and eating out, a high demand for fast-food services and take-home meals, especially among the urban employed, will also prevail.

About 25–30 percent of the population is estimated to be in the college-age group, undertaking studies full-time directly after graduating from their secondary (high) school. As 53 percent of the total population in 2000 were in the fifteen to sixty-four age group, with education positioned as lifelong learning, the potential adult education market is tremendous. It is no wonder that the local demand for quality tertiary education will surpass the capacity of the nation to internally produce a sufficient pool of educators, for several generations in the future. While there were only three public universities (University of Malaya, Universiti Kebangsaan Malaysia, and Universiti Sains Malaysia) in 1970, there are now eighteen universities and university colleges, both public and private, and over 600 private colleges nationwide. By 2000, the number of students pursuing tertiary education was estimated to be over 380,000, comprising approximately 170,000 enrolled in local public universities and 200,000 attending private institutions (*Sunday Star* 2002, 3).

Increasing Women's Role in Purchasing Decisions

Women make up approximately half of the population, and although 49 percent of these fall within the working age group of fifteen to sixty-four years, they only comprise one-third of the total labor force. However, since its independence, women's entry into the labor force has been dramatic, from 30.8 percent in 1957 to 47.1 percent in 1995 (*Seventh Malaysia Plan 1996–2000*). Three main reasons have accounted for this increase: (1) greater educational opportunities available for women; (2) implementation of the New Economic Policy by the government in 1969; and (3) rapid economic development and industrialization, which have created jobs for women within labor-intensive industries, such as electronics and textiles (Noraini 1999). Due to these educational opportunities, which have direct impact on employment and upward social mobility, the role of women has undergone marked changes and has become much more significant.

Even the early study by M. Z. Osman and Aliah H. M. Salleh (1986) on marital role consensus in twenty-two household purchases found evidence that the wife has more say over major household decisions when she has a career outside the home (thus contributing to the family income), compared to situations in which she is a full-time homemaker. There was high consensus between husbands and wives that the following purchasing decisions have been made jointly: forms of savings, family medical care, children's schooling, home entertainment equipment, children's toys, and the hiring of domestic help. While purchasing decisions on wives' cosmetics and personal items were clearly the wives' domains, surprisingly, Malaysian wives were found to exert a strong influence even on the purchases of their husbands' clothes and personal items. Another well-established behavior evidenced in the study is that automobile purchase was clearly a male domain, with the wife's influence being felt only in the choice of the automobile's color. Perhaps this explains why an earlier attempt by a local auto distributor employing female sales personnel to sell cars received a lukewarm response from the predominantly male car purchasers. Yet another interesting finding of this study is the prevalence of more Malay (therefore, Muslim) couples that made purchase decisions jointly, vis-à-vis other ethnic (religious) families.

Another study by Sidin and Anjang (1996) provided further evidence that wives exert more influence in furniture purchasing, compared to car purchasing. (Malay wives had significantly more influence in furniture purchases vis-à-vis wives of other ethnic groups.) A greater degree of involvement in the decision-making process was found among wives with higher incomes, among older wives, among families with higher incomes, and among career wives, consistent with past studies based on Western culture. Studies by Md. Nor Othman and Aik Shian Heng (1997) and Lee and Hendon (1999) discovered in different contexts that Malaysian married couples tended to make joint decisions with their spouses, prior to purchase, and that this was related to length of marriage. This trend of growing equality is being accelerated by education and rising incomes.

Knowing precisely which household member is relatively more dominant in a particular decision stage in the purchase of specific products can help marketers devise more targeted promotional campaigns and make other marketing mix decisions more effectively. Nik Rahimah Yacob and Ismail Rejab (1984) found evidence that role specialization in purchasing decisions among Malaysian families tends to vary by product type. The stage of the family life cycle can also be useful in indicating the demand patterns within categories (Bakar 1991). In the study by Ismail Rejab and Nik Rahimah Yacob (1986), eight distinct Malaysian women's lifestyles were found using the AIO (activities, interests, opinions) inventory:

1. *Traditional mothers* (believe that children bring a husband and a wife closer together; believe that drug pushers should be punished severely; believe that mothers should give attention to their sick children)
2. *Fashion-conscious women* (keep informed of latest fashions; wear clothes of the latest fashion)
3. *Innovative opinion leaders* (try new products before others; provide friends with new brand referrals)
4. *Feminine women* (agree to "arranged" marriage; often sew clothes for their family; visit their relatives more than friends)
5. *Liberated women* (believe that women can perform multiple roles; believe that women are exploited in advertisements)
6. *Economically conscious women* (compare prices before purchasing and go for cost savings)
7. *Socially active women* (like to get involved in social work; keep in touch with current affairs)
8. *Women with basic role orientation* (believe that they are good cooks; like to cook children's favorites; like to try out new recipes)

This study showed that the conceptualization of the AIO items that are consistent with local culture not only portrays the complexity of lifestyle dimensions, but also generates new findings regarding behavioral attributes specific to Malaysian women. Besides the need to be sensitive to local cultural variations in conceptualizing research variables, international marketers ought to view women in distinct segments, identifiable through lifestyle dimensions or any other feasible base(s) of segmentation. Unfortunately, no recent study on Malaysian women has emerged to indicate whether these identified lifestyles remain or have evolved into other new women's lifestyles within the last five years.

Further, women's shopping behavior has been profiled by Sofiah A. Rahman (2001), who used consumer retail brand lifestyle orientations to differentiate the profiles of women shoppers into seven segments:

1. *Sophisticated shoppers* (rather young, aged twenty to thirty-five years old; highest education levels; self-driven women)
2. *Value shoppers* (older women; slightly less educated than sophisticated shoppers; government employees including many Chinese)

3. *Dreamers* (many married women, but still young; least educated; less likely to be employed; lowest income earner; mostly Malay)
4. *Fashion enthusiasts* (young shoppers; mostly in private employment, but many still not employed; various education levels, but many with diplomas; rather low income)
5. *Career women* (slightly older than fashion enthusiasts; various education levels, with the highest of those working in the private sector; average income; many Malays)
6. *Ruthless shoppers* (many married women but rather young; low levels of employment; various levels of education; many Chinese)
7. *Status shoppers* (many married with children; a large percentage of highest income levels; average education levels)

Knowledge of these profiles of Malaysian shoppers offers an opportunity and a challenge to marketers to reach and serve these segments more effectively. Malaysian women have progressed, and with gains in social mobility acquired through higher educational attainment, they have significant influence on the economy. For successful marketing in Malaysia, it is imperative that this be recognized by management.

Ethnically Segmented and Differentiated Consumer Markets

The multicultural nature of Malaysia demands that the associated cultural and religious differences be considered for segmentation and differentiated marketing strategies. This translates to usage of language-specific brand names and different colored packaging and labeling for food products appealing to either Muslim, non-Muslim, or other specific ethnic groups. For example, goods packaged in black-colored material are not readily accepted by the Chinese (as this color signifies death or mourning), compared to packaging using red or gold (which signifies prosperity and good fortune). The traditional Chinese also favor the number eight. Psychological pricing tactics incorporating the digit 8 are used widely, including project bids and property pricing. Other examples include Aminah Hassan chili sauce, Babas and Adabi spices, Tamin black soya sauce, and Buruh cooking oil, which cater more for Malay households, while Maggi instant mee and sauces and Mazola cooking oil, popular national brands, are positioned for the larger market for all ethnic groups. Lingam sauce, though originally Indian by inspiration, has been geared for the export market, in view of the insufficient size of the domestic market of Malaysian Indians, and other market considerations. Perniagaan Orang Kampung is an exception, where the company using a Malay brand name has been heavily using radio advertising on an English-language music station to promote to all ethnic groups its tongkat Ali and kacip Fatimah health beverages.

Because the majority of the Malaysian population is Muslim, the government is very sensitive to the needs of the Muslim majority. Muslims consume only *halal* foods, or those deemed permissible by Islamic standards (in terms of ingredients and the production processes used). As such, halal and non-halal sections of dairy and meat counters are clearly demarcated and labeled. The basic premise is to offer these halal goods and services to Muslims and non-Muslims alike, thus benefiting all consumers with a wider product selection. Malaysia is noted to be the only Asian country besides those in the Saudi Arabian subcontinent and a few other Middle Eastern nations, operating globally renowned fast-food franchised restaurants certified halal by the Islamic Religious Affairs Department under the office of its Prime Minister's Department. Many other large restaurant establishments are also legislatively bound to serve halal food with no alcoholic drinks served in the premises, unless under specially restricted licenses. All international fast-food franchised services are gazetted under Malaysian law to serve only halal food and nonalcoholic beverages.

The pious, in addition, will also not allow themselves to earn profits from investments or trading in convertible unsecured loan stocks and other debt-financing instruments that bear interest (usury) (*Asian Business* 1994). These are among pertinent consumer-driven demand issues to consider, now that Malaysia is making a bid to become the Islamic banking capital of the world. Bank Islam Malaysia (BIMB) symbolizes the beginning of the efforts of Malaysian Muslims to develop an integrated Islamic financial system in the country and globally. Since its establishment on March 1, 1983, BIMB has been pioneering innovative Islamic banking products and operations within the country's banking system. In conjunction with the Securities Commission (SC), Bank Negara, the Malaysian Central Bank, is working to set up a more formal framework to develop the Islamic capital market, since 1994, when BIMB Securities, Malaysian's first Islamic stockbroking company, was formed. Muslim investors have been able to invest directly in halal counters. More recently, conventional securities firms have also set up their own Islamic stockbroking on halal stocks, just as there exist Islamic banking counters alongside conventional banking systems and products in most commercial banks since the Islamic interest-free banking system was first propagated twenty years ago.

As of July 1996, 364 stocks out of 633 stocks listed on the Kuala Lumpur Stock Exchange (KLSE) were considered halal (*Asiamoney* 1996). The list, which is updated regularly, is based on the set of criteria determined by BIMB's religious supervisory council and is widely regarded as the benchmark for Islamic investors. Halal stock must confirm with Syariah (Islamic jurisprudence) principles and exclude companies with activities that involve gambling, alcohol, interest-based banking and finance, and conventional insurance, as well as other *haram* (forbidden) sectors, such as non-halal food products. This prevents blue-chip stocks such as Maybank, Genting, and Malaysian Airlines from being included in an Islamic fund managers' portfolio (as the national carrier Malaysian Airlines serves alcohol on its flights, Genting group's core business revolves on gambling income, and Maybank also manages the conventional usury-tied banking alongside interest-free counters). Pioneering an integrated Islamic financial system has opened an entirely new window of opportunity for new financial instruments in Malaysia's banking and capital market. This includes a wide range of corporate financial instruments and retail products, including savings (such as *al-wadiah* "savings with a guarantee" bank savings account), lending (such as the *al-baithamin ajal* home loan), and deposit instruments, as well as *takaful* (insurance) and unit trust products for the entire financial industry, where the usury elements have been eliminated.

Changing Malaysian Lifestyles

The large-scale survey of 2,214 Malaysian conducted by Rejab and Nik Rahimah (1986) described earlier, although its focus was on women, led to pioneering work on Malaysian lifestyles and their marketing implications. Kiu (1991) reported a psychographic study capturing the following Malaysian lifestyles: *yesterday people, village trendsetters, chameleons, loners, new breed, yuppies,* and *sleepwalkers.* There emerged a first attempt to examine lifestyle tied to a specific Malaysian product (i.e., credit card usage); this study also contributed to an understanding of men's lifestyles and their associated impact on credit card usage (Kaur and Othman 1995). Recently, Ramayah, Noor, Nasurdin, and Choo (2002) validated attributes influencing the differences in attitudes among active and inactive credit card holders in Malaysia. Among thirteen attributes, acceptance level, credit limit, interest-free repayment period, ancillary functions, handling of cardholders' complaints, bank image, and bank advertising were the factors distinguishing between active and nonactive cardholders in Malaysia. To stimulate higher usage levels, the authors suggest that banks issuing credit cards should work closer with retailers, provide adequate credit limit, and implement strategic alliances with firms in travel, leisure, insurance, and telecommunications besides obtaining wider advertising exposure to build their brand image.

Since the first large-scale Malaysian Lifestyle Study (MLS) in 1993, Malaysia has undergone major changes in its marketing environment, which called for an updated profile tracking of current lifestyles. To gain in-depth insights of relevant new marketing issues to be examined, the most recent MLS study by ACNielsen (1998) held four focus group discussions (with four panelists per group) and held discussions with respondents to pretest the 277–variable structured questionnaire inclusive of 125 AIO statements. ACNielsen's Media Index ($n = 2,551$), deemed the largest syndicated study in Malaysia, was used as a base study while incorporating inputs from other ACNielsen studies in other countries. Stratified random probability sampling was used to generate the sample size obtained of 2,358 adults, representing 58 percent Malays, 32 percent Chinese, and 10 percent Indians and others, the ethnic composition being consistent with the population structure (Hew 2000). This 1998 MLS study identified seven distinct lifestyle clusters, which are as follows:

1. *Generasi era baru* (estimated to comprise 16 percent of the population; mainly male; average age of twenty-nine; Malay dominant; medium–high income; students/white-collar workers; patriotic; religious; sensible about money; striving to improve; health conscious)

2. *Struggling fatalists* (estimated to comprise 20 percent of the population; mainly female; average age of thirty-six; Chinese skewed; medium income; blue-collar workers; they despise their jobs; they are superstitious; they feel restricted by family/social pressures)

3. *Boleh believers* (estimated to comprise 14 percent of the population; mainly male; average age of thirty-six; Malay dominant; lower–middle income; tradition-bound but want to try new things; fun-loving; not in control of their money but are brand conscious)

4. *Respectable providers* (estimated to comprise 16 percent of the population; more female; average age of thirty-six; Malay dominant; medium income; optimistic; nationalistic; love their jobs; family-focused; proud of their homes; religious; bargain hunters)

5. *Silver spoons* (estimated to comprise 11 percent of the population; mainly male; average age of thirty-three; higher income; Chinese dominant; "Western"; leisure-oriented; in control over their money; plan their future; not religious but have strong filial piety, brand loyal)

6. *Quiet country homebodies* (estimated to comprise 12 percent of the population; mainly female; average age of forty-five; housewives/retirees; lowest income; tradition-bound and family-focused; not ambitious; cannot save; price-sensitive; low-involvement shopping)

7. *Happy-go-lucky kampongists* (estimated to comprise 11 percent of the population; average age of thirty-six; skewed Malay; laborers; lower–middle income; proud of their homes; religious; money as status quo; spenders; enjoy leisure; health-conscious; bargain-hunters)

The seven clusters that emerged are distinctly different from the set of lifestyles identified only five years earlier. This reflects the lifestyle changes that are expected to happen in the advent of a higher quality of life and after surviving the aftermath of the 1997–98 financial crisis. From the above seven lifestyles, three segments are Malay dominant, while the silver spoons are largely

Chinese, but a fair mix of both Chinese and Malays are members of the struggling fatalists. Hew and Salleh (2001) explored the use of psychographic and demographic profiles in determining potential target segments for CELCOM, a leading mobile telephone service provider. It was found that the two profiles between the potential user and the nonpotential user of mobile telephone services are different in Malaysia. The targeted new user segments for this category are found to be respectable providers, generasi era baru, and silver spoons. Certainly, knowledge of these lifestyle segments offers both an opportunity as well as a challenge to marketers to reach and serve these segments more effectively than do their competitors.

The capitalist transformation process has accompanied many social, cultural, and other changes relating to attitudes and values. Noticeable changes have been occurring in the area of family structure. With the introduction of the market system, the extended family structure is slowly disappearing and is being replaced by a nuclear family structure. A sizeable proportion of those in the twenty-five through twenty-nine age group choose to delay marriage. More males than females below the age of twenty-five are still singles—"staying single" has become more common among educated young urbanites. At the same time, the total fertility rate declined from seven children in the 1960s to 3.4 children in 1995. Another important social change is that almost half of the labor force is comprised of women, and Malaysians are becoming more and more urbanized. The labor force participation rates for women are drastically increasing, especially in the urban areas, and women are becoming better educated to enter the job market. The influx of career women has visibly affected the lifestyles of the middle- and upper-class consumers, with a growing demand for more leisure time and quality family time. This is not surprising, but is typical of an economy undergoing rapid transformation (Ghosh 1998).

Increasing Number of "Internet Savvy" Consumers

Statistics compiled by the Economic Planning Unit of the Prime Minister's Department revealed that in 1997, Malaysia, with 46.1 personal computers per 1,000 people, was ranked highest among the ASEAN-6 countries, behind South Korea, Hong Kong, and Singapore. In 1999, the above source further reported Malaysia's standing as second to Brunei among the ASEAN-6, with 2.13 Internet hosts per 1,000 people (against Japan's figure of 13.40, Singapore's figure of 21.00, and the United States's figure of 113.20). It is observed that Malaysia is in the early adoption and trial stages in the diffusion of adoption cycle of the Internet, going through what the United States faced in the mid-1990s.

Tih Sio Hong (1998) explored Internet adoption, focusing on demographic characteristics of the Internet user and the function of the Internet as an advertising tool in Malaysia. She found that Internet usage is highly correlated with higher education and income levels, and users are predominantly male, students, researchers, professionals, and related to the technical/computer sciences. However, advertising through the Internet still has very far to go in its likely impact on the country's marketing practices. With the number of Internet subscribers increasing tremendously from 810 "Jaring" subscribers in 1994 to 275,000 subscribers in 1998, mushrooming of other popular Internet servers, such as TMNet, Hotmail, and other institutionally based servers, vast potential for advertising through the Internet is foreseen in the future.

A survey of 202 online purchasers by Tih (1998) revealed that 82 percent of respondents surf the Internet at home for ten hours a week on average, and 62.4 percent purchased once a month through the Internet for items up to RM400 per purchase. Most popular online purchases revolve around books and magazines, music items, compact discs, and greeting cards; 71.8 percent of these purchases are made through credit card payments. However, no significant variances on their purchasing behavior were detected based on gender, age, and education. This exploratory study indicated the potent role of the Internet in influencing the information search and overall product selection stages in the consumer buying decision process at this stage of its adoption cycle in Malaysia.

Norzalita Abd. Aziz (2000) sought to identify characteristics of local Internet users in relation to travel information, tourism Web sites, and motivation to travel. A survey of 120 respondents in the Kelang Valley using a questionnaire with fifty-one measures revealed that a majority of these tourism Web site users are in the twenty- to thirty-five-year age group, are highly educated, earning monthly incomes of RM3,000 to RM5,000. Most pertinent information needed is location and accommodation details, while the desired features are real pictures with animated video clips. Creative marketing strategies using effective promotional tactics of information presentation are suggested to increase the awareness and frequency of using Web sites for travel, consistent with the government's efforts to boost both the ICT and tourism industries. Ezlika Ghazali and Md.Nor Othman (2001), in their study on demographic and pyschographic profiles of active and passive investors in urban Malaysia, found the Internet to be one of the main information sources appealing to active investors inclined to be knowledge seekers and, thus, information hungry. This further supports the prominent role of the Internet that grants greater empowerment to consumers to make purchase decisions, thereby reducing their overdependence on intermediaries such as travel agents and remisiers or stockbrokers, especially in the information search stage of the consumer buying process.

A sample of 150 vacation travelers in the Kelang Valley was recently surveyed, capturing psychographic, lifestyle, vacation-style dimensions, and vacation purchasing patterns (Chow 2000). Three segments emerged. One segment, named "the joy luck club" was found to use the Internet more actively as a prime information source, as a stimulant for the need for a vacation and as a medium for travel reservations and payment transactions. The Internet's role was more significant for this particular segment, relative to the two other segments. This vacationer segment is predominantly aged thirty-five years and below, comprising single Chinese females with relatively higher income. A majority of this segment takes at least three vacations a year within Malaysia, works in the private sector, and is drawn by the attractive locations of the vacation destinations, rather than motivated by other reasons to make the trip. The profile of this Internet-savvy group is notably different, specifically in the active vacationer market, relative to the largely male-skewed profile of the general Internet user across the population. This may signal the need for more extensive research for particular service markets to better fine-tune differentiated marketing strategies for particular segments, rather than assuming a mass-marketing approach. More research on online shopping, e-commerce, and specifically on the Internet's role on consumer buying behavior and business-to-business marketing alliances are vital for providing business practitioners with an empirically rooted basis for engineering effective strategies and forging best practices in relationship marketing. Asian consumer behavior, relationship networks, and service connections cannot be assumed to be similar to the best practices we are exposed to, on predominantly Western culture (Salleh and Chow 2001).

The local universities and university-colleges with constrained teaching and physical resources have spurred the development of "e-learning" in Malaysia. (In 1999, 288,693 secondary school-leavers in Malaysia entered institutions of higher learning [IHLs], and this figure is bound to increase yearly.) By 2000, there were already four IHLs offering e-learning (i.e., learning using material distributed by electronic media), culminating with the recent intake of hundreds of teachers into several degree programs operated by the newly established Open University Malaysia. Other forces driving e-learning in Malaysia include shortage of knowledge workers to meet the nation's

Table 10.7

Opinions in Search of "Institutional Success" for E-Learning and Their Implications

Statement	Number of respondents	Performance dimension
The Internet is a level playing field, so quality with cost competitiveness is a must for survival.	6	Market responsiveness
The role of the teacher will change, i.e., to a facilitator rather than the center of knowledge. The shift is toward student-centered learning.	5	Operational excellence
It means increased competition. Conventional universities need to be proactive about this intensified international competition.	5	Managerial imperative
Universities need to be globally competitive, and the offer needs to be world-class.	5	Managerial imperative
Students of higher learning are increasingly demanding and discerning. If a university does not use quality staff to produce quality products, they will go elsewhere. The customers demand value-for-money.	5	Operational excellence
The university needs to focus on its market niche—what segment it can serve best and what it can do best—and to leverage on its strength.	4	Managerial imperative
Teachers need to be retrained, retooled, and updated with new ICT.	3	Operational excellence
The IT infrastructure needs to be made ready.	3	Market responsiveness
In the shrinking and borderless marketplace, those who do not have an Internet strategy will be left behind; only the fittest will survive.	3	Managerial imperative
Currently, competition is not a worry, as demand exceeds supply, and our costs (incurred by the students) are relatively low.	2	Operational excellence

Note: The number of experts interviewed ($n = 13$) who shared similar comments on the issue, is shown in the second column. The third column denotes the category assigned under each of the three performance dimensions developed. (The relatively most dominant category is selected.)

Vision 2020, skills upgrading, and the MSC's smart school flagship project, targeted to produce 158,000 Internet-savvy smart school graduates (Salleh and Teh 2000). Teh (2000) interviewed a panel of thirteen e-learning industry experts to define what constitutes institutional success for an IHL providing e-learning for the Malaysian market. Three performance dimensions were identified: managerial imperatives, market responsiveness, and operational excellence generated by thirty-one success factors that emerged, with a common thread being total quality management and relationship marketing playing a dual role integral to this success. Table 10.7 shows a sample of expert opinions generated by the interviews when defining institutional success in delivering e-learning. Not only is e-learning a dynamically changing industry that hopes to supply enough knowledge workers for the success of Malaysia's MSC project, with ICT, it is also among the best placed industries to benefit from the MSC project, besides the electronic government, the smart card (*Mykad*), and the smart school projects.

CONCLUSION

There are two formidable challenges that multicultural Malaysia has to confront as progress is made. These challenges are the need to arrest the racial divide and the digital divide.

The infamous racial riot of May 13, 1969 was a milestone in Malaysian history. This incident has been analyzed by politicians and community leaders, with the New Economic Policy and the National Educational Policy as the products of such studies. The intention was for Malaysia to portray the kind of harmonious multicultural and multiracial mix that makes for a vibrant emerging nation. However, in reality, thirty years later, Malaysians in general are still segregated along racial, social, and religious lines, with certain groups still living within their cocoons (Jaffar 2002, 10). To what extent this has resulted from the "ethnically" structured nature of the political parties and balance of shared political power is difficult to gauge. But several indicators, such as the option to attend either government/national (hence, Malay-medium) or Chinese or Tamil school systems for precollege education, have been speculated to lead to disturbingly rampant racial polarizations among university student life in the last decade. (This is compared to university campus life in the 1970s, when there was more racial integration with English language as the common bond.) Such a racial polarization during student life, if not addressed to some extent, is bound to prevail in work settings and later adult life. However, racial polarization is not necessarily negative. This is perhaps one contributory factor toward the prevalence of ethnically differentiated customer segments for some retail products, thus further enriching the culturally diverse feature of the Malaysian consumer market.

Much of Malaysia's success story over two decades of recent development has been correlated with the dynamism of its fourth prime minister, Tun Dr. Mahathir Mohamad. In the mind-set of international Muslim circles, "Malaysia" has been synonymously and analogously perceived to be linked to "Mahathir." His vision and determination to drag this country into the modern age was much maligned and misunderstood by many (Noor 2002a, 10). Malaysia under Tun Dr. Mahathir has experienced significant changes to its social, economic, and political culture. He has successfully shifted the Malaysian economy from relying solely on agriculture to becoming industrial-based and now gearing for a knowledge base. He has courageously stopped foreign attempts to colonize the economy, successfully handled the devastating impact caused by it, and reconstructed it using Malaysia's own model. At the same time, he has been the respected spokesman for other nations (including Muslim and developing countries). This visionary statesman talked against uncontrolled "globalization" by the Western economic giants and expressed concern over its likely impact of making poorer nations even poorer (Faisal 2002, 11).

To understand Malaysia's market behavior is to appreciate the vital balance of racial harmony and political stability delicately fostered in this nation since independence from the British in 1957. The political will obviously rests on the strength of UMNO, even within a framework of an ethnically represented multicomponent political party system. Tun Dr. Mahathir, when he was the nation's top CEO, had preoccupations with the creation of a proud, independent, and dynamic nation. These preoccupations

> are an act of historical imagination that not only made it possible for us to fathom the nightmares of a downtrodden nation in colonial times, but also to dream the glories of a resurrected nation. The gift of self-esteem, the power of imagination and the means to be all that we can possibly be—Tun Dr. Mahathir imparted these to generations of Malaysians. . . . Based on the party's track record, political finesse and pragmatism, we can expect post-Mahathir UMNO to further strengthen its deeply held values that are deemed to underpin Malaysia's stability and viability. . . ." (*New Straits Times* 2002b, 10)

Table 10.8

Malaysia versus ASEAN Key Economic Indicators, 2000–2004

	Real GDP growth (%)	GDP per capita at nominal value (US$)	Growth in consumer prices (%)	Current account balance of the balance of payments (US$ million)	Gross international reserves[c] (US$ million)	Total external debt (US$ billion)	Unemployment rates (% of labor force)
Brunei Darussalam							
2000	2.8	12,751	1.6	4,007	n.a	n.a	4.7
2001	3.0	12,245	-3.1	3,765	n.a	n.a	5.6
2002	3.2	n.a	-0.3	3,708	n.a	n.a	4.6
2003[a]	5.0–6.0	n.a	1.0	n.a	n.a	n.a	n.a
2004[b]	n.a	n.a	1.3	n.a	n.a	n.a	n.a
Indonesia							
2000	4.9	740	9.3	7,985	29,394	0.14	6.1
2001	3.4	691	12.5	6,899	28,017	0.13	8.1
2002	3.7	n.a	10.0	7,257	31,571	0.13	9.1
2003[a]	3.5–4.0	n.a	9.0	n.a	28,004	n.a	n.a
2004[b]	4.0	n.a	8.4	n.a	n.a	n.a	n.a
Malaysia							
2000	8.5	3,837	1.5	8,487	29,886	0.042	3.1
2001	0.3	3,664	1.4	7,286	30,848	0.045	3.6
2002	4.1	3,870	1.8	7,190	34,583	0.048	3.5
2003[a]	4.5	4,053	1.2	9,676	38,669[c]	0.048	3.5
2004[b]	5.5–6.0	4,229	n.a	10,543	n.a	n.a	3.4
Philippines							
2000	4.4	981	6.6	9,349	15,024	0.052	10.1
2001	4.5	914	4.1	1,323	15,658	0.052	9.8
2002	4.4	n.a	2.6	4,197	16,299	0.054	11.4
2003[a]	4.2–5.2	n.a	4.0	n.a	n.a	n.a	10.0
2004[b]	4.0	n.a	4.0	n.a	n.a	n.a	10.0
Singapore							
2000	9.4	23,071	2.1	13,291	80,362	0.22	3.1
2001	-2.4	20,659	-0.6	16,114	75,800	0.22	3.3

2002	2.2	n.a	0.4	18,740	82,276	0.23	4.4
2003[a]	0.0–1.0	n.a	0.9	n.a	n.a	n.a	4.5
2004[b]	3.0	n.a	1.7	n.a	n.a	n.a	4.0
Thailand							
2000	4.6	1,968	1.4	9,328	32,661	0.079	3.6
2001	1.9	1,831	0.8	6,236	23,048	0.067	3.3
2002	5.3	n.a	1.6	7,647	38,924	0.059	2.4
2003[a]	4.2	n.a	1.0–2.0	n.a	n.a	n.a	n.a
2004[b]	4.3	n.a	0.9	n.a	n.a	n.a	n.a
Vietnam							
2000	6.76	403	–0.6	–354	3,417	n.a	6.4
2001	6.93	416	0.5	–682	3,675	n.a	6.3
2002	7.04	n.a	4.0	–870	4,121	n.a	n.a
2003[a]	6.2	n.a	3.8	n.a	n.a	n.a	n.a
2004[b]	7.0	n.a	3.3	n.a	n.a	n.a	n.a
Myanmar							
2000	13.7	142	–6.3	–243.0	223.5	–6	n.a
2001	9.9	151	51.0	–309.5	410.2	n.a	n.a
2002	n.a	n.a	n.a	n.a	n.a	n.a	n.a
2003[a]	n.a	n.a	n.a	n.a	n.a	n.a	n.a
2004[b]	n.a	n.a	n.a	n.a	n.a	n.a	n.a
Laos, PDR							
2000	5.8	328	10.6	–12.1	140.9	0.001	7.3
2001	5.8	330	7.5	–78.6	133.4	0.001	n.a
2002	5.9	n.a	15.2	–32.8	191.0	0.001	n.a
2003[a]	n.a	n.a	n.a	n.a	n.a	n.a	n.a
2004[b]	n.a	n.a	n.a	n.a	n.a	n.a	n.a

Source: IMF World Economic Outlook, April 2002.
[a]Estimate.
[b]Forecast.
[c]As of August 30, 2003.

ACKNOWLEDGMENTS

The authors wish to thank Bianca Teo for her contribution to Salleh, Teo, and Pecotich (1998).

REFERENCES

ACNielsen. 1998. *Malaysian Lifestyle Survey*. Malaysia: ACNielsen.

Ariffin, Ahmad Azmi Mohd. 1999. "Motivasi dan Implikasi Pemasaran Pelancongan ke Pulau Peranginan di Kalangan Segmen Eksekutif Muda" (Motivation and Tourism Implications of Marketing Island Resorts to Young Executive Segmen). *Jurnal Pengurusan* (Penerbit Universiti Kebangsaan Malaysia) 18 (July): 89–107.

Asiamoney. 1996. "Islamic Banking Boost," October: 14.

Asian Business. 1994. "Malaysia: Model Banking for Muslim, Hong Kong," January: 6.

Asian Development Bank. 1992. *Key Indicators of Developing Asian and Pacific Countries*, vol. 23, July. Manila, Philippines: Asian Development Bank.

———. 2003. *Asian Development Outlook 2003*. Hong Kong: Oxford University Press.

Asia Times Online Co., Ltd. 2003. "Abdullah Badawi: Malaysia's Tinker Man." Available at www.atimes.com.

Aziz, Norzalita Abd. 2000. "Penggunaan Internet Sebagai Sumber Maklumat Industri Pelancongan Di Malaysia" (Internet Usage as Information Source for the Malaysian Tourism Industry). *Jurnal Pengurusan* (Universiti Kebangsaan Malaysia) 19 (July): 41–60.

Bair, F. E. (ed.). 1988. *International Marketing Handbook*, 3rd ed., vol. 2. Detroit, MI: Gale Research Company.

Bakar, Zaharah. 1991. "Ciri-ciri kitaran hayat keluarga: suatu tinjauan keatas keluarga-keluarga diLembah Kelang" (Family Life Cycle Characteristics: A Survey of Families in the Kelang Valley). *Jurnal Pengurusan* (Universiti Kebangsaan Malaysia) 10 (July): 75–94.

Bank Negara Malaysia. 2002. "Economic and Financial Developments in the Malaysian Economy in the First Quarter of 2002." Available at www.bnm.gov.my.

———. 2003. "Economic and Financial Data for Malaysia (2003)." Available at www.bnm.gov.my.

Beng-Huat, Chua. 2000. *Consumption in Asia: Lifestyles and Identities*. London: Routledge.

Berita Harian—Ekonomi. 1995. "Proton yakin jual hingga 160,000 unit," February 11: 17.

Celcom. 2002. *Utusan Malaysia Online—Korporat*. DIGI. Com jalin usaha sama, March 14.

Chin, Cristine B. N. 2000. "The State of the 'State' in Globalization: Social Order and Economic Restructuring in Malaysia." *Third World Quarterly* 21: 10–35.

Chow, Sook Woon. 2000. "Pemetakan Pasaran Untuk Industri Hospitaliti di Malaysia—Pemasaran Melalui Internet" (Market Segmentation for the Hospitality Industry in Malaysia—Marketing through the Internet). Unpublished MBA Master's Project, Universiti Kebangsaan Malaysia, Faculty of Business Management, Bangi.

Damhoeri, Khairudin, Fuat Mashori, Jaafar Muhamad, and Kamaruddin Sharif. 1994. "Corporate Leadership and the Myth of the Incompetent Malay Chief Executive Officer: Evidence from the Malaysian General Insurance Industry." *Jurnal Pengurusan* (Universiti Kebangsaan Malaysia) 13 (July): 47–62.

Danamodal Nasional Berhad. 2002. *Annual Report 2001*. Available at www.danamodal.com.my.

De Mooiji, Marieke K., and Warren Keegan. 1996. "Lifestyle Research in Asia." In *Marketing Lifestyles for the Asia-Pacific*, eds. S. M. Leong, S. H. Ang, and C. T. Tan, pp. 87–98. Singapore: Heinemann.

Demaine, Harvey. 1994. "Malaysia: Physical and Social Geography," In *The Far East and Australasia*, 25th ed., ed. L. Daniel, p. 518. London: Europa Publications.

Department of Statistics, Malaysia. 2000. "Preliminary Count Report: Population and Housing Census 2000." Available at www.statistics.gov.my.

———. 2002. "Population Distribution and Basic Demographic Characteristics Report, Population and Housing Census 2002." Available at www.statistics.gov.my.

———. 2003. Available at www.statistics.gov.my.

Economic Planning Unit. 1999. *Malaysian Quality of Life 1999*. Malaysia: Prime Minister's Department.

———. 2000. *The Malaysian Economy in Figures—2000*. Malaysia: Prime Minister's Department.

Economic Report 1999/2000. 1999. Kuala Lumpur: Percetakan Nasional Malaysia Berhad.

Economic Report 2002/2003. 2002. Kuala Lumpur: Percetakan Nasional Malaysia Berhad.

Economic Report 2003/2004. 2003. Kuala Lumpur: Percetakan Nasional Malaysia Berhad.

The Economist. 2003. "The Changing of the Guard: A Survey of Malaysia," April 5: 3–14.

Eighth Malaysia Plan 2001–2005. Kuala Lumpur: Percetakan Nasional Malaysia Berhad.

Elegant, Simon. 2000. "Bound by Tradition." *Far Eastern Economic Review*, July 27: 65.

Engel, J. F., R. D. Blackwell, and P. W. Miniard. 1993. *Consumer Behaviour*, 7th ed. Sydney: The Dryden Press.

Euromoney. 1990. *Asia Pacific: An Investment Guide.* London: Euromoney Publications PLC.

Faisal, I. A. 2002. "Orderly Leadership Transition Will Help Prevent Any Disunity." *New Straits Times*, June 27: 11.

Far Eastern Economic Review. 1993. *Asia 1993 Yearbook: A Review of the Events of 1992.* Hong Kong: Review Publishing Company Ltd.

Funston, John. 2000. "Malaysia's Tenth Elections: Status Quo, Reformasi or Islamization?" *Contemporary Southeast Asia: A Journal of International & Strategic Affairs* 22 (1): 23–60.

Ghazali, Ezlika, and Md. Nor Othman. 2001. "Demographic and Psychographic Profile of Active and Passive Investors in Urban Malaysia." In *The Fourth Asian Academy of Management (AAM) Conference 2001 Proceedings*, Vol. 1, pp. 515–26. Universiti Sains Malaysia.

Ghosh, B. N. 1998. *Malaysia: The Transformation Within.* Selangor, Malaysia: Addision Wesley Longman Malaysia Sdn. Bhd.

Handbook of the Nations, 6th ed. 1986. Detroit, MI: Gale Research Co.

Harris, P. R., and R. T. Moran. 1987. *Managing Cultural Differences.* Houston: Gulf Publishing.

Hew, Lee Fing, Heida. 2000. "Segmentation, Targeting and Positioning Strategy for CELCOM Based on Psychographic Profile and Lifestyle." MBA Unpublished Master's Project, Universiti Kebangsaan Malaysia, Faculty of Business Management, Bangi.

Hew, Lee Fing, Heida, and Aliah Hanim M. Salleh. 2001. "Lifestyle Clustering for Targeted Segmentation —The Case of Malaysia's Mobile Telephone Users." Paper presented at *The National Seminar on Consumer and Consumerism: Issues and Challenges*, School of Management, Universiti Utara Malaysia, Sintok, Kedah, October 24.

The Hong Kong and Shanghai Banking Corporation. 1991. *Business Profile Series: Malaysia*, 6th ed. Hong Kong.

Hult, G. Tomas, Bruce D. Keillor, and Roscoe Hightower. 2000. "Valued Product Attributes in an Emerging Market: A Comparison between French and Malaysian Consumers." *Journal of World Business* 35: 206–222.

Information Malaysia 2000 Yearbook. 2000. Kuala Lumpur: Berita Publishing Sdn Bhd.

Jaffar, Johan. 2002. "The Drift Must Be Arrested." *New Straits Times*, June 17: 10.

Jayasakaran, S. 2000. "Merger Muddle." *Far Eastern Economic Review*, August 10: 51.

Jeannet, J. P., and H. Hennessey. 1988. *International Marketing Management.* New York: Houghton Mifflin.

Kaur, Indar d/o Dan Singh and Md. Nor Othman. 1995. "Psychographic and Demographic Profiles of Credit Card and Non-Credit Cardholders in Urban Malaysia." *Juranal Pengurusan* 14: 59–80.

Keat, Guah Poh, and Gan Boon Phin. 1998. "Malaysia's Multimedia Super Corridor." *The International Tax Journal* (Winter): 89–95.

Kiu, Victor. 1991. "The Use of Psychographic Research for Advertising." In *Advertising Worldwide: Concepts, Theories, and Practice of International, Multinternational, and Global Advertising*, ed. Marieke K. de Mooij and Warren Keegan. Singapore: Prentice Hall.

Kreutzer, Ralf T. 1988. "Key Factors for the Development of Marketing Strategies for West Asia." *Singapore Marketing Review* 3: 61–70.

Lee, Kiyau Loo, and Donald W. Hendon. 1999. "Decision Making on Consumer Purchases for Malaysian Married Couples and Others." In *Tun Abdul Razak International Conference—Part 2 Proceedings*, pp. 249–359. Penang: Universiti Sains Malaysia and Ohio University.

Malar, Deva, and M. I. Ahmad. 1997. "The Perception of Viewers on Female Role Portrayals in Malaysian Television Advertisements." In *Proceedings of the Eighth Biennial World Marketing Congress*, vol. VIII, pp. 347–49. Academy of Marketing Science USA, held at Kuala Lumpur.

The Malay Mail. 2001a. "Oracle Promotes IT Learning in Asia Pacific," March 28: 24.

———. 2001b. "Winning the Name Game on the Web," March 28: 25.

"Malaysia in 2000." 2002. *Asian Survey* 14 (1; January/February): 189–201.

The Malaysian Economy in Figures 2000. 2000. Kuala Lumpur: Percetakan Nasional Malaysia Berhad.

Mid-Term Review of the Sixth Malaysia Plan, 1991–1995. 1993. Kuala Lumpur: Percetakan Nasional Berhad.

Mohamad, Mahathir. 1999. *Jalan Ke Puncak.* Selangor, Malaysia: Pelanduk Publication (M) Sdn Bhd.

Mohamad, Osman, Zafar U. Ahmed, Earl D. Honeycutt, Jr., and Tyebkhan, Taizoon Hyder. 2000. "Does 'Made in . . .' Matter to Consumers? A Malaysian Study of Country of Origin Effect." *Multinational Business Review* 8 (2; Fall): 69–73.

Moore, Spencer. 1994. "Malaysia: Economy." In *The Far East and Australasia*, 25th ed., ed. L. Daniel, pp. 526–32. London: Europa Publications Ltd.

Munan, H., and F. Yuk Yee. 1990. *Cultures of the World Malaysia* (Times Editions). Singapore: Marshall Cavendish.

Navaratnam, Ramon V. 1997. *Managing the Malaysian Economy: Challenges and Prospects.* Selangor, Malaysia: Pelanduk Publications (M) Sdn. Bhd.

———. 2001. *Malaysian Economic Recovery: Policy Reforms for Economic Sustainability.* Selangor, Malaysia: Pelanduk Publications (M) Sdn. Bhd.

New Straits Times. 1995a. "Comprehensive Study to Chart Industrialisation," February 22: 14, 18–19.

———. 1995b. "Of Success, Glory and Prosperity," February 18: 10.

———. 1995c. "One-Stop Centre for Interest-Free Banking," February 22: 14.

———. 1995d. "Malaysia Gets Excellent Rating," April 13.

———. 1995e. "Higher Growth Forecast," March 30 (front page).

———. 2001a. "Eighth Malaysia Plan: 2001–2005," April 24: 1–10.

———. 2001b. "Perodua's New Gameplan," April 23: 1.

———. 2001c. "Malaysia Proves Critics Wrong," March 11: 10.

———. 2001d. "Telekom Should Get Its Priorities Right in Serving Customer," April 18: 13.

———. 2002a. "Fight Price Hike with Parallel Imports," March 13: 12.

———. 2002b. "Letting Go, Moving On [Editorial]," June 26: 10.

New Straits Times—Management. 2000. "Survey Reveals Malaysians Are Still Cautious Purchasers," September 25.

New Straits Times—Management Times. 2001. "Incentives to Attract More Tech Investment," July 16.

New Sunday Times. 2002a. "Advertisers Beginning to Eye Malay Market," January 13: F2.

———. 2002b. "English Media Still Has the Edge," January 13: F1.

Noor, Noraini M. 1999. "Roles and Women's Well-Being: Some Preliminary Findings from Malaysia." *Sex Roles: A Journal of Research* 41 (3–4; August): 123–45.

———. 2002a. "Thoughts of Dr. M in a Zanzibar Café," *New Straits Times* June 25:10.

———. 2002b. "Comment." *New Straits Times,* June 26:10.

Okposin, S. B., and Cheng Ming Yu. 2000. *Economic Crisis in Malaysia: Causes, Implications & Policy Prescriptions.* Selangor, Malaysia: Pelanduk Publications (M) Sdn. Bhd.

Osman, M. Z. 1994. "The Influence of Lifestyles on Loyalty Patronage Behaviour." In *Pascasidang Seminar Antarabangsa Prospek dan Cabaran Ekonomi dan Pengurusan dalam Pembangunan Abad ke-21*, ed. Nik Hashim Mustapha, Jaafar Muhamad, Aliah Hanim Mohd. Salleh and Zaini Mahbar. Universiti Kebangsaan Malaysia and Universitas Syiah Kuala, Indonesia.

Osman, M. Z., and Aliah Hanim M. Salleh. 1986. "Husband–Wife Influence in Purchasing Decisions: A Research Using the Delphi Technique." In *Emerging International Strategic Frontiers—Proceedings of the American Marketing Association International Marketing Conference in Singapore*, ed. Chin Tiong Tan et al., pp. 331–36. American Marketing Association.

Othman, Md. Nor, and Aik Shian Heng. 1997. "Brand Selection Decisions for the Purchase of Electrical Appliances: A Cross-Cultural Study of Urban Malaysian Consumers." In *Proceedings of the Eighth Biennial World Marketing Congress*, vol. VIII, pp. 291–96. Academy of Marketing Science, held in Kuala Lumpur.

Pengurusan Danaharta Nasional Berhad. 2001. "Operations Report for Six Months Ended 30 June 2001." www.danaharta.com.my.

"The Political Scene." 2001. *Malaysia Country Report* (10; October): 14–19.

Rafferty, Kevin. 1990. "Malaysia: Country Profile." In *The Asia and Pacific Review*, 11th ed. Edison, NJ: Hunter.

Rahman, Sofiah Abd. 2001. "Profiling Malaysian Shoppers Through Retail Brand Lifestyle Orientation—What Went Wrong." In *The Fourth Asian Academy of Management (AAM) Conference 2001 Proceeding*, vol. 1, pp. 376–82.

Ramayah, T., Nasser Noor, Aizzat Mohd. Nasurdin, and Lee Hee Choo. 2002. "Cardholders' Attitude and Bank Credit Card Usage in Malaysia: An Exploratory Study." *Asian Academy of Management Journal* 1 (7; January): 75–102.

Rejab, Ismail, and Nik Rahimah Nik Yacob. 1986. "An Application of AIO Inventory in Delineating Patterns of Women's Lifestyles in a Non-Western Culture." In *Emerging International Strategic Frontiers— Proceedings of the American Marketing Association International Marketing Conference in Singapore*, ed. Chin Tiong Tan et al. American Marketing Association.

Rowell, Jonathan. 1996. *Malaysia: A Study of an Economically Developing Country.* East Sussex, UK: Wayland.

Salleh, Aliah Hanim M., and Sook Woon Chow. 2001. "Marketing Hospitality Services Through the Internet— Which Malaysian Segments to Target?" In *Proceedings of the Asia Pacific Management Conference 2001:* 505–20. Kuala Lumpur.

Salleh, Aliah Hanim M., and Heida Hew Lee Fing. 2001. "From Lifestyle Clustering to Marketing Strategy (Celcom Malaysia's Market Selection Process)." Unpublished paper.

Salleh, Aliah Hanim M., and Siew Choo Teh. 2000. "In Search of Key Success Factors in E-Learning: An Exploratory Industry Study on Malaysian Universities." In *Proceedings of the International Conference On Electronic Commerce—Emerging Trends in E-Commerce*, pp. 1–5. Multimedia University and Telekom Malaysia Berhad, November 21–23, Kuala Lumpur.

Salleh, Aliah Hanim Mohd., Bianca Teo, and Anthony Pecotich. 1998. "Malaysia: Consumer Behavior and the Future." In *Marketing and Consumer Behaviour in East and South-East Asia*, ed. A. Pecotich and C. Shultz, pp. 451–92. Sydney: McGraw-Hill.

Selvarajah, C. T. 1993. "The Opening of Strategic Windows for Australia and New Zealand in the Asia-Pacific: Focus on Malaysia: The Tiger with a Vision." In *Proceedings of the International Symposium on Gaining Competitive Advantage Through Marketing—Current Issues and Future Challenges for Small and Medium-Scale Enterprises*, ed. Nik Yacob et al., pp. 29–42. Kuala Lumpur.

———. 1999. "Guest Commentary: Globalisation and Emerging Nations—Conceptualization of the Asian Crisis." *Jurnal Pengurusan* (Universiti Kebangsaan Malaysia) 18 (July): 3–23.

Seventh Malaysia Plan 1996–2000. Kuala Lumpur: Percetakan Nasional Malaysia Berhad.

Sidin, Samsinar Md., and Mary Anjang. 1996. "Wives' Involvement and the Effects of Sex Role Orientation in Family Decision Making." *Proceedings of Multicultural Marketing*, Virginia, USA.

Singh, Hari. 1998. "Tradition, UMNO and Political Succession in Malaysia." *Third World Quarterly* 19 (2; June): 241–55.

Singh, Indar Kaur d/o Dan, and Md. Nor Othman. 1995. "Psychographic and Demographic Profiles of Credit Card and Non-Credit Cardholders in Urban Malaysia." *Jurnal Pengurusan* 14: 59–79.

The Star. 1995. "Little Big Spenders," March 27: 2–4.

———. 2001a. "Eighth Malaysia Plan 2001–2005," April 24: 1–16.

———. 2001b. "Layman's Guide to Our Economy," April 10: 4.

———. 2002a. "Building an East Asian Community," March 11: 31.

———. 2002b. "Developing Islamic Securities Instruments Essential, Say BIMB," March 28: 8.

———. 2002c. "Dollah: We're not Filling Up Gender Quota," March 9: 21.

———. 2002d. "Government subsidises 80% of Real Cost of Exam Fees," March 27.

———. 2002e. "Higher Economic Growth Expected," March 28.

———. 2002f. "Islamic Banking can Hit 20%: Azman," March 28.

———. 2002g. "Islamic Banking Industry Sustains Its Expansion Despite Slower Economic Growth," March 23.

———. 2002h. "Malaysia Needs to Further Develop Islamic Market," March 27: 9.

———. 2002i. "More Females in Varsities, say Shafie," March 22.

———. 2002j. "Pragmatism in Islamic Finance," March 27.

———. 2002k. "Promoting the Islamic Capital Market," March 26: 7.

———. 2002l. "Some of UKM's Courses to be in English," March 28: 3.

———. 2002m. "The Pain of Being Different," March 27: 20.

———. 2002n. "Zeti: Economy in Early Recovery," March 27.

The Star—Business. 2002a. "Investors Interest in Malaysian Dollar Bonds Likely to Strengthen. March 18: 3.

The Star—Business. 2002b. "Proton Expects Boost from New Engine," March 27: 5.

Subramanian, Surain. 2001. "The Dual Narrative of 'Good Governance': Lessons for Understanding Political and Cultural Changes in Malaysia and Singapore." *Contemporary Southeast Asia: A Journal of International & Strategic Affairs* 23 (1): 65–81.

Sunday Star. 2002. Education supplement, June 16: 3.

Survey Research Malaysia. 1990. "The Malaysian Lifestyle Study." Kuala Lumpur: Survey Research Malaysia.

Tan, Cheng Leong, and Terence T. S. Lim. 1992. *Malaysia: Business and Investment Opportunities.* Singapore: Cassia Communications.

Teh, Siew Choo. 2000. "Towards Developing E-Learning Strategies for Malaysian Universities to Leapfrog Competition in the Information Age." Unpublished MBA Master's Project, Universiti Kebangsaan Malaysia, Faculty of Business Management, Bangi.

Tih, Sio Hong. 1998. "Tinjauan Terhadap Pengunaan Internet di Malaysia" (Exploring Internet Usage in Malaysia). *Jurnal Pengurusan* (Universiti Kebangsaan Malaysia) 17 (July): 93–106.

Utusan Malaysia. 2002. "PM: Rakyat harus teruskan budaya berkongsi kekayaan," March 11.

Utusan Malaysia Online. 2002. "Malaysia Berupaya Hadapi Tekanan Ekonomi Dunia," January 23. Available at www.utusan.com.my.

Utusan Malaysia Online—Parlimen. 2002. "Malaysia catat lebihan dagangan RM53.7b tahun lalu," March 28. Available at www.utusan.com.my.

Utusan Malaysia Online—Rencana. 2002. "Malaysia Berupaya Hadapi Tekanan Ekonomi Dunia," January 23. Available at www.utusan.com.my.

Utusan Malaysia Online—Rencana, January 23, 2002, and *Bank Negara Malaysia*, 2002. Available at www.bnm.gov.my.

Vatikiotis, Michael. 1990a. "A Mirage Market." *Far Eastern Economic Review* 148, May 17: 48.

———. 1990b. "The Late Starter." *Far Eastern Economic Review* 148, May 17: 46–48.

———. 1994a. "A Matter of Identity." *Far Eastern Economic Review* 157, March 17: 18.

———. 1994b. "Morality Plays." *Far Eastern Economic Review* 157(March 10): 40–41.

Vittachi, Nury. 2000a. "Asian Lifestyles." *Far Eastern Economic Review*, September 7: 73–78.

———. 2000b. "Ready to Shop; Asian Lifestyles." *Far Eastern Economic Review*, July 27: 60–63.

———. 2000c. "Rewarding Lifestyles; Asian Lifestyles." *Far Eastern Economic Review*, August 17: 53–58.

Wall Street:Finance. 2002. "Malaysia Meets Foreign Investment Target." *World Bank Magazine,* March 29.

The World Bank Annual Report. 1993. Washington, DC: The World Bank.

Xinhua News Agency. 2001a. "Foreign Investors Have Confidence in Malaysia: Badawi," July 2.

———. 2001b. "Malaysia Continues to Attract Foreign Investors," July 12.

———. 2001c. "Malaysia Targeting Knowledge-Based Foreign Direct Investment," March 28.

Yacob, Nik Rahimah Nik. 1991. "Gender and Ethnic-Subcultural Influences on Product Symbolism." *Jurnal Pengurusan* (Universiti Kebangsaan Malaysia) 10(July): 13–26.

Yacob, Nik Rahimah Nik, and Ismail Rejab. 1984. "Pemilihan responden bagi mengukur struktur peranan keluarga dalam keputusan membeli." *Jurnal Pengurusan* 3 (July): 77–84.

Yacob, Nik Rahimah Nik, and Sallehuddin M. Noor. 1993. "Influences of Women's Lifestyle Patterns on Family Role Structure." *Malaysian Management Review* 28(December, 2): 8–15.

Zabid Md., Abdul Rashid, and Jainthy Nallamuthu. 2001. "Consumers' Perceptions of Advertising Branded Products by Celebrities: A Cross-Cultural Comparison," In *Proceedings of the Seventh Asia Pacific Management Conference*, vol. II, pp. 445–58. Kuala Lumpur.

Zabid Md., Abdul Rashid, Sidin Samsinar, and Daud Siti Hawa. 1996. "Malaysian Consumer Attitudes and Purchases Toward Local versus Foreign Made Products." *Proceedings of the Academy of Marketing Science Annual International Conference on Cross-Cultural Marketing*, pp. 95–101. Norfolk, VA: Old Dominion University.

Zain, Osman, Zahir A. Quraeshi, and Mohd Ashaari Idris. 2000. "Direct Selling in Malaysia." *Journal of Asia-Pacific Business* 2 (4): 83–101.

CHAPTER 11

MYANMAR

Foreign Brands Trickling Through

MAY LWIN, ANTHONY PECOTICH, AND VICKI THEIN

OVERVIEW

Myanmar's emergence from a period of inward-looking economic policies has been met with mixed international response. The nation is, nonetheless, proceeding with reforms directed toward the opening of its economy so as to improve the economic and social conditions of the people. This chapter provides an overview of the historical nature of these developments as well as evaluates some of the present conditions, which may be responsible for shaping the future.

INTRODUCTION

The Union of Myanmar (known until 1989 as Burma or the Socialist Republic of Burma—we will use the names Myanmar and Burma interchangeably) is a Southeast Asian (SEA) nation that, after a postcolonial period of devastation and poverty, is moving forward with the hope of taking its place as one of the strong, progressive nations of the region. It was admitted as a full-fledged member into the Association of Southeast Asian Nations (ASEAN) in July 1997. This was partly a result of the ASEAN belief in "constructive engagement" toward their neighbor, in view of objections by the Western nations, namely, the United States and some European countries. These governments had sought to delay Myanmar being admitted into ASEAN based on political uncertainties that were expected to influence ASEAN's dialogues with Western partners. These political reservations are best illustrated by a statement in *The Economist*:

> There is no international consensus about how best to influence the regime. America, which at present imposes mild sanctions on trade and investment in Myanmar, recently threatened to strengthen them unless the government took more vigorous steps to restore democracy. But Sergio Pinheiro, who monitors the human-rights situation in Myanmar for the UN, says that the generals respond better to engagement than to ostracism. There is, of course, a third possibility: that the behavior of outsiders, friendly or hostile, has no effect on the regime at all. (*The Economist* 2003)

447

Myanmar is located between China and India, and also shares borders with Bangladesh, Thailand, and Laos. Within Asia, Myanmar is seen as one of the most promising markets. In terms of mineral and agricultural resources, Myanmar is one of the region's richest and least exploited countries. In the 1950s, it was among the most economically promising Southeast Asian nations and the largest exporter of rice in the world. These strengths are accentuated by the strong emphasis on market reform as the country moves its economy into a transitional phase. In the past six years, Myanmar has undergone radical changes that have transformed the once sleepy underdeveloped backwater to a budding economy capable of giving tough competition to neighboring markets such as those of Vietnam and Cambodia.

Our purpose in this chapter is to evaluate how such disparate responses have influenced the Myanmar consumer market. As an introduction, the nation's background, economic circumstances, and, in particular, the consumer habits and the marketing conditions will be discussed, followed by an evaluation of the potential for future development and challenges facing marketing managers during this confusing period within the nation.

HISTORICAL BACKGROUND

Prior to World War II and subsequent independence in 1948, Myanmar was under the influence of Britain, its colonial ruler since 1885. In 1962, political turmoil led the military to seize power and introduce "the Burmese Way to Socialism," a unique blend of self-reliance, socialism, and national ethos. Hence, for the past three decades, Myanmar has been in a state of self-imposed isolation described as a period of hibernation by many outsiders. It has been described as a place "where people haven't heard of Pepsi-Cola" and "East Asia's last frontier after Vietnam" (Moreau 1995). During this period, the country faced decreasing levels of economic output coupled with falling imports and exports. Across towns and villages, consumers coped with product shortages by turning to the emerging black market. Although the once-thriving economy has been reduced to one of the most backward in the world, change is under way since the State Law and Order Restoration Council (SLORC) took over the government in 1988. While the country continues to face internal political problems and external pressure, the SLORC has attempted to move the economy from one based on a socialist command philosophy to one driven more by market forces, so hoping to create in Myanmar a land of opportunity. This "open-market" policy attracted foreign investment that is inevitably changing the nature of Myanmar society (Lwin and Lan 2000). On November 15, 1997, the SLORC was replaced by a State Peace and Development Council (SPDC) with nineteen members who were almost exclusively military personnel. Since then, attempts at a political rapprochement have been made both internally and externally, culminating with admission to the ASEAN grouping. Despite the continuation of political problems (most clearly manifested by the changing status of Aung San Suu Kyi), for tourists, Myanmar retains the fascination of a backward step in time not only into a world of another generation, but also into one of unique cultural and environmental beauty.

ENVIRONMENT

To fully comprehend the consumers of Myanmar requires an open mind and empathy for a people who, although relatively advanced in the 1950s, were then isolated from the rest of the world. Unlike other parts of Southeast Asia, which are still recovering from the ravages of recent wars, Myanmar went through a unique period of self-imposed isolation. Today, this is reflected in the aged look of the intact cities and the timeless character of the environment, which have contributed to Myanmar people's particular pattern of consumer behavior. In the following, we describe the recent natural, economic, demographic, and cultural factors that are critical in understanding the nature of the Myanmar market.

Natural Environment

Myanmar is strategically located overlooking the Bay of Bengal and the Andaman Sea, and also bordering Bangladesh, China, India, Laos, and Thailand. Surrounded by mountains, it is also blessed with great alluvial lowlands through which the river Ayeyarwady (previously Irrawaddy) with its two tributaries (Chindwinn and Sittoung) flows, so forming the cultural and economic center of the nation (Demaine 1994, 611). Although its climate may be classified as "tropical monsoonal," it has important climatic variations, including a dry zone caused by a rain shadow area from the southwestern monsoons.

Traditionally, Myanmar has been most dependent on its agricultural resources. Although rice exports have diminished, Myanmar was once the world's greatest rice exporter. About 33 percent of the population is still employed in agriculture, which includes the production of oil-seed and cotton as well as rice. On the mountainsides, the greatest treasures are timber and the variety of metallic minerals, such as silver and zinc. Similar to the rest of Asia, the timber holdings are under pressure, and although almost half of Myanmar is forested, if present rates of depletion (legal and illegal) continue, an environmental disaster could result. Due to the nation's long period of isolation, the mineral resources have not been fully exploited, and prospects for the petroleum and related industries are bright.

Economic Environment

During the 1970s and the 1980s, Myanmar was economically poor and considered among the least developed nations of the world. As recently as the mid-1990s, based on the traditional measure of development, Myanmar, with a per capita income of about US$200, was still considered among the forty-six lowest-income countries with per capita income below US$500 (Kyaw 1995). While its Southeast Asian neighbors Singapore and Brunei lead the gross domestic product (GDP) Purchasing Power Parity Dollars (PPP$) index, followed by Malaysia, Thailand, the Philippines, and Indonesia, Myanmar lags behind with a PPP$ figure of 659. Generally, though, accurate figures are hard to obtain. *The Economist*, for example, describes the situation as follows:

> One Yangon-based ambassador calls Myanmar an information black hole, where the Internet is seen as a tool of subversion which ordinary people—including most doctors, journalists and students—are not permitted to use. Very few statistics on health, education or much else have been published since 1997. (2002, 28)

Therefore, although the official figures for, say, unemployment may be as low as 4.1 percent (Asian Development Bank 2003), there is evidence to suggest that unemployment and underemployment may be quite high in both urban and rural areas, and depending on the season. Further, estimates based on population projections suggest that as much as one-third of the labor pool may be unemployed.

In an attempt to remedy this situation, the SLORC initiated, in October 1988, economic reforms with the aim of decontrolling and deregulating a wide spectrum of economic activities. The SLORC enacted new liberalizing laws and regulations designed to encourage economic activity by enabling extensive private-sector participation (Kyaw 1995). The main components of this policy were (1) adoption of a market economy, (2) encouragement of private investment and entrepreneurial activity, and (3) allowance of foreign trade and investment. This resulted in a turnaround of the Myanmar economy, as the country entered into an era of a "Market Economy System." After two years of negative growth, a recovery followed in 1989–90. Growth of Myanmar's GDP initially declined to 2.7 percent in 1990–91 and to 1.3 percent in 1991–92, before rising to 10.9 percent in 1992–93 (Vokes 1997), and in 1993–94 this figure was a respectable 6 percent. Myanmar's GDP peaked in the following year at 7.5 percent but faced a steady decline from 1994–95 to 1997–98, when it dropped to about 5.7 percent. Since then, it has been reported to be over 11 percent, reaching 11.1 percent in 2001 (Asian Development Bank 2003). The government's target for the fiscal year from April 2003 to March 2004 of about 10 percent was not likely to be met because of the impact of sanctions, slower growth in natural gas production, and manufacturing output. Progress is made difficult by shortages of power and critical imported inputs (Asian Development Bank 2003, 71). Social conditions also improved as measured by various indicators, such as the crude death rate that fell from 15 in 1970 to 11.8 in 2000, the life expectancy that increased from 44 in 1960 to 57.2 in 2001, and the infant mortality rate that fell from 121 per thousand live births in 1970 to 77 in 2001 (Asian Development Bank 2003; The Economist Intelligence Unit Quarter 1 1998; United Nations 2000; World Bank 2003).

The greatest economic impact on Myanmar has emanated from foreign trade and investment. Despite sanctions and political problems, the entry of potential foreign investors exploring possibilities has increased from 1990 to 2003, and deals have been struck on hotel, gas, and oil projects. Conventional trade (export and import) has also been promoted to a great extent. From 1989, exports have steadily grown in almost all sectors (Table 11.1); however, in 1995 exports fell 7.4 percent. This could be due to the oil embargo imposed by the United States in 1994. The export growth has continued but slowed from 45 percent in 2001 to 28 percent in 2003, and a further decline is expected. However, imports have not been strong also due to restrictions, foreign exchange shortages, and weak domestic demand, so that the trade account is expected to be in surplus (Asian Development Bank 2003).

Foreign direct investment has grown more than ten times since 1992, when economic reforms began in earnest, to US$2.6 billion in 1994 and to US$3 billion as of August 1995 (Kyaw 1995). The oil and gas sectors have attracted the most foreign investment. Six multinational oil and gas companies are involved in production sharing projects in seven offshore and five onshore areas (see Table 11.2). One of the most visible investments is a US$1 billion natural-gas pipeline being built by France's Total with an American partner, Unocal. It is expected to bring in annual revenues of US$400 million—enough to balance the country's current account deficit (Hirsh and Moreau 1995). Following the energy sector is the hotels and tourism sector, which alone has the most ongoing projects (thirty-one) with a forecasted addition of over 5,000 rooms when all projects are completed. However, the agriculture sector, the mainstay of Myanmar's economy in the past, has attracted only one major investment so far.

Investment in Myanmar is headed by Singapore with US$1.35 billion (Table 11.3), which actually leads in terms of the total number of sixty-seven investments, followed closely by the United Kingdom with US$1.34 billion. In fact, regional neighbors such as Singapore, Thailand, Malaysia, and Hong Kong make up the bulk of investors in Myanmar in terms of the number of investments. Given the colonial history, investment from the United Kingdom may have been expected, but the high proportion emanating from the SEA region not only provides a new economic facade for Myanmar (a more Asian character as opposed to a Western profile), but also

Table 11.1

Value of Foreign Trade (kyat millions)

Year	Export	Import	Balance of trade
1983–84	3,386.4	5,197.3	−1,810.9
1984–85	3,134.3	5,041.2	−1,906.9
1985–86	2,566.1	4,802.0	−2,235.9
1986–87	2,418.5	3,936.1	−1,517.6
1987–88	1,655.2	4,065.7	−2,410.5
1988–89	2,168.9	3,443.0	−1,274.1
1989–90	2,834.1	3,395.0	−560.9
1990–91	2,952.6	5,522.8	−2,570.2
1991–92	2,925.9	5,336.7	−2,410.8
1992–93	3,590.0	5,365.3	−1,775.3
1993–94	4,227.8	7,923.3	−3,695.5
1994–95	5,405.2	8,332.3	−2,927.1
1995–96	5,032.7	10,301.6	−5,268.9
1996–97	5,487.7	11,778.8	−6,291.1
1997–98	6,446.8	14,366.1	−7,919.3
1998–99	6,755.8	16,871.7	−10,115.9
1999–2000	7,103.3	16,264.8	−9,161.5
2000–2001	12,262.0	14,900.0	−1,638.0

Source: Statistical Yearbook 2000 (Yangon: The Government of the Union of Myanmar, Ministry of National Planning and Economic Development, Central Statistical Organization, 2000); Asian Development Bank, *Asian Development Outlook 2003* (Hong Kong: Oxford University Press [China], 2003).

Table 11.2

Foreign Investment in Myanmar by Sector (as of August 31, 1995)

Sector	Numbers	Foreign capital (US$ million)
Oil and gas	24	1,435.42
Hotels and tourism	31	603.88
Fisheries	15	252.04
Real estate	5	224.45
Mining	25	192.51
Manufacturing	51	178.30
Transport	5	113.21
Agriculture	1	2.69
Total	157	3,002.50

Source: Thane Kyaw, eds., "Golden Opportunities for Investment in Myanmar," *Golden Myanmar* 2, no. 4 (1995).

underlines a newfound regional confidence. The increase in foreign-related businesses is also more clearly visible from six-year data showing the number of registered companies (Table 11.4).

However, it is not just foreign-related companies that have developed. Business enterprises appear to have mushroomed in all sectors too. For example, domestic Myanmar Limited companies increased by over 30 percent in 1994 alone, while tour guide businesses more than doubled. This resulted because the government has encouraged the private sector and foreign investment in an unprecedented manner. As a result, many private companies, enterprises, and agencies have

Table 11.3

Foreign Investment in Myanmar by Country of Origin (as of March 31, 2000)

Sector	Numbers	Foreign capital (US$ million)
United Kingdom	33	1,343.8
Singapore	67	1,352.3
France	3	470.4
Thailand	48	1,188.8
United States	16	582.1
Malaysia	25	587.2
Japan	23	229.3
The Netherlands	5	237.8
Australia	14	82.1
Hong Kong	24	133.0
Others	69	707.3
Total	327	6,914.1

Source: Statistical Yearbook 2000 (Yangon: The Government of the Union of Myanmar, Ministry of National Planning and Economic Development, Central Statistical Organization, 2000), p. 251.

Table 11.4

Number of Registered Exporters, Importers, Limited Companies, Partnerships, and Joint-Venture Companies Limited

Enterprises	1989–90	1994–95	1999–2000
Exporters/importers	986	4,277	13,780
Business representatives	183	1,509	2,170
Myanmar companies ltd.	174	4,786	14,146
Partnerships	376	1,055	1,247
Foreign companies and branches	39	442	1,340
Joint-venture companies ltd. (not under foreign investment law)	15	31	59
State-owned economic enterprises and private entrepreneurs	7	18	44
State-owned economic enterprises and foreign companies	8	13	15
Joint-venture companies ltd. (under foreign investment law)	0	54	114
Other organizations	3	31	39
Tourist enterprises	0	288	567
Tourist transport business	0	825	404
Hotel business	0	112	334
Lodging house business	0	102	181
Tour guide business	0	600	4,402
Total	1,776	14,112	38,783

Source: Statistical Yearbook 2000 (Yangon: The Government of the Union of Myanmar, Ministry of National Planning and Economic Development, Central Statistical Organization, 2000).

emerged, and 38,783 of them were registered by December 31, 2000, at the Ministries of Trade, and National Planning and Development. More specifically, there are 13,780 exporters/importers; 2,170 business representatives; 1,247 partnerships; 14,146 Myanmar Companies Limited; 1,340 foreign companies and branches; 242 joint ventures (Myanmar and foreign organizations), and 39 other organizations.

Table 11.5

Number of Tourist Arrivals at Yangon

Nationality	1981	1986	1991	1994	2000
North America					
American	2,730	5,875	677	3,052	5,746
Canadian	673	1,400	132	536	993
Europe					
British	1,934	3,694	491	2,240	4,255
French	4,960	4,726	870	2,254	1,116
German	4,258	5,943	1,606	2,355	11,651
Italian	—	2,680	1,213	1,930	6,192
Russian	—	25	1	16	65
Swiss	1,385	2,524	453	820	2,192
Asia					
Chinese	—	93	6	322	2,737
Indian	352	389	4	271	981
Korean	—	104	51	1,633	2,196
Japanese	3,164	2,999	1,051	4,557	16,096
Singapore	—	—	56	567	5,427
Thai	—	913	172	4,684	7,159
Australian	1,846	2,043	174	745	1,128
Others	6,546	6,931	1,145	13,548	46,006
Total	28,079	40,605	8,061	39,403	113,940

Source: Statistical Yearbook 2000 (Yangon: The Government of the Union of Myanmar, Ministry of National Planning and Economic Development, Central Statistical Organization, 2000).

Heeding advice from the World Bank and International Monetary Fund, the government has installed foreign investment laws that make it attractive for foreign businesses to venture into Myanmar. For example, foreign firms are eligible for a three-year tax holiday. Although inflation remains high (35 percent) and the local currency, kyat, is pegged to artificial levels, the government has instituted foreign-exchange certificates similar to those once used by China to facilitate capital flows. Border trade was also legalized in connection with Thailand, China, India, and Bangladesh. This has resulted in a wide range of commodities (except some that are prohibited) being traded across these borders.

Another noteworthy fact is that foreigners of all nationalities are now commonly seen in both Yangon and smaller cities. This increase in foreign visitors (Table 11.5) has given further momentum to the hotel and tourism business, which was boosted further when the Ministry of Hotels and Tourism was instituted in September 1992. Prior to this, there were four foreign companies that had signed contracts to build and operate hotels in Myanmar. Since September 18, 1995, the "total number of licenses issued to local entrepreneurs to operate motels and inns" totaled 248, while at the same time, thirty-two "foreign invested hotel projects worth over US$1 billion and providing over 8,000 rooms" have also been approved (*Business Indochina* 1996, 13). Such well-known giants as the Shangri-la and Idris Hydraulic are involved in large projects worth well over US$200 million (Naw 1994). The government has sought to increase tourism by facilitating various activities, such as opening border areas with China and Thailand, extending a tourist visa from fourteen to twenty-eight days, and simplifying entry formalities. This has resulted in an increase in the arrivals of tourists and business travelers that is sure to place great pressure on the hotel and tourism industry. Between 1989 and 1996, the number of hotels and motels rose from 22 to 402, while the number of hotel rooms increased from 978 to an estimated 20,000.

Despite the Visit Myanmar Year (VMY) promotional campaign from November 1996 to August 1997, tourist arrivals for those years were disappointing, at only half of the expected figure of 500,000. Although tourist arrivals have continued to grow, the growth rate has slowed dramatically. Even with the fall of the kyat, visitors have been deterred by international boycotts and the regional currency crisis.

Table 11.5 shows that much of the visitor growth stems from Asian countries, such as Thailand and Korea. While separate figures are not available for Singapore and other ASEAN countries, it is anticipated that a great deal of the growth in the "others" group is from these sources. Figures also show that in 1995, 81,428 foreigners entered Myanmar through the Yangon airport alone. International promotions such as the VMY 1996 attracted attention, and the number of visitors is expected to continue to rise in the future. Over one-third of the visitors are businesspeople intent on exploring business opportunities.

These activities have resulted in a transforming economic and demographic environment, the signs of which can most clearly be seen in large cities like Yangon. Cities that over the last few decades appeared as sleepy unchanging hollows are now bustling with activity, as the construction of hotels, new buildings, and roads accelerates. Observers have noted some signs of increasing affluence (Thein and Than 1995), such as the following:

1. An increasing number of motor cars in Yangon, Mandalay, and other big towns
2. Widened roads and highways with advertising billboards lining them at intervals
3. New buildings and private houses in urban centers and new satellite towns
4. New stores stacked with imported goods
5. New and more sophisticated advertisements on television and in the press
6. The appearance of numerous satellite dishes in many cities

New shops stocked with Western products now line city streets; and many people have found employment with foreign businesses. These economic changes are, however, not as obvious in the rural areas, except in towns on the border trade route that show signs of newfound prosperity. Examples are cities such as Mandalay, which provides the perfect transshipment point for Chinese merchandise to Yangon and overseas. While Mandalay's city business center largely features Chinese immigrants, Monywa, linked to the Indian border trade, is thriving in trade with India (Moreau 1995). These activities have resulted in a variety of cheap consumer goods swamping the market.

Political Environment

The United States and many European nations have imposed a policy of partial, or in some instances, complete, political and economic isolation. The most important actor in organizing international political opposition to the ruling military regime and relative economic isolation in terms of trade and investment with Myanmar has been the United States. In response to sustained pressure by various human rights and pro-democracy campaigners, the Clinton Administration imposed sanctions against Myanmar on April 22, 1997 (Finch 1997). In the view of Schermerhorn (1997), former U.S. President Bill Clinton should have banned all American investment in Myanmar, instead of banning only "future" investments by American companies in the country. Some European countries introduced a ban on issue of visas to Myanmar officials (*The Economist* 1997). While the United States and the European Union (EU), to some extent, adopted a policy of "isolationism" in regard to Myanmar, ASEAN governments and business communities have encouraged constructive engagement (*Business Asia* 1996). ASEAN admitted Myanmar as a member in 1997 despite the policy of "isolation" adopted by the United States and EU governments (Masaki 1997). The ASEAN took a different stance from the West, because it considered "the West as posturing over Myanmar, trying to impose its own, inappropriate values on an Asian country" (*The Economist* 1996).

Supporters of isolating Myanmar, including Nobel laureates such as the Dalai Lama and Desmond Tutu, often quoted South Africa as an example whereby economic sanctions brought about significant measures toward democratization (*Global Investor* 1995). Oil and gas companies operating in Myanmar have attracted a great deal of criticism from human rights activists because of claims that their investment in Myanmar has supported the military government in Myanmar and damaged the environment ("Green Light Given for Myanmar's First Offshore Development" 1995).

Concerned investors have increasingly pushed for shareholder resolutions demanding that companies investing in Myanmar "should develop guidelines about their policies there" (Fulman 1997). Social investors have called for global corporations not to do business with governments that do not respect human rights.

It is a highly complex issue to ascertain to what extent the U.S. sanctions on Myanmar are effective. Technically, the effect of the U.S. sanctions in Myanmar was limited, as it only prohibits "new investment" made by U.S. companies in Myanmar, and it only applies to U.S. citizens and companies registered in the United States (Finch 1997). Because U.S. sanctions apply only to companies registered in the United States and to U.S. citizens, this raises the question as to whether or not "a U.S. person could circumvent the sanctions simply by operating in Myanmar through a company registered in a third country." It also does not preclude a U.S. company operating in Myanmar under a different name or through a local business partner (Finch 1997). The effectiveness of economic sanctions was best described as follows: "economic sanctions—porous at best, divisive at worst rarely work. But life can be made harder for the generals [in Myanmar]" (*The Economist* 1996).

Nonetheless, following the imposition of the sanctions, many Western companies, especially those dealing with consumer goods and those that had retail businesses, pulled out of Myanmar. Notably, this withdrawal occurred despite the fact that most of these companies were not technically required to do so by the U.S. trade sanctions. The most publicized case was that of Pepsi's withdrawal from Myanmar. PepsiCo responded to protests made by college students on campuses in the United States by pulling out of Myanmar (*Business Asia* 1997). Other major U.S. retail and consumer goods companies, such as Liz Claiborne, Macy's, Reebok, Eddie Bauer, Levi Strauss, J. Crew, and Apple Computer, soon followed suit by pulling out of Myanmar (*Global Investor* 1995; Schermerhorn 1997). Around the same time, two European beer companies, Carlsberg and Heinekin, also pulled out of Myanmar (Humphreys 1996).

Many of these companies cited apparent political threats and an increasing international demand to isolate Myanmar's military government as reasons for the decision to withdraw (*Global Investor* 1995). In addition to consumer goods companies, oil and gas companies were also pressured to pull out of Myanmar. Some of the manufacturers or brand owners and retailers of consumer goods made a point in stating that their withdrawal was a response to calls from human rights activists. For example, Levi Strauss ended its operations in Myanmar in 1992, because it believed that "it is not possible to do business in Burma without directly supporting the military government and its pervasive violations of human rights" (*Global Investor* 1995).

Table 11.6

Population by Age, Group, and Sex

Age group	1973	1983	1993	1997
0–4	28,083	4,502	5,319	5,786
5–9	3,929	4,388	4,984	4,959
10–14	3,481	4,268	4,698	4,708
15–19	2,931	3,735	4,627	4,593
20–24	2,309	3,286	4,353	4,299
25–29	1,795	2,763	3,832	3,952
30–34	1,664	2,152	3,244	3,555
35–39	1,594	1,667	2,700	3,060
40–44	1,470	1,480	2,147	2,594
45–49	1,159	1,414	1,688	2,131
50–54	1,043	1,299	1,415	1,747
55–59	781	995	1,260	1,466
60–64	662	830	1,066	1,202
65+	1,031	1,340	1,796	2,350
Total	28,083	34,119	43,116	46,402

Source: Statistical Yearbook 2000 (Yangon: The Government of the Union of Myanmar, Ministry of National Planning and Economic Development, Central Statistical Organization, 2000), p. 24.

Demographic Environment

The population of the country was estimated to be 51.14 million at the end of 2001 (Asian Development Bank 2003). With a population growth rate of about 2.01 percent, there appears to be a steady increase in numbers at every lower cohort level (Table 11.6). For example, in 1996, 33 percent of the population was younger than the age of fourteen. This increase in numbers of younger age groups is expected to have significant impact on marketing trends in Myanmar. Unlike other countries in SEA, the rate of urbanization in Myanmar has been slow. Only 28 percent of the population was classified as urban in 2001, compared to 33 percent in 1992 and 23 percent in 1970. Unless Myanmar bucks the trend, this is likely to accelerate as the nation develops.

The numbers enrolled at institutes of higher education (see Table 11.7) have remained relatively constant over the past ten years, especially in the professional institutions. Since April 1997, all universities have been capped; thus, enrollment has remained constant. The total enrollment of 354,511 in 1996–97 is more than the 1985–86 figure of 117,246, indicating that the population has become more literate. Thus, the percentage of graduates for the entire population has actually increased over the last decade. A comparison with the regional countries (Table 11.8) shows that while Myanmar lags behind its neighbors in absolute GDP indicators, the literacy rate of 85 percent in 2001 (an increase from 71 percent in 1970) is high when compared to countries such as India (58 percent) and some of the less-developed SEA countries (Table 11.8). This is a result of a government policy that has sought to eradicate illiteracy by implementing innovative programs such as encouraging students to spend their holidays in rural literacy programs. Despite problems, the tertiary education system appears to be expanding (e.g., in 1993, Yangon's second arts and science university opened), and the public expenditure on the educational sector appears to be increasing.

In Myanmar, about 135 ethnically different groups of nationalities exist. The Bamah, Kachin, Kaya, Kayin, Chin, Mon, Rakhine, and Shan are the predominant groups. Among them, Bamah is

Table 11.7

Enrollment at Institutes of Higher Education

Professional institutes	1983–84	1990–91	1999–2000
Medicine 1	2,303	1,434	2,013
Medicine 2	932	684	1,302
Medicine Mandalay	1,085	736	1,293
Dental medicine	313	291	571
Paramedical school	61	70	475
Institute of Nursing	—	—	497
Institute of Pharmacy	—	—	417
Technology	5,324	—	6,102
Economics	5,447	—	1,120
Education	515	—	1,290
Agriculture	1,574	—	1,139
Forestry	—	—	276
Animal husbandry and veterinary science	873	—	611
Computer science and technology	—	818	—
Subtotal	18,427	4,033	17,106
Others: Arts and science	65,790	—	70,716

Source: Statistical Yearbook 2000 (Yangon: The Government of the Union of Myanmar, Ministry of National Planning and Economic Development, Central Statistical Organization, 2000), p. 350.

the majority (69 percent of the total population), mainly inhabiting the large cities like Yangon and Mandalay. While a great deal of attention is paid to the preservation of the culture of each group, the language of the Bamah is the official language. This is a monosyllabic tonal language that Westerners find difficult to hear correctly (Maung 1991). About 89.4 percent of the population, mainly Bamahs, Shans, Mons, Rakhines, and some Kayins, are Buddhists, while the rest are Christians, Muslims, Hindus, and Animists. The Christian population is composed mainly of Kayins, Kachins, and Chins. People of Indian origin mainly practice Islam and Hinduism.

Cultural Environment

The Myanmar society has developed from about fifteen centuries of a rural, agricultural way of life in which the village, and, within the village, the family was the controlling unit (Khaing 1994). The Myanmar national character is distinct, produced through interaction with the peaceful landscape of green paddy fields, palm groupings, low roofs, high pagodas, and monasteries. Some of the key ingredients of Myanmar's culture include those discussed next.

Dominance/Influence of Religion

Myanmar is one of the few places where pure Buddhism is still practiced. Over 85 percent of the citizens are practicing Therevada Buddhists, and the lives and values of the people are greatly intertwined with the Buddhist religion. Every Myanmar Buddhist tries to live a life based on the Buddhist principles of a simple lifestyle and tries to fulfill the requirements of merit. It is, indeed, a religion that affects both the social and psychological aspects of life in Myanmar. The belief in karma, that of present life being due to deeds in past lives, is also strong. The Myanmar Buddhists hold all persons, places, or things associated with religion in much veneration (Pe 1996). In order

Table 11.8

Comparison of Vital Statistics among Selected Countries for 2001

Country	Population (m)	Population growth (%)	Physician (per 100,000)	Literacy rate (%)	GDP (per cap)	GDP growth (%)	Consumer price index change (%)
Bangladesh	140.9	1.8	20	40.6	1,610	3.1	1.1
Cambodia	13.5	2.2	30	68.7	1,860	2.2	-0.6
India	1,033.4	1.3	48	58.0	2,840	4.0	3.7
Laos	5.4	2.1	61	65.6	1,620	3.9	7.8
Malaysia	23.5	1.6	68	87.9	8,750	3.9	1.4
Myanmar	48.2	1.0	30	85.0	1,027	5.7	21.1
Philippines	77.2	1.6	124	95.1	3,840	1.0	6.1
Singapore	4.1	1.0	135	92.5	22,680	4.4	1.0
Thailand	61.6	0.9	24	95.7	6,400	3.0	1.7
Vietnam	79.2	1.3	52	92.7	2,070	6.0	-0.4

Source: United Nations Human Development Report 2003.

to avoid seeming disrespectful, marketing managers should be aware of certain codes of conduct to which Buddhists adhere. For example, Buddha images or photographs of pagodas should not be used in advertisements except for tourism purposes. Uniforms or cloth of saffron color should be avoided, as they are used for religious purposes only. This is a mistake that can be made even by academic publishers and the most sympathetic of observers. A book review (Thein 2001) of *Economic Development of Burma, a Vision and a Strategy* illustrates this point. The reviewer commented that she had a personal problem with the book's cover, which sported the picture of Shwedagon Pagoda (the most sacred in Burma) as seen through a window from outside. Although the image captured the spirit of the analysis, she considered that, as a practicing Buddhist brought up in Burma, such religious images were far too sacred to be used on a book cover.

Strength of Family Ties

The components of a Myanmar family are mirrored in the three ages that Buddhist teaching apportions to a human being: the first of acquiring knowledge, the second of building up material resources, and the third of devotion to more spiritual things. Family ties in Myanmar are strong—not so much from rigid traditions as from natural affections allowed full play. Thus, in a typical family are included the children, the parents, usually both of them working to support the home, and the old men and women giving much time to prayer and daily offerings at the altar for the entire family. The family structure is loosely defined, with its membership varying with circumstances. Sons and daughters and sisters, aunts, and uncles acquired by marriage may be incorporated. The Bamar word for "relative" has the same root as "friend," and most Myanmar people have a warmhearted wish for as many relatives as possible. Such a concept extends the family naturally to friends and neighbors—in the country to the village, and in the city to *yatkwet* (residential districts). The community elders share with the heads of family the privileges of giving guidance and being kept informed. Marketers should, therefore, mirror such values in advertising concepts.

Advertisements for household electrical appliances, for instance, often feature a housewife or a mother, who lives in a modern house, condominium, or apartment, happily cooking and looking after her children and her working husband. According to a marketing manager in Yangon, it is important for advertisements for household goods to highlight family units and family values. For example, for an average Burmese family, shopping for a TV set is an important occasion that is shared by the whole family. Mature-aged children, their spouses, and even grandchildren, are likely to accompany the parents on a shopping trip to buy a major household appliance such as a TV set. The purchase of a major "luxury" item is often a source of collective family pride, and it is likely that many family members will be consulted and that the family will choose the most popular brand, in part, because their neighbor(s) have the same brand. The family will then happily take the item home, perhaps in a taxi, without waiting for delivery.

Customs and Beliefs

Within the Myanmar society, a great deal of respect is accorded to the elders, teachers (*sayah*), and religious authority. There exists a nexus of obligations due by the young to the old and the old to the young that bonds all generations of Myanmar people (Pe 1996). Many unspoken rules exist with respect to interaction between various types of people. For example, one should not offer to shake hands with monks but should instead observe *gadaw*, with clasped palms at forehead level.

One should not touch any person on the head or step over any part of a person. One should also seek permission before retrieving an article above a person's head. In addition, when using the Myanmar language, suitable words or phrases should be used when addressing others based upon the relative relationships and social position. There is a very strong sense of *ar-nah* among the Myanmar. Loosely, this refers to a feeling of being beholden, and as such, the Myanmar people shy away from imposing on another and from actions that require a favor. Care is often taken not to create the loss of "face." This is somewhat, though not exactly, similar to the Thai concept of *krenjai*. Spiritual beliefs are also strong and harmoniously blend with religious beliefs. These include giving offering to the *Nats* or spirits before any ceremony or major undertaking, for example, purchase of a car.

Myanmar people are superstitious. For example, entering a building from an entrance facing west is commonly considered to bring bad luck, especially on occasions such as weddings. One recent example of this was evident in the renovation of a major hotel in Yangon, which, for many years, had been considered to be the most prestigious wedding venue in the city. The new Western management changed the entrance of the hotel's reception hall. Unfortunately, according to locals, the new entrance was designed in such a way that people were perceived to be entering the reception hall from the back, which was considered to bring bad luck to the people. Because of this, many people no longer booked the reception hall for weddings. A similar example was a new development for condominiums on the outskirts of Yangon, initially hailed as one of the most promising property investments for years. In this case, a cemetery had to move (making way for a hotel construction, according to locals), and the new venue for the cemetery happened to be near the condominium development. This resulted in a dramatic fall in the sales of the condominiums, as Myanmar people do not wish to live in the vicinity of a cemetery.

Ceremonies and Festivals

There is hardly any activity, apart from routine work, in which all neighbors do not participate. Myanmar life is rich in opportunities for communal experience. Due to the semitropical climate, the Myanmar people enjoy being outdoors, with the exception of during the monsoon months, and cultural traditions provide many opportunities to join festival processions to the monastery or to the pagoda, with each person dressed in their best and bearing gifts or offerings. The Myanmar calendar is lunar and liberally sprinkled with holidays such as Thingyan, the New Year Water Festival, Kason, the watering festival of the Bodhi tree, and Thadingyut, the festival of lights. Thingyan is celebrated merrily and noisily, while Kason is a more somber religious occasion (Thein 1996). At Thadingyut, the young pay respect to the elders. For example, it is common for the young to wash the hair of the elderly. Recently, the distributor of a Western shampoo brand took advantage of this opportunity by sponsoring this hair-washing event at Thingyan, where the young women used the shampoo brand to wash the hair of the elderly. Thingyan is also a strategic moment for promotions and sponsors. In particular, cigarette marketers have seized the opportunity for sales promotions. The promoter of an international cigarette brand brought in a musical act from the United States, which was mainly made up of African Americans, and put on a stage show during Thingyan in Yangon. It was considered to be a big success. According to the promoter, the event was seen to be unique, as many Burmese were impressed and excited by a touch of foreign "glamour" during this festive period.

At the festivals such as Thadingyut, it is also a time for donations and gift giving to elders, teachers, employers, senior managers, and monks. Consumer goods marketers tend to step up marketing campaigns in the lead up to these festivals. The type of gifts will depend on who the receiver is and, more importantly, how significant or powerful the individual or the family is to the giver.

Gift giving is practiced widely in Burmese culture. It is very important in business, because gifts are expected in many situations—when one receives an introduction or a promotion or wins a lucrative contract, etc. Popular gift items for business interactions with senior managers are golf clubs and accessories, up-market beverages (Chivas Regal, blue or black label whiskey), and cigarettes (555 appears to be the most popular brand within business circles). Also popular is men's clothing, such as polo shirts, smart casual shirts, jackets, and so forth. There are a few essential rules in regard to gift giving. One must choose popular international brands—preferably from the West. If possible, it is advisable to find out which international brands are currently best-known in Myanmar. If a recipient is not familiar with the brand, it is likely that they will not appreciate it, regardless of how expensive it is overseas. It is also better to choose items with labeling that indicates that it was made in major Western and developed Asian countries (i.e., "Made in USA," "Made in UK," "Made in Germany," "Made in Japan"). One must also remember to leave the price tag on the item (and any other tags or labels; even the shopping bags are desirable), as this assures the recipient that the items were purchased overseas from an up-market retailer.

There are myriad sports activities and cultural events almost every month of the year, ranging from boat racing festivals to soccer matches. In addition to such occasions, there are many reasons for social get-togethers. For example, there will always be a gathering for the naming ceremony for a month-old child, when the baby's hair is cut and washed for the first time. Far more elaborate preparations will be made for the ceremonies that mark the passing from childhood into adolescence. Almost all young boys go through a *shinpyu* ceremony, where they spend a period of time as novice monks. Other occasions of celebration include housewarmings, weddings, birthdays, paying gratitude to the dead, or anytime one is in good spirits, or, alternatively, in low spirits and needing the blessings of a righteous deed done.

Historical Characteristics

As present-day Myanmar history stretches back many centuries, at least to the Pyu Kings in the fifth century C.E., there is an invisible web of cultural pride, awareness of legends and folklore, and strong sense of history that binds the people. Myanmar people are proud of their history, of which the greatest period of cultural activity began with King Anawratha in the eleventh century. His legacy can be seen in the ruins of Bagan, with its magnificent temples and pagodas. This was a time from which Theravada Buddhism and Myanmar language, art, and culture flourished (Thein 1996). Since then, a long list of kings, queens, heroes, battles, conquests, and legends have embraced the Myanmar collective past. After the fall of Bagan to the Mongols in the thirteenth century, the Ava Dynasty (1364–1555) was followed by the Toungoo Dynasty (1486–1752). The most prominent member of the latter dynasty was King Bayinnaung, who forged Myanmar into a strong respected nation. In the final days of this dynasty, Myanmar was at war with neighboring Thailand and there occurred the infamous sacking of the Thai capital of Ayutthaya in 1767. Another dynasty followed under King Alaungpaya in 1752. During this time, the Myanmar kingdom conquered farther away regions such as Arakan, Manipur, and Assam. These victories were followed by the wars with the British in the early nineteenth century, leading to Myanmar's defeat and eventual annexation of Burma. In 1886, King Thibaw, the last king of the dynasty, was deported to India. Myanmar did not gain its independence until January 4, 1948, after the tumultuous World War I and World War II.

The strong influence of history is apparent not only in the Myanmar religious and cultural systems but also in the more tangible aspects, such as in architecture, arts and crafts, dance and drama, and the Myanmar language and literature. There are 2,217 historic monuments and temples under the care of the Archaeological Department in Bagan alone. For example, large audiences, even in small towns of today, enjoy the performance of Ramayana in Myanmar drama, said to be adopted from the Thais in the eighteenth century.

Role of Women

Compared to other Third World and even some more developed Asian nations, Myanmar women enjoy a fairly high status in society. A single woman is not necessarily considered an "old spinster." Myanmar women also enjoy an active say in household and purchase decisions. In most cases, affairs concerning the household, including managing money earned by the husband, are overseen by women. Gender bias against women is neither apparent nor acute (Thein 1996). In the cities and the countryside, there is a fair share of participation in the economic activities, such as production, service, and agriculture. Myanmar women also enjoy shopping of any nature and, therefore, are an important target for marketing activities. Myanmar's society puts a great deal of emphasis on women's beauty and appearance, and Myanmar women are very interested in beauty products. Since the adoption of the market economy, more cosmetics and beauty products have been presented in the market than ever before, and many brands, including many international brands from the West, have been doing well. A U.S. cosmetic brand was highly promoted, and its marketers often sponsored fashion shows held in up-market shopping centers. A night cream distributed by a Thailand-based distributor has also been selling well. The distributor of an international soap brand that was promoted in Myanmar as a beauty soap was a proud sponsor of a beauty contest, which was a nationwide event.

Modeling (which was nonexistent in the socialist era) has become a new "career" for some young women aspiring to be movie stars. With the opening of the economy since the early 1990s, movie stars, singers, and models have enjoyed much higher incomes and profiles than ever before. One unique aspect of promoting cosmetics and beauty products in Myanmar is that, in most cases, advertising requires "localization," meaning that it must use local celebrities. Myanmar people love their own celebrities (this aspect will be discussed in more detail later in the chapter). However, other international brands often strive to maintain their "international" image and so use standard Western-type brochures and posters.

Nevertheless, as stated in the Buddhist doctrine, women are considered to be on a plane of "lesser existence" than men. Education and choice of profession are regarded as less important for a girl than for a boy. Child rearing and food preparation are still mainly in the domain of women.

Overall, the Myanmar life is seen to be one of goodwill and fraternity, with its spirit of generosity and relaxation due to the different elements' being well adjusted to each other (Khaing 1994). For instance, the elderly neither feel unwanted nor have an urge to behave like the young when there is a definite function for them in every festivity and in the home routine. Both sexes also have traditional roles. There exists a pride in an isolated inland culture that saw no real superiority in anything from the outside world for many centuries. This pride will be hard to eradicate, even with the introduction of Western materialism. Despite the economic difficulties, the people of Myanmar live within a social system that allows a sense of both spiritual and worldly fulfillment. Regardless of their economic hardships, the people of Myanmar believe in their way of life, and so do not feel inferior to other better-off people.

Consumer Behavior

The economic, cultural, and demographic environment has an important bearing on the consumer behavior of the Myanmar people. Class structures exist within Myanmar, and consumers can be roughly divided into two types: the well-educated and wealthy upper class, and the much larger and poorer lower class. Unlike most other developing countries, a large middle class of consumers did not exist in Myanmar until recently. With the influx of foreign capital and growth in the economy, there appears to be the beginning of a middle class of consumers who have most directly benefited from the economic reforms. This phenomenon, however, is confined mainly to the cities and certain rural areas. For example, a village called Ywatharnyunt near Nyaungdon, with approximately 275 households relying mainly on the cultivation of beans and pulses, had about thirty radios and two bicycles before 1988. Now it has a television set, over eighty radios, and about sixty bicycles (see also Thein and Than 1995).

The small upper class consists of the ruling elite, the traditional nobility that remains a vestige of the past, a handful of newly rich businesspeople, and some wealthy families of overseas workers who have repatriated their earnings back home. They mostly dwell in the cities, such as Yangon, Mandalay, and Mawlamyaing, own property, and have the means to buy any of the array of consumer products that are available in these large cities.

The new car market targets these wealthy people, and four-wheel-drive vehicles seem to be particularly popular for two apparent reasons: (1) for image (the ruling elite are often seen on television in four-wheel-drive vehicles) and (2) for "up-country" driving on difficult terrain to destinations such as Mandalay, Taungyi, and Bagan. In fact, since the opening of the market economy, the new car market in Myanmar has been a highly visible symbol of change. The availability of brand new cars, especially in Yangon, has been a new phenomenon. Previously, most cars in the market were secondhand or reconditioned Japanese cars, and new cars were driven only by foreign embassy staff and senior government ministers. New cars sold in showrooms these days have, therefore, been something of a novelty to Myanmar consumers. However, there have been two major problems associated with the sluggish sale of the new cars: (1) A permit to import passenger cars (new or old) is extremely difficult to obtain; and (2) only the upper end of the Myanmar elite can afford to buy these new cars. In many ways, this is indicative of some underlying and generalized difficulties with Myanmar as a market for consumer goods—serious bureaucratic obstacles and limited demand due to the restricted size and purchasing power of the middle class.

The wealthy, the powerful, and the newly rich, also, these days, have more up-market venues in which to shop for their groceries. There are now a few mini supermarkets around Yangon, a market characteristic that did not exist before the so-called open-door market policy. Another aspect of upper class consumer behavior is that some items considered essential in developed countries are not seen as essential in Myanmar. For example, washing machines are not essential in Myanmar, as domestic helpers are commonplace. Similarly, microwave ovens are even less useful because of frequent power shortages, and because Burmese housewives, unlike working women in other countries, are able to cook more regularly. For these reasons, there is also less need/demand to store food in refrigerators and freezers. However, some rich consumers have purchased these items, more for the sake of image than for convenience or out of necessity.

The lower class consists of both city dwellers and farmers. In the city, they tend to be small traders, manual and salaried workers, and the unemployed; while the rural areas are made up mainly of farm workers. While the nominal incomes of the city workers have probably just kept pace with the increase in general level of prices, some of the workers are able to earn additional wages by moonlighting. The lower, middle, and upper-middle classes make up the largest consumer groups, but, at present, they do not have purchasing power large enough to consume foreign international brands. Through television advertisements and billboards, they may well recognize and aspire to these brands, yet few can afford to actually purchase such products. Marketers have had to modify their product strategies to suit the needs of this group. For example, products such as shampoos and detergents are repackaged in small packets for single use to make them more affordable for everyday consumers.

As for the farm workers, those who do not have surplus to sell on the open market have little discretionary income. Their purchase cycles also tend to be seasonal, with harvest period late in the year being a good time for targeting marketing activities. For example, electronic products were heavily advertised and promoted in country areas around rice harvesting time, when farmers realized the monetary value of their crops by selling rice. However, rural consumers are unlikely primary targets of Western consumer marketing at present. It may be of greater value to concentrate on city consumers, principally those in Yangon and Mandalay.

It is interesting to note that although many international consumer packaged products are beyond the reach of the majority of consumers, especially those in small towns outside of Yangon and Mandalay, these consumers are sometimes selectively targeted by marketers. For example, in the late 1990s, an international shampoo brand staged a sales promotion in very remote country areas by driving around in a van, demonstrating to country people how to use shampoo and distributing free samples of their product. In country areas, there is a strong appetite for products such as soft drinks, cigarettes, and beer. For example, Marlboro and 555 were distributed so extensively that they were available in every small shop and cafe around the country. However, most consumers cannot afford these international brands and turn instead to cheaper Chinese-made brands and a locally manufactured brand with an international name, "London" cigarettes.

Perhaps because of many decades of isolation, Myanmar consumers' thirst for famous international brands, especially brands from the West, is insatiable. Rumors have it that Coke, although not locally bottled in Myanmar and where the brand is not advertised at all, is more popular than Pepsi, a brand that, until its withdrawal under political pressure in the mid-1990s, was locally bottled and heavily advertised in Myanmar.

One trait of elite Burmese consumers is that, as acknowledged by many marketing managers, they like to buy the same brand as do their neighbors. This has resulted in popular brands being replaced regularly. For example, in the electronics market, Daewoo enjoyed popularity first, followed by Toshiba and later Sony. Marketing managers admit that it is often very difficult to change perceptions as to which brand is currently popular or prestigious. This trait is particularly pronounced in country areas, where product knowledge is often low; consumers buy the product that works for people they know. Burmese consumers are price sensitive and love bargains. There is an expression to describe this bargain-loving nature. In Burmese, it is called *Paw, Chong, Kaung*. Paw means "cheap price," Chong means "good bargain," and Kaung means "good quality."

Despite the barriers to external influences, the Myanmar city dwellers are surprisingly well informed, if somewhat dated, in their knowledge of the outside world. This infiltration of foreign influences has been aided by the factors discussed below.

Myanmar People Abroad

There is a large number of Myanmar emigrants working and living abroad. Unlike the refugees originating from Indochina, they are mostly professionals with high levels of skill and education.

Most of them send food, clothing, and other necessities to relatives and friends in Myanmar, thus keeping the recipients in touch with foreign goods. This has created a latent demand for foreign brands.

Additionally, the newly rich in Myanmar often travel overseas, mostly for the purpose of shopping for international consumer goods. Bangkok and Singapore are the two most popular shopping destinations, and the United States is the most desired destination. Women from this elite class are very aware and conscious of famous international brands. Brands hotly sought after by rich women include Estée Lauder cosmetics, Opium perfume, Gucci handbags, and Bailey shoes, while men desire Chivas Regal, golf clubs and golf apparel. Because the Myanmar elite are so blindly brand conscious, one must be aware of these popular brands when giving gifts. Gift giving is extremely popular when doing business in Myanmar, and a step beyond gift giving is an offer of shopping trips overseas. What people learn from these shopping trips can be of considerable influence on people back home. For instance, white gold is a new fashion in the jewelry market in Myanmar, a trend that has been picked up by actresses during shopping trips abroad. However, white gold has been so new in Myanmar that many jewelers have not yet mastered the art of its production, and inferior imitations abound. The newly rich also learn of brands through advertising featured on programs broadcast into the country by satellite television channels.

Like the newly rich, most consumers within Myanmar are also brand conscious, despite the fact that many brands are beyond the majority of consumers' means. However, when it comes to purchases relating to entertainment and "aspirational" items, even those with relatively low purchasing power will sometimes save money to indulge in these products. For instance, some products that fall into this category include popular brands such as Sony TVs and VCRs, Toyota cars, OMO washing detergent, and Coke soft drinks.

For the lower middle class, there are also more affordable brands, and many are locally manufactured. For example, while brands such as Marlboro, Lucky Strike, and 555 may be every smoker's first choice, most cannot afford it. To make up for this gap, "London" cigarettes are produced locally. Locals like the London brand because it is new, it has a foreign image, and prices are much lower than those of big international brands. Similarly, there are locally brewed beers (e.g., Mandalay beer) to satisfy local demand. In consumer electronics, Daewoo products are a cheaper option, while a majority of households use OSO detergent powder, a Chinese clone, instead of the more internationally recognized OMO brand.

Knowledge of English

One of the most striking features about the Myanmar people, especially the older generation, is their ability to understand English. Most Myanmar schooling was conducted in English until 1962, when it was banned as "representative of a degenerate and decadent culture" (Maung 1991, 222). Nonetheless, the decades of British rule have ensured that many older people are fluent in the English language. After a lapse of about thirty years, English has been introduced in schools again as a second language. In the cities, there is a great demand for English books, CDs, magazines, videotapes, and movies.

Many foreign advertisements are used unaltered or unadapted to the local language, while others are replayed with a mere voiceover. There are two reasons for this approach. The first is that expatriate marketing managers often tend to resist complete localization (some strongly oppose using a completely localized TV advertising strategy featuring a popular "song and dance" format). The second is that, although many consumers cannot understand English, marketers often believe that advertisements in English create a much desired foreign image that will give the brand prestige in the local market. This is why, for example, newspaper advertising for consumer electronic products quite often features a mix of English and Burmese.

Intact Brand Profiles

The Myanmar consumer is surprisingly brand conscious. The British influence created consumer habits that many of the upper class retained and that have recently started to reappear. Therefore, brands that were strongly represented in Myanmar from the 1940s to the 1960s continue to have strong "share of mind" and are widely popular on the international consumer goods market. For example, food giant Nestle has been in Myanmar homes for generations, and even today, consumers' preference leans toward Nestle products, such as Nescafe for coffee, if they can afford it. There is also a preference for well-known brands from the United States (for instance, the popularity of Coca Cola). In some ways, this is surprising, as Myanmar is a country under U.S. trade sanctions. However, Myanmar consumers do not seem to bear any resentment toward the United States, in fact, if anything, the opposite applies.

Brand Consciousness

Contrary to popular belief, many products and brands are available in Myanmar, imported through an official container trade, or a semi-official border trade. For example, in the Mingala Bazaar in Yangon town center, there exists a large mall of small shops where almost any Western item, from toothpaste to television sets, can be bought. The strong presence of these markets has provided consumers with a continuous link to the products and fashions of the outside world despite the years of isolation.

Given the above knowledge, Myanmar consumers tend to be selective in their shopping habits. They tend to prefer well-known labels over cheaper versions and familiar makes over newer ones. For example, a "Made in England" label would be perceived to be better than a "Made in Hong Kong" label. Similarly, they prefer Japanese-made products over those made in Korea. In fact, they so highly regard Japanese-made products that one automobile marketer has confessed that Myanmar consumers prefer a secondhand car that has been made in Japan for the Japanese market and then imported to Myanmar, over a brand-new made-in-Japan export model. Consumers tend to believe that products made for Japanese markets are much better in quality. However, because of tight budget constraints, the consumers often settle for a cheaper, less desirable brand of the product. Marketers also respond to this need by selling smaller-sized or single use packets (e.g., shampoos and detergents). Given budget constraints, Myanmar shoppers tend to be very careful in selecting a product to meet their needs. While some forms of impulse purchases exist, consumers tend to consider all aspects of product benefits before a purchase decision is made, often going back to the shop for a second look. In addition, close social ties create an environment in which entire clans remain faithful to a brand, as compared to a Western family where each individual in the same household may prefer or use a different brand. Also, Myanmar consumers tend to follow their neighbors' purchase decisions, making word-of-mouth advertising crucial. Furthermore, word-of-mouth recommendation plays an important role in determining the success of a product, especially from family members or neighbors. Women especially play an important role as decision makers and influencers. There is a great deal of receptivity to foreign goods and advertising. This has been explained by suggesting that Myanmar is in the initial stages of development, and therefore, its consumers tend to be less cynical toward marketing practices. Recent studies have indicated that Myanmar consumers tend to have a much stronger positive response to advertising than consumers in more developed countries (Lwin 1997).

Many consumers in Myanmar prefer viewing advertisements (most of them in a song-and-dance format) more than watching the actual programs. Advertisement breaks are the most popular times for viewers, and the whole family (including domestic helpers, drivers, and maybe some not-so-affluent neighbors who do not own a TV set) gathers to watch them. It is common for consumers (especially in out-of-town places) to go to shops and ask for a product by the name of the actor or actress who appears in the TV advertisement for the product. So, although consumers may not necessarily remember the brand name, they remember the entertainer associated with that product. However, one problem in the Myanmar advertising industry is that popular entertainers are often used for a vast range of products. It is common for popular actors to appear in advertisements for more than one brand in the same product category. For example, at one point, the most popular actress appeared in a majority of television advertisements. Nonetheless, given the strong popular following of movie stars, many expatriate marketing managers should perhaps rethink their anti-localization approaches to advertising.

TRENDS IN MARKETING MIX

Consumer Products

Surprisingly, it is not an overstatement to suggest that almost anything and everything a consumer could want is quite easily available in Myanmar—at a price. Imported cooking tools, food, toiletries, electrical goods, and many other products are available not only at the central Mingala Market but in any small provision store, even on the outskirts of Yangon. Most imports appear to have originated from Thailand, Hong Kong, and Singapore, although of late, cheap products from China and India have infiltrated the market as well. In Yangon and Mandalay, larger department stores carry various types of foreign goods.

Of the products that have been brought into the country, either via border trade (unofficially or semi-officially) or the more official container trade via the Yangon port, a majority of them are not made specifically for the Myanmar market. As a result, the products still carry, for instance, Thai language on the packaging if the good is from Bangkok. It is rare that one will find an international brand manufactured specifically for the Myanmar market. Moreover, overdue/expired products are often found in the Myanmar market. This is either because traders deliberately import expired goods (e.g., unsold goods from Bangkok) or because products have been on the shelf for too long in the country. For example, it is not unusual to find cigarettes in the market that are stale simply because they are outdated. This is one of the reasons why the locally manufactured London cigarette brand is so popular—it is relatively fresh.

One of the problems in the market is a lack of consistency within brands—there are many different makes of the same brand selling for different prices. For example, an international film brand (one of the top-selling brands of film in Myanmar) was imported from Japan and also from China (made for the Chinese market). This presented serious problems for the brand's importer/distributor in Myanmar, who handled only those made-in-Japan, because the company was competing against itself with the same brand.

A wide variety of local products are also available, a few of which are direct imitations of foreign goods, right down to the packaging. The products available in the markets follow a clear trend, with market leaders being the most visible and well stocked. Lesser-known brands, imitations, and even totally unknown brands are also widely available. For example, among cigarette brands, 555 and Marlboro appeared to be the best sellers. The consumer outlook has been so good that foreign companies like Rothmans of Pall Mall are jointly manufacturing the locally made mega-successful "London" brand. "Duya," another local brand, is also very popular, because it is much cheaper than the foreign brands. Besides these brands, locally produced cigarettes by joint-venture companies, such as "Polo" and "Sampoena," were also selling well. In addition, a typical cigarette seller might stock virtually unknown brands such as "KKK" and "American Club." The clear market leaders, however, are always present at shops, sidewalk stalls, homes, and the black market. This exclusive club includes Colgate toothpaste, Ovaltine beverage, Johnny Walker Red Label, and Nescafe instant coffee. There is also a great demand for electrical and high technology products, such as computers. As Myanmar opens to the outside world, most consumers are eager to show their modernity through acquisition of products such as television sets, cameras, video recorders, and even home computers, which ten years ago had almost no penetration in the market. In addition to selling to the consumer market, there is also a sizeable and potentially lucrative market in selling to government departments. Government ministries and departments regularly buy products such as heavy machinery, construction materials, fertilizers, medicines, raw materials, office equipment, and so on. In fact, for products such as computers, the domestic consumer market is still too small to target. Instead, government departments are the obvious targets for products such as computers. According to local sources, the distributor of a major international computer brand has supplied a vast quantity of computers to schools in Myanmar.

Pricing

Pricing of foreign goods follows similar processes. Prices that are usually quite uniform across institutions may fluctuate, sometimes daily, due to the erratic supply situation. Inflation in Myanmar presents a huge problem for marketers, because goods are often sold on credit or on consignment. By the time the money is paid, the Myanmar kyat is worth less than it was at the time of the sale. Also, many traders pay for goods in U.S. dollars and sell in the country in kyats. As a result, during one particular time in 1997, when inflation went out of control, many shopkeepers decided to close their doors. Retailers also had to change prices almost everyday, and many priced the goods in Foreign Exchange Certificates (FECs), or they carried a chart comparing FECs to the prevailing market rate and when customers paid for a product, they worked out the equivalent rate.

In addition to inflation, marketers often faced supply problems, mainly due to government restrictions on imports and permits. Supply difficulties with products in high demand, such as cigarettes and electronics, presented major time-consuming problems for marketers/importers. Local managers complained that they were so busy worrying about how to get the supply into the country, that they had little time to concentrate on developing sophisticated marketing strategies. Taking into consideration the official exchange rate of approximately US$1 to 6 kyats and a black market rate of US$1 to over 800 kyats, a few black market selections are priced approximately as shown in Table 11.9.

Pricing of local produce such as food and many other commodities, has been much more predictable. With the high inflation rates, the consumer price index (CPI) has shown rising costs over the years (see Table 11.10). Since 1986, the CPI rose over fivefold to 571.5 in 1994. This problem is even more acute in the food and beverages category (CPI = 658.4) and fuel and light category (CPI = 613.6), while tobacco and education have been more controlled at lower CPIs of 244.7 and 113.7, respectively.

Table 11.9

Average Pricing of Consumer Products in Yangon (kyats)

Colgate toothpaste (large)	2,000
Darlie toothpaste (small)	1,000
Lux soap (bar)	500
Kleenex tissue (box)	500
Carnation evaporated milk	800
Nescafe (large tin)	5,000

Table 11.10

Consumer Price Index of Selected Items (base year 1997 = 100)

Particulars	1998	1999	2000
General consumer price index	102.6	133.5	154.4
Food and beverages	102.6	133.3	154.1
Tobacco	102.8	134.0	155.0
Fuel and light	102.5	130.2	136.1
Clothing and apparel	102.5	130.2	136.1
House rent and repairs	101.4	117.1	131.8
Education	101.2	114.0	124.3
Medical care	102.0	122.3	131.0
Conveyance	102.6	133.7	148.4
Cleansing and toiletries	106.3	183.5	259.2
Annual change in CPI (%)	n.a.	30.1	15.7

Source: Statistical Yearbook 2000 (Yangon: The Government of the Union of Myanmar, Ministry of National Planning and Economic Development, Central Statistical Organization, 2000).

Recently, the influx of foreign goods through legal retail outlets has made many consumer products readily available to consumers. While these products are readily available, their prices place them out of reach of ordinary citizens whose household incomes are well below 2,000 kyats per month. Nevertheless, sales have been brisk due to the possibility that many households have supplementary incomes from second jobs or part-time work. Thus, marketers are advised to consider the total household income, including secondary incomes, when deciding on pricing issues rather than simple individual incomes (Bin et al. 1996).

Distribution: The Retail Market

Traditionally, there existed only two types of distribution outlets: government-run stores and small private bazaars. Most of the private bazaars sold illegal black market goods. At the government stores, a quota was often set for each family for the purchase of products. However, with the opening of the economy, there has been a systematic entry of larger trading houses cum stores as well as provision shops. There is a blurred division among the various types of establishments. The government-run stores continue to be poorly stocked. These mainly sell commodities (sugar, rice, unbranded soap, textiles). In some outlets, foreign goods, imported by the government, are available. For example, Medicines and Medical Equipment Trading imports large quantities of pharmaceuticals and medical supplies that are available through hospital outlets. Many consumers continue to purchase items from this source, as prices are stabilized and way below market costs.

The busy bazaars continue to thrive. They range from open-air market stalls and provision shops that are family owned and operated to the newer department stores. Many stock both local and Western products, while some specialize in only a few types of products. Before the opening of the economy to international trade in the early 1990s, their supply of merchandise used to emanate from seamen, foreign returnees, and foreigners, as well as from direct illegal imports over the border from Thailand, China, and India. However, recently, a new channel of import by official container trade has been added to the previous channels. Also, as the Myanmar government has quasi-legalized the previously illegal border trade, more goods have flown in from over the borders. A number of these stores are housed in a few major shopping centers in Mingala Zay, Bogyoke Zay (old), and Bogyoke Zay (new) areas. Newer and more modern shopping complexes exist around Yangon, including FMI Centre and Yuzana Plaza.

There has been a proliferation of new stores run by Myanmar traders or foreign investors. Many of these have sprouted in recent years due to the government's more liberal trade and investment policies. The market they aim at is comprised of local consumers. Their pricing structure sometimes varies to accommodate taxes and other costs. However, the bottom line is the same, and at many of the stores, items for sale can be paid for in U.S. dollars, by credit cards, or by FECs. As ordinary citizens are allowed to handle FECs (U.S. dollars being illegal for locals), an FEC market has been created in which FECs can be traded. Local shoppers have the option of paying in FEC or in kyats, and, in either case, the conversion rate used is the prevailing black market rate rather than the official rate of 6 kyats to US$1.

Examples of new retailing developments include the Myanmar–Singapore Emporium run by Singapore entrepreneurs; Sony Electronics; Samsung and the Toshiba outlets, showrooms, and service centers; new car showrooms selling Toyota, Nissan, Mitsubishi, and Volkswagen; clothing stores such as Hang Ten and Giordano; Konica photo services; and so on. Even though this channel may not provide large short-term profits, investors obviously see it as a good and legitimate way to enter the market to establish their presence and leadership. It is important, however, to note that many of the aforementioned operations are not handled directly by brand manufacturers or owners. Many are handled by authorized distributors or agents. In some cases, the so-called agent in Myanmar has no official relationship with owners of the brands. In such a case, the agent simply brings the goods in officially or unofficially and sells them in Myanmar. Thus, it is common for official importers to face competition from black marketers or smugglers or self-appointed unofficial agents.

These stores are run in a more Western manner compared to black market outlets. Products such as refrigerators, television sets, and household appliances are "departmentalized" by product category, and prices are fixed. One notable aspect of these modern stores is that there are many more salespersons in the shop than are seen in most other countries. The same also applies for up-market restaurants. Most also provide product guarantees and after-sales service. Toshiba, for example, boasts of having over thirty technicians among its after-sales service staff.

Promotion and Advertising

The major media (TV, radio, and newspapers) are state owned. There is a wide number of private publications—mainly feature journals, magazines, comics, cartoons, and novels. The local media, the majority of which are in the Myanmar language, dominate the general communication scene in Myanmar. In a survey done in 1994, the "Top Ten" lists of best-selling books, magazines, videos and LDs, cassettes, and CDs found that locally produced Myanmar-language titles take up all ten positions in each category (*Myanma Dhana* 1994). Myanmar Television and Radio Department is in charge of radio and television broadcasting. It has five divisions: Information, Radio Broadcasting, Engineering, Television, and Administrative. Television, at present, airs approximately three to five hours of programs on weekdays and seven hours on weekends. TV transmissions are now beamed to almost every corner of the vast country through a network of recently built repeater stations. It is the most effective media for creating advertising impact if cost is not a factor. A thirty-second TV spot of advertising, exclusive of agency commission that can be discussed on a project basis, ranges from US$360 to US$760, with prime time slots commanding the highest premiums.

Myanmar people love entertainment. Given that there is little in terms of modern forms of entertainment (night clubs, bars, shows, etc.), people, young and old, turn to entertainment such as TV and video viewing and reading local publications. In fact, TV advertisements are sometimes more popular with viewers than the actual programs. The ads are shown for about forty-five minutes after the news and before the feature film. During the feature film, the ads come on every twenty to thirty minutes, and each ad break lasts around twenty minutes. This phenomenon is perhaps to be expected in a country where TV advertising is relatively new. Television advertisements are so popular that many local marketers believe that the sure way to launch a number one selling brand is to advertise on TV using a top-notch star in a song-and-dance-style advertisement. Most advertisements in Myanmar feature a song-and-dance format, and many marketers believe that this approach is almost certain to guarantee success. Although this is changing as the market becomes more sophisticated, with an increasing number of brands and marketing campaigns penetrating the country, this advice still seems to be valid for the time being.

However, there are several drawbacks related to television advertising. The first is that the news program, which starts at 8 P.M., is quite long and takes up most of the prime time viewing hours, and no advertisements are shown during the news. The main content of the news program is coverage of the activities of ministers of government ministries (e.g., ministers inspecting irrigation dams and construction projects, paying homage to temples, attending various award ceremonies, etc.). The second, and biggest, drawback is frequent power cuts that interrupt programming. In fact, some expatriate marketing managers have begun to think that TV advertising is not that effective because of the extent of this problem. However, this problem is not as acute as it sounds, because many households nowadays use what are called "invertors," which convert D.C. current (from battery) to A.C. current from 12 volts to 110 or 230 volts.

According to official figures, TV reaches 80 percent of the country's households at present. Within six months, this is expected to grow to 90 percent. Ownership of TVs, however, is much smaller and limited to better-off consumers, totaling 225,477 in 1994. However, in the suburbs, it is common for people to join their neighbors to watch TV and video programs. Radio has a much higher reach of 95 percent, airing approximately ten hours a day in English and Myanmar. At present, there are an estimated 50,000 video sets in Yangon, representing a 150 percent increase over the 20,000 sets in 1988; and ownership is fast increasing due to aggressive marketing campaigns by foreign brands. Radio, however, is not very popular, especially in Yangon, as the music played by radio stations is often classical Myanmar music, rather than more popular film songs and modern Western-tuned "pop" songs. Because Myanmar people love listening to music, cassettes of songs are very popular, many of which are straight copies of modern Western songs (e.g., there is a Burmese version of a song from the movie *Titanic*). Recorded advertisements on cassette tapes and print advertisements on the covers of the tapes have also begun to be featured as effective tools for advertising. Myanmar television technical data are as follows: video system—

Umatic—NTSC 3.58–525 lines with audio frequency of 4.5 megahertz. Print media such as journals, magazines, and newspapers are very popular. Journals, as many marketers claimed, are a very good medium, as the cost is reasonable, they have fast turnaround, and they are available in color. The journals are a new thing in Myanmar, and their readership is widespread.

Myanmar television broadcasts both English and Myanmar programs, although documentaries, variety shows, and dramas are mainly in the Myanmar language. There are two TV broadcasting stations—the TV Myanmar (state-owned) and the Myawaddy (owned by the military). Weekday programs on television are mainly confined to evenings, with the highlight being an hour-long news program at 8 P.M. The world news program broadcasts for about twenty minutes, while Myanmar news items are broadcast between one and one and a half hours. The news is repeated twice—once in Burmese and once in English, which is simply a direct translation of Myanmar news. No advertising is allowed during this news period. Most TV advertisements are shown during commercial breaks during the prime time periods. For example, advertisements are shown before and during movies. The majority of commercials are locally produced, although some foreign advertisements also appear. Western television commercials are allowed as long as approval is obtained from the censorship board. The Myanmar Television and Radio Department also runs radio advertisements. These are mostly in Myanmar, with the range of products advertised similar to that on television. Prime time for radio is 8 A.M. to 9 A.M., before work, and 7 P.M. to 8 P.M. after work.

Chinese TV series are the most popular in Myanmar. Viewers are "addicted" to Chinese shows, which feature historic martial arts with love stories. There are also Japanese TV series. There are no Western movie/TV series currently shown in Myanmar. However, every weekend, English Premier League soccer is shown on TV, and this program is sponsored by Loi Hain Company, the local manufacturer of soft drink brands and cigarettes. Tiger Beer was the past sponsor of soccer's 2002 World Cup and World Cup qualifiers.

The News and Periodicals Corporation publishes and distributes national and international news as well as periodicals, books, and other literature. Newspaper advertising is the most far-reaching and cost-effective medium available in Myanmar at present. There are only three newspapers in the country, all of which have a wide readership. At present, *The New Light of Myanmar* (NLM) is the only English-language newspaper. There are two Myanmar-language newspapers—*Kyemon Daily* and NLM's version in Myanmar language known as *Myanmar A-Lin*. Daily newspaper circulation figures show that there was a tremendous increase in circulation between 1990 and 1995, even surpassing the pre-1988 figures when more newspapers were available. However, the English newspaper circulation makes up only a small percentage of the versions in Myanmar language. The approximate circulation is as follows: *The New Light of Myanmar* (English)—24,000+; *Kyemon* (Myanmar)—180,000+; and *Myanma Alin* (Myanmar)—220,000+. The base rate for newspaper advertising is US$15 per inch per column. Thus, the base rate for a half-page advertisement in *The New Light of Myanmar* is about US$1,100, and a half-page advertisement in the tabloid-sized *Kyemon* is about US$700. Discounted rates are available from the official advertising agents.

There is a wide range of local reading material. Materials published by the government-controlled Printing and Publishing Corporation include *Forward Magazine*, *People's Army Magazine*, *Workers Journal*, *Shwe Thway Journal* (comics and features for the young people), texts, schoolbooks, and many local magazines. The Myanmar people and visitors read many magazines, especially as the TV viewing time is limited. There are about forty monthly magazines ranging from children's magazines to magazines devoted to selective translations of *Time* and *Newsweek* magazines. The majority of publishers are private. The magazine publishers are often flexible and willing to discuss various promotional ideas. All printers and publishers are required to register annually with the General Administration Department, Ministry of Home Affairs, for permission to operate. They also have to submit regular information on the books and magazines published to the Registration Office. Registered books are classified under nine subjects, and authors wishing to publish books have to obtain permission.

Print advertising is abundant in local magazines, although both print and paper quality are poor. For newspapers and magazines, the printing is acceptable, but the paper used is often of inferior quality. Color is available for both newspaper and magazine advertisements. However, magazines provide great flexibility in terms of color and space and seem to be favored by the smaller local advertisers.

The Motion Picture Corporation is the state agency responsible for the operation of cinemas in major cities as well as for the procurement of films. There are over twenty cinemas in Yangon showing local films and a potpourri of English, Indian, Chinese, and Japanese movies. It is a popular entertainment medium; a large cinema complex that can show five movies simultaneously has recently opened. In addition, locally produced video movies are equally popular, if not more popular, than cinema movies.

In Myanmar, billboards are a popular and effective advertising medium, especially in strategic locations. Before Myanmar adopted open market economy in 1988, these were almost nonexistent in Yangon, but today, billboards are present in major towns, especially in Yangon, Mandalay, and Taungyi. Billboards can serve as a year-round awareness generator on major roads and intercity "highways." Although billboard advertising is highly effective, the cost of it is phenomenal for foreign brands, as rates for advertising foreign brands are much higher than those charged for local brands. Billboard advertising is available at specific sites in the cities in a wide variety of sizes. The jurisdiction of these sites falls under city municipalities. While most of the billboards are in Myanmar language, some foreign products and services, such as airlines, beer, cigarettes, soft drinks, and films, are advertised in English. One disadvantage of billboard advertising is that it attracts unwanted attention from foreign tourists and journalists. This scares many foreign advertisers (especially from Western countries) who do not wish to broadcast their presence in Myanmar to the outside world, for fear of attracting consumer boycotts in their home markets. For instance, one billboard in a prime location in Yangon was left vacant for some time, because a foreign advertiser decided to withdraw its ad and kept the spot vacant for the rest of the prepaid term. Another similar case occurred when a distributor of an alcohol brand had the lights of its billboard switched off at night in order to avoid unwanted attention from foreign tourists.

An important factor to note is the overall lack of regulation on advertising claims. This has created many advertising opportunities for advertisers of products ranging from tobacco to alcohol to medicinal products to skincare products, who face restrictions in other countries. In some cases, the product benefits are simply exaggerated or consumers take the claims too literally or seriously. For example, an up-market international brand of bottled water is believed to give the drinker an extraordinarily beautiful complexion. Similarly, an eye cream is believed to wipe out black circles around the eyes overnight, and gassy soft drinks are sometimes thought to be good for those who suffer from stomach indigestion.

Other popular promotional activities include sports sponsorships (the most popular being soccer and golf), beauty contests or pageants, festival participation, and celebrity endorsements. Most of the events tend to be seasonal, to take advantage of the cool dry season (October to February) and to avoid the monsoon or the wet season (July to September). Some of the important festivals include the New Year Water Festival (Thingyan) in April and the Light Festival (Thadingyut) in October.

Sales promotion is one of the most popular and widely used promotional tools for two important reasons. The first reason is that Burmese consumers respond very well to sales promotions such as "buy one, get one free," free gifts, and lucky draws. Lucky draws give out very expensive prizes including gold coins, cars, and even overseas trips. Competitions, however, are so popular that they have been somewhat overused. One new promotional tool is what is known as SPGs (Sales Promotion Girls), who are used extensively to promote international cigarette brands. SPGs go around to places like tea shops (where men gather) and persuade men to buy cigarettes from them.

The second reason relates to the isolationist stance taken by the Western governments and human rights campaigners on the Myanmar government. Due to the imposition of U.S. trade sanctions on Myanmar, many advertisers do not want to expose their advertising to the outside world. In this respect, TV advertising scores higher than billboard advertising, as foreign tourists or journalists are less likely to tune into Myanmar TV's dull programming. Sales promotions, on the other hand, are considered to be best because of their "below the line" nature and the fact that they can be launched at strategic moments, such as festivals. Furthermore, sales promotions are particularly useful in out of the way towns where there is a lack of infrastructure for other kinds of advertising.

CONCLUSION

There is little doubt that potential for marketing of foreign products exists in Myanmar with its relatively large population and attractive location. Initially, however, consumer markets may have to be confined to the major cities. Certainly, the Myanmar people are aware of many Western brands and are anxious to purchase them, provided the price is within their means. In the early 1990s, the United Nations Development Programme worked out a Human Development Index (HDI) combining life expectancy, education, literacy, and GDP to show how well people live in 130 different countries. According to the HDI ranking, Myanmar, with a life expectancy at birth of 61.8 years, adult literacy rate of 80.6 percent, 2.5 mean years of schooling, and an adjusted real GDP per capita of PPP$ 659 rates an HDI of 0.390 and ranks number 123 among 197 countries (Tun 1995). The index ranked Myanmar only just behind Indonesia and Vietnam and much further ahead than India, Laos, and Cambodia. In fact, many businessmen we have spoken with consider Myanmar to have as good a potential, although less developed than, Vietnam.

On the downside, managers need to be aware of the risk factors involved in marketing in Myanmar. There exists a host of uncertainties ranging from:

- The risk of consumer boycotts in home markets
- Lack of market intelligence and other consumer information
- Inflation
- Profit repatriation and payment for goods from overseas because the Myanmar currency (kyats) is nonconvertible
- Handling of a three-tier currency system (the official exchange rate, the black market rate, and the FEC)
- "Unfair" competition from black marketeers and border traders
- Dealings with the bureaucracy and ever-changing laws and regulations
- Poor infrastructure
- Relatively expensive advertising costs

The interested marketers are advised to familiarize themselves with various business and social issues involved in marketing to the Myanmar people. Despite the presence of many private companies and enterprises engaged in various kinds of trade, it is obvious that much remains to be done. Investment by foreign organizations so far has been small when compared to the available resources and investment potential. The SEA region has taken a pragmatic approach toward Myanmar with the hope that economic development will lead to other social and political improvements. In particular, in welcoming Myanmar into their forum, the members of ASEAN have indicated their faith in the nation's future. If the political situation remains stable and continues to develop along democratic lines, and, especially, if mineral deposits such as oil are discovered by the major foreign oil companies, then the life of the people will become much better, and consumer marketing in the Western sense will blossom. Hopefully, economic development will provide an opportunity for a peaceful transition and prosperity.

NOTE

This is a revised and expanded version of the earlier article by May Lwin and Anthony Pecotich, "Myanmar: From an Isolated Past to a Golden Future?" in *Marketing and Consumer Behavior in East and South-East Asia*, ed. A. Pecotich and C. Shultz II (Sydney: McGraw-Hill, 1998), pp. 493–520.

REFERENCES

Asian Development Bank. 2003. *Asian Development Outlook 2003*. Hong Kong: Oxford University Press (China) Ltd.
Asiaweek. 1995. October 13: 78.
Bin, Hee Jun, Kenneth Kwok, Kok Chiang Lau, Joon Boo Then, and Kuan Sze Yap. 1996. "Marketing in Myanmar." In *Business Opportunities in Myanmar* (Nanyang Business Report Series), ed. Teck Meng Tan, Low Aik Meng, John J. Williams, and Ivan P. Polunin, pp. 217–230. Englewood Cliffs, NJ: Prentice Hall.
Burma Trade Guide. 1983. Rangoon: Trade Information Service, Directorate of Trade, with the assistance of International Trade Centre UNCTAD/GATT and the United Nations Development Programme (UNDP).
Business Asia. 1996. "Inexorably, the Tide Turns," 28: 24.
———. 1997. "Country Watchlist," 29.
Business Indochina. 1996. "Special Issue on Myanmar." Hong Kong: Indochina Project Management Ltd.
Demaine, Harvey. 1994. "Myanmar: Physical and Social Geography." In *The Far East and Australasia*, 25th ed., ed. L. Daniel, pp. 611–33. London: Europa Publications.
The Economist. 1996. "More Repression in Myanmar," 341: 17.
———. 1997. "Cook's Orders," September 6: 344.
———. 2002. "Myanmar: The Black Hole of Yangon," March 28: 28.
———. 2003. "Myanmar: Investing in a Misruled Land," April 10: 30.
The Economist Intelligence Unit (EIU). 1995. *EIU Country Profile—Myanmar,* pp. 1–71. London: EIU.
Finch, J. 1997. *East Asian Executive Reports,* 19: 9–13.
Fulman, R. 1997. *Pensions and Investments,* 25: 38.
Global Investor. 1995. "Burma a Pariah," 84: 7–8.
"Green Light Given for Myanmar's First Offshore Development." 1995. *Oil and Gas Journal,* 93: 28–30.
Hirsh, Michael, and Ron Moreau. 1995. "Risky Business," *Newsweek Magazine,* June 19: 10.
Humphreys, J. 1996. *International Business,* 9: 48.
Insight Guide to Burma. 1994. Hong Kong: APA Publications.
Investing in Myanmar. 1994. The Union of Myanmar Foreign Investment Commission, p. 2.
Khaing, Mi Mi. 1994. "Myanmar Character and Customs." *Golden Myanmar* (Uniforce Co. Ltd.), 1 (4): 3.
Khin, Maung Kyi. 1994. "Myanmar: Will Forever Flow the Ayeyerwady?" In *Southeast Asian Affairs*, ed. Chan Heng Chee. Singapore: Institute of Southeast Asian Studies.
Kyaw, Thane, ed. 1995. "Golden Opportunities for Investment in Myanmar." *Golden Myanmar* (Uniforce Co. Ltd.), 2 (4): 5.

Lwin, May. 1990. *Myanmar: Coming Out of Its Shell*. New York: Ogilvy & Mather Worldwide.

———. 1997. "The Effect of an Audio Stimulus: Accents in English Language on Cross-Cultural Consumer Response to Advertising." Unpublished doctoral thesis, National University of Singapore.

Lwin, May, and L.L. Lan. 2000. "DBI: Doing Business in Myanmar." *Thunderbird International Business Review* 43 (2; March): 269–87.

Lwin, May, and Anthony Pecotich. 1998. "Myanmar: From an Isolated Past to a Golden Future?" In *Marketing and Consumer Behaviour in East and South-East Asia*, ed. A. Pecotich and C. Shultz II, pp. 493–520. Sydney: McGraw-Hill.

Masaki, H. 1997. *Japan Times Weekly International Edition,* 37: 10–11.

Maung, Mya. 1991. *The Burma Road to Poverty*. New York: Praeger.

Moreau, Ron. 1995. "Mandalay: The Next Chinese Province?" *Newsweek,* June 19: 13.

Myanma Dhana. 1994. "Top Ten Survey," May (47): 10.

Naw, Angeline. 1994. "Hotel Fever," *Today Magazine,* April: 55.

Pe, Win. 1996. *Dos and Don'ts in Myanmar*. Bangkok: Amarin Printing and Publishing.

Review of the Financial, Economic and Social Conditions for 1993/94. 1994. Yangon: The Government of the Union of Myanmar, Ministry of National Planning and Economic Development, Central Statistical Organization.

Schermerhorn, J.R.J. 1997. *Bangkok Post,* May 23: 9–10.

Statistical Abstract 1995. 1995. Yangon: The Government of the Union of Myanmar, Ministry of National Planning and Economic Development, Central Statistical Organization.

Statistical Yearbook 2000. 2000. Yangon: The Government of the Union of Myanmar, Ministry of National Planning and Economic Development, Central Statistical Organization.

Than, Mya. 1995. " Economic Outlook, Myanmar 1994–95." In *Regional Outlook Southeast Asia 1994–95*, ed. Chan Heng Chee. Singapore: Institute of Southeast Asian Studies.

Thein, Mya, and Mya Than. 1995. "Transitional Economy of Myanmar: Performance, Issues and Problems." In *Asian Transitional Economies—Challenges and Prospects for Reform and Transformation*, ed. Seiji Finch Naya and Joseph L.H. Tan, pp. 211–61. Singapore: Institute of Southeast Asian Studies.

Thein, Myat. 1996. "Socio-Economic and Cultural Background of Myanmar." In *Business Opportunities in Myanmar*, ed. Teck Meng Tan, Low Aik Meng, John J. Williams and Ivan P. Polunin, pp. 17–24. Englewood Cliffs, NJ: Prentice Hall.

Thein, V. 2001. "Book Review." In *Economic Development of Burma, a Vision and a Strategy: A Study by Burmese Economists*, ed. Khin Maung Kyi, Ronald Findlay, R.M. Sundrum, Mya Maung, Myo Nyunt, Zaw Oo, et al. Olof Palme International Center, Stockholm, Sweden: Singapore University Press; *Journal of Asian Business*, 17.1: 113–15.

Tun, Thet. 1995. "International and Regional Perspective for the Development of Myanmar." *Myanmar Business and Economic Review* 1.1 (5; May–June).

United Nations. 2000. *World Population Prospects: The 2000 revision.*

Vokes, Richard. 1997. "Myanmar: Economy." In *The Far East and Australasia,* 27th ed., ed. L. Daniel, pp. 644–55. London: Europa Publications.

World Bank. 2003. *World Development Indicators 2003*. CD-ROM. Washington, DC; aggregates calculated for the Human Development Report Office by the World Bank.

CHAPTER 12

<hr>

NEW ZEALAND

Consumers in Their Market Environment—Profiles and Predictions

ROGER MARSHALL, MIKE POTTER, AND CHRISTINA KWAI CHOI LEE

OVERVIEW

New Zealand is a small, island country, in the southernmost part of the South Pacific region. It is a country dominated by its British heritage, the multiethnic nature of its population, its larger, more powerful northern neighbors, as well as by its geographical isolation. Marketers coming into the region will find the country is distinctly different from any other, even her closest neighbor, Australia. This chapter provides an overview of the New Zealand environment and a profile of the New Zealand consumer. First, the economic, demographic, and cultural environments are discussed, then implications are drawn from the trends noted, in order to provide a guide for potential marketers.

THE ECONOMIC ENVIRONMENT

New Zealand has, historically, provided a stable, small, democratic commercial arena in which market forces have been able to function. This has proved both advantageous and disadvantageous, in that the country is generally attractive to investors, but that the small, open economy has been very susceptible to external shocks. It is mainly for this reason that there have, from time to time, been swings toward protectionism. The latest and most powerful protectionist lobby dominated the nation's politics and economy for many years, up to the late 1970s. During this time, New Zealand's international trade consisted largely of unprocessed agricultural products, sold mostly to the United Kingdom. Inefficient import-substitution activities were supported, and the national debt figures began to climb alarmingly.

Although strongly democratic in orientation, New Zealand has always had a "first-past-the-post" party-based voting system, which gives full powers to one of the two major political parties for a three-year term. Traditionally, this political system has tended toward a stable, strong government. It was the agriculture-based, traditional, right-wing National Party that led the protectionist movement mentioned above, while the left-wing Labor Party was dedicated to the maintenance of the welfare state established by Labor Party in the immediate postwar (1945–1950) years. Ironically, it was the Labor Party that, when it gained power in the 1980s, began massive restructuring to make New Zealand a more competitive economy. This restructuring embraced the privatization (or, at least, the corporatization) of many public utilities, including the welfare-state establishments of health and education. The irony of this is even more poignant if we consider that when the National Party regained power and continued the economic restructuring process during the second half of the decade, this led inevitably to a massive loss of the collective bargaining power of the labor unions.

New Zealand's political system has undergone dramatic change, however, following a national referendum in 1993, after which the country abandoned the "first-past-the-post" system in favor of proportional representation. This system came into effect in October 1996. Since that time, it has been harder for elected governments to push through strong, radical changes, because the coalitions that have formed have not had the same mandate of power accorded the victor in the two-party system. The inability to make radical, rapid change in the near future is rather more a comfort than a worry in short-run economic terms, as the present economic direction seems successful and will probably be continued. It is only in the reaction to external shocks or internal pressure groups that the new form of governance could, in the longer run, be less positive for the economy than the old.

New Zealand is now in the midst of a long, steady economic recovery. Twin economic shocks were sustained when England joined the European Common Market—the traditional outlet for New Zealand's vital agricultural exports consequently disappeared—and when intense pressure was exerted on the country to remove protectionist measures. Both have led to a trade (and attitudinal) realignment toward the Asia-Pacific region. The transition of New Zealand from a Euro-focused to an Asia-focused economy, from unprocessed agricultural exports to technological, processed agricultural and light manufactured exports, involving such significant and painful restructuring, is seen by most to have been successfully managed to date.

Gross domestic product (GDP) growth over recent years peaked at 6 percent in 1966, but a number of negative factors have come into play since then, including the recent Asian crisis, drought, tax increases, rising import prices, and tightened monetary policy. In spite of these, the indicators for the New Zealand economy are generally positive, and it is still predicted to average between 2 percent and 3 percent in 2002–4 (Reserve Bank 2001).

Over the next few years, the largest contributors to annual growth are expected to be forestry and logging, financial and insurance services, tourism, communications, construction, nonmetallic mineral products, and electricity. Generally, the lower-performing sectors tend to be those producing commodity-type goods (agriculture, basic metals, mining, and fishing), while higher-performing sectors are those with a higher value-added content. This trend is indicative of a country moving from an agricultural-based economy to a manufacturing- and service-based economy. A cost of this planned sectoral evolution is that New Zealand's longer-term track record of socioeconomic policies toward privatization and private enterprise is now being tempered with certain short-term measures that are diluting and delaying that process, and this has consequences for the much-needed investor confidence to stimulate and support diversification and growth.

New Zealand has had operating surpluses from 1994–95 (NZ$2.6 billion) to 2000–1 ($1.4 billion), largely as the result of an overhauled taxation system, significant growth in both company taxation and source deductions, and a nominal decline in financial net expenditure. Economic observers, however, suggest that these figures belie the real financial position of the government, due to planned capital expenditure, signaled contributions to the Treasurer's Superannuation Fund, and the refinancing of Air New Zealand in 2001, following the collapse of the airlines investment in Ansett Australia. This level of fiscal commitment means that any further expenditure will need to be financed by debt. Despite this, the economy is expected to grow modestly as a result of the capital expenditure program, which includes expenditure on core infrastructure components such as health and transportation.

Trading

The volume of exports of goods and services rose by 7.4 percent in the 2000 calendar year, assisted by a weak New Zealand dollar, which reached a historic low of 39 cents to the U.S. dollar in October 2000. This growth is expected to weaken somewhat in the short run, due to declining world commodity prices and the continued general slowdown in the world economy. The major contributors to export returns have been dairy products, wool, basic metals, noncommodity manufacturing goods, and tourism. Optimism among exporters is high, particularly in the agricultural sector, which has been buoyed by strong returns and predictions of positive outcomes from trade negotiations. Tourism is expected to continue to be an important driver of growth, although annual visitor numbers are expected to be down 3 percent to 10 percent in 2001–2. The dramatic decline in world tourism that stemmed from the September 11, 2001 terrorist attacks on the United States have been offset to a point in New Zealand, which is seen by many to be a safe destination for tourists and a viable alternative for Asians frightened to travel to the United States for holidays. Increasing costs have slowed the growth in imports of goods and services to 1 percent in the year ending 2000 (National Bank 2001).

Finance

New Zealand's Reserve Bank plays the important role of adjusting interest rates so as to maintain sufficient levels of growth in competitive sectors. It is a delicate operation, as it must balance the need to attract foreign investment with the need for economic growth and an inflation target of less than 2 percent, without allowing the economy to overheat resulting in direct government assistance to struggling sectors.

The 2001–2 global slowdown has been, in part, evaded by New Zealand, thanks to the Reserve Bank reducing interest rates, a low New Zealand dollar, and solid income returns, particularly in agriculture. These factors have contributed to reduced pressure on inflation, which is predicted to remain less than 2 percent in 2002 and 2003. Despite a downturn in world commodity prices and pressure on employment, New Zealanders are generally optimistic toward investment in the domestic economy, particularly in the construction industry, where building completions increased 4.3 percent in the September Quarter 2001 (National Bank 2001).

Regional Differences

It is still too early to fully predict the consequences of September 11, 2001, and the threat of international terrorism for the New Zealand economy. Sectors most at risk to further downturns in global demand, however, include those strongly dependent on global trade and international commodity prices. Agriculture, tourism, commodity manufacturing, transportation, forestry, and fishing are all important sectors that are considered high risk at this time (National Bank 2001). As a result, the regions that rely on these sectors for growth are most likely to be affected. Softer primary-sector incomes will weigh on Northland and Southland, although, interestingly enough, Southland was demonstrating the highest level of growth of any region in June 2001 (5.5 percent), largely as a result of innovative policies by local government to sponsor free education and create job opportunities within the region. The Nelson-Marlborough and Bay of Plenty areas are also at risk, through their strong orientations toward tourism and primary-sector exports; yet both have grown substantially through migration over the past decade. The areas of the country seen to be least influenced by a global downturn are Auckland (because of continued inward migration and domestic growth), Taranaki (gas and oil production), Manawatu (education and defense activity), and Wellington (government activity).

Auckland is by far the largest city in New Zealand, the most vigorous business center, and the strongest in the growing service sector (employment is expected to come through increased tourism from, inter alia, the country's first casino, and from running further America's Cup yacht races in 2002–3). For the country overall, growth, of course, continues to be heavily dependent—in a regional sense—on the success of specific, local investments already made. Hence, the West Coast (with the Reefton Gold Mine), Southland (with the Tiwai Point smelter and the Rayonier fibreboard plant in Matura), and Gisborne (with a Juken Nissho fiberboard plant) are heavily dependent on their success for ongoing regional growth. Provinces without such specific investments are more reliant on growth from agricultural products and, possibly, tourism, and are thus likely to experience much slower growth in both employment and exports.

Employment

Employment has been a key economic, social, and political factor for the country for the last three decades. The immediate effect of the depression that struck the country after the British realignment to Europe was widespread unemployment. This had a strong impact on the financially strapped social services; these services have been deliberately pruned in recent years, and more public money has been spent on job-creation schemes and retraining exercises.

The reduction of unemployment to the current, more acceptable, levels has been a major achievement. The unemployment rate as of March 1994 was 9 percent, in December 2001, it was 5.5 percent. One of the key devices used to achieve economic efficiency in labor markets—required to support New Zealand's economic recovery—was the Employment Contracts Act (ECA) of 1991. This act effectively curtailed the collective bargaining power of organized labor and created a more flexible employment environment that was advantageous to business in a general sense. The Labor/Alliance Coalition Government of 1999 altered the ECA, however, restrengthening the influence of trade unions in wage negotiations. In addition, the same Labor/Alliance government awarded a significant rise in the minimum wage, renationalized accident compensation insurance, ceased state asset sales, and increased the marginal tax rate for incomes over NZ$60,000 to 39 percent.

Income

Rising employment, combined with moderate wage increases and a significant rise in the minimum wage in 2000, has led to a growth in household incomes. Household nominal disposable income grew by almost 6 percent in 2000–1, well in excess of the 4.3 percent consumption expenditure growth. Large tax cuts, previously announced in 1996–97, have been largely responsible for this predicted growth, as they were intended by the government to provide an internal stimulus to growth without fueling import-led inflation.

The Residential Sector

Housing activity collapsed over 2000 and early 2001, but dwelling authorizations have now firmed from that trough. Low interest rates and improving migration are conducive to a solid upturn in 2002–3. Growth in the residential real estate market has not been evident in all parts of New Zealand but is manifest chiefly in the main cities, Auckland, in particular. With the current trend toward inner-city living, many office blocks have been converted into apartments, although the New Zealand

Table 12.1

New Zealand Retail Sales (in NZ$ million)

Store type	1995	1996	1997	1998	1999	2000
Food retailing	7,758	7,878	8,253	8,672	9.086	9,534
Footwear	253	246	224	227	229	242
Clothing and soft goods	1,480	1,441	1,384	1,391	1,393	1,501
Furniture and floor coverings	997	957	1,001	1,044	1,071	1,134
Appliance retailing	1,348	1,368	1,325	1,271	1,307	1,365
Hardware	768	732	810	807	766	775
Chemists	997	1,073	1,103	1,254	1,211	1,272
Department	1,835	1,839	1,870	1,952	2,161	2,421
Recreational goods	1,346	1,414	1,542	1,609	1,592	1,654
Accommodation, hotels, and liquor	3,320	3,372	3,487	3,524	3,573	3,641
Cafes, restaurants, and takeouts	1,940	2,247	2,414	2,529	2,596	2,896
Personal and household services	931	964	1,020	1,065	1,079	1,172
Other	2,098	2,092	2,012	2,038	2,083	2,273
Subtotal	25,071	25,623	26,445	27,383	28,148	29,866
Motor vehicle retailing	6,663	7,196	6,872	6,040	5,833	6,071
Motor vehicle services	4,654	5,015	5,227	5,369	5,325	5,796
All stores total	36,388	37,834	38,544	38,793	39,306	41,732
Per head of population by total	10,061	10,301	10,337	10,286	10,351	10,903

Source: New Zealand Official Yearbook 2000 (Wellington: Statistics New Zealand, 2000).

dream of a suburban house remains. Nevertheless, the trend toward inner-city living is steady, as inner-city living is attractive to investors, young professionals without children, and older couples.

The Retail Sector

As previously mentioned, retailing is fairly buoyant in New Zealand at this time, with consumer spending set to rise still further in the near future. The nature of shopping has changed, both in concert with the economy and with the new internationalism experienced by the country as a whole. Economic pressure has forced retailers into competitive innovation, and often into out-right price competition, all of which work to the consumer's advantage. The entry of overseas competitors such as FAL, the Australian retail food giant, has also added to the intense competition in this sector. Table 12.1 shows that supermarket sales are still growing—at the expense of smaller food retailers, whose sales are being further eroded as pharmacists and gas stations continue to encroach on their traditional, convenience-type general merchandise territory.

The country's most successful retailer, The Warehouse, is a Wal-Mart-like operation claiming one square foot of retail space for every New Zealander (almost four million square meters across seventy stores), with the largest retail distribution system in Australasia. Australian category killer chains have also seen success, making life difficult for the likes of broader department stores such as Kmart (which withdrew from the market in 2001) and the traditional Farmers department store, which have struggled of late to compete.

As in other developed nations, information technology has allowed retailers unprecedented opportunities to understand their customers, and local companies have not been slow to take advantage. Similarly, the style of retailing has developed to satisfy not only local customers with increasingly sophisticated tastes, but also the many shopping-oriented Asian tourists. Perhaps as a consequence of the increased participation of women in the workforce, retail shopping hours have been extended. Indeed, weekend shopping—not so long ago an impossibility even in the large cities—is now a major leisure activity. Legislation in 2002 extended trading hours to enable shopping on many public holidays, such as Easter and Labor weekend in October.

THE DEMOGRAPHIC ENVIRONMENT

Population

Population growth over the past decade has been steady at just under 1 percent annual growth rate, relatively faster than that experienced in the 1980s. The volatility in this rate is mainly due to migration. The 1991 Amendment to the Immigration Act allowed a target number of new residents to be set; this is currently set at 25,000 persons per annum. Although, of course, there are outflows, permanent and long-term arrivals are expected to exceed departures over the next five years. By the year 2031, the present population of 3.8 million is projected to increase to 4.5 million (assuming medium fertility and mortality, and a net migration of 5,000). Growth rates are expected to slow steadily in the future.

Although predominantly European, New Zealand is a multiethnic society, with the subcultures consisting mainly of Maoris (15.1 percent of the total population), Pacific Islanders (5.0 percent), and Asians (Chinese 2.2 percent, Indians 1.2 percent). The influx of Asian immigrants over the past five years has made this a significant group in the community; between 1986 and 1991, the Chinese population increased by 92 percent, and between 1991 and 1996, this group grew by a further 97 percent, or 12 percent per year.

The population of New Zealand follows a pattern typical of maturing societies, with an increasing number of people in the older age group. This is not, however, true for the Maori and Pacific Island subpopulations, with age distributions that are less mature (see Figure 12.1). The younger age group, those under fifteen years, has shrunk from 27.8 percent of the population in 1980 to 23.8 percent in 1999. In the next twenty years, the older age group will move toward retirement age, putting more stress on the social system. Department of Statistics figures indicate that the dependency ratio (the number of dependent people of ages up to fourteen and ages sixty-five and above for each working-age person between the ages of fifteen and sixty-four) will double from eighteen per one hundred in 1999 to forty-three per one hundred by 2040. In 1999, the median age of the population was thirty-four years; this is set to increase to forty-one by the year 2031 and to forty-six by the year 2101.

Household Size

The growth rate for households in New Zealand is very slow. The total number of households in New Zealand grew 8.4 percent between 1991 and 1996. Significant growth was recorded for nonfamily households, which increased by 31 percent, while for sole-person households, the increase was 8.7 percent (see Table 12.2). Although families are still an important unit in New Zealand, the composition of a "typical" family has changed—families are smaller than in the past, there are more families without children, and one in four families with children are headed by a single parent.

Figure 12.1   **New Zealand Age Distribution by Ethnicity**

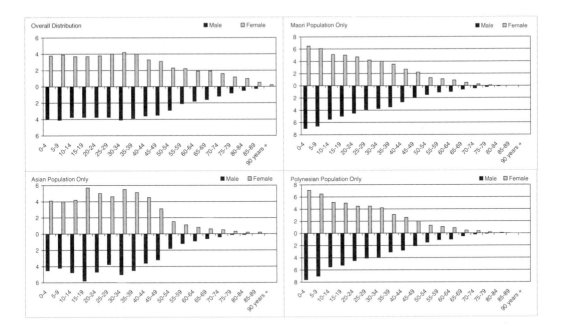

Source: New Zealand Department of Statistics 2000.

Table 12.2

Household Types in New Zealand, 1991–1996

Household type	1991	Percent of total	1996	Percent of total
One family only	775,557	65.9	803,994	63.0
One family plus other people	66,387	5.6	78,909	6.2
Two or more families	19,818	1.7	32,193	2.5
Other multiperson household	68,820	5.8	66,360	5.2
One-person household	235,986	20.0	256,572	20.1
Not elsewhere classified	11,097	1.0	38,304	3.0

Source: New Zealand Official Yearbook 2000 (Wellington: Statistics New Zealand, 2000).

Housing continues to be the most significant item of household expenditure (19 percent of household spending in 1997–98), closely followed by transportation (18 percent) and food (17 percent), which are closely followed by health, education, insurance, and other services. The percentage of households with major amenities and access to entertainment services continues to rise. In 1997–98, 33 percent of households had a computer, 21 percent had at least one cell phone, and 20 percent had subscriber television decoders.

Sales of take-out foods and restaurant meals indicate a growing trend in consumption of food outside the home, from NZ$1.05 billion in 1986 to NZ$2.25 billion in 1996 and NZ$2.27 billion in 2000. This is a result of the increase in the number of double-income families, time pressures, and affordability of food outside the home. The influence of the overseas trend of cafés and breakfast bars is also evident, especially in the major cities of New Zealand.

THE CULTURAL ENVIRONMENT

New Zealand has been described in the past as an "England of the South," but this is even less true today than it was previously. Although it is dominantly English, the earliest settlers were, of course, the Maori people. There were also Scottish, Dutch, French, and Scandinavian settlers; several areas in New Zealand still recognize their non-English roots and have a distinctly non-English flavor.

It is true that the Maori were not considered New Zealanders in the early recorded history of the country, but this has changed significantly over the last few decades. Toward the turn of the twentieth century, at the cessation of the Maori Wars, the Treaty of Waitangi was drawn up between Queen Victoria's New Zealand representative and a consortium of Maori chiefs. The Treaty was designed to safeguard Maori interests from exploitation. As a result of legal action, it has recently been re-recognized, and a series of lawsuits have brought large settlements (mostly in terms of land, but also cash and shares) to various Maori tribes. The question of a Maori identity within the national identity is being vigorously pursued at this time by both Maori and non-Maori New Zealanders.

Another potent agent for cultural change has been the economic imperative that has turned New Zealand increasingly toward Asia for new trading partners. Consequently, New Zealand businesspeople travel more frequently than ever before within the region, both inbound and out-bound Asian tourism has mushroomed, and there have been significant increases in Asian immigration. This has all led to the development of a less ethnocentric New Zealander, and a more cosmopolitan shopping and living environment, particularly in the larger cities.

Women in New Zealand

There is an increase in women's participation in the workforce overall, and a corresponding deferral of childbearing to a later age. In 1994, for the first time ever, more women than men graduated from New Zealand universities. The percentage of professional women in the workforce has increased in recent years, with women now comprising over 54 percent of professionals. Women, therefore, are an important force in the marketplace, both as consumers and as a major influence in family decisions. This recognition of total equality is also reflected in their direct political influence over the country. In the years 2000 and 2001, women held the roles of governor general, prime minister, leader of the opposition, and chief justice. Moreover, a high percentage of single-parent families is headed by females.

It is important that marketers do not neglect to target women in their product advertising, even

Figure 12.2   **Highest Educational Attainments of New Zealand School Leavers**

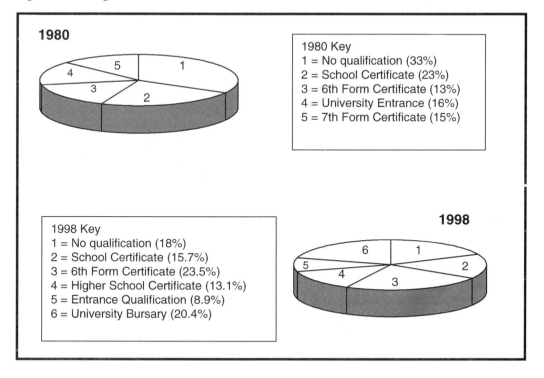

1980

1980 Key
1 = No qualification (33%)
2 = School Certificate (23%)
3 = 6th Form Certificate (13%)
4 = University Entrance (16%)
5 = 7th Form Certificate (15%)

1998 Key
1 = No qualification (18%)
2 = School Certificate (15.7%)
3 = 6th Form Certificate (23.5%)
4 = Higher School Certificate (13.1%)
5 = Entrance Qualification (8.9%)
6 = University Bursary (20.4%)

1998

Source: New Zealand Ministry of Education.

for product categories not traditionally targeted toward women. The increase in the level of education attained by this gender group and the emergence of active consumer-rights groups have also brought about an increasing awareness of consumer rights in terms of quality, service, sales, and purchases of goods and services.

Education

New Zealand has a strong tradition of accessible education (see Figure 12.2) and follows the British model. One repercussion of changes in the government's competitive philosophy and policy is that schools have been given more autonomy to manage their own affairs. This has meant, though, that different standards of equipment and teaching have emerged for schools located in suburbs with differing degrees of wealth among their population. Thus, the quality of education depends, to a point, on the financial status of parents. However, teenagers are being encouraged to stay in school to receive further training because of the government's stated intention not to provide unemployment benefits to persons under eighteen years of age. This move is in response to the growing need for a more skilled and educated labor force.

Similar changes are being made to the tertiary system. The open-door university policy of the 1960s and 1970s no longer pertains, and there are clear differences in the standards of degrees awarded by various universities—often reflected in the stringency, or otherwise, of entry requirements.

Social-Class Structure

In the 1950s, Keith Sinclair (1959) expressed the sentiment that New Zealand is a relatively classless society. But this has long been forgotten—although New Zealand's society is egalitarian in nature, the society is becoming more and more stratified. As with other Western cultures, a person's social class is measured in terms of economic success—that is, the amount of wealth and property owned, either inherited or through one's occupation. Although this is not directly related to any hierarchy of social class, Statistics New Zealand uses the International Standard Classification of Occupations (ISCO) to provide information on the different sectors of New Zealand. The most prominent work on socioeconomic status measurement is that of Elley and Irving (1976; 1985), who have produced an index of occupational status using census data based upon incomes and education levels of the people in various occupations. This categorizes a person into the upper, middle, or lower socioeconomic class. However, New Zealand is predominantly middle class—Johnston (1983) notes that more than 54 percent of New Zealanders can be categorized as part of this class.

The significance of social class in consumer behavior has been questioned (Coleman 1983), and interest in this issue has waxed and waned over the past thirty years. In any event, the importance of social class as a marketing tool will continue to increase in New Zealand, given both the current and predicted social and economic environments. Social class is related to attitudinal differences. Martineau (1958), and later Coleman (1983), proposed that social class reflects psychological differences in consumers and is, therefore, better, in some circumstances at least, as a predictor of behavior than of income. Lawson and Winzar's (1994) study on social class in New Zealand and Australia shows that there are real and significant attitudinal differences between social classes in New Zealand. In this study, social class was measured using the Elley and Irving scale. The authors found that lower classes were oriented to the shorter term, for example, they were less career motivated and less focused on the local community. Table 12.3 presents the attitudinal differences among differing social classes in New Zealand, based on the findings of Lawson and Winzar (1994) that families in the lower social class are more conservative about roles within the family. In the view of this class, the father should be "boss," and the woman's place is at home. This finding is confirmed by Lee (1994), who notes that fathers in the lower social class have more influence in family decisions when their wives do not have paid employment outside the home.

THE MARKETING ENVIRONMENT

Distribution

The geography of the country makes trade awkward. Although it is impossible to be more than 75 kilometers from the sea anywhere in New Zealand, its five main centers are strung across two large islands, from Auckland in the north to Dunedin some 1,358 road kilometers to the south. More than half of the population lives in the relatively industrialized northern half of the North Island. Other than the capital (Wellington) at the southern extremity of the North Island, and the South Island cities of Christchurch and Dunedin, the rest of the country is fundamentally rural; hence, distributional possibilities are constrained.

A recurring theme running through this chapter has been the increasing competitiveness in all facets of New Zealand business life, and the transport sector is no exception. Rail services for freight are excellent, along the north–south axis at least, and the roads and road services are well developed. Rail and road compete directly on most major routes, and this keeps service and price strategies to the fore. Similarly, air services have moved away from a monopoly situation, in

Table 12.3

Attitudes of New Zealand Social Classes

Social class category	Attitudinal differences
Upper	• Feel less alienated in society than middle and lower classes • Are more likely to regard themselves as leaders • Are less conservative • Feel less attracted to simplicity and more drawn to sophistication • Attach higher importance to education • Attach less importance to children's obedience
Middle	• Are less concerned with appearance and fashion than upper and lower classes
Lower	• Are less career minded • Are more likely than middle and upper classes to be "do-it-yourselfers" • Are more interested in local, community events than national or international events • Exhibit more traditional attitudes toward roles within the family

Source: Rob Lawson and Hume Winzar, "Social Class and Consumer Behavior in Australia and New Zealand," paper presented at the New Zealand Marketing Educators Conference, Hamilton, New Zealand, November (1994).

which the government-backed national carrier provided the only regular internal freight and passenger services, to a competitive situation, in which two major international carriers compete in an open market.

The major cost problem associated with transportation comes back to the population density and the small size of the country. Hence, at this time, and under some conditions, it is cheaper to airfreight goods from Auckland to Sydney (Australia) than from Auckland to Dunedin. The Cook Strait acts as an impediment to the flow of vehicles and trains between the North and South Islands. Even though ferries ply the route regularly, waiting is inevitable at peak demand periods, and there has been a long history of industrial action plaguing the ferry services. However, with the introduction of two new fast ferries and the threat of further competition, this situation has improved.

Pricing

At various points above, we have referred to price-related factors—New Zealand's generally low inflation rate, its relatively low and stable labor rates, and the generally competitive environment. All of these have acted to keep prices in check. However, the low (but slowly appreciating) value of the New Zealand dollar is countering this pressure on prices. Although the low "Kiwi" (dollar) assists exporters, and, consequently, makes a major contribution to the overall economic welfare of the country, it also makes the cost of imported goods high. This becomes particularly significant when imports have to be freighted over great distances.

Consumer watchdog organizations are active, and the government has enacted strong legislation—The Consumer Guarantees Act, 1994—that can affect manufacturers' approaches to pricing. For instance, all consumers are guaranteed financial redress if they are not satisfied with their purchases, and traders are not permitted to trade off this legislated right within their pricing strategies. The government levies a 12.5 percent goods and services tax on all goods and services, and this tax must be included in the advertised price of the item. The tax was introduced in an effort to lower income tax, introduce more equity into the system, and make taxation changes more readily visible to the constituency.

Communications

Communication technology is well advanced in New Zealand. At least fifteen companies were offering telecommunications services as of January 2000. There is also a very competitive national and local radio network, a thriving print-media industry, and many television services, including two government and three private contractors, as well as several regional and special-interest services. All of the television services are available via digital satellite coverage. The technological advances in telecommunications have had their most visible marketing impact in the areas of direct mail and telemarketing. Addressed direct mail comprises a huge 8.7 percent of total media advertising expenditures (ACNeilsen) and continues to grow, and telemarketing is thought to be growing at an even faster rate, although no comparable figures are available.

As it is in most developed countries, the advertising industry is generally thriving in New Zealand, despite temporary setbacks caused by exogenous impacts, such as the global turndown around late 2001. There have been tremendous changes in structure and levels of advertising expenditure, with growth from NZ$997 million in 1990 to NZ$1.4 billion in 1999, according to the New Zealand Association of Advertising Agencies (Nielsen Media Research 2001). Globalization and international alignments have created a smaller number of large agencies and encouraged the growth of independent media buying houses as well as creative and strategic agencies. Advertising expenditure by industry, reported in Table 12.4, reflects both local patterns (home improvement and agricultural advertising, for instance) and the more typical, international pattern (high expenditures by retailers, fast-moving consumer goods, foodstuffs, automotive marketers, and the telecommunications, leisure, travel, and entertainment sectors).

It is worthy of note that New Zealanders read a great deal—twenty-six daily newspapers are published in the country, although two large publishing groups account for 90 percent of their ownership. In addition, there are over 6,000 magazines available, of which over 600 are published locally. Of these, only seventeen had circulation exceeding 5,000 (as of December 2000). Again, there is a typical (Western) pattern in the type of magazine publications available as well as a more unique, New Zealand pattern. For instance, women's magazines are very popular in the country, as they are in so many others. Titles include the *Australian Women's Weekly* (circulation 75,538), *Cleo New Zealand* (circulation 23,701), *NZ Women's Day* (circulation 143,420), and the *NZ Women's Weekly* (circulation 94,000). Similarly, family publications, such as the *Reader's Digest* (circulation 115,467), are popular, as are the regional lifestyle magazines such as *North & South* (circulation 37,061), and local versions of international magazines such as *TIME Magazine* (circulation 36,013). This small, well-developed magazine market, though, also boasts a plethora of small-circulation specialist magazines, from *Boating New Zealand* (circulation 13,444) and *NZ Fishing news* (circulation 25,384) to *Pet New Zealand* (circulation 13,464) and *NZ Historic Places* (circulation 20,379). For a nation with a population of under four million, these are interesting figures. They show that New Zealanders, on the one hand, seem to be aware of their isolation, and thus seek to follow the news and trends of the rest of the world, but, on the other, this suggests a highly segmented, sophisticated local market catering to many small, special-interest groups. Under these conditions, although there are strong efforts to keep markets competitive, concentrations of marketing power are not unusual.

Table 12.4

**Advertising Expenditure, by Medium and Selected Industry,
December 2000–November 2001**

Medium	Expenditure (NZ$ million)	Percent share	Industry	Expenditure (NZ$ million)
Newspapers	596	40.1	Agricultural/industrial/office	35
Television	501	22.7	Automotive	117
Radio	190	11.5	Beverages	94
Magazines	157	6.4	Business services	31
Outdoor	28	1.9	Clothing	30
Cinemas	13	.09	Computers	51
Total	1,485	100	Foodstuffs	222
			Government	130
			Home improvements	68
			Household	144
			Insurance	27
			Investment/finance/banking	81
			Leisure/entertainment	265
			Travel	74
			Telecommunications	74
			Pharmaceuticals	66
			Retail	180
			Toiletries/cosmetics	90

Source: Advertising Standards Authority (available at www.asa.co.nz) and ACNielsen Advertising Expenditure Measurement.

Product

The Consumer Guarantees Act mentioned above also affects product issues, in that all providers of goods and services must meet basic quality standards—although it has yet to be decided by the courts exactly what the concept of "what reasonable people might reasonably expect to receive for the amount they pay" actually means (Mackay 1994). Whatever else the act achieves, it has placed a spotlight on consumer rights with respect to product quality standards; these rights cannot be ignored by marketers. The consumer protection legislation being implemented in Singapore is modeled on that of Australia and New Zealand.

Also mentioned above is the high level of mass-communication integration enjoyed by the country. This factor contributes to the high rate of adoption of new technologies in New Zealand. There is also a high level of general education and a large middle class; these factors all contribute to a positive attitude to change and a willingness to try new products. The latter trait has been noted by both the local media (Young 1993) and some multinationals, who have chosen to test their new products in New Zealand before rolling them out to the rest of the world.

CONSUMER LIFESTYLES

This topic has already been introduced in the discussion above about social class in New Zealand. However, specific research, carried out over a number of years, is also of interest because of the trends that can be extrapolated from it. New Zealand researchers are challenged by the small market size, as there is an important trade-off between more detailed (but smaller) segments and larger (but more generalized) groups. Otago University conducted Lifestyle Surveys in 1989 (sponsored by *Readers Digest*), 1995, and 2000 (sponsored by Fisher and Paykel, the New Zealand white-goods manufacturer), and ACNielsen (which merged with AGB McNair in 1998) utilizes a Target Audience Grouping System (TAGS), which is a media-linked segmentation-based lifestyle, attitude, and media consumption study.

Although these studies are interesting and valuable enough in themselves as a guide to local marketers, they show a roughly similar lifestyle base to that of other Western countries. There is also evidence in these studies of a social phenomenon readily observed in the everyday life of the country—the growing divide between rich and poor. Although this division still falls far short of that evident in the United States and many of the neighboring Southeast Asian countries, it is particularly obvious to New Zealand social observers because of the contrast with the extreme egalitarianism that has been a feature of New Zealand society for so many years under welfare economics regimes. The data in the AGB McNair study (Table 12.5) show the divide particularly clearly. For consumer durables, purchasing power clearly lies with the 28 percent of the population ("Liberal Sophisticates," "Affluent Acquirers," and "Comfortable Full Nesters") that is heavily overrepresented by the professions, the top income earners, and those with a higher education level. It should also be noted, however, that personal debt in New Zealand has grown significantly through the 1990s and into the new century, as consumers in other segments have utilized credit cards and home mortgages to keep up with their relatively affluent segments. The Otago studies (Table 12.6) confirm this view, noting that there is also an emerging group of young people with a focus on consumption that could be classed as hedonistic.

THE INTERNET

New Zealand has an excellent Internet structure, and the diffusion of the Internet into households, although not as spectacularly fast as it has been in some other countries, is quite rapid and appears to be steadily climbing (see Figure 12.3, p. 493). The good distribution and financial structure of the country, allied with a high general level of education and geographical factors such as the existence of a number of scattered cities with low-density urban areas separated by large rural areas, would seem ideal for an Internet-purchasing culture to prosper in time, and all the signs are that this is happening already.

Even more supportive of the belief that the Internet is becoming an integral part of the New Zealand lifestyle are the data in Figure 12.4 (p. 493) concerning usage patterns within the general population. Although teenagers are the major users, there seems to be little difference in Internet usage between the ages of twenty and sixty years, and the increase in usage, noted in the previous chart, can be seen to be common to all age groups. This is not a phenomenon unique to a single age group or generation cohort, so it can be reasonably stated that half the working population is Internet connected.

CONCLUSION

New Zealand business has to operate in a dynamic social, demographic, technological, and economic environment, and, as a result, any new entry into the marketplace will find at least basic market research a necessity. In reality, it is somewhat artificial to discuss these environments

Table 12.5

Eight Identified New Zealand Lifestyles

"Liberal sophisticates" (10%)	"Young hopefuls" (16%)
• High demographics, innovative	• Comprises half of the 15–24 year olds, mainly male
• Low TV and radio use, but high readership	• Low personal income, many beneficiaries
• Set opinions on environment, Maori culture, youth, education, and women	• High TV and radio usage, low readership
• Active lifestyle (health, fitness, restaurants, arts, and culture)	• Strong desire for success, often not realized
	• Extrovert lifestyle (away-from-home focus, high takeout food and beer consumption
"Affluent acquirers" (8%)	"Struggling young families" (11%)
• Younger (15–39 years of age)	• Family, children-centric
• High disposable incomes, no children	• Budget-conscious
• Active consumers	• High church attendance
• Low TV, high radio and readership	• Low career aspirations
• Concerned with contemporary life issues	• Low media-users—only interested in local news
"The settled seniors" (18%)	"Comfortable full-nesters" (10%)
• Many retired, married, empty-nesters	• Family-oriented, with older children, higher incomes
• Low incomes but manage well	• Combine home activities (e.g., gardening) with out-of-home activities (e.g., restaurants)
• Very high TV, high radio and newspaper usage, low magazine readers	• Very high magazine, newspaper readership, VCR and radio usage, but low TV use
• High sporting interests	• Innovative purchasers, environmental concerns
• Conservative, suspicious, brand loyal	
"Lonely and dissatisfied" (19%)	The "next generation" (9%)
• Many older and retired, but one-third are 15–39 years	• Seen as an eighth segment
• Many lonely, no sense of purpose in life	• Ages 10–14 years
• Interests either in raising a family or work	• TV-dominated
• Low media usage	• Very active

Source: AGB McNair "Target Audience Grouping System" (1998).

separately, as they interact so closely. The economic drive and the changing immigration patterns that have forced New Zealanders to become world citizens have resulted in a less ethnocentric attitude in all walks of life. Again, the advances in communications technology that have created such a strong marketing tool for advertisers, researchers, and marketers, also influence the shopping habits of consumers.

What are the important trends that will change the face of consumer behavior in New Zealand over the next few decades? Technology changes will clearly have further impact—on advertisers,

Table 12.6

Seven Identified New Zealand Lifestyles

"Accepting mid-lifers" (19.4%)
• Acceptance of status quo
• Content
• Observe rather than partake

"Traditional values" (18.8%)
• Family and community focus
• Traditional principles
• Conservative outlook

"Success-driven extroverts" (13.2%)
• Actively ambitious
• Self-oriented
• Value free enterprise

"Social strivers" (13%)
• Outer-directed
• Conformist
• Feel life is a struggle

"Pragmatic strugglers" (11.8%)
• Politically conservative
• Determined
• Family survival focus

"Educated liberals" (10.3%)
• Progressive
• Egalitarian
• Enjoy variety and diversity

"Young pleasure seekers" (13.5%)
• Few opinions on social issues
• Think money buys happiness
• Live for today

Source: S. Todd, R. Lawson, and T. Jamieson, "New Zealand Beyond 2000: A Consumer Lifestyles Study," University of Otago, Marketing Department (2001).

retailers, researchers, and consumers. This is a worldwide phenomenon, however, and is by no means unique to New Zealand. The drives toward privatization and internationalization are also shared by many other countries, although it is hard to find an example of another country that has moved from the extremes of protectionism and isolationism to open markets and globalization quite so quickly and dramatically.

The economic signs are positive. New Zealand seems to be on a sustainable economic growth curve that is founded in a competitive attitude and a willingness to seek business wherever it comes from, rather than a desire simply to tag along as a protected little speck of pink on England's trade map.

The demographic trends noted are also of interest and importance but, again, are hardly unique. That the population is aging, that the structure of family groups is changing, even that the (in this case, northward) urban drift does not seem to be slowing much, are all significant trends, but they are also prevalent in other developed nations in some form or another.

In contrast, however, it seems probable that the social trends identified in this chapter are unique to New Zealand. The struggle to find a clear national identity has been going on for many years. The peculiar local aspects of this problem lie with the indigenous Maori people, the immigrant Asians, and a new awareness by the population at large that the country really is more a part of the Asia-Pacific region than of any other grouping of nations.

Talk of "the browning of New Zealand" seems to suggest that the country may go through some melting-pot cultural transformation. This cry, however, echoes the words of Sir Keith Holyoak, Prime Minister in the 1950s, which were succeeded by louder cries from the Maori people for a separation of the Maori from the dominant European culture in order to retain and develop their fast-disappearing cultural identity. The Chinese, too, are hardly noted for a ten-

Figure 12.3 **Access to the Internet in New Zealand**

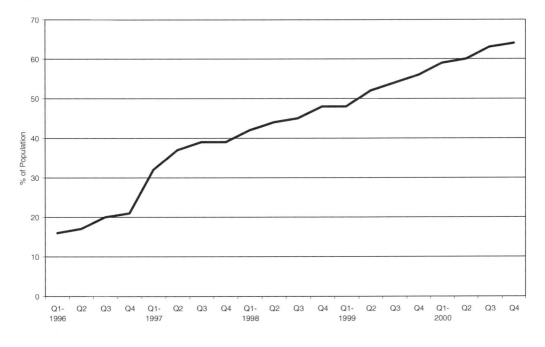

Figure 12.4 **Internet Usage in New Zealand**

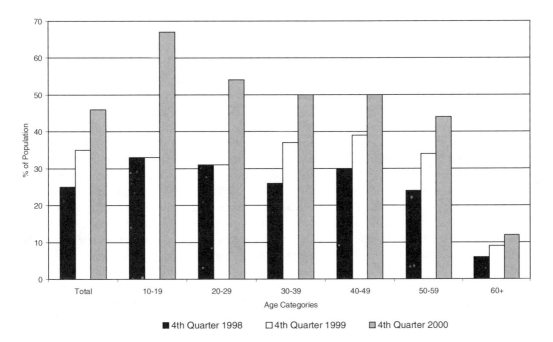

dency to compromise with their cultural values and habits, so the views of the melting-pot theorists lack conviction.

Whatever the outcome, in the coming years, businesspeople interested in the New Zealand market will not only (as always) have to complete their segmentation studies before launching their products or services, but will also have to pay attention to ensure that the supersensitive cultural dimension is not neglected.

Concern for the environment is another issue that echoes some overseas trends and has a unique local flavor. The general international issues pertaining to the balance between economic growth and the need for constant economic growth, so often accompanied by environmental degradation, are evident in New Zealand. The same micro-issues are also present. So, although there is a strong movement to eschew genetic modification (GM), which has even been evinced in retail boycotts, there is also a strong government and private-sector push to develop GM applications for commercial purposes.

Local dimensions include the major issue of Maori claims to fishing rights and land, and the increasing number of tourists tramping through the country. The Green lobby is strong, reflected in the growth in size of the Green Party in New Zealand politics, which plays an active role in the government of the country. The demographic profile of the "Educated liberals" in Table 12.6 shows clearly that the Liberals are indeed educated, and that they have considerable political leverage in terms of both their ability to understand and work the system and their possession of enough money to back their concerns with action. What is not shown in the table is the fundamental concern with the environment that is part of the Maoris' cultural-value system—the group of citizens concerned with what happens to New Zealand's waterways and forests is far larger than the numbers reveal.

New Zealand has a long sporting tradition. Sir Edmund Hillary, a New Zealander, was the first to climb Mount Everest; the America's Cup, which resided in the United States for so many years, is now proudly displayed in Auckland; the "All Blacks" is arguably the best-known and most successful rugby football team in the World; the list goes on through Olympic successes, equestrian victories, and accomplishments in cricket, rowing, and so many other sporting arenas. No change is apparent in the importance accorded to sports in the lives of most New Zealanders, but there is a strong wind of change with regard to the relative status of amateur and professional in sports. Professionals are making their presence felt very strongly in many sporting areas where amateurism was the unquestionable norm a very short time ago. This has led to the spawning of a vigorous sports marketing industry, which is becoming adept at not only event marketing but also of sustained marketing endeavors—involving quite sophisticated promotion, sponsorship deals, and public relations—to support sporting and cultural activities on a professional, ongoing basis.

The trend in which New Zealand began to turn toward the Asia-Pacific region for trade is likely to continue to strengthen. The New Zealand–Australia Free Trade Agreement has been in place for some time, and New Zealand has already begun negotiations with Singapore to establish a bilateral trade agreement that could result in improved access for New Zealand businesses to the ASEAN group. Recently, however, the Chinese Premier has suggested that an expanded ASEAN should include China as well as Australia and New Zealand; such an arrangement could offer huge benefits to New Zealand and further strengthen an Asian-Pacific focus in the country. No doubt, kinship ties and a common cultural heritage with Britain and other Western countries will always play an important role in shaping New Zealanders' cultural makeup. But, increasing immigration from Asia allied with increasing trade-related tourism and the rapid economic and social development of many neighboring Asian countries will surely all play a part in expanding an Asian-Pacific orientation in New Zealand.

Probably the only trend that can be predicted with any real degree of confidence is that the rate of change enjoyed (or suffered, perhaps) by New Zealanders will continue to increase. This is a small, rapidly maturing nation blessed with a well-educated, positive-thinking, competitive population and a fundamentally sound economy. The country is poised to make a significant contribution to the Asia-Pacific region, to which it so clearly belongs.

REFERENCES

Boland, Mary J. 1994. "Teens in the Marketplace." *New Zealand Herald*, August 6, section 3:3.

Business and Economic Research Limited. 1994. *BERL Monthly Monitor*, November.

Coleman, Richard P. 1983. "The Continuing Significance of Social Class to Marketing." *Journal of Consumer Research* 1 (10; December): 265–79.

Craig, Duncan. 1994. "Banks Warn Clients to Dump Apartments." *National Business Review* 2 (December).

Deutsche Bank New Zealand. 2001. *Bond Report*, October.

Elley, W. B., and J. C. Irving. 1976. "Revised Socio-Economic Index for New Zealand." *New Zealand Journal of Educational Studies* 11 (2): 25–30.

———. 1985. "The Elley–Irving Socio-Economic Index 1981 Census Revision." *New Zealand Journal of Educational Studies* 20 (2): 115–28.

Johnston, Raylee. 1983. *A Revision of Socio-economic Indices for New Zealand*. Wellington: New Zealand Council for Educational Research.

Lawson, Rob, and Hume Winzar. 1994. "Social Class and Consumer Behaviour in Australia and New Zealand." Paper presented at the New Zealand Marketing Educators Conference, Hamilton, New Zealand, November.

Mackay, R. 1994. *Foodbanks in* New Zealand: *Patterns of Growth and Usage*. Wellington: Social Policy Agency.

Martineau, Pierre. 1958. "Social Class and Spending Behavior." *Journal of Marketing* 23: 121–41.

National Bank of New Zealand. 2001. *National Business Outlook* (November). Wellington: National Bank of New Zealand.

New Zealand Official Yearbook 2000. 2000. Wellington: Statistics New Zealand.

Nielsen Media Research. 2001. www.acnielsen.co.nz

Reserve Bank of New Zealand. 2001. *Monetary Policy Statement*, November.

Sinclair, Keith. 1959. *A History of* New *Zealand*. Harmondsworth, New Zealand: Penguin Books.

Teutenburg, Penny. 1994. "Fast Forward-Focus on the Future." *Marketing* (a Market Research Conference Report), October: 37–42.

Walters, C. 2001. *Marketing Principles in New Zealand*, 2nd ed. Auckland: Pearson.

Young, Christine. 1993. "The New Megatrends: What's in Store for Business." *New Zealand Business*, October: 12–20.

Web sites

www.acnielsen.co.nz
www.asa.co.nz
www.nbnz.co.nz
www.nzherald.co.nz
www.statistics.govt.nz

CHAPTER 13

PAPUA NEW GUINEA

Marketing and Consumer Behavior

RONALD A. FULLERTON

OVERVIEW

Papua New Guinea is a rugged land, and its economy is not well developed, though some signs of a more modern economy exist in urban areas. Several historical events constrained—and more contemporary forces still seem to constrain—more optimal growth and development. This chapter provides an analysis of those forces that affect socioeconomic dynamics and then provides insightful thoughts on marketing opportunities and future trends.

INTRODUCTION

Papua New Guinea occupies the eastern half of the large Pacific island of New Guinea, outer islands such as New Britain, New Ireland, the Bismarck Archipelago, and several hundred small islands adjacent to the coasts. The other half of New Guinea, Irian Jaya, belongs to Indonesia at the time that this is written. New Guinea is divided by the rugged Owen Stanley mountain range, in which some elevations approach 5,000 meters. With a land area of 462,840 square kilometers, Papua New Guinea is slightly larger than California. The country lies about 160 kilometers (98 miles) north of Australia's northeastern tip.

The population has more than doubled since the country gained independence from Australia in 1975, to an estimated five million at the time of this writing. Human settlement in Papua New Guinea goes back 60,000 years (Central Intelligence Agency 2000)—three to four times as long as that in the Americas—and yet for most of this time, there was little contact with people from elsewhere. Similarly to the Aborigines of Australia, the people of Papua New Guinea have evolved institutions and belief systems over far longer time spans than has most of humanity. This may help to explain their reactions to economic modernity as exemplified by Australian colonizers and, later, market economists and the World Bank.

Historical Overview

The earliest humans were the Papuans, hunter-gathers who came by boat from Southeast Asia. Somewhat later, the dark-skinned Melanesians arrived, who today make up the majority of Papua New Guinea's population and who later settled the Solomon Islands, Vanuatu, and Fiji. There was considerable intermingling of the Papuans and Melanesians, to the point that most indigenous people refer to themselves as Melanesians. The resultant population had developed settled agriculture by about the same time as the Neolithic revolution in Anatolia and Mesopotamia seven to ten thousand years ago. Within the last several thousand years, small populations of Polynesians and Micronesians arrived by water to Papua New Guinea and settled on some of the country's coastal areas and smaller islands. Although Spanish and Portuguese explorers noticed the area of Papua New Guinea in the sixteenth century, there was little activity by Europeans until three hundred years later. Britain and Germany staked claims to different sections of New Guinea in 1884, at the height of the European colonization push. The Germans were pushed out at the start of World War I in 1914, when Britain handed over most of the colonial administration to its Australian colony.

The Western—including Australian—presence was minimal for decades. The vast central Highlands were not explored, because it was felt that neither humans nor anything of value could exist in such wet and rugged terrain. In the 1930s, as Australian mining engineers pushed into the Highlands searching for gold and other metal minerals, they found, to their surprise, that literally hundreds of societies were flourishing there, each with its own language, albeit with extremely "primitive" living circumstances from their perspectives. Use of metal and the wheel had never developed in pre-European Papua New Guinea. The indigenous societies had, however, highly evolved social structures, behavioral patterns, and belief systems (Narokobi 1983).

Melanesian Culture

Marketing and consumer behavior in Papua New Guinea have been strongly influenced by the Melanesian culture, which, in turn, has been largely determined by long isolation—not only from the outside but also from one Melanesian group to another. Forbidding mountainous terrain and jungle conditions made contact among the Melanesian settlements difficult. There was certainly trade among communities, especially in coastal areas (Malinowski 1922; Narokobi 1983), but it did not eliminate antagonism. Frequent warfare, especially in the Highlands, reinforced differences. As a consequence, many languages developed; no country in the world today has more distinct languages—eight hundred is the figure usually given. Linguists and anthropologists are as enthralled by Papua New Guinea as market economists are appalled, and studies of it are among the classics of anthropology (e.g., Lawrence 1964; Malinowski 1922). English and Pidgin are the only languages understood across the country, with English being the language of government and most of the media. Motu, which was originally a dialect of the capital, Port Moresby, is also used across much of the country.

Wantok: Kinship in Melanesian Culture

Historically, one's identity grew from, and one's loyalty was to, others in the same vicinity who considered themselves part of the same community and who spoke the same language—the *wantok* or people of "one talk." The wantok makes demands but also provides support; no Melanesian exists as an isolated individual, as might be the case in the West. (See Narokobi, passim, for a good exposition.) A person with means would be expected to support his or her immediate family as well as needy members of the extended family (Narokobi 1983). Such expectations are, of course, widespread among "developing" societies in Oceania, Asia, and Africa. They are the glue that holds these societies together, often with less hostility and tension than the social welfare programs of the "developed" nations.

Although wantok have separate identities, certain core assumptions are held by all of them.

The most fundamental is that land is communally owned and cannot be bought or sold by individuals—private property simply does not and should not exist. Ninety-seven percent of the land in Papua New Guinea is communally held. Another core assumption is that certain men will have more of the community wealth at their dispersal, and they enjoy deference and other privileges but, in turn, *should* use their largesse to help other members of the community. Today such men (this is a single gender phenomenon) are called "Big Men." Even if they seem to be indulging themselves—in overseas junkets, imported beer, mistresses, new vehicles, and so forth—the kin group could participate vicariously in the consumption. It is a particular thrill to the wantok if the Big Man's indulgences are funded by AusAid (Australian Foreign Aid) and other foreign sources, because opportunistic gain at the expense of outsiders is valued.

A central tenet of Papua New Guinea's present-day Melanesian culture is that most problems are caused by outsiders, who abuse and mistreat the gentle indigenous people (Narokobi 1983; Filer and Sekhran 2001).

Spirituality in Melanesian Culture

People are deeply spiritual (Counts 1994). Most Papua New Guineans are profoundly religious in a way that has not existed in Western societies for a century or more. They reflexively seek spiritual explanations even for phenomena that in Western cultures would be explained in terms of natural science. Some core values reflect a profoundly pantheistic belief that God or gods are everywhere and everything—plants, animals, streams, clouds, landforms. One's surroundings are God or gods, alive and spiritually infused. The spirits of one's ancestors are alive and present. The pantheistic perspective is beautifully expounded by Narokobi (1983, especially 19, 32–34).

Other core values come from Christianity, which is the only European belief system to have been seriously embraced by Melanesians. Two-thirds or more adhere to one of several Christian churches, while the remainder follow traditional polytheistic religious beliefs ("Papua New Guinea—Land of the Unexpected" ca. 1997). Among Christians, long-established pantheistic beliefs and rituals have been assimilated, just as pre-Christian beliefs were into European Christianity 1,500 years ago.

Silence and Sharing: A Different Way of Being

The culture values quietness, as opposed to constant speech, and passivity as opposed to self-assertion; to acquire without sharing with family and wantok members was, and generally still is, considered inappropriate. The traditional wantok sensibilities, the Big Men, and the spiritual mentalities combine to make Papua New Guineans most exasperating to the World Bank officials and other devotees of economic modernity. Were it not for the size and enormous natural resources of Papua New Guinea, agents of modernity would have stayed away, and Melanesian societies would have been left to their own.

An Unfortunate Colonial Legacy

Contact with economic—and political—modernity has wrought great change, not all of it beneficial. Papua New Guinea had the misfortune to be administered as a Crown colony by Australia, which showed less appreciation for the ethnic and cultural differences and essential humanity of its colonists than, say, France or Portugal in their colonies. Australia was the colonial power in Papua New Guinea at the same time as its official state policy mandated forcefully taking Aborigine children from their parents and putting them in "good" White homes. Earlier, the Australian government had encouraged "blackbirding"—bringing Melanesians to work the plantations of Queensland under conditions of forced indentured servitude. The author remembers Australian academics joking about the "assgrass"-wearing savages of Papua New Guinea in the mid-1970s. Australian labor market policies reflecting that country's pugnacious trade union sector have been disastrous in Papua New Guinea. Adoption of Australian policies that discourage development of informal enterprises has retarded what has been a major growth sector in some developing countries. Aid, much but hardly all from Australia, has fostered dependency and a self-perpetuating aid consultant syndrome that has had little, if any, real benefit to most citizens of Papua New Guinea. The Japanese conquest and rule during the early 1940s was an even more unpleasant colonial experience.

The Westminister (i.e., British)-style constitution bequeathed by Australia at Independence in 1975 has proven durable over more than a quarter century, yet has given the country neither stable nor effective government. In modern urban environments like Port Moresby and Lae, behavioral constraints have disintegrated, giving the country one of the worst crime problems in the world. Crime is a major economic activity and colors much consumer behavior. Both provincial and central government are the playgrounds of corrupt Big Men, whose conspicuous consumption rivals that of Saudi princes and central African politicians—and which, of course, leads to interesting episodes of consumer behavior.

Most citizens of Papua New Guinea live more peacefully and modestly in traditional, basically subsistence circumstances in the vast rural sectors. They are increasingly marginalized in their own country, partly as a consequence of the adherence to communal landholding, partly because of their traditional passivity, and all too much because some of their own leaders are susceptible to bribes from overseas businesspeople. Much of the modern economic sector is in the hands of over 40,000 expatriates. Australians dominate the large mining sector; Asian families dominate more and more of distribution and retailing. Growth in the modern sector has slowed during the past ten years as declining world prices for gold and copper have made the expenses and difficulties of operating in Papua New Guinea bulk larger.

Natural Resources

Many of the businesses that have invested in Papua New Guinea have been drawn by its rich endowments of mineral resources—gold, silver, copper, natural gas, and oil. Known oil deposits are small, but it is likely that larger ones will be found. The mining sector contributed slightly more than two-thirds of the country's export revenue in 1996 (Aka 2001). However, the intensity and scope of mining activity fluctuate with world prices. Because the investment required and frustrations encountered for mining are high in Papua New Guinea, mining activity there is particularly prone to slowdown if prices drop as they have in recent years. In addition to forbidding terrain and poor transportation, mining companies have to deal with bribe-hungry government officials, cumbersome procedures, extremely high expatriate salaries to lure skilled workers, and incessant quarrels with the kinship groups that own the land upon which mining takes place. In business terms, the return does not always justify the investment and effort.

The country has extensive fisheries. Given the enormous and ever-growing appetite for fish in China, South Korea, Japan, and other Asian countries, Papua New Guinea's fish resources are very valuable. They are also vulnerable to short-sighted exploitation.

Extensive tracts of tropical timber cover about 60 percent of the country's land area. Some lies in plantations. Ninety-nine percent of the timber is on communally owned land. Royalty distribution to communities by government has been a contentious issue (Filer and Sekhran [2001] provide an excellent discussion), as has the willing corruption of chiefs and government officials in exchange for bribes from Asian firms. Although up to 7,000 Papua New Guineans are employed in the industry, nearly all hold low-level positions. Timber distribution networks and financing are controlled by large Japanese trading firms; management of the logging operations is in the hands of a handful of Malaysian firms. Revenue from log exports peaked in 1994. Since then, prices have gone down, and considerable timber was lost to fires during the 1998 drought.

Environmental Issues

Papua New Guinea's great size and forbidding terrain have thus far protected it from the worst environmental disasters, but there are realistic concerns about deforestation, land degradation, species extinction, and pollution (Aka 2001). Holzknecht (2002) argues that influential indigenous Papua New Guineans have, in return for bribes, become front men for rapacious logging operations that will sacrifice future timber possibilities for destructive logging in the here and now. At current cutting rates, the forests could be gone in less than ten years. Concerns about excessive cutting have been raised by international ecology organizations (Friends of the Earth 2001). Pollution comes from human wastes—the beach as toilet and garbage dump—mine tailings, and widespread illegal use of dynamite to "fish" along coastal areas. Soil erosion is the biggest land degradation problem.

Demographic Conditions

Papua New Guinea has the highest birthrate but lowest life expectancy in the South Pacific. Life expectancy at birth is fifty-seven years for males and fifty-nine years for females, hence, fifty-nine years overall. While higher than the figures at independence, these are low numbers for a country without a raging AIDS epidemic. The unusually small difference between male and female life expectancy is due, in part, to the high rate of gender violence directed at females. According to the United Nations Development Programme (UNDP 1997), only four countries in the world have higher maternal mortality rates. But a birthrate of 2.27 percent a year pushes up the overall number of the living, from about two million at independence in 1975 to about five million now. About 40 percent of the people live in the Highlands. Approximately 570,000 households are currently found in the country's rural areas. About two-thirds keep livestock, especially pigs, that in good years number one for each two humans. The highest percentage of pig ownership— nearly 80 percent of households—is in the Highlands.

Approximately two-thirds of the workforce is said to be involved in agriculture (Macfarlane 2002), but the percentage is doubtless higher; official figures are weak on the subsistence part of the economy, which is largely agricultural.

The Expatriate Community

There is a substantial expatriate community—more than 40,000 people, most residing in the largest cities, Port Moresby and Lae, and the remainder in the smaller cities. Australians constitute the largest number of expatriate residents in a community that also includes Japanese, Malays, New Zealanders, Americans, Filipinos, Britons, Singaporeans, South Koreans, and overseas Chinese. Given the severe crime conditions that these expatriates face, they live in high security areas and command high "combat pay" salaries. Freedom of movement and the ability to observe and enjoy a different environment are simply not actions available to the country's expatriates.

Urban Areas

The urban areas, according to the 2001 *Papua New Guinea Business and Street Directory,* are as follows:

- Moresby, 220,000 people
- Lae, 90,000 people
- Mt. Hagen, 45,000 people
- Madang, 30,000 people
- Goroka, 25,000 people
- Wewak, 23,000 people

STRUCTURE OF THE ECONOMY/ECONOMIC ENVIRONMENT

A Dualistic Economy

Papua New Guinea has a pronounced dualistic economy. Approximately 85 percent of the country's estimated five million people practice a subsistence way of village life in rural areas, growing and handcrafting most of what they require to live, and only occasionally participating in the cash market economy. Most of the time, they neither buy nor sell for cash; they may exchange with each other things they have grown or created. The available figures on the country's gross domestic product (GDP) do not include the subsistence sector and, hence, are misleading (Macfarlane 2002).

The Market Sector

The remaining 15 percent of the country's population, including the expatriates, participates in the cash market economy, buying most of what they consume. Their money income is generated in large mineral extraction ventures (gold, copper, oil, natural gas), in domestic market or export-oriented agriculture (coffee, cocoa, tea, palm oil, copra), in timber production, in retail and service businesses, in a few manufacturing operations (e.g., fish canning in Lae), in government service, and in crime. The market part of the economy is driven by the attractiveness of the country's enormous natural resources. When people are wealthy in Papua New Guinea, they are wealthy. Distribution of wealth runs to extremes.

According to the latest available figures, those for 1996, commercial agriculture accounts for 26.4 percent, industry (including mining) 41 percent, and services 32.6 percent of Papua New Guinea's GDP. After growing at an annual rate of 7 percent between 1980 and 1993, GDP has since faltered, with annual rates of −6.5 percent to +5.2 percent (Macfarlane 2002). The principal agricultural exports are coffee, cocoa, tea, palm oil, copra, and natural rubber. Mining and mineral exports include copper, gold, silver, oil, and natural gas.

Papua New Guinea exports agricultural and mineral commodities and imports finished products, above all those from Australia and New Zealand, countries that enjoy preferential status as well as relative proximity. Devaluation of the Papua New Guinea kina a few years ago, however, has made Australian and New Zealand imports costlier.

While production of pigs and chickens is protected from outside competition, and the government subsidizes a few manufacturing ventures, such as a large fish cannery at Lae, much of the economy of Papua New Guinea is open. The country has joined with other South Pacific countries, such as Fiji and Vanuatu, in the Melanesian Spearhead economic union. Duty-free imports of beef from Vanuatu have substantially replaced those from Australia.

Papua New Guinea is heavily dependent on its former colonial possessor, Australia, for manufactured goods, wheat and rice for urban areas, financial services, mining investment, and regular doses of aid money. The timber trade is controlled by Malaysian and Japanese holdings (Filer and Sekhran 2001). As in other South Pacific countries, there has developed in Papua New Guinea what I will term the "Aid Donor/Developing Country Syndrome," in which political elites and aid consultants foster each other without ever fostering substantial economic development.

Restraints on the Economy

By the market-oriented economic orthodoxies most widely held today, Papua New Guinea's economy is severely restrained in almost every conceivable way, by:

- high wages and low productivity;
- restrictions on the (noncriminal) informal economy's development;
- poor education;
- a large, corrupt and generally ineffectual government sector;
- poor infrastructure;
- rampant and violent crime in urban areas; and
- a communal land ownership system that makes long-term leases difficult for businesses and property ownership near impossible.

Wages and Productivity

Wages have been out of proportion to productivity in Papua New Guinea since before independence, a legacy of Australian colonial policies (McGavin 1998). Just as the 1991 decision by the West German government to raise wages to Western standards in the former East Germany made the former Communist area unappealing to investors, so too has the 1972 decision by Australian administrators to set generous minimum wages in urban Papua New Guinea hampered business development. The idea was well intended, heavily influenced by Australian labor union leaders who (as the author has often observed) love to look after their brothers and sisters in the South Pacific Island countries. The minimum urban wage, however, was set far too high in view of employee productivity. Businesses voted with their feet. Urban private-sector employment was lower in 1992 than it had been twenty years before, though the urban populations had grown fourfold. Government employment grew to include 60 percent of all formal nonagricultural employment, but this was not enough to employ all of the new urbanites. Crime thus blossomed as an occupation (Jowitt 2001; Levantis and Fane 1998).

In 1992, realizing that the wage policy was disastrous, the government slashed the urban minimum wage by two-thirds—but only for hires subsequent to that date. The continued employment of older hires, as well as the continuation of relatively generous government salaries, has had the effect of keeping prevailing urban wages too high to make the place attractive to business (Levantis and Fane 1998). In 1992, the percentage of urban people with formal employment was 24.5 percent, about half the percentage it had been in 1971.

Restrictions on the Informal Economy

One of the most disastrous legacies of Australian rule has been the restrictions placed on Papua New Guineans who would attempt to establish informal businesses—street vending, small backyard workshops, and so forth. Legislation designed to protect rate-paying shop and restaurant owners in Queensland was put in force in Papua New Guinea to thwart street vendors of food and sundries and has remained in force over a quarter century of independence (Pitts 2001). Informal employment, which has blossomed in many developing areas of South America, Asia, and Africa—and is one of the hottest mantras of today's development consultants—has not blossomed in Papua New Guinea. Not only are opportunities to be honorably self-employed foreclosed, but also consumers have far fewer choices from which to purchase fruit, candies, prepared meals, cigarettes, reading matter, and other products commonly sold by informal economy vendors. The limitations hit hardest at low-income consumers in urban areas.

Poor Education

At independence, the University of Papua New Guinea in Port Moresby attracted talented students from around the South Pacific. Few have come in recent years. Only a tiny proportion of Papua New Guineans have ever attended. In the mid-1980s, the participation rates were 2 percent for high school and 2 percent for university (Gibson and Fatai 2001). Illiteracy remains significantly higher than in such South Pacific countries as Fiji, Tonga, or Samoa.

To be sure, educational reforms begun in 1995 have expanded access to secondary school. A recent government decision to make education free for all may raise literacy if it can be successfully implemented throughout the country. But in Papua New Guinea, government decisions are seldom successfully implemented, not least because many of them are drafted by foreign consultants flown in for the work and only dimly aware of the Melanesian ethos (Filer and Sekhran 2001). Moreover, it is not certain that school fees account for the country's unusually high rate of attrition and dropouts at the primary school level. Only six of ten primary students complete primary studies (World Bank 2002). Most of the primary and secondary schools in rural areas are run by Christian church organizations on a nonprofit basis. Even these had to curtail services in 1998 and 1999 when funding was cut by the government of Prime Minister Bill Skate.

Unemployment is extremely high in Papua New Guinea's cities. Highly skilled and educated local people are in such short supply that both business and government have no recourse except to bring in expatriates (Gibson and Fatai 2001).

Ineffective Government

Papua New Guinea has representative government, regular and reasonably honest elections, free and open political debate, a stable constitution, and formal adherence to the rule of law. Queen Elizabeth II is the titular sovereign, as she is to so many former British colonies. The current prime minister, Sir Mekere Morauta, is by all accounts honest and sincere. No ethnic group within the country has disproportionate political power. However, the performance of the government has been increasingly ineffectual and corrupt. Accountability appears irrelevant in practice, despite vibrant dirt-slinging debates by politicians and citizens in the country's open press. As in other Melanesian countries, such as Vanuatu and the Solomon Islands, elections can act as a revolving door through which dishonest and inept politicians may go out but usually come back in at some not-too-distant date. Jail terms for corruption are rare and are no deterrent to future reelection when they are applied (Mana 1999). Among civil servants, spectacular, widely known failures cannot stop the career progress of those with well-connected friends and relatives (Pitts 2001). Bribe taking is practiced on a grand scale by senior officials, on a petty scale by lesser officials. Projects do not get completed, and policies do not get implemented. The government cannot provide decent infrastructure or basic security.

Rampant Crime

For many, violent crime is the overshadowing force in today's Papua New Guinea. It impacts all aspects of economic activity, and hence, marketing and consumer behavior. The violence of crime in Papua New Guinea exceeds that of almost any other country. People are routinely murdered for small amounts of money. In a typical story, the *Sydney Morning Herald* (2001b) told how a sixty-two-year-old Dutch priest who had served in Papua New Guinea for thirty years was murdered by a gang that then robbed him of 45 kina, about US$12; thousands came to mourn at his funeral. Three months earlier, a sixty-four-year-old cleric was murdered in his bed by a gang. Both men were killed by head shots, a specialty among Papua New Guinea's violent criminals. Armed robbery, burglary, and gang rape are the most common crimes. A recent international study of victimization in developing countries in Asia, Africa, and Latin America found Papua New Guinea's urban centers the absolute worst, especially for violent crime (Pitts 2001). Firearms are readily available, some siphoned off during the civil war with Bougainville, others acquired in exchange for drugs (Dinnen 1998). They are used readily, often indiscriminately, with shoot-outs between gangs or between gangs and police being common.

Papua New Guinea leads the world in incidence of sexual assaults against women and children (Levantis 2000). Shootings on the University of Papua New Guinea campus in Port Moresby are regular, random, and deadly, despite armed guards who escort people. Hence, the university has lost many talented researchers to Australia, New Zealand, and the University of the South Pacific. Established to provide highly educated citizens, it is unable to fulfill its promise.

Crime as Employment. Crime has itself become a widespread economic activity—a career choice for thousands in urban areas; Levantis (2000) estimates that nearly 15 percent of the urban workforce is involved in crime full time. Such criminals are known as "rascals" (*raskols*), and their work is known as *raskolism*. Drawing upon the well-known argument of Becker that much crime is the result of economically rational decisions, Chand and Levantis (1998) argue that crime is an economically viable occupational option—the most economically viable choice available to many urban dwellers. Informal businesses are discouraged, formal employment has been static to declining for twenty years, even as urban populations have grown, and policing is sporadic and overall ineffectual—those who are jailed find it easy to escape. Two high-profile commissions have documented the theft of millions by politicians involved in a major scandal five years ago; not a single fine has been paid, and not a single day has been spent in jail (Pitts 2001).

Though brutal, most of Papua New Guinea's crime is not mindless but rather is highly organized along hierarchical lines, often with political figures and other Big Men in top leadership roles. In 1997, Australian TV ran videotapes in which the then-prime minister, Bill Skate, discussed gangland killings with his top deputy (Standish 1999). (Mr. Skate explained later that it had not been him talking on the tape but rather the whiskey that he had drunk.) Gang fights for "payback" (revenge) or major robberies can be large-scale events. In some ways, raskolism recapitulates the incessant warfare of precolonial Highland Papua New Guinea. Big communal battles over land claims still roil parts of the Highlands today (Australian Department of Foreign Affairs and Trade 2001).

Effects of Crime on Other Economic Activity. Crime on the scale experienced in Papua New Guinea thwarts other economic activities. Nearly two-thirds of the businesses responding to a 1997 study said that security was the biggest impediment to fruitful daily activity (Pitts 2001). Well-founded fears discourage potential tourists who otherwise would be drawn to the country's spectacular diving, unspoiled and dramatic scenery, and possibilities for ecotourism and adventure tourism. Chand and Levantis (1998, 33) note that the country attracts only one-twentieth the number of tourists that Fiji does. Fiji is a considerably smaller, partly Melanesian country that has its own crime problems, yet its violent crime rate is one-sixth that of Papua New Guinea's rate.

Businesses that operate in Port Moresby complain about the onerous costs of acquiring effective security against car theft, assaults, bag thefts, truck hijackings, and other robberies. Those who come to the cities for business can move about during the day—but not by taxi or public transport. They must stay in barred hotels at night (Dyce 2001). The environment is suffocating, unpleasant, and dangerous.

Another kind of crime that thwarts business is government corruption, at both the national and provincial levels, which has soared to levels comparable to those in Pakistan and Nigeria. Foreign and domestic firms must pay bribes to get routine access to natural resources; ongoing bribery is the only way to ensure electricity and telephone service for urban businesses (Mana 1999; Pitts 2001).

Outside the urban areas crime is less in evidence. Pitts (2001) reports that people strive to maintain order in most rural villages. Roughly 70 percent of crimes are not reported but rather resolved through traditional ways, especially compensation and gift giving to the victims, the amounts bestowed depending upon victims' status. Village court arbitration works, because it expresses the community's values. Arbitration by respected people—religious figures, elders—is also common and effective. In the Highland provinces, however, violent crime is common. Gang rapes go along with tribal fighting and help males to assert their solidarity and superiority (Standish 1999). Peachin (1997) reports that adventure tourists are welcome to observe payback battles in the Southern Highlands.

Because the urban areas, particularly the port cities of Lae and Port Moresby, are hubs of business activity from finance through distribution, the severe crime there dampens economic life in the entire market as opposed to the subsistence sector of the economy. Tourists or mining engineers going to reasonably safe destinations would likely have to pass through Port Moresby, which is not safe at all. Papua New Guinea offers a poor environment for business development.

Communal Land Ownership

As noted above, communal land ownership is the overwhelming norm in Papua New Guinea. Enshrined in the country's constitution, the existence and value of communally owned land are deeply held beliefs by Papua New Guineans—as least as deeply held as the belief among American Republicans that private property is an inalienable right. For Melanesians, the key point is that the land is communally owned; whether or not the land is used for productive projects or revenue generation is not necessarily important. The American legal maxim that land should be put to its "highest and best use"—its most economically remunerative use—is alien to Melanesian thinking. The anthropologist Counts (1994) found a strong belief that moral behavior is that such as reinforces ties of community and kinship. Moral behavior, in other words, requires that the land be communally owned.

Businesses seeking to acquire property in Papua New Guinea will find that nearly impossible. Even the 3 percent of the land that is freehold is frequently disputed by communal groups claiming that it was taken inappropriately from them in the past. Such disputes are expensive to settle and, once settled, can be reopened (Ward 2000).

Stable long-term leasing of communal land, which is well developed (although not without periodic contention about past wrongs) in Fiji, is extremely difficult in Papua New Guinea because it is nearly impossible to determine who represents the village with regard to land issues. Agreements reached with one group of spokespeople may be renounced by another. Conflicting claims to speak for the community are legion. Authority can best be described as fluid. In the Highlands, violence is routinely threatened if new demands are not met; given the government's inability to curb violence, such claims must be taken seriously. This appears to show that the cohesiveness of rural villages and clans has weakened; but it could also reflect both the villagers' unwillingness to discuss or negotiate land ownership issues with outsiders, and a mischievously opportunistic attitude toward foreign wealth. In a growing number of cases, communities have exploited the money value of property claims settlements with foreign businesses, by howling out claims of grievance with the intent of forcing a cash award (Ward 2000). Moreover, Australian nongovernmental organizations (NGOs) are said to love weighing in to fan the flames to prove their own importance in the fight against exploitation and globalization (Callick 1995).

In such a difficult business climate, only the lure of extraordinary profits can justify investment in Papua New Guinea. Lea (2001) argues that there can be no economic progress in Papua New Guinea unless individual title to land becomes reality. And yet, to change the rules about land ownership would tear apart the Melanesian culture and provoke paralyzing violence. Even the perceived threat to indigenous land rights has led to three military coups in Fiji since 1987. It should be noted, however, that Asian logging companies have been able to make the system work for them by paying local Big Men to be cooperative community representatives. (A similar pattern is found in the Melanesian Solomon Islands.) The Big Men are lackeys, but very well-bribed lackeys (Holzknecht 2002; World Rainforest Movement 2001). Western companies with greater inhibitions (and legal restrictions) about corrupt payments are at a competitive disadvantage.

The OK Tedi Mine Case. Although the locus of blame in this case will be long disputed, it illustrates some of the challenges facing a large investment in Papua New Guinea. The OK Tedi copper mine was opened in 1984 and, within a few years, was contributing 9 percent of the country's GDP and 35 percent of its export revenue. It was developed and operated by Australia's Broken Hill Mining Company, one of that country's largest firms, which had a 52 percent share of ownership. Other owners were the government of Papua New Guinea, with 30 percent, and another mining company. During the 1990s, there were incessant disputes about the mine. Was it dumping trainings that polluted streams so as to threaten the livelihood of 30,000 villagers (ECA Watch ca. 2001)? Was Broken Hill Mining cheating the government of revenue? Broken Hill met a 1994 lawsuit filed by the villagers by using its political influence to threaten the villagers with immense fines. That backfired, and a large (A\$82 million) compensation program for the villagers was enacted by the provincial legislature. Eventually, the mine was shut down for a spell. Were cutbacks in mine operations efforts to punish landowners for exercising their rights, or were they necessitated by low world prices for copper?

Broken Hill baled out of the venture in late 2001 by transferring its ownership to something called the "Papua New Guinea Sustainable Development Company" (Inmet Mining Corporation 2001). This new company, as its name suggests, will deal with all of the politically correct themes, while keeping the mine operating with the previous senior managers. The company has agreed to make payments to eight regional trust funds that have been established to manage current and future payments to landowners, according to the article "OK Tedi Regional Trusts Are Set Up"

(*Post-Courier* 2002a). Given the corruption and instability that characterize institutions in Papua New Guinea, it is difficult to place too much credence in this solution.

A Paucity of Entrepreneurship

Exceptions do exist, yet, in general, Papua New Guineans do not exhibit the sort of business entrepreneurship that creates new and enlarges older economic institutions. As an example, demand for domestically produced beef exists, yet little has been done to develop better husbandry (Macfarlane 2002). Another example, from the March 26, 2002 Papua New Guinea *Post-Courier*: world prices for cocoa soared recently; the cocoa raised in Papua New Guinea is highly prized, yet growers have not increased production. Entrepreneurship is restrained by several strong forces described throughout this paper—adherence to tradition, communal land holding, claims upon gains by family and kin, and a tendency to attribute constructive activity to spiritual rather than human efforts. Keeping ruminants such as cattle and sheep was not traditional.

POLITICAL ENVIRONMENT

An Unfortunate Rush to Independence

If any colony was not ready for viable independence, it was Papua New Guinea. The few educated people related more to Australia than to their own country. There was absolutely no sense of national identity; people identified with their own linguistic group and place—of which there were eight hundred or so. The Australian colonial government had never unified administration of the former German section with the British Crown section (Narokobi 1983, 21). The Westminister system of government did not represent an indigenous approach to governance but rather was arbitrarily grafted upon the collection of disparate groups that constituted the new country.

By 1970, however, the rush to get rid of colonies was as frenetic as had been that to acquire them eighty years before. The large island of Bougainville was put with Papua New Guinea, although its inhabitants voiced a preference to become joined to the Solomon Islands, with independence that was imminent at the time. The Bougainville Civil War from 1988–97 was costly and humiliating for the government of Papua New Guinea. Prime Minister Sir Julius Chan was forced out of office in 1997 when he tried to employ the South African Sandline mercenary organization to do what Papua New Guinea's army could not. Eventually, the Papua New Guinea government relinquished its claims, but the country had been flooded with weapons and thousands of poorly disciplined and violent ex-soldiers who, in turn, swelled the ranks of the raskols.

Papua New Guinea's political parties developed differently from their supposed models in Australia and Britain. Rather than being enduring institutions with relatively coherent political ideologies, they are essentially personal factions that wax and wane with the prospects of various political leaders—the man who can deliver the most money is always the favorite of the day. Ten different parties were involved in the government between 1997 and 1999, none large enough to constitute a majority (Standish 1999). Party switching is common. Party discipline hardly exists. In such an environment, it is exceedingly difficult to enact sustained legislative programs that might lead to more effective government.

Papua New Guinean political leaders differ in style from distinguished statesmanship (Sir Julius Chan, Sir Mekere Morauta) to hard-talking buffoonery (Bill Skate). But none seem able to provide effective government. A tidal wave disaster in 1998 took 2,000 lives, yet the government proved unable to provide help; instead, help came from NGOs and from donations from church congregations throughout the South Pacific. Disillusion with government institutions and the governing elite has grown in recent years. And it is voiced: there are lively, often scathing discussions in the press and even on the Internet (Papua New Guinea Women's Forum 2000a; Standish 1999). A March 2002 parliamentary debate in which former Prime Minister Bill Skate used the "F" word against current Prime Minister Sir Mekere Morauta—and drew loud applause—was reported in both the *National Online* and the *Post-Courier* on March 28.

Women and religious leaders have mounted huge demonstrations against violent, misogynistic, crime. In was no secret when, a few years ago, a videotape of a high minister having sex with an underage girl was tabled in Parliament (Standish 1999). In Papua New Guinea, at any rate, open debate is no guarantee of effective government. Politicians who are currently out of power eloquently denounce the corruption and moral degeneracy of those who are in—then revel in these when they come into power.

Government corruption has reached a point where it seriously hinders the economic welfare of the country. For example, ruthless clear-cutting of tropical timber by Malaysian logging companies endangers the long-term viability of one of the country's major resources, but this is, as noted above, sheltered by Big Men on the take.

The Aid Donor/Developing Country Syndrome

During over four years at the University of the South Pacific (1995–99) the author both participated in, and observed, the South Pacific variant of the behaviors and assumptions that make up this syndrome, an elaborate yet ultimately unproductive minuet involving aid consultants, aid donors, NGO administrators, and South Pacific politicians and government leaders. Aid donors, above all Australia, provide the financial resources, as do some NGOs. Consultants provide the content—consultant reports, meetings for discussion and debate, and training opportunities. Papua New Guinea's government provides the people who receive all of this content.

A sizeable group of the consultants thrives by providing studies, training programs, and advice to government ministries and regional (e.g., South Pacific Forum Secretariat) as well as global (e.g., UN agencies) organizations dedicated to fostering economic and human development. The consultants represent the intellectual talent of Western Europe, Australia, and North America—at least in economics. Little use is made of anthropology, although anthropologists' studies could help formulate considerably more relevant and actionable development projects. Little use is made of applied disciplines in management.

As the largest, most populous, and resource-rich country in the South Pacific, Papua New Guinea is a major customer for aid consultants. In addition to reports—some normative, others describing multiyear projects that have been completed—aid consultants provide training, training, and yet more training. Many government employees are sent to international training events in Fiji or Australia. Ministers look forward to high-level international "study" tours to advanced market economies.

Those sent for training expect to be, and usually are, paid for attending. They are frequently selected because they are the cronies and favorites of government ministers rather than because they might learn something. In Suva, Fiji, owners of nightclubs and brothels look forward to such events, especially those heavily attended by Papua New Guineans. Cairns, Australia, is another favored venue, because wives and other ladies like the amenities and the shopping there. Originally idealistic trainers soon realize that their efforts will amount to little.

Similarly, idealistic consultants soon realize that their project reports will seldom lead to sustained action, if they are even read. One reason for this is that key government figures are rarely in their offices in Papua New Guinea, but rather they are almost constantly jetting to international meetings in posh venues. Conference and "study" travel takes up a great deal of the time of top ministers in Papua New Guinea (Pitts 2001). If it did not, their prestige would suffer, as prestige rises proportionately with the amount of time that one is outside the country. These are often intelligent and vibrant people, shaped by this syndrome into people who simply lack the time to act upon even the most brilliant consultant report or insight acquired during an international meeting in Paris.

Aside from foreign travel, the well-connected also look forward to another inevitable component of nearly every aid project—new vehicles, including rugged Toyota Kijangs and Hilux pick-ups for the lower ranking and Land Cruisers and equally costly large vehicles for the Big Men. White is the favored color for these vehicles; dark-tinted windows are a must-have feature.

There are always new projects. As this is being written in March 2002, there is a frenzied push to increase aid to developing countries as a way of curtailing the appeal of terrorist militants. Given the unstable state of Muslim Indonesia—which includes separatist urges in Irian Jaya— Papua New Guinea can count on being favored with some unexpected new projects as well as the regular infusions from AusAid and other usual donors. Some projects will reflect the current fashionable concerns in the development pantheon—good governance, biodiversity, micro-enterprise, certified timber, anything that promises sustainable development, and so forth. Any of these themes would be relevant to Papua New Guinea, yet they would be funded mainly because they are favored by, and will shower favors upon, overseas consultants and their sleek codependents among Papua New Guinea's elites. Because projects perforce have finite time horizons, each with a beginning, middle, and end, they tend to be forgotten once completed. The South Pacific is a museum for completed then forgotten projects—few of which have ever led to transfer of know-how or continuing progress.

The syndrome has been thriving for decades and, given the material and psychological benefits it showers upon aid consultants and aid recipients, should continue to thrive into the indeterminate future. The probability that any of this activity will promote sustained development, is, of course, slight. On the other hand, it does enable continued conspicuous consumption by elites.

Did Outsiders Ruin Papua New Guinea's Social Structure?

Melanesian writers such as Narokobi (1983) extol traditional society as truly collective and communal, an idyllic human structure in which clan ties and village life provide wonderfully supportive social networks in which altruism and gentleness can flourish. Problems have been inflicted upon Papua New Guinea, according to this line of thought, by foreigners, especially the colonial masters. The Port Moresby crime problem is the fault of the Australians, etc. Blaming foreigners for problems has become part of Papua New Guinean culture; Asians have recently surpassed Australians as the biggest devils in popular thinking (Dyce 2001; Filer and Sekhran 2001).

Did the foreigners from overseas really ruin a gentle and peaceful precolonial society? Certainly, Narokobi and others ignore the constant warfare and cannibalism of precolonial Melanesian society, as well as today's viciousness toward women and internecine strife in rural as well as urban Papua New Guinea. Narokobi's views have been disputed by native citizens, especially women, who have argued that too many Papua New Guinean men are irresponsible and brutal (see Narokobi 1983, chap. 14). Filer and Sekhran (2001) show instances in which supposedly communal-minded and nonmaterialistic villagers can be opportunistic, conflict-prone within clans, and grasping.

The high incidence of violence toward women is deeply rooted in long-established beliefs and social practices in the Highlands (Gilmore 2001, chap. 1; Counts 1994). In many if not all of the Highland village societies, women traditionally lived in separate dwellings from the men, even when married, and have been feared as possible sorceresses. Even today, there are some villages that retain the large men's house surrounded by women's huts. Although men relish sexual intercourse, they believe women's bodies to be dangerously polluted, their menstrual discharges highly toxic for males. Male antagonism toward females is stronger in Papua New Guinea's Highlands than anywhere else on earth; urban drift has brought the antagonism to Port Moresby, Lae, and other urban areas. There are, it should be noted, places within the country where women receive greater respect, for example, the Trobriand Islands (Weiner 1988).

Resilience of Papua New Guinean Society and Culture

Despite decades of exposure to the very different mentalities of developed country people, and despite continual exposure to commercial radio and television fare, anthropological studies show that people in rural Papua New Guinea retain much of their traditional ways (e.g., Kempf 1996; Weiner 1988). In particular, Papua New Guineans still tend to perceive most phenomena in spiritual/ supernatural terms. Kempf (1996) found that his subjects attributed the ascendance of Whites not to racial superiority or advanced culture, but rather to secret ritual knowledge about circumcision —which once discovered could be easily copied by Melanesians. The old culture is durable, as Weiner (1988) found to her surprise in comparing her participant observations in the Trobriand Islands with those done six decades previously by Malinowski (1922). Anthropological studies focus upon specific communities and are not intended to be generalized across the whole country, yet they cumulate in a way that makes the durability and resilience of received ways seem true for the entire society, particularly the rural majority.

MARKETING INSTITUTIONS

Infrastructure and Distribution

Product distribution within the country is costly. Roads in much of Papua New Guinea are few and poor. There are wide paved boulevards in Port Moresby and other urban areas, and good roads on the large islands of New Britain and New Ireland. A cross-country highway is being constructed, yet existing roads are not well maintained. Lae is connected to the interior Highlands by a reasonably good road that is sometimes closed because of tribal warfare and other disputes. Mining companies develop their own infrastructures, at great cost, but these are not open to other traffic. There are no railroads. Much of the interior is not reachable by water. It is frequently cheaper to import food products, such as rice and beef from Australia, than to produce and ship them within the country. Because Papua New Guinea is not on the main sea or air routes, it is costly to bring in imports from Europe or North America (*Papua New Guinea Food Market Report* 1995).

Advertising

There is a lively English-language press in urban areas that carries advertising. Illiteracy and semiliteracy constrain the reach of print media even in urban Papua New Guinea. Radio has the widest reach countrywide, yet television is available to the communities in many rural villages. Communities that have gotten royalties from mining, commercial agriculture, or logging will certainly have the ability to acquire television. Electronic media are the best ways to reach large numbers of people, although one has to bear in mind that most people are only fitfully in the cash economy, and that hundreds of different languages are used. As noted above, English, Pidgin, and Motu are understood in different parts of the country, but hardly by everyone.

CONSUMER LIFE IN PAPUA NEW GUINEA

To understand consumer life, it is necessary to understand the perceptual frameworks within which people in Papua New Guinea operate. These have been influenced by the tide of developed country thinking, yet in many ways, retain far older structures.

Awareness of Western Goods: Cargo Cults

People in coastal areas were stupefied by the material abundance with which early colonial officials and other Westerners surrounded themselves. Papua New Guineans interpreted that materialism within typically supernatural and spiritual frameworks, leading to the earliest of the "cargo cults." Cult members believed that the plethora of goods were gifts from their own ancestors that had been intercepted and stolen by the cunning white settlers. By building symbolic representations of the ships (and later airplanes) that the whites had used to deceive the Papua New Guinean ancestors, it would be possible to attract the "cargo" of goods to those for whom they were intended. The cargo cults exploded during and after World War II as a result of exposure to the material-rich U.S. soldiers fighting to dislodge the Japanese from New Guinea. A few cargo cults still exist today in Papua New Guinea (on cargo cults, see Lawrence 1964; Steinbauer 1971; Whitehouse 1995).

Cargo cults were ridiculed by the Australian colonial administrators as the simple-minded fantasies of hopeless primitives. Today, many Papua New Guineans are embarrassed by the cults. Yet the thinking behind cargo cults reflected a highly developed spiritual mentality by means of which Papua New Guineans interpreted the unimagined spectacle of industrial affluence. Western goods joined some traditional items—pigs, shells, stone axe blades, clay pots, yams—in the pantheon of prized possessions, in some cases being assigned meaning and significance far beyond anything that Western advertising creative directors could envision. Such items could not conceivably come from an economic system grounded in utility maximization and ceaseless toil but had to have spiritual and supernatural origin. Such thinking makes sense to people who believe that most deaths are caused by human sorcery rather than by "natural causes" (Weiner 1988).

The Rural Majority

As noted above, approximately 85 percent of Papua New Guinea's five million inhabitants live in rural villages on a basically subsistence basis. Their lives take place largely outside of the market economy. Subsistence means self-providing, and this is what most people do, albeit on a collective level across the village. Growing conditions are usually good in most of the country, with plentiful crops, especially yams, to support both people and pigs. Pigs represent wealth. In villages where females dwell apart from men, they often live with the pigs. Shelter, clothing, and artifacts are created from local materials, although cloth and manufactured clothing bought in village trading stores are being used more and more. Descriptions by anthropologists and adventure tourists indicate some density of material goods as well as exchange rituals, largely involving self-created objects. In the much-studied Trobriand Islands, bundles of banana leaves are valuable for some ritual occasions, and yams are valued far beyond their food worth (Weiner 1988). Men may purchase store items and then exchange them for banana leaf bundles.

(If these practices seem primitive, one should study the monetary values assigned to items such as cereal boxes, beer cans, and barbed wire by Western collectors dealing on Internet auction sites.)

Villagers make occasional forays into the cash economy, for example, by selling coffee beans, cocoa beans, or copra for cash that, in turn, might be used to acquire products such as cloth, clothing, pots, canned fish, canned corned beef, rice, beverages, beer, or cigarettes in a small village store. Formerly owned by people of European descent, the stores are increasingly owned and operated by Asian families. Weiner (1988) observed that Johnson's Baby Powder was purchased for use as a male body decoration in the Trobriand Islands. Cash might be used to acquire religious literature or artifacts from one of the country's nine Christian bookstores. Anthropologists report seeing Western T-shirts and other clothing being worn by men even in remote areas.

Limited use of cash money and high distribution costs mean that the retail "trading" stores of rural areas are spartan in appearance and have limited product arrays. Store names, however, may reflect higher aspirations—Peachin (1997) found one rural shack store calling itself "K-Mart." Fresh vegetables are sold at village vegetable markets.

Rural Elites

Rural elites command large wealth. Some people have always had more wealth in rural Papua New Guinea, although they also had greater responsibilities to help others. Weiner (1988) found that chiefs could have multiple wives and openly lust after still more, while commoner males had to restrict themselves to one and lust discretely. Since independence, the unbalanced distribution of mining and logging royalties has led to more pronounced—and disputed—imbalances of wealth in rural areas. Today's rural Big Man may have multiple ostentatious large dwellings, possibly including one in Port Moresby and perhaps another in Cairns, Australia, have at least one 4×4 luxury vehicle, and travel frequently. His children will enjoy similar consumption experiences. He will bestow largesse upon his friends and followers, but not necessarily as generously as did traditional leaders. He may neglect kin with whom he disagrees (Narokobi 1983).

The Urban Minority

In urban areas, extremes of wealth and consumption are strikingly evident. The lifestyles of the expatriate communities and Papua New Guinea's economic elite are materially lavish—and protected by elaborate human and other security. Unless given substantial combat pay, few expatriates would come to crime-ridden Papua New Guinea. When there, they expect to have lavish apartments with swimming pools, satellite dish television, upscale Western appliances, and soft-spoken domestic help. Luxury apartment complexes are now favored over detached houses, because they can provide more security against attacks by raskol gangs. Expatriates expect new and luxurious sport-utility vehicles. They expect to be able to buy the packaged foods and health and beauty aids to which they are accustomed. They expect frequent rest and recuperation trips to Australia and other developed countries. Many expect to have their own yachts or, at the minimum, ocean-worthy motorized boats.

Expatriates tend to acquire much of their clothing, shoes, and electronic goods overseas, either before coming to Papua New Guinea or during overseas trips. These items are sold in the country but at high prices. Few books are sold there, making these another item to be acquired overseas

(UNDP 1997). An Australian consultant with considerable experience in Papua New Guinea has recently observed that the lifestyle of the expatriate community is heavily influenced by that of rural areas of Australia's Queensland Province (Dyce 2001). It is considerably different from the cosmopolitan lifestyles common in Sydney or Melbourne. Styles that were popular in Sydney and Melbourne in the 1970s remain popular among expatriates in Papua New Guinea today. An example is restaurant menus so laden with spectacular flambé dishes that the dining room experience becomes like a bonfire and fireworks show. Expatriates consume mainly Western-style foods: frozen TV diners, frozen imported beef, local chicken, cold cereals, temperate climate fruits (apples, pears), imported juices, confectionary and snack foods, spices, sauces, and dressings (*Papua New Guinea Food Market Report* 1995). Several supermarket chains cater to urban expatriates, generally, familiar names from Australia but at least one run by overseas Chinese.

Papua New Guinea's own economic elite consists of government ministers and other high officials and Big Men from the provinces as well as the urban areas. Some Big Men are full-time crime bosses. These people have adopted most of the same imported foodstuffs as the expatriates, particularly the Australians. The indigenous elite expect all that the expatriates have and more, although boats and yachts hold less interest. They too do much of their shopping for clothes, footwear, and appliances in developed countries overseas; the fact that a product was purchased in a rich overseas country adds immeasurably to its value. They also expect to have sufficient funds to pay bride prices that will get the finest brides. Their vehicles should be white, with tinted windows. The elite also expect to have a substantial presence overseas, especially in Australia, by means of property acquisition, private education for their children, private bank accounts, and frequent overseas junkets to luxurious venues. Tastes run to the ostentatious; a shop in one of the high-security luxury hotels in Port Moresby recently featured photo albums with puffy covers in bright pink acrylic (Dyce 2001).

Urban Papua New Guineans of modest means are increasingly reliant on fast food, retail, and service businesses operated by newly migrated Asian families who rely on family members for labor and exploit their native supply contacts for cheap overseas imports. They thus have weak roots in Papua New Guinea and yet appear to thrive more than do indigenous urban people. There is a rising feeling among Papua New Guineans that they are being marginalized in their own country (Dyce 2001). In the author's own experience, Asian merchants can be arrogant and condescending toward Melanesians in ways that are much more offensive than, say, crude behavior by Australian mining expatriates. In Papua New Guinea as in the Melanesian Solomon Islands, dark interiors and overpriced shoddy products characterize many Asian retail stores.

Among urban Papua New Guineans, rice has become a staple food, most of it currently imported from Australia. Research by Gibson (2001a; 2001b) indicates, however, that urban dwellers with Highland roots tend to stick to yams long after migrating to urban settlements—still another example of the persistence of past practice among Papua New Guineans. Tinned fatty corned beef and fish are popular edibles. As do their rural fellow citizens, many urban men chew betel nut, a traditional mild intoxicant that stains teeth red and results in the expectoration of copious red spittle. Just as drinking kava is fundamental to Melanesian life in Fiji, so too is chewing betel nut fundamental to the Melanesian way of life in Papua New Guinea, according to the journalist and current Leader of the Opposition Narokobi (1983).

Marketing Opportunities

Resentful of the shoddy merchandise they are often presented, Papua New Guineans of moderate incomes would respond enthusiastically to retail establishments offering good-quality products at affordable prices. There are a few models for such stores operating in urban areas in Fiji, stocking products such as decent-quality kitchenware, cosmetics for dark-skinned curly-haired people, linens, and small ceramic pieces suitable for decoration or gift giving. However, efforts to establish such stores would be resisted by entrenched merchants and the government officials under their (paid) control.

There is a huge demand for religious literature, pictures, and other items across all income levels in Papua New Guinea.

Papua New Guineans have been adept at figuring out their own uses for familiar manufactured products, such as textiles and baby powder—they clearly have their own ways of responding to and assigning meaning to products. Well-informed and subtle promotional efforts might encourage more new uses for products. Well-informed means using market research grounded in cultural anthropological methods, which are labor intensive but offer a proven way to understand Papua New Guinean situations. Long interviews might work well with the educated urban elite. Conventional surveys as well as focus groups elicit far too many demand artifacts and too much whimsical role-playing.

The country's indigenous elites as well as expatriates do much of their buying overseas and will continue to do so. For expatriates, overseas purchases seem more trustworthy; for indigenous elites, they offer prestige. To reach such people, marketers should think about distribution outlets in Cairns, Australia, and other favored spots.

There are some elite sector market opportunities that can be pursued by means of distribution within Papua New Guinea. The shops in high-security hotels in Port Moresby and Lae are also good places from which to sell to Big Men and their ladies. Products targeted at such consumers gain in appeal as they gain in flamboyance and ostentation—if it would have appealed to Liberace, it will likely appeal to them. These are consumers for whom conspicuous consumption is a joyful experience, to be relished without shame or scruple. Stretched versions of already-enormous sport-utility vehicles should be attractive to some expatriates and Big Men alike. The rampant crime creates market opportunities for security services and devices as well as weapons. Callick (2000) reports on a gun manufacturer in the Highlands who puts production in overtime to meet the demand surges that accompany national and provincial elections.

FUTURE TRENDS

The Morauta government has not been able to energize the economy, cut crime, or develop a system of secure land use that would be acceptable to communities as well as investors (Duncan 2001). It has no control over world mineral prices, which so heavily influence foreigners' willingness to develop the gold, silver, and copper mines. It has no control over coffee prices, which are considerably below historic peaks. Among Australians—traditionally the largest investors in the country—the *Sydney Morning Herald* (2002b) story "Caution Reigns Over PNG Gas" reports skepticism that even the large natural gas deposits will represent a viable *business*. Given investor attitudes toward Papua New Guinea, only major increases in world commodity prices would justify substantial investments. The influx of Asian families seeking to operate small businesses, however, will continue, because prior families have done well by their standards. Similarly, larger Asian firms, which have mastered the art of buying officials, should also continue to come. At some point in the not-too-distant future, the perceived "Asianization" of the economy may provoke popular violence, just as it did in Indonesia a few years ago.

The dependency of the governing elite on overseas aid money has been accentuated in recent months by the Australian government's humiliating demand that Papua New Guinea and other

South Pacific aid recipients must "temporarily" house the Afghan and other refugees who are seeking asylum in Australia. As the respected *Sydney Morning Herald* reported (2001a), "PNG (has been) Urged to Get a Wiggle Over Camp." Papua New Guinea has, in fact, recently agreed to take in several hundred more refugees, according to the article "Not a Solution" in the *Sydney Morning Herald* (2002a).

On the positive side, the government has been proceeding to implement its promise of free education. A tax cut in November 2001 benefited the lowest-paid workers in the cash economy (Papua New Guinea *Post-Courier* November 23, 2001). Papua New Guinea has accepted the loss of Bougainville and not attempted to thwart that island's movement toward full autonomy. Political discussion remains open and uninhibited. World cocoa prices are soaring as this is written, which will bring more spending cash for some rural citizens. The country's newspapers carry optimistic stories about indigenous business growth. In "Agarwood Spurs New 'Gold Rush,'" *The National Online* for March 28, 2002, reported a growing demand for the country's aromatic agarwood. In "Lufa Cashes in on Mushroom Sales," the *Post-Courier* for March 28–April 2, 2002 describes entrepreneurial mushroom growing for cash sales in the Eastern Highlands. At best, however, these ventures will help a few hundred families. Gradual improvements in the country's infrastructure, especially progress on a paved North–South highway across the main island, are counterbalanced by poor maintenance and deterioration of some other infrastructure. The Papua New Guinea *Post-Courier* for March 26 reported that a main highway had been severed by recent washouts.

On balance, no radical change in economic life seems likely over the next several years. Elections will jiggle the political lineup; but for every scoundrel swept out, a previous scoundrel is likely to be voted back in. The winners will want to stock up on expensive kitsch at home and, especially, overseas. The usual marketing opportunities, including, of course, first-class air tickets to Cairns and other favored spots, should continue. Aid consultants and their happy clients will have opportunities to fly to international summits to discuss the latest hot issue of this community—good governance.

CONCLUSION

Papua New Guinea is a different place, a place where highly evolved societies have been dragged into economic modernity by colonial powers and then by the expectations of the development community. The people have taken on some aspects of economic modernity, but usually in their own unique ways. Much of what is conventionally taught about marketing and consumer behavior shows up as ethnocentric and irrelevant in this environment. Papua New Guinea is not on the verge of becoming the latest Southeast Asian "tiger." It is not on the verge of becoming a marketer's consumer paradise, as are sections of China and India. By standards grounded in Western development experience, Papua New Guinea is a disappointment. Most of its people think differently and have profoundly different values; they are not ready, and do not want to become ready, to become consumers such as those who populate Australia, the United States, Japan, or other consumer societies. In their deep and pervasive spirituality, they have more in common with other South Pacific people as well as Sub-Saharan Africans. Papua New Guineans certainly enjoy some products and services typical of "developed" country life, especially big vehicles and jet travel— yet many may not value these any higher than they do pigs, shells, or banana bundles. The crime and political racketeering that so anger aid donors, World Bank types, and the country's own Westernized minorities are, in a sense, a way of mocking the outsiders who burst in uninvited upon this unique world two centuries ago.

REFERENCES

Aka, Joseph R. 2001. "Papua New Guinea Country Report." Report presented to ESCAP Workshop on Environmental Studies, Port Vila, Vanuatu.

Australian Department of Foreign Affairs and Trade. 2001. "Travel Information: Papua New Guinea."

Callick, Rowan. 1995. "Papua New Guinea: The Cargo Cult is on the Way Back." *Australian Financial Review,* December 22.

————. 2000. "Pacific Observed." *Australian Financial Review,* August 16.

Central Intelligence Agency. 2000. *The World Factbook.* Washington, DC: Central Intelligence Agency.

Chand, Satish, ed. 1998. *Productivity Performance in the South Pacific Islands.* Canberra: National Centre for Development Studies.

Chand, Satish, and Theodore Levantis. 1998. "The Nexus Between Crime and Productivity in Papua New Guinea." In *Productivity Performance in the South Pacific Islands*, ed. Satish Chand, pp. 33–46. Canberra: National Centre for Development Studies.

Counts, Dorothy Ayers. 1994. "Snakes, Adulterers, and the Loss of Paradise in Kaliai." *Pacific Studies* 17: 109–51.

Dinnen, Sinclair. 1998. "Criminal Justice Reform in Papua New Guinea." National Briefing Paper, Canberra: National Centre for Development Studies.

Duncan, Ron. 2001. "PNG Economic Survey: A Scorecard for the Morauta Administration." *Pacific Economic Bulletin* 16(2).

Dyce, Tim. 2001. Personal communication to the author, November 24.

ECA Watch. ca. 2001. "Case Study: BHP's OK Tedi Copper and Gold Mine—Papua New Guinea." Available at www.eca-watch.org.

Filer, Colin, and Nikhil Sekhran. 2001. *Loggers, Donors, and Resources Owners: Papua New Guinea.* IIED: International Institute for Environment and Development.

Friends of the Earth (FOE). 2001. "UK Govt Funding Forest Destruction." Press release, July 30, London.

Gibson, John. 2001a. "Food Demand in Rural and Urban Sectors of Papua New Guinea." Working paper, University of Waikato, Hamilton, New Zealand.

————. 2001b. "New Town, Old Diet? Highlanders and the Demand for Staples in Urban Papua New Guinea." Working paper, University of Waikato, Hamilton, New Zealand.

Gibson, John, and Osaiasi Fatai. 2001. "Subsidies, Selectivity and the Returns to Education in Urban Papua New Guinea." Working paper, University of Waikato, Hamilton, New Zealand.

Gilmore, David D. 2001. *Misogyny: The Male Malady.* Philadelphia: University of Pennsylvania Press.

Holzknecht, Hartmut. 2002. "Policy Reform, Customary Tenure and Stakeholder Clashes in Papua New Guinea's Rainforests." South Pacific Information Network, Customary Tenure Seminar, paper no. 1.

Inmet Mining Corporation. 2001. "Inmet Announces PNG Approval of OK Tedi Arrangements." Press release, December 12.

Jowitt, Anita. 2001. "Review of Theodore Levantis' Papua New Guinea: Employment, Wages, and Economic Development." *Journal of South Pacific Law* 5.

Kempf, Wolfgang. 1996. *Das Innere des Aeusseren.* Berlin: Dietrich Reimer.

Lawrence, Peter. 1964. *Road Belong Cargo: A Study of the Cargo Movement in the Southern Madang District, New Guinea.* Melbourne: Melbourne University Press.

Lea, David. 2001. "Resolving the Complexity of Land Mobilization Issues in Papua New Guinea." *Pacific Economic Bulletin* 16(2).

Levantis, Theodore, and George Fane. 1998. "Labour Market Reform in Papua New Guinea." In *Productivity Performance in the South Pacific Islands*, ed. Satish Chand, pp. 47–64. Canberra: National Centre for Development Studies.

————. 2000. "Crime Catastrophe—Reviewing Papua New Guinea's Most Serious Social and Economic Problem." *Pacific Economic Bulletin* 15(2): 130–42.

Macfarlane, David. 2002. *Grassland and Pasture Crops Country Pasture/Forage Resource Profiles: Papua New Guinea.* Rome: Food and Agriculture Organization of the United Nations (FAO).

Malinowski, Bronislaw. 1922. *Argonauts of the Western Pacific.* New York: E.P. Dutton.

Mana, Bui. 1999. "An Anti-Corruption Policy for Provincial Government in Papua New Guinea." Working paper Gov99–5, Asia Pacific School of Economics and Management, Australian National University, Canberra.

McGavin, Paul. 1998. "Building Productivity Culture in Papua New Guinea." In *Productivity Performance in the South Pacific Islands*, ed. Satish Chand, pp. 65–86. Canberra: National Centre for Development Studies.

Narokobi, Bernard. 1983. *The Melanesian Way*, revised ed. Boroko, Papua New Guinea: Institute of Papua New Guinea Studies.

The National Online. 2002. "Agarwood Spurs New 'Gold Rush,'" March 28.

Papua New Guinea Business and Street Directory. 2001. Available at www.nationwidepngpages.com.

Papua New Guinea Food Market Report. 1995. Singapore: Agricultural Trade Office of the Foreign Agricultural Service/USDA.

"Papua New Guinea—Land of the Unexpected." ca. 1997. Available at www.geocities.com/Hot Springs.

Papua New Guinea Women's Forum. 2000a. "Hey, What's Our First Ladies Up To???" (www.network/54.com).

———. 2000b. Available at www.pngbd.com/forum/

Peachin, Mary L. 1997. "Adventuring in Papua New Guinea." *The Private, Selective Newsletter for the Active/Adventure Traveler* 1(6).

Pitts, Maxine. 2001. "Crime and Corruption—Does Papua New Guinea Have the Capacity to Control It?" *Pacific Economic Bulletin* 16(2): 127–34.

Post-Courier. 2002a. "OK Tedi Regional Trusts Are Set Up," March 28.

———. 2002b. "Lufa Cashes In on Mushroom Sales," March 28–April 2.

Standish, Bill. 1999. "Papua New Guinea 1999: Crisis of Governance." Research paper 4 (1999–2000), Parliament of Australia.

Steinbauer, F. 1971. *Melanesische Cargo-Kulte*. Munich: Delp.

Sydney Morning Herald. 2001a. "PNG (has been) Urged to Get a Wiggle Over Camp," October 16.

———. 2001b. "Dutch Priest Robbed and Shot in PNG," November 25.

———. 2002a. "Not a Solution," January 22.

———. 2002b. "Caution Reigns Over PNG Gas," March 28.

United Nations Development Programme (UNDP). 1997. "Briefing Report: Papua New Guinea."

Ward, Michael. 2000. "Cooling Emotions with Money: Compensation Policy Reform in Papua New Guinea." *Pacific Economic Bulletin* 15(1):119–25.

Weiner, Annette B. 1988. *The Trobrianders of Papua New Guinea*. Fort Worth: Harcourt Brace.

Whitehouse, Harvey. 1995. *Inside the Cult*. Oxford: Oxford University Press.

World Bank. 2002. Papua New Guinea Country Report. Washington: World Bank Group.

World Rainforest Movement (WRM). 2001. "Papua New Guinea: Social and Environmental Destruction by Logging." WRM Bulletin no. 43. Available at www.wrm.org.uy/index.html.

CHAPTER 14

THE PHILIPPINES

Marketing and Consumer Behavior—Past, Present, and Future

ALBERT F. CELOZA, JANE HUTCHISON, AND ANTHONY PECOTICH

OVERVIEW

The Philippines, an Asian nation with strong connections to the West, was established through colonialism, first by Spain and then by the United States. The Philippines is emerging from a period of political and economic unrest to join the ranks of fast-growing, developing nations. The journey, however, is not yet complete, and although the most recent signs are very promising, the nation still faces many political and economic problems. In this chapter, an attempt is made to provide a brief historical introduction to the marketing, consumer, and economic environments of this evolving nation that has the potential to provide a positive model of successful economic development by a democratic Asian nation.

INTRODUCTION

Not so long ago, the Philippines was being cast as the "sick man" of Asia. But by weathering the 1997 financial crisis comparatively well, and thereafter returning to modest economic growth sooner than Thailand, Indonesia, or Malaysia, its regional status has improved markedly. Indeed, with the consolidation of democratic institutions in the last decade, the Philippines is looking to offer a unique example of "development with democracy" in East and Southeast Asia. Yet, despite these positive developments, other troubling national features have not changed considerably. The recent return to modest economic growth has not reduced the high levels of poverty and inequality; nor has the restoration of democracy seen a significant lessening of public- and private-sector corruption (Asian Development Bank 2003; World Bank 2001, 2002). In this chapter, we outline how these and other aspects of the Philippines' political and economic development have shaped the environment for marketing, as well as briefly enumerate the elements of the environmental structure.

THE PHYSICAL ENVIRONMENT

The Philippines consists of 7,107 islands (the combined land area of which amounts to 300,000 square kilometers), about 880 of which are inhabited. The two largest islands, Luzon in the north (covering 104,688 square kilometers), and Mindanao (94,630 square kilometers) in the south, account for 66.4 percent of its territory (Europa 1994). The climate is maritime and tropical, the seasons varying more in the amount of rainfall than in temperature. Because of its mountainous character and its alignment, the Philippines has considerable regional variation in both the total amount and the seasonal incidence of rainfall. The climatic vagaries between the wet and dry seasons, typhoons, and high temperatures (rarely much below 26.7°C) places considerable pressure on the farming community, as many members of this community lead a marginal existence (Europa 1995). About a third of the total land area is arable and under permanent crops (Economic and Social Commission for Asia and the Pacific [hereafter ESCAP], 2001). The best food-producing region is in the central lowlands of Luzon, although many of the smaller lowlands are also intensively cultivated, despite poor soil quality (Europa 1995).

Since the 1940s, the only substantial areas of lowland offering scope for any extension of cultivation have been in the southern island of Mindanao. However, the population growth in recent years has placed great pressure on the resources of this island, where such treasures as the tropical hardwoods are rapidly disappearing (Europa 1995). Rice is the most important single crop, although on some of the islands, because of low rainfall, maize is the leading food crop. Major export crops are coconut products, bananas, and canned pineapples. A wide range of metallic mineral deposits exists, the most important of which are copper, chromate, and nickel. Unfortunately, the country is deficient in energy-producing minerals, with 60 percent of the energy requirements (mostly petroleum) imported in 1990. Increasing costs of oil-based imports motivated the search for and discovery of petroleum on the island of Palawan in 1977. The energy sector's reliance on petroleum decreased significantly by 2003 with the development of new sources of power (Asian Development Bank 2003; Europa 2003, 2004).

THE CONSUMER ENVIRONMENT

Demographics

The population of the Philippines reached 77.9 million by mid-2001, compared with 48.3 million in 1980 (Asian Development Bank 2003; Europa 2003, 2004; ESCAP 2001). The population growth rate of 2.3 percent in 2000 remains one of the highest in the region, despite its decrease from the 3.1 percent rate of the 1960s. Indonesia, by contrast, had a 1.5 percent population growth rate in 2000 (ESCAP 2001). The influence of the Catholic church means that family planning programs are not well developed and tend to depend on foreign assistance (World Bank 2000, 32). As a consequence, at the end of the twentieth century, Filipino women were still bearing, on average, one more child than they wanted (World Bank 2000, 29). At current growth rates, this means that the population of the Philippines is expected to double by 2029 (National Statistical Office 2002).

In 2001, the average population density was 259.8 persons per square kilometer. This is well above the density of all other Southeast Asian nations, except Singapore, which is a city state (Asian Development Bank 2003; Europa 2003, 2004; ESCAP 2001). This existing density and the high rate of population growth are placing increasingly severe pressure on the available productive land resources, particularly in central Luzon (Europa 1995, 2003, 2004). Though the majority still live in rural areas, there has been an ever-increasing urban drift since the mid-1970s. The proportion of the population in urban areas in 2000 was 58.6 percent compared with 37.3 percent twenty years earlier (ESCAP 2001). Manila, the nation's capital, is the core of an extensive, densely populated area called the National Capital Region (NCR) of Metropolitan Manila.

The NCR had 9.9 million inhabitants and a population density of 15,617 per square kilometer in 2000 (National Statistical Office 2002). It is thus one of the busiest and most congested cities of Southeast Asia. Other major urbanized macro regions are Cebu City (2.4 million) in the Central Visayas, Davao City (1.1 million) in Southern Mindanao, and Zamboanga City (601,794) in Western Mindanao (National Statistical Office 2002).

In 2001, the size of the workforce was estimated at some 29.5 million (National Economic and Development Authority [NEDA] 2002). Unemployment was officially at 11 percent, compared to 9 percent in 1990 (National Statistical Office 2002). Underemployment was officially at 16 percent, with the figure much higher in rural areas (National Statistical Office 2002). However, unemployment and underemployment levels would be even greater if there were not many Filipinos looking for work overseas. According to the Asian Development Bank, the Philippines is the region's largest exporter of labor, and the world's second largest, after Mexico (Tigno 1997, 2). In 2001 alone, 866,590 individuals left to find temporary employment, four times the number that departed in a year twenty years earlier (NEDA 2002). While, typically, women in their mid- to late twenties become domestic workers in Hong Kong, men in their early thirties obtain work in construction in the Middle East. The wages these workers send back to their families kept the growth in private consumption ahead of that for gross domestic product (GDP) for all of the 1990s (World Bank 2000, 25). In 2001, the value of remittances sent through official channels was US$6,235 million (NEDA 2002).

In part because of the historical failure of the economy to grow apace with the population, the incidence of poverty is high. Just before the 1997 financial crisis, a quarter of the population was living below the official poverty line in that their spending was below the cost of basic needs (World Bank 2000, 6–7). This figure is a marked improvement on the 41 percent figure for 1985, yet since the 1997 financial crisis, "poverty reduction has stagnated" (World Bank 2002, 4). Agriculture is the area of greatest poverty, and the one where improvements have been slowest (World Bank 2000, 21–22). While poverty declined in the mid-1990s, inequality did not. Families in all income groups gained between 1994 and 1997, but those with the highest incomes gained more purchasing power than the rest (World Bank 2000, 26).

Education

In spite of the poverty and inequality, Filipinos are comparatively well educated. In 1999, the adult literacy rate for men and women was 95 percent (ESCAP 2001). In the same year, just under 20 percent of government spending went to education (ESCAP 2001). Compulsory elementary education begins at seven and lasts for six years, with instruction in English and Filipino. In 2001, 96 percent of all children in the relevant age group were enrolled in primary schools and 70 percent in secondary schools (NEDA 2002). Participation rates are increasing, and so too are the number of dropouts. Nearly a third of students who enroll do not complete their primary schooling, while less than half who begin secondary school get to the end of their fourth year (World Bank 2002, 6). In technical training at the tertiary level, the Philippines is doing relatively well. A higher proportion of students in technical courses can be found in this country than in Malaysia, Indonesia, and Thailand. This has done much to create a skilled workforce that is attractive to foreign investment (World Bank 2000, 24). In higher education, the most popular fields are business, education, engineering, math, and computer sciences (Villegas 2001, 67). Philippine institutions of higher learning, as well as vocational and technical schools, are turning out skilled workers ready to take on jobs and work opportunities at home and abroad.

Culture and Religion

Although the majority of the population is Malay, Philippine culture is a product of diverse ethnic and historical influences (Bair 1988). The major cultural influences initially emanated from Chinese and Hindu-Arab merchants who gained a foothold for trading purposes. In the sixteenth century, the Chinese began to settle in the Philippines and quickly gained influence in the economy by accumulating capital to dominate commerce, trade, and the market for skilled labor. The Spaniards, in turn, dominated the islands for 300 years, followed by U.S. colonial rule that lasted for another fifty years. During the postcolonial period, U.S. language and cultural forces remained highly influential, despite strong nationalistic tendencies.

The Philippines is the only predominantly Christian state in Asia (*The Asia and Pacific Review* 1990). Reflecting the country's past as a former Spanish colony, over 80 percent of the population practices the Roman Catholic faith. Around two million Muslims (about 5 percent of the total population) live in the southern islands (*Asian Economic Handbook* 1987; Europa 1995). The influence of the Catholic church on social policy is reflected in the slow efforts of government with regards to family planning and the continued ban on divorce. There are also a number of much smaller communities of animist hill peoples, principally in the more remote parts of Luzon and Mindanao, who together contribute perhaps 6 percent of the total (Europa 1995). The Chinese population in the Philippines is minimal, accounting for only about 1 percent of the total (Europa 1995), but this population's share in business and financial activities is proportionately greater than their number. Through intermarriage with the native population, the Chinese have contributed to the country's customs and traditions.

Despite the existence of several regional languages, the lowland Filipinos, who form the great majority of the population, share a common culture based on Roman Catholicism. In recent decades, considerable progress has been made in developing Tagalog, the language of central Luzon, as a national language (Filipino). English is widely used, particularly among the largely mestizo elite elements and for practically all business and political transactions (Europa 1995). Eleven Malayo-Polynesian languages and eighty-seven dialects are spoken, with over 90 percent of the population speaking one of their native tongues, such as Tagalog, Cebuano, Hiligaynon, Bicolano, Waray-Waray, Pampangan, Ilocano, and Pangasinan (Dolan 1993).

In general, Filipinos are often claimed to be highly personalistic in their social orientation. That is, they place great importance on the maintenance of strong interpersonal relations (see Library of Congress 1991). This is argued to shape public institutions in two ways. First, with regards to elections and political representation, "the overriding importance of interpersonal linkages" is said to hamper "the emergence of any group loyalties on which cohesive political parties or policy-oriented activities might be based" (Wurfel 1988, 35). Second, the primacy of personal relations is seen to conflict with the rational, "public service" requirements of a modern bureaucracy (Hutchcroft 1994). The "cronyism" and corruption that result are argued to lower state capacities with regards to business governance and the delivery of social services. In these terms, successive governments have been characterized as "weak" (Rivera 1996). Yet, as the next section explains, these features of public life are not the product of an immutable culture. They are a product of historical events with relatively enduring legacies that, nevertheless, are subject to some of the social changes that arise with economic complexity.

GOVERNMENT AND POLITICS

The constitution, which was approved by a national referendum on February 2, 1987, provides for a bicameral congress comprised of a directly elected, twenty-four-member senate, and a house of representatives (with a three-year mandate) that has a maximum of 250 members (200 are directly elected). Executive authority is vested in the president and cabinet, but power is separated under the constitution, with legislative power held by the elected congress, and judicial power placed with the supreme court and lower courts. Local government exists in the thirteen regions, with provincial, city, and municipal councils (*The Asia and Pacific Review* 1990). The president is head of state, chief executive of the Republic, and commander-in-chief of the armed forces (Europa 1994). The presidential term (six years without further eligibility) and other powers are limited to prevent the rise of another autocrat.

Historical Background

The precolonial era was a period of fragmented political organization incapable of resisting Spanish colonial conquest (Brown 1995). Under the Spanish regime, the Philippines became the bridge for the China–Acapulco trade, as goods crossed the Pacific until Mexico became independent in 1821. From these colonial initiatives, there emerged the production and export of crops such as sugar, coconuts, Manila hemp (abaca), and tobacco, that were to become the foundation of the economy during colonial rule and into the post-independence period (Brown 1995). These economic changes had important repercussions, both socially and politically. An increase in agricultural production, from the middle of the nineteenth century onwards, encouraged the settlement of a vigorous Chinese entrepreneurial class from which the mestizo, or half-caste, elite developed (sons of Chinese fathers and native mothers, brought up as natives and Roman Catholics). The mestizo derived their wealth and influence from land ownership, and frequently sent their children, born of native mothers and known as *ilustrados* (enlightened ones), to universities in Manila and Europe (Brown 1995).

The principal aim of Spanish rule in the Philippines was religious conversion. In this, Spain exerted a profound influence over the indigenous population, although the Muslims of Mindanao and Sulu effectively resisted conversion to Roman Catholicism, and animist beliefs were by no means exterminated. The ilustrados became the channels for Spanish culture and liberal thought, but by the end of the nineteenth century, they were challenging the repressive orthodoxy and exclusiveness of Spanish rule (Brown 1995). They sought reform through a so-called Propaganda Movement, but the mass of rural and urban Filipinos, impoverished by loss of land and exploitation, were moving toward armed revolt against the colonial power (Brown 1995). The Philippine revolution erupted in 1896, launched by a secret society, the Katipunan (Association of Sons of the People). After the entry of the United States into the war, General Emilio Aguinaldo, leader of the revolutionary movement, proclaimed Philippine independence on June 12, 1898, with the support of the United States (Europa 1994). However, from this time onwards, a rift developed between the United States and its Filipino "allies." In December 1898, the Spanish ceded the Philippines to the United States for the payment of US$20 million under the terms of the Treaty of Paris (Brown 1995). On January 23, 1899, the Philippine Republic was inaugurated, and for a year after, the new republic resisted the U.S. forces (Brown 1995). However, though President Aguinaldo took his oath of allegiance to the United States in 1900 and urged his fellow Filipinos to do the same, sporadic fighting by guerrillas continued.

Rule by the United States

Under U.S. dominance, the Philippines became even more heavily dependent on agricultural exports, and the rural masses found no relief from the exploitative conditions of tenancy. Superficially, the U.S. political administration appeared to constitute a decisive break with the past (Brown 1995), for while the Spanish had denied Filipinos even the prospect of political advancement, the new U.S. administration moved rapidly to make political and bureaucratic positions accessible to them. By 1903, Filipinos occupied 49 percent of bureaucratic positions. By 1928, virtually the whole colonial government was controlled by Filipinos (Brown 1995). However, these appointees were almost exclusively ilustrados, and as a result, land reform that would have destroyed the foundation of their wealth and influence was out of the question. Without such reform, the early introduction of democracy resulted in wealthy landowners dominating the legislature.

Philippine independence was secured less by Filipino agitation than by U.S. domestic rejection of its colonial role, due to its heritage of independence and democratic traditions (Brown 1995). A new constitution, ratified by plebiscite in May 1935, gave the Philippines internal self-government and provided for independence after ten years (Europa 1994). During World War II in early 1942, Manila was invaded and occupied by the Japanese (Brown 1995). But, after Japan's surrender in 1945, U.S. rule was restored. The political and bureaucratic elite remained largely intact during this occupation (Brown 1995).

The Republic of the Philippines and the Marcos Years

The occupation and liberation resulted in a severely damaged physical capital infrastructure and an export economy that was in urgent need of rehabilitation. However, this was difficult to achieve with the Filipino political life full of conflict and chaos, and it was inevitable that the movement toward independence (attained on July 4, 1946) was going to be a difficult process (Brown 1995). A succession of presidents effectively constrained by the Filipino land-owning class did little to help the peasant majority or to curb the resultant unrest and violence in the countryside. Ferdinand E. Marcos was elected president in 1965 on a pledge to restore the economy after the obstructionist political wrangling of his predecessors. In his early years of power, he had many successes, transforming the economy with agricultural improvements and initiating the process of industrialization (*Asian Economic Handbook* 1987; Brown 1995). However, by the end of the 1960s, the country faced a balance of payments crisis that was aggravated by massive election spending and vote buying in the 1969 election. Marcos won the presidential election for the second and supposedly last time.

Economic problems and civil unrest plagued President Marcos's second term, and the social fabric of the Republic became unraveled. To restore order and entrench his personal power, Marcos declared martial law in September 1972, claiming the existence of a subversive conspiracy between right-wing oligarchies and Maoist revolutionaries (Brown 1995; Europa 1994). The economic rhetoric of the Marcos administration was strongly behind a shift to export-oriented industrialization. It passed a number of legislative incentives to encourage the rapid growth of manufactured exports like garments and electronics. But while this growth did occur, the government's incentives program was largely not responsible (Lindsey 1992). Instead, in keeping with "weak" governmental capacities, the main thrust of the administration was the economic advancement of the president's family and cronies (Hutchcroft 1994). To support the resultant unsustainable drain on public resources, the administration was forced to rely upon heavy foreign borrowing.

Opposition leader Benigno Aquino's assassination in 1983 (in which Marcos appeared implicated) precipitated a major political crisis (Brown 1995). Domestic political instability caused foreign creditors to suspend the short-term loans that had sustained the economy from the late 1970s onwards (Brown 1995). The U.S. government brought pressure to bear on Marcos, urging him to hold a "snap election" in early 1986 to establish the legitimacy of his regime. But the writing was already on the wall, as the splintered opposition rallied behind Corazon Aquino, widow of the opposition leader. Marcos' claim of electoral victory drew little domestic and international support. The regime fell after a group of reformist military officers withdrew their support and hundreds of thousands protested in the streets in a demonstration of "people power." Marcos, with his family and friends, fled to the United States (Celoza 1992; Celoza and Sours 1993), and he died there in exile three years later. Corazon Aquino was sworn to office as president of the Republic.

After Marcos

Political and economic developments in the Philippines in the 1990s were profoundly shaped by the experience of authoritarian rule under Marcos. On the political front, democratic elections were reintroduced, and the bicameral legislature was restored. However, the new administration's early efforts at political consolidation did not extend to any serious attempt at more fundamental socioeconomic reforms. Despite concerns over the president's ability to produce cohesive policy and the almost bankrupt condition of the economy, popular support for redemocratization was strong. This was demonstrated in February 1987, when the new constitution was approved in a national referendum by 76 percent of voters (Brown 1995). Nevertheless, the subsequent congressional elections in May showed that much had not changed. Overwhelmingly, the candidates elected were from families belonging to the traditional political and economic elite (Bello and Gershman 1990).

Yet, toward the end of her presidency, Aquino made some effort to enlarge the political space for popular participation in government. In particular, the 1991 Local Government Code devolved decision making and resources to the level of local government, while enshrining nongovernmental organization (NGO) representation. In general, this legislation is thought to have left the state "less completely captive of elite interests" than before (Silliman and Noble 1988, 306). Later in the decade, "people power" was again at the fore. Aquino's two successors each proposed changes to the constitution that would allow them to run for the presidency more than twice. However, each was also thwarted in their plans by a number of large public demonstrations in the streets. On these accounts, political processes in the Philippines have become "decidedly more populist than was the case before martial law, and also one that is less confined to the ballot box" (Pinches 1997, 116).

In economic terms, the disastrous example of authoritarianism under Marcos helped to drive the liberalization agenda of the 1990s (de Dios 1998). Initially, in the late 1980s, the Philippine economy was still crippled by large foreign debt repayment obligations and breakdowns in the power supply. Yet, among other moves, the Aquino administration quickly dismantled the marketing monopolies in agriculture, reformed the banking sector, and introduced a program of privatization to reduce debt and encourage private investment (Europa 1994). Also, the administration made headway in trade liberalization. Debt restructuring by the country's commercial creditors and new funds from official sources in the late 1980s reduced both total debt and the cost of servicing it (Hodgkinson 1995). However, the economy continued to struggle, in part because of the additional factors of a couple of failed coup attempts, drought, a major earthquake, and a volcanic eruption (Hodgkinson 1995).

Ramos and Economic Liberalization

General Fidel Ramos was elected president in 1992 with a mandate to right the economy through further market liberalization. Market liberalization was being looked to as the antidote to Marcos-style cronyism (de Dios 1998), but it was also in line with pressures from the World Bank and

International Monetary Fund (IMF). Immediately, the Ramos administration lifted controls on the entry and repatriation of foreign investment. In 1993, the administration's liberalization agenda was locked in with the launch of the "Philippine 2000" plan to see the country become Asia's next tiger economy by the end of the century. Reforms arising from this included the ending of the telephone monopoly, the rehabilitation of the Central Bank, and entry of foreign banks. The Philippines joined the ASEAN Free Trade Area (AFTA), ratified the Uruguay Round of GATT, and thereby, was a founding member of the World Trade Organization (WTO) (WTO 1999). In part as a consequence of these developments, trade liberalization proceeded over the decade, with the average nominal tariff falling from 28 percent in 1990 to about 9 percent in 2000 (World Bank 1999, 22).

A feature of the Philippines' economic performance in the 1990s was the "outstanding" growth in exports (World Bank 1999, 47). The strongest growth came from the electronics industry, semiconductor production in particular. Between 1991 and 1997, 84 percent of the increase in value of exports was from electronics. As a result of this, the structure of Philippine exports are now more high-tech than those of Malaysia, Singapore, South Korea, and Taiwan (World Bank 1999, 47). The Philippines was firmly integrated into transnational production arrangements in the 1990s as a result of the new policies to attract foreign investment. However, an important contributing factor in this was "the ample supply of relatively skilled and English-speaking workers who could quickly adapt to the high-tech production methods" (World Bank 2000, 24). In contrast to electronics, exports of labor-intensive consumer products have declined in importance. For example, garments exports have suffered from "lags in the upgrading of technology and product quality" (World Bank 1999, 53).

But after just three years of strong growth, the Philippine economy was caught up in the 1997 regional financial crisis. Remarkably, given its past poor record, it came through better than its neighbors in Southeast Asia. One reason was that its financial sector was "in better shape than others around the region" (Noland 2000, 402). Commercial banks were better capitalized and so had a lower proportion of nonperforming loans. Also, there was less investment exposure to real estate, and the corporate sector had a lower debt-to-equity ratio (Noland 2000). Because of its past poor performance, in the decade before the crisis, the Philippines had "had relatively less exposure to international 'hot money' flows" than other countries in the region (Noland 2000, 411).

In short, developments that caused the crisis elsewhere in Asia were less prevalent in the Philippines (World Bank 1999, 16). Nevertheless, President Ramos and his successor were able to claim some of the credit for the country's relatively strong performance (Hutchison 2001). President Estrada took office in June 1998, committing himself to further market liberalization, while embracing the populist position as a "friend of the poor." However, very soon into his first term, Estrada's main modus operandi was one of old-style cronyism (Wurfel 1999). In late 2000, a former crony switched allegiances and revealed lucrative, corrupt practices committed by President Estrada, and an impeachment trial was begun. Eventually, in the wake of more public demonstrations, in January 2001, Estrada was forced to resign. He was replaced by the vice president, Dr. Gloria Macapagal-Arroyo, a U.S.-trained economist and a former president's daughter. The midterm elections held in May 2001 were violent, but Arroyo achieved a clear victory through the election of her supporters.

In 2000, Estrada had declared "all-out-war" on Muslim militants on the southern island of Mindanao after the well-publicized kidnappings of foreign tourists and some locals. President Arroyo first attempted to pursue peace negotiations with the Moro Islamic Liberation Front (MILF). However, in May, another separatist organization, the Abu Sayyaf, staged a second tourist kidnapping, and the government responded militarily. Then, after September 11, 2001, the U.S.–Philippine bilateral relationship was rekindled. President Bush responded to Arroyo's quick support for the "war on terrorism" by providing substantial military and financial assistance (Labrador 2002). Thus, a decade after the withdrawal of U.S. military bases from the Philippines, serving troops were back in the country.

ECONOMIC ENVIRONMENT

The Philippines has a postwar history of squandering the advantages of plentiful natural resources, a skilled labor force, and a potentially enormous domestic market. Also, development has long been handicapped by the tendency of wealth acquisition to occur through ownership of monopolistic privileges and patronage, rather than through productivity and efficiency (Hodgkinson 1995). But as the World Bank (2000, 58) points out, the economic environment "has changed dramatically over the last decade under the combined influence of trade liberalization and heightened domestic competition." Despite this, there remains a particularly high concentration of ownership across firms in the corporate sector. The conglomerates in existence resemble Japanese *zaibatsu* in that they are family-owned, have interlocking directorates that include banks, and are politically influential (World Bank 2000, 44). However, further domestic and foreign competition is predicted to reduce the spread of these conglomerates "by forcing the owners of a group to focus on core activities and divest of non-core businesses" (World Bank 2000, 54).

In other respects, the economic environment continues to be shaped by the persistence of "deep-seated" corruption in both public and private arenas (World Bank 2001). Events surrounding the trial and eventual resignation of President Estrada have brought this issue to the fore, to the point that in 2000, it was found to be diminishing investor confidence in the country. President Arroyo named corruption as a top priority of her administration, but this has not been generally matched by strong actions (World Bank 2001). Corruption has been and will continue to be a major political issue in the Philippines. Both the Marcos and the Estrada cases highlighted the extent of the problem and the need to address it.

OVERVIEW OF MAJOR INDUSTRIAL SECTORS

Agriculture

The agriculture, forestry, and fishing sector contributed 22.5 percent of GDP in early 2002 and employed 37.1 percent of the working population (National Statistical Office 2002). The farming system is extremely diverse. It includes a large number of rice, maize, and coconut holdings that are farmed by agricultural tenants or workers, as well as sugar haciendas and large agribusiness plantations, devoted mainly to nontraditional export crops such as bananas and pineapples. Rice, maize, and cassava are the main subsistence crops. The principal crops cultivated for export are coconuts, bananas, and pineapples. The Philippines is a predominantly agricultural country, with 47 percent of total land area (about 13 million hectares) devoted to it; and the sector accounted for 20 percent of GDP, about half of the total labor force, and registered growth of 3.9 percent in the year 2000. To achieve development, the government is determined to make agriculture a modern, dynamic, and competitive sector. Growth has not kept up with demand, so the Philippines remains a net importer of agricultural products such as wheat, rice, milk, and cream products (Trade Partners UK 2002).

Coconuts are the most important crop (involving about 35 percent of the population) and are grown over about the same area as rice. The Philippines is the world's leading exporter of coconut products, supplying up to three-quarters of total world demand (Hodgkinson 1995). In the past, the sugar industry was of great importance, but by 2000, the value of exports of coconut products and bananas was, respectively, ten and five times greater than the value for sugar (NEDA 2002).

Trade liberalization in agriculture has fallen behind that in manufacturing. The effective rate of protection in agriculture fell only from 26.4 percent in 1990 to 22.5 percent in 2000 (World Bank 2000, 13). Since 1995, the sector has been more protected than manufacturing (World Bank 2000, 15).

Since independence, the landed elite has continually resisted pressure for land reform. Marcos commenced a program of land reform in 1972, but it was limited to areas growing rice and corn. The scope of land reform was significantly increased under the Aquino administration's Comprehensive Agrarian Reform Program (CARP). Not only was CARP to cover all agricultural lands, "the range of potential beneficiaries was considerably expanded to include, at least in principle, the landless" (World Bank 2000, 55). However, more than a decade after its introduction in 1988, the targets have not been met. Moreover, there are concerns that in fact the program has disadvantaged the poor and landless by reducing the area of land that is available for rent. The resultant loss of access to land is estimated to mean a reduction in total household income of "up to 30 percent" (World Bank 2000, 57). On the other hand, the beneficiaries of land reform have been shown to have gained in areas like per capita consumption and the number of years their children are at school (World Bank 2000).

In December 1997, President Ramos enacted the Agriculture and Fisheries Modernization Act (AFMA), a law that aims to modernize and increase the productivity of the agriculture and fisheries sector by transforming the sector from being resource-based to technology-based. This provided the Macapagal-Arroyo administration with a framework to address the following areas: agricultural productivity programs, irrigation systems, farm-to-market roads, post harvest and other related infrastructure, research and development, rural finance, and education (Trade Partners UK 2002).

Fishing

The Philippines has extensive fishing resources in both marine and inland waters. Its sea area is about seven times larger than its land area and ranks eleventh among eighty fish-producing countries in the world. The industry contributes 3.8 percent to the GDP and employs 5 percent of the labor force. The fishing sector produces an important source of animal protein and is an important source of foreign-exchange earnings, principally through the export of shrimp and prawns to Japan. While both freshwater ponds and most of the marine waters have not been fully developed, productivity in some areas has deteriorated because of poor infrastructure and pollution (NEDA 2002; Hodgkinson 1995).

Forestry

Philippines' forests contain a large quantity of valuable nonconiferous hardwood trees covering 51 percent of the land area and containing an estimated 1,454m cubic meters of hardwood (*The Asia and Pacific Review* 1990). The forests have suffered severe depletion as the result of population pressure, shifting cultivation, severe illegal logging (from the end of WWII to the 1970s), and inadequate reforestation (Hodgkinson 1995; Wong and Chau 2001). The export of logs, an important source of foreign exchange, was suspended in 1986 due to the effect of deforestation (Europa 1994). In 1989, exports of sawn wood were banned in an attempt to increase the value of forestry-related exports through encouraging the manufacture of wood products. Deforestation continues at a high rate, however, due to illegal logging and to slash-and-burn farming techniques or clear-cutting. In the late 1980s, illegal exports were estimated to total about US$800 million (Hodgkinson 1995). Though the reforestation program is seriously behind schedule, it is now being accelerated (*The Asia and Pacific Review* 1990). The urgency of reforestation is dramatized by its effects on the high rate of species endangerment and extinction as well as to indigenous populations who are losing their livelihoods and are being displaced by commercial and illegal loggers (Wong and Chau 2001).

Mining

The minerals industry accounted for over 20 percent of Philippine exports in the 1980s; it decreased to 1.24 percent of total country exports in the year 2000 (Macapagal-Arroyo 2002). Mining contributed 1.6 percent of GDP in 1990 and engaged 0.4 percent of the employed labor force in early 2002 (National Statistical Office 2002). The Philippines has extensive deposits of gold, silver, copper, nickel, iron, lead, and chromium. Lesser, but still important, products include zinc, cobalt, limestone, and manganese (Hodgkinson 1995). However, by 1994, around one-quarter of the land area remained to be surveyed, and some of the richest deposits have yet to be exploited. The Philippines is the world's eighth largest gold producer. Output is largely a by-product of copper mining, and thus tends to reflect trends in the copper sector, as well as in world prices. Overall, there is a need to combine industrial efficiency with sensitivity to the environmental aspects and consequences of production of minerals. In a 1992 speech, President Macapagal-Arroyo said, "this is an opportune time to review and re-explore the opportunities for a resurgence in our mineral exports, when the economic development agenda is a top priority of government" (Macapagal-Arroyo 2002).

Energy

During the early 1990s, there were frequent and prolonged losses of power, due to a severe shortage of generating capacity. In 1993, however, eleven new plants, with a total capacity of 1,074 MW, became operational. In 1999, the total system capacity was 12,050 MW, compared to 6,683 MW in 1992. As well as the growth in generating capacity, the reliance on hydro- and oil-powered sources has fallen, while the contribution from coal and gas has increased. In 1992, hydro and oil sources made up 33 percent and 45 percent of the total system capacity, respectively, whereas seven years later, they were contributing 19 percent and 21 percent, respectively. In contrast, the contributions from coal and gas have increased from 6 percent and 0 percent to 32 percent and 12 percent, respectively. The other source of generating capacity is geothermal, at 16 percent in 1999 (NEDA 2002).

Significantly, the growth in system capacity has mostly come from the expansion of private operations under the government's build, operate, transfer (BOT) program. In 1993, private operations contributed only 11 percent of the total, whereas by 1999, they were contributing 55 percent (NEDA 2002). Also, the reduced dependence on oil means a reduced dependence on imported sources. In the early 1990s, oil was the country's major import, accounting for over 15 percent of total imports and mainly sourced from the Middle East. In 1973, at the time of the first major increase in international petroleum prices, the Philippines was dependent on imported oil for 95 percent of its energy supply (Hodgkinson 1995).

Reforms in the Philippines' energy sector are underway, "as are projects to electrify isolated villages, to reduce the Philippines' dependence on imported oil, and to change the relative composition of fuel consumption" (Energy Information Administration, Department of Energy, U.S. Government, 2003). The government has created the Philippine Energy Plan (PEP) 2000–2009 that aims to increase domestic petroleum production to become at least 50 percent energy self-sufficient by 2004, to accelerate completion of the rural electrification program, to increase private-sector investment, and to continue to deregulate the downstream oil sector. The Philippines' downstream oil industry is dominated by three companies: Petron, Pilipinas Shell (Royal Dutch/Shell's Philippine subsidiary), and Caltex (Philippines). Petron is the Philippines' largest oil refining and marketing company. The company was a wholly owned subsidiary of the state-owned Philippine National Oil Company (PNOC) until 1994. Currently, the Philippine government and Saudi Aramco each own 40 percent of the company, with the remaining 20 percent held by portfolio and institutional investors, making it the only publicly listed firm among the three oil majors (Energy Information Administration, Department of Energy, U.S. Government 2003).

Manufacturing

Manufacturing employed 10.3 percent of the labor force in early 2002 (National Statistical Office 2002). Based on the value of output, the principal branches of manufacturing are food products, petroleum refineries, chemical products, electrical machinery (mainly telecommunications equipment), beverages, metals and metal products, and textiles. Exports of manufactures are highest in electronics, automotive parts, and garments. The contribution of these and other manufactures to total exports increased from 76.6 percent in 1992 to 86 percent in 1997 (WTO 1999). In the 1990s, the effective rate of protection in manufacturing was more than halved from 31 percent in 1990 to 14.5 percent in 2000 (World Bank 2000, 13).

Services

Economist Bernardo Villegas noted that "the year 2001 saw the coming of age of the service sector as the engine of growth of the economy" (Villegas 2001, 11). In early 2002, 47.5 percent of the workforce was employed in the services sector. Tourism is notable in this sector.

Tourism

The Philippines prides itself on being a member of the informal "one million club" of the region's countries that attract over a million tourists a year. The shadow that hangs over the lucrative development of the Philippines as a popular destination for tourists is the political uncertainty. Tourist numbers have fluctuated widely, largely in response to the political instability of the Philippines since the 1980s. In 1973–78, arrivals were rising by an average of 33 percent a year (Hodgkinson 1995). There was a reduction in growth for the following four years, and a sharp decline thereafter. After a leveling out in 1986 and 1987, the numbers were back to the 1980 level by 1988, reflecting both the improvement in the political situation and marketing efforts by the Philippine tourist industry. While the Gulf War and the Mt. Pinatubo eruption adversely affected numbers for most of 1991, when they registered 961,365 tourist arrivals, the number increased by 20 percent in 1992 and 22 percent in 1993, to a new record of 1.4 million. Tourist receipts were equivalent to one-fifth of total merchandise export earnings (Hodgkinson 1995). Around one-tenth of tourist visitors are overseas Filipinos (Balikbayan), while the United States and Japan each account for around one-quarter of arrivals. As in the past, terrorist threats and kidnapping for ransom by various groups increased the level of insecurity of some tourist destinations. External events like the September 11, 2001 and Bali terrorist attacks have also reduced the Philippines' attractiveness to Western visitors. These ongoing trends are exacerbated by the political climate that is perceived to be unstable.

INTERNATIONAL TRADE

Between 1985 and 1998, the Philippines doubled its export share of world markets from 0.3 percent to 0.6 percent (World Bank 2000, 17). As we have seen, this growth was largely the result of multinational corporation investment in the electronics industry. Consequently, export growth was stronger to the industrialized world. The United States continued to dominate the picture, taking 32 percent of Philippine exports in 2001, compared to Japan's share of 19 percent (NEDA 2002).

Trade with other ASEAN countries has grown in importance due to increasing liberalization (Hodgkinson 1995). The commodity composition of the Philippines' export trade has been transformed since the 1970s, when four primary commodities—coconut products, sugar, timber, and copper—accounted for about one-half of the total (Hodgkinson 1995). The general decline in world prices of these commodities and the fall in the volume of production coincided with the development of the export manufacturing sector and the diversification of agricultural production. The result was that by 2001, the four traditional exports accounted for only 2 percent of the total, while manufactures accounted for 70 percent (NEDA 2002; cf. Hodgkinson 1995). In that year, electronic equipment and parts accounted for 41 percent of total exports. Garments, a leading export earner in the early 1990s, had fallen to 6 percent of the total. Other principal exports were agricultural products (particularly fruit and products derived from coconuts), shrimp and prawns, and copper (NEDA 2002).

Changes in imports have been less marked, although the fall in world prices and some contribution from domestic production have halved the proportions represented by crude petroleum from the 23 percent recorded in 1983 (Hodgkinson 1995). Imports of capital equipment and intermediates increased in significance in response to the post-1986 economic recovery and were largely responsible for the sharp increase in the import bill in 1988–90. The principal imports for 1991 were mineral fuels and lubricants, electronics and components, nonelectric machinery and equipment, textiles, and electrical machinery and appliances (Europa 1994). The trade deficit of the Philippines continues to surge, as imports increase in volume. The biggest import items are electronic products used as inputs for the country's electronic industry. Mineral fuels, lubricants, and related materials are second to electronics. The rise in imports in 2003 has been interpreted as a possible indication of surge in economic activity and expansion.

INVESTMENT CLIMATE: ELEMENTS OF THE MARKETING MIX

Product

With certain exceptions, every imported or locally manufactured product must be labeled to indicate brand, trademark, or trade name; country of manufacturer; physical or chemical composition; net weight and measure, if applicable; and address of manufacturer or re-packer. The country-of-origin lettering must be permanent enough to appear on the article at least until it reaches the ultimate purchaser. The lettering, which may be abbreviated, should be Filipino, English, or Spanish. If the article cannot be marked prior to shipment without injury or prohibitive expense, is a crude substance, is incapable of being marked, is imported for use of the importer and not intended for resale in its imported form, or was produced twenty years prior to importation, the product will be exempt from the marketing requirement. However, the container must indicate the country of origin. Any article (or its container) that does not bear a proper mark of origin at the time of importation is subject to a marking duty of 5 percent. Misleading, misrepresenting, or misbranding may subject the entire shipment to seizure and disposal (see also Bair 1988).

Channels of Distribution

A major disincentive for direct foreign investment in the Philippines, political instability apart, is the poor state of the Filipino infrastructure. The country's physical infrastructure is characterized by marked regional disparity, which both reflects and reinforces the concentration of modern economic activity in Metropolitan Manila and the regions immediately adjacent. Infrastructure has been declining in efficiency as the result of reductions in budget expenditure under the mid-1980s austerity program, and the early tendency to concentrate on new installations, rather than maintenance (Hodgkinson 1995).

The road network, which accommodates about 60 percent of freight and 80 percent of passenger traffic, was comprised of 160,633 kilometers of roads in 1992 (Hodgkinson 1995). Only about 14 percent is paved, and many roads are in very poor condition, which is the result of inferior construction, inadequate maintenance, and use by overloaded vehicles. Precious resources are being distributed to improve the situation. As of April 1988, six major highway projects costing P4.5 billion were in various stages of implementation under a highways development program that aimed by 1992 to improve the road density, to increase the percentage of all-weather roads to 60 percent, and to raise the percentage of paved national roads to 55 percent.

The rail system is similarly limited, with only 740 kilometers of single-line track in Luzon, and it is also in a poor state of repair (Hodgkinson 1995). Due to the fragmentation of land areas and the high amount of investment needed to build railroads, they are not a significant mode of transportation (Bair 1988). A light railway system (LRT), which became operational in December 1984, was built to minimize the traffic problem in Manila's main thoroughfares by servicing the Baclaran, Caloocan, and Metro Manila routes—railroads carrying freight and passengers are limited to other parts of Luzon and Panay (Bair 1988). Improvements in the mass transport and highway system are projected to meet increasing transportation needs. These projects are being carried out through the BOT scheme.

Because of its insular character, the Philippines is heavily dependent on marine transport, with the seaport network servicing about 40 percent of freight and carrying 10 percent of passenger traffic (Hodgkinson 1995). The Philippines has 473 ports, eighty-one of which are national and the remainder of which are municipal. Unfortunately, less than half of the national ports are open to international shipping (Bair 1988). The most important ports are Manila and Cebu, but while both have container facilities (Hodgkinson 1995), Manila is the busiest national port, with approximately 85 percent of Philippine foreign trade passing through. Ninety percent of imports enter this port. Consequently, a number of expansion and rehabilitation projects to reduce congestion in the Manila port area (which had been shelved during the economic crisis in 1983) have been revived. To add to this problem of congestion, the interisland fleet is old, safety regulations are poor, and maritime navigational aids are inadequate.

There are eighty-four national airports (including two main international ones, at Manila and Cebu) that handle about 9 percent of passenger travel (Hodgkinson 1995). There are plans to develop an alternative site for Manila's international airport, and Clark Air Base, from which the United States withdrew its forces in 1991, is under consideration. Airport improvement projects were approved by loans from the Asian Development Bank to upgrade standards; promote increased trade with Indonesia, Malaysia, and Brunei; and support the Philippine government's peace and development initiatives in Mindanao and Palawan. Air freight and air express shipments are becoming more economical for some imported merchandise.

The Philippines' telephone density ratio of 9.12 landlines per 100 Filipinos at the end of 1999 indicates one of the lowest in Asia. Telephone services in rural areas remain at even lower levels. While infrastructure improvements account for a significant portion of government spending, it is envisaged that foreign investors and the private sector will also be important contributors. Philippine Long Distance Telephone Co. (PLDT), for instance, is investing heavily in improving communications.

According to Trade Partners UK, "as of August 2000, there were an estimated 4.2 million cellular subscribers from only 2.85 million at the end of 1999. Keen competition between major operators (PLDT's subsidiary Smart and Globe Telecom) led to hefty price cuts on handsets and airtime rates." The cell phone boom has contributed to improvement in other areas, such as Internet services. In 2000, there were an estimated thirty-three Internet service providers (ISPs) and 4.5 million Internet users.

The Philippines is linked with other countries by satellite communications, telex lines, and microwave relay stations. Underwater cable systems link the country with the United States, Hong Kong, and other locations in the Pacific area. Telecommunications services in the Philippines are provided mostly by private companies that operate on the basis of franchises obtained from the Philippine government and permits from the National Telecommunications Commission. Telephone services are dominated by the Philippine Long Distance Telephone Co., a private company that accounts for more than 90 percent of all available telephone installations in the country (Bair 1988). The remaining telephone subscribers are served by some fifty-five small local enterprises. The government-owned Bureau of Telecommunications (BUTEL) also provides very limited telephone and telegraph services in rural areas.

There are seven domestic record carriers and three data communications carriers (Bair 1988). There are 2,131 telegraph main stations and substations, and 122 telex main stations and substations. In addition, there are four international record carriers and two domestic and international satellite systems. Surface and airmail facilities are provided and include postal money order service and registered and special delivery mail service (mail is handled by a government bureau, as well as a number of private firms). Courier service is recommended for transmittal of important documents to the Philippines.

For administrative purposes, the country is subdivided into thirteen regions: Ilocos, Cagayan Valley, Central Luzon, Southern Tagalog, Bicol, Western Visayas, Central Visayas, Eastern Visayas, Western Mindanao, Northern Mindanao, Southern Mindanao, Southwestern Mindanao, and the National Capital Region (Metro Manila). The country's national center is Manila, which provides a variety of specialized central services (Bair 1988). It also serves as an interregional center for all the northern provinces, is a major center for a large immediate hinterland, and is the nerve center of industrial activity; transportation; communications; trade, educational, and developmental services; governmental services; and various administrative and social services (Bair 1988).

About 90 percent of all Philippine industries are located in the greater Manila area in three major locations. The first, an area of heavy industries, is situated along the banks of the Pasig River, which flows through the city and the port area into Manila Bay. Cargo discharged from vessels in the bay is often loaded onto barges and lighters for transport via Pasig to the industrial area. The second industrial district, containing medium-sized plants, is located about fifteen miles outside of Manila at Antipolo, in the Marikina Valley. Supplies and raw materials are generally carried from the port area by truck. The third major industrial area is located in Makati City, currently the main business and financial area in the country. In addition to small manufacturing plants, a considerable number of distribution centers, trading firms, and banks are located here. Makati City is also a popular shopping area of the higher-income residents (cf. Bair 1988).

In addition to Manila, the other major interregional centers are Cebu City, Iloilo, Davao, and Zamboanga. Cebu City, the third largest city in the Philippines, is the prime trading center in the southern part of the archipelago, its hinterland being mainly accessible by boat. Iloilo shares with Cebu the servicing of the country's central area. Davao, the second largest city in the Philippines, enjoys a trade monopoly in Southern Mindanao, due mainly to the presence of land and water connections with its nearby provinces. Zamboanga also functions partly as an interregional center (cf. Bair 1988).

Transportation to the hinterland is almost entirely by water, as there are only a few roads along the peninsula. Furnishing the archipelago with basic economic, political, and social services are about forty major and thirty-five secondary centers situated throughout the Philippines. These are similar to retail outlets and are relatively small, with populations of up to 60,000. Their importance lies in the fact that they render essential urban services to their respective territories (cf. Bair 1988).

Advertising

The Philippines is a brand-conscious market. Advertising thus plays a significant part in promoting the sale of most goods, particularly nondurable consumer goods. Most advertising agencies (of which there are currently forty-four accredited agencies and 104 others) have patterned their organizations after U.S. advertising agencies, and many advertising contracts go to multinational agencies or agencies with multinational links. The estimated overall national breakdown of total media expenditures indicates approximately 50 percent going to television, 29 percent to print, 20 percent to radio, and the remaining 1 percent to cinema and outdoor advertising. The availability of inexpensive mass-produced transistorized radio receivers and the growth of radio stations throughout the country have made radio the unrivaled mode of communications in the Philippines (Bair 1988). Radio is the cheapest way to reach the rural population, as almost two-thirds of all families own one or more radios. There are 599 commercial and noncommercial broadcasting radio stations, with some 3.6 million radio sets. In 2000, the broadcast sector was made up of 108 television stations, 270 AM radio stations, and 329 FM radio stations (*2000 Philippine Media Factbook*; cf. Bair 1988).

Media are increasingly influential. Metro Manila has thirteen major TV stations, and the provinces are served by relay stations. But, while television use has grown rapidly, it is concentrated mostly in Manila and other urban centers. Almost half of Manila's families own a television set, but only 5 percent of all Filipino families own a television. By 1997, fifty-two Filipinos per 1,000 owned a television set. The high cost of television sets and the absence of television stations in many parts of the country still make television viewing a remote possibility in the rural areas. Twenty-two percent of print media is published in the NCR (Metropolitan Manila). Thirteen major newspapers, seventeen tabloids, thirty-two comics, and five Chinese dailies are published in Manila (*2000 Philippine Media Factbook*). The major newspapers are in English. These publications provide domestic and international news, as well as an expanding standard medium for advertising. The *Philippine Daily Inquirer,* the *Manila Bulletin,* and *The Philippine Star* are some of the newspapers with the widest reach. These newspapers are also accessible online. Daily business newspapers and periodicals cover most fields, with trade journals on almost every trade and profession (*The Asia and Pacific Review* 1990). There are forty-five magazines, some of which are supplements of Sunday newspapers, while others are independent publications (*2000 Philippine Media Factbook*). Magazines and newspapers are the major advertisement outlets.

CONCLUSION

The Philippines was considered one of the promising countries in Asia in the early 1960s. It had the region's most advanced educational infrastructure, a vibrant economy, and a stable political system. In 1965, it was ahead of South Korea in economic terms and was second only to Japan (Celoza and Sours 1993). However, disturbances and upheavals in the 1970s and 1980s put the Philippines behind its Asian neighbors in terms of economic progress. With the demise of the Marcos dictatorship and the revitalization of democratic structures, optimism was restored in the 1990s. In 2001, protests in the streets of Manila resulted in the ousting of President Joseph Estrada. His vice president, Gloria Macapagal-Arroyo, assumed the presidency and offered renewed hope for positive change. The Philippine economy weathered the Asian financial crisis of the late 1990s, the turmoil of the Estrada presidency, and the impact of terrorist threats. The story of the past decades indicate that the goals of achieving development and maintaining a democratic polity are not elusive but are subject to complex environmental factors.

ACKNOWLEDGMENTS

The authors wish to express their gratitude to Bianca Teo for her contributions to the earlier work by Teo, Pecotich, and Celoza (1998).

REFERENCES

The Asia and Pacific Review: Fifty-eight Countries, from New Zealand to China to Afghanistan. 1990. Edison, NJ: Hunter Publishing Inc., pp. 195–99.

Asian Development Bank. 2003. *Asian Development Outlook 2003.* Hong Kong: Oxford University Press (China) Ltd.

Asian Economic Handbook. 1987. London: Euromonitor Publications Ltd., pp. 70–127.

Bair, F. E. 1988. *International Marketing Handbook,* pp. 2030–71. Detroit, MI: Gale Research Company.

Bello, Walden, and Gershman, John. 1990. "Democratization and Stabilization in the Philippines." *Critical Sociology* 17 (1): 35–56.

Brown, I. 1995. "History." In *The Far East and Australasia,* 26th ed., ed. L. Daniel. London: Europa Publications.

Celoza, Albert F. 1992. "The Ambiguities of Modernization: The Political Class and Regime Change in the Philippines." In *Modernization in East Asia: Political, Economic and Social Perspectives,* ed. R. Brown and W. Liu, pp. 93–111. New York: Praeger.

Celoza, Albert F., and Sours, Martin. 1993. "Philippine and South Korean International Relations in Post-Cold War Asia Pacific." In *Asia Pacific in the New World Politics,* ed. J. Hsiung, pp. 133–45. Boulder, CO, and London: Lynne Rienner.

de Dois, Emmanuel S. 1998. "Philippine Economic Growth: Can It Last?" In *The Philippines: New Directions in Domestic Policy and Foreign Relations,* ed. David G. Timberman, pp. 49–84. New York: The Asia Society.

Dolan, Ronald. 1993. *The Philippines: A Country Study.* Washington, DC: Federal Research Division, Library of Congress.

Europa. 1994. *The Europa World Yearbook 1994,* 35th ed. London: Europa Publications.

———. 1995. *The Far East and Australasia,* 26th ed. London: Europa Publications.

———. 2003. *The Europa World Yearbook 2003,* 44th ed. London: Europa Publications.

———. 2004. *The Far East and Australasia,* 35th ed. London: Europa Publications.

Economic and Social Commission for Asia and the Pacific (ESCAP). 2001. Various data available at United Nations website, www.unescap.org.

Energy Information Administration, Department of Energy, U.S. Government. 2003. Various data available at www.cia.doe.gov.

Hodgkinson, E. 1995. "Economy." In *The Far East and Australasia*, 26th ed., ed. L. Daniel. London: Europa Publications.

Hutchcroft, Paul. 1994. "Booty Capitalism: Business–Government Relations in the Philippines." In *Business and Government in Industrialising Asia*, ed. Andrew J. MacIntyre, pp. 216–43. St. Leonards, NSW: Allen and Unwin.

Hutchison, Jane. 2001. "Crisis and Change in the Philippines." In *The Political Economy of South-East Asia: Conflicts, Crises, and Change*, eds. Garry Rodan, Kevin Hewison, and Richard Robison, pp. 42–70. New York: Oxford University Press.

Labrador, Mel C. 2002. "The Philippines in 2001." *Asian Survey* 42 (1): 141–50.

Library of Congress. 1991. *Philippines: Social Values and Organization.* Washington, DC: Federal Research Division, Library of Congress. Available at http://lcweb2.10c.gov/frd/cs/phtoc.html, accessed August 2002.

Lindsey, Charles. 1992. "The Political Economy of International Economic Policy Reform in the Philippines: Continuity and Restoration." In *The Dynamics of Economic Policy Reform in South-east Asia and the South-west Pacific*, eds. Andrew J. MacIntyre and Kanishka Jayasuriya, pp. 74–93. Singapore: Oxford University Press.

Macapagal-Arroyo, Gloria. 2002. Data from Department of Environment and Natural Resources, The Philippines.

National Economic and Development Authority (NEDA). 2002. "Economic Indicators Online." Available at www.neda.gov.ph, accessed 2004.

National Statistical Office. 2002. "Manila." Available at www.census.gov.ph, accessed 2004.

Noland, Marcus. 2000. "The Philippines in the Asian Financial Crisis: How the Sick Man Avoided Pneumonia." *Asian Survey* 40 (3): 401–12.

Pinches, Michael. 1997. "Elite Democracy, Development and People Power: Contending Ideologies and Changing Practices in Philippine Politics." *Asian Studies Review* 21 (2–3): 104–20.

Rivera, Temario C. 1996. *State of the Nation Philippines.* Singapore: Institute of Southeast Asian Studies.

Silliman, G. Sidney, and Lela Ganer Noble. 1998. "Introduction." In *Organizing for Democracy: NGOs, Civil Society, and the Philippine State*, ed. G. Sidney Silliman and Lela Ganer Noble, pp. 1–25. Honolulu: University of Hawai'i Press.

Teo, Bianca, Anthony Pecotich, and Albert F. Celoza. 1998. "The Philippines Marketing and Consumer Behavior: Past, Present and the Future." In *Marketing and Consumer Behavior in East and South-East Asia*, ed. A. Pecotich and C. Shultz II, pp. 561–84. Sydney: McGraw-Hill.

Tigno, Jorge V. 1997. "Ties That Bind: The Past and Prospects of Philippine Labor Outmigration." *Pilipinas* 29: 1–18.

Trade Partners UK. 2002. Available at www.tradepartners.gov.uk/agriculture/philippines/profile/overview.shtml.

2000 Philippine Media Factbook. 2000. Manila: Philippine Information Agency.

Villegas, Bernardo M. 2001. *The Philippine Advantage.* Manila: University of Asia and the Pacific.

Wong, Ansely, and Chau, Kathleen. 2001. "Rainforests of the Philippines." Available at www.forestry.utoronto.ca/for201.

World Bank. 1999. *Philippines: The Challenge of Economic Recovery.* Washington, DC: Poverty and Economic Management Sector Unit, East Asia and Pacific Regional Office.

———. 2000. *Philippines Growth with Equity: The Remaining Agenda.* Report No. 20066–PH. Washington, DC: Poverty and Economic Management Sector Unit, East Asia and Pacific Regional Office.

———. 2001. *Combating Corruption in the Philippines: An Update.* Report No. 23687–PH. Washington, DC: East Asia and Pacific Regional Office.

———. 2002. *Philippines Development Policy Review: An Opportunity for Renewed Poverty Reduction.* Report No: 23629–PH. Washington, DC: Poverty and Economic Management Sector Unit, East Asia and Pacific Regional Office.

World Factbook. 2003. Central Intelligence Agency, Washington DC. Available at www.cia.gov/cia/publications/factbook/geos/cb.html.

World Trade Organization (WTO). 1999. *Trade Policy Review: The Philippines: September 1999.* Geneva: WTO. Available at www.wto.org/wto/english/tratop_e/tpr_e/tp114_e.htm.

Wurfel, David. 1988. *Filipino Politics: Development and Decay.* Quezon City: Ateneo de Manila University Press.

———. 1999. "Convergence and Divergence Amidst Democratization and Economic Crisis: Thailand and the Philippines Compared." *Philippine Political Science Journal* 20 (43): 1–44.

CHAPTER 15

SINGAPORE

Marketing, Macro Trends, and Their Implications for Marketing Management for 2005 and the Years Beyond

JOCHEN WIRTZ AND CINDY M.Y. CHUNG

OVERVIEW

This chapter analyzes trends in Singapore's marketing environment in terms of economy, demographics, and culture, as well as from a consumer-behavior and marketing-mix perspective. The analysis shows a fairly wealthy society with good future prospects. The main demographic trends follow those of more developed nations. Singapore has an interesting mix of cultures with distinct languages, religions, and customs. Macro trends are reflected in consumption behavior with increasing overall consumption, an increasing share of higher-level goods, such as recreational, education, and health services, as well as changing consumer values and lifestyles, which show that Singaporeans have become more brand and status conscious, more discerning, quality oriented, technologically savvy, and health conscious. Trends in the marketing mix are a direct reflection of the macro environment. The chapter concludes with implications for marketing strategies.

INTRODUCTION

Singapore is a small city-state of approximately 648 square kilometers in area, consisting of the main island of Singapore and some sixty islets within its territorial waters. Singapore has a tropical climate, which is warm and humid. The temperature is uniform throughout the year, ranging between 24°C and 32°C, moderated by sea breezes.

Singapore was founded in 1819 by Sir Stamford Raffles as a trading post for the East India Company, and it became a British colony in 1867. It was an important British trading post and military center in 1900, with a population of about 220,000. At the end of World War II, its population was still less than one million. The economy showed little development from the end of the war until the early 1960s under British rule, and in 1970, its gross domestic product (GDP) per capita was still only US$950.

In 1963, Singapore joined Malaya as one of the constituent states of a new Federation of Malaysia, with virtual freedom from colonial rule. In 1965, Singapore was separated from Malaysia by mutual agreement and became a fully independent republic (Ministry of Information, Communications, and the Arts 1994). Its astonishing transformation into a modern industrial society began in the early 1970s. Since then, Singapore has enjoyed impressive rates of economic growth and achieved higher GDP per capita (e.g., US$21,220 by 2001) than some developed countries such as Canada, England, and Australia. In fact, the World Bank ranked Singapore number nine in its list of the world's richest countries measured in purchasing power parity (1995). This has been achieved with full employment, budget surpluses, low pollution, and by standards of most industrial countries, with few social problems. In May 1997, Singapore was reclassified by the International Monetary Fund (IMF) in its semiannual publication, *World Economic Outlook*, as an "advanced economy" (Ministry of Information, Communications, and the Arts 1998, 10). IMF's reclassification of Singapore was recognition of how far Singapore has traveled since its independence.

POLITICAL AND HISTORICAL BACKGROUND INFORMATION

Singapore's political structure, its position in the Association of Southeast Asian Nations (ASEAN) and the region, and an analysis for the reasons behind Singapore's success are discussed in the subsequent sections to provide a platform for a more detailed analysis of trends in the economic, demographic, and cultural environments.

Political Structure

Singapore is a parliamentary democracy. The executive branch, which consists of the prime minister, at present, Goh Chok Tong, and fourteen ministers, is appointed by the president and is responsible to the parliament. The head of state, the incumbent President S. R. Nathan, is elected directly by the citizens of Singapore for a five-year term. The president has certain veto powers primarily related to appointments of senior civil servants, protection of reserves, internal security detentions, investigations into corruption, and restraint orders connected with the maintenance of religious harmony.

The national legislature is a unicameral parliament consisting of nine members who are directly elected from single-member constituencies, and seventy-four who are elected in teams of four to six to represent the fifteen-group representation constituencies (GRCs). At least one member of any GRC must be from an ethnic minority, usually Malay or Indian. The ruling People's Action Party (PAP), which has been in power since the separation from Malaysia, won 75.3 percent of the 2001 valid votes and presently holds eighty-two of eighty-four seats in parliament (*The Sunday Times* 2001). The parliamentary opposition consists of the Worker's Party (WP), which holds one seat, and the Singapore Democratic Alliance (SDA), with another seat in parliament.

The judicial power is vested in the supreme court and the subordinate courts. The judiciary administers the law independently from the executive. The chief justice and the other judges of the supreme court are appointed by the president, acting on the advice of the prime minister, who, in turn, consults the chief justice for appointments of judges other than the chief justice.

Some Explanations for Singapore's Rapid Economic Development

The reasons for Singapore's rapid economic development are manifold and closely related. At least four factors have to be considered. They are (1) good governance and political stability, including efficient and effective institutions and a policy of export orientation; (2) favorable starting conditions in comparison to other developing economies; (3) external factors, such as world market developments and geopolitical constellations; and finally, (4) cultural values (Wirtz and Menkhoff 1998).

First, good governance and a high level of political stability are important factors for Singapore's success. Singapore has managed to achieve political stability and macroeconomic management, which can effectively and efficiently implement policy changes and address problems. These are probably made easier by Singapore's small size. This stability has enabled Singapore to pursue an export- and growth-oriented development strategy, and as the World Bank formulated it, "getting the basics right" (1993, 5). The World Bank concluded that the success of high-performing Asian economies is largely due to private investment financed by high levels of savings—both initiated and fostered by various government policies, such as opening the economy to attract foreign direct investment, integrating into world trade, high savings via the Central Provident Fund (CPF)—and a rapidly growing human capital (mainly via substantial investment into housing, health, and education).

Good governance is also reflected in the low level of corruption. In contrast to other developing countries, corruption, which is vigorously policed, is not a concern in Singapore. Civil servants receive competitive salaries, which are pegged and automatically adjusted to those in the private sector (Lee 2000). The level of corruption in Singapore is lower than in most American and European countries, including in the United States, the United Kingdom, and Germany, as shown by a joint research report by Transparency International and the University of Göttingen (Sim 1995). Berlin-based Transparency International, a nongovernmental agency dedicated to fighting graft, has also rated Singapore among the top ten in its list of the world's least corrupt nations (Ministry of Information, Communications, and the Arts 1998, 7).

McRae suggests that the level of efficiency of an economy as a whole has to be considered when looking at its long-term international competitiveness (1995, 3). One important factor, of course, is the efficiency and effectiveness of public services. In recent years, Singapore's civil service has been a forerunner to local firms in terms of service quality. Here, Singapore seems to be at the same level as, if not higher than, many developed countries. The latest knowledge and technologies in quality management are applied, ranging from overall quality programs such as the Public Service 21st Century (PS 21) initiative, to micro issues such as advanced queue management systems in hospitals or the immigration office, and increasingly to service provision via telecommunications and other electronic means, such as ATM-type interfaces, services provided through the Internet, or services provided via dedicated networks (e.g., Tradenet for import/export transactions). This dedication to public service quality has been reflected by evaluations of international bodies, which awarded the number one position in quality in their respective industries to a number of Singapore's services. Examples include the Singapore Port, Changi Airport, mass rapid transport system, and Singapore Airlines (which is still more than 50 percent state owned). A poll conducted by a regional financial magazine, *FinanceAsia*, has found that Singapore has the most competent government in Asia (*The Straits Times* 2001a).

A discussion of the efficiency and effectiveness of the Singapore government would be incomplete without mentioning its unceasing effort in taking "online" initiatives. The government has received the accolade for being the most advanced in providing full online services to its citizens (Holmes 2001). Its e-Citizen Centre that was started in 1997 organizes public services by life events rather than by various ministries or departments. The Centre demonstrates how a government can provide integrated and citizen-centric electronic services with efficiency. By April 1999, the Centre included forty-nine life events with 150 transactions (Holmes 2001). Also, government regulations on the whole are favorable for the development and adoption of the Internet and e-commerce. Since October 1998, the IDA has led major efforts in providing greater quality, availability, and more competitive prices for Internet access. Singapore has been listed as a "wired" capital, along with San Francisco, London, Seoul, Sydney, Hong Kong, and Amsterdam, by a global study undertaken by Euro RSCG, an advertising-agency network (*The Straits Times* 2001b). To maintain and further enhance this image, the government also drew up a ten-year master plan, Information and Communication Technology 21 (ICT21), in August 2000 to position the country as a global capital of information and communication technology by 2010. The government also provides subsidies to encourage businesses to use IT and the Internet. One recent example is that the Singapore Productivity and Standards Board offers subsidies of 50 percent, or a maximum of $20,000, to small and medium-size enterprises to initiate or improve their e-commerce capabilities (*The Straits Times* 2001c).

In conclusion, looking at past performance, it appears that the Singapore government has been doing a good job in supporting and managing the astonishing transformation of the city-state into a modern industrial economy (Wirtz and Menkhoff 1998). The country is therefore deserving of its second position in global competitiveness in both 2000 and 2001 (*The Global Competitiveness Report* 2000; *The World Competitiveness Yearbook* 2001).

A second reason for Singapore's success has been its favorable geographic conditions, such as being centrally located on world trade routes for shipping, air transport, and trade, as well as its natural deep-sea port. These factors were the key reasons for British interest in establishing Singapore as a trading post in 1819 in the first place. Other important favorable conditions include the well-functioning public administration structures and the civil service, which were left behind by the British and were developed further after independence, and the traditional free trade status, including its ideology of a liberal economic order and free market orientation. Furthermore, in contrast to many other Asian developing countries, Singapore as a city-state has had no socioeconomic problems with rural populations pushing into its city. The immigration of workers from Malaysia, Thailand, Indonesia, Bangladesh, and other countries has been effectively controlled since independence. As a city-state, no economic conflicts of interest between regions with different levels of development have existed. Another of Singapore's advantages has been its population of largely dynamic and achievement-oriented immigrants.

Third, external factors such as world market developments and geopolitical constellations have also contributed to Singapore's success. Singapore's outward-oriented policies with respect to trade and FDI attracted multinational corporations with tax concessions, good infrastructure, and low wages. These were pursued at a favorable world historical time when world trade grew rapidly. U.S. foreign policy and its interests in the region were additional factors. The United States provided substantial support to the founding of ASEAN in 1967. Singapore, one of the founding members of this alliance against communism, received much economic and military support from the United States.

Finally, cultural values have to be considered when explaining Singapore's advance. It is easier for a government to successfully encourage savings and education, if these are already ingrained in the value system of its people. Singaporeans show strong commitment to education, high savings, and evident discipline and industriousness. These factors are considered important drivers of economic development (World Bank 1993; McRae 1995, 70).

Singapore's Position in the Region

Singapore's foreign policy emphasizes the enhancing of security and prosperity through regional cooperation, of which ASEAN remains a central pillar. The government also aims to consolidate its relationship with other ASEAN countries, especially its immediate and by far larger neighboring countries, Malaysia and Indonesia (Economist Intelligence Unit [EIU] 1994, 7–8). In July 1995, the ASEAN Regional Forum (ARF) was inaugurated, which laid the groundwork for regional security cooperation. In 1992, ASEAN countries also agreed to establish a free trade area (FTA) for the purpose of increasing competitive advantage of the region as a product base. This was to be achieved through elimination of tariff and nontariff barriers. In response to the 1997 Asian financial crisis, ASEAN countries agreed to speed up the completion of the FTA by 2002 (it was originally scheduled to complete by 2008), whereby more than 80 percent of goods have 0 percent to 5 percent of tariffs (ASEAN Secretariat 1999). High on the agenda for ASEAN countries is the creation of an ASEAN–China Free Trade Area within the next ten years, which will open up a combined market of 1.7 billion people with a GDP of about $3.7 trillion (*The Straits Times* 2001d). An FTA, as such, will also enhance peace and stability in the region. Other ambitious schemes such as an ASEAN–South Korea Free Trade Area and ASEAN–India Free Trade Area are also under conception.

On the backdrop of an increasingly import-oriented Asia-Pacific in the global economy, a major objective of Singapore's foreign policy will continue to be the strengthening of economic relationships with those regional countries that Singapore sees as important future export markets or investment locations. The emphasis is on regional direct investments, projects, and initiatives, with the underlying objective of generating economic spin-offs in Singapore (Ministry of Information, Communications, and the Arts 1995, 106). This is hoped to be achieved by promoting Singapore as a regional gateway for mainly Western companies, by encouraging private local firms to invest in the region, and by supporting relationships between multinational corporations (MNCs) and leading local firms for regional investments (Menkhoff and Wirtz 1999).

Background Information: Summary and Conclusions

The background information presented here puts the recent economic developments described in the next section into a wider perspective and also indicates future directions. Singapore's stable democracy is expected to continue providing a favorable political environment for further economic growth. The success factors of the past will remain important drivers of growth in the future. They include, first, good governance, political stability, and a public sector that works vigorously toward efficiency and service quality; second, favorable base conditions such as its natural deep-sea port, and its British-inherited free trade mentality with its liberal economic attitude; third, a favorable timing of its development efforts during a period of rapidly increasing world trade and, now, increasing focus on Asia; and finally, its cultural values, which emphasize saving, education, and discipline and industriousness. Singapore's recent significantly increased efforts to use its expertise and capital to build an external wing of its own economy in the region will also impact its economy. Low value-added jobs will be increasingly exported into low-cost countries in the region, and more highly skilled jobs will be created in Singapore.

The next section describes key economic variables at a more micro level. Trends in income, employment, and inflation, as well as trade policy and future developments are discussed.

ECONOMIC ENVIRONMENT

The economic environment has been improving rapidly over the past two decades. Table 15.1 provides an overview of selected macroeconomic variables, such as GDP growth, gross national product (GNP) per capita, unemployment rates, and the like. The first half of the 1990s has seen generally high positive economic growth in Singapore. The advent of the Asian currency crisis has rendered growth to a mere 0.1 percent in 1998. There was dramatic improvement in the following two years, with the GDP growth rate rising to 9.9 percent in 2000. However, with the onset of economic uncertainty and a recession in 2001, the growth slowed. The economy shrank by 2.1 percent. The worsening disruptions and slowdown in the U.S. economy aggra-

Table 15.1

Developments in Selected Macro-Economic Variables

	1990	1995	1996	1997	1998	1999	2000	2001
Population in '000[a]	3,047.1	3,525.6	3,670.4	3,793.7	3,922.0	3,950.9	4,017.7	4,131.2
Change in % to year before	2.9	3.1	4.1	3.4	3.4	0.7	1.7	2.8
GDP growth (real) in %	9	8	7.6	8.5	0.1	5.9	9.9	−2.1
GNP per capita in S$ (at current prices)	22,411.0	34,420.0	35,454.0	39,394.0	37,193.0	36,323.0	40,051.0	37,433.0
Labor Force in '000	1,562.8	1,749.3	1,801.9	1,876.0	1,931.8	1,976.0	2,192.3	2,119.7
Change in % to year before	—	3.3	3	4.1	3	2.3	10.9	-3.3
Unemployment rate in %	1.7	2.7	3	2.4	3.2	4.6	4.4	3.4
Private consumption (at current market prices in S$ million)[b]	30,846.5	48,839.5	52,741.3	56,456.3	54,197.6	57,429.2	63,564.9	64,758.0
Change in private consumption (real) in %	—	6	8	7	−4	6	10.7	1.9
Consumer price index	3.4	1.7	1.4	2	-0.3	0	1.3	1.0

Sources: Singapore Statistical Highlights (Singapore: Department of Statistics, 2001 and 2002); *Yearbook of Statistics* (Singapore: Department of Statistics, 2001, 2002); Euromonitor International, *Global Market Information Database, National Statistics* (London: Euromonitor International, 2002); *Annual Manpower Statistics* (Singapore: Ministry of Manpower, 2001).

[a] Population comprises all citizens and permanent residents with local residence and foreigners staying in Singapore for 1 year or more.

[b] Private consumption excludes residents' expenditure abroad and includes non-residents' expenditure locally.

Table 15.2

Recent Economic Developments

	1st Quarter (2001)	2nd Quarter (2001)	3rd Quarter (2001)	4th Quarter (2001)	1st Quarter (2002)	2nd Quarter (2002)	3rd Quarter (2002)
GDP growth (real) in %	5	−0.5	−5.4	−6.6	−1.6	3.7	3.7
Consumer price index change (%)	1.7	1.7	0.8	−0.2	−0.9	−0.4	−0.4

Sources: Economic Survey of Singapore, "First, Second and Third Quarter Reports" (Singapore: Ministry of Trade and Industry, 2002).

vated by the September 11, 2001, terrorist attacks on New York and Washington, D.C., could trigger economic downturn worldwide.

The Asian Economic Crisis and Recession in 2001

The Asian economic crisis began as a currency crisis in the middle of 1997, triggered by Thailand's inability to defend its baht against a sustained attack by speculators. The crisis soon spread across the Asian region, with currencies from the Korean won to the Indonesian rupiah plunging dramatically by as much as 70 percent. The impact of the crisis on Singapore was initially muted, as Singapore had strong economic fundamentals, with the Singapore currency losing only 26 percent of its original value against the U.S. dollar. However, Singapore soon felt the impact of the crisis toward the end of 1997, as total trade with Southeast Asian neighbors contributed to 27 percent of exports, and foreign investors started withdrawing their investments, thinking that this was affected by the region's crisis. GDP growth dropped from 6.2 percent in the first quarter to −0.8 percent in the fourth quarter, clearly showing the economy's recessionary effects. After growing by 0.7 percent in the first half of 1998, the consumer price index for the second half shrank by 1.2 percent, showing the deflationary pressures as a result of the economic slowdown. To worsen the situation, the firm Singapore dollar dampened imported inflationary pressures. As a result, the GDP growth for 1998 turned out to be a mere 0.1 percent. However, Singapore showed a healthy rebound of 5.9 percent growth in 1999, despite general pessimism and conservative forecasts, as evidenced by the IMF's projection of a 0.2 percent GDP growth for that year (IMF 1998, 172).

Singapore's economy shrank by 2.1 percent in 2001 (see Table 15.2). This had been the first contraction since the 1.8 percent shrinkage in 1985. The main causes were believed to be the heavy downturns in the electronics cycle and the downturn in the U.S. economy.

The recession in 2001 resulted in widespread layoffs and pay cuts. The government had taken several measures to ease the pain. The off-budget packages announced during the year that amounted to $11.3 billion were expected to stimulate economic growth (*The Straits Times* 2001e). Various schemes and measures have been formulated to help the retrenched workers and to ease the crisis. Along with these short-term measures, long-term policies are being chalked out to strengthen the fundamentals, like educational standards and infrastructure. The government in-

Table 15.3

Income Distribution

Gross monthly income ($)	1990 (%)	2000 (%)	Change in percentage points from 1990 to 2000
Below 1,000	16.0	12.6	−3.4
1,000–1,999	27.1	14.0	−13.1
2,000–2,999	20.1	14.7	−5.4
3,000–3,999	13.0	13.1	+0.1
4,000–4,999	8.2	10.3	+2.1
5,000–5,999	5.1	8.2	+3.1
6,000–6,999	3.3	6.2	+2.9
7,000–7,999	2.1	4.6	+2.5
8,000–8,999	1.4	3.5	+2.1
9,000–9,999	1.0	2.5	+1.5
10,000 and over	2.8	10.3	+7.5
Total workforce	100.0	100.0	—

Sources: Singapore Census of Population, "Advance Data Release No. 7" (Singapore: Census of Population Office, Department of Statistics, 2001b).

tends to promote services like medical care, biotechnology, and education to attract new investments. The authorities remain cautious, as other risk factors exist in the Asian region: the weakening Japanese economy, the turmoil in Indonesia, and the recent reduction of FDI in ASEAN. For instance, Singapore attracted $11.5 billion in FDI in 2000, down from $13 billion in 1999 (*The Straits Times* 2001f).

Income

There was a significant improvement in the income of the workforce in the last decade (Table 15.3). The average household income increased from $3,076 in 1990 to $4,943 in 2000. The percentage of households earning less than $3,000 continued to fall. Half of the households earned at least $3,600 in 2000, compared to $2,300 in 1990. One in ten households earned $10,000 or more and represented the greatest increase among all the income categories.

Incomes of skilled workers and professionals seemed to increase faster than did those of unskilled workers. Abeysinghe (1994) showed that Singapore has a wider earnings gap between department managers and workers in various occupational groups than cities in all other countries examined, which included not only key Western cities, but also Asian cities, such as Hong Kong, Seoul, and Taipei. Although hampered by a lack of data, the author argues that the available evidence suggests that this wide gap may be explained by the fact that professionals and executives in Singapore earn internationally competitive remuneration packages (Union Bank of Switzerland 1991), whereas wages of low-skilled workers are held back by foreign workers coming to Singapore from largely low-income countries in Asia (Abeysinghe 1994). The earning capacity of low-skill workers will have to be raised through the retraining and upgrading of skills rather than salary growth over and above productivity increases.

Table 15.4

Wage Costs (US$)

	Singapore	Penang	West Malaysia	Shanghai	Thailand
Direct labor costs per hour excluding bonus	7.00	2.00	1.40	1.60	1.20

Source: The Straits Times, November 5 (1998): 3.

During economic downturns, wage costs in Singapore can become considerably higher relative to other ASEAN countries (see Table 15.4 for wage costs during the 1998 economic crisis). This can hamper Singapore's ability to attract new investments and to stay competitive in the global market. As a result, the government has taken firm steps to address this issue by having the public sector cut the variable component of wages and forgoing 1998 and 1999 pay adjustments. The government has also introduced a 10 percent cut in the compulsory employer contribution of employees' pension funds, the Central Provident Fund (CPF), to help reduce labor costs and save jobs. This cut in the CPF contribution rate from 20 percent to 10 percent reduced payrolls without affecting the immediate disposable income, thereby avoiding any economic aggravation by the crisis.

Employment

Singapore has one of the highest labor participation rates in the world, higher than in any Asian newly industrialized economies (NIEs), and also higher than the three developed countries (Japan, the United States, and the United Kingdom), which were included in a study by the Ministry of Labor (*The Straits Times* 1995a). Despite its high level, the overall labor force participation rate kept edging upwards until the currency crisis in 1998, when it dropped to 63.9 percent in that year (Table 15.5). It soon recovered and reached 68.6 percent in 2000. It had dropped to 65.4 percent in 2001. The participation rate of females has been increasing steadily throughout the last decade and was at 54.3 percent in 2001. Additionally, the labor force participation rate of the fifteen- to nineteen-year age group decreased from 30.9 percent in 1990 to 17.6 percent in 2001 (Table 15.5). This decline could be mainly attributed to an increase in the proportion of teenagers who remained in the educational system.

Unemployment has generally not been a problem in Singapore. The unemployment rate of 3.4 percent in 2001 (and in other years) shown in Table 15.1, has been somewhat inflated by university, polytechnic, and school leavers who entered the labor market during May and June of the year, which coincided with the annual survey period. With the current economic downturn, however, the unemployment rate is expected to rise.

The Singaporean government has been supportive of its people in the face of rising unemployment. It has taken steps to ensure that retrenched workers are given the opportunity to retrain, and thus be able to be redeployed to other jobs. One of such steps introduced is a scheme sponsored by the Chinese Development Assistance Council, in which retrenched and unemployed workers are given a monthly allowance of $500 to sustain them as they are completing a National Technical Certificate Grade 3 course (Koh 1998).

Inflation

Inflation has been below 3.5 percent per annum for the last decade (Table 15.1). With the economic crisis of 1997, the consumer price index actually dropped to –0.3 percent in 1998,

Table 15.5

Labor Force Participation

Labor force participation rate (%)	1990	1995	1996	1997	1998	1999	2000	2001	Change in % points from 1990 to 2001
Total	66.0	64.4	64.6	64.2	63.9	64.7	68.6	65.4	−0.6
Male	79.0	78.4	78.7	78.3	77.5	77.8	81.1	77.8	−1.2
Female	53.0	50.1	51.5	51.1	51.3	52.7	55.5	54.3	+1.3
Youth labor participation rate									
15–19 years	30.9	19.9	20.1	16.8	14.7	17.2	19.1	17.6	−13.3
20–24 years	82.5	76.9	76.1	73.5	71.5	74.0	77.4	73.7	−8.8
25–29 years	86.4	86.6	88.1	88.2	87.9	87.1	91.1	88.8	+2.4

Sources: Singapore Statistical Highlights (Singapore: Department of Statistics, 2002); *Yearbook of Statistics* (Singapore: Department of Statistics, 2002); *Annual Manpower Statistics* (Singapore: Ministry of Manpower, 2001).

suggesting that inflation would not pose a problem in Singapore in the short term. In the long run, inflation is expected to remain low, supported by public budget surpluses and sustained, high private saving rates.

Trends in Trade Policy

The movement of goods, services, and capital in and out of the country is not hampered by trade or exchange controls. A few exceptions are restrictions on the import of goods mainly for health, safety, or security reasons. Singapore is essentially a free port, and most goods can be imported and exported freely. This situation is unlikely to change, because Singapore has derived considerable benefits from its role as the regional trading center. Rather, continued efforts are being made toward making trading in Singapore more efficient and cost-effective, for example, by further simplifying trade documentation and rationalizing customs operations. Since January 1994, items from furniture to biscuits have been entering Singapore duty-free, bringing the total number of duty-free goods to 5,736 items and representing 96 percent of all goods entering the country. Import duties are mainly revenue duties on items such as alcoholic beverages and tobacco to discourage their consumption, and motor vehicles to discourage car ownership and control traffic congestion (Asia Business Network 1997).

As a result of the liberal trade policy, Singapore already enjoys a competitive market environment in most consumer markets. An opening of the markets in its neighboring ASEAN countries, particularly with the ASEAN Free Trade Area, will, therefore, not have much impact on Singapore's consumers, who already enjoy a full range of goods from all over the world at competitive international market prices.

Long-Term Trends in the Economic Environment

Singapore recovered from the Asian economic crisis and achieved an amazing growth of 9.9 percent in 2000. The country is expected to recover from the current evolving recession. Singapore still seems very competitive, with the cuts in wages and CPF (especially with the measures taken to cope with the economic crisis), and as many companies place a high premium on efficient air and sea transport, telecommunications, and other supporting services and facilities, which Singapore adequately provides. In fact, U.S.-based Business Environment Risk Intelligence (BERI) ranked Singapore as the world's number two investment spot after Switzerland, but before countries such as Japan, the United States, and Germany (Business Environment Risk Intelligence S.A. 1999). Singapore was also ranked as the world's most competitive country since 1996, according to the World Economic Forum's *Global Competitiveness Report* (2000), even with the economic downturn.

High wages and other business-related costs relative to other countries in the region have to be seen against a backdrop of Singapore working rigorously toward increasing the value-added worth of its small workforce. The Singapore Government sets economic master plans every year, into which a range of other plans fit. For instance, it launched a $7 billion Science and Technology Plan for 2001–2005 and announced a long-term initiative to develop Life Sciences as a pillar of Singapore industries (Ministry of Trade and Industry 2001). These plans affect economic growth and international competitiveness and maximize the value-added generated by Singapore's labor, land, and capital resources.

To achieve the objective of adding value to Singapore's various resources, investments are made to upgrade skills and education levels of the country's workforce and to add to and improve its infrastructure. In its endeavor to become the information and communications hub in the Asia Pacific, IDA is offering up to $2 million per year to sponsor information technology (IT) students for academic exchanges that will provide them with overseas working experience (*The Straits Times Interactive* 2001a). More broadly, in 2000, Singapore pumped in a record $3.01 billion into research and development (R&D), representing a 13 percent increase from 1999, and 1.89 percent of the country's GDP, which is close to the 2–3 percent of that of developed nations (*The Straits Times Interactive* 2001b). Other strategies include attracting skilled workers and professionals to Singapore to supplement its workforce. Minister for Trade and Industry George Yeo emphasized the importance of foreign talent and the government's encouragement of their immigration (2001a). It will, therefore, remain easy to hire expatriates and to obtain employment passes for professionals and skilled workers in Singapore.

The strategy toward higher value-added per employee can be seen in Singapore's recent effort to attract global companies and highly accomplished scientists to enter the life science industry and business in Singapore. Senior Minister Lee Kuan Yew has pointed out that partnering with global players to bring in new technology will be a way to deal with greater economic competition (*The Straits Times Interactive* 2001c). *New Scientist,* a scientific publication, has referred to Singapore as "every researcher's dream," with great career prospects and state-of-the-art labs and equipment, and, in general, as a great place in which to live and work (*The Straits Times* 2001g). Key initiatives such as the Singapore Genomics Programme and the Bioinformatics Institute are expected to attract hundreds of local and foreign researchers to the field. Long-term efforts to nurture talent have also been made. Through 2005, US$500 million has been set aside for Ph.D. scholarship and fellowship awards, and some local tertiary institutes are geared toward training scientists and engineers that are high in demand in the field. Other grand schemes are also planned for the near future. The Biopharmaceutical Manufacturing Technology Centre that makes and tests drugs using living cells is up and running as of January 2003. A $300 million biomedical city in the heart of Singapore's Science Hub at Buona Vista was launched in 2003. A national "bank," the Singapore Tissue Network, which will store healthy and diseased human tissues, was established in 2002 and subsequently was located at the Biopolis at Buona Vista (*The Straits Times Interactive* 2001d, e, f).

To add value, another long-term strategy aims to take advantage of resources in Asia. Singapore possesses capital and specialist management skills in some areas, where many other Asian countries are capital-short but have the land and labor resources Singapore lacks. Furthermore, they represent markets that are larger and will, in the longer term, grow faster than Singapore's. One example of government initiatives to take advantage of these factors is the use of government-linked companies to develop flagship projects, which put in place the infrastructures required by private-sector companies before moving to these countries. Examples of such projects are the Batam Industrial Park in Indonesia, the industrial park being developed in the Fujian Province in China, and the technology park under development in Bangalore in India. One of the objectives of these projects is to move labor-intensive operations out of Singapore, while retaining high-value-added, skill-intensive operations (EIU 1994).

The upgrading of Singapore's workforce and value-added jobs coupled with the outsourcing of low-end labor-intensive work to other countries should result in increased competitiveness of Singapore as a whole.

Summary: Economic Environment

Singapore's economic environment experienced a negative growth in 2001. However, recovery is expected. The Singaporean government has launched many well-publicized and bold measures to tackle the local downturn. Initiatives on various economic master plans, the development of information technology, and life science research are expected to help the economy reduce its reliance on the electronics sector. In addition, Singapore has the advantage of a well-trained and equipped workforce (albeit leading to relatively higher labor costs), a high labor participation rate, low unemployment, and an almost negligible inflation rate. These factors play an important role in the country's recovery from economic challenges and also in its long-term prosperity.

DEMOGRAPHIC ENVIRONMENT

Long-term demographic developments are powerful change agents in any society. Changes in size of population and age distribution have profound impacts on any economy and its consumption patterns. Singapore seems to follow demographic trends of developed nations. The population grows slowly and is aging fast. Both trends seem to be due partially to a tendency toward delayed marriage and childbirth, as well as a sharply reduced fertility rate. An increasing life expectancy contributes further to the aging of the population. These trends are discussed in more detail below.

Population Size

Singapore is a small city-state with a population of only approximately 4 million (including citizens, permanent residents, and foreigners who have lived in the country for a year or more). Its population has been growing slowly at no higher than 4 percent per annum for the past decade, mainly through immigration (Table 15.1). The government allows large numbers of skilled workers, professionals, and their families to migrate to Singapore. In recent years, the government, long concerned about a sluggish birthrate, put in place a number of incentives for couples to have more children, earlier in life.

The expatriate population tends to increase faster than the resident population. In 1995, the total population growth, including that of foreigners, was 3.1 percent. This was in direct contrast to the growth of the resident population, which was only 1.8 percent (*Yearbook of Statistics* 2001). In 2000, the total population growth was 2.8 percent, and the resident population grew by only 1.7 percent. Singapore will continue to use such expatriates and foreign workers for specialized skills not locally available and for unskilled work, such as work on construction sites and basic assembly work in electronics factories.

Age Distribution

Singapore is one of the fastest-aging countries in the world. The proportion of elderly residents ages sixty and above increased from 9 percent in 1990 to 11.1 percent in mid-2002. A slight drop was also observed for the fifteen- to fifty-nine-year age group in the same period. In contrast, residents ages zero to fourteen decreased from 23 percent to 21.2 percent (Table 15.6). These trends are reflected in an increase in the median age of the population from 29.8 years in 1990 to 34.6 years in 2001 (Table 15.7).

Some reasons for the aging of Singapore's population are an increased life expectancy, lower reproduction rates, as well as trends toward delaying marriage and childbirth. Life expectancy of Singaporeans has increased dramatically from 63 years in 1957 to 78.4 years in 2001 (*Yearbook of Statistics* 1998, 2001), and the gross reproduction rate continued to drop (from about 1.18

Table 15.6

Age Profile of the Resident Population

	Age Distribution in %			
	0–14	15–59	60+	Total
1990	23	68	9	100
1995	22.8	67.5	9.7	100
1996	22.6	67.6	9.8	100
1997	22.4	67.8	9.8	100
1998	22.1	67.9	10	100
1999	21.8	67.8	10.4	100
2000	21.5	67.8	10.7	100
2002 (End of June)	21.2	67.7	11.1	100
Change in percentage points from 1990 to 2002	–1.8	–0.3	2.1	—

Source: Yearbook of Statistics (Singapore: Department of Statistics, 2002): Advanced data released.

Table 15.7

Median Age and Life Expectancy

	Life Expectancy in Years			
	Male	Female	Total	Median age
1990	73.1	77.6	75.3	29.8
1995	74.2	78.6	76.3	31.9
1996	74.5	78.9	76.6	32.4
1997	74.9	79.1	76.9	32.8
1998	75.3	79.4	77.3	33.2
1999	75.6	79.7	77.6	33.7
2000	76.1	80.1	78.1	34.2
2001	76.4	80.4	78.4	34.6
Change in years from 1990 to 2001	3.3	2.8	3.1	4.8

Sources: Yearbook of Statistics (Singapore: Department of Statistics, 2002).

per female age fifteen to forty-four in 1990 to only 0.94 in 2000) (*Trends in Singapore Resident Population* 2000). Finally, mean marriage age increased from 28.7 to 29.9 years for males from 1990 to 2001, and from 25.9 to 26.8 years for females during the same period (*Yearbook of Statistics* 2001). Shantakumar projects that the aging process will continue for at least the next forty years, peaking in the years 2020 to 2030, when between 24 percent and 27 percent of the total population will be sixty years and older (Fernandez 1995).

In summary, Singapore's demographic environment resembles that of older industrialized societies, with a stagnating or only slowly growing and rapidly aging population.

Table 15.8

Ethnicity in Singapore

In % of resident population	1990	1996	1997	1998	1999	2000	2002 (end of June)
Chinese	77.8	77.3	77.2	77	77.7	76.8	76.5
Malays	14	14	14.1	13.9	14.1	13.9	13.8
Indians	7.1	7.4	7.4	7.7	7.1	7.9	8.1
Others	1.1	1.3	1.3	1.4	1.1	1.4	1.6
Total	100	100	100	100	100	100	100

Sources: Yearbook of Statistics (Singapore: Department of Statistics, 1994, 1998, 2002).

CULTURAL ENVIRONMENT

Singapore's people are largely descendants of immigrants from China, the Malay Peninsula, the Indian subcontinent, and Sri Lanka. They have gradually developed a Singaporean identity, while, at the same time, retaining their cultural heritage (Ministry of Information, Communications, and the Arts 1995, 29). As a result, Singapore has become a multicultural society, dominated by Chinese, with Malays and Indians as its two other main ethnic groups. Each ethnic group has its own cultural background that includes its languages and religions. The main religions remain Buddhism, Chinese traditional beliefs/Taoism, Islam, and Christianity. Other aspects of Singapore's cultural developments resemble those of older industrialized countries in the past forty years. In particular, there are rapidly improving education levels, with more and more entrants into the workforce having university and postsecondary education; reducing household sizes; and an increasing workforce participation rate to one of the highest in the world. These cultural trends are detailed further in the sections below.

Ethnicity

The population in Singapore is predominantly Chinese, constituting some 76.5 percent of the population, followed by 13.9 percent Malays and 7.9 percent Indians. The racial mix has been relatively stable over the past decade (Table 15.8).

Singapore seems to show that the various groups have learned to be quite tolerant of one another (Lai 1995; Chua 1995). An analysis of interethnic contacts during activities, such as daily marketing, eating in the hawker centers, chatting, playing in public places, and other similar activities, suggests a harmonious society. This interracial harmony in everyday life also shows the tolerance for one another's festivals and ritual practices, as well as in the preference for multiracial living (although the main reason seems to be the wish to escape excessive, even claustrophobic, closeness of one's own community). However, Lai concludes that Singaporeans have not achieved much depth of mutual cultural understanding, which was manifested in interviewee statements on wedding customs: "We have our own way of doing ours, they have theirs."

Languages

The official languages are English, Chinese (Mandarin), Malay, and Tamil. English is the language of administration, and Malay is the national language. Mandarin is being increasingly used

Table 15.9

Literacy of Ethnic Groups in Various Languages in Singapore

In % of resident population aged 15 years and older	1990	2000	Change in percentage points from 1990 to 2000
Chinese	100.0	100.0	—
English only	19.8	16.4	−3.4
Chinese only	40.6	32.0	−8.6
English and Chinese	37.8	48.3	+10.5
Others	1.9	3.3	+1.4
Malays	100.0	100.0	—
English only	3.2	2.0	−1.2
Malay only	27.3	19.8	−7.5
English and Malay	68.1	76.7	+8.6
Others	1.4	1.5	+0.1
Indians	100.0	100.0	—
English only	22.1	21.5	−0.6
Tamil only	14.5	8.9	−5.6
English and Tamil	31.5	37.5	+6.0
English and Malay	19.1	17.4	−1.7
Others	12.8	14.6	+1.8

Sources: Singapore Census of Population, "Advance Data Release No. 3" (Singapore: Census of Population Office, Department of Statistics, 2000c).

among Chinese in place of Chinese dialects such as Hokkien, Teochew, Cantonese, Hakka, Hainanese, and Foochow. Most Malays speak Malay, while Indians speak mainly Tamil but also other Indian dialects such as Telegu, Malayalam, Punjabi, Hindi, and Bengali.

Singaporeans are becoming increasingly multilingual. The proportion of people speaking only their own language or dialect has decreased sharply. More and more people speak their own dialect plus English and/or Mandarin (Table 15.9). In particular, the literacy in English (English only, or English and another language) increased significantly, and English has become the most widely spoken language. This was the result of wider usage of English in commerce and the adoption of English as the main medium of instruction in schools and other educational institutions. Also, English is used almost exclusively for communications across ethnic groups. As Senior Minister Lee Kuan Yew pointed out:

> English as our working language has prevented conflicts arising between our different races and given us a competitive advantage because it is the international language of business and diplomacy, of science and technology. Without it, we would not have many of the world's multinationals and over 200 of the world's top banks in Singapore. Nor would our people have taken so readily to computers and the Internet. (Lee 2000, 181)

Greater usage of Mandarin instead of Chinese dialects reflects the success of the government's "speak Mandarin" campaign for a month every year, as well as the emphasis on Mandarin as the second language among Chinese pupils (Lee 2000).

The household language refers to the language or dialect that is used most frequently among

Table 15.10

Household Language Spoken

In % of residents households age five and older	1980	1990	2000	Change in percentage points from 1980 to 2000
English	11.6	18.8	23.0	+11.4
Mandarin	10.2	23.7	35.0	+24.8
Chinese dialects	59.5	39.6	23.8	−35.7
Malay	13.9	14.3	14.1	+0.2
Tamil	3.1	2.9	3.2	+0.1
Others	1.7	0.8	0.9	−0.8
Total	100.0	100.0	100.0	—

Sources: Singapore Census of Population, "Statistical Release 3: Literacy, Languages Spoken and Education" (Singapore: Census of Population Office, Department of Statistics, 1990b); *Singapore Census of Population*, "Advance Data Release No. 3" (Singapore: Census of Population Office, Department of Statistics, 2000c).

family members. In general, the use of English has become more prevalent when speaking to family members (Table 15.10). Among Chinese, there was a significant shift away from the use of dialects toward English and Mandarin as the predominant household languages. English-speaking households increased from 11.6 percent in 1980 to 23 percent in 2000, while those using Mandarin increased from 10.2 percent to 35 percent. Consequently, the use of Chinese dialects dropped from 59.5 percent in 1980 to 23.8 percent in 2000 (*Singapore Census of Population* 2000c).

Religions

The religious backgrounds are closely related to the various ethnic groups. Many Chinese follow Buddhism and, increasingly, Christianity. The vast majority of Malays are Muslims, and Indians are predominantly Hindus but also Buddhists and Muslims. With Chinese comprising almost 77 percent of the resident population, Buddhism is the predominant religion in Singapore, followed by Islam and Christianity (Table 15.11).

In the last two decades, a drastic shift has been seen toward Buddhism, mainly among the Chinese population, wherein 54 percent identified themselves as Buddhists in 2000, and clearly at the expense of traditional beliefs/Taoism, which are commonly perceived as superstitious and antiquated (*The Straits Times* 1995b). In particular, the number of followers of Chinese traditional beliefs/Taoism had reduced to less than one-third of its 1980 level. The increase in the proportion of Christians has been gradual, from about 10 percent in 1980 to about 15 percent in 2000. The increase mainly comes from the better-educated Chinese.

Education

Current education levels in Singapore are still lagging behind those in developed countries. Only about 12 percent of its residents ages fifteen and above have tertiary education (Table 15.12; *Singapore Census of Population* 2000a). This is in contrast to about one-third of the population

Table 15.11

Religion

In % of resident population ages 10 and over	1980	1990	2000	Change in percentage points from 1990 to 2000
Buddhism	27.0	31.2	42.5	+15.5
Chinese traditional beliefs/Taoism	30.0	22.4	8.5	−21.5
Islam	15.7	15.3	14.9	−0.8
Christianity	10.1	12.7	14.6	+4.5
Hinduism	3.6	3.7	4.0	+0.4
Other religions	0.5	0.6	0.6	+0.1
No religion/free thought	13.0	14.1	14.8	+1.8

Source: Singapore Census of Population, "Statistical Release 6: Religion, Childcare and Leisure Activities" (Singapore: Census of Population Office, Department of Statistics, 1990); *Singapore Census of Population*, "Advance Data Release, No. 2" (Singapore: Census of Population Office, Department of Statistics, 2000).

with tertiary education in the United States or Japan, and 22 percent in Germany. Nevertheless, education levels in Singapore are improving fast. For example, the proportion of the workforce with primary education or less decreased 15.6 percentage points from 58.5 percent in 1990 to 42.7 percent in 2000, whereas the proportion of the workforce with university degrees increased more than twofold from 4.5 percent to 11.7 percent (Table 15.12). The rise in educational levels indicates that new entrants to the workforce will continue to be better educated and well skilled.

Households

Households in Singapore are getting smaller. The average number of persons per household declined from 4.9 in 1980 to 3.7 in 2000 (Table 15.13). This is due to the decline in number of children per family and the desire of young couples to set up homes of their own rather than to stay with their parents (Department of Statistics 2001).

The participation rate of females in the labor force continued to increase gradually from 53.5 percent in 1990 to 54.3 percent in 2001 (Table 15.5), indicating that the trend towards dual income households goes on. The participation rate of married females continued to rise from 1990 to 2000, particularly for two age groups (*Singapore Census of Population* 2001a). Married females in the first age group (twenty-five to twenty-nine years old) tend to stay in the workforce and delay childbirth, at which time they may withdraw from their work. More married women are also reentering the workforce at ages between forty-five and forty-nine, when their children grow older. Furthermore, the availability of retired parents, other relatives, a large number of foreign maids, and a wide variety of child care centers allow Singaporean women to continue working after having children (Kau, Yeong, and Richmond 1993, 26).

Other Aspects of Singapore's Cultural Environment

There are other aspects of Singapore's cultural background that are less well documented in statistical data but still have significant impact on values systems, consumer behavior, and mar-

Table 15.12

Education

Highest qualification attained	1990	2000	Change in percentage points from 1990 to 2000
Primary and below	58.3	42.7	−15.6
Secondary	26.5	24.6	−1.9
Upper secondary	7.3	14.9	+7.6
Polytechnic	3.5	6.2	+2.7
University	4.5	11.7	7.2
Total	100.0	100.0	—
Literacy rate (% of population 15 years and over)	89.1	92.5	+3.4

Sources: Singapore Census of Population, "Advance Data Release, No. 1" (Singapore: Census of Population Office, Department of Statistics, 2000a); *Yearbook of Statistics* (Singapore: Department of Statistics 2001).

Table 15.13

Private Household by Size (in percent)

Household size (persons)	1980	1990	2000	Change in percentage points from 1980 to 2000
1	5.7	5.2	8.2	+2.5
2–3	23.8	28.5	36.3	+12.5
4–5	36.7	45.6	43.5	+6.8
6 and more	33.8	20.7	12.0	−21.8
Total	100.0	100.0	100.0	—
Average household size	4.9	4.2	3.7	−1.2

Source: Singapore Census of Population, "Statistical Release 2: Household and Housing" (Singapore: Census of Population Office, Department of Statistics, 1990a); *Singapore Census of Population*, "Advance Data Release, No. 6: Key Indicators on Households and Population" (Singapore: Census of Population Office, Department of Statistics, 2001a).

keting management. Some of these features include the lifestyle of Singaporeans in a high-density city-state with no hinterland. This means nearly all the population lives in high-rises (more than 95 percent), and leisure activities are shaped by the urban environment and the surrounding sea. The tropical weather is another aspect of life in Singapore, which discourages strenuous outdoor activities but allows sitting outside at one of the many hawker centers all year round. The confluence of rich and diverse cultural influences has endowed Singaporeans with an outlook that is both traditional and contemporary, and this is reflected in many aspects of local life, including the wide variety of food available at almost every street corner, the architectural styles ranging from traditional Chinese to hypermodern skyscrapers, and the arts and cultural scene encompassing both Singapore's Asian heritage and Western plays and music. A flavor of the diversity of Singapore's cultural environment is presented to show some of the features of life in this city-state. Where considered important, these features are elaborated in the following sections on consumer behavior and marketing.

Cultural Environment: Summary and Conclusions

This section discussed the cultural environment of Singapore, which is characterized by its population of descendants of immigrants mainly from Asia. Chinese constitutes the main ethnic group, with Malays and Indians as its two other important groups. Singapore has managed to create a social environment of racial harmony and mutual acceptance. The various groups have kept their cultural heritage, which includes their languages and dialects, religions, and customs. The main languages spoken are Mandarin and various Chinese dialects by the Chinese, Malay by the Malays, Tamil and other Indian dialects by the Indians, and English across all ethnic groups. The extent of cultural identity by the various groups is reflected in use of their own languages and dialects at home, whereby only 23 percent use English as their household language. Nevertheless, Singaporeans are becoming increasingly multilingual, with an increasing proportion of people speaking English (71 percent), the language of administration and main medium of instruction in educational institutions, and an increasing number of Chinese speaking Mandarin (65 percent of total population) on top of their own dialects. The religious backgrounds are also closely related to the various ethnic groups, with many Chinese following Buddhism and, recently, Christianity; the vast majority of Malays practicing Islam; and Indians following mainly Hinduism. Other developments in the cultural environment resemble those of older industrialized countries over the past forty years. In particular, education levels show rapid improvement, with more and more entrants into the workforce who have tertiary education (although the proportion of the total population with tertiary education is still far below those of older developed countries), household sizes getting smaller, and the workforce participation rate edging up to one of the highest in the world.

CONSUMER BEHAVIOR

Singapore is becoming an increasingly affluent society. This is reflected in high real growth rates of private consumption, as well as an increasing share of higher-level goods, such as recreational, educational, and health services, and a declining share of basic goods, such as food and beverages, on total consumption. The increasing affluence is also reflected in recent consumer value and lifestyle studies that show that Singaporeans have become more brand and status conscious and more discerning and health-conscious consumers. Increases in consumer spending and the trends observed in values and lifestyles are expected to continue for the coming years and are discussed in more detail in the sections below. Relative to its population, Singapore welcomes a large number of visitors, many with substantial spending power. Therefore, key data on Singapore's visitors are also presented.

Consumption

Private consumption has been growing rapidly in real terms. Between 1990 and 2000, the annual increase was between 6 percent and 10.7 percent (Table 15.1). It is expected that the consumption growth will continue. There was negative growth in 1998 because of the Asian economic crisis, but private consumption recovered and increased by 6.4 percent and 10.7 percent in 1999 and

Table 15.14

Consumer Durables

% of Households	1995	1996	1997	1998	1999	2000	2001
Refrigerator	98.3	98.5	98.7	98.8	98.8	99.0	99.1
Washing machine	85.6	88.1	90.7	91.7	92.0	92.3	93.9
Air conditioner	44.2	48.7	53.2	54.2	55.2	55.4	55.7
TV	97.9	98.3	98.4	98.3	98.4	98.5	98.5
VCR	74.0	77.6	78.2	78.7	79.3	79.8	80.4
Piano/organ	11.1	10.7	10.3	10.3	10.0	9.8	9.6
PC	30.6	35.7	40.9	45.9	50.9	56.0	57.1
Car	33.5	34.7	35.9	36.9	38.0	39.1	40.2
Microwave oven	30.3	34.5	38.7	42.7	46.8	50.8	52.2

Source: Euromonitor International, "Global Market Information Database, National Statistics" (London: Euromonitor International, 2002).

2000, respectively, which was well in line with the EIU expectation of an average annual rate of nearly 7 percent until the year 2000. The main driving force has likely been the continuing rapidly rising income per capita (EIU 1994, 13), as discussed in the section on the economic environment. Private consumption is expected to suffer from the current recession, with more households taking a conservative outlook and putting more emphasis on saving their incomes.

Tangible evidence for the increasing wealth is household penetration rates of consumer durables, which have generally increased significantly during the years 1988 to 2000. The most noticeable increases were in the proportion of households with washing machines, air conditioners, microwave ovens, and PCs (Table 15.14). For example, the penetration rate for PCs increased from 30.6 percent in 1995 to a stunning 57.1 percent in 2001.

Increasing affluence is also reflected in changing consumption patterns. The share of total consumption of basic goods, such as food and beverages, furniture and household equipment, and clothing and footwear has been declining from 1990 to 2000. For example, food and beverages had a share of 25.1 percent of total consumption in 1983, which fell to 13.8 percent by 2000 (Table 15.15). In contrast, services such as rent and utilities and medical services showed increases in their shares of total private consumption. As Singapore's real wages are set to keep rising, these trends can be expected to continue, and private consumption growth will tend to be driven by spending on services rather than on goods.

The household penetration with cars is low in comparison with countries of similar GDP per head. This is mainly due to an excellent public transport infrastructure but probably more due to the world's heaviest taxation of car ownership (a customs duty of 42 percent plus a so-called additional registration fee of 150 percent of the value of the car) and car usage (relatively high road and petrol taxes, high parking fees throughout the city, and the recent introduction of the Electronic Road Pricing system). Furthermore, to avoid the heavy costs of traffic jams to the economy as a whole, as can be observed in many other cities in the region, the Singapore government controls the car population via a license system. Every month, a fixed number of licenses for new car registrations are released. Prospective car owners then have to bid for such a license, called the Certificate of Entitlement (to buy a car), in a monthly auction before being able to purchase an automobile. The prices for these licenses vary by engine size. Though the prices for these certificates have been dropping since June 2001, they are still expensive. For instance, in December 2001, a certificate cost some $27,000 for cars with engines of 1,600 cc or less (*The*

Table 15.15

Consumer Expenditure in Singapore

Private consumption in % of total (at current market prices)	1990	1995	1996	1997	1998	1999	2000
Food and beverages	20.1	16.0	15.6	15.1	15.2	14.7	13.8
Clothing and footwear	8.5	6.0	5.7	5.3	4.6	4.8	4.9
Rent and utilities	14.2	14.0	14.0	14.1	15.6	15.1	14.5
Furniture and household equipment	9.4	8.6	8.6	8.5	8.5	8.4	8.1
Medical services	5.0	5.1	5.3	5.4	5.8	5.9	5.6
Transport and communications	18.2	21.8	19.9	18.8	18.1	19.9	21.9
Recreation and education	19.4	17.5	16.5	15.9	15.6	15.6	16.0
Other goods and services	24.2	22.9	22.4	22.8	20.5	20.3	20.2
Add: Residents' expenditure abroad	8.6	10.8	12.4	11.0	11.6	10.9	10.9
Less: Nonresidents' expenditure locally	27.6	22.7	20.2	17.0	15.4	15.6	15.9
Total	100.0	100.0	100.0	100.0	100.0	100.0	100.0
Consumer expenditure (in '000,000)	30,847	48,840	52,741	56,456	54,198	57,429	63,565

Sources: Yearbook of Statistics (Singapore: Department of Statistics, 2001).
Note: Consumer expenditure includes residents' expenditure abroad and excludes nonresidents' expenditure locally (e.g., tourists' spending).

Straits Times 2001h). The government policy of encouraging usage of public transport and discouraging usage of private cars is unlikely to change in the foreseeable future.

Unlike in many Western industrialized countries, private consumption does not seem to be driven much by credit availability and affordability. Rather, Singaporeans tend to save up enough before making purchases. The saving rate in Singapore is high. For example, a study on saving behavior in various Asian countries shows that in 1996, saving in Singapore was 35.2 percent of GDP (Rojthamrong 2000). On the whole, Singaporeans can be described as financially sober, if not conservative. In the same study, the saving–investment gap (defined as saving as a percentage of GDP minus investment as a percentage of GDP) was consistently at 0 percent. This conservatism is further supported by the government's ideological promotion of so-called Asian values as social ethos, with frugality being promoted as one of the highest virtues.

With the current economic downturn, short-term consumer expenditure is expected to change. However, the above consumption trends are projected long-term trends that are expected to continue after the downturn. With the downturn in place, consumers have less disposable income, and therefore, consumption expenditure is expected to focus more on staple and necessity goods. Few changes would be expected in consumer expenditure for the food and beverage category, as this category, being a staple good, is resilient in an economic downturn. Because the transport and communication category includes vehicles, consumer expenditure in this category is expected to decrease, as consumers have less spending power and may switch to public transport. This is reflected in the drop in private consumption on transport and communications from a high of 19.9 percent in 1996 to 18.8 percent in 1997, and finally to only 18.1 percent in 1998 as a result of the Asian economic crisis in 1997. The expenditure has increased in 1999 and 2000, but it is expected to again decrease with the downturn in 2001.

Expectations on Consumer Values and Lifestyles

Kau et al. (1993) conducted a Delphi study with 150 participants. The authors concluded that future Singaporeans will:

- become more individualistic. The increasing affluence and living in a highly urbanized society is felt to make consumers want to differentiate themselves from the general society;
- remain very status conscious and materialistic. This is reflected in the infamous "5 Cs" said to be aspired by all young professionals: career, cash, credit card (the issue of credit cards is strictly regulated, and they are only issued to individuals with an annual income of S$30,000 or more, an amount difficult to achieve for many nonuniversity graduates); condominium (instead of the state-subsidized Housing Development Board flats in which more than 90 percent of the population lives); and a car (see previous section on car population regulation to appreciate the costs of car ownership in Singapore);
- become more brand conscious. Respondents believed that future consumers will be increasingly concerned with buying well-known brands across a wide range of product categories, from cosmetics and food to jewelry and cookware. It appears that brands associated with high income, status, and sophistication will show the highest growth;
- become more discerning. For example, consumers are expected to increasingly value and be willing to pay for higher-quality products, increasingly want detailed and accurate product information (e.g., materials used in clothes, expiration dates, and ingredients in food), and will increasingly appreciate art and culture;
- become more health conscious. As the population ages and affluence grows, consumers are expected to pay more attention to their health. For example, this will show in an increased demand for fitness and health clubs, as well as for health food with lower cholesterol, fat, salt, and sugar content, but with more vitamins, fiber, and natural ingredients;
- put more emphasis on leisure activities, such as traveling, water sports, golfing, and cultural activities; and
- be more pressed for time. The continuous increase in the labor participation rate of women will lead to more time pressures, particularly for working women. However, time pressures will not reach levels such as in the United States, as Singaporeans frequently live within an extended family, and maids and other household helpers are readily available.

All the above trends would be affected by the economic downturn, as there is less disposable income for spending in the short term. However, in the long run, Singaporeans are expected to continue following these trends.

Lifestyle Structures

A large-scale lifestyle study conducted in 1998 identified the following seven major clusters of Singaporeans based on lifestyle and value systems (Jung, Wirtz, Kau, and Tan 1999; Kau, Tan, and Wirtz 1998). A more detailed description of the seven clusters is presented in Table 15.16.

Table 15.16

Values Orientation of the Seven Clusters

Clusters	% of Respondents	Values orientation
Traditional family oriented	16.1	Least materialistic; low pecuniary adherence; spender; high moral standards; very pro-family and religious
New age family oriented	13.9	Women should have own career; lifelong learning is important; environmentally conscious, concerned about moral decay; pro-family
Entrepreneurs	13.1	Like stimulation and changes; value education; work smart rather than work hard; sense of accomplishment is important; nontraditional; more liberal about premarital sex and divorce
Aspirers	18.4	Early adopters of new ideas/products; would rather fight than compromise; materialistic; enjoy attention; highly pro-family; observe traditions
Materialists	14.3	Not environmentally conscious; materialistic; financial security very important; not society conscious; less trusting of others
Pragmatists	11.1	Least adventurous; low entrepreneurial spirit; dislike attention and do not worry about social status; low respect for authority; pro-Westernization
Independents	13.1	Pro-feminism; low value for education; not too concerned about financial security; liberal moral standards; not too pro-family

Source: Kwon Jung, Jochen Wirtz, Ah Keng Kau, and Soo Jiuan Tan, "The Seven Faces of Singaporeans: A Typology of Consumers Based on a Large-Scale Lifestyle Study," *Asia Pacific Journal of Management* 16, no. 2 (1998): 17.

Traditional Family Oriented

This cluster characterizes those who are high on both family and traditional value orientations. This group also shows nonmaterialistic tendencies. Demographically, it has relatively more women (58.9 percent) and Malays (31.1 percent).

New Age Family Oriented

This cluster characterizes those who are high on family orientation, but low on traditional value orientation. This group is somewhat status oriented and society conscious, but not too materialistic. This group seems to pursue both status and societal harmony as well as family values, but without much concern for traditional values. Demographically, this group has relatively more teens (54.5 percent) and women (62.3 percent).

Entrepreneurs

This group represents those who have high entrepreneurial sprit and low traditional values and status orientation. It has relatively more respondents in their twenties (40.3 percent) who are better educated (32.7 percent have tertiary education), tend to have high income, do not seem very religious (39.2 percent have no religion), and are mostly Chinese (93 percent).

Aspirers

This category represents those who have entrepreneurial spirit and want status but yet adhere to traditional values. They are also somewhat materialistic and society conscious. This group aspires to excel in every aspect possible. Demographically, this group has relatively more Malays (27.1 percent) and Indians (17.1 percent) than other clusters.

Materialists

This cluster characterizes those who are high on materialism and low on society orientation. This group is so named, because it tends to seek materialistic values in a selfish way. It does not exhibit any distinct demographic characteristics.

Pragmatists

This group represents those who are high on materialistic and society orientations but low on status orientation. This group tries to balance materialistic pursuit with societal considerations. It has relatively more respondents in their thirties (40.1 percent), with the majority being Chinese (92.4 percent). Most of them are married (76.3 percent) with children (72.4 percent).

Independents

This group characterizes those who are low on family orientation and about average on all other aspects. People in this group do not care much about things around them. This group of people is quite uniformly distributed across all age groups.

Tourism

Singapore has almost two visitors per annum for every resident (see Table 15.17). The number of visitors increased steadily from 4.2 million in 1988 to 7.5 million in 2001. The majority of visitors (69.2 percent) come from Asia, with ASEAN, Japan, and Taiwan being the most important markets. The share of Asian visitors has increased significantly from 57.4 percent in 1988 to 69.4 percent in 2001, while the European share fell from 24.4 percent to 14.8 percent in the same time frame. These data suggest a shift for businesses targeting tourists to offer more goods and services that meet the tastes and preferences of Asian tourists rather than Westerners.

The 1998 economic crisis drove total visitor arrivals down to 6.2 million during that year. This decrease was likely attributable to the fall in visitor arrivals from Asia, as most Asian economies were badly hit by the crisis. It is notable that the share of visitor arrivals from all other continents showed an increase, with those from Europe and Oceania being the most significant. These tourists might have taken the opportunity to obtain cheaper airfares and lower exchange rates to travel to this region. The total arrivals have since increased back to the regular level. The worldwide economic slowdown in 2001 coupled with the September 11, 2001, terrorist attacks on New York and Washington, D.C., have taken their toll on tourism in Singapore. According to statistics from the Singapore Tourism Board (STB), the total visitor arrivals in 2001 dropped by 2.2 percent compared to the previous year (2001a).

Table 15.17

Tourism

	1995	1996	1997	1998	1999	2000	2001	2002 (end of September)
Visitor arrival in '000	7,136.5	7,292.4	7,197.9	6,242.2	6,958.2	7,691.3	7,522.2	5,629.00
Growth in % to year before	3.4	2.2	–1.3	–13.3	11.5	10.5	–2.2	—
Share of arrivals by continent (%)								
Asia	73.3	72.9	72.3	67.7	68.9	69.2	69.4	—
Europe	13.5	13.7	13.7	15.7	15.1	14.7	14.8	—
United States	6	6.3	6.4	6.8	6.4	6.3	5.8	—
Oceania	6	5.9	6.4	8.3	8.1	8	8.7	—
Others	1.2	1.1	1.2	1.4	1.5	1.9	1.3	—
Total	100	100	100	100	100	100	100	—
Share of arrivals by key countries (%)								
ASEAN	30.7	30.9	32.3	30.1	31.9	31.6	33.5	32.2
Japan	16.5	16.1	15.2	13.5	12.4	12.1	10.1	9.8
United Kingdom	4	4.3	4.6	5.7	5.8	5.8	6.1	6.1
Taiwan	7.9	7.2	6.9	5.8	4.6	3.8	3	3
Australia	4.9	4.8	5.3	6.8	6.7	6.6	7.3	7.4
United States	4.8	5.1	5.2	5.5	5.1	5	4.6	4.4
Other countries	31.2	31.5	30.4	32.6	33.5	35.1	35.4	37.1
Total	100	100	100	100	100	100	100	100
Purpose of visit								
Holiday only	55.5	53.2	47.8	45.3	49	48.1	46.4	46.7
Business only	14.2	14.6	16.1	16.5	16.3	16.4	15.6	15.2
Business and holiday	3	2.9	2.9	2.8	2.6	2.5	2.5	2.4
In transit	10	9.4	9.3	9.8	10.1	10.1	10.6	8
Others	17.3	19.9	24	25.6	22	22.9	24.9	18.9
Total	100	100	100	100	100	100	100	100

Sources: Singapore Tourist Promotion Board, "Survey of Overseas Visitors in Singapore" (Singapore: Market Planning Department, Singapore Tourist Promotion Board, 1994); *Yearbook of Statistics* (Singapore: Department of Statistics, 1993, 2001); *Annual Report on Tourism Statistics* (Singapore: Competitive Analysis Department, Planning Division, Singapore Tourism Board, 2001); *Tourism Focus* (Singapore: Singapore Tourism Board, 2002).

Note: The data exclude arrivals of Malaysians by land.

The majority of visitors (almost half) come for a holiday, and about 16 percent come exclusively for business purposes. The average length of stay is relatively short, at around three to four days, which indicates the stopover character of most visits (*Yearbook of Statistics* 2001).

Despite an increasing number of visitors since 1988, the importance of tourist spending to Singaporean retailers has been declining. Singapore is no longer the shopping paradise that it once was for Asian tourists, mainly because of a strengthening Singapore dollar. Taiwanese tourists complain that Singapore has become just as expensive as Taipei, and Japanese save only about 20 to 25 percent in comparison to prices back home rather than 50 percent as it was in the past. It seems that retailers will have to focus increasingly on local business and less on tourist dollars.

Although there has been a slowdown in the tourism industry, the World Travel and Tourism Council and the World Tourism Organization have both forecasted that tourist arrivals in East Asia and the Pacific regions will increase from 84 million in 1995 to 190 million in 2010 (*Enterprise* 1996a), a compound annual growth rate in arrivals of slightly less than 6 percent. Against this backdrop of a region with sustained growth in tourist numbers, STB has formulated Tourism 21, a strategic plan that aims at creating new scope for growth of Singapore's tourism industry. The targets set by Tourism 21 include attracting 10 million visitors, bringing in $16 billion of revenue in the year 2000 (*Enterprise* 1996b). This target growth rate of slightly more than 7 percent per annum of arrivals is higher than the expected growth rate for the region as a whole. To achieve this, Singapore has integrated nearby attractions and regional holiday destinations in Malaysia, Indonesia, Thailand, and other countries in its tourism strategy (Brady 1996). However, with the crisis, the number of tourists to Singapore, especially tourists from Asian countries, has decreased considerably. To attract tourist dollars and to stem the fall in tourist arrivals during these hard times, STB introduced a scheme that gave free gifts to Singaporeans and expatriates who invited their friends or families to Singapore (*The Straits Times* 1998). In addition, in 1999, the Board also launched "Live It Up!"— a campaign that aimed at telling potential visitors to Singapore that the city would offer them the holiday of a lifetime (Singapore Tourism Board 2001b). The postcrisis high tourist receipts of $11 billion and a record high of 7.7 million visitors in 2000 are indicators of the success of campaigns such as "Live It Up!" and other marketing activities.

Consumer Behavior: Summary

Macroeconomic trends of increasing prosperity are reflected in the consumption behavior of Singaporeans. Overall consumption has been increasing fast, with a declining share of basic goods, such as food and clothing, and increasing shares of higher-level goods and services, such as recreational as well as educational and health services. Increasing affluence is also reflected in changing consumer values and lifestyles, which show that Singaporeans have become more brand and status conscious, more discerning, quality oriented, and health conscious. However, due to the economic downturn, these behaviors are partially affected, as there is a decrease in consumers' disposable income and higher unemployment rates. The number of Asian tourists has been decreasing partially due to a lower price differential to their home countries and the higher exchange rates of the Singapore dollar as compared to the rest of the currencies in the region. It seems tourist shopping is becoming less important.

CHANGES IN THE MACROMARKETING MIX

This section examines past and anticipated changes in the macromarketing mix based on statistical data and anecdotal evidence. Many of the trends identified are a direct reflection of and are shaped by the macro environment discussed in previous sections. Long-term product and service trends emphasize the upmarket shift identified in previous sections, reflecting the increasing so-phistication and educational levels of Singaporeans, as well as rising incomes. Pricing strategies go hand-in-hand with the higher quality of goods and services offered. Distribution becomes more competitive, with retail space increases far outpacing sales increases, continuing concentration on retail outlets in supermarket and other retail store chains and discount stores gaining share from a low level. The importance of advertising in the marketing mix is set to increase further. With increasing competitiveness and sales volume, market research will increase in importance and sophistication. These trends are presented below in more detail.

Products and Services

Trends identified in the previous sections have profound impacts on the types of products and services gaining share and being launched in the Singapore market. It is expected that in the long term, rising incomes and increasing status brought about by rising educational levels will bring with them more discerning and informed consumers who ask for more information-technology oriented, healthy, and environmentally friendly products.

Consumer demand for and usage of such information and technology oriented products/services as mobile phones, Internet dial-up services, and home computers, have increased severalfold in the past few years. According to figures provided by the IDA (2001a), the mobile phone penetration rate increased from 24 percent of the total population in 1997 to 75.8 percent by October 2002 (Table 15.18). Even more stunningly, the Internet dial-up penetration rate increased from 7 percent to 48.3 percent in the same time period. These technologies have been flourishing at the expense of more traditional means of communication, as seen from the practically stagnant or even shrinking penetration rates of fixed phone lines (55.4 percent in 1998 to 46.9 percent by October 2002) and pagers (42.3 percent in 1997 to 8 percent in 2002). Also, more than half of the households in Singapore now own at least one computer, and almost one in four households owns at least two (IDA 2001b). In the 1,500 households interviewed in 2000, 50 percent of them access the Internet regularly, compared to only 14 percent in 1997. This percentage is higher than house-holds in countries such as the United States, Australia, and Hong Kong, where regular access is 42 percent, 37 percent, and 36 percent, respectively, in the same time frame (IDA 2001b).

The health aspects of products will continue to receive greater consumer attention. In the past, health food showed relatively low growth rates of around 10 percent per year. Taste seems to be the main hindering factor, as a perception exists among consumers that health food does not taste as good as less healthy food but is more expensive. The perceptions of health food among Singaporeans, however, seem to be changing. Foods with reduced sugar, salt, fat, and cholesterol content and increased natural and vitamin contents are expected to increase in market shares. For example, hawker center stalls started displaying stickers reading "no monosodium glutamate (MSG)," "no added meat fat" (which is being replaced by vegetable oils), and "reduced sugar." This program was promoted by the Ministry of Health and has been shown to be popular with hawkers and customers. More organic food outlets are opening, as more consumers are willing to spare 30–50 percent more in grocery expenditure for pesticide-free food. Despite the lack of official figures, most of these retailers have reported an annual growth of 5–20 percent (*The Straits Times Interactive* 2001g). As another example, the sales of bottled water in Singapore continued to rise steadily over the last five years from an annual sale of $22.6 million in 1995 to $28.3 million in 2000 (Euromonitor International 2001). It is now considered trendy among the young and more educated in the population to get knowledgeable with and purchase health-related products. These trends are expected to accelerate further.

Table 15.18

Subscription to and Penetration of Telecomm Services

Number of people ('000) from % of the total population	1997	1998	1999	2000	2001	2002 (end of October)	Change in percentage points (1997 to October 2002)
Mobile phone subscribers	743	1,020.0	1,471.3	2,442.1	2,858.8	3,131.9	+321.5
Mobile phone penetration rate	24	32.3	45.7	74.8	69.2	75.8	+51.8
Pager subscribers	1,300.00	1,309.40	1,199.70	839.1	481.6	330.7	−94.2
Pager penetration rate	42.3	41.4	37.3	25.7	11.7	8.0	−34.3
Fixed line subscribers	—	1,751.50	1,850.70	1,935.90	1,948.50	1,937.3	+10.3
Fixed line penetration rate	—	55.4	57.5	59.3	47.2	46.9	−8.5
Internet dial-up subscribers	267.4	393.6	582.6	1,940.30	1,917.90	1,994	+645.7
Internet dial-up penetration rate	7	10	18.1	59.5	46.4	48.3	+41.3

Source: Infocomm Development Authority (IDA), *Statistics on Telecom Services* (Singapore: IDA, 2002).

Although environmental consciousness is not yet strong in Singapore, the market for environmentally friendly products is expected to grow from its existing small base. There is increasing environmental awareness among Singaporeans, and there is immediate and growing concern of the government about environmental issues translating into proenvironmental legislation. The Green Labeling System, which sets specific guidelines pertaining to the manufacture, distribution, usage, and disposal of products, and campaigns such as the Clean and Green Week have been in effect since the early 1990s. The government also encourages businesses to promote environmental protection through such awards as Singapore Environmental Achievement Award and Green Leaf Award. Efforts from bodies like the Environment Ministry and Singapore Retailers Association also help to increase consumer awareness of green issues. Results from these efforts are remarkable. The Clean Green Week in 2001, for example, was the most successful so far, with 820 "green" activities and 240,000 participants, compared to 450 activities and 110,000 participants in 2000 (*The Straits Times* 2001i). Recycling activities among households in densely populated residential estates have been introduced since July 1999, whereby household recyclables are collected every fortnight. It is found that one in five households recycles garbage regularly, in response to the National Recycling Program that was launched in April 2001 (*The Straits Times* 2001i). This rate is expected to double within two years. Manufacturers of environmentally safe products and packaging are expected to gain from this shift in consumer values.

Religious and ethnic background idiosyncrasies often have to be considered when designing and marketing new products. For example, nonhalal food is not acceptable to the Muslim community, which, for instance, led gourmet shops to offer halal fruitcakes that have no brandy. Kau and Yang (1991) conducted a lifestyle analysis with 2,126 respondents and found significant differences between the ethnic and religious backgrounds on nearly all aspects of consumer behavior and the marketing mix, including need perceptions, leisure activities, media exposure, and shopping center and department store patronage. It is not expected that cultural and religious differences will assimilate much over the near future, and therefore they will remain a key consideration in any marketing mix.

The region's weakening currencies provide an opportunity for cash-rich firms to source new products, as currency fluctuations may result in vendors offering low wholesale prices. Consumers are expected to buy good-quality products at reasonable prices; thus, highly priced, branded products would not do well in the present situation.

Consumer Reactions to Price and Promotions

Low-income households and affluent households will coexist for the foreseeable future in Singapore. This means we will continue to see highly priced, high-quality and expensive products for high-income households alongside low-priced, low-quality products for low-income households. However, it can be expected that the high-quality segment will grow significantly, whereas the low-quality segment may actually see a decline due to the decreasing number of low-income households. Education and skill upgrading will improve the earning power of many currently low-income households.

However, consumers patronize high-quality brands such as BMW and Mercedes-Benz or five-star hotels such as Ritz Carlton and Shangri-La because they feel that they are getting good value for their money (*The Straits Times* 2001j). Consumer price consciousness has led to a large number of sales (after Christmas, Chinese New Year, The Great Sale in August, and numerous store-wide sales) and promotional activities (ranging from lucky draws, patronage rewards to tie-in promotions). Whether this perception of extreme price-consciousness is right is somewhat questionable. A recent study comparing Singaporean and U.S. shoppers showed that Singaporeans were less sensitive to price-related costs and more sensitive to certain non–price-related costs (e.g., time, effort, and risk) than were U.S. shoppers (Funkhouser, Parker, and Chatterjee 1994). Although the samples are not representative of the two countries (a convenience sample of 315 undergraduates, MBA students, and their family members and friends), it clearly contradicts the general perception of Singapore's practitioners. There are grounds to suggest that in the future, the focus should be shifted from sales and promotions to reducing nonmonetary costs.

During the recession, price promotions are expected to be even more popular with consumers. Consumers are expected to be more price conscious and will, therefore, be slightly more sensitive to price-related costs. More promotional strategies may be needed to attract customers. This may include promoting products by advertising over the Internet and through mass e-mail promotions to customers.

Distribution

The Singapore retail market experienced a contraction due to the economic crisis in 1998, with total sales falling by almost 11 percent from 1997 to 1998. Since then, there has been an encouraging recovery. Retail sales growth in 1999 and 2000 was at 5.7 percent and 4.6 percent, respectively (Euromonitor International 2001). Despite steady recovery for two consecutive years, retailer profits will be under pressure because of the highly competitive nature of the market, and the general caution that consumers take in the face of economic downturn in 2001.

The Singapore retail scene is experiencing a concentration of market share, with larger supermarket and retail store chains growing at the expense of smaller independent shops. For example, the number of provision shops fell from 2,438 in 1987 to only 1,528 in 1997 (*The Straits Times* 1999), and the number of independent grocers has experienced a steady decrease since 1997 (Table 15.19). Many of these are small independent shops with low efficiency and productivity, and they offer a rather similar range of goods. On the other hand, the number of supermarkets, most of which belong to chains, increased sharply from sixty stores in 1987 to 181 in 2000 (Euromonitor International 2001; *The Straits Times* 1999; see also Table 15.19). Apart from supermarkets, there is also an increasing number of department stores and convenience stores (e.g., 7–Eleven, Shell Select, and Esso Tigermarts). The number of electronic and computer outlets have also increased by an impressive 20 percent (Table 15.19), indicating a response to the surging demand from the techno-savvy population.

Shop rents in the downtown Orchard area and suburban areas have gone down considerably since the economic crisis in the late 1990s. This is an opportunity for foreign competitors, such as U.S. supermarket chains, to come into the Singapore retail scene. The emergence of these competitors would hasten the demise of Asian retailers. For example, Tokyu has already closed down its Funan Mall store. The shakeout during the 1998 economic crisis also resulted in an almost 30 percent reduction in the number of department store outlets. More foreigner-owned chain stores are expected to be set up during this period, as product sourcing is much more focused on value for money.

It is expected that the more competitive environment as well as the availability of more retail space will eventually lead to shops with a sharper merchandising mix, including an increasing number of specialty shops. Loh of the Retail Promotion Board anticipates that more specialized shops will show good growth potential in the future (Yap 1995). Even in the hard times, niche marketing has proven to be successful. Borders Books and Music, which opened in November

Table 15.19

Trends in Type of Retail Outlets

	1996	1997	1998	1999	2000	Change in percentage points (1996 to 2000)
Hypermarkets	0	1	1	1	2	—
Major supermarkets	154	163	175	182	181	+17.5
Convenience stores	194	209	224	244	292	+5.1
Independent grocers	2,687	2,759	2,657	2,567	2,477	−7.8
Electronics/computer outlets	677	761	753	779	811	+19.8
Booksellers	1,002	981	916	920	920	−8.2
Department store outlets	53	49	39	39	38	−28.3

Source: Euromonitor International, "Global Market Information Database, National Statistics" (London: Euromonitor International, 2001).

1997, managed to survive the retail slump in Singapore and even made profits. This shows that retailers can still be profitable if they hit the right combination of novelty, affordability, and smart marketing (Dolven 1998).

There are three trends that exist or are emerging in the retail market in Singapore. First and foremost is the increasing popularity of one-stop suburban shopping malls, which are located near mass regional transit (MRT) stations and close to densely populated residential estates. With a relatively low car ownership and increasing demand for convenient locations decentralization of shopping made possible by these malls will continue to increase in significance. Regional centers have been developed in the east, north, northwest, and west of the island; and each has a self-contained mini-downtown, which provides similar quality facilities to those available in the central area. The year 2002 will see the establishment of yet another shopping mall, Compass Point Mall, in Sengkang in the northeastern part of the island, with 27,900 square meters of floor space (*Retail Trade International* 2001).

Another retail phenomenon in Singapore is the entry into the market of two hypermarkets. French retailer Carrefour opened business in Suntec City in late 1997. Giant, a Malaysian-based retailer owned by Dairy Farm International (DFI), established its first overseas outlet in Singapore in June 2000. While both hypermarkets offer consumers a spacious environment in which to select a whole range of products from grocery items to home appliances, the two differ in both pricing and targeting strategies. Carrefour conveys a more European taste; Giant's goods are normally priced at about 10 percent to 30 percent below competitors' prices. The store caters to the masses and has a strong Asian bazaar-style appeal. DFI has strong logistics and IT support due to its operation in Malaysia. Moreover, it possesses rich local knowledge from its experience in operating the local Cold Storage supermarkets and 7–Eleven convenience store chains. It is expected to have a strong edge over competitors and foresees the potential of another two to three Giant hypermarkets in the city.

Finally, with the general increase in education level and extreme receptiveness toward technology, many welcome the idea of electronic or even mobile shopping. These new forms of shopping initially experienced slower growth than expected, despite the continuous increase in computer ownership and Internet access, as seen in the previous sections, and a high awareness of

Table 15.20

Awareness and Usage of Internet Services (percent*)

Internet services	Awareness	Use
E-mail/chat	98.2	91.6
Information retrieval	89.2	74.6
Online shopping	81.1	16.2
News/web cast	80.1	39.8
Government transaction	78.9	31.9
Download online music	78.6	37.4
Job search	77.5	24.3
Online games	77.0	29.2
Watch movies/VCD	68.0	15.5
Library services	58.6	15.8

Source: Infocomm Development Authority (IDA), Survey on Infocomm Usage in Households (Singapore: IDA, 2001).

* Percent of the 1,500 households interviewed by IDA in 2000.

the available range of online transactions and activities (Table 15.20). This may be attributable to various reasons, such as the leisurely elements of shopping in Singapore (Shamdasani and Ong 1995), convenience, competitive prices, comprehensively stocked retail shops in most housing estates, and the small size of the island combined with an excellent public transport system. Additionally, security concerns relating to the release of credit card and other personal information online negatively affect the willingness to shop via the Internet, especially for consumers who have never used this channel.

Despite these initial inhibitions, consumers seem to be warming up to the idea of e-commerce or m-commerce, partly due to retailers' efforts to familiarize consumers with the necessary know-how and support. Some e-retailers are now perceived as being more sophisticated, offering better services than those in shopping malls (*The Straits Times* 2001k). The number of companies that use e-commerce increased by 30 percent from 1999 to 2000 (*The Straits Times* 2001l), and many also promote their products or offer discounts through SMS (short message service). Online shopping increased from $200 million in 1999 to $1.17 billion in 2000 (*The Straits Times* 2001k). Many consumers access the Internet to retrieve information on products and purchasing to facilitate decision making. Also, the use of SMS has become a part of many mobile phone owners' daily routine. The penetration rates of Teleview (videotex) and the Internet are expected to grow rapidly, and more and more retailers, such as Cold Storage and NTUC FairPrice supermarkets and Courts furniture store, are offering their products via these electronic shopping facilities.

In summary, Singapore's retail environment will become increasingly competitive, with rapidly increasing retail space combined with only moderate sales volume growth, as well as continuing concentration of the marketplace, with chains and supermarkets gaining share. The increased competition and increasing demand for higher-end and more specialized goods will induce smaller stores and chains to move toward sharper and deeper merchandise mixes. Low levels of car ownership, demand for convenience, and retail saturation in the central business district will move shopping from downtown areas to the densely populated housing estates. In-house shopping via the phone, the Internet, and the like is expected to grow slowly from a low level.

Table 15.21

Share of Advertising Expenditure by Media

Share of advertising revenue (%)	1996	1997	1998	1999	2000	2001	Change in percentage points from 1996 to 2001
Print[a]	58.6	55.7	53.4	51.7	54.7	51.1	−7.5
Television	32.1	34.4	36.6	38.4	33.5	36.1	+4
Outdoor[b]	3.0	3.5	4.1	4.6	5.2	6.0	+3
Radio	5.4	5.2	4.5	3.9	5.1	5.3	−0.1
Cinema	0.9	1.2	1.3	1.3	1.5	1.5	+0.4
Total	100.0	100.0	100.0	100.0	100.0	100.0	—
In $'000,000	1,135.0	1,273.0	1,185.0	1,219.0	1,503.0	1,460.0	—
Change in % from year before	—	+12.2	−6.9	+2.9	+23.3	−2.9	—

Sources: Euromonitor International, "Global Market Information Database, National Statistics" (London: Euromonitor International, 2002).
[a]Print includes predominantly newspaper, and also periodicals.
[b]Outdoor includes posters and bus-back/taxi-top advertising.

Advertising

Advertising has become an important variable in the marketing mix. Spending on advertising has increased from $407.5 million in 1988 to $1,157.7 million in 1995 and to $1,460 million in 2001 (Table 15.21) (Euromonitor International 2002). This trend is set to continue.

No major shifts in the usage of media could be observed over the period from 1996 to 2001 (Table 15.21). The print category, which contains predominantly newspapers, is the biggest recipient of advertising dollars. The largest increase in share of total advertising expenditure was achieved by television, which increased its share slightly from 32.1 percent in 1996 to 36.1 percent in 2001. This may be attributed to the introduction of cable TV, with an increase in the number of channels available. The big increase in the number of households subscribing to cable TV from 33,000 (about 5 percent of all households) in 1995 to 153,800 (21.3 percent) in 1999 indicates the popularity of this service among Singaporeans. Outdoor media also increased, including posters and bus-back/taxi-top, and cinema.

Two emerging trends in advertising are observed. First, there has been an advertising boom for Singapore dot-com companies, despite the demise of many dot-com businesses worldwide. In the first quarter in 2000 alone, for example, an ACNielsen advertising expenditure report showed an astronomical leap of 6,500 percent in ad spending from around $1,800 to almost $12 million for Singapore dot-com and Internet-related companies (ACNielsen 2000). The interesting point to note here is that the traditional media, namely, newspapers, TV, and radio, have been heavily used to advertise this new medium of conducting business. This trend is expected to continue, with more dot-com companies penetrating the market.

The second trend relates to the full deregulation of the telecommunication market in April 2000. The telecomm sector has since been the top advertising product category. In the first nine

Table 15.22

Newspaper Circulation

In % of total by language	1995	1996	1997	1998	1999	2000	2001
English	47.8	47.7	48	47.9	47.5	46.1	62
Chinese	45.9	46.2	45.8	45.7	46	47.7	33.4
Malay	5.7	5.4	5.4	5.5	5.6	5.4	4
Tamil	0.6	0.7	0.8	0.9	0.9	0.8	0.6
Total	100	100	100	100	100	100	100
Number of copies sold daily in '000	1,063	1,072	1,093	1,126	1,148	1,197	1,586
Change in %	—	0.1	2	3.1	2	4.3	+32.5

Sources: Yearbook of Statistics (Singapore: Department of Statistics, 2002); Euromonitor International, "Global Market Information Database, National Statistics" (London: Euromonitor International, 2002).

months of 2000, the advertising expenditure in this sector increased by 132 percent to reach $116 million (ACNielsen 2000). Singtel, Starhub, and MobileOne lead the pack in adspend. According to Lennart Bengtsson, managing director, ACNielsen Singapore/Malaysia, the three companies had provided the growth impetus in Singapore's advertising industry. This sector will continue to provide major spenders in advertising due to the fully deregulated, increasingly competitive telecomm market.

The main languages for advertising in TV and newspapers are English and Mandarin (Table 15.22). The role of English seems to be similar to that of Mandarin. The content of advertisements will have to continue to incorporate cultural sensitivities. They include a general sense of modesty with relation to using sexual stimuli; a wide variety of superstitious beliefs, such as lucky and unlucky numbers; and the prohibition of consumption of alcoholic beverages by Muslims. Although some of these sensitivities seem to be reducing (such as sexual explicitness in advertisements), others such as showing alcoholic beverages when targeting Muslims, or showing dogs (which are considered impure) to Malays, are still taboos.

Market Research

It is generally expected that scanner data will be more efficiently used in market research. With available technology and the introduction of the Goods and Services Tax in 1994 (which produced the need to keep track of tax due on various categories), scanning has become widespread among all retailers. The majority of products sold in Singapore now have a bar code affixed and are source-marked by manufacturers. The Singapore Article Numbering Council has started trials using electronic data interchange (EDI) to retrieve bar code data at the point-of-sale to predict demand, track stock levels, and order electronically. The rapid penetration of bar code scanning and the introduction of advanced market research products and services will further improve the availability and also reduce the price of market information, thereby increasing the application of more formal and reliable market research tools.

This trend may have a positive impact on the utilization of market research data and tools in Singapore. Currently, Singaporean firms tend to use informal market research, such as feedback from the sales force and customers for identifying market opportunities, and hardly any quantitative techniques (Shamdasani, Wirtz, and Chong 1995). Also, when monitoring the performance of their products, many firms, probably the smaller and medium-size ones, still rely mainly on informal checks with their distributors rather than supplementing their current data with more formalized and quantitative research.

Marketing Mix: Summary

Trends observed in the marketing mix are a direct reflection of and are shaped by the macro environment. Product and service trends emphasize the upmarket shift identified in previous sections on consumer behavior, the increasing sophistication and education of consumers, as well as rising income levels. Pricing strategies will go hand-in-hand with the higher quality of goods and services offered, and nonmonetary price reduction strategies may become increasingly attractive. The retail environment will become more competitive, with growth in retail space far outpacing sales growth, continuing concentration of retail outlets in supermarket and other retail store chains, and discount stores gaining share from a low level. The importance of advertising in the marketing mix is set to increase further and will continue to be highly localized to Singapore's cultural environment. Market research is expected to become more formalized and sophisticated in its application.

CONCLUSIONS AND IMPLICATIONS FOR MARKETING MANAGEMENT

Trends in Singapore's marketing environment were described and analyzed in previous parts of this chapter. This final section brings together the main themes in Singapore's marketing environment, which include trends in the economic, demographic, and cultural environments, and trends in consumer behavior and the marketing mix. The findings are integrated, and key implications for marketing management derived are discussed in the following two subsections. The first deals with implications for the marketing mix; the second derives more general marketing strategies.

Future Developments of Singapore's Marketing Environment

With high literacy rates, relatively young populations, open economies, and vast untapped hinterlands, Asia was expected to recover from the economic crisis. Singapore survived the 1997–98 crisis, because it had good fundamentals, such as high political stability, good governance, and strong monetary policies. Singapore also has the ability to harness its debt-free national reserves to stimulate the economy by increasing infrastructure spending.

We have identified four key sets of conclusions on long-term future developments in Singapore's marketing environment that will have important bearing on marketing management.

First, when the region eventually recovers, Singapore's economic environment is expected to reach the level of a developed country and is expected to remain favorable, with continuing high increases in personal income, virtually full employment, and low inflation rates.

Second, Singapore's demographic environment will continue to follow the same trends of older industrialized countries. The population will grow slowly, due to low fertility rates, late marriages, and delayed childbirth. These factors and an increasing life expectancy contribute to rapid aging of the population.

Third, Singapore will remain a multicultural society, with Chinese, Malays, and Indians as the dominant ethnic groups, each with its own strong cultural background, including languages, religions, and customs. This cultural diversity is particularly distinct because of Singapore's tiny geographic size and small population of only some four million. Nevertheless, Singaporeans are becoming increasingly multilingual, with more people speaking their own dialects plus English and Mandarin. Significant changes will also occur in other aspects of Singapore's cultural environment. In particular, education levels will continue to improve rapidly, with more Singaporeans receiving university and postsecondary education; the female workforce participation rate, which has increased to one of the highest in the world, will remain at high levels; and household sizes will continue to become smaller.

Fourth, Singapore is expected to continue developing into an increasingly affluent society. This will have substantial impact on trends in consumer behavior. Real growth rates of private consumption will be high, with the declining share of basic goods, such as food and clothing, on total consumption. Consumers will become more and more brand and status conscious, more discerning, and more health conscious.

A summary of the detailed economic, demographic, cultural, and consumer trends is provided in Table 15.23. For ease of reference, these trends are presented in the same order as they were discussed in the main body of the paper. Anticipated impacts of each of these trends on marketing management are outlined in the same table. These implications for marketing are summarized and discussed in the next section. Here, the discussion is organized broadly into two groups: first, implications for the marketing mix, and second, marketing strategies.

Implications for Marketing Mix

Trends in the marketing mix are a direct reflection of and are shaped by changes in the macro environment presented in the previous sections. In general, the implications presented here fit into the overall picture of a steady growth environment with a focus on quality and upgrading rather than just more of the same. Implications for the marketing mix are presented below.

Product

Although Singapore's private consumption continues to grow, this does not apply equally to all segments of the market. Table 15.23 shows a number of trends in the environment that will have significant impact on the growth prospects for various product types. For example, high-quality, high-end, and more sophisticated product markets are anticipated to grow faster than the overall market, while low-quality, low-end, and basic product markets are expected to decline. Drivers of this trend include increasing disposable incomes combined with improving education levels, and consumers becoming more discerning. Shifts in consumer values and demand emphasizing technology and health and environmental concerns will lead to high growth for technology-oriented, health improving, and environmentally friendly products, whereas low growth or declining markets can be expected for goods being perceived as low-tech, unhealthy, and environmentally unfriendly. Table 15.24 (p. 576) provides an overview of product types that are expected to show higher growth than the overall market. The information in the table is based on trends highlighted in Table 15.23.

Service Quality

With the consumer market becoming more competitive, marketers will eventually have to realize the importance of value-added services. It has been criticized that there is no tradition in Singapore for value-added services. Many businesses lack a positive attitude toward serving their customers

Table 15.23

Changes of the Marketing Environment and Implications for Marketing Management

Marketing environment when recovered from economic downturn	Long term implications for marketing management
Economic Environment • Increasing wages • Continuing full employment • Low inflation	Increasing disposable income and high consumer confidence should set the scene for marketing strategies aimed at achieving high growth
Demographic environment • Small population	The small market size may suggest that economies of scale, such as in advertising, distribution, import/logistics will drive toward a more competitive environment with a focus on obtaining volume and market share
• Low population growth	A limited number of new consumers may suggest marketing strategies aimed at creating loyal customers or even enter more formalized relationships with one's customers
• Aging population	Marketing strategies targeted at older customers will be placed in fast-growing markets, whereas those targeted at babies, children and young adults have to work in low growth if not stagnating markets
Cultural environment • Improving education levels	Marketing strategies aimed at more sophisticated segments will be placed in fast-growing markets
• Increasing proficiency in English and Mandarin	The majority of the population can be increasingly communicated to in English and Mandarin
• Smaller household sizes	Smaller package sizes and perhaps convenient retail locations become more important
• High female participation rate in the workforce	Products that deliver time saving (ready made meals, laundry services, etc.) and convenient retail locations (to reduce shopping time) become more important
• Three main ethnic groups with their own languages and religions	Marketing strategies will have to continue to take cultural, language, and religious variables into account
Consumer behavior • Increasing total consumption • Declining share of basic goods on overall consumption	All main goods categories will show growth, but basic goods such as food and beverages, grow slower than those goods satisfying higher level needs. For example, entertainment, education and health have been increasing their share on total consumption

- Increasingly discerning consumers

More sophisticated products will gain market share among techno-savvy consumers

- Increasingly health conscious consumers

Health products (health food, exercise equipment, sports clothes, etc.) will gain market share

- Declining importance of tourist shopping due to declining price differential to their home countries

Sales to tourists will grow slower than overall consumption; marketing strategies based predominantly on price advantage over tourist home countries will become increasingly infeasible

Trends in marketing mix
Product

- Consumers have become more quality conscious

Marketing strategies targeting at high quality segments are in high-growth areas, whereas the low quality end will at best stagnate

- High price/high quality segments will grow fast

- Low price/low quality segments will decline but not vanish altogether

- Consumers are becoming more techno-savvy

High-tech products/services (mobile phones, computers, Internet dial-ups) will increase in penetration rate

- Consumers are becoming more health conscious

Health products (health food, exercise equipment, sports clothes, etc.) will gain market share

- Consumers are becoming somewhat more environmentally conscious

Environmentally friendly product-attributes will become more important in consumer decision making

- Cultural differences will remain and not assimilate much

Segmentation along cultural dimensions will remain important

Service quality

- Service quality needs to be boosted for competing better

Companies will spend more on educating staff on value-added services

Price and promotion

- Anecdotal evidence seems to suggest that consumers are more sensitive to non-monetary costs

Sales and promotions will remain important components of the marketing mix

- Sales and promotions remain an important component of the marketing mix, as marketers, whether rightly or not, perceive their consumers as very price-sensitive

Strategies reducing non-monetary costs rather than prices may be employed more than in the past

Distribution

- Retail floor space will continue to grow from a relatively low level

Specialist retailers will grow and increasingly serve the sophisticated/high end of many markets

- Shopping as leisure activity will remain important

Creating a shopping and entertainment atmosphere will remain important

- More shopping centers will be opened in suburbs

  Demand for larger and more spacious shopping environment will be better satisfied

- Hypermarkets will make further inroads

  Consumers will welcome the product selection, competitive price offers, and bazaar-style ambience that are offered

- Penetration of direct marketing channels is low and will not grow significantly over the coming years

  Direct marketing will not become an important channel in the medium-term future

- Awareness of these channels is high, consumers may gradually warm up to shopping on-line, particularly when security guarantee is further pushed

Advertising

- Advertising expenditure will continue to grow faster than total consumer expenditure

  The role of advertising in the marketing mix will become more important as the importance of branding increases

- No major shifts are expected in media shares of advertising revenue in the medium term

  Newspaper and TV advertising will remain the most important media

- Dot.com and Internet-related companies increase in advertising expenditure

  Traditional advertising media (e.g., newspaper and TV) facilitate advertising of technology or knowledge-driven businesses

- Telecomm sector leads in advertising expenditure

  Telecomm industry will become increasingly competitive, rendering rigorous advertising indispensable

- Cultural segmentation, beliefs, sensitivities and superstitions remain important

  Culturally targeted and sensitive advertising will remain crucial

Market research

- Scanner data will become increasingly available (publicly)

  Marketing decisions will be increasingly based on more quantitative market research; the methods employed will become more sophisticated

- More sophisticated research methods will be introduced to the Singapore market place

- Indigenous Singaporean firms may increasingly use market research techniques

---

well, and simply see providing good service as contributing to extra costs. Despite Singapore's global competitiveness, its customer orientation was ranked sixteenth (Yeo 2001b). However, the government has been working toward building awareness among businesses of the value of good services. Public bodies, such as the Singapore Retailers Association, the Retail Promotion Centre, and the Productivity and Standards Board, are contributing efforts to such events as courtesy campaigns, Retail 21, and Service Quality 21, all aimed at encouraging companies to do friendly business and also devising standards for gauging service quality.

Table 15.24

Trends in Consumption

Expected high-growth products	Expected low-growth products
Cater to needs of older consumers	Cater to needs of younger consumers
High quality	Low quality
Branded	Not branded
Sophisticated	Basic, coarse
Convenient purchase, consumption, and disposal	Inconvenient
Help to save time	Do not help to save time
Maintain or improve health	Do not help to maintain or improve health
Environmentally friendly	Environmentally unfriendly

Pricing and Price Promotions

It is not clear whether Singaporeans are actually more price sensitive than, for example, U.S. consumers. However, preliminary evidence suggests that if there was a difference, Singaporeans seemed to be more sensitive toward nonmonetary costs than U.S. consumers. Combining this with anticipated trends toward higher-quality products, one may expect that pricing may not increase in importance. Strategies focusing on lower nonmonetary costs may be increasingly attractive to follow rather than continuing to focus predominantly on monetary pricing, as is currently being done.

Distribution

Convenience, specialist, and discount shopping are expected to show strong growth. Convenient shopping locations are important in Singapore, as more than two-thirds of all households do not own cars and are unlikely to be able to acquire cars in the foreseeable future due to government regulation. Large shopping complexes are currently being built in the suburbs, to benefit from the trend toward decentralized retail locations. Specialist retailers will develop, as demand for more high-end sophisticated products increases. Hypermarkets may also grow in sales and outlets, as consumers seem to welcome the idea of a one-stop grocery shopping experience.

Many more marketing mix implications could be discussed for each of the trends shown in Table 15.23. These general trends, of course, trickle down from market segmentation and product development to packaging, pricing, distribution, advertising, and promotions. For example, an increase in demand for healthier products and a more educated consumer base will require food marketers to display much more information on ingredients on their packaging and to focus advertising and promotions to help position these products as health improving. Or, smaller household sizes may require smaller package sizes, and so on. The implications are numerous and often product-category specific, but it is hoped that this chapter provides interested readers with necessary background information to ease the first steps of developing and assessing their own specific marketing mix for the Singapore marketplace.

Implications for Overall Marketing Strategies

A number of implications for overall marketing strategies can be derived from the environmental analysis. Three main implications that refer to growth with caution strategies in higher-end market segments, high volume/market leader strategies in a tiny marketplace with country-specific costs, and to customer retention strategies in a market with declining numbers of new customers entering the market are presented below.

First, marketers in Singapore can expect to operate in cautiously growing markets for some time to come, and this is mainly fueled by disposable income of cautious consumers in the face of economic uncertainties. This suggests the pursuit of slow and steady growth strategies in general, but with a focus on growth in quality rather than quantity. It will be reasonable growth in better-quality products, and products that are consistent with a higher standard of living, rather than a growth in numbers of units sold. For example, this will not mean more television sets, but more better-quality home entertainment sets.

Second, the Singapore market in absolute terms is small, with fewer than four million consumers. This is further aggravated by the existence of very distinct cultural differences, which often requires segmentation along cultures (e.g., food preferences of Malays and Chinese can vary substantially). There are a number of country-specific costs that cannot be shared with neighboring country markets. These costs can include advertising costs in Singapore's media, sales force expenditure, and logistics costs. Trends toward branded goods, and, often related, increased advertising, channel management, and market research expenditures, will further increase country-specific costs. However, worldwide future markets are expected to become more competitive, with continuing pressure on both prices and costs (Lazer et al. 1990, 102, 140), and Singapore will be no exception. This has to be seen in the light of the current competitive environment, which is, by far, not as harsh as in more developed economies, such as the U.S. and European countries, and margins for all channel members can still be considered quite generous. Nevertheless, it seems clear that for long-term profitability in an increasingly competitive marketplace, economies of scale on those country-specific costs will become more important. This is particularly so, as the small volume achievable in Singapore's market may mean that many firms are actually quite high on the sales volume/unit cost curve with strong incentives to increase volume. Therefore, higher volume and market leader strategies seem to be even more attractive than in larger economies, and for many products. "Follower" or "me too" strategies with low market share may become unsustainable, as country-specific unit costs can render those players uncompetitive. It seems that, similarly to Singapore's retail sector, further concentration of market shares can be expected. Exceptions to this rule may be high-end, sophisticated image products in which margins remain high and snob-appeal favors low volumes.

Third, similar to many older industrialized countries, the pool of new consumers entering the market is getting smaller due to the aging population, markets serving basic needs are becoming increasingly saturated, and as is generally known, it is expensive to switch consumers from competitors. Although not yet to the same extent as in more saturated older industrialized economies, marketing strategies achieving customer retention and loyalty will also become increasingly important in Singapore for maintaining market share and profitability. An increased pursuit of membership and relationship marketing strategies combined with competitive strategies aimed at switching customers from competition seem appropriate. Most major department stores, for example, issue loyalty cards at their openings and offer their frequent customers discounts on goods and advance information on upcoming sales and promotions. Other retailers also issue store cards, either in partnership with major credit card companies like Visa, or with a group of other retailers. Despite being initiated more for retailers' profits, store cards also serve the function of persuading customers to repatronize businesses in which these store cards can be used.

In conclusion, prospects remain excellent, in general, and for goods and service categories catering to higher needs, in particular. However, the environment will become more competitive, although it is still a far way off from the intensely competitive markets in the United States and Europe. Nevertheless, it will no longer be sufficient to merely appoint importers for Singapore. Integrated marketing strategies, with increasing investment into brand equity, increasingly sophisticated channel management, supported by cost-effective logistics and market research, will increasingly be needed to ensure success.

Summary of Implications for Marketing Management

Trends observed in implications for the marketing mix are a direct reflection and are shaped by the macro environment presented in this chapter. Product and service trends emphasize the upmarket shift identified in previous paragraphs on consumer behavior, increasing sophistication and education, as well as rising income levels. Pricing strategies should go hand-in-hand with the higher quality of goods and services offered, and nonmonetary price reduction strategies may become increasingly attractive to follow. The distribution environment will become more competitive, with retail space increases far outpacing sales increases, a continued concentration of retail outlets in supermarket and other retail store chains, and the share of discount stores increasing from low levels. The importance of advertising in the marketing mix is set to increase further.

Three main implications for overall marketing strategies were proposed. First, marketers in Singapore can expect to operate in slowly, steadily growing markets for some time to come, which is mainly fueled by increased disposable income rather than population growth. This suggests the pursuit of growth strategies, in general, with a focus on growth in quality and upgrading rather than in terms of quantity. Second, the marketplace will remain small, and there are substantial country-specific costs that cannot be shared with neighboring countries. Therefore, it seems clear that for long-term profitability, economies of scale will become more important, suggesting the pursuit of higher volume and market leader strategies. Finally, customer retention strategies combined with competitive strategies aimed at switching customers will become more important in a market with declining numbers of new customers entering the market. The last two implications suggest an increasingly competitive marketing environment in the years to come.

REFERENCES

Abeysinghe, Tilak. 1994. "Why a Wider Wage Gap in Singapore?" Paper presented at the *ESU Mid-Year Review of the Singapore Economy*, eds. Tilak Abeysinghe, Ng Hock Guan, Anthony Ngerng, and Amina Tyabji. Singapore: Economic Studies Unit, Department of Statistics, National University of Singapore, and Economics Society of Singapore.

ACNielsen. 2000. ACNielsen Media International.

Annual Manpower Statistics. 2001. Singapore: Ministry of Manpower.

Annual Report on Tourism Statistics. 2001. Singapore: Competitive Analysis Department, Planning Division, Singapore Tourism Board.

ASEAN Secretariat. 1999. *ASEAN Free Trade: An Update. ASEAN Information Series*. Jakarta: ASEAN.

Asia Business Network (ABISNET). 1997. *Trade Regulations—Singapore*. Singapore: ABISNET.

Brady, Diane. 1996. "Asian Travel: Tourism Promoters are Lumping Together Regional Packages." *The Asian Wall Street Journal*, May 1: 8.

Business Environment Risk Intelligence S.A. 1999. *1999 Report*. Friday Harbor, WA: Business Environment Risk Intelligence S.A.

Chua, Beng-Huat. 1995. "Ethnic Groups Tolerant but Lack Mutual Understanding." *The Straits Times*, September 23: 28.

Department of Statistics. 2001. *Key Indicators of Households and Population*. Singapore: Department of Statistics.

Dolven, Ben. 1998. "Finding the Niche." *Far Eastern Economic Review*, March 26: 58–59.

Economic Survey of Singapore. 2002. "First, Second & Third Quarter Reports." Singapore: Ministry of Trade and Industry.

Economist Intelligence Unit (EIU). 1994. *Country Forecast Singapore* (Main Report 4th Quarter 1994). London: EIU.

Enterprise. 1996a. "Making Singapore a 'Tourism Capital,'" October 12.

———. 1996b. "Tourism 21: Let's Work Together to Achieve Targets, Says Minister (T&I)," August 1.

Euromonitor International. 2001. *Global Market Information Database, National Statistics*. London: Euromonitor International.

———. 2002. *Global Market Information Database, National Statistics*. London: Euromonitor International.

Fernandez, Warren. 1995. "Those 'Vulnerable Years' Ahead." *The Straits Times*, April 8: 32.

Funkhouser, G. Ray, Richard Parker, and Anindya Chatterjee. 1994. "A Cross-Cultural Comparison of Source and Brand Choice as a Function of Consumer Price and Non-price Cost Sensitivities." In *Asia Pacific Advances in Consumer Research*, Vol. 1, ed. Joseph A. Cote and Siew Meng Leong, pp. 140–47. Provo, UT: Association for Consumer Research.

The Global Competitiveness Report. 2000. Geneva: World Economic Forum.

Holmes, Douglas. 2001. *eGov–eBusiness Strategies for Government*. London: Nicholas Brealey.

Infocomm Development Authority (IDA). 2001a. *Statistics on Telecom Services*. Singapore: IDA.

———. 2001b. *Survey on Infocomm Usage in Households* (August). Singapore: IDA.

———. 2002. *Statistics on Telecom Services*. Singapore: IDA.

International Monetary Fund (IMF). 1998. *World Economic Outlook*. Washington, DC: IMF.

Jung, Kwon, Jochen Wirtz, Ah Keng Kau, and Soo Jiuan Tan. 1999. "The Seven Faces of Singaporeans: A Typology of Consumers Based on a Large-Scale Lifestyle Study." *Asia Pacific Journal of Management* 16(2): 229–48.

Kau, Ah Keng, and Charles Yang. 1991. *Values and Lifestyles of Singaporeans*. Singapore: Singapore University Press, National University of Singapore.

Kau, Ah Keng, Soo Jiuan Tan, and Jochen Wirtz. 1998. *Seven Faces of Singaporeans—Their Values, Aspiration, and Lifestyles*. Singapore: Prentice Hall.

Kau, Ah Keng, Yeong Wee Yong, and Daleen Richmond. 1993. *A Delphi Study of Future Lifestyles and Consumption Patterns in Singapore*. Singapore: Singapore Center for Business Research and Development, National University of Singapore, DNC Advertising.

Koh, Leslie. 1998. "Unemployed Will Be Trained, and Paid as Well." *The Strait Times*, December 4.

Lai, Ah Eng. 1995. *Meaning of Multiethnicity: A Case-Study of Ethnicity and Ethnic Relations in Singapore*. Oxford: Oxford University Press.

Lazer, William, Priscilla LeBarbera, James M. MacLachlan, and Allen E. Smith. 1990. *Marketing 2000 and Beyond*. Chicago: American Marketing Association.

Lee, Kuan Yew. 2000. *From Third World to First—The Singapore Story: 1965–2000*. Singapore: Singapore Press Holdings (Times Edition).

McRae, Hamish. 1995. *The World in 2020—Power, Culture and Prosperity*. Boston: Harvard Business School Press.

Menkhoff, Thomas, and Jochen Wirtz. 1999. "Local Responses to Globalisation—The Case of Singapore." Working Paper No. 142, Department of Sociology, National University of Singapore.

Ministry of Information, Communications, and the Arts. 1994. Singapore: Ministry of Information and the Arts.

———. 1995. *Singapore 1995*. Singapore: Ministry of Information and the Arts.

———. 1998. *Singapore 1998*. Singapore: Ministry of Information and the Arts.

———. 2002. *Singapore 2002*. Singapore: Ministry of Communication, Information and the Arts.

Ministry of Trade and Industry. 2001. Singapore: Ministry of Trade and Industry.

Retail Trade International. 2001. July.

Rojthamrong, Sophton. 2000. *Saving Culture*. Bangkok: Information and Public Relations Group, Bank of Thailand.

Shamdasani, Prem, and Ong Geok Yeow. 1995. "An Exploratory Study of In-Home Shoppers in a Concentrated Retail Market." *Journal of Retailing and Consumer Services* 2(1).

Shamdasani, Prem, Jochen Wirtz, and Michael Chong. 1995. "An Exploratory Study on New Product Development Activities of Singapore Firms." In *Proceedings of the Academy of International Business Conference on Asia-Pacific Business*, pp. 327–30. Perth: Murdoch University.

Sim, Susan. 1995. "Corruption Index Based on 7 Polls of Businessmen, Newsmen." *The Straits Times,* August 26: 2.

Singapore Census of Population. 1990a. "Statistical Release 2: Household and Housing." Singapore: Census of Population Office, Department of Statistics.

———. 1990b. "Statistical Release 3: Literacy, Languages Spoken and Education." Singapore: Census of Population Office, Department of Statistics.

———. 1990c. 1 "Statistical Release 6: Religion, Childcare and Leisure Activities." Singapore: Census of Population Office, Department of Statistics.

———. 2000a. "Advance Data Release No. 1." Singapore: Census of Population Office, Department of Statistics.

———. 2000b. "Advance Data Release No. 2." Singapore: Census of Population Office, Department of Statistics.

———. 2000c. "Advance Data Release No. 3." Singapore: Census of Population Office, Department of Statistics.

———. 2001a. "Advance Data Release, No. 6: Key Indicators on Households and Population." Singapore: Census of Population Office, Department of Statistics.

———. 2001b. "Advance Data Release No. 7." Singapore: Census of Population Office, Department of Statistics.

Singapore Statistical Highlights. 2002. Singapore: Department of Statistics.

Singapore Tourism Board. 2001a. *Fact Sheet of 2001.* Singapore: Singapore Tourism Board.

———. 2001b. *Twin Accolades for the Singapore Tourism Board* (April 11). Singapore: Singapore Tourism Board.

———. 2002. *Fact Sheet of 2002.* Singapore: Singapore Tourism Board.

Singapore Tourist Promotion Board. 1994. *Survey of Overseas Visitors in Singapore.* Singapore: Market Planning Department, Singapore Tourist Promotion Board.

The Straits Times. 1995a. "Christianity Here Has Strong 'Social, Political Influence,'" April 26: 25.

———. 1995b. "Singapore Has Highest Rate of Labor Participation Among NIEs, Other Economies," September 13: 38.

———. 1998. "Get Freebies for Bringing Visitors Here," October 28: 33.

———. 1999. "Small Grocery Shops Hang On," May 25: 35.

———. 2001a. "Poll Finds S'pore Govt Best in Asia," September 23: 6.

———. 2001b. "S'pore Stands out in Survey as a Wired Capital," September 26: H14.

———. 2001c. "Easing Retailers into e-Business," September 29: H1.

———. 2001d. "Asean, China Plan FTA," November 7: 1.

———. 2001e. "Economy Could Grow by 4.4% Next Year: NUS," October 24: S12.

———. 2001f. "Big Investors Skipping Asean," September 19: 4.

———. 2001g. "S'pore Gets International Praise for Biomed Push," September 29: H15.

———. 2001h. "December COE Results." December: L20.

———. 2001i. "One in Five S'pore Homes Recycles Waste," November 12: H8.

———. 2001j. "Wanted: Value-for-Money Brands," May 1: H10.

———. 2001k. "E-asy Way to Shop," July 21: H2.

———. 2001l. "Net Transactions up Fivefold," May 10.

The Straits Times Interactive. 2001a. "IT Students Get $2m Boost to Work Abroad," September 22.

———. 2001b. "S'pore R&D Spending Tops $3b," September 19.

———. 2001c. "Partners for Products Needed," September 20.

———. 2001d. "Centre Here to Turn Living Cells into Drug 'Factories,'" September 22.

———. 2001e. "Biomed Hotbed on the Cards," September 20.

———. 2001f. "Tissue 'Bank' to Boost Research Here," September 20.

———. 2001g. "Back to Nature: Organic Food," May 21.

The Sunday Times. 2001. "75.3% Resounding Win for PAP," November 4: 1.

Tourism Focus. 2002. Singapore: Singapore Tourism Board.

Trends in Singapore Resident Population 1990–2000. 2000. Singapore.

Union Bank of Switzerland. 1991. *Prices and Earnings Around the Globe 1991.*

Wirtz, Jochen, and Thomas Menkhoff. 1998. "From Entrepôt to NIC—Economic and Structural Policy Aspects of Singapore's Development." *Sasin Journal of Management* 4: 1–12.

World Bank. 1993. *The East Asian Miracle: Economic Growth and Public Policy.* Oxford: Oxford University Press for the World Bank.

The World Competitiveness Yearbook. 2001. International Institute for Management Development.

Yap, Evelyn. 1995. "HDB Shopping to Change by Year 2000." *The Sunday Times*, February 12: 2.

Yearbook of Statistics. 1993. Singapore: Department of Statistics.

———. 1994. Singapore: Department of Statistics.

———. 1998. Singapore: Department of Statistics.

———. 2001. Singapore: Department of Statistics.

———. 2002. Singapore: Department of Statistics.

Yeo, George. 2001a. Minister for Trade and Industry, Speech at Media Briefing on the Release of Census 2000 Population Publication, February 20.

———. 2001b. Minister for Trade and Industry, Speech at the launch of the Robinsons Institute For Service Excellence (RISE), October 1.

CHAPTER 16

TAIWAN

Euphoria and Paranoia on the Emerging Greater China Economy

YINGCHAN EDWIN TANG

OVERVIEW

Taiwan has become an economic powerhouse in East and Southeast Asia. Its growth and development over the past fifty years have been remarkable and have resulted in increased standards of living and economic resources that also drive development in other countries throughout the region. Recent political changes, demographic trends, and forces inherent to the emerging process of Greater China create new challenges and opportunities. This chapter provides a systemic overview of Taiwan, with particular emphasis on Taiwan's notable socioeconomic evolution and detailed analysis of current marketing dynamics, with probable trends for the future.

INTRODUCTION

Greater China (China, Taiwan, and Hong Kong Special Administrative Region together) is well on its way to becoming an economic superpower. With both China and Taiwan entering the World Trade Organization (WTO) in 2001, the combined volume of total international trade from Greater China is expected to be the second largest in the world, only next to that of the United States. Together, Taiwan's entrepreneurial and technological know-how as well as high-standard quality control and management skills, Hong Kong's well reputed legal and physical infrastructure as well as financial and marketing skills, China's massive supply of labor, research and development (R&D) expertise, land, natural resources, and a huge potential market, are destined to drive this great economic frontier in the twenty-first century (WTO 2001).

While the economic boundary between Taiwan and China is fading, no one can foresee whether or not Greater China will become politically integrated. Taiwan has dropped the myth that it is China's sole legitimate government and has begun to seek its own independent identity from international organizations such as the Asia-Pacific Economic Cooperation (APEC), International Monetary Fund (IMF), and United Nations (UN). Former president Lee Teng-hui's "Two States" remark, with its implication of independence for Taiwan, has infuriated Beijing, which regards Taiwan as a renegade province of China. The March 2000 election of a pro-independence president from the Democratic Progressive Party (DPP) has further sparked renewed fears in Beijing that Taiwan is definitely seeking independence. China asserts that Taiwan's refusal of reunification might force it "to adopt all drastic measures possible, including the use of force, to safeguard China's sovereignty and territorial integrity." The political tensions between the Taiwan Strait make the Taiwan issue "the most intractable and dangerous East-Asia flashpoint" (Carlucci, Hunter, and Khalilzad 2000).

With the opposite development of economic boom and political tension with China, Taiwan lives in a state of euphoria and paranoia. To capitalize on China's cheap labor and massive land, Taiwanese companies, most of them without governmental approval, have invested US$18 billion (unofficial estimate is US$70 billion) with a total of 24,000 manufacturers in the last decade. The mainland investment mania has caused the hollowing out of the Taiwan economy, with the closure of 5,000 plants, and unemployment reaching a postwar high of 5.5 percent in 2001. On the other hand, Taiwan maintains an annual defense budget of $10 billion and has more than four million soldiers. In fear of military invasion by China, Taiwan has proposed to deploy theater missile defense (TMD) and national missile defense (NMD) systems with United States.

The mixed signals from economic and political development make it difficult to gauge business opportunity in Taiwan. The optimistic view is that China will resolve the political conflicts in a peaceful way instead of through military attacks. In this chapter, we present an overview of the Taiwanese market as an independent regime, presuming that China will agree to peacefully resolve the reunification issue. Because of its complicated political and economic background, we begin this chapter with an analysis of history. We then move to economic environment and discuss how the economy has evolved. In particular, we discuss how the economy has benefited from relationships with three major trading partners—Japan, the United States, and China. Next, we discuss demographic and sociocultural influences, and then move to the marketing executive and infrastructural environment. This is followed by analysis of marketing mix variables and their development in Taiwan. We conclude the final section with future market trends and recommendations for marketing strategies for this country.

HISTORY

Taiwan has a unique and rich history. Once connected to the Chinese mainland during the Ice Ages, Taiwan was first populated by those of Malay–Polynesian descent in prehistoric times. Beginning in the thirteenth century and continuing into the eighteenth century, large numbers of Chinese settlers from the Hoklo-speaking province of Fujian and the Hakka-speaking province of Guangdong arrived in Taiwan. Sixteenth-century Portuguese traders christened the island *Isla Formosa*, or "beautiful island," a name that has been popularly referred to until recently. Because of its strategic location along the lucrative trade route to the Far East, Portuguese, Spaniards, and Dutch all struggled for colonial control of the island. The Dutch won out and colonized Taiwan in 1624 (while Portuguese settled in Macau and Spaniards in the Philippines). The Dutch colony was short lived. In 1662, Cheng Cheng-kung (Koxinga) expelled the Dutch from Taiwan. In 1887, the Ching Dynasty granted Taiwan's provincial status under China, which still holds, in principle, to this date.

As a consequence of its defeat in the Sino–Japanese War, China ceded Taiwan to Japan "in perpetuity," as outlined in the Treaty of Shimonoseki. Taiwan was occupied by Japan from 1895 to 1945, the longest period in history that Taiwan was governed by a foreign nation. During the Japanese colonization, tremendous economic progress was made, as Taiwan underwent rapid industrialization to feed the Japanese war machine.

In China, the ending of dynastic rule and the establishment of the Republic of China (ROC) in 1911 led to civil war from the 1920s to 1949, between the Nationalists Kuomintang (KMT) under Generalissimo Chiang Kai-shek and the Chinese Communists under Mao Zedong. Although the two sides briefly fought together to expel the Japanese from China, they resumed civil war in 1945. Interestingly, both Chinese leaders once supported the independence of Taiwan. Chiang Kai-shek stated in 1938, "We must restore the independence and freedom of the brethren in Korea and Taiwan." Mao Zedong stated, " . . . we will extend them [Koreans] our enthusiastic help in their struggle for independence. The same thing applies for Formosa" (Snow 1948). In 1951, with the San Francisco Peace Treaty, Japan surrendered Taiwan to the ROC. Chiang Kai-shek and his KMT regime dominated national politics until 2000, when the Democratic Progressive Party's candidate, Chen Shiu-bian, won the presidency through democratic election. This landmark event ended fifty years of KMT supremacy and culminated in a peaceful transfer of power. Today, Taiwan maintains a strong tradition of multiparty, representative democracy (*Taiwan Yearbook* 2003; *World Factbook* 2003). While Taiwan may well be part of "Greater China," it has never been part of the People's Republic.

GEOGRAPHY

Taiwan is a mountainous island in the Western Pacific Ocean, some 100 miles southeast of mainland China and separated from it by the Taiwan Strait. It extends 394 kilometers long and 144 kilometers at its widest point (shaped like a sweet yam). With a total area of nearly 36,000 square kilometers, the island is equilateral in area to Hong Kong and Shanghai. Mountains cover nearly two-thirds of the island. There are sixty-two peaks of more than 10,000 feet, the tallest being Mount Jade (Yushan), the highest in northeast Asia.

Marketers usually segment Taiwan into four areas: north, south, middle, and east, with five principal cities associated with them. The northern area is the most important segment, with Taipei City, the provisional capital; Keelung City, the major harbor city since Japanese colonial time; and Hsinchu City, the Industrial Science Park. The southern area includes Kaohsiung City, the largest harbor in Taiwan, and Tainan City, the new industrial center in the south. The middle area includes Taichung City, the second largest harbor in Taiwan. The east coast is a less developed area that includes Taitung and Hualien counties.

ECONOMIC ENVIRONMENT

From Colonial Vestige to Little Dragon

Having few natural resources and arable land, Taiwan has astonished the world in creating an economic miracle. In 1950, Taiwan was one of the world's poorest countries. But by the present decade, it now holds the world's third largest currency reserves (exceeded only by Japan and China). The story of Taiwan's modern-day success begins with Japanese colonization. Under Japanese rule, Taiwan was first looked upon as an agricultural colony and later as an industrial supplier to support the Japanese war efforts during World War II (Barclay 1954). The infrastructure, including manufacturing, transportation, education, banking, and finance, put in place during the colonization period enabled postwar Taiwan to make such spectacular economic progress.

The fast pace of economic growth in postwar Taiwan has dramatically transformed it from a relatively impoverished agricultural economy to a relatively affluent industrial and service economy. This transitional growth can be characterized by four distinct phases: the agriculture and import substitution phase from the end of War World II to the 1950s, the export-oriented industrialization (EOI) phase from 1960 to 1973, the technologically sensitive external orientation phase from 1973 to 1986, and the small and medium-size enterprise promotion and easing of

Table 16.1

Major Taiwan Trade Partners (in US$ million)

		Hong Kong		Japan		United States	
	Trade surplus	Exports	Imports	Exports	Imports	Exports	Imports
1993	8,030	18,453	1,729	8,977	23,186	23,587	16,723
1996	13,572	26,788	1,705	13,659	27,493	26,866	19,972
1999	10,901	26,012	2,093	11,900	30,591	30,902	19,693
2000	8,310	31,336	2,187	16,599	38,558	34,815	25,126
2002	18,070	30,850	1,740	11,970	27,280	26,760	18,090
2004	6,120	29,880	2,090	13,230	43,650	28,130	22,390

Source: Monthly Statistics of Exports and Imports in Taiwan Area, January 2005, Ministry of Finance, Republic of China, www.mof.gov.tw/engWeb/default.asp

barriers to entry into the global market from 1986 to the present (Ariff and Khalid 2000). Right now, 64 percent of Taiwan's gross domestic product (GDP) is generated by the service sector, followed by 33 percent from industry, and less than 3 percent in the agricultural sector. This economic structure is similar to that of many postindustrializing and high-income countries (World Bank 2000).

As many have claimed, the EOI strategy was the basic factor determining the rapid growth of Asia's "Four Little Dragons": Taiwan, South Korea, Hong Kong, and Singapore. But for Taiwan, two additional forces were essential to economic success. First, there were no strong opposition groups to the ex-ruling party, thus enabling the KMT government to pursue effective growth and export-oriented policies. Second, a large amount of foreign aid, including military support, has been received from the United States in the 1960s and 1970s, thus helping Taiwan to obtain the necessary financial capital and military protection during the transitional growth period (Gulati 1992).

Japan and the United States not only assisted with Taiwan's transformation into an industrialized nation, they have also become Taiwan's top two trading partners in the last several decades. Taiwan's large foreign currency exchange reserves have largely emanated from the trade surplus with the United States. Exports to the United States were US$34.8 billion, and imports from Japan were US$38.6 billion in 2000 (Table 16.1). Its major exports are electronics, computer and communication products, textiles, machinery, articles of iron and steel, chemical, and plastic and rubber products, while the major imports are electronics, machinery, auto parts, telecommunications, transportation, and optical products (China External Trade Development Council [CETRA] 2001).

The EOI strategy and massive holdings of foreign reserves are two key factors that protected Taiwan from the 1997 Asian financial crisis (Naughton 2000). Yet Taiwan's trade surplus with the United States has also reached an all-time high. To keep pace with the economic growth and to diversify its export markets, Taiwan is gradually emphasizing trade with China. In 1988, the KMT government lifted its ban on martial law and allowed cross-strait exchanges; that strategic move not only relieved trade tension with the United States but also created more favorable conditions for reunification. A major beneficiary was Hong Kong, a third-party gateway for indirect trade with China. As a result, in ten years' time, Taiwan's total exports to the United States have declined from 40 percent to 25 percent. Major items exported to or via Hong Kong include electrical and electronic equipment and peripherals, machinery, accessories, raw plastic materials, and textiles. Currently, China (via Hong Kong) is the second largest trade surplus source for Taiwan.

Table 16.2

Economic and Income Profile

	Real GNP		Per capita income
	Amount ($US Million)	Annual change (%)	Amount (US$)
1993	228,578	6.66	10,964
1996	283,599	6.10	13,260
1999	289,277	5.32	13,177
2000	312,265	5.78	14,114
2002	288,544	3.94	12,884
2004	316,704	5.71	14,032

Source: Statistical Abstract of National Income, Taiwan Area, Republic of China, June 2005. Directorate General of Budget, Accounting and Statistics, Executive Yuan, Republic of China, http://eng.stat.gov.tw

Per Capita Income

Continuous economic growth with massive holdings of foreign reserves means that Taiwanese consumers enjoy a moderately stable and high income. Taiwan's per capita income was US$14,188 in 2000 (Table 16.2), higher than South Korea's and slightly equivalent to New Zealand (APEC 2001). This has risen from approximately US$150 five decades ago, at the period of Japanese colonization. The rapid rise of income and subsequent purchasing power make Taiwanese consumers receptive to newly introduced products and services.

Equitable distribution of income has accompanied economic growth. The ratio of income share of the highest 20 percent of wage earners to that of the lowest 20 percent is about fivefold (5.55 in year 2000). This relatively small difference compared to many Asian nations (e.g., 8.96 in Hong Kong, 9.27 in Singapore, and 11.96 in Malaysia) has contributed greatly to social and political stability, which, in return, creates the necessary conditions for still more economic development. For marketers, the equitable distribution of income also makes the income figure a very meaningful guide to the configuration of the market.

Changes in Disposable Income, Savings Rate, and Credit Spending

Household disposable income and consumption expenditures have increased nearly fourfold in the past twenty years (Table 16.3). Yet even with such a rapid rise in income, Taiwanese consumers still embrace a "spend less and save more" philosophy. Over 25 percent of household income goes into savings; this translates into an average US$45 billion capital flow annually for the banking, financial, and investment industries. Most savings are invested in long-term savings accounts, stocks and mutual funds, and "one-stop shopping" financial service companies. The savings and investments are primarily intended for children's college or overseas education, real estate purchases, investments in businesses, and gifts and other forms of financial support customary when sons and daughters marry. The minor investment outlets are cars, holiday traveling, retirement funds, and new TVs or computers.

Because the overall expenditure level on consumption has increased, one noticeable trend for Taiwanese consumers is an increasing tendency to buy on credit. This makes incumbent card issuers, such as Citibank and American Express, the beneficiaries of the Taiwanese spending

Table 16.3

Disposable Income and Consumption Expenditure (NT$ per Household)

	Disposable income	Consumption expenditure	Savings rate (%)
1970	40,929	3,558	8.00
1975	86,849	15,173	14.87
1980	179,687	54,204	23.17
1985	246,277	75,749	23.52
1990	370,323	149,824	28.80
1995	591,035	220,303	27.15
2000	662,722	228,723	25.66
2004	891,249	692,648	22.28

Source: The Survey of Family Income and Expenditure, Taiwan Area, Republic of China, 2004. Directorate General of Budget, Accounting and Statistics, Executive Yuan, Republic of China, http://eng.stat.gov.tw

spree. Citibank alone has issued more than one million cards to Taiwanese, second only to the U.S. market in the number of cards issued. Many department stores and major Taiwanese banks have also issued their own credit cards that offer high credit limits. There are 539 financial institutions with 6,245 branches in Taiwan, including the central banks, monetary institutions, the postal savings system, and nonmonetary institutions, all poised to capitalize on opportunities presented by rising incomes and consumer spending.

Changes in Consumer Consumption Patterns

Given such rapid growth in disposable income, consumer consumption patterns also have changed, which, subsequently, has a large impact on the economy and the overall marketplace. Similar to trends in the other "tiger economies," the most significant changes are allocations for food spending, which have declined from 51 percent of income in 1961 to 20.85 percent in 2000; spending on transportation and telecommunications, recreation, entertainment, education, and cultural services has risen the most, while spending on necessities such as clothing, footwear, fuel, and water has remained constant. The sevenfold increase in transportation and telecommunications is the most drastic. The changes in Taiwan's consumption patterns are consistent with classic economic predictions (e.g., Engel's Law). That is, Taiwan's rise in family incomes has generally evinced declines in the percentage spent on food, beverages, and tobacco; the percentage spent on housing remains constant; and the percentage spent on other items such as transportation, communication, education, and recreation has increased, as generally shown in Table 16.4. One exception has been the housing expenditures on rent and water that are rising at a constant rate. One possible explanation is that the housing expenditure share has not fully grown to a state of equilibrium (the ratio in the United States, for example, is about 24 percent for all income levels). In addition, the dense population in Taiwan has contributed to increased housing costs; this incremental rate is expected to grow, as there is no long-term solution for the problem of high population density in Taiwan.

Structural Change of the Economy, Inflation and Unemployment

Rapid economic growth was accomplished with little inflation or unemployment in the 1970s and 1980s. This reflects well on the tightly controlled political system as well as on the effort by the

Table 16.4

Consumption Expenditure (% of Household Spending at Current Prices)

Consumption items	1951	1961	1971	1981	1991	2000
Food	55.80	51.02	41.72	33.55	23.34	20.85
Beverage	1.93	3.02	3.70	4.33	3.56	2.81
Tobacco	4.08	4.77	4.45	2.78	1.58	0.97
Clothing and footwear	5.43	5.21	5.20	5.05	4.83	4.15
Fuel and power	4.19	4.86	4.10	4.43	2.83	2.14
Rent and water charge	—	10.52	12.69	12.34	15.89	16.15
Furniture/household equipment	11.64	0.90	2.78	3.05	2.79	3.04
Household operation	—	1.65	2.07	2.10	2.04	2.71
Medical and health expenses	2.58	4.21	4.25	5.07	6.64	8.53
Recreation, entertainment, education, and culture	6.09	5.45	8.11	12.80	16.26	18.95
Transport and communication	1.72	1.74	3.45	7.58	13.16	11.79
Miscellaneous goods/services	6.54	6.65	7.48	6.92	7.08	7.91

Source: The Survey of Family Income and Expenditure, Taiwan Area, Republic of China, 2001. Directorate General of Budget, Accounting and Statistics, Executive Yuan, Republic of China, http://eng.stat.gov.tw/

government to promote financial stability and foster economic development. The consumer price index (CPI) hovered around 3.5 percent per year, while the unemployment rate remained at 2 percent (Table 16.5). An important vehicle to help control inflation and generate employment opportunities has been high-yield government bonds, which have been designated for land reform, massive infrastructure spending, and monetary stabilization (Chang 1994). High interest rates, furthermore, have not only encouraged high saving rates and a choice of investments that have high returns, they have also contributed to the choice of labor-intensive industries that have contributed to Taiwan's comparative advantage and have led to an equitable distribution of income (Balassa 1991).

In the 1990s, the labor-intensive industries were adjusted and upgraded to technology and capital-intensive products, due to the global trade liberalization and the emerging new economy. High-tech products, such as computer monitors, optical scanners, and memory chips, accounted for 24 percent of total exports in 1989. By 1998, this figure had risen to 45 percent. Booming high-tech exports have altered the structure of the manufacturing sector as well as the labor market. The shares of heavy industry and electrical/electronic machinery rose from 44.5 percent and 33 percent, respectively, to 64.4 percent and 52 percent, respectively. High-tech and heavy industries now account for more than 75 percent of total industrial output (CETRA 2001).

This structural change of the manufacturing sector, however, does not substantially improve Taiwan's domestic economy. Because of heavy reliance on high-tech exports, the technology downturn and the weakening U.S. economy have hit Taiwan's economy doubly hard. The increasing numbers of Taiwanese manufacturers—most of them looking for low-cost operation in order to compete in the global market—migrate to mainland China. Among those ventures, a great portion came from the heavy and high-technology industries. As a result, the newly registered new companies plunged 40 percent since 1996, while the unemployment rate hit a postwar high of 5.5 percent in October 2001 (Table 16.5). These outgoing mainland-based manufacturers not only will hollow out investment in the domestic industrial sector and hence decrease employment opportunities, but they will also sack domestic manufacturers and the local labor force even further.

Table 16.5

Consumer Price Index and Unemployment Rate

	Consumer price index (%)	Unemployment (%)	New registered company		Mainland investment	
			Total number	Capital (NT$ million)	Volume (US$10,000)	Electronics and appliances
1991	3.63	1.51	46,326	356,418	17,416	3,157
1993	2.94	1.45	51,716	391,743	316,841	44,351
1996	3.07	2.60	43,638	480,005	122,924	27,686
1999	0.18	2.92	35,367	348,111	125,278	53,775
2000	1.26	2.99	34,404	581,875	260,714	146,477
2003	−0.28	4.99	40,837	314,147	769,878	233,003

Source: Consumer Price Index are from Commodity-Price Statistics Monthly in Taiwan Area of the Republic of China, 2004; Unemployment rates are from *Yearbook of Manpower Statistics,* Taiwan Area, Republic of China, 2004; Bureau of Foreign Trade, Ministry of Economic Affairs (www.moea.gov.tw).

Table 16.6

Population Growth in Taiwan

	Population size (million)	Annual growth (%)	Male/female ratio
1970	14.6	2.2	111
1980	17.8	1.9	109
1990	20.4	1.1	107
1995	21.36	0.85	106.02
1999	22.09	0.75	104.95
2000	22.28	0.83	104.66
2004	22.69	0.36	103.54

Source: Monthly Bulletin of Interior Statistics, June 2005. Ministry of the Interior, www.moi.gov.tw/stat/english/index.asp

DEMOGRAPHIC AND SOCIOCULTURAL ENVIRONMENT

Population

Table 16.6 reveals population trends; at the time of this writing, Taiwan has a population of approximately twenty-three million people. The earliest census recorded the island's population at 3.12 million in 1905. After forty years, the figure had nearly doubled to 6.02 million. The population further increased to 7.39 million in 1949 due to the influx of migrants from the Chinese mainland. The baby boom in the postwar years put excessive population pressure on Taiwan's economy, and the government has encouraged family planning. The population growth rate had dropped from 3.8 percent in the 1950s to 1 percent in recent times, and zero growth is forecasted by 2035. With 618 people per square kilometer, however, Taiwan has one of the highest population densities in the world, second only to Bangladesh. This population density has put a lot of pressure on the environment, infrastructure, and public education and health systems.

Table 16.7

Percentage of Income Recipients by Age

	Number of income recipients	Under 20 years	21–34 Years	35–54 Years	55 Years and above
1976	5,027,156	9.38%	36.65%	44.24%	9.73%
1980	6,637,376	8.87	41.68	38.30	11.69
1985	7,271,473	5.16	42.00	38.15	14.80
1990	8,574,546	3.99	38.25	42.42	16.11
1995	9,744,267	2.76	33.99	45.54	17.71
2000	10,914,109	1.84	31.33	46.80	20.03
2004	11,642,237	0.72	29.00	48.56	21.71

Source: The Survey of Family Income and Expenditure, Taiwan Area, Republic of China, 2004. Directorate General of Budget, Accounting and Statistics, Executive Yuan, Republic of China, www.stat.gov.tw/

One unique characteristic of the population is the sex ratio. The current ratio of males to females is 104 to 100, which has declined from 111 to 100 in 1970. This reflects an interesting Chinese traditional value in that sons, in general, have more favorable status than do daughters (Parish and Willis 1993). Because modern medical technology provides the means to detect the sex of a fetus in early pregnancy, some parents, by choice, abort baby girls before birth. Such preference has created an unbalanced gender structure problem. Among the 284,073 births registered in 1999, there were 109.47 boys for every 100 baby girls. In addition, in the population of those age twenty and above, the sex ratio for singles is 137 males to 100 females. Finding a mate is often a highly skillful and complex task for Taiwanese singles and their associated parents. Unbalanced gender structure, delayed marriages, increased female labor, a dismally high divorce rate, and comparatively fewer potential mothers between the ages of twenty-five and thirty-four have reduced the birthrate. The population increase rate was 0.392 percent in September 2001.

Age Distribution and Income Segment

In Taiwan, the age structure can be classified according to Taiwan's historical and economic development. People who were born before 1945, referred to as the "Japanese Colonial generation," hold most of the personal wealth, land, and political power. Because of the Japanese cultural influence, the value system, the living habits, as well as the consumption behavior patterns, this group tends to be pro-Japanese. The second group is Taiwan's "Baby Boomers," now thirty-five to fifty-five years old, who comprise the bulk of the Taiwanese population. The majority of today's workforce and corporate leaders come from this group. The third group is the "Bean Sprout" generation, with members who were born after 1971, the year Taiwan was exiled from the United Nations. This group is the counterpart of the "Generation X" or "Quarter-Life Crisis" in the United States, and its members were raised with MTV, Nintendo, and Nike, and enjoy better economic and material lives than did their parents. The term "Bean Sprout" implies that this youngest group is like a greenhouse-nurtured bean sprout: well-protected, yet feeble and vulnerable to high pressure. As indicated in Table 16.7, nearly 10 percent of Taiwanese under the age of twenty were income receivers in 1970s; the figure has dropped to 1.8 percent in 2000.

Similar to the "demographic imperative" scenario that most industrialized nations are now facing, the "graying" of the population will also present a threat to Taiwan (Table 16.8). This is due to the decreasing fertility rate, which has dropped from an average number of 5.5 children per

Table 16.8

Age Distribution (%)

| | Age-specific distribution (%) | | | |
	0–14 Years	15–64 Years	65+ Years	Median age (years)
1975	35.3	61.2	3.5	21
1985	29.9	65.2	4.9	25
1995	24.9	67.8	7.3	30
2000	21.11	70.27	8.62	32.1
2020	18.3	67.8	13.9	39

Source: Monthly Bulletin of Statistics of the Republic of China, October 2001. Directorate General of Budget, Accounting and Statistics, Executive Yuan, Republic of China, www.stat.gov.tw/

couple in the 1960s to the current rate of 1.3. However, the graying of the population is rather modest. In 2020, the estimated graying percentage will be 13.9 percent, which is considered small compared to other developed countries, such as Great Britain and Japan. The market demand for the graying market in Taiwan is typically for products and services related to overseas traveling, health expenses, pension funds, and children's education.

Household Size

The average Taiwanese household size is shrinking. In 1976, the average household contained 5.5 people. In 2000, the figure stood at 2.33, the percentage of three to four people per household size rose from 27.2 percent to 43.3 percent, while the size of seven and above declined from 22.6 percent to 4.79 percent (Table 16.9). This metamorphosis has resulted in a growing number of small families—including young families having only one or two children, single-parent families, senior citizens living alone, and couples without children. In 2000, there were 6,682,000 family households, a 60 percent increase since 1976. The reason behind the shrinking of household size is because the traditional concept of the "big family," whereby all the members of an extended family live together in one household, has been challenged by the emergence of a modern, postagricultural economy. Many young people have left family farms to establish nuclear families in urban areas.

Although the number of small families has increased, the percentage of people who live in households of more than five people remains high. One reason for this high percentage is due to the traditional concept of "family-derived nurturing" that still exists; therefore, many young families still prefer to live with their parents and share the same dwelling. Another reason is economic. Due to high real estate prices, the ideal ratio of one person to one bedroom is still considered a luxury by many young families. The housing problem is especially serious in big cities, such as Taipei and Kaohsiung. Expensive real estate and housing are also causing the erosion of the equitable distribution of income. To separate the rich from the poor in Taiwan, one easy way is to classify them according to "have" and "have not" categories on real estate and house ownership. Last, social pressures assured that the divorce rate and the number of single-parent households was low in the past, but this too has changed; the growth of single-parent families has become a noticeable social phenomenon. Prior to 1975, the divorce rate was around 0.04 percent; the figure increased about sixfold to 0.237 percent in 2000.

Table 16.9

Family Household Size

	Number of households	Household size (occupants/household)				
		Average	2 or less	3 to 4	5 to 6	7+
1976	3,470,000	5.5	8.6%	27.2%	41.6%	22.6%
1986	4,165,000	4.3	14.5	36.5	36.7	12.3
1996	5,800,000	3.6	19.2	43.0	31.0	7.0
2000	6,682,000	2.3	29.1	43.3	22.8	4.8

Source: Monthly Bulletin of Statistics of the Republic of China, October 2001. Directorate General of Budget, Accounting and Statistics, Executive Yuan, Republic of China, www.stat.gov.tw/

Table 16.10

Increasing Ratio of Higher Education

	Literacy (over 15 years old)	First level (junior high & below)	Second level (senior high & vocational)	Third level (college*)
1986	90.82	52.56	37.60	9.84
1990	92.42	49.57	38.29	12.14
1995	94.01	42.32	41.55	16.13
1999	95.28	41.20	37.54	21.26
2000	95.55	40.71	36.21	23.08
2004	94.75	29.32	33.52	31.91

Source: Yearbook of Manpower Statistics, Taiwan Area, Republic of China, 2004.
*Refers to education at colleges and universities, excluding the first three years of education at five-year junior colleges.

Education

Because the Chinese culture looks upon education as a symbol of respectful status, the pursuit of higher-level education for children has never ceased to be a major concern of parents. Currently, the literacy rate is around 95 percent, a significant increase from 58 percent in 1952. There are 1.93 million students attending 2,600 primary schools; 1.71 million students attending 1,174 secondary schools; and more than one million students enrolled in 150 colleges and universities (Table 16.10).

A more highly educated labor force is one of the most important determinants of economic growth in Taiwan. To increase productivity for economic growth, the educational system in Taiwan is focused on developing the workforce with sound basic education and vocational skills. The development of education can be tracked as follows. During the 1950s and 1960s, the emphasis was on the popularization of primary education. Following the rapid growth of the economy and the high demand for a technically skilled labor force, emphasis in the 1970s shifted from academic to vocational education at the more senior institutions. To meet the growing demand for more highly educated workers and to keep pace with the development of high-tech industries, and partly to keep students from going abroad to study for their degrees, in the late 1980s and the early 1990s, the focus was on the development of higher education. As a result, a large number of scholars and professionals have returned from abroad, and the brain-drain problem has been somewhat halted.

Table 16.11

Income Segmentation by Education Level (NT$)

Educational level	2000 Disposable income	2004 Disposable income
Graduate school	1,039,590	750,773
University	790,030	582,130
Junior college	612,467	481,919
Senior high school	502,345	515,622
Junior high school	434,643	438,039
Primary school	326,937	371,930
Supplementary school and illiteracy	127,241	256,385

Source: The Survey of Family Income and Expenditure, Taiwan Area, Republic of China, 2000, 2004. Directorate General of Budget, Accounting and Statistics, Executive Yuan, Republic of China, www.stat.gov.tw/

For income segmentation, there is a positive correlation between education and annual income levels. The graduate-level labor force commands the highest annual income (Table 16.11). For income change rate, the tendency, not surprisingly, is that better-educated people are getting richer, while the less well-educated are getting poorer. So, in Taiwan, education is doubly practical: it is a symbol of social status, and it generates higher incomes (which also enhances one's chances of finding an ideal mate).

Ethnicity and Language

The majority of the people in Taiwan are ethnic Chinese who settled on the island to avoid civil wars in the mainland during the past four hundred years. In the sequence of settlement, four broad groups were developed. The Aborigines are a minority, with an estimated population of 402,452 in 2000 (less than 2 percent of total population). The Aborigines belong to nine tribes—Atayal, Saisiyat, Bunun, Tsou, Paiwan, Rukai, Pinuyumayan (or Punuyumayan), Amis, and Yami—and live scattered in the island's mountain areas. The earliest immigrants were Hoklo people from Fujian coastal districts and Hakka people from the Guangdong hinterland in the seventeenth century; most of them were peasants and merchants. Hoklo and Hakka make up about 65 percent and 20 percent of the total population, respectively. The third wave of immigrants came in the late 1940s, when the ROC government withdrew from China; some two million Chinese, predominantly military officials, bureaucrats, and businesspeople, settled on the island. These mainland Chinese now make up about 15 percent of the population.

The ethnic groups originally were notably different in their dialects, living habits, socioeconomic status, and political ideology. However, after fifty years of integration efforts by means of government propaganda, the educational system, and interethnic relations, ethnic differences have diminished. A noticeable ethnic unity movement was proposed by former president Lee Teng-hui in 1998 on the concept of the "new Taiwanese." It retains the principle that people in the Taiwan area are ethnically and culturally Chinese but emphasizes the attachment and commitment of the people to their homeland.

Women's Liberation

Similar to liberalization of other parts of Taiwanese culture, the newly awakened awareness of women's rights emerged after the lifting of martial law and the eruption of Sunism (Sun Yat-sen's "Three Principles of the People") in the late 1980s (Lu 1994). The rise of women's liberation came with their greater participation in the labor force, economic activities, and even politics. A great number of well-educated and well-trained women now make their competitiveness keenly felt in every business sector. In 1999, 56 percent of junior college graduates, 51 percent of university and college graduates, and 27 percent of graduate school graduates were women. In the labor force, 37 percent of women are regular wage earners and help support their families financially.

However, in the traditional Confucian and male-dominant Chinese culture, the economic autonomy and self-independence of women is always associated with rebellion, liberated sex, and irresponsible motherhood. The stereotypical role expectation of grocery shopping, cooking, and nursing remains high, and the idea of androgyny for either female or male is still difficult to come by. The economic role of Taiwanese women may be drastically modernized, but social and family roles remain traditional. The government has adopted measures to protect women's welfare by setting up a women's protection hotline and women's rights promotion and sexual violation prevention committees. Many local governments have also organized regional coalitions to help women generate public awareness about gender issues, and provided legal, psychological, educational, and vocational assistance.

Chinese Culture

The Chinese culture promotes hard work, industriousness, thrift, and relationship networking, all of which contribute to entrepreneurial activity. The doctrine of Confucianism values education, individual responsibility, unity of the family, and the harmony of society—all of these are deeply imbedded in the mainstream of the nation's social norm. Without doubt, these social and cultural factors played a significant role in the success of the entrepreneur in Taiwan. In addition, limited natural resources combined with a large number of state-controlled conglomerates in the infrastructural sector (banking, telecommunication, and transportation), as well as the "islander" personality, have pushed out many adventurous and risk-taking businessmen to seek overseas opportunities.

MARKETING INFRASTRUCTURE SYSTEM

Mass Media

The demise of martial law has spawned the transformation of mass media in Taiwan (Chai 2000). The media have shifted their role from governmental control tool to democratization, industrialization, globalization, and knowledge-generating vehicles for Taiwanese consumers. There are seventy foreign mass media organizations stationed along with 260 domestic news agencies in Taiwan, compared with thirty-six before the lift of the ban in 1987. The number of newspapers increased from the regulated thirty-one to 445 in 2000, whereas the number of registered magazines nearly doubled from 3,132 to 6,641 (Table 16.12). Broadcast media have experienced spectacular growth as well. Cable television now reaches 80 percent of the residents in Taiwan, the highest penetration rate in Greater China nations (91 percent in Taipei, 53 percent in Hong Kong, and 46 percent in Singapore). As of May 2001, a total of fifty-four domestic and fourteen foreign companies were offering 141 satellite channels, including a number of foreign channels, such as NHK from Japan; Star-TV from Hong Kong; CNN and ESPN from the United States; and local media conglomerates including Eastern Multimedia Group, Sanlih Entertainment Television, and Videoland.

Table 16.12

Number of Newspapers, Magazines, and Radio Stations

	Newspapers	Magazines	News agencies	Radio stations	Movie theaters
1986	31	3,027	44	33	577
1991	237	4,282	190	33	343
1996	362	5,493	242	41	285
1997	344	5,676	251	65	233
1998	360	5,884	238	89	234
1999	384	6,463	242	143	226
2000	445	6,641	260	176	206
2003	602	4,405	841	172	188

Source: Taiwan Year Book 2004, Governmental Information Office, www.gio.gov.tw/taiwan-website/5-gp/yearbook/index.htm

Similar to the "Three Blind Mice" of the United States that are out of touch with market demand and competition, Taiwan's ex-ruling party Kuomintang-owned commercial TV stations, TTV, CTV, and CTS are equally out of touch and face several challenges. First, because of the pressure from the public, the government agreed to allow a fourth private-owned TV station, Formosa Television (owned by current ruling party, the Democratic Progressive Party) which began broadcasting in the late 1990s. Second, because the three original stations are controlled by the ex-ruling party, the TV news looked more like propaganda. This opened a huge market for the Taiwan audiences looking for other alternatives and perspectives such as those provided by TVBS, FTV, and CNN. Third, the growing satellite channels, such as Discovery and HBO, offer a variety of programming, which is refreshing to the Taiwanese. The most popular cable channels are HBO, TVBS-N, TVBS, ETTV News, Discovery, National Geographic, FTV news, and Star Chinese (Government Information Office [GIO] 2001).

Until fairly recently, there were only thirty-three radio broadcasting companies, most of them controlled by the ex-ruling party KMT. By October 2001, the number had increased to 176. The radio industry has led to a proliferation of interactive call-in programs, principally because of increasing social diversity and growing public assertiveness. Call-in programs cover a wide range of topics, ranging everything from debates about unification with mainland China to Taiwan's suburban legends. Among radio listeners, 70 percent are employed, and 19 percent are students. Workers prefer news, traffic updates, information technology, and current affairs programs, while students are attracted to music, movie star gossip, entertainment, and travel-related programs (Rainmaker 2001).

Telecommunications and the Internet

As with broadcast media, the telecommunications industry used to be controlled fully by the KMT's subsidiary ChungHwa Telecom Co., which provides a full spectrum of services, including local, long-distance, and international telephone, as well as mobile communications, radio paging, and Internet services. The market has been gradually liberalized after the Telecommunications Act was revised in 1996. At the time of this writing, 66 percent of ChungHwa's total equity shares are released to employees, overseas investors, and the public.

Table 16.13

Internet and Telecommunication Service (unit: 1,000)

	Number of subscriberspublic					Public phone sets	Outgoing int'l. calls (minutes)
	Local phone	Mobile phone	Radio paging	xDSL	Internet		
1993	7,951	539	1,352	—	—	117	442,308
1994	8,503	584	1,729	—	—	122	501,849
1995	9,175	770	2,083	1	21	122	593,023
1996	10,011	970	2,301	3	165	126	700,502
1997	10,862	1,492	2,641	8	429	128	789,061
1998	11,500	4,727	4,261	15	1,665	135	860,878
1999	12,044	11,541	3,873	28	2,874	145	958,264
2000	12,642	17,874	2,813	87	4,650	150	1,058,378
2005	13,600	20,659	1,153	4024	8,277	N.A.	284,000

Source: Monthly Statistics of Transportation and Communications, June 2005. The Ministry of Transportation and Communications, www.motc.gov.tw

One drastic change after the liberalization of the telecommunications industry was the growth of mobile phone services, which opened to the private sector in early 1998. Mobile phone subscribers have increased from 1.49 million at the end of 1997 to 20.48 million by October 2001, a sharp penetration increase from 6.88 percent to 92 percent. The number of mobile phone subscribers has also surpassed local telephone subscribers by 35 percent (Table 16.13).

As of September 2001, active Internet users totaled 7.50 million. This represents an online penetration rate of 34 percent in Taiwan. Among those Internet users, 5.25 million access the Internet via telephone modem, 2.85 million via TANet (campus network), 710,000 via ADSL, and 180,000 via cable modem (Focus on Internet News and Data [FIND] 2001). These figures are increasing steadily with the availability of broadband services. According to IDC's Information Society Index (ISI), Taiwan, along with the United States, Japan, and Hong Kong, is classified as a "skater," an advanced information society (the other three categories are striders, sprinters, and strollers). The ranking is based on IT spending per capita, and computer, information, social, and Internet infrastructures (Bruno 2001).

Transportation

The motorcycle has been the major transportation vehicle in Taiwan. With eleven million motorcycles and a population of twenty-two million, Taiwan boasts more motorcycles per capita than any other country in the world (Table 16.14). In the late 1970s when the North–South Freeway was completed, the demand for automobiles began to grow. In recent years, higher living standards and the redistribution of wealth promoted by the booming stock and real estate markets have further stimulated the automobile market. The percentage of families owning cars increased from 5 percent in 1980 to 71 percent in 2000. The high percentage of car ownership has benefited the retailing industry (in particular, superstores and shopping malls) and Taiwan's travel industry.

Although the demand for automobiles remains strong, factors such as limited car parks, poor road traffic design, and inflated gasoline prices have hindered such growth. Also, with a near tenfold increase in automobile usage, most road systems are overloaded. Bicycles are seldom

Table 16.14

Registered Automobile and Motorcycle (1,000 vehicles)

	Passenger car	Bus and truck	Motorcycle
1980	424	254	3,966
1985	916	429	6,589
1989	1,969	595	7,619
1993	3,239	800	9,284
1999	4,509	804	10,958
2000	4,716	833	11,423
2005	5,398	967	12,972

Source: Monthly Statistics of Transportation and Communications, June 2005. The Ministry of Transportation and Communications, www.motc.gov.tw/

considered as transportation vehicles in Taiwan; their use is considered suicidal, especially on the chaotic road systems in metro cities.

The 373-kilometer-long North–South national freeway was built in 1978 and is still Taiwan's primary highway. It links the two largest harbors, Keelung and Kaohsiung, by connecting Taipei as the transit center. To release the traffic loads and congestion problems in Taipei, several subroutes have been built. These include two viaducts parallel to the North–South freeway from Hsichih to Wuku, southbound Chungho to Hsinchu (where the Science Industrial Park is located), and westbound Hsichih to Mucha and Chungho. In addition to the highway systems, Taiwan has an extensive rail network and bus system throughout main cities and the countryside. Overall, the infrastructure system in Taiwan is quite efficient and effective.

Environmental Protection

During the martial law period, the KMT government's slogan was "Construct Taiwan, Retrieve Mainland China," which clearly indicates its interest was to use Taiwan as a stepping stone in building up economic and military power to retaliate against mainland China, as opposed to protect the island's environment. After decades of virtually unheeded environmental regulations, Taiwan is among the most polluted countries in the world. Despite the public outcry and many grassroots environmental movements, the government has been slow to awaken to the need for policy change. It was not until 1987 that the government promoted its Bureau of Environmental Protection Administration (EPA) to cabinet level in order to oversee environmental issues. An estimated US$1.5 billion was spent on cleanup efforts by the end of the 1990s. Given the degradation and despite such a large expenditure, however, it is not an easy task, to clean up the environment, and there is no quick fix. Environment nuisance petitions do not seem to have improved. The most serious problems are noise and water pollution (Table 16.15). The dense small and medium-size manufacturing factories, heavy vehicular exhaust, inadequate sewage systems, and industrial waste and wastewater are the main sources of pollutants.

The tension between the government and the general public is constantly high. Many foreign companies, such as Bayer (petrochemical), GE (nuclear plant), and DuPont (CFC), and local companies including Taiwan Electricity (radioactive waste), China Petroleum (naphtha cracker), and Formosa Plastics (hazardous waste) have frequently found themselves caught at the center of the public debate on environmental issues.

Table 16.15

Nuisance Petition on Environment (cases)

	Waste disposal	Air	Noise	Water	Odors
1993	15,576	18,719	19,378	4,820	8,361
1996	40,120	10,996	19,567	5,718	12,770
1999	32,135	14,411	22,036	5,021	18,324
2000	32,875	11,091	26,158	7,498	24,087

Source: Statistical Yearbook of the Republic of China, 2001. Environmental Protection Administration (EPA), http://cemnt.epa.gov.tw/eng

Table 16.16

Health and Medical System and Major Diseases (persons)

	Medical care facilities	Number of physicians	Top five causes of death				
			Malignant neoplasm	Cerebro vascular	Accidents	Heart disease	Diabetes mellitus
1986	12,037	15,767	16,559	14,862	12,187	9,953	2,970
1991	13,661	21,115	19,630	14,137	13,636	12,026	4,210
1996	16,645	24,790	27,961	13,944	12,422	11,273	7,525
2000	18,082	29,585	31,554	13,332	10,515	10,552	9,450
2003	18,777	32,390	35,201	12,404	8,191	11,785	10,013

Source: Statistical Yearbook of the Republic of China, 2004. Department of Health, www.doh.gov.tw/statistic/index.htm

To sustain sales and market growth, marketers have started to pay more attention to environmental claims for their products. For instance, Acer green PC, which is configured to use power more efficiently, has been a big hit in the PC market. Other peripheral products such as recyclable printer cartridges and laptop PC batteries were made greener to win over Taiwanese consumers.

Public Health System

The life expectancy in Taiwan is 72.01 years for men and 77.39 for women. Rapid industrialization and urbanization as well as a growing aging population have highlighted the need for better health care services. Thus, in 1985, the government mandated a fifteen-year project designated the Establishment of Medical Network. At the end of 2000, a total of 18,082 public and private hospitals and clinics provided comprehensive health care service (Table 16.16). On average, there was one doctor of Western medicine for every 783 persons. There are currently eleven medical schools, thirteen paramedical junior colleges, and fourteen paramedical vocational schools in Taiwan.

The top five causes of death are cancer (25.4 percent), cerebrovascular diseases (10.7 percent), accidents (8.5 percent), heart disease (8.5 percent), and diabetes mellitus (7.6 percent). Cancer, with an average 6 percent increase rate, has been the leading cause of death since 1982. The five most common forms of cancer for men are liver, lung, colorectal, stomach, and oral; while women are mainly affected by lung, liver, colorectal, breast, and cervical cancers. Lung cancer is due to bad air quality and a large number of cigarette smokers, while liver cancer can be attributed to smoking, hepatitis (perhaps because of dining out frequently), alcohol drinking habits, and high working pressures. The causes of death somehow reflect Taiwanese consumers' living environment, lifestyle, and drinking and eating habits.

Trademark and Patent Protection

Taiwan has been identified by the U.S. Trademark Association as one of the most problematic countries for protecting trademark rights. Being prodded by threats of Super 301 trade sanctions from the United States, as well as the motive for continued access to Western markets, Taiwan has implemented extensive regulations on intellectual property rights. The most recent amendment to the Trademark Law, which became effective in December 1993, was intended to overhaul the old system to meet international standards. The International Classification of Goods and Services under the Nice Agreement has been adopted in the new Enforcement Rules, which became effective in July 1994. This new law intends to protect rights holders on a par with international standards. In addition, intellectual property protection is provided by the Fair Trade Law, the Integrated Circuit Protection Law, the Industrial Design Law, the Cable TV Law, the Video Reproduction Law, and the Trade Secrets Law.

The enforced intellectual property protection laws not only help foreign companies, but many domestic firms have benefited as well. Consumers are now paying more for higher-quality publications. Companies and authorized dealers need no longer fear competition from "pirate" versions of cheaper and low-quality products. Higher royalties and profit margins have helped publishers to reinvest in R&D and to produce more new products. The immediate impact is visible in Taiwan's information and communication technology (ICT) industry. Taiwan currently ranks number one for global market share in six categories of ICT products, including the notebook PC, mouse, scanner, monitor, interface card, and modem. Most of the ICT products were registered with Taiwanese patents. According to the U.S. Patent and Trademark Office (USPTO), the U.S. government issued 5,984 new patents to Taiwan manufacturers in 2000. This makes Taiwan the third largest patent holder (next to Japan and Germany) in the United States. The number of patents awarded to a country by the United States has long served as an indicator of that country's level of scientific and technological advancement and global competitiveness. The most active research areas from Taiwanese high-tech companies are semiconductors, electrical connectors, transistors, and information storage and retrieval devices (USPTO 2004).

CHANGES IN CONSUMPTION BEHAVIOR

The average household consumption expenditure was NT$662,772 (US$19,490) in 2000. As indicated in Table 16.3, the salient trend is that the consumption percentage spent in the nondurable goods category, including foods, beverages, and grocery products, has declined; whereas, the percentage spent on durable goods, including entertainment, education, transportation, and telecommunication, has increased. The penetration rates of color TVs, telephones, and washing machines are above 95 percent for Taiwanese households, whereas automobile and personal computers have reached 50 percent (Table 16.17). As a whole, durable goods, which were considered symbols of family wealth thirty years ago, are now necessities for Taiwanese families.

Following the worldwide trend, DVD players, video games, personal computers, cellular phones, and Internet facilities are now the new status symbols for younger-generation families. According to the Family Income and Expenditure Survey (Directorate General of Budget, Accounting and Statistics [DGBAS] 2001), the penetration rates of those IT-related products were 14 percent,

Table 16.17

Percentages of Households with Household Appliances

	Color TV	Telephone	Air conditioner	Videotape recorder	Washing machine	Sedan car	Motorcycle	Home PC
1964	—	1.50	—	—	—	—	2.87	—
1970	—	4.37	—	—	6.95	—	19.15	—
1975	16.42	15.76	3.42	—	31.16	1.27	43.37	—
1980	69.29	51.09	14.40	1.45	64.73	5.11	63.51	—
1985	92.31	82.12	23.95	20.70	77.84	11.91	71.87	2.32
1990	98.26	93.08	47.26	63.56	88.79	29.07	77.51	6.77
1995	99.29	96.70	67.08	62.19	92.83	47.95	79.88	18.54
2000	99.45	98.04	79.46	46.72	95.36	55.58	79.37	46.49
2004	99.47	97.56	85.71	25.42	96.91	58.04	80.78	62.37

Source: The Survey of Family Income and Expenditure, Taiwan Area, Republic of China, 2004. Directorate General of Budget, Accounting and Statistics, Executive Yuan, Republic of China, www.stat.gov.tw/

15 percent, 47 percent, 76 percent, and 34 percent, respectively (Table 16.18). City consumers have higher ownership rates than do town and village consumers in all categories. The only exceptions for which township consumers have higher ownership were motorbikes and sedan vehicles; this partly reflects the traffic congestion and parking problems in cities.

The low percentage of disposable income spent on the nondurable goods category, including foods, beverages, and grocery items, does not imply that Taiwanese consumers eat less or drink less. To the contrary, because of the real purchasing power from increasing discretionary income, Taiwanese consumers consume and demand more in both quantity and quality. The popularity of American fast-food chains and more Western cuisines, such as cheese, beef, and wine, in the daily diet, indicate that Western foods are gradually changing dietary consumption patterns. In addition, because of changing lifestyles, Taiwanese eat out frequently. Cafés, snack bars, bubble-tea houses, food stalls, and street vendors are popular outlets for family lunches and dinners.

CHANGES IN THE MACROMARKETING MIX

Products

Imported products have long dominated Taiwan's luxury goods market. High-price-tag consumer items—including cognac and perfumes from France; leather and clothing from Italy; video games, small appliances, and automobiles from Japan; computer and IT-related products from the United States—have long dominated this elite segment. Coinciding with the further opening of the Taiwanese market and the increasing number of retailing channels, the demand for foreign goods will continue to grow. Taiwanese consumers are highly fashion conscious and somewhat insensitive to price. Innovative Western products with strong brand images will continue to fulfill such needs, if consumers can be assured of reasonable quality.

A study on women's sweaters indicated that the country-of-origin significantly influenced Taiwanese consumers' perception of product quality. The sweater with the "Made in Japan" label received the highest evaluation, while the sweater labeled "Made in Taiwan" got the lowest. "Made in the USA" and "Made in Italy" were rated between these two countries' labels (Chang

Table 16.18

Percentages of Household Appliances by Urbanization Levels

Household equipment	Average	City	Town	Village
Color TV sets	99.45	99.60	99.26	99.12
DVD player	13.47	17.04	9.78	3.79
Video camera	8.57	10.90	5.60	3.39
Stereo	50.43	54.99	47.72	33.88
Piano	10.80	13.74	7.75	2.87
Video game	15.28	17.60	14.10	6.40
Videotape recorder	46.72	51.99	42.19	30.54
Cable TV	71.96	81.10	64.15	43.71
Personal computer	46.49	54.19	40.51	21.48
Telephone	98.04	98.67	97.50	96.13
Cell phone	76.03	80.03	74.71	59.33
Answering machine	4.69	6.78	1.84	0.51
Internet facility	33.91	40.81	27.82	12.98
Fax machine	10.51	13.60	6.75	3.32
Sedan vehicle	55.58	54.93	61.14	47.10
Motor-bicycle	79.37	76.74	83.86	82.82
Electromagnetic oven	41.95	48.59	35.57	22.91
Air conditioner	79.46	86.88	73.56	55.63
Dehumidifier	24.93	30.89	19.86	6.42
Washing machine	95.36	96.16	94.65	92.97
Drier	20.50	22.48	20.50	10.84
Air-cleaning machine	7.90	10.54	4.48	2.13
Water filter machine	27.85	30.90	25.66	17.55
Vacuum cleaner	40.27	46.65	34.89	20.41
Geyser	94.49	95.80	93.46	90.26
Hot- and warm-water fountain	54.21	51.60	59.52	55.82
Microwave oven	44.78	53.17	36.73	20.75
Newspaper	43.61	47.64	40.01	31.55
Magazine	14.12	16.74	11.59	6.65

Source: The Survey of Family Income and Expenditure, Taiwan Area, Republic of China, 2000. Directorate General of Budget, Accounting and Statistics, Executive Yuan, Republic of China, www.stat.gov.tw/

and Sternquist 1993). Although the result cannot be generalized to cover all goods, the demand for snob-appeal goods in Taiwan remains at an all-time high.

The private label started with a local company, the Far East Department Store, selling men's shirts some thirty years ago. Today, many foreign-invested retailers, such as Watson's personal stores (offering mainly body care, toiletries, and facial tissue products), Wellcome supermarkets, and 7–Eleven convenience stores have introduced their own private labels (No Frills by Wellcome and Cold Storage by 7–Eleven) at a fairly aggressive pace. One local supermarket chain, Xiao Bei, has also become active in this field. Xiao Bei's private label products range from disposable paper products to breakfast cereals, cooking oil, bread, and diapers. Its private label products are also available at 7–Eleven.

The costs of pollution were very rarely taken into account in the past. However, environmental awareness has now arrived, bringing with it new pressures on the government and business sectors. This awareness and pressures to address the issue will likely result in more green products and services. Several demonstrations have been held by environmental groups against polluters such as nuclear-power reactors and landfill sites. Yet, green marketing is still on a self-regulatory basis, as the government has not enforced any mandatory programs on the business sector.

The concern for a healthy diet has long been a tradition in Chinese culture, but the definition of "healthy" is very different from that held by Westerners. The Western standards of low-calories, low-sodium, low-cholesterol, low-caffeine, high-fiber, and GM (genetically modified)-free are well accepted among many consumers, but in Taiwan, the philosophy of choosing healthy food is Taoism or yin and yang oriented. Many people believe that any natural foods, from the mountains or the sea, have tonic and curing effects, while products with artificial colors and flavors, chemical additives, preservatives, and special treatments are not considered healthy.

Changes in Retailing Channel

Taiwan has experienced tremendous growth and modernization in its retailing sector in the last five years. Due to changes in consumers' lifestyles and shopping patterns, many mom-and-pop corner grocery stores are now giving way to clean, convenient, and efficiently run Western-style chain stores. A large proportion of independent grocers has disappeared in the urban area, with many of them being converted to franchises of large convenience stores or supermarket chains (see also Lee 1995; Liu 1992). In the retail structural change, the sales share of independent grocers has declined from 25.3 percent in 1996 to 19.8 in 2000, whereas the "one-stop shopping" hypermarket, which takes most of the gains from all other retail types, has expanded from 11.7 percent to 22.1 percent. The average retail sale of the hypermarket is also the highest, with sales volume near one billion NT dollars per store (Table 16.19). The major hypermarket chains in Taiwan are Carrefour, Makro, RT Mart, and Aimai Hypermarket (owned by Far East Department Stores).

Convenience stores have become the second fastest-growing type of retailing. This trend is primarily because of the limited availability of store sites, high real estate prices, and the high population density. The number of convenience stores has expanded almost twofold, from 3,123 in 1996 to 6,000 in 2000. Major players are 7–Eleven (owned by President Chain Store), Circle K, and Family Mart.

Supermarkets are the third largest category. They have had a stable sales share of 15 percent over the years. There were 1,100 supermarkets, which took in average sales of NT$60 million per store in 2000. Major players are Wellcome, Xiao Bei, and Ding Hao. Supermarkets are located mainly in big cities.

Wet markets remain a major force in the retailing business. With the leading sales share of 27 percent in 2000, wet markets still enjoy thriving business. One reason, perhaps, is that the traditional shopping habit is not easily changed, particularly within the older generation and suburban segments. For Taiwanese consumers, the wet market and corner store still offer the highest utility in convenience, shopping efficiency, and friendliness.

The last category is cooperatives retailing. Referred to as "PX stores," they are a specialty in Taiwan. These stores are a legacy of the martial law period, when military personnel, government officials, and public school educators were given certain privileges in terms of tax relief and purchasing. Many of the PX stores can be found on military bases and at government agencies, such as schools and hospitals, and they sell mainly staples, such as vegetable oil, rice, milk powder, and detergent. The major attractiveness of PX stores is exemption from value-added tax; some prices of goods can be 25 percent lower than retail prices. Many PX stores are slowly being converted to regular supermarkets.

Similar to the development of food retailing businesses, nonfood retailing is also undergoing major revamping. The number of shopping malls, department stores, and large-scale specialty stores, such as clothing and footwear outlets, booksellers, furnishing outlets, and computer

Table 16.19

Establishments and Sales Volumes of Food Retailers (NT$1,000)

	Supermarkets	Hypermarkets	Cooperatives	Convenience stores	Independent grocers	Wet markets	Food specialists
1996	827[a]	48	52	3,123	15,900	635	487
	$68,319[b]	$895,833	$101,923	$15,145	$5,862	$193,071	$3,900
	15.3%[c]	11.7%	1.4%	12.8%	25.3%	33.2%	0.3%
1997	930	56	58	3,623	16,000	632	493
	$64,624	$985,714	$87,931	$14,601	$5,875	$196,202	$3,762
	15.3%	14.1%	1.3%	13.5%	24%	31.6%	0.3%
1998	1,013	72	62	4,348	16,200	631	499
	$61,204	$1,048,611	$83,871	$13,616	$5,889	$202,536	$4,079
	14.5%	17.7%	1.2%	13.9%	22.4%	30%	0.3%
1999	1,055	95	65	5,217	15,900	630	498
	$61,042	$936,842	$83,076	$12,613	$5,931	$199,365	$4,787
	14.4%	20%	1.2%	14.8%	21.1%	28.2%	0.3%
2000	1,100	111	70	6,000	15,200	631	509
	$60,182	$924,324	$80,000	$12,100	$6,053	$195,563	$6,006
	14.3%	22.1%	1.2%	15.6%	19.8%	26.6%	0.4%

Source: Euromonitor International, "Retail Trade in Taiwan" (London: Euromonitor International, 2001).
[a]Number of food retailers by outlet type.
[b]Average retail sales (NT$1,000) through food outlets.
[c]Retail sales share through food retails by outlet type.

stores, are expanding. Major newly launched shopping malls are Breeze Centre and Core Pacific City in Taipei, and TaiMall and Metro Walk in Taoyuan. Major players in the department store business are Yuan Tung (Far East Department Store), Xing Guan San Yue, and Sogo. Taiwan had 73,971 nonfood retail outlets with estimated sales of US$22 billion in 2000 (Euromonitor International 2001).

Advertising

Mass communication media in Taiwan has shown unprecedented growth since martial law deregulation. The new services, including satellite and cable broadcasts, offer viewers more diversified and privileged programming than that shown by the three homogeneous state-controlled TV stations. The repeal of the Publication Law in 1999 has produced spectacular growth in the number of newspapers and magazines. Furthermore, with advanced information and telecommunication technology, both electronic media and printed media are entering another new frontier. All these changes are resulting in more varied advertising.

Advertising expenditure has grown significantly, with an average growth rate of 20 percent, though expenditures leveled off during the Asian financial crisis (Rainmaker 2001). The total advertising expenditure in 1999 was US$2.5 billion (NT$81 billion) for TV, newspapers, and magazines alone. Among the five major media, television, due to high cable TV subscription rates, remains the leading advertising medium. When combining commercial TV and cable TV, television commands a leading share of 54.5 percent in advertising expenditure. The Internet is a new medium, holding a 0.6 percent share (Table 16.20).

Table 16.20

Advertising Spending by Media

Media*	Share (%)	Ad spending (US$ million)
Terrestrial TV	29.8	535.5
Cable TV	24.7	441.2
Newspaper	31.7	571.5
Magazine	10.2	184.8
Radio	3.6	65.2
Internet	0.6	10.8

Source: "Adspending of in Top Five Media," Rainmaker Adspending Report, 2001. Rainmaker, www.rainmaker.com.tw.

*These include 4 Terrestrial TV stations, 65 cable TV channels, 67 newspapers, 91 magazines, and 8 radio stations.

Products and services on which companies spend the most to advertise include real estate, automobiles, mobile phones, shampoos, and telecommunication service providers. Television remains the major medium for advertising grocery products, such as shampoo, chewing gum, detergent, and toiletries, and emotional appeal products, such as mobile phones and credit cards. Newspapers are a major medium for high involvement products and shopping goods, such as property, cars, furniture, and Internet service providers. Magazines account for a smaller share of adspend but remain a major medium for fashion goods and cosmetics. Radio is the major outlet for musical records and tapes (Table 16.21).

For creative appeals, the traditional Chinese cultural values (collectivism, oneness with nature, and emphasis on family and societal harmony), Western-style appeals (e.g., individualism, hedonism, and promise of American lifestyle), and universal appeals (e.g., global villager, "new mankind") coexist (Shao, Raymond, and Taylor 1999). This is due to Taiwan's history of accepting foreign cultures (Japanese and American), an adoration of foreign products, and the impact of global advertising agencies. In addition, Taiwan has undergone tremendous economic development, which affects a societal shift toward materialism and nontraditional values (e.g., product comparisons, humorous ad copy, and status appeals), which now are more acceptable to Taiwanese consumers.

Internet Shopping and Direct Marketing

Although the advertising spending on the Internet is relatively small, the growing impact of the Internet on marketing communications cannot be ignored. Because of security and logistics problems, the Internet is yet to be a shopping tool in Taiwan. But for the youth segment, the Web is a viable communication tool, such as for virtual marketing and permission marketing. According to the government "Internet Usage" survey in 1999, 3,979 (39 percent) out of 11,098 respondents have visited the Web (Ministry of Transportation and Communication [MOTC] 1999). Among the Web users, 53.4 percent were male, and 46.6 percent were female. Respondents are generally young, with 42 percent between the ages of twenty and twenty-nine, followed by 36.1 percent between the ages of twelve and nineteen, and 23.9 percent between the ages of thirty and thirty-nine. The majority of them are new users, with the largest category having been online for less than six months (28.4 percent), and the second largest category six months to one year (22.6 percent).

Table 16.21

Adspending of Top Twenty Product Categories in Top Five Media

Product category	Adspend (NT$000)	Terres. TV (%)	Cable TV (%)	Newspaper (%)	Magazine (%)	Radio (%)
Residential/estate/ property sales	275,717	0.00	3.04	93.53	2.29	1.14
Cars	231,899	17.16	31.76	39.39	7.02	4.68
Mobile phone	142,335	18.68	48.94	24.80	5.57	2.02
Shampoo	135,415	55.54	42.48	0.00	1.51	0.47
Communication equipment/service	91,465	28.72	25.95	39.93	3.31	2.09
Credit card	90,526	18.90	48.39	25.35	4.85	2.51
Internet service provider	86,583	8.03	22.00	34.51	27.06	8.41
Department store	85,094	2.85	15.59	76.91	1.05	3.59
Records and tapes	72,776	4.54	32.30	0.32	8.23	54.61
Newspaper	70,943	0.29	4.70	90.13	2.25	2.63
Telecom service	67,241	18.77	26.88	44.81	5.95	3.60
Financial service	65,642	16.05	19.38	48.64	8.35	7.58
Cosmetics	65,325	2.01	18.97	36.58	42.16	0.28
Supermarket/superstore	60,602	39.39	43.24	12.70	0.38	4.28
Beauty salon	56,518	8.60	7.35	77.53	5.53	0.99
Chewing gum	54,324	30.86	67.90	0.00	0.17	1.07
Toiletries	53,977	39.45	40.63	8.29	9.91	1.71
Detergent/softener	53,782	54.44	41.11	2.45	1.17	0.83
Furniture	52,984	4.50	8.17	75.59	10.57	1.18

Source: "Adspending of Top 20 Product Categories in Top Five Media," Rainmaker Adspending Report 2001. Rainmaker, www.rainmaker.com.tw.

The most popular Web sites were Kimo (acquired by Yahoo), Yam, Sina, Yahoo, PC Home, Hinet, 104 Job Bank, and Seed Net. The major concerns when browsing the Web were traffic jams (74.8 percent), disconnections (27.8 percent), too much garbage information (17 percent), expensive connection fees (15.2 percent), poor content (14.6 percent), viruses (5 percent), and privacy issues (3.7 percent). The purposes for going online were for searching for information (80 percent), accessing databases or software (27 percent), chatting or playing games online (26 percent), sending/receiving e-mail (22 percent), looking for business opportunities or jobs (3.9 percent), distance learning (2.8 percent), and online shopping (2.8 percent).

There are several reasons why direct marketing and Internet shopping have not yet become mainstream in Taiwan. In terms of business customs, personal contact and familiarity are important in earning trust and acceptance from customers. Electronic commerce and online marketing are viewed as a nuisance and are considered untrustworthy in Chinese business culture. Second, direct marketing relies heavily on frequently updating customer databases and other back-office supports. The necessary marketing databases, such as single-source data, credit card purchase records, and online log files, simply do not exist or are not easily accessible. Third, there is no significant cost advantage in operating direct marketing as compared to traditional mass media and retail outlets. The so-called last one mile cost, such as parcel delivery, is relatively expensive.

Marketing Research

Increased foreign participation has transformed the advertising and marketing research industries in recent years. Global giants, such as Dentsu, Ogilvy & Mather, Saatchi & Saatchi, and McCann-Erickson, have all rushed to capitalize on Taiwan's growing market. Along with the booming number of foreign advertising agencies are the marketing concepts they brought with them. Many companies increased their emphasis on the significance of marketing as a driving force for business operations and strategic planning. As a result, more companies now appreciate the importance of marketing research, consumer studies, advertising research, and media habits research. The major players in Taiwan are ACNielsen, Burke, INRA (International Research Associates), and SRG (Survey Research Group).

Because Taiwan has an international trade-oriented economy, business-to-business marketing research is essential. The China External Trade Development Council, a nonprofit, independent trade promotion organization supported by government and local business associations, offers market information to companies doing business in Taiwan. Information on how to do business with Taiwan, Taipei International trade shows, Taiwan trade opportunities, and trade inquiry services can be found.

FUTURE TRENDS AND EXPECTATIONS

Internationalization

Taiwan depended on its close relationship with the United States to create its "economic miracle" in the 1960s and 1970s. This era is drawing to an end, as dependence on the U.S. market diminishes, and the need to remedy U.S. trade deficits becomes more urgent. The development in China's coastal provinces and in various other Southeast Asian nations combined these places into a singular region of economic growth. Taiwan has poured capital, technology, people, and international trade know-how into this new economic region, where cultural, religious, ethnic, linguistic, and subregional identity are often similar to its own.

However, the reasons for Taiwan's success could also portend its downfall. Taiwan has created many new competitors in labor-intensive industries, such as textiles, apparel, lumber, furniture, toys, computer keyboards, and agricultural products, in neighboring nations. The low-cost pressure from the region will become greater, as bilateral trading between those nations increases. As a result, Taiwan has been forced to upgrade its manufacturing and service sectors to be more capital-, technology-, and service-oriented, and to promote itself as a manufacturing and logistics center in the region. The *Global Logistics Development Plan*, as proposed by the Executive Yuan, is seeking to form strategic alliances, mainly with Western companies, using Taiwan as a foothold into mainland China and Southeast Asia markets (Executive Yuan 2001).

Although China is included as part of the strategic plan, Taiwan's relationship with China remains a wild card. Taiwan stood calm during the Asian financial crisis but is now facing the new growing power of not-so-friendly neighbor China, which has sucked out the needed investment capital and management professionals. As both the ROC and the People's Republic of China (PRC) are in the WTO, the only hope is that Beijing, which still insists on a "One China" policy, will play the game by the same rules as other members, that is, admitting Taiwan as a separate entity and leaving all the trade spats to WTO's Dispute Settlement Board in Geneva (Clifford 2001). The new DPP-led Taiwan government overall, and the Taiwanese businessmen in general, are cautious about investing in China. The main concerns are not political, but legal and economic. Political instability, out-of-control regional governments, insufficient legal guarantees, frequently changing legal and tax policies, wage hikes, and inflation have stirred up the fearfulness and uncertainty of doing business with China (Mainland Affairs Council [MAC] 2001).

Economic Liberalization

Economic growth in Taiwan has been projected at less than 4 percent per year for the period 2002–5. This is lower than the boom period of 10 percent plus in 1960–89 and 7 percent in the 1990s. The appearance of this new growth rate suggests that Taiwan has passed through the high growth phases of a labor-intensive manufacturing period and is now heading toward a mature service- and technology-oriented economy.

With the economic miracle losing its magic, the question for Taiwan is how to restructure the economy and to get out of the stagnancy rut. Similar to most of the transitional economies, the bottleneck of Taiwan's stagnancy rests on governmental interference (Flannery 2001). A unique industrial feature in Taiwan is the existence of state-run companies, including more than 100 companies with total estimated assets of US$600 billion. These state-run conglomerates, with some management by the ex-ruling party KMT, operate in industries such as petroleum, construction, telecommunications, steel, transportation, electronic mass media, real estate, and financial services that control more than 20 percent of Taiwan's gross national product (GNP). Taiwan enacted the Fair Trade Law (similar to the Antitrust Law) in 1991 to prohibit monopolistic and oligopolistic enterprises from unfairly excluding others from the market and thus maintaining unfair pricing policies. Yet, the majority of state-run companies have been excluded from the Fair Trade Law.

The new DPP-led government, which took administrative office in May 2000, has made several attempts to privatize the state-run companies since coming to power. The targets were Taiwan Motor Transport Corp., Taiwan Machinery Manufacturing, Chung Hsing Paper, Taiwan Power Company, Chinese Petroleum Corp., and most recently, the financial and banking institutions. For marketers, privatization means the opening of lucrative business opportunities in Taiwan, especially in the telecommunications, transportation, financing, and banking industries.

Demographic Trends

The major demographic trends in Taiwan include (1) suburbanization, (2) declining population growth, and (3) aging population. Suburbanization is a major trend in Taiwan, especially for those young families who live in northern Taiwan and the greater Taipei area. This will be accomplished by Taipei's mass transit system and the new island-wide highway system that were recently completed. This change will mean success for most business sectors, including durable goods, housing and construction, financing, retailing, and other services.

A declining population growth and an aging population are not as alarming as they sound. Taiwan will remain a very densely populated country even with a zero growth rate in the future. Yet aging may be a problem after 2030, when the proportion of citizens ages sixty-five and above is predicted to reach 20 percent, from the current 8 percent. This could lead to a buildup of a financial burden, in that the elderly social subsidy must be met by the government. Contrary to past family planning programs aimed at trimming population growth, the government now proposes a moderate theme, "two is just right, and three is not too many" to boost the fertility rate.

Consumption

Expenditures on housing and gross rent will continue to grow because of population pressure and the increasing number of new families. The growing number of working women, single families, and new families in suburban areas means that the demand for child care, twenty-four-hour convenience stores, transit services, and other services will increase. Along with this emerging population segment is the teenage market. The youth segment, between the ages of ten and nineteen, represents 18 percent of the total population. Teens influence family purchases. In Taiwan, in particular, the highly fickle and fashion-oriented teens influence broader consumption trends for clothing and footwear, recreation, entertainment, and other services.

Another noticeable shift is that Taiwanese are now traveling internationally in large numbers. Favored destinations are China (via Hong Kong), Japan, the United States, Thailand, Canada, and Australia. The overseas shopping experience not only creates demand for more variety, including Western foods and international brand names, but it has also influenced lifestyle, consumption, and shopping habits back home (see also Clancy 1988).

Products

As the country-of-origin effect continues to be important in Taiwanese consumers' purchasing, it is expected that foreign brands will become more important in the twenty-first century. Furthermore, with greater protection of intellectual property rights, it is expected that demand for upscale goods, sophisticated capital goods, and franchised products and services will continue to grow. Entertainment and cultural services, telecommunications, finance, education and training, medical and hygiene services, and information services are expected to have the highest growth.

Distribution

Superstores, warehouse clubs, and wholesaling outlets will enjoy continuous growth. This is due to the increasing automobile ownership in Taiwan, the completion of the public transit system, and the increasing average size of household dwellings that will enhance consumers' shopping efficiency. The expansion trend will be toward suburban areas in metropolitan Taipei and big cities in middle and south Taiwan.

The growth of convenience stores will level off. It is estimated that a population of 3,500 is needed to support one convenience store in Taiwan. There were 6,000 stores in 2000, which is close to the maximum level of 6,500 stores. The future of supermarkets and department stores may not be bright either. With the average revenue per store continuing to slide, both sectors would seem to be at the stage of maturity and decline. In addition to the saturation factor, the increasing numbers of shopping malls, which provide the same shopping function plus entertainment, will affect the share of supermarket and department stores, which is expected to drop further.

As the retailing industry is in a transition period, wholesaling and physical distribution are changing as well. In Taiwan, five popular physical distribution systems are TDC (Distribution Center built by Trucker), MDC (Distribution Center built by Maker), RDC (Retailer Distribution Center), WDC (Distribution Center built by Wholesaler), and PDC (Process Distribution Center). In terms of industry trends, the wholesaling industry has developed automated product distribution centers that have the potential to increase customer service capabilities while simultaneously decreasing operating costs. The nation has intensified application of the bar code system, the electronic ordering and inventory system, the point-of-sale system, and the computer-aided picking system (Lee 1995).

Marketing Management

Marketing managers must prepare themselves to deal with the consequences of a regional economy and the reality of global competition. These new business ventures are accompanied by a new marketing management philosophy. Rapid changes in manufacturing and design technologies have led to a shorter product life cycle. Growing computer network integration and advancements in decision support systems have made the distribution channel more efficient and compact. The efficiency of mass distribution systems will drive the already low price even lower. For large and small companies alike, the traditional view that assumes labor is the major cost component should be changed. More emphasis should be placed on the changing competitive and technological environments, and also on the importance of marketing value-added services such as customer needs, product quality, distribution efficiency, and relationship marketing.

REFERENCES

Ariff, Mohamed, and A. M. Khalid. 2000. *Liberalization, Growth and the Asian Financial Crisis: Lessons for Developing and Transitional Economies in Asia*. Northampton, MA: Edward Elgar.

Asia-Pacific Economic Cooperation (APEC). 2001. *Members' Economics Indicators*. Singapore: APECSEC. Available at www.apecsec.org.sg/member/indi.html.

Balassa, Bela. 1991. *Economic Policies in the Pacific Area Developing Countries*. London: MacMillan.

Barclay, George W. 1954. *Colonial Development and Population in Taiwan*. Princeton, NJ: Princeton University Press.

Bruno, Ludovica. 2001. *Measuring the Evolution of Information Society: Information Society Index Report*. Framingham, MA: IDC Inc. Available at www.idc.com.

Carlucci, F., R. Hunter, and Z. Khalilzad. 2000. *Taking Charge: A Bipartisan Report to the President Elect on Foreign Policy and National Security*. Santa Monica, CA: The RAND Corporation.

Chai, Winberg. 2000. "The Transformation of Mass Media in Taiwan Since 1950: Introduction." *Asian Affair, An American Review* 27 (3): 133.

Chang, Hua-Jen. 1994. "Impact of Inflation, Output, Employment, and Income Effect in Budget Deficits for Taiwan: A Forecast of Regional Input–Output Approach." *Journal of Policy Modeling* 16 (June): 345–51.

Chang, Li Dong, and B. Sternquist. 1993. "Taiwanese Department Store Industry: An Overview." *International Journal of Retail & Distribution Management* 21 (1):26–34.

China External Trade Development Council (CETRA). 2001. "Summary of Taiwan External Trade Performance, Taipei, Taiwan." Available at www.taiwantrade.com.tw.

Clancy, Michael. 1988. *The Business Guide to Taiwan*. Singapore: B-H Asia.

Clifford, Mark L. 2001. "Can Two Chinas Live Together in the WTO?" *Business Week*, November 19: 20.

Directorate General of Budget, Accounting and Statistics (DGBAS). 2001. "Executive Yuan," Taipei, Taiwan. Available at http://eng.dgbas.gov.tw.

Euromonitor International. 2001. Retail Trade International (Taiwan): Global Market Information Database. London: Euromonitor International. Available at www.euromonitor.com.

Executive Yuan. 2001. "Global Logistics Development Plan." Taipei, Taiwan: Center for Economic Deregulation and Innovation, Council for Economic Planning and Development. Available at www.cedi.cepd.gov.tw/eng/

Flannery, Russell. 2001. "The Ghosts of Chiang Kai-shek: The Taiwan Economy Can Get Out of Its Rut Only if the Government Meddles Less in Business." *Forbes*, September 17: 22–23.

Focus on Internet News and Data (FIND). 2001. *Internet Subscribers in Taiwan*. Taiwan: Internet Society. Available at www.isoc.org.tw.

Government Information Office (GIO). 2001. "ROC Snapshot," Taipei, Taiwan. Available at www.gio.gov.tw/taiwan-website/4–oa/index.html#3.

Gulati, Umesh C. 1992. "The Foundations of Rapid Economic Growth: The Case of the Four Tigers." *American Journal of Economics & Sociology* 51 (April): 161–72.

Lee, Zen-fung. 1995. *Seven-Eleven Takes over Taiwan.* Taipei, Taiwan: Yuan-liu Publishing, Inc. (in Chinese).

Liu, Shuei-Shen. 1992. "Seven-Eleven in Taiwan." In *Taiwan's Enterprises in Global Perspective*, ed. N.T. Wang. Armonk, NY: M.E. Sharpe.

Lu, Hsiu-Lien A. 1994. "Women Liberation: The Taiwanese Experience." In *The Other Taiwan, 1945 to the Present*, ed. M.A. Rubinstein. Armonk, NY: M.E. Sharpe.

Mainland Affairs Council (MAC). 2001. "Statistics on Cross-Strait Exchanges." Available at www.mac.gov.tw/english/index1-e.htm.

Ministry of Transportation and Communication (MOTC). 1999. *Internet Users Survey*, Vol. 42. Taipei: Taiwan Census Bureau. Available at www.motc.gov.tw/en.

Naughton, Tony. 2000. "Taiwan: An Island State with Economic Insulation?" In *The Causes and Impact of the Asian Financial Crisis*, ed. T.V. Ho and C. Harvie. New York: Palgrave Macmillan.

Parish, William L., and Robert J. Willis. 1993. "Daughters, Education, and Family Budgets: Taiwan Experiences." *Journal of Human Resources* 28 (4): 863–98.

Rainmaker. 2001. "Adspending of Top 20 Product Categories in Top Five Media." Available at www.rainmaker.com.tw.

ROC Yearbook. 2001. Government Information Office, Taiwan. Available at www.gio.gov.tw/taiwan-website/5–gp/yearbook/index.htm.

Shao, A. T., M. A. Raymond, and C. Taylor. 1999. "Shifting Advertising Appeals in Taiwan." *Journal of Advertising Research* 39 (November/December): 61–69.

Snow, Edgar. 1948. *Red Star over China.* New York: Random House.

Taipei Association of Advertising Agencies (TAAA). Available at www.taaa.org.tw.

Taiwan Yearbook. 2003. Available at www.gio.gov.tw/taiwan-website/5–gp/yearbook/chpt05.htm#2.

U.S. Patent and Trademark Office (USPTO). 2004. "PTMD Special Report: All Patents, All Types, January 1977–December 2004." Office of Electronic Information Products/PTMD, Washington, D.C. Available at www.uspto.gov/web/offices/ac/ido/oeip/taf/apat.pdf.

World Bank. 2000. "Beyond Economic Growth, Meeting the Challenges of Global Development." Available at www.worldbank.org/depweb/beyond/beyond.htm.

World Factbook. 2003. Central Intelligence Agency, Washington DC. Available at www.cia.gov/cia/publications/factbook/geos/tw.html#Govt.

World Trade Organization (WTO). 2001. "International Trade Statistics," Geneva, Switzerland. Available at www.wto.org/english/res_e/statis_e/its2001_e/its01_toc_e.htm.

CHAPTER 17

THAILAND

Consumer Behavior and Marketing

NITTAYA WONGTADA, BUSAYA VIRAKUL, AND ANUSORN SINGHAPAKDI

OVERVIEW

Changes in consumer behavior and marketing practices in Thailand are the main focus of this chapter. Thailand enjoyed an economic boom during the late 1980s and early 1990s. In 1997, the country was strongly affected by the economic crisis that hit many Southeast Asian nations. The crisis created an awareness of the importance of globalization and the urgent need to make social institutions and business operations internationally competitive. To cope with the rapidly emerging global environment, many changes occurred in policies, focus, structures, and strategies within both the government and private sector. After 2000, although not fully recovered from the crisis, Thailand resumed development activities at full pace. The market is vibrant with new activities of both large and small operations. Subsequently, increased competition is unavoidable. Large businesses exploit their advantages in the market while smaller ones retract to niche strategies. Some, though not many, prominent local brands have started to appear. It is expected that the second half of the current decade will see even more intense competition as the country opens up to goods, services, and investment from China. Thailand's keys to survival in this new environment will be more precise targeting of markets, more innovative marketing strategies, and improved efficiency.

INTRODUCTION

Geography

Thailand has a total land area of 514,000 square kilometers, which makes it about the same size as France. It is situated in the center of the Indochina Peninsula and is bordered by Myanmar (Burma), Cambodia, Laos, Malaysia, the Gulf of Thailand, and the Andaman Sea. Its population of approximately sixty million is predominantly ethnic Thai. The Chinese, who make up about 15 percent of the population, form the largest non-Thai ethnic group, with most living in the commercial center of Bangkok. Through successive waves of immigration and intermarriage, however, the ethnic Chinese are little different from ethnic Thais in terms of cultural practices and national identity.

Approximately 70 percent of the Thai population lives in rural areas, and the rest lives in the capital city, Bangkok, its surroundings, and other major provincial cities. Bangkok is located in the lower Central Plains, and the traditional language of this region has been adopted as the national tongue. The Thai language is tonal; that is, the same word can have different meanings if the tone differs.

Bangkok serves as the administrative, financial, industrial, and commercial center of the country, with a population varying from six million to as many as ten million after harvesting season, when agricultural labor migrates into the city seeking work to supplement income from farming. The other major regional centers are Chiang Mai in the north, Na Korn Ratchasima in the northeast, and Songkla/Hat Yai in the south.

History

Throughout its history, Thailand has been influenced by foreign cultures. The Thais are descended from an ethnic group closely related to the Chinese. They originated in South China and then migrated southward in successive waves into Southeast Asia during the eleventh and twelfth centuries (US-ASEAN Business Council 2002). Their social and cultural influences interacted with the society and culture of the Khmers, Mons, Malays, and other regional ethnic groups, and eventually evolved into the one homogeneous Thai culture today. The first Thai Empire, Sukhothai, was established in the thirteenth and fourteenth centuries. The Thai monarchy and Buddhism are as old as the Thai nation. Starting from King Ramkhamhaeng, who led Sukhothai to growth and prosperity, to the current Chakri dynasty, the monarchy has continued to lead the country and to patronize Buddhism. The status of the monarchy has changed, however, from absolute monarchy to a constitutional one since 1932.

The capital city of Thailand moved from Sukhothai to Ayutthaya, then to Thonburi, and eventually to Bangkok, the current capital city. By the time Bangkok became the capital in 1782, contacts between the Europeans and Thais had already begun. During this Western colonial era, Thailand was the only Southeast Asian country that retained its independence. However, part of its historic territory was forfeited in treaties that assured its sovereignty. During the nineteenth century, the Thai monarchy started programs and policies to modernize the nation. The influence of Western culture was evident. The abolition of slavery, the end of the absolute monarchy, and the modernization of the educational system are some examples of Western influences on Thai culture.

Prevailing Culture

The following traits and institutions may be used to define the modern Thai culture.

Buddhism

Approximately 95 percent of Thais practice Buddhism, a religion that emphasizes coexistence, tolerance, and individual initiative. As a result of this open-mindedness, other religions are also freely practiced. There is a large Muslim community in the south, and the precepts of Christianity, Confucianism, Hinduism, and Sikhism are celebrated and practiced by various minorities throughout the nation (US-ASEAN Business Council 2002). The influence of Buddhism on daily life in Thailand is evident. The many temples, the saffron-robed monks making their daily early-morning alms rounds, and the medallions bearing Buddha images worn by most Thais, are but a few indications of their strong faith. Although Thais use the Western calendar, they also use a Buddhist calendar. Many of their holidays reflect the influence of Buddhism.

Monarchy

Currently, Thailand is governed by a constitutional monarchy with the king as head of state. Sovereignty is derived from the Thai people and exercised by the king through the National Assembly, the Council of Ministers (Cabinet), and the courts under the constitution. Despite the many changes in the country's political scene, the royal family provides a unifying and stabilizing force in Thailand.

Thailand developed into a constitutional monarchy in 1932 when King Prajadhipok (Rama VII) introduced a more democratic form of government. The present monarch, Rama IX, is a direct descendant of Rama V, who began the modernization of many Thai institutions in the nineteenth century. Rama IX, crowned on May 5, 1950, is the longest reigning monarch in Thai history.

Hierarchy and Seniority

Thai society is organized in a hierarchical fashion: people occupy differently ranked positions (Mulder 1992). Superior versus inferior relationships, therefore, characterize most relationships. There are several overlapping hierarchies in Thai culture, based on such factors as age, social class, education, and position. Examples of hierarchy relationships include parent–child, teacher–student, and patron–client. In all cases, people of lower status are expected to pay courtesy to those of higher status (Aufrecht and Ractham 1991; Mulder 1992). When dealing with new acquaintances, most Thai will try to place them in the hierarchy of social status. As a result, Thais tend to be respectful in order to avoid misplacing status (US-ASEAN Business Council 2002).

Loyalty

Within the Thai culture, the sense of reciprocal loyalty and responsibility for family and close friends is strong (Aufrecht and Ractham 1991). This obligation means that a person must be available, when asked, to offer assistance within his or her ability. Similarly, family and friends are obligated to reciprocate when the person is in need.

Avoiding Confrontation

Open disagreement among Thais is rare. Thais are supposed to be polite and to avoid open conflict (Mulder 1992). "Face" is important; therefore, conciliatory compromise is always the best approach when conflict exists.

Resilience

Thais believe that they may be able to interact with foreign influences without diminishing the role of their own culture. They also believe their history shows that they have successfully achieved this balance in the past (US-ASEAN Business Council 2002).

Thailand was the only free country in Southeast Asia during the Western colonial era. The nation emerged victorious after World War II, even though it declared war on the allies. These events have convinced many Thais that their culture is resilient enough to be able to incorporate and accommodate any foreign influence (Mulder 1992).

CHANGES IN THE ENVIRONMENT

Economic Environment

From the 1980s to the early 1990s, the Thai economy grew rapidly. However, in the latter half of the 1990s, the country faced a severe economic recession. As shown in Table 17.1, the Thai economy is still in the process of recovering after having plunged into negative growth in 1997 and 1998. The global economic slump that started at the beginning of 2001 has slowed the Thai economy, which depends heavily on exports. This section will describe the changes in some important economic variables that directly influence the consumption of Thai consumers. These variables are economic growth, the 1997 economic crisis and recovery, changes in real income, the employment rate, international trade, and infrastructure.

Economic Growth

Thailand had impressive economic growth from the middle of the 1980s until the middle of the 1990s. The national growth rates, ranging from 8 percent to 12 percent, ranked Thailand among the fastest-growing economies in the world. This economic success was recognized as a result of Thai government policies that focused on generating national income through producing goods for export and tourism (Dixon 1996; Office of the National Economic and Social Development Board [NESDB], 2000). With this rapid economic growth, the country's gross national product (GNP) almost doubled from US$1,292 in 1989 to US$2,371 in 1994 (*BOI Investment Review* 1994). It was forecast (see *Bangkok Post* 1994) that the future of the Thai economy would continue to be vibrant. Moreover, Thailand was anticipated to achieve newly industrializing country status before 2000 (*Consumers of Southeast Asia* 1994).

The 1997 Economic Crisis

Thailand's impressive economic growth came to a drastic halt in 1997 when the country encountered the financial crisis experienced simultaneously by other countries in Asia, such as Malaysia, South Korea, and Indonesia. The cause of the crisis was largely due to mismanagement, particularly in the finance and banking industry, which placed Thailand's economy in heavy reliance on external funds. It can be argued that the cause of this crisis dates back to the early 1990s, when Thai governments followed the International Monetary Fund (IMF) guidelines and liberalized the financial market. The Bangkok International Banking Facility (BIBF) was established in 1992 to allow local and foreign banks to engage in onshore and offshore lending and to accept deposits and to lend foreign currencies (United Nations Development Programme [UNDP] 1999). Unfortunately, there was no effective financial monitoring system implemented as part of BIBF. As a result, companies in Thailand rushed to take advantage of cheap foreign credit, creating a significant amount of foreign debt. Furthermore, a large portion of the money was borrowed for speculations in such nonproductive sectors as real estate, private hospitals, and the stock market.

Following the massive influx of foreign capital was the combination of "superficial" or "bubble" high economic growth, an overvalued currency, and overconsumption of imported luxury items. Due to higher wage rates as a result of the dramatic economic growth, Thailand began to lose its competitiveness to emerging competitors, including China and Vietnam, in some traditional industries such as textiles, garments, and footwear. The strengthening of the U.S. dollar against

Table 17.1

Thailand's Key Economic Indicators, 1998–2000

% Change compared with the previous year	1998	1999P	2000E
GDP at current year price	−1.9	1.1	6.6
GDP at 1988 prices	−10.2	4.2	4.5
Agricultural sector	−1.4	3.9	2.1
Nonagricultural sector	−11.2	4.2	5.4
Industry	−10.8	11.1	7.0
Domestic demand	−23.9	5.4	7.0
Overall investment	−44.2	−3.7	8.5
Overall consumption	−10.5	3.4	5.3
Exports and services	6.7	8.9	6.8
Imports and services	−22.3	20.2	12.7
Inflation (Consumer price index: average)	8.1	0.3	2.5–3.0
External sector			
Export value (in US$)	−6.8	7.4	9.6
Export volume	8.1	11.5	8.0
Export prices	−13.8	−3.7	1.5
Merchandised imports (in US$)	−33.8	17.7	19.0
Volume	−27.4	23.8	16.3
Import prices	−8.8	−4.9	2.3
Monetary sector			
Commercial bank credits (including BIBF*)	−3.2	−2.8	2.0
Commercial bank deposit	8.8	−0.5	3.0
Broad money (M2a)	6.1	1.3	7.5
Money base	0.3	30.8	−10.5
Public finance			
Expenditures (billions of baht)	830.0	825.0	860.0
% Change	−10.3	−0.6	4.2
Government cash balance (% of GDP)	−5.2	−5.3	−5.0

Source: From Bank of Thailand, *Economic and Financial Report 1999* (Bangkok: Bank of Thailand, 2000).
Note: P = preliminary; E = estimated; * = Excluding the valuation change from exchange rate changes on BIBF (Bangkok International Banking Facility) credits (exchange rate on June 30, 1997).

other currencies also caused Thai exports to be uncompetitive in the world market. Thailand was facing a large government deficit and sharp export declines that led many foreign currency dealers to become increasingly nervous about persistent rumors of a baht devaluation. There were two massive attacks on the baht in the first six months of 1997. The government, with the encouragement of financial companies, banks, and many large enterprises with large debts in foreign currencies, sought to defend the dollar-pegged baht. Following the government's policy, the Bank of Thailand had to draw heavily upon the nation's foreign reserves (see more about the 1997 Thai economic crisis in UNDP 1999).

The depletion of foreign reserves forced the Bank of Thailand to announce a "manage float" policy on July 2, 1997, the first day of the crisis. The depreciation of the baht pushed nonperforming loans denominated in foreign currency to skyrocket. Many businesses plunged into negative balance sheets. Thailand was in a big crisis because of the shortage of cash flow and severe credit crunch, both of which contributed to drastic economic contraction. Industrial production and retail sales fell. In all, the crisis left the country in 1997 with debts to foreign institutes of around US$109 billion or 70 percent of gross domestic product (GDP) (Bank of Thailand 2001).

Table 17.2

Vulnerable Indicators Benchmark of Foreign Debt

	Indicator benchmarks[a]			Thailand[b]		
	Low	Medium	High	1998	1999	2000
Debt/GDP[c] (%)	<46	48–80	>80	93.1	77.8	65.1
Debt/export goods and services (XGS)[c] (%)	<132	132–220	>220	155.6	130.4	95.5
Debt service ratio[d] (%)	←	Less than 20	→	21.4	19.4	15.4
Reserve/short-term debt (%)	←	More than 150	→	103.9	178.0	222.3

[a]Data from Supanich Tientip and Regina Woraurai, "Financial Liberalization Policy: Towards a New Paradigm," paper presented at the Bank of Thailand Symposium, Bangkok (2001).

[b]Data from Bank of Thailand, *Economic and Financial Statistics (January 2002)* (Bangkok: Bank of Thailand, 2002a).

[c]Average GDP and XGS in three years.

[d]Does not include advanced debt payment.

Economic Recovery

The first two years after the 1997 crisis were perhaps the most difficult economic time in Thailand's history. Thai economic growth figures were negative: –0.4 percent in 1997 and –10.2 percent in 1998. The Thai economy started its recovery in 1999. The economic growth rose to 4.2 percent in 1999 and 4.3 percent in 2000 (Bank of Thailand 2000; NESDB 2001b). Reforms and changes in policy and structures were implemented in many areas that were critical in helping to alleviate the depth of the economic crisis. Some important measures included:

1. government interventions in domestic demand by accelerating expenditures to stimulate the economy (which resulted in an expansion in both public and private spending);
2. changes in government and business strategies to promote export-oriented industries (e.g., vehicles and parts, food and beverages, iron and steel) to help generate income;
3. a debt-restructuring policy and plans to help Thai businesses revive their operations;
4. reinforcement of the financial sector reform policy to help upgrade and maintain the competitiveness of the Thai financial system internationally;
5. implementation of effective monetary policy to help attract foreign investment, facilitate international trading, and stabilize economic growth; and
6. organizational restructuring of the Bank of Thailand to help improve its effectiveness in supervising the country's financial institutions.

Table 17.2 illustrates the benchmark of foreign debt in relation to the economic conditions. It also shows some improvements in Thailand's debt management performance three years after the crisis. At the end of 2001, Thailand owed around US$76 billion to foreign institutions. The debt accounted for approximately 63 percent of the nation's GDP (Bank of Thailand 2002a). Exports and tourism are anticipated to be the country's major income-producing areas. However, Thailand's economy also depends on the influence of the global economy. The adverse impact of the global economic downturn in 2001 caused the amount of Thai exports to decline for the entire year (Bank of Thailand 2002b). Thailand's economic recovery, therefore, could face some delays if the global economy does not improve.

Table 17.3

Thailand's Consumer Price Index and Inflation Rate, 1996–2000

	1996	1997	1998	1999	2000
Consumer price index (1994 = 100)	112.0	118.2	127.8	128.2	130.2
Consumer price index (Δ%)	5.9	5.6	8.1	0.3	1.6
Food and beverages	8.9	7.0	9.6	−0.9	−1.1
Nonfood and beverages	3.7	4.6	7.3	1.0	3.2

Source: From Bank of Thailand, *Annual Economic Report* (Bangkok: Bank of Thailand, 1998, 1999, 2000, 2001).

Inflation

Before 1997, while high inflation was a problem for Thailand, this did not hinder the rise of real income, because the country's productivity exceeded its inflation rate. As compared with the expected rate of inflation of 2.5–2.6 percent for developed countries, Thailand's overall inflation level was relatively high: 3.3 percent in 1993, 5 percent in 1994, and 5.8 percent in 1995. However, because the country's GNP growth rate had been higher than its inflation rate—8.5 percent, 8.9 percent, and 8.8 percent in 1994, 1995, and 1996, respectively—its real gain income was substantial (Schwartz 1994; Bank of Thailand 1997, 1998).

During and after the economic crisis of 1997, despite the fact that the baht had been devalued by 50 percent, the annual inflation rates were below expectations—they had been estimated to be around 10–12 percent (*Bangkok Post Economic Review* 1998). This is due to such important factors as strong price competition among businesses as a result of shrinking market demand. Moreover, given that Thailand is a major producer and exporter of agricultural products, its strong agricultural sector has helped to keep food prices down. The monetary discipline that helped to stabilize the baht and the governments' effort to prevent stockpiling and exploitative price increases also contributed as major conditions keeping the inflation rate lower than expected (see Table 17.3).

International Trade

International trade has always been crucial to Thailand's economy. Table 17.4 provides a summary of Thailand's export and import figures in recent years. During the past two decades, high economic growth has been credited, in part, to Thailand's international trade, which had moved away from traditional, mostly agricultural products toward high-value-added goods. In 1993, Thailand's top five exports were electronics and components, textiles, frozen seafood, canned and processed foods, and gems and jewelry. Traditional exports, such as rubber, rice, and tapioca, became less important. Agricultural products faired poorly in 1993, bringing a total value of 13.3 percent (*BOI Investment Review* 1994).

At the same time, the country imported more high-tech goods, such as telecommunication equipment, computer equipment, medical equipment, and food-processing and packaging machinery in preparation for future exports (*Consumers of Southeast Asia* 1994). During the peak time, the volume of exports and imports expanded at a rate of more than 100 percent annually. As a whole, the country continued to have a negative trade balance. Nevertheless, the Thai balance of payments remained positive for two reasons. First, the Thai government deliberately encour-

Table 17.4

Thailand's Exports and Imports

	1997	1998	1999	2000	2001
Exports					
Total exports (billions of US$) f.o.b.	56.7	52.9	56.8	67.9	63.2
Total exports (Δ%)	4.4	−6.8	7.4	19.6	−6.9
Imports					
Total imports (billions of US$) c.i.f.	61.3	40.6	47.5	62.4	60.7
Total imports (Δ%)	−13.2	−33.8	16.9	31.3	−2.8

Source: Bank of Thailand, *Annual Economic Report* (Bangkok: Bank of Thailand, 1998, 1999, 2000, 2001); Bank of Thailand, *Economic and Financial Statistics (January 2002)* (Bangkok: Bank of Thailand, 2002a); Office of the National Economic and Social Development Board, *Economic Conditions of Thailand in 2000 and Trends for 2001* [in Thai] (Bangkok: NESDB, 2001b).

aged more foreign investment by liberalizing international trade and investment regulations (Thai Military Bank 1995). The government was aggressively courting foreign investors by using different strategies (Pinkerton 1992). For example, in 1991, Thailand implemented several economic reforms, including tariff reduction and foreign-exchange liberalization, as part of its overall national economic and social development plan. The removal of such foreign trade and investment barriers greatly accelerated foreign direct investment and the concomitant economic growth. Second, after the introduction of the Securities and Stock Exchanges Act and the establishment of the Securities and Exchange Commission in 1992, confidence in the Thai market increased. This led more large foreign financial institutions to invest in the Thai financial market (*Bangkok Post Economic Review* 1993).

Unfortunately, the situation has changed dramatically since the beginning of the 1997 economic crisis (*Bangkok Post Economic Review* 1998). Foreign capital has dried up and imports of both consumer and industrial goods slowed for the first time. Exports of agricultural products and other previously noncompetitive manufactured goods, such as textiles and leather goods, surged. This led to a reassessment of the country's international trade policy. The agricultural sector has been the country's economic backbone and depends very little on imported raw materials. Therefore, it has benefited significantly from the devaluation of the baht. As a result, the Thai government has reassessed the development plans of this sector to try to make it a sustainable, competitive advantage for Thailand. For example, encouraging Thai businesses to export agricultural products (canned or processed foods and fruits and vegetables) to international markets has been recognized as one of the government's strategies to restore the country's economic strength (Bank of Thailand 2001; NESDB 2001b).

Manufactured products, such as vehicles and parts, electrical appliances, computers, integrated circuits and other computer parts, as well as other electronics, were among Thailand's top exports in 1999 and 2000 and are still considered the country's leading export products (NESDB 2001b). However, there are some changing situations that may impede Thailand's international trade. For example, the country's export markets may be strained by strong competition from other countries, such as China and Vietnam, where agriculture and labor are becoming more favorable for producing the important exports that Thailand has. The problems are further compounded given that China has now been admitted to the World Trade Organization, and Vietnam has secured a bilateral trade agreement with the United States; these recent events will definitely help facilitate

Table 17.5

Thailand's Labor Market Condition, 1997–2000 (million persons)

	1997	1998	1999	2000
Population	60.82	61.47	61.66	61.88
Labor force	32.57	32.46	32.72	33.22
Employment	31.52	30.10	30.66	31.29
Agriculture	14.20	13.45	13.88	13.89
Nonagriculture	17.33	16.65	16.79	17.40
Unemployment	0.49	1.41	1.37	1.19
Unemployment rate (%)	1.5	4.4	4.2	3.6
Seasonal unemployment	0.56	0.89	0.69	0.74
Seasonal unemployment rate (%)	1.7	2.7	2.1	2.2

Source: From Bank of Thailand, *Economic and Financial Statistics (January 2002)* (Bangkok: Bank of Thailand, 2002).

both China's and Vietnam's exports, especially to the United States. Moreover, the global economy will always have a major influence on Thailand's exports. It is widely acknowledged that Thailand's economic recovery depends significantly on how well Thai businesses can reap benefit from global demand (Bank of Thailand 2002b; NESDB 2001b). Reforms in corporate and industrial sectors to improve export competitiveness are strongly recommended by Thai policy makers so that Thailand will continue to be one of the important exporters in the Southeast Asian region.

Employment

During the period of economic prosperity, the unemployment rate in Thailand was less than 1 percent (*Bangkok Post* 1994). An employment rate this low created a labor-scarcity problem, especially in skilled labor. In the past, the country's growth had been based on industries that required low skill levels, such as textiles, food processing, and canning. Industry's labor needs were satisfied by transferring people from the agricultural to the industrial sectors. However, several industries had evolved into new higher-technology production and services that required a better-trained labor force (Thai Military Bank 1995).

In the first two years after the 1997 economic crisis, there was a sharp reduction in labor demand. Unemployment rates rose sharply to 4.4 percent in 1998 and remained at 4.2 percent in 1999 (see Table 17.5). Unemployment was not limited to unskilled labor but was also composed of highly educated groups who lost their jobs as a result of the closing of financial institutions and of corporate failures and downsizing. Many unskilled laborers who had moved to urban areas to work in factories or low-paying service jobs before the economic crisis, however, could be reabsorbed by the resurging agricultural sector. The skilled laborers, on the contrary, had a tougher time finding compatible jobs. Many were forced to accept lower-paid positions or became petty cash vendors. As a result, average individual earnings had been declining, and this resulted in a much weaker consumer spending rate in recent years.

As described earlier in this chapter, the Thai economy showed signs of recovery from the crisis in 1999. The unemployment rate declined slightly. Employment expansion was found in hotel and restaurant sectors in 2001, in line with a tourism increase, and also in the construction sector. However, even though there have been some positive indicators, the global economic

Table 17.6

Annual Household Income (in Baht) and Income Distribution

(a) Annual household income[a]

	1994	1996	1998
Whole country	99,144	129,348	149,904
North	75,120	99,972	117,348
Northeast	67,188	88,656	102,552
Central	104,688	238,884	151,716
South	96,168	118,152	137,532
Bangkok Metro area	197,016	263,364	299,148

(b) Gini index[b] (per capita welfare) and percentage share of income[c]

	1990	1992	1994	1996	1998
Gini index	48.1	49.9	48.6	47.7	48.1
Lowest 20%	4.9	4.5	4.6	4.8	4.8
Second 20%	8.4	7.9	8.3	8.5	8.4
Third 20%	12.7	12.2	12.7	12.9	12.7
Fourth 20%	19.9	19.8	20.3	20.5	20.2
Highest 20%	54.1	55.6	54.1	53.3	53.9

[a]Data from Alpha Research, *Thailand in Figures 2000–2001* (Bangkok: Alpha Research, 2000).

[b]See more of the Gini index in The World Bank, *2001 World Development Indicator* (Washington, DC: The World Bank, 2001), pp. 70–73.

[c]Data from Office of the National Economic and Social Development Board, *Evaluation Report of the First Half of the Eighth National Economic and Social Development Plan 1997–1998* (Bangkok: NESDB, 2000).

---

slump from the beginning of 2001 has been a significant factor in making the Thai government, social and economic specialists, and businesspeople cautious about expecting major improvements in labor employment.

Income Distribution

The previous rapid industrialization in Thailand resulted in more household income nationwide, but this was not equally distributed. The most significant increase occurred in the Bangkok metropolitan area. The gap between the lowest 20 percent and the top 20 percent income brackets was wide. While the income of the lowest 20 percent was only 4.8 percent of the nation's total income, the income of the highest 20 percent accounted for 53.9 percent (see Table 17.6). The 1997 economic crisis affected most Thais, but the effect was felt mostly among people who had an income near or lower than the poverty line. Making income distribution more even among various groups in the country has been one of the main national policies of most Thai governments.

Before the 1997 economic crisis, the income of workers in the manufacturing sector increased more than in other sectors. A comparison of the figures for the year 2000 with those for 1990 suggests that the average per capita income of workers in the manufacturing sector increased by 87.8 percent compared to 30.9 percent and 62.1 percent for the agricultural and service sectors, respectively. However, the impact of the economic crisis could change this income pattern. Although the average income of employees in the manufacturing sector will continue to be higher than in other sectors, the agricultural sector could see some improvements. The Thai government has recognized the importance of the agricultural sector both to the strength of the nation and to the country's exports. Policies supporting agricultural-based trade development have always been part of the National Development Plans (NESDB 1997, 2000). The importance of the agricultural sector is increasingly visible considering the current national development policy (NESDB 2001b; Bank of Thailand 2001, 2002b). Because at least 45 percent of employed Thai workers and 25 percent of the country's households are involved in agriculture (National Statistical Office 2002), a government policy intended to improve the average income of people in the agricultural sector could prove to be beneficial to the stability and growth of the Thai economy.

Infrastructure

Rapid economic growth in Thailand has created a drain on the country's infrastructure. Power shortages, an inadequate telecommunications system, chronic urban traffic problems, and port congestion are among the main problems (see also Ungpakorn 1993; Thai Military Bank 1995). These problems are most acute in Bangkok and are appearing in other major cities as well. Traffic in Bangkok approaches gridlock. The city has only 112 main roads, with a total length of 524 kilometers, and 4,280 smaller roads. Its road surface is less than 11 percent of the city's land area—road surface in New York is less than 23.2 percent of New York's land area; in Tokyo, it is 13.6 percent of Tokyo's land area. The number of vehicles in Bangkok increased from 1.1 million in 1984 to 1.7 million in 1989. In 1999, there were 2.3 million cars, vans, and pickup trucks, and 1.7 million motorcycles registered in Bangkok (Alpha Research 2000). The rapid increase in the number of automobiles causes chronic traffic jams in Bangkok and other large provinces. For instance, the average speed of traffic in business areas is less than seven kilometers per hour and is less than twenty kilometers per hour in other parts of Bangkok (*Consumers of Southeast Asia* 1994).

Communication services were improved by new telephone line installations. In 1993, there were only three lines per 100 people in Bangkok (Chantranontwong 1993); that number increased to 8.5 lines per 100 people in 1999 (Alpha Research 2000). However, with the construction expansion, water and utility shortages are still common problems. According to the 2001 *World Competitiveness Yearbook*'s (Institute for Management Development [IMD] 2001) ranking of forty-nine countries on their international competitiveness, Thailand was placed at number forty in terms of basic infrastructure (see Table 17.7).

Pollution

Another problem associated with rapid economic development is pollution. Over the past decade, the environment of the country's large cities has deteriorated. Air pollution, water pollution, solid waste, and excessive noise are the most acute environmental problems (Thailand Development Research Institute 1990; Clifton 1994). Because of heavy traffic congestion, air pollution has worsened in the big cities. Noise pollution in Bangkok also exceeds, by several times, the recommended environment standard. Water has become heavily polluted due to the waste discarded from households and factories. Solid waste frequently accumulates faster than the collection capacity. More than 5,000 tons of waste are generated daily in Bangkok, whereas its collection capacity is about 400 tons per day (cf. Petmark and Unksutanasombat 1990). The uncollected solid waste is often disposed of in undesignated

Table 17.7

Ranking of Competitiveness in Infrastructure

Ranking	Country	Score	Ranking	Country	Score
1	United States	75.20	14	Hong Kong	50.20
2	Finland	67.72	16	Taiwan	48.42
3	Sweden	65.37	19	Japan	47.30
4	Iceland	64.42	23	United Kingdom	41.97
5	Singapore	63.51	34	South Korea	29.74
6	Australia	62.67	38	Malaysia	23.58
7	The Netherlands	60.07	39	China	23.01
8	Canada	59.32	40	Thailand	20.13
9	Switzerland	58.29	41	Philippines	18.41
10	Germany	56.58	49	Indonesia	8.35

Source: Institute for Management Development (IMD), *World Competitiveness Yearbook* (Infrastructure Ranking as of April 2001) (Lausanne, Switzerland: IMD, 2001).

areas, including canals. Pollution in Bangkok's canals and of the canals of the large provinces has killed off the fish and other water animals. Table 17.8 illustrates some indicators used for monitoring the country's pollution situation.

Corruption

In addition to producing congested streets, strained communications, and inadequate infrastructure, the nation's economic advancement has also affected corruption. The acceptance of widespread corruption by rising middle-class Thais has declined, because such practices have frightened off large foreign investment (cf. Stone and Janssen 1991). This group, which has gained the most from the decade of economic prosperity, views the corruption as a roadblock to economic advancement.

The uprising against the Thai military government in 1992 by the middle-class workers indicates this attitude change (Crossette 1992). The majority of the demonstrators were middle-class workers, who carried cellular phones and used facsimile machines to spread news when other mass media were censored. The following year marked the first time in Thailand's political history that the country elected a prime minister who was not tainted by either corruption or authoritarian tactics (Tasker 1993).

Paradoxically, the economic downturn has resulted in increased public disapproval of corruption. After the strong resistance, the government eventually yielded to widespread public pressure, and the Thai parliament successfully passed a new Constitution in 1997 (*Bangkok Post Economic Review* 1998). Under this constitution, the government's cabinet members must report their financial status and sources of wealth. Those suspected of being corrupt will be investigated and prosecuted.

Relative to the political and social climate before 1990, there has been a reduction in corruption partly due to establishment of the new constitution and overall public attitudes. Strategies to reduce corruption in Thailand have been widely studied and well-documented (Poapongsakorn, Yavaprabhas, Phongpaichit, and Thairungroj 2000). Implementing the anticorruption principle and policy into effective practices, however, requires time and effort. According to the 2001 survey by Transparency International (TI) (2002), Thailand's image in corruption is still significantly less impressive

Table 17.8

Pollution Indicators, 1995–1999

	Standard	1995	1996	1997	1998	1999
(a) Average water quality of the Chao Praya River						
Lower Chao Praya River						
OD	>2.0	1.0	0.7	0.5	1.0	1.8
BOD	<4.0	3.5	6.2	3.1	2.8	3.3
Coliform	—	959,000	85,000	46,000	14,500	44,160
Middle Chao Praya River						
OD	>4.0	5.7	4.6	4.1	4.5	4.7
BOD	<2.0	1.4	1.0	1.5	0.8	1.8
Coliform	<20,000	76,000	12,000	2,000	2,700	7,805
Upper Chao Praya River						
OD	>6.0	6.5	5.8	6.4	5.7	6.3
BOD	<1.5	1.6	1.1	1.2	0.9	2.1
Coliform	<5,000	402,000	20,000	20,000	1,300	3,000
(b) Air quality at measurement stations in Bangkok metropolis						
Office of Environment Policy and Planning						
Carbon monoxide	34.20	1.24	1.00	1.10	1.00	1.50
Suspended particulates	0.10	0.14	0.17	0.12	0.08	0.08
Lead	10.00	0.11	0.07	0.07	0.05	0.03
Meteorological Department						
Carbon monoxide	34.20	8.93	18.10	0.60	0.70	1.50
Suspended particulates	0.10	0.12	0.09	0.10	0.08	n.a.
Lead	10.00	0.39	0.43	0.15	0.20	n.a.
(c) Sound levels at measurement stations in Bangkok metropolis						
Chulalongkorn Hospital	<70	80.40	77.80	74.45	n.a	n.a.
Ministry of Science, Technology, and Environment	<70	75.70	73.00	70.05	75.30	n.a.
Odian Circle	<70	69.70	66.00	70.50	n.a.	79.60
Din Daeng Road	<70	—	75.65	74.70	75.95	74.35

Sources:
1. Office of the National Economic and Social Development Board (NESDB), *Social Indicators 1995–1999* (Bangkok: NESDB, 2001).
2. (a) Standard values of oxygen content dissolving in water (OD) in the lower, middle, and upper Chao Praya River are not less than 2.0, 4.0, and 6.0 milligrams per liter, respectively; standard values of bacteria enabled to dissolve (BOD) at the lower, middle, and upper Chao Praya River are less than 4.0, 2.0, and 1.5 milligrams per liter, respectively; standard values of coliform at specific areas of the middle and upper Chao Praya River are not more than 20,000 and 5,000 MPN per milliliter, respectively.
3. (b) Standard value of carbon monoxide in the air is 34.2 milligrams per cubic meter per hour; standard value of suspended particulates in the air is 0.1 milligram per cubic meter per year; standard value of lead in the air is 10 micrograms per cubic meter per twenty-four hours.
4. (c) Standard sound level value is not to exceed 70 decibels A.

Table 17.9

Corruption Perceptions Index and Social and Economic Indicators of Selected Countries

Country	CPI (2001)[a]		HDI (1999)[b]		Competitiveness[c]		GDP per capita
	Ranking	Index	Ranking	Index	Ranking	Score	(PPP US$)[d]
Indonesia	88	1.9	102	0.677	49	8.35	2,857
Japan	21	7.1	9	0.928	19	47.30	24,898
Malaysia	36	5.0	56	0.774	38	23.58	8,209
Philippines	66	2.9	70	0.749	41	18.41	3,805
Singapore	5	9.2	26	0.876	5	63.51	20,767
Thailand	61	3.2	66	0.757	40	20.13	6,132
United Kingdom	13	8.3	14	0.923	23	41.97	22,093
United States	17	7.6	6	0.934	1	75.2	31,872

[a]Corruption Perceptions Index; Best ranking is 1; Best index is 9.9 (Finland); From Transparency International, *The Global Corruption Report 2001 (2001 Corruption Perceptions Index)* (Berlin: Transparency International, 2002).

[b]Best ranking is 1; Best index is 0.939; From United Nations, *Human Development Indicators* (New York: United Nations, 2001).

[c]Best ranking is 1; From Institute for Management Development (IMD), *World Competitiveness Yearbook* (Infrastructure Ranking as of April 2001) (Lausanne, Switzerland: IMD, 2001).

[d]Gross domestic product per capita in 1999 expressed in an internationally comparable "Purchasing Power Parity" scheme; From United Nations, *Human Development Indicators* (New York: United Nations, 2001).

than the images of neighboring business competitors, such as Malaysia and Singapore. In particular, out of the ninety-one countries surveyed, Thailand ranks sixty-first, while Malaysia ranks thirty-sixth, and Singapore ranks fourth. Interestingly, the data in Table 17.9 seem to indicate that the lower the corruption level, the better the social and economic indicators (i.e., in terms of human development and country's competitiveness as well as its GDP).

Demographic Environment

The demographic structure of Thailand is moving closer to the pattern that is commonly found in developed countries. That is, the country is experiencing slower population growth, and now has a larger number of older people, a larger number of urban residents, and a smaller household size.

Population Size

Thailand's population was approximately sixty-two million in 1999 and is estimated to reach seventy million (Office of the Prime Minister 1999) or 72.5 million (UNDP 2001) in 2015. The population growth rate in Thailand at the end of the last decade averaged about 1.5 percent yearly. Even though this average is considered high by Western standards, the country's population growth rate declined drastically from 2.27 percent in 1986 to 0.32 percent in 1999 (see Table 17.10). It is estimated that from 1999 to 2015, Thailand will see its population increase at a rate of 1 percent annually (UNDP 2001).

Approximately 31.2 percent of the population reside in urban areas (see Table 17.11). More

Table 17.10

Population and Population Distribution

(a) Population

	1986	1995	1996	1997	1998	1999
Total population (millions)	52.97	59.46	60.12	60.82	61.47	61.66
Growth rate (%)	2.27	0.62	1.10	1.16	1.07	0.32
Male/female ratio	101.2	99.7	99.4	99.3	99.1	98.8
Population per square kilometer						
Whole country	103	116	117	119	120	120
Bangkok	3,450	3,559	3,568	3,581	3,608	3,618

(b) Population distribution (%)

	1994	1995	1996	1997	1998	1999
Bangkok	9.4	9.4	9.3	9.2	9.2	9.2
Vicinity of Bangkok	5.5	5.6	5.7	5.8	5.8	5.9
Central	4.8	4.8	4.8	4.8	4.8	4.8
East	6.5	6.6	6.7	6.7	6.7	6.7
West	5.9	5.9	5.9	5.9	5.8	5.8
North	20.2	20.0	19.9	19.9	19.8	19.7
Northeast	34.8	34.8	34.7	34.7	34.7	34.7
South	12.9	13.0	13.0	13.1	13.2	13.2
Whole country	100.0	100.0	100.0	100.0	100.0	100.0

Source: Alpha Research, *Thailand in Figures 2000–2001* (Bangkok: Alpha Research, 2000).

Table 17.11

Percentage of Population in Urban Areas

Area	1986[a]	1987[a]	1988[a]	1989[a]	1990[a]	1999[b]
Whole country	26.2	26.6	27	27.4	27.8	31.2
North	16.4	16.7	17	17.3	17.6	20.3
Northeast	10.3	10.5	10.7	10.8	11.0	14.9
Central	29	29.9	30.9	31.9	32.8	33.8
South	15.6	15.8	16	16.2	16.4	20.9

[a]Data from Office of the National Economic and Social Development Board (NESDB), *Social Indicators 1990* (Bangkok: NESDB, Human Resource Planning Division, 1990).

[b]Data from National Statistical Office, *Report of the Household Socio-economic Survey 1998–1999* [in Thai] (Bangkok: National Statistical Office, Statistical Techniques Division, 2000).

people in the central region of the country live in urban areas. Bangkok, the nation's business and industrial center, is located in the central portion of the country.

Age Distribution

Thai demographic trends mimic those of many Western countries, such as the United States and European countries, where the population is getting older due to a slowdown in the birthrate and

Table 17.12

Population by Age Group and Population Projection

(a) Population by age group ('000 persons)[a]

Age group	1995	1996	1997	1998	1999
Total	58,935	59,602	60,273	60,941	61,644
0–14	14,873	14,719	14,603	14,530	14,540
% change	−10.69	−1.04	−0.79	−0.50	0.07
% of total	25.24	24.70	24.23	23.84	23.59
15–59	39,263	39,871	40,448	40,986	41,479
% change	4.51	1.55	1.44	1.33	1.20
% of total	66.62	66.90	67.11	67.26	67.29
60+	4,799	5,012	5,222	5,425	5,625
% change	2.70	4.44	4.19	3.89	3.69
% of total	8.14	8.41	8.66	8.90	9.12

(b) Composition of Thailand population projection, 2000–2015[b]

Age group	2000	2005	2010	2015
0–14	23.4	22.2	20.7	19.0
15–24	17.4	15.2	14.2	14.0
25–44	35.6	35.1	33.2	30.5
45–59	14.3	17.0	20.0	22.0
Over 60	9.4	10.4	12.0	14.4
Total	100.0	100.0	100.0	100.0
Total population ('000 persons)	62,320	65,299	67,681	69,567

[a]Data from Office of the National Economic and Social Development Board (NESDB), *Social Indicators 1995–1999* (Bangkok: NESDB, 2001).

[b]Data from Office of the Prime Minister, *Thailand Population Projection 1999–2016* (Bangkok: Office of the National Education Commission, Population Projection Working Group, 1999).

an increasing life expectancy. As shown in Table 17.12, the population group under age fifteen has decreased slightly, while the older population group over age sixty has experienced an increase of almost 4 percent annually.

Household Size

Although the average household size in Thailand is large by Western standards, family size is shrinking. Information on average household size for different geographical areas of Thailand is given in Table 17.13. The average household size for the whole country was 4.9 persons per household in 1990. It decreased to 3.8 persons per household in 1999. It is estimated that Thai households will decline to an average size of 3.1 members by 2015 (*Consumers of Southeast Asia* 1994).

Change in the Cultural Environment

Rapid economic development and changes in the socioeconomic situation have dramatically altered Thai culture. These changes have resulted in a large number of educated consumers, more

Table 17.13

Population per Household (number of persons)

Area	1995	1996	1997	1998	1999
Whole country	4.0	3.9	3.9	3.9	3.8
Bangkok	3.4	3.3	3.1	3.1	3.0
Vicinity of Bangkok	2.9	2.8	2.7	2.7	2.7
Central	3.9	3.8	3.8	3.8	3.8
East	3.4	3.3	3.2	3.2	3.2
West	4.0	3.9	3.9	3.9	3.8
North	3.8	3.7	3.8	3.7	3.7
Northeast	4.9	4.8	4.8	4.7	4.6
Southern	4.4	4.2	4.2	4.1	4.0

Source: Office of the National Economic and Social Development Board (NESDB), *Social Indicators 1995–1999* (Bangkok: NESDB, 2001).

liberalization of modern practices, the increase of materialism, the deterioration of the environment, and for some Thais, deterioration in health.

Education

Literacy in Thailand has improved significantly because of governmental educational policies and a widespread belief in the value of education. Thailand's adult literacy rate was 95.3 percent in 1999 (UNDP 2001). The Thai government policy has been to promote education. As seen in Table 17.14, more than 95 percent of Thais finished sixth grade to satisfy the compulsory requirement. However, the enrollment rate drops to less than the 60 percent range for high school. After graduating from high school, many students will take the national entrance exam in order to be accepted at one of the national universities. The competition is high, and the number of places is limited. Only 50 percent of high school graduates are accepted at universities.

Fortunately, Thai government policy is trying to improve this situation. The current national economic and social development plan (2002–6) will extend basic education from six to nine years for all school-aged children and will work toward the further extension of basic education to twelve years (NESDB 2002). The government plans to further foster higher education by sponsoring open universities and allowing private universities to compete with the national universities. High school graduates who are not accepted into the national universities or who do not want to compete in the entrance examination can enroll in one of two governmental open universities. As shown in Table 17.15, more than half of Thai students who continued their education enrolled at open universities

The value attached to education by the family also contributes to the higher literacy rate. Education is perceived as the major avenue to advancement in career, income, and social status. Thai parents who can afford the expense often place their children in the best elementary schools so that they have a better chance of entering the national universities. Spending the summer abroad attending school is now common among the younger generation of the wealthy. And parent responsibility does not end at basic education. Many Thai students are sponsored by their parents for Master's and Ph.D. degrees, pursued either domestically or abroad.

Table 17.14

Enrollment and School-Age Population Ratio (%)

Age group	1995	1996	1997	1998	1999
Total	54.30	56.71	60.32	60.60	62.36
Pre-primary (3–5)	80.39	85.80	99.39	94.52	96.96
Primary (6–11)	103.45	103.03	103.09	102.60	103.56
Lower secondary (12–14)	73.05	78.25	81.79	83.41	83.94
Higher secondary (15–17)	39.23	43.99	49.26	51.92	58.50
Higher education (18–24)*	9.01	10.27	11.97	12.92	13.12

Source: Office of the National Economic and Social Development Board (NESDB), *Social Indicators 1995–1999* (Bangkok: NESDB, 2001).
*Excluding the students of open universities.

Table 17.15

Enrollment at Higher Education Institutions (%)

Ministry of University Affairs	1990	1991	1993	1994	1996
Public institutions	83.0	81.8	80.5	79.2	80.0
University	19.9	21.3	23.5	24.0	24.9
Open university	63.1	60.5	57.0	55.2	55.1
Private institutions	17.0	18.2	19.5	20.8	20.0
Total	100.0	100.0	100.0	100.0	100.0
Total number ('000 persons)	783.5	809.7	799.8	855.0	929.3

Source: Alpha Research, *Thailand in Figures 2000–2001* (Bangkok: Alpha Research, 2000).

Social Liberalization

Thailand's extensive economic growth has most certainly caused changes in the ways many Thais view their environment and consequent consumption patterns in the country. Two major forces account for the movement toward Western-style liberalization. First, with their higher disposable income, many Thais have traveled or studied abroad, especially in the United States and Europe. As a result of their international exposure, they have adopted Western values, including egalitarianism and individualism. According to Komin (1990), liberal Thais differ from their conservative counterparts. They place less emphasis on obedience and respect for traditional ways, and more on egalitarian and intellectual values.

The second force influencing liberalization is the increasing number of working women. With high economic growth and the labor shortage, women have gained more income, and more freedom. Those who are less educated have shifted from working in the field or household to employment in factories. For women with more education, management and other professions are more accessible, even though bias toward males is still prevalent. This movement allows women financial independence and provides additional financial support for their families.

However, the increase in the number of women in the workforce does not mean that liberalization of women follows. Social values and gender-role expectations requiring women to take charge of the household remain strong (Siengthai and Leelakulthanit 1994). Thai working women have searched for ways to cope with this dual responsibility. When housemaids or part-time helpers cannot be found or are too expensive, they delegate household responsibilities to their children or use more time-saving equipment, such as washing machines and other kitchen gadgets. Some working women prolong their single status or avoid marriage entirely. Others divorce their spouses to gain freedom from being a wife. The divorce rate increased approximately 30 percent, from 9.7 percent in 1990 to 13.4 percent in 2000. In fact, many women in Thailand find that being single is as fulfilling as being married (Leelakulthanit and Day 1992).

Materialism

Materialism has been a part of the Thai social structure, and the rise in wealth has accentuated this and allowed people to consume even more conspicuously. As previously stated, Thai society is not stratified with simple upper-/middle-/working-class distinctions. Rather, a person's social status depends on the perception of his or her status in relation to the person with whom he or she is interacting (Terwiel 1984; Cooper and Cooper 1990). To behave appropriately, a person must accurately assess the other's social position. When introduced to someone new, a Thai will quickly try to establish the relative status of the person he or she is meeting. The first impression will often dictate the relationship between both people.

Appearance and material possessions are commonly used as assessment criteria. In the West, a person has freedom in choosing his or her attire, especially during leisure time. In Thailand, however, a person's ranking is expressed through his or her attire, actions, mannerisms, and speech (Cooper and Cooper 1990). It is not surprising to see Thais who place great pride in "conspicuous consumption" (Thorelli and Santell 1982). Thais are particular about their appearances (Komin 1990). They buy many outfits and often dress themselves in quality clothes with designer labels. Such material possession–oriented behaviors are evident in all social classes. Rich people buy what they do not really need, just to show their wealth. Those who cannot afford genuine items buy imitation merchandise. Material possession brings satisfaction in life to Thais (Leelakulthanit and Day 1992).

The 1997 economic crisis impacted Thai materialism. It curbed many Thais' financial ability to spend lavishly on brand-name luxury goods. In the early 1990s, Thais became known as "global shoppers par excellence." Signs in the Thai language could be seen posted on shop windows in Switzerland, France, and Hong Kong. However, possessing foreign luxury items is no longer unilaterally seen as positive, since it was cited as a fundamental reason for the current economic crisis (*Bangkok Post Economic Review* 1998). An extravagant demonstration of wealth by using foreign products is partly blamed for the depletion of foreign currencies. It is not certain, however, that Thais' materialism will not reemerge if the country's economy becomes strong again.

Health

Economic expansion has occurred to the detriment of the Thai environment and the general health of many Thais. Modern Thailand has many pollution problems. The effect of pollution on the nation's health is apparent. Close to one-eighth of Bangkok residents suffered from respiratory illness in 1989 because of air pollution. In 1994, it was reported that 60 percent of Bangkok's traffic police had serious hearing loss and respiratory illness because of exposure to noise and air pollution in the course of their duties (*Consumers of Southeast Asia* 1994).

Thais are aware of these problems, especially those who have a higher education and a higher income (Leelakulthanit and Wongtada 1993). Health issues are considered important and influence consumption. With their increased knowledge about the harmful effects of certain products, educated Thais are willing to purchase environmentally friendly products, even when they have to pay higher prices or sacrifice quality (Leelakulthanit and Wongtada 1993; Wongtada, Leelakulthanit, and Rice 1994).

Enormous market opportunities exist for products and services for individual use that prevent or treat environmental problems. For example, home and automobile air-purification devices are popular items. There is increasing demand for better health care in Thailand. Modern hospitals with the latest medical equipment are being built. Many Thai physicians who were working abroad have moved back to the country to provide expensive but advanced medical services.

Another important health issue that should be discussed here is the AIDS epidemic in Thailand, as well as its potential impact on the Thai economy. It is believed that few countries outside Africa face the potential public-health catastrophe that Thailand does with the AIDS epidemic (*The Economist* 1990). One of the commonly cited causes of the AIDS problem and its rapid spread is the thriving sex industry in Thailand (e.g., Handley 1989; Lintner and Lintner 1992). Although Thailand has made great strides in building AIDS awareness in recent years, the disease is still considered to be a serious health problem in the country; perhaps the biggest problem facing the health profession in Thailand (Chow 1994). The more recent reports from international organizations (e.g., Joint United Nations Programme on HIV/AIDS [UNAIDS] 2002; UNDP 1999) also verify the potentially detrimental effect of AIDS to Thailand and other countries in Asia and the need to remedy the problem.

The number of HIV-infected people has been increasing. The known cases of people infected with HIV/AIDS, accumulating since its first report in 1984, were nearly one million in 2000. Of those infected, approximately 300,000 have died. At least 90 percent of the deaths occurred among the population group of those between the ages of twenty and forty-four, which is in the prime of their working lives. Between 2002 and 2006, it is estimated that at least 55,000 Thais will die of AIDS each year (Ministry of Public Health 2001). AIDS is viewed by most Thais as an incurable disease, which is associated with improper sexual behavior such as prostitution. Therefore, many Thais who are HIV positive or are suffering from AIDS complications will keep their illness unknown to others for fear of rejection or discrimination. The magnitude of the AIDS problem has been recognized by the government and social leaders in Thailand. For example, the National AIDS Prevention and Control Master Plan (1992–96) was formulated by the National AIDS Prevention and Control Committee chaired by the prime minister. Every Thai government since the beginning of the 1990s has addressed AIDS control as an important national policy.

CHANGES IN CONSUMER BEHAVIOR

Naturally higher income and liberalization from traditional practices as well as the current economic recession have led to changes in consumption behavior in Thailand. In particular, new behavior can be observed in terms of the increase in consumer credit usage, the changes in consumption patterns, and the favorable attitude toward locally made products.

Consumer Credit Usage

Traditionally, the use of credit was limited. Most transactions were accomplished using cash and, to a lesser extent, personal checks. However, in recent years, credit cards have gained popularity among Thai consumers because of their convenience and because they grant freedom from carrying cash. It is estimated that US$6.2–6.5 million was spent daily by holders of credit cards in 1991 (*Bangkok*

Table 17.16

Personal Income, Personal Outlay, and Personal Savings (in Baht)

	1995	1996	1997	1998	1999
Personal income per capita	44,104	47,528	49,192	49,619	49,306
% change	13.5	7.8	3.5	0.9	−0.6
Personal outlay per capita	38,600	42,770	44,284	42,098	42,820
% change	12.3	10.8	3.5	−4.9	1.7
Personal saving per capita	5,505	4,758	4,908	7,521	6,486
% change	22.7	−13.6	3.2	53.2	−13.8

Source: Office of the National Economic and Social Development Board (NESDB), *Social Indicators 1995–1999* (Bangkok: NESDB, 2001).

Post 1992). Sixty percent of Bangkok residents and 40 percent of the non-Bangkok population use credit cards (Yeedin 1994). Credit card consumption for all Thais is expected to be on the increase due both to the predicted rise in income for all segments and aggressive strategies by banks.

Consumption

Consumer confidence in the country's economic growth has led to increased consumer spending. During the late 1980s, Thai consumer purchasing power averaged only US$8–12 per shopping trip. In 1992, each shopper increased his or her spending to an average of US$24–32 per purchase in upscale department stores, and US$20 in general department stores (*Business Review* 1992). Before 1995, the growth rate of spending in Thailand exceeded that for earning as well as saving. The saving rate declined in 1990 despite the fact that disposable income increased by 10 percent. However, many Thais managed to adjust their consuming behavior through economic growth and economic crisis. Personal income and spending increased on the yearly average of 5 percent and 4.7 percent, respectively, from 1995 to 1999. Therefore, the personal saving of Thais for the second half of the 1990s increased at an average of 10.3 percent per year (see Table 17.16).

Existing studies suggest that there are three consumption patterns for Thais. First, Thais are spending more on imports. In 1993, Thailand imported about 46 billion worth of foreign goods, about 37 percent of its GNP. In 2004, the figure jumped to US$95 billion, amounting to 66 percent of GNP (www.moc.go.th, accessed on March 29, 2005 and www.worldbank.org/data/countrydata/aag/tha_aag.pdf, accessed on March 29, 2005). Second, the changes in the Thai economic and demographic environments have caused some items previously regarded as luxuries and as a display of wealth to be seen as necessities. For instance, the rapid sales growth of cellular phones is due to the desire of the people to be accessible. This is especially important, because the public telephone system is unreliable and inadequate (*Bangkok Post Economic Review* 1993). Many businesspeople, housewives, students, and food vendors now have cellular phones, where in the past, owning such a phone was an indication of status. Likewise, the labor-shortage problem is severe. Families find it difficult to get domestic help. Using their increased income, many middle-class households have bought kitchenware and electrical appliances to ease daily domestic chores. The sales of electric kitchenware reached an estimated US$100 million in the early 1990s and this category generally continues to show strong growth (*Business Review* 1992).

The worsening pollution problems have increased the health concerns of many Thais. As a result, they are spending money on health foods, vitamins, exercise, and vacations to less-polluted areas. Interestingly, a study on beverage consumption found that milk, unusual as a table staple in the past, was the top ready-to-drink beverage in a consumer survey (*Consumers of Southeast Asia* 1994). Furthermore, milk has become the most commonly available beverage in Thai households—50 percent of households surveyed kept milk on hand, while 42 percent had soft drinks.

Third, for most Thais, the higher-priced consumer goods are still out of reach. Despite the fact that personal income has risen, Thailand is still a long way from achieving Western-style standards of living as in Hong Kong and Singapore. Moreover, income distribution is skewed toward certain consumer groups and industry sectors. Therefore, the majority of Thais have experienced only limited benefits from the country's economic progress. They can only afford, for example, standard electrical appliances, and items at the lower end of the toiletries and cosmetics range (*Consumers of Southeast Asia* 1994).

This does not indicate that a wealthier segment cannot be found. Survey Research Group Ltd. (*Consumers of Southeast Asia* 1994) carried out a survey in the seven capital cities in the region—Hong Kong, Singapore, Jakarta, Manila, Kuala Lumpur, Taipei, and Bangkok—on the consumer behavior of the elite segment defined as "men and women aged 25 and older who are currently employed in senior positions in business, the professions, government, and education, and who live in the capital cities." The survey found that this group is fairly young: 55 percent of this segment is less than forty years old, and highly educated; 44 percent have a university degree. The Thai elites seem to possess consumer durables that are similar to those of the elites of the neighboring nations. The Thai elite also travel abroad frequently and bring back items that cannot be found in the country. This segment is familiar with the latest fashion trends, new electronic gadgets, and other popular items in the West and Japan. Therefore, its consumption patterns are closer to its counterpart in the other countries than they are to the consumption patterns of other Thai market segments.

CHANGES IN MARKETING PRACTICES

The Asian economic crises have caused some changes in marketing practices in Thailand. Initially, consumers were afraid to spend money, because they were uncertain about their future financial well-being. Many businesses and factories were closed down, and people were out of work. Companies fought hard to keep their businesses by utilizing numerous techniques to make their prices affordable. Charging only marginal costs, reducing product size, and substituting import with local contents were just a few examples.

After these initial adjustments, new marketing practice patterns have emerged, in response to tougher competition. Brand strategy has become the most important aspect of product management. Various modern retailers dominate the resale industry, and the channel of distribution has been shortening due to integration strategies adopted by these retailers. Promotion expenditure must provide the return on investment that quickly forces advertisers to be more creative and to rely on diverse media mixes. Price and nonprice strategies have often been combined to obtain stronger customer appeal.

Products

New products and services from around the world, especially from the United States, Europe, and Japan, entered into the Thai market in the early 1990s. Existing manufacturers churned out new products to satisfy nouveau riche Thais. Thai consumers found that new products and services were flooded into the market, making their daily lives easier. Personal portable toilets used in passenger vehicles, cellular phones, and air- and water-purification products were some examples of products intended to help individual city dwellers cope with overcrowding, heavy traffic, and pollution in larger cities—especially Bangkok. Food containers were designed to make consumption convenient in motor vehicles. Mobile fast-food vans parked at business centers during lunch hours and at closing times to cater to the needs of working people. Many companies used product quality guarantees to gain customer trust. If the product was unsatisfactory, the consumer could return the unused portion for a refund.

Entering the new millennium, brand turns out to be the most important aspect of products. The "survival of the fittest" rule manifests itself: there are only a few leading brands dominating many industries. Large-scale retailers also compete by using private labels. Consumers trust their ability to deliver quality products with lower prices. Smaller companies also emphasize brand as a key component of strategy. Finally, the "Made in Thailand" label, for some products, is valuable and should be protected. More details of these changes will be discussed next.

Fewer Leading Brands

During the economic expansion, more companies and brands entered the market. However, the stiff competition during the economic downturn wiped out weaker brands or caused many companies to downsize their businesses. For example, Subway's three outlets in Thailand and AM/PM convenience stores were closed down (Lee and Karkoviata 2001). As another example, after sixteen years in the supermarket business, Siam Jusco supermarkets reduced food areas and added nonfood lines to avoid direct competition with large discount chains (Rungfapaisarn 2001c).

The current competition occurs among a few major brands. For example, in the body moisturizer market, only four brands have sizable market shares. In particular, Nivea has 29 percent; Citra, 24 percent; Vaseline, 19 percent; and Johnson, 15 percent. The liquid soap market is dominated by Lux with 62 percent market share followed by Shugubushi and Protex. In the beer industry, Chang is the market leader, with 60 percent, and Singha follows with 30 percent (Rungfahpaisarn and Limsamarnphun 2001). For the cellular phone market, Nokia is the market leader, followed by Motorola, Siemens, and Ericsson (Mongkolporn 2001). Similarly, in the entertainment industry, Grammy is the largest music studio, with the lion's share of 60 percent, and trailing far behind is RS Promotion (*Bangkok Post* 2002).

Because only a few major brands dominate the market, retail vendors with sophisticated stock control systems realize that they do not have to carry all brands to satisfy the needs of most of their customers. As a consequence, consumers see fewer brands. Nevertheless, consumers can still be satisfied with the available product assortment, as each brand has numerous product variations to meet the needs of specific segments. Nokia (Thailand), for instance, has different mobile phones to serve different consumer lifestyles (Mongkolporn 2001). Similarly, in addition to having the Singha brand to serve the upper market, Leo for the low-priced segment, Tai for the high-alcohol content market, and Mittweida for foreign beer drinkers, Boon Rawd Brewery launched ES, a new bottled drink mixing tequila and beer, to please the premixed-drink market (Thongrung 2001a).

Private Labels

While brand leaders are dominating the market, private labels are gaining momentum. In particular, private branding is becoming a more common strategy for large, well-established resale businesses that do not have their own production facilities. Prominent retailers, such as Central department store, Makro wholesale warehouse, and 7–Eleven convenience stores, were among the first to use this strategy in Thailand. They also used various brands to indicate different levels of product quality.

With the effectiveness of modern stock control systems, large-scale retailers have the ability to assess the popularity of each product. This helps them spot the potential for private brand. That is, they may notice that consumers are willing to switch to any brand, as long as these brands offer similar benefits. For instance, in the instant noodle section, the sales volumes of different brands are about the same (see also examples in the beer industry, as discussed in Rungfahpaisarn and Limsamarnphun 2001). This indicates that consumers do not always perceive differences among available brands. A retailer, therefore, could contact seemingly any instant noodle manufacturer to produce this product and could ultimately enhance margins.

When consumers are very price conscious, private label brands are more vital to business success and are an effective competitive strategy. In this light, Casino Group, the French-based hypermarket operator of Big C supermarket, launched its "Leader Price" stores in Thailand. These new outlets sell the company's private brands (Rungfapaisarn 2001b). Currently, Big C has about 600 different house brand products, compared to the total of 60,000 items handled by the chain. Thus, there are more opportunities to expand in this direction.

Building Local Brands

Brand leader and private label are primarily strategies of multinational companies operating in Thailand. The influence of these brands on the purchasing behavior of Thai consumers receives attention from local brand owners. Even though Thais have preferred many foreign products and services for quite some time, the economic recession has dampened this foreign-brand loyalty. Expensive foreign products are no longer easily affordable, causing many Thai consumers to switch to locally made products, especially to those imitating successful marketing techniques of international companies. For example, with attractive packaging and a savvy advertising campaign, Mistin became a well-known cosmetic brand. Likewise, other local brands, such as S&P bakery and restaurant, MK Suki restaurant, and Twin Lotus toothpaste, are popular Thai brands that have employed a modern marketing strategy.

The success of some Thai brands in the global market has also built up the confidence in local products for Thai businesses. Once a lowly health tonic drunk by taxi drivers in Thailand, Red Bull is now the epitome of cool in Europe—a favorite of the hip young e-crowd (Yoon 2000). Following the success of Red Bull, family-owned Thai company Otsotspa launched Shark in an effort to challenge Red Bull's domination of the energy drink market in Europe (*Marketing* 2002). Building or strengthening brands has become a primary focus for many Thai managers, and this strategy has led to domestic and international successes in several categories (Phuangkanok 2001b).

Intellectual Property Rights and the Value of "Made in Thailand"

The surge to build local brands coincides with awareness of the value of local products sold in international markets. Violation of intellectual property rights (IPR) has been a problem between Thai and foreign companies. Thai manufacturers have often been accused of copying famous international brands, leading to claims by U.S. companies and other brand-holders that Thailand has insufficient protection of IPR. The U.S. administration has pressured the Thai government to protect IPR by threatening to cut some Thai goods from its generalized system of preferences (GSP). Thai brands, however, have also become well known enough to be copied by entrepreneurs in other nations. Thai claims of intellectual property infringement for common brands have become more common and vocal. The local tuk-tuk (the three-wheeled taxi), jasmine rice, and pad Thai fried noodles are vulnerable to commercial exploitation by businesses in Western nations. Also, businesses in China have registered famous Thai brand names, such as Cotto, Karat, and Mama ("China Infringe Thai Brand" 2005). As a result, the Thai Intellectual Property Department has warned Thai inventors and businesspeople to protect local creations against "opportunists" from abroad (Pongvuthitham 2002).

With pressure from the U.S. government and the intention to protect the interest of the country, the Thai government passed numerous IPR protection regulations. In the area of copyright protection, for example, there are nine main areas that are subject to copyright-fee collection: literature, fine art, drama, music, recording products, visual audio items, and movies, public playing of music, and the showing of films and other works concerning drama, science, and fine arts. A copyright owner could collect copyright fees from the operators of restaurants, karaoke houses, lounges, or hotels that play music for their guests (Pongvuthitham 2001a).

On the broad issue of IPR, both copyright holders and abusers cry foul. Some copyright violators, for example, argue that counterfeiting software or music makes products more affordable and available to the majority of Thais, with little real damage to the copyright holders. The equity debate will not subside, but sensitivities to the issues will increase as Thailand continues to develop its own quality brands, patents, and other forms of IPR, which likely will be subjected to violations and requests for protection.

Channels of Distribution

In the 1990s, Thailand experienced the entrance of modern distribution systems from advanced economic countries. Because of the backward retail system in the country and increased spending power of consumers, Thai entrepreneurs recognized opportunities inherent to modern retail operations. Many formed joint ventures with foreign enterprises to transfer know-how. New types of retail outlets mushroomed, allowing Thai consumers to have entirely new shopping experiences. Hypermarket outlets, convenience stores, and category killers were no longer alien concepts to them. Modern wholesale operations have also entered the market in order to facilitate implementations of the new retail systems. Unfortunately, these novel entities nibbled the share of existing businesses and generally rendered the retailing environment more competitive.

Weakened by the economic crash in 1997, several Thai companies surrendered controls of operations to their foreign counterparts. With limited budgets, consumers tended to favor the lower prices offered by modern retail outlets, allowing the new retailers to open even more branches. Seeing their sales plunge, local businesses moved to serve niche markets, requested assistance from the government, or went out of business. Some of these important changes are described below.

More Modern Retail Outlets

An average Bangkok consumer may spend as much as six hours a day in traffic, traveling to and from the workplace. With growing pressures on time and more disposable income, Thais spend less time on daily shopping. Many Thais have switched from open-air markets to the convenience of shopping at department stores and supermarkets for their everyday grocery needs. New retail methods are being developed to help consumers reduce their shopping time. Three patterns of development have become obvious in recent years: one-stop shopping, convenience-store shopping, and home shopping or home delivery.

One-Stop Shopping

One-stop shopping can reduce the amount of travel time spent searching for products and ser-vices. Consumers can find everything they need in a large retail complex. A large department store, beauty salon, dentistry practice, movie theater, computer school, playground, billiards hall, and car repair shop, for example, are commonly located in a complex (Plubpleng 1991). Between 1986 and 1994, thirty-seven such new large-scale retail centers were opened in the Bangkok area (*Consumers of Southeast Asia* 1994). Most of these new shopping centers were constructed in the suburb residential areas. The largest one, Seacon Square, opened at the end of 1994, and was advertised as one of the five largest shopping centers in the world. However, after the economic crisis in 1997, many of them closed down, especially the smaller shopping centers.

A hypermarket is another form of one-stop shopping. Unlike a large retail complex, where numerous independent retailers are located, a hypermarket is a single large retail operation. This type of retailing was developed to reduce the difficulties, for a retail store, of accommodating a large number of customers shopping at one time during certain hours of the weekday, weekends, and holidays. This causes long delays at checkouts, out-of-stock product problems, and disgruntled consumers. To fill this void, hypermarkets offer a larger variety of products and more checkouts than are found in existing supermarkets. Online inventory control and order are implemented to help consumers easily find more brands and more sizes in a store (Plubpleng 1991).

Convenience Stores

While one-stop shopping outlets reduce travel time by making the retail operation larger, conve-nience stores provide the ease of shopping closer to home. Convenience stores such as 7–Eleven and Family Mart have seemingly sprung up on every corner street, particularly in big cities (Upananchai 1994). As in the United States, these convenience stores are open twenty-four hours and carry only necessary grocery items. However, because of the intense competition among modern retailers, convenience store operators have to adjust their strategies. Although ready-to-eat food, snacks, and beverages are the most popular items in these stores, books, CDs, VCDs, and IT products are now available to reduce the store's dependence on income from food items. Selling via catalogs is an-other strategy for convenience stores (Srisongkrot 2001). After selecting items from the store's catalog, consumers place their orders at 7–Eleven and usually can pick them up in a few days.

Direct Marketing

Unlike one-stop shopping and convenience stores, direct marketing allows consumers to elimi-nate traveling entirely. Although the sales volume of direct marketing in Thailand is still relatively small, the industry has grown rapidly. The sales volume increased from only US$20 million in 1994 (Upananchai 1994) to US$500 million in 1997 (Chom-in 1998). Direct marketing will grow even faster in the future as more major manufacturers, such as Unilever and Sahapat, use it to counter the power of modern retailers (Sooksiriserikul 2000).

Mail order is another form of direct marketing found in Thailand. American Express (Thai) Company was the first to introduce mail order to the Thai market, as a service provided to its card holders (Upananchai 1994). Other credit card companies and department stores have followed because of the attractive growth potential. However, most Thai consumers are still unfamiliar with the practice of purchasing through mail order. As in other countries, some common misperceptions limit buying from mail-order houses (Wongtada and Zerio 1993). For Thai consumers, the limitations of the system include the inability to observe the product prior to the purchase, the perceived difficulty of returning unsatisfactory items, and time delays between placing an order and receiving a product. Mail-order companies have tried to solve these problems by offering more extensive warranties, providing generous return policies, and charging no interest for purchase on credit (Gatedee 1994a).

Multilevel marketing (MLM) is another popular method of direct marketing in Thailand. Independent salespeople join together in a form of a pyramid, where each sales representative solicits more sales members. The commission generated from the sales of each member is divided between the member and the original sales representative. The company that sets up the MLM pyramid develops an elaborate scheme to encourage independent representatives to work hard. For instance, a representative can put part of his or her commission into a savings account managed by the company to buy a house.

E-Commerce and M-Business

E-Commerce offers another venue for the modern distribution channel. Selling through the Internet is still in the early stages of development in Thailand. Approximately three million Thais were Internet users in 2001, and the transaction volume was US$90 million in 2000. Gems and jewelry, books, flowers, and the souvenir industry outperform all other products and services in e-commerce.

One of the problems that hinders the growth of e-commerce is in the demographic of the Internet users. In Thailand, Internet users are mostly male, between the ages of twenty and thirty-four and live in Bankok ("The Internet and Electronic Commerce in ASEAN and Thailand and Overview of the Present Situation and Future Prospects" 2005). Their income is relatively low, and therefore, a larger number of them do not have credit cards, which are more efficient for Internet purchases. Although they like the idea of shopping online, they have to pay cash. According to a survey by the National Electronics and Computer Technology Center (NECTEC), only 18.4 percent of Thai Internet users have ever made a purchase of goods or services online. Hence, most companies use the Internet only as an advertising venue (Kittikanya 2000). Interestingly, Internet cafés have sprung up seemingly everywhere in big cities to cater to young consumers who have access at home. The café may serve as a new outlet for products and services targeting this group. Coca-Cola, for instance, just announced its intention to penetrate this outlet (*Prachachart Business* 2002).

Thais are more likely to own cellular phones than to have computers with Internet access (Kittikanya 2000). Furthermore, the cellular phone market covers a wider range of consumers than does the Internet. These consumers are also older and have more income. For most of them, the possession of cellular phones is no longer an indicator of status. Rather, cellular phones are a display of one's personality. These cellular phone users like to decorate their handsets, adjust ringing sounds, and show pictures on the display panel to suit their lifestyle (Wittuhattakit 2001). Since cellular phones have become integrated into the daily life of many Thais, e-commerce is very likely to find its way into cellular phones. Users are already able to download their e-mail and listen to music. Given the affinity for this product, it is reasonable to conclude that Thais will be comfortable ordering products and services through it.

Intense Competition

Because there are more types of retail outlets, and each intends to expand its operations, intense competition is inevitable. The modern retail trade has grown at double-digit growth rates even during the economic recession. Discount stores, for example, increased their outlets by more than 30 percent in one year (see Table 17.17). The expansion of discount stores has not only affected

Table 17.17

Store Numbers by Category in Thailand, 1995–2001

Category	1995	1996	1997	1998	1999	2000	2001	% Change from 2000 to 2001
Department	105	109	110	111	112	103	106	4.8
Discount store	9	20	37	48	45	59	79	33.8
Supermarket	61	98	116	124	136	150	170	13.3
Convenience	1,129	1,672	2,260	2,504	4,500	5,537	5,570	3.8
Cash-and-carry	12	16	17	18	18	19	21	10.5
Category killer	14	31	54	58	150	206	239	16.0
Total	1,130	1,946	2,550	2,869	4,964	6,047	6,387	4.82

Source: Bangkok Post Mid-Year Economic Review 2001 (available at www.bangkokpost.com/yearend2001).

traditional shops but also other modern outlets. The obvious losers are small traditional retailers and modern retail outlets operated by Thai management, such as Super T of Tang Hua Seng and Supersave of the Imperial Group, that closed down because of substantial losses. The number of family-owned retailers was projected to decline by 10 percent from about 300,000 nationwide. The impact has been most pronounced in major cities.

Given the increasing competition among modern trade retailers, to survive and grow in this tough environment, modern retailers have adjusted their strategies (Jitpleecheep 2001). Some hypermarket discount stores expand rapidly to untapped areas of the provincial market. Others seek different outlets in larger cities by operating convenience stores in gas stations or setting up smaller stores in the inner city. In addition to regular items, convenience stores offer catalog sales, handle bill payments, and serve as movie ticket outlets.

Department stores respond to the intense competition by investing heavily on renovations to create a more attractive shopping atmosphere to combat discount stores' convenience advantage. The Mall Supermarket, for example, mimics the fresh market shopping environment by stressing fun, excitement, and service, as well as discount prices. It also sells some basic grocery items at heavily discounted prices. Category killers or specialty stores, such as Power Buy and Super Sport, are another strategy used by department stores to concentrate on specific product lines to lure back Thai customers.

The evolution of modern retail trade, especially in the grocery category, has also been adopted in other sectors. For instance, the construction industry starts to see the emergence of large do-it-yourself (DIY) outlets, the franchise of construction material stores, and category killers. Home Paint Store, for example, which opened in early 2002, has positioned itself as the paint center where consumers will find everything concerning home paint (Tesnork 2002).

Niche Market for Local Retailers

Since Thai shoppers have been abandoning traditional grocery stores for newer hypermarket outlets that offer lower prices and modern shopping environments, the number of traditional retailers has been decreasing. The head-on strategy proves to be unsuccessful for local retailers when competing with large modern retail trade because of the lack of capital and sophisticated management systems. However, some local retailers find their niches in the crowded market. Thai consumers still prefer to buy perishable items from small vendors. According to Kujalearnpaisarn

(2001), Thai consumers tend to divide their shopping list into two categories. Items such as household cleaning, personal hygiene, and nonperishable products are bought from modern retail outlets. They are willing to travel far to acquire these products, because they believe that modern outlets offer cheaper prices, more choices, pleasant shopping environments, and sufficient parking space. However, for perishable items such as vegetable, fruit, meat, poultry, and ready-to-eat food, Thais still buy these items daily and prefer to deal with local vendors.

The stringent stock control system of modern retailers also allows local retailers to find a niche. Because modern retailers offer a wide variety of products, slow-moving items are discarded or sold at discount. Therefore, seasonal items are often not available during off-season. Modern retailers will not carry products appealing to small segments. Their product assortment tends to consist of national or international brands and their own brands. As previously discussed, these large-scale retailers select to offer their own brands only for the products that have high volume as well as for products to which consumers are not brand loyal.

Home delivery seems to be another potential niche for smaller retail operators. By offering only popular items and brand names, they can compete with large-scale retailers by providing home delivery. Their prices are slightly higher, but consumers do not mind, because their services are more convenient. These retailers usually employ a troop of deliverymen who deliver products by using motorcycles in the heavy traffic of Bangkok. Logistics and warehousing are crucial to succeed in this area. Smaller retailers capable of managing them can survive successfully. Grocery home delivery retailers such as DSTmart Company are able to fill most orders within two hours.

Growth Control

Although some smaller retailers can compete in this stiff competition, the majority cannot. Furthermore, foreign companies operate almost all discount stores, which creates social friction. Discount stores had about 40–45 percent of retail sales in 2002. The rapid expansion and the fall of traditional retailers raised sentiment to protect local business (*The Nation* 2001d).

Small retailers have tried to fight back by pressuring the government to implement strong discriminatory measures against modern retailers. Although avoiding being labeled as antiforeigners, Thai authorities looked into various control measures, including zoning regulations, limiting operating hours, and unfair pricing. However, putting these into practice has been slow, if not impossible. Large-scale retailers have mushroomed and advanced into the town centers in major provinces. Therefore, zoning will not alleviate the problem facing small retailers. Limiting operating hours was seen as selective implementation. Investigating the real costs of goods sold was not practical. Instead, the government chose to nurture small and medium-size enterprises to become more innovative and more marketing oriented. However, the pressure to control the operation of modern retailers will not disappear. For instance, after protests from local stores, Tesco Lotus "limited" its hours of operation to between 6 A.M. and midnight.

Modern Wholesale Distribution

Similar to the retailing industry, wholesaling has experienced rapid changes. The conventional wholesaling method of distribution has given way to a more integrated one. Traditionally, wholesalers operated independently from manufacturers and retailers (Wongtada 1993). Retailers place an order at the wholesaler's office and pay for the transaction. Retailers may patronize a wholesaler, because the latter may extend generous credit terms, and also because they may trust the wholesaler as a result of prior association.

As a result of the changes in wholesaling methods, the relationship among channel members has changed. Personal relationships between retailers and wholesalers were disrupted. Retailers no longer know their wholesalers personally, because they buy from cash-and-carry wholesalers. On the other hand, because of the surge in channel integration, a formal association has replaced the informal association among trade members.

Cash-and-Carry Wholesale

This type of establishment operates in a large modern warehouse. Only retailers with membership cards are allowed to enter the premises. Members purchase from these warehouses and immediately pay cash. The personal relationship between wholesalers and retailers is not a part of this distribution, because retailers do not get in touch directly with the management of the wholesale operation. The main contact is through cashier clerks at checkout points similar to supermarket checkouts.

These cash-and-carry wholesalers can offer a wide assortment and lower prices. There are only a few players in this category, and Siam Makro is the most successful operation in Bangkok and provincial markets (Srisongkrot 2001). Some cash-and-carry wholesalers, however, aim at a narrow product assortment. For example, OfficeMax concentrates only on wholesaling office-supply products and Home Depot only on home construction and furnishing items.

Vertical Integration

While cash-and-carry wholesaling reduces the connection between trade members, many channel members try to formalize their trade relations. Some manufacturers prefer working closely with a few wholesalers, who will distribute their products. In this situation, wholesalers own warehouses, manage inventory, and provide credits to retailers, while the manufacturers handle the shipping and manage the sales force that will restock products for retailers. Wholesalers receive compensation of 2–3 percent of the total sales volume.

Some variations of this relationship exist. For example, Colgate Palmolive Company has required its wholesalers to invest in vehicles and salespeople (Loawakul 1991). Others demanded that their wholesalers and retailers handle their product lines, exclusively. For example, the beer market leader, Boon Rawd Brewery, which had controlled the domestic market for almost six decades with Singha beer, adjusted its strategy as the result of the challenge from Carlsberg, a Danish brewer (*Bangkok Post Economic Review* 1993). Boon Rawd strengthened its distribution with agents nationwide by asking them to form regional clubs to ensure that Boon Rawd agents would not sell beer made by other companies. A violation led to an end to the right to distribute Boon Rawd products. In addition, the company urged its agents to adopt more consumer-oriented marketing by being more aggressive in selling and attending more to servicing their clients.

Similar to manufacturers, many wholesalers attempt to integrate vertically by strengthening their relationships with their retailers. Some wholesalers provide new services to their retail clients so that their clients will not switch to cash-and-carry rivals. Several wholesalers even offer consulting services to their retail clients who want to modernize their operations. These services include investment analysis, equipment selection, inventory control, and use of computers.

Rise in Horizontal Integration

In addition to the emergence of vertical integration, horizontal integration is found among traditional channel members. In fact, the integration among members of the same channel level has been increasing rapidly. Some traditional retailers combine their orders to increase their bargaining power with suppliers (Siam Turakit 2003). Winstore Company, for example, acts as an agent by offering services to smaller retailers who want to benefit from combining their purchases. Retailers place their orders through the Internet, which links them with distribution centers and suppliers. When shelf stocks fall below a set level, electronic purchase orders for retail stores are automatically generated and sent over the Internet to distribution centers that, in turn, automatically make contact with the appropriate suppliers.

For those retailers who are uncomfortable with high-tech, MotivationAsia (Thailand) Company Ltd. offers a similar program by bringing suppliers together to share expenses, ideas, and benefits in distributing their products to traditional mom-and-pop stores (Rungfapaisarn 2002a). Mom-and-pop stores will see few changes, because they still order from salespeople. However, the level of services that these stores get will be more limited given that the number of salespeople will be reduced, and each represents more product items.

Promotion

As with other marketing mix practices in Thailand, businesses have experienced changes in terms of promotion. These changes are discussed below.

More Innovative Commercials

In the 1990s, the advertising sector in Thailand was among the largest in the ASEAN countries. During this period, commercials were effective because Thais were receptive to advertising. Most Thais believed that commercials were a valuable source of information on new products, styles, and trends (*Consumers of Southeast Asia* 1994). Advertisers could target the audience relatively easily, because channel surfing was not as common, and consumers tended to be more loyal to particular television programs, magazines, and newspapers.

During the economic downturn, Thais were still exposed to a lot of commercials. Despite the fact that the economy has been troubled, Thailand continues to be the biggest advertising market in Southeast Asia. According to ACNielsen, the advertising expenditure in Thailand exceeded that in other countries in Southeast Asia in 2000 (see Table 17.18).

Consumer media habits, however, have changed. Viewing advertising no longer translates into consumer belief. Thais are starting to behave as do consumers in more economically advanced nations; they are becoming ad resistant (Rungfapaisarn 2001a). They tend to change channels or leave the room during commercial breaks, or turn pages without looking at the advertisements in newspapers and magazines. They tend to tune to a different station during radio commercial breaks. Accordingly, to capture Thai consumers' attention, today's commercials must be more innovative and segment specific. A department store, for instance, employed a "moving ad" concept by having attractive female models dance in a trolley along main streets to promote its store (*Thai Post* 2002a); Unilever Company hired 1,000 women to be in its commercial called "Thousand Stars" for its Sunsilk shampoo. Both of these creative commercials received much media attention.

The Increased Importance of Nontelevision Media

Although TV in Thailand is still the most popular medium, other media can be better utilized to target particular market segments. For example, it seems that the economic downturn did not

Table 17.18

Asia Pacific Advertising Growth (January–June 2000)

	US$ million	Annual growth % (based on local currencies)
North		
China	3,978	44
South Korea	2,672	35
Hong Kong	1,646	20
Southeast Asia		
Thailand	723	27
Philippines	634	17
Singapore	414	28
Indonesia	361	46
Malaysia	357	29
Vietnam	47	38
Pacific		
Australia	1,775	15
New Zealand	383	9
Total	12,990	

Source: ACNielsen Media International, "Asia Pacific Advertising in Full Upswing: Double-digit Growth in First Half of 2002," www.acnielsen.com/news/asiapacific/hk/2000/20001016.htm.

drastically reduce the traffic congestion in Bangkok. Therefore, most Bangkok residents still spend a considerable amount of time waiting for buses, using buses, and sitting in their vehicles. Accordingly, outdoor advertisements, such as different types of billboards, still have wider exposure in this urban market. Bangkok also has a relatively large portion of young people and a growing number of professionals who like to read about both local and world events. Newspapers and magazines have, accordingly, been launched to serve these market segments. Moreover, many radio stations concentrate on specific interests, such as traffic reports or teenager talks, and, therefore, have been used to help reach particular segments.

Currently, the TV advertising industry experiences further pressure. Companies, facing hard times, have cut their advertising budget and demanded immediate results. They shift media spending to marketing events, public relations, and trade promotions to target niche segments and save on costs (Amnatcharoenrit 2001). The less popular media are expected to suffer the most, while the leading medium in each category was not likely to be much affected by this shift (Intarakomalyasut and Amnatcharoenrit 2001). For example, on-screen advertising expenses increased approximately 40 percent (Phuangkanok 2001a).

New Appeals in Commercials

Not only will the advertising media shift, the content of commercials will become more sophisticated, in line with the changes in consumers' tastes. Many Thai consumers prefer the Japanese style of advertising to that of the United States. That is, they respond best to the use of visual impact with emotional content, rather than to written text and logical reasoning (Chumunee 1994). With more women in the workplace, smaller family sizes, and marriage at a later age (Shawsotikul 2002), the advertisements in Thailand for many products, including furniture, tour packages, cars, and microwave ovens, are now appealing more to both genders. Also, given that soccer is very popular in Thailand, commercials associated with international soccer matches will tend to capture the attention of Thai consumers, especially male audiences.

Price

Intense Price Competition

Recent economic hardships have rendered many Thais more price sensitive; they also demand more from sellers. In fact, Thais are more responsive to price reductions than are consumers in neighboring countries (Huff and Alden 1998). Thais, for example, favor sales promotions, particularly coupons, while Malaysians fear being embarrassed or losing face if they use coupons. In addition to being more price sensitive, Thais also have become less brand conscious. Nowadays, less than half of Thai consumers buy based on brand name. Furthermore, first-time buyers often buy on price alone (U.S. Commercial Service 2002). Thai consumers are quite fond of free gifts or extra options with their purchases. As a result, since special sales events occur quite often, Thai consumers tend to postpone their purchases until the price is right. Because of these changing behaviors of Thai consumers, modern retail stores employ loss–leader pricing strategies for popular products to lure shoppers to their stores. As mentioned earlier, supermarkets and hypermarkets sell some items below cost, while traditional retailers lament the consumer's willingness to switch to any discount store, even when the price difference is small. Some retailers tend to compare the shopping costs at their store to those of competitors to try to convince the consumers that their prices are lower. The current intense price competition will likely continue.

Value for Money

Not all groups of Thai consumers are willing to trade a quality product for a lower price. This is especially true for the middle-class buyers. In the 1990s, middle-class Thais already knew how to be smart shoppers. They looked for the best value for their money. They searched for good-quality products with low prices, and delayed their purchases until they got a price reduction (Gatedee and Upananchai 1993). The recession did not wipe out the middle-class and high-class consumers entirely. Although these groups of Thai consumers still have their wealth, they tend to be reluctant to spend, because they feel uncertain of their future. Nevertheless, when there is a good bargain available, they are likely to be the first to grasp the offer. The stocks of PTT, a petroleum company, for instance, offered to domestic and foreign investors were all sold in less than five minutes. Nearly US$14 million were raised from domestic investors alone (Thongrung 2001). Over 8,000 new vehicles were sold at the Twenty-third Motor Show in Bangkok, because consumers were attracted by sales promotions ranging from interest-free installment plans to low down payments and free options (*The Nation* 2002a).

Different Forms of Price Promotion

Although an immediately available price discount on an item is the most effective way to entice consumers to buy, especially during economic hardship, other forms of price discounts are commonly practiced. Retailers offer membership cards that give discounts on many purchases. In addition, if a consumer buys up to a target amount, he or she can purchase promoted items at discount prices. Free premiums are often provided with purchases. Motor-vehicle dealers use several strategies, including buying a house and receiving a free automobile, low down payments and low monthly payments, and sweepstakes to win an automobile (Mekruengassamee 1994).

Marketing Management into the Future

Perpetual change and competition seem to be the operative terms for future marketing management in Thailand. The ability to target segments accurately is a key to win over Thai customers. Efficiency improvement and appropriate strategic partnership will enhance a company's competitive advantage. Moreover, the integration of Thailand into the global economies will change the business landscape. Each of these important trends in marketing management is described below.

Precise Demographic Segments

In order to be more competitive, marketers will have to position their products and services to cater to specific requirements of a target market. Strategies must be developed to deal with cautious Thai consumers who are uncertain about their economic futures and to compete with formidable competitors who are willing to cut prices below their costs. Boon Rawd Brewery, for example, recently revamped its beer portfolio to appeal to specific market niches. In particular, Super Lion brand was dropped, and Thai Beer was added to regain its share in the low-cost beer segment (Rungfapaisarn 2002b).

Demographic segmentation will be extremely useful, because it reflects the different consumption patterns found in the market for many products. Children, teenagers, and seniors, in particular, are important as market segments and deserve closer attention from marketers.

The Children Market

During the economic prosperity in the 1990s, many Thai parents had more disposable income and few children and, as a result, tended to pamper their offspring. From about five years old, children start to influence their parents' choice of products bought for them (Doungmanee 1993). The older they become, the more influence they have. Even during economic downturn, this consumption pattern has not altered much. Many parents continue to devote their time and efforts to please their children, even though they have to cut down on their own personal spending. Tutoring schools, extracurricular activities, amusement parks, and cartoon character shows remain very popular among families with young children.

The behavior of this market segment differs from that of other age groups, because children are heavily influenced by premiums and promotional associations that come with products; in fact, they may be the key buying decision factors for this segment. Thai children are exposed to entertainment programs and cartoon characters such as Mickey Mouse, Ultraman, and Pokemon. These personalities are popular product presenters. When a character is in fashion, Thai children want to own the products associated with the character in order to "fit in" with their group (see also Gatedee 1993b).

The Teenager Market

Thai parents indulge their teenagers as well as their younger children. Teen consumers, however, often make their own buying decisions, and their peers strongly influence their choice of brands (Lee and Lim 2001). Even though the teenager market is large in size and in purchasing power, it is not easy to please this market, because its preferences tend to change rapidly. In many ways, teen behavior in Thailand is similar to that observed in Western countries. Thai teens have disposable income mainly from allowances, although a few can earn money by working part-time. Thai teens are quite fashion conscious, do not think about long-term utility of products, and prefer to possess several items to suit different occasions. Marketers who can predict the needs of this market accurately are likely to see sales increase rapidly, but only for short periods and until the next fashion-trend arrives (Gatedee 1994b).

Interestingly, although a large number of Thai teens behave similarly to their counterparts in the Western world, many of them can be classified as achievers who value anonymity and prefer to be somewhat inconspicuous (*Brandweek* 2000). These teens tend to conform to traditional morals—to be bookish and well disciplined, and to prefer to study long hours to earn good grades in order to attend good universities. Their career advancement is often predetermined by their parents, who are eager for their children to do well, by instilling in their children the importance of discipline and the value of homework. Although these teens rarely go out in the evening and tend to avoid parties and drinking, they are prime consumers of CDs, stereo equipment, and education-related products. The parents of these teens often have sufficient wealth to reward them. Moreover, the parents will place higher priority on their children's product needs when products, for example, computers and other technological products, facilitate education.

The Senior Market

Thais traditionally take care of their aging parents. However, the lifestyle of the present generation makes it difficult to fulfill this responsibility. Urban Thais who work spend little time at home during the week. Many young people migrate to and live in Bangkok, where there are more economic opportunities, but frequently, their aging parents stay in provinces. These factors are forcing senior consumers to take care of themselves and to rely less on their children. However, the younger generation still provide financial supports that allow most senior citizens to make their purchases of products and services.

Compared to the child and teenager segments, the senior segment is relatively small. However, this segment has been growing. In the year 2000, this segment grew by double digits, while the child segment experienced negative growth, and the teenage segment saw only single-digit growth (see Table 17.19). This pattern will continue throughout this decade, leading to an accelerated "graying" of Thai society.

Health-Oriented Marketing

High industrial growth, urbanization, and pollution continue to dominate the Bangkok scene as well as other major cities in Thailand. In the 1990s, green marketing was a popular marketing appeal. Biodegradable plastic bags, recycled packages, and nonpolluting detergents were offered by department stores (Weerakultewan 1994). Unfortunately, the green marketing appeal did not last. Since the economic slump, Thai consumers tend to pay more attention to only nongreen factors (Johri and Sahasakmontri 1998). As a result, businesses now hardly address environmental issues in their marketing strategies. Nevertheless, environmental problems in Thailand have not disappeared, and consumers are still worried about their negative impacts.

Thais' environmental concern appears to have transformed into health concerns. More Thai consumers are now interested in purchasing products with natural ingredients in order to improve their health. Organic food, herbal drinks, and natural ingredient cosmetics are a few examples of

Table 17.19

The Population of Thailand

Age group	1990	2000	% Change 1990–2000
0–4	6,240,000	4,362,398	(30.1)
5–9	6,357,000	4,785,879	(24.7)
10–14	6,207,000	4,563,973	(26.5)
15–19	6,156,000	5,046,845	(18.0)
20–24	6,008,000	5,416,372	(9.8)
25–29	5,169,000	5,586,662	8.1
30–34	4,453,000	5,623,738	26.3
35–39	3,634,000	5,250,822	44.5
40–44	2,775,000	4,496,700	62.0
45–49	2,246,000	3,578,623	59.3
50–54	2,029,000	2,718,420	34.0
55–59	1,645,000	2,023,519	23.0
60–64	1,285,000	1,802,902	40.3
65–69	893,000	1,418,505	58.8
70–74	607,000	993,406	63.7
75+	636,000	4,209,982	561.9
All ages	56,340,000	61,878,746	9.8

Source: National Statistical Office, *Key Statistics of Thailand* (Bangkok: National Statistical Office), www.nso.go.th/pop2000/table/eadv_tab1.pdf.

these products (Lapsarupong 2001; Tetnok 2002). Not only have local companies taken advantage of this trend, but also multinational enterprises have jumped at this opportunity. For example, Colgate Palmolive Company recently launched Colgate Herbal toothpaste and Protex Herbal soap after observing the rapid sales growth of the local herbal toiletry market (Phuangkanok 2002a). McDonald's offers "Mc Som-Tum Shaker" (Thai Northeastern-style papaya salad) to cater to health-conscious customers (*Krungtepturakit* 2002).

Increased Efficiency

Thai managers increasingly emphasize efficiency (Keawkumnurdpong 2001a). Different techniques have been employed to achieve low-cost production without sacrificing quality. Meeting International Organization for Standardization (ISO) requirements, reengineering, balance scorecard, six sigma, supply chain management, electronic data interchange (EDI), and customer relationship management (CRM) are among many new management techniques that up-to-date managers need to know (Kanoksilp 2001; Toomgum 2001a; *The Nation* 2002b). However, only a few of these new techniques have been successfully implemented. Among these techniques, meeting ISO requirements seems to be accepted most widely. Initially, only export companies that were worried about being left out of the European Union (EU) market applied for ISO standards. Lately, entities that have nothing to do with exporting have also applied for ISO standards. Schools, hospitals, and government agencies proudly announce to the world that they too are certified by ISO. CRM, on the other hand, is a very new revolutionary marketing practice. Targeting an individual customer instead of using mass marketing requires some changes in data collection and analysis, new software, and, above all, different ways of thinking. Thai firms, because of these changes, have been slow to apply this concept (Toomgum 2001a).

Increasing efficiency may lead to higher costs for some channel members. Traditionally, space allocation and display decisions are based on the hunches of a store manager as well as his or her relationship with the supplier. However, the current decision on what products to be displayed is typically based on a calculation of sales per square meter and a setting of daily targets for sales of each product. Any product with a low turnover rate and a low margin will be quickly discarded. Manufacturers have to compete to maintain their brands on the top selling list if they want to keep their brands on retail shelves. New products made by small manufacturers will have difficulties finding shelf space in major retail stores (Plubpleng and Upananchai 1995). Manufacturers must build product demand at the consumer level by encouraging product trial, prior to placing the product in a retail store. At the same time, they have to pay various fees, such as product placement fees and in-store promotion charges, to ensure that their products will be promoted by the store.

Strategic Alliance

Though Thai companies have been cooperating for some time (e.g., Gatedee 1993a), there are greater pressures to form strategic partnerships to be competitive. Alliances take several forms: copromotion, cobranding, and sharing distribution networks. Copromotion between well-known brands is the most common arrangement. By combining their promotional budgets, strategic partners have a larger budget to spend and, therefore, have greater impact.

A common trend is to form a long-lasting strategic alliance. Asian Life, a company selling cosmetics through direct selling, signed a contract with 7–Eleven Company (*Business.Com* 2001). 7–Eleven Company differentiates itself from other convenience outlets by selling Thai cosmetics, while the cosmetic company benefits from an extensive network of convenience stores. Similarly, McDonald's chain teamed up with One-2–Call, a prepaid service to distribute phone cards through McDonald's outlets (Toomgum 2001b). Perhaps the most unusual strategic alliance was formed between Grammy, the leader in the entertainment industry, and Saha Group, the owner of the famous "Mama" instant noodle brand. These two companies established a new company; their first product was "4 ME" instant noodle, aimed at the teenage market by using famous entertainers from Grammy as spokespersons (Sunsompak 2002).

Global Integration

In the 1990s, globalization was considered to be an opportunity to integrate Thai society into the international community—to modernize the Thai way of life. Satellite systems and other forms of global mass communication enabled Thais to view international programs from the likes of CNN, BBC, MTV, and other networks, creating new awareness. Preferences for many ideas and foreign-made goods from the United States and Europe are now rooted in Thai society, especially among older customers from the middle and upper classes. Japanese culture has also influenced Thai preferences, perhaps because of increasing trade between the two countries. Japanese fashion is especially popular among younger Thais. However, traditional Japanese culture is not winning over young Thai consumers; rather, it is Japanese popular culture in the forms of products, images, and brands blended with Western influences. It should be noted that artifacts of globalization reach provincial cities as well as Bangkok. Shopping at large discount stores or at convenience stores, Internet cafés, CNN, and large movie complexes have become part of the lifestyles of many Thai consumers. The process of integrating rural consumers into the modern consumption system is expected to continue.

If the 1990s were a time for embracing globalization, the new millennium will make Thais more aware of its negative impact as well as its benefits. As mentioned earlier, uncountable numbers of small retailers and wholesalers have gone out of business, as they cannot compete with modern retailers. Businesses and factories have closed; workers have lost jobs. Many Thai teenagers, perhaps influenced by some movies from Hollywood, behave in manners unacceptable to their elders. IMF is synonymous with the nation's huge debt that will take years to repay. Privatization of the telecommunication industry and oil and gas operations brings an outcry for giving away profitable national operations to foreign investors. Then, there are issues with Thailand's increasingly powerful neighbor to the north. China's full membership in the WTO has stirred worries from many Thai businesses (Kanjanasupak 2002); even before China was admitted to the WTO, several business sectors of Thailand lost their competitiveness in terms of cheap labor. Thai businesses fear that they could lose out in a number of industries, particularly those that are labor intensive, such as textiles, computers, air conditioners, footwear, and toys (*The Nation* 2001e). Furthermore, direct foreign investment may be diverted to China (*The Nation* 2001b). However, the positive side of all these trends is that the Chinese market will open for some Thai products, such as livestock, seafood, and other processed food for which Thailand still has competitive advantages over China.

The aforementioned trends have forced Thai government and businesses to make adjustments. Developing closer ties with countries in ASEAN is an example. Interregional trade should increase, and the combined markets of the member countries should still make the region attractive for foreign investment (Pongvuthitham 2001b). Many far-sighted Thai businessmen have already prepared for this situation. Thai apparel manufacturers, for example, have expanded their operations into China's coastal areas in the past decade. However, they are not abandoning their Thai operations. Their factories in Thailand produce higher-value-added items, while their plants in China produce lower-valued-added, low-cost apparel (*The Nation* 2001a).

The impacts of globalization and the competitiveness of Thailand are likely to be crucial to marketing well into this decade and beyond. Marketing managers will see new competitors entering the domestic market and will confront competitors' new strategies in responding to the changing environment in Thailand. The Thai government will devise numerous policies to cope with the changing environment. Inevitably, globalization will certainly have significant impacts on Thai businesses when conducting business domestically and internationally.

Small and Medium-Size Enterprises

The impact of globalization is very powerful and difficult to manage. Accordingly, the Thai government has attempted to balance the reliance on large corporate exporters and multinationals by also promoting small to medium enterprises (SMEs). The SME Promotion Act, passed on February 18, 2000, set up a venture capital fund to support SMEs that have good potential but lack capital. State financial institutions were to provide SMEs with financial support, while an Institute for Small and Medium Enterprise Development was established to assist SMEs with technology and advice. Furthermore, the government plans to set up the country's first national design center to help improve product design for SME exporters.

SMEs have become an integral part of business. Newspapers, trade magazines, and trade shows have special sections for them. Universities offer courses and even degrees in entrepreneurship and SMEs business management. These activities have begun to yield results. Newspapers publicize the success of SMEs, especially those established in the crisis years. For example, natural soaps using local materials are exported to the United States, Canada, Japan, South Africa, Russia, and elsewhere (Keawkumnurdpong 2001b). Gazebo manufacturer Sala-Tanum Company formed when many Thai companies went bankrupt at the beginning of the 1997 financial crisis, and the company is now thriving by offering various East-meets-West styles of gazebos.

Intending to encourage entrepreneurial spirit even at the grassroots level, the Thai government implemented a "one tambon one product" project. This project encourages each village to offer a product or service (Phuangkanok 2002b). With more experience in this industry, the Japanese government has offered some assistance. In particular, the Japan External Trade Organization (JETRO) held an exhibition in Tokyo featuring 600 items from the "One Village One Product" program, as part of its attempt to help promote Thai products in the Japanese market. If the SMEs promotional programs are successful, other businesses will be stimulated, and competition will increase.

Transparency in Business

In addition to promoting SMEs, the Thai government realizes the importance of business management transparency as another key to help improve the country's competitiveness. It is believed that the low level of investment in Thailand's financial market is partly due to the lack of transparency in business operations. The Institute of Management and Development of Switzerland ranked Thailand as one of the lowest good-governance countries in Asia (*Poo Chad Karn* 2002). This prompted the government to launch various programs to help promote more transparency in business practice. The programs include establishing the guideline for good business practices, establishing a corporate governance rating agency, and awarding tax privileges. Also, through its Thai Research Fund program, the government has provided grants to conduct studies of different factors of ethical decisions of Thai managers (Singhapakdi, Salyachivin, Virakul, and Veerayangkur 2000); in the future, it expects that a company will not only publicize its ISO certification but also its achievement as a good corporate citizen.

MARKETING IMPLICATIONS

Marketing practices in Thailand are currently at a stage of flux. As previously mentioned, the Asian economic crisis caused several business sectors to collapse. This event changed the behavior of many Thai consumers, as many went from being able to afford expensive brands to being concerned about their ability to pay for anything. Many consumers became price conscious. As a result, large-scale discount stores cater to greater price sensitivity and, at the same time, offer shopping convenience; they use their bargaining power from volume purchases to drive down their costs. This creates some conflicts between manufacturers and retailers. When confronted with the possibility that the Thai government would limit their venues of operation, these discount stores moved into the territory of convenience stores and created additional marketing channel conflict.

Given evolving dynamics, to be successful, marketing companies should use some or all of the following strategies. First, brand building and loyalty are vital to fend off competitors. Even though brand loyalty for expensive items is in decline, Thai consumers still like to buy recognizable brand names to assure a certain status level. Thus, a well-known name for a product or a retail operation will bolster bargaining power. As in the United States, retailers have to offer certain brands, because consumers prefer them. Likewise, the name of a well-known retail establishment serves as a quality indicator that consumers tend to use. Without a strong brand, many manufacturers and retail outlets will vanish or will be dominated by emerging channel captains.

Second, given that the marketing war is intensifying and does not have boundaries, appropriate strategic alliance will become more important. In Thailand's current business environment, the classification of retailing and industry type has almost no meaning. Large-scale discount stores enter the convenience store territory, and the convenience stores expand into catalog retailing. Manufacturers set up their own direct marketing network. Accordingly, strategic partners could be many companies that serve the same groups of customers. Competitors and alliances can come from any industry. As we have seen, an entertainment company forms an unlikely strategic alliance with a food company to produce an instant noodle product aimed at the teenager market.

Third, effectiveness and efficiency in business operation are perhaps two more important requirements for survival in Thailand. There are greater pressures for businesses to rid any inefficiency their systems, because they lead to higher prices. Shortening the channel of distribution, therefore, is an increasingly favored technique to reduce costs and prices.

CONCLUSIONS

The evolution from traditional marketing management to modern practices in Thailand has continued and will evolve further. This development could be categorized into three stages. The first stage was the introduction of modern management in the retail sector to satisfy Thai customers with high disposable income. Numerous retailers from triad countries, namely, the United States, Europe, and Japan, rushed to set up their operations in Thailand. The domination of modern marketing management over indigenous management practices had begun. However, this was noticed by few people because the market expanded rapidly (there was enough business for everyone). This change could have happened gradually if the economic burst had not occurred.

The economic downturn has accelerated the evolution of marketing management in Thailand, leading to the second stage. Winners and losers have quickly appeared. Armed with strong financial backing from abroad and with better management techniques, modern large-scale retailers and wholesalers have easily undercut the prices of smaller independent traders, which were the first casualties. Local laws and the government were not adequate for this situation and, therefore, were ineffective in helping small retailers. The second group that lost out was weaker modern operations. They are, generally, Japanese retail stores and large local department stores. The European retailing and wholesaling systems are winning in the supermarket industry, while the U.S. food franchising operations are dominating the fast-food business. This stage of evolution is not yet complete. The modern marketing practice is spreading into other trading sectors, such as the construction industry and the electronics market. It is not the U.S. or European companies or entrepreneurs who caused the change in these sectors, but it is local entrepreneurs who see opportunity widely open there.

The final stage of the marketing management evolution in Thailand could be similar to the situation in the United States, where the wheel of retailing fully operates. Hypersupermarkets and category killers increasingly dominate the U.S. market. Other distribution systems, such as direct marketing and convenience stores, seem to be carving out or holding onto market share; small entrepreneurs will survive mainly in niche markets.

Although large-scale operations will likely eventually dominate in Thailand, their marketing strategies will probably be modified to fit the changing environment. Unlike in the United States— where traffic congestion tends not to parallel the extreme situation in, say, Bangkok—traffic problems in Thailand can significantly influence Thai consumers' buying patterns. As a result, some large-scale retailers already have started to set up smaller outlets in the inner cities and to offer home delivery. It is uncertain whether large-scale retailers will continue to compete based on standardized sizes and forms, or whether they will evolve to be conglomerate operations of various sizes and forms. Under the latter scenario, they might see that their competitive advantage lies in their ability to source products and to deliver them effectively and efficiently to Thai consumers; they will evolve into other classes of retail outlets and take on new channel functions. If their diversification extends beyond their core competencies, surely we will see the wheel of retailing turning again. Other forms of retailing and marketing practices will emerge and control the industry. Regardless of the precise tack, consumer behavior and marketing in Thailand will continue a multifaceted, interactive, and rapidly changing dynamism.

REFERENCES

Alpha Research. 2000. *Thailand in Figures 2000–2001*. Bangkok: Alpha Research.
———. 2001. *Thailand in Figures 2001*. Bangkok: Alpha Research.
Amnatcharoenrit, Bamrung. 2001. "Ad Spending Expectations Cut." *Bangkok Post Economic Review Year-End 2001*, December 28: 44.
Aufrecht, Steven, and Arun Ractham. 1991. "Traditional Thai Values and the Thai Bureaucracy's Ability to Change." In *Public Management in 1990s: Challenges and Opportunities*, ed. Goraksha Bohadur, N. Pradham and Mila A. Reforma, pp. 51–62. Quezon City, Philippines: EROPA Secretariat General.
Bangkok Post. 1992. "Plastic Money: Card Use Continues to Soar." *Bangkok Post Economic Review Mid Year 1992*, June 30: 72–74.
———1993. *Bangkok Post Economic Review*, December 30. Available at www.bangkokpost.com, accessed April 30, 2003.
———. 1994. "Thailand Set to Rank 4 in Asian Growth." *Bangkok Post Weekly Review*, December 30: 11.
———. 1998. *Bangkok Post Economic Review*, December 30. Available at www.bangkokpost.com, accessed April 30, 2003.
———. 2002. "Sony, BEC to Make Thai Music," April 18: 1.
Bank of Thailand. 1997. *Annual Economic Report 1996*. Bangkok: Bank of Thailand.
———. 1998. *Annual Economic Report 1997*. Bangkok: Bank of Thailand.
———. 1999. *Annual Economic Report 1998*. Bangkok: Bank of Thailand.
———. 2000. *Annual Economic Report 1999*. Bangkok: Bank of Thailand.
———. 2001. *Annual Economic Report 2000*. Bangkok: Bank of Thailand.
———. 2002a. *Economic and Financial Statistics (January 2002)*. Bangkok: Bank of Thailand.
———. 2002b. *Quarterly Bulletin December 2001*, 4 (4). Bangkok: Bank of Thailand.
BOI Investment Review. 1994. 3 (4); November.
Brandweek. 2000. "The Six Value Segments of Global Youth," 41 (21), May 22: 38–50.
Business.com. 2001. "Loxley Joins with 7–Eleven to Increase Outlets for Cosmetics," 13 (150), August: 28.
Business Review. 1992. "Spend . . . Spend . . . Spend." *Consumerism*, September: 59–61.
Chantranontwong, Pattanapong. 1993. "Satellite, Phones Ring in New Era" [in Thai]. *Bangkok Post Economic Review, Year End 1993*, December 30: 36–37.
Chom-in, Pornparit. 1998. "Direct Sales of Thailand in 1997 Worth 20,000 Million Baht." *Thai Farmer Bank*, April 9. Available at www.kasikornresearch.com, accessed April 30, 2003.
"China Infringe Thai Brand." 2005. *Post Today Newspaper*, Business Market Section, February 16: B1
Chumunee, Narisa. 1994. "Next Century . . . Advertising in Thailand." *Kookengkaan*, September: 50–54.
Consumers of Southeast Asia. 1994. Volume 1, Dynamic Markets Reprint Series. Ithaca, NY: W-Two Publication.
Chow, Dominic Cheung. 1994. "AIDS in Thailand: A Medical Student Perspective." *Journal of Community Health* 19 (6): 417–31.
Clifton, Tony. 1994. "Dark Satanic Mills." *Newsweek*, May 9: 18–22.
Cooper, Roberts and Nathapa Cooper. 1990. *Culural Shock*. Singapore: Times Books International.
Crossette, Barbara. 1992. "Across Southeast Asia, Awakenings to Democracy." *The New York Times*, May 24: 3.
Dixon, C. 1996. "Thailand's Rapid Economic Growth: Causes, Sustainability and Lessons." In *Uneven Development in Thailand*, ed. M. J. G. Parnwell, pp. 28–48. Aldershot: Avebury.

Doungmanee, Kokeit. 1993. "Power of Children in Clothing Business." *Kookengkaan*, September: 201–8.

The Economist. 1990. "Thailand: The New Leaper," September 15: 44.

Gatedee, Rampai. 1993a. "Symbiotic Marketing, Strategy in Co-operating Strengths." *Kookengkaan*, May: 210–16.

———. 1993b. "Kid Power." *Kookengkaan*, September: 195–200.

———. 1994a. "Enter the Era of Home Shopping When Goods Are Available at Consumer Home." *Kookengkaan*, March: 199–204.

———. 1994b. "Teen . . . Boom, Win Over Teenager Segment." *Kookengkaan*, October: 142–54.

Gatedee, Rampai, and Sutinee Upananchai. 1993. "Value for the Money, Consumer's Dream Comes True." *Kookengkaan*, February: 46–51.

Handley, Paul. 1989. "The Lust Frontier." *Far Eastern Economic Review* 148, November 2: 44–45.

Huff, Lenard C., and Dana L. Alden. 1998. "An Investigation of Consumer Response to Sales Promotions in Developing Markets: A Three-Country Analysis." *Journal of Advertising Research* 38 (3), May–June: 47–56.

Institute for Management Development (IMD). 2001. *World Competitiveness Yearbook* (Infrastructure ranking as of April 2001). Lausanne, Switzerland: IMD. Available at www02.imd.ch/wcy/factors/f4.cfm, accessed April 5, 2002.

Intarakomalyasut, Nondhanada, and Bamrung Amnatcharoenrit. 2001. "Spending Forecast to Fall Sharply 4thQ." *Bangkok Post*, October 18. Available at www.bangkokpost.com, accessed April 30, 2003.

"The Internet and Electronic Commerce in ASEAN and Thailand and Overview of the Present Situation and Future Prospects." 2005. Conducted by Foundation for MultiMedia Communications of Japan. Available at www.maxcyber.com, accessed March 30, 2005.

Jitpleecheep, Sukanya. 2001. "Giants Force Rivals to Innovate." *Bangkok Post Economic Review Mid Year 2001*, June 29: 36–37.

Johri, Lalit M., and Kanokthip Sahasakmontri. 1998. "Green Marketing of Cosmetics and Toiletries in Thailand." *Journal of Consumer Marketing* 15 (3), March 15: 265–81.

Joint United Nations Programme on HIV/AIDS (UNAIDS). 2002. *Report on the Global HIV/AIDS Epidemic—June 2000* (Table of Country-Specific HIV/AIDS Estimates and Data). April 29. Geneva: UNAIDS. Available at www.aids.org/wad2004/report.html.

Kanjanasupak, Luxana. 2002. "China, Not Just One Big Market." *The Nation*, February 25: 2B.

Kanoksilp, Jiwamol. 2001. "TFB Aims for 'Balance.'" *The Nation*, December 25: 8B.

Keawkumnurdpong, Jirapreeya. 2001a. "Companies Advised to Adapt Quickly." *The Nation*, November 23: 3B.

———. 2001b. "SME: Architect Designs a Natural Success." *The Nation*, December 10: 3B.

Kittikanya, Charoen. 2000. "Electronic Commerce, Uptake Remains Relatively Slow." *Bangkok Post Economic Review Year End 2000*. Available at www.bangkokpost.com/yearend2000, accessed April 30, 2003.

Komin, Suntaree. 1990. *Psychology of the Thai People: Values and Behavioral Patterns*. Bangkok: Magenta.

Krungtepturakit. 2002. "McDonald Sends Mc Som-tum to Compete in Fast Food Business," March 14: 29.

Kujalearnpaisarn, Pranee. 2001. "Consumer Satisfaction of Traditional Retail Outlets; the Case of Bangkok Metropolitan and Chiang Mai Consumers." *Journal of Business Administration* 1 (1): 49–56.

Lapsarupong, Pranee. 2001. "Thai Cosmetics, Bright Future and Profitable?" *Make Money*, February 23: 42–44.

Lee, James, and Karkoviata Leonie. 2001. "Fast Tract to Growth." *Asian Business* 1.37 (12) December: 29–36.

Lee Soo Hoon, and Vivien K.G. Lim. 2001. "Attitudes Towards Money and Work: Implications for Asian Management Style Following the Economic Crisis." *Journal of Managerial Psychology* 16 (2): 159–72.

Loawakul, Somchai. 1991. "Build New Barriers for Wholesalers All Over the Country." *Kookengkaan*, June: 247–54.

Leelakulthanit, Orose, and Day, Ralph. 1992. "Quality of Life in Thailand." *Social Indicator Research* 27 (41): 1–57.

Leelakulthanit, Orose, and Wongtada, Nittaya. 1993. "Thai Consumer Behavior: Reponses in Conserving the Environment," in *Fourth Symposium* on *Cross-Cultural Consumer & Business Studies*, ed. Gerald S. Albaum et al., pp. 313–19, Hong Kong.

Lintner, Bertil, and Lintner, Hseng Noung. 1992. "Immigrant Viruses." *Far Eastern Economic Review* 155, February 20: 31.

Loawakul, Somchai. 1991. "Build New Barriers for Wholesalers All over the Country." *Kookengkaan*, June: 247–54.

Marketing. 2002. "Shark UK Launch to Challenge Red Bull's Dominance," February 28: 6.

Mekruengrassamee, Wanida. 1994. "Price War in Other Markets." *Kookengkaan*, September: 146–48.

Ministry of Public Health. 2001. "A Review of the Eighth National Conference on AIDS" [in Thai]. *AIDS Newsletter* 14 (2): 1–8. Bangkok: Ministry of Public Health, Department of Communicable Diseases, Division of AIDS.

Mongkolporn, Usanee. 2001. "Nokia to Defend Its Supremacy." *The Nation*, December 17: 1B–2B.

Mulder, Niles. 1992. *Inside Southeast Asia: Thai, Japanese, and Filipino Interpretation of Everyday Life*. Bangkok: Duang Kamol.

The Nation. 2001a. "China and the WTO: Facing the Juggernaut," September 3: 2B.

———. 2001b. "China's WTO Entry Will Hit Investment Here," September 6: 3B.

———. 2001c. "Editorial: Reining in the Hypermarkets," August 9: 4A.

———. 2001d. "Editorial: Retail Zoning: What's Needed," September 3: 4A.

———. 2001e. "What China Will Mean," November 13: 5A.

———. 2002a. "Cars Sold Like Hot Cakes at 23rd Motor Show," April 8. Available at www.nationmultimedia.com.

———. 2002b. "Supply-Chain Management: A Key Tool for Competitiveness," January 7: 3B.

National Statistical Office. 2000. *Report of the Household Socio-economic Survey 1998–1999* [in Thai]. Bangkok: National Statistical Office, Statistical Techniques Division.

———. 2002. *Preliminary Report of the 2000 Household Socio-economic Survey*. Bangkok: National Statistical Office, Statistical Techniques Division.

Office of the National Economic and Social Development Board (NESDB). 1990a. *Social Indicators* [in Thai]. Bangkok: NESDB, Office of the Prime Minister.

———. 1990b. *Social Indicators 1990*. Bangkok: NESDB, Human Resource Planning Division.

———. 1997. *The Eighth National Economic and Social Development Plan (1997–2001)*. Bangkok: NESDB

———. 2000. *Evaluation Report of the First Half of the Eighth National Economic and Social Development Plan 1997–1998* [in Thai]. Bangkok: NESDB.

———. 2001a. *Social Indicators 1995–1999*. Bangkok: NESDB.

———. 2001b. *Economic Conditions of Thailand in 2000 and Trends for 2001* [in Thai]. Bangkok: NESDB.

———. 2002. *The Ninth National Economic and Social Development Plan (2002–2006)*. Bangkok: NESDB.

Office of the Prime Minister. 1999. *Thailand Population Projection 1999–2016*. Bangkok: Office of the National Education Commission, Population Projection Working Group.

Petmark, Puntip and Unksutanasombat, Kanika. (1990). *The Relationship between the Informal Sector in Dense Areas and City Economic System: A Study of Professions in Collecting and Buying Trash in Bangkok* [in Thai]. Center for Information Distribution, Foundation for Development of Housing, Bangkok.

Phuangkanok, Naranart. 2001a. "Advertisers are Moving Outdoors." *The Nation*, November 23. Available at www.nationmultimedia.com, accessed April 30, 2003.

———. 2001b. "Brand-Building Vital to S&P." *The Nation*, October 27: 1B–2B.

———. 2001c. "Retail Survey: Supercentres Now No. 1." *The Nation*, August 6: 3B.

———. 2002a. "Colgate Palmolive High Hopes for Herbal Products." *The Nation*, January 11: 3B.

———. 2002b. "Tokyo Hosts 'One Tambon One Product.'" *The Nation*, March 29: 2B.

Pinkerton, Stewart. 1992. "A Second South Korea?" *Forbes*, December 21: 149–58.

Plubpleng, Patikom. 1991. "Hyper-market, New Strategy for Retailers." *Kookengkaan*, December: 271–78.

Plubpleng, Patikom, and Sutinee Upananchai. 1995. "Superretailers." *Kookengkaan*, June: 128–31.

Poapongsakorn, Nipon, Supachai Yavaprabhas, Pasuk Phongpaichit, and Sauwanee Thairungroj. 2000, November. *Anti-corruption Strategy in Thailand in the Year 2000*. Bangkok: The Office of the Civil Service Commission.

Pongvuthitham, Achara. 1999. "U.S. Focuses on Thai Piracy Ahead of GSP." *The Nation*, March 22. Available at www.nationmultimedia.com, accessed April 30, 2003.

———. 2001a. "Analysis: Who Should Collect Copyright Fees?" *The Nation*, November 5: 1B.

———. 2001b. "China and WTO: Boost for Region–Supachai." *The Nation*, August 17: 3B.

———. 2002. "Battle over the Tuk-Tuk: Efforts to Protect National Symbol." *The Nation*, January 3: 2A.

Poo Chad Karn. 2002. "Foreigner Gives Thailand Poor Mark on Corporate Good Governance," March 15: 17–18.

Prachachart Business. 2002. "@ Coca Cola Moves into Internet Café, a New Outlet for University Students and Teenagers," March 14–17: 17–18.

Rungfapaisarn, Kwanchai. 2001a. "Ad Avoidance: Bangkok Viewers Switch Off." *The Nation*, September 17. Available at www.nationmultimedia.com, accessed April 30, 2003.

———. 2001b. "Big C Plans Outlets for Own Brands." *The Nation*, October 16: 2B.

———. 2001c. "Retail Strategy: Jusco Tries a New Tack." *The Nation*, November 10: 2B.

———. 2002a. "Retail Sector: Mom and Pop Stores Get a Break." *The Nation*, March 8: 3B.

———. 2002b. "Something Brewing, Beer Will Pack Punch." *The Nation*, April 6: 1B–2B.

Rungfahpaisarn, Kwanchai, and Nophakhun Limsamarnphun. 2001. "Champ Hits Big C Shelves." *The Nation*, October 25: 1B–2B.

Schwarz, Adam. 1994. "Just Fine, for Now." *Far Eastern Economic Review*, June 16: 68.

Shawsotikul, Pattarin. 2002. "Women Power Changes Business Tide." *Krungtepturakit*, March 20: 34.

Siam Turakit. 2003. "Way out for Small Retailers," May 4–10. Available at www.ifd.or.th/clippingoneline, accessed March 29, 2004.

Siengthai, Sunanta and Orose Leelakulthanit. 1994. "Women in Management in Thailand," in *Competitive Frontiers: Women Managers in a Global Economy*, ed. Nancy J. Adler and Dafna N. Izraeli, p. 160. Cambridge, MA: Blackwell Publishers.

Singhapakdi, Anusorn, Somboon Salyachivin, Busaya Virakul, and Vinich Veerayangkur. 2000. "Some Important Factors Underlying Ethical Decision Making of Managers in Thailand." *Journal of Business Ethics* 27 (3): 271–84.

Sooksiriserikul, Trungjai. 2000. "Tough Competition in the Grocery Section in 2000 . . . Retailing Moves Direct Selling." *Thai Farmer Bank*, no. 23(April–June). Available at www.kasikornresearch.com, accessed April 30, 2003.

Srisongkrot, Busakorn. 2001. "Business Strategy: 7–Eleven." *Business.Com* 13 (147): 115–18.

Stone, Eric and Janssen, Peter. 1991. "Thailand: Indecision Comes Home to Roost." *Asian Business*, March: 32–44.

Sunsompak, Chanaiya. 2002. "Co-branding Strategy, Put Signers in an Instant Noodle Pack." *Krungtepturakit*, February 25: 1–3.

Supanich, Tientip, and Regina Woraurai. 2001. "Financial Liberalization Policy: Towards a New Paradigm." Paper presented at the Bank of Thailand (BOT) Symposium 2001, Bangkok, Thailand.

Tasker, Rodney. 1993. "Thailand: The Straight and Narrow." *Far Eastern Economic Review*, August 5: 18–19.

Terweil, Barend J. 1984. "Formal Structure and Informal Rules: An Historical Perspective on Hierarchy, Bondage and the Patron-Client Relationship," in *Strategies and Structures in Thai Society*, ed. Han Ten Brummelhuis and Jerry H. Kemp. Amsterdam: Department of Southeast Asian Studies, University of Amsterdam.

Tesnork, Preeya. 2002. "Semi-Modern Trade—Innovation in Paint Store." *Krungtepturakit*, March 6: 30, 32.

Tetnok, Preeya. 2002. "Principle Enhances the Value of Herbal with Modern Package." *Krungtepturakit*, March 2: 23.

Thailand Development Research Institute (TDRI). 1990. *Urbanization and Environment: Managing the Conflicts.* Research Report no. 6, TDRI.

Thai History. 2003. "Ratanakosin Period." Available at www.asia-discovery.com/thai_history.htm, accessed March 10, 2005.

Thai Military Bank. 1995. *Summary on Economic Situation in 1994 and Trends in 1995.* Bangkok: Thai Military Bank, Research Department.

Thai Post. 2002a. "New Advertising Move of Department Store," March 26. Available at www.thaipost.net, accessed April 30, 2005.

———. 2002b. "Congregation of 1,000 Hair Beauty in a Commercial," March 11. Available at www.thaipost.net, accessed April 30, 2003.

Thongrung, Watcharapong. 2001a. "Boon Rawd Mixes Its Drinks." *The Nation*, December 8: 1B.

———. 2001. "PTT's IPO Success 'Will Reignite SET.'" *The Nation*, November 24. Available at www.nationmultimedia.com.

Thorelli, Hans B. and Sentell, Gerald D. 1982. *Consumer Emancipation and Economic Development: The Case of Thailand.* London: JAI Press.

Toomgum, Sirivish. 2001a. "Local Firms Dragging Their Feet." *The Nation*, September 5: 3B.

———. 2001b. "McDonald's, One-2–Call Team Up." *The Nation*, October 2: 2B.

Transparency International. 2002. *The Global Corruption Report 2001* (2001 Corruption Perceptions Index). Berlin: Transparency International. www.globalcorruptionreport.org, accessed April 5, 2002.

Ungphakorn, Peter Mytri. 1993. Can We Manage This Pace? [in Thai]. *Bangkok Post Economic Review Year End 1993,* December 30: 11.

United Nations. 2001. *Social Indicators.* New York: UN Statistics Division, Department of Economic and Social Affairs of the UN Secretariat. Available at http://unstats.un.org/unsd/demographic/products/socind, accessed April 5, 2002.

United Nations Development Programme (UNDP). 1999. *Human Development Report of Thailand 1999.* New York: UNDP.

———. 2001. *Human Development Indicators.* New York: UNDP. Available at www.undp.org/hdr2001/ indicator, accessed April 5, 2002.

Upananchai, Sutinee. 1994. "Changes in Marketing Strategies in Response to Traffic Jam." *Kookengkaan,* October: 140–49.

US-ASEAN Business Council. 2002. "Doing Business in Thailand." Washington, DC: US-ASEAN Business Council. Available at www.us-asean.org/arthur/Thailand/The_Business_Enviroment.htm.

U.S. Commercial Service. 2002. *Market Commercial Guide 2002.* Washington, DC: U.S. Commercial Service, Department of Commerce. www.buyusa.gov/thailand.

Weerakultewan, Sotida. 1994. "Environment Today . . . Lip Service." *Rayngang Piset,* January: 1–2.

Wittuhattakit, Saruktorn. 2001. "M-Life." *BrandAge* 2 (9): 126–30.

Wongtada, Nittaya. 1993. "Forces Controlling the Compliance of the Gentlemen's Agreement Among Overseas Chinese Businessmen." *Journal of International Consumer Marketing* 5 (2): 69–83.

Wongtada, Nittaya, and John Zerio. 1993. "Toward a Conceptual Model of Japanese Consumer Response to Direct Marketing." In *The Japanese Distribution System Handbook,* ed. Michael R. Czinkota and Misaki Kotabe, pp. 191–208. Chicago: Probus.

Wongtada, Nittaya, Orose Leelakulthanit, and Gillian Rice. 1994. "An Investigation of Attitudes and Environmentally Concerned Behavior of Thai Consumers." Paper delivered at the 1994 Asia Pacific Advances in Consumer Research Conference, June 13–16, Singapore.

The World Bank. 2001. *2001 World Development Indicator.* Washington, DC: The World Bank.

Yeedin, Apison. 1994. "Credit-Card Strategies in 1994: Penetration in Rural Market" [in Thai]. *Kookengkaan* 162 (March): 109–12.

Yoon, Suh-kyung. 2000. "Bull's-Eye." *Far Eastern Economic Review* 163, October 12: 42–43.

CHAPTER 18

VIETNAM

Expanding Market Socialism and Implications for Marketing, Consumption, and Socioeconomic Development

CLIFFORD J. SHULTZ II, DAVID DAPICE, ANTHONY PECOTICH, AND DOAN HUU DUC

OVERVIEW

Vietnam continues its transition. A growing and diversifying economy, greater reforms, a rapidly emerging and increasingly sophisticated consumer society, new trade agreements, and sheer market potential all make Vietnam one of the most compelling markets in Southeast Asia. Global marketers must have a presence in Vietnam, yet many unique challenges remain that must be addressed with keen awareness and sensitivity by investors and managers. In this chapter, we present a synopsis of the social, political, economic, marketing, and consumer behavior trends and phenomena that make Vietnam both an attractive and frustrating market. We articulate the challenges that must be overcome and share insights on strategies currently being implemented by successful marketing firms competing in Vietnam.

INTRODUCTION

> Trying to stop a market is like trying to stop a river.
> —Vietnamese Proverb (McMillan 2002, 15)

Vietnam continues to distance itself from war and privation and is demonstrating a remarkable economic, marketing, and consumption renaissance. Reforms initiated in 1986, followed by the restoration of U.S.–Vietnam diplomatic relations in 1995, and the bilateral trade agreement (BTA) signed with the United States in November 2002 have expanded Vietnam's interpretations of market socialism and firmly anchored the country in the global economy. Vietnam is a country of enormous potential, and despite its troubled past, progressive analysts, investors, and other stakeholders are looking to the future. Former U.S. Ambassador to Vietnam, Douglas "Pete" Peterson, embodied this sentiment when stating, "I can't do anything about what happened yesterday, but I can help move forward positively and constructively on what happens tomorrow" (in Lamb 2002,

189). This statement represents well the forward-thinking orientation of those who wish to invest in and to trade with this transitioning country.

Much of Vietnam's rebirth can be explained by the country's natural wealth, its strategic location, the perseverance of the Vietnamese people, as well as the domestic and international policies that have enabled Vietnam to leverage its human and natural resources, to access markets, and thus to grow its economy and to improve the lot of its people. With cultural wealth that includes the traditions and artifacts of four thousand years of national identity, the Vietnamese people are industrious, optimistic, and increasingly joining the consumer society. However, despite considerable foreign investment and a more positive business environment, understanding the interactions of land, culture, political, and economic dynamics, and, in turn, competing effectively in this market as it continues to evolve, remain challenging. The purpose of this chapter is to help investors and managers better understand the relevant and interactive forces that are shaping Vietnam now and into the foreseeable future. To that end, we synthesize and extend streams of research on economics, marketing, and consumer behavior (e.g., Dapice 2000, 2003; Dapice et al. 1994; Dapice and Vallely 1996; Pecotich and Shultz 1993; Shultz 1994; Shultz and Ardrey 1997; Shultz, Ardrey, and Pecotich 1995; Shultz and Le 1993; Shultz and Pecotich 1994; Shultz, Pecotich, and Le 1994; Shultz, Nguyen, Pecotich, and Ardrey 1998; Shultz, Speece, and Pecotich 2000), with the objective to provide insights that managers can leverage to be successful in the arcane market that is Vietnam.

LAND OF THE VIET

Geography and Population

Vietnam is located on the South China Sea—or East Sea, as the Vietnamese claim—and borders China, Laos, and Cambodia; it has a coastline of over 3,444 kilometers (longer than the distance between Seattle and San Diego). The total land area is estimated to be roughly 330,000 square kilometers, or about the size of California. The topography is dominated by hills and mountains—only 20 percent of the land is level, hills comprise approximately 40 percent, and mountains comprise approximately 40 percent. Throughout most of the country, the climate is tropical and monsoonal; there are essentially two seasons: rainy and dry, but unique tendencies can be found. In the northwest mountainous regions, for example, where the summit of Phan Si Pan exceeds 3,200 meters, temperatures can dip below freezing and light snow can be seen during the winter months. The country is long, North to South, and comparatively narrow, East to West. In one stretch of Quang Binh Province, Vietnam is only about 35 kilometers wide (see also Le 1997; *World Factbook* 2004).

Geography is a strong predictor for the movement and location of people and societal practices in transitional Southeast Asia, including in Vietnam (Shultz and Pecotich 1997). The population of Vietnam now exceeds eighty million people, the majority of whom reside in the northern and southern watersheds of the Red and Mekong Rivers, respectively. The dominant contributions of agriculture, and the ensuing urbanization and commercial activity, are greatly determined by lowland and midland fertile planes and watersheds. People living in them historically have grown wet rice and other agricultural products and still wear the customary and practical *Non La* (conical hat) when working the fields. In the mountainous areas, people grow wet rice in valleys and develop terraces for dry crops, such as corn, and they live in houses built on stilts. In the northern uplands and central highlands, slash-and-burn farming still exists; people here grow multiple crops suited to the climate, though the growth, processing, and export of more systemic agricultural enterprises (e.g., coffee and pepper), have become increasingly important to this and other regions (Hoang, Shultz, and Pecotich 2001; see also Tran 1998; Son 2004). Along the coastline, people traditionally organize their lives around fishing, shipping, and tourism (Hoang Nam 2000). More broadly, the country can be categorized into three regions: North, Central, and South, each with distinct geographical, meteorological, and cultural tendencies. The country is generally administered with these fairly distinct regions in mind, though remote mountainous areas and the ethnic minorities that tend to inhabit them create unique administrative challenges.

In its pristine state, most of Vietnam would be covered by rain forest. Urbanization, defoliation, and intensive agricultural practices have denuded substantial tracts of the forest, but dense vegetation still covers much of the country, and deforestation-prevention policies are increasingly a subject of concern. Nearly 75 percent of Vietnamese still reside in rural areas. Urbanization, paramount to economic transformation from an agrarian economy, is increasing and creating ecological and social challenges as well as economic growth (e.g., Dapice 1996, 2003).

The most commercially and politically influential urban centers include the following cities. Hanoi, located on the Red River, with a population of approximately three million people, is the political capital, as well as a growing industrial center. Haiphong, a port and industrial city of nearly two million people, is the other dominant commercial center in northern Vietnam. Ho Chi Minh City, formerly Saigon, located in southern Vietnam on the Saigon River, is the country's commercial capital. By most accounts, Ho Chi Minh City is Vietnam's most cosmopolitan city and remarkably accounts for 23 percent of the nation's gross domestic product (GDP)—the entire region, including Ho Chi Minh City, accounts for 40 percent. Official population statistics indicate that approximately five million people live in Ho Chi Minh City, but responses from multiple interviews by the authors suggest this figure may actually be as large as eight million people. Can Tho, the "rice bowl" on the Mekong, is an agribusiness and aquaculture center. Vung Tau and Danang are key coastal ports. In the central highlands, Da Lat, a mountainous refuge from tropical heat, and Buon Ma Thuot, the coffee capital, are important tourism and agribusiness centers. Hue, located in the central region, is the former capital of Imperial Vietnam and has been classified as a World Heritage Site by the United Nations Educational, Scientific, and Cultural Organization (UNESCO). Ha Long—an abstruse geological phenomenon of 3,000 islands sprinkling the sea—My Son, Hoi An, and Phong Nha have also been classified as such. All are testimony to Vietnam's varied geography, complex cultural heritage, and multisector economic contributions.

In summary, Vietnam's natural assets include a diverse, primarily tropical landscape, which is increasingly being parlayed into economic value. Its fisheries and its vast oil, gas, coal, bauxite, and other mineral reserves contribute to Vietnam's economic expansion. Its fertile soil and the people who till it have enabled Vietnam to become among the two or three largest rice, coffee, pepper, and seafood exporters, depending upon any given year's harvest. Its geographic shape, long coastline, and strategic location at the mouth of the Mekong Basin and bordering China, Laos, and Cambodia indicate that Vietnam is well placed to participate in regional commerce.

Political Structure

Officially the Socialist Republic of Vietnam, the nation is administered by the Communist Party of Vietnam (CPV)—"the force leading the State and society" (Embassy of Vietnam 2003)—and its politburo, which controls both the electoral process and the executive branch. CPV holds a national congress every five years; these meetings formalize policies and generally outline the country's direction and future course. The executive branch is constitutionally responsible to the National Assembly and is elected for a five-year term; primary members of the cabinet include the prime minister and the deputy prime ministers. Key ministries include agriculture and rural development; construction; culture and information; education and training; finance; foreign affairs; industry; interior; justice; labor, war invalids and social affairs; marine products; national defense; planning and investment; public health; science, technology and environment; trade; transport and communications. There is also a central bank governor. The president serves as head of state. The legislature or national assembly is the 498-member *Quoc Hoi*; it meets biannually. The assembly appoints the president and the cabinet. Local government is, ultimately, centrally controlled but has some degree of local accountability and is becoming more autonomous, particularly on matters of economic and business policy (see also Abruza 2002). Ho Chi Minh City and Binh Duong Province, for example, have been reform leaders in policy change and implementation. The judiciary is administered by regional people's courts and military courts; the supreme court is the pinnacle of the legal system (see also Economist Intelligence Unit 2003). Increasingly important foci for the government are how, or to what extent, to administer the evolving reform process; which stakeholders should be included (see also Nguyen in PRS Group 2002, 218); and how best to optimize Vietnam's socioeconomic development. All issues are earnestly debated within the government and among the Vietnamese people.

Ascent of Modern Vietnam and Its People

Vietnam's national character, cultural institutions, and present borders—truly, its birth and present existence—came about from centuries-long persistence and at the price of incessant wars (e.g., Karnow 1991; McAlister and Mus 1970; Nguyen 1987; Taylor 1983). Most archaeological records indicate the first Vietnamese were a homogeneous linguistic group that inhabited the fertile Red River valley, establishing a wet-rice culture, about four thousand years ago. Over the centuries, Vietnam has engaged a nearly continuous battle for sovereignty, while expanding its own territory. Vietnamese history is replete with famous warriors who fought for independence: the Trung Sisters, Ngo Quyen, Le Loi, and others, including, of course, Ho Chi Minh. These wars were also a source of cultural infusion, most notably by China, the Cham and Khmer kingdoms, the Mongols, France, and the United States, which shaped and continues to shape Vietnamese culture. The remnant of this struggle is immense national pride, determined independence, and, some might argue, tendencies toward xenophobia. It is not by chance that one of the most visible aphorisms one sees on landmarks throughout Vietnam is Ho Chi Minh's exhortation: "Nothing is more precious than independence and freedom."

China ruled Vietnam for nearly a thousand years until 939 C.E. and, despite signed agreements and a new spirit of cooperation, particularly concerning border trade and investment, Vietnam continues to keep a wary eye on its formidable rival to the north (e.g., Chen 1987; see also Shultz and Ardrey 1995; Roper 2000).[1] Historical antipathies aside, Chinese influence provided the impetus for a loose adaptation of Taoism, Confucianism, and a mandarin system of administration that Vietnamese feudal rulers used to expand southward in the fifteenth, sixteenth, and seventeenth centuries to conquer the Chams of present-day central Vietnam and the Khmers of the South. The southern expansion led to a fusion of Confucian and Buddhist values that are endemic to Vietnamese culture. Unlike many Southeast Asian states, by the seventeenth century and the arrival of the Europeans, Vietnam had a well-formed culture and language and effective political and economic systems (Williams 1992). These developments helped to shape the Vietnamese view of the world, which, in turn, influences many consumer activities today.

In traditional Vietnam, an amalgam of early animistic beliefs, Taoism, Mahayana Buddhism,

and Confucianism forms the world view based on the existence of two all-encompassing forces—
the Yin and the Yang—the sources of all creation. Jamieson explains their nature as follows:

> Yang is defined by a tendency toward male dominance, high redundancy, low entropy,
> complex and rigid hierarchy, competition, and strict orthodoxy focused on rules for behav-
> ior based on social roles. Yin is defined by a tendency toward greater egalitarianism and
> flexibility, more female participation, mechanisms to dampen competition and conflict,
> high entropy, low redundancy, and more emphasis on feeling, empathy, and spontaneity.
> (1995, 12–13 and 399–400)

It is the desire for harmony and balance between these two coexisting, interlocking forces that
leads to social change, particularly when the Yang dominance is too strong and a Yin reaction is
necessary. Based on this foundation, the Vietnamese developed a core set of traditional values
described by Jamieson as follows:

- *Ly* (reason or the nature of things)—An overarching principle intended to provide a harmonious conformity to structural, universal governing principles by specifying the proper form
  of relationships.
- *Hieu* (filial piety) and *On* (moral debt)—The parent–child relationship forms a core of the
  culture—children must obey, respect, and honor parents and endeavor to repay (unpayable)
  moral debt.
- *De* (the basis of a proper relationship between brothers)—This is the model for societal
  roles, where the older brother should "teach, nurture, and protect" the younger brother, who,
  in turn, should "respect, obey, and support." This is an important principle, as "blood family
  ties" are a critical factor in social action and to disregard them is to act contrary to the natural
  order. Vietnamese children traditionally learn dependence, nurturance, and submissiveness
  rather than assertiveness and independence.
- Sex roles—Even in the traditional context, there was social tension in the roles expected of
  women (the Yin as opposed to the Yang). While the Vietnamese narrative includes heroic, intelligent, and successful women (e.g., the aforementioned Trung Sisters), the general role expectation is submissive and subordinate. Marriages were primarily transactions between two families
  with care needed not to lose face. A wife's primary obligation (*hieu*) was to provide a male heir.
- *Nghia* (the righteous path)—This emphasized duty, justice, and the fulfilling of obligations
  in social relations, regardless of circumstances or preferences.
- *Tinh* (emotionalism, spontaneity or love) and *Nhan* (compassion)—These two values, although
  subordinate to *Nghia*, provide balance to the rationality embodied in the other values.
- *Dieu* (relative versus absolute harmony)—This moderates the absolute standards of *Ly* and
  emphasizes a relativist, reasonable, moderate position in social affairs.
- Abstention versus participation—A good citizen must strive to land between these two extremes of social involvement.
- The power of the natural order—The moral justice by which the universe operates guarantees return to the natural order.
- The family—This basic unit reinforced by ancestral worship forms the fundamental element
  of natural order. Marriage, birth, death, and other complex social interactions all occur within
  the family and the wider context of the village-based hierarchical society. The social and
  economic structures involved both "solidarity and competition," with emphasis on "face and
  status." *Tet*, or the "family ritual of renewal," requires atonement, forgiveness, and philan-

thropy; this annual festival forms a central part of Vietnamese culture and coincides with the commencement of the lunar New Year (Jamieson 1995, 16–41 and 397–400).

This traditional order, briefly articulated, forms the basic fabric of Vietnamese society or, more accurately, the order of the majority ethnic group of Vietnam, the *Kinh* or *Viet,* whose members comprise more than 80 percent of the current population. Vietnam is also home to fifty-three other ethnic groups, with unique languages and cultures. Preponderant among them are the Tay, Thai, Muong, Hoa or ethnic Chinese, Khmer, and Nung; the smallest minorities (numbering in the few hundreds) are the Brau, Romam, and Odu. Economic development, variances in values, and a shift to a consumer society are having a profound impact on the traditional order.

Western influence began with exposure to maritime European powers, particularly the French. The cultural impact of over 100 years of French colonial rule was significant in shaping many Vietnamese institutions. The influence was particularly strong in urban areas and among the Mandarin class, intellectuals, and other elite elements of Vietnamese society. This impact is still seen today in the architecture, the Latin alphabet (i.e., *quoc ngu*), education, some social attitudes, the arts, Roman Catholicism (practiced by about 10 percent of the population), and even in Caodaism, a religion unique to Vietnam, practiced by about three million worshippers in southern Vietnam. However, the French, as the Chinese before them, had a precarious coexistence with the Vietnamese. Given the failures of the traditional system, the Yang domination, the economic hardships, repression, and the resulting cultural disorientation, not surprisingly, by the 1930s, voices were raised questioning traditional values. This was the beginning of the ideological struggle among traditional values, Western ideas, and revolutionary ideals (Jamieson 1995).[2] Following a sustained insurrection, the French were finally expelled from Vietnam after their defeat at Dien Bien Phu in 1954, which, in turn, led to the North–South/Communist–Capitalist division of Vietnam.

U.S. engagement was evident early in American history, when Thomas Jefferson explored the feasibility of importing Vietnamese rice seedlings to Virginia. More direct involvement began in World War II, when the Office of Strategic Services (OSS) worked cooperatively with Ho Chi Minh to repel Japanese forces from Indochina. Viewed by the Eisenhower, Kennedy, Johnson, and Nixon administrations as a beachhead to prevent the spread of communism, the U.S. military involvement increased steadily during the 1960s. By 1968, the influence of Western popular culture reached its peak, with the presence of over 500,000 U.S., Australian, and other allied troops in South Vietnam. During this period, southern, urban Vietnam had become a service economy greatly catering to the American war effort; the departure of Americans created severe economic and psychological challenges for urban economies, particularly Saigon (Williams 1992).

The final withdrawal of the United States and the capitulation of the southern regime on April 30, 1975, resulted in the unification of Vietnam and the emergence of the Socialist Republic. War devastation and unification presented the national leadership with the immense problems of reconstruction and peacetime government. From 1975 to 1986, attempts to rebuild Vietnam, ravaged by two generations of uninterrupted war, were derailed by devastating Marxist–Leninist plans and neo-Stalinist social policies, a protracted border conflict with China, and Vietnam's military expansion into Cambodia, which further depleted social and economic resources.

ECONOMIC ENVIRONMENT

Vietnam clearly faced a crisis in the mid-1980s, as it became one of the poorest countries in the world. The catastrophe was most evident in the forms of hyperinflation, food shortages, boat people, and the prospect that the Soviet Union, its main trading partner and donor, would collapse. The response to that challenge was economic renovation or *Doi Moi*, a far-reaching set of reform policies. By decollectivizing agriculture, moving toward market prices, and bringing inflation under control, the stage was set for a period of rapid economic growth from 1991 to 1997. The Asian Crisis did not have as large an impact on Vietnam as it did on its Association of Southeast Asian Nations (ASEAN) neighbors, but GDP growth slowed from 8 to 9 percent to an official 6.2 percent rate from 1998 to 2002. (The estimates for the post-crisis period from the International Monetary Fund [IMF] are only 4.8 percent.[3]) In either case, Vietnam is in a good position to the extent that it capitalizes upon the economic potential that has been created. The BTA with the United States should open a huge market to manufactured exports and draw in larger amounts of job-creating foreign investment. The Enterprise Law, which took effect in January 2000, makes it much easier to register a domestic private firm and has resulted in a flood of new registrations. If the key issues of improving the legal system, reforming the banking and financial system, and improving the efficiency of public investment can be resolved, then a further period of rapid and poverty-reducing growth should be possible.

Changing Course: The 1980s

Vietnam began the 1980s by having to recover from a Chinese punitive invasion in its north and also facing a lengthy conflict in Cambodia with the Khmer Rouge. The economy was heavily dependent upon the Soviet Union for aid and planned trade. The government imposed a central planning system on a fundamentally agrarian economy, and the result was some growth, but there were enormous distortions. Inflation averaged 160 percent per year from 1980 to 1985 and more than double that from 1986 to 1988. Because the exchange rate and most prices were meaningless, except as accounting prices, the more important fact was that from 1982 to 1987, grain output rose only 5 percent or less than half as much as the population (see Table 18.1). Even though the CPV had given agriculture top priority in the 1981–85 plan, hunger began to appear in several areas. (In the 1976–80 period, the emphasis was on industry and large-scale agriculture. This resulted in declining paddy production and overall output per capita.) While some policies were meant to favor agriculture, the high rate of tax and a substantial labor levy on farmers meant that it was difficult to raise output per capita. Industry did somewhat better, but it was a modest portion of total output, and vital items such as construction materials for living quarters badly lagged behind. But even this unsatisfactory and precarious situation was threatened, as it became clear that there were limits to the extent to which the Soviet Union would be able to continue its support—support that was economically and strategically crucial to Vietnam. Thus, there began to be a reevaluation of the economic policies (e.g., Vo 1990). The fruit of this reappraisal was announced in several meetings culminating in the Sixth National Party Congress in December 1986.

The Party concluded that better economic policy was a matter of life and death. There had been too much emphasis on heavy industry and too little on creating conditions for favorable agricultural growth. There had to be less bureaucratic subsidy-led development and corruption and more use of the full potential of all people. In practice, this meant decollectivization of agriculture; that is, allowing a return to family farms. In principle and increasingly in practice, farmers would be allowed to plant what they wanted and sell it to whomever they wanted, at a market price. However, these changes were phased in gradually, and at different rates in different parts of the country. Indeed, in some places, the policies merely confirmed what local authorities had done on their own. In others, it created real changes on the ground. This marked a huge departure in itself, as it sanctioned petty capitalism in the rural sector where three-quarters of the people lived and farmed. However, this was also accompanied by a decontrol of most prices, including

Table 18.1

Some Basic Economic Indicators, post Doi Moi: 1986–1990

	1986	1987	1988	1989	1990
Inflation (%)	487	301	308	74	36
Grain output (million tons)	18.4	17.5	19.6	21.5	21.5
Grain per capita (kg)	301	281	307	332	323
Exports ($ million)	495	610	733	1,320	1,731
Oil	0	30	79	200	390
Nonoil exports	495	580	654	1,120	1,341
Imports ($ million)	1,121	1,184	1,412	1,670	1,772

Source: World Bank, Report 13143-VN, 9/26 (Washington, DC: World Bank, 1994), pp. 118–19 and 129–30.

the exchange rate. Trade was freed up and foreign investment welcomed. This was a profound change in ideological terms. In practical terms, the first impact was felt in agriculture and petty services, and inflation dropped in 1989 and later years as food output rose.

Perhaps the most surprising aspect of the reforms was the fast and impressive response of the various sectors to the opportunities created by the reduction in planning related controls (see also Cima 1989; Do Duc Dinh 1993; General Statistical Office 1992). There was declining Soviet aid, almost no Western aid, and little foreign investment outside the oil sector. Yet by the time the changes had taken hold in the early 1990s, in spite of the collapse of its main trading partner, Vietnam managed to begin a period of rapid growth marked by progress in exports, agriculture, and industry. Real GDP data for this period are not exact, but growth probably averaged less than 4 percent a year in 1986–87 and more than 6 percent in 1988–90. The removal of restrictions on trade and transport, the freeing up of foreign trade, the shift to a market-based exchange rate, and a partial move toward "normal" commercial banking instead of plan-based enterprise credits all helped the supply response. There was even a formal recognition of a "multisector economy," meaning that private firms were allowed, if not encouraged. Another point, not always noted, is that the completion of the huge Hoa Binh hydroelectric facility allowed electricity production to grow by 54 percent from 1986 to 1990. This provided a critical input.

The rapid increase in exports, which allowed strong growth in imports despite a phasing down of aid, was a key element in the success of this period. While oil went from nothing to nearly $400 million, the nonoil sectors contributed over $800 million. Rice and marine and other agricultural products were major items, as exports to nonsocialist economies rose very quickly. The ability of agriculture and fisheries to adjust was essential to this early success. Beyond the increased food output, the freeing up of restrictions on the movement of both goods and people also had a major beneficial impact on the population. This increased support for subsequent steps.

The First Transition: 1991–1993

By 1991, it became clear that economic reforms would not be suppressed, and the Seventh Party Congress solidified them (Communist Party of Vietnam 1991); it also became apparent that supporting reform would likely consolidate the party's power (Erlanger 1991; see also *Quan Doi Nhan Dan* 1992). However, despite the initial successes, there was a lot of unfinished business. Inflation flared

Table 18.2

Some Basic Economic Indicators during the First Transition, 1991–1993

	1991	1992	1993
Real GDP growth (%)	6.0	8.6	8.1
Inflation (%)	83	38	8.4
Money supply growth (%)	79	34	19
Exports ($ million)	$2,042	$2,475	$2,850
Imports ($ million)	$2,105	$2,535	$3,505
Revenue/GDP (%)	13.5	19.0	22.3
Spending/GDP (%)	14.2	19.8	25.8
Deficit*/GDP (%)	1.5	1.7	4.8
Savings/GDP (%)	13.1	16.3	11.2

*The government budget deficit includes interest paid, while the spending variable does not. Interest paid is less than interest due. In 1990, the government's cash deficit was 5.8 percent of GDP, and savings were 7.4 percent of GDP (World Bank, Report 14645-VN [Washington, DC: World Bank, 1995], Appendix Table 5.1).

up in late 1990 and 1991, reaching a year-over-year increase of 83 percent in 1991. Budget deficits had to be brought down, money supply growth reined in, and domestic savings raised and then allocated more efficiently. The oil sector helped by growing from $390 million in exports in 1990 to $844 million in 1993, providing both foreign exchange and tax revenue. However, nonoil exports also increased over 50 percent from 1990 to 1993, reaching the $2 billion level. Garments began to play a major role, along with raw materials. The Vietnamese authorities responded fairly well to these challenges. Certainly, the data show an impressive further decline in inflation, even while GDP and export growth continued or even improved. Table 18.2 outlines major variables.

During this period, the exchange rate was allowed to depreciate, but not as fast as inflation. The nominal exchange rate was 5,800 dong to the dollar during 1990, and this rose to 10,640 dong in 1993, an increase of 83 percent. Yet, prices rose 160 percent in the same period. To the extent that the export supply curve was improving due to continued restructuring, this real appreciation was appropriate. However, to the extent that increasing oil exports, borrowing, or remittances allowed this, there may have been a kind of "Dutch Disease" effect. (This refers to a case of mineral exports causing a real appreciation of the exchange rate that harms nonoil sectors, though other sources of foreign exchange can cause the problem.) Many would argue that because exports were growing at nearly 20 percent a year—though nonoil exports grew only 15 percent a year—there could not be any problem. Others, concerned that farmers were most of the poor and were most hurt by the appreciation, would argue the opposite. In any case, Vietnam in 1993 remained a very poor nation, with less than $200 per capita income, and only $12 billion in total GDP. In spite of continuing growth in agriculture and industry, Vietnam was still isolated from the United States, a recipient of little nonoil foreign investment and unable to get significant aid levels.

The Boom Years: 1994–1997

The economic slowdown during the mid-1990s in Europe and Japan meant that there were substantial savings in those places looking for investments. Asia was one of the primary desti-

Table 18.3

Some Basic Economic Indicators During the Boom Years, 1994–1997

	1994	1995	1996	1997
Real GDP (%)	8.8	9.5	9.3	8.2
Inflation (%)	9.4	17.4	5.7	3.2
Investment/GDP (%)	26	27	28	28
Exchange rate ('000)	11	11	11	11.7
Exports ($ billion)	4.0	5.2	7.3	9.1
Imports ($ billion)	5.8	8.4	11.6	11.6
FDI commitments (U.S.$ billion)	3.8	7.5	9.3	4.8
FDI, actual inflow	1.5	2.3	1.8	2.1

Source: International Monetary Fund data. Imports are c.i.f.

nations, and Vietnam was among the recipients, if only a relatively minor one. The major form of inflow was foreign direct investment (FDI). It rose from $260 million in 1992 to over $1 billion in 1994, and then averaged $2 billion in 1995–97. Transfers (gifts, both private and official, and family investments from abroad) were $123 million in 1992, rising to over $300 million in 1994 and an average of $900 million in 1995–97. Foreign aid and other loans also grew, multiplying by a factor of four to $1 billion by 1997. These flows allowed imports to skyrocket far beyond exports, which themselves tripled from $3 to over $9 billion from 1993 to 1997 (Table 18.3). The result was a small increase in the proportion of investment, but a strong overall rise in spending and output. These were heady years, producing high growth rates and significant reductions in poverty. However, there was an element of a bubble in some of the capital flows, especially since about three-quarters of the FDI in industry was aimed at high-cost import-substituting industries. With high tariffs and other trade barriers, the prices of many products were well above world levels.

It is noteworthy that the FDI commitments were so much higher than the actual inflows, at least as estimated by the IMF. This is a complicated matter, for many of the initial FDI partnerships were with state enterprises—it was often hard for a foreign firm to enter an industry unless one selected a state-owned firm as a joint-venture partner. (This was not true for exporting, especially from export-processing zones.) Because the state-owned enterprise effectively got a 30 percent share of ownership for contributing land, the foreign firm would often overstate the value of its own contribution, typically machinery. This would create higher nominal depreciation and reduce profits, thus reducing the need for profit sharing. The official data include the overstated value of land and of machinery. This is why the IMF figures are used.

Export growth in US$ was 30 percent per year from 1993 to 1997, with 35 percent per year for nonoil exports. The manufactured exports, such as garments, shoes, and electronic goods, finally began to take a considerable share of output, and their share grew very quickly. Coffee also grew very fast, at 61 percent per year. Oil (14 percent), rice (26 percent), coal (24 percent), and rubber (31 percent) also continued to grow but at a slower pace than manufactured goods and coffee. In 1997, the combination of garments, shoes, electronics, and handicrafts accounted for over $3 billion in exports, or a third of all exports. In 1993, all light industrial good exports had totaled only $526 million, so there was a sixfold increase in four years. Yet, for many of these exports, the domestic value added was only 10–20 percent of the export value. That is, materials would come in, get processed with low-cost labor, and the final product would be exported. Relatively little of the export value came from or went to the Vietnamese. There was not yet the development of supplier industries. Most inputs were imported.

The ownership structure of industry began to be measured in its current form—that is, by breaking out the foreign sector separately—only in 1995. In 1995, the state sector accounted for 50 percent of output, the local nonstate sector for 25 percent, and the foreign sector (including oil) for 25 percent. Both the state and the domestic private sectors saw their shares drop by 1 percent per year, while the foreign sector's share grew by 2 percent per year until 1997. There was almost no real movement on state-owned enterprise reform during this period. Very few firms were "equitized" or put into a joint-stock company structure with a board of directors and some outside shareholders. (Most shares continued to be held by the government, other state enterprises, and employees.) Because much of the FDI output was protected and high-cost, the competitiveness of the economy may have been impaired during this growth spurt, despite the gains in labor productivity. Employment in industry of any kind scarcely grew at all, though real output was growing by 13–14 percent per year.

The banking system continued to lend mostly to state enterprises, though the private loan share approached 50 percent as farmers began to get production loans. Credit-to-GDP ratios rose from 19 percent in 1994 to 21 percent in 1997, suggesting a backward and slowly developing financial sector. Credit/GDP in Thailand exceeded 100 percent, and it was nearly 100 percent in China. One reason for this was that legal reforms, especially with respect to bankruptcy laws and procedures, continued to lag. It was difficult for a bank to be sure that pledged collateral would, in fact, be made available on an overdue loan, as collection procedures were lengthy and expensive.

Because exports were growing so quickly, there was no reason to depreciate the exchange rate during this period. It stayed close to 11,000 dong to the dollar, even though inflation averaged 9 percent per year over this period. Again, a massive increase of investment may have allowed exports to be created at existing cost levels. But real income gains for farmers were harder to come by, as export prices did not rise, though consumer prices did. Agriculture continued to grow by over 4 percent per year, so real income gains, while low, were positive. Poverty had declined to about three-eighths of the population by 1997. This was about half the poverty rate in 1987. Most poor people (90 percent) were rural.

Government revenues and grants remained at around 21–23 percent of GDP in this period, and spending was normally a bit higher, though in 1997, the fiscal balance (including onlending) rose to 3.9 percent of GDP, mostly financed by foreign loans. Public capital spending and onlending rose from 5.4 percent of GDP in 1994 to 8.4 percent in 1997. Perhaps because of the ample supplies of capital, many public investments were quite capital intensive (e.g., Yali, the 720 megawatt hydropower project), even though other alternatives were available and would have been cheaper at market interest rates.

Asian Crisis and Its Aftermath: 1998–2001

The collapse of a number of Asian economies in 1997–98 had a distinct impact on the Vietnamese economy. FDI declined, and exports and total growth slowed. Because the level of imports, while not increasing until after 1999, was still well above that of exports, it became necessary to require the surrender of foreign exchange. At first, 80 percent of foreign exchange earnings had to be turned in for local currency, though this was lowered in steps to 40 percent by 2001. However, the prospect of extra difficulty in converting local currency profits to foreign exchange for repatria-

Table 18.4

Some Basic Economic Indicators During Asian Crisis and Its Aftermath, 1998–2001

	1998	1999	2000	2001
Real GDP—official	5.8%	4.8%	6.8%	6.8%
Real GDP—IMF	3.5%	4.2%	5.5%	5.0%
Inflation	7.3%	4.1%	−1.7%	1.0%
M2/GDP	28%	40%	50%	57%
Credit/GDP	22%	29%	35%	40%
Investment/GDP	29%	28%	30%	31%
Exports ($ billion)	9.4	11.5	14.4	15.2
Imports ($ billion)	11.5	11.7	15.6	16.2

Sources: World Bank, *Vietnam: Delivering on Its Promise* (Washington, DC: World Bank, 2002); International Monetary Fund (IMF), Reports 02/5 and 02/151 (Washington, DC: IMF, 2002).

tion meant that import-substituting investment declined. The decline in commitments was very large, from $9.3 billion in 1996 to $1.7 billion in 1999, with only a slight recovery to $2.1 billion in 2000. IMF estimates of FDI disbursements dropped from $2.1 billion in 1997 to $700–800 million per year in 1998–2000 and $1 billion in 2001. This decline was partly offset by an increase in transfers from $900 million in 1997 to $1.5 billion in 2001. Official development assistance (ODA) loans similarly rose from $550 million to $1 billion. Because the dong was not convertible, and there had been relatively little short-term debt, the overall impact of the decline in private capital flows was much less than in other economies, but it was big enough to be noticed, as Table 18.4 indicates.

To be specific, the growth rate of GDP was officially estimated at an average 6 percent per year from 1998 through 2001. However, the IMF estimated GDP growth at only 4.5 percent, and other estimates were also lower than the official one. Since investment remained at around 28–30 percent of GDP, it appears that the required investment for a unit of continuing output rose from three to five or six. This is partly due to the unexpected slowdown, and may also be partly due to the poor project selection by both high-cost FDI and public investments.

Even exports, which have held up fairly well, have slowed. They rose from $9 billion to $15 billion from 1997 to 2001, a growth rate of 14 percent per year. Coffee exports actually declined in value, as prices fell for robusta coffee. The huge increase in Vietnam's production (and Brazil's too) created excess supply and a virtual market collapse for that kind of coffee. Rice, rubber, and crude oil faced similar problems of declining prices, though not due to unreasonably high export volumes from Vietnam. Meanwhile, gains in labor-intensive manufactured exports were harder to achieve, as competition from other ASEAN economies (who had devalued in real terms) and China proved troublesome. It is also true that with a soft global economy and a larger export base, the conditions were tougher, but a lack of domestic reforms and slow development of local supplier networks also played a role. In particular, it was still difficult for many private firms to get bank loans, especially longer-term loans.

The virtual collapse in approvals of FDI and the slower rate of GDP growth pushed the government into making several key reforms. The surrender of foreign exchange requirement was cut from 80 percent to 40 percent. It became possible for ordinary citizens to save foreign exchange in banks. The foreign exchange could also be withdrawn on demand. This sparked an extremely rapid increase in bank deposits in foreign exchange, with a fivefold increase measured in dong from the end of 1997 to 2001. Dong deposits only tripled in the same period, so the share of foreign currency deposits surpassed 45 percent and is heading toward half. However, in part because of continuing difficulties with legal procedures,[4] much of the increase in deposits in Vietnamese banks was passed offshore to Singapore and Hong Kong bank deposits, where the dollars earned only about 1 percent per year at the end of 2001. This amounted to billions of dollars. Meanwhile, thousands of private firms were hampered by a lack of access to capital. However, credit rose to 40 percent of GDP by the end of 2001—nearly double the ratio of 1997. The problems lie in the ability to lend effectively, more than in lack of demand. Interest rates have been gradually freed and are not a major burden on the ability of banks to attract deposits or lend.

The need to create jobs and economic growth prompted another major step in 1999. An Enterprise Law was debated and passed, taking effect in early 2000. This law allowed private firms above the household level to register easily, with a minimum of red tape. Small firms had always been allowed, as they were really a way for families to survive. However, as a firm got larger and started to employ numbers of nonfamily labor, they had historically faced many barriers. Land, outside of that owned for housing, was difficult to get for a firm's location—unless it was insecurely rented from a state enterprise. However, such renting could be revoked at any time, so building on the plot was inadvisable. Bank loans, as has been mentioned, were, and remained, difficult to arrange except for very short-term loans. The registration process had been very complicated and lengthy, often involving considerable expense. The law reduced the registration period from one to two months to ten days or less, with similar reductions in expenses. In 2000–2001, thirty thousand new firms were registered. Some of these had certainly existed previously as large firms with (incorrect) household registrations, but others had been small and expanded or were totally new. It is likely that several hundred thousand new jobs were created and perhaps $2 billion in new investment created. This change, especially if backed up by further financial and land reforms, is one of the largest since the initial Doi Moi reforms of the 1980s. It is especially important if it allows the development of supplier industries to exporters, reducing input costs and boosting competitiveness. Vietnam's current manufactured exports of $5 billion are tiny compared to those of Guangdong province in China. With the same population as Vietnam, it has $100 billion in exports, nearly all of them manufactured. FDI inflows are roughly ten times as high, as well.

The flip side of private-sector development is a rationalization and shrinkage in the state enterprise sector. Many state enterprises are inefficient, either losing money or making money only with the implicit subsidies from free land and other advantages. The bad loans in the state banking system are officially 12–15 percent of total loans, but probably double to triple that level in fact. If the state firms are not reformed, the banking system will continue to produce bad loans, and there will be constant problems of an "uneven playing field" relative to the private sector. Vietnam is fortunate in that only about 5 percent of the labor force works in state enterprises, and aid is available to ease the retirement or retraining of surplus state employees, and to restructure the banks. (The problem in China is comparatively much larger.) In March 2001, a plan was adopted to equitize, divest, close, or merge 2,000 out of 5,500 state enterprises. Most of these are small to medium-size enterprises, with only a tenth of loans or capital. However, they account for nearly one-third of all jobs. This will leave the major state enterprises in capital-intensive industries much as they are. Because many of them are unable to produce competitive goods at world prices, they tend to create conflicts with the reductions in tariffs and other protectionist measures, which the Vietnamese government has already negotiated within the ASEAN Free Trade Area and with the United States in the BTA. There is thus an urgent need to find ways to deal with these larger state enterprises.

While the banking system has grown rapidly, so has another financing mechanism. This is called the Development Assistance Fund. Its increase in credit outstanding in 2000 was as large as that of the entire banking system. It gathers funds from aid, government bonds, and pension funds, and lends them at below-market rates (almost entirely) to government projects. Thus, the effective supply of credit is skewed more toward the public sector than the banking data alone would indicate. This is a concern for several reasons. One is that this mechanism can end up supporting state enterprises with hidden subsidies, prolonging the expensive period of transition. Another is that draining off long-term capital for low-yield public investments reduces the supply of longer-term funds for private firms. There are literally billions of dollars in infrastructure and heavy industry investment projects that would not pass any basic economic analysis but are supported by various constituencies. Unless the investment selection system is strengthened, these projects will increase debt and reduce the competitiveness of the economy. For example, Vietnam's telephone company has long-distance calls that cost three or four times those of China, even though their rates have dropped somewhat. This makes it difficult for Vietnamese firms to market their exports.

Another macroeconomic challenge has come from the change in government finances. In 1996, revenue was 22.4 percent of GDP, and grants were 0.6 percent. This nearly matched spending, if onlending is excluded. However, revenues have generally fallen to about 20 percent, and grants have also slipped to 0.4 percent of GDP, while spending has risen to the 23–25 percent range. Thus, the budget deficit has risen to 2–4 percent of GDP. While a budget deficit of 2 percent of GDP could probably be sustained, the long-term viability of higher debts is more problematic. Because income relies on international trade taxes, which are declining as tariffs are reduced, and other revenues rely on volatile oil prices, an improvement in tax design and enforcement is needed, especially the value-added tax. Local governments might also make greater use of real estate taxes. Personal income taxes generate little income, because they quickly climb to 50 percent of income (even though recently reduced) and are widely evaded or avoided by legal means. Ironically, a lower tax rate might actually generate more tax revenue. The other approach is to reduce spending, and here the restraint on expensive but low-return public investments would be crucial, as would faster equitization. To the extent that state-owned enterprise reform or bank restructuring uses soft ODA loans, the repayment burdens should be manageable. Debt-service ratios are modest (12 percent of exports), especially since the Russian debt was reduced via negotiations.

The exchange rate has been allowed to depreciate from about 12,300 to the dollar at the end of 1997 to 15,000 by the end of 2001. Inflation was only 10 percent over the entire period, so the real exchange rate depreciated, though not so much as it did in some other Asian nations. The slippage in the exchange rate is one reason why dollar deposits became more popular, especially as interest rates on local currency became so low after 1998 that they were barely able to cover the rate of depreciation against the dollar. The faster growth of trade than output has meant that the ratio of imports and exports to GDP now exceeds 100 percent. Thus, Vietnam is a highly and increasingly open economy, with further scope for integration into the global economy on increasingly favorable terms.

Current Conditions

In 2002–3, Vietnam has distinguished itself by continuing brisk growth in exports (11 percent per year from 2001–3) and GDP (6–7 percent, official estimates). Private-sector business registrations continue to soar, with twenty thousand a year forming in 2001 and 2002. FDI has grown, especially in response to gas and electrical generation projects. The IMF estimates FDI inflows at just over $1 billion (2–3 percent of GDP) in 2001–2. The trade deficit in 2003 began to run at a high $4 billion annual rate (10 percent of GDP), although the exchange rate is stable against the dollar, albeit with rising interest rates on dong deposits and loans. Other concerns are slow movement in financial liberalization, sluggish reform of state enterprises, poor-quality and high-cost public investment, and a continuing lag in various international comparisons with other economies. Progress is being made—the cost of international telephone calls is now below $1 a minute for those who know the cheapest way—but falling costs in other countries mean that Vietnam remains a high-cost economy for many items. High-cost data lines make Internet use lag well behind China or Thailand. In short, Vietnam has come a long way but has a long way left to go, as others also improve, but from a more advanced initial position.

Still, considering where it started, Vietnam has made remarkable economic progress. Though its per capita income is still only about $400, that is double in real terms what it was when reforms started. Inflation, at the time of this writing, has ceased to be a factor, and both interest and exchange rates are close to their scarcity values. Major problems in legal and financial reform lie ahead, and there are further challenges to formulating better tax and spending policies. But these should be less difficult than the steps taken thus far. Perhaps tougher will be the transformation of the state enterprises from cost centers representing economic liabilities to competitive or, at least, not-deficit firms that do not crowd out efficient companies that generate growth and jobs. Job creation will require that private firms continue to grow, and that will require the further removal of barriers to acquiring land, credit, information, and permission to operate; at the time of this writing, such changes are occurring at a rapid pace. Still, with the approval of the BTA and access to the U.S. market, and with a push to join the WTO by 2005, it is likely that FDI and exports will increase, and with that, there will be opportunity for further growth by domestic firms. With the macroeconomic fundamentals close to right, further equitable growth mainly requires that the momentum and logic of the past reforms be pushed forward. Because of competitive pressure from its neighbors, it is likely that any Vietnamese administration will conclude that such a path is necessary, even if it is difficult. Thus, even if Vietnam is not bound to succeed, most likely, it can and will, as it continues to transition and "to catch up with the rest of the world" (the stated objective of so many Vietnamese), and to become an industrialized country by the year 2020, the stated objective of the government (Economist Intelligence Unit 2003).

MARKETING ENVIRONMENT

Vietnam is recreating its national identity as a country that is open for business, while distancing itself from the images of war devastation and ineffectual policies. The tendencies and trends discussed above, coupled with latent consumer demand, underscore the vast potential that is Vietnam. Despite its market potential, however, Vietnam is not soon likely to become an "easy" market, not even for investors with successful experience in Southeast Asia and other transitional economies. Some key market tendencies to consider are discussed in the following subsections.

Marketing Institutions and Infrastructure

If the reforms are to succeed fully, Vietnam needs to develop marketing institutions; not only for Vietnam to fulfill its strategic plan to grow through export development, but also to meet the increasing demands of the domestic market. Infrastructure development and technology transfer are requisite drivers of this process (cf. *Vietnam News* 2003), and the foundation for an integrated modern marketing system is, in fact, emerging. Air- and seaports are being refurbished, and the Internet is more accessible, as broad examples. To enhance efficiencies, considerable emphasis has been placed on special economic zones, which abets integrated infrastructure development and, in turn, enables more seamless interaction with global markets. Still, there is much work to be done throughout the value chain, particularly to roads, railways, and seaports. Telecommunications, banking, construction, universities, water treatment facilities, medical centers, dams, power plants, and other institutions necessary for the establishment of a modern marketing system, while on many measures are improved, remain suboptimal. Yet, precisely because the marketing infrastructure is still relatively nascent and challenging, as compared to many other investment destinations in the region, there are good opportunities to seize, if investors understand the unique dynamism of the market.

Consumers and Their Consumption

The Vietnamese people will ultimately determine the long-term success of the country's renaissance. The new (consumption-driven) world order for them has changed dramatically since the implementation of Doi Moi. These changes include population migrations; emerging class stratification and greater market segmentation; brand, advertising, and retail proliferation; variety and competition; fundamental changes in societal values; and in essence, the unremitting desires, uncertainties, anxieties, and general frustrations and opportunities most "capitalists" expect from a relatively unrestricted free market economy. The vast majority of Vietnamese, however, still have very modest purchasing power. The average urban consumer counts on an annual per capita income of under $800 per year, similar to Chinese urban incomes in 2000. This is less than a quarter of the income earned by consumers in Thailand. Vietnam, therefore, is still a poor, albeit developing, country, which creates problems for marketers and investors.

Reforms, nevertheless, are creating more wealth; many Vietnamese have shifted from the grind of daily subsistence and, as a consumer culture continues to diffuse through society, specific trends and segments are becoming more evident. Initial attempts to understand Vietnamese consumers resulted in rudimentary segmentation profiles: traditional versus nontraditional, rural versus urban, north versus south, and younger versus older (Shultz, Pecotich, and Le 1994). Attempts have also been made to discern tendencies among particular city-dwellers and rural residents, suggesting, for example, that Hanoians tend to be more serious, scrutinizing, demanding, value conscious, trend followers; while Saigonese tend to be more playful, casual, compromising, and outspoken trend setters; and rural consumers tend to focus more on family, product utility, personal relationships, and general happiness (cf. Vietnam Consulting Group 2002). More recently, consumer panels have been formed, providing more detailed market tendencies. What follows is an examination of Vietnam's emerging consumer class.

The consumer class in Vietnam has been defined as individuals reporting annual income greater than 54 million dong (US$3,600).[5] While clearly a minority, accounting for no more than 25 percent of all consumers in either Hanoi or Ho Chi Minh City, it is important to measure and to understand this cluster, members of which will likely be opinion leaders for the entire country and thus will predict future, larger-scale consumption patterns of interest to marketers.

Who comprises the consumer class? Fifty-six percent of them are under the age of thirty. (Note too that over half the *entire* Vietnamese population is under the age of thirty.) Fifty-three percent are male. They are relatively well educated: over 40 percent have at least attended college; another 45 percent have completed at least the tenth grade. They tend to be students, professionals, businesspersons, and skilled laborers. The number of people entering the consumer class has grown 14 percent in two years, indicating an increase in spending power for the entire country, and certainly, the principal urban areas. In what could be considered the contemporary Vietnamese standard package (cf. Keyfitz 1982), virtually everyone in this class now can afford and does, in fact, own relatively expensive items, such as motorcycles, color televisions, and stereo equipment; most own washing machines, and many own air conditioners and karaoke machines. They also tend to be technologically aware and savvy. In only two years, ownership of mobile phones and home-access to the Internet has increased 200 percent. Preferences have shifted from VCR to DVD players, and this group has access to satellite and cable television, which gives access to Australian, Japanese, Thai, Korean, Singaporean, Indonesian, Chinese, American, British, French, German, Malaysian, Pakistani, and Indian programming.[6] As evidence of their longer-term focus and concern for security and financial planning, life insurance sales have increased dramatically, and multinational underwriters have entered the market. A small, but growing upper class has emerged. This group of consumers is purchasing luxury items, including expensive automobiles, villas, and high-fashion products, and is traveling the world (e.g., Dao Loan 2003).

Consumption of global products and services and exposure to the media from other parts of the world inevitably will have a greater influence on everyone in Vietnam. Yet, while a consumption ethos definitely has emerged, some of the pillars of Vietnamese values reportedly remain, such as an obligation to live up to others' expectations, health consciousness, thrift and financial savings, and working hard to the benefit of the next generation. Two-thirds of the consumer class think holding onto traditional Vietnamese values is important, especially respecting the elderly and being humble and altruistic. Family attachments remain very important, and concern for money rather than family reportedly has decreased since 1999. Nevertheless, a growing number of consumers under the age of thirty choose to spend time with friends rather than family and increasingly describe their attitudes as different from their parents; they also are willing to spend more to have "finer things." The entire consuming class has raised its sights. More than half now want to own a car and to have an "expensive" foreign vacation; many want a new home and new computers. They also believe the economic, marketing, and consumption environment and the quality of life, generally, will improve, though they have concerns about the environment.

Subsumed in the consumer class is the post-Doi Moi generation, or "Po-Dois," as we have labeled them. They are between eighteen and twenty-three years of age and are attuned to the marketing environment, both in Vietnam and more globally. Self-confident, setting their own agenda, and improving their financial independence, Po-Dois manage to balance newly found freedom and opportunities with traditional Vietnamese norms. Qualitative research enabled psychographic categorizations, which, upon further analysis, we have labeled and described as subsequently discussed (cf. *Vietnam Economic Times* 2000a).

Hip 'n' Cool

They live for the moment and are less concerned about the future. They tend to come from wealthy families and focus their time and energies on having fun. Marketers should view them as trendsetters for fashion, conspicuous consumption, and hedonic lifestyle, including what, where, how, how much, and when they buy, spend, and recreate.

Neo-Trads

The largest subset of Po-Dois, Neo-Trads view education, career, and social status as key drivers for their lives. They have traditional values, but they see new ideas and opportunities as mechanisms to enhance their station in life and those values. Dedicating most of their time to self-improvement, they also spend their time in nightclubs, bars, and other fashionable venues, but not as much as do the Hip 'n' Cool. Friends and "safer" social activities are meant to justify playtime, which will enhance their work and professional goals. Neo-Trads are keen to maintain the traditional social and family roles and values in ways that are harmonious with modern life.

Hard Chargers

The second largest group, Hard Chargers, devote their time to work and to building their careers. Stable financial conditions and fast-track management must come before marriage. Secure with larger disposable income, they spend money on items and brands that strengthen their social status. For a brighter future, honor, and to achieve newly attainable goals in life, strivers will sacrifice social life, entertainment, and play.

Satisfieds

Mostly female and earning lower incomes, members of this segment are more conservative in their orientation toward life's goals and their behavior. They focus on caring for family and striving for a stable marriage, preferably to a rich man. Less individualistic and opinioned, they are reluctant to take advantage of new and emerging opportunities. They also tend not to be key decision makers for many products and services; rather, they tend to rely on one or many influencers in their referent group.

Again, though still a minority, the preceding segments—a younger subset of the consumer class—are a precursor for Vietnamese consumer trends and the future orientation of Vietnamese society.

Retailing and Shopping Revolution

A dynamic relationship exists between consumers and retailers. Consumers want more goods and services, have higher expectations for their performance, and want more modern venues in which to purchase and to consume them; retailers respond to these expectations and demands, and also drive them. A retailing and shopping revolution, therefore, has accompanied the consumer boom. Product proliferation and expansion of the wholesaling and retailing sectors indicate that shopping, in addition to being utilitarian, has become a hedonic pastime. Indeed, going to markets, supermarkets, and coffee shops accounts for nearly half of the reported leisure time for the consumer class. The following text provides a glimpse into this revolution.

Modern retail outlets have been mushrooming, offering more products, better service, and more pleasant shopping ambiance. These outlets also threaten the existence of hundreds, perhaps thousands, of traditional or wet markets and state-run retail shops. Five predominant types of retail establishments have emerged in Ho Chi Minh City and Hanoi, which are likely to serve as predictors for other urban areas. These types include niche retailers, restaurants/cafés, supermarkets, department stores, and hypermarkets.

Niche markets, such as clothing shops, other consumer retailers, and parts suppliers, were among the first to emerge in the wake of Doi Moi. Primarily labor intensive, they have grown on every conceivable dimension: there are more of them, with better variety, including globally recognized and authentic brands, in better physical venues, with better service, catering to many, more diverse segments of the market. Restaurants and cafés similarly emerged and evolved. Perhaps the bellwether, however, has been the emergence of large retailers and hypermarkets. Some leaders included Coopmart, Diamond Plaza, and Metro.

Coopmart, which we categorize as a supermarket, opened in the late 1990s, principally focused on food and household-goods retailing. Consumers initially tended to visit simply for window shopping. Supermarkets were places to view new products or fashions that visitors then would attempt to purchase at other, more affordable establishments. Over time, air-conditioning, selection, service, merchandising, and hygiene became competitive advantages; furthermore, Coopmart gained bargaining power by increasing purchase volume to manufacturers. Management focused on fast-moving local consumer goods, with certified quality. Coopmart then leveraged facing capacity by selling prime racks or location to international manufacturers, who wanted to merchandise their global brands in more up-market venues with more controls and facings. Coopmart management also sought corporate sponsorship for weekend events or periodic store promotions. By the end of 2000, Coopmart was recognized as the largest supermarket chain. Other stores with similar market targets and positioning have begun operation, with hopes of mimicking Coopmart's success.

Diamond Plaza, a modern department store, further expanded and developed the retail sector. A mid- to high-end retailer, the store originally operated by leasing spaces and booths to various subcontract retailers and their brands. This model was similar to the long-standing administrative practices in the large, older markets, such as Ben Thanh and Dong Xuan—it was intended to minimize investment risks. However, the resulting disorganization in floor layout and inconsistency in retail practices confused shoppers. Diamond Plaza management adjusted. All booths were redesigned to create a unified theme and harmony. Lights and merchandising were carefully used to optimize consumer interfaces. Floor maps and signs were made more clear and easy to find. Staffs of each booth were carefully trained and wore uniforms of similar, fashionable design. All retailers who lease space and booths can participate in store promotion to their advantage. The design of the building, per se, was new, modern, and attractive; management placed carts and attractive promotional materials outside the store to entice customers. Clearance-sales areas were administered at corners to direct traffic and to create an image of value- rather than price-orientation. As a multifloor facility, booths and products were placed strategically. The first two floors featured fashion products, including branded clothes, cosmetics, sport shops, and jewelry; the third floor featured home appliances, kitchenwares, audio and video equipment, and a convenience market; the fourth floor focused on entertainment in the forms of video games, bowling and billiards, and a fast-food court featuring a U.S. fast-food franchise. Consumer prices tend to be higher than outside shops by 25–50 percent, given the rent was US$70–US$80 per square meter, and the retailers were attempting to position themselves as value-added shopping venues.

Despite the premium look and the prime location, some visitors said it coincided too closely with Korean tastes, including the absence of a parking lot for motorbikes, the most popular form of transportation for Vietnamese. In fact, Diamond Plaza was a joint venture between a Korean Steel company and Vietnam Steel Corporation. Further adjustments are being made, including the recent addition of a modern cinema. Diamond Plaza remains popular and has spurred similar shopping venues in District 1 of Ho Chi Minh City, but it is also important to note that, similar to activity seen at Coopmart, many consumers only window-shop there and then purchase products from other retailers.

There also is a revolution in the wholesale and wholesale-retail markets, as evidenced by the German Metro-Cash & Carry and French Cora hypermarkets that have entered Vietnam. Hypermarkets, which typically have considerable bargaining power over suppliers, will lower prices and render consumer channels more efficient.

Most of the aforementioned developments in the distribution system have occurred in less than five years. From a consumer's perspective, they have positively affected variety, efficiency, prices, hygiene, service, shopping and consumption experiences, and life quality. Additional changes and streamlines are rapidly forthcoming that will strongly affect marketing processes, shopping, and consumption.

Products and Brands

Given Vietnam's stage of development and the contributions from particular sectors, products and services intended to improve agribusiness and infrastructure are still in great demand, but the emerging consumer market in Vietnam is compelling. All types and brands of end-user products and services are rapidly diffusing throughout the country. Consumers are increasingly brand aware, loyal, and willing to pay price premiums for favored brands. International brands are equated with quality and prestige. In 1999, among the top most recollected international brands were familiar names in electronics and beverages; in 2001, those brands/products were still popular, but personal luxury items were recalled more readily, reflecting a growing interest in luxury, recreational, and personal care items, as well as high-quality, more utilitarian products and brands.

Our early research indicated that while many Vietnamese welcomed new products, some were concerned about their country being little more than an export market for other countries' brands, as experienced global marketers entered Vietnam (e.g., Hoang, Thanh Xuan 1993). In a number of cases, Vietnamese consumer product manufacturers have successfully responded to the new marketing competition. Not only are some Vietnamese brands capturing (or recapturing) market share, evidence suggests that some young consumers may now actually prefer domestic fashion, music, and other local interpretations of global pop culture, compared to 1999. One interesting twist on brand perception and loyalty is the belief by many Vietnamese that Omo (laundry detergent) is a Vietnamese brand, when, in fact, it is a brand owned by Unilever. However, it is important to note that such brand "Vietnamization" is a factor contributing to Unilever's success in the market and possibly is a brand strategy to be considered by other firms as well. Other companies, for example, Pierre Cardin and An Phuoc, have formed brand alliances to leverage global prestige and local loyalties.

Though branding has become increasingly important, it has some drawbacks. Even though globally recognized brand names are very popular among Vietnamese, brand authenticity is a secondary consideration. Consequently, one drawback is a flourishing brand piracy industry, whereby Vietnamese manufacture or distribute counterfeit items. Brands associated with pop culture are favorite targets for brand pirates. Counterfeiting and other violations of intellectual property rights (IPR) used to be viewed as the foreign investor's problem, but as Vietnamese brands become more successful and prominent, they too are falling prey to brand pirates. The successes of Trung Nguyen (coffee), Kinh Do (baked goods), Miss Saigon (cosmetics), Vinamilk (dairy products), Lac Viet (software), and Khai Silk (clothing), for example, have created a cottage industry of remarkably similar knockoffs and copies, much to the chagrin of the Vietnamese brand owners; even artists, particularly Le Thanh Son and Le Quan, have seen their works copied and mass produced.

Brands and other forms of registered intellectual property are now being taken more seriously than before by Vietnamese authorities and businesses. Vietnam's inclusion in the WTO in 2005 will further mobilize their efforts to respect and to protect IPR. A second drawback is concern by the CPV and domestic manufacturers that many Vietnamese products are being squeezed out of the marketplace. Consequently, domestic producers regularly call on the government to protect industries. Despite rhetoric to the contrary, trends and trade agreements will likely make Vietnam more open, and thus, industries will be less protected.[7]

The success of foreign products, brands, and services is occasionally accompanied by seemingly capricious and arbitrary crackdowns on "social evils," though these crackdowns may be a crude form of industry protection, rather than policy driven by higher moral standards. Companies that tend to maintain good relations with the government also tend to be unaffected or less affected by such crackdowns. Stating the situation more succinctly, conventional wisdom in Vietnam indicates that the authorities interpret the law for friends and enforce it for strangers (Shultz and Ardrey 1997). Nevertheless, karaoke bars, discos, various advertisements, and other institutions and activities that sometimes are and sometimes are not categorized as social evils occasionally draw the attention of the authorities, making business difficult for some companies. Although the government does not expect demand for popular brands, non-Vietnamese ideas, or even blatantly illicit activities to disappear, it periodically takes steps to avoid dominance by foreign products, moral turpitude, and cultural disintegration.

Government rhetoric, however, cannot affect the reality that the market is the way to prosperity and that the consumer is now king in Vietnam. Truly, there is no stopping or even slowing the marketing and consumer revolution. Rising incomes, diffusion of telecommunications, exposure to popular culture, brand awareness, and product availability are making shopping and consumption popular pastimes in Vietnam. Indeed, just about every cultural and physical artifact is now viewed as a marketable commodity. The legendary Cu Chi tunnels, for example, have been made into a tourist attraction: for a fee, tourists can book air-conditioned buses to the Cu Chi District on the periphery of Ho Chi Minh City. Upon arrival, they are greeted by smiling tour guides who lead them through the tunnels of the former Viet Cong stronghold. At well-spaced, convenient locations, visitors are invited to sip American soft drinks at the snack shop and to shoot a Soviet-era rifle. For the more up-market visit to Cu Chi, tourists are invited to play a round of golf on the adjacent course.

MULTI-INSTITUTIONAL MARKET TRANSFORMATION

Vietnam's transition affects many institutions, in addition to the economy, markets, and marketing. Policy changes and trends affecting the shift toward a consumer culture are deeply affecting the social structure of Vietnam. The changes are so systemic that we refer to them as a multi-institutional market revolution, which is principally driven by the following trends.

Globalization and Pluralism

Vietnam's reforms have opened the doors to businesspersons, multilateral aid workers, educators, and tourists, all of which have descended upon the country in growing numbers. Accompanying these visitors are new capital, ideas, products, consumer expectations, and demands; their involvement reshapes many business, governmental, and cultural institutions. Enterprise development zones, housing projects, international schools, restaurants of various ethnic hues, hotels, modern retailers, transportation services, discos, cinemas, local and foreign newspapers and magazines, golf courses, promotions campaigns, satellite TV, and the Internet, are now common to urban Vietnam; they are increasingly evident in smaller towns and more remote rural areas. Vietnamese now more freely travel internationally to recreate, to study, and to work in more parts of the world, further adding to the infusion of new ideas, technologies, beliefs, and practices.

Reintegrating Viet Kieu and Ethnic Chinese

Unique to Vietnam in this infusion of new people, ideas, and technologies is the participation of the overseas Vietnamese or "Viet Kieu." The term is used both admiringly and disparagingly. Viet Kieu typically refers to the Vietnamese who fled Vietnam during the 1970s and 1980s; over 70 percent of them now reside in the United States, France, Australia, and Canada. In the late 1980s, many of them began to return to Vietnam, making substantial contributions to the country's renaissance. Official statistics indicate that each year Viet Kieu contribute more than US$1 billion to the Vietnamese economy, which is equivalent to the annual amount of development aid contributed by forty-five countries; the actual figure is believed to be much higher (*Vietnam Economic Times* 2000b). Many of them return annually to celebrate the Tet Holiday, which incites massive consumer spending and gift giving, to begin a fresh start in a new year.

Viet Kieu were viewed by the Vietnamese government and people as a bridge to the world, and many local Vietnamese admired them for their relative sophistication and wealth; multinational firms also sought assistance from them, believing they had unique skills and cultural sensibilities that would be helpful to business start-ups in transitioning Vietnam. In many cases, Viet Kieu were helpful; in other cases, they were exploitive and insensitive. In time, it became apparent to both local Vietnamese and foreign investors that their inclusion in business endeavors should be predicated on a healthy balance of project-specific expertise, cultural awareness, and integrity. The Resolution of the Party's Ninth Congress considers Viet Kieu vital to development of the country and has issued many policies to encourage them to return and also to establish Vietnamese business associations in their adopted countries. These associations are intended to enhance cooperation and to boost Vietnamese exports, a key to further economic development.

As in many countries throughout Southeast Asia, Vietnam has an influential Chinese community. This community, deeply ingrained in the commercial sector for generations, particularly in Saigon, was depleted after many fled Vietnam during the socialist transformation and the most recent border war with China, in the late 1970s. A more receptive political and economic environment has enticed many of them to return and new Chinese investors to participate in Vietnam's growth. FDI totaling nearly US$2 billion a year originates from overseas Chinese.[8]

Urbanization

Vietnam is still an agrarian society, with approximately 75 percent of the population living in the countryside, but there is large-scale migration to the cities. Many fringe areas around cities are growing rapidly. They are virtual extensions of the major city but are still categorized as rural. This migration is the result of economic growth and opportunities afforded by extensive foreign investment in Hanoi, Ho Chi Minh City, Buon Ma Thuot, Danang, Can Tho, Hue, and Haiphong. Special economic zones such as Vung Tau and Binh Duong, and even smaller and sometimes remote tourist destinations such as Hoi An and Sapa, draw Vietnamese in search of opportunities. As part of this urbanization process, Vietnamese are increasingly exposed to the new consumption ethos found in the cities.

Families, Education, Opportunity

Other institutions principally affected include the family and education; they reciprocally affect each other and markets, consumption, businesses, and socioeconomic development. The Vietnamese family remains the core institution. The population growth rate is declining to just above

1 percent (see Economist Intelligence Unit 2003), but families still tend to be large, extended, and share a small house. The types of dwellings available to them in the housing market continue to diversify (Trinh, Nguyen, Wiesman, and Leaf 2000). Although each family member may not earn more than a few hundred dollars each year, households are often "income pooling units" (Vu, Tran, and McGee 2000, 128); therefore, income usually exceeds expenses, even when those expenses may include luxury items. Children typically live at home until marriage, contributing to the family income in addition to their own needs. Viet Kieu also contribute to their immediate and extended families and friends. So, while individual purchasing power is modest for the average individual or family, pooled resources create purchasing clout.

To carve their way in the new Vietnam, to acquire skills needed to thrive in the new global economy, Vietnamese demand more of education. Indeed, Vietnamese revere education, and teachers and learning institutions are afforded considerable prestige. An ancient Vietnamese aphorism conveys that prestige: "Honor the King, the Teacher, the Father" (in that order). Vietnamese, therefore, will sacrifice considerably to attend better schools and universities. In response to market demand, curricula are changing and foreign institutions are entering the market to collaborate with local universities or to commence independent programs anchored in the foreign country. Australian, non-Vietnamese Asian, European, and American universities all have a presence in Vietnam. This engagement provides new educational opportunities to meet the growing needs for higher-quality education and to make the workforce more competitive. Somewhat ironically, at the time of this writing, there is speculation that public education may receive less government support, thus pressuring families and education institutions to find resources to educate a population that hungers to learn and to become more skilled; if at all possible, Vietnamese will find these resources.

Add to these dynamics unemployment, underemployment, and the addition of 1.4 million new workers—each year—to the labor pool, and one can envision enormous policy challenges. In the middle is the government. Trends suggest Vietnam will remain a single-party state, administered by the CPV, though the party leaders will increasingly be forced to deal with more robust influences from other institutions, including the growing private sector and middle class, foreign investors, and even subsets of the government, which are gaining more autonomy and authority (see also Gainsborough 2002, 707; Abrami 2003). These changes will put more pressure on the government to deliver the goods, literally. Corruption and inefficiencies will be less tolerated (e.g., Quan 2000; *The New York Times* 2003). In many respects, Vietnam is at yet another crossroad (cf. Pike 1992), and more extensive reforms that affect virtually all institutions, even the most sacrosanct, will be required.

Entrepreneurial Nation

Multi-institutional market transformation has unleashed an entrepreneurial spirit that is seemingly intrinsic to the Vietnamese people. The process essentially evolved in three stages. The mid-1980s evinced the emergence of small, family-owned and operated retailers and manufacturers of Vietnamese products, such as food commodities, lacquerware, ceramics, rattan, and simple metal parts. A second type of entrepreneurship emerged but was driven by technocrats, usually trained in Eastern Europe, trying to render state-owned enterprises more effective through difficult restructuring of state enterprises and joint ventures with foreign companies. Export markets for commodities and minerals and some machinery and processed goods to countries of the former Soviet bloc and countries that tried to circumvent the U.S.-led trade embargo were the targets. During the late 1990s and into the new millennium, a young executive core emerged. Trained locally and in Western countries, they earned business degrees, worked for multinational firms, and returned to Vietnam to start new enterprises. We have interviewed scores of these new entrepreneurs, over the years. The following representative cases—two of many we have studied—capture their purpose and spirit. The names are fictitious.

Phuong, female, twenty-five years of age, resides in Hanoi, and is from a traditional family. Her father was a high-ranking administrator in higher education. Formerly a graduate student, she seldom ventured beyond Hanoi, but eventually did travel to Thailand, China, and Hong Kong to learn about international trade. Rejecting offers from prestigious design companies upon her return, she wanted to set up her own business. Phuong then established a clothing design company, targeting teenagers. She also got involved in mobile phone distribution across the country and entered the first duck export business in the Mekong Delta, all while preparing her long-term project of redesigning a major zoological park. When asked about the future, she stated her dream was to build an interior design house, targeting the "new rich." Reflecting upon working in Vietnam, she indicated, "We cannot afford to lose opportunities, which come and go everyday, but must focus on something we can do better than others to sustain (us) in the long run" (Doan 2002).

Khanh, early thirties, from Ho Chi Minh City, set up his small workshop with three workers in Tan Binh district, a midtown area of Ho Chi Minh City, where most immigrants from other provinces settled. The firm made industrial metal racks and shelves for warehouses. Khanh carefully developed his firm, competing against six international rivals, and in ten years he captured about 80 percent of the market. He now has a new factory in an industrial park and employs seventy workers. The keys to his success were a focus on international standards of design and performance, cost management, and after-sales services. Khanh now has his sights on future opportunities, particularly logistics. His dream is to build a warehouse system across the country with transport fleets to distribute products made by small and medium-size enterprises that either do not have the capability to have their own sales forces and distribution mechanisms or simply have limited knowledge of rapidly evolving distribution processes.

Entrepreneurship is now regarded as so important to Vietnam's development and welfare that reformists and conservatives have come together to conclude, as expressed by the prime minister, that private entrepreneurs are "creating glorious victory for the country and the nation" (Associated Press Newswires in Abrami 2003, 96). Such pragmatism by the country's leadership, which is so counter to the genesis and purported ideology of the CPV, is perhaps the quintessential example of the transformation unfolding in so many Vietnamese institutions.

IMPLICATIONS FOR MARKETING MANAGEMENT

Vietnam is an increasingly promising market, but to succeed there, investors and managers must have more than a rudimentary understanding of economic dynamics and marketing principles. The management milieu is a series of enigmas and seemingly illogical confounds; management in Vietnam is as much art, nuance, persuasion, and sheer perseverance, as science. Regardless of the generally favorable impressions of Vietnam's market potential, particularly in Ho Chi Minh City and other urban hubs, such as Hanoi, Hue, Danang, and Can Tho, it is easy to forget that transition is ongoing, and some still resist its pace and scope or are not yet fully equipped to participate in a more globally embedded, market-oriented Vietnam. The management environment has been likened to a playing field with moving goalposts, suggesting that just when it seems one is about to "score," the goalposts move. That is, the rules seem to change, just when a firm is about to be profitable (e.g., Shultz and Ardrey 1997). The goalposts, fortunately, now tend to remain fixed longer, and the field is easier to play on, but scoring remains difficult. This practical reality may be explained by many factors, including, for example, government insecurities, bureaucracy, poor infrastructure, corruption, and cultural variances vis-à-vis professionalism, urgency, time management, gift-giving, social roles, and "face." Despite greater involvement by foreign investors and chambers of commerce, newly signed agreements, and increasingly shared values of generally accepted best practices for business, managing people and things in Vietnam can be daunting.

It would be easy for a person charged with introducing and managing an enterprise in Vietnam to become disheartened by the preceding text. We believe many of the problems one now witnesses in Vietnam, however, are manifestations of growing pains, which many policy makers in the central government and certainly the growing business community are keen to remedy (cf. PRS Group 2002). After more than fifteen years of reforms, the direction, if not always the pace, of Doi Moi is irreversible. We have conducted numerous case studies in country, across many sectors of the economy, over the last decade. The essence of our findings: projects largely do not fail because of poor market demand, but because managers and investors simply cannot come to grips with the arcane conditions of Vietnam's business environment. The overarching themes from those cases are captured in the following text and are presented here as factors to consider during the process of entry and marketing management.

Research the Market

Initial research must address the entry strategy and the extent to which locals should be involved. Entry and eventual success require diligence, commitment, perseverance, and faith in the long-term future of the country. Potential investors also need to recognize that Vietnam continues its process of rebuilding a nation—its way—despite investors' concerns that the development plans and administrative practices frequently may seem economically irrational (Shultz, Speece, and Pecotich 2000). An active and connected local presence and official support are necessary to succeed. Many investors regrettably still view Vietnam as a generic Southeast Asian market or a smaller version of transitioning China, for which operations can be managed indirectly from offices or regional centers in, for example, Singapore or Hong Kong. This approach generally proves to be an unsuccessful strategy. Local partners may facilitate successful entry, and the partner-selection process must be included as part of one's market research. Individuals and groups truly committed to the project and not concerned with undue favors and quick returns have typically proven to be good partners. In addition to understanding local customs and procedures, there is an ongoing, strong economic incentive to pick good partners: they are likely to be charged ten times less than foreigners when paying "facilitation fees" and other gratuities frequently required to expedite business processes.

Good partnerships are enhanced by nurturing relationships. If a good partner has been chosen, the social institutions of honor and saving face will often suffice when no contract is available or is being negotiated. Because of these social institutions, a company can be successful, even without an intricate legal system familiar to Westerners. Instead of standard institutions of accepted business practices that Westerners tend to think are requisites for success, in Vietnam, a confederation of loosely cooperative networks and relationships exist, and these help to provide much of the institutional framework.

Private and government intermediaries can help investors find partners, but circumspection should be used here. Current Vietnamese law still requires most firms to work cooperatively with government intermediaries, such as city and local authorities, and the Ministry for Planning and Investment (MPI), an agency ostensibly responsible for "streamlining" the business application process. Agents and enterprises engaged in processing operations or shipping concerns may also be helpful, but investors will still need to work cooperatively with local authorities. Any "large" or "strategic" project, in other words, a project that even remotely hints at national security, will require MPI approval.

More specific market research vis-à-vis one's product or service has been and always will be important in Vietnam. But the dynamics of the market and the research requirements have changed considerably. The previously discussed segmentation trends support this assertion, and urban consumers have become much more sophisticated as a result of the deluge of products and promotions. For many Vietnamese, attitudes and beliefs have changed. Understanding how they have changed, of course, will affect how one manipulates the marketing mix and manages marketing relationships. Also, the competition across product categories has become much more intense. These changes collectively shape how one might now administer, for example, a promotions campaign. Now, the battle for many segments is to differentiate rather than to make consumers aware. Furthermore, where once simple outdoor advertisements and point-of-purchase materials sufficed, many managers now must administer integrated marketing communications. Several globally recognized market research and advertising firms have established operations to assist with the market research process; successful local market research firms also have emerged, but there is still no substitution for sending multiskilled employees to Vietnam to thoroughly examine the market conditions and to determine the viability of one's product or service offering and the appropriate management of pricing, distribution, and promotion.

Channel Considerations

As indicated earlier, Vietnam is generally divided into three basic cultural/commercial zones: north, central, and south. Most investors have opted to establish commercial operations in or near Ho Chi Minh City on the Saigon River, the largest, most cosmopolitan urban center and Vietnam's commercial hub. The city is booming by any standards and is generally considered to be so because of its intrinsic market size and the marketing acumen and consumption ethos of its population. Not surprisingly, it is usually favored by foreign investors. The government does, however, frequently provide incentives to invest in other parts of the country, including remote rural areas. There are other promising locations in Vietnam that should not be overlooked. Hanoi, for example, the capital and second-largest city of Vietnam, has a large metropolitan population. The city is located on the Red River, and while most of Vietnam is tropical, its latitude causes significant changes in seasons: hot and steamy summers; cooler (10 to 15 degrees Celsius) and damp winters. Although Doi Moi has brought new life to Hanoi, its development lags behind that of Ho Chi Minh City; Hanoi and the north are generally more conservative. Nevertheless, Hanoi is the political nerve center of the country and a viable market in its own right. The Vietnamese government is eager to develop the north and the countryside and often offers incentives to foreigners interested in investing in these areas. Moreover, while the urban sprawl of Ho Chi Minh City may make it an attractive consumer market, rent and wage increases may make it less desirable for manufacturing. Consequently, Haiphong, Vung Tau, Danang (all of which also happen to be ports), Binh Duong and other special economic development zones, may be more attractive sites for factories and distribution centers.

Develop Human Resources

Vietnamese have earned a reputation as hard workers. As a population, they enjoy one of the highest literacy rates in Asia. They are also very keen to learn contemporary business practices and often prefer to work for Western and developed-Asian companies. There is some evidence to suggest that there are variances in the quality of the workforce, from north to south (cf. Ralston, Nguyen, and Napier 1999), but a more competitive environment is inspiring many Vietnamese to acquire relevant skills needed to thrive in the new millennium. Toward this objective, leading universities have changed their curricula in response to new needs of the labor force. Some are working in cooperation with foreign universities to offer non-Marxist economics, business courses, and MBA programs. The net result is an emerging pool of managers able to excel in a global economy. While many Vietnamese now have functional mastery of English, computer skills, marketing, and accounting skills, the operative word for this prospective management pool is "emerging." To date, that workforce is still lacking a critical mass of middle managers and even administrative assistants. The problem, in the short run, can only be remedied with substantial investments in corporate-sanctioned training. No matter how great the demand for a company's product or service, employee selection, training, and management remain critical.

Problems accompany promise. Demand for qualified employees creates employee-retention problems. Thus, managers must not only train personnel, but must also provide incentives to keep them. Finally, while it is possible to administer an office using the customs of the normative work setting in the investing country or company, most managers have learned that deference to Vietnamese customs is advantageous. For example, woe to the manager who fails to share gifts during Tet or fails to appreciate the Vietnamese preference for an early-afternoon "siesta." Perhaps more problematic is a failure simply to adjust to the realities of life in Vietnam and to commit fully to one's organization and its people. We address these issues below.

Move with the Goalposts

Managers must accept that the goalposts in Vietnam will continue to shift, and they, accordingly, must move with them. Asian and some European investors seem more willing to accept this fact and are more willing to allocate considerable amounts of time nurturing relationships with partners, associates in the value chain in which they participate, and government authorities (note, too, that sometimes these entities are synonymous). Consequently, they are able to predict and to adjust to goalpost movements. More importantly, they often discover that because of their efforts to nurture relationships, (1) the goalposts have not moved at all for them, and (2) new opportunities emerge from the process. As a case in point, one European brewer was pleased to discover it would not have to remove or repaint its billboards in response to the social evils campaign in the mid-1990s. Its country representatives attributed this time- and cost-savings solely to its good relationship with government authorities.

Managers in Vietnam constantly struggle to balance home-country laws, Vietnamese laws, and vested interests of various Vietnamese stakeholders, in addition to their responsibilities for managing the firm. With WTO on the horizon and extant pressures from the ASEAN Free Trade Area (AFTA), the business landscape is becoming more predictable. The most encouraging changes from the perspective of foreign investors include investment guarantee measures, assurances of rights and obligations of foreign organizations and individuals, contract guidelines, procedures for resolution of disputes, export and import regulations, labor regulations, contracts on leases of land and water, insurance contracts and credit, and banking and financial contracts. However, recent trends suggest the legal code is changing so rapidly that it is difficult for foreign managers to keep pace, even those with considerable experience in Vietnam. Thus, somewhat counterintuitively, efforts to codify policy have rendered relationship management more, rather than less, important. The upshot of this evolution—and we cannot emphasize this too strongly—

despite progress on law reform, as with other Vietnamese institutions, the legal system is comparatively new and in transition. That is, the management playing field is still evolving, and managers must deal with this reality.

Avoid the Sisyphus Syndrome

Vietnam remains an exceptionally challenging market, where strategic focus and sound, consistent commitment to projects are the greatest predictors of success. Companies that come to Vietnam for a week of meetings, leave for three weeks, return, switch representatives, and repeat this cycle time and again are likened to Sisyphus (the ancient king of Corinth condemned perpetually to roll a huge stone up a hill only to have it roll back down the hill after he reached the top), in that their representatives not only work arduously with little to show for their efforts, but they are also constantly replicating unsuccessful strategies. There are good examples of large and small firms that have avoided the Sisyphus syndrome and have done very well in Vietnam.

A frequently cited large-firm success story is that of PepsiCo. Typically second in market share in the cola wars around the globe, PepsiCo arrived in Vietnam within hours after the U.S. embargo was lifted. They thoroughly researched all relevant aspects of the market and, in so doing, determined demand and found an optimal partner and appropriate manufacturing sites. They kept the initial investment low, established quality controls, offered professional training and cash resources, and effectively used *Su Lua Cua The He Moi* ("The choice of a new generation") as their promotional tag line. In one year, this joint venture had sales revenue of US$33 million and a profit of US$2.5 million. In the process, PepsiCo solidified their relationship with the government by paying US$6 million in taxes and employing 1,200 people. In the twenty-first century, PepsiCo has remained nimble and market focused. They solidified an alliance with IBC (a local beverage company), have implemented their global marketing campaign, including the "Generation Next" tag line (exclusively in English), and more recently, have employed popular European soccer stars to promote their products and brands. They have also been a large and visible sponsor of Vietnam's national soccer league. In soccer-mad Vietnam, such promotional endeavors are particularly effective.

A second case, involving a European beverage company, provides another illustration of this strategy. First, the company acquired a clear understanding of consumer demand for a specific product. Second, the company entered a cooperative agreement with a Singaporean company that had many synergies with the European firm; moreover, the Singaporeans had established regional distribution and manufacturing capabilities and good working relationships with appropriate gatekeepers in Vietnam. Third, once a "go" decision was made, the European company sent a plant manager to Vietnam during the earliest stages of the plan. This person was involved in every aspect of the project, including negotiations, site location, and employment decisions. This person's "staying power" and commitment to the project were vital. Last, the company used an extensive top-of-mind-awareness campaign via outdoor advertising and sponsorship of local events, as well as point-of-purchase items such as mugs, coasters, posters, and so on. The firm maintains a very favorable brand image, and consumers are willing to pay premium prices for the product. The firm also developed new brands to target emerging segments, willingly shared technology and management practices with locals, employs a well-trained and loyal workforce, makes important tax contributions, and more broadly is seen as a good corporate citizen in the form of community involvement. In other words, it has met objectives of the Vietnamese government as well as corporate objectives.

Small-firm success typically involves young, energetic entrepreneurs who are attacking newly emerging niche markets. From coffee production and real estate brokerage to trading companies

and language centers, these pioneers are making a mark in Vietnam. There are interesting commonalities among these success stories. They include low overhead, focus with flexibility, pragmatism, an ability to see opportunities where others only saw stumbling blocks, enthusiasm, and
a sense of adventure. All of these successful firms made a total commitment: they moved to
Vietnam and immersed themselves in the environment; many learned the language, and they
made market-opportunity discoveries that enabled them to leverage their skills. Upon reflection,
these commonalities, in many ways, were demonstrated by successful multinational firms as well.

CONCLUSION

The combination of policy changes, market reforms, extant consumer demand, and the reemer-
gence of local entrepreneurs and multinational corporations, has dramatically changed the lives
of Vietnamese. The magnitude of the change is placed in perspective when one considers that
little more than a decade ago, most Vietnamese struggled simply to survive. Now many, especially in urban areas, struggle to make sense of the multitude of products and brands that have
flooded their markets, the obtrusiveness of advertising, retail proliferation, and the confusion of
consumer choice. As a result, we are witnessing an unprecedented social as well as economic
transformation in Vietnam, including poverty reduction, emerging class stratification, fundamental changes in societal values, and, for many Vietnamese, new experiences with the hopes, desires,
uncertainties, anxieties, general frustrations, and opportunities one expects from a relatively unrestricted market economy.

Most Vietnamese believe the sweeping changes have enhanced their quality of life. Increases
in the availability, variety, and quality of consumer goods contribute to this belief, as does the
government's successful efforts to control inflation. These beliefs can only be sustained, of course,
if consumers have access to desirable goods and can afford to purchase them. As living standards
rise, so do expectations; the mechanisms that enable the influx of desirable consumer goods also
give Vietnamese greater access to information from other market economies, especially their
more affluent Asian neighbors who provide benchmarks by which Vietnam measures its progress.
Ironically, the successes of Doi Moi, in conjunction with better information about living standards elsewhere, raises consumer expectancies and, in turn, challenges the constraints of current
government policies, which often seem to be a step behind consumer desires.

The transformation from a society in which harmony and collectivism were importuned—
sometimes with harsh measures—into one in which individuals are now encouraged to compete
and to be profitable does not occur without some social costs. Corruption, anxiety about class
stratification, and the erosion of social programs also accompany the emerging consumption
ethos and the state's shift toward the market and entrepreneurship. A society of haves and want-
to-haves, winners and losers, is likely to become more apparent. And, not surprisingly, in addition to having more material possessions or being able to purchase them, the extent to which
Vietnamese are satisfied with the current stage of economic reforms and consumer conditions is
usually affected by their social role, access to capital, relationship with the government, marketable skills, age, health, personal or familial well-being, and geographic location.

All these changes spell opportunity, and Vietnam provides opportunities for marketing enterprises of numerous sizes and specialties. The initial reforms favored only well-capitalized or
well-connected businesses that could rebuild infrastructure, resurrect agribusiness, export oil, or
generate hard currency. Vietnam's transformation has created a growing appetite among Vietnamese and the growing expatriate community for all kinds of goods and services.

Vietnam should also be recognized for its links to other promising markets in the region. Its strategic location in the Greater Mekong subregion makes it possible for firms to enter Vietnam as part of a larger plan to market products to the 200 million consumers in this emerging trade bloc. But as promising as the Vietnam market may be, it is still perilous. Bureaucratic encumbrances and other constraints one would expect to find in any developing economy are inevitable. Problems especially relevant to Vietnam include poor infrastructure, a dearth of qualified managers and other human resources, and nebulous yet continually evolving legal, tax, and accounting systems. Rent extractions and other forms of corruption by national and local authorities can still be problematic; so too are occasional reactionary movements within the government as Vietnam makes its unique transition to a market economy. Now fierce competition has become a factor, as many companies struggle to penetrate the market and to establish brand dominance.

Similar to the marketing environments in other transition economies in Southeast Asia—Cambodia, Laos, and Myanmar—any serious marketing manager in Vietnam should add prudence, patience, and persistence to the classic "4 Ps" of the marketing mix. In Vietnam, relationships take time to nurture. Favorable brand and company images must be built, maintained, and protected. Flexibility, good contacts, understanding the market, incremental growth, and sound business practices that address the unique Vietnamese condition will pay off in the long term. Although the Vietnamese government's policies can be confusing, the government has attempted to address the concerns of foreign investors over problems that need longer-term solutions. Even with desirable growth rates, however, it will be more than a decade before Vietnam joins the ranks of the "tiger" economies. Trends suggest that Vietnam will eventually join them, and failing to have a presence in the market now will be costly to companies that intend to position themselves as significant players in Vietnam and the region as a whole.

NOTES

The authors acknowledge the support and assistance of the Marley Foundation, the Harvard-Fulbright Economics Teaching Program, Taylor Nelson Sofres, the Ho Chi Minh City Economics University, the Vietnam Ministry of Agriculture and Rural Development, the Vietnam Ministry of Foreign Affairs, the General Statistics Office of Vietnam, Berthold Heinemann, and Mai AB, Ltd., Vietnam. This chapter expands Shultz, Nguyen, Pecotich, and Ardrey (1998).

1. Though trade and commerce are now integral to Chinese–Vietnamese relations, some Vietnamese resentment has emerged, as China's products stream into Vietnam, legally and illegally, pressuring Vietnamese producers (e.g., *The Economist* 2002a).

2. This struggle, in many ways, continues to the present and now includes forces endemic to globalization and market-oriented societies.

3. International Monetary Fund, *World Economic Outlook*, April 2003, p. 179.

4. This is a complicated problem. Many private firms have unreliable financial accounts. The banks are not skilled at loan evaluation. The law itself is not strong, and enforcement procedures are weak and variable. There is also a risk that if dollars were loaned to firms that earn mainly local currency, they would be vulnerable to bankruptcy in the event of devaluation. No single policy will fix the problem.

5. The data were collected from panelists and a representative sample of 1,232 respondents residing in Hanoi and Ho Chi Minh City (Taylor Nelson Sofres 2002). These figures are incomes reported to the field researchers, which are not necessarily the numbers consumers report to the government. As in other developing or transitional economies, many consumers in Vietnam underreport income and function in the parallel economy.

6. The government remains ambivalent about allowing access to international programming and periodically cracks down on personal television satellites and access to cable. Most observers, however, believe this policy shift may go the way of the "helmet law," legislation implemented to force motorcycle riders to wear helmets—consumers scrambled to buy helmets, and then, after a rather brief period, the law was and remains largely ignored.

7. Protectionism is not unique to Vietnam, of course, and it has been a sore point between Vietnam and

some of its trading partners, as evidenced by the "catfish wars," in which U.S. growers effectively lobbied to limit catfish imports from Vietnam (*The Economist* 2002b); Japan and Vietnam have had similar disagreements over motorcycle parts (Abrami 2003).

8. There was and still is a high rate of intermarriage between Vietnamese and ethnic Chinese, with 30 percent of Chinese marrying non-Chinese partners (Economist Intelligence Unit 2003), so readers should note that measures of Viet Kieu and ethnic Chinese, particularly vis-à-vis population and investments, may overlap.

REFERENCES

Abrami, Regina. 2003. "Vietnam in 2002." *Asian Survey* 43 (1): 91–100.

Abruza, Zachary. 2002. "The Lessons of Le Khai Phieu: Changing Rules in Vietnam Politics." *Contemporary Southeast Asia* 24 (1): 121–43.

Associated Press Newswires. 2002. "Communist Vietnam's Prime Minister Says Capitalist Success Is Glorious." April 1.

Chen, King C. 1987. *China's War with Vietnam, 1979.* Stanford, CA: Hoover Institution Press.

Cima, Ronald J. 1989. "Vietnam's Economic Reform: Approaching the 1990s.'" *Asian Survey* 29 (8; August): 786–99.

Communist Party of Vietnam. 1991. *Seventh National Congress Documents.* Hanoi: Foreign Language Press.

Dao Loan. 2003. "Young and Hopefully Rich." *The Saigon Times,* January 11: 24–25.

Dapice, David O. 1996. *Catching Up.* New York: United Nations Development Program.

———. 2000. "Choices and Opportunities." Unpublished monograph, Harvard University, Cambridge, MA.

———. 2003. "Vietnam's Economy: Success or Weird Dualism?" Working paper, Harvard University, Cambridge, MA.

Dapice, David O., and Thomas J. Vallely. 1996. "Vietnam's Economy: Will It Get and Stay on the Dragon's Trail." Research report, Harvard Institute for International Development, Cambridge, MA.

Dapice, David O., Jonathan Haughton, and Dwight Perkins. 1994. *Theo Huong Rong Bay* (also: *In Search of the Dragon's Trail: Economic Reform in Vietnam*). Ho Chi Minh City: Harvard Institute for International Development/Fulbright Economics Teaching Program.

Do, Duc Dinh. 1993. "Vietnam's Economic Renovation to the Market Mechanism." *Journal of Asian Business,* 9(Summer): 17–33.

Doan, Huu Duc. 2002. Personal interview, Hanoi.

The Economist. 2002a. "Trading Places," March 23: 67.

———. 2002b. "Case of the Ghostly Catfish," December 14–20: 35.

Economist Intelligence Unit. 2003. *Vietnam Country Profile.* London: The Economist Group.

Embassy of Vietnam. 2003. Available at www.vietnamembassy-usa.org.

Erlanger, Stephen. 1991. "Vietnam's Gains Slip Away." *International Herald Tribune,* February 19.

Gainsborough, Martin. 2002. "Political Change in Vietnam: In Search of the Middle Class Challenge to the State." *Asian Survey* 52 (5): 694–707.

General Statistical Office. 1992. Raw data. Hanoi.

Hoang, Nam. 2000. *Viet Nam.* Ha Noi: The Ethnic Cultures Publishing House.

Hoang, Thanh Xuan. 1993. Personal interview, Ministry of Trade and Economic Development, January 18, Hanoi.

Hoang, Thuy Bang, Clifford J. Shultz II, and Anthony Pecotich. 2001. "Challenges of Market Development: Some Issues in the Vietnamese Coffee Industry." In *Proceedings of the 26th Annual Macromarketing Conference,* ed. D. Rahtz and P. McDonagh, pp. 247–52, Madison, WI: Omnipress.

International Monetary Fund (IMF). 2002. Reports 02/5 and 02/151. Washington, DC: IMF.

———. 2003. *World Economic Outlook.* Washington, DC: IMF.

Jamieson, Neil L. 1995. *Understanding Vietnam.* Berkeley: University of California Press.

Karnow, Stanley. 1991. *Vietnam: A History.* New York: Penguin.

Keyfitz, Nathan. 1982. "Development and the Elimination of Poverty." *Economic Development and Cultural Change* 30 (6): 346–55.

Lamb, David. 2002. *Vietnam, Now.* New York: PublicAffairs.

Le, Ba Thao. 1997. *Viet Nam: The Country and Its Geographical Regions.* Hanoi: The Gioi Publishers.

McAlister, John T. Jr., and Paul Mus. 1970. *The Vietnamese and Their Revolution.* New York: Harper and Row.

McMillan, John. 2002. *Reinventing the Bazaar.* New York: Norton.

The New York Times. 2003. "Vietnam Puts 155 on Trial in Graft Case." Associated Press, February 26: 6.

Nguyen, Khach Vien. 1987. *Vietnam: A Long History.* Hanoi: Foreign Language Publishing House.

Nguyen, Tan Dung. 2002. *International Country Risk Guide* (The PRS Group) 23 (9): 214–19.

Pecotich, Anthony, and Clifford J. Shultz II. 1993. "Vietnam Revisited: Observations and Emergent Themes in Consumer Behavior Since the Implementation of Market Reforms." In *European Advances in Consumer Research*, pp. 1423–26, ed. G. Bamossy and W. F. van Raaij. Amsterdam: Association for Consumer Research.

Pike, Douglas. 1992. "Vietnam: 1991 the Turning Point." *Asian Survey* 32 (1): 74–81.

The PRS Group. 2002. *International Country Risk Guide* 23 (9): 214–19.

Quan, Xuan Dinh. 2000. "The Political Economy of Vietnam's Transformation Process." *Contemporary Southeast Asia* 22 (2): 360–88.

Quan Doi Nhan Dan. 1992, February. Hanoi: The People's Army of Vietnam.

Ralston, David A., Van Thong Nguyen, and Nancy K. Napier. 1999. "A Comparative Study of the Work Values of North and South Vietnamese." *Journal of International Business Studies* 30 (4): 655–72.

Roper, Christopher. 2000. "Sino-Vietnamese Relations and the Economy of Vietnam's Border Region." *Asian Survey* 40 (6): 1019–41.

Shultz, Clifford J. II. 1994. "Balancing Policy, Consumer Desire and Corporate Interests: Considerations for Market Entry in Vietnam." *Columbia Journal of World Business* 29(Winter): 42–53.

Shultz, Clifford J. II, and William J. Ardrey. 1995. "Future Prospects for Sino-Vietnamese Relations: Are Trade and Commerce the Critical Factors for Sustainable Peace?" *Contemporary Southeast Asia* 17 (September): 126–46.

———. 1997. "Asia's Next Tiger? Vietnam is Fraught with Promise and Peril for Marketers." *Marketing Management* 5 (Winter): 26–37.

Shultz, Clifford J. II, and Khai Le. 1993. "Vietnam's Inconsistencies between Political Structure and Socio-economic Practice, and Implications for the Future." *Contemporary Southeast Asia* 15 (September): 179–94.

Shultz, Clifford J. II, and Anthony Pecotich. 1994. "Vietnam: New Assessments of Consumption Patterns in a (Re)Emergent Capitalist Society." In *Asia Pacific Advances in Consumer Research*, ed. J. Cote and Siew Meng Leong, pp. 222–27. Provo, UT: Association for Consumer Research.

———. 1997. "Marketing and Development in the Transition Economies of Southeast Asia: Policy Explication, Assessment and Implications." *Journal of Public Policy and Marketing* 16 (1): 55–68.

Shultz, Clifford J. II, William J. Ardrey, and Anthony Pecotich. 1995. "American Involvement in Vietnam, Part II: Prospects for US Business in a New Era." *Business Horizons* 38 (March–April): 21–27.

Shultz, Clifford J. II, Anthony Pecotich, and Khai Le. 1994. "Changes in Marketing Activity and Consumption in the Socialist Republic of Vietnam." In *Research in Consumer Behavior*, Vol. 7, ed. C. Shultz, R. Belk, and G. Ger, pp. 225–57. Greenwich, CT: JAI Press.

Shultz, Clifford J. II, Nguyen Xuan Que, Anthony Pecotich, and William Ardrey. 1998. "Vietnam: Market Socialism, Marketing and Consumer Behavior." In *Marketing and Consumer Behavior in East and Southeast Asia*, ed. A. Pecotich and C. Shultz II, pp. 715–43. Sydney: McGraw Hill.

Shultz, Clifford J. II, Mark Speece, and Anthony Pecotich. 2000. "The Evolving Investment Climate in Vietnam and Subsequent Challenges to Foreign Investors." *Thunderbird International Business Review* 42 (6): 735–54.

Son, Dang Kim. 2004. Interview with author, November 25, Hanoi.

Taylor, Keith Weller. 1983. *The Birth of Vietnam.* Berkeley: University of California Press.

Taylor Nelson Sofres plc. 2002. Unpublished data, Ho Chi Minh City.

Tran, Thi Que. 1998. *Vietnam's Agriculture: The Challenges and Achievements.* Singapore: Institute of Southeast Asian Studies.

Trinh, Duy Luan, Quang Vinh Nguyen, Brahm Wiesman, and Michael Leaf. 2000. "Urban Housing." In *Socioeconomic Renovation in Vietnam*, ed. Peter Boothyard and Pham Xuan Nam, pp. 51–100. Singapore: International Development Research Centre.

Vietnam Consulting Group. 2002. Raw data, based on fieldwork in Ho Chi Minh City, Da Nang, Ha Noi, and rural communities.

Vietnam Economic Times. 2000a. "Birth of the Cool," March: 18–19.

———. 2000b. "Return of the Natives," March: 22–24.

Vietnam News. 2003. "Infrastructure Projects Pave Way for Growth," January 11: 1–2.

Vo, Nhan Tri. 1990. *Vietnam's Economic Policy Since 1975.* Sydney: Allen and Unwin.

Vu, Tuan Anh, Thi Van Anh Tran, and Terry G. McGee. 2000. "Household Economy." In *Socioeconomic Renovation in Vietnam*, ed. Peter Boothyard and Pham Xuan Nam, pp. 101–35. Singapore: International Development Research Centre.

Williams, Michael C. 1992. *Vietnam at the Crossroads.* London: Pinter Publishers Ltd.

World Bank. 1994. Report 13143–VN, 9/26/1994. Washington, DC: World Bank.

———. 1995. Report 14645–VN. Washington, DC: World Bank.

———. 2002. *Vietnam: Delivering on its Promise.* Washington, DC: World Bank.

World Factbook. 2004. Central Intelligence Agency, available at www.cia.gov/cia/publications/factbook/geos/vm.html.

ABOUT THE EDITORS AND CONTRIBUTORS

THE EDITORS

Anthony Pecotich (Ph.D., University of Wisconsin–Madison) is associate professor of marketing at the University of Western Australia. He has considerable academic and consulting experience in marketing and economic development in Australia, the United States, Europe, and Asia. He currently serves on several editorial and policy boards and has published extensively on a wide array of marketing and management topics, for which he has earned distinction for "best papers," and other scholarly awards for contributions as author and scholarly service to the academy.

Clifford J. Shultz II (Ph.D., Columbia University) is Professor and Marley Foundation Chair at the Morrison School of Agribusiness at the Arizona State University. He holds an appointment in the Program for Southeast Asian Studies and is a Fellow at the Harvard-Fulbright Program in Vietnam. He has administered numerous marketing and development projects in Southeast Asia and the Balkans. He has published widely on consumer, marketing, and development phenomena in recovering economies, particularly in Indochina, and serves as editor of the *Journal of Macromarketing.*

THE CONTRIBUTORS

William J. Ardrey (Ph.D., University of Western Australia) is senior lecturer at the Center for Entrepreneurial Management and Innovation, University of Western Australia Graduate School of Management. He has counseled the United Nations and World Bank on entrepreneurship and economic development and has led numerous banking capacity building projects in Southeast Asia, especially in Vietnam and Laos, funded by these organizations. He also serves on the boards of companies in the United States, Australia, and Southeast Asia.

Albert Celoza is faculty and chair of Liberal Arts at Phoenix College, and affiliate faculty with the Program for Southeast Asian Studies at Arizona State University where he teaches Business Environment of Asia. He taught at the University of the Philippines and the Thunderbird Garvin School of International Management. He studied at Claremont Graduate University, University of San Francisco and the University of the Philippines. He is author of *Marcos and the Philippines: Political Economy of Authoritarianism* (1997).

Seungwoo Chun is a marketing doctoral student at the University of Nebraska–Lincoln. His dissertation research involves the learning of sport fan rituals, specifically looking at that process in the context of professional baseball in the United States and in Japan. He has presented papers at the Association for Consumer Research and published an article in the *AMS Review.*

Cindy M.Y. Chung is assistant professor in marketing at the Nanyang Business School. She obtained her Ph.D. in business at the University of British Columbia in Vancouver, Canada. Her research interests include word-of-mouth behavior, price–quality relationship, and cross-cultural consumer behavior. She teaches consumer behavior to undergraduates and postgraduates.

Steven Cornish-Ward is a senior lecturer in marketing at Murdoch University, Western Australia. He has published twenty-five refereed papers in leading international journals, books, and conference proceedings. His research interests are varied and include body image, innovation, pharmaceutical marketing, country of origin, global branding, wine marketing, and privacy research.

David Dapice (Ph.D., Harvard) is associate professor of economics at Tufts University and has also been chief economist of the Vietnam Program at Harvard University's Kennedy School since 1990. He has worked on a variety of development issues, primarily in Southeast Asia, since 1971. He spent a year working at the World Bank as a Brookings Policy Fellow, the Rockefeller Foundation, and worked with several other foundations and donors on development strategy and policy, as well as a number of applied fields.

Doan Huu Duc owns Vietnam Consulting Group, which focuses on small and medium-size enterprises, corporate structure and design, and mechanisms to enhance competitive advantages in Vietnam's emerging industries. Duc has taught at the Fulbright Economics Teaching Program in Ho Chi Minh City and is the first and youngest Vietnamese from the private sector who was awarded a Fulbright Scholarship to study for the MBA, which he earned from Northwestern University's Kellogg School. He has degrees in economics and literature from the National University of Ho Chi Minh City.

Tan Siew Ee is associate professor at the University of Brunei Darussalam, where he also served as head of the Economics Department. His scholarly focus is development, labor economics, and the economies of ASEAN, and he has about fifty publications in the form of books, articles, and research papers. He has served as a consultant to several leading agencies and institutes. Formerly, he was associate professor at Universiti Sains Malaysia and a Research Fellow at Regensburg Universität.

Ronald A. Fullerton is professor of marketing at the American University of Cairo. His previous experience in developing countries includes professorships at the University of Botswana, Al Akhawayn University in Morocco, and at the University of the South Pacific, where his interest in Papua New Guinea developed. He has published widely on the topic of marketing, serves on editorial boards, and is a leading scholar on marketing history as well as marketing and development.

N. Clay Gary has lived and worked as a marketer in Japan for sixteen years. His career includes seven years as an account planner for foreign multinationals and a six-year stint as director of marketing for Callaway Golf K.K. (Japan). He is currently an independent marketing consultant in Tokyo.

James W. Gentry is the Maurice J. and Alice Hollman Professor in Marketing at the University of Nebraska–Lincoln. He earned his doctorate from Indiana University and has taught at Kansas State University, Oklahoma State University, and the University of Wisconsin, as well as University of Nebraska. He is the North American editor of the *Journal of Consumer Behaviour* and the editor of the *AMS Review*. His primary research areas are cross-cultural differences in consumer behavior and family decision making.

Jane Hutchison lectures in politics and international studies in the School of Social Sciences and Humanities at Murdoch University in Western Australia. She has research interests in the Philippines and has coedited a book on labor and globalization in Asia.

Sunkyu Jun is associate professor of marketing at Hongik University in Seoul. He obtained his doctorate at the University of Nebraska, and taught previously at Han Nam University. His research interests include consumer acculturation, expatriation processes, gender research, and how consumers process information in advertisements. His research has appeared in the *Journal of International Business Studies,* the *Journal of Business Research,* the *Journal of Advertising,* the *International Business Review,* the *AMS Review,* and the *Journal of Current Issues and Research in Advertising.*

Hee Suk Kang is assistant professor at WooSuk University in Chonju. She earned her doctorate at Chonbuk National University. Recently, she completed a sabbatical at Shandong National University. Her research interests are in consumer research.

Michael Keane (B.A., University of Southern California, MBA University of Chicago, J.D., University of Texas School of Law) is currently managing director at Wedbush Morgan Securities in Los Angeles, California. He is also a visiting professor at the Marshall School of Business at the University of Southern California. He has authored numerous peer-reviewed and business press articles and monographs on strategy, finance, and Southeast Asian business.

Gyungtai Ko (now deceased) was formerly an assistant professor at Chonbuk National University in Chonju. He earned his doctorate from the University of Nebraska–Lincoln. His research involved cross-cultural differences in decision making.

Tony Lapsley (B.A., Dip.Ed., B.Ed., M.A., Ph.D., Grad. Cert. Bus. Admin.) is a former Australian civil servant and lecturer in the School of Asian Studies at the University of Western Australia. He has worked for three UN missions in East Timor—UNAMET, UNTAET, and UNMISET. In 2000–2001, he was administrator of the district of Liquiça, west of Dili, and is now an adviser to the National Institute of Public Administration of Timor Leste.

Christina Kwai Choi Lee (Ph.D., M. Com, University of Auckland) is Senior Lecturer in the Department of Marketing at the University of Auckland Business School. Christina's areas of research interest are principally in consumer behavior, specifically, household and family influence and decision making processes, cross-cultural research, and social marketing issues related to adolescents. Her work has been published in *Asia Pacific Advances in Consumer Research, Journal of Advertising, Australasian Journal of Marketing, European Journal of Marketing* and other scholarly outlets.

May Lwin (Ph.D., National University of Singapore) is assistant professor of marketing at the National University of Singapore Business School. Having previously worked for Citibank N.A. and as account planner and Myanmar manager for Ogilvy & Mather, her research has largely dealt with social and regulatory issues in international markets. Her publications include the best-selling *Clueless* books and publications in *Marketing Letters, Journal of Public Policy & Marketing, Journal of Current Issues in Research & Advertising,* and *Journal of Business Law.*

Roger Marshall is Associate Professor of Marketing and International Business, Director of the MBA Marketing Programme. He teaches marketing management and consumer behavior. Dr. Marshall enjoyed a first career as a businessman in New Zealand, working for a retail chain, and as a marketing manager for a stainless steel fabrication company, that marketed products throughout the Asia-Pacific region. He also has taught at the University of Auckland.

Janet R. McColl-Kennedy is professor of marketing at University of Queensland Business School. Her primary scholarly interest is services marketing, and she has over seventy research publications, including articles in *Journal of Service Research, Journal of Business Research, The Leadership Quarterly, Journal of Services Marketing, Advances in Consumer Research, Australasian Marketing Journal, Journal of International Consumer Marketing, International Journal of Human–Computer Studies,* and *Marketing Intelligence and Planning.*

Tsutomu Okahashi has been with Dentsu Inc. since 1970 and is currently deputy director of the Integrated Marketing Communications Planning Division. His main focus has been on consumer studies and strategic planning for clients in Japan and in Asian markets. He has a B.A. in aesthetics and psychology from the University of Tokyo.

John O'Shaughnessy is professor emeritus of business at the Graduate School of Business, Columbia University, New York, and Senior Associate of the Judge Institute of Management Studies, Cambridge University. He has published thirteen books, most recently, *The Marketing Power of Emotion* (Oxford University Press, 2003) and *Persuasion in Advertising* (Routledge, 2004). He has been a marketing research manager and has extensive international consulting experience.

Pia Polsa is assistant professor, Department of Marketing and Corporate Geography at the Swedish School of Economics and Business Administration, Helsinki. Her expertise is Chinese consumer behavior and distribution channels. She teaches "Doing Business in China" courses at several universities and has taught at the Nankai University in the People's Republic of China. Her research has been presented at numerous conferences and published in several academic publications, including *Journal of Services Marketing, International Marketing Review,* and *Supply Chain Management.*

Mike Potter is a Senior Lecturer in Marketing and Advertising at the Auckland University of Technology, Auckland, New Zealand. His expertise and consulting interests are in strategic marketing, marketing research, cross-cultural marketing, consumer behavior and global marketing.

Don R. Rahtz (Ph.D., Virginia Tech) is professor of marketing at The College of William and Mary. His expertise is integrated marketing communications, marketing research, and market assessment. He has worked extensively in South Asia and Southeast Asia, primarily in Bangladesh,

Cambodia, Thailand, and Vietnam. He has a particular interest in environmental issues, economic sustainable development, transitional economies, business/community interface evaluation, and health systems, and he has written a number of publications regarding these topics that have appeared in books, academic journals, and the popular press.

Sharyn Rundle-Thiele (BBus., MBus., University of South Australia) is a marketing lecturer at the Graduate School of Management, Griffith University. She has lectured at the University of Queensland, Bond University, and the University of South Australia. She has extensive marketing experience in several Australian industries, including food manufacturing and marketing, telecommunications, electricity, engineering, and professional services. She has consulted for private organizations, such as Wine Australia Pty. Ltd., and government organizations, such as Telstra and various South Australian government departments.

Aliah Hanim M. Salleh is Associate Professor of Marketing at Universiti Kebangsaan Malaysia School of Business Management, Faculty of Economics and Business. Her tertiary degrees include in B.S. in Agribusiness, M.B.A. (Ohio University) and Ph.D. (Manchester). She teaches Marketing, Business Communications and Research Methods at the Doctoral, MBA and undergraduate levels. Her current research interests however, focus more on Services Marketing and New Product Development.

Leong Vai Shiem (Dip. QA [Kent], B.BA [UBD], M.Mktg [Griffith]) is a lecturer at the Department of Business and Management of University Brunei Darussalam. Her current research interests are advertising appeals of the financial services industry and marketing applications for the small and medium enterprises in Brunei Darussalam.

Ignas G. Sidik is a faculty member at the Prasetiya Mulya Business School in Jakarta, Indonesia, where he teaches marketing and strategy courses in its MBA programs. He is an active observer of the Indonesian consumer market. His research interests include strategic marketing, competitive strategy, and brand management. He is also a consultant to leading companies in Indonesia. He holds degrees from the Institut Teknologi Bandung, the Wharton School of the University of Pennsylvania, and Boston University.

Anusorn Singhapakdi is professor and coordinator of marketing at Old Dominion University. He has published over forty journal articles and has received numerous recognitions for his work. His 1996 article on moral intensity was cited as the second most influential article published in the *Journal of Business Research* for the 1995–99 period . He is an active member of various professional organizations and is a current member of the board of directors for the International Society for Quality of Life Studies.

Stella Lai Man So is marketing professor at the Chinese University of Hong Kong. She teaches marketing management and advertising and promotional management. She received her MBA and her B.Sc. from Aston University at Birmingham in England. She was formerly research manager for *Reader's Digest* and *Asiaweek* in Hong Kong, market information systems manager of Union Carbide Eastern Inc., and has extensive consulting experience in China. Before returning to Hong Kong, she was a lecturer at European University in Antwerp, Belgium.

Mark Speece is professor at University of Alaska Southeast. He previously worked in Thailand for ten years, principally at the Asian Institute of Technology; two years in Singapore; five years at the Chinese University of Hong Kong, including consulting on China markets. His research and consulting has focused on marketing and development issues in Asia and the Middle East. He earned a Ph.D. in marketing from the University of Washington and a Ph.D. in Middle East economic geography from the University of Arizona.

Yingchan E. Tang is associate professor of marketing at National Chiao Tung University (Taiwan). He holds a Ph.D. in Marketing from University of Texas at Dallas. His current research deals with online shopping behavior and channel distribution in China. He has publications appearing in many books and journals, including *Journal of Marketing, Journal of Consumer Marketing, Journal of Management, PacPacific Management Review,* and the monograph *One-to-One Marketing: The Core Strategy to CRM.*

Htwe Htwe (Vicki) Thein is associate lecturer in the School of Management of Curtin Business School, Curtin University of Technology. She was born in Myanmar and has research and consulting experience in that nation.

Busaya Virakul holds a B.Sc. and a D.V.M. from the School of Veterinary Medicine, Chulalongkorn University, Bangkok, Thailand. She continued study in the United States and earned an M.Ed. and Ph.D. in Agricultural Education from the University of Minnesota. Before taking up teaching, she spent six years working with agribusiness companies. She now teaches research methodology, business ethics, and human resources classes at the Graduate Program in Human Resource Development, The National Institute of Development Administration (NIDA), Bangkok.

Che Aniza Che Wel, DBS, BBA (Universiti Teknologi Mara, Malaysia) holds a M.Sc. degree in Marketing from Universiti Putra Malaysia. As a lecturer at UKM's School of Business Management, her teaching and research areas revolve around consumer behavior, sales management, marketing research and internet marketing. She is currently pursuing her doctoral degree.

Jochen Wirtz (Ph.D., London Business School) is associate professor of marketing, academic director, APEX-MBA Program, and academic codirector, UCLA-NUS Executive MBA Program, National University of Singapore. He is a leading authority in services marketing in Asia. His latest book, *Services Marketing—People, Technology, Strategy* (fifth edition, 2004), coauthored with Christopher Lovelock, is one of the top two services marketing texts in the world. He has published some fifty academic papers in journals. And, he has received several teaching awards.

Nittaya Wongtada is a faculty member at the Graduate School of Business Administration, National Institution of Development Administration (NIDA), Thailand. Her primary scholarly focus is entrepreneurship, marketing, and public policy.

INDEX